Psychology
Themes and Variations

8TH EDITION

W9-CCM-964

Briefer Version

Psychology
Themes and Variations

Briefer Version

© Maurizio Rellini/Grand Tour/Corbis

Wayne Weiten
University of Nevada, Las Vegas

WADSWORTH
CENGAGE Learning™

Australia • Brazil • Japan • Korea • Mexico • Singapore • Spain • United Kingdom • United States

Psychology: Themes and Variations, Briefer Version, Eighth Edition
Wayne Weiten

Senior Publisher: Linda Schreiber

Executive Editor, Psychology: Jon-David Hague

Senior Developmental Editor: Kristin Makarewycz

Assistant Editor: Trina Tom

Editorial Assistant: Kelly Miller

Media Editor: Lauren Keyes

Marketing Manager: Elisabeth Rhoden

Executive Marketing Communications Manager: Talia Wise

Senior Content Project Manager: Pat Waldo

Creative Director: Rob Hugel

Senior Art Director: Vernon Boes

Senior Print Buyer: Judy Inouye

Rights Acquisitions Account Manager, Text: Bob Kauser

Rights Acquisitions Account Manager, Images: John Hill

Production Service: Joan Keyes, Dovetail Publishing Services

Text Designer: Tani Hasegawa

Photo and Text Permissions: Linda L Rill

Copy Editor: Jackie Estrada

Illustrators: Carol Zuber-Mallison and Fred Harwin

Cover Designer: Irene Morris Design

Cover Image: Basque Provinces, Pais Vasco Bilbao, Zubizuri Bridge, Cambo Volantin Footbridge. © Maurizio Rellini/Grand Tour/Corbis

Compositor: Thompson Type

For product information and technology assistance, contact us at **Cengage Learning Customer & Sales Support, 1-800-354-9706.**

For permission to use material from this text or product, submit all requests online at **www.cengage.com/permissions.** Further permissions questions can be e-mailed to **permissionrequest@cengage.com.**

Library of Congress Control Number: 2009932084

Student Edition:
ISBN-10: 0-495-81310-9
ISBN-13: 978-0-495-81310-1

Paper Edition:
ISBN-10: 0-495-81133-5
ISBN-13: 978-0-495-81133-6

Loose-leaf Edition:
ISBN-10: 0-495-81334-6
ISBN-13: 978-0-495-81334-7

Wadsworth
20 Davis Drive
Belmont, CA 94002-3098
USA

Cengage Learning is a leading provider of customized learning solutions with office locations around the globe, including Singapore, the United Kingdom, Australia, Mexico, Brazil, and Japan. Locate your local office at **www.cengage.com/global.**

Cengage Learning products are represented in Canada by Nelson Education, Ltd.

To learn more about Wadsworth, visit **www.cengage.com/Wadsworth.** Purchase any of our products at your local college store or at our preferred online store **www.ichapters.com.**

Printed in the United States of America
1 2 3 4 5 6 7 13 12 11 10 09

In memory of Mother Publisher, Claire Verduin (1932–2008),
a cherished friend, inspirational mentor, and legendary editor

ABOUT THE AUTHOR

Wayne Weiten is a graduate of Bradley University and received his Ph.D. in social psychology from the University of Illinois–Chicago, in 1981. He currently teaches at the University of Nevada, Las Vegas. He has received distinguished teaching awards from Division Two of the American Psychological Association (APA) and from the College of DuPage, where he taught until 1991. He is a Fellow of Divisions 1 and 2 of the American Psychological Association. In 1991, he helped chair the APA National Conference on Enhancing the Quality of Undergraduate Education in Psychology and in 1996-1997 he served as President of the Society for the Teaching of Psychology. Weiten has conducted research on a wide range of topics, including educational measurement, jury decision making, attribution theory, stress, and cerebral specialization. His recent interests have included pressure as a form of stress and the technology of textbooks. He is also the co-author of *Psychology Applied to Modern Life* (Wadsworth, 2009) and the creator of an educational CD-ROM titled *PsykTrek: A Multimedia Introduction to Psychology.*

TO THE INSTRUCTOR

Psychology is an exciting, dynamic discipline that has grown by leaps and bounds in recent decades. This progress has been reflected in the field's introductory texts, which have grown longer and longer. However, the length of the introductory psychology course generally has not changed. Hence, an increasing number of professors are reporting that they find it difficult to cover the wealth of material found in the typical introductory text. With this situation in mind, I decided to write a briefer version of *Psychology: Themes and Variations* to help meet the needs of those teachers who would like a challenging, but concise, introductory text.

If I had to sum up in a single sentence what I hope will distinguish this text, the sentence would be this: I have set out to create a *paradox* instead of a *compromise*.

Let me elaborate. An introductory psychology text must satisfy two disparate audiences: professors and students. Because of the tension between the divergent needs and preferences of these audiences, textbook authors usually indicate that they have attempted to strike a compromise between being theoretical versus practical, comprehensive versus comprehensible, research oriented versus applied, rigorous versus accessible, and so forth. However, I believe that many of these dichotomies are false. As Kurt Lewin once remarked, "What could be more practical than a good theory?" Similarly, is rigorous really the opposite of accessible? Not in my dictionary. I maintain that many of the antagonistic goals that we strive for in our textbooks only *seem* incompatible and that we may not need to make compromises as often as we assume.

In my estimation, a good introductory textbook is a paradox in that it integrates characteristics and goals that appear contradictory. With this in mind, I have endeavored to write a text that is paradoxical in three ways. First, in surveying psychology's broad range of content, I have tried to show that our interests are characterized by diversity *and* unity. Second, I have emphasized both research *and* application and how they work in harmony. Finally, I have aspired to write a book that is challenging to think about *and* easy to learn from. Let's take a closer look at these goals.

Goals

1. *To show both the unity and the diversity of psychology's subject matter.* Students entering an introductory psychology course often are unaware of the immense diversity of subjects studied by psychologists. I find this diversity to be part of psychology's charm, and throughout the book I highlight the enormous range of questions and issues addressed by psychology. Of course, our diversity proves disconcerting for some students, who see little continuity between such disparate areas of research as physiology, motivation, cognition, and abnormal behavior. Indeed, in this era of specialization, even some psychologists express concern about the fragmentation of the field.

However, I believe that there is considerable overlap among the subfields of psychology and that we should emphasize their common core by accenting the connections and similarities among them. Consequently, I portray psychology as an integrated whole rather than as a mosaic of loosely related parts. A principal goal of this text, then, is to highlight the unity in psychology's intellectual heritage (the themes), as well as the diversity of psychology's interests and uses (the variations).

2. *To illuminate the process of research and its intimate link to application.* For me, a research-oriented book is not one that bulges with summaries of many studies but one that enhances students' appreciation of the logic and excitement of empirical inquiry. I want students to appreciate the strengths of the empirical approach and to see scientific psychology as a creative effort to solve intriguing behavioral puzzles. For this reason, the text emphasizes not only *what* we know (and don't know) but *how* we attempt to find out. It examines methods in some detail and encourages students to adopt the skeptical attitude of a scientist and to think critically about claims regarding behavior.

Learning the virtues of research should not mean that students cannot also satisfy their desire for concrete, personally useful information about the challenges of everyday life. Most researchers believe that psychology has a great deal to offer those outside the field and that psychologists should share the practical implications of their work. In this text, practical insights are carefully qualified and closely tied to data, so that students can see the interdependence of research and application. I find that students come to appreciate the science of psychology more when they see that worthwhile practical applications are derived from careful research and sound theory.

3. *To make the text challenging to think about and easy to learn from.* Perhaps most of all, I have sought to create a book of ideas rather than a compendium of studies. I consistently emphasize concepts and theories over facts, and I focus on major issues and

tough questions that cut across the subfields of psychology (for example, the extent to which behavior is governed by nature, nurture, and their interaction), as opposed to parochial debates (such as the merits of averaging versus adding in impression formation). Challenging students to think also means urging them to confront the complexity and ambiguity of our knowledge. Hence, the text doesn't skirt gray areas, unresolved questions, and theoretical controversies. Instead, readers are encouraged to contemplate open-ended questions, to examine their assumptions about behavior, and to apply psychological concepts to their own lives. My goal is not simply to describe psychology but to stimulate students' intellectual growth.

However, students can grapple with "the big issues and tough questions" only if they first master the basic concepts and principles of psychology—ideally, with as little struggle as possible. In my writing, I never let myself forget that a textbook is a tool for teaching. Accordingly, I have taken great care to ensure that the book's content, organization, writing, illustrations, and pedagogical aids work in harmony to facilitate instruction and learning.

Admittedly, these goals are ambitious. If you're skeptical, you have every right to be. Let me explain how I have tried to realize the objectives I have outlined.

Special Features

This text has a variety of unusual features, each contributing in its own way to the book's paradoxical nature. These special features include unifying themes, Personal Application sections, Critical Thinking Application sections, a didactic illustration program, Web Links, an integrated running glossary, Concept Checks, Key Learning Goals, interim Reviews of Key Learning Goals, and Practice Tests.

Unifying Themes

Chapter 1 introduces seven key ideas that serve as unifying themes throughout the text. The themes serve several purposes. First, they provide threads of continuity across chapters that help students see the connections among various areas of research in psychology. Second, as the themes evolve over the course of the book, they provide a forum for a relatively sophisticated discussion of enduring issues in psychology, thus helping to make this a "book of ideas." Third, the themes focus a spotlight on a number of basic insights about psychology and its subject matter that should leave lasting impressions on your students. In selecting the themes, the question I asked myself (and other professors) was, "What do I really

want students to remember five years from now?" The resulting themes are grouped into two sets.

THEMES RELATED TO PSYCHOLOGY AS A FIELD OF STUDY

Theme 1: Psychology is empirical. This theme is used to enhance the student's appreciation of psychology's scientific nature and to demonstrate the advantages of empiricism over uncritical common sense and speculation. I also use this theme to encourage the reader to adopt a scientist's skeptical attitude and to engage in more critical thinking about information of all kinds.

Theme 2: Psychology is theoretically diverse. Students are often confused by psychology's theoretical pluralism and view it as a weakness. I don't downplay or apologize for our field's theoretical diversity, because I honestly believe that it is one of our greatest strengths. Throughout the book, I provide concrete examples of how clashing theories have stimulated productive research, how converging on a question from several perspectives can yield increased understanding, and how competing theories are sometimes reconciled in the end.

Theme 3: Psychology evolves in a sociohistorical context. This theme emphasizes that psychology is embedded in the ebb and flow of everyday life. The text shows how the spirit of the times has often shaped psychology's evolution and how progress in psychology leaves its mark on our society.

THEMES RELATED TO PSYCHOLOGY'S SUBJECT MATTER

Theme 4: Behavior is determined by multiple causes. Throughout the book, I emphasize, and repeatedly illustrate, that behavioral processes are complex and that multifactorial causation is the rule. This theme is used to discourage simplistic, single-cause thinking and to encourage more critical reasoning.

Theme 5: People's behavior is shaped by their cultural heritage. This theme is intended to enhance students' appreciation of how cultural factors moderate psychological processes and how the viewpoint of one's own culture can distort one's interpretation of the behavior of people from other cultures. The discussions that elaborate on this theme do not simply celebrate diversity. They strike a careful balance—that accurately reflects the research in this area—while highlighting both cultural variations and similarities in behavior.

Theme 6: Heredity and environment jointly influence behavior. Repeatedly discussing this theme permits me to explore the nature versus nurture issue in all its complexity. Over a series of chapters, students gradually learn how biology shapes behavior, how experience shapes behavior, and how scientists estimate the relative importance of each. Along the way, students will gain an in-depth appreciation of what we mean when we say that heredity and environment interact.

Theme 7: Our experience of the world is highly subjective.

All of us tend to forget the extent to which we view the world through our own personal lens. This theme is used to explain the principles that underlie the subjectivity of human experience, to clarify its implications, and to repeatedly remind readers that their view of the world is not the only legitimate view.

After introducing all seven themes in Chapter 1, I discuss different sets of themes in each chapter as they are relevant to the subject matter. The connections between a chapter's content and the unifying themes are highlighted in a standard section near the end of the chapter, in which I reflect on the "lessons to be learned" from the chapter. The discussions of the unifying themes are largely confined to these sections, titled "Reflecting on the Chapter's Themes." I have not tried to make every chapter illustrate a certain number of themes. Rather, the themes were allowed to emerge naturally, and I found that two to five surfaced in any given chapter. The chart below shows which themes are highlighted in each chapter. Color-coded icons near the beginning of each "Reflecting on the Chapter's Themes" section indicate the specific themes featured in each chapter.

Unifying Themes Highlighted in Each Chapter

Chapter	THEME						
	1 Empiricism	2 Theoretical Diversity	3 Sociohistorical Context	4 Multifactorial Causation	5 Cultural Heritage	6 Heredity and Environment	7 Subjectivity of Experience
1. The Evolution of Psychology	●	●	●	●	●	●	●
2. The Research Enterprise in Psychology	●						●
3. The Biological Bases of Behavior	●			●		●	
4. Sensation and Perception		●			●		●
5. Variations in Consciousness		●	●	●	●		●
6. Learning			●			●	
7. Human Memory		●		●			●
8. Cognition and Intelligence	●		●		●	●	●
9. Motivation and Emotion		●	●	●	●	●	
10. Human Development Across the Life Span		●	●	●	●	●	
11. Personality: Theory, Research, and Assessment		●	●		●		
12. Stress, Coping, and Health				●			●
13. Psychological Disorders			●	●	●	●	
14. Treatment of Psychological Disorders		●			●		
15. Social Behavior	●			●	●		●

Personal Applications

To reinforce the pragmatic implications of theory and research stressed throughout the text, each chapter includes a Personal Application section that highlights the practical side of psychology. Each Personal Application devotes two to five *pages* of text (rather than the usual box) to a single issue that should be of special interest to many of your students. Although most of the Personal Application sections have a "how to" character, they continue to review studies and summarize data in much the same way as the main body of each chapter. Thus, they portray research and application not as incompatible polarities but as two sides of the same coin. Many of the Personal Applications—such as those on finding and reading journal articles, understanding art and illusion, and improving stress management—provide topical coverage unusual for an introductory text.

Critical Thinking Applications

A great deal of unusual coverage can also be found in the Critical Thinking Applications that follow the Personal Applications. Conceived by Diane Halpern (Claremont McKenna College), a leading authority on critical thinking, these applications are based on the assumption that critical thinking skills can be taught. They do not simply review research critically, as is typically the case in other introductory texts. Instead, they introduce and model a host of critical thinking skills, such as looking for contradictory evidence or alternative explanations; recognizing anecdotal evidence, circular reasoning, hindsight bias, reification, weak analogies, and false dichotomies; evaluating arguments systematically, and working with cumulative and conjunctive probabilities.

The specific skills discussed in the Critical Thinking Applications are listed in the accompanying table (on the next page), where they are organized into five categories using a taxonomy developed by Halpern (1994). In each chapter, some of these skills are applied to topics and issues related to the chapter's content. For instance, in the chapter that covers drug abuse (Chapter 5), the concept of alcoholism is used to highlight the immense power of definitions and to illustrate how circular reasoning can seem so seductive. Skills that are particularly important may surface in more than one chapter, so students see them applied in a variety of contexts. For example, in Chapter 7 students learn how hindsight bias can contaminate memory and in Chapter 11 they see how hindsight can distort analyses of personality. Repeated practice across chapters should help students spontaneously recognize the relevance of specific critical thinking skills when they encounter certain types of information. The skills approach taken to critical thinking and the content it has spawned are unprecedented for an introductory psychology text.

A Didactic Illustration Program

When I first outlined my plans for this text, I indicated that I wanted every aspect of the illustration program to have a genuine didactic purpose and that I wanted to be deeply involved in its development. In retrospect, I had no idea what I was getting myself into, but it has been a rewarding learning experience. In any event, I have been intimately involved in planning every detail of the illustration program. I have endeavored to create a program of figures, diagrams, photos, and tables that work hand in hand with the prose to strengthen and clarify the main points in the text.

The most obvious results of our didactic approach to illustration are the eight Illustrated Overviews that combine tabular information, photos, diagrams, and sketches to provide exciting overviews of key ideas in the areas of history, methods, sensation and perception, learning, development, personality theory, psychopathology, and psychotherapy. But I hope you will also notice the subtleties of the illustration program. For instance, diagrams of important concepts (conditioning, synaptic transmission, EEGs, experimental design, and so forth) are often repeated in several chapters (with variations) to highlight connections among research areas and to enhance students' mastery of key ideas. Numerous easy-to-understand graphs of research results underscore psychology's foundation in research, and photos and diagrams often bolster each other (for example, see the treatment of classical conditioning in Chapter 6). Color is used carefully as an organizational device, and visual schematics help simplify hard-to-visualize concepts (see, for instance, the figure explaining reaction range for intelligence in Chapter 8). All of these efforts have gone toward the service of one master: the desire to make this an inviting book that is easy to learn from.

Web Links

The Internet is rapidly altering the landscape of modern life, and students clearly need help dealing with the information explosion in cyberspace. To assist them, I recruited web expert Vincent Hevern (Le Moyne College), formerly the Internet Editor for the Society for the Teaching of Psychology, to evaluate hundreds of psychology-related sites on the web and come up with some recommended sites that appear to provide reasonably accurate, balanced, and empirically sound information. Short descriptions of these recommended websites (called Web Links) are dispersed throughout the chapters, adjacent to

Taxonomy of Skills Covered in the Critical Thinking Applications

Verbal Reasoning Skills

Understanding the way definitions shape how people think about issues	Chapter 5
Identifying the source of definitions	Chapter 5
Avoiding the nominal fallacy in working with definitions and labels	Chapter 5
Recognizing and avoiding reification	Chapter 8

Argument/Persuasion Analysis Skills

Understanding the elements of an argument	Chapter 9
Recognizing and avoiding common fallacies, such as irrelevant reasons, circular reasoning, slippery slope reasoning, weak analogies, and false dichotomies	Chapters 9 and 10
Evaluating arguments systematically	Chapter 9
Recognizing and avoiding appeals to ignorance	Chapter 8
Understanding how Pavlovian conditioning can be used to manipulate emotions	Chapter 6
Developing the ability to detect conditioning procedures used in the media	Chapter 6
Recognizing social influence strategies	Chapter 15
Judging the credibility of an information source	Chapter 15

Skills in Thinking as Hypothesis Testing

Looking for alternative explanations for findings and events	Chapters 1, 8, and 10
Looking for contradictory evidence	Chapters 1, 3, and 8
Recognizing the limitations of anecdotal evidence	Chapters 2 and 14
Understanding the need to seek disconfirming evidence	Chapter 7
Understanding the limitations of correlational evidence	Chapters 10 and 12
Understanding the limitations of statistical significance	Chapter 12
Recognizing situations in which placebo effects might occur	Chapter 14

Skills in Working with Likelihood and Uncertainty

Utilizing base rates in making predictions and evaluating probabilities	Chapter 12
Understanding cumulative probabilities	Chapter 13
Understanding conjunctive probabilities	Chapter 13
Understanding the limitations of the representativeness heuristic	Chapter 13
Understanding the limitations of the availability heuristic	Chapter 13
Recognizing situations in which regression toward the mean may occur	Chapter 14
Understanding the limits of extrapolation	Chapter 3

Decision-Making and Problem-Solving Skills

Using evidence-based decision making	Chapter 2
Recognizing the bias in hindsight analysis	Chapters 7 and 11
Seeking information to reduce uncertainty	Chapter 12
Making risk-benefit assessments	Chapter 12
Generating and evaluating alternative courses of action	Chapter 12
Recognizing overconfidence in human cognition	Chapter 7
Understanding the limitations and fallibility of human memory	Chapter 7
Understanding how contrast effects can influence judgments and decisions	Chapter 4
Recognizing when extreme comparitors are being used	Chapter 4

related topical coverage. Because URLs change frequently, we have not placed the URLs for these Web Links in the book itself. Insofar as students are interested in visiting these sites, we recommend that they do so through the *Psychology: Themes & Variations, Briefer Version* home page at the Wadsworth/Cengage Learning website (www.cengage.com/psychology/weiten). Links to all the recommended sites are maintained there, and the webmaster periodically updates the URLs. Of course, students can also use a search engine, such as Google, to locate recommended websites that interest them.

Integrated Running Glossary

An introductory text should place great emphasis on acquainting students with psychology's technical language—not for the sake of jargon, but because a great many of our key terms are also our cornerstone concepts (for example, *independent variable, reliability, and cognitive dissonance*). This text handles terminology with a running glossary embedded in the prose itself. The terms are set off in **blue boldface italics**, and the definitions follow in **blue, boldface roman type**. This approach retains the two advantages of a conventional running glossary: vocabulary items are made salient, and their definitions are readily accessible. However, it does so without interrupting the flow of discourse, while eliminating redundancy between text matter and marginal entries.

Concept Checks

To help students assess their mastery of important ideas, Concept Checks are sprinkled throughout the book. In keeping with my goal of making this a book of ideas, the Concept Checks challenge students to apply ideas instead of testing rote memory. For example, in Chapter 6 the reader is asked to analyze realistic examples of conditioning and identify conditioned stimuli and responses, reinforcers, and schedules of reinforcement. Many of the Concept Checks require the reader to put together ideas introduced in different sections of the chapter. For instance, in Chapter 4 students are asked to identify parallels between vision and hearing. Some of the Concept Checks are quite challenging, but students find them engaging, and they report that the answers (available in Appendix A in the back of the book) are often illuminating.

Key Learning Goals and Reviews of Key Learning Goals

To help students organize, assimilate, and remember important ideas, each major section of every chapter begins with a succinct, numbered set of Key Learning Goals and ends with a detailed, numbered Review of Key Learning Goals. The Key Learning Goals are found adjacent to the level-one headings that begin each major section; the Reviews of Key Learning Goals are found at the end of each major section, just before the next level-one heading. The Key Learning Goals are thought-provoking learning objectives that should help students focus on the key issues in each section. Each Review of Key Learning Goals is an interim summary that addresses the issues posed in the preceding Learning Goals. Interspersing these reviews throughout the chapters permits students to check their understanding of each section's main ideas immediately after finishing the section instead of waiting until the end of the chapter. This approach also allows students to work with more modest-sized chunks of information.

Practice Tests

Each chapter ends with a 12-item multiple-choice Practice Test that should give students a realistic assessment of their mastery of that chapter and valuable practice taking the type of test that many of them will face in the classroom (if the instructor uses the Test Bank). This feature grew out of some research that I conducted on students' use of textbook pedagogical devices (see Weiten, Guadagno, & Beck, 1996). This research indicated that students pay scant attention to some standard pedagogical devices. When I grilled my students to gain a better understanding of this finding, it quickly became apparent that students are very pragmatic about pedagogy. Essentially, their refrain was "We want study aids that will help us pass the next test." With this mandate in mind, I devised the Practice Tests. They should be useful, as I took most of the items from Test Banks for previous editions.

In addition to the special features just described, the text includes a variety of more conventional, "tried and true" features as well. The back of the book contains a standard *alphabetical glossary*. Opening *outlines* preview each chapter, and a *chapter recap* appears at the end of each chapter. I make frequent use of *italics for emphasis,* and I depend on *frequent headings* to maximize organizational clarity. The preface for students describes these pedagogical devices in more detail.

Content

The text is divided into 15 chapters, which follow a traditional ordering. The chapters are not grouped into sections or parts, primarily because such groupings can limit your options if you want to reorganize the order of topics. The chapters are written in a way that facilitates organizational flexibility, as I always assume that some chapters might be omitted or presented in a different order.

The topical coverage in the text is relatively conventional, but there are some subtle departures from the norm. For instance, Chapter 1 presents a relatively "meaty" discussion of the evolution of ideas in psychology. This coverage of history lays the foundation for many of the crucial ideas emphasized in subsequent chapters. The historical perspective is also my way of reaching out to the students who find that psychology isn't what they expected it to be. If we want students to contemplate the mysteries of behavior, we must begin by clearing up the biggest mysteries of them all: "Where did these rats, statistics, synapses, and genes come from, what could they possibly have in common, and why doesn't this course bear any resemblance to what I anticipated?" I use history as a vehicle to explain how psychology evolved into its modern form and why misconceptions about its nature are so common.

I also devote an entire chapter (Chapter 2) to the scientific enterprise—not just the mechanics of research methods but the logic behind them. I believe that an appreciation of the nature of empirical evidence can contribute greatly to improving students' critical thinking skills. Ten years from now, many of the "facts" reported in this book will have changed, but an understanding of the methods of science will remain invaluable. An introductory psychology course, by itself, isn't going to make a student think like a scientist, but I can't think of a better place to start the process.

As its title indicates, this book is a condensed version of my introductory text, *Psychology: Themes and Variations*. I have reduced the word count of this book to 70% of the word count of the full-length version. How was this reduction in size accomplished? It required a great many difficult decisions, but fortunately, I had excellent advice from a team of professors who served as consultants. About 40% of the reduction came from deleting entire topics, such as psychophysics, mental retardation, blocking in classical conditioning, and so forth. However, the bulk of the reduction was achieved by compressing and simplifying coverage throughout the book. I carefully scrutinized the parent book sentence by sentence and forced myself to justify the existence of every study, every example, every citation, every phrase. The result is a thoroughly *rewritten* text, rather than one that was *reassembled* through "cut and paste" techniques.

Changes in the Eighth Edition

A good textbook must evolve with the field of inquiry it covers. Although the professors and students who used the first seven editions of this book did not clamor for alterations, there are some changes. Perhaps the most noticeable is the replacement of the Preview Questions from previous editions with the numbered Key Learning Goals. The new learning goals are more precise and more thorough than the Preview Questions, which functioned more like "teasers" than learning objectives. Moreover, numbering both the Key Learning Goals and the material in the Review of Key Learning Goals makes it easier for students to see the relation between these companion features. The greater precision in this framework also led me to make the Reviews of Key Learning Goals longer and more detailed than interim reviews usually are.

You will also find a variety of other changes in this edition, such as three new Illustrated Overviews (in Chapters 2, 4, and 10) that were not in the previous edition and two new chapter introductions (in Chapters 2 and 11). The graphic design of the text has been improved in a variety of ways. For instance the level-one headings have been reworked in a refreshing way. We have also revised our thematic and *PsykTrek* icons and our treatment of theorist photos in the margins. And we have strived to make the photo program more engaging.

Another major change is the addition of 15 new Concept Checks that focus on the chief contributions and ideas of major theorists and researchers in the field. These Concept Checks now appear near the end of the main body of each chapter. They challenge students to match major theorists' names with their key innovations or accomplishments. These Concept Checks essentially replace the list of "key people" formerly found in the chapter recap at the end of the chapter. This feature will enable students to quickly and conveniently review "who did what" in a way that should be far superior to the old list of names.

We have also added two new appendixes. The first of these is a discussion of careers in psychology (Appendix C). I have come to the conclusion that this is an overlooked topic that we should try to address in introductory courses. This appendix also provides brief profiles of the various areas in psychology. Students can read about nine major research areas in psychology, as well as six applied specialties. The second new appendix focuses on the timely issue of sustainability (Appendix D). It explains how sustainability depends on changes in individuals' behavior more than any other single factor. It focuses on the cognitive and behavioral processes that tend to impede environmentally responsible behavior, as well as the alterations in behavior that will be necessary to sustain the world's natural resources for future generations.

Since the publication of the previous edition we have released a completely revised version of *Psyk-Trek*, the multimedia learning tool designed to help students master the key concepts covered in introductory psychology. I will discuss the new *PsykTrek* momentarily, but let me first note a change in the book related to *PsykTrek*. In this edition we have strived to improve the integration of the text with *PsykTrek*. To that end, we have added a preview of relevant *PsykTrek* content at the end of each chapter. Each preview shows four screenshots accompanied by brief captions intended to entice students into exploring the visually rich, highly interactive domain of *PsykTrek*. These previews are intended to give students concrete illustrations of how using *PsykTrek* can increase their understanding of important concepts and provide enjoyable opportunities for active learning.

Of course, the book has been thoroughly updated to reflect recent advances in the field. One of the exciting things about psychology is that it is not a stagnant discipline. It continues to move forward at what seems a faster and faster pace. This progress has necessitated a host of specific content changes that you'll find sprinkled throughout the chapters. Of the roughly 3600 references cited in the text, just under 1000 are new to this edition. Following is a partial list of specific changes in each chapter of the eighth edition.

Chapter 1: The Evolution of Psychology

• Elaborated coverage of William James's ideas and contributions
• Discussion of Pavlov's discovery of classical conditioning integrated into coverage of Watson and the emergence of behaviorism
• New data on rankings of the most important contributors to psychology
• New data on the popularity of the psychology major
• Revised coverage of areas of specialization in psychology featuring several areas not mentioned previously, including health psychology, clinical neuropsychology, and forensic psychology
• Expanded discussion of the concept of culture
• New discussion in the Application of how effective text marking can enhance students' reading
• Additional advice on improving note taking in lectures

Chapter 2: The Research Enterprise in Psychology

• New introduction to the chapter focusing on more engaging empirical questions about behavior
• Greatly expanded coverage of the peer-review process for journal submissions

• In coverage of naturalistic observation, new emphasis on its importance to studies of animal behavior and new discussion of reactivity
• New discussion of the recent decline in response rates to surveys
• New example of placebo effects in studies of the effects of alcohol
• New Illustrated Overview comparing major research methods in psychology
• Added section on how research is increasingly conducted via the Internet
• New discussion of the advantages and disadvantages of Internet-mediated research
• In Application on library research, elaboration on the nature of technical journals and mention of the phase-out of *Psychological Abstracts*

Chapter 3: The Biological Bases of Behavior

• Expanded coverage of glial cells' functions and significance
• Added discussion of acetylcholine depletion in Alzheimer's disease
• Added coverage of dopamine pathways' role in the experience of reward and addiction
• New coverage of the role of GABA and glutamate in behavioral processes
• Expanded and revised table summarizing various neurotransmitters' functions and characteristics
• New coverage of the discovery of mirror neurons and their possible significance
• More elaborated discussion of the plasticity of the brain and neurogenesis
• New discussion of fMRI research on hemispheric specialization
• New research on how elevated stress hormones undermine immune response and neurogenesis in the hippocampus
• New coverage of variations in testosterone levels and individual differences in aggression
• New coverage of testosterone levels as related to cognitive functioning

Chapter 4: Sensation and Perception

• New discussion of recent research related to the concept of a "grandmother cell"
• New findings on how "face-detector" neurons can learn from experience
• Expanded discussion of inattentional blindness and its practical implications
• New discussion of how perception of forms can be influenced by motivational forces
• Added coverage of how judgments of distance can be skewed by people's goals and physical states
• New discussion of how supertasters and nontasters exhibit different consumption habits that affect their health
• Reports new research on the effects of subliminal odors on behavior

- Six new figures
- New Illustrated Overview comparing the five major senses

Chapter 5: Variations in Consciousness

- New data quantifying how often people's minds wander from the task at hand
- New discussion of the 17-year cycle in cicadas as an example of an extremely influential and unusual biological rhythm
- Coverage of new findings on individual differences in sleep architecture
- New discussion of sleep loss as related to physical health
- New research suggesting a curvilinear relationship between typical sleep duration and mortality
- Revised coverage of the treatment of insomnia
- Expanded discussion of sleep apnea
- Expanded discussion of sleepwalking
- New discussion of Kihlstrom's reconciliation of the role-playing and altered state views of hypnosis
- New coverage of the OxyContin epidemic
- Coverage of new research linking cannabis use to vulnerability to psychotic disorders
- New emphasis on additional text theme (multifactorial causation)

Chapter 6: Learning

- Revised take on the degree to which a conditioned response tends to be similar to the unconditioned response that it is based on
- New discussion of why fear conditioning is not automatic in the wake of traumatic conditioning experiences
- New discussion of the renewal effect and its contribution to the difficulty inherent in extinguishing conditioned fears
- New discussion questioning the value of the distinction between positive and negative reinforcement
- Reinstated section on preparedness and phobias
- New discussion of Öhman & Mineka's concept of an evolved module for fear learning
- Expanded discussion of the effects of violent video games and why they may be more problematic than violent movies or TV shows
- New data on the strength of the association between exposure to media violence and aggression

Chapter 7: Human Memory

- Expanded discussion of the costs of divided attention in relation to the controversy about cell phones and driving performance
- New discussion of Cowan's view that short-term memory capacity may only be four plus or minus one
- Expanded coverage of individual differences in working memory capacity
- Updated analysis of whether flashbulb memories are special
- New research on how the goal-directed retelling of stories introduces errors into memory

- New discussion of how forgetting can be adaptive, including recent brain-imaging research on the issue
- Updated discussion of recovered memories, including studies using doctored photos to create false memories
- New discussion of long-term potentiation as a physiological basis for memory
- New research on how neurogenesis may contribute to sculpting neural circuits that underlie memories
- New research on the testing effect, the finding that testing on material enhances retention
- New data on the effects of spaced practice as a function of retention interval

Chapter 8: Cognition and Intelligence

- New analysis of the difficulties inherent in problems requiring insight
- New coverage of the hill-climbing heuristic in problem solving
- Recent research on the extent to which people depend on analogies in everyday problem-solving efforts
- Added discussion of the theory that people in modern society are overwhelmed by decision overload
- Added coverage of loss aversion in decision making
- Coverage of new findings reporting strong relationship between intelligence and educational achievement
- New research on the association between students' self-discipline and academic performance
- New findings on the modest relationship between IQ and income
- New meta-analytic findings on IQ increments following adoption
- Coverage of new data on narrowing of cultural disparities in IQ scores
- New data on the relationship between creativity and intelligence

Chapter 9: Motivation and Emotion

- New discussion of the role of the arcuate nucleus of the hypothalamus in the regulation of hunger
- Revised coverage of neurotransmitters and hunger with new discussion of the importance of ghrelin
- Revised discussion of hormonal regulation of hunger incorporating findings on ghrelin and CCK
- New findings relating to gender differences in orgasmic consistency
- New cross-cultural data on gender disparities in mating priorities and preferences
- Coverage of new research on the degree to which males and females pay attention to potential partners' willingness to invest in children
- New data supporting the idea that sexual orientation should be viewed as a continuum
- New findings on cultural disparities in the experience of socially engaging versus disengaging emotions
- New discussion of the modest association between actual wealth and subjective perceptions of finances, and other new research on income and happiness

- New coverage of the heritability of subjective well-being
- New discussion of Gilbert's work on how people are surprisingly bad at predicting what will make them happy

Chapter 10: Human Development Across the Life Span

- Expanded coverage of the effects of normal drinking during pregnancy on subsequent development
- New discussion of the stability of individual differences in patterns of attachment
- New three-part section on language development
- New discussion of the constricted focus of Kohlberg's theory
- New take on generational decreases in the age of onset of puberty
- New discussion of adolescent risk taking in relation to susceptibility to peer influence
- Condensed coverage of identity development in adolescence
- New discussion of emerging adulthood as a distinct stage of development
- Expanded discussion of Roberts' work on personality trends in the adult years
- Revised discussion of male menopause
- Expanded coverage of age trends in intelligence to include the distinction between fluid and crystallized intelligence
- New discussion of the "use it or lose it hypothesis" as related to aging and cognitive decline
- Reinstated four-page Illustrated Overview of human development

Chapter 11: Personality: Theory, Research, and Assessment

- New introduction to the chapter focusing on the fascinating life of Richard Branson
- New discussion of how the Big Five traits are predictive of important life outcomes, such as occupational attainment and mortality
- Expanded discussion of the relationship between self-efficacy and specific aspects of behavior
- Expanded critique of behavioral theories to include new discussion of the dilution of the behavioral approach
- New discussion of Nettle's evolutionary analysis of the adaptive implications of the Big Five traits
- New research on cross-cultural variations in scores on the Big Five traits
- New research on the inaccuracy of national character stereotypes
- New section on personality testing over the Internet
- New explanation of how hindsight bias distorts thinking

Chapter 12: Stress, Coping, and Health

- New discussion of how pressure is often self-imposed
- New coverage of Fredrickson's broaden-and-build theory of positive emotions
- New findings on the effects of positive emotions on mental and physical health
- Profile of recent study linking positive emotional style to enhanced immune response

- New discussion of how stress can suppress the process of neurogenesis in the hippocampus
- New research on the adaptive value of giving up the pursuit of unattainable goals
- New findings indicating that resilience in the face of traumatic stress is not as rare as assumed
- Discussion of new findings on how transient mental stress can trigger inflammatory responses
- New coverage of how stress can lead to immune system dysregulation that promotes chronic inflammation
- New research on the relationship between social support and reduced mortality
- New discussion of the relationship between conscientiousness and longevity
- New research on how exercise can reduce chronic inflammation and promote neurogenesis
- New study of how often HIV-positive individuals are unaware of their HIV status

Chapter 13: Psychological Disorders

- New discussion of the process to develop DSM-V
- Added discussion of how normality and abnormality exist on a continuum
- New discussion of anxiety sensitivity as an etiological factor in anxiety disorders
- New information on the prevalence of PTSD and concerns about PTSD in veterans of the Iraq war
- New discussion of Öhman & Mineka's notion of an evolved module for fear learning in relation to the acquisition of phobias
- Revised estimates of the prevalence of depressive disorders
- Expanded discussion of gender differences in depression
- New section on the association between mood disorders and suicide
- New figure presenting advice on suicide prevention
- Revised discussion of the course and outcome of schizophrenic disorders
- New data linking marijuana use to increased vulnerability to schizophrenia
- New emphasis on how dangerous and debilitating eating disorders are
- Updated coverage of the prevalence of eating disorders among college students and males

Chapter 14: Treatment of Psychological Disorders

- New findings on the efficacy of psychodynamic therapies
- Added section on innovative insight therapies inspired by the positive psychology movement
- New discussion of the cost effectiveness of atypical antipsychotics in comparison to conventional antipsychotics
- Discussion of how antidepressant medications are not as effective for bipolar patients (in comparison to patients with unipolar depression)
- New coverage of serotonin-norepinephrine reuptake inhibitors
- Updated coverage of whether antidepressants elevate suicide risk in adolescents

- Added coverage of transcranial magnetic stimulation as a psychiatric treatment
- New coverage of direct brain stimulation as a psychiatric treatment
- New discussion on the impact of poverty on psychotherapy
- New information on the importance of a strong therapeutic alliance and the value of adapting treatments for ethnic minority clients

Chapter 15: Social Behavior

- New findings on how perceptions of facial appearance predict election results
- New research on how social perceptions based on facial features are formed in the blink of an eye
- New study of how familiarity with a situation reduces observers' tendency to make the fundamental attribution error
- New research on culture and attributional tendencies
- New brain-imaging research suggesting that passionate love activates the same dopamine circuits activated by addictive drugs
- Expanded discussion of attachment style and patterns of sexual interaction
- New coverage of how the Internet can contribute to the development of close relationships
- New discussion of the differences between online and face-to-face relationships
- Coverage of new evolutionary research on women's mating preferences
- New evolutionary research relating women's menstrual cycles to their mate preferences and men's reactions to these changes
- Discussion of new research using Milgram's obedience paradigm
- New findings on moderators of the social loafing effect

Concept Charts for Study and Review

To help your students organize and assimilate the main ideas contained in the text, I have created a unique supplement—a booklet of Concept Charts. This booklet contains a two-page Concept Chart for each chapter. Each Concept Chart provides a detailed visual map of the key ideas found in the main body of that chapter. These color-coded, hierarchically organized charts create snapshots of the chapters that should allow your students to quickly see the relationships among ideas and sections.

PsykTrek: A Multimedia Introduction to Psychology

PsykTrek is a multimedia supplement that will provide students with new opportunities for active learning and reach out to "visual learners" with greatly increased efficacy. *PsykTrek* is intended to give students a second pathway to learning much of the content of introductory psychology. Although it does not cover all of the content of the introductory course, I think you will see that a great many key concepts and principles can be explicated *more effectively* in an interactive audiovisual medium than in a textbook.

PsykTrek consists of four components. The main component is a set of 65 *Interactive Learning Modules* that present the core content of psychology in a whole new way. These tutorials include thousands of graphics, hundred of photos, hundreds of animations, approximately four hours of narration, 40 carefully selected videos, and about 160 uniquely visual concept checks and quizzes. The ten *Simulations* allow students to explore complex psychological phenomena in depth. They are highly interactive, experiential demonstrations that will enhance students' appreciation of research methods. The *Multimedia Glossary* allows students to look up over 800 psychological terms, access hundreds of pronunciations of obscure words, and pull up hundreds of related diagrams, photos, and videos. The *Video Selector* permits students (or faculty) to directly access the video segments that are otherwise embedded in the Interactive Learning Modules.

The key strength of *PsykTrek* is its ability to give students new opportunities for active learning outside of the classroom. For example, students can run themselves through re-creations of classic experiments to see the complexities of data collection in action. Or they can play with visual illusions on screen in ways that will make them doubt their own eyes. Or they can stack color filters on screen to demonstrate the nature of subtractive color mixing. *PsykTrek* is intended to supplement and complement *Psychology: Themes & Variations*. For instance, after reading about operant conditioning in the text, a student could work through three interactive tutorials on operant principles, watch four videos (including historic footage of B. F. Skinner shaping a rat), and then try to shape Morphy, the virtual rat, in one of the simulations.

This edition of the text is accompanied by a brand new version (3.0) of *PsykTrek*. The new version has been re-created from the bottom up. It has a more modern look and has been designed to run more effectively on today's personal computers. Moreover, for the first time, *PsykTrek* is available in an online format that can make student access easier than ever. *PsykTrek* 3.0 includes three new Interactive Learning Modules: Attachment, Forgetting, and Conformity and Obedience. All of the modules now include a multiple-choice test, as well as an interactive quiz. We have also incorporated unit-level multiple-choice exams to permit students to better assess their mastery of content. And each unit includes a critical thinking exercise, written by Jeffry Ricker (Scottsdale Community College). Finally, the new version of PsykTrek contains additional videos, including historically noteworthy segments showing B. F. Skinner's shaping of pigeons to play Ping-Pong, Albert Bandura's Bobo doll study, and Stanley Milgram's legendary study of obedience.

Other Supplementary Materials

The teaching/learning package that has been developed to supplement *Psychology: Themes and Variations, Briefer Version* also includes many other useful tools. The development of all its parts was carefully coordinated so that they are mutually supported.

Study Guide (by Richard Stalling and Ronald Wasden)

For your students, there is an exceptionally thorough *Study Guide* available to help them master the information in the text. It was written by two of my former professors, Richard Stalling and Ronald Wasden of Bradley University. They have over 40 years of experience as a team writing study guides for introductory psychology texts, and their experience is readily apparent in the high-quality materials that they have developed.

The review of key ideas for each chapter is made up of an engaging mixture of matching exercises, fill-in-the-blank items, free-response questions, and programmed learning. Each review is organized around the Key Learning Goals. The *Study Guide* is closely coordinated with the *Test Bank,* as the same Key Learning Goals guided the construction of the questions in the *Test Bank.* The *Study Guide* also includes a review of key terms, a review of key people, and a self-test for each chapter in the text.

Instructor's Resource Manual (coordinated by Randolph A. Smith and Benjamin R. Smith)

A talented roster of professors have contributed to the *Instructor's Resource Manual (IRM)* in their respective areas of expertise. The *IRM* was developed under the guidance of Randolph Smith, the former editor of the journal *Teaching of Psychology,* and Benjamin R. Smith. It contains a diverse array of materials designed to facilitate efforts to teach the introductory course and includes the following sections.

• The *Instructor's Manual,* by Randolph A. Smith (Lamar University) and Benjamin R. Smith, contains a wealth of detailed suggestions for lecture topics, class demonstrations, exercises, discussion questions, and suggested readings, organized around the content of each chapter in the text. It also highlights the connections between the text coverage and *Psyk-Trek* content and features an expanded collection of masters for class handouts.

• *Strategies for Effective Teaching,* by Joseph Lowman (University of North Carolina), discusses practical issues such as what to put in a course syllabus, how to handle the first class meeting, how to cope with large classes, and how to train and organize teaching assistants.

• *AV Media for Introductory Psychology,* by Russ Watson (College of DuPage), provides a comprehensive, up-to-date, critical overview of educational films relevant to the introductory course.

• *The Use of Computers in Teaching Introductory Psychology,* by Susan J. Shapiro (Indiana University–East), offers a thorough listing of computer materials germane to the introductory course and analyzes their strengths and weaknesses.

• *Introducing Writing in Introductory Psychology,* by Dana Dunn (Moravian College), discusses how to work toward enhancing students' writing skills in the context of the introductory course and provides suggestions and materials for specific writing assignments chapter by chapter.

• *Crossing Borders/Contrasting Behaviors: Using Cross-Cultural Comparisons to Enrich the Introductory Psychology Course,* by Ginny Zahn, Bill Hill, and Michael Reiner (Kennesaw State University), discusses the movement toward "internationalizing" the curriculum and provides suggestions for lectures, exercises, and assignments that can add a cross-cultural flavor to the introductory course.

• *Teaching Introductory Psychology with the World Wide Web,* by Michael R. Snyder (University of Alberta), discusses how to work Internet assignments into the introductory course and provides a guide to many psychology-related sites on the World Wide Web.

• *Using InfoTrac in Introductory Psychology,* by Randolph Smith, discusses how to make effective use of the *InfoTrac* subscription that is made available to students with this text. *InfoTrac College Edition* is an online database of recent full-text articles from hundreds of scholarly and popular periodicals.

Test Bank (by Joseph Morrissey, Christopher J. Barnum, & Kelly Dickerson)

Joseph Morrisey, Christopher J. Barnum, and Kelly Dickerson (all from SUNY-Binghamton) have assembled a large, diversified, and carefully constructed *Test Bank* to accompany this text. The questions are closely tied to the Key Learning Goals found in both the text and the *Study Guide*. The items are categorized as (a) factual, (b) conceptual/applied, (c) integrative, or (d) critical thinking questions. The test bank also includes a separate section that contains about 600 multiple-choice questions based on the content of *PsykTrek's* Interactive Learning Modules. Data on item difficulty are included for many questions. Electronic versions of the *Test Bank* are available for a variety of computer configurations. The *ExamView* software is user-friendly and allows teachers to insert their own questions and to customize those provided.

PowerLecture with JoinIn™ and ExamView®

This one-stop lecture and class preparation tool makes it easy for you to assemble, edit, and present customized, media-enhanced lectures for your course using Microsoft® PowerPoint®. It includes chapter-specific lecture outlines and art from the text on PowerPoint slides as well as video clips and other integrated media. It also contains the Instructor's Resource Manual and Test Bank in Microsoft® Word format; ExamView®, which lets you create, deliver, and customize tests (both print and online) in minutes using all questions from the Test Bank in electronic format; and JoinIn™ content, which allows you to pose book-specific questions and display students' answers seamlessly within the PowerPoint slides of your lecture, in conjunction with the clicker hardware and student response system software of your choice.

Challenging Your Preconceptions: Thinking Critically About Psychology, Second Edition (by Randolph A. Smith)

This brief paperback book is a wonderful introduction to critical thinking as it applies to psychological issues. Written by Randolph Smith (Lamar University), this book helps students apply their critical thinking skills to a variety of topics, including hypnosis, advertising, misleading statistics, IQ testing, gender differences, and memory bias. Each chapter ends with critical thinking challenges that give students opportunities to practice their critical thinking skills.

Using YouTube in Psychology (by Jeremy A. Houska)

An entirely new ancillary, available on eBank, has been developed to help instructors make use of the ever-growing collection of psychology-related videos available online at the popular YouTube website. As is often the case with my books, this new idea emerged from my classroom experience. Each year I teach a seminar for graduate students in psychology who are teaching for the first time. Among other things, the seminar requires each graduate student to develop extensive teaching materials for a specific topic in the field, including audio-visual materials that they think would be worthwhile for classroom use. About three years ago, I noticed an unexpected trend, as the students started incorporating more and more videos from YouTube in their recommended audio-visual materials. I was surprised to learn that YouTube contains an amazing diversity of videos that can be relevant to a host of psychological topics. These include educational videos posted by psychology teachers, interviews with prominent psychologists, TV clips profiling recent research, historically important footage from classic studies, and all sorts of creative, sometimes wacky, videos that can be used to stimulate discussion of an endless variety of topics.

After developing a new appreciation for the treasure trove of valuable videos available via YouTube, I recruited one of my graduate students to compile a catalog of videos that would be potentially useful to introductory psychology instructors. Jeremy A. Houska (University of Nevada, Las Vegas) has done an outstanding job in researching and creating this compilation. It is organized by chapter, and by specific topics within each chapter. Each entry identifies the video's title, posting, length, and URL. This information is followed by a list of psychological concepts covered, a brief description of the video, and suggestions for discussion questions. I think many instructors will be surprised by the educational potential of YouTube (I know I was).

ACKNOWLEDGMENTS

Creating an introductory psychology text is a complicated challenge, and a small army of people have contributed to the evolution of this book. Foremost among them are the psychology editors I have worked with—Claire Verduin, C. Deborah Laughton, Phil Curson, Eileen Murphy, Edith Beard Brady, Michele Sordi, and Jon-David Hague—and the developmental editor for the first edition of this book, John Bergez. They have helped me immeasurably, and each has become a treasured friend along the way. I am especially indebted to Claire, who educated me in the intricacies of textbook publishing, and to John, who has left an enduring imprint on my writing. I am dedicating this edition to Claire, who passed away in 2008. "Mother Publisher" was a legend in the field of textbooks and I will always cherish her memory.

The challenge of meeting a difficult schedule in producing this book was undertaken by a talented team of people coordinated by Joan Keyes, who did a superb job of pulling it all together. Credit for the text design goes to tani hasegawa, who was very creative in building on the previous design. Linda Rill handled permissions and photo research with enthusiasm and extraordinary efficiency, and Jackie Estrada did an outstanding job once again in copyediting the manuscript. Fred Harwin and Carol Zuber-Mallison made stellar contributions to the artwork, and the team at Thompson Type efficiently oversaw the composition process.

A number of psychologists deserve thanks for the contributions they made to this book. I am grateful to Diane Halpern for her work on the Critical Thinking Applications; to Vinny Hevern for contributing the original Web Links; to Marky Lloyd for writing the appendix on careers in psychology; to Susan Koger and Britain Scott for crafting a compelling appendix on sustainability; to Rick Stalling and Ron Wasden for their work on the *Study Guide;* to Bill Addison and Shirley Hensch for their work on the previous editions of the *Test Bank;* to Randy Smith, Ben Smith, Joseph Lowman, Russ Watson, Dana Dunn, Ginny Zahn, Bill Hill, Michael Reiner, Susan Shapiro, and Michael Snyder for their contributions to the *Instructor's Resource Manual;* to Jeffry Ricker for devising *PsykTrek's* critical thinking exercises; to Randy Smith, David Matsumoto, and Jeremy Houska for contributing ancillary books; to Jim Calhoun for providing item analysis data for the test items; to Harry Upshaw, Larry Wrightsman, Shari Diamond, Rick Stalling, and Claire Etaugh for their help and guidance over the years; and to the chapter consultants listed on page xxi and the reviewers listed on page xxii, who provided insightful and constructive critiques of various portions of the manuscript.

Many other people have also contributed to this project, and I am grateful to all of them for their efforts. Bill Roberts, Tom Dorsaneo, Nancy Sjoberg, John Odam, Fiorella Ljunggren, Jim Brace-Thompson, Susan Badger, Sean Wakely, Eve Howard, and Margaret Parks helped with varied aspects of previous editions. At Wadsworth, Michelle Julet, Linda Schreiber, Vernon Boes, Pat Waldo, Kristin Makarewycz, Kim Russell, Liz Rhoden, Lauren Keyes, Trina Tom, and Kelly Miller made valuable contributions to the current edition. At the College of DuPage, where I taught until 1991, all of my colleagues in psychology provided support and information at one time or another, but I am especially indebted to Barb Lemme, Alan Lanning, Pat Puccio, and Don Green. I also want to thank my former colleagues at Santa Clara University (especially Tracey Kahan, Tom Plante, and Jerry Burger), and my current colleagues at UNLV who have been fertile sources of new ideas. And I am indebted to the many graduate students that I have worked with at UNLV, and to Neda Raymond who helped complete the reference entries.

My greatest debt is to my wife, Beth Traylor, who has been a steady source of emotional sustenance while enduring the rigors of her medical career, and to my son T. J., for making dad laugh all the time.

Wayne Weiten

CHAPTER CONSULTANTS

Chapter 1
David Baker
University of Akron
Charles L. Brewer
Furman University
C. James Goodwin
Wheeling Jesuit University
David Hothersall
Ohio State University
E. R. Hilgard
Stanford University
Michael G. Livingston
St. John's University

Chapter 2
Larry Christensen
Texas A & M University
Francis Durso
University of Oklahoma
Donald H. McBurney
University of Pittsburgh
Wendy Schweigert
Bradley University

Chapter 3
Nelson Freedman
Queen's University at Kingston
Michael W. Levine
University of Illinois, Chicago
Corinne L. McNamara
Kennesaw State University
James M. Murphy
Indiana University–Purdue University at Indianapolis
Paul Wellman
Texas A & M University

Chapter 4
Stephen Blessing
University of Tampa
Nelson Freedman
Queen's University at Kingston
Kevin Jordan
San Jose State University
Michael W. Levine
University of Illinois, Chicago
John Pittenger
University of Arkansas, Little Rock

Lawrence Ward
University of British Columbia
Chrislyn E. Randell
Metropolitan State College of Denver

Chapter 5
Frank Etscorn
New Mexico Institute of Mining and Technology
Tracey L. Kahan
Santa Clara University
Charles F. Levinthal
Hofstra University
Wilse Webb
University of Florida

Chapter 6
A. Charles Catania
University of Maryland
Michael Domjan
University of Texas, Austin
William C. Gordon
University of New Mexico
Russell A. Powell
Grant MacEwan College
Barry Schwartz
Swarthmore College
Deborah L. Stote
University of Texas, Austin

Chapter 7
Tracey L. Kahan
Santa Clara University
Ian Neath
Purdue University
Tom Pusateri
Loras College
Stephen K. Reed
San Diego State University
Patricia Tenpenny
Loyola University, Chicago

Chapter 8
John Best
Eastern Illinois University
David Carroll
University of Wisconsin, Superior

Charles Davidshofer
Colorado State University
Shalynn Ford
Teikyo Marycrest University
Richrd J. Haier
University of California, Irvine
Tom Pusateri
Loras College
Stephen K. Reed
San Diego State University
Timothy Rogers
University of Calgary
Dennis Saccuzzo
San Diego State University

Chapter 9
Robert Franken
University of Calgary
Russell G. Geen
University of Missouri
Douglas Mook
University of Virginia
D. Louis Wood
University of Arkansas, Little Rock

Chapter 10
Ruth L. Ault
Davidson College
John C. Cavanaugh
University of Delaware
Claire Etaugh
Bradley University
Doug Friedrich
University of West Florida
Barbara Hansen Lemme
College of DuPage

Chapter 11
Susan Cloninger
Russel Sage College
Caroline Collins
University of Victoria
Howard S. Friedman
University of California, Riverside
Christopher F. Monte
Manhattanville College

Ken Olson
Fort Hays State University

Chapter 12
Robin M. DiMatteo
University of California, Riverside
Jess Feist
McNeese State University
Regan A. R. Gurung
University of Wisconsin, Green Bay
Chris Kleinke
University of Alaska, Anchorage

Chapter 13
David A. F. Haaga
American University
Richard Halgin
University of Massachusetts, Amherst
Chris L. Kleinke
University of Alaska, Anchorage
Elliot A. Weiner
Pacific University

Chapter 14
Gerald Corey
California State University, Fullerton
Herbert Goldenberg
California State University, Los Angeles
Jane S. Halonen
Alverno College
Thomas G. Plante
Santa Clara University

Chapter 15
Jerry M. Burger
Santa Clara University
Stephen L. Franzoi
Marquette University
Donelson R. Forsyth
Virginia Commonwealth University
Cheryl Kaiser
Michigan State University

Reviewers for Briefer Version

Marcelle Bartolo Abela
Southern New Hampshire University

Elizabeth S. Athens
Kennesaw State University

Bart Bare
Caldwell Community College

Mitchell Berman
University of Southern Mississippi

Chris A. Bjornsen
Longwood University

Charles B. Blose
MacMurray College

Frederick Bonato
Saint Peter's College

Edward Brady
Belleville Area College

Kate Byerwalter
Grand Rapids Community College

James F. Calhoun
University of Georgia

Cheryl Camenzuli
Hofstra University

Elaine Cassel
Lord Fairfax Community College

Heather Chabot
New England College

Monica Chakravertti
Mary Washington College

Jennifer Clark
University of North Carolina

Elizabeth Coccia
Austin Community College

Thomas Collins
Mankato State University

Luis Cordon
Eastern Connecticut State University

Christopher Cronin
Saint Leo University

Robert DaPrato
Solano Community College

Peggy A. DeCooke
Purchase College SUNY

Joan Doolittle
Anne Arundel Community College

Kimberley Duff
Cerritos College

David Eckerman
University of North Carolina

Kenneth Elliott
University of Maine, Augusta

Meredyth Fellows
West Chester University

Bob Fletcher
Truckee Meadows Community College

Christina Frederick
Southern Utah University

Barry Fritz
Quinnipiac College

Ronald Gage-Mosher
Imperial Valley College

Linda Gibbons
Westark College

Amber Gilewski
Burlington County College

Richard Griggs
University of Florida

Robert Guttentag
University of North Carolina, Greensboro

Cheryl Hale
Jefferson College

Jane Halonen
James Madison University

Kevin B. Handey
Germanna Community College

Patricia Hinton
Cumberland College

Jeremy Ashton Houska
Nevada State University

Stephen Hoyer
Pittsburgh State University

Allen I. Huffcutt
Bradley University

Nancy Jackson
Johnson & Wales University

Cindy Kamilar
Pikes Peak Community College

Margaret Karolyi
University of Akron

Sheila Kennison
Oklahoma State University

Mark Krause
University of Portland

Charles F. Levinthal
Hofstra University

Gary Levy
University of Wyoming

Laura Madson
New Mexico State University

Kathleen Malley-Morrison
Boston University

Deborah R. McDonald
New Mexico State University

Marisa McLeod
Santa Fe Community College

Le'Ann Milinder
New England College

Antoinette R. Miller
Clayton State University

Jack J. Mino
Holyoke Community College

Joel Morogovsky
Brookdale Community College

Dirk W. Mosig
University of Nebraska at Kearney

David R. Murphy
Waubonsee Community College

Bonnie J. Nichols
Mississippi County Community College

Bonnie Nicholson
University of Southern Mississippi

Susan Nolan
Seton Hall University

Caroline Olko
Nassau Community College

Gayle Pitman
Sacramento City College

Edward I. Pollack
West Chester University of Pennsylvania

Rose Preciado
Mount San Antonio College

Bryan Raudenbush
Wheeling Jesuit University

Elizabeth A. Rider
Elizabethtown College

Alysia Ritter
Murray State University

Vicki Ritts
St. Louis Community College, Meramec

James Rodgers
Hawkeye Community College

Jayne Rose
Augustana College

Lori Rosenthal
Lasell College

Ana Ruiz
Alvernia College

H. R. Schiffman
Rutgers University

Heide Sedwick
Mount Aloysius College

George Shardlow
City College of San Francisco

Randolph A. Smith
Ouachita Baptist University

Thomas Smith
Vincennes University

James L. Spencer
West Virginia State College

Tim Tomczak
Genesee Community College

Iva Trottier
Concordia College

Travis Tubre
University of Southern Mississippi

Jim Turcott
Kalamazoo Valley Community College

Mary Ann Valentino
Reedley College

Doris C. Vaughn
Alabama State University

Paul Vonnahme
New Mexico State University

Shelly Watkins
Modesto Junior College

Will Wattendorf
Adirondack Community College

Carol Winters-Smith
Bay Path College

Randall Wight
Ouachita Baptist University

Brief Contents

1

The Evolution of Psychology 1

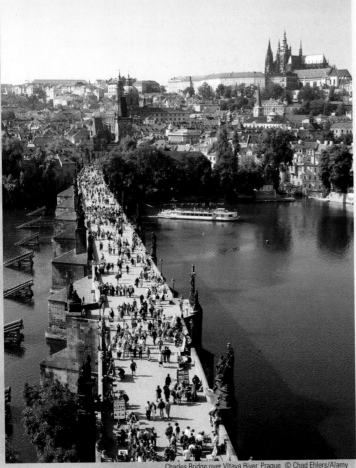

Charles Bridge over Vltava River, Prague © Chad Ehlers/Alamy

2

The Research Enterprise in Psychology 34

Capilano suspension bridge, Vancouver, Canada © UrbanEye/Alamy

3
The Biological Bases of Behavior 68

Congress Street Bridge, Austin, Texas © Patrick Byrd/Science Faction/Getty Images

4

Sensation and Perception 106

Okinawa prefecture, Japan Ikema Bridge © DAJ/Getty Images

5

Variations in Consciousness 150

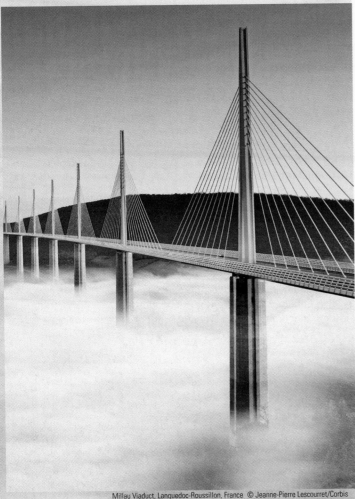

Millau Viaduct, Lanquedoc-Roussillon, France © Jeanne-Pierre Lescourret/Corbis

6

Learning 186

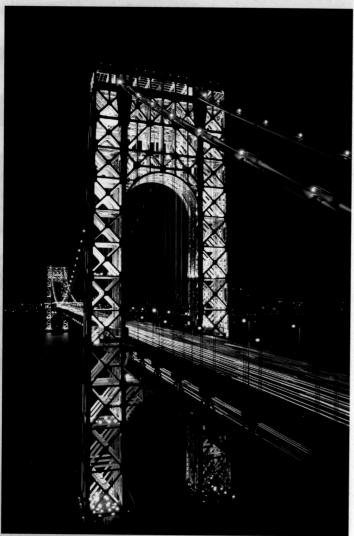

George Washington Bridge, New York © Richard Berenholtz/Corbis

7

Human Memory 224

Venice, Italy © Hermera Technologies/Jupiter Images

8

Cognition and Intelligence 258

The Pythonbrug, or "Python Bridge," connecting the Sporenburg Peninsula with Borneo Island, Amsterdam © Bruno Ehrs/Corbis

9

Motivation and Emotion 298

Golden Gate Bridge, San Francisco © Philip Coblentz/JupiterImages/Brand X/Alamy

12

Stress, Coping, and Health 414

A bridge in Kondus Valley, Pakistan © Jimmy Chin/National Geographic/Getty Images

13

Psychological Disorders 448

Sunshine Skyway Bridge, St. Petersburg, FL © Pete Turner/Image Bank/Getty Images

14

Treatment of Psychological Disorders 484

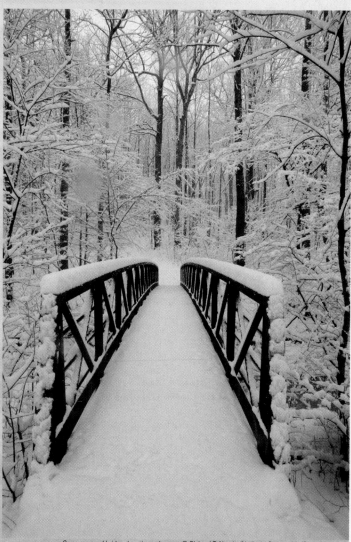

Snow-covered bridge, location unknown © Richard T. Nowitz/National Geographic/Getty Images

15

Social Behavior 518

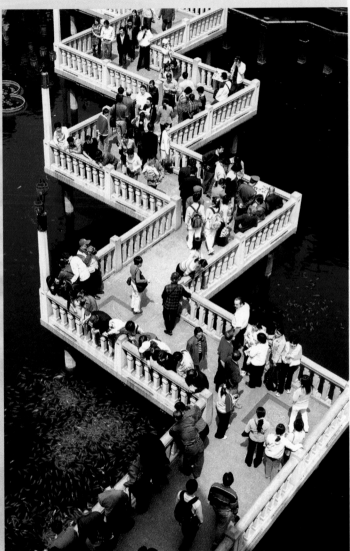

Zigzag Footbridge, Yu Yan Gardens, Shanghai, China © Jose Fuste Raga/Corbis

TO THE STUDENT

Welcome to your introductory psychology textbook. In most college courses, students spend more time with their textbooks than with their professors, so it helps if students *like* their textbooks. Making textbooks likable, however, is a tricky proposition. By its very nature, a textbook must introduce students to many complicated concepts, ideas, and theories. If it doesn't, it isn't much of a textbook, and instructors won't choose to use it. Nevertheless, in writing this book I've tried to make it as likable as possible without compromising the academic content that your instructor demands. I've especially tried to keep in mind your need for a clear, well-organized presentation that makes the important material stand out and yet is interesting to read. Above all else, I hope you find this book challenging to think about and easy to learn from.

Before you plunge into your first chapter, let me introduce you to the book's key features. Becoming familiar with how the book works will help you to get more out of it.

Key Features

You're about to embark on a journey into a new domain of ideas. Your text includes some important features that are intended to highlight certain aspects of psychology's landscape.

Unifying Themes
To help you make sense of a complex and diverse field of study, I introduce seven themes in Chapter 1 that reappear in a number of variations as we move from chapter to chapter. These unifying themes are meant to provoke thought about important issues and to highlight the connections between chapters. They are discussed at the end of each chapter in a section called "Reflecting on the Chapter's Themes." Icons for the specific themes covered in a chapter appear near the beginning of these sections to help make the book's thematic structure more prominent.

Personal Applications
Toward the end of each chapter you'll find a Personal Application section that shows how psychology is relevant to everyday life. Some of these sections provide concrete, practical advice that could be helpful to you in your educational endeavors, such as those on improving academic performance, improving everyday memory, and achieving self-control. So, you may want to jump ahead and read some of these Personal Applications early.

Critical Thinking Applications
Each Personal Application is always followed by a two-page Critical Thinking Application that teaches and models basic critical thinking skills. I think you will find that these sections are refreshing and interesting. Like the Personal Applications, they are part of the text's basic content and should be read unless you are told otherwise by your instructor. Although the "facts" of psychology will gradually change after you take this course (thanks to scientific progress), the critical thinking skills modeled in these sections should prove valuable for many years to come.

Web Links
To help make this book a rich resource guide, we have included dozens of Web Links, which are recommended websites that can provide you with additional information on many topics. The recommended sites were selected by Professor Vincent Hevern, who sought out resources that are interesting and that provide accurate, empirically sound information. The Web Links are dispersed throughout the chapters, adjacent to related topical coverage. Because web addresses change frequently, we have *not* placed the URLs for the Web Links in the book. If you are interested in visiting these sites, we recommend that you do so through the *Psychology: Themes & Variations* book companion site at www.cengage.com/psychology/weiten. Links to all the recommended websites are maintained there and the Wadsworth webmaster periodically updates the URLs. Of course, you can also track down the recommended websites by using a web search engine, such as Google.

Appendix on Careers in Psychology
Many students who take the introductory psychology course are intrigued by the possibility of pursuing a career in psychology. If you think you might be interested in a psychology-related career, you should consider reading Appendix C, which provides a succinct overview of career options in the field, written by Professor Marky Lloyd.

Learning Aids

This text contains a great deal of information. A number of learning aids have been incorporated into the book to help you digest it all.

An *outline* at the beginning of each chapter provides you with an overview of the topics covered in that chapter. Think of the outlines as road maps, and bear in mind that it's easier to reach a destination if you know where you're going.

Headings serve as road signs in your journey through each chapter. Four levels of headings are used to make it easy to see the organization of each chapter.

Key Learning Goals, found at the beginning of major sections, can help you focus on the important issues in the material you are about to read.

Reviews of Key Learning Goals, found at the end of major sections, are interim summaries that permit you to check your understanding of a section's main ideas immediately after finishing the section. The numbered paragraphs in these reviews address the learning objectives outlined in the Key Learning Goals.

Italics (without boldface) are used liberally throughout the text to emphasize crucial points.

Key terms are identified with ***italicized blue boldface*** type to alert you that these are important vocabulary items that are part of psychology's technical language.

An *integrated running glossary* provides an on-the-spot definition of each key term as it's introduced in the text. These formal definitions are printed in **blue boldface** type. Becoming familiar with psychology's terminology is an essential part of learning about the field. The integrated running glossary should make this learning process easier.

Concept Checks are sprinkled throughout the chapters to let you test your mastery of important ideas. Generally, they ask you to integrate or organize a number of key ideas, or to apply ideas to real-world situations. Although they're meant to be engaging and fun, they do check conceptual *understanding,* and some are challenging. But if you get stuck, don't worry; the answers (and explanations, where they're needed) are in the back of the book in Appendix A.

Illustrations in the text are important elements in your complete learning package. Some illustrations provide enlightening diagrams of complicated concepts; others furnish examples that help flesh out ideas or provide concise overviews of research results. Careful attention to the tables and figures in the book will help you understand the material discussed in the text.

A *Chapter Recap* at the end of each chapter provides a summary of the chapter's key ideas. It's wise to read over these review materials to make sure you've digested the information in the chapter.

Each chapter ends with a 12-item *Practice Test* that should give you a realistic assessment of your mastery of that chapter and valuable practice in taking multiple-choice tests.

An *alphabetical glossary* is provided in the back of the book. Most key terms are formally defined in the integrated running glossary only when they are first introduced. So if you run into a technical term a second time and can't remember its meaning, it may be easier to look it up in the alphabetical glossary.

A Few Footnotes

Psychology textbooks customarily identify the studies, theoretical treatises, books, and articles that information comes from. These *citations* occur (1) when names are followed by a date in parentheses, as in "Smith (2008) found that . . ." or (2) when names and dates are provided together within parentheses, as in "In one study (Burke, Martinez, & Jones, 2005), the researchers attempted to . . ." All of the cited publications are listed by author in the alphabetized *References* section in the back of the book. The citations and references are a necessary part of a book's scholarly and scientific foundation. Practically speaking, however, you'll probably want to glide right over them as you read. You definitely don't need to memorize the names and dates. The only names of people you may need to know are the handful whose contributions are profiled in the last Concept Check for each chapter.

Concept Charts for Study and Review

Your text should be accompanied by a booklet of Concept Charts that are designed to help you organize and master the main ideas contained in each chapter. Each Concept Chart provides a detailed visual map of the key ideas found in the main body of that chapter. Seeing how it all fits together should help you to better understand each chapter. You can use these charts to preview chapters, double-check your mastery of chapters, and memorize the crucial ideas in chapters.

PsykTrek: A Multimedia Introduction to Psychology

PsykTrek is a multimedia CD-ROM developed to accompany this textbook. It is an enormously powerful learning tool that can enhance your understanding of many complex processes and theories, provide you with an alternative way to assimilate many crucial concepts, and add a little more fun to your journey through introductory psychology. *PsykTrek* has been designed to supplement and complement your textbook. I strongly encourage you to use it. The *PsykTrek* icons that you will see in many of the headings in the upcoming chapters refer to the content of *PsykTrek*. An icon indicates that the textbook topic referred to in the heading is covered in the Interactive Learning Modules or Simulations found on *PsykTrek*. The relevant simulations (Sim1, Sim2, and so forth) and the relevant Interactive Learning Modules (1a, 1b, 1c, and so forth) are listed to the left of the icons. Some of the more intriguing learning activities in *PsykTrek* are also previewed at the end of each chapter.

A Word About the Study Guide

A *Study Guide* is available to accompany this text. It was written by two of my former professors, who introduced me to psychology years ago. They have done a great job of organizing review materials to help you master the information in the book. I suggest that you seriously consider using it to help you study.

A Final Word

I'm pleased to be a part of your first journey into the world of psychology, and I sincerely hope that you'll find the book as thought provoking and as easy to learn from as I've tried to make it. If you have any comments or advice on the book, please write to me in care of the publisher (Wadsworth/Cengage Learning, 20 Davis Drive, Belmont, CA 94002). You can be sure I'll pay careful attention to your feedback. Finally, let me wish you good luck. I hope you enjoy your course and learn a great deal.

Wayne Weiten

1

The Evolution of Psychology

Charles Bridge over Vltava River, Prague © Chad Ehlers/Alamy

What is psychology, and why is it worth your time to study? Let me approach these questions by sharing a couple of stories with you.

In 2005, Greg Hogan, a college sophomore, briefly achieved national notoriety when he was arrested for a crime. Greg wasn't anybody's idea of a likely criminal. He was the son of a Baptist minister and the president of his class. He played cello in the university orchestra. He even worked part-time in the chaplain's office. So it shocked everybody who knew Greg when police arrested him at his fraternity house for bank robbery.

It seems that Greg had faked having a gun and made away with over $2800 from a local bank. His reason? Over a period of months he had lost $5000 playing poker on the Internet. His lawyer said Greg's gambling habit had become "an addiction" (Dissell, 2005; McLoughlin & Paquet, 2005).

Greg eventually entered a clinic for treatment of his gambling problem. In a way, he was lucky—at least he got help. Moshe Pergament, a 19-year-old community college student in Long Island, New York, wasn't so fortunate. Moshe was shot to death after brandishing a gun at a police officer. The gun turned out to be plastic. On the front seat of his car was a note that began, "Officer, it was a plan. I'm sorry to get you involved. I just needed to die." Moshe had just lost $6000 betting on the World Series. His death was what people in law enforcement call "suicide by cop" (Lindsay & Lester, 2004).

These stories are at the extreme edge of a trend that concerns many public officials and mental health professionals: The popularity of gambling—from lotteries to sports betting to online poker—is booming, especially among the young (D. F. Jacobs, 2004). College students seem to be leading the way. To some observers, gambling on college campuses has become an "epidemic." Student bookies on some campuses make tens of thousands of dollars a year taking sports bets from other students. Television shows such as *The World Series of Poker* are marketed squarely at college-student audiences. Poker sites on the web invite students to win their tuition by gambling online.

For most people, gambling is a relatively harmless—if sometimes expensive—pastime. However, estimates suggest that 5%–6% of teens and young adults develop serious problems with gambling—two to four times the rate for older adults (Jacobs, 2004; Petry, 2005; Winters et al., 2004). The enormous growth of pathological gambling among young people raises a number of questions. Is gambling dangerous? Can it really be addictive? What is an addiction, anyway? If pathological gamblers abuse drugs or commit crimes, is gambling the cause of their troubles, or is it a symptom of a deeper problem? Perhaps most critically of all, why do some people become patho-

logical gamblers while the great majority do not? Every day millions of people in the United States play the lottery, bet on sports, or visit casinos without apparent harm. Yet others can't seem to stop gambling until they have lost everything—their savings, their jobs, their homes, and their self-respect. Why? What causes such perplexing, self-destructive behavior?

Psychology is about questions like these. More generally, psychology is about understanding *all* the things we do. All of us wonder sometimes about the reasons underlying people's behavior—why it's hard to diet, why we procrastinate about studying, why we fall in love with one person rather than another. We wonder why some people are outgoing while others are shy. We wonder why we sometimes do things that we know will bring us pain and anguish, whether it's clinging to a destructive relationship or losing our tuition money in a game of Texas Hold 'Em. The study of psychology is about all these things, and infinitely more.

Many of psychology's questions have implications for people's everyday lives. For me, this is one of the field's major attractions—*psychology is practical*. Consider the case of gambling. Pathological gamblers suffer all kinds of misery, yet they can't seem to stop. Listen to the anguish of a gambler named Steve: "Over the past two years I have lost literally thousands . . . I have attempted to give up time after time after time, but failed every time. . . . I have debts around my neck which are destroying mine and my family's life. . . . I just want a massive light to be turned on with a message saying, 'This way to your old life, Steve'" (SJB, 2006).

What is the best way to help someone like Steve? Should he join a group like Gamblers Anonymous? Would counseling work? Are there drugs that can help? By probing the whys and hows of human behavior, psychology can help us find answers to pressing questions like these, as well as better understand issues that affect each of us every day. You

The perplexing problem of pathological gambling, which has increased dramatically among college students in recent years, raises a host of complicated questions. As you will see throughout this text, psychologists investigate an infinite variety of fascinating questions.

will see the practical side of psychology throughout this book, especially in the Personal Applications at the ends of chapters. These Applications focus on everyday problems, such as coping more effectively with stress, improving self-control, and dealing with sleep difficulties.

Beyond its practical value, psychology is worth studying because it provides a powerful *way of thinking.* All of us make judgments every day about why people do the things they do. For example, we might think that pathological gamblers are weak willed, or irrational, or just too dumb to understand that the odds are stacked against them. Or we might believe they are in the grip of an addiction that simply overpowers them. How do we decide which of these judgments—if any—are right?

Psychologists are committed to investigating questions about human behavior in a scientific way. This means that they seek to formulate precise questions about behavior and then test possible answers through systematic observation. This commitment to testing ideas means that psychology provides a means of building knowledge that is relatively accurate and dependable. It also provides a model for assessing the assertions we hear every day about behavior, as you'll see in upcoming chapters' Critical Thinking Applications.

In the case of gambling, for example, researchers have designed careful studies to probe the relationship of gambling problems to any number of possible influences, from childhood experiences to membership in a college fraternity. They have compared the way slot machines are set to reward players with frequent small payoffs to the way rats and pigeons learn to earn food rewards in the laboratory. They have used state-of-the-art brain-imaging techniques to study the brains of people performing tasks similar to placing bets. They have even looked at whether some people are predisposed by their genes to develop problems with gambling (Petry, 2005; Rockey et al., 2005; Szegedy-Maszak, 2005).

If there is one clear conclusion that emerges from these studies, it is that there is no simple answer to the mystery of pathological gambling. Instead, a full explanation of gambling problems will likely involve many influences that interact in complex ways (Derevensky & Gupta, 2004; Petry, 2005). As you'll see throughout this course, the same is true of most aspects of behavior. In my opinion, this is yet another reason to study psychology: It teaches us a healthy respect for the *complexity* of behavior. In a world that could use more understanding—and compassion—this can be an invaluable lesson.

As you go through this course, I hope you'll come to share my enthusiasm for psychology as a fascinating and immensely practical field of study. Let's begin our exploration by seeing how psychology has evolved from early speculations about behavior to a modern science. By looking at this evolution, you'll better understand psychology as it is today, a sprawling, multifaceted science and profession. We'll conclude our introduction with a look at seven unifying themes that will serve as connecting threads in the chapters to come. The chapter's Personal Application reviews research that provides insights into how to be an effective student. Finally, the Critical Thinking Application discusses how critical thinking skills can be enhanced.

Key Learning Goals

1.1 Summarize Wundt's accomplishments and contributions to psychology.

1.2 Describe the chief tenets of structuralism and functionalism and their impact on the development of psychology.

1.3 Articulate Freud's principal ideas and why they inspired controversy.

1.4 Trace the development of behaviorism and assess Watson's impact on the evolution of psychology.

1.5 Summarize Skinner's key insights and why they were controversial.

1.6 Explain the impetus for the emergence of humanism and its underlying philosophy.

Psychology's Early History

Psychology's story is one of people groping toward a better understanding of themselves. As the discipline has evolved, its focus, methods, and explanatory models have changed. Let's look at how psychology has developed from philosophical speculations about the mind into a modern research-based science.

The term *psychology* comes from two Greek words, *psyche,* meaning the soul, and *logos,* referring to the study of a subject. These two Greek roots were first put together to define a topic of study in the 16th century, when *psyche* was used to refer to the soul, spirit, or mind, as distinguished from the body (Boring, 1966). Not until the early 18th century did the term *psychology* gain more than rare usage among scholars. By that time it had acquired its literal meaning, "the study of the mind."

Of course, people have always wondered about the mysteries of the mind. In that sense, psychology is as old as the human race. But it was only about 130 years ago that psychology emerged as a scientific discipline.

A New Science Is Born

1a

Psychology's intellectual parents were the disciplines of *philosophy* and *physiology.* By the 1870s a small number of scholars in both fields were actively exploring questions about the mind. How are bodily sensations turned into a mental awareness of the outside world? Are our perceptions of the world accurate reflections of reality? How do mind and body interact? The philosophers and physiologists who were interested in the mind viewed such questions as fascinating issues *within* their respective fields. It was a German professor, Wilhelm Wundt (1832–1920), who eventually changed this view. Wundt mounted a campaign to make psychology an independent discipline rather than a stepchild of philosophy or physiology.

The time and place were right for Wundt's appeal. German universities were in a healthy period of expansion, so resources were available for new disciplines. Furthermore, the intellectual climate favored the scientific approach that Wundt advocated. Hence, his proposals were well received by the academic community. In 1879 Wundt succeeded in establishing the first formal laboratory for research in psychology at the University of Leipzig. In recognition of this landmark event, historians have christened 1879 as psychology's "date of birth." Soon after, in 1881, Wundt established the first journal devoted to publishing research on psychology. All in all, Wundt's campaign was so successful that today he is widely characterized as the founder of psychology.

Wundt's conception of psychology dominated the field for two decades and was influential for several more. Borrowing from his training in physiology, Wundt (1874) declared that the new psychology should be a science modeled after fields such as physics and chemistry. What was the subject matter of the new science? According to Wundt, it was *consciousness*—the awareness of immediate experience. *Thus, psychology became the scientific study of conscious experience.* This orientation kept psychology focused squarely on the mind. But it demanded that the methods used to investigate the mind be as scientific as those of chemists or physicists.

Wundt was a tireless, dedicated scholar who generated an estimated 54,000 pages of books and articles in his career (Bringmann & Balk, 1992). Studies in his laboratory focused on attention, memory, sensory processes, and reaction-time experiments that provided estimates of the duration of various mental processes (Fuchs & Milar, 2003). His hard work and provocative ideas soon attracted attention. Many outstanding young scholars came to Leipzig to study under Wundt. Many of his students then fanned out around the world, establishing laboratories that formed the basis for the new, independent science of psychology. The growth of this new science was particularly rapid in North America, where some 23 new psychological research laboratories sprang up between 1883 and 1893 at the universities shown in **Figure 1.1** (Benjamin, 2000). Although psychology was born in Germany, it blossomed into adolescence in North America. Like many adolescents, however, the young science was about to enter a period of turbulence and turmoil.

The Battle of the "Schools" Begins: Structuralism Versus Functionalism   1a

When you read about how psychology became a science, you might have imagined that psychologists became a unified group of scholars who busily added new discoveries to an uncontested store of "facts." In reality, no science works that way. Competing schools of thought exist in most scientific disciplines. Sometimes the disagreements among these schools are sharp. Such diversity in thought is

Wilhelm Wundt

"Physiology informs us about those life phenomena that we perceive by our external senses. In psychology, the person looks upon himself as from within and tries to explain the interrelations of those processes that this internal observation discloses."

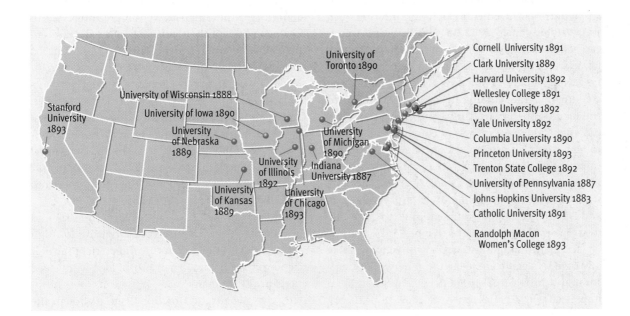

Figure 1.1

Early research laboratories in North America. This map highlights the location and year of founding for the first 23 psychological research labs established in North American colleges and universities. Many of these labs were founded by the students of Wilhelm Wundt. (Based on Benjamin, 2000)

University of Toronto 1890
University of Wisconsin 1888
University of Iowa 1890
Stanford University 1893
University of Nebraska 1889
University of Michigan 1890
University of Illinois 1892
Indiana University 1887
University of Kansas 1889
University of Chicago 1893

Cornell University 1891
Clark University 1889
Harvard University 1892
Wellesley College 1891
Brown University 1892
Yale University 1892
Columbia University 1890
Princeton University 1893
Trenton State College 1892
University of Pennsylvania 1887
Johns Hopkins University 1883
Catholic University 1891
Randolph Macon Women's College 1893

web link 1.1

Mind and Body: René Descartes to William James

Designed originally to celebrate psychology's first century as an independent discipline, this online exhibition traces three historical themes: the mind-body problem posed in the 17th century by philosopher René Descartes, the rise of experimental psychology, and the beginnings of psychology in America. **Note: The URLs (addresses) for the Web Links can be found on the website for this text (www .cengage.com/psychology/ weiten), or you can find them using a search engine such as Google.**

William James

"It is just this free water of consciousness that psychologists resolutely overlook."

natural and often stimulates enlightening debate. In psychology, the first two major schools of thought, *structuralism* and *functionalism,* were entangled in the first great intellectual battle in the field.

Structuralism emerged through the leadership of Edward Titchener, an Englishman who emigrated to the United States in 1892 and taught for decades at Cornell University. Although Titchener earned his degree in Wundt's Leipzig laboratory and expressed great admiration for Wundt's work, he brought his own version of Wundt's psychology to America (Hilgard, 1987; Thorne & Henley, 1997). *Structuralism* **was based on the notion that the task of psychology is to analyze consciousness into its basic elements and investigate how these elements are related.** Just as physicists were studying how matter is made up of basic particles, the structuralists wanted to identify the fundamental components of conscious experience, such as sensations, feelings, and images.

Although the structuralists explored many questions, most of their work concerned sensation and perception in vision, hearing, and touch. To examine the contents of consciousness, the structuralists depended on the method of *introspection,* **or the careful, systematic self-observation of one's own conscious experience.** As practiced by the structuralists, introspection required training to make the *subject*—the person being studied—more objective and more aware. Once trained, participants were typically exposed to auditory tones, optical illusions, and visual stimuli such as pieces of fruit and were asked to analyze what they experienced.

The functionalists took a different view of psychology's task. *Functionalism* **was based on the belief that psychology should investigate the function or purpose of consciousness, rather than its structure.** The chief architect of functionalism was William James (1842–1910), a brilliant American scholar (and brother of novelist Henry James). James's formal training was in medicine. However, he was too sickly to pursue a medical practice (he couldn't imagine standing all day long), so he joined the faculty of Harvard University to pursue a less grueling career (Ross, 1991). Medicine's loss proved to be a boon for psychology, as James quickly became an intellectual giant in the field. James's landmark book, *Principles of Psychology* (1890), became standard reading for generations of psychologists and is perhaps the most influential text in the history of psychology (Weiten & Wight, 1992).

James's thinking illustrates how psychology, like any field, is deeply embedded in a network of cultural and intellectual influences. James had been impressed with Charles Darwin's (1859, 1871) theory

of *natural selection.* According to the principle of *natural selection,* inherited characteristics that provide a survival or reproductive advantage are more likely than alternative characteristics to be passed on to subsequent generations and thus come to be "selected" over time. This cornerstone notion of Darwin's evolutionary theory suggested that the typical characteristics of a species must serve some purpose. Applying this idea to humans, James (1890) noted that consciousness obviously is an important characteristic of our species. Hence, he contended that psychology should investigate the *functions* rather than the *structure* of consciousness.

James also argued that the structuralists' approach missed the real nature of conscious experience. Consciousness, he argued, consists of a continuous *flow* of thoughts. In analyzing consciousness into its "elements," the structuralists were looking at static points in that flow. James wanted to understand the flow itself, which he called the *stream of consciousness.* Today, people take this metaphorical description of mental life for granted, but at the time it was a revolutionary insight. As Leary (2003) put it, "No longer was consciousness depicted as some kind of encompassing mental container more or less full of such 'contents' as sensations, images, ideas, thoughts, feelings, and the like; rather it was now portrayed as a continually ongoing, wholistic experience or process" (p. 25). James went on to provide enormously influential analyses of many crucial issues in the emerging field of psychology. Among other things, his discussions of how people acquired *habits* laid the groundwork for progress in the study of learning, and his conception of the *self* provided the foundation for subsequent theories of personality (Leary, 2003).

Whereas structuralists naturally gravitated to the laboratory, functionalists were more interested in how people adapt their behavior to the demands of the real world around them. This practical slant led them to introduce new subjects into psychology. Instead of focusing on sensation and perception, functionalists such as G. Stanley Hall, James McKeen Cattell, and John Dewey began to investigate mental testing, patterns of development in children, the effectiveness of educational practices, and behavioral differences between the sexes. These new topics may have played a role in attracting the first women into the field of psychology (see **Figure 1.2**).

The impassioned advocates of structuralism and functionalism saw themselves as fighting for high stakes: the definition and future direction of the new science of psychology. Their war of ideas continued energetically for many years. Who won? Most historians give the edge to functionalism. Although the

Figure 1.2

Mary Whiton Calkins (1863–1930)

Mary Calkins, who studied under William James, founded one of the first dozen psychology laboratories in America at Wellesley College in 1891, invented a widely used technique for studying memory, and became the first woman to serve as president of the American Psychological Association in 1905. Ironically, however, she never received her Ph.D. in psychology. Because she was a woman, Harvard University only reluctantly allowed her to take graduate classes as a "guest student." When she completed the requirements for her Ph.D., Harvard would only offer her a doctorate from its undergraduate sister school, Radcliffe. Calkins felt that this decision perpetuated unequal treatment of the sexes, so she refused the Radcliffe degree.

Margaret Floy Washburn (1871–1939)

Margaret Washburn was the first woman to receive a Ph.D. in psychology. She wrote an influential book, *The Animal Mind* (1908), which served as an impetus to the subsequent emergence of behaviorism and was standard reading for several generations of psychologists. In 1921 she became the second woman to serve as president of the American Psychological Association. Washburn studied under James McKeen Cattell at Columbia University, but like Mary Calkins, she was only permitted to take graduate classes unofficially, as a "hearer." Hence, she transferred to Cornell University, which was more hospitable toward women, and completed her doctorate in 1894. Like Calkins, Washburn spent most of her career at a college for women (Vassar).

Leta Stetter Hollingworth (1886–1939)

Leta Hollingworth did pioneering work on adolescent development, mental retardation, and gifted children. Indeed, she was the first person to use the term *gifted* to refer to youngsters who scored exceptionally high on intelligence tests. Hollingworth (1914, 1916) also played a major role in debunking popular theories of her era that purported to explain why women were "inferior" to men. For instance, she conducted a study refuting the myth that phases of the menstrual cycle are reliably associated with performance decrements in women. Her careful collection of objective data on gender differences forced other scientists to subject popular, untested beliefs about the sexes to skeptical, empirical inquiry.

Women pioneers in the history of psychology. Women have long made major contributions to the development of psychology (Milar, 2000; Russo & Denmark, 1987), and today nearly half of all psychologists are female. As in other fields, however, women have often been overlooked in histories of psychology (Furumoto & Scarborough, 1986). The three psychologists profiled here demonstrate that women have been making significant contributions to psychology almost from its beginning—despite formidable barriers to pursuing their academic careers.

Photos courtesy of the Archives of the History of American Psychology, University of Akron, Akron, Ohio.

---

structuralists can be credited with strengthening psychology's commitment to laboratory research, functionalism left a more enduring imprint on psychology. Indeed, Buxton (1985) has remarked that "nowadays no one is called a functionalist in psychology, and yet almost every psychologist is one" (p. 138). Functionalism eventually faded as a school of thought, but its practical orientation fostered the development of two important descendants— behaviorism and applied psychology—that we will discuss momentarily.

Freud Brings the Unconscious into the Picture

1a, 10a

Sigmund Freud (1856–1939) was an Austrian physician who early in his career dreamed of achieving fame by making an important discovery. His determination was such that in medical school he dis-

sected 400 male eels to prove for the first time that they had testes. His work with eels did not make him famous, but his subsequent work with people did. Indeed, his theories made him one of the most influential—and controversial—intellectual figures of modern times.

Freud's (1900, 1933) approach to psychology grew out of his efforts to treat mental disorders. In his medical practice, Freud treated people troubled by psychological problems such as irrational fears, obsessions, and anxieties with an innovative procedure he called *psychoanalysis* (described in detail in Chapter 14). Decades of experience probing into his patients' lives provided much of the inspiration for Freud's theory. He also gathered material by looking inward and examining his own anxieties, conflicts, and desires.

His work with patients and his own self-exploration persuaded Freud of the existence of what he called the *unconscious*. According to Freud, **the *unconscious* contains thoughts, memories, and**

Sigmund Freud

"The unconscious is the true psychical reality; in its innermost nature it is as much unknown to us as the reality of the external world."

desires that are well below the surface of conscious awareness but that nonetheless exert great influence on behavior. Freud based his concept of the unconscious on a variety of observations. For instance, he noticed that seemingly meaningless slips of the tongue (such as "I decided to take a summer school curse") often appeared to reveal a person's true feelings. He also noted that his patients' dreams often seemed to express important feelings that they were unaware of. Knitting these and other observations together, Freud eventually concluded that psychological disturbances are largely caused by personal conflicts existing at an unconscious level. More generally, his *psychoanalytic theory* attempts to explain personality, motivation, and mental disorders by focusing on unconscious determinants of behavior.

Freud's concept of the unconscious was not entirely new (Rieber, 1998). However, it was a major departure from the prevailing belief that people are fully aware of the forces governing their behavior. In arguing that behavior is governed by unconscious forces, Freud made the disconcerting suggestion that people are not masters of their own minds. Other aspects of Freud's theory also stirred up debate. For instance, he proposed that behavior is greatly influenced by how people cope with their sexual urges. At a time when people were far less comfortable discussing sexual issues than they are today, even scientists were offended and scandalized by Freud's emphasis on sex. Small wonder, then, that Freud was soon engulfed in controversy.

In part because of its controversial nature, Freud's theory was slow to gain influence. However, he was a superb and prolific writer who campaigned vigorously

for his psychoanalytic movement (Messer & McWilliams, 2003). As a result, his approach gradually won acceptance within medicine, attracting prominent followers such as Carl Jung and Alfred Adler. Important public recognition from psychology came in 1909, when G. Stanley Hall invited Freud to give a series of lectures at Clark University in Massachusetts.

By 1920 psychoanalytic theory was widely known around the world, but it continued to meet with considerable resistance in psychology (Fancher, 2000). Why? The main reason was that it conflicted with the spirit of the times in psychology. Many psychologists were becoming uncomfortable with their earlier focus on conscious experience and were turning to the less murky subject of observable behavior. If they felt that conscious experience was inaccessible to scientific observation, you can imagine how they felt about trying to study *unconscious* experience. Most psychologists viewed psychoanalytic theory as unscientific speculation that would eventually fade away (Hornstein, 1992).

They turned out to be wrong. Psychoanalytic ideas steadily gained acceptance around the world, influencing thought in medicine, the arts, and literature (Rieber, 1998). Then, in the 1930s and 1940s, more and more psychologists found themselves becoming interested in areas Freud had studied: personality, motivation, and abnormal behavior. As they turned to these topics, many of them saw merit in some of Freud's notions (Rosenzweig, 1985). Although psychoanalytic theory continued to generate heated debate, it survived to become an influential theoretical perspective. Today, many psychoanalytic concepts have filtered into the mainstream of psychology (Luborsky & Barrett, 2006; Westen, 1998).

---

concept check 1.1

Understanding the Implications of Major Theories: Wundt, James, and Freud

Check your understanding of the implications of some of the major theories reviewed in this chapter by indicating who is likely to have made each of the statements quoted below. Choose from the following theorists: (a) Wilhelm Wundt, (b) William James, and (c) Sigmund Freud. You'll find the answers in Appendix A in the back of the book.

_____ 1. "He that has eyes to see and ears to hear may convince himself that no mortal can keep a secret. If the lips are silent, he chatters with his fingertips; betrayal oozes out of him at every pore. And thus the task of making conscious the most hidden recesses of the mind is one which it is quite possible to accomplish."

_____ 2. "The book which I present to the public is an attempt to mark out a new domain of science. . . . The new discipline rests upon anatomical and physiological foundations. . . . The experimental treatment of psychological problems must be pronounced from every point of view to be in its first beginnings."

_____ 3. "Consciousness, then, does not appear to itself chopped up in bits. Such words as 'chain' or 'train' do not describe it fitly. . . . It is nothing jointed; it flows. A 'river' or 'stream' are the metaphors by which it is most naturally described."

Watson Alters Psychology's Course as Behaviorism Makes Its Debut

PSYK TREK

1a, 5b

The debate between structuralism and functionalism was only the prelude to other fundamental controversies in psychology. In the early 1900s, another major school of thought appeared that dramatically altered the course of psychology. Founded by John B. Watson (1878–1958), *behaviorism* is a theoretical orientation based on the premise that scientific psychology should study only observable behavior. It is important to understand what a radical change this definition represents. Watson (1913, 1919) was proposing that psychologists *abandon the study of consciousness altogether* and focus exclusively on behaviors that they could observe directly. In essence, he was redefining what scientific psychology should be about.

Why did Watson argue for such a fundamental shift in direction? Because to him, the power of the scientific method rested on the idea of *verifiability*. In principle, scientific claims can always be verified (or disproved) by anyone who is able and willing to make the required observations. However, this power depends on studying things that can be observed objectively. Otherwise, the advantage of using the scientific approach—replacing vague speculation and personal opinion with reliable, exact knowledge—is lost. In Watson's view, mental processes are not a proper subject for scientific study because they are ultimately private events. After all, no one can see or touch another's thoughts. Consequently, if psychology was to be a science, it would have to give up consciousness as its subject matter and become instead the *science of behavior*.

Behavior refers to any overt (observable) response or activity by an organism. Watson asserted that psychologists could study anything that people do or say—shopping, playing chess, eating, complimenting a friend—but they could *not* study scientifically the thoughts, wishes, and feelings that might accompany these behaviors. Obviously, psychology's shift away from the study of consciousness was fundamentally incompatible with psychoanalytic theory. By the 1920s Watson had become an outspoken critic of Freud's views (Rilling, 2000b). Behaviorism and psychoanalysis would go on to generate many heated theoretical debates in the ensuing decades.

Watson's radical reorientation of psychology did not end with his redefinition of its subject matter. He also took an extreme position on one of psychology's oldest and most fundamental questions: the issue of *nature versus nurture*. This age-old debate is concerned with whether behavior is determined mainly by genetic inheritance ("nature") or by environment and experience ("nurture"). To oversimplify, the question is this: Is a great concert pianist or a master criminal born, or made?

Watson argued that each is made, not born. He discounted the importance of heredity, maintaining that behavior is governed entirely by the environment. Indeed, he boldly claimed:

Give me a dozen healthy infants, well-formed, and my own special world to bring them up in and I'll guarantee to take any one at random and train him to become any type of specialist I might select—doctor, lawyer, artist, merchant-chief, and yes, even beggar-man and thief, regardless of his talents, penchants, tendencies, abilities, vocations and race of his ancestors. I am going beyond my facts and I admit it, but so have the advocates of the contrary and they have been doing it for many thousands of years. (1924, p. 82)

For obvious reasons, Watson's tongue-in-cheek challenge was never put to a test. Although this widely cited quote overstated and oversimplified Watson's views on the nature-nurture issue (Todd & Morris, 1992), his writings contributed to the environmental slant that became associated with behaviorism (Horowitz, 1992).

The gradual emergence of behaviorism was partly attributable to an important discovery made around the turn of the century by Ivan Pavlov, a Russian physiologist. As you'll learn in Chapter 6, Pavlov (1906) showed that dogs could be trained to salivate in response to an auditory stimulus such as a tone. This deceptively simple demonstration of the *conditioned reflex* provided insight into how stimulus-response bonds are formed. Such bonds were exactly what behaviorists wanted to investigate, so Pavlov's discovery paved the way for their work. Watson (1925), for instance, embraced Pavlov's model as a new way of thinking about learning (Rilling, 2000a), and the behaviorists eventually came to view psychology's mission as an attempt to relate overt behaviors (responses) to observable events in the environment (stimuli). Because the behaviorists investigated stimulus-response relationships, the behavioral approach is often referred to as *stimulus-response (S-R) psychology*.

Behaviorism's stimulus-response approach contributed to the rise of animal research in psychology. Having deleted consciousness from their scope of concern, behaviorists no longer needed to study human subjects who could report on their mental processes. Many psychologists thought that animals

John B. Watson

"The time seems to have come when psychology must discard all references to consciousness."

web link 1.2

History & Philosophy of Psychology Web Resources

Professor Christopher Green of York University in Canada has assembled a wide range of web-based materials relating to psychology's theoretical and historical past, including a collection of sites focused on specific individuals. Webpages devoted to key figures mentioned in this chapter (such as Mary Whiton Calkins, William James, B. F. Skinner, and Margaret Floy Washburn) can be accessed here.

would make better research subjects anyway. One key reason was that experimental research is often more productive if experimenters can exert considerable *control* over their subjects. Otherwise, too many complicating factors enter into the picture and contaminate the experiment. Obviously, a researcher can exert much more control over a laboratory rat or pigeon than over a human subject, who arrives at a lab with years of uncontrolled experience and who will probably insist on going home at night. Thus, the discipline that had begun its life a few decades earlier as the study of the mind now found itself heavily involved in the study of simple responses made by laboratory animals.

Skinner Questions Free Will as Behaviorism Flourishes   1a, 10b

The advocates of behaviorism and psychoanalysis tangled frequently during the 1920s, 1930s, and 1940s. As psychoanalytic thought slowly gained a foothold within psychology, many psychologists softened their stance on the acceptability of studying internal mental events. However, this movement toward the consideration of internal states was dramatically reversed in the 1950s by the work of B. F. Skinner (1904–1990), an American psychologist whose thinking was influenced by the work of Ivan Pavlov and John B. Watson (Dinsmoor, 2004; Moore, 2005). Skinner (1953) championed a return to Watson's strict stimulus-response approach. Skinner did not deny the existence of internal mental events. However, he insisted that they could not be studied scientifically. Moreover, he maintained, there was no need to study them. According to Skinner, if the stimulus of food is followed by the response of eating, we can fully describe what is happening without making any guesses about whether the animal is experiencing hunger. Like Watson, Skinner also emphasized how environmental factors mold behavior. Although he repeatedly acknowledged that an organism's behavior is influenced by its biological endowment, he argued that psychology could understand and predict behavior adequately without resorting to physiological explanations (Delprato & Midgley, 1992).

The fundamental principle of behavior documented by Skinner is deceptively simple: *Organisms tend to repeat responses that lead to positive outcomes, and they tend not to repeat responses that lead to neutral or negative outcomes.* Despite its simplicity, this principle turns out to be quite powerful. Working primarily with laboratory rats and pigeons, Skinner showed

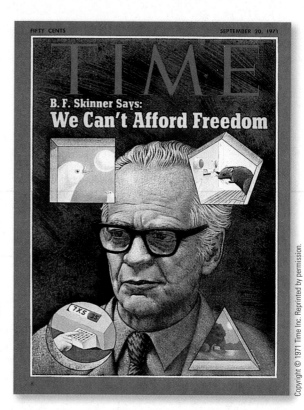

B. F. Skinner created considerable controversy when he asserted that free will is an illusion.

that he could exert remarkable control over the behavior of animals by manipulating the outcomes of their responses. He was even able to train animals to perform unnatural behaviors. For example, he once trained some pigeons to play a respectable version of table tennis (they pecked the ball back and forth on the Ping Pong table). Skinner's followers eventually showed that the principles uncovered in their animal research could be applied to complex human behaviors as well. Behavioral principles are now widely used in factories, schools, prisons, mental hospitals, and a variety of other settings.

Skinner's ideas had repercussions that went far beyond the debate among psychologists about what they should study. Skinner spelled out the full implications of his findings in his book *Beyond Freedom and Dignity* (1971). There he asserted that all behavior is fully governed by external stimuli. In other words, your behavior is determined in predictable ways by lawful principles, just as the flight of an arrow is governed by the laws of physics. Thus, if you believe that your actions are the result of conscious decisions, you're wrong. According to Skinner, we are all controlled by our environment, not by ourselves. In short, Skinner arrived at the conclusion that *free will is an illusion.*

B. F. Skinner

"I submit that what we call the behavior of the human organism is no more free than its digestion."

As you can readily imagine, such a disconcerting view of human nature was not universally acclaimed. Like Freud, Skinner was the target of harsh criticism. Much of this criticism stemmed from misinterpretations of his ideas that were reported in the popular press (Rutherford, 2000). Despite the controversy, however, behaviorism flourished as the dominant school of thought in psychology during the 1950s and 1960s (Gilgen, 1982). And even today, when experts are asked to nominate psychology's most important contributors, Skinner's name is typically found at the top of the list (see **Figure 1.3**).

The Humanists Revolt

1a, 10c

By the 1950s behaviorism and psychoanalytic theory had become the most influential schools of thought in psychology. However, many psychologists found these theoretical orientations unappealing. The principal charge hurled at both schools was that they were "dehumanizing." Psychoanalytic theory was attacked for its belief that behavior is dominated by primitive, sexual urges. Behaviorism was criticized for its preoccupation with the study of simple animal behavior. Both theories were criticized because they suggested that people are not masters of their own destinies. Above all, many people argued, both schools of thought failed to recognize the unique qualities of *human* behavior.

Beginning in the 1950s, the diverse opposition to behaviorism and psychoanalytic theory blended into a loose alliance that eventually became a new school of thought called "humanism" (Bühler & Allen, 1972). In psychology, *humanism* is a theoretical orientation that emphasizes the unique qualities of humans, especially their freedom and their potential for personal growth. Some of the key differences between the humanistic, psychoanalytic, and behavioral viewpoints are summarized in **Table 1.1** on page 10, which compares six contemporary theoretical perspectives in psychology.

Humanists take an *optimistic* view of human nature. They maintain that people are not pawns of either their animal heritage or environmental circumstances. Furthermore, these theorists say, because humans are fundamentally different from other animals, research on animals has little relevance to the understanding of human behavior. The most prominent architects of the humanistic movement have been Carl Rogers (1902–1987) and Abraham Maslow (1908–1970). Rogers (1951) argued that human behavior is governed primarily by each individual's sense of self, or "self-concept"—which animals presumably lack. Both he and Maslow (1954) maintained that to fully understand people's behavior, psychologists must take into account the human drive toward personal growth. They asserted that people have a basic need to continue to evolve as human beings and to fulfill their potentials.

Fragmentation, dissension, and a distaste for conducting research have reduced the influence of humanism in recent decades, although some advocates are predicting a renaissance for the humanistic movement (Taylor, 1999). To date, the humanists' greatest contribution to psychology has probably been their innovative treatments for psychological problems and disorders. For example, Carl Rogers pioneered a new approach to psychotherapy—called *client-centered therapy*—that remains influential today, as you will see in Chapter 14 (Kirschenbaum & Jourdan, 2005).

web link

Museum of the of Psychologic Instrumentation

You can examine inst and complex apparatus by psychological research in the discipline's early decades in this "cybermuseum" maintained at Montclair State University.

Two Rankings of Important Figures in the History of Psychology			
Estes et al. (1990)		Haggbloom et al. (2002)	
Rank	Name	Rank	Name
1	B. F. Skinner	1	B. F. Skinner
2	Sigmund Freud	2	Jean Piaget
3	William James	3	Sigmund Freud
4	Jean Piaget	4	John B. Watson
5	G. Stanley Hall	5	Albert Bandura
6	Wilhelm Wundt	6	William James
7	Carl Rogers	6	Ivan Pavlov
8	John B. Watson	8	Kurt Lewin
9	Ivan Pavlov	9	Carl Rogers
10	E. L. Thorndike	9	E. L. Thorndike

Figure 1.3

Influential contributors in the history of psychology. The results of two surveys regarding the most important people in the history of psychology are shown here. In the 1990 survey, 93 chairpersons of psychology departments ranked psychology's most influential contributors (Estes, Coston, & Fournet, 1990, as cited in Korn et al., 1991). In the 2002 survey, a sample drawn from the membership of the Association for Psychological Science was asked to identify the greatest psychologists of the 20th century (Haggbloom et al., 2002). As you can see, B. F. Skinner earned the top ranking in both surveys. Although these ratings of scholarly eminence are open to debate, these data should give you some idea of the relative impact of various figures discussed in this chapter.

Carl Rogers

"It seems to me that at bottom each person is asking, 'Who am I, really? How can I get in touch with this real self, underlying all my surface behavior? How can I become myself?'"

Table 1.1 Overview of Six Contemporary Theoretical Perspectives in Psychology

Perspective and Its Influential Period	Principal Contributors	Subject Matter	Basic Premise
Behavioral (1913–present)	John B. Watson Ivan Pavlov B. F. Skinner	Effects of environment on the overt behavior of humans and animals	Only observable events (stimulus-response relations) can be studied scientifically.
Psychoanalytic (—present)	Sigmund Freud Carl Jung Alfred Adler	Unconscious determinants of behavior	Unconscious motives and experiences in early childhood govern personality and mental disorders.
Humanistic (1950s–present)	Carl Rogers Abraham Maslow	Unique aspects of human experience	Humans are free, rational beings with the potential for personal growth, and they are fundamentally different from animals.
Cognitive (1950s–present)	Jean Piaget Noam Chomsky Herbert Simon	Thoughts; mental processes	Human behavior cannot be fully understood without examining how people acquire, store, and process information.
Biological (1950s–present)	James Olds Roger Sperry David Hubel Torsten Wiesel	Physiological bases of behavior in humans and animals	An organism's functioning can be explained in terms of the bodily structures and biochemical processes that underlie behavior.
Evolutionary (1980s–present)	David Buss Martin Daly Margo Wilson Leda Cosmides John Tooby	Evolutionary bases of behavior in humans and animals	Behavior patterns have evolved to solve adaptive problems; natural selection favors behaviors that enhance reproductive success.

concept check 1.2

Understanding the Implications of Major Theories: Watson, Skinner, and Rogers

Check your understanding of the implications of some of the major theories reviewed in this chapter by indicating who is likely to have made each of the statements quoted below. Choose from the following: (a) John B. Watson, (b) B. F. Skinner, and (c) Carl Rogers. You'll find the answers in Appendix A at the back of the book.

_____ 1. "In the traditional view, a person is free. . . . He can therefore be held responsible for what he does and justly punished if he offends. That view, together with its associated practices, must be reexamined when a scientific analysis reveals unsuspected controlling relations between behavior and environment."

_____ 2. "I do not have a Pollyanna view of human nature. . . . Yet one of the most refreshing and invigorating parts of my experience is to work with [my clients] and to discover the strongly positive directional tendencies which exist in them, as in all of us, at the deepest levels."

_____ 3. "Our conclusion is that we have no real evidence of the inheritance of traits. I would feel perfectly confident in the ultimately favorable outcome of careful upbringing of a healthy, well-formed baby born of a long line of crooks, murderers and thieves, and prostitutes."

REVIEW of Key Learning Goals

1.1 Psychology became an independent discipline when Wilhelm Wundt established the first psychological research laboratory in 1879 at Leipzig, Germany. Wundt, who is widely characterized as the founder of psychology, viewed psychology as the scientific study of consciousness. The new discipline grew rapidly in North America in the late 19th century.

1.2 The structuralists, led by Edward Titchener, believed that psychology should use introspection to analyze consciousness into its basic elements. The functionalists, inspired by the ideas of William James, believed that psychology should focus on the purpose and adaptive functions of consciousness. Functionalism paved the way for behaviorism and applied psychology and had more of a lasting impact than structuralism.

1.3 Sigmund Freud was an Austrian physician who invented psychoanalysis. His psychoanalytic theory emphasized the unconscious determinants of behavior and the importance of sexuality. Freud's ideas were controversial, and they met with resistance in academic psychology. However, as more psychologists developed an interest in personality, motivation, and abnormal behavior, psychoanalytic concepts were incorporated into mainstream psychology.

1.4 Behaviorists, led by John B. Watson, argued that psychology should study only observable behavior. Thus, they campaigned to redefine psychology as the science of behavior. Emphasizing the importance of the environment over heredity, the behaviorists began to explore stimulus-response relationships, often using laboratory animals as subjects.

1.5 Working with laboratory rats and pigeons, American behaviorist B. F. Skinner demonstrated that organisms tend to repeat responses that lead to positive consequences and not to repeat responses that lead to neutral or negative consequences. Based on the belief that all behavior is fully governed by external stimuli, Skinner argued that free will is an illusion. His ideas were controversial and often misunderstood.

1.6 Finding both behaviorism and psychoanalysis unsatisfactory, advocates of a new theoretical orientation called humanism became influential in the 1950s. Humanism, led by Abraham Maslow and Carl Rogers, emphasized the unique qualities of human behavior and humans' freedom and potential for personal growth.

Psychology's Modern History

The principal storyline of psychology's early history was its gradual maturation into a research-based science. The seminal work of Wundt, James, Watson, Pavlov, Skinner, and a host of other pioneers served to establish psychology as a respected scientific discipline in the halls of academia. As you will learn momentarily, the principal storyline of psychology's modern history has been its remarkable growth into a multifaceted scientific and professional enterprise. In more recent decades psychology's story has been marked by expanding boundaries and broader interests.

Psychology Comes of Age as a Profession

As you know, psychology is not all pure science. It has a highly practical side. Many psychologists provide a variety of professional services to the public. Their work falls within the domain of *applied psychology,* **the branch of psychology concerned with everyday, practical problems.** This branch of psychology, so prominent today, was actually slow to develop. Although a small number of early psychologists dabbled in various areas of applied psychology, it remained on the fringes of mainstream psychology until World War II (Benjamin et al., 2003).

The first applied arm of psychology to achieve any prominence was *clinical psychology.* As practiced today, *clinical psychology* **is the branch of psychology concerned with the diagnosis and treatment of psychological problems and disorders.** In the early days, however, the emphasis was almost exclusively on psychological testing and adjustment problems in schoolchildren. Although the first psychological clinic was established as early as 1896, by 1937 only about one in five psychologists reported an interest in clinical psychology (Goldenberg, 1983). Clinicians were a small minority in a field devoted primarily to research.

That picture was about to change with dramatic swiftness. During World War II (1939–1945), many academic psychologists were pressed into service as clinicians. They were needed to screen military recruits and to treat soldiers suffering from trauma. Many of these psychologists (often to their surprise) found the clinical work to be challenging and rewarding, and a substantial portion continued to do clinical work after the war. More significantly, some 40,000 American veterans, many with severe psychological scars, returned to seek postwar treatment in Veterans Administration (VA) hospitals. With the demand for clinicians far greater than the supply, the VA stepped in to finance many new training programs in clinical psychology. These programs, emphasizing training in the treatment of psychological disorders as well as in psychological testing, proved attractive. Within a few years, about half of the new Ph.D.'s in psychology were specializing in clinical psychology (Goldenberg, 1983). Assessing the impact of World War II, Routh and Reisman (2003) characterize it as "a watershed in the history of clinical psychology. In its aftermath, clinical psychology received something it had not received before: enormous institutional support" (p. 345). Thus, during the 1940s and 1950s the prewar orphan of applied/professional psychology rapidly matured into a robust, powerful adult.

Since the 1950s, the professionalization of psychology has continued at a steady pace. In fact, the trend has spread into additional areas of psychology. Today the broad umbrella of applied psychology covers a variety of professional specialties, including school psychology, industrial/organizational psychology, counseling psychology, and emerging new areas, such as forensic psychology (Benjamin & Baker, 2004). Whereas psychologists were once almost exclusively academics, the vast majority of today's psychologists devote some of their time to providing professional services.

Psychology Returns to Its Roots: Renewed Interest in Cognition and Physiology

While applied psychology has blossomed in recent years, scientific research has continued to progress. Ironically, two of the latest trends in research hark back more than a century to psychology's beginning, when psychologists were primarily interested in consciousness and physiology. Today psychologists are showing renewed interest in consciousness (now called "cognition") and the biological bases of behavior.

Cognition **refers to the mental processes involved in acquiring knowledge.** In other words, cognition involves thinking or conscious experience. For many decades, the dominance of behaviorism discouraged investigation of "unobservable" mental processes, and most psychologists showed little interest in cognition (Mandler, 2002). During the 1950s and 1960s, however, research on cognition

Key Learning Goals
1.7 Discuss how historical events contributed to the emergence of psychology as a profession.

1.8 Describe two trends emerging in the 1950s–1960s that represented a return to psychology's intellectual roots.

1.9 Explain why Western psychology has shown an increased interest in cultural variables in recent decades.

1.10 Discuss the emergence and basic ideas of evolutionary psychology.

1.11 Explain the development and principal tenets of the positive psychology movement.

slowly began to emerge (Miller, 2003). Major progress in the study of cognitive development (Piaget, 1954), memory (Miller, 1956), language (Chomsky, 1957), and problem solving (Newell, Shaw, & Simon, 1958) sparked a surge of interest in cognitive psychology.

Cognitive theorists argue that psychology must include the study of internal mental events to fully understand human behavior (Gardner, 1985; Neisser, 1967). Advocates of the *cognitive perspective* point out that our mental processes surely influence how we behave. Consequently, focusing exclusively on overt behavior yields an incomplete picture of why we behave as we do. Equally important, psychologists investigating decision making, reasoning, and problem solving have shown that methods *can* be devised to study cognitive processes scientifically. Although the methods are different from those used in psychology's early days, recent research on the inner workings of the mind has put the *psyche* back in contemporary psychology. In fact, many observers maintain that the cognitive perspective has become the dominant perspective in contemporary psychology—and some interesting data support this assertion, as can be seen in **Figure 1.4** (Robins, Gosling, & Craik, 1999).

The 1950s and 1960s also saw many discoveries that highlighted the interrelations among mind, body, and behavior (Thompson & Zola, 2003). For example, researchers demonstrated that electrical stimulation of the brain could evoke emotional responses such as pleasure and rage in animals (Olds, 1956). Other work, which eventually earned a Nobel prize for Roger Sperry (in 1981), showed that the right and left halves of the brain are specialized to handle different types of mental tasks (Gazzaniga, Bogen, & Sperry, 1965). The 1960s also brought the publication of David Hubel and Torsten Wiesel's (1962, 1963) Nobel prize–winning work on how visual signals are processed in the brain. These and many other findings stimulated an increase in research on the biological bases of behavior. Advocates of the *biological perspective* maintain that much of human and animal behavior can be explained in terms of the bodily structures and biochemical processes that allow organisms to behave. As you know, in the 19th century the young science of psychology had a heavy physiological emphasis. Thus, the renewed interest in the biological bases of behavior represents another return to psychology's heritage.

Although advocates of the cognitive and biological perspectives haven't done as much organized campaigning for their viewpoint as proponents of the older, traditional schools of thought, these newer perspectives have become important theoretical orientations in modern psychology. They are increasingly influential viewpoints regarding what psychology should study and how. The cognitive and biological perspectives are compared to other contemporary theoretical perspectives in **Table 1.1**.

Psychology Broadens Its Horizons: Increased Interest in Cultural Diversity

1a

Throughout psychology's history, most researchers have worked under the assumption that they were seeking to identify general principles of behavior that would be applicable to all of humanity (Smith, Spillane, & Annus, 2006). In reality, however, psychology has largely been a Western (North American and European) enterprise with a remarkably provincial slant (Gergen et al. 1996; Norenzayan & Heine, 2005). The vast majority of research has been conducted in the United States by middle- and upper-class white psychologists who have used mostly middle- and upper-class white males as participants (Hall, 1997; Norenzayan & Heine, 2005). Traditionally, Western psychologists have paid scant attention to how well their theories and research might apply to

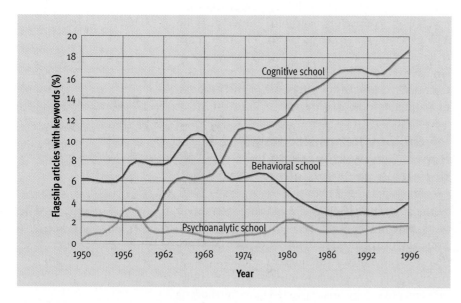

Figure 1.4

The relative prominence of three major schools of thought in psychology. To estimate the relative influence of various theoretical orientations in recent decades, Robins, Gosling, and Craik (1999) analyzed the subject matter of four prestigious general publications in psychology, measuring the percentage of articles relevant to each school of thought. Obviously, their approach is just one of many ways one might gauge the prominence of various theoretical orientations in psychology. Nonetheless, the data are thought provoking. Their findings suggest that the cognitive perspective surpassed the behavioral perspective in influence sometime around 1970. As you can see, the psychoanalytic perspective has always had a modest impact on the mainstream of psychology.

SOURCE: Adapted from Robins, R. W., Gosling, S. D., & Craik, K. H. (1999). An empirical analysis of trends in psychology. *American Psychologist, 54,* 117–128. Copyright © 1999 by the American Psychological Association. Reprinted by permission of the author.

non-Western cultures, to ethnic minorities in Western societies, or even to women as opposed to men.

However, in recent years Western psychologists have begun to recognize that their neglect of cultural variables has diminished the value of their work, and they are devoting increased attention to culture as a determinant of behavior. What brought about this shift? The new interest in culture appears mainly attributable to two recent trends: (1) Advances in communication, travel, and international trade have "shrunk" the world and increased global interdependence, bringing more and more Americans and Europeans into contact with people from non-Western cultures; and (2) the ethnic makeup of the Western world has become an increasingly diverse multicultural mosaic (Brislin, 1993; Hermans & Kempen, 1998; Mays et al., 1996).

These trends have prompted more and more Western psychologists to broaden their horizons and incorporate cultural factors into their theories and research (Adamopoulos & Lonner, 2001; Matsumoto & Yoo, 2006). These psychologists are striving to study previously underrepresented groups of subjects to test the generality of earlier findings and to catalog both the differences and similarities among cultural groups. They are working to increase knowledge of how culture is transmitted through socialization practices and how culture colors one's view of the world. They are seeking to learn how people cope with cultural change and to find ways to reduce misunderstandings and conflicts in intercultural interactions. In addition, they are trying to enhance understanding of how cultural groups are affected by prejudice, discrimination, and racism. In all these efforts, they are striving to understand the unique experiences of culturally diverse people *from the point of view of those people*. These efforts to ask new questions, study new groups, and apply new perspectives promise to enrich the discipline of psychology (Fowers & Davidov, 2006; Lehman, Chiu, & Schaller, 2004; Matsumoto, 2003; Sue, 2003).

Psychology Adapts: The Emergence of Evolutionary Psychology 1a

A relatively recent development in psychology has been the emergence of *evolutionary psychology*, a new theoretical perspective that is likely to be influential in the years to come. Evolutionary psychologists assert that the patterns of behavior seen in a species are products of evolution in the same way that anatomical characteristics are. *Evolutionary psychology*

The praying mantis has an astonishing ability to blend in with its environment, along with remarkably acute hearing and vision that permit it to detect prey up to 60 feet away and powerful jaws that allow it to devour its prey. They are so deadly they will eat each other, which makes sex quite a challenge, but males have evolved a reflex module that allows them to copulate successfully while being eaten (even after decapitation)! These physical characteristics obviously represent adaptations that have been crafted by natural selection over the course of millions of generations. Evolutionary psychologists maintain that many patterns of behavior seen in various species are also adaptations that have been shaped by natural selection.

examines behavioral processes in terms of their adaptive value for members of a species over the course of many generations. The basic premise of evolutionary psychology is that natural selection favors behaviors that enhance organisms' reproductive success—that is, passing on genes to the next generation. Thus, if a species is highly aggressive, evolutionary psychologists argue that it's because aggressiveness conveys a survival or reproductive advantage for members of that species, so genes that promote aggressiveness are more likely to be passed on to the next generation. Although evolutionary psychologists have a natural interest in animal behavior, they have not been bashful about analyzing the evolutionary bases of human behavior. As La Cerra and Kurzban (1995) put it, "The human mind was sculpted by natural selection, and it is this evolved organ that constitutes the subject matter of psychology" (p. 63).

Looking at behavioral patterns in terms of their evolutionary significance is not an entirely new idea (Graziano, 1995). As noted earlier, William James and other functionalists were influenced by Darwin's concept of natural selection over a century ago. However, in the ensuing decades applications of evolutionary concepts to *psychological* processes were piecemeal, half-hearted, and not particularly well received. The 1960s and 1970s brought major breakthroughs in the field of evolutionary *biology* (Hamilton, 1964; Trivers, 1971, 1972; Williams, 1966), but these advances had little immediate impact in

web link 1.4

The Archives of the History of American Psychology (AHAP)

The Archives of the History of American Psychology (AHAP) at the University of Akron is a huge repository of information and materials on the history of psychology. Its website provides a well-organized overview of the archive's holdings and access to a number of photos of instruments and equipment used in psychological research.

psychology. The situation began to change in the middle to late 1980s. A growing band of evolutionary psychologists—led by David Buss (1985, 1988, 1989), Martin Daly and Margo Wilson (1985, 1988), and Leda Cosmides and John Tooby (Cosmides & Tooby, 1989; Tooby & Cosmides, 1989)—published widely cited studies on a broad range of topics, including mating preferences, jealousy, aggression, sexual behavior, language, decision making, personality, and development. By the mid-1990s, it became clear that psychology was witnessing the birth of its first major, new theoretical perspective since the cognitive revolution in the 1950s and 1960s.

As with all prominent theoretical perspectives in psychology, evolutionary theory has its critics (Gould, 1993; Lickliter & Honeycutt, 2003; Plotkin, 2004; Rose & Rose, 2000). They argue that many evolutionary hypotheses are untestable and that evolutionary explanations are post hoc, speculative accounts for obvious behavioral phenomena (see the Critical Thinking Application for this chapter). However, evolutionary psychologists have articulated persuasive rebuttals to these and other criticisms (Buss & Reeve, 2003; Conway & Schaller, 2002; Hagen, 2005), and the evolutionary perspective has become increasingly influential.

Psychology Moves in a Positive Direction

1a

Shortly after Martin Seligman was elected president of the American Psychological Association in 1997, he experienced a profound insight that he characterized as an "epiphany." This pivotal insight came from an unusual source—Seligman's 5-year-old daughter, Nikki. She scolded her overachieving, task-oriented father for being "grumpy" far too much of the time. Provoked by his daughter's criticism, Seligman suddenly realized that his approach to life *was* overly and unnecessarily negative. More important, he recognized that the same assessment could be made of the field of psychology—that, it too, was excessively and needlessly negative in its approach (Seligman, 2003). This revelation inspired Seligman to launch an influential new initiative within psychology that came to be known as the *positive psychology movement.*

Seligman went on to argue convincingly that the field of psychology had historically devoted too much attention to pathology, weakness, and damage, and ways to heal suffering. He acknowledged that this approach had yielded valuable insights and progress, but he argued that it also resulted in an unfortunate neglect of the forces that make life worth living. Seligman convened a series of informal meetings with

influential psychologists and then more formal conferences to gradually outline the philosophy and goals of positive psychology. Other major architects of the positive psychology movement have included Mihaly Csikszentmihalyi (2000), Christopher Peterson (2000, 2006), and Barbara Fredrickson (2002, 2005). Like humanism before it, positive psychology seeks to shift the field's focus away from negative experiences. As Seligman and Csikszentmihalyi (2000) put it, "The aim of positive psychology is to begin to catalyze a change in the focus of psychology from preoccupation with only repairing the worst things in life to also building positive qualities" (p. 5). Thus, *positive psychology* **uses theory and research to better understand the positive, adaptive, creative, and fulfilling aspects of human existence.**

The emerging field of positive psychology has three areas of interest (Seligman, 2003). The first is the study of *positive subjective experiences,* or positive emotions, such as happiness, love, gratitude, contentment, and hope. The second focus is on *positive individual traits*—that is, personal strengths and virtues. Theorists are working to identify, classify, and analyze the origins of such positive traits as courage, perseverance, nurturance, tolerance, creativity, integrity, and kindness. The third area of interest is in *positive institutions and communities.* Here the focus is on how societies can foster civil discourse, strong families, healthful work environments, and supportive neighborhood communities.

Although it has proven far less controversial than evolutionary psychology, positive psychology also has critics (La Torre, 2007; Sugarman, 2007). For example, Richard Lazarus (2003) has argued that it is an oversimplification to divide human experience into positive and negative domains and that the line between these two domains is not as clear and obvious as most have assumed. Lazarus expresses concern that positive psychology may be little more than "one of the many fads that come and go in our field" (p. 93). Only time will tell, as positive psychology is still in its infancy. It will be fascinating to see whether and how this new movement reshapes psychology's research priorities and theoretical interests in the years to come.

Our review of psychology's past has shown how the field has evolved. We have seen psychology develop from philosophical speculation into a rigorous science committed to research. We have seen how a highly visible professional arm involved in mental health services emerged from this science. We have seen how psychology's focus on physiology is rooted in its 19th-century origins. We have seen how and why psychologists began conducting research on lower animals. We have seen how psychology has evolved from the study of mind and body to the study of behavior. And we have seen how the investigation of mind and body has been welcomed back into the mainstream of modern psychology. We have seen how different theoretical schools have defined the scope and mission of psychology in different ways. We have seen how psychology's interests have expanded and become increasingly diverse. Above all else, we have seen that psychology is a growing, evolving intellectual enterprise.

Psychology's history is already rich, but its story has barely begun. The century or so that has elapsed since Wilhelm Wundt put psychology on a scientific footing is only an eyeblink of time in human history. What has been discovered during those years, and what remains unknown, is the subject of the rest of this book.

REVIEW of Key Learning Goals

1.7 Stimulated by the demands of World War II, clinical psychology grew rapidly in the 1950s. Thus, psychology became a profession as well as a science. This movement toward professionalization eventually spread to other areas in psychology.

1.8 During the 1950s and 1960s advances in the study of cognition led to renewed interest in mental processes, as psychology returned to its roots. Advocates of the cognitive perspective argue that human behavior cannot be fully understood without considering how people think. The 1950s and 1960s also saw advances in research on the physiological bases of behavior. Advocates of the biological perspective assert that human and animal behavior can be explained in terms of the bodily structures and biochemical processes that allow organisms to behave.

1.9 In the 1980s, Western psychologists, who had previously been rather provincial, developed a greater interest in how cultural factors influence behavior. This trend was sparked in large part by growing global interdependence and by increased cultural diversity in Western societies.

1.10 The 1990s witnessed the emergence of a new theoretical perspective called evolutionary psychology. The central premise of this new school of thought is that the patterns of behavior seen in a species are products of evolution in the same way that anatomical characteristics are and that the human mind has been sculpted by natural selection.

1.11 Around the beginning of the 21st century, the positive psychology movement became an influential force. Advocates of positive psychology argue that the field has historically devoted too much attention to pathology, weakness, and ways to heal suffering. Positive psychology seeks to better understand the adaptive, creative, and fulfilling aspects of human existence.

Psychology Today: Vigorous and Diversified

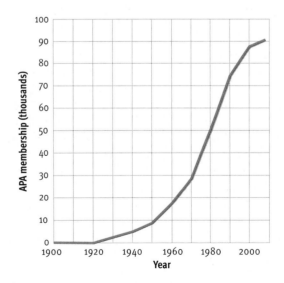

We began this chapter with an informal description of what psychology is about. Now that you have a feel for how psychology has developed, you can better appreciate a definition that does justice to the field's modern diversity: *Psychology* is the science that studies behavior and the physiological and cognitive processes that underlie behavior, and it is the profession that applies the accumulated knowledge of this science to practical problems.

Contemporary psychology is a thriving science and profession. Its growth has been remarkable. One simple index of this growth is the dramatic rise in membership in the American Psychological Association (APA), a national organization devoted to the advancement of psychology. The APA was founded in 1892 with just 26 members. Today, the APA has over 90,000 members. Moreover, as **Figure 1.5** shows, APA membership has increased ninefold since 1950. In the United States, psychology is the second most popular undergraduate major (see **Figure 1.6** on the next page), and the field accounts for nearly 10% of all doctoral degrees awarded in the sciences and humanities. Of course, psychology is an international enterprise.

Figure 1.5

Membership in the American Psychological Association, 1900–2008. The steep rise in the number of psychologists in the APA since 1950 testifies to psychology's remarkable growth as a science and a profession. If graduate student members are also counted, the APA has over 150,000 members. (Adapted from data published by the American Psychological Association.)

Key Learning Goals

1.12 Discuss the growth of psychology, and identify the most common work settings for contemporary psychologists.

1.13 List and describe nine major research areas in psychology.

1.14 List and describe six professional specialties in psychology.

Figure 1.6

Psychology's place among leading college majors. This graphic lists the twelve most popular undergraduate majors in the United States, based on the number of bachelor's degrees awarded in 2004–2005. As you can see, psychology ranked second only to business administration and management in the number of degrees awarded. (Data from U.S. Department of Education, National Center for Education Statistics, *Digest of Education Statistics: 2006*)

Today, over 2100 technical journals from all over the world publish research articles on psychology. Thus, by any standard of measurement—the number of people involved, the number of degrees granted, the number of studies conducted, the number of journals published—psychology is a healthy, growing field.

Psychology's vigorous presence in modern society is also demonstrated by the great variety of settings in which psychologists work. The distribution of psychologists employed in various categories of settings can be seen in **Figure 1.7**. They were once found almost exclusively in academia. However, today only about one-fourth of American psychologists work in colleges and universities. The remaining three-fourths work in hospitals, clinics, police departments, research institutes, government agencies, business and industry, schools, nursing homes, counseling centers, and private practice.

Clearly, contemporary psychology is a multifaceted field, a fact that is especially apparent when we consider the many areas of specialization within psychology today. Let's look at the current areas of specialization in both the science and the profession of psychology.

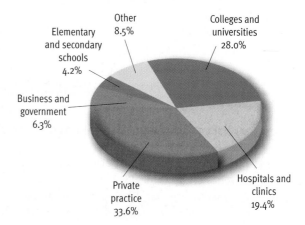

Figure 1.7

Employment of psychologists by setting. The work settings in which psychologists are employed have become very diverse. Survey data on the primary employment setting of APA members indicates that one-third are in private practice (compared to 12% in 1976), while only 28% work in colleges and universities (compared to 47% in 1976). (Based on *2000 APA Directory Survey*)

Research Areas in Psychology

Although most psychologists receive broad training that provides them with knowledge about many areas of psychology, they usually specialize when it comes to doing research. Such specialization is necessary because the subject matter of psychology has become so vast over the years. Today it is virtually impossible for anyone to stay abreast of the new research in all specialties. Specialization is also necessary because specific skills and training are required to do research in some areas.

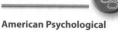

web link 1.5

American Psychological Association (APA)

The APA website is a treasure trove of resources on psychology in all its rich diversity. The section for the public includes electronic pamphlets on practical topics such as depression, aging, and anger. A wealth of information on career possibilities in the field can also be found here.

The seven major research areas in modern psychology are (1) developmental psychology, (2) social psychology, (3) experimental psychology, (4) physiological psychology, (5) cognitive psychology, (6) personality, and (7) psychometrics, (8) educational psychology, and (9) health psychology. **Figure 1.8** briefly describes each of these areas of inquiry. They are elaborated on in more detail in Appendix C.

Professional Specialties in Psychology

Applied psychology consists of four well-established areas of specialization and a couple of new, emerging specialties. The four established professional specialties are (1) clinical psychology, (2) counseling psychology, (3) school psychology, and (4) industrial/organizational psychology. The two emerging specialties are clinical neuropsychology and forensic psychology. Descriptions of all six of these specialties can be found in **Figure 1.9** (on page 20), as well as Appendix C. Clinical psychology is currently the most widely practiced professional specialty.

Although it is useful to distinguish between research and professional specialties in psychology, it is important to note that many psychologists work on *both* research and application. Some academic psychologists work as consultants, therapists, and counselors on a part-time basis. Similarly, some applied psychologists conduct basic research on issues related to their specialty. For example, many clinical psychologists are involved in research on the nature and causes of abnormal behavior.

web link 1.6

Marky Lloyd's Career Page
For those who think they might want to find a job or career in psychology or a related field, Marky Lloyd of Georgia Southern University has put together a fine set of resources to help in both planning and making choices.

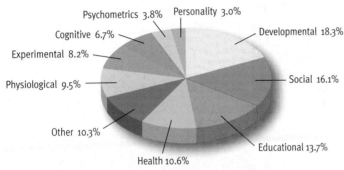

Psychometrics 3.8% — Personality 3.0%
Cognitive 6.7%
Experimental 8.2%
Physiological 9.5%
Other 10.3%
Health 10.6%
Developmental 18.3%
Social 16.1%
Educational 13.7%

Figure 1.8
Major research areas in contemporary psychology. Most research psychologists specialize in one of the nine broad areas described here. The figures in the pie chart reflect the percentage of academic and research psychologists belonging to APA who identify each area as their primary interest. (Based on data published by the American Psychological Association)

Area	Focus of research
Developmental psychology	Looks at human development across the life span. Developmental psychology once focused primarily on child development, but today devotes a great deal of research to adolescence, adulthood, and old age.
Social psychology	Focuses on interpersonal behavior and the role of social forces in governing behavior. Typical topics include attitude formation, attitude change, prejudice, conformity, attraction, aggression, intimate relationships, and behavior in groups.
Educational psychology	Studies how people learn and the best ways to teach them. Examines curriculum design, teacher training, achievement testing, student motivation, classroom diversity, and other aspects of the educational process.
Health psychology	Focuses on how psychological factors relate to the promotion and maintenance of physical health and the causation, prevention, and treatment of illness.
Physiological psychology	Examines the influence of genetic factors on behavior and the role of the brain, nervous system, endocrine system, and bodily chemicals in the regulation of behavior.
Experimental psychology	Encompasses the traditional core of topics that psychology focused on heavily in its first half-century as a science: sensation, perception, learning, conditioning, motivation, and emotion. The name experimental psychology is somewhat misleading, as this is not the only area in which experiments are done. Psychologists working in all the areas listed here conduct experiments.
Cognitive psychology	Focuses on "higher" mental processes, such as memory, reasoning, information processing, language, problem solving, decision making, and creativity.
Psychometrics	Is concerned with the measurement of behavior and capacities, usually through the development of psychological tests. Psychometrics is involved with the design of tests to assess personality, intelligence, and a wide range of abilities. It is also concerned with the development of new techniques for statistical analysis.
Personality	Is interested in describing and understanding individuals' consistency in behavior, which represents their personality. This area of interest is also concerned with the factors that shape personality and with personality assessment.

ILLUSTRATED OVERVIEW OF PSYCHOLOGY'S HISTORY

1870 **1880** **1890** **1900** **1910** **1920** **1930**

1875

First demonstration laboratories are set up independently by **William James** (at Harvard) and Wilhelm Wundt (at the University of Leipzig).

1905
Alfred Binet develops first successful intelligence test in France.

1914–1918

Widespread intelligence testing is begun by military during World War I.

1879

Wilhelm Wundt establishes first research laboratory in psychology at Leipzig, Germany.

1908

Margaret Washburn publishes *The Animal Mind*, which serves as an impetus for behaviorism.

1916
Lewis Terman publishes Stanford-Binet Intelligence Scale, which becomes the world's foremost intelligence test.

1920s
Gestalt pychology nears its peak influence.

1933
Sigmund Freud's influence continues to build as he publishes *New Introductory Lectures on Psychoanalysis*.

1881

Wilhelm Wundt establishes first journal devoted to research in psychology.

1909

Sigmund Freud's increasing influence receives formal recognition as G. S. Hall invites Freud to give lectures at Clark University.

1890
William James publishes his seminal work, *The Principles of Psychology*.

1913

John B. Watson writes classic behaviorism manifesto, arguing that psychology should study only observable behavior.

1883
G. Stanley Hall establishes America's first research laboratory in psychology at Johns Hopkins University.

1892
G. Stanley Hall founds American Psychological Association.

1904

Ivan Pavlov shows how conditioned responses are created, paving the way for stimulus-response psychology.

1914

Leta Hollingworth publishes pioneering work on the psychology of women.

1940   **1950**   **1960**   **1970**   **1980**   **1990**   **2000**

1941–1945

Rapid growth in clinical psychology begins in response to huge demand for clinical services created by World War II and its aftermath.

1953

B. F. Skinner publishes his influential *Science and Human Behavior,* advocating radical behaviorism similar to Watson's.

1954

Abraham Maslow's *Motivation and Personality* helps fuel humanistic movement.

1956

The cognitive revolution is launched at watershed conference where Herbert Simon, George Miller, and Noam Chomsky report three major advances in just one day.

1947

Kenneth and Mamie **Clark** publish work on prejudice that is cited in landmark 1954 Supreme Court decision outlawing segregation.

1963

Stanley Milgram conducts controversial study of obedience to authority, which may be the most famous single study in psychology's history.

1950

Erik Erikson writes *Childhood and Society* in which he extends Freud's theory of development across the life span.

1951

Carl Rogers helps launch humanistic movement with publication of *Client-Centered Therapy.*

1961–1964

Roger Sperry's split-brain research and work by David Hubel and Torsten Wiesel on how cortical cells respond to light help rejuvenate the biological perspective in psychology.

1971

B. F. Skinner creates furor over radical behaviorism with his controversial book *Beyond Freedom and Dignity.*

1974

Eleanor Maccoby and Carol Jacklin publish their landmark review of research on gender differences, which galvanizes research in this area.

1978

Herbert Simon wins Nobel prize (in economics) for research on cognition.

1980s

Increased global inter-dependence and cultural diversity in Western societies spark surge of interest in how cultural factors mold behavior.

1981

Roger Sperry wins Nobel prize (in physiology and medicine) for split-brain studies.

1988

Research psychologists form American Psychological Society (APS) to serve as an advocate for the science of psychology.

Early 1990s

Evolutionary psychology emerges as a major new theoretical perspective.

1990s

The repressed memories controversy stimulates influential research by **Elizabeth Loftus** and others on the malleability and fallibility of human memory.

Late 1990s

Martin Seligman launches the positive psychology movement.

2000

Eric Kandel wins Nobel Prize (in physiology and medicine) for his research on the biochemistry of memory.

2002

Daniel Kahneman wins Nobel Prize (in economics) for his research on decision making.

Note:
The credits for copyrighted photos and illustrations on pages 18–19 can be found on page CR-1.

Figure 1.9

Principal professional specialties in contemporary psychology. Most psychologists who deliver professional services to the public specialize in one of the six areas described here. The figures in the pie chart reflect the percentage of APA members delivering professional services who identify each area as their chief specialty. (Based on data published by the American Psychological Association)

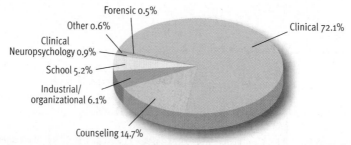

Forensic 0.5%
Other 0.6%
Clinical Neuropsychology 0.9%
School 5.2%
Industrial/organizational 6.1%
Counseling 14.7%
Clinical 72.1%

Specialty	Focus of professional practice
Clinical psychology	Clinical psychologists are concerned with the evaluation, diagnosis, and treatment of individuals with psychological disorders, as well as treatment of less severe behavioral and emotional problems. Principal activities include interviewing clients, psychological testing, and providing group or individual psychotherapy.
Counseling psychology	Counseling psychology overlaps with clinical psychology in that specialists in both areas engage in similar activities—interviewing, testing, and providing therapy. However, counseling psychologists usually work with a somewhat different clientele, providing assistance to people struggling with everyday problems of moderate severity. Thus, they often specialize in family, marital, or career counseling.
Industrial and organizational psychology	Psychologists in this area perform a wide variety of tasks in the world of business and industry. These tasks include running human resources departments, working to improve staff morale and attitudes, striving to increase job satisfaction and productivity, examining organizational structures and procedures, and making recommendations for improvements.
School psychology	School psychologists strive to promote the cognitive, emotional, and social development of children in schools. They usually work in elementary or secondary schools, where they test and counsel children having difficulties in school and aid parents and teachers in solving school-related problems.
Clinical neuropsychology	Clinical neuropsychologists are involved in the assessment and treatment of people who suffer from central nervous system dysfunctions due to head trauma, dementia, stroke, seizure disorders, and so forth.
Forensic psychology	Forensic psychologists apply psychological principles to issues arising in the legal system, such as child custody decisions, hearings on competency to stand trial, violence risk assessments, involuntary commitment proceedings, and so forth.

concept check 1.3

Understanding the Major Research Areas in Contemporary Psychology

Check your understanding of the various research areas in psychology reviewed in this chapter by indicating which type of psychologist would be most likely to perform each of the investigations described below. Choose from the following: (a) physiological psychology, (b) cognitive psychology, (c) developmental psychology, (d) psychometrics, and (e) personality. You'll find the answers in Appendix A at the back of the book.

1. Researchers interviewed the parents of 141 children (all born in 1956) every few months throughout childhood. Questions dealt with various aspects of the children's temperaments. The conclusion was that most children fall into one of three temperamental categories: "easy," "difficult," or "slow to warm up."

_____

2. It was discovered that rats will work extremely hard (pressing a lever, for instance) to earn small amounts of electrical stimulation directed to specific areas of their brains. Research indicates that the human brain may also contain similar "pleasure centers."

_____

3. The Sensation Seeking Scale (SSS) was developed to measure individual differences in the extent to which people prefer high or low levels of sensory stimulation. People such as skydivers tend to score high on the SSS, while someone whose idea of a good time is settling down with a good book would tend to score low.

_____

Seven Unifying Themes

The enormous breadth and diversity of psychology make it a challenging subject for the beginning student. In the pages ahead you will be introduced to many areas of research and a multitude of new ideas, concepts, and principles. Fortunately, not all ideas are created equal. Some are far more important than others. In this section, I will highlight seven fundamental themes that will reappear in a number of variations as we move from one area of psychology to another in this text. You have already met some of these key ideas in our review of psychology's past and present. Now we will isolate them and highlight their significance. In the remainder of the book these ideas serve as organizing themes to provide threads of continuity across chapters and to help you see the connections among the various areas of research in psychology.

In studying psychology, you are learning about both behavior and the scientific discipline that investigates it. Accordingly, our seven themes come in two sets. The first set consists of statements highlighting crucial aspects of psychology as a way of thinking and as a field of study. The second set consists of broad generalizations about psychology's subject matter: behavior and the cognitive and physiological processes that underlie it.

Themes Related to Psychology as a Field of Study

Looking at psychology as a field of study, we see three crucial ideas: (1) psychology is empirical, (2) psychology is theoretically diverse, and (3) psychology evolves in a sociohistorical context. Let's look at each of these ideas in more detail.

Theme 1: Psychology Is Empirical

Everyone tries to understand behavior. Most of us have developed our own personal answers to such questions as why some people are hard workers, why some are overweight, and why others stay in demeaning relationships. If all of us are amateur psychologists, what makes scientific psychology any different or better? The critical difference is that psychology is *empirical.*

What do we mean by empirical? ***Empiricism* is the premise that knowledge should be acquired through observation.** This premise is crucial to the scientific method that psychology embraced in the late 19th century. To say that psychology is empirical means that its conclusions are based on direct observation rather than on reasoning, speculation, traditional beliefs, or common sense. Psychologists are not content with having ideas that sound plausible. They conduct research to test their ideas. Is intelligence higher on the average in some social classes than in others? Are men more aggressive than women? Psychologists find a way to make direct, objective, and precise observations to answer such questions.

The empirical approach requires a certain attitude—a healthy brand of skepticism. Empiricism is a tough taskmaster. It demands data and documentation. Psychologists' commitment to empiricism means that they must learn to think critically about generalizations concerning behavior. If someone asserts that people tend to get depressed around Christmas, a psychologist is likely to ask, "How many people get depressed? In what population? In comparison to what baseline rate of depression? How is depression defined and measured?" Their skeptical attitude means that psychologists are trained to ask, "Where's the evidence? How do you know?" If psychology's empirical orientation rubs off on you (and I hope it does), you will be asking similar questions by the time you finish this book.

Theme 2: Psychology Is Theoretically Diverse

Although psychology is based on observation, a string of unrelated observations would not be terribly enlightening. Psychologists do not set out to collect isolated facts; they seek to explain and understand what they observe. To achieve these goals they must construct theories. A *theory* is a system of interrelated ideas used to explain a set of observations. In other words, a theory links apparently unrelated observations and tries to explain them. As an example, consider Sigmund Freud's observations about slips of the tongue, dreams, and psychological disturbances. On the surface, these observations appear unrelated. By devising the concept of the *unconscious*, Freud created a theory that links and explains these seemingly unrelated aspects of behavior.

Our review of psychology's past should have made one thing abundantly clear: Psychology is marked by theoretical diversity. Why do we have so many competing points of view? One reason is that no single theory can adequately explain everything that is known about behavior. Sometimes different theories focus on different aspects of behavior—that is, different collections of observations. Sometimes there is simply more than one way to look at something. Is the glass half empty or half full? Obviously, it is both. To take an example from another science, physicists wrestled for years with the nature of light. Is it a wave, or is it a particle? In the end, it proved useful to think of light sometimes as a wave and sometimes as a particle. Similarly, if a business executive lashes out at her employees with stinging criticism, is she releasing pent-up aggressive urges (a psychoanalytic view)? Is she making a habitual response to the stimulus of incompetent work (a behavioral view)? Or is she scheming to motivate her employees with "mind games" (a cognitive view)? In some cases, all three of these explanations might have some validity. In short, it is an oversimplification to expect that one view has to be right while all others are wrong. Life is rarely that simple.

Students are often troubled by psychology's many conflicting theories, which they view as a weakness. *However, contemporary psychologists increasingly recognize that theoretical diversity is a strength rather than a weakness* (Hilgard, 1987). As we proceed through this text, you will learn how clashing theories have often stimulated productive research. You will also

see how approaching a problem from several theoretical perspectives can often provide a more complete understanding than could be achieved by any one perspective alone.

Theme 3: Psychology Evolves in a Sociohistorical Context

Science is often seen as an "ivory tower" undertaking, isolated from the ebb and flow of everyday life. In reality, however, psychology and other sciences do not exist in a cultural vacuum. Dense interconnections exist between what happens in psychology and what happens in society at large (Altman, 1990; Danziger, 1990; Runyan, 2006). Trends, issues, and values in society influence psychology's evolution. Similarly, progress in psychology affects trends, issues, and values in society. To put it briefly, psychology develops in a *sociohistorical* (social and historical) context.

Psychology's past is filled with examples of how social trends have left their imprint on psychology. For example, Sigmund Freud's groundbreaking ideas emerged out of a specific sociohistorical context. Cultural values in Freud's era encouraged the suppression of sexuality. As a result, people tended to feel guilty about their sexual urges to a much greater extent than is common today. This situation clearly contributed to Freud's emphasis on unconscious sexual conflicts. As another example, consider how World War II sparked the rapid growth of psychology as a profession.

If we reverse our viewpoint, we can see that psychology has in turn left its mark on society. Consider, for instance, the pervasive role of mental testing in modern society. Your own career success may depend in part on how well you weave your way through a complex maze of intelligence and achievement tests made possible (to the regret of some) by research in psychology. As another example of psychology's impact on society, consider the influence that various theorists have had on parenting styles. Trends in childrearing practices have been shaped by the ideas of John B. Watson, Sigmund Freud, B. F. Skinner, and Carl Rogers—not to mention many more psychologists yet to be discussed. In short, society and psychology influence each other in complex ways. In the chapters to come, we will frequently have occasion to notice this dynamic relationship.

Themes Related to Psychology's Subject Matter

Looking at psychology's subject matter, we see four additional crucial ideas: (4) behavior is determined

web link 1.7

Encyclopedia of Psychology

This "encyclopedia," developed by psychology faculty at Jacksonville State University, is actually a collection of over 2000 links to webpages around the world on psychological matters. The links related to the history of the field and careers in psychology are extensive, as are the links relating to theories and publications in psychology.

by multiple causes, (5) behavior is shaped by cultural heritage, (6) heredity and environment jointly influence behavior; and (7) people's experience of the world is highly subjective.

Theme 4: Behavior Is Determined by Multiple Causes

As psychology has matured, it has provided more and more information about the forces that govern behavior. This growing knowledge has led to a deeper appreciation of a simple but important fact: Behavior is exceedingly complex, and most aspects of behavior are determined by multiple causes.

Although the complexity of behavior may seem self-evident, people usually think in terms of single causes. Thus, they offer explanations such as "Andrea flunked out of school because she is lazy." Or they assert that "teenage pregnancies are increasing because of all the sex in the media." Single-cause explanations are sometimes accurate insofar as they go, but they usually are incomplete. In general, psychologists find that behavior is governed by a complex network of interacting factors, an idea referred to as the *multifactorial causation of behavior.*

As a simple illustration, consider the multiple factors that might influence your performance in your introductory psychology course. Relevant personal factors might include your overall intelligence, your reading ability, your memory skills, your motivation, and your study skills. In addition, your grade could be affected by numerous situational factors, including whether you like your psychology professor, whether you like your assigned text, whether the class meets at a good time for you, whether your work schedule is light or heavy, and whether you're having any personal problems. As you proceed through this book, you will learn that complexity of causaton is the rule rather than the exception. If we expect to understand behavior, we usually have to take into account multiple determinants.

Theme 5: Behavior Is Shaped by Cultural Heritage

Among the multiple determinants of human behavior, cultural factors are particularly prominent. Just as psychology evolves in a sociohistorical context, so, too, do individuals. Our cultural backgrounds exert considerable influence over our behavior. As Markus and Hamedani (2007) put it, "The option of being *a*social or *a*cultural—that is, living as a neutral being who is not bound to particular practices and socioculturally structured ways of behaving—is not available. People eat, sleep, work, and relate to one another in culture-specific ways" (p. 5). What

Cultural background has an enormous influence on people's behavior, shaping everything from modes of dress to sexual values and norms. Increased global interdependence brings more and more people into contact with cultures other than their own. This increased exposure to diverse cultures only serves to underscore the importance of cultural factors.

is *culture?* Theorists have argued about the exact details of how to define culture for over a century, and the precise boundaries of the concept remain a little fuzzy (Matsumoto & Yoo, 2006). Broadly speaking, *culture* **refers to the widely shared customs, beliefs, values, norms, institutions, and other products of a community that are transmitted socially across generations.** Culture is a broad construct, encompassing everything from a society's legal system to its assumptions about family roles, from its dietary habits to its political ideals, from its technology to its attitudes about time, from its modes of dress to its spiritual beliefs, and from its art and music to its unspoken rules about sexual liaisons.

Triandis (2007) emphasizes that culture has a dual nature, existing both outside and inside people. Culture lies outside of people in that one can identify various customs, practices, and institutions that mold people's behavior. Culture lies inside people in that everything that happens to them is viewed through a cultural lens—a way of thinking—that cannot be set aside. The fact that culture lies within people means that much of a person's cultural heritage is invisible (Brislin, 2000). Assumptions, ideals, attitudes, beliefs, and unspoken rules exist in people's minds and may not be readily apparent to outsiders. Moreover, because our cultural background is widely shared, we feel little need to discuss it with others, and we often take it for granted. For example, you probably don't spend much time thinking about the importance of living in rectangular rooms, trying to minimize body odor, limiting yourself to one spouse at a time, or using credit cards to obtain material goods and services. We often fail to appreciate its influence, but our cultural heritage has a pervasive impact on our thoughts, feelings, and behavior (Matsumoto & Juang, 2008; Triandis, 2007).

Although the influence of culture is everywhere, generalizations about cultural groups must always be tempered by the realization that great diversity exists within any society or ethnic group (Markus & Hamedani, 2007). Researchers may be able to pinpoint genuinely useful insights about Ethiopian, Korean American, or Ukrainian culture, for example, but it would be foolish to assume that all Ethiopians, Korean Americans, or Ukrainians exhibit identical behavior. It is also important to realize that *both differences and similarities in behavior occur across cultures.* As we will see repeatedly, psychological processes are characterized by both cultural variance and invariance. Caveats aside, if we hope to achieve a sound understanding of human behavior, we need to consider cultural determinants.

Theme 6: Heredity and Environment Jointly Influence Behavior

Are we who we are—athletic or artistic, quick-tempered or calm, shy or outgoing, energetic or laid back—because of our genetic inheritance or because of our upbringing? This question about the importance of nature versus nurture, or heredity versus environment, has been asked in one form or another since ancient times. Historically, the nature versus nurture question was framed as an all-or-none proposition. In other words, theorists argued that personal traits and abilities are governed entirely by heredity or entirely by environment. John B. Watson, for instance, asserted that personality and ability depend almost exclusively on an individual's environment. In contrast, Sir Francis Galton, a pioneer in mental testing, maintained that personality and ability depend almost entirely on genetic inheritance.

Today, most psychologists agree that heredity and environment are both important. A century of research has shown that genetics and experience jointly influence individuals' intelligence, temperament, personality, and susceptibility to many psychological disorders (Grigerenko & Sternberg, 2003; Plomin, 2004). If we ask whether people are born or made, psychology's answer is "Both." This response does not mean that nature versus nurture is a dead issue. Lively debate about the *relative influence* of genetics and experience continues unabated. Furthermore, psychologists are actively seeking to understand the complex ways in which genetic inheritance and experience interact to mold behavior.

Theme 7: People's Experience of the World Is Highly Subjective

Our experience of the world is highly subjective. Even elementary perception—for example, of sights and sounds—is not a passive process. We actively process incoming stimulation, selectively focusing on some aspects of that stimulation while ignoring others.

Moreover, we impose organization on the stimuli that we pay attention to. These tendencies combine to make perception personalized and subjective.

The subjectivity of perception was demonstrated nicely in a study by Hastorf and Cantril (1954). They showed students at Princeton and Dartmouth universities a film of a hotly contested football game between the two rival schools. The students were told to watch for rules infractions. Both groups saw the same film, but the Princeton students "saw" the Dartmouth players engage in twice as many infractions as the Dartmouth students "saw," and vice versa. The investigators concluded that the game "actually was many different games and that each version of the events that transpired was just as 'real' to a particular person as other versions were to other people" (Hastorf & Cantril, 1954). This study showed how people sometimes see what they *want* to see. Other studies have demonstrated that people also tend to see what they *expect* to see (Kelley, 1950).

Human subjectivity is precisely what the scientific method is designed to counteract. In using the scientific approach, psychologists strive to make their observations as objective as possible. Left to their own subjective experience, people might still believe that the earth is flat and that the sun revolves around it. Thus, psychologists are committed to the scientific approach because they believe it is the most reliable route to accurate knowledge.

Now that you have been introduced to the text's organizing themes, let's turn to an example of how psychological research can be applied to the challenges of everyday life. In our first Personal Application, we'll focus on a subject that should be highly relevant to you: how to be a successful student. In the Critical Thinking Application that follows it, we discuss the nature and importance of critical thinking skills.

Identifying the Contributions of Major Theorists and Researchers

Check your recall of the principal ideas of important theorists and researchers covered in this chapter by matching the people listed on the left with the appropriate contributions described on the right. If you need help, the crucial pages describing each person's ideas are listed in parentheses. Fill in the letters for your choices in the spaces provided on the left. You'll find the answers in Appendix A.

Major Theorists and Researchers

_____ 1. Mary Whiton Calkins (p. 5)

_____ 2. Sigmund Freud (pp. 5–6)

_____ 3. Leta Stetter Hollingworth (p. 5)

_____ 4. William James (p. 4)

_____ 5. Carl Rogers (p. 9)

_____ 6. B. F. Skinner (pp. 8–9)

_____ 7. Margaret Floy Washburn (p. 5)

_____ 8. John B. Watson (pp. 7–8)

_____ 9. Wilhelm Wundt (p. 3)

Key Ideas and Contributions

a. This theorist was the founder of behaviorism. He proposed that psychologists should abandon the study of consciousness altogether.

b. This individual, who authored *The Animal Mind* (1908), was the first woman to receive a Ph.D. in psychology.

c. This influential American researcher showed that organisms tend to repeat responses that lead to positive outcomes. He also argued that free will is an illusion.

d. Widely viewed as the founder of psychology, this person established the first laboratory for research in psychology in 1879.

e. This person was the first woman to serve as president of the American Psychological Association.

f. This Harvard scholar was the chief architect of functionalism, arguing that psychology should investigate the functions rather than the structure of consciousness.

g. This advocate of humanism took an optimistic view of human nature and was a major critic of psychoanalytic and behavioral theories.

h. This pioneer was the first person to use the term *gifted* to refer to youngsters who scored extremely high on intelligence tests.

i. This theorist focused on the unconscious and sexuality, causing considerable controversy. He also invented psychoanalytic theory.

Improving Academic Performance

Key Learning Goals

1.17 Review three important considerations in designing a program to promote adequate studying.

1.18 Discuss some strategies for improving reading comprehension.

1.19 Summarize advice provided on how to get more out of lectures.

1.20 Summarize advice provided on improving test-taking strategies.

Answer the following "true" or "false."

___ **1** If you have a professor who delivers chaotic, hard-to-follow lectures, there is little point in attending class.

___ **2** Cramming the night before an exam is an efficient method of study.

___ **3** In taking lecture notes, you should try to be a "human tape recorder" (that is, write down everything your professor says).

___ **4** You should never change your answers to multiple-choice questions, because your first hunch is your best hunch.

All of the above statements are false. If you answered them all correctly, you may have already acquired the kinds of skills and habits that facilitate academic success. If so, however, you are not typical. Today, many students enter college with poor study skills and habits, and it's not entirely their fault. Our educational system generally provides minimal instruction on good study techniques. In this first Personal Application, I will try to remedy this situation to some extent by reviewing some insights that psychology offers on how to improve academic performance. We will discuss how to promote better study habits, how to enhance reading efforts, how to get more out of lectures, and how to improve test-taking strategies. You may also want to jump ahead and read the Personal Application for Chapter 7, which focuses on how to improve everyday memory.

Developing Sound Study Habits

Effective study is crucial to success in college. Although you may run into a few classmates who boast about getting good grades without studying, you can be sure that if they perform well on exams, they do study. Students who claim otherwise simply want to be viewed as extremely bright rather than as studious.

Learning can be immensely gratifying, but studying usually involves hard work. The first step toward effective study habits is to face up to this reality. You don't have to feel guilty if you don't look forward to studying. Most students don't. Once you accept the premise that studying doesn't come naturally, it should be apparent that you need to set up an organized program to promote adequate study. According to Siebert & Karr (2003), such a program should include the following considerations:

1. *Set up a schedule for studying.* If you wait until the urge to study strikes you, you may still be waiting when the exam rolls around. Thus, it is important to allocate definite times to studying. Review your various time obligations (work, chores, and so on) and figure out in advance when you

can study. When allotting certain times to studying, keep in mind that you need to be wide awake and alert. Be realistic about how long you can study at one time before you wear down from fatigue. Allow time for study breaks; they can revive sagging concentration.

It's important to write down your study schedule. A written schedule serves as a reminder and increases your commitment to following it. You should begin by setting up a general schedule for the quarter or semester, like the one in **Figure 1.10**. Then, at the beginning of each week, plan the specific assignments that you intend to work on during each study session. This approach to scheduling should help you avoid cramming for exams at the last minute. Cramming is an ineffective study strategy for most students (Underwood, 1961; Wong, 2006; Zechmeister & Nyberg, 1982). It will strain your memorization capabilities, can tax your energy level, and may stoke the fires of test anxiety.

In planning your weekly schedule, try to avoid the tendency to put off working on major tasks such as term papers and reports. Time-management experts, such as Alan Lakein (1996), point out that many of us tend to tackle simple, routine tasks first, saving larger tasks for later when we sup-

posedly will have more time. This common tendency leads many of us to repeatedly delay working on major assignments until it's too late to do a good job. You can avoid this trap by breaking major assignments down into smaller component tasks that can be scheduled individually.

2. *Find a place to study where you can concentrate.* Where you study is also important. The key is to find a place where distractions are likely to be minimal. Most people cannot study effectively while the TV is on or music is playing or while other people are talking. Don't depend on willpower to carry you through such distractions. It's much easier to plan ahead and avoid the distractions altogether.

3. *Reward your studying.* One reason that it is so difficult to be motivated to study regularly is that the payoffs often lie in the distant future. The ultimate reward, a degree, may be years away. Even more short-term rewards, such as an A in the course, may be weeks or months away. To combat this problem, it helps to give yourself immediate, tangible rewards for studying, such as a snack, TV show, or phone call to a friend. Thus, you should set realistic study goals for yourself and then reward yourself when you meet them. The systematic manipulation of rewards involves harnessing the principles of behavior modification described by B. F. Skinner and other behavioral psychologists. These principles are covered in the Chapter 6 Personal Application.

Improving Your Reading

Much of your study time is spent reading and absorbing information. The keys to improving reading comprehension are to preview reading assignments section by section, work hard to actively process the meaning of the information, strive to identify the key ideas of each paragraph, and carefully review these key ideas after each section. Modern textbooks often contain a variety of learning aids that you can use to improve your reading. If a book provides a chapter outline, chapter summary, or learning objectives, don't ignore them. They can help you recognize the important points in the chapter. Graphic organizers (such as the Concept Charts available for this text) can also enhance understanding of text mate-

Weekly Activity Schedule

	Monday	Tuesday	Wednesday	Thursday	Friday	Saturday	Sunday
8 A.M.						Work	
9 A.M.	History	Study	History	Study	History		
10 A.M.	Psychology	French	Psychology	French	Psychology		
11 A.M.	Study		Study		Study		
Noon	Math	Study	Math	Study	Math		Work
1 P.M.							
2 P.M.	Study	English	Study	English	Study		
3 P.M.							
4 P.M.							
5 P.M.							
6 P.M.	Work	Study	Study	Work			Work
7 P.M.							
8 P.M.							
9 P.M.							
10 P.M.							

Figure 1.10

One student's general activity schedule for a semester. Each week the student fills in the specific assignments to work on during each study period.

Some locations are far more conducive to successful studying than others.

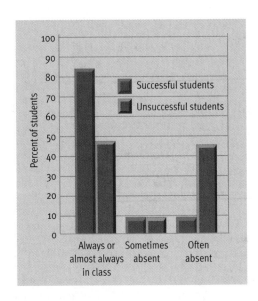

Figure 1.11

Attendance and grades. When Lindgren (1969) compared the class attendance of successful students (B average or above) and unsuccessful students (C– average or below), he found a clear association between poor attendance and poor grades.

rial (Nist & Holschuh, 2000). A lot of effort and thought go into formulating these and other textbook learning aids. It is wise to take advantage of them.

Another important issue related to textbook reading is whether and how to mark up one's reading assignments. Many students deceive themselves into thinking that they are studying by running a marker through a few sentences here and there in their text. If they do so without thoughtful selectivity, they are simply turning a textbook into a coloring book. This situation probably explains why some professors are skeptical about the value of highlighting textbooks. Nonetheless, research suggests that highlighting textbook material *is* a useful strategy—if students are reasonably effective in focusing on the main ideas in the material and if they subsequently review what they have highlighted (Caverly, Orlando, & Mullen, 2000).

When executed effectively, highlighting can foster active reading, improve reading comprehension, and reduce the amount of material that one has to review later (Van Blerkom, 2006). The key to effective text marking is to identify (and highlight) only the main ideas, key supporting details, and technical terms (Daiek & Anter, 2004). Most textbooks are carefully crafted such that every paragraph has a purpose for being there. Try to find the sentence or two that best captures the purpose of each para-

graph. Text marking is a delicate balancing act. If you highlight too little of the content, you are not identifying enough of the key ideas. But if you highlight too much of the content, you are not going to succeed in condensing what you have to review to a manageable size.

Getting More out of Lectures

Although lectures are sometimes boring and tedious, it is a simple fact that poor class attendance is associated with poor grades. For example, in one study (see **Figure 1.11**), Lindgren (1969) found that absences from class were much more common among "unsuccessful" students (grade average C– or below) than among "successful" students (grade average B or above). Even when you have an instructor who delivers hard-to-follow lectures, it is still important to go to class. If nothing else, you can get a feel for how the instructor thinks, which can help you anticipate the content of exams and respond in the manner expected by your professor.

Fortunately, most lectures are reasonably coherent. Studies indicate that attentive note taking is associated with enhanced learning and performance in college classes (Titsworth & Kiewra, 2004; Williams & Eggert, 2002). However, research also shows that many students' lecture notes are surprisingly incomplete, with the average student often recording less than 40% of

the crucial ideas in a lecture (Armbruster, 2000). Thus, the key to getting more out of lectures is to stay motivated, stay attentive, and expend the effort to make your notes as complete as possible. Books on study skills (Longman & Atkinson, 2005; McWhorter, 2007) offer a number of suggestions on how to take good-quality lecture notes, some of which are summarized here:

• Extracting information from lectures requires *active listening*. Focus full attention on the speaker. Try to anticipate what's coming and search for deeper meanings.

• When course material is especially complex, it is a good idea to prepare for the lecture by *reading ahead* on the scheduled subject in your text. Then you have less new information to digest.

• You are not supposed to be a human tape recorder. Insofar as possible, try to write down the lecturer's thoughts *in your own words*. Doing so forces you to organize the ideas in a way that makes sense to you.

• In taking notes, pay attention to clues about what is most important. These clues may range from subtle hints, such as an instructor repeating a point, to not-so-subtle hints, such as an instructor saying "You'll run into this again."

• In delivering their lectures most professors follow an organized outline, which they may or may not share with the class (on the blackboard or via a presentation tool, such as PowerPoint). Insofar as you can decipher the outline of a lecture, try to organize your notes accordingly. When you go back to review your notes later, they will make more sense and it should be easier to identify the most important ideas.

• *Asking questions* during lectures can be helpful. Doing so keeps you actively involved in the lecture and allows you to clarify points that you may have misunderstood. Many students are more bashful about asking questions than they should be. They don't realize that most professors welcome questions.

Improving Test-Taking Strategies

Let's face it—some students are better than others at taking tests. *Testwiseness* is the ability to use the characteristics and for-mat of a cognitive test to maximize one's score. Students clearly vary in testwiseness, and such variations are reflected in performance on exams (Geiger, 1997; Rogers & Yang, 1996). Testwiseness is *not* a substitute for knowledge of the subject matter. However, skill in taking tests can help you show what you know when it is critical to do so (Flippo, Becker, & Wark, 2000).

A number of myths exist about the best way to take tests. For instance, it is widely believed that students shouldn't go back and change their answers to multiple-choice questions. Benjamin, Cavell, and Shallenberger (1984) found this to be the dominant belief among college *faculty* as well as students (see **Figure 1.12**). However, the old adage that "your first hunch is your best hunch on tests" has been shown to be wrong. Empirical studies clearly and consistently indicate that, over the long run, changing answers pays off. Benjamin and his colleagues reviewed 20 studies on this issue; their findings are presented in **Figure 1.13**. As you can see, answer changes that go from a wrong answer to a right answer outnumber changes that go from a right answer to a wrong one by a sizable margin. The popular belief that answer changing is harmful is probably attributable to painful memories of right-to-wrong changes. In any case, you can see how it pays to be familiar with sound test-taking strategies.

General Tips

The principles of testwiseness were first described by Millman, Bishop, and Ebel (1965). Here are some of their general ideas:

• If efficient time use appears crucial, set up a mental schedule for progressing through the test. Make a mental note to check whether you're one-third finished when a third of your time is gone.

• Don't waste time pondering difficult-to-answer questions excessively. If you have no idea at all, just guess and go on. If you

Figure 1.12

Beliefs about the effects of answer changing on tests. Ludy Benjamin and his colleagues (1984) asked 58 college faculty whether changing answers on tests is a good idea. Like most students, the majority of the faculty felt that answer changing usually hurts a student's test score, even though the research evidence contradicts this belief (see **Figure 1.13**).

Figure 1.13

Actual effects of changing answers on multiple-choice tests. When the data from all the relevant studies were combined by Benjamin et al. (1984), they indicated that answer changing on tests generally *increased* rather than *reduced* students' test scores. It is interesting to note the contrast between beliefs about answer changing (see **Figure 1.12**) and the actual results of this practice.

need to devote a good deal of time to the question, skip it and mark it so you can return to it later if time permits.

• Adopt the appropriate level of sophistication for the test. Don't read things into questions. Sometimes students make things more complex than they were intended to be. Often, simple-looking questions are just what they appear to be.

• If you complete all of the questions and still have some time remaining, review the test. Make sure that you have recorded your answers correctly. If you were unsure of some answers, go back and reconsider them.

Tips for Multiple-Choice Exams

Sound test-taking strategies are especially important with multiple-choice (and true-false) questions. These types of questions often include clues that may help you converge on the correct answer (Mentzer, 1982; Weiten, 1984). You may be able to improve your performance on such tests by considering the following points (Flippo, 2000; Millman et al., 1965; Smith, 2005; Van Blerkom, 2006):

• Always read each question completely. Continue reading even if you find your anticipated answer among the options. There may be a more complete option farther down the list.

• Learn how to quickly eliminate options that are highly implausible. Many questions have only two plausible options, accompanied by "throwaway" options for filler. You should work at spotting these implausible options so that you can quickly discard them and narrow your choices.

• Be alert to the fact that information relevant to one question is sometimes given away in another test item.

• On items that have "all of the above" as an option, if you know that just two of the options are correct, you should choose "all of the above." If you are confident that one of the options is incorrect, you should eliminate this option and "all of the above" and choose from the remaining options.

• Options that represent broad, sweeping generalizations tend to be incorrect. You should be vigilant for words such as *always, never, necessarily, only, must, completely, totally,* and so forth that create these improbable assertions.

• In contrast, options that represent carefully qualified statements tend to be correct. Words such as *often, sometimes, perhaps, may,* and *generally* tend to show up in these well-qualified statements.

In summary, sound study skills and habits are crucial to academic success. Intelligence alone won't do the job (although it certainly helps). Good academic skills do not develop overnight. They are acquired gradually, so be patient with yourself. Fortunately, tasks such as reading textbooks, writing papers, and taking tests get easier with practice. Ultimately, I think you'll find that the rewards—knowledge, a sense of accomplishment, and progress toward a degree—are worth the effort.

REVIEW of Key Learning Goals

1.17 To foster sound study habits, you should devise a written study schedule, find a place to study where you can concentrate, and reward yourself for following your study schedule. Try to avoid the tendency to put off working on major tasks.

1.18 You should use active reading techniques to select the most important ideas from the material you read. Highlighting textbook material is a useful strategy—if students are reasonably effective in focusing on the main ideas in the material and if they subsequently review what they have highlighted.

1.19 The key to good note taking is to strive to make lecture notes as complete as possible. It's important to use active listening techniques and to record lecturers' ideas in your own words. It also helps if you read ahead to prepare for lectures and ask questions as needed.

1.20 In taking tests, it's a good idea to devise a schedule for progressing through an exam, to adopt the appropriate level of sophistication, to avoid wasting time on troublesome questions, and to review your answers. On multiple-choice tests it is wise to anticipate answers, to read questions completely, and to quickly eliminate implausible options.

Psychology's Early History

▌ Psychology's intellectual parents were 19th-century philosophy and physiology, which shared an interest in the mysteries of the mind. Psychology was born as an independent discipline when Wilhelm Wundt established the first psychological research laboratory in 1879 at Leipzig, Germany. He argued that psychology should be the scientific study of consciousness. The new discipline grew rapidly in North America in the late 19th century.

▌ The structuralists believed that psychology should use introspection to analyze consciousness into its basic elements. Functionalists such as William James believed that psychology should focus on the purpose and adaptive functions of consciousness. Functionalism left a more enduring imprint on psychology.

▌ Sigmund Freud's psychoanalytic theory emphasized the unconscious determinants of behavior and the importance of sexuality. Freud's controversial ideas were met with resistance in academic psychology. However, as more psychologists developed an interest in personality, motivation, and abnormal behavior, psychoanalytic concepts were incorporated into mainstream psychology.

▌ Behaviorists, led by John B. Watson, argued that psychology should study only observable behavior. Thus, they campaigned to redefine psychology as the science of behavior. Emphasizing the importance of the environment over heredity, they often used laboratory animals as research subjects.

▌ The influence of behaviorism was boosted greatly by B. F. Skinner's research. Like Watson before him, Skinner asserted that psychology should study only observable behavior, and he generated controversy by arguing that free will is an illusion.

▌ Finding both behaviorism and psychoanalysis unsatisfactory, advocates of humanism, such as Carl Rogers and Abraham Maslow, became influential in the 1950s. Humanism emphasizes the unique qualities of human behavior and humans' potential for personal growth.

Psychology's Modern History

▌ Stimulated by the demands of World War II, clinical psychology grew rapidly in the 1950s. Thus, psychology became a profession as well as a science. This movement toward professionalization eventually spread to other areas in psychology. During the 1950s and 1960s advances in the study of cognitive processes and the physiological bases of behavior led to renewed interest in cognition and physiology.

▌ In the 1980s, Western psychologists, who had previously been rather provincial, developed a greater interest in how cultural factors influence thoughts, feelings, and behavior. This trend was sparked in large part by growing global interdependence and by increased cultural diversity in Western societies.

▌ The 1990s witnessed the emergence of a new theoretical perspective called evolutionary psychology. The central premise of this new school of thought is that patterns of behavior are the product of evolutionary forces, just as anatomical characteristics are shaped by natural selection. The turn of the century brought the emergence of the positive psychology movement.

Psychology Today: Vigorous and Diversified

▌ Contemporary psychology is a diversified science and profession that has grown rapidly in recent decades. Major areas of research in modern psychology include developmental psychology, social psychology, experimental psychology, physiological psychology, cognitive psychology, personality, psychometrics, health psychology, and educational psychology. Applied psychology encompasses four established professional specialties: clinical psychology, counseling psychology, educational and school psychology, and industrial and organizational psychology. Clinical neuropsychology and forensic psychology are two emerging professional specialties.

Seven Unifying Themes

▌ As we examine psychology in all its many variations, we will emphasize seven key ideas as unifying themes. Looking at psychology as a field of study, our three key themes are (1) psychology is empirical, (2) psychology is theoretically diverse, and (3) psychology evolves in a sociohistorical context.

▌ Looking at psychology's subject matter, the remaining four themes are (4) behavior is determined by multiple causes, (5) behavior is shaped by cultural heritage, (6) heredity and environment jointly influence behavior, and (7) people's experience of the world is highly subjective.

PERSONAL APPLICATION Improving Academic Performance

▌ To foster sound study habits, you should devise a written study schedule and reward yourself for following it. You should also try to find places for studying that are relatively free of distractions. You should use active reading techniques to select the most important ideas from the material you read. Highlighting textbook material is a useful strategy—if students are reasonably effective in focusing on the main ideas in the material and if they subsequently review what they have highlighted.

▌ Good note taking can help you get more out of lectures. It's important to use active listening techniques and to record lecturers' ideas in your own words. It also helps if you read ahead to prepare for lectures and ask questions as needed.

▌ Being an effective student also requires sound test-taking skills. In general, it's a good idea to devise a schedule for progressing through an exam, to adopt the appropriate level of sophistication, to avoid wasting time on troublesome questions, and to review your answers whenever time permits.

CRITICAL THINKING APPLICATION Developing Critical Thinking Skills: An Introduction

▌ Critical thinking refers to the use of cognitive skills and strategies that increase the probability of a desirable outcome. Critical thinking is purposeful, reasoned thinking. A critical thinker is flexible, persistent, able to admit mistakes, and mindful of the thinking process.

▌ Evolutionary psychologists have attributed contemporary sex differences in spatial abilities to the sex-based division of labor in hunting-and-gathering societies. However, there are alternative explanations for these differences that focus on the sex-typed activities that modern males and females engage in. There also are contradictory data regarding the adaptive pressures faced by females and males in hunting-and-gathering societies.

PSYKTREK PREVIEW

Visit Module 1a (*Psychology's Timeline*) to see a multimedia overview of psychology's evolution as a discipline.

Go to the Video Selector or Module 5c (*Overview of Operant Conditioning*) to see pigeons playing ping-pong—the famous example of behavioral control by B. F.

1. For which of the following is Wilhelm Wundt primarily known?
   A. The establishment of the first formal laboratory for research in psychology
   B. The distinction between mind and body as two separate entities
   C. The discovery of how signals are conducted along nerves in the body
   D. The development of the first formal program for training in psychotherapy

2. Which of the following approaches might William James criticize for examining a movie frame by frame instead of seeing the motion in the motion picture?
   A. Structuralism
   B. Functionalism
   C. Dualism
   D. Humanism

3. Fred, a tennis coach, insists that he can make any reasonably healthy individual into an internationally competitive tennis player. Fred is echoing the thoughts of:
   A. Sigmund Freud.
   B. John B. Watson.
   C. Abraham Maslow.
   D. William James.

4. Which of the following is a statement with which Skinner's followers would agree?
   A. The whole is greater than the sum of its parts.
   B. The goal of behavior is self-actualization.
   C. Nature is more influential than nurture.
   D. Free will is an illusion.

5. Which of the following approaches has the most optimistic view of human nature?
   A. Humanism
   B. Behaviorism
   C. Psychoanalysis
   D. Structuralism

6. Which of the following historical events created a demand for clinicians that was far greater than the supply?
   A. World War I
   B. The Depression
   C. World War II
   D. The Korean War

7. _____ psychology examines behavioral processes in terms of their adaptive value for a species over the course of many generations.
   A. Clinical
   B. Cognitive
   C. Evolutionary
   D. Physiological

8. The study of the endocrine system and genetic mechanisms would most likely be undertaken by a:
   A. clinical psychologist.
   B. physiological psychologist.
   C. social psychologist.
   D. educational psychologist.

9. A multifactorial causation approach to behavior suggests that:
   A. Most behaviors can be explained best by single-cause explanations.
   B. Most behavior is governed by a complex network of interrelated factors.
   C. Data need to be analyzed by the statistical technique called factor analysis in order for the data to make sense.
   D. Explanations of behavior tend to build up from the simple to the complex in a hierarchical manner.

10. Psychology's answer to the question of whether we are "born" or "made" tends to be that:
    A. we are "born."
    B. we are "made."
    C. we are both "born" and "made."
    D. neither is correct.

11. In regard to changing answers on multiple-choice tests, research indicates that _____ changes tend to be more common than other types of changes.
    A. wrong to right
    B. right to wrong
    C. wrong to wrong

12. Critical thinking skills:
    A. are abstract abilities that cannot be identified.
    B. usually develop spontaneously through normal content instruction.
    C. usually develop spontaneously without any instruction.
    D. need to be deliberately taught because they often do not develop by themselves with standard content instruction.

Answers

1 A p. 3
2 A p. 4
3 B p. 7
4 D p. 8
5 A p. 9
6 C p. 11
7 C p. 13
8 B p. 17
9 B p. 23
10 C p. 24
11 A pp. 28–29
12 D p. 30

PsykTrek Preview

The limbic system is one of the areas in the brain that appears to contain emotion-tinged pleasure centers. Using an apparatus like the one shown here, James Olds and Peter Milner discovered that rats would press a lever thousands of times per hour to send brief bursts of electrical stimulation to certain spots in the brain where an electrode was implanted.

Critical Thinking

Scientific research is generally guided by theories. A theory is a system of interrelated ideas used to explain a set of observations. Theories are used to generate specific predictions, or *hypotheses*, that can be tested through research. Because theories consist of claims about the causes of phenomena, we test theories in the same way that we test other claims. To test a theory, we need to do two things: (a) make a prediction about what should be observed if the theory is true, and (b) make the relevant observations. To illustrate this process, let's examine the theory tested in a legendary study of classical conditioning conducted by John B. Watson and Rosalie Rayner (see Module 5b).

Watson (1878–1958) was the founder of behaviorism, an influential school of thought in psychology since the 1920s. Watson argued that humans have inborn reflexive fears of only a few events, such as loud noises or a loss of physical support. He developed a theory that attempted to explain why people eventually develop fears of many other events. He speculated that most fear responses are learned through a process that today is called *classical conditioning*. To be specific, in Watson's theory, a neutral event initially eliciting no fear is paired with a second event that elicits fear reflexively, such as a loud noise (the unconditioned stimulus, or UCS). After a number of pairings of the neutral stimulus and the UCS, the neutral stimulus becomes a conditioned stimulus (CS) that elicits the fear response (the conditioned response or CR). Watson's theory suggested that, over a number of years, this process is repeated many times with a range of conditioned stimuli until a person develops fears of a number of events.

Go to the VIdeo Selector or Module 2e (*The Forebrain: Subcortical Structures*) to see historic footage of James Olds's discovery of "pleasure centers" in the brain

Check out the Critical Thinking Exercise for Unit 5 (*Theory Development and the Testing of Theories*) for an enlightening discussion of how one can evaluate the

2

The Research Enterprise in Psychology

Capilano suspension bridge, Vancouver, Canada © UrbanEye/Alamy

• Does sleeping less than seven hours a day reduce how long you will live?
• Do violent video games make people more aggressive?
• Can you make better decisions by not deliberating about them?
• Can women judge men's testosterone level in just one glance?
• Do IQ scores predict how long people will live?

Questions, questions, questions—everyone has questions about behavior. Investigating these questions is what psychology is all about.

Some of these questions pop up in everyday life. Many a parent, for example, has wondered whether violent video games might be having a harmful effect on their children's behavior. Other questions explored by psychologists might not occur to most people. For example, you may never have wondered what effects your sleeping habits or IQ could have on your life expectancy or whether women can judge men's testosterone levels. Of course, now that you've been exposed to these questions, you may be curious about the answers!

In the course of this book, you'll find out what psychologists have learned about the five questions asked above. Right now I want to call your attention to the most basic question of all—namely, how should we go about investigating questions like these? How do we find answers to our questions about behavior that are accurate and trustworthy?

As noted in Chapter 1, *psychology is empirical.* Psychologists are committed to addressing questions about behavior through formal, systematic observation. This commitment to the empirical method is what makes psychology a scientific endeavor. Many people may have beliefs about the effects of playing violent video games based on personal opinion, a feeling of aversion toward violence, a generally permissive attitude toward children's games, anecdotal reports from parents, or other sources. As scientists, however, psychologists withhold judgment on questions like these until they have objective evidence based on valid, reproducible studies. Even then, their judgments are likely to be carefully qualified so that they do not go beyond what the evidence actually shows.

Gathering and evaluating that empirical evidence is an exercise in creative problem solving. As scientists, psychologists have to figure out how to make observations that will shed light on the puzzles they want to solve—and stand up to the critical scrutiny of their peers. In this endeavor psychologists rely on a large toolkit of research methods because different kinds of questions call for different strategies of investigation. In this chapter, you'll learn about some of the principal methods used by psychologists in their research.

Why should you care about psychologists' research methods? There are at least two good reasons. First, having a good grasp of these methods will enhance your ability to understand the information you will be reading in the rest of this book, all of which is based on research. Second, becoming familiar with the logic of the empirical approach will improve your ability to think critically about claims concerning behavior. This ability is important because you are exposed to such claims—in conversations with friends, in advertising, in the news media—nearly every day. Learning how to evaluate the basis of these claims can make you a more skilled consumer of psychological information.

We'll begin our introduction to the research enterprise in psychology by examining the scientific approach to the study of behavior. From there we'll move to the specific research methods that psychologists use most frequently. Although scientific methods have stood the test of time, individual scientists are human and fallible. For this reason we'll conclude our discussion with a look at some common flaws in research. This section alone can make you a more skilled evaluator of claims that are said to be based on psychological studies. Then, in the Personal Application, you'll learn how to find and read journal articles that report on research. Finally, in the Critical Thinking Application, we'll examine the perils of a type of evidence people are exposed to all the time—anecdotal evidence.

Does a person's average sleep time influence how long they will live? Questions such as these are the point of departure for scientific investigations. Answering empirical questions is what science is all about. Consult Chapter 5 to learn what recent studies have discovered about the relationship between typical sleep duration and longevity.

Key Learning Goals

2.1 Explain science's main assumption, and describe the goals of the scientific enterprise.

2.2 Clarify the relations between theory, hypotheses, and research.

2.3 Outline the steps in a scientific investigation.

2.4 Identify the advantages of the scientific approach.

Looking for Laws: The Scientific Approach to Behavior

Whether the object of study is gravitational forces or people's behavior under stress, *the scientific approach assumes that events are governed by some lawful order.* As scientists, psychologists assume that behavior is governed by laws or principles, just as the movement of the earth around the sun is governed by the laws of gravity. The behavior of living creatures may not seem as lawful and predictable as the "behavior" of planets. However, the scientific enterprise is based on the belief that there are consistencies or laws that can be uncovered. Fortunately, the value of applying this fundamental assumption has been supported by the discovery of a great many such consistencies in behavior, some of which provide the subject matter for this text.

Goals of the Scientific Enterprise

Psychologists and other scientists share three sets of interrelated goals: measurement and description, understanding and prediction, and application and control.

1. *Measurement and description.* Science's commitment to observation requires that a researcher figure out a way to measure the phenomenon under study. For example, a psychologist could not investigate whether men are more or less sociable than women without first developing some means of measuring sociability. Thus, the first goal of psychology is to develop measurement techniques that make it possible to describe behavior clearly and precisely.

2. *Understanding and prediction.* A higher-level goal of science is understanding. Scientists believe that they understand events when they can explain the reasons for their occurrence. To evaluate such understanding, scientists make and test predictions called hypotheses. A *hypothesis* is a tentative statement about the relationship between two or more variables. *Variables* are any measurable conditions, events, characteristics, or behaviors that are controlled or observed in a study. If we predicted that putting people under time pressure would lower the accuracy of their time perception, the variables in our study would be time pressure and accuracy of time perception.

3. *Application and control.* Ultimately, most scientists hope that the information they gather will be of some practical value in helping to solve everyday problems. Once people understand a phenomenon,

they can often exert more control over it. Today, the profession of psychology attempts to apply research findings to practical problems in schools, businesses, factories, and mental hospitals. For example, a school psychologist might use findings about the causes of math anxiety to devise a program to help students control their math phobias.

How do theories help scientists to achieve their goals? As noted in Chapter 1, psychologists do not set out to just collect isolated facts about relationships between variables. To build toward a better understanding of behavior, they construct theories. A *theory* is a system of interrelated ideas used to explain a set of observations. For example, using a handful of concepts, such as natural selection and reproductive fitness, evolutionary theory (Buss, 1995, 1996) purports to explain a diverse array of known facts about mating preferences, jealousy, aggression, sexual behavior, and so forth (see Chapter 1). Thus, by integrating apparently unrelated facts and principles into a coherent whole, theories permit psychologists to make the leap from the *description* of behavior to the *understanding* of behavior. Moreover, the enhanced understanding afforded by theories guides future research by generating new predictions and suggesting new lines of inquiry (Fiske, 2004; Higgins, 2004).

A scientific theory must be testable, as the cornerstone of science is its commitment to putting ideas to an empirical test. Most theories are too complex to be tested all at once. For example, it would be impossible to devise a single study that could test all the many aspects of evolutionary theory. Rather, in a typical study, investigators test one or two specific hypotheses derived from a theory. If their findings support the hypotheses, confidence in the theory the hypotheses were derived from grows. If their findings fail to support the hypotheses, confidence in the theory diminishes, and the theory may be revised or discarded. Thus, theory construction is a gradual, iterative process that is always subject to revision.

Steps in a Scientific Investigation

Curiosity about a question provides the point of departure for any kind of investigation, scientific or otherwise. Scientific investigations, however, are *systematic.* They follow an orderly pattern, which is outlined in **Figure 2.1**. Let's look at how this standard series of steps was followed in a study of *naive realism* conducted by David Sherman, Leif Nelson, and Lee Ross (2003). Sherman and his colleagues wanted to investigate whether adversaries in political debates overestimate the gap between their views.

Step 1: Formulate a Testable Hypothesis

The first step in a scientific investigation is to translate a theory or an intuitive idea into a testable hypothesis. Sherman et al. (2003) noted that in heated disputes people seem to assume that they see matters as they really are—that their perceptions are objective and accurate—and that their opponents' views must be distorted by self-interest, ideology, or some other source of bias. The researchers call this belief in one's own objectivity and opponents' subjectivity "naive realism." Based on their concept of naive realism, Sherman and his colleagues speculated that in political debates people on both sides would tend to characterize their opponents as extremists and to overestimate the extent of their mutual disagreement. To explore this line of thinking, they chose to examine individuals' views on the contentious issue of affirmative action. Thus, they hypothesized that proponents of affirmative action would overestimate opponents' conservativism and that opponents of affirmative action would overestimate proponents' liberalism.

To be testable, scientific hypotheses must be formulated precisely, and the variables under study must be clearly defined. Researchers achieve these clear formulations by providing operational definitions of the relevant variables. An *operational definition* de-

Step 1
Formulate a hypothesis

Proponents of affirmative action will overestimate opponents' conservatism and opponents of affirmative action will overestimate proponents' liberalism.

Step 2
Design the study

Use survey method with undergraduate participants. Devise hypothetical affirmative action proposal and appropriate rating scales.

Step 3
Collect the data

Administer questionnaire to 78 students at Stanford University in exchange for small nonmonetary gift.

Step 4
Analyze the data and draw conclusions

Calculate average ratings of proposal by supporters and rejectors and compare to subjects' estimates of opponents' ratings. Data are consistent with the prediction that adversaries overestimate the gap between their views.

Step 5
Report the findings

Publish report of the study (and two companion studies) in a 2003 issue of the journal *Basic and Applied Social Psychology*.

Figure 2.1

Flowchart of steps in a scientific investigation. As illustrated in the study by Sherman, Nelson, and Ross (2003), a scientific investigation consists of a sequence of carefully planned steps, beginning with the formulation of a testable hypothesis and ending with the publication of the study, if its results are worthy of examination by other researchers.

scribes the actions or operations that will be used to measure or control a variable. Operational definitions—which may be quite different from dictionary definitions—establish precisely what is meant by each variable in the context of a study.

To illustrate, let's see how Sherman and his colleagues operationalized their variables. They decided that the issue of affirmative action is too complex and multifaceted to ask people about their views of affirmative action *in general*. Each person would be judging something different, based on his or her highly varied exposure to affirmative action initiatives. To circumvent this problem they asked students to respond to a specific affirmative action

"IT MAY VERY WELL BRING ABOUT IMMORTALITY, BUT IT WILL TAKE FOREVER TO TEST IT."

program that supposedly had been proposed for their university. To get a precise measurement of participants' views, they asked the students to indicate their degree of support for the proposal on a 9-point scale anchored by the descriptions *definitely adopt* and *definitely reject*. Those checking 1 to 4 on the scale were designated as *supporters* of the proposal, while those checking 6 to 9 on the scale were designated as *rejectors* (those who checked the midpoint of 5 were classified as *neutral*).

Step 2: Select the Research Method and Design the Study

The second step in a scientific investigation is to figure out how to put the hypothesis to an empirical test. The research method chosen depends to a large degree on the nature of the question under study. The various methods—experiments, case studies, surveys, naturalistic observation, and so forth—each have advantages and disadvantages. The researcher has to ponder the pros and cons, then select the strategy that appears to be the most appropriate and practical. In this case, Sherman and colleagues decided that their question called for *survey* research, which involves administering questionnaires or interviews to people.

Once researchers have chosen a general method, they must make detailed plans for executing their study. Thus, Sherman and associates had to decide how many people they needed to survey and where they would get their participants. *Participants,* or *subjects,* are the persons or animals whose behavior is systematically observed in a study. For their first study, Sherman et al. chose to use 78 undergraduates (45 women and 29 men) at Stanford University. Sherman and his colleagues also had to devise a plausible-sounding affirmative action proposal that students could evaluate. And they had to craft rating scales that would permit the assessment of subjects' political ideology and the subjects' perceptions of their opponents' political ideology.

Step 3: Collect the Data

The third step in the research enterprise is to collect the data. Researchers use a variety of *data collection techniques,* which are procedures for making empirical observations and measurements. Commonly used techniques include direct observation, questionnaires, interviews, psychological tests, physiological recordings, and examination of archival records (see **Table 2.1**). The data collection techniques used in a study depend largely on what is being investigated. For example, questionnaires are well suited for studying attitudes, psychological tests for studying personality, and physiological recordings for studying the biological bases of behavior. Depending on the nature and complexity of the study, data collection can often take months, and it sometimes requires years of work. One advantage of the survey method, however, is that data can often be collected quickly and easily, which was true in this case. Sherman and his colleagues simply had their subjects complete a carefully designed questionnaire in their dorm rooms in exchange for a small nonmonetary gift.

Step 4: Analyze the Data and Draw Conclusions

The observations made in a study are usually converted into numbers, which constitute the raw data of the study. Researchers use *statistics* to analyze their data and to decide whether their hypotheses have been supported. Thus, statistics play an essential role in the scientific enterprise. Based on their statistical analyses, Sherman et al. (2003) concluded that their data supported their hypothesis. As predicted, they found that supporters of the affirmative action proposal greatly overestimated the conservatism of the rejectors and that the rejectors of the proposal

Table 2.1 Key Data Collection Techniques in Psychology

Technique	Description
Direct observation	Observers are trained to watch and record behavior as objectively and precisely as possible. They may use some instrumentation, such as a stopwatch or video recorder.
Questionnaire	Subjects are administered a series of written questions designed to obtain information about attitudes, opinions, and specific aspects of their behavior.
Interview	A face-to-face dialogue is conducted to obtain information about specific aspects of a subject's behavior.
Psychological test	Subjects are administered a standardized measure to obtain a sample of their behavior. Tests are usually used to assess mental abilities or personality traits.
Physiological recording	An instrument is used to monitor and record a specific physiological process in a subject. Examples include measures of blood pressure, heart rate, muscle tension, and brain activity.
Examination of archival records	The researcher analyzes existing institutional records (the archives), such as census, economic, medical, legal, educational, and business records.

greatly overestimated the liberalism of the supporters (see **Figure 2.2**). The data indicated that the actual (average) attitudes of the two groups really were not all that far apart, but each group *assumed* that their opponents held very dissimilar views. Obviously, insofar as this may be true of political debates in general, it sheds light on (1) why it is often so difficult for opposing sides to bridge the (perceived) gap between them, and (2) why people often have such pervasively negative views of their adversaries.

Step 5: Report the Findings

Scientific progress can be achieved only if researchers share their findings with one another and with the general public. Therefore, the final step in a scientific investigation is to write up a concise summary of the study and its findings. Typically, researchers prepare a report that is delivered at a scientific meeting and submitted to a journal for publication. A *journal* is a periodical that publishes technical and scholarly material, usually in a narrowly defined area of inquiry. The study by Sherman and his colleagues (2003) was published, along with two companion studies, in a journal called *Basic and Applied Social Psychology*.

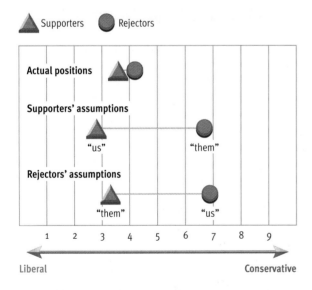

Figure 2.2

Results of the Sherman et al. (2003) study. As you can see, the actual positions of the supporters and rejectors of the affirmative action proposal were not all that far apart (top row). However, when supporters of the proposal were asked to estimate the political ideology of other supporters as well as of those who rejected the proposal, they assumed that there was a huge gap between the two groups (middle row). Similarly, when those who were against the proposal were asked to make the same estimates (bottom row), they also overestimated the disparity between the two groups.

SOURCE: Sherman, D. K., Nelson, L. D., & Ross, L. D. (2003). Naive realism and affirmative action: Adversaries are more similar than they think. *Basic and Applied Social Psychology, 25*, 275–289. Copyright © 2003 Lawrence Erlbaum Associates, Inc. Reprinted by permission.

The process of publishing scientific studies allows other experts to evaluate and critique new research findings. When articles are submitted to scientific journals they go through a demanding *peer review process* that is summarized in **Figure 2.3**. Experts thoroughly scrutinize each submission. They carefully evaluate each study's methods, statistical analyses, and conclusions, as well as its contribution to knowledge and theory. The peer review process is so demanding, many top journals reject over 90% of submitted articles! The purpose of the peer review process is to ensure that journals publish reliable

Figure 2.3

The peer review process for journal submissions. Scientists use an elaborate peer review process to determine whether studies merit publication in a technical journal. The goal of this process is to maximize the quality and reliability of published scientific findings.

Peer Review of Scientific Articles

Researcher or research team authors manuscript that describes the methods, findings, and implications of an empirical study or series of related studies.

Manuscript is submitted to the editor of a professional journal (such as *Journal of Abnormal Psychology* or *Psychological Science*) that seems appropriate given the topic of the research. A manuscript can be submitted to only one journal at a time.

The journal editor sends the manuscript to two to four experts in the relevant area of research who are asked to serve as reviewers. The reviewers provide their input anonymously and are not paid for their work.

The reviewers carefully critique the strengths, weaknesses, and theoretical significance of the research and make a recommendation as to whether it is worthy of publication in that specific journal. If the research has merit, the reviewers usually offer numerous suggestions for improving the clarity of the manuscript.

The editor reads the manuscript and expert reviews and decides whether the submission deserves publication. Most journals reject a substantial majority of submissions. The editorial decision, the reasoning behind it, and the expert reviews are sent to the author.

If the manuscript is accepted, the author may incorporate suggestions for improvement from the reviews, make final revisions, and resubmit the article to the journal editor.

If the manuscript is rejected, the author may (a) abandon the publication effort, or (b) use reviewers' suggestions to make revisions and then submit the article to another journal.

The article is published in a professional journal usually three to six months after final acceptance.

Following rejection, researchers sometimes give up on a line of research, but often they go back to the drawing board and attempt to design a better study.

findings based on high-quality research. The peer review process is a major strength of the scientific approach because it greatly reduces the likelihood of publishing erroneous findings.

Advantages of the Scientific Approach

Science is certainly not the only method that can be used to draw conclusions about behavior. We all use logic, casual observation, and good old-fashioned common sense. Because the scientific method requires painstaking effort, it seems reasonable to ask what advantages make it worth the trouble.

Basically, the scientific approach offers two major advantages. The first is its clarity and precision. Commonsense notions about behavior tend to be vague and ambiguous. Consider the old adage "Spare the rod and spoil the child." What exactly does this generalization about childrearing amount to? How severely should children be punished if parents are not to "spare the rod"? How do we assess whether a child qualifies as "spoiled"? A fundamental problem is that such statements have different meanings, depending on the person. In contrast, the scientific approach requires that people specify *exactly* what they are talking about when they formulate hypotheses. This clarity and precision enhance communication about important ideas.

The second and perhaps greatest advantage offered by the scientific approach is its relative intolerance of error. Scientists are trained to be skeptical. They subject their ideas to empirical tests. They also inspect one another's findings with a critical eye. They demand objective data and thorough documentation before they accept ideas. When the findings of two studies conflict, the scientist tries to figure out why, usually by conducting additional research. In contrast, commonsense analyses involve little effort to verify ideas or detect errors.

All this is not to say that science has an exclusive copyright on truth. However, the scientific approach does tend to yield more accurate and dependable information than casual analyses and armchair speculation do. Knowledge of scientific data can thus provide a useful benchmark against which to judge claims and information from other kinds of sources.

Now that we have had an overview of how the scientific enterprise works, we can focus on how specific research methods are used. *Research methods* **consist of differing approaches to the observation, measurement, manipulation, and control of variables in empirical studies.** In other words, they are general strategies for conducting studies. No single research method is ideal for all purposes and situations. Much of the ingenuity in research involves selecting and tailoring the method to the question at hand. The next two sections of this chapter discuss the two basic types of methods used in psychology: *experimental research methods* and *descriptive/correlational research methods*.

REVIEW of Key Learning Goals

2.1 The scientific approach assumes that there are laws of behavior that can be discovered through empirical research. The goals of the science of psychology include (1) the measurement and description of behavior, (2) the understanding and prediction of behavior, and (3) the application of this knowledge to the task of controlling behavior.

2.2 By integrating apparently unrelated facts into a coherent whole, theories permit psychologists to make the leap from the description of behavior to the understanding of behavior. Confidence in a theory increases when hypotheses derived from it are supported by research.

2.3 A scientific investigation follows a systematic pattern that includes five steps: (1) formulate a testable hypothesis, (2) select the research method and design the study, (3) collect the data, (4) analyze the data and draw conclusions, and (5) report the findings.

2.4 One major advantage of the scientific approach is its clarity in communication, which is promoted by its use of operational definitions. Another key advantage is its relative intolerance of error, which is promoted by scientists' constant testing of hypotheses and skeptical scrutiny of research findings.

Looking for Causes: Experimental Research

Does misery love company? This question intrigued social psychologist Stanley Schachter. When people feel anxious, he wondered, do they want to be left alone, or do they prefer to have others around? Schachter's review of relevant theories suggested that in times of anxiety people would want others around to help them sort out their feelings. Thus, his hypothesis was that increases in anxiety would cause increases in the

desire to be with others, which psychologists call the *need for affiliation*. To test this hypothesis, Schachter (1959) designed a clever experiment.

The *experiment* **is a research method in which the investigator manipulates a variable under carefully controlled conditions and observes whether any changes occur in a second variable as a result.** The experiment is a relatively powerful procedure that allows researchers to detect cause-and-effect relationships. Psychologists depend on this method more than any other. To see how an experiment is designed, let's use Schachter's study as an example.

Independent and Dependent Variables

SIM1, 1b

The purpose of an experiment is to find out whether changes in one variable (let's call it *X*) cause changes in another variable (let's call it *Y*). To put it more concisely, we want to find out *how X affects Y*. In this formulation, we refer to *X* as the *independent variable* and to *Y* as the *dependent variable*.

An *independent variable* is a condition or event that an experimenter varies in order to see its impact on another variable. The independent variable is the variable that the experimenter controls or manipulates. It is hypothesized to have some effect on the dependent variable, and the experiment is conducted to verify this effect. The *dependent variable* is the variable that is thought to be affected by manipulation of the independent variable. In psychology studies, the dependent variable is usually a measurement of some aspect of the subjects' behavior. The independent variable is called *independent* because it is *free* to be varied by the experimenter. The dependent variable is called *dependent* because it is thought to *depend* (at least in part) on manipulations of the independent variable.

In Schachter's experiment, *the independent variable was the participants' anxiety level*. He manipulated anxiety level in a clever way. Subjects assembled in his laboratory were told by a "Dr. Zilstein" that they would be participating in a study on the physiological effects of electric shock. They were further informed that during the experiment they would receive a series of electric shocks from an intimidating-looking apparatus while their pulse and blood pressure were being monitored. Half of the participants were warned that the shocks would be very painful. They made up the *high-anxiety* group. The other half of the participants (the *low-anxiety* group) were told that the shocks would be mild and painless. In reality, there was no plan to shock anyone at any time. These orientation procedures were simply intended to evoke various levels of anxiety. After the orientation, the experimenter indicated that there would be a delay while he prepared the shock apparatus for use. The participants were asked whether they would prefer to wait alone or in the company of others. *The subjects' desire to be with others was the dependent variable.*

concept check 2.1

Recognizing Independent and Dependent Variables

Check your understanding of the experimental method by identifying the independent variable (IV) and dependent variable (DV) in the following investigations. Note that one study has two IVs and another has two DVs. You'll find the answers in Appendix A in the back of the book.

1. A researcher is interested in how heart rate and blood pressure are affected by viewing a violent film sequence as opposed to a nonviolent film sequence.
   IV _____
   DV _____

2. An organizational psychologist develops a new training program to improve clerks' courtesy to customers in a large chain of retail stores. She conducts an experiment to see whether the training program leads to a reduction in the number of customer complaints.
   IV _____
   DV _____

3. A researcher wants to find out how stimulus complexity and stimulus contrast (light/dark variation) affect infants' attention to stimuli. He manipulates stimulus complexity and stimulus contrast and measures how long infants stare at various stimuli.
   IV _____
   DV _____

4. A social psychologist investigates the impact of group size on subjects' conformity in response to group pressure.
   IV _____
   DV _____

Experimental and Control Groups

SIM1, 1b

In an experiment the investigator typically assembles two groups of subjects who are treated differently with regard to the independent variable. These two groups are referred to as the *experimental group* and the *control group*. The *experimental group* consists of the subjects who receive some special treatment in regard to the independent variable. The *control group* consists of similar subjects who do not receive the special treatment given to the experimental group.

In the Schachter study, the participants in the high-anxiety condition constituted the experimental group. They received a special treatment designed to create an unusually high level of anxiety. The participants in the low-anxiety condition constituted the control group. They were not exposed to the special anxiety-arousing procedure.

It is crucial that the experimental and control groups in a study be very similar, except for the different treatment that they receive in regard to the independent variable. This stipulation brings us to the logic that underlies the experimental method.

If the two groups are alike in all respects *except for the variation created by the manipulation of the independent variable,* then any differences between the two groups on the dependent variable *must be due to the manipulation of the independent variable.* In this way researchers isolate the effect of the independent variable on the dependent variable. Schachter, for example, isolated the impact of anxiety on the need for affiliation. As predicted, he found that increased anxiety led to increased affiliation. As **Figure 2.4** indicates, the percentage of participants in the high-anxiety group who wanted to wait with others was nearly twice that of the low-anxiety group.

Extraneous Variables   SIM1, 1b

As we have seen, the logic of the experimental method rests on the assumption that the experimental and control groups are alike except for their treatment in regard to the independent variable. Any other differences between the two groups can cloud the situation and make it difficult to draw conclusions about how the independent variable affects the dependent variable.

In practical terms, of course, it is impossible to ensure that two groups of subjects are exactly alike in *every* respect. The experimental and control groups have to be alike only on dimensions that are relevant to the dependent variable. Thus, Schachter did not need to worry about whether his two groups were similar in hair color, height, or interest in bal-

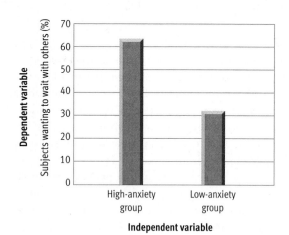

Figure 2.4

Results of Schachter's study of affiliation. The percentage of people wanting to wait with others was higher in the high-anxiety (experimental) group than in the low-anxiety (control) group, consistent with Schachter's hypothesis that anxiety would increase the desire for affiliation. The graphic portrayal of these results allows us to see at a glance the effects of the experimental manipulation on the dependent variable.

let. Obviously, these variables weren't likely to influence the dependent variable of affiliation behavior.

Instead, experimenters concentrate on making sure that the experimental and control groups are alike on a limited number of variables that could have a bearing on the results of the study. These variables are called extraneous, secondary, or nuisance variables. *Extraneous variables* are any variables other than the independent variable that seem likely to influence the dependent variable in a specific study.

In Schachter's study, one extraneous variable would have been the participants' tendency to be sociable. Why? Because subjects' sociability could affect their desire to be with others (the dependent variable). If the participants in one group had happened to be more sociable (on the average) than those in the other group, the variables of anxiety and sociability would have been confounded. A *confounding of variables* occurs when two variables are linked in a way that makes it difficult to sort out their specific effects. When an extraneous variable is confounded with an independent variable, a researcher cannot tell which is having what effect on the dependent variable.

Unanticipated confoundings of variables have wrecked innumerable experiments. That is why so much care, planning, and forethought must go into designing an experiment. A key quality that separates a talented experimenter from a mediocre one is the ability to foresee troublesome extraneous variables and control them to avoid confoundings.

Experimenters use a variety of safeguards to control for extraneous variables. For instance, subjects are usually assigned to the experimental and control groups randomly. *Random assignment* of subjects occurs when all subjects have an equal chance of being assigned to any group or condition in the study. When experimenters distribute subjects into groups through some random procedure, they can be reasonably confident that the groups will be similar in most ways.

To summarize the essentials of experimental design, **Figure 2.5** provides an overview of the elements in an experiment, using Schachter's study as an example.

Variations in Designing Experiments   SIM1, 1b

We have discussed the experiment in only its simplest format, with just one independent variable and one dependent variable. Actually, many variations are possible in conducting experiments. *Sometimes it is advantageous to use only one group of subjects who*

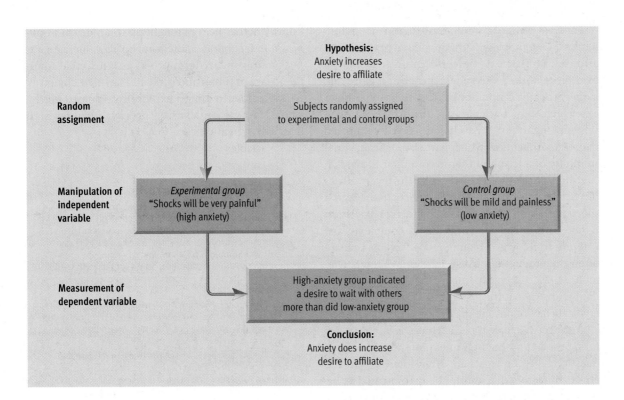

Figure 2.5

The basic elements of an experiment. As illustrated by the Schachter study, the logic of experimental design rests on treating the experimental and control groups exactly alike (to control for extraneous variables) except for the manipulation of the independent variable. In this way, the experimenter attempts to isolate the effects of the independent variable on the dependent variable.

Hypothesis:
Anxiety increases desire to affiliate

Random assignment — Subjects randomly assigned to experimental and control groups

Manipulation of independent variable — *Experimental group* "Shocks will be very painful" (high anxiety) / *Control group* "Shocks will be mild and painless" (low anxiety)

Measurement of dependent variable — High-anxiety group indicated a desire to wait with others more than did low-anxiety group

Conclusion:
Anxiety does increase desire to affiliate

serve as their own control group. The effects of the independent variable are evaluated by exposing this single group to two different conditions: an *experimental condition* and a *control condition*. For example, imagine that you wanted to study the effects of loud music on typing performance. You could have a group of participants work on a typing task while loud music was played (experimental condition) and in the absence of music (control condition). This approach would ensure that the participants in the experimental and control conditions would be alike on any extraneous variables involving their personal characteristics, such as motivation or typing skill. After all, the same people would be studied in both conditions.

It is also possible to manipulate more than one independent variable or measure more than one dependent variable in a single experiment. For example, in another study of typing performance, you could vary both room temperature and the presence of distracting music as independent variables (see **Figure 2.6**), while measuring two aspects of typing performance (speed and accuracy) as dependent variables.

Advantages and Disadvantages of Experimental Research

The experiment is a powerful research method. Its principal advantage is that it permits conclusions about cause-and-effect relationships between variables. Researchers are able to draw these conclusions

Distracting music
Present — Absent

Room temperature: Normal / High

Figure 2.6

Manipulation of two independent variables in an experiment. As this example shows, when two independent variables are manipulated in a single experiment, the researcher has to compare four groups of subjects (or conditions) instead of the usual two. The main advantage of this procedure is that it allows an experimenter to see whether two variables interact.

about causation because the precise control allows them to isolate the relationship between the independent variable and the dependent variable, while neutralizing the effects of extraneous variables. No other research method can duplicate this strength of the experiment. This advantage is why psychologists usually prefer to use the experimental method whenever possible.

For all its power, however, the experiment has limitations. One problem is that experiments are often artificial. Because experiments require great control over proceedings, researchers must often construct simple, contrived situations to test their hypotheses experimentally. For example, to investigate decision making in juries, psychologists have conducted many experiments in which participants read a brief summary of a trial and then record their individual "verdicts" of innocence or guilt. However, critics have pointed out that having a participant read a short case summary and make an individual decision is quite artificial in comparison to the complexities of real jury trials, which require group verdicts that are often the product of heated debates (Weiten & Diamond, 1979). When experiments are highly artificial, doubts arise about the applicability of findings to everyday behavior outside the experimental laboratory.

Another disadvantage is that the experimental method can't be used to explore some research questions. Psychologists are often interested in the effects of factors that cannot be manipulated as independent variables because of ethical concerns or practical realities. For example, you might want to know whether being brought up in an urban as opposed to a rural area affects people's values. An experiment would require you to assign similar families to live in urban and rural areas, which obviously is impossible to do. To explore this question, you would have to use descriptive/correlational research methods, which we turn to next.

Looking for Links: Descriptive/Correlational Research

Key Learning Goals

2.8 Distinguish between positive and negative correlations.

2.9 Discuss correlation in relation to prediction and causation.

2.10 Explain the role of naturalistic observation, case studies, and surveys in psychological research.

2.11 Evaluate the major advantages and disadvantages of descriptive/correlational research.

As we just noted, in some situations psychologists cannot exert experimental control over the variables they want to study. In such situations, investigators must rely on *descriptive/correlational research methods*. What distinguishes these methods is that the researcher cannot manipulate the variables under study. This lack of control means that these methods cannot be used to demonstrate a cause-effect relationship between variables. *Descriptive/correlational methods permit investigators to see only whether there is a link or association between the variables of interest.* Such an association is called a *correlation*, and the results of descriptive research are often summarized with a statistic called the *correlation coefficient*. In this section, we'll take a close look at the concept of correlation and then examine three specific approaches to descriptive research: naturalistic observation, case studies, and surveys.

The Concept of Correlation   1d

In descriptive research, investigators often want to determine whether there is a correlation between two variables. A *correlation* exists when two variables are related to each other. A correlation may be either positive or negative, depending on the nature of the association between the variables measured. A *positive* correlation indicates that two variables covary (change together) in the *same* direction. This means that high scores on variable *X* are associated with high scores on variable *Y* and that low scores on variable *X* are associated with low scores on variable *Y*. For example, there is a positive correlation between high school grade point average (GPA) and subsequent college GPA. That is, people who do well in high school tend to do well in college, and those who perform poorly in high school tend to perform poorly in college (see **Figure 2.7**).

In contrast, a *negative* correlation indicates that two variables co-vary in the *opposite* direction. This means that people who score high on variable *X* tend to score low on variable *Y*, whereas those who score low on *X* tend to score high on *Y*. For example, in most college courses, there is a negative correlation between how frequently students are absent and how well they perform on exams. Students who have a high number of absences tend to get low exam scores, while students

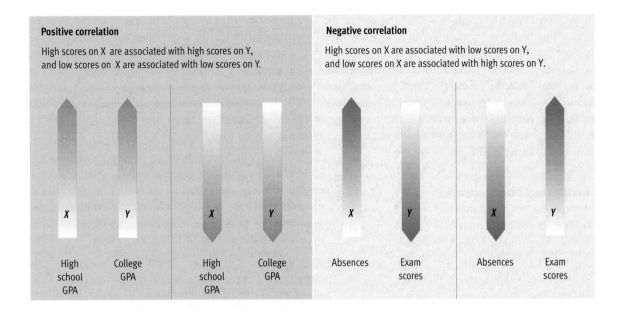

Positive correlation

High scores on X are associated with high scores on Y, and low scores on X are associated with low scores on Y.

High school GPA   College GPA   High school GPA   College GPA

Negative correlation

High scores on X are associated with low scores on Y, and low scores on X are associated with high scores on Y.

Absences   Exam scores   Absences   Exam scores

Figure 2.7
Positive and negative correlation. Notice that the terms *positive* and *negative* refer to the direction of the relationship between two variables, not to its strength. Variables are positively correlated if they tend to increase and decrease together and are negatively correlated if one tends to increase when the other decreases.

who have a low number of absences tend to earn higher exam scores (see **Figure 2.7**).

Strength of the Correlation   1d

The strength of an association between two variables can be measured with a statistic called the correlation coefficient. The *correlation coefficient* is **a numerical index of the degree of relationship between two variables.** This coefficient can vary between 0 and +1.00 (if the correlation is positive) or between 0 and –1.00 (if the correlation is negative). A coefficient near zero indicates no relationship between the variables. That is, high or low scores on variable *X* show no consistent relationship to high or low scores on variable *Y*. A coefficient of +1.00 or –1.00 indicates a perfect, one-to-one correspondence between the two variables. Most correlations fall between these extremes.

The closer the correlation is to either –1.00 or +1.00, the stronger the relationship (see **Figure 2.8**). Thus, a correlation of .90 represents a stronger tendency for variables to be associated than a correlation of .40. Likewise, a correlation of –.75 represents a stronger relationship than a correlation of –.45. Keep in mind

that the *strength* of a correlation depends only on the size of the coefficient. The positive or negative sign simply indicates the direction of the relationship. Therefore, a correlation of –.60 reflects a stronger relationship than a correlation of +.30.

Correlation and Prediction   1d

You may recall that one of the key goals of scientific research is accurate *prediction*. There is a close link between the magnitude of a correlation and the power it gives scientists to make predictions. *As a correlation increases in strength (gets closer to either –1.00 or +1.00), the ability to predict one variable based on knowledge of the other variable increases.*

To illustrate, consider how college admissions tests (such as the SAT or ACT) are used to predict college performance. When students' admissions test scores and college GPA are correlated, researchers generally find moderate positive correlations in the .40s and .50s (Gregory, 1996). Because of this relationship, college admissions committees can predict with modest accuracy how well prospective students will do in college. Admittedly, the predictive power of these admissions tests is far from perfect.

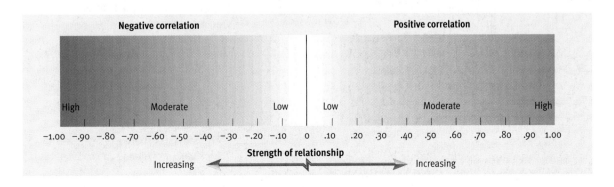

Negative correlation

High   Moderate   Low

Positive correlation

Low   Moderate   High

–1.00 –.90 –.80 –.70 –.60 –.50 –.40 –.30 –.20 –.10   0   .10 .20 .30 .40 .50 .60 .70 .80 .90 1.00

Strength of relationship

Increasing ←   → Increasing

Figure 2.8
Interpreting correlation coefficients. The magnitude of a correlation coefficient indicates the strength of the relationship between two variables. The sign (plus or minus) indicates whether the correlation is positive or negative. The closer the coefficient comes to +1.00 or –1.00, the stronger the relationship between the variables.

But it's substantial enough to justify the use of the tests as one factor in making admissions decisions. However, if this correlation were much higher, say .90, admissions tests could predict with superb accuracy how students would perform. In contrast, if this correlation were much lower, say .20, the tests' prediction of college performance would be so poor that considering the test scores in admissions decisions would be unreasonable.

Correlation and Causation   1d

Although a high correlation allows us to predict one variable on the basis of another, it does not tell us whether a cause-effect relationship exists between the two variables. The problem is that variables can be highly correlated even though they are not causally related.

When we find that variables X and Y are correlated, we can safely conclude only that X and Y are related. We do not know *how* X and Y are related. We do not know whether X causes Y or Y causes X, or whether both are caused by a third variable. For example, survey studies have found a positive correlation between smoking and the risk of experiencing a major depressive disorder (Johnson & Breslau, 2006; Kinnunen et al., 2006). Although it's clear that there is an association between smoking and depression, it's hard to tell what's causing what. The investigators acknowledge that they don't know whether smoking makes people more vulnerable to depression or whether depression increases the tendency to smoke. Moreover, they note that they can't rule out the possibility that both are caused by a third variable (Z). Perhaps anxiety and neuroticism increase the likelihood of both taking up smoking and becoming depressed. The plausible causal relationships in this case are diagrammed in **Figure 2.9**, which illustrates the "third variable problem" in interpreting correlations. This is a common problem in research,

and you'll see this type of diagram again when we discuss other correlations. Thus, it is important to remember that *correlation is not equivalent to causation*.

Naturalistic Observation

Does the pace of everyday life vary substantially from one culture to the next? Do people operate at a different speed in say, Germany, as opposed to Canada or Brazil? Are factors such as economic vitality and climate related to differences in the pace of life? These are the kinds of questions that intrigued Robert V. Levine and Ara Norenzayan (1999), who compared the pace of life in more than two dozen countries around the world. Perhaps they could have devised an experiment to examine this question, but they wanted to focus on the pace of life in the real world rather than in the laboratory.

To study the pace of life, Levine and Norenzayan had to come up with concrete ways to measure it—their operational definition of the concept. The mea-

"CONTRARY TO THE POPULAR VIEW, OUR STUDIES SHOW THAT IT IS REAL LIFE THAT CONTRIBUTES TO VIOLENCE ON TELEVISION."

© ScienceCartoonsPlus.com

---

concept check 2.2

Understanding Correlation

Check your understanding of correlation by interpreting the meaning of the correlation in item 1 and by guessing the direction (positive or negative) of the correlations in item 2. You'll find the answers in Appendix A.

1. Researchers have found a substantial positive correlation between youngsters' self-esteem and their academic achievement (measured by grades in school). Check any acceptable conclusions based on this correlation.
   _____ **a.** Low grades cause low self-esteem.
   _____ **b.** There is an association between self-esteem and academic achievement.
   _____ **c.** High self-esteem causes high academic achievement.
   _____ **d.** High ability causes both high self-esteem and high academic achievement.
   _____ **e.** Youngsters who score low in self-esteem tend to get low grades, and those who score high in self-esteem tend to get high grades.

2. Indicate whether you would expect the following correlations to be positive or negative.
   _____ **a.** The correlation between age and visual acuity (among adults).
   _____ **b.** The correlation between years of education and income.
   _____ **c.** The correlation between shyness and the number of friends one has.

Figure 2.9

Three possible causal relations between correlated variables. If variables *X* and *Y* are correlated, does *X* cause *Y*, does *Y* cause *X*, or does some hidden third variable, *Z*, account for the changes in both *X* and *Y*? As the relationship between smoking and depression illustrates, a correlation alone does not provide the answer. We will encounter this problem of interpreting the meaning of correlations frequently in this text.

sure they chose depended on *naturalistic observation.* In ***naturalistic observation*** a researcher engages in careful observation of behavior without intervening directly with the subjects. In this instance, the researchers observed (1) the average walking speed in downtown locations, (2) the accuracy of public clocks, and (3) the speed with which postal clerks completed a simple request. Their collection of data on walking speed illustrates the careful planning required to execute naturalistic observation effectively. In the main downtown area of each city, they had to find two flat, unobstructed, uncrowded 60-foot walkways where they could unobtrusively time pedestrians during normal business hours. Only adult pedestrians walking alone and not window shopping were timed. In most cities, the observations continued until 35 men and 35 women had been timed.

Levine and Norenzayan conducted their naturalistic observations in 31 countries, typically using the largest city in each country as the locale for their research. Their findings, based on all three measures, are summarized in **Figure 2.10** which ranks the pace of life in the countries studied. Their data suggest

Naturalistic observation can be complex and challenging, as the study by Levine and Norenzayan (1999) illustrates. One of their measures of the pace of life in 31 cultures involved estimating people's walking speed in downtown locations. To reduce the influence of confounding factors, they had to find sidewalks that were unobstructed, uncrowded, not dominated by window shoppers, and so forth. Moreover, they had to find reasonably comparable locations in 31 very different types of cities.

Rank	Country	Rank	Country	Rank	Country
1	Switzerland	11	France	21	Greece
2	Ireland	12	Poland	22	Kenya
3	Germany	13	Costa Rica	23	China
4	Japan	14	Taiwan	24	Bulgaria
5	Italy	15	Singapore	25	Romania
6	England	16	United States	26	Jordan
7	Sweden	17	Canada	27	Syria
8	Austria	18	S. Korea	28	El Salvador
9	Netherlands	19	Hungary	29	Brazil
10	Hong Kong	20	Czech Republic	30	Indonesia
				31	Mexico

Figure 2.10

Ranking the pace of life in 31 cultures. Using naturalistic observation to collect their data, Levine and Norenzayan (1999) calculated estimates of the pace of life in 31 countries. Their rankings—from fastest to slowest—are shown here. As you can see, their findings indicate that the pace of life is fastest in Western Europe and Japan.

SOURCE: Adapted from Levine, R. V., & Norenzayan, A. (1999). The pace of life in 31 countries. *Journal of Cross-Cultural Psychology, 30* (2), 178–205. Copyright © 1999 by Sage Publications. Reprinted by permission.

RESEARCH METHOD	DESCRIPTION	EXAMPLE APPLIED TO RESEARCH ON AGGRESSION

EXPERIMENT

Manipulation of an independent variable under carefully controlled conditions to see whether any changes occur in a dependent variable

Example: Schachter's (1959) study of whether increased anxiety leads to increased affiliation

Hypothesis: Anxiety increases affiliation

Random assignment → Subjects randomly assigned to experimental and control groups

Manipulation of independent variable → Experimental group "Shocks will be very painful" (high anxiety) — Control group "Shocks will be mild and painless" (low anxiety)

Measurement of dependent variable → High-anxiety group indicated a desire to wait with others more than did low-anxiety group

Youngsters are randomly assigned to watch a violent or nonviolent film (manipulation of the independent variable), and some aspect of aggression (the dependent variable) is measured in a laboratory situation.

NATURALISTIC OBSERVATION

Careful, usually prolonged observation of behavior in its natural setting, without direct intervention

Example: Levine and Norenzayan's (1999) study comparing the pace of life in 31 countries

© Rob Crandall/Alamy

Youngsters' spontaneous acts of aggression during recreational activities on their playground are recorded unobtrusively by a team of carefully trained observers.

CASE STUDIES

In-depth investigation of a single individual using direct interview, direct observation, review of records, interviews of those close to the person, and other data sources

Example: The Isometsa et al. (1995) study of all known suicide cases in Finland for an entire year

© David Buffinton/Photodisc Green/Getty Images

Detailed case histories are worked up for youngsters referred to counseling because of excessive aggressive behavior in school. The children are interviewed, as are their parents and teachers.

SURVEYS

Use of questionnaires or interviews to gather information about specific aspects of participants' behavior, attitudes, and beliefs

Example: Judge and Cable's (2004) analysis of questionnaire data on the correlation between height and income

© Studio DL/Corbis/Photolibrary

A large sample of youngsters are given a questionnaire describing hypothetical scenarios that might be expected to trigger aggressive behavior and are asked about how they think they would respond in the situations.

ADVANTAGES

DISADVANTAGES

Precise control over variables can eliminate alternative explanations for findings.

Researchers are able to draw conclusions about cause-and-effect relationships between variables.

Confounding of variables must be avoided.

Contrived laboratory situations are often artificial, making it risky to generalize findings to the real world.

Ethical concerns and practical realities preclude experiments on many important questions.

© Michael Nichols/National Geographic Image Collection

Artificiality that can be a problem in laboratory studies is minimized.

It can be a good place to start when little is known about the phenomena under study.

Unlike other descriptive/correlational methods, it can be used to study animal as well as human behavior.

It can be difficult to remain unobtrusive; even animal behavior may be altererd by the observation process.

Researchers are unable to draw causal conclusions.

Observational data are often difficult to quantify for statistical analyses.

Case studies are well suited for study of psychological disorders and therapeutic practices.

Individual cases can provide compelling illustrations to support or undermine a theory.

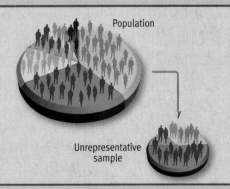

Population

Unrepresentative sample

Subjectivity makes it easy to see what one expects to see based on one's theoretical slant.

Researchers are unable to draw causal conclusions.

Clinical samples are often unrepresentative and suffer from sampling bias.

Data collection can be relatively easy, saving time and money.

Researchers can gather data on difficult-to-observe aspects of behavior.

Questionnaires are well suited for gathering data on attitudes, values, and beliefs from large samples.

Self-report data are often unreliable, due to intentional deception, social desirability bias, response sets, memory lapses, and poor wording of questions.

Researchers are unable to draw causal conclusions.

methods, since they can't control where subjects grow up. Thus, *descriptive research broadens the scope of phenomena that psychologists are able to study.*

Unfortunately, descriptive methods have one significant disadvantage: Investigators cannot control events to isolate cause and effect. *Consequently, descriptive/correlational research cannot demonstrate conclusively that correlated variables are causally related.* As an example, consider the cross-cultural investigation of the pace of life that we discussed earlier. Although Levine and Norenzayan (1996) found an association between colder climates and a faster pace of life, their data do not permit us to conclude that a cold climate causes a culture to move at a faster pace. Too many factors were left uncontrolled in the study. For example, we do not know how similar the cold and warm cities were. Climate could co-vary with some other factors, such as modernization or economic vitality, that might have led to the observed differences in the pace of life.

REVIEW of Key Learning Goals

2.8 Correlations may be either positive (when two variables co-vary in the same direction) or negative (when two variables co-vary in the opposite direction). The closer a correlation is to either +1.00 or –1.00, the stronger the association is.

2.9 As a correlation increases in strength, the ability to predict one variable based on knowledge of the other variable increases. However, a correlation is no assurance of causation. When variables are correlated, we do not know whether *X* causes *Y*, *Y* causes *X*, or a third variable causes both.

2.10 Naturalistic observation involves careful, prolonged observation of behavior in its natural setting without any intervention. Clinical research depends heavily on case studies, which involve in-depth investigations of individuals. In a survey, researchers interview participants or administer questionnaires to gather information on specific aspects of attitudes or behavior. Each approach has its unique strengths and weaknesses.

2.11 Descriptive/correlational research methods allow psychologists to explore issues that might not be open to experimental investigation because the variables of interest cannot be manipulated. However, these research methods cannot demonstrate cause-effect relationships.

concept check 2.3

Matching Research Methods to Questions

Check your understanding of the uses and strengths of various research methods by figuring out which method would be optimal for investigating the following questions about behavioral processes. Choose from the following methods: (a) experiment, (b) naturalistic observation, (c) case study, and (d) survey. Indicate your choice (by letter) next to each question. You'll find the answers in Appendix A in the back of the book.

_____ 1. Are people's attitudes about capital punishment related to their social class or education?

_____ 2. Do people who suffer from anxiety disorders share similar early childhood experiences?

_____ 3. Do troops of baboons display territoriality—that is, do they mark off an area as their own and defend it from intrusion?

_____ 4. Can the presence of food-related cues (delicious-looking desserts in advertisements, for example) cause an increase in the amount of food that people eat?

Looking for Flaws: Evaluating Research

Key Learning Goals

2.12 Articulate the importance of replication in research.

2.13 Recognize sampling bias and placebo effects in research.

2.14 Recognize problems with self-report data and experimenter bias in research.

Scientific research is a more reliable source of information than casual observation or popular belief. However, it would be wrong to conclude that all published research is free of errors. Scientists are fallible human beings, and flawed studies do make their way into the body of scientific literature.

That is one of the reasons that scientists often try to replicate studies. ***Replication* is the repetition of a study to see whether the earlier results are duplicated.** The replication process helps science identify and purge inaccurate findings. Of course, the replication process sometimes leads to contradictory results. You'll see some examples in later chapters. Fortunately, one of the strengths of the empirical approach is that scientists work to reconcile or explain conflicting results. In fact, scientific advances often emerge out of efforts to explain contradictory findings.

Like all sources of information, scientific studies need to be examined with a critical eye. This section describes a number of common methodological problems that often spoil studies. Being aware of these pitfalls will make you more skilled in evaluating research.

Sampling Bias

A *sample* is the collection of subjects selected for observation in an empirical study. In contrast, the *population* is the much larger collection of animals or people (from which the sample is drawn) that researchers want to generalize about. For example, when political pollsters attempt to predict elections, all of the voters in a jurisdiction represent the population, and the voters who are actually surveyed constitute the sample. If researchers were interested in the ability of 6-year-old children to form concepts, those 6-year-olds actually studied would be the sample, and all similar 6-year-old children (perhaps those in modern, Western cultures) would be the population.

The strategy of observing a limited sample in order to generalize about a much larger population rests on the assumption that the sample is reasonably *representative* of the population. A sample is representative if its composition (its demographic makeup in terms of age, sex, income, and so forth) is similar to the composition of the population (see **Figure 2.11**). *Sampling bias* exists when a sample is not representative of the population from which it was drawn. When a sample is not representative, generalizations about the population may be inaccurate. For instance, if a political pollster were to survey only people in posh shopping areas frequented by the wealthy, the pollster's generalizations about the voting public as a whole would be off the mark.

Limits on available time and money often prevent researchers from obtaining as representative a sample as they would like. In general, when you

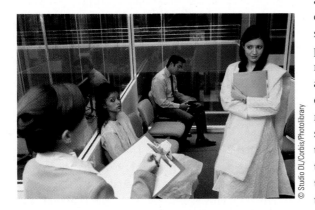

Before accepting the results of a survey poll, one should know something about how the poll was conducted. A polling could, for instance, contain sampling bias. Opinions collected solely from middle-class people but generalized to the voting public as a whole would be an example of such bias.

Population

Representative sample

Unrepresentative sample

have doubts about the results of a study, the first thing to examine is the composition of the sample.

Placebo Effects

A *placebo* is a substance that resembles a drug but has no actual pharmacological effect. In studies that assess the effectiveness of medications, placebos are given to some participants to control for the effects of a treacherous extraneous variable: subjects' expectations. Placebos are used because researchers know that participants' expectations can influence their feelings, reactions, and behavior (Stewart-Williams, 2004). Thus, *placebo effects* occur when participants' expectations lead them to experience some change even though they receive empty, fake, or ineffectual treatment. In medicine, placebo effects are well documented (Quitkin, 1999). Many physicians tell of patients being "cured" by prescriptions of sugar pills. Similarly, psychologists have found that participants' expectations can be powerful determinants of their perceptions and behavior when they are under the microscope in an empirical study. For example, placebo effects have also been seen in laboratory experiments on the effects of alcohol. In these studies, some of the participants are led to believe that they are drinking alcoholic beverages when in reality the drinks only appear to contain alcohol. Many of the subjects show effects of intoxication even though they haven't really consumed any alcohol (Assefi & Garry, 2003). If you know someone who shows signs of intoxication as soon as they start drinking, before their alcohol intake could take effect physiologically, you have seen placebo effects in action.

Figure 2.11
The relationship between the population and the sample. The process of drawing inferences about a population based on a sample works only if the sample is reasonably representative of the population. A sample is representative if its demographic makeup is similar to that of the population, as shown on the left. If some groups in the population are overrepresented or underrepresented in the sample, as shown on the right, inferences about the population may be skewed or inaccurate.

Researchers should guard against placebo effects whenever participants are likely to have expectations that a treatment will affect them in a certain way. The possible role of placebo effects can be assessed by including a fake version of the experimental treatment (a placebo condition) in a study.

Distortions in Self-Report Data

Research psychologists often work with *self-report data*, made up of participants' verbal accounts of their behavior. This is the case whenever questionnaires, interviews, or personality inventories are used to measure variables. Self-report methods can be quite useful, taking advantage of the fact that people have a unique opportunity to observe themselves full-time (Baldwin, 2000). However, self-reports can be plagued by several kinds of distortion.

One of the most problematic of these distortions is the *social desirability bias,* which is a tendency to give socially approved answers to questions about oneself. Subjects who are influenced by this bias work overtime trying to create a favorable impression, especially when they are asked about sensitive issues (Tourangeau & Yan, 2007). For example, many survey respondents will report that they voted in an election or gave to a charity when in fact it is possible to determine that they did not (Granberg & Holmberg, 1991; Hadaway, Marler, & Chaves, 1993). Interestingly, people who answer questions in socially desirable ways take slightly longer to respond to the questions, suggesting that they are carefully "editing" their responses (Holtgraves, 2004).

Other problems can also produce distortions in self-report data (Krosnick, 1999; Schuman & Kalton, 1985). Respondents misunderstand questionnaire items surprisingly often, and the way questions are worded can shape participants' responses (Schwarz, 1999). Memory errors can undermine the accuracy of verbal reports. In responding to certain kinds of scales, some people tend to agree with nearly all of the statements, while others tend to disagree with nearly everything (Krosnick & Fabrigar, 1998). Obviously, distortions like these can produce inaccurate results. Although researchers have devised ways to neutralize these problems, we should be especially cautious in drawing conclusions from self-report data (Schaeffer, 2000).

Experimenter Bias

As scientists, psychologists try to conduct their studies in an objective, unbiased way so that their own views will not influence the results. However, objectivity is a *goal* that scientists strive for, not an accomplished fact that can be taken for granted (MacCoun, 1998). In reality, most researchers have an emotional investment in the outcome of their research. Often they are testing hypotheses that they have developed themselves and that they would like to see supported by the data. It is understandable, then, that *experimenter bias* is a possible source of error in research.

Experimenter bias occurs when a researcher's expectations or preferences about the outcome of a study influence the results obtained. Experimenter bias can slip through to influence studies in many subtle ways. One problem is that researchers, like others, sometimes *see what they want to see.* For instance, when experimenters make apparently honest mistakes in recording subjects' responses, the mistakes tend to be heavily slanted in favor of supporting the hypothesis (O'Leary, Kent, & Kanowitz, 1975).

Research by Robert Rosenthal (1976) suggests that experimenter bias may lead researchers to unintentionally influence the behavior of their subjects. In one study, Rosenthal and Fode (1963) recruited undergraduate psychology students to serve as the "experimenters." The students were told that they would be collecting data for a study of how participants rated the success of people portrayed in photographs. In a pilot study, photos were selected that generated (on the average) neutral ratings on a scale extending from −10 (extreme failure) to +10 (extreme success). Rosenthal and Fode then manipulated the expectations of their experimenters. Half of them were told that they would probably obtain average ratings of −5. The other half were led to expect average ratings of +5. The experimenters were forbidden from conversing with their subjects except for reading some standardized instructions. Even though the photographs were exactly the same for both groups, the experimenters who *expected* positive ratings *obtained* significantly higher ratings than those who expected negative ones.

How could the experimenters have swayed the participants' ratings? According to Rosenthal, the experimenters unintentionally influenced their subjects by sending subtle nonverbal signals as the experiment progressed. Without realizing it, they sometimes smiled, nodded, or sent other positive cues when participants made ratings that were in line with their expectations. Thus, experimenter bias may influence both researchers' observations and their subjects' behavior (Rosenthal, 1994, 2002).

The problems associated with experimenter bias can be neutralized by using a double-blind procedure. The *double-blind procedure* is a research strategy in which neither subjects nor experimenters know which subjects are in the experimental or

Robert Rosenthal

"Quite unconsciously, a psychologist interacts in subtle ways with the people he is studying so that he may get the response he expects to get."

control groups. It's not particularly unusual for subjects to be "blind" about their treatment condition. However, the double-blind procedure keeps the experimenter in the dark as well. Of course, a member of the research team who isn't directly involved with subjects keeps track of who is in which group.

concept check 2.4

Detecting Flaws in Research

Check your understanding of how to conduct sound research by looking for methodological flaws in the following studies. You'll find the answers in Appendix A.

Study 1. A researcher announces that he will be conducting an experiment to investigate the detrimental effects of sensory deprivation on perceptual-motor coordination. The first 40 students who sign up for the study are assigned to the experimental group, and the next 40 who sign up serve in the control group. The researcher supervises all aspects of the study's execution. Experimental subjects spend two hours in a sensory deprivation chamber, where sensory stimulation is minimal. Control subjects spend two hours in a waiting room that contains magazines and a TV. All subjects then perform ten 1-minute trials on a pursuit-rotor task that requires them to try to keep a stylus on a tiny rotating target. The dependent variable is their average score on the pursuit-rotor task.

Study 2. A researcher wants to know whether there is a relationship between age and racial prejudice. She designs a survey in which respondents are asked to rate their prejudice against six different ethnic groups. She distributes the survey to over 500 people of various ages who are approached at a shopping mall in a low-income, inner-city neighborhood.

Check the flaws that are apparent in each study.

Methodological flaw	Study 1	Study 2
Sampling bias	_____	_____
Placebo effects	_____	_____
Distortions in self-report	_____	_____
Confounding of variables	_____	_____
Experimenter bias	_____	_____

Looking into the Future: The Internet and Psychological Research

The Internet is revolutionizing many aspects of modern life. Some experts compare the emergence of the World Wide Web to the shift from speech to writing, the invention of the printing press, and the widespread distribution of electricity (Weiten, 2002). Small wonder then, that the Internet is gradually altering the ways in which psychological research is conducted.

Internet-mediated research refers to studies in which data collection occurs over the web. All of the different methods that we have discussed in this chapter can be used in Internet-mediated research. Mostly, investigators have conducted online experiments and distributed online surveys. An example of a web experiment is a study by Göritz (2006) that compared various cash lottery incentives to see which would yield the highest response rates in online studies. An example of a Web survey is a study by Tower and Krasner (2006) in which over 1100 online participants responded to measures of marital

web link 2.5

Psychological Research on the Net

This site, sponsored by the Association for Psychological Science, is a launching point for people interested in participating in ongoing research projects that are collecting data over the Internet. Visitors will find a host of opportunities for taking part in genuine research.

closeness and depressive symptoms to explore the correlation between marital adjustment and depression. Although experiments and surveys have dominated Internet-mediated research, the web has also afforded psychologists enlightening opportunities to engage in naturalistic observation of social interaction in online communities, such as chatrooms and newsgroups (Glaser & Kahn, 2005; McKenna & Bargh, 2000; McKenna & Seidman, 2005).

Why have researchers been drawn to the web? Because the Internet offers some very enticing advantages in the data collection process. For example, studies conducted via the Internet can often obtain samples that are much larger and much more diverse than the samples typically used in laboratory research (Buchanan, 2000; Reips, 2007). If a researcher is interested in some special population, whether it be gamblers, steroid users, atheists, dentists, elderly marathon runners, or lesbians living in rural areas, creative recruitment via the Internet can yield sizable samples that would be difficult or impossible to obtain through traditional research procedures (Mathy et al., 2002; Skitka & Sargis, 2005). Moreover, once an online survey or experiment is set up, data can be collected effortlessly 24 hours a day, 7 days a week. Thus, Internet-mediated research can reduce costs and save time (Göritz, 2007; Skitka & Sargis, 2006).

As you can see, Internet-mediated research offers many attractive benefits, but this approach also has some weaknesses that concern researchers. One major concern is the potential for sampling bias. Although access to the Internet grows daily, web users tend to be younger, brighter, and more affluent than nonusers (Lenert & Skoczen, 2002). A related issue is that web studies tend to have lower participation rates than conventional studies (Skitka & Sargis, 2005). In laboratory studies, although subjects can always elect to not participate, the vast majority generally tend to go along with whatever study they are assigned to. In most web studies, broad invitations to participate are issued via e-mail or posted announcements, and only a small minority of potential subjects typically choose to volunteer their time. Researchers worry that their self-selected volunteers might be systematically different from the majority of people who, for one reason or another, choose not to participate.

Another issue in Internet-mediated research is that data are collected under far less controlled conditions than in traditional studies (Buchanan, 2007; Hewson, 2003). Laboratory studies are conducted under carefully controlled conditions that are held constant for all participants. In contrast, subjects in web studies usually participate from home where environmental circumstances are uncontrolled and unknown. Some participants may be distracted by TV; some may sit around and discuss their data input with friends; some may provide data while intoxicated.

Although web studies have created some new complexities related to sampling bias and experimental control, research findings suggest that these issues may be less problematic than feared (Birnbaum, 2004b; Hewson, 2003). Thus, it appears that the Internet will gradually alter the landscape of psychological research, just as it has altered the landscape of communication, shopping, politics, real estate, entertainment, and many other aspects of modern life.

REVIEW of Key Learning Goals

2.15 Internet-mediated research has grown in recent years because it offers access to larger and more diverse samples and to specialized samples while reducing costs and saving time. However, Internet-mediated research raises its own concerns about sampling bias and uncontrolled conditions during data collection.

Looking at Ethics: Do the Ends Justify the Means?

Key Learning Goals

2.16 Contrast the pros and cons of deception in research with human subjects.

2.17 Discuss the controversy about the use of animals as research subjects.

Think back to Stanley Schachter's (1959) study on anxiety and affiliation. Imagine how you would have felt if you had been one of the participants in Schachter's high-anxiety group. You show up at a research laboratory, expecting to participate in a harmless experiment. The room you are sent to is full of unusual electronic equipment. An official-looking man in a lab coat announces that this equipment will be used to give you a series of painful electric shocks. His statement that the shocks will leave "no permanent tissue damage" is hardly reassuring. Surely, you think, there must be a mistake. All of a sudden, your venture into research has turned into a nightmare! Your stomach knots up in anxiety. The researcher explains that there will be a delay while he prepares his apparatus. He asks you to fill out a short questionnaire about whether you would prefer to wait alone or with others. Still reeling in dismay at the prospect of being shocked, you fill out the questionnaire. He takes it and then announces that you won't be shocked after all—it was all a hoax! Feelings of relief wash over you, but they're mixed with feelings of anger. You feel as though the experimenter has just made a fool out of you, and you're embarrassed and resentful.

Should researchers be allowed to play with your feelings in this way? Should they be permitted to deceive participants in such a manner? Is this the cost that must be paid to advance scientific knowledge? As these questions indicate, the research enterprise sometimes presents scientists with difficult ethical dilemmas. *These dilemmas reflect concern about the possibility for inflicting harm on subjects.* In psychological research, the major ethical dilemmas center on the use of deception and the use of animals.

The Question of Deception

Elaborate deception, such as that seen in Schachter's study, has been fairly common in psychological research since the 1960s, especially in the area of social psychology (Epley & Huff, 1998; Korn, 1997). Over the years, psychologists have faked fights, thefts, muggings, faintings, epileptic seizures, rapes, and automobile breakdowns to explore a number of issues. Researchers have led subjects to believe that they (the subjects) were hurting others with electrical shocks, had homosexual tendencies, and were overhearing negative comments about themselves. Why have psychologists used so much deception in their research? Quite simply, they are trying to deal with the methodological problems discussed earlier. They often misinform participants about the purpose of a study to reduce problems resulting from placebo effects, the unreliability of self-reports, and the like that can undermine the scientific value and validity of research (Berghmans, 2007).

Critics argue against the use of deception on several grounds (Baumrind, 1985; Kelman, 1982; Ortmann & Hertwig, 1997). First, they assert that deception is only a nice word for lying, which they see as inherently immoral. Second, they argue that by deceiving unsuspecting participants, psychologists may undermine many individuals' trust in others. Third, they point out that many deceptive studies produce distress for participants who were not forewarned about that possibility. Specifically, participants may experience great stress during a study or be made to feel foolish when the true nature of a study is explained.

Those who defend the use of deception in research maintain that many important issues could not be investigated if experimenters were not permitted to mislead subjects (Bröder, 1998). They argue that most research deceptions involve "white lies" that are not likely to harm participants. A review of the relevant research by Larry Christensen (1988) suggests that deception studies are *not* harmful to participants. Indeed, most subjects who participate in experiments involving deception report that they enjoyed the experience and that they didn't mind being misled. Moreover, the empirical evidence does not support the notions that deceptive research undermines subjects' trust in others or their respect for psychology or scientific research (Kimmel, 1996; Sharpe, Adair, & Roese, 1992). Curiously, the weight of the evidence suggests that researchers are more concerned about the negative effects of deception on participants than the participants themselves are (Fisher & Fyrberg, 1994; Korn, 1987). Finally, researchers who defend deception argue that the benefits—advances in knowledge that often improve human welfare—are worth the costs.

The Question of Animal Research

Psychology's other major ethics controversy concerns the use of animals in research. Psychologists use animals as research subjects for several reasons. Sometimes they simply want to know more about the behavior of a specific type of animal. In other instances, they want to identify general laws of behavior that apply to both humans and animals. Finally, in some cases psychologists use animals because they can expose them to treatments that clearly would be unacceptable with human participants. For example, most of the research on the relationship between deficient maternal nutrition during pregnancy and the incidence of birth defects has been done with animals.

It's this third reason for using animals that has generated most of the controversy. Some people maintain that it is wrong to subject animals to harm or pain for research purposes. Essentially, they argue that animals are entitled to the same rights as humans (Regan, 1997; Ryder, 2006). They accuse researchers of violating these rights by subjecting animals to unnecessary cruelty in many "trivial" studies (Bowd & Shapiro, 1993; Hollands, 1989). They also argue that most animal studies are a waste of time because the results may not even apply to humans (Millstone, 1989; Norton, 2005). Some of the more militant animal rights activists have broken into laboratories, destroyed scientists' equipment and research records, and stolen experimental animals. The animal rights movement has enjoyed considerable success. For example, membership in People for the Ethical Treatment of Animals (PETA) grew from 8,000 in 1984 to 750,000 in 2003 (Herzog, 2005). Johnson (1990) noted that "the single issue citizens write about most often to their congresspersons and the president is not homelessness, not the drug problem, not crime. It is animal welfare" (p. 214).

In spite of the great furor, only 7%–8% of all psychological studies involve animals (mostly rodents and birds). Relatively few of these studies require

web link 2.6

Office of Research Integrity

Anyone who needs a comprehensive, up-to-date overview of ethical concerns in research from the perspective of the U.S. government should consider visiting this site. Although the Office of Research Integrity (ORI) deals with research sponsored by the U.S. Public Health Service, it also offers links to parallel offices and resources in many other agencies.

web link 2.7

Bad Blood: The Tuskegee Syphilis Study

The enduring damage of unethical scientific and medical research—here seen in the infamous 1932–1972 Tuskegee Syphilis Study among 399 poor African American men in Alabama—is detailed in several government reports and a rare presidential apology to the victims.

web link 2.8

Animal Welfare Information Center

This site, maintained by the U.S. Department of Agriculture, is an excellent jumping-off point for information relating to all aspects of how animals are (and should be) cared for in research, laboratory, and other settings.

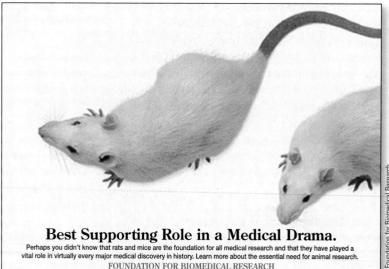

Best Supporting Role in a Medical Drama.

Perhaps you didn't know that rats and mice are the foundation for all medical research and that they have played a vital role in virtually every major medical discovery in history. Learn more about the essential need for animal research.

FOUNDATION FOR BIOMEDICAL RESEARCH
www.fbresearch.org

Many important scientific discoveries have been achieved through animal research, as the advertisement on the right notes. But many people remain vigorously opposed to animal research. The animal liberation activist shown here was covered in fake blood and strapped to a giant vivisection board as part of a protest against animal research in Melbourne, Australia. Clearly, the ethics of animal research is a highly charged controversy.

Neal Miller

"Who are the cruel and inhumane ones, the behavioral scientists whose research on animals led to the cures of the anorexic girl and the vomiting child, or the leaders of the radical animal activists who are making an exciting career of trying to stop all such research and are misinforming people by repeatedly asserting that it is without any value?"

subjecting the animals to painful or harmful manipulations (American Psychological Association, 1984). Psychologists who defend animal research point to the major advances attributable to psychological research on animals, which many people are unaware of (Baldwin, 1993; Compton, Dietrich, & Smith, 1995). Among them are advances in the treatment of mental disorders, neuromuscular disorders, strokes, brain injuries, visual defects, headaches, memory defects, high blood pressure, and problems with pain (Carroll & Overmier, 2001; Domjan & Purdy, 1995). To put the problem in context, Neal Miller (1985), a prominent psychologist who has done pioneering work in several areas, noted the following:

At least 20 million dogs and cats are abandoned each year in the United States; half of them are killed in pounds and shelters, and the rest are hit by cars or die of neglect. Less than 1/10,000 as many dogs and cats were used in psychological laboratories. . . . Is it worth sacrificing the lives of our children in order to stop experiments, most of which involve no pain, on a vastly smaller number of mice, rats, dogs, and cats? (p. 427)

As you can see, the manner in which animals can ethically be used for research is a highly charged controversy. Psychologists are becoming increasingly sensitive to this issue. Although animals continue to be used in research, strict regulations have

Figure 2.12

Ethics in research. Key ethical principles in psychological research, as set forth by the American Psychological Association (2002), are summarized here. These principles are meant to ensure the welfare of both human and animal subjects.

APA Ethical Guidelines for Research

1 A subject's participation in research should be voluntary and based on informed consent. Subjects should never be coerced into participating in research. They should be informed in advance about any aspects of the study that might be expected to influence their willingness to cooperate. Furthermore, they should be permitted to withdraw from a study at any time if they so desire.

2 Participants should not be exposed to harmful or dangerous research procedures. This guideline is intended to protect subjects from psychological as well as physical harm. Thus, even stressful procedures that might cause emotional discomfort are largely prohibited. However, procedures that carry a modest risk of moderate mental discomfort may be acceptable.

3 If an investigation requires some deception of participants (about matters that do not involve risks), the researcher is required to explain and correct any misunderstandings as soon as possible. The deception must be disclosed to subjects in "debriefing" sessions as soon as it is practical to do so without compromising the goals of the study.

4 Subjects' rights to privacy should never be violated. Information about a subject that might be acquired during a study must be treated as highly confidential and should never be made available to others without the consent of the participant.

5 Harmful or painful procedures imposed upon animals must be thoroughly justified in terms of the knowledge to be gained from the study. Furthermore, laboratory animals are entitled to decent living conditions that are spelled out in detailed rules that relate to their housing, cleaning, feeding, and so forth.

6 Prior to conducting studies, approval should be obtained from host institutions and their research review committees. Research results should be reported fully and accurately, and raw data should be promptly shared with other professionals who seek to verify substantive claims. Retractions should be made if significant errors are found in a study subsequent to its publication.

been imposed that regulate nearly every detail of how laboratory animals can be used for research purposes (Ator, 2005; Garnett, 2005).

The ethics issues that we have discussed in this section have led the APA to develop a set of ethical standards for researchers (American Psychological Association, 2002). Although most psychological studies are fairly benign, these ethical principles are intended to ensure that both human and animal subjects are treated with dignity. Some of the key guidelines in these ethical principles are summarized in **Figure 2.12**.

REVIEW of Key Learning Goals

2.16 Critics argue that deception in research is unethical because it is inherently immoral, may undermine participants' trust in others, and may expose them to high levels of stress. Those who defend deception in research argue that many important issues could not be investigated without misleading subjects and that the negative effects of deception on participants have been overestimated.

2.17 Critics of animal research argue that it violates animals' rights and that the findings of animal studies may not generalize to humans. Psychologists who defend animal research argue that it has brought major advances that are worth the costs.

Reflecting on the Chapter's Themes

Two of our seven unifying themes have emerged strongly in this chapter. First, the entire chapter is a testimonial to the idea that psychology is empirical. Second, the discussion of methodological flaws in research provides numerous examples of how people's experience of the world can be highly subjective. Let's examine each of these points in more detail.

As explained in Chapter 1, the empirical approach entails testing ideas, basing conclusions on systematic observation, and relying on a healthy brand of skepticism. All of those features of the empirical approach have been apparent in this chapter. As you have seen, psychologists test their ideas by formulating clear hypotheses that involve predictions about relations between variables. They then use a variety of research methods to collect data, so they can see whether their predictions are supported. The data collection methods are designed to make researchers' observations systematic and precise. The entire venture is saturated with skepticism. In planning and executing their research, scientists are constantly on the lookout for methodological flaws. They publish their findings so that other experts can subject their methods and conclusions to

critical scrutiny. Collectively, these procedures represent the essence of the empirical approach.

The subjectivity of personal experience became apparent in the discussion of methodological problems, especially placebo effects and experimenter bias. When research participants report beneficial effects from a fake treatment (the placebo), it's because they expected to see these effects. The studies showing that many subjects start feeling intoxicated just because they think that they have consumed alcohol are striking demonstrations of the enormous power of people's expectations. As pointed out in Chapter 1, psychologists and other scientists are not immune to the effects of subjective experience. Although they are trained to be objective, even scientists may see what they expect to see or what they want to see. This is one reason that the empirical approach emphasizes precise measurement and a skeptical attitude. The highly subjective nature of experience is exactly what the empirical approach attempts to neutralize.

The publication of empirical studies allows us to apply our skepticism to the research enterprise. However, you cannot critically analyze studies unless you know where and how to find them. In the

3

The Biological Bases of Behavior

Congress Street Bridge, Austin, Texas © Patrick Byrd/Science Faction/Getty Images

If you have ever visited an aquarium, you may have encountered one of nature's more captivating animals: the octopus. Although this jellylike mass of arms and head appears to be a relatively simple creature, it is capable of a number of interesting behaviors. The octopus has highly developed eyes that enable it to respond to stimuli in the darkness of the ocean. When threatened, it can release an inky cloud to ward off enemies while it makes its escape by a kind of rocket propulsion. If that doesn't work, it can camouflage itself by changing color and texture to blend into its surroundings. Furthermore, the animal is surprisingly intelligent. In captivity, an octopus can learn, for example, to twist the lid off a jar with one of its tentacles to get at a treat that is inside.

Despite its talents, there are many things an octopus cannot do. An octopus cannot study psychology, plan a weekend, dream about its future, or discover the Pythagorean theorem. Yet the biological processes that underlie these uniquely human behaviors are much the same as the biological processes that enable an octopus to escape from a predator or forage for food. Indeed, some of science's most important insights about how the nervous system works came from studies of a relative of the octopus, the squid.

Organisms as diverse as humans and squid share many biological processes. However, the unique behavioral capacities of various organisms depend on the differences in their physiological makeup. You and I have a larger repertoire of behaviors than the octopus because we come equipped with a more complex brain and nervous system. The activity of the human brain is so complex that no computer has ever come close to duplicating it. Your nervous system contains as many cells busily integrating and relaying information as there are stars in our galaxy. Whether you are scratching your nose or composing an essay, the activity of those cells underlies what you do. It is little wonder, then, that many psychologists have dedicated themselves to exploring the biological bases of behavior.

How do mood-altering drugs work? Are the two halves of the brain specialized to perform different functions? What happens inside the body when you feel a strong emotion? Are some mental illnesses the result of chemical imbalances in the brain? To what extent is intelligence determined by biological inheritance? These questions only begin to suggest the countless ways in which biology is fundamental to the study of behavior.

Communication in the Nervous System

Imagine that you are watching a scary movie. As the tension mounts, your palms sweat and your heart beats faster. You begin shoveling popcorn into your mouth, carelessly spilling some in your lap. If someone were to ask you what you are doing at this moment, you would probably say, "Nothing—just watching the movie." Yet some highly complex processes are occurring without your thinking about them. A stimulus (the light from the screen) is striking your eye. Almost instantaneously, your brain is interpreting the light stimulus, and signals are flashing to other parts of your body, leading to a flurry of activity. Your sweat glands are releasing perspiration, your heartbeat is quickening, and muscular movements are enabling your hand to find the popcorn and, more or less successfully, lift it to your mouth.

Even in this simple example, you can see that behavior depends on rapid information processing. Information travels immediately from your eye to your brain, from your brain to the muscles of your arm and hand, and from your palms back to your brain. In essence, your nervous system is a complex communication network in which signals are constantly being received, integrated, and transmitted. The nervous system handles information, just as the circulatory system handles blood. In this section, we take a close look at communication in the nervous system.

Nervous Tissue: The Basic Hardware

PSYK TREK 2a

Your nervous system is living tissue composed of cells. The cells in the nervous system fall into two major categories: *glia* and *neurons*. Let's look at neurons first.

Neurons

PSYK TREK 2a

Neurons are individual cells in the nervous system that receive, integrate, and transmit information. They are the basic links that permit communication within the nervous system. The vast majority of them communicate only with other neurons. However, a small minority receive signals from outside the nervous system (from sensory organs) or carry

Key Learning Goals

3.1 Identify the various parts of the neuron and the main functions of glial cells.

3.2 Describe the neural impulse.

3.3 Explain how neurons communicate at chemical synapses.

3.4 Discuss some of the functions of acetylcholine, the monoamine neurotransmitters, amino acid transmitters, and endorphins.

messages from the nervous system to the muscles that move the body.

A highly simplified drawing of two "typical" neurons is shown in **Figure 3.1**. Actually, neurons come in such a tremendous variety of types and shapes that no single drawing can adequately represent them. Trying to draw the "typical" neuron is like trying to draw the "typical" tree. Despite this diversity, the drawing in **Figure 3.1** highlights some common features of neurons.

The *soma*, **or cell body, contains the cell nucleus and much of the chemical machinery common to most cells** (*soma* **is Greek for "body"). The** rest of the neuron is devoted exclusively to handling information. The neurons in **Figure 3.1** have a number of branched, feelerlike structures called *dendritic trees* (*dendrite* is a Greek word for "tree"). Each individual branch is a *dendrite*. **Dendrites are the parts of a neuron that are specialized to receive information.** Most neurons receive information from many other cells—sometimes thousands of others—and so have extensive dendritic trees.

From the many dendrites, information flows into the cell body, then travels away from the soma along the *axon* (from the Greek for "axle"). **The** *axon* **is a long, thin fiber that transmits signals away from the soma to other neurons or to muscles or glands.** Axons may be quite long (sometimes several feet), and they may branch off to communicate with a number of other cells.

In humans, many axons are wrapped in cells with a high concentration of a white, fatty substance called *myelin*. **The** *myelin sheath* **is insulating material that encases some axons.** It functions to speed up the transmission of signals that move along axons. If an axon's myelin sheath deteriorates, signals may not be transmitted effectively. The loss of muscle control seen with the disease *multiple*

sclerosis is due to a degeneration of myelin sheaths (Schwartz & Westbrook, 2000).

The axon ends in a cluster of *terminal buttons,* **which are small knobs that secrete chemicals called neurotransmitters.** These chemicals serve as messengers that may activate neighboring neurons. The points at which neurons interconnect are called *synapses.* **A** *synapse* **is a junction where information is transmitted from one neuron to another** (*synapse* is from the Greek for "junction").

To summarize, information is received at the dendrites, is passed through the soma and along the axon, and is transmitted to the dendrites of other cells at meeting points called synapses. Unfortunately, this nice, simple picture has more exceptions than the U.S. Tax Code. For example, some neurons do not have an axon, while others have multiple axons. Also, although neurons typically synapse on the dendrites of other cells, they may also synapse on a soma or an axon.

Glia

Glia are cells found throughout the nervous system that provide various types of support for neurons. Glia (literally "glue") tend to be much smaller than neurons, but they outnumber neurons by about 10 to 1, so glial cells appear to account for over 50% of the brain's volume. Among other things, glial cells supply nourishment to neurons, help remove neurons' waste products, and provide insulation around many axons. The myelin sheaths that encase some axons are derived from special types of glial cells. Glia also play a complicated role in orchestrating the development of the nervous system in the human embryo.

These functions, which have been known for many years, made glial cells the unsung heroes of

Figure 3.1
Structure of the neuron.
Neurons are the communication links of the nervous system. This diagram highlights the key parts of a neuron, including specialized receptor areas (dendrites), the cell body (soma), the axon fiber along which impulses are transmitted, and the terminal buttons, which release chemical messengers that carry signals to other neurons. Neurons vary considerably in size and shape and are usually densely interconnected.

Dendrites

Soma

Myelin sheath

Axon

Terminal buttons and synapses

the nervous system. Until recently, it was thought that the "glamorous" work in the nervous system—the transmission and integration of informational signals—was the exclusive province of the neurons. New research, however, suggests that glia may also send and receive chemical signals (Fields, 2004; Fields & Stevens-Graham, 2002). Some types of glia can detect neural impulses and send signals to other glial cells. Surprised by this discovery, neuroscientists are now trying to figure out how this signalling system interfaces with the neural communication system. Some of the preliminary findings and theorizing have proven very interesting. For example, recent research suggests that glial cells may play an important role in memory formation (Bains & Oliet, 2007) and that gradual deterioration of glial tissue might contribute to Alzheimer's disease (Streit, 2005). Other research suggests that glial cells play a crucial role in the experience of chronic pain (Banks & Watkins, 2006) and that impaired neural-glial communication might contribute to psychological disorders, such as schizophrenia (Hashimoto, Shimizu, & Iyo, 2005) and mood disorders (Lee et al., 2007).

Although glia may contribute to information processing in the nervous system, the bulk of this crucial work is handled by the neurons. Thus, we need to examine the process of neural activity in more detail.

The Neural Impulse: Using Energy to Send Information   2a

What happens when a neuron is stimulated? What is the nature of the signal—the *neural impulse*—that moves through the neuron? These were the questions that Alan Hodgkin and Andrew Huxley set out to answer in their groundbreaking experiments with axons removed from squid. Why did they choose to work with squid axons? Because squid have a pair of "giant" axons that are about a hundred times larger than those in humans (which still makes them only about as thick as a human hair). This large size permitted Hodgkin and Huxley to insert fine wires called *microelectrodes* into the axons. By using the microelectrodes to record the electrical activity in individual neurons, Hodgkin and Huxley unraveled the mystery of the neural impulse.

The Neuron at Rest: A Tiny Battery   2a

Hodgkin and Huxley (1952) learned that the neural impulse is a complex electrochemical reaction. Both inside and outside the neuron are fluids containing electrically charged atoms and molecules called *ions*. Positively charged sodium and potassium ions and

negatively charged chloride ions flow back and forth across the cell membrane, but they do not cross at the same rate. The difference in flow rates leads to a slightly higher concentration of negatively charged ions inside the cell. The resulting voltage means that the neuron at rest is a tiny battery, a store of potential energy. The *resting potential* of a neuron is its stable, negative charge when the cell is inactive. As shown in **Figure 3.2(a)**, this charge is about –70 millivolts, roughly one-twentieth of the voltage of a flashlight battery.

The Action Potential   2a

As long as the voltage of a neuron remains constant, the cell is quiet, and no messages are being sent. When the neuron is stimulated, channels in its cell membrane open, briefly allowing positively charged sodium ions to rush in. For an instant, the neuron's charge is less negative and eventually positive, creating an action potential (Koester & Siegelbaum, 2000). An *action potential* is a very brief shift in a neuron's electrical charge that travels along an axon. The firing of an action potential is reflected in the voltage spike shown in **Figure 3.2(b)**. Like a spark traveling along a trail of gunpowder, the voltage change races down the axon.

web link   3.1

Neuropsychology Central

This content-rich site, maintained by Professor Jeffrey Browndyke of Louisiana State University, is dedicated to all aspects of human neuropsychology from the perspectives of the experimental research laboratory as well as the applied clinical setting of the hospital and professional office.

Figure 3.2.

The neural impulse. The electrochemical properties of the neuron allow it to transmit signals. The electric charge of a neuron can be measured with a pair of electrodes connected to an oscilloscope, as Hodgkin and Huxley showed with a squid axon. Because of its exceptionally thick axons, the squid has frequently been used by scientists studying the neural impulse. **(a)** At rest, the neuron's voltage hovers around –70 millivolts. **(b)** When the axon is stimulated, there is a brief jump in a neuron's voltage, resulting in a spike on the oscilloscope recording of the neuron's electrical activity. This change in voltage, called an action potential, travels along the axon like a spark traveling along a trail of gunpowder.

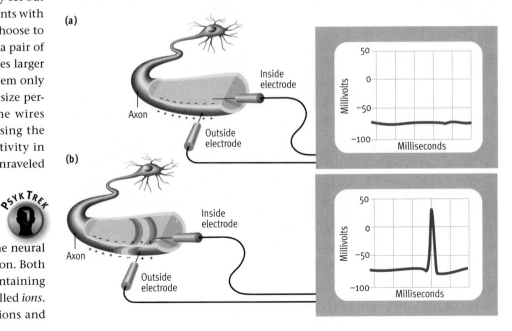

After the firing of an action potential, the channels in the cell membrane that opened to let in sodium close up. Some time is needed before they are ready to open again, and until that time the neuron cannot fire. The *absolute refractory period* is the minimum length of time after an action potential during which another action potential cannot begin. This "down time" isn't very long, only 1 or 2 milliseconds.

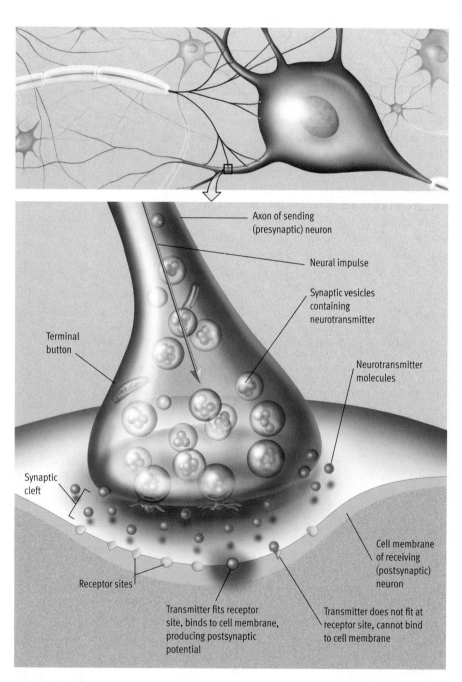

Figure 3.3

The synapse. When a neural impulse reaches an axon's terminal buttons, it triggers the release of chemical messengers called neurotransmitters. The neurotransmitter molecules diffuse across the synaptic cleft and bind to receptor sites on the postsynaptic neuron. A specific neurotransmitter can bind only to receptor sites that its molecular structure will fit into, much like a key must fit a lock.

The All-or-None Law 2a

The neural impulse is an all-or-none proposition, like firing a gun. You can't half-fire a gun. The same is true of the neuron's firing of action potentials. Either the neuron fires or it doesn't, and its action potentials are all the same size (Kandel, 2000). That is, weaker stimuli do not produce smaller action potentials and stronger stimuli do not evoke larger action potentials.

Even though the action potential is an all-or-nothing event, neurons *can* convey information about the strength of a stimulus. They do so by varying the *rate* at which they fire action potentials. In general, a stronger stimulus will cause a cell to fire a more rapid volley of neural impulses than a weaker stimulus will.

Various neurons transmit neural impulses at different speeds. For example, thicker axons transmit neural impulses more rapidly than thinner ones do. Although neural impulses do not travel as fast as electricity along a wire, they *are* very fast, moving at up to 100 meters per second, which is equivalent to more than 200 miles per hour. The entire complicated process of neural transmission takes only a few thousandths of a second. In the time it has taken you to read this description of the neural impulse, billions of such impulses have been transmitted in your nervous system!

The Synapse: Where Neurons Meet 2b

In the nervous system, the neural impulse functions as a signal. For that signal to have any meaning for the system as a whole, it must be transmitted from the neuron to other cells. As noted earlier, this transmission takes place at special junctions called *synapses*, which depend on *chemical* messengers.

Sending Signals: Chemicals as Couriers 2b

A "typical" synapse is shown in **Figure 3.3**. The first thing that you should notice is that the two neurons don't actually touch. They are separated by the *synaptic cleft,* a microscopic gap between the terminal button of one neuron and the cell membrane of another neuron. Signals have to cross this gap to permit neurons to communicate. In this situation, the neuron that sends a signal across the gap is called the *presynaptic neuron,* and the neuron that receives the signal is called the *postsynaptic neuron.*

How do messages travel across the gaps between neurons? The arrival of an action potential at an axon's terminal buttons triggers the release of *neuro-*

transmitters—chemicals that transmit information from one neuron to another. Within the buttons, most of these chemicals are stored in small sacs, called *synaptic vesicles*. The neurotransmitters are released when a vesicle fuses with the membrane of the presynaptic cell and its contents spill into the synaptic cleft. After their release, neurotransmitters diffuse across the synaptic cleft to the membrane of the receiving cell. There they may bind with special molecules in the postsynaptic cell membrane at various *receptor sites*. These sites are specifically "tuned" to recognize and respond to some neurotransmitters but not to others.

Receiving Signals: Postsynaptic Potentials

 2b

When a neurotransmitter and a receptor molecule combine, reactions in the cell membrane cause a *postsynaptic potential* (*PSP*), a voltage change at a receptor site on a postsynaptic cell membrane. Postsynaptic potentials do *not* follow the all-or-none law like action potentials do. Instead, postsynaptic potentials are *graded*. That is, they vary in size and they increase or decrease the *probability* of a neural impulse in the receiving cell in proportion to the amount of voltage change.

Two types of messages can be sent from cell to cell: excitatory and inhibitory. An *excitatory PSP* is a positive voltage shift that *increases* the likelihood that the postsynaptic neuron will fire action potentials. An *inhibitory PSP* is a negative voltage shift that *decreases* the likelihood that the postsynaptic neuron will fire action potentials. The direction of the voltage shift, and thus the nature of the PSP (excitatory or inhibitory), depends on which receptor sites are activated in the postsynaptic neuron (Kandel, 2000).

The excitatory or inhibitory effects produced at a synapse last only a fraction of a second. Then neurotransmitters drift away from receptor sites or are inactivated by enzymes that metabolize (convert) them into inactive forms. Most are reabsorbed into the presynaptic neuron through *reuptake*, a process in which neurotransmitters are sponged up from the synaptic cleft by the presynaptic membrane. Reuptake allows synapses to recycle their materials. Reuptake and the other key processes in synaptic transmission are summarized in **Figure 3.4**.

Integrating Signals: A Balancing Act

2b

Most neurons are interlinked in complex, dense networks. In fact, a neuron may receive a symphony of signals from *thousands* of other neurons. That same neuron may pass its messages along to thousands of other neurons as well. Thus, a neuron must do a great

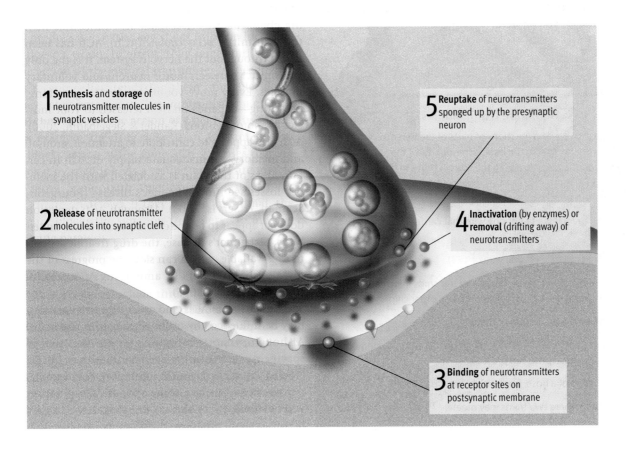

1 Synthesis and **storage** of neurotransmitter molecules in synaptic vesicles

2 Release of neurotransmitter molecules into synaptic cleft

3 Binding of neurotransmitters at receptor sites on postsynaptic membrane

4 Inactivation (by enzymes) or **removal** (drifting away) of neurotransmitters

5 Reuptake of neurotransmitters sponged up by the presynaptic neuron

Figure 3.4
Overview of synaptic transmission. The main processes in synaptic transmission are summarized here. The five key processes involved in communication at synapses are (1) synthesis and storage, (2) release, (3) binding, (4) inactivation or removal, and (5) reuptake of neurotransmitters. As you'll see in this chapter and the remainder of the book, the effects of many phenomena—such as pain, drug use, and some diseases—can be explained in terms of how they alter one or more of these processes (usually at synapses releasing a specific neurotransmitter).

various types of mental tasks, neuroscientists are increasingly using *functional magnetic resonance imaging (fMRI)*, which consists of several new variations on MRI technology that monitor blood flow and oxygen consumption in the brain to identify areas of high activity (Song, Huettel, & McCarthy, 2006). This technology is exciting because, like PET scans, it can map actual *activity* in the brain over time, but with vastly greater precision. For example, using fMRI scans, researchers have identified patterns of brain activity associated with cocaine craving in cocaine addicts (Wexler et al., 2001), the learning of specific motor skills (Poldrack & Willingham, 2006), the recognition and comprehension of verbal stimuli (Wise & Price, 2006), and the contemplation of risky gambles (Tom et al., 2007).

Another new research tool in neuroscience is **transcranial magnetic stimulation (TMS)**, a technique that permits scientists to temporarily enhance or depress activity in a specific area of the brain. With TMS, a magnetic coil mounted on a small paddle is held over a specific area of a subject's head (see **Figure 3.11**). By varying the timing and duration of magnetic pulses, a researcher can either increase or decrease the excitability of neurons in the local tissue (George, Bohning et al., 2007; Nahas et al., 2007). Thus far, researchers have mostly been interested in temporarily deactivating discrete areas of the brain to learn more about their functions. In essence, this technology allows scientists to create "virtual lesions" in human subjects for short periods of time, using a painless, noninvasive method. This approach has been used to explore whether specific areas of the brain are involved in visuospatial processing (Sack et al., 2002), memory for objects (Oliveri et al., 2001), and language (Knecht et al., 2002). Scientists are also studying whether TMS might have potential as a therapeutic treatment for anxiety disorders (Greenberg, 2007), depression (Mantovani & Liasanby, 2007), and schizophrenia (Hoffman, 2007).

Now that we have discussed a few approaches to brain research, let's look at what scientists have discovered about the functions of various parts of the brain. The brain is divided into three major regions: the hindbrain, the midbrain, and the forebrain. The principal structures found in each of these regions are listed in the organizational chart of the nervous system in **Figure 3.5**. You can see where these regions are located in the brain by looking at **Figure 3.12**. They can be found easily in relation to the *brainstem*. The brainstem looks like its name—it appears to be a stem from which the rest of the brain "flowers," like a head of cauliflower. At its lower end the stem is contiguous with the spinal cord. At its higher end it lies deep within the brain. We'll begin at the brain's lower end, where the spinal cord joins the brainstem. As we proceed upward, notice how the functions of brain structures go from the regulation of basic bodily processes to the control of "higher" mental processes.

The Hindbrain

The *hindbrain* includes the cerebellum and two structures found in the lower part of the brainstem: the medulla and the pons. The *medulla*, which attaches to the spinal cord, controls largely unconscious but essential functions, such as breathing, maintaining muscle tone, and regulating circulation. The *pons* (literally "bridge") includes a bridge of fibers that connects the brainstem with the cerebellum. The pons also contains several clusters of cell bodies involved with sleep and arousal.

The *cerebellum* ("little brain") is a relatively large and deeply folded structure located adjacent

Figure 3.11

Transcranial magnetic stimulation (TMS). In TMS, magnetic pulses are delivered to a localized area of the brain from a magnet mounted on a small paddle **(a)**. The magnetic field only penetrates to a depth of 2 centimeters **(b)**. This technique can be used to either increase or decrease the excitability of the affected neurons. The inset at bottom right depicts neurons near the surface of the brain being temporarily activated by TMS **(c)**.

SOURCE: Adapted from Bremner, J. D. (2005). *Brain imaging handbook.* New York: W. W. Norton, p. 34. Illustration © Bryan Christie Design.

The left column text is largely cut off at the edge:

T
emot
possi
stimu
Miln
would
electr
where
They
the ra
later
planta
hypot
comir
Subse
would
stimul
mente
it, the
some s
Wh
brain?
system
tion ap
bundle
The me
releasir
self-stin
activati

Figure 3.12

Structures and areas in the human brain. (Top left) This photo of a human brain shows many of the structures discussed in this chapter. (Top right) The brain is divided into three major areas: the hindbrain, midbrain, and forebrain. These subdivisions actually make more sense for the brains of other animals than of humans. In humans, the forebrain has become so large it makes the other two divisions look trivial. However, the hindbrain and midbrain aren't trivial; they control such vital functions as breathing, waking, and maintaining balance. (Bottom) This cross section of the brain highlights key structures and some of their principal functions. As you read about the functions of a brain structure, such as the corpus callosum, you may find it helpful to visualize it.

Forebrain

Midbrain

Hindbrain

Wadsworth Collection

Cerebrum
Responsible for sensing, thinking, learning, emotion, consciousness, and voluntary movement

Amygdala
Part of limbic system involved in emotion and aggression

Corpus callosum
Bridge of fibers passing information between the two cerebral hemispheres

Thalamus
Relay center for cortex; handles incoming and outgoing signals

Cerebellum
Structure that coordinates fine muscle movement, balance

Hypothalamus
Responsible for regulating basic biological needs: hunger, thirst, temperature control

Pituitary gland
"Master gland" that regulates other endocrine glands

Hippocampus
Part of limbic system involved in learning and memory

Pons
Involved in sleep and arousal

Medulla
Responsibe for regulating largely unconscious functions such as breathing and circulation

Reticular formation
Group of fibers that carry stimulation related to sleep and arousal through brainstem

Spinal cord
Responsible for transmitting information between brain and rest of body; handles simple reflexes

to the back surface of the brainstem. The cerebellum is involved in the coordination of movement and is critical to the sense of equilibrium, or physical balance (Ghez & Thach, 2000). Although the actual commands for muscular movements come from higher brain centers, the cerebellum plays a key role in the execution of these commands. It is your cerebellum that allows you to hold your hand out to the side and then smoothly bring your finger to a stop on your nose. This exercise is a useful roadside test for drunken driving because the cerebellum is one of the structures first depressed by alcohol. Damage to the cerebellum disrupts fine motor skills, such as those involved in writing, typing, or playing a musical instrument.

The Midbrain

2d

The *midbrain* is the segment of the brainstem that lies between the hindbrain and the forebrain. The midbrain contains an area that is concerned with integrating sensory processes, such as vision and

Communication in the Nervous System

▮ Cells in the nervous system receive, integrate, and transmit information. Neurons are the basic communication links. They normally transmit a neural impulse (a change in electrical charge, called an action potential) along an axon to a synapse with another neuron. Glial cells provide various types of support for neurons and may contribute to signal transmission in the nervous system.

▮ Action potentials trigger the release of chemicals called neurotransmitters that diffuse across a synapse to communicate with other neurons. Most neurons are linked in neural pathways, circuits, and networks. A variety of neurotransmitters function by binding at specific receptor sites according to a lock-and-key model.

Organization of the Nervous System

▮ The nervous system can be divided into two main subdivisions, the central nervous system and the peripheral nervous system. The central nervous system consists of the brain and spinal cord. The brain plays a crucial role in virtually all aspects of behavior.

▮ The peripheral nervous system consists of the nerves that lie outside the brain and spinal cord. It can be subdivided into the somatic nervous system, which connects to muscles and sensory receptors, and the autonomic nervous system, which connects to blood vessels, smooth muscles, and glands.

The Brain and Behavior

▮ Neuroscientists use a variety of invasive and noninvasive techniques to study the living brain. These methods include lesioning, electrical stimulation, CT scans, MRI scans, PET scans, fMRI scans, and transcranial magnetic stimulation. The brain has three major regions: the hindbrain, midbrain, and forebrain. Structures in the hindbrain and midbrain handle essential functions such as breathing, circulation, and coordination of movement.

▮ The forebrain includes many structures that handle higher functions. The thalamus is primarily a relay station. The hypothalamus is involved in the regulation of basic biological drives such as hunger and sex. The limbic system is a network of loosely connected structures involved in emotion, motivation, and memory.

▮ The cerebrum is the brain area implicated in most complex mental activities. The cortex is the cerebrum's convoluted outer layer, which is subdivided into four areas. These areas and their primary known functions are the occipital lobe (vision), the parietal lobe (touch), the temporal lobe (hearing), and the frontal lobe (movement of the body). The organization of the brain is more plastic than widely appreciated. The process of neurogenesis is a key contributor to this plasticity.

Right Brain/Left Brain: Cerebral Specialization

▮ The cerebrum is divided into right and left hemispheres connected by the corpus callosum. Studies have revealed that the right and left halves of the brain each have unique talents, with the right hemisphere being specialized to handle visual-spatial functions, while the left hemisphere handles verbal processing.

The Endocrine System: Another Way to Communicate

▮ The endocrine system consists of the glands that secrete hormones, which are chemicals involved in the regulation of basic bodily processes. The control centers for the endocrine system are the hypothalamus and the pituitary gland. Variations in testosterone levels may correlate with variations in aggression and cognitive functioning.

Heredity and Behavior: Is It All in the Genes?

▮ The basic units of genetic transmission are genes housed on chromosomes. Most behavioral qualities appear to involve polygenic inheritance. Researchers assess hereditary influence through family studies, twin studies, and adoption studies. These studies indicate that most behavioral traits are influenced by a complex interaction between heredity and environment.

The Evolutionary Bases of Behavior

▮ Darwin argued that if a heritable trait contributes to an organism's survival or reproductive success, organisms with that trait should produce more offspring than those without the trait and that the prevalence of the trait should gradually increase over generations—thanks to natural selection.

▮ Adaptations sometimes linger in a population even though they no longer provide a survival or reproductive advantage. Darwin recognized from the beginning that natural selection was applicable to behavioral traits, as well as physical traits.

Reflecting on the Chapter's Themes

▮ Three of the book's unifying themes stand out in this chapter. First, we saw how heredity interacts with experience to govern behavior. Second, the discussions of biological factors underlying schizophrenia highlighted the multifactorial causation of behavior. Third, we saw how innovations in research methods often lead to advances in knowledge, underscoring the empirical nature of psychology.

PERSONAL APPLICATION Thinking Critically About the Concept of "Two Minds in One"

▮ The cerebral hemispheres are specialized for handling different cognitive tasks, but only to a degree, and people vary in their patterns of specialization. Evidence on whether people vary in brainedness and whether the two hemispheres vary in cognitive style is inconclusive. There is no evidence that exercising a hemisphere of the brain is useful.

CRITICAL THINKING APPLICATION Building Better Brains: The Perils of Extrapolation

▮ Although some education and childcare reformers have used neuroscience as the basis for their campaigns, research has not demonstrated that birth to 3 is a critical period for human neural development or that specific enrichment programs can enhance brain development. These assertions are highly conjectural overextrapolations from existing data.

PSYKTREK PREVIEW

The arrival of an action potential at an axon's terminal buttons triggers the release of neurotransmitters. They are released when a vesicle fuses with the membrane of the presynaptic neuron and releases its contents into the synaptic cleft.

Visit Module 2b (*Synaptic Transmission*) to see animations of varioius aspects of the neural impulse.

Positron emission tomography, or the PET scan, maps activity in the brain over time. In PET scans, radioactively tagged chemicals are introduced into the brain. They serve as markers of metabolic activity or blood flow in the brain, which can be monitored with X- rays, as shown here.

Go to Module 2c (*Looking Inside the Brain: Research Methods*) to learn how electrical stimulation, lesioning, CT scans, PET scans, and MRI scans are used to investigate brain function.

1. A neural impulse is initiated when a neuron's charge momentarily becomes less negative, or even positive. This event is called:
   A. an action potential.
   B. a resting potential.
   C. impulse facilitation.
   D. neuromodulation.

2. Neurons convey information about the strength of stimuli by varying:
   A. the size of their action potentials.
   B. the speed of their action potentials.
   C. the rate at which they fire action potentials.
   D. all of the above.

3. Alterations in activity at dopamine synapses have been implicated in the development of:
   A. anxiety.
   B. schizophrenia.
   C. Alzheimer's disease.
   D. nicotine addiction.

4. Jim has just barely avoided a head-on collision on a narrow road. With heart pounding, hands shaking, and body perspiring, Jim recognizes that these are signs of the body's fight-or-flight response, which is controlled by the:
   A. empathetic division of the peripheral nervous system.
   B. parasympathetic division of the autonomic nervous system.
   C. somatic division of the peripheral nervous system.
   D. sympathetic division of the autonomic nervous system.

5. The thalamus can be characterized as:
   A. a regulatory mechanism.
   B. the consciousness switch of the brain.
   C. a relay system.
   D. a bridge between the two cerebral hemispheres.

6. The _____ lobe is to hearing as the occipital lobe is to vision.
   A. frontal
   B. temporal
   C. parietal
   D. cerebellar

7. The scientist who won a Nobel prize for his work with split-brain patients is:
   A. Walter Cannon.
   B. Paul Broca.
   C. Roger Sperry.
   D. James Olds.

8. In people whose corpus callosums have not been severed, verbal stimuli are identified more quickly and more accurately:
   A. when sent to the right hemisphere first.
   B. when sent to the left hemisphere first.
   C. when presented to the left visual field.
   D. when presented auditorally rather than visually.

9. Hormones are to the endocrine system as _____ are to the nervous system.
   A. nerves
   B. synapses
   C. neurotransmitters
   D. action potentials

10. Adopted children's similarity to their biological parents is generally attributed to _____ ; adopted children's similarity to their adoptive parents is generally attributed to _____ .
    A. heredity; the environment
    B. the environment; heredity
    C. the environment; the environment
    D. heredity; heredity

11. In evolutionary theory, *fitness* refers to:
    A. the ability to survive.
    B. the ability to adapt to environmental demands.
    C. reproductive success.
    D. the physical skills necessary for survival.

12. For which of the following assertions is the empirical evidence strongest?
    A. The two cerebral hemispheres are specialized to handle different types of cognitive tasks.
    B. Schools should be reformed to better educate the right hemisphere.
    C. Each hemisphere has its own cognitive style.
    D. Some people are right-brained, while others are left-brained.

Answers

1 A p. 71
2 C p. 72
3 B pp. 75–76
4 D p. 79
5 C p. 84
6 B pp. 86–87
7 C p. 89
8 B pp. 90–91
9 C p. 92
10 A p. 95
11 C p. 97
12 A pp. 100–101

PSYKTREK PREVIEW

BIOLOGICAL BASES OF BEHAVIOR
2f   The Cerebral Cortex

Motor homunculus

If we remove the strip of cortex that houses the left hemisphere's primary motor cortex, we can create a diagram called the motor homunculus, which maps out how specific areas in the motor cortex are devoted to the control of various muscles and limbs.

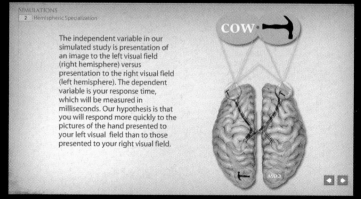

SIMULATIONS
2   Hemispheric Specialization

COW

The independent variable in our simulated study is presentation of an image to the left visual field (right hemisphere) versus presentation to the right visual field (left hemisphere). The dependent variable is your response time, which will be measured in milliseconds. Our hypothesis is that you will respond more quickly to the pictures of the hand presented to your left visual field than to those presented to your right visual field.

Explor Modules 2d (*The Hindbrain and Midbrain*), 2e (*The Forebrain: Subcortical Structures*), and 2f (*The Cerebral Cortex*) for detailed tours of how various areas

Go to Simulation 2 (*Hemispheric Specialization*) to participate in an experiment on the abilities of your right brain versus your left brain

4

Sensation and Perception

Okinawa prefecture, Japan Ikema Bridge © DAJ/Getty Images

Take a look at the photo in the margin on the right. What do you see? You probably answered, "a rose" or "a flower." But is that what you really see? No, this isn't a trick question. Let's examine the odd case of "Dr. P." It shows that there's more to seeing than meets the eye.

Dr. P was an intelligent and distinguished music professor who began to exhibit some worrisome behaviors that seemed to be related to his vision. Sometimes he failed to recognize familiar students by sight, though he knew them instantly by the sound of their voices. Sometimes he acted as if he saw faces in inanimate objects, cordially greeting fire hydrants and parking meters as if they were children. On one occasion, reaching for what he thought was his hat, he took hold of his wife's head and tried to put it on! Except for these kinds of visual mistakes, Dr. P was a normal, talented man.

Ultimately Dr. P was referred to Oliver Sacks, a neurologist, for an examination. During one visit, Sacks handed Dr. P a fresh red rose to see whether he would recognize it. Dr. P took the rose as if he were being given a model of a geometric solid rather than a flower. "About six inches in length," Dr. P observed, "a convoluted red form with a linear green attachment."

"Yes," Sacks persisted, "and what do you think it is, Dr. P?"

"Not easy to say," the patient replied. "It lacks the simple symmetry of the Platonic solids . . ."

"Smell it," the neurologist suggested. Dr. P looked perplexed, as if being asked to smell symmetry, but he complied and brought the flower to his nose. Suddenly, his confusion cleared up. "Beautiful. An early rose. What a heavenly smell" (Sacks, 1987, pp. 13–14).

What accounted for Dr. P's strange inability to recognize faces and familiar objects by sight? There was nothing wrong with his eyes. He could readily spot a pin on the floor. If you're thinking that he *must* have had something wrong with his vision, look again at the photo of the rose. What you see *is* "a convoluted red form with a linear green attachment." It doesn't occur to you to describe it that way only because, without thinking about it, you instantly perceive that combination of form and color as a flower. This is precisely what Dr. P was unable to do. He could see perfectly well, but he was losing the ability to assemble what he saw into a meaningful picture of the world. Technically, he suffered from a condition called *visual agnosia,* an inability to recognize ovbjects through sight. As Sacks (1987) put it, "Visually, he was lost in a world of lifeless abstractions" (p. 15).

As Dr. P's case illustrates, without effective processing of sensory input, our familiar world can become a chaos of confusing sensations. To acknowledge the needs to both take in and process sensory information, psychologists distinguish between sensation and perception. *Sensation* **is the stimulation of sense organs.** *Perception* **is the selection, organization, and interpretation of sensory input.** Sensation involves the absorption of energy, such as light or sound waves, by sensory organs, such as the eyes and ears. Perception involves organizing and translating sensory input into something meaningful. For example, when you look at the photo of the rose, your eyes are sensing the light reflected from the page, including areas of low reflection where ink has been deposited in an irregular shape. What you *perceive,* however, is a picture of a rose.

The distinction between sensation and perception stands out in Dr. P's case of visual agnosia. His eyes were doing their job of registering sensory input and transmitting signals to the brain. However, damage in his brain interfered with his ability to put these signals together into organized wholes. Thus, Dr. P's process of visual *sensation* was intact, but his process of visual *perception* was severely impaired.

Dr. P's case is unusual, of course. Normally, the processes of sensation and perception are difficult to separate because people automatically start organizing incoming sensory stimulation the moment it arrives. The distinction between sensation and perception has been useful in organizing theory and research, but in actual operation the two processes merge.

We'll begin our discussion of sensation and perception with a long look at vision, then take a briefer look at the other senses. As we examine each of the sensory systems, we'll see repeatedly that people's experience of the world depends on both the physical stimuli they encounter (sensation) and their active processing of stimulus inputs (perception). The chapter's Personal Application explores how principles of visual perception come into play in art and illusion. The Critical Thinking Application discusses how perceptual contrasts can be manipulated in persuasive efforts.

The Visual System: Essentials of Sight

Key Learning Goals

4.1 List the three properties of light and the aspects of visual perception that they influence.

4.2 Describe the role of the lens and pupil in the functioning of the eye.

4.3 Explain how the retina contributes to visual information processing.

4.4 Trace the routing of signals from the eye to the brain, and explain the brain's role in visual information processing.

4.5 Distinguish two types of color mixing and compare the trichromatic and opponent process theories of color vision.

"Seeing is believing." Good students are "bright," and a good explanation is "illuminating." This section is an "overview." Do you see the point? As these common expressions show, humans are visual animals. People rely heavily on their sense of sight, and they virtually equate it with what is trustworthy (seeing is believing). Although it is taken for granted, you'll see (there it is again) that the human visual system is amazingly complex. Furthermore, as in all sensory domains, what people "sense" and what they "perceive" may be quite different.

The Stimulus: Light

 3a

For people to see, there must be light. *Light* is a form of electromagnetic radiation that travels as a wave, moving, naturally enough, at the speed of light. As **Figure 4.1(a)** shows, light waves vary in *amplitude* (height) and in *wavelength* (the distance between

peaks). Amplitude affects mainly the perception of brightness, while wavelength affects mainly the perception of color. The lights humans normally see are mixtures of different wavelengths. Hence, light can also vary in its *purity* (how varied the mix is). Purity influences perception of the *saturation,* or richness, of colors. Saturation refers to the relative amount of whiteness in a color. As whiteness declines, saturation increases (see **Figure 4.2**). Of course, most objects do not emit light, they reflect it (the sun, lamps, and fireflies being some exceptions).

What most people call light includes only the wavelengths that humans can see. But as **Figure 4.1(c)** shows, the visible spectrum is only a slim portion of the total range of wavelengths. Vision is a filter that permits people to sense only a fraction of the real world. Other animals have different capabilities and so live in a quite different visual world. For example, many insects can see shorter wavelengths than humans can see, in the *ultraviolet* spectrum,

Figure 4.1

Light, the physical stimulus for vision. (a) Light waves vary in amplitude and wavelength. **(b)** Within the spectrum of visible light, amplitude (corresponding to physical intensity) affects mainly the experience of brightness. Wavelength affects mainly the experience of color, and purity is the key determinant of saturation. **(c)** If white light (such as sunlight) passes through a prism, the prism separates the light into its component wavelengths, creating a rainbow of colors. However, visible light is only the narrow band of wavelengths to which human eyes happen to be sensitive.

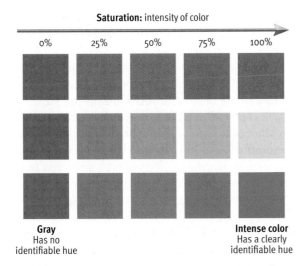

Saturation: intensity of color

0% 25% 50% 75% 100%

Gray
Has no
identifiable hue

Intense color
Has a clearly
identifiable hue

Figure 4.2

Saturation. Saturation refers to the amount of whiteness in a color. As you can see in these examples, as the amount of whiteness declines (moving to the right), the saturation or richness of a color increases.

whereas many fish and reptiles can see longer wavelengths, in the *infrared* spectrum.

Although the sense of sight depends on light waves, in order for people to see, incoming visual input must be converted into neural impulses that are sent to the brain. Let's investigate how this transformation is accomplished.

The Eye: A Living Optical Instrument

3a

The eyes serve two main purposes: They channel light to the neural tissue that receives it, called the *retina,* and they house that tissue. The structure of the eye is shown in **Figure 4.3**. Each eye is a living optical instrument that creates an image of the visual world on the light-sensitive retina that lines its inside back surface.

Light enters the eye through a transparent "window" at the front, the *cornea.* The cornea and the

web link 4.1

Vision Science: An Internet Resource for Research in Human and Animal Vision

Numerous online sites are devoted to the sense of sight and visual processes. Vision Science provides a convenient guide to the best of these sites, especially for online demonstrations and tutorials.

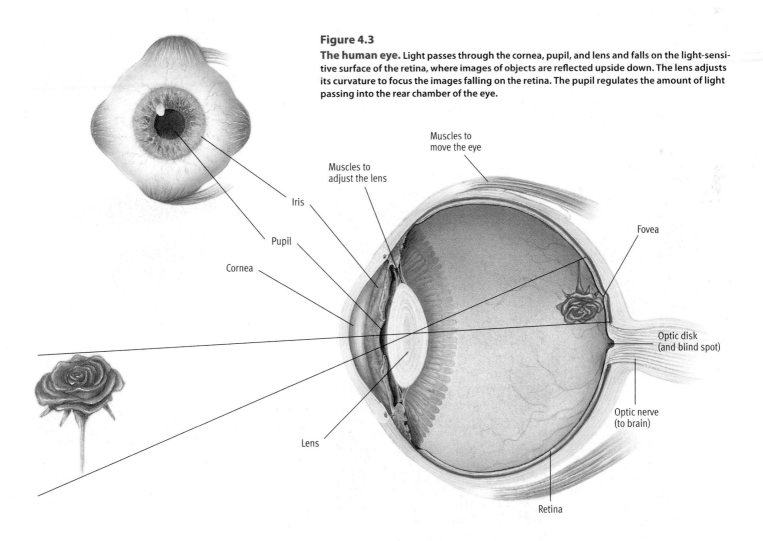

Figure 4.3

The human eye. Light passes through the cornea, pupil, and lens and falls on the light-sensitive surface of the retina, where images of objects are reflected upside down. The lens adjusts its curvature to focus the images falling on the retina. The pupil regulates the amount of light passing into the rear chamber of the eye.

crystalline *lens,* located behind it, form an upside down image of objects on the retina and adjust the focus of the image. It might seem disturbing that the image is upside down, but the arrangement works. It doesn't matter how the image sits on the retina, as long as the brain knows the rule for relating positions on the retina to the corresponding positions in the world. **The *lens* is a transparent eye structure that focuses the light rays falling on the retina.** The lens is made up of relatively soft tissue, capable of adjustments that facilitate a process called accommodation. *Accommodation* occurs when the curvature of the lens adjusts to alter visual focus. When you focus on a close object, the lens of your eye gets fatter (rounder) in order to give you a clear image. When you focus on distant objects, the lens flattens out to give you a better image of them.

A number of common visual problems are caused by focusing problems or defects in the lens (Guyton, 1991). For example, in *nearsightedness,* close objects are seen clearly but distant objects appear blurry because the focus of light from distant objects falls a little short of the retina (see **Figure 4.4**). This focusing problem occurs when the cornea or lens bends light too much or when the eyeball is too long. In *farsightedness,* distant objects are seen clearly but close objects appear blurry because the focus of light from close objects falls behind the retina (again, see **Figure 4.4**). This focusing problem typically occurs when the eyeball is too short. A

cataract is a lens that is clouded. This defect occurs mainly in older persons, affecting three out of four people over the age of 65.

The eye also makes adjustments to alter the amount of light reaching the retina. The *iris* is the colored ring of muscle surrounding the *pupil,* or black center of the eye. **The *pupil* is the opening in the center of the iris that helps regulate the amount of light passing into the rear chamber of the eye.** When the pupil constricts, it lets less light into the eye, but it sharpens the image falling on the retina. When the pupil dilates (opens), it lets more light in, but the image is less sharp. In bright light, the pupils constrict to take advantage of the sharpened image. But in dim light, the pupils dilate. Image sharpness is sacrificed to allow more light to fall on the retina so that more remains visible.

The Retina: The Brain's Envoy in the Eye 3b

The *retina* is the neural tissue lining the inside back surface of the eye; it absorbs light, processes images, and sends visual information to the brain. You may be surprised to learn that the retina *processes* images. But it's a piece of the central nervous system that happens to be located in the eyeball. Much as the spinal cord is a complicated extension of the brain, the retina is the brain's envoy in the eye. About half as thick as a credit card, this thin sheet of neural tissue contains a complex network of specialized cells arranged in layers (Rodieck, 1998), as shown in **Figure 4.5**.

The axons that run from the retina to the brain converge at a single spot where they exit the eye. At that point, all the fibers dive through a hole in the retina called the *optic disk.* Since the optic disk is a *hole* in the retina, you cannot see the part of an image that falls on it. It is therefore known as the *blind spot.* Most people are not aware that they have a blind spot in each eye. Why? Because each eye compensates for the blind spot of the other and because the brain somehow "fills in" the missing part of the image (Churchland & Ramachandran, 1996).

Visual Receptors: Rods and Cones 3b

The retina contains millions of receptor cells that are sensitive to light. Surprisingly, these receptors are located in the innermost layer of the retina (see **Figure 4.5**). Hence, light must pass through several layers of cells before it gets to the receptors that actually detect it. Only about 10% of the light arriving at the cornea reaches these receptors (Leibovic, 1990). The

Figure 4.4
Nearsightedness and farsightedness. The pictures on the right simulate how a scene might look to nearsighted and farsighted people. Nearsightedness occurs because light from distant objects focuses in front of the retina. Farsightedness results from the opposite situation—light from close objects focuses behind the retina.

Nearsightedness

Normal eye shape
Retina
Focus point falls in front of retina

Farsightedness

Normal eye shape
Retina
Focus point falls behind retina

Figure 4.5

The retina. The close-up shows the several layers of cells in the retina. The cells closest to the back of the eye (the rods and cones) are the receptor cells that actually detect light. The intervening layers of cells receive signals from the rods and cones and form circuits that begin the process of analyzing incoming information before it is sent to the brain. These cells feed into many optic fibers, all of which head toward the "hole" in the retina where the optic nerve leaves the eye—the point known as the optic disk (which corresponds to the blind spot).

retina contains two types of receptors, *rods* and *cones*. Their names are based on their shapes, as rods are elongated and cones are stubbier. Rods outnumber cones by a huge margin, as humans have 100–125 million rods, but only 5–6.4 million cones (Frishman, 2001).

Cones **are specialized visual receptors that play a key role in daylight vision and color vision.** The cones handle most of people's daytime vision, because bright lights dazzle the rods. The special sensitivities of cones also allow them to play a major role in the perception of color. However, cones do not respond well to dim light, which is why you don't see color very well in low illumination. Nonetheless, cones provide better *visual acuity*—that is, sharpness and precise detail—than rods. Cones are concentrated most heavily in the center of the retina and quickly fall off in density toward its sides. The *fovea* **is a tiny spot in the center of the retina that contains only cones; visual acuity is greatest at this spot** (consult **Figure 4.3** again). When you want to see something in sharp focus, you usually move your eyes to center the object in the fovea.

Rods **are specialized visual receptors that play a key role in night vision and peripheral vision.** Rods handle night vision because they are more sensitive than cones to dim light. They handle the lion's share of peripheral vision because they greatly outnumber cones in the periphery (outer areas) of the retina. The density of the rods is greatest just outside the fovea and gradually decreases toward the periphery of the retina. Because of the distribution of rods, when you want to see a faintly illuminated object in the dark, it's best to look slightly above or below the place it should be. Averting your gaze this way moves the image from the cone-filled fovea, which requires more light, to the rod-dominated area just outside the fovea, which requires less light. This trick of averted vision is well known to astronomers, who use it to study dim objects viewed through the eyepiece of a telescope.

Dark and Light Adaptation   3b

You've probably noticed that when you enter a dark theater on a bright day, you stumble about almost blindly. But within minutes you can make your way about quite well in the dim light. This adjustment is called *dark adaptation*—the process in which the eyes become more sensitive to light in low illumination. **Figure 4.6** maps out the course of this process. It shows how, as time passes, you require less and less light to see. Dark adaptation is virtually complete in about 30 minutes, with considerable progress occurring in the first 10 minutes. The curve in **Figure 4.6** that charts this progress consists of

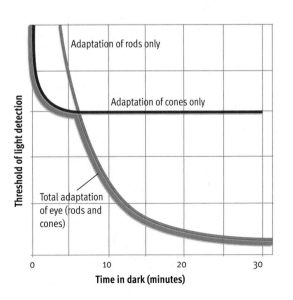

Figure 4.6

The process of dark adaptation. The declining thresholds over time indicate that your visual sensitivity is improving, as less and less light is required to see. Visual sensitivity improves markedly during the first 5 to 10 minutes after entering a dark room, as the eye's bright-light receptors (the cones) rapidly adapt to low light levels. However, the cones' adaptation, which is plotted in purple, soon reaches its limit, and further improvement comes from the rods' adaptation, which is plotted in red. The rods adapt more slowly than the cones, but they are capable of far greater visual sensitivity in low levels of light.

two segments because cones adapt more rapidly than rods (Walraven et al., 1990).

When you emerge from a dark theater on a sunny day, you need to squint to ward off the overwhelming brightness, and the reverse of dark adaptation occurs. *Light adaptation* is the process in which the eyes become less sensitive to light in high illumination. As with dark adaptation, light adaptation improves your visual acuity under the prevailing circumstances.

Information Processing in the Retina   3b

In processing visual input, the retina transforms a pattern of light falling onto it into a very different representation of the visual scene. Light striking the retina's receptors (rods and cones) triggers the firing of neural signals that pass into the intricate network of cells in the retina. Thus, signals move from receptors to bipolar cells to ganglion cells, which in turn send impulses along the *optic nerve*—a collection of axons that connect the eye with the brain (see **Figure 4.5**). These axons, which depart the eye through the optic disk, carry visual information, encoded as a stream of neural impulses, to the brain.

A great deal of complex information processing goes on in the retina itself before visual signals are sent to the brain. Ultimately, the information from as many as 130 million rods and cones converges to travel along "only" 1 million axons in the optic nerve (Slaughter, 1990). This means that the bipolar and ganglion cells in the intermediate layers of the retina integrate and compress signals from many receptors. The collection of rod and cone receptors that funnel signals to a particular visual cell in the retina (or ultimately in the brain) make up that cell's *receptive field*. Thus, **the *receptive field* of a visual cell is the retinal area that, when stimulated, affects the firing of that cell.**

Receptive fields in the retina come in a variety of shapes and sizes. Particularly common are circular fields with a center-surround arrangement (Tessier-Lavigne, 2000). In these receptive fields, light falling in the center has the opposite effect of light falling in the surrounding area (see **Figure 4.7**). For example, the rate of firing of a visual cell might be *increased* by light in the center of its receptive field and *decreased* by light in the surrounding area. Other visual cells may work in just the opposite way. Either way, when receptive fields are stimulated, retinal cells send signals toward the brain.

Vision and the Brain   3c

Light falls on the eye, but you see with your brain. Although the retina does a lot of information processing for a sensory organ, visual input is meaningless until it is processed in the brain.

Visual Pathways to the Brain   3c

How does visual information get to the brain? Axons leaving the back of each eye form the optic nerves, which travel to the *optic chiasm,* the point at which the axons from the inside half of each eye cross over and then project to the opposite half of the brain (as we first discussed in Chapter 3—refer to **Figure 3.17**). This arrangement ensures that signals from both eyes go to both hemispheres of the brain. Thus, as **Figure 4.8** shows, axons from the left half of each retina carry signals to the left side of the brain, and axons from the right half of each retina carry information to the right side of the brain.

After reaching the optic chiasm, the optic nerve fibers split along two pathways. The main pathway projects into the thalamus, the brain's major relay station. Here, about 90% of the axons from the retinas synapse in the lateral geniculate nucleus (LGN) (Pasternak, Bisley, & Calkins, 2003). Visual signals are processed in the LGN and then distributed to areas in the occipital lobe that make up the *primary visual cortex.* After the initial cortical processing of visual input takes place here, signals are typically sent to the temporal and parietal lobes for additional processing. The second visual pathway leaving the optic chiasm branches off to an area in the midbrain (the *superior colliculus*) before traveling through the

concept check 4.1

Understanding Sensory Processes in the Retina

Check your understanding of sensory receptors in the retina by completing the following exercise. Consult Appendix A for the answers.

The receptors for vision are rods and cones in the retina. These two types of receptors have many important differences, which are compared systematically in the chart below. Fill in the missing information to finish the chart.

Dimension	Rods	Cones
1. Physical shape	*Elongated*	
2. Number in the retina		*5–6.4 million*
3. Area of the retina in which they are dominant receptor	*Periphery*	
4. Critical to color vision		
5. Critical to peripheral vision		*No*
6. Sensitivity to dim light	*Strong*	
7. Speed of dark adaptation		*Rapid*

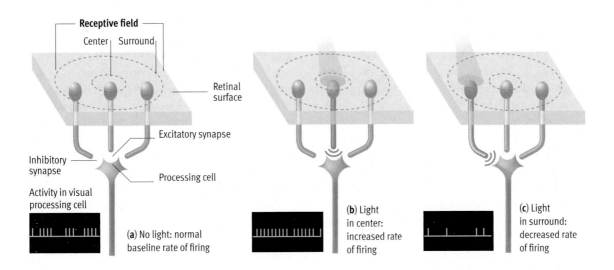

Receptive field
Center | Surround
Retinal surface
Excitatory synapse
Inhibitory synapse
Processing cell
Activity in visual processing cell

(a) No light: normal baseline rate of firing

(b) Light in center: increased rate of firing

(c) Light in surround: decreased rate of firing

Figure 4.7
Receptive fields in the retina. Visual cells' receptive fields in the retina are often circular with a center-surround arrangement, so that light striking the center of the field produces the opposite result of light striking the surround. In the receptive field depicted here, light in the center produces increased firing in the visual cell (symbolized by green at the synapse), whereas light in the surround produces decreased firing (symbolized by red at the synapse). The arrangement in other receptive fields may be just the opposite.

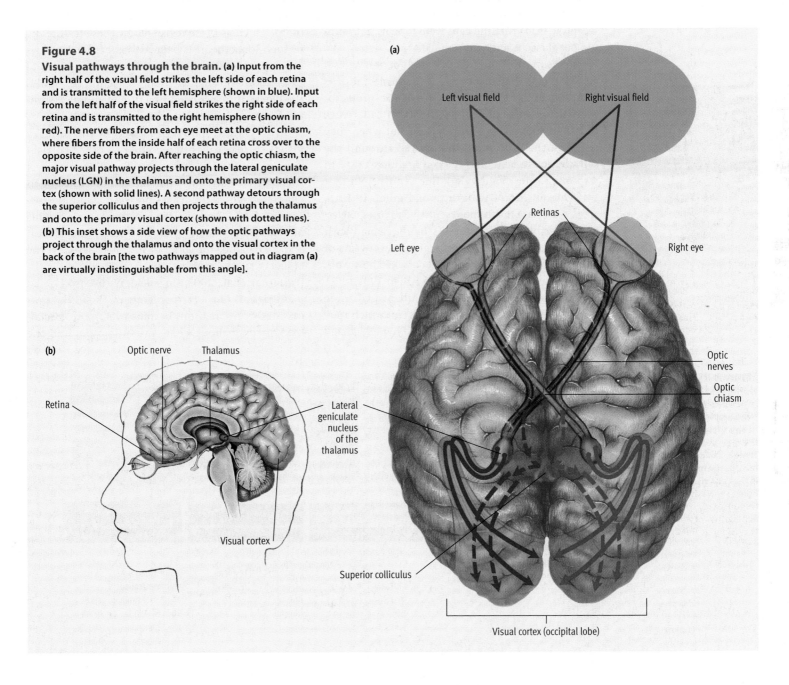

Figure 4.8
Visual pathways through the brain. (a) Input from the right half of the visual field strikes the left side of each retina and is transmitted to the left hemisphere (shown in blue). Input from the left half of the visual field strikes the right side of each retina and is transmitted to the right hemisphere (shown in red). The nerve fibers from each eye meet at the optic chiasm, where fibers from the inside half of each retina cross over to the opposite side of the brain. After reaching the optic chiasm, the major visual pathway projects through the lateral geniculate nucleus (LGN) in the thalamus and onto the primary visual cortex (shown with solid lines). A second pathway detours through the superior colliculus and then projects through the thalamus and onto the primary visual cortex (shown with dotted lines). **(b)** This inset shows a side view of how the optic pathways project through the thalamus and onto the visual cortex in the back of the brain [the two pathways mapped out in diagram (a) are virtually indistinguishable from this angle].

(a)
Left visual field | Right visual field
Retinas
Left eye | Right eye
Optic nerves
Optic chiasm
Superior colliculus
Visual cortex (occipital lobe)

(b)
Optic nerve | Thalamus
Retina
Lateral geniculate nucleus of the thalamus
Visual cortex

thalamus to the occipital lobe. However, the second pathway projects into different areas of the thalamus and the occipital lobe than the main visual pathway does. The principal function of the second pathway appears to be the coordination of visual input with other sensory input (Casanova et al., 2001; Stein & Meredith, 1993).

Information Processing in the Visual Cortex

3c

Visual input ultimately arrives in the primary visual cortex located in the occipital lobe. How these cortical cells respond to light used to pose a perplexing problem. Researchers investigating the question placed microelectrodes in the visual cortex of animals to record action potentials from individual cells. They would flash spots of light in the retinal receptive fields that the cells were thought to monitor, but the cells rarely responded.

According to David Hubel and Torsten Wiesel (1962, 1963), they discovered the solution to this mystery quite by accident. One of the projector slides they used to present a spot to a cat had a crack in it. The spot elicited no response, but when they removed the slide, the crack moved through the cell's receptive field, and the cell fired like crazy in response to the moving dark line. It turns out that cortical cells don't really respond much to little spots—they are much more sensitive to lines, edges, and other more complicated stimuli. Armed with new slides, Hubel and Wiesel embarked on years of painstaking study of the visual cortex. Their work eventually earned them a Nobel prize in 1981.

Hubel and Wiesel (1979, 1998) identified three major types of visual cells in the cortex, which they called simple cells, complex cells, and hypercomplex

cells. *Simple cells* are quite specific about which stimuli will make them fire. A simple cell responds best to a line of the correct width, oriented at the correct angle, and located in the correct position in its receptive field (see **Figure 4.9**). *Complex cells* also care about width and orientation, but they respond to any position in their receptive fields. Some complex cells are most responsive if a line sweeps across their receptive field—but only if it's moving in the "right" direction. *Hypercomplex* cells are cells that are particularly fussy about the length of a stimulus line.

The key point of all this is that the cells in the visual cortex seem to be highly specialized. They have been characterized as **feature detectors, neurons that respond selectively to very specific features of more complex stimuli.** Ultimately, most visual stimuli could be represented by combinations of lines such as those registered by these feature detectors. Some theorists believe that feature detectors are registering the basic building blocks of visual perception and that the brain somehow assembles the blocks into a coherent picture of complex stimuli (Maguire, Weisstein, & Klymenko, 1990).

After visual input is processed in the primary visual cortex, it is often routed to other cortical areas for additional processing. These signals travel through two streams that have sometimes been characterized as the *what* and *where pathways* (see **Figure 4.10**). The *ventral stream* processes the details of *what* objects are out there (the perception of form and color), while the *dorsal stream* processes *where* the objects are (the perception of motion and depth) (Pasternak et al., 2003; Ungerleider & Haxby, 1994).

As signals move farther along in the visual processing system, neurons become even more specialized or fussy about what turns them on, and the

David Hubel

"One can now begin to grasp the significance of the great number of cells in the visual cortex. Each cell seems to have its own specific duties."

Figure 4.9
Hubel and Wiesel's procedure for studying the activity of neurons in the visual cortex. As the cat is shown various stimuli, a microelectrode records the firing of a neuron in the cat's visual cortex. The figure shows the electrical responses of a visual cell apparently "programmed" to respond to lines oriented vertically.

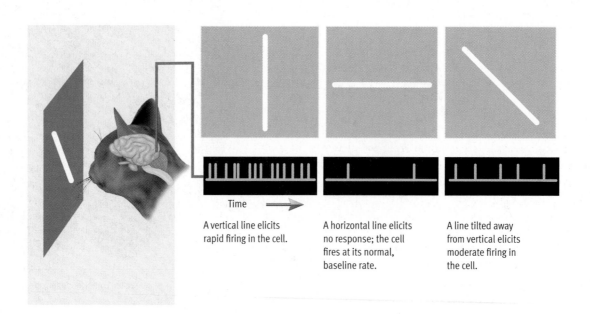

Time →

A vertical line elicits rapid firing in the cell.

A horizontal line elicits no response; the cell fires at its normal, baseline rate.

A line tilted away from vertical elicits moderate firing in the cell.

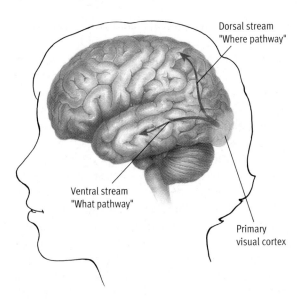

Figure 4.10

The *what* and *where* pathways from the primary visual cortex. Cortical processing of visual input is begun in the primary visual cortex. From there, signals are shuttled onward to a variety of other areas in the cortex along a number of pathways. Two prominent pathways are highlighted here. The dorsal stream, or *where* pathway, which processes information about motion and depth, moves on to areas of the parietal lobe. The ventral stream, or *what* pathway, which processes information about color and form, moves on to areas of the temporal lobe.

© Steve Granitz/WireImage/Getty Images   © Doane Gregory/Warner Bros./Bureau L. A. Collection/Corbis

Figure 4.11

Examples of stimuli used by Quiroga et al. (2005). Quiroga and colleagues exposed participants to varied views of specific objects, buildings, animals, faces, and random photos while monitoring activity in selected brain cells. They discovered neurons in the hippocampal area that were uniquely responsive to certain famous people, such as Halle Berry. These cells apparently were responding to the *concept* of Halle Berry rather than to her *face* because they responded not only to facial photos, but also to pictures of the actress in a Catwoman costume and to the words HALLE BERRY. Similar results were observed for diverse stimuli related to other famous people.

stimuli that activate them become more and more complex. For example, researchers have identified cells in the temporal lobe (along the what pathway) of monkeys and humans that are especially sensitive to pictures of faces (Levine, 2001; Rolls & Tovee, 1995). These neurons respond even to pictures that merely suggest the form of a face (Cox, Meyers, & Sinha, 2004).

This incredible specificity led researchers to joke that they might eventually find a neuron that only recognizes one's grandmother (Cowey, 1994). Although the concept of a "grandmother cell" was meant to be humorous, researchers recently have discovered the equivalent, albeit in areas of the brain that handle memory rather than vision (Gaschler, 2006). Using pictures of famous people as stimuli, Quiroga et al. (2005) found individual neurons in the hippocampal area that would respond only to photos of Bill Clinton, others that would respond only to Halle Berry, and still others that were activated only by Jennifer Aniston. Interestingly, these cells would also respond to the words BILL CLINTON or HALLE BERRY (see **Figure 4.11**), so it appears that they are activated by concepts rather than visual forms. Thus, these ultraspecific cells probably have more to do with memory than vision. Nonetheless, it is fascinating that the frequently mocked concept of a "grandmother cell" is not as preposterous as once assumed.

Another dramatic finding in this area of research is that the neurons in the what pathway that are involved in perceiving faces can learn from experience (Gauthier & Curby, 2005; Palmeri & Gauthier, 2004). In one eye-opening study, participants were given extensive training in discriminating among similar artificial objects called Greebles (**see Figure 4.12**). After this training, neurons that are normally sensitive to faces were found to be almost as sensitive to Greebles as to faces (Gauthier et al., 1999). In other words, neurons that usually serve as face detectors were "retuned" to be responsive to other visual forms. Like many findings discussed in Chapter 3, these results demonstrate that the functional organization of the brain is somewhat "plastic" and that the brain can be rewired by experience.

Figure 4.12

Distinguishing Greebles. Gauthier et al. (1999) gave subjects seven hours of training in the recognition of novel stimuli called Greebles, four of which are shown here. As the text explains, this training was conducted to explore whether neurons that normally respond to faces could be retuned by experience.

SOURCE: Reproduced by permission of Isabel Gauthier. Copyright © 2008 by Isabel Gauthier.

Viewing the World in Color 3d

So far, we've considered only how the visual system deals with light and dark. Let's journey now into the world of color. Of course, you can see perfectly well without seeing in color. Many animals get by with little or no color vision, and no one seemed to suffer back when photographs, movies, or TV shows were all in black and white. However, color adds not only spectacle but information to perceptions of the world. The ability to identify objects against a complex background is enhanced by the addition of color (Tanaka, Weiskopf, & Williams, 2001). Thus, some theorists have suggested that color vision evolved in humans and monkeys because it improved their abilities to find food through foraging, to spot prey, and to quickly recognize predators (Spence et al., 2006). Although the purpose of color vision remains elusive, scientists have learned a great deal about the mechanisms underlying the perception of color.

The Stimulus for Color 3d

As noted earlier, the lights people see are mixtures of different wavelengths. Perceived color is primarily a function of the dominant wavelength in these mixtures. In the visible spectrum, lights with the longest wavelengths appear red, whereas those with the shortest appear violet. Notice the word *appear*. Color is a psychological interpretation. It's not a physical property of light itself.

Although wavelength wields the greatest influence, perception of color depends on complex blends of all three properties of light. Wavelength is most closely related to hue, amplitude to brightness, and purity to saturation. These three dimensions of color are illustrated in the *color solid* shown in **Figure 4.13**.

As a color solid demonstrates systematically, people can perceive many different colors. Indeed, ex-

perts estimate that humans can discriminate among roughly a million colors (Boynton, 1990). Most of these diverse variations are the result of mixing a few basic colors. There are two kinds of color mixture: subtractive and additive. *Subtractive color mixing works by removing some wavelengths of light, leaving less light than was originally there.* You probably became familiar with subtractive mixing as a child when you mixed yellow and blue paints to make green. Paints yield subtractive mixing because pigments *absorb* most wavelengths, selectively reflecting back specific wavelengths that give rise to particular colors. Subtractive color mixing can also be demonstrated by stacking color filters. If you look through a sandwich of yellow and blue cellophane filters, they will block out certain wavelengths. The middle wavelengths that are left will look green.

Additive color mixing works by superimposing lights, putting more light in the mixture than exists in any one light by itself. If you shine red, green, and blue spotlights on a white surface, you'll have an additive mixture. As **Figure 4.14** shows, additive and subtractive mixtures of the same colors produce different results.

White light actually includes the entire visible spectrum, as you can demonstrate by allowing white light to pass through a prism (consult **Figure 4.1** once again). Accordingly, when all wavelengths are mixed additively, they yield natural white light. Human processes of color perception parallel additive color mixing much more closely than subtractive mixing, as you'll see in the following discussion of theories of color vision.

Trichromatic Theory of Color Vision 3d

The trichromatic theory of color vision (*tri* for "three," *chroma* for "color") was first stated by

Figure 4.13

The color solid. The color solid shows how color varies along three perceptual dimensions: brightness (increasing from the bottom to the top of the solid), hue (changing around the solid's perimeter), and saturation (increasing toward the periphery of the solid).

Courtesy of BASF

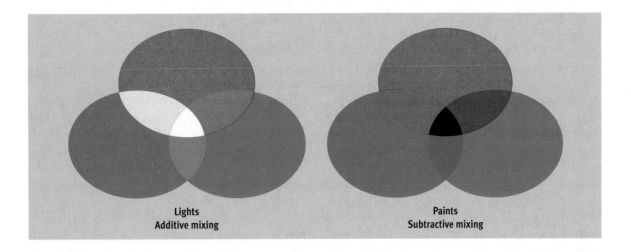

Lights
Additive mixing

Paints
Subtractive mixing

Figure 4.14
Additive versus subtractive color mixing. Lights mix additively because all the wavelengths contained in each light reach the eye. If red, blue, and green lights are projected onto a white screen, they produce the colors shown on the left, with white at the intersection of all three lights. If paints of the same three colors were combined in the same way, the subtractive mixture would produce the colors shown on the right, with black at the intersection of all three colors.

Thomas Young and modified later by Hermann von Helmholtz (1852). The *trichromatic theory* holds that the human eye has three types of receptors with differing sensitivities to different light wavelengths. Helmholtz believed that the eye contains specialized receptors sensitive to the wavelengths associated with red, green, or blue. According to this model, people can see all the colors of the rainbow because the eye does its own "color mixing" by varying the ratio of neural activity among these three types of receptors.

The impetus for the trichromatic theory was the demonstration that a light of any color can be matched by the additive mixture of three *primary colors.* (Any three colors that are appropriately spaced out in the visible spectrum can serve as primary colors, although red, green, and blue are usually used.) Does it sound implausible that three colors should be adequate for creating all other colors? If so, consider that this phenomenon is exactly what happens on your color TV screen. Additive mixtures of red, green, and blue fool you into seeing all the colors of a natural scene.

Most of the known facts about color blindness also meshed well with trichromatic theory. *Color blindness* encompasses a variety of deficiencies in the ability to distinguish among colors. Color blindness occurs much more frequently in males than in females. Actually, the term color *blindness* is somewhat misleading, as complete blindness to differences in colors is quite rare. Most people who are color blind are *dichromats;* that is, they make do with only two color channels. There are three types of dichromats, and each type is insensitive to a different color (red, green, or blue, although the latter is rare) (Gouras, 1991). The three deficiencies seen among dichromats support the notion that there are three channels for color vision, as proposed by trichromatic theory.

Opponent Process Theory of Color Vision 3d

Although trichromatic theory explained some facets of color vision well, it ran aground in other areas. Consider complementary afterimages, for instance. *Complementary colors are pairs of colors that produce gray tones when mixed together.* The various pairs of complementary colors can be arranged in a *color circle,* such as the one in **Figure 4.15**. If you stare at a strong color and then look at a white background, you'll see an *afterimage*—a visual image that persists after a stimulus is removed. The color of the afterimage will be the *complement* of the color you originally stared at. Trichromatic theory cannot account for the appearance of complementary afterimages.

Here's another peculiarity to consider. If you ask people to describe colors but restrict them to using three names, they run into difficulty. For example, using only red, green, and blue, they simply don't feel comfortable describing yellow as "reddish green." However, if you let them have just one more name, they usually choose yellow. Then they can

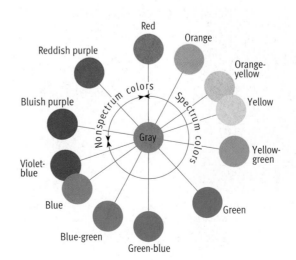

Figure 4.15
The color circle and complementary colors. Colors opposite each other on this color circle are complements, or "opposites." Additively mixing complementary colors produces gray. Opponent process principles help explain this effect as well as the other peculiarities of complementary colors.

describe any color quite well (Gordon & Abramov, 2001). If colors are reduced to three channels, why are four color names required to describe the full range of possible colors?

In an effort to answer questions such as these, Ewald Hering proposed the *opponent process theory* of color vision in 1878. **The *opponent process theory* holds that color perception depends on receptors that make antagonistic responses to three pairs of colors.** The three pairs of opponent colors he hypothesized were red versus green, yellow versus blue, and black versus white. The antagonistic processes in this theory provide plausible explanations for complementary afterimages and the need for four names (red, green, blue, and yellow) to describe colors. Opponent process theory also explains some aspects of color blindness. For instance, it can explain why dichromats typically find it hard to distinguish either green from red or yellow from blue.

Reconciling Theories of Color Vision

PSYK TREK

3d

Advocates of trichromatic theory and opponent process theory argued about the relative merits of the two models for almost a century. Most researchers assumed that one theory must be wrong and the other must be right. In recent decades, however, it has become clear that *it takes both theories to explain color vision.* Eventually a physiological basis for both theories was found. Research that earned George Wald a Nobel prize demonstrated that *the eye has three types of cones,* with each type being most sensitive to a different band of wavelengths, as shown in **Figure 4.16** (Lennie, 2000; Wald, 1964). The three types of cones represent the three different color receptors predicted by trichromatic theory. Interestingly, the three types

of cones are distributed in a seemingly random fashion in the central area of the retina where cones predominate (Solomon & Lennie, 2007).

Researchers also discovered a biological basis for opponent processes. They found cells in the retina, the thalamus, and the visual cortex *that respond in opposite ways to red versus green and blue versus yellow* (DeValois & Jacobs, 1984; Zrenner et al., 1990). For example, some ganglion cells in the retina are excited by green and inhibited by red. Other ganglion cells in the retina work in just the opposite way, as predicted by opponent process theory.

In summary, the perception of color appears to involve stages of information processing (Hurvich, 1981). The receptors that do the first stage of processing (the cones) seem to follow the principles outlined in trichromatic theory. In later stages of processing, cells in the retina and the brain seem to follow the principles outlined in opponent process theory. As you can see, vigorous theoretical debate about color vision produced a solution that went beyond the contributions of either theory alone.

Figure 4.16

Three types of cones. Research has identified three types of cones that show varied sensitivity to different wavelengths of light. As the graph shows, these three types of cones correspond only roughly to the red, green, and blue receptors predicted by trichromatic theory, so it is more accurate to refer to them as cones sensitive to short, medium, and long wavelengths.

SOURCE: Wald, G., & Brown, P. K. (1965). Human color vision and color blindness. *Symposium Cold Spring Harbor Laboratory of Quantitative Biology, 30,* 345–359 (p. 351). Copyright © 1965. Reprinted by permission of the author.

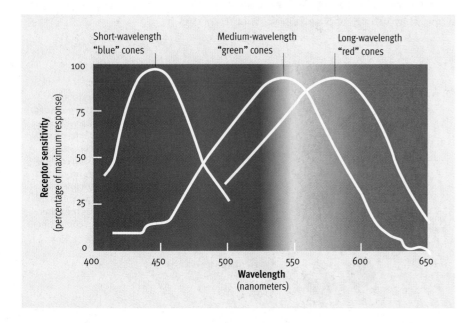

REVIEW of Key Learning Goals

4.1 Light varies in terms of wavelength, amplitude, and purity. Perceptions of color (hue) are primarily a function of light wavelength, while amplitude mainly affects brightness and purity mainly affects saturation.

4.2 Light enters the eye through the cornea and pupil and is focused upside down on the retina by the lens. Distant objects appear blurry to nearsighted people and close objects appear blurry to farsighted people. The pupils control the amount of light entering the eye.

4.3 The retina is the neural tissue in the eye that absorbs light, processes images, and sends visual signals to the brain. Cones, which are concentrated in the fovea, play a key role in daylight vision and color perception. Rods, which have their greatest density just outside the fovea, are critical to night vision and peripheral vision. Dark adaptation and light adaptation both involve changes in the retina's sensitivity to light. Receptive fields are areas in the retina that affect the firing of visual cells.

4.4 The optic nerves from the inside half of each eye cross at the optic chiasm and then project to the opposite half of the brain. Two visual pathways send signals to different areas of the primary visual cortex. The main pathway is routed through the LGN in the thalamus. After processing in the primary visual cortex, visual information is shuttled along the what and where pathways to other cortical areas. Research suggests that the visual cortex contains cells that function as feature detectors. The what pathway has neurons inside it that are especially sensitive to faces and other highly specific stimuli.

4.5 There are two types of color mixing: additive and subtractive. Human color perception depends on processes that resemble additive color mixing. The trichromatic theory holds that people have three types of receptors that are sensitive to wavelengths associated with red, green, and blue. The opponent process theory holds that color perception depends on receptors that make antagonistic responses to red versus green, blue versus yellow, and black versus white. The evidence now suggests that both theories are necessary to account for color vision.

Comparing Theories of Color Vision

Check your understanding of the differences between the trichromatic and opponent process theories of color vision by filling in the blanks below. The answers are in Appendix A.

	Trichromatic theory	Opponent process theory
1. Theory proposed by	_____	_____
2. Can/can't account for complementary afterimages	_____	_____
3. Explains first/later stage of color processing	_____	_____
4. Does/doesn't account for need for four terms to describe colors	_____	_____

The Visual System: Perceptual Processes

We have seen how sensory receptors in the eye transform light into neural impulses that are sent to the brain. We focus next on how the brain makes sense of it all—how does it convert streams of neural impulses into perceptions of chairs, doors, friends, automobiles, and buildings? In this section we explore perceptual processes in vision, such as the perception of forms, objects, depth, and so forth.

Perceiving Forms, Patterns, and Objects   3c, 3e

The drawing in **Figure 4.17** is a poster for a circus act involving a trained seal. What do you see?

No doubt you see a seal balancing a ball on its nose and a trainer holding a fish and a whip. But suppose you had been told that the drawing is actually a poster for a costume ball. Would you have perceived it differently?

If you focus on the idea of a costume ball (stay with it a minute if you still see the seal and trainer), you will probably see a costumed man and woman in **Figure 4.17**. She's handing him a hat, and he has a sword in his right hand. This tricky little sketch was made ambiguous quite intentionally. It's a *reversible figure,* **a drawing that is compatible with two different interpretations that can shift back and forth.** Another classic reversible figure is shown in **Figure 4.18** on the next page. What do you see? A rabbit or a duck? It all depends on how you look at the drawing.

The key point is simply this: *The same visual input can result in radically different perceptions.* There is no one-to-one correspondence between sensory input and what you perceive. *This is a principal reason that people's experience of the world is subjective.* Perception

Figure 4.17
A poster for a trained seal act. Or is it? The picture is an ambiguous figure, which can be interpreted as either of two scenes, as explained in the text.

Key Learning Goals

4.6 Discuss the subjectivity of form perception, the phenomenon of inattentional blindness, and the concept of feature analysis.

4.7 State the basic premise of Gestalt psychology and describe Gestalt principles of visual perception.

4.8 Clarify how form perception can be a matter of formulating perceptual hypotheses.

4.9 Describe the monocular and binocular cues used in depth perception and cultural variations in depth perception.

4.10 Describe perceptual constancies and illusions in vision, and discuss cultural variations in susceptibility to certain illusions.

Figure 4.18
Another ambiguous figure. What animal do you see here? As the text explains, two very different perceptions are possible. This ambiguous figure was devised around 1900 by Joseph Jastrow, a prominent psychologist at the turn of the 20th century (Block & Yuker, 1992).

Figure 4.19
Ambiguous stimulus used by Balcetis and Dunning (2006). Participants saw brief presentations of this stimulus, which could be viewed as a letter (B) or as a number (13). The study demonstrated that motivational factors influence what people tend to see.

involves much more than passively receiving signals from the outside world. It involves the *interpretation* of sensory input.

In this case, your interpretations result in two different "realities" because your *expectations* have been manipulated. Information given to you about the drawing has created a *perceptual set*—a readiness to perceive a stimulus in a particular way. A perceptual set creates a certain slant in how you interpret sensory input.

Like expectations, motivational forces can foster perceptual sets, as demonstrated in one recent study (Balcetis & Dunning, 2006) using reversible figures as stimuli. Participants were told that a computer would flash a number or a letter to indicate whether they were assigned to a pleasant or unpleasant experimental task (trying some orange juice or a nasty-looking health food drink). Each of the subjects briefly saw the same ambiguous stimulus (see **Figure 4.19**), which could be viewed as either a number (13) or a letter (B), then the computer appeared to crash. Participants were then asked what they had seen before the computer crashed. Subjects hoping for a letter were much more likely to interpret the stimulus as a B, and those hoping for a number were much more likely to view the stimulus as a 13. Thus, we see once again, that people have a tendency to see what they want to see.

Form perception also depends on the *selection* of sensory input—that is, what people focus their attention on (Chun & Wolfe, 2001). A visual scene may include many objects and forms. Some of these may capture viewers' attention while others may not. This fact has been demonstrated in dramatic fashion in studies of *inattentional blindness*, which **involves the failure to see fully visible objects or events in a visual display because one's attention is focused elsewhere.** In one such study (Simons & Chabris, 1999), participants watched a video of a group of people in white shirts passing a basketball laid over another video of people in black shirts passing a basketball (the two videos were partially transparent). The observers were instructed to focus on one of the two teams and press a key whenever that team passed the ball. Thirty seconds into the task, a woman carrying an umbrella clearly walked through the scene for four seconds. You might guess that this bizarre development would be noticed by virtually all the observers, but 44% of the participants failed to see the woman. Moreover, when someone in a gorilla suit strolled through the same scene even more subjects (73%) missed the unexpected event!

Additional studies using other types of stimulus materials have demonstrated that people routinely overlook obvious forms that are unexpected (Most

et al., 2005). Inattentional blindness has been attributed to subjects having a perceptual set that leads them to focus most of their attention on a specific feature in a scene (such as the basketball passes) while neglecting other facets of the scene (Most et al., 2001). Consistent with this analysis, recent research has shown that the likelihood of inattentional blindness increases when people work on tasks that require a lot of attention or create complicated perceptual demands (Cartwright-Finch & Lavie, 2007). Inattentional blindness may account for many automobile accidents, as accident reports often include the statement "I looked right there, but never saw them" (Shermer, 2004). Although this phenomenon can happen to an attentive and unimpaired driver, research shows that inattentional blindness increases when people talk on a cell phone or are even slightly intoxicated (Clifasefi, Takarangi, & Bergman, 2006; Strayer & Drews, 2007). The idea that we see much less of the world than we think we do surprises many people, but there is an auditory parallel that people take for granted (Mack, 2003). Think of how often you have had someone clearly say something to you, but you did not hear a word of what was said because you were "not listening." Inattentional blindness is essentially the same thing in the visual domain.

An understanding of how people perceive forms, patterns, and objects also requires knowledge of how people *organize and interpret* visual input. Several influential approaches to this question emphasize *feature analysis*.

Feature Analysis: Assembling Forms

3c

The information received by your eyes would do you little good if you couldn't recognize objects and forms—ranging from words on a page to mice in your cellar and friends in the distance. According to some theories, perceptions of form and pattern entail *feature analysis* (Lindsay & Norman, 1977; Maguire et al., 1990). **Feature analysis is the process of detecting specific elements in visual input and assembling them into a more complex form.** In other words, you start with the components of a form, such as lines, edges, and corners, and build them into perceptions of squares, triangles, stop signs, bicycles, ice cream cones, and telephones. An application of this model of form perception is diagrammed in **Figure 4.20**.

Feature analysis assumes that form perception involves *bottom-up processing,* a progression from individual elements to the whole (see **Figure 4.21**). The plausibility of this model was bolstered greatly when Hubel and Wiesel showed that cells in the

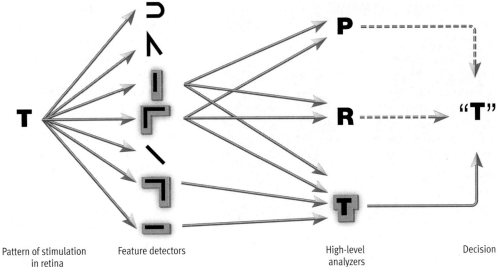

Figure 4.20

Feature analysis in form perception. One vigorously debated theory of form perception is that the brain has cells that respond to specific aspects or features of stimuli, such as lines and angles. Neurons functioning as higher-level analyzers then respond to input from these "feature detectors." The more input each analyzer receives, the more active it becomes. Finally, other neurons weigh signals from these analyzers and make a "decision" about the stimulus. In this way perception of a form is arrived at by assembling elements from the bottom up.

Pattern of stimulation in retina — Feature detectors — High-level analyzers — Decision

visual cortex operate as highly specialized feature detectors. Indeed, their findings strongly suggested that at least some aspects of form perception involve feature analysis.

Can feature analysis provide a complete account of how people perceive forms? Clearly not. A crucial problem for the theory is that form perception often does not involve bottom-up processing. In fact, there is ample evidence that perceptions of form frequently involve *top-down processing,* a progression from the whole to the elements (see **Figure 4.21**). For example, there is evidence that people can perceive a word before its individual letters, a phenomenon that has to reflect top-down processing (Johnston & McClelland, 1974). If readers depended exclusively on bottom-up processing, they would have to analyze the features of letters in words to recognize them and then assemble the letters into words. This task would be time-consuming and would slow down reading speed to a snail's pace.

Looking at the Whole Picture: Gestalt Principles

PSYK TREK

3e

Sometimes a whole, as we perceive it, may have qualities that don't exist in any of the parts. This insight—*that the whole can be greater than the sum of its parts*—became the basic assumption of *Gestalt psychology,* an influential school of thought that emerged out of Germany during the first half of the 20th century (*Gestalt* is a German word for "form" or "shape").

A simple example of this principle, which you have experienced countless times, is the *phi phenomenon,* first described by Max Wertheimer in 1912. The *phi phenomenon* is the illusion of movement created by presenting visual stimuli in rapid succession. You encounter examples of the phi phe-

nomenon nearly every day. For example, movies and TV consist of separate still pictures projected rapidly one after the other. You *see* smooth motion, but in reality the "moving" objects merely take slightly different positions in successive frames. Viewed as a whole, a movie has a property (motion) that isn't evident in any of its parts (the individual frames).

The Gestalt psychologists formulated a series of principles that describe how the visual system organizes a scene into discrete forms. Let's explore some of these principles.

Figure and Ground   Take a look at **Figure 4.22** on the next page. Do you see the figure as two silhouetted faces against a white background, or as a white vase against a black background? This reversible figure illustrates the Gestalt principle of *figure*

Archives of the History of American Psychology, University of Akron

Max Wertheimer

"The fundamental 'formula' of Gestalt theory might be expressed in this way: There are wholes, the behaviour of which is not determined by that of their individual elements."

Figure 4.21

Bottom-up versus top-down processing. As explained in these diagrams, bottom-up processing progresses from individual elements to whole elements, whereas top-down processing progresses from the whole to the individual elements.

Figure 4.22

The principle of figure and ground. Whether you see two faces or a vase depends on which part of this drawing you see as figure and which as background. Although this reversible drawing allows you to switch back and forth between two ways of organizing your perception, you can't perceive the drawing both ways at once.

web link 4.3

Sensation and Perception Tutorials

John Krantz of Hanover College has assembled a collection of quality tutorials on sensation and perception. Topics covered include receptive fields, depth perception, Gestalt laws, and the use of perceptual principles in art.

and ground. Dividing visual displays into figure and ground is a fundamental way in which people organize visual perceptions (Baylis & Driver, 1995). The figure is the thing being looked at, and the ground is the background against which it stands. The figure seems to have substance and appears to stand out in front of the ground. Other things being equal, an object is more likely to be viewed as a figure when it is smaller in size, higher in contrast, or greater in symmetry (Palmer, 2003), and especially when it is lower in one's frame of view (Vecera & Palmer, 2006). More often than not, your visual field may contain many figures sharing a background. The following Gestalt principles relate to how these elements are grouped into higher-order figures (Palmer, 2003).

The illusion of movement in a highway construction sign is an instance of the phi phenomenon, which is also at work in motion pictures and television. The phenomenon illustrates the Gestalt principle that the whole can have properties that are not found in any of its parts.

Proximity Things that are near one another seem to belong together. The black dots in **Figure 4.23(a)** could be grouped into vertical columns or horizontal rows. However, people tend to perceive rows because of the effect of proximity (the dots are closer together horizontally).

Closure People often group elements to create a sense of *closure,* or completeness. Thus, you may "complete" figures that actually have gaps in them. This principle is demonstrated in **Figure 4.23(b)**.

Similarity People also tend to group stimuli that are similar. This principle is apparent in **Figure 4.23(c)**, where elements of similar darkness are grouped into the number 2.

Simplicity The Gestaltists' most general principle was the law of *Pragnanz,* which translates from German as "good form." The idea is that people tend to group elements that combine to form a good figure. This principle is somewhat vague in that it's often difficult to spell out what makes a figure "good" (Biederman, Hilton, & Hummel, 1991). Some theorists maintain that goodness is largely a matter of simplicity, asserting that people tend to organize forms in the simplest way possible (see **Figure 4.23(d)**).

Continuity The principle of continuity reflects people's tendency to follow in whatever direction they've been led. Thus, people tend to connect points that result in straight or gently curved lines that create "smooth" paths, as shown in **Figure 4.23(e)**.

Although Gestalt psychology is no longer an active theoretical orientation in modern psychology, its influence is still felt in the study of perception (Banks & Krajicek, 1991). The Gestalt psychologists raised many important questions that still occupy researchers, and they left a legacy of many useful insights about form perception that have stood the test of time (Sharps & Wertheimer, 2000).

Formulating Perceptual Hypotheses

The Gestalt principles provide some indications of how people organize visual input. However, scientists are still one step away from understanding how these organized perceptions result in a representation of the real world. In visual perception, the images projected on the retina are distorted, two-dimensional versions of their actual, three-dimensional counterparts. For example, consider the stimulus of a square such as the one in **Figure 4.24**. If the square is lying on a desk in front of you, it is actually projecting a trapezoid on your retinas, because the top of the square is farther from your eyes than the bottom. Obviously, the

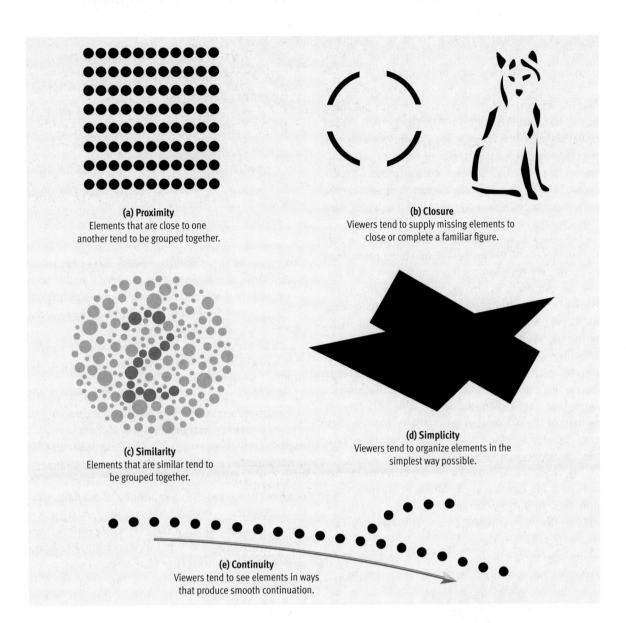

(a) Proximity
Elements that are close to one
another tend to be grouped together.

(b) Closure
Viewers tend to supply missing elements to
close or complete a familiar figure.

(c) Similarity
Elements that are similar tend to
be grouped together.

(d) Simplicity
Viewers tend to organize elements in the
simplest way possible.

(e) Continuity
Viewers tend to see elements in ways
that produce smooth continuation.

Figure 4.23
Gestalt principles of perceptual organization. Gestalt principles help explain some of the factors that influence form perception. **(a) Proximity:** These dots might well be organized in vertical columns rather than horizontal rows, but because of proximity (the dots are closer together horizontally), they tend to be perceived in rows. **(b) Closure:** Even though the figures are incomplete, you fill in the blanks and see a circle and a dog. **(c) Similarity:** Because of similarity of color, you see dots organized into the number 2 instead of a random array. If you did not group similar elements, you wouldn't see the number 2 here. **(d) Simplicity:** You could view this as a complicated 11-sided figure, but given the preference for simplicity, you are more likely to see it as an overlapping rectangle and triangle. **(e) Continuity:** You tend to group these dots in a way that produces a smooth path rather than an abrupt shift in direction.

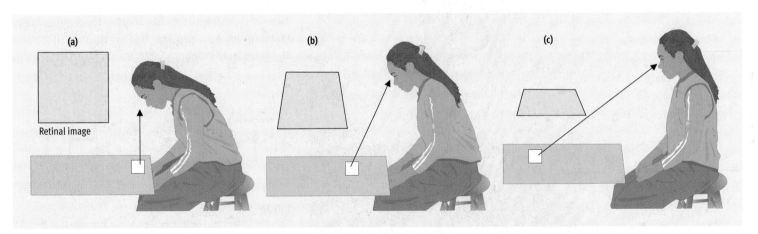

Retinal image

Figure 4.24
Perceptual hypotheses. The images projected on the retina are often distorted, shifting representations of stimuli in the real world, requiring ongoing perceptual hypotheses about what form could be responsible for a particular pattern of sensory stimulation. For example, if you look directly down at a small, square piece of paper on a desk **(a)**, the stimulus (the paper) and the image projected on your retina will both be square. But as you move the paper away on the desktop, as shown in **(b)** and **(c)**, the square stimulus projects an increasingly trapezoidal image on your retina.

trapezoid is a distorted representation of the square. If what people have to work with is so distorted, how do they get an accurate view of the world?

One explanation is that people are constantly making and testing *hypotheses* about what's out there in the real world (Gregory, 1973). Thus, a *perceptual hypothesis* is an inference about what form could be responsible for a pattern of sensory stimulation. The square in **Figure 4.24** may project a trapezoidal image on your retinas, but your perceptual system "guesses" correctly that it's a square—and that's what you see.

Let's look at another ambiguous drawing to further demonstrate the process of making a perceptual hypothesis. **Figure 4.25** is a famous reversible figure, first published as a cartoon in a humor magazine. Perhaps you see a drawing of a young woman looking back over her right shoulder. Alternatively, you might see an old woman with her chin down on her chest. The ambiguity exists because there isn't enough information to force your perceptual system to accept only one of these hypotheses. Incidentally, studies show that people who are led to *expect* the young woman or the old woman generally see the one they expect (Leeper, 1935). This is another example of how perceptual sets influence what people see.

Psychologists have used a variety of reversible figures to study how people formulate perceptual hypotheses. Another example can be seen in **Figure 4.26**, which shows the *Necker cube*. The shaded surface

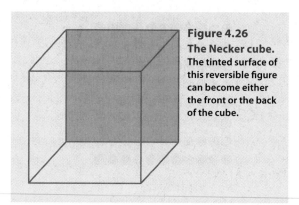

Figure 4.26
The Necker cube. The tinted surface of this reversible figure can become either the front or the back of the cube.

can appear as either the front or the rear of the transparent cube. If you look at the cube for a while, your perception will alternate between these possibilities.

The *context* in which something appears often guides our perceptual hypotheses. To illustrate, take a look at **Figure 4.27**. What do you see? You probably saw the words "THE CAT." But look again; the middle characters in both words are identical. You identified an "H" in the first word and an "A" in the second because of the surrounding letters, which shaped your expectations. The power of expectations explains why typographical errors like those in this sentence often pass unoberved (Lachman, 1996).

Our perceptual hypotheses clearly are guided by our experience-based expectations. For example, subjects recognize everyday objects more quickly when they are presented from familiar viewpoints as opposed to unfamiliar viewpoints (Enns, 2004; see **Figure 4.28**). We also realize that certain objects and settings generally go together. We expect to see a sofa sitting in a living room, but not on a beach. When subjects are given very brief glimpses of objects in typical versus unusual settings, the objects that appear in typical settings are identified more accurately (Davenport & Potter, 2004). This finding illustrates the importance of both context and experience.

Figure 4.25
A famous reversible figure. What do you see? Consult the text to learn what the two possible interpretations of this figure are.

Figure 4.27
Context effects. The context in which a stimulus is seen can affect your perceptual hypotheses. The middle character in the word on the left is assumed to be an "H," whereas in the word on the right the same character is assumed to be an "A." In addition to showing the potential influence of context, this example shows the power of expectations and top-down processing.

Figure 4.28

Effect of viewpoint on form perception. Research on object recognition shows that the time needed to recognize an object depends on the perspective from which it is viewed (Enns, 2004). Subjects recognize familiar, prototypical views of everyday objects (such as the tricycle on the left) more quickly than atypical views of the same objects (such as the tricycle on the right) (Palmer, Rosch, & Chase, 1981). This finding shows that our perceptual hypotheses are guided by our experience.

SOURCE: Enns, J. T. (2004). *The thinking eye, the seeing brain: Explorations in visual cognition.* New York: W. W. Norton. Copyright © 2004 by W. W. Norton & Company. Used by permission.

Perceiving Depth or Distance 3f

More often than not, forms and figures are objects in space. Spatial considerations add a third dimension to visual perception. *Depth perception* involves **interpretation of visual cues that indicate how near or far away objects are.** To make judgments of distance, people rely on quite a variety of clues, which can be classified into two types: binocular cues and monocular cues (Hochberg, 1988; Proffitt & Caudek, 2003).

Binocular Cues 3f

Because they are set apart, the eyes each have a slightly different view of the world. *Binocular depth cues* **are clues about distance based on the differing views of the two eyes.** "Stereo" viewers like the Viewmaster toy you may have had as a child make use of this principle by presenting slightly different flat images of the same scene to each eye. The brain then supplies the "depth," and you perceive a three-dimensional scene.

The principal binocular depth cue is *retinal disparity,* which refers to the fact that objects within 25 feet project images to slightly different locations on the right and left retinas, so the right and left eyes see slightly different views of the object. The closer an object gets, the greater the dis-

parity between the images seen by each eye. Thus, retinal disparity increases as objects come closer, providing information about distance.

Monocular Cues 3f

Monocular depth cues **are clues about distance based on the image in either eye alone.** There are two kinds of monocular cues to depth. One kind is the result of active use of the eye in viewing the world. For example, as an object comes closer, you may sense the accommodation (the change in the curvature of the lens) that must occur for the eye to adjust its focus.

The other kind of monocular cues are *pictorial depth cues*—cues about distance that can be given in a flat picture. There are many pictorial cues to depth, which is why paintings and photographs can seem so realistic that you feel you can climb right into them. Six prominent pictorial depth cues are described and illustrated in **Figure 4.29** on the next page. The first of these, *linear perspective,* is a depth cue reflecting the fact that lines converge in the distance. Because details are too small to see when they are far away, *texture gradients* can also provide information about depth. If an object comes between you and another object, it must be closer to you, a cue called *interposition. Relative size* is a cue because closer objects appear larger. *Height in plane* reflects the fact that distant objects appear higher in a picture. Finally, the familiar effects of shadowing make *light* and *shadow* useful in judging distance.

Linear perspective Parallel lines that run away from the viewer seem to get closer together.

Texture gradient As distance increases, a texture gradually becomes denser and less distinct.

Interposition The shapes of near objects overlap or mask those of more distant ones.

Relative size If separate objects are expected to be of the same size, the larger ones are seen as closer.

Height in plane Near objects are low in the visual field; more distant ones are higher up.

Light and shadow Patterns of light and dark suggest shadows that can create an impression of three-dimensional forms.

Figure 4.29

Pictorial cues to depth.
Six pictorial depth cues are explained and illustrated here. Although one cue stands out in each photo, in most visual scenes several pictorial cues are present. Try looking at the light-and-shadow picture upside down. The change in shadowing reverses what you see.

Some cultural differences appear to exist in the ability to take advantage of pictorial depth cues in two-dimensional drawings. These differences were first investigated by Hudson (1960, 1967), who presented pictures like the one in **Figure 4.30** to various cultural groups in South Africa. Hudson's approach was based on the assumption that subjects who indicate that the hunter is trying to spear the elephant instead of the antelope don't understand the depth cues (interposition, relative size, height in plane) in the picture, which place the elephant in the distance. Hudson found that subjects from a rural South African tribe (the Bantu), who had little exposure at that time to pictures and photos, frequently misinterpreted the depth cues in his pictures. Similar difficulties with depth cues in pictures have been documented for other cultural groups who have little experience with two-dimensional representations of three-dimensional space (Berry et al., 1992). Based on this evidence, Deregowski (1989) concluded that

the application of pictorial depth cues to pictures is partly an acquired skill that depends on experience.

Recent studies have shown that estimates of distance can be skewed by transient changes in people's goals and their physical and emotional states (Proffitt, 2006a). For example, the effort required to walk to a target destination influences how far away the target appears to be. Participants wearing a heavy backpack estimate that target destinations are farther away than subjects not burdened with the backpack (Proffitt et al., 2003). Similarly, when participants are asked to throw a ball at targets, those throwing a heavy ball estimate that the targets are farther away than those throwing a light ball (Witt, Proffitt, & Epstein, 2004). And when they are standing on a high balcony, the more anxious participants are about heights, the more they tend to overestimate the distance to the ground (Proffitt, 2006b). Thus, like other perceptual experiences, judgments of distance can be highly subjective.

Figure 4.30
Testing understanding of pictorial depth cues. In his cross-cultural research, Hudson (1960) asked subjects to indicate whether the hunter is trying to spear the antelope or the elephant. He found cultural disparities in subjects' ability to make effective use of the pictorial depth cues, which place the elephant in the distance and make it an unlikely target.

SOURCE: Adapted by permission from an illustration by Ilil Arbel in Deregowski, J. B. (1972, November). Pictorial perception and culture. *Scientific American, 227* (5), p. 83. Copyright © 1972 by Scientific American, Inc. All rights reserved.

Perceptual Constancies in Vision

When a person approaches you from the distance, his or her image on your retinas gradually changes in size. Do you perceive that person as growing right before your eyes? Of course not. Your perceptual system constantly makes allowances for this variation in visual input. In doing so, it relies in part on perceptual constancies. A *perceptual constancy* is a tendency to experience a stable perception in the face of continually changing sensory input. Among other things, people tend to view objects as having a stable size, shape, brightness, hue (color), and location in space. Perceptual constancies such as these help impose some order on the surrounding world.

The Power of Misleading Cues: Visual Illusions   SIM3, 3g

In general, perceptual constancies, depth cues, and principles of visual organization (such as the Gestalt laws) help people perceive the world accurately. Sometimes, however, perceptions are based on inappropriate assumptions, and *visual illusions* can result. A *visual illusion* involves an apparently inexplicable discrepancy between the appearance of a visual stimulus and its physical reality.

One famous visual illusion is the *Müller-Lyer illusion,* shown in **Figure 4.31**. The two vertical lines in this figure are equally long, but they certainly don't look that way. Why not? Several mechanisms probably play a role (Day, 1965; Gregory, 1978). The figure on the left looks like the outside of a building, thrust toward the viewer, while the one on the right looks like an inside corner, thrust away (see **Figure 4.32** on the next page). The vertical line in the left figure therefore seems closer. If two lines cast equally long retinal images but one seems closer, the closer one is

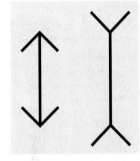

Figure 4.31
The Müller-Lyer illusion. Go ahead, measure them: The two vertical lines are of equal length.

concept check 4.3

Recognizing Pictorial Depth Cues

Painters routinely attempt to create the perception of depth on a flat canvas by using pictorial depth cues. **Figure 4.29** describes and illustrates six pictorial depth cues, most of which are apparent in Vincent van Gogh's colorful piece titled *Corridor in the Asylum* (1889). Check your understanding of depth perception by trying to spot the depth cues in the painting.

In the list below, check off the depth cues used by van Gogh. The answers can be found in Appendix A. You can learn more about how artists use the principles of visual perception in the Personal Application at the end of this chapter.

_____ 1. Interposition   _____ 4. Relative size

_____ 2. Height in plane   _____ 5. Light and shadow

_____ 3. Texture gradient   _____ 6. Linear perspective

Vincent van Gogh, *A Corridor in the Asylum,* 1889. Oil color and essence over black chalk on pink laid (Ingres) paper, 25-5/8 x 19-5/16 in. (65.1 x 49.1 cm): The Metropolitan Museum of Art, Bequest of Abby Aldrich Rockfeller, 1948 (48.190.2). Image © 1998 The Metropolitan Museum of Art. Reproduced by permission.

Figure 4.32

Explaining the Müller-Lyer illusion. The figure on the left seems to be closer, since it looks like an outside corner, thrust toward you, whereas the figure on the right looks like an inside corner thrust away from you. Given retinal images of the same length, you assume that the "closer" line is shorter.

assumed to be shorter. Thus, the Müller-Lyer illusion may be due largely to a combination of size constancy processes and misperception of depth.

The *Ponzo illusion,* shown in **Figure 4.33**, appears to result from the same factors (Coren & Girgus, 1978). The upper and lower horizontal lines are the same length, but the upper one appears longer. This illusion probably occurs because the converging lines convey linear perspective, a key depth cue

suggesting that the upper line lies farther in the distance. **Figure 4.34** is a drawing by Stanford University psychologist Roger Shepard (1990) that creates a similar illusion. The second monster appears much larger than the first, even though they are really identical in size. This variation on the Ponzo illusion and the other geometric illusions shown in **Figure 4.33** demonstrate that visual stimuli can be highly deceptive.

Impossible figures create another form of illusion. *Impossible figures* are objects that can be represented in two-dimensional pictures but cannot exist in three-dimensional space. These figures may look fine at first glance, but a closer look reveals that they are geometrically inconsistent or impossible. Three classic impossible figures are shown in **Figure 4.35**. Notice that you perceive specific features of the figure as acceptable but are baffled when they are built into a whole. Your perceptual hypothesis about one portion of the figure turns out to be inconsistent with your hypothesis about another portion.

Obviously, impossible figures involve a conspiracy of cues intended to deceive the viewer. Many visual illusions, however, occur quite naturally and are part of everyday life. A well-known example is the *moon illusion.* The full moon appears to be much

Figure 4.33

Four geometric illusions. Ponzo: The horizontal lines are the same length. **Poggendorff:** The two diagonal segments lie on the same straight line. **Upside-down T:** The vertical and horizontal lines are the same length. **Zollner:** The long diagonals are all parallel (try covering up some of the short lines if you don't believe it).

Figure 4.34

A monster of an illusion. The principles underlying the Ponzo illusion also explain the striking illusion seen here, in which two identical monsters appear to be quite different in size.

SOURCE: Explaining Ponzo illusion from *Mind Sights* by Roger N. Shepard. Copyright © 1990 by Roger N. Shepard. Reprinted by arrangement with Henry Holt & Co., LLC.

Figure 4.35
Three classic impossible figures. The figures are impossible, yet they clearly exist—on the page. What makes them impossible is that they appear to be three-dimensional representations yet are drawn in a way that frustrates mental attempts to "assemble" their features into possible objects. It's difficult to see the drawings simply as lines lying in a plane—even though this perceptual hypothesis is the only one that resolves the contradiction.

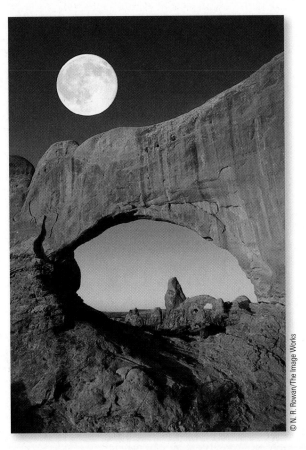

A puzzling perceptual illusion common in everyday life is the moon illusion: the moon looks larger when at the horizon than when overhead.

© N. R. Rowan/The Image Works

web link 4.5

The Moon Illusion Explained
Don McCready, professor emeritus at the University of Wisconsin (Whitewater), addresses the age-old puzzle of why the moon appears much larger at the horizon than overhead. He uses a helpful collection of illustrations in a comprehensive review of alternative theories.

smaller when overhead than when looming over the horizon. As with many of the other illusions we have discussed, the moon illusion appears to result mainly from size constancy effects coupled with the misperception of distance (Coren & Aks, 1990; Kaufman & Rock, 1962), although other factors may also play a role (Suzuki, 2007).

Cross-cultural studies have uncovered some interesting differences among cultural groups in their tendency to see certain illusions. For example, Segall, Campbell, and Herskovits (1966) found that people from Western cultures are more susceptible to the Müller-Lyer illusion than people from some non-Western cultures. The most plausible explanation is that in the West, we live in a "carpentered world" dominated by straight lines, right angles, and rectangular rooms, buildings, and furniture. Thus, our experience prepares us to readily view the Müller-Lyer figures as inside and outside corners of buildings, inferences that help foster the illusion (Segall et al., 1990).

What do illusions reveal about visual perception? They drive home the point that people go through life formulating perceptual hypotheses about what lies out there in the real world. The fact that these are only hypotheses becomes especially striking when the hypotheses are wrong, as they are with illusions. Visual illusions also show how context factors such as depth cues shape perceptual hypotheses. Finally, like ambiguous figures, illusions clearly demonstrate that human perceptions are not simple reflections of objective reality. Once again, we see that perception of the world is subjective.

These insights do not apply to visual perception only. We will encounter these lessons again as we examine other sensory systems, such as hearing, which we turn to next.

Unlike people in Western nations, the Zulus live in a culture where straight lines and right angles are scarce. Thus, they are not affected by such phenomena as the Müller-Lyer illusion nearly as much as people raised in environments that abound with rectangular structures.

© Alan Evrard/Robert Harding/Getty Images

REVIEW of Key Learning Goals

4.6 Reversible figures and perceptual sets demonstrate that the same visual input can result in very different perceptions. Form perception depends on both the selection and interpretation of sensory inputs. Inattentional blindness involves the failure to see readily visible objects. According to feature analysis theories, people detect specific elements in stimuli and build them into recognizable forms through bottom-up processing, but form perception also involves top-down processing.

4.7 Gestalt psychology emphasized that the whole may be greater than the sum of its parts (features), as illustrated by the phi phenomenon. Objects are more likely to be viewed as figure rather than ground when they are smaller, higher in contrast or symmetry, and lower in one's frame of view. Gestalt principles of form perception include proximity, similarity, continuity, closure, and simplicity.

4.8 Other approaches to form perception emphasize that people develop perceptual hypotheses about the external

stimuli that could be responsible for various patterns of sensory stimulation. These perceptual hypotheses are influenced by context and guided by experience-based expectations.

4.9 Binocular cues such as retinal disparity can contribute to depth perception. But depth perception depends primarily on monocular cues, including pictorial cues such as texture gradient, linear perspective, light and shadow, interposition, relative size, and height in plane. People from pictureless societies have some difficulty in applying pictorial depth cues to two-dimensional pictures.

4.10 Perceptual constancies in vision help viewers deal with the ever-shifting nature of sensory input. Visual illusions demonstrate that perceptual hypotheses can be inaccurate and that perceptions are not simple reflections of objective reality. Researchers have found some interesting cultural differences in susceptibility to the Müller-Lyer and Ponzo illusions.

The Auditory System: Hearing

Key Learning Goals

4.11 List the three properties of sound and the aspects of auditory perception that they influence.

4.12 Summarize information on human hearing capacities, and describe how sensory processing occurs in the ear.

4.13 Compare the place and frequency theories of pitch perception, and discuss the resolution of the debate.

web link 4.6

American Speech-Language-Hearing Association

The site for this national organization of audiologists and speech pathologists has a useful section intended for the public that provides information on the dangerous effects of loud noise, detection of hearing loss, the utility of hearing aids, and other topics related to hearing.

Stop reading for a moment, close your eyes, and listen carefully. What do you hear?

Chances are, you'll discover that you're immersed in sounds: street noises, a dog barking, the buzzing of a fluorescent lamp, perhaps some background music you put on a while ago but forgot about. As this little demonstration shows, physical stimuli producing sound are present almost constantly, but you're not necessarily aware of these sounds.

Like vision, the auditory (hearing) system provides input about the world "out there," but not until incoming information is processed by the brain. An auditory stimulus—a screech of tires, someone laughing, the hum of the refrigerator—produces sensory input in the form of sound waves reaching the ears. The perceptual system must somehow transform this stimulation into the psychological experience of hearing. We'll begin our discussion of hearing by looking at the stimulus for auditory experience: sound.

The Stimulus: Sound   3h

Sound waves are vibrations of molecules, which means that they must travel through some physical medium, such as air. They move at a fraction of the speed of light. Sound waves are usually generated by vibrating objects, such as a guitar string, a loudspeaker cone, or your vocal cords. However, sound waves can also be generated by forcing air past a

chamber (as in a pipe organ), or by suddenly releasing a burst of air (as when you clap).

Like light waves, sound waves are characterized by their *amplitude,* their *wavelength,* and their *purity* (see **Figure 4.36**). The physical properties of amplitude, wavelength, and purity affect mainly the perceived (psychological) qualities of *loudness, pitch,* and *timbre,* respectively. However, the physical properties of sound interact in complex ways to produce perceptions of these sound qualities (Hirsh & Watson, 1996).

Human Hearing Capacities   3h

Wavelengths of sound are described in terms of their *frequency,* which is measured in cycles per second, or *hertz* (Hz). For the most part, higher frequencies are perceived as having higher pitch. That is, if you strike the key for high C on a piano, it will produce higher-frequency sound waves than the key for low C. Although the perception of pitch depends mainly on frequency, the amplitude of the sound waves also influences it.

Just as the visible spectrum is only a portion of the total spectrum of light, so, too, what people can hear is only a portion of the available range of sounds. Humans can hear sounds ranging in frequency from a low of 20 Hz up to a high of about 20,000 Hz. Sounds at either end of this range are harder to hear, and sensitivity to high-frequency tones declines as adults grow older. Other organisms have different capabilities. Low-frequency sounds under 10 Hz are audible to homing pigeons, for example. At the other extreme, bats and porpoises can hear frequencies well above 20,000 Hz.

In general, the greater the amplitude of sound waves, the louder the sound perceived. Whereas frequency is measured in hertz, amplitude is measured in *decibels* (dB). The relationship between decibels (which measure a physical property of sound) and loudness (a psychological quality) is complex. A rough rule of thumb is that perceived loudness doubles about every 10 decibels (Stevens, 1955). Very loud sounds can have negative effects on the quality of your hearing. Even brief exposure to sounds over 120 decibels can be painful and may cause damage to your auditory system (Henry, 1984). As shown in **Figure 4.37**, the weakest sound a person can hear depends on its frequency. The human ear is most sensitive to sounds at frequencies near 2000 Hz. Thus, loudness ultimately depends on an interaction between amplitude and frequency.

People are also sensitive to variations in the purity of sounds. The purest sound is one that has only a single frequency of vibration, such as that produced by a tuning fork. Most everyday sounds are complex mixtures of many frequencies. The purity or complexity of a sound influences how *timbre* is perceived. To understand timbre, think of a note with precisely the same loudness and pitch played on a piano and then on a violin. The difference you perceive in the sounds is a difference in timbre.

Sensory Processing in the Ear

PsykTrek 3h

Like your eyes, your ears channel energy to the neural tissue that receives it. **Figure 4.38** on the next page shows that the human ear can be divided into three sections: the external ear, the middle ear, and the inner ear. Sound is conducted differently in each section. The external ear depends on the *vibration of air molecules*. The middle ear depends on the *vibration of movable bones*. And the inner ear depends on *waves in a fluid*, which are finally converted into a stream of neural signals sent to the brain (Moore, 2001).

The *external ear* consists mainly of the *pinna*, a sound-collecting cone. When you cup your hand behind your ear to try to hear better, you are augmenting that cone. Many animals have large external ears that they can aim directly toward a sound source. However, humans can adjust their aim only crudely, by turning their heads. Sound waves collected by the pinna are funneled along the auditory canal toward the *eardrum*, a taut membrane that vibrates in response.

Figure 4.36
Sound, the physical stimulus for hearing. (a) Like light, sound travels in waves—in this case, waves of air pressure. A smooth curve would represent a pure tone, such as that produced by a tuning fork. Most sounds, however, are complex. For example, the wave shown here is for middle C played on a piano. The sound wave for the same note played on a violin would have the same wavelength (or frequency) as this one, but the "wrinkles" in the wave would be different, corresponding to the differences in timbre between the two sounds. **(b)** The table shows the main relations between objective aspects of sound and subjective perceptions.

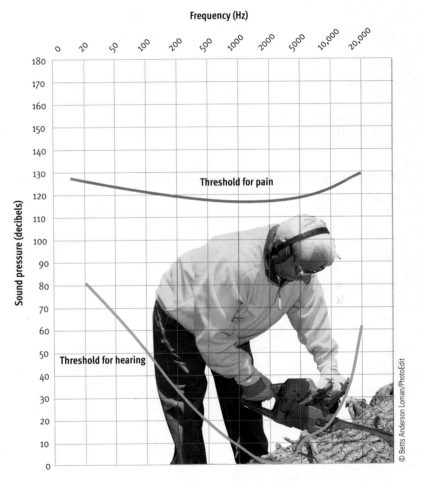

Figure 4.37
Sound pressure and auditory experience. The threshold for human hearing (graphed in green) is a function of both sound pressure (decibel level) and frequency. Human hearing is keenest for sounds at frequencies around 2000 Hz; at other frequencies, higher decibel levels are needed to produce sounds people can detect. On the other hand, the human threshold for pain (graphed in red) is almost purely a function of decibel level.

In the *middle ear*, the vibrations of the eardrum are transmitted inward by a mechanical chain made up of the three tiniest bones in your body (the hammer, anvil, and stirrup), known collectively as the *ossicles*. The ossicles form a three-stage lever system

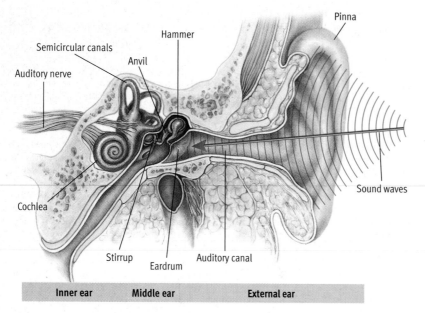

Figure 4.38
The human ear. Converting sound pressure to information processed by the nervous system involves a complex relay of stimuli. Waves of air pressure create vibrations in the eardrum, which in turn cause oscillations in the tiny bones in the inner ear (the hammer, anvil, and stirrup). As they are relayed from one bone to the next, the oscillations are magnified and then transformed into pressure waves moving through a liquid medium in the cochlea. These waves cause the basilar membrane to oscillate, stimulating the hair cells that are the actual auditory receptors (see **Figure 4.39**).

web link 4.7

The Cochlea: Graphic Tour of the Inner Ear's Machinery

The dynamics of hearing and the workings of the inner ear are graphically demonstrated at this site maintained by the Laboratory of Biophysics at the International School of Advanced Studies (Trieste, Italy). The collection of links to other laboratories studying hearing make this a fine jumping-off point.

that converts relatively large movements with little force into smaller motions with greater force. The ossicles serve to amplify tiny changes in air pressure.

The *inner ear* consists largely of the *cochlea,* a fluid-filled, coiled tunnel that contains the receptors for hearing. The term *cochlea* comes from the Greek word for a spiral-shelled snail, which this chamber re-

sembles (see **Figure 4.38**). Sound enters the cochlea through the *oval window,* which is vibrated by the ossicles. The ear's neural tissue, which is functionally similar to the retina in the eye, lies within the cochlea. This tissue sits on the basilar membrane that divides the cochlea into upper and lower chambers. The *basilar membrane,* which runs the length of the spiraled cochlea, holds the auditory receptors, called hair cells. Waves in the fluid of the inner ear stimulate the hair cells. Like the rods and cones in the eye, the hair cells convert this physical stimulation into neural impulses that are sent to the brain (Hudspeth, 2000). These signals are routed through the thalamus to the auditory cortex, which is located mostly in the temporal lobes of the brain.

Auditory Perception: Theories of Hearing

Theories of hearing need to account for how sound waves are physiologically translated into perceptions of pitch, loudness, and timbre. To date, most of the theorizing about hearing has focused on the perception of pitch, which is reasonably well understood. Researchers' understanding of loudness and timbre perception is primitive by comparison. Consequently, we'll limit our coverage to theories of pitch perception.

Place Theory

There have been two influential theories of pitch perception: *place theory* and *frequency theory*. You'll be able to follow the development of these theories more eas-

---

concept check 4.4

Comparing Vision and Hearing

Check your understanding of both vision and hearing by comparing key aspects of sensation and perception in these senses. The dimensions of comparison are listed in the first column below. The second column lists the answers for the sense of vision. Fill in the answers for the sense of hearing in the third column. The answers can be found in Appendix A in the back of the book.

Dimension	Vision	Hearing
1. Stimulus	Light waves	
2. Elements of stimulus and related perceptions	Wavelength/hue	
	Amplitude/brightness	
	Purity/saturation	
3. Receptors	Rods and cones	
4. Location of receptors	Retina	
5. Main location of processing in brain	Occipital lobe, Visual cortex	

ily if you can imagine the spiraled cochlea unraveled, so that the basilar membrane becomes a long, thin sheet, lined with about 25,000 individual hair cells (see **Figure 4.39**). Long ago, Hermann von Helmholtz (1863) proposed that specific sound frequencies vibrate specific portions of the basilar membrane, producing distinct pitches, just as plucking specific strings on a harp produces sounds of varied pitch. Thus, *place theory* holds that perception of pitch corresponds to the vibration of different portions, or places, along the basilar membrane. Place theory assumes that hair cells at various locations respond independently and that different sets of hair cells are vibrated by different sound frequencies. The brain then detects the frequency of a tone according to which area along the basilar membrane is most active.

Frequency Theory

Other theorists in the 19th century proposed an alternative theory of pitch perception, called frequency theory (Rutherford, 1886). *Frequency theory* holds that perception of pitch corresponds to the rate, or frequency, at which the entire basilar membrane vibrates. This theory views the basilar membrane as more like a drumhead than a harp. According to frequency theory, the whole membrane vibrates in response to sounds. However, a particular sound frequency, say 3000 Hz, causes the basilar membrane to vibrate at a corresponding rate of 3000 times per second. The brain detects the frequency of a tone by the rate at which the auditory nerve fibers fire.

Reconciling Place and Frequency Theories

The competition between these two theories is similar to the dispute between the trichromatic and opponent process theories of color vision. Like that argument, the debate between place and frequency theories generated roughly a century of research. Although both theories proved to have some flaws, *both turned out to be valid in part.*

Helmholtz's place theory was basically on the mark except for one detail. The hair cells along the basilar membrane are not independent. They vibrate together, as suggested by frequency theory. The ac-

Figure 4.39
The basilar membrane. This graphic shows how the cochlea might look if it were unwound and cut open to reveal the basilar membrane, which is covered with thousands of hair cells (the auditory receptors). Pressure waves in the fluid filling the cochlea cause oscillations to travel in waves down the basilar membrane, stimulating the hair cells to fire. Although the entire membrane vibrates, as predicted by frequency theory, the point along the membrane where the wave peaks depends on the frequency of the sound stimulus, as suggested by place theory.

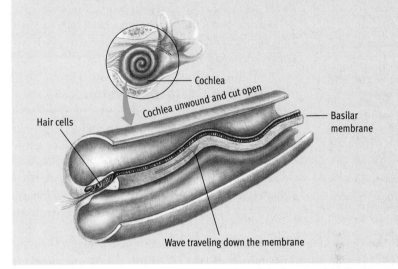

tual pattern of vibration, described in Nobel prize–winning research by Georg von Békésy (1947), is a traveling wave that moves along the basilar membrane. Place theory is correct, however, in that the wave peaks at a particular place, depending on the frequency of the sound wave.

Although the original theories had to be revised, the current thinking is that pitch perception depends on both place and frequency coding of vibrations along the basilar membrane (Goldstein, 1996). Sounds under 1000 Hz appear to be translated into pitch through frequency coding. For sounds between 1000 and 5000 Hz, pitch perception seems to depend on a combination of frequency and place coding. Sounds over 5000 Hz seem to be handled through place coding only. Again we find that theories that were pitted against each other for decades are complementary rather than contradictory.

REVIEW of Key Learning Goals

4.11 Sound varies in terms of wavelength (frequency), amplitude, and purity. Wavelength mainly affects perceptions of pitch, amplitude mainly influences perceptions of loudness, and purity is the key determinant of timbre.

4.12 The human ear can detect sounds between 20 and 20,000 Hz, but it is most sensitive to sounds around 2000 Hz. Even brief exposure to sounds over 120 decibels can be painful and damaging. Sound is transmitted through the external ear via air conduction to the middle ear, where sound waves are translated into the vibration of tiny bones called ossicles. In the inner ear, fluid conduction vibrates hair cells along the basilar membrane in the cochlea. These hair cells are the receptors for hearing.

4.13 Place theory proposed that pitch perception depends on where vibrations occur along the basilar membrane. Frequency theory countered with the idea that pitch perception depends on the rate at which the basilar membrane vibrates. Modern evidence suggests that these theories are complementary rather than incompatible.

The Other Senses: Taste, Smell, and Touch

Are the elaborate wine-tasting rituals of wine lovers just a pretentious tradition, or do they make sense in light of what science has revealed about the gustatory system? Your text answers this question in this section.

Psychologists have devoted most of their attention to the visual and auditory systems. Although less is known about the senses of taste, smell, and touch, they also play a critical role in people's experience of the world. Let's start by taking a brief look at what psychologists have learned about the *gustatory system*—the sensory system for taste.

Taste: The Gustatory System

True wine lovers go through an elaborate series of steps when they are served a good bottle of wine. Typically, they begin by drinking a little water to cleanse their palate. Then they sniff the cork from the wine bottle, swirl a small amount of the wine around in a glass, and sniff the odor emerging from the glass. Finally, they take a sip of the wine, rolling it around in their mouth for a short time before swallowing it. At last they are ready to indicate their approval or disapproval. Is all this activity really a meaningful way to put the wine to a sensitive test? Or is it just a harmless ritual passed on through tradition? You'll find out in this section.

The physical stimuli for the sense of taste are chemical substances that are soluble (dissolvable in water). The gustatory receptors are clusters of taste cells found in the *taste buds* that line the trenches around tiny bumps on the tongue. When these cells absorb chemicals dissolved in saliva, neural impulses are triggered that are routed through the thalamus to the cortex. Interestingly, taste cells have a short life, spanning only about 10 days, and they are constantly being replaced (Cowart, 2005). New cells are born at the edge of the taste bud and migrate inward to die at the center.

It's generally (but not universally) agreed that there are four *primary tastes:* sweet, sour, bitter, and salty (Buck, 2000). Sensitivity to these tastes is distributed somewhat unevenly across the tongue. However, Linda Bartoshuk (1993b), a leading authority on taste research, emphasizes that these variations in sensitivity are quite small and very complicated (see **Figure 4.40**). Although most taste cells respond to more than one of the primary tastes, they typically respond best to a specific taste (Di Lorenzo & Youngentob, 2003). Taste signals are routed through the thalamus and sent on to the insular cortex in the frontal lobe, where the initial cortical processing takes place.

Some basic aspects of taste perception may be inborn, but taste preferences are largely learned and are heavily influenced by social processes (Rozin, 1990). Most parents are aware of this reality and intentionally try—with varied success—to mold their children's taste preferences early in life (Patrick et al., 2005). This strong social influence contributes greatly to the striking ethnic and cultural disparities found in taste preferences (Kittler & Sucher, 2008). Foods that are a source of disgust in Western cultures—such as worms, fish eyes, and blood—may be delicacies in other cultures. To a large degree, variations in taste preferences depend on what one has been exposed to (Capaldi & VandenBos, 1991). Exposure to particular foods varies along ethnic lines because different cultures have different traditions in food preparation, different agricultural resources, different climates to work with, and so forth.

Research reveals that people vary considerably in their sensitivity to certain tastes. Bartoshuk (1993a) notes that these differences depend in part on the density of taste buds on the tongue, which appears

Linda Bartoshuk

"Good and bad are so intimately associated with taste and smell that we have special words for the experiences (e.g., repugnant, foul). The immediacy of the pleasure makes it seem absolute and thus inborn. This turns out to be true for taste but not for smell."

to be a matter of genetic inheritance. People characterized as *nontasters,* as determined by their insensitivity to PTC (phenythiocarbamide), or its close relative, PROP (propylthiouracil), tend to have about one-quarter as many taste buds per square centimeter as people at the other end of the spectrum, who are called *supertasters* (Miller & Reedy, 1990). Supertasters also have specialized taste receptors that are not found in nontasters (Bufe et al., 2005). In the United States, roughly 25% of people are nontasters, another 25% are supertasters, and the remaining 50% fall between these extremes and are characterized as *medium tasters* (Di Lorenzo & Youngentob, 2003).

Supertasters and nontasters respond similarly to many foods, but supertasters are much more sensitive to certain sweet and bitter substances. For example, supertasters react far more strongly to the chemical (capsaicin) in hot peppers (Tepper & Nurse, 1997). Supertasters also respond more intensely to many fatty substances (Bartoshuk, 2000). These differences in taste sensitivity influence people's eating habits in ways that can have important repercussions for their physical health. For example, supertasters are less likely to be fond of sweets (Yeomans et al., 2007) and tend to consume fewer high-fat foods, both of which are likely to reduce their risk for cardiovascular disease (Duffy, Lucchina, & Bartoshuk, 2004). Supertasters also tend to react more negatively to alcohol and smoking, thereby reducing their likelihood of developing drinking problems or nicotine addiction (Duffy, Peterson, & Bartoshuk, 2004; Snedecor et al., 2006). The only health disadvantage identified for supertasters thus far is that they respond more negatively to many vegetables, which seems to hold down their vegetable intake (Basson et al., 2005; Dinehart et al, 2006). Overall, however, supertasters tend to have better health habits than nontasters, thanks to their strong reactions to certain tastes (Duffy, 2004).

Women are more likely to be supertasters than men (Bartoshuk, Duffy, & Miller, 1994). Some psychologists speculate that the gender gap in this trait may have evolutionary significance. Over the course of evolution, women have generally been more involved than men in feeding children. Increased reactivity to sweet and bitter tastes would have been adaptive in that it would have made women more sensitive to the relatively scarce high-caloric foods (which often taste sweet) needed for survival and to the toxic substances (which often taste bitter) that hunters and gatherers needed to avoid.

When you eat, you are constantly mixing food and saliva and moving it about in your mouth, so the stimulus is constantly changing. However, if you place a flavored substance in a single spot on

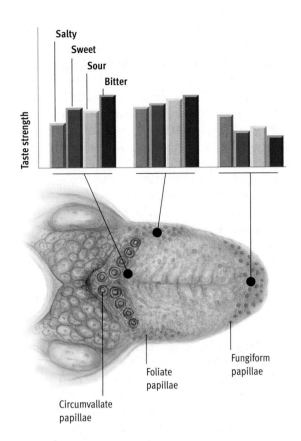

Figure 4.40

The tongue and taste. Taste buds are clustered around tiny bumps on the tongue called papillae. There are three types of papillae, which are distributed as shown here. The taste buds found in each type of papilla show slightly different sensitivities to the four basic tastes, as mapped out in the graph at the top. Thus, sensitivity to the primary tastes varies across the tongue, but these variations are small and all four primary tastes can be detected wherever there are taste receptors. (Data adapted from Bartoshuk, 1993a)

your tongue, the taste will fade until it vanishes (Krakauer & Dallenbach, 1937). This fading effect is an example of *sensory adaptation*—a gradual decline in sensitivity to prolonged stimulation. Sensory adaptation is not unique to taste. This phenomenon occurs in other senses as well. In the taste system, sensory adaptation can leave aftereffects (Bartoshuk, 1988). For example, adaptation to a sour solution makes water taste sweet, whereas adaptation to a sweet solution makes water taste bitter.

Now that we've explored the dynamics of taste, we can return to our question about the value of the wine-tasting ritual. This elaborate ritual is indeed an authentic way to put wine to a sensitive test. The aftereffects associated with sensory adaptation make it wise to cleanse one's palate before tasting the wine. Sniffing the cork, and the wine in the glass, is important because odor is a major determinant of flavor. Swirling the wine in the glass helps release the wine's odor inside the glass. Rolling the wine around in your mouth is especially critical because it distributes the wine over the full range of taste cells. It also forces the wine's odor up into the nasal passages. Thus, each action in this age-old ritual makes a meaningful contribution to the tasting.

Smell: The Olfactory System

The *olfactory system*, the sensory system for smell, resembles the sense of taste in many ways. The phys-

web link 4.8

The ChemoReception Web
This site is devoted to the sensory and biological aspects of the chemical senses of taste and smell. It includes abstracts of relevant research, book reviews, and links to many other useful websites.

ical stimuli are chemical substances—volatile ones that can evaporate and be carried in the air. These chemical stimuli are dissolved in fluid—specifically, the mucus in the nose. The receptors for smell are *olfactory cilia,* hairlike structures located in the upper portion of the nasal passages (Getchell & Getchell, 1991) (see **Figure 4.41**). They resemble taste cells in that they have a short life and are constantly being replaced (Buck, 2000). Olfactory receptors have axons that synapse with cells in the olfactory bulb and then are routed directly to the olfactory cortex in the temporal lobe and other areas in the cortex. This arrangement is unique. *Smell is the only sensory system that is not routed through the thalamus before it projects onto the cortex.*

Odors cannot be classified as neatly as tastes, since efforts to identify primary odors have proven unsatisfactory (Doty, 1991). If primary odors exist, there must be a fairly large number of them. Perhaps that is why humans have about 350 different types of olfactory receptors (Buck, 2004). Most olfactory receptors respond to a wide range of odors (Doty, 2001). Hence, the perception of various odors probably depends on a great many types of receptors that are uniquely responsive to specific chemical structures (Bartoshuk & Beauchamp, 1994). Like the other senses, the sense of smell shows sensory adaptation. The perceived strength of an odor usually fades to less than half its original strength within about 4 minutes (Cain, 1988). For example, let's say you walk into your kitchen and find that the garbage has started to smell.

If you stay in the kitchen without removing the garbage, the stench will soon start to fade.

Humans can distinguish a great many odors, with estimates of the number of distinct odors ranging from 10,000 (Axel, 1995) to 100,000 (Firestein, 2001). However, when people are asked to identify the sources of specific odors (such as smoke or soap), their performance is rather mediocre (Engen, 1987). For some unknown reason, people have a hard time attaching names to odors (Cowart & Rawson, 2001). Gender differences have been found in the ability to identify odors, with females tending to be somewhat more accurate than males on odor recognition tasks (de Wijk, Schab, & Cain, 1995).

Although smell is often viewed as an unimportant sense in humans, ample evidence demonstrates that odors can have profound effects on people's mood and cognition (Herz & Schooler, 2002; Jacob et al., 2002). The $4 billion spent on perfumes annually in the United States shows how motivated people are to enjoy pleasant fragrances. Interestingly, recent research indicates that subtle background odors that people are unaware of can influence their behavior. In one study, subliminal exposure to a citrus-scented cleaning solution led participants to keep their immediate environment cleaner (Holland, Hendriks, & Aarts, 2005). In another study, subjects' ratings of the likeability of a series of faces were swayed by the subliminal introduction of pleasant versus unpleasant odors (Li et al., 2007). Small wonder, given these results, that "environmental fragrancing" is a growing industry (Gilbert & Firestein, 2002; Peltier, 1999).

Touch: Sensory Systems in the Skin

The physical stimuli for touch consist of mechanical, thermal, and chemical energy that comes into contact with the skin. These stimuli can produce perceptions of tactile stimulation (the pressure of touch against the skin), warmth, cold, and pain. The human skin is saturated with at least six types of sensory receptors, four of which are depicted in **Figure 4.42**. To some degree, these different types of receptors are specialized for different functions, such as the registration of pressure, heat, cold, and so forth. However, these distinctions are not as clear as researchers had originally thought (Sinclair, 1981).

If you've been to a mosquito-infested picnic lately, you'll appreciate the need to quickly know where tactile stimulation is coming from. The sense of touch is set up to meet this need for tactile localization with admirable efficiency. Cells in the nervous system that respond to touch are sensitive to specific patches of skin. These skin patches, which vary considerably in size, are the functional equivalents of *receptive*

Figure 4.41
The olfactory system. Odor molecules travel through the nasal passages and stimulate olfactory cilia. An enlargement of these hairlike olfactory receptors is shown in the inset. The olfactory axons transmit neural impulses through the olfactory bulb to the brain.

Olfactory bulb   Olfactory axons

Olfactory cilia
(receptor cells)

Nasal
passage

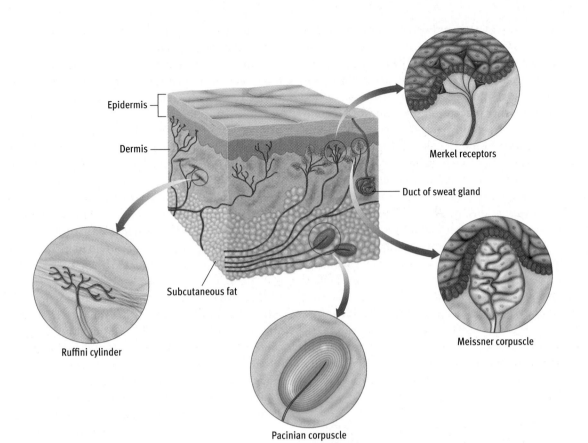

Figure 4.42
Receptors in the skin. Human skin houses quite a variety of receptors in a series of layers. The four types of receptors shown in this diagram all respond to various aspects of pressure, stretching, and vibration. In addition to these receptors, free nerve endings in the skin respond to pain, warmth, and cold, and hair-follicle receptors register the movement of hairs.

SOURCE: Goldstein, E. B. (2007). *Sensation and perception.* Belmont, CA: Wadsworth.

Epidermis

Dermis

Merkel receptors

Duct of sweat gland

Subcutaneous fat

Ruffini cylinder

Meissner corpuscle

Pacinian corpuscle

fields in vision. Like visual receptive fields, they often involve a center-surround arrangement (Kandel & Jessell, 1991). If a stimulus is applied continuously to a specific spot on the skin, the perception of pressure gradually fades. Thus, *sensory adaptation* occurs in the perception of touch as it does in other sensory systems.

The nerve fibers that carry incoming information about tactile stimulation are routed through the spinal cord to the brainstem. The tactile pathway then projects through the thalamus and onto the *somatosensory cortex* in the brain's parietal lobes. The entire body is sensitive to touch. However, in humans the bulk of the somatosensory cortex is devoted to processing signals coming from the fingers, lips, and tongue. Some cells in the somatosensory cortex function like the *feature detectors* discovered in vision (Gardner & Kandel, 2000). They respond to specific features of touch, such as a movement across the skin in a particular direction.

The receptors for pain are mostly free nerve endings in the skin. Pain messages are transmitted to the brain via two pathways that pass through different areas in the thalamus (Willis, 1985) (see **Figure 4.43**). One is a *fast pathway* that registers localized pain and relays it to the cortex in a fraction of a second. This is the system that hits you with sharp pain when you first cut your finger. The second system uses a *slow pathway,* routed through the limbic

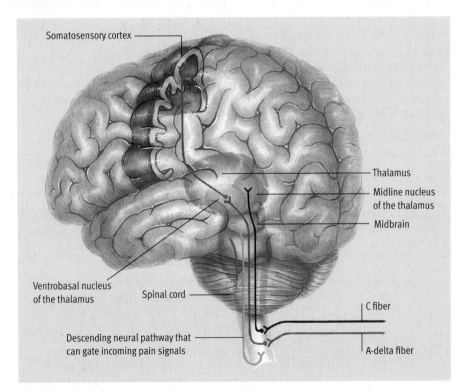

Somatosensory cortex

Thalamus

Midline nucleus of the thalamus

Midbrain

Ventrobasal nucleus of the thalamus

Spinal cord

C fiber

Descending neural pathway that can gate incoming pain signals

A-delta fiber

Figure 4.43
Pathways for pain signals. Pain signals are sent inward from receptors to the brain along the two ascending pathways depicted here in red and black. The fast pathway, shown in red, and the slow pathway, shown in black, depend on different types of nerve fibers and are routed through different parts of the thalamus. The gate control mechanism hypothesized by Melzack and Wall (1965) apparently depends on signals in a descending pathway (shown in green) that originates in an area of the midbrain.

system, that lags a second or two behind the fast system. This pathway (which also carries information about temperature) conveys the less localized, longer-lasting aching or burning pain that comes after the initial injury.

As with other perceptions, pain is not an automatic result of certain types of stimulation. Some people with severe injuries report little pain, whereas other people with much more modest injuries report agonizing pain (Coderre, Mogil, & Bushnell, 2003). The perception of pain can be influenced greatly by beliefs, expectations, personality, mood, and other factors involving higher mental processes (Turk & Okifuji, 2003). The subjective nature of pain is illustrated by placebo effects. As we saw in Chapter 2, many people suffering from pain report relief when given a placebo—such as an inert "sugar pill" that is presented to them as if it were a painkilling drug (Stewart-Williams, 2004; Vase, Riley, & Price, 2002).

Cultural variations in the experience of pain provide further evidence for the subjective quality of pain (Ondeck, 2003). Melzack and Wall (1982) have described a number of anecdotal examples of remarkable pain tolerance in non-Western cultures. Moreover, systematic empirical comparisons have found ethnic and cultural differences in the experience of chronic pain (Bates, Edwards, & Anderson, 1993) and the pain associated with childbirth (Jordan, 1983). It appears that culture doesn't affect the process of pain perception so much as the willingness to tolerate certain types of pain (Zatzick & Dimsdale, 1990).

As you can see, then, tissue damage that sends pain impulses on their way to the brain doesn't necessarily result in the experience of pain. Cognitive and emotional processes that unfold in higher brain centers can sometimes block pain signals coming from peripheral receptors.

How are incoming pain signals blocked? In an influential effort to answer this question, Ronald Melzack and Patrick Wall (1965) devised the gate-control theory of pain. *Gate-control theory holds that incoming pain sensations must pass through a "gate" in the spinal cord that can be closed, thus blocking ascending pain signals.* The gate in this model is not an anatomical structure but a pattern of neural activity that inhibits incoming pain signals. Melzack and Wall suggested that this imaginary gate can be closed by signals from peripheral receptors or by signals from the brain. They theorized that the latter mechanism can help explain how factors such as attention and expectations can shut off pain signals. As a whole, research suggests that the concept of a gating mechanism for pain has merit (Craig & Rollman, 1999; Sufka & Price, 2002). However, relatively little support has been found for the neural circuitry originally hypothesized by Melzack and Wall. Other neural mechanisms, discovered after gate-control theory was proposed, appear to be responsible for blocking the perception of pain.

One of these discoveries was the identification of endorphins. As discussed in Chapter 3, *endorphins* are the body's own natural morphinelike painkillers, which are widely distributed in the central nervous system (Pert, 2002). The other discovery involved the identification of a descending neural pathway that mediates the suppression of pain (Basbaum & Jessell, 2000). This pathway appears to originate in an area of the midbrain (see **Figure 4.43**). Neural activity in this pathway is probably initiated by endorphins. The circuits in this pathway synapse in the spinal cord, where they inhibit the activity of neurons that would normally transmit incoming pain impulses to the brain. The painkilling effects of morphine appear to be at least partly attributable to activity in this descending pathway, as cutting the fibers in this pathway reduces the analgesic effects of morphine

concept check 4.5

Identifying the Contributions of Major Theorists and Researchers

Check your recall of the principal ideas of important theorists and researchers covered in this chapter by matching the people listed on the left with the appropriate contributions described on the right. If you need help, the crucial pages describing each person's ideas are listed in parentheses. Fill in the letters for your choices in the spaces provided on the left. You'll find the answers in Appendix A.

Major Theorists and Researchers

_____ 1. Linda Bartoshuk (pp. 134–135)

_____ 2. Hermann von Helmholtz (pp. 117, 133)

_____ 3. David Hubel and Torsten Wiesel (p. 114)

_____ 4. Ronald Melzack and Patrick Wall (p. 138)

_____ 5. Max Wertheimer (p. 121)

Key Ideas and Contributions

a. This 19th-century theorist developed both the trichromatic theory of color vision and the place theory of pitch perception.

b. In the 1960s, these theorists developed the gate-control theory of pain, which holds that incoming pain signals can be blocked by neural mechanisms.

c. This person has conducted a great deal of influential research on the gustatory system, including pioneering work comparing supertasters and nontasters.

d. This advocate of Gestalt psychology, who was the first person to describe the phi phenomenon, asserted that in perception, the whole is often greater than the sum of its parts.

e. This research team won a Nobel prize for discovering three types of specialized visual cells in the occipital lobe, which have been characterized as feature detectors.

(Jessell & Kelly, 1991). Clearly, this pathway plays a central role in gating incoming pain signals.

Scientific understanding of the experience of pain continues to evolve. The newest discovery is that certain types of *glial cells* may contribute to the modulation of pain (Watkins, 2007). As noted in Chapter 3, it is only recently that neuroscientists have realized that glial cells contribute to signal transmission in the nervous system (Fields, 2004). Two types of glia in the spinal cord appear to play an important role in chronic pain (Watkins & Maier, 2002). These glia are activated by immune system responses to infection or by signals from neurons in pain pathways. Once activated, these glial cells appear to "egg on neurons in the pain pathway," thus amplifying the experience of chronic pain (Watkins & Maier, 2003; Watkins et al., 2007). The discovery that glia play a role in the human pain system may eventually open up new avenues for treating chronic pain.

web link 4.10

Seeing, Hearing, and Smelling the World

Hosted by the Howard Hughes Medical Institute, this site provides a graphically attractive review of what scientific research has discovered about human sensory systems, with suggestions about where research will be moving in the future.

REVIEW of Key Learning Goals

4.14 The taste buds are sensitive to four basic tastes: sweet, sour, bitter, and salty. Sensitivity to these tastes is distributed unevenly across the tongue, but the variations are small. Some basic taste preferences appear to be innate, but taste preferences are largely learned as a function of what one is exposed to. Taste preferences are also heavily influenced by cultural background.

4.15 Supertasters are much more sensitve to some tastes than nontasters, with medium tasters falling in between these extremes. Nontasters tend to be more susceptible to the lure of sweets, high-fat foods, alcohol, and smoking, which means their consumption habits tend to be less healthy than those of supertasters.

4.16 Like taste, smell is a chemical sense. Chemical stimuli activate receptors, called olfactory cilia, that line the nasal passages. Most of these receptors respond to more than one odor. Smell is the only sense that is not routed through the thalamus. Humans can distinguish many different odors, but their performance on odor identification tasks tends to be surprisingly mediocre. Ambient odors can influence mood and cognition—even when they are subliminal.

4.17 The skin houses many types of sensory receptors. They respond to pressure, temperature, and pain. Tactile localization depends on receptive fields similar to those seen for vision. Some cells in the somatosensory cortex appear to function like feature detectors.

4.18 Pain signals are sent to the brain along two pathways that are characterized as fast and slow. The perception of pain is highly subjective and may be influenced by personality and mood. Placebo effects in pain treatment and cultural variations in pain tolerance also highlight the subjective nature of pain perception.

4.19 Gate-control theory holds that incoming pain signals can be blocked in the spinal cord. Endorphins and a descending neural pathway appear responsible for the suppression of pain by the central nervous system. Recent studies indicate that glial cells contribute to the modulation of chronic pain.

Reflecting on the Chapter's Themes

In this chapter, three of our unifying themes were highlighted: (1) psychology is theoretically diverse, (2) people's experience of the world is highly subjective, and (3) our behavior is shaped by our cultural heritage. Let's discuss the value of theoretical diversity first.

Contradictory theories about behavior can be disconcerting and frustrating for theorists, researchers, teachers, and students alike. Yet this chapter provided two dramatic demonstrations of how theoretical diversity can lead to progress in the long run. For decades, the trichromatic and opponent process theories of color vision and the place and frequency theories of pitch perception were viewed as fundamentally incompatible. These competing theories generated and guided the research that now provides a fairly solid understanding of how people perceive color and pitch. As you know, in each case the evidence eventually revealed that the opposing theories were not really incompatible. Both were needed to fully explain the sensory processes that each sought to explain individually. If it hadn't been for these theoretical debates, our current understanding of color vision and pitch perception might be far more primitive.

This chapter should have also enhanced your appreciation of why human experience of the world is highly subjective. As ambiguous figures and visual illusions clearly show, there is no one-to-one correspondence between sensory input and perceived experience of the world. Perception is an active process in which people organize and interpret the information received by the senses. Small wonder, then, that people often perceive the same event in very different ways. Thus, individuals' experience of the world is subjective because the process of perception is inherently subjective.

Finally, this chapter provided numerous examples of how cultural factors can shape behavior—in an area of research where one might expect to find little cultural influence. Most people are not surprised to learn that there are cultural differences in attitudes,

Key Learning Goals

4.20 Identify the three unifying themes that were highlighted in this chapter.

 Theoretical Diversity

 Subjectivity of Experience

 Cultural Heritage

ILLUSTRATED OVERVIEW OF FIVE MAJOR SENSES

SENSE	STIMULUS	ELEMENTS OF THE STIMULUS

The Visual System: SIGHT

Light is electromagnetic radiation that travels in waves. Humans can register only a slim portion of the total range of wavelengths, from 400 to 700 nanometers.

© John White Photos/Alamy

Light waves vary in *amplitude, wavelength,* and *purity,* which influence perceptions as shown below.

Physical properties	Related perceptions
Wavelength	Hue (color)
Amplitude	Brightness
Purity	Saturation

The Auditory System: HEARING

Sound waves are vibrations of molecules, which means that they must travel through some physical medium, such as air. Humans can hear wavelengths between 20 and 20,000 Hz.

© Photodisc/Getty Imagesz

Sound waves vary in *amplitude, wavelength,* and *purity,* which influence perceptions, as shown below.

Physical properties	Related perceptions
Amplitude	Loudness
Frequency	Pitch
Purity	Timbre

The Gustatory System: TASTE

The stimuli for taste generally are chemical substances that are soluble (dissolvable in water). These stimuli are dissolved in the mouth's saliva.

© Lisa Woollett/Photofusion Picture Library/Alamy

It is generally, but not universally, agreed that there are four primary tastes: *sweet, sour, bitter,* and *salty.*

The Olfactory System: SMELL

© Blend Images/Jamie Grill

The stimuli are volatile chemical substances that can evaporate and be carried in the air. These chemical stimuli are dissolved in the mucus of the nose.

Efforts to identify primary odors have proven unsatisfactory. If primary odors exist, there must be a great many of them.

The Tactile System: TOUCH

The stimuli are mechanical, thermal, and chemical energy that impinge on the skin.

© IS713/ Image Source Pink/Alamy

Receptors in the skin can register *pressure, warmth, cold,* and *pain.*

NATURE AND LOCATION OF RECEPTORS

BRAIN PATHWAYS IN INITIAL PROCESSING

The *retina*, which is neural tissue lining the inside back surface of the eye, contains millions of receptor cells called *rods* and *cones*. Rods play a key role in night and peripheral vision; cones play a key role in daylight and color vision.

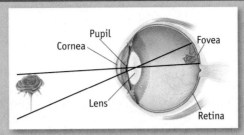

Cornea
Pupil
Fovea
Lens
Retina

Neural impulses are routed through the *LGN* in the *thalamus* and then distributed to the *primary visual cortex* at the back of the *occipital lobe.*

Primary visual cortex

The receptors for hearing are tiny *hair cells* that line the *basilar membrane* that runs the length of the *cochlea*, a fluid-filled, coiled tunnel in the inner ear.

Semicircular canals
Pinna
Auditory nerve
Cochlea
Sound waves
Eardrum

Neural impulses are routed through the *thalamus* and then sent to the *primary auditory cortex*, which is mostly located in the *temporal lobe.*

Primary auditory cortex

The gustatory receptors are clusters of *taste cells* found in the *taste buds* that line the trenches around tiny bumps in the tongue. Taste cells have a short life span (about 10 days) and are constantly being replaced.

Tongue
Fungiform papillae
Taste buds
Circumvallate papillae
Foliate papillae

Neural impulses are routed through the *thalamus* and on to the *insular cortex* in the frontal lobe.

Primary taste cortex (insula)

The receptors for smell are *olfactory cilia*, hairlike structures in the upper portion of the nasal passages. Like taste cells, they have a short lifespan (about 30–60 days) and are constantly being replaced.

Olfactory bulb
Olfactory axons
Nasal passage
Olfactory cilia (receptor cells)

Neural impulses are routed through the *olfactory bulb* and then sent directly to the *olfactory cortex* in the *temporal lobe* and other cortical areas. Smell is the only sensory input not routed through the thalamus.

Primary olfactory cortex

The human skin is saturated with at least six types of sensory receptors. The four types shown here respond to pressure, whereas *free nerve endings* in the skin respond to pain, warmth, and cold.

Epidermis
Ruffini cylinder
Meissner corpuscle
Merkel receptors
Pacinian corpuscle

Neural impulses are routed through the *brainstem* and *thalamus* and on to the *somatosensory cortex* in the *parietal lobe.*

Primary somatosensory cortex

values, social behavior, and development. But perception is widely viewed as a basic, universal process that should be invariant across cultures. In most respects it is, as the similarities among cultural groups in perception far outweigh the differences. Nonetheless, we saw cultural variations in depth perception, susceptibility to illusions, taste preferences, and pain tolerance. Thus, even a fundamental, heavily physiological process such as perception can be modified to some degree by one's cultural background.

The following Personal Application highlights the subjectivity of perception once again. It focuses on how painters have learned to use the principles of visual perception to achieve a variety of artistic goals.

REVIEW of Key Learning Goals

4.20 This chapter provided two dramatic demonstrations of the value of theoretical diversity. It also provided numerous examples of how and why people's experience of the world is highly subjective. Finally, it highlighted the importance of cultural background.

Appreciating Art and Illusion

Key Learning Goals

4.21 Discuss how the Impressionists, Cubists, and Surrealists used various principles of visual perception.

4.22 Discuss how Escher, Vasarely, and Magritte used various principles of visual perception.

Answer the following multiple-choice question.

Artistic works such as paintings

___ **a** render an accurate picture of reality.

___ **b** create an illusion of reality.

___ **c** provide an interpretation of reality.

___ **d** make us think about the nature of reality.

___ **e** do all of the above.

The answer to this question is (e), "all of the above." Historically, artists have had many and varied purposes, including each of those listed in the question (Goldstein, 2001). To realize their goals, artists have had to use a number of principles of perception—sometimes quite deliberately, and sometimes not. Here we'll use the example of painting to explore the role of perceptual principles in art and illusion.

The goal of most early painters was to produce a believable picture of reality. This goal immediately created a problem familiar to most of us who have attempted to draw realistic pictures: The real world is three-dimensional, but a canvas or a sheet of paper is flat. Paradoxically, then, painters who set out to re-create reality had to do so by creating an *illusion* of three-dimensional reality.

Prior to the Renaissance, these efforts to create a convincing illusion of reality were awkward by modern standards. Why? Because artists did not understand how to use depth cues. This fact is apparent in **Figure 4.44**, a religious scene painted around 1300. The painting clearly lacks a sense of depth. The people seem paper-thin. They have no real position in space.

Although earlier artists made *some* use of depth cues, Renaissance artists manipulated the full range of pictorial depth cues and really harnessed the crucial cue of linear perspective (Solso, 1994). **Figure 4.45** dramatizes the resulting transition in art. This scene, painted by Italian Renaissance artists Gentile and Giovanni Bellini, seems much more realistic and lifelike than the painting in **Figure 4.44** because it uses a number of pictorial depth cues. Notice how the buildings on the sides converge to make use of linear perspective. Additionally, distant objects are smaller than nearby ones, an application of relative size. This painting also uses height in plane, as well as interposition. By taking advantage of pictorial depth cues, an artist can enhance a painting's illusion of reality.

In the centuries since the Renaissance, painters have adopted a number of view-

Figure 4.44

Master of the Arrest of Christ **(detail, central part) by S. Francesco, Assisi, Italy (circa 1300).** Notice how the absence of depth cues makes the painting seem flat and unrealistic.

Scala/Art Resource, New York

points about the portrayal of reality. For instance, the French Impressionists of the 19th century did not want to re-create the photographic "reality" of a scene. They set out to interpret a viewer's fleeting perception or impression of reality. To accomplish this end, they worked with color in unprecedented ways.

Consider, for instance, the work of Georges Seurat, a French artist who used a technique called pointillism. Seurat carefully studied what scientists knew about the composition of color in the 1880s, then applied this knowledge in a calculated, laboratory-like manner. Indeed, critics in his era dubbed him the "little chemist." Seurat constructed his paintings out of tiny dots of pure, intense colors. He used additive color mixing, a departure from the norm in painting, which usually depends on subtractive mixing of pigments. A famous result of Seurat's "scientific" approach to painting was *Sunday Afternoon on the Island of La Grande Jatte* (see **Figure 4.46**). As the work of Seurat illustrates, modernist painters were moving away from attempts to re-create the world as it is literally seen.

If 19th-century painters liberated color, their successors at the turn of the 20th century liberated form. This was particularly true of the Cubists. Cubism was begun in 1909 by Pablo Picasso, a Spanish artist who

Figure 4.45

A painting by the Italian Renaissance artists Gentile and Giovanni Bellini (circa 1480). In this painting a number of depth cues—including linear perspective, relative size, height in plane, and interposition—enhance the illusion of three-dimensional reality.

went on to experiment with other styles in his prolific career. The Cubists didn't try to portray reality so much as to reassemble it. They attempted to reduce everything to combinations of geometric forms (lines, circles, triangles, rectangles, and such) laid out in a flat space, lacking depth. In a sense, they applied the theory of feature analysis to canvas, as they built their figures out of simple features.

The resulting paintings were decidedly unrealistic, but the painters would leave realistic fragments that provided clues about the

subject. Picasso liked to challenge his viewers to decipher the subject of his paintings. Take a look at the painting in **Figure 4.47** (on the next page) and see whether you can figure out what Picasso was portraying.

The work in **Figure 4.47** is titled *Violin and Grapes*. Note how Gestalt principles of perceptual organization are at work to create these forms. Proximity and similarity serve to bring the grapes together in the bottom right corner. Closure accounts for your being able to see the essence of the violin.

Figure 4.46

Georges Seurat's *Sunday Afternoon on the Island of La Grande Jatte* (without artist's border) (1884–1886). Seurat used thousands of tiny dots of color and the principles of color mixing (see detail); the eye and brain combine the points into the colors the viewer actually sees.

Georges Seurat, French, 1859–1891, *Sunday Afternoon on the Island of La Grande Jatte* (and detail), oil on canvas, 1884–1886, 207.6 X 308 cm, Helen Birch Bartlett Memorial Collection, 1926.224, © 1990 The Art Institute of Chicago. All rights reserved.

The Visual System: Essentials of Sight

▌ Light varies in terms of wavelength, amplitude, and purity. Light enters the eye through the cornea and pupil and is focused on the retina by the lens. Rods and cones are the visual receptors found in the retina. Cones play a key role in daylight vision and color perception, while rods are critical to night vision and peripheral vision. Dark adaptation and light adaptation both involve changes in the retina's sensitivity to light.

▌ The retina transforms light into neural impulses that are sent to the brain via the optic nerve. Receptive fields are areas in the retina that affect the firing of visual cells. They vary in shape and size, but center-surround arrangements are common.

▌ Two visual pathways send signals through the thalamus to the primary visual cortex. From there, visual signals are shuttled along pathways that have been characterized as the *what* and *where* pathways. The visual cortex contains cells that appear to function as feature detectors. The *what pathway* has neurons inside it that are especially sensitive to faces and other highly specific stimuli.

▌ Perceptions of color (hue) are primarily a function of light wavelength, while amplitude affects brightness and purity affects saturation. Perceptions of colors depend on processes that resemble additive color mixing. The accumulated evidence suggests that both the trichromatic and opponent process theories of color perception are partly correct.

The Visual System: Perceptual Processes

▌ Reversible figures and perceptual sets demonstrate that the same visual input can result in very different perceptions. Inattentional blindness involves the failure to see readily visible objects. According to feature analysis theories, people detect specific elements in stimuli and build them into recognizable forms.

▌ Gestalt psychology emphasized that the whole may be greater than the sum of its parts (features). Other approaches to form perception emphasize that people develop perceptual hypotheses about the stimuli that could be responsible for sensory inputs. These perceptual hypotheses are guided by experience-based expectations.

▌ Depth perception depends primarily on monocular cues such as linear perspective, texture gradient, interposition, relative size, height in plane, and light and shadow. Binocular cues such as retinal disparity can also contribute to depth perception. Cultures may vary in their use of pictorial depth cues.

▌ Perceptual constancies in vision help viewers deal with the ever-shifting nature of sensory stimuli. Visual illusions demonstrate that perceptual hypotheses can be inaccurate and that perceptions are not simple reflections of objective reality. Researchers have found some interesting cultural variations in the susceptibility to certain illusions.

The Auditory System: Hearing

▌ Sound varies in terms of wavelength (frequency), amplitude, and purity. These properties affect mainly perceptions of pitch, loudness, and timbre, respectively.

▌ Sound is transmitted through the external ear via air conduction to the middle ear. In the inner ear, fluid conduction vibrates hair cells along the basilar membrane in the cochlea. These hair cells are the receptors for hearing. Modern evidence suggests that the place and frequency theories of pitch perception are complementary rather than incompatible.

The Other Senses: Taste, Smell, and Touch

▌ The taste buds are sensitive to four basic tastes: sweet, sour, bitter, and salty. Sensitivity to these tastes is distributed somewhat unevenly across the tongue, but the variations in sensitivity are quite small. Taste preferences are shaped by experience and culture. Supertasters are more sensitive to bitter and sweet tastes than other people are, which helps to make their consumption habits relatively healthy.

▌ Like taste, smell is a chemical sense. Chemical stimuli activate olfactory receptors lining the nasal passages. Most of these receptors respond to more than one odor. Smell is the only sense that is not routed through the thalamus. Humans can distinguish many different odors, but their performance on odor identification tasks tends to be surprisingly mediocre.

▌ Sensory receptors in the skin respond to pressure, temperature, and pain. Pain signals are sent to the brain along two pathways that are characterized as fast and slow. The perception of pain is highly subjective. Gate-control theory holds that incoming pain signals can be blocked in the spinal cord. Endorphins and a descending neural pathway appear responsible for the suppression of pain.

Reflecting on the Chapter's Themes

▌ This chapter underscored three of our unifying themes: the value of theoretical diversity, the subjective nature of experience, and the importance of one's cultural heritage.

PERSONAL APPLICATION Appreciating Art and Illusion

▌ The principles of visual perception are often applied to artistic endeavors. Painters routinely use pictorial depth cues to make their scenes more lifelike. Color mixing, feature analysis, Gestalt principles, reversible figures, and impossible figures have also been used in influential paintings.

CRITICAL THINKING APPLICATION Recognizing Contrast Effects: It's All Relative

▌ The study of perception often highlights the relativity of experience. This relativity can be manipulated by carefully arranging for contrast effects. Critical thinking is enhanced by an awareness of how comparitors can distort many types of judgments.

PsykTrek Preview

Visit Modules 3b (*The Retina*) and 3c (*Vision and the Brain*) to see animations of how visual signals are transmitted from the eye to the brain.

Play with color filters in Module 3d (*Perception of Color*) to see subtractive color mixing in action, or try manipulating an example of the phi phenomenon in Module 3e (*Gestalt Psychology*).

1. The term used to refer to the stimulation of the sense organs is:
   A. sensation.
   B. perception.
   C. transduction.
   D. adaptation.

2. Perception of the brightness of a color is affected mainly by:
   A. the wavelength of light waves.
   B. the amplitude of light waves.
   C. the purity of light waves.
   D. the saturation of light waves.

3. In farsightedness:
   A. close objects are seen clearly but distant objects appear blurry.
   B. the focus of light from close objects falls behind the retina.
   C. the focus of light from distant objects falls a little short of the retina.
   D. both A and B occur.
   E. both A and C occur.

4. The collection of rod and cone receptors that funnel signals to a particular visual cell in the retina make up that cell's:
   A. blind spot.
   B. optic disk.
   C. opponent process field.
   D. receptive field.

5. The primary visual cortex is located in the:
   A. occipital lobe.
   B. temporal lobe.
   C. parietal lobe.
   D. frontal lobe.

6. Which theory would predict that the American flag would have a green, black, and yellow afterimage?
   A. Subtractive color mixing
   B. Opponent process theory
   C. Additive color mixing
   D. Trichromatic theory

7. A readiness to perceive a stimulus in a particular way is referred to as (a):
   A. Gestalt.
   B. feature analysis.
   C. perceptual set.
   D. congruence.

8. In a painting, train tracks may look as if they go off into the distance because the artist draws the tracks as converging lines, a monocular cue to depth known as:
   A. interposition.
   B. texture gradient.
   C. relative size.
   D. linear perspective.

9. Perception of pitch can best be explained by:
   A. place theory.
   B. frequency theory.
   C. both place theory and frequency theory.
   D. neither theory.

10. In what way(s) is the sense of taste like the sense of smell?
    A. There are four primary stimulus groups for both senses.
    B. Both systems are routed through the thalamus on the way to the cortex.
    C. The physical stimuli for both senses are chemical substances dissolved in fluid.
    D. All of the above.
    E. None of the above.

11. The fact that theories originally seen as being incompatible, such as the trichromatic and opponent process theories of color vision, are now seen as both being necessary to explain sensory processes illustrates:
    A. that psychology evolves in a sociohistorical context.
    B. the subjectivity of experience.
    C. the value of psychology's theoretical diversity.
    D. the nature-nurture controversy.

12. In the study by Kenrick and Gutierres (1980), exposing male subjects to a TV show dominated by extremely beautiful women:
    A. had no effect on their ratings of the attractiveness of a prospective date.
    B. increased their ratings of the attractiveness of a prospective date.
    C. decreased their ratings of the attractiveness of a prospective date.
    D. decreased their ratings of their own attractiveness.

Answers

1 A p. 107	5 A pp. 112–113	9 C p. 133
2 B p. 108	6 B p. 117	10 C pp. 134–136
3 B p. 110	7 C p. 120	11 C p. 139
4 D p. 112	8 D pp. 125–126	12 C p. 147

PSYKTREK PREVIEW

SENSATION AND PERCEPTION
3g | Visual Illusions

Here's a similar illusion created by Stanford University psychologist, Roger Shepard. To prove to yourself that the monsters are in fact the same size, drag the one in the foreground on top of the one in the background.

SIMULATIONS
3 | The Poggendorff Illusion

Trial 2

Drag the line on the right to the correct position, then click the DONE button.

DONE

Go to Module 3g (*Visual Illusions*) to play with stunning illusions and watch a video on the Ames room in which people appear to change size right before your eyes.

Try Simulation 3 (*The Poggendorff Illusion*) in which you get to tinker with a classic illusion to see how various factors enhance or diminish the illusion.

5

Variations in Consciousness

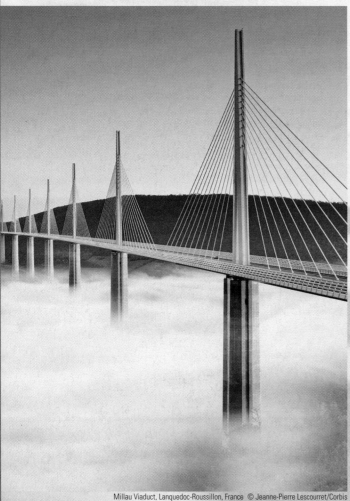

Millau Viaduct, Lanquedoc-Roussillon, France © Jeanne-Pierre Lescourret/Corbis gests that melatonin can reduce the effects of jet lag by helping travelers resynchronize their biological clocks, but the research results are inconsistent (Arendt & Skeen, 2005; Monk, 2006). One reason for the inconsistent findings is that when melatonin is used to ameliorate jet lag, the timing of the dose is crucial; because calculating the optimal timing is rather complicated, it is easy to get it wrong (Czeisler, Cajochen, & Turek, 2000).

Researchers have also tried carefully timed exposure to bright light as a treatment to realign circadian rhythms in rotating shift workers in industrial settings. Positive effects have been seen in some studies (Lowden, Akerstedt, & Wibom, 2004). This treatment can accelerate workers' adaptation to a new sleep-wake schedule, leading to improvements in sleep quality and alertness during work hours. However, the effects of bright-light administration have been modest and somewhat inconsistent (Rogers & Dinges, 2002), and it isn't a realistic option in many work settings. Another strategy to help shift workers involves carefully planning their rotation schedules to reduce the severity of their circadian

The Sleep and Waking Cycle

Although it is a familiar state of consciousness, sleep is widely misunderstood. Historically, people have thought of sleep as a single, uniform state of physical and mental inactivity, during which the brain is "shut down" (Dement, 2003). In reality, sleepers experience quite a bit of physical and mental activity throughout the night. Scientists have learned a great deal about sleep since the landmark discovery of REM sleep in the 1950s.

The advances in our understanding of sleep have been the result of hard work by researchers who have spent countless nighttime hours watching other people sleep. This work is done in sleep laboratories, where volunteer participants come to spend the night. Sleep labs have one or more "bedrooms" in which the subjects retire, usually after being hooked up to a variety of physiological recording devices. In addition to an EEG, these devices typically include an *electromyograph* (*EMG*), which records muscular activity and tension; an *electrooculograph* (*EOG*), which records eye movements; and an *electrocardiograph* (*EKG*), which records the contractions of the heart (Carskadon & Rechtschaffen,

Nathaniel Kleitman and Eugene Aserinsky couldn't believe their eyes—or their subject's eyes, either. It was the spring of 1952, and Kleitman, a physiologist and prominent sleep researcher, was investigating the slow, rolling eye movements displayed by subjects at the onset of sleep. Kleitman had begun to wonder whether these slow eye movements would show up during later phases of sleep. The trouble was that watching a participant's closed eyelids all night long was a surefire way to put the *researcher* to sleep. Cleverly, Kleitman and Aserinsky, a graduate student, came up with a better way to document eye movements. They hooked subjects up to an apparatus that was connected to electrodes pasted near the eyes. The electrodes picked up the small electrical signals generated by moving eyeballs. In turn, these signals moved a pen on a chart recorder, much like an electroencephalograph (EEG) traces brain waves (see Chapter 3). The result was an objective record of sleepers' eye movements that could be studied at leisure (Dement, 1992).

One night, while one of their subjects was asleep, the researchers were astonished to see a tracing in the recording that suggested a different, much more rapid eye movement. This result was so unexpected that they at first thought the recording device was on the blink. "It was a rickety old thing, anyway," a technician in Kleitman's lab recalled (Coren, 1996, p. 21). Only when they decided to walk in and personally observe sleeping subjects were they convinced that the eye movements were real. The subjects were deeply asleep, yet the bulges in their closed eyelids showed that their eyeballs were moving laterally in sharp jerks, first in one direction and then in the other. It was almost as if the sleeping participants were watching a chaotic movie. The researchers wondered—what in the world was going on?

In retrospect, it's amazing that no one had discovered these rapid eye movements before. It turns out that periods of rapid eye movement are a routine characteristic of sleep in humans and many animals. In fact, you can observe them for yourself in your

pet dog or cat. The phenomenon had been there for everyone to see for eons, but anyone who noticed must not have attached any significance to it.

Kleitman and Aserinsky's discovery might have remained something of an oddity, but then they had a brainstorm. Could the rapid eye movements perhaps be related to dreaming? With the help of William Dement, a graduate student who was interested in dreams, they soon found the answer. When Dement woke up subjects during periods of rapid eye movement, about 80% reported that they had just been having a vivid dream. By contrast, only a small minority of participants awakened from other phases of sleep reported that they had been dreaming. Dement knew that he was on to something. "I was overwhelmed with excitement," he wrote later (1992, pp. 24–25). Subsequently, EEG recordings showed that periods of rapid eye movement were also associated with marked changes in brain-wave patterns. What Kleitman and his graduate students had stumbled on was considerably more than an oddity. It was a window into the most private aspect of consciousness imaginable—the experience of dreaming. As you will learn in this chapter, the discovery of rapid eye movement (REM) sleep blossomed into a number of other fascinating insights about what goes on in the brain during sleep. This is just one example of how modern psychologists have tried to come to grips with the slippery topic of consciousness.

We'll begin our tour of variations in consciousness with a few general points about the nature of consciousness. After that, much of the chapter will be a "bedtime story," as we take a long look at sleep and dreaming. We'll continue our discussion of consciousness by examining hypnosis, meditation, and the effects of mind-altering drugs. The Personal Application addresses a number of practical questions about sleep and dreams. Finally, the Critical Thinking Application returns to the topic of drugs and looks at the concept of alcoholism to highlight the power of definitions.

On the Nature of Consciousness

What is consciousness? *Consciousness* is the awareness of internal and external stimuli. Your consciousness includes (1) your awareness of external events ("The professor just asked me a difficult question about medieval history"), (2) your awareness of your internal sensations ("My heart is racing and I'm beginning to sweat"), (3) your awareness of your *self* as the unique being having these experiences ("Why me?"), and (4) your awareness of your thoughts about these experiences ("I'm going

Key Learning Goals

5.1 Discuss the nature and evolution of consciousness.

5.2 Articulate the relationship between consciousness and EEG activity.

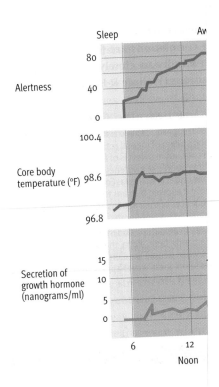

Figure 5.1
Examples of circadian rhythms. These graphs show how core body temperature and the secretion of growth hormone typically fluctuate in a 24-hour rhythm. Circadian rhythms are also seen for many other physiological functions.

SOURCE: Circadian rhythms adapted from *Wide Awake at 3:00 AM* by Richard M. Coleman. Copyright © 1986 by Richard M. Coleman. Reprinted by arrangement of Henry Holt & Company, LLC.

Sleep   Aw

Alertness 80 40 0

Core body temperature (°F) 100.4 98.6 96.8

Secretion of growth hormone (nanograms/ml) 15 10 5 0

6   12
Noon

Ignoring Circadian Rhyth

What happens when you ignor
clock and go to sleep at an unusu
the quality of your sleep suffers. C
with your circadian rhythms a
When you fly across several tim
logical clock keeps time as usua
ficial clock time changes. You the
"wrong" time and are likely to ex
falling asleep and poor-quality s
sleep, which can continue to occ
can make you feel fatigued, slug
during the daytime (Arendt, Stor

People differ in how quickly t
biological clocks to compensate
speed of readjustment depend
traveled. Generally, it's easier t
lengthen your day than it is to
shorten it (Arendt et al., 2005). T
ity in jet lag is sizable enough to
the performance of sports teams
that teams flying westward pe
better than teams flying eastw
baseball (Recht, Lew, & Schwar
football (Worthen & Wade, 19
thumb for jet lag is that the re
takes about a day for each time
flying eastward and about two
time zone when flying westwar

---

web link 5.1

SleepNet

This extensive website offers a wealth of information on sleep disorders, sleep labs, sleep aids, and sleep research. It also includes links to other sites dedicated to the topic of sleep.

---

a night to adapt to the strange bedroom and the recording devices and to return to their normal mode of sleeping (Carskadon & Dement, 2005).

Cycling Through the Stages of Sleep 4b

Not only does sleep occur in a context of daily rhythms, but subtler rhythms are evident within the experience of sleep itself. During sleep, people cycle through a series of five distinct stages. Let's take a look at what researchers have learned about the many types of changes that occur during these sleep stages (Carskadon & Dement, 2005; Rosenthal, 2006).

Stages 1–4   4b
Although it may only take a few minutes, the onset of sleep is gradual, with no obvious transition point between wakefulness and sleep (Rechtschaffen, 1994). The length of time it takes people to fall asleep varies considerably, but the average in a recent study of over 35,000 people from 10 countries

Figure 5.2
EEG patterns in sleep and wakefulness. Characteristic brain waves vary depending on one's state of consciousness. Generally, as people move from an awake state through deeper stages of sleep, their brain waves decrease in frequency (cycles per second) and increase in amplitude (height). However, brain waves during REM sleep resemble "wide awake" brain waves.

SOURCE: Adapted from Hauri, P. (1982). *Current concepts: The sleep disorders*, Kalamazoo, MI. The Upjohn Company. Reprinted by permission.

Awake
Low-voltage, high-frequency beta waves

1 second   50 μV

Drowsy
Alpha waves prominent

Theta waves

Stage 1 sleep
Theta waves prominent

Sleep spindle

Stage 2 sleep
Sleep spindles and mixed EEG activity

Slow-wave sleep (stage 3 and stage 4 sleep)
Progressively more delta waves (stage 4 shown)

REM sleep
Low-voltage, high-frequency brain waves

---

was 25 minutes (Soldatos et al., 2005). This time length depends on quite an array of factors, including how long it has been since the person has slept, where the person is in his or her circadian cycle, the amount of noise or light in the sleep environment, and the person's age, desire to fall asleep, boredom level, recent caffeine or drug intake, and stress level, among other things (Broughton, 1994). In any event, stage 1 is a brief transitional stage of light sleep that usually lasts only 10–12 minutes (Rama, Cho, & Kushida, 2006). Your breathing and heart rate slow as your muscle tension and body temperature decline. The alpha waves that probably dominated your EEG activity just before you fell asleep give way to lower-frequency EEG activity in which theta waves are prominent (see **Figure 5.2**).

As you descend through stages 2, 3, and 4 of the sleep cycle, your respiration rate, heart rate, muscle tension, and body temperature continue to decline. Gradually, your brain waves become higher in amplitude and slower in frequency, as you move into a deeper form of sleep, called slow-wave sleep (see **Figure 5.2**). *Slow-wave sleep* consists of sleep stages 3 and 4, during which low-frequency delta waves become prominent in EEG recordings. Typically you reach slow-wave sleep in less than an hour and stay there for roughly a half-hour. Then the sleep cycle reverses itself and you gradually move upward through lighter stages of sleep. That's when things start to get interesting.

REM Sleep 4b
When you reach what should be stage 1 once again, you usually go into the fifth stage of sleep, which is most widely known as *REM sleep*. REM is the abbreviation for rapid eye movements, which are prominent during this stage. In a sleep lab, researchers use an electrooculograph to monitor these lateral movements that occur beneath the sleeping person's closed eyelids. However, they can be seen with the naked eye if you closely watch someone in the REM stage of sleep (little ripples move back and forth across his or her closed eyelids).

As we discussed at the beginning of the chapter, the discovery of REM sleep was made accidentally in the 1950s in Nathaniel Kleitman's lab at the University of Chicago (Aserinsky & Kleitman, 1953; Dement, 2005). The term *REM sleep* was coined by William Dement, a student in Kleitman's lab, who went on to become one of the world's foremost sleep researchers. The REM stage tends to be a "deep" stage of sleep in the conventional sense that it is relatively hard to awaken a person from it (although arousal thresholds vary during REM). The REM stage is also marked by irregular breathing and pulse rate. Muscle tone is extremely relaxed—so much so that bodily movements are minimal and the sleeper is virtually paralyzed. Although REM is a relatively deep sleep stage, EEG activity is dominated by high-frequency beta waves that resemble those observed when people are alert and awake (see **Figure 5.2** again).

This paradox is probably related to the association between REM sleep and dreaming. When researchers systematically awaken subjects from various stages of sleep to ask them whether they were dreaming, most dream reports come from awakenings during the REM stage (Dement, 1978; McCarley, 1994). Although decades of research have revealed that some dreaming occurs in the non-REM stages, dreaming is most frequent, vivid, and memorable during REM sleep (Pace-Schott, 2005).

To summarize, *REM sleep* is a deep stage of sleep marked by rapid eye movements, high-frequency brain waves, and dreaming. It is such a special stage of sleep that the other four stages are often characterized simply as "non-REM sleep." *Non-REM (NREM) sleep* consists of sleep stages 1 through 4, which are marked by an absence of rapid eye movements, relatively little dreaming, and varied EEG activity.

REM sleep is not unique to humans. Nearly all mammals and birds exhibit REM sleep. The only known exceptions among warm-blooded vertebrates are dolphins and some whales (Morrison, 2003). Dolphins are particularly interesting, as they sleep while swimming, resting one hemisphere of the brain while the other hemisphere remains alert.

Repeating the Cycle   4b

During the course of a night, people usually repeat the sleep cycle about four times. As the night wears on, the cycle changes gradually. The first REM period is relatively short, lasting only a few minutes. Subsequent REM periods get progressively longer, peaking at around 40–60 minutes. Additionally, NREM intervals tend to get shorter, and descents into NREM stages usually become more shallow. These trends can be seen in **Figure 5.3** on the next page, which provides an overview of a typical night's sleep cycle. These trends mean that most slow-wave sleep occurs early in the sleep cycle and that REM sleep tends to pile up in the second half of the sleep cycle. Summing across the entire cycle, young adults typically spend about 15%–20% of their sleep time in slow-wave sleep and another 20%–25% in REM sleep (Rama et al., 2006).

What we have described thus far is the big picture—the typical structure of sleep averaged over many people. However, recent research by Tucker, Dinges, and Van Dongen (2007) has shown that the "architecture" of sleep—how quickly one falls asleep, how long one sleeps, how one cycles through the various stages—varies from one person to the next more than sleep researchers initially realized. And these personal variations are pretty stable from one night to the next, meaning that each of us has a signature sleep pattern. Tucker et al. (2007) believe that these signature patterns are mostly shaped by biological factors rather than personal habits, although much more research is needed on this issue.

concept check 5.1

Comparing REM and NREM Sleep

A table here could have provided you with a systematic comparison of REM sleep and NREM sleep, but that would have deprived you of the opportunity to check your understanding of these sleep phases by creating your own table. Try to fill in each of the blanks below with a word or phrase highlighting the differences between REM and NREM sleep with regard to the various characteristics specified. As usual, you can find the answers at the back of the book in Appendix A.

Characteristic	REM sleep	NREM sleep
1. Type of EEG activity	_____	_____
2. Eye movements	_____	_____
3. Dreaming	_____	_____
4. Depth (difficulty in awakening)	_____	_____
5. Percentage of total sleep (in adults)	_____	_____
6. Increases or decreases (as percentage of sleep) during childhood	_____	_____
7. Timing in sleep cycle (dominates early or late)	_____	_____

Figure 5.3

An overview of the cycle of sleep. The white line charts how a typical, healthy young adult moves through the various stages of sleep during the course of a night. This diagram also shows how dreams and rapid eye movements tend to coincide with REM sleep, whereas posture changes occur in between REM periods (because the body is nearly paralyzed during REM sleep). Notice how the person cycles into REM four times, as descents into NREM sleep get shallower and REM periods get longer. Thus, slow-wave sleep is prominent early in the night, while REM sleep dominates the second half of a night's sleep. Although these patterns are typical, keep in mind that sleep patterns vary from one person to another and that they change with age.

Posture shifts

Wakefulness — A fast low-voltage brain wave characterizes wakefulness

Stage 1 sleep or REM sleep — REM — REM

Stage 2

Stage 3

Stage 4

Dreams

Eye movements

web link 5.2

SleepQuest

Leading sleep researcher William Dement of Stanford University—the founder of sleep medicine—is the chief scientific advisor for this site. Visitors can access an archive of "columns" written by Dr. Dement and a diverse array of resources on sleep disorders.

Age, Culture, and Sleep

 4b

Now that we have described the basic architecture of sleep, let's take a look at a couple of factors that contribute to variations in patterns of sleeping: age and culture.

Age Trends   4b

Age alters the sleep cycle. What we have described so far is the typical pattern for young to middle-aged adults. Children, however, display different patterns (Bootzin et al., 2001; Roffwarg, Muzio, & Dement, 1966). Newborns will sleep six to eight times in a 24-hour period, often exceeding a total of 16 hours of sleep (see **Figure 5.4**). Fortunately for parents, during the first several months much of this sleep begins to get unified into one particularly long nighttime sleep period (Webb, 1992a). Interestingly, infants spend much more of their sleep time than adults do in the REM stage. In the first few months, REM accounts for about 50% of babies' sleep, as compared to 20% of adults' sleep. During the remainder of the first year, the REM portion of infants' sleep declines to roughly 30% (Ohayon et al., 2004). The REM portion of sleep continues to decrease gradu-

ally until it levels off at about 20% during adolescence (see **Figure 5.4**).

During adulthood, gradual, age-related changes in sleep continue. Although the proportion of REM sleep remains fairly stable (Floyd et al., 2007), the percentage of slow-wave sleep declines and the percentage of time spent in stage 1 increases slightly, with these trends stronger in men than women (Bliwise, 2005). These shifts toward lighter sleep *may* contribute to the increased frequency of nighttime awakenings seen among the elderly (Klerman et al., 2004). As **Figure 5.4** shows, the average amount of total sleep time also declines with advancing age. However, these averages mask important variability, as total sleep *increases* with age in a substantial portion of older people (Webb, 1992a).

Cultural Variations

Although age clearly affects the nature and structure of sleep itself, the psychological and physiological experience of sleep does not appear to vary much across cultures. For example, a recent cross-cultural survey (Soldatos et al., 2005) found relatively modest differences in the average amount of time that people sleep, or the time that it takes for them to fall asleep (see **Figure 5.5** on page 160). Cultural disparities in

REM

REM

The last REM period of the night has the fastest eye movements and may be the period from which dreams are best remembered.

Figure 5.4

Changes in sleep patterns over the life span. Both the total amount of sleep per night and the portion of sleep that is REM sleep change with age. Sleep patterns change most dramatically during infancy, with total sleep time and amount of REM sleep declining sharply in the first two years of life. After a noticeable drop in the average amount of sleep in adolescence, sleep patterns remain relatively stable, although total sleep and slow-wave sleep continue to decline gradually with age.

SOURCE: Adapted from an updated revision of a figure in Roffwarg, H. P., Muzio, J. N., & Dement, W. C. (1966). Ontogenetic development of human sleep-dream cycle. *Science, 152,* 604–609. Copyright © 1966 by the American Association for the Advancement of Science. Adapted and revised by permission of the authors.

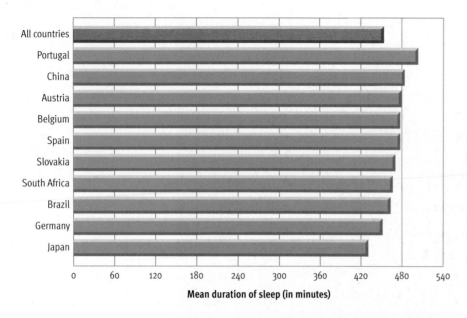

Mean duration of sleep (in minutes)

Figure 5.5

Cultural variations in how long people tend to sleep. A recent study (Soldatos et al., 2005) surveyed over 35,000 people in 10 countries about various aspects of their sleep habits. This graph shows the average duration of nighttime sleep reported by the respondents in each country. Although Japan was a bit of an "outlier," the cultural differences are rather modest. Cultural variability in the average time required to fall asleep was also modest. Consistent with previous findings, the results of this study suggest that the basic architecture of sleep does not vary much across cultures.

sleep are limited to more peripheral matters, such as sleeping arrangements and napping customs. For instance, there are cultural differences in co-sleeping, the practice of children and parents sleeping together (McKenna, 1993). In modern Western societies, co-sleeping is actively discouraged. As part of their effort to foster self-reliance, American parents teach their children to sleep alone. In contrast, co-sleeping is more widely accepted in Japanese culture, which emphasizes interdependence and group harmony (Latz, Wolf, & Lozoff, 1999). Around the world as a whole, co-sleeping is normative (Ball, Hooker, & Kelly, 2000). Strong pressure against co-sleeping appears to be largely an urban, Western phenomenon.

Napping practices also vary along cultural lines. In many societies, shops close and activities are curtailed in the afternoon to permit people to enjoy a 1- to 2-hour midday nap. These "siesta cultures" are found mostly in tropical regions of the world (Webb & Dinges, 1989). There, this practice is adaptive in that it allows people to avoid working during the hottest part of the day. As a rule, the siesta tradition is not found in industrialized societies, where it conflicts with the emphasis on productivity and the philosophy that "time is money."

The Evolutionary Bases of Sleep

What is the evolutionary significance of sleep? The fact that sleep is seen in a highly diverse array of organisms and that it appears to have evolved independently in birds and mammals suggests that sleep has considerable adaptive value (Zepelin, 1993). But theorists disagree about *how* exactly sleep is adaptive. One hypothesis is that sleep evolved to conserve organisms' energy. According to this notion, sleep evolved

millions of years ago in service of warmbloodedness, which requires the maintenance of a constant, high body temperature by metabolic means. An alternative hypothesis is that the immobilization associated with sleep is adaptive because it reduces exposure to predators and other sources of danger. A third hypothesis is that sleep is adaptive because it helps animals restore energy and other bodily resources depleted by waking activities. But what, exactly, sleep restores is not readily apparent (Frank, 2006). Overall, the evidence seems strongest for the energy conservation hypothesis, but there is room for extensive debate about the evolutionary bases of sleep (Zepelin, Siegel, & Tobler, 2005). Complicating the picture more, many theorists believe that the function and evolutionary roots of REM sleep and NREM sleep may be quite different (Siegel, 2005).

Doing Without: Sleep Deprivation

Scientific research on sleep deprivation presents something of a paradox. On the one hand, some studies suggest that sleep deprivation is not as detrimental as most people subjectively feel it to be. On the other hand, evidence suggests that sleep deprivation may be a major social problem, undermining efficiency at work and contributing to countless accidents.

Research has mostly focused on *partial sleep deprivation,* or *sleep restriction,* which occurs when people make do with substantially less sleep than normal over a period of time. Many sleep experts believe that much of American society chronically suffers from partial sleep deprivation (Walsh, Dement, & Dinges, 2005). It appears that more and more people are trying to squeeze additional waking hours out of their days as they attempt to juggle conflicting work, family, household, and school responsibilities, leading William Dement to comment that "Most Americans no longer know what it feels like to be fully alert" (Toufexis, 1990, p. 79).

How serious are the effects of partial sleep deprivation? Research findings and expert opinions on this matter have varied over recent decades. One reason for this variability is that the effects of sleep restriction will vary depending on the amount of sleep lost, where subjects are in their circadian cycles when tested, and the nature of the task (Bonnet, 2000; Dorrian & Dinges, 2006). Moreover, recent research has also found variability among individuals in how sensitive they are to sleep restriction. Over a series of three carefully controlled sleep-deprivation episodes, Van Dongen et al. (2004) found that some subjects were more vulnerable to the negative effects of sleep deprivation than others.

Caveats aside, the emerging consensus is that sleep restriction has far more negative effects than most people assume. Studies indicate that sleep restriction can impair individuals' attention, reaction time, motor coordination, and decision making and may also have negative effects on endocrine and immune system functioning (Dinges, Rogers, & Baynard, 2005). Evidence suggests that sleep deprivation contributes to errors in medical treatment by physicians in training (medical residents), who often work 80–100 hours a week without adequate rest (Weinger & Ancoli-Israel, 2002). Sleep deprivation has also been blamed for a large proportion of transportation accidents and mishaps in the workplace (Walsh et al., 2005). For example, sleepiness appears to be a contributing factor in roughly 20% of motor vehicle accidents (MacLean, Davies, & Thiele, 2003). Sleep deprivation seems to be particularly problematic among young drivers, truck drivers, and drivers who work late or rotating shifts (Durmer & Dinges, 2005).

Studies also suggest that nighttime workers in many industries frequently fall asleep on the job (Roehrs et al., 2005). Obviously, for a person running a punch press, driving a bus, or working as an air traffic controller, a momentary lapse in attention could be very, very costly. In recent decades, a number of major disasters, such as the nuclear accidents at Three Mile Island and Chernobyl, the running aground of the Exxon Valdez in Alaska, and the Challenger space shuttle tragedy, have been blamed in part on lapses in judgment and attention resulting from sleep deprivation (Doghramji, 2001). Experts have estimated that accidents attributed to drowsiness induced by sleep deprivation cost the U.S. economy as much as $56 billion annually (Durmer & Dinges, 2005).

The unique quality of REM sleep led researchers to look into the effects of a special type of partial sleep deprivation—*selective deprivation*. In a number of laboratory studies, participants were awakened over a period of nights whenever they began to go into the REM stage. These subjects usually got a decent amount of sleep in NREM stages, but they were selectively deprived of REM sleep.

What are the effects of REM deprivation? The evidence indicates that it has little impact on daytime functioning and task performance, but it *does* have some interesting effects on subjects' patterns of sleeping (Bonnet, 2005). As the nights go by in REM deprivation studies, it becomes necessary to awaken the participants more and more often to deprive them of their REM sleep, because they spontaneously shift into REM more and more frequently. Whereas most subjects normally go into REM about four times a night, REM-deprived participants start slipping into REM every time the researchers turn around. Furthermore, when

a REM-deprivation experiment comes to an end and participants are allowed to sleep without interruption, they experience a "rebound effect." That is, they spend extra time in REM periods for one to three nights to make up for their REM deprivation (Bonnet, 2005).

Similar results have been observed when subjects have been selectively deprived of slow-wave sleep (Borbely & Achermann, 2005). What do theorists make of these spontaneous pursuits of REM and slow-wave sleep? They conclude that people must have specific *needs* for REM and slow-wave sleep—and rather strong needs, at that.

Why do we need REM and slow-wave sleep? Some influential studies suggest that REM and slow-wave sleep contribute to firming up learning that takes place during the day—a process called memory consolidation (Gais & Born, 2004; Stickgold, 2001). Efforts to explore this hypothesis have led to some interesting findings in recent years. For example, in one study participants were given training on a perceptual-motor task and then retested 12 hours later. Those who slept during the 12-hour interval showed substantial improvement in performance that was not apparent in participants who did not sleep (Walker et al., 2002). A number of similar studies have shown that sleep seems to enhance subjects' memory of specific learning activities that occurred during the day (Walker & Stickgold, 2004). These studies also find that the length of time spent in REM and SWS correlates with subjects' learning and memory performance (Walker

Courtesy of William Dement

William Dement

"Sleep deprivation is a major epidemic in our society.... Americans spend so much time and energy chasing the American dream, that they don't have much time left for actual dreaming."

Many traffic accidents occur because drivers get drowsy or fall asleep at the wheel. Although the effects of sleep deprivation seem innocuous, sleep loss can be deadly.

& Stickgold, 2006). The theoretical meaning of these findings is still being debated, but the most widely accepted explanations center on how time spent in specific stages of sleep may stabilize or solidify memories formed during the day (Stickgold, 2005). The practical meaning of these results, however, should be rather obvious: Sound sleep habits should facilitate learning.

Sleep Loss and Health

In recent years, researchers have begun to investigate the notion that sleep deprivation might have serious health consequences. Accumulating evidence suggests that sleep loss can affect physiological processes in ways that may undermine physical health. For example, sleep restriction appears to trigger hormonal changes that increase hunger (Spiegel et al., 2004). Consistent with this finding, studies have found a link between short sleep duration and increased obesity, which is a risk factor for a variety of health problems (Kohatsu et al., 2006). Researchers have also found that sleep loss leads to impaired immune system functioning (Motivala & Irwin, 2007) and increased inflammatory responses (Irwin et al., 2006), which are likely to heighten vulnerability to a variety of diseases. Thus, it is not surprising that studies have uncovered links between short sleep duration and an increased risk for diabetes (Gottlieb et al., 2005), hypertension (Gangwisch et al., 2006), and coronary disease (Ayas et al., 2003).

These findings have motivated researchers to explore the correlation between habitual sleep time and overall mortality. The results of this research have provided a bit of a surprise. As expected, people who consistently sleep less than 7 hours exhibit an elevated mortality risk, but so do those who routinely sleep more than 8 hours, and mortality rates are especially high among those who sleep over 10 hours (see **Figure 5.6**; Patel et al., 2004; Tamakoshi et al., 2004). Researchers are now scrambling to figure out why long sleep duration is correlated with elevated mortality. It could be that prolonged sleep is a "marker" for other problems, such as depression or a sedentary lifestyle, that have negative effects on health (Patel et al., 2006). Bear in mind, also, that the studies linking typical sleep duration to mortality have depended on participants' self-report estimates of how long they normally sleep, which could be inaccurate.

The evidence linking sleep duration to mortality has inspired new research intended to determine exactly how much people really sleep. Using a wristwatch-like device that can record sleep data around the clock, Lauderdale and colleagues (2006) monitored the sleep habits of 669 participants for three days. They found that while their subjects spent an average of 7.51 hours in bed each day, actual sleep time was only 6.06 hours. This finding suggests that self-estimates of sleep duration may be distorted, which will greatly complicate the effort to clarify the association between sleep patterns and mortality. In any event, the relationship between sleep and health is an emerging area of research that probably will yield some interesting findings in the years to come.

Problems in the Night: Sleep Disorders

Not everyone is able to consistently enjoy the luxury of a good night's sleep. In this section we will briefly discuss what is known about a variety of sleep disorders.

Insomnia

Insomnia is the most common sleep disorder. *Insomnia* refers to chronic problems in getting adequate sleep. It occurs in three basic patterns: (1) difficulty in falling asleep initially, (2) difficulty in remaining asleep, and (3) persistent early-morning awakening. Insomnia may sound like a minor problem to those who haven't struggled with it, but it can be a very unpleasant malady. Moreover, insomnia is associated with daytime fatigue, impaired functioning, an elevated risk for accidents, reduced productivity, absenteeism at work, depression, and increased health problems (Benca, 2001; Edinger & Means, 2005).

How common is insomnia? Nearly everyone suffers occasional sleep difficulties because of stress, disruptions of biological rhythms, or other temporary circumstances. Fortunately, these problems

Figure 5.6
Mortality rates as a function of typical sleep duration. In a study of over 100,000 subjects followed 10 years, Tamakoshi et al. (2004) estimated mortality rates in relation to typical sleep duration. The lowest mortality rate was found among those who slept 7 hours, so that figure was arbitrarily set to 1.00 and the mortality rates for other sleep lengths were calculated relative to that baseline. The rates shown here are averaged for males and females. As you can see, higher mortality rates are associated with both shorter sleep durations and longer sleep durations. Mortality rates were especially elevated among those who reported that they slept 10 or more hours per night.

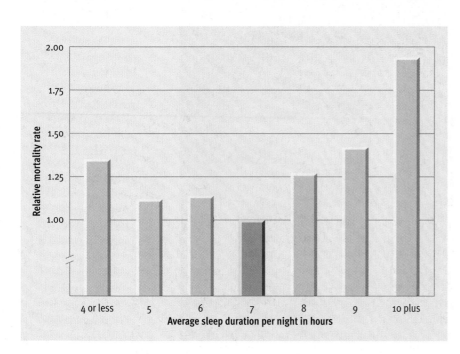

clear up spontaneously for most people. However, studies suggest that about 30%–35% of adults report chronic problems with insomnia, and about half to two-thirds of these people suffer from severe or frequent insomnia (Brown, 2006; Zorick & Walsh, 2000). The prevalence of insomnia increases with age and is about 50% more common in women than in men (Partinen & Hublin, 2005).

A huge portion of people suffering from insomnia do not pursue professional treatment (Sivertsen et al., 2006). Many of them probably depend on over-the-counter sleep aids, which have questionable value (Mahowald & Schenck, 2005). The most common approach in the medical treatment of insomnia is the prescription of two classes of drugs: benzodiazepine sedatives (such as Dalmane, Halcion, and Restoril), which were originally developed to relieve anxiety, and newer nonbenzodiazepine sedatives (such as Ambien, Sonata, and Lunesta), which were designed primarily for sleep problems (Mendelson, 2005). Both types of sedative medications are fairly effective in helping people fall asleep more quickly, and they reduce nighttime awakenings and increase total sleep (Lee-Chiong & Sateia, 2006; Mendelson, 2005).

Nonetheless, sedatives are a poor long-range solution for insomnia, for a number of reasons (Roehrs & Roth, 2000; Wesson et al., 2005). It is possible to overdose on sleeping pills and some people become dependent on sedatives to fall asleep. Sedatives also have carryover effects that can make people drowsy and sluggish the next day and impair their functioning (Vermeeren, 2004). Moreover, with continued use sedatives gradually become less effective, so people need to increase their dose to more dangerous levels, creating a vicious circle of escalating dependency (Lader, 2002; see **Figure 5.7**). Another problem is that when people abruptly discontinue their sleep medication, they can experience unpleasant withdrawal symptoms and increased insomnia (Lee-Chiong & Sateia, 2006). Fortunately, the newer generation of nonbenzodiazepine sedatives have reduced (but not eliminated) many of the problems associated with previous generations of sleeping pills (Sanger, 2004). People suffering from insomnia can also turn to melatonin, the hormone that has been used to treat jet lag (see pp. 154–155), which is available over the counter in the United States. Research indicates that melatonin can function as a mild sedative and that it has some value in the treatment of insomnia (Turek & Gillete, 2004).

Other Sleep Problems

Although insomnia is the most common difficulty associated with sleep, people are plagued by many other types of sleep problems as well. Let's briefly look at the symptoms, causes, and prevalence of three additional sleep problems, as described by Kryger, Roth, and Dement (2005) and Bootzin et al. (2001).

Narcolepsy is a disease marked by sudden and irresistible onsets of sleep during normal waking periods. A person suffering from narcolepsy goes directly from wakefulness into REM sleep, usually for a short period (10–20 minutes). This is a potentially dangerous condition, as some victims fall asleep instantly, even while walking across a room or driving a car (Pelayo & Lopes, 2006). Narcolepsy is relatively uncommon, as it is seen in only about 0.05% of the population (Partinen & Hublin, 2005). Its causes are not well understood, but some individuals appear to be genetically predisposed to the disease (Mignot, 2005). Stimulant drugs have been used to treat this condition with modest success (Guilleminault & Fromherz, 2005). But as you will see in our upcoming discussion of drugs, stimulants carry many problems of their own.

Sleep apnea involves frequent, reflexive gasping for air that awakens a person and disrupts sleep. Some victims are awakened from their sleep hundreds of times a night. Apnea occurs when a person literally stops breathing for a minimum of 10 seconds. This disorder, which is usually accompanied by loud snoring, is seen in about 2% of women and about 4% of men, with a higher incidence among older adults, postmenopausal women, and those who are obese (Sanders & Givelber, 2006). As you might expect, sleep apnea can have a disruptive effect on sleep, leading to excessive daytime sleepiness. Sleep apnea is a more serious disorder than widely appreciated because it increases vulnerability to hypertension, coronary disease, and stroke (Hahn, Olson, & Somers, 2006). Apnea may be treated via lifestyle modifications (weight loss, reduced alcohol intake,

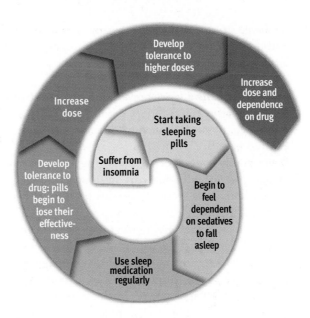

Figure 5.7
The vicious circle of dependence on sleeping pills. Because of the body's ability to develop tolerance to drugs, using sedatives routinely to "cure" insomnia can lead to a vicious circle of escalating dependency as larger and larger doses of the sedative are needed to produce the same effect.

web link 5.3

National Sleep Foundation
This attractive, well-organized website houses a great deal of information on sleep. Highlights include an interactive test to assess your sleep habits; electronic pamphlets on practical sleep topics, such as strategies for shift workers, the dangers of drowsy driving, and reducing jet lag; and extensive coverage of the full range of sleep disorders.

improved sleep hygiene), drug therapy, special masks and oral devices that improve airflow, and upper airway and craniofacial surgery (Phillips & Kryger, 2005; Strollo, Atwood, & Sanders, 2005).

Somnambulism, or sleepwalking, occurs when **a person arises and wanders about while remaining asleep.** About 15% of children and 3% of adults exhibit repetitive sleepwalking (Cartwright, 2006). Sleepwalking tends to occur during the first 3 hours of sleep, when individuals are in slow-wave sleep. Episodes may last from 15 seconds to 30 minutes (Aldrich, 2000). Sleepwalkers may awaken during their journey, or they may return to bed without any recollection of their excursion. The causes of this unusual disorder are unknown, although it appears to have a genetic predisposition (Keefauver & Guilleminault, 1994) and episodes may be more likely in people who use nonbenzodiazepine sedatives, especially Ambien (Gunn & Gunn, 2006). Sleepwalking does not appear to be a manifestation of underlying emotional or psychological problems (Mahowald,

1993). However, while sleepwalking, some people have engaged in inappropriate aggressive or sexual behavior (Cartwright, 2006). Sleepwalkers are prone to accidents, including life-threatening incidents (Gunn & Gunn, 2006). In this regard, contrary to popular myth, it is best to awaken people (gently) from a sleepwalking episode—awakening them is much safer than letting them wander about.

"Wait! Don't! It can be dangerous to wake them!"

REVIEW of Key Learning Goals

5.5 When people fall asleep, they pass through a series of stages in cycles of approximately 90 minutes. Slow-wave sleep consists of stages 3 and 4, during which delta waves are prominent. During the REM stage, sleepers experience rapid eye movements, brain waves that are characteristic of waking thought, and vivid dreaming. The sleep cycle tends to be repeated about four times a night, as REM sleep gradually becomes more predominant and NREM sleep dwindles. People vary somewhat in their signature sleep architecture.

5.6 The REM portion of sleep declines during childhood, leveling off at around 20%. During adulthood, slow-wave sleep tends to decline. Total sleep time decreases for most elderly people. Culture appears to have little impact on the physiological experience of sleep, but it does influence napping patterns and sleeping arrangements, such as co-sleeping. Hypotheses about the evolutionary bases of sleep focus on energy conservation, reduced exposure to predators, and restoration of resources depleted by waking activity.

5.7 The effects of sleep restriction depend on a variety of factors, but partial sleep deprivation tends to impair attention, motor coordination, decision making, and immune functioning. Increased sleepiness can be a significant problem that appears

to contribute to many transportation accidents and mishaps at work. Research on selective sleep deprivation suggests that people need REM sleep and slow-wave sleep. These stages of sleep may contribute to memory consolidation.

5.8 Short sleep duration is associated with a variety of health problems, including obesity, impaired immune function, and increased inflammation. People who sleep 7–8 hours per day have lower mortality rates than individuals who are long or short sleepers. Self-estimates of sleep duration may not be all that accurate.

5.9 Roughly 30%–35% of people suffer from insomnia, which is associated with impaired functioning, depression, and health problems. Sedative drugs can increase sleep time, but sleeping pills generally are a poor solution for insomnia. Sedatives can lead to overdose, dependency, and problems when sleep medication is discontinued.

5.10 Narcolepsy is an infrequent but dangerous disease marked by sudden, irresistible onsets of sleep during normal waking periods. Sleep apnea involves frequent gasping for air, which occurs when people stop breathing. It is a more serious disorder than widely appreciated. Somnambulism (sleepwalking) typically occurs during slow-wave sleep. Sleepwalkers are prone to accidents and should be awakened.

The World of Dreams

For the most part, dreams are not taken very seriously in Western societies. Paradoxically, though, Robert Van de Castle (1994) points out that dreams have sometimes changed the world. For example, Van de Castle describes how René Descartes's philosophy of dualism, Frederick Banting's discovery of insulin, Elias Howe's refinement of the sewing

machine, Mohandas Gandhi's strategy of nonviolent protest, and Lyndon Johnson's withdrawal from the 1968 U.S. presidential race were all inspired by dreams. He also explains how Mary Shelley's *Frankenstein* and Robert Louis Stevenson's *The Strange Case of Dr. Jekyll and Mr. Hyde* emerged out of their dream experiences. In his wide-ranging discussion,

Van de Castle also relates how the Surrealist painter Salvador Dali characterized his work as "dream photographs" and how legendary filmmakers Ingmar Bergman, Orson Welles, and Federico Fellini all drew on their dreams in making their films. Thus, Van de Castle concludes that "dreams have had a dramatic influence on almost every important aspect of our culture and history" (p. 10).

The Contents of Dreams

What do people dream about? Overall, dreams are not as exciting as advertised. Perhaps dreams are seen as exotic because people are more likely to remember their more bizarre nighttime dramas (De Koninck, 2000). After analyzing the contents of more than 10,000 dreams, Calvin Hall (1966) concluded that most dreams are relatively mundane. They tend to unfold in familiar settings with a cast of characters dominated by family, friends, and colleagues. People are more tolerant of logical discrepancies and implausible scenarios in their dreams than in their waking thought (Kahn, 2007), but in dreams they generally move through coherent virtual worlds with a coherent sense of self (Nielsen & Stenstrom, 2005).

Certain themes tend to be more common than others in dreams. **Figure 5.8** lists the most common dream themes reported by 1181 college students in a recent study of typical dream content (Nielsen et al., 2003). If you glance through this list, you will see that people dream quite a bit about sex, aggression, and misfortune. According to Hall, dreams tend to center on classic sources of internal conflict, such as the conflict between taking chances and playing it safe. Hall was struck by how little people dream about public affairs and current events. Typically, dreams are self-centered; people dream mostly about themselves.

Though dreams seem to belong in a world of their own, what people dream about is affected by what is going on in their lives (Kramer, 1994). If you're struggling with financial problems, worried about an upcoming exam, or sexually attracted to a classmate,

Rank	Dream content	Total prevalence
1	Chased or pursued, not physically injured	81.5
2	Sexual experiences	76.5
3	Falling	73.8
4	School, teachers, studying	67.1
5	Arriving too late, e.g., missing a train	59.5
6	Being on the verge of falling	57.7
7	A person now alive as dead	54.1
8	Trying again and again to do something	53.5
9	Flying or soaring through the air	48.3
10	Vividly sensing . . . a presence in the room	48.3
11	Failing an examination	45.0
12	Physically attacked (beaten, stabbed, raped)	42.4
13	Being frozen with fright	40.7
14	A person now dead as alive	38.4
15	Being a child again	36.7
16	Being killed	34.5
17	Swimming	34.3
18	Insects or spiders	33.8
19	Being nude	32.6
20	Being inappropriately dressed	32.5
21	Discovering a new room at home	32.3
22	Losing control of a vehicle	32.0
23	Eating delicious foods	30.7
24	Being half awake and paralyzed in bed	27.2
25	Finding money	25.7

Figure 5.8

Common themes in dreams. Studies of dream content find that certain themes are particularly common. The data shown here are from a study of 1181 college students in Canada (Nielsen et al., 2003). This list shows the 25 dreams most frequently reported by the students. Total prevalence refers to the percentage of students reporting each dream.

SOURCE: Nielsen, T. A., Zadra, A. L., Simard, V., Saucier, S., Stenstrom, P, Smith, C., & Kuiken, D. (2003). The typical dreams of Canadian university students. *Dreaming, 13,* 211–235. Copyright © 2003 Association for the Study of Dreams. [from Table 1, p. 217]

SLEEP DISORDER RESEARCH

ScienceCartoonsPlus.com

Sigmund Freud

"[Dreams are] the royal road to the unconscious."

National Library of Medicine

these themes may very well show up in your dreams. Freud noticed long ago that the contents of waking life tend to spill into dreams. He labeled this spill-over the *day residue.*

On occasion, the contents of dreams can also be affected by external stimuli experienced while one is dreaming (De Koninck, 2000). For example, William Dement sprayed water on one hand of sleeping subjects while they were in the REM stage (Dement & Wolpert, 1958). Subjects who weren't awakened by the water were awakened by the experimenter a short time later and asked what they had been dreaming about. Dement found that 42% of the participants had incorporated the water into their dreams. They said that they had dreamt that they were in rainfalls, floods, baths, swimming pools, and the like. Some people report that they occasionally experience the same phenomenon at home when the sound of their alarm clock fails to awaken them. The alarm is incorporated into their dream as a loud engine or a siren, for instance.

Culture and Dreams

Striking cross-cultural variations occur in beliefs about the nature of dreams and the importance attributed to them (Lohmann, 2007). In modern Western society, we typically make a distinction between the "real" world we experience while awake and the "imaginary" world we experience while dreaming. Some people realize that events in the real world can affect their dreams, but few believe that events in their dreams hold any significance for their waking life. Although a small minority of individuals take their dreams seriously, in Western cultures dreams are largely written off as insignificant and meaningless (Tart, 1988).

In many non-Western cultures, however, dreams are viewed as important sources of information about

oneself, about the future, or about the spiritual world (Kracke, 1991). Although no culture confuses dreams with waking reality, many view events in dreams as another type of reality that may be just as important as, or perhaps even more important than, events experienced while awake. In some instances, people are even held responsible for their dream actions. Among the New Guinea Arapesh, for example, an erotic dream about someone may be viewed as the equivalent of an adulterous act. In many cultures, dreams are seen as a window into the spiritual world, permitting communication with ancestors or supernatural beings (Bourguignon, 1972). People in some cultures believe that dreams provide information about the future—good or bad omens about upcoming battles, hunts, births, and so forth (Tedlock, 1992).

The tendency to remember one's dreams varies across cultures. In modern Western societies where little significance is attributed to dreams, dream recall tends to be mediocre. Many people remember their dreams only infrequently. In contrast, dream recall tends to be much better in cultures that take dreams seriously (Kracke, 1992). In regard to dream content, both similarities and differences occur across cultures in the types of dreams that people report (Domhoff, 2005b; Hunt, 1989). Some basic dream themes appear to be nearly universal (falling, being pursued, having sex). However, the contents of dreams vary some from one culture to another because people in different societies deal with different worlds while awake.

Theories of Dreaming

Many theories have been proposed to explain the purposes of dreaming. Sigmund Freud (1900), who analyzed clients' dreams in therapy, believed that the principal purpose of dreams is *wish fulfillment.* He thought that people fulfill ungratified needs from waking hours through wishful thinking in dreams. For example, if you were feeling unconscious guilt about being rude to a friend, you might dream about the incident in a way that renders you blameless. Freud asserted that the wish-fulfilling quality of many dreams may not be readily apparent because the unconscious attempts to censor and disguise the true meaning of dreams. Freud's influential theory sounded plausible when it was proposed over 100 years ago, but research has not provided much support for Freud's conception of dreaming (Fisher & Greenberg, 1996). That said, efforts are under way to modernize and rehabilitate the Freudian view of dreams (Solms, 2000b, 2004). Whether these efforts will prove to be influential remains to be seen.

Other theorists, such as Rosalind Cartwright, have proposed that dreams provide an opportunity to work through everyday problems (Cartwright, 1977; Cartwright & Lamberg, 1992). According to her cognitive, *problem-solving view,* there is considerable continuity between waking and sleeping thought. Proponents of this view believe that dreams allow people to engage in creative thinking about problems because dreams are not restrained by logic or realism. Recent research showing that REM sleep can enhance learning (Walker & Stickgold, 2004) adds new credibility to the problem-solving view of dreams (Cartwright, 2004).

J. Allan Hobson and colleagues argue that dreams are simply the by-product of bursts of activity emanating from subcortical areas in the brain. Their activation-synthesis model (Hobson & McCarley, 1977; McCarley, 1994) and its more recent revisions (Hobson, 2007; Hobson, Pace-Schott, & Stickgold, 2000) propose that dreams are side effects of the neural activation that produces the beta brain waves during REM sleep that are associated with wakefulness. According to this model, neurons firing periodically in lower brain centers (especially the pons) send random signals to the cortex (the seat of complex thought). The cortex supposedly synthesizes

(constructs) a dream to make sense out of these signals. In contrast to the theories of Freud and Cartwright, this theory obviously downplays the role of emotional factors as determinants of dreams. Like other theories of dreams, the activation-synthesis model has its share of critics. They point out that the model has a hard time accommodating the fact that dreaming occurs outside of REM sleep, that damage to the pons does not eliminate dreaming, and that the contents of dreams are considerably more meaningful than the model would predict (Domhoff, 2005a; Foulkes, 1996; Solms, 2000a).

These theories, which are summarized in **Figure 5.9**, are only three of numerous ideas about the functions of dreams. All of these theories are based more on conjecture than research. In part, this is because the private, subjective nature of dreams makes it difficult to put the theories to an empirical test. Thus, the purpose of dreaming remains a mystery.

We'll encounter more unsolved mysteries in the next two sections of this chapter as we discuss hypnosis and meditation. Whereas sleep and dreams are familiar to everyone, most people have little familiarity with hypnosis and meditation, which both involve deliberate efforts to temporarily alter consciousness.

Rosalind Cartwright

"One function of dreams may be to restore our sense of competence.... It is also probable that in times of stress, dreams have more work to do in resolving our problems and are thus more salient and memorable."

J. Allan Hobson

"Activation-synthesis ascribes dreaming to brain activation in sleep. The principal engine of this activation is the reticular formation of the brainstem."

Dreams as wish fulfillment (Freud)

The day residue shapes dreams that satisfy unconscious needs in a disguised fashion.

The problem-solving view (Cartwright)

We mull over major problems in our lives with reduced logical constraints.

Activation-synthesis model (Hobson)

The cortex constructs a story to make sense of internal signals from lower brain centers.

Figure 5.9

Three theories of dreaming. Dreams can be explained in a variety of ways. Freud stressed the wish-fulfilling function of dreams. Cartwright emphasizes the problem-solving function of dreams. Hobson asserts that dreams are merely a by-product of periodic neural activation. All three theories are speculative and have their critics.

REVIEW of Key Learning Goals

5.11 Dreams are not taken very seriously in Western cultures, but Van de Castle argues persuasively that dreams have influenced many important events. Dreams are not as bizarre as widely assumed, although people are more tolerant of logical discrepancies and implausible scenarios. People dream mostly about themselves. The content of one's dreams may be affected by what is going on in one's life and by external stimuli that are experienced during the dream.

5.12 In many non-Western cultures, dreams are viewed as important sources of information. Cultures vary in beliefs about

the nature of dreams, dream content, and dream interpretation. Dream recall tends to be greater in cultures that take dreams seriously.

5.13 Freud argued that the principal purpose of dreams is wish fulfillment. Cartwright has articulated a problem-solving view, which asserts that dreams allow people to engage in creative thinking. Hobson and colleagues assert that dreams are simple side effects of the neural activation seen during REM sleep that have relatively little meaning.

Hypnosis: Altered Consciousness or Role Playing?

Key Learning Goals

5.14 Discuss hypnotic susceptibility, and list some prominent effects of hypnosis.

5.15 Compare the role-playing and altered-state theories of hypnosis.

Hypnosis has a long and checkered history. It all began with a flamboyant 18th-century Austrian by the name of Franz Anton Mesmer. Working in Paris, Mesmer claimed to cure people of illnesses through an elaborate routine involving a "laying on of hands." Mesmer had some complicated theories about how he had harnessed "animal magnetism." However, we know today that he had simply stumbled onto the power of suggestion. Eventually he was dismissed as a charlatan and run out of town by the local authorities. Although officially discredited, Mesmer inspired followers—practitioners of "mesmerism"—who continued to ply their trade. To this day, our language preserves the memory of Franz Mesmer: When we are under the spell of an event or a story, we are "mesmerized."

Eventually, a Scottish physician, James Braid, became interested in the trancelike state that could be induced by the mesmerists. It was Braid who popularized the term *hypnotism* in 1843, borrowing it from the Greek word for sleep. Braid thought that hypnotism could be used to produce anesthesia for surgeries. However, just as hypnosis was catching on as a general anesthetic, more powerful and reliable chemical anesthetics were discovered, and interest in hypnotism dwindled.

Since then, hypnotism has led a curious dual existence. On the one hand, it has been the subject of numerous scientific studies. Furthermore, it has enjoyed considerable use as a clinical tool by physicians, dentists, and psychologists for over a century and has empirically supported value in the treatment of a variety of psychological and physical maladies (Lynn et al., 2000; Maldonado & Spiegel, 2003). On the other hand, an assortment of entertainers and quacks have continued in the less respectable tra-

dition of mesmerism, using hypnotism for parlor tricks and chicanery. It is little wonder, then, that many myths about hypnosis have come to be widely accepted (see **Figure 5.10**).

Hypnotic Induction and Phenomena

Hypnosis is a systematic procedure that typically produces a heightened state of suggestibility. It may also lead to passive relaxation, narrowed attention, and enhanced fantasy. If only in popular films, virtually everyone has seen a *hypnotic induction* enacted with a swinging pendulum. Actually, many techniques can be used (Meyer, 1992). Usually, the hypnotist will suggest to the subject that he or she is relaxing. Repetitively, softly, subjects are told that they are getting tired, drowsy, or sleepy. Often, the hypnotist vividly describes bodily sensations that should be occurring. Subjects are told that their arms are going limp, that their feet are getting warm, that their eyelids are getting heavy. Gradually, most subjects succumb and become hypnotized.

People differ in how well they respond to hypnotic induction. About 10%–20% of the population doesn't respond well at all. At the other end of the continuum, about 10%–15% of people are exceptionally good hypnotic subjects (Hilgard, 1965). As Kihlstrom (2007) notes, "the most dramatic phenomena of hypnosis—the ones that really count as reflecting alterations in consciousness—are generally observed in those 'hypnotic virtuosos' who comprise the upper 10 to 15 % of the distribution of hypnotizability" (p. 446). Among people who are susceptible to hypnosis, many interesting effects can be produced. Some of the more prominent hypnotic phenomena include:

web link 5.6

States of Consciousness

PsychWeb, Russ Dewey's (Georgia Southern University) superb resource page, hosts this fine collection of scientifically grounded guides to three topics that too often provoke nonsensical claims: hypnosis, out-of-body experiences, and dreaming.

1. *Anesthesia.* Drugs are more reliable, but hypnosis can be surprisingly effective in the treatment of both acute and chronic pain (Boly et al., 2007; Patterson & Jensen, 2003). Although the practice is not widespread, some physicians and dentists use hypnosis as a substitute for anesthetic drugs.

2. *Sensory distortions and hallucinations.* Hypnotized subjects may be led to experience auditory or visual hallucinations (Spiegel, 2003b). They may hear sounds or see things that are not there, or fail to hear or see stimuli that are present (Spiegel et al., 1985). Subjects may also have their sensations distorted so that something sweet tastes sour or an unpleasant odor smells fragrant.

3. *Disinhibition.* Hypnosis can sometimes reduce inhibitions that would normally prevent subjects from acting in ways that they would see as immoral or unacceptable. In experiments, hypnotized subjects have been induced to throw what they believed to be nitric acid into the face of a research assistant. Similarly, stage hypnotists are sometimes successful in getting people to disrobe in public. This disinhibition effect may occur simply because hypnotized people feel that they cannot be held responsible for their actions while they are hypnotized.

4. *Posthypnotic suggestions and amnesia.* Suggestions made during hypnosis may influence a participant's later behavior (Barnier, 2002). The most common posthypnotic suggestion is the creation of posthypnotic amnesia. That is, subjects are told that they will remember nothing that happened while they were hypnotized. Such subjects usually remember nothing, as ordered.

Theories of Hypnosis

Although a number of theories have been developed to explain hypnosis, it is still not well understood. One popular view is that hypnotic effects occur because participants are put into a special, altered state of consciousness, called a hypnotic trance (Christensen, 2005). Although hypnotized subjects may feel as though they are in an altered state, they do not seem to show reliable alterations in brain activity that are unique to hypnosis (Burgess, 2007; Lynn et al., 2007). The failure to find special changes in brain activity that are consistently associated with hypnosis has led some theorists to conclude that hypnosis is a normal state of consciousness that is characterized by dramatic role playing.

Hypnosis as Role Playing

The role-playing view asserts that hypnosis produces a normal mental state in which suggestible people act out the role of a hypnotic subject and behave as

Hypnosis: Myth and Reality	
If you think . . .	**The reality is . . .**
Relaxation is an important feature of hypnosis.	It's not. Hypnosis has been induced during vigorous exercise.
It's mostly just compliance.	Many highly motivated subjects fail to experience hypnosis.
It's a matter of willful faking.	Physiological responses indicate that hypnotized subjects generally are not lying.
It has something to do with a sleeplike state.	It does not. Hypnotized subjects are fully awake.
Responding to hypnosis is like responding to a placebo.	Placebo responsiveness and hypnotizability are not correlated.
People who are hypnotized lose control of themselves.	Subjects are perfectly capable of saying no or terminating hypnosis.
Hypnosis can enable people to "relive" the past.	Age-regressed adults behave like adults play-acting as children.
When hypnotized, people can remember more accurately.	Hypnosis may actually muddle the distinction between memory and fantasy and may artificially inflate confidence.
Hypnotized people do not remember what happened during the session.	Posthypnotic amnesia does not occur spontaneously.
Hypnosis can enable people to perform otherwise impossible feats of strength, endurance, learning, and sensory acuity.	Performance following hypnotic suggestions for increased muscle strength, learning and sensory acuity does not exceed what can be accomplished by motivated subjects outside hypnosis.

Figure 5.10

Misconceptions regarding hypnosis. Mistaken ideas about the nature of hypnosis are common. Some widely believed myths about hypnosis are summarized here, along with more accurate information on each point, based on an article by Michael Nash (2001), a prominent hypnosis researcher. Many of these myths and realities are discussed in more detail in the text.

they think hypnotized people are supposed to. Theodore Barber (1979), Nicholas Spanos (1986, 1991), and Irving Kirsch (2000; Kirsch & Lynn, 1998) have been the leading advocates of this view, which emphasizes the social context of hypnosis. According to this notion, it is subjects' role expectations that produce hypnotic effects, rather than a special trancelike state of consciousness.

Two lines of evidence support the role-playing view. First, many of the seemingly amazing effects of hypnosis have been duplicated by nonhypnotized subjects or have been shown to be exaggerated (Kirsch, 1997; Kirsch, Mazzoni, & Montgomery, 2007). For example, much has been made of the fact that hypnotized subjects can be used as "human planks" (see the photo on the next page), but it turns out that nonhypnotized subjects can easily match

Theodore Barber

"Thousands of books, movies, and professional articles have woven the concept of 'hypnotic trance' into the common knowledge. And yet there is almost no scientific support for it."

Some feats performed under hypnosis can be performed equally well by nonhypnotized subjects. Here "the Amazing Kreskin" demonstrates that proper positioning is the only requirement for the famous human plank feat.

Ernest Hilgard

"Many psychologists argue that the hypnotic trance is a mirage. It would be unfortunate if this skeptical view were to gain such popularity that the benefits of hypnosis are denied to the numbers of those who could be helped."

this and other hypnotic feats (Barber, 1986). This finding suggests that no special state of consciousness is required to explain hypnotic feats.

The second line of evidence involves demonstrations that hypnotized participants are often acting out a role. For example, Martin Orne (1951) regressed hypnotized subjects back to their sixth birthday and asked them to describe it. They responded with detailed descriptions that appeared to represent great feats of hypnosis-enhanced memory. However, instead of accepting this information at face value, Orne compared it with information that he had obtained from the participants' parents. It turned out that many of the subjects' memories were inaccurate and invented! Many other studies have also found that age-regressed subjects' recall of the distant past tends to be more fanciful than factual (Green, 1999). Thus, the role-playing explanation of hypnosis suggests that situational factors lead suggestible subjects to act out a certain role in a highly cooperative manner.

Hypnosis as an Altered State of Consciousness

Despite the doubts raised by role-playing explanations, many prominent theorists still maintain that hypnotic effects are attributable to a special, altered state of consciousness (Fromm, 1979, 1992; Hilgard, 1986; Naish, 2006; Spiegel, 1995, 2003a). These theorists argue that it is doubtful that role playing can explain all hypnotic phenomena. For instance, they assert that even the most cooperative subjects

are unlikely to endure surgery without a drug anesthetic just to please their physician and live up to their expected role. They also cite studies in which hypnotized participants have continued to display hypnotic responses when they thought they were alone and not being observed (Perugini et al., 1998). If hypnotized participants were merely acting, they would drop the act when alone. The most impressive research undermining the role-playing view has come from recent brain-imaging studies, which suggest that hypnotized participants experience changes in brain activity that appear consistent with their reports of hypnosis-induced hallucinations (Spiegel, 2003b) or pain suppression (Hofbauer et al., 2001).

The most influential explanation of hypnosis as an altered state of awareness has been offered by Ernest Hilgard (1986, 1992). According to Hilgard, hypnosis creates a *dissociation* in consciousness. ***Dissociation* is a splitting off of mental processes into two separate, simultaneous streams of awareness.** In other words, Hilgard theorizes that hypnosis splits consciousness into two streams. One stream is in communication with the hypnotist and the external world, while the other is a difficult-to-detect "hidden observer." Hilgard believes that many hypnotic effects are a product of this divided consciousness. For instance, he suggests that a hypnotized subject might appear unresponsive to pain because the pain isn't registered in the portion of consciousness that communicates with other people.

One appealing aspect of Hilgard's theory is that *divided consciousness* is a common, normal experience. For example, people will often drive a car a great distance, responding to traffic signals and other cars, with no recollection of having consciously done so. In such cases, consciousness is clearly divided between driving and the person's thoughts about other matters. Interestingly, this common experience has long been known as *highway hypnosis*. In summary, Hilgard presents hypnosis as a plausible variation in consciousness that has continuity with everyday experience.

John Kihlstrom (2007) takes the position that the role-playing and altered-state views of hypnosis are not entirely incompatible. He maintains that hypnotic phenomena involve both alterations in consciousness and complex social interactions that are shaped by role expectations. Kihlstrom (2005) also argues that the role-playing versus altered-state debate has been a "distraction." Although his view seems to have some merit, it appears likely that the grand debate of hypnosis will continue for the foreseeable future (Kirsch, 2004). As you will see momentarily, a similar debate has dominated the scientific discussion of meditation.

REVIEW of Key Learning Goals

5.14 Hypnosis has had a long and curious history since the era of mesmerism in the 18th century. People vary in their susceptibility to hypnosis. About 10%-15% of people are exceptionally good hypnotic subjects. Hypnosis can produce anesthesia, sensory distortions, disinhibition, and posthypnotic amnesia.

5.15 One approach to hypnosis is to view it as a normal state of consciousness in which subjects play the role of being hypnotized. Another approach asserts that hypnosis leads to an altered state in which consciousness is split into two dissociated streams of awareness. Kihlstrom argues that these opposing views of hypnosis are not entirely incompatible.

Meditation: Pure Consciousness or Relaxation?

Recent years have seen growing interest in the ancient discipline of meditation. *Meditation* refers to a family of practices that train attention to heighten awareness and bring mental processes under greater voluntary control. In North America, the most widely practiced approaches to meditation are those associated with yoga, Zen, and transcendental meditation (TM). All three are rooted in Eastern religions (Hinduism, Buddhism, and Taoism). However, meditation has been practiced throughout history as an element of all religious and spiritual traditions, including Judaism and Christianity (Walsh & Shapiro, 2006). Moreover, the practice of meditation can be largely divorced from religious beliefs. In fact, most Americans who meditate have only vague ideas regarding its religious significance. Of interest to psychology is the fact that meditation involves a deliberate effort to alter consciousness.

Most meditative techniques are deceptively simple. For example, in TM a person is supposed to sit in a comfortable position with eyes closed and silently focus attention on a *mantra*. A mantra is a specially assigned Sanskrit word that is personalized for each meditator. This exercise in mental self-discipline is to be practiced twice daily for about 20 minutes. The technique has been described as "diving from the active surface of the mind to its quiet depths" (Bloomfield & Kory, 1976, p. 49). Most proponents of TM believe that it involves an altered state of "pure consciousness." Many skeptics counter that meditation is simply an effective relaxation technique. Let's look at the evidence.

What happens when an experienced meditator goes into the meditative state? One intriguing finding is that alpha and theta waves become more prominent in EEG recordings (Cahn & Polich, 2006). Many studies also find that subjects' heart rate, skin conductance, respiration rate, oxygen consumption, and carbon dioxide elimination decline (see **Figure 5.11**; Dillbeck & Orme-Johnson, 1987; Fenwick,

1987; Travis, 2001). Taken together, these changes suggest that meditation leads to a potentially beneficial physiological state characterized by suppression of bodily arousal. However, some researchers have argued that a variety of systematic relaxation training procedures can produce similar results (Holmes, 1987; Shapiro, 1984). Mere relaxation hardly seems like an adequate explanation for the transcendent experiences reported by many meditators. Thus, debate continues about whether there are physiological changes associated with meditation that are unique to a special state of consciousness (Shear & Jevning, 1999; Travis & Pearson, 2000).

What about the long-term benefits that have been claimed for meditation? Research suggests that meditation may have some value in reducing the effects of stress (Grossman et al., 2004; Salmon et al., 2004). In particular, regular meditation is associated with lower levels of some "stress hormones" (Infante et al., 2001) and enhanced immune response

Key Learning Goals

5.16 Explain the nature of meditation, and describe its physiological correlates.

5.17 Assess the evidence on the long-term benefits of meditation.

Figure 5.11

The suppression of physiological arousal during transcendental meditation. The physiological changes shown in the graph are evidence of physical relaxation during the meditative state. However, critics argue that similar changes may also be produced by systematic relaxation procedures.

SOURCE: Adapted from Wallace, R. K., and Benson, H. (1972, February). The physiology of meditation, *Scientific American, 226*, 85–90. Graphic redrawn from illustration on p. 86 by Lorelle A. Raboni. Copyright © 1972 by Scientific American, Inc.

concept check 5.2

Relating EEG Activity to Variations in Consciousness

Early in the chapter we emphasized the intimate relationship between brain activity and variations in consciousness. Check your understanding of this relationship by indicating the kind of EEG activity (alpha, beta, theta, or delta) that would probably be dominant in each of the following situations. The answers are in Appendix A.

_____ 1. You are playing a video game.

_____ 2. You are deep in meditation.

_____ 3. You have just fallen asleep.

_____ 4. You are in the midst of a pleasant dream.

_____ 5. You are a novice typist, practicing your typing.

(Davidson et al., 2003a). Research also suggests that meditation can improve mental health while reducing anxiety and drug abuse (Alexander et al., 1994). Other studies report that meditation may have beneficial effects on self-esteem (Emavardhana & Tori, 1997), mood and one's sense of control (Easterlin & Cardena, 1999), depression (Kabat-Zinn, 2003), eating disorders (Kristeller, Baer, & Quillian-Wolever, 2006), and overall well-being (Reibel et al., 2001). In the physiological domain, research has suggested that meditation may help to control blood pressure (Barnes, Treiber, & Davis, 2001), improve cardiovascular health (Walton et al., 2004), and reduce chronic pain (Orme-Johnson et al., 2006). Finally, although more difficult to measure, some theorists assert that meditation can enhance human po-

tential by improving concentration, heightening awareness, building emotional resilience, and fostering moral maturity (Walsh & Shapiro, 2006). At first glance these results are impressive, but they need to be viewed with some caution. At least some of these effects may be just as attainable through systematic relaxation or other mental focusing procedures (Shapiro, 1984; Smith, 1975). Critics also wonder whether placebo effects, sampling bias, and other methodological problems may have exaggerated some of the reported benefits of meditation (Bishop, 2002; Canter, 2003; Caspi & Burleson, 2005).

In summary, it seems safe to conclude that meditation is a potentially worthwhile relaxation strategy. And it's entirely possible that meditation involves much more than mere relaxation, as meditation advocates insist. Certainly, it is hard to envision mere relaxation providing such a diverse constellation of benefits. At present, however, there is great debate about the notion that meditation produces a unique state of "pure consciousness" and healthy skepticism about some of its alleged long-term benefits.

REVIEW of Key Learning Goals

5.16 Meditation refers to a family of practices that train attention to heighten awareness and bring mental processes under greater voluntary control. Studies suggest that meditation leads to a potentially beneficial physiological state characterized by suppression of bodily arousal.

5.17 Evidence suggests that meditation may reduce stress hormones, enhance self-esteem and well-being, and reduce vulnerability to a variety of diseases. However, some critics suggest that these benefits are not unique to meditation and are a product of any effective relaxation procedure.

Altering Consciousness with Drugs

Key Learning Goals

5.18 Identify the major types of abused drugs and their main effects.

5.19 Understand why drug effects vary and how drugs affect the brain.

5.20 Contrast psychological and physical dependence.

5.21 Summarize evidence on the major health risks associated with drug abuse.

Like hypnosis and meditation, drugs are commonly used in deliberate efforts to alter consciousness. In this section, we focus on the use of drugs for nonmedical purposes, commonly referred to as "recreational drug use." Recreational drug use involves personal, moral, political, and legal issues that are not matters for science to resolve. However, the more knowledgeable you are about drugs, the more informed your decisions and opinions about them will be. Accordingly, this section describes the types of drugs that are most commonly used for recreational purposes and summarizes their effects on consciousness, behavior, and health.

Principal Abused Drugs and Their Effects

4c

The drugs that people use recreationally are termed *psychoactive*. *Psychoactive drugs* are chemical substances that modify mental, emotional, or behavioral functioning. Not all psychoactive drugs produce effects that lead to recreational use. Generally, users prefer drugs that elevate their mood or produce other pleasurable alterations in consciousness. The principal types of recreational drugs are described in **Table 5.2**. The table lists representative drugs in each of six categories. It also summarizes how the

Table 5.2 Psychoactive Drugs: Methods of Ingestion, Medical Uses, and Effects

Drugs	Methods of Ingestion	Principal Medical Uses	Desired Effects	Potential Short-Term Side Effects
Narcotics (opiates) Morphine Heroin	Injected, smoked, oral	Pain relief	Euphoria, relaxation, anxiety reduction, pain relief	Lethargy, drowsiness, nausea, impaired coordination, impaired mental functioning, constipation
Sedatives Barbiturates Benzodiazepines	Oral, injected	Sleeping pill, anticonvulsant	Euphoria, relaxation, anxiety reduction, reduced inhibitions	Lethargy, drowsiness, severely impaired coordination, impaired mental functioning, emotional swings, dejection
Stimulants Amphetamines Cocaine	Oral, sniffed, injected, freebased, smoked	Treatment of hyperactivity and narcolepsy, local anesthetic (cocaine only)	Elation, excitement, increased alertness, increased energy, reduced fatigue	Increased blood pressure and heart rate, increased talkativeness, restlessness, irritability, insomnia, reduced appetite, increased sweating and urination, anxiety, paranoia, increased aggressiveness, panic
Hallucinogens LSD Mescaline Psilocybin	Oral	None	Increased sensory awareness, euphoria, altered perceptions, hallucinations, insightful experiences	Dilated pupils, nausea, emotional swings, paranoia, jumbled thought processes, impaired judgment, anxiety, panic reaction
Cannabis Marijuana Hashish THC	Smoked, oral	Treatment of glaucoma and chemotherapy-induced nausea and vomiting; other uses under study	Mild euphoria, relaxation, altered perceptions, enhanced awareness	Elevated heart rate, bloodshot eyes, dry mouth, reduced short-term memory, sluggish motor coordination, sluggish mental functioning, anxiety
Alcohol	Drinking	None	Mild euphoria, relaxation, anxiety reduction, reduced inhibitions	Severely impaired coordination, impaired mental functioning, increased urination, emotional swings, depression, quarrelsomeness, hangover

drugs are taken, their medical uses, their effects on consciousness, and their common side effects (based on Julien, Advokat, & Comaty, 2008; Levinthal, 2008; Lowinson et al., 2005). The six categories of psychoactive drugs that we will focus on are narcotics, sedatives, stimulants, hallucinogens, cannabis, and alcohol. We will also discuss "ecstasy," which has surged in popularity in recent years.

Narcotics, or *opiates,* are drugs derived from opium that are capable of relieving pain. The main drugs in this category are heroin and morphine, although less potent opiates such as codeine, Demerol, and methadone are also abused. The emerging problem in this category is a new drug called oxycodone (trade name: OxyContin). It's time-release format was supposed to make it an effective analgesic with less potential for abuse than the other opiates (Cicero, Inciardi, & Munoz, 2005). But people quickly learned that they could grind it up and gain a powerful high, leading to a new epidemic of serious drug abuse, especially in rural areas of the United States (Tunnell, 2005). In sufficient dosages these drugs can produce an overwhelming sense of euphoria or well-being. This euphoric effect has a relaxing, "Who cares?" quality that makes the high an attractive escape from reality.

Sedatives are sleep-inducing drugs that tend to decrease central nervous system activation and behavioral activity. Historically, the most widely abused sedatives have been the *barbiturates.* But in recent decades stricter controls have reduced their availability and people have turned to the *benzodiazepine* sedatives, which, fortunately, have notably less appeal as a drug of abuse. People abusing sedatives, or "downers," generally consume larger doses than are prescribed for medical purposes. The desired effect is a euphoria similar to that produced by drinking large amounts of alcohol. Feelings of tension or dejection are replaced by a relaxed, pleasant state of intoxication, accompanied by loosened inhibitions.

Stimulants are drugs that tend to increase central nervous system activation and behavioral activity. Stimulants range from mild, widely available drugs, such as caffeine and nicotine, to stronger, carefully regulated ones, such as cocaine. We will focus on cocaine and amphetamines. Cocaine is a natural substance that comes from the coca shrub. In contrast, amphetamines ("speed") are synthesized in a pharmaceutical laboratory. Cocaine and amphetamines have fairly similar effects, except that cocaine produces a briefer high. Stimulants produce a euphoria very different from that created by narcotics or sedatives. They produce a buoyant, elated, energetic, "I can conquer the world!" feeling accompanied by increased alertness. In recent years, cocaine and amphetamines have become available in much more potent (and dangerous) forms than before. "Crack" consists of relatively pure chips of cocaine that are

web link 5.7

Web of Addictions

From the earliest days of the World Wide Web, this page at The Well has been regularly recognized as a primary source for accurate and responsible information about alcohol and other drugs.

"JUST TELL ME WHERE YOU KIDS GET THE IDEA TO TAKE SO MANY DRUGS."

Alcohol encompasses a variety of beverages containing ethyl alcohol, such as beers, wines, and distilled spirits. The concentration of ethyl alcohol varies from about 4% in most beers to 40% in 80-proof liquor—and occasionally more in higher-proof liquors. When people drink heavily, the central effect is a relaxed euphoria that temporarily boosts self-esteem, as problems seem to melt away and inhibitions diminish. Common side effects include impairments in mental and motor functioning, mood swings, and quarrelsomeness. Alcohol is the most widely used recreational drug in our society. Because alcohol is legal, many people use it casually without even thinking of it as a drug.

MDMA, or "ecstasy," is a compound drug that is related to both amphetamines and hallucinogens, especially mescaline. MDMA was originally formulated in 1912 but was not widely used in the United States until the 1990s, when ecstasy became popular in the context of "raves" and dance clubs. MDMA produces a short-lived high that typically lasts a few hours or more. Users report that they feel warm, friendly, euphoric, sensual, insightful, and empathetic, but alert and energetic. Problematic side effects include increased blood pressure, muscle tension, sweating, blurred vision, insomnia, and transient anxiety.

Factors Influencing Drug Effects

The drug effects summarized in **Table 5.2** are the *typical* ones. Drug effects can vary from person to person and even for the same person in different situations. The impact of any drug depends in part on the user's age, mood, motivation, personality, previous experience with the drug, body weight, and physiology. The dose and potency of a drug, the method of administration, and the setting in which a drug is taken also are likely to influence its effects (Leavitt, 1995). Our theme of *multifactorial causation* clearly applies to the effects of drugs.

So, too, does our theme emphasizing the *subjectivity of experience*. Expectations are potentially powerful factors that can influence the user's perceptions of a drug's effects. You may recall from the discussion of placebo effects in Chapter 2 that some people who are misled to *think* that they are drinking alcohol show signs of intoxication (Assefi & Garry, 2003). If people expect a drug to make them feel giddy, serene, or profound, their expectation may contribute to the feelings they experience.

A drug's effects can also change as the person's body develops a *tolerance* to the chemical. *Tolerance*

usually smoked. Amphetamines are increasingly sold as a crystalline powder, called "crank," or "crystal meth" (short for methamphetamine), that may be snorted or injected intravenously.

Hallucinogens are a diverse group of drugs that have powerful effects on mental and emotional functioning, marked most prominently by distortions in sensory and perceptual experience. The principal hallucinogens are LSD, mescaline, and psilocybin. These drugs have similar effects, although they vary in potency. Hallucinogens produce euphoria, increased sensory awareness, and a distorted sense of time. In some users, they lead to profound, dreamlike, "mystical" feelings that are difficult to describe. The latter effect is why they have been used in religious ceremonies for centuries in some cultures. Unfortunately, at the other end of the emotional spectrum hallucinogens can also produce nightmarish feelings of anxiety and paranoia, commonly called a "bad trip."

Cannabis is the hemp plant from which marijuana, hashish, and THC are derived. Marijuana is a mixture of dried leaves, flowers, stems, and seeds taken from the plant. Hashish comes from the plant's resin. Smoking is the usual route of ingestion for both marijuana and hashish. THC, the active chemical ingredient in cannabis, can be synthesized for research purposes (for example, to give to animals, which can't very well smoke marijuana). When smoked, cannabis has an immediate impact that may last several hours. The desired effects of the drug are a mild, relaxed euphoria and enhanced sensory awareness.

Table 5.3 Psychoactive Drugs: Tolerance, Dependence, Potential for Fatal Overdose, and Health Risks

Drugs	Tolerance	Risk of Physical Dependence	Risk of Psychological Dependence	Fatal Overdose Potential	Health Risks
Narcotics (opiates)	Rapid	High	High	High	Infectious diseases, accidents, immune suppression
Sedatives	Rapid	High	High	High	Accidents
Stimulants	Rapid	Moderate	High	Moderate to high	Sleep problems, malnutrition, nasal damage, hypertension, respiratory disease, stroke, liver disease, heart attack
Hallucinogens	Gradual	None	Very low	Very low	Accidents, acute panic
Cannabis	Gradual	None	Low to moderate	Very low	Accidents, lung cancer, respiratory disease, pulmonary disease, increased vulnerability to psychosis
Alcohol	Gradual	Moderate	Moderate	Low to high	Accidents, liver disease, malnutrition, brain damage, neurological disorders, heart disease, stroke, hypertension, ulcers, cancer, birth defects

refers to a progressive decrease in a person's responsiveness to a drug as a result of continued use. Tolerance usually leads people to consume larger and larger doses of a drug to attain the effects they desire. Most drugs produce tolerance, but some do so more rapidly than others. For example, tolerance to alcohol usually builds slowly, while tolerance to heroin increases much more quickly. **Table 5.3** indicates whether various categories of drugs tend to produce tolerance rapidly or gradually.

Mechanisms of Drug Action 4d

Most drugs have effects that reverberate throughout the body. However, psychoactive drugs work primarily by altering neurotransmitter activity in the brain. As we discussed in Chapter 3, *neurotransmitters* are chemicals that transmit signals between neurons at junctions called synapses.

The actions of amphetamines illustrate how drugs have selective, multiple effects on neurotransmitter activity. Amphetamines exert their main effects on two neurotransmitter systems: norepinephrine (NE) and dopamine (DA). Amphetamines appear to have two key effects at DA and NE synapses (Koob & Le Moal, 2006). First, they increase the release of dopamine and norepinephrine by presynaptic neurons. Second, they interfere with the reuptake of DA and NE from synaptic clefts. These actions serve to increase the levels of dopamine and norepinephrine at the affected synapses. Cocaine shares some of these actions, which is why cocaine and amphetamines produce similar stimulant effects.

Although specific drugs exert their initial effects in the brain on a wide variety of neurotransmitter systems, many theorists believe that virtually all abused drugs eventually increase activity in a particular neural pathway, called the mesolimbic dopamine pathway (Nestler & Malenka, 2004). This neural circuit—which runs from an area in the midbrain, through the nucleus accumbens, and on to the prefrontal cortex (see **Figure 5.12**)—has been characterized as a "reward pathway" (Pierce & Kumaresan, 2006). Large and rapid increases in the release of dopamine along this pathway are thought to be the neural basis of the reinforcing effects of most abused drugs (Volkow, Fowler, & Wang, 2004).

Figure 5.12

The "reward pathway" in the brain. The neural circuits shown here in blue make up the *mesolimbic dopamine pathway*. Axons in this pathway run from an area in the midbrain through the medial forebrain bundle to the *nucleus accumbens* and on to the prefrontal cortex. Recreational drugs affect a variety of neurotransmitter systems, but theorists believe that heightened dopamine activity in this pathway—especially the portion running from the midbrain to the nucleus accumbens—is responsible for the reinforcing effects of most abused drugs.

Dopamine projections to prefrontal cortex

Nucleus accumbens

Medial forebrain bundle (a path of axons that release dopamine)

Area in midbrain

Drug Dependence   4c

People can become either physically or psychologically dependent on a drug. Physical dependence is a common problem with narcotics, sedatives, and alcohol and is an occasional problem with stimulants. *Physical dependence* exists when a person must continue to take a drug to avoid withdrawal illness. The symptoms of withdrawal illness depend on the specific drug. Withdrawal from heroin, barbiturates, and alcohol can produce fever, chills, tremors, convulsions, vomiting, cramps, diarrhea, and severe aches and pains. Withdrawal from stimulants leads to a more subtle syndrome, marked by fatigue, apathy, irritability, depression, and disorientation.

Psychological dependence exists when a person must continue to take a drug to satisfy intense mental and emotional craving. Psychological dependence is more subtle than physical dependence, but the need it creates can be powerful. Cocaine, for instance, can produce an overwhelming psychological need for continued use. Psychological dependence is possible with all recreational drugs, although it seems rare for hallucinogens.

Both types of dependence are established gradually with repeated use of a drug. Drugs vary in their potential for creating either physical or psychological dependence. **Table 5.3** provides estimates of the risk of each kind of dependence for the six categories of recreational drugs covered in our discussion.

Drugs and Health   4c

Recreational drug use can affect physical health in a variety of ways. The three principal risks are overdose, tissue damage (direct effects), and health-impairing behavior that results from drug abuse (indirect effects).

Overdose   4c

Any drug can be fatal if a person takes enough of it, but some drugs are much more dangerous than others. **Table 5.3** shows estimates of the risk of accidentally consuming a *lethal* overdose of each listed drug. Drugs that are CNS depressants—sedatives, narcotics, and alcohol—carry the greatest risk of overdose. It's important to remember that these drugs are synergistic with each other, so many overdoses involve lethal *combinations* of CNS depressants. What happens when a person overdoses on these drugs? The respiratory system usually grinds to a halt, producing coma, brain damage, and death within a brief period. Fatal overdoses with CNS stimulants usually

In 2008, actor Heath Ledger died from an accidental overdose of prescription drugs. Subsequent investigation revealed that he had overmedicated himself in an effort to deal with chronic sleep problems. The toxicology report found traces of two narcotic painkillers, two antianxiety agents, and two sedative medications. His tragic death illustrates how dangerous combinations of CNS depressants can be.

involve a heart attack, stroke, or cortical seizure. Years ago, deaths attributable to overdoses of stimulant drugs used to be relatively infrequent. However, cocaine overdoses have increased sharply as more people have experimented with smoking crack and using other more dangerous modes of ingestion (Repetto & Gold, 2005).

Direct Effects   4c

In some cases, drugs cause tissue damage directly. For example, chronic snorting of cocaine can damage nasal membranes. Cocaine use can also foster cardiovascular disease and crack smoking is associated with a number of respiratory problems (Gold & Jacobs, 2005; Gourevitch & Arnsten, 2005). Long-term, excessive alcohol consumption is associated with an elevated risk for a wide range of serious health problems, including liver damage, ulcers, hypertension, stroke, heart disease, neurological disorders, and some types of cancer (Johnson & Ait-Daoud, 2005; Mack, Franklin, & Frances, 2003).

The health risks of marijuana have generated considerable debate in recent years. The available evidence suggests that chronic marijuana use increases the risk for respiratory and pulmonary disease (Aldington et al., 2007; Tashkin et al., 2002). Some studies have also found a link between long-term marijuana use and the risk for lung cancer, although the data are surprisingly inconsistent (Aldington et al., 2008; Mehra et al., 2006). Finally, there have been a rash of recent studies that report an unexpected link between cannabis use and severe, psychotic disorders, including schizophrenia (Degenhardt & Hall, 2006; DiForti et al., 2007). Obviously, the vast majority of marijuana users do not develop psychoses, but it appears that cannabis may trigger psychotic illness in individuals who have a genetic vulnerability to such disorders (D'Souza, 2007; Murray et al., 2007). Although these dangers are real, some other widely publicized dangers have been exaggerated by the popular press. For instance, contrary to popular reports, it appears that cannabis does *not* produce meaningful reductions in immune system responding (Bredt et al., 2002; Klein, Friedman, & Specter, 1998) or any significant effects on male smokers' fertility or sexual functioning (Grinspoon, Bakalar, & Russo, 2005).

Indirect Effects 4c

The negative effects of drugs on physical health are often indirect results of the drugs' impact on behavior. For instance, people using stimulants often do not eat or sleep properly. Sedatives increase the risk of accidental injuries because they severely impair motor coordination. People who abuse downers often trip down stairs, fall off stools, and suffer other mishaps. Many drugs, such as marijuana, impair driving ability, increasing the risk of automo-

concept check 5.3

Recognizing the Unique Characteristics of Commonly Abused Drugs

From our discussion of the principal psychoactive drugs, it is clear that considerable overlap exists among the categories of drugs in terms of their methods of ingestion, medical uses, desired effects, and short-term side effects. Each type of drug, however, has at least one or two characteristics that make it different from the other types. Check your understanding of the unique characteristics of each type of drug by indicating which of them has the characteristics listed below. Choose from the following: (a) narcotics, (b) sedatives, (c) stimulants, (d) hallucinogens, (e) cannabis, and (f) alcohol. You'll find the answers in Appendix A.

_____ **1.** Increases alertness and energy, reduces fatigue.

_____ **2.** No recognized medical use. May lead to insightful or "mystical" experiences.

_____ **3.** Used as a "sleeping pill" because it reduces CNS activity.

_____ **4.** Increases one's risk for a number of diseases, including liver disease and neurological disorders.

_____ **5.** Derived from opium; used for pain relief.

_____ **6.** One likely health risk is respiratory and pulmonary disease.

bile accidents (Ramaekers et al., 2004). Alcohol, for instance, may contribute to roughly 40% of all automobile fatalities (Hingson & Sleet, 2006). Intravenous drug users risk contracting infectious diseases that can be spread by unsterilized needles. In recent years, acquired immune deficiency syndrome (AIDS) has been transmitted at an alarming rate through the population of intravenous drug users (Des Jarlais, Hagan, & Friedman, 2005).

The major health risks (other than overdose) of various recreational drugs are listed in the sixth column of **Table 5.3**. As you can see, alcohol appears to have the most diverse negative effects on physical health. The irony, of course, is that alcohol is the only recreational drug listed that is legal.

REVIEW of Key Learning Goals

5.18 The principal categories of abused drugs are narcotics, sedatives, stimulants, hallucinogens, cannabis, and alcohol. Narcotics are opium derivatives that are capable of relieving pain. Sedatives decrease CNS activity, whereas stimulants increase activation in the central nervous system. Hallucinogens produce emotional changes and distortions in sensory experience. Cannabis use is associated with relaxed euphoria and enhanced sensory awareness. Alcohol produces a mild euphoria accompanied by reduced inhibitions.

5.19 Although it's possible to describe the typical effects of various drugs, the actual effects on any individual depend on a host of factors, including subjective expectations and tolerance to the drug. Psychoactive drugs exert their main effects in the brain, where they selectively alter neurotransmitter activity at synaptic sites in a variety of ways. For example, amphetamines increase the release of DA and NE and slow reuptake at DA and NE synapses. The mesolimbic dopamine pathway may mediate the reinforcing effects of most abused drugs.

5.20 Physical dependence exists when people must continue drug use to avoid withdrawal. Psychological dependence involves intense mental and emotional craving for a drug. Both types of dependence develop gradually with continued use of a drug.

5.21 Recreational drug use can prove harmful to health by producing an overdose, by causing tissue damage, or by increasing health-impairing behavior. The chances of accidentally consuming a lethal overdose are greatest for the CNS depressants and cocaine. Direct tissue damage occurs most frequently with alcohol and cocaine. Cannabis may increase risk for respiratory disease, lung cancer, and psychotic disorders, but some other concerns appear to be exaggerated. Many drugs impair driving ability and increase automobile accidents.

Key Learning Goals

5.22 Identify the five unifying themes highlighted in this chapter.

Sociohistorical Context

Subjectivity of Experience

Cultural Heritage

Multifactorial Causation

Theoretical Diversity

Reflecting on the Chapter's Themes

This chapter highlighted five of our unifying themes. First, we saw how psychology evolves in a sociohistorical context. Research on consciousness dwindled to almost nothing after John B. Watson (1913, 1919) and others redefined psychology as the science of behavior. However, in the 1960s, people began to turn inward, showing a new interest in altering consciousness through drug use, meditation, hypnosis, and biofeedback. Psychologists responded to these social trends by beginning to study variations in consciousness in earnest. This shift shows how social forces can have an impact on psychology's evolution.

A second theme that surfaced in this chapter is the idea that people's experience of the world is highly subjective. We encountered this theme toward the end of the chapter when we discussed the subjective nature of drug effects, noting that the alterations of consciousness produced by drugs depend significantly on personal expectations.

Third, we saw once again how culture molds some aspects of behavior. Although the basic physiological process of sleep appears largely invariant from one society to another, culture influences certain aspects of sleep habits and has a dramatic impact on whether people remember their dreams and how they interpret and feel about their dreams. If not for space constraints, we might also have discussed cross-cultural differences in patterns of recreational drug use, which vary considerably from one society to the next.

Fourth, we learned once again that behavior is governed by multifactorial causation. For example, we discussed how the effects of jet lag, sleep deprivation, and psychoactive drugs depend on a number of interacting factors.

Finally, the chapter illustrated psychology's theoretical diversity. We discussed conflicting theories about dreams, hypnosis, meditation, and the evolutionary bases of sleep and consciousness. For the most part, we did not see any of the opposing theories converging toward reconciliation, as we did in the previous chapter. However, it's important to emphasize that rival theories do not always merge neatly into tidy models

concept check 5.4

Identifying the Contributions of Major Theorists and Researchers

Check your recall of the principal ideas of important theorists and researchers covered in this chapter by matching the people listed on the left with the appropriate contributions described on the right. If you need help, the crucial pages describing each person's ideas are listed in parentheses. Fill in the letters for your choices in the spaces provided on the left. You'll find the answers in Appendix A.

Major Theorists and Researchers

_____ **1.** Rosalind Cartwright (p. 167)

_____ **2.** William Dement (pp. 151, 156, 161)

_____ **3.** Sigmund Freud (pp. 152, 166, 181)

_____ **4.** Ernest Hilgard (p. 170)

_____ **5.** J. Alan Hobson (p. 167)

_____ **6.** William James (p. 152)

Key Ideas and Contributions

a. According to this theorist's view, the principal purpose of dreams is wish fulfillment. He also distinguished between the manifest content and latent content of dreams.

b. According to this theorist's activation-synthesis model, dreams are side effects of the neural activation that produces beta waves during REM sleep.

c. This theorist emphasized that the contents of consciousness are always changing. He referred to this continuous flow of thought as the *stream of consciousness*.

d. According to this theorist's cognitive, problem-solving view, dreams provide an opportunity to work through everyday problems unrestrained by logic.

e. This person contributed to the discovery of REM sleep. He has also argued that chronic sleep deprivation is a major problem in modern society.

f. This theorist uses the concept of dissociation to explain many of the effects of hypnosis.

of behavior. While it's always nice to resolve a theoretical debate, the debate itself can advance knowledge by stimulating and guiding empirical research.

Indeed, our upcoming Personal Application demonstrates that theoretical debates need not be resolved in order to advance knowledge. Many theoretical controversies and enduring mysteries remain in the study of sleep and dreams. Nonetheless, researchers have accumulated a great deal of practical information on these topics, which we'll discuss next.

Addressing Practical Questions About Sleep and Dreams

Indicate whether the following statements are "true" or "false."

____ **1** Naps rarely have a refreshing effect.

____ **2** Some people never dream.

____ **3** When people cannot recall their dreams, it's because they are trying to repress them.

These assertions were drawn from the Sleep and Dreams Information Questionnaire (Palladino & Carducci, 1984), which measures practical knowledge about sleep and dreams. Are they true or false? You'll see in this Application.

Common Questions About Sleep

How much sleep do people need? The average amount of daily sleep for young adults is 7.5 hours. However, people vary considerably in how long they sleep. Based on a synthesis of data from many studies, Webb (1992b) estimates that sleep time is distributed as shown in **Figure 5.13**. These data suggest that sleep needs vary from person to person. That said, many sleep experts believe that most people would function more effectively if they increased their amount of sleep (Banks & Dinges, 2007; Maas, 1998). Bear in mind, too, that research suggests that people who sleep 7–8 hours per night have the lowest mortality rates (Patel et al., 2004; Tamakoshi et al., 2004).

Can short naps be refreshing? Some naps are beneficial and some are not. The effectiveness of napping varies from person to person. Also, the benefits of any specific nap depend on the time of day and the amount of sleep one has had recently (Dinges, 1993). In general, naps are not a very efficient way to sleep because you're often just getting into the deeper stages of sleep when your nap time is up. Nonetheless, naps can enhance subsequent alertness and task performance and reduce sleepiness (Takahashi & Kaida, 2006). Many highly productive people, including Thomas Edison, Winston Churchill, and John F. Kennedy, have made effective use of naps. In conclusion, naps can be refreshing for many people, so the first statement opening this Application is false.

What is the significance of snoring? Snoring is a common phenomenon that is seen in roughly 30%–40% of adults (Hoffstein, 2005). Snoring increases after age 35, occurs in men more than women, and is more common among people who are overweight (Kryger, 1993; Stoohs et al., 1998). Many factors, including obesity, colds, allergies, smoking, and some drugs, can contribute to snoring, mainly by forcing people to breathe through their mouths while sleeping. Some people who snore loudly disrupt their own sleep as well as that of their bed

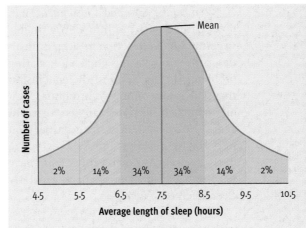

Figure 5.13

Variation in sleep needs. Based on data from a variety of sources, Webb (1992b) **estimates that average sleep length among young adults is distributed normally, as shown here. These data suggest that some people need more or less sleep than others. However, most sleep experts agree that a great many people could benefit from longer sleep.**

SOURCE: Adapted from Webb, W. B. (1992). *Sleep, the gentle tyrant* (2nd Ed.). Bolton, MA: Anchor Publishing. Copyright © 1992 by Anker Publishing Co. Adapted by permission.

partners. It can be difficult to prevent snoring in some people, whereas other people can reduce their snoring by losing weight or sleeping on their side instead of their back (Lugaresi et al., 1994). Snoring may seem like a trivial problem, but it is associated with sleep apnea and cardiovascular disease, and it may have more medical significance than most people realize (Dement & Vaughn, 1999; Olson & Park, 2006).

What can be done to avoid sleep problems? There are many ways to improve your chances of getting satisfactory sleep (see **Figure 5.14**). Most of them involve developing sensible daytime habits that won't interfere with sleep (see Foldvary-Schaefer, 2006; Maas, 1998; Stepanski & Wyatt, 2003). For example, if you've been having trouble sleeping at night, it's a good idea to avoid daytime naps, so that you'll be tired when bedtime arrives. Some people find that daytime exercise helps them fall asleep more readily at bedtime (King et al., 1997).

It's wise to minimize consumption of stimulants such as caffeine and nicotine. Because coffee and cigarettes aren't prescription

People typically get very upset when they have difficulty falling asleep. Unfortunately, this emotional distress tends to make it even harder for people to get to sleep.

1. Reduce stress as much as possible.
2. Exercise to stay fit.
3. Keep mentally stimulated during the day.
4. Eat a proper diet.
5. Stop smoking.
6. Reduce caffeine intake.
7. Avoid alcohol near bedtime.
8. Take a warm bath before bed.
9. Maintain a relaxing atmosphere in the bedroom.
10. Establish a bedtime ritual.
11. Have pleasurable sexual activity.
12. Clear your mind at bedtime.
13. Try some bedtime relaxation techniques.
14. Avoid trying too hard to get to sleep.
15. Learn to value sleep.

Figure 5.14
Suggestions for better sleep. In his book *Power Sleep,* **James Maas (1998) offers this advice for people concerned about enhancing their sleep. Maas argues convincingly that good daytime habits can make all the difference in the world to the quality of one's sleep.**

SOURCE: Adapted from Maas, J. B. (1998). *Power sleep.* New York: Random House. Copyright © 1998 by James B. Maas, Ph.D. Reprinted by permission of Villard Books, a division of Random House, Inc.

drugs, people don't appreciate how much the stimulants they contain can heighten physical arousal. Many foods (such as chocolate) and beverages (such as cola drinks) contain more caffeine than people realize. Also, bear in mind that ill-advised eating habits can interfere with sleep. Try to avoid going to bed hungry, uncomfortably stuffed, or soon after eating foods that disagree with you. It's also a good idea to try to establish a reasonably regular bedtime. This habit will allow you to take advantage of your circadian rhythm, so you'll be trying to fall asleep when your body is primed to cooperate.

What can be done about insomnia? First, don't panic if you run into a little trouble sleeping. An overreaction to sleep difficulties can begin a vicious circle of escalating problems. If you jump to the conclusion that you are becoming an insomniac, you may approach sleep with anxiety that will aggravate the problem. The harder you work at falling asleep, the less success you're likely to have. As noted earlier, temporary sleep problems are common and generally clear up on their own.

One sleep expert, Dianne Hales (1987), lists 101 suggestions for combating insomnia in her book *How to Sleep Like a Baby.*

Many involve "boring yourself to sleep" by playing alphabet games, reciting poems, or listening to your clock. Another recommended strategy is to engage in some not-so-engaging activity. For instance, you might try reading your dullest textbook. It could turn out to be a superb sedative.

It's often a good idea to simply launch yourself into a pleasant daydream. This normal presleep process can take your mind off your difficulties. Whatever you think about, try to avoid ruminating about the current stresses and problems in your life. Research has shown that the tendency to ruminate is one of the key factors contributing to insomnia (Kales et al., 1984). Anything that relaxes you—whether it's music, meditation, prayer, a warm bath, or a systematic relaxation procedure—can aid you in falling asleep.

Common Questions About Dreams

Does everyone dream? Yes. Some people just don't remember their dreams. However, when these people are brought into a sleep lab and awakened from REM sleep, they report hav-

FRANK AND ERNEST

FRANK AND ERNEST © 2006 Byb Thaves/
Distributed by Newspaper Enterprise
Association, Inc.

ing been dreaming—much to their surprise (statement 2 at the start of this Application is false). Scientists have studied a small number of people who have sustained brain damage in the area of the pons that has wiped out their REM sleep, but even these people report dreams (Klosch & Kraft, 2005).

Why don't some people remember their dreams? The evaporation of dreams appears to be quite normal. Given the lowered level of awareness during sleep, it's understandable that memory for dreams is mediocre. Dream recall is best when people are awakened during or soon after a dream (Goodenough, 1991). Most of the time, people who *do* recall dreams upon waking are remembering either their *last* dream from their final REM period or a dream that awakened them earlier in the night. Hobson's (1989) educated guess is that people probably forget 95%–99% of their dreams. This forgetting is natural and is not due to repression (statement 3 is also false). People who never remember their dreams probably have a sleep pattern that puts too much time between their last REM/dream period and awakening, so even their last dream is forgotten.

Do dreams require interpretation? Yes, but interpretation may not be as difficult as generally assumed. People have long believed that dreams are symbolic and that it is necessary to interpret the symbols to understand the meaning of dreams. Freud, for instance, made a distinction between the *manifest content* and the *latent content* of a dream. The **manifest content** consists of the plot of a dream at a surface level. The **latent content** refers to the hidden or disguised meaning of the events in the plot. Thus, a Freudian therapist might equate such dream events as walking into a tunnel, mounting a horse, or riding a roller coaster with sexual intercourse. Freudian theorists assert that dream interpretation is a complicated task requiring considerable knowledge of symbolism.

However, many dream theorists argue that symbolism in dreams is less deceptive and mysterious than Freud thought (Faraday, 1974; Foulkes, 1985; Hall, 1979). Calvin Hall makes the point that dreams require some interpretation simply because they are more visual than verbal. That is, pictures need to be translated into ideas. According to Hall, dream symbolism is highly

personal and the dreamer may be the person best equipped to decipher a dream. Unfortunately, you'll never know whether you're "correct," because there is no definitive way to judge the validity of different dream interpretations.

Could a shocking dream be fatal? According to folklore, if you fall from a height in a dream, you'd better wake up on the plunge downward, because if you hit the bottom the shock to your system will be so great that you will actually die in your sleep. Think about this one for a moment. *If it were a genuine problem, who would have reported it?* You can be sure that no one has ever testified to experiencing a fatal dream. This myth presumably exists because many people do awaken during the downward plunge, thinking they've averted a close call. A study by Barrett (1988–1989) suggests that dreams of one's own death are relatively infrequent. However, people do have such dreams—and live to tell about them.

Key Learning Goals

5.25 Recognize the influence of definitions and understand the nominal fallacy.

Is Alcoholism a Disease? The Power of Definitions

Alcoholism is a major problem in most—perhaps all—societies. It destroys countless lives, tears families apart, and is associated with an elevated risk for a variety of physical maladies (Johnson & Ait-Daoud, 2005). With roughly 15 million problem drinkers in the United States (Mack et al., 2003), it seems likely that alcoholism has touched the lives of a majority of Americans.

In almost every discussion about alcoholism someone will ask, "Is alcoholism a disease?" If alcoholism is a disease, it is a strange one, because the alcoholic is the most direct cause of his or her own sickness. If alcoholism is *not* a disease, what else might it be? Over the course of history, alcoholism has been categorized under many labels, from a personal weakness to a crime, a sin, a mental disorder, and a physical illness (Meyer, 1996). Each of these definitions carries important personal, social, political, and economic implications.

Consider, for instance, the consequences of characterizing alcoholism as a disease. If that is the case, alcoholics should be treated like diabetics, heart patients, or victims of other physical illnesses. That is, they should be viewed with sympathy and should be given appropriate medical and therapeutic interventions to foster recovery from their illness. These treatments should be covered by medical insurance and delivered by health care professionals. Just as important, if alcoholism is defined as a disease, it should lose much of its stigma. After all, we don't blame people with diabetes or heart disease for their illnesses. Yes, alcoholics admittedly contribute to their own disease (by drinking too much), but so do many victims of diabetes and heart disease who eat all the wrong foods, fail to control their weight, and so forth (McLellan et al., 2000). And, as is the case with many physical illnesses, one can inherit a genetic vulnerability to alcoholism (Lin & Anthenelli, 2005),

so it is difficult to argue that alcoholism is caused solely by one's behavior.

Alternatively, if alcoholism is defined as a personal failure or a moral weakness, alcoholics are less likely to be viewed with sympathy and compassion. They might be admonished to quit drinking, put in prison, or punished in some other way. These responses to their alcoholism would be administered primarily by the legal system rather than the health care system, as medical interventions are not designed to remedy moral failings. Obviously, the interventions that would be available would not be covered by health insurance, which would have enormous financial repercussions (for both health care providers and alcoholics).

The key point here is that definitions lie at the center of many complex debates, and they can have profound and far-reaching implications. People tend to think of definitions as insignificant, arbitrary sets of words found buried in the obscurity of thick dictionaries compiled by ivory tower intellectuals. Much of this characterization may be accurate, but definitions are not insignificant. They are vested with enormous power to shape how people think about important issues. And an endless array of issues boil down to matters of definition. For example, the next time you hear people arguing over whether a particular movie is pornographic, whether the death penalty is cruel and unusual punishment, or whether spanking is child abuse, you'll find it helps to focus the debate on clarifying the definitions of the crucial concepts.

The Power to Make Definitions

So, how can we resolve the debate about whether alcoholism is a disease? Scientists generally try to resolve their debates by conducting research to achieve a better understanding of the phenomena under study. You may have noticed already that "we need more research on this issue" is a frequent refrain in this text. Is more research the answer in this case? For once, the answer is "no." There is no conclusive way to deter-

mine whether alcoholism is a disease. It is not as though there is a "right" answer to this question that we can discover through more and better research.

The question of whether alcoholism is a disease is a *matter of definition:* Does alcoholism fit the currently accepted definition of what constitutes a disease? If you consult medical texts or dictionaries, you will find that disease is typically defined as *an impairment in the normal functioning of an organism that alters its vital functions.* Given that alcoholism clearly impairs people's normal functioning and disrupts a variety of vital functions (see **Figure 5.15**), it seems reasonable to characterize it as a disease, and this view has been the dominant one in the United States since the middle of the 20th century (Maltzman, 1994; Meyer, 1996). This view has only been strengthened by recent evidence that addiction to alcohol (and other drugs) is the result of dysregulation in key neural circuits in the brain (Cami & Farre, 2003). Still, many critics express vigorous doubts about the wisdom of defining alcoholism as a disease (Peele, 1989, 2000). They often raise a question that comes up frequently in arguments about definitions: Who should have the power to make the definition? In this case, the power lies in the hands of the medical community, which seems sensible, given that disease is a medical concept. But some critics argue that the medical community has a strong bias in favor of defining conditions as diseases because doing so creates new markets and fuels economic growth for the health industry (Nikelly, 1994). Thus, debate about whether alcoholism is a disease seems likely to continue for the indefinite future.

To summarize, definitions generally do not emerge out of research. They are typically crafted by experts or authorities in a specific field who try to reach a consensus about how to best define a particular concept. Thus, in analyzing the validity of a definition, you need to look not only at the definition itself but at where it came from. Who decided what the definition should be? Does the source of the definition seem legitimate and appropriate? Did the author-

Figure 5.15

Physiological malfunctions associated with alcoholism. This chart amply demonstrates that alcoholism is associated with a diverse array of physiological maladies. In and of itself, however, this information does not settle the argument about whether alcoholism should be regarded as a disease. It all depends on one's definition of what constitutes a disease.

SOURCE: Edlin, G. and Golanty, E. (1992). *Health and wellness: A holistic approach.* Boston: Jones & Bartlett. Copyright © 1992 by Jones & Bartlett Publishers, Inc., Sudbury, MA. www.jbpub.com. Reprinted by permission.

Table 5.4 Critical Thinking Skills Discussed in This Application

Skill	Description
Understanding the way definitions shape how people think about issues	The critical thinker appreciates the enormous power of definitions and the need to clarify definitions in efforts to resolve disagreements.
Identifying the source of definitions	The critical thinker recognizes the need to determine who has the power to make specific definitions and to evaluate their credibility.
Avoiding the nominal fallacy in working with definitions and labels	The critical thinker understands that labels do not have explanatory value.

ities who formulated the definition have any biases that should be considered?

Definitions, Labels, and Circular Reasoning

One additional point about definitions is worth discussing. Perhaps because definitions are imbued with so much power, people have an interesting tendency to incorrectly use them as *explanations* for the phenomena they describe. This logical error, which equates *naming* something with *explaining* it, is sometimes called the *nominal fallacy*. Names and labels that are used as explanations often sound quite reasonable at first. *But definitions do not really have any explanatory value; they simply specify what certain terms mean.* Consider an example. Let's say your friend, Frank, has a severe drinking problem. You are sitting around with some other friends discussing why Frank drinks so much. Rest assured, at least one of these friends will assert that "Frank drinks too much because he is an alcoholic." This is *circular reasoning,* which is just as useless as explaining that Frank is an alcoholic because he drinks too much. It tells us nothing about *why* Frank has a drinking problem.

The diagnostic labels that are used in the classification of mental disorders—labels such as schizophrenia, depression, autism, and obsessive-compulsive disorder (see Chapter 13)—also seem to invite this type of circular reasoning. For example, people often say things like "That person is delusional because she is schizophrenic," or "He is afraid of small, enclosed places because he is claustrophobic." These statements may sound plausible, but they are no more logical or insightful than saying "She is a redhead because she has red hair." The logical fallacy of mistaking a label for an explanation will get us as far in our understanding as a dog gets in chasing its own tail.

> **REVIEW of Key Learning Goals**
>
> **5.25** Like many questions, the issue of whether alcoholism should be regarded as a disease is a matter of definition. In evaluating the validity of a definition, one should look not only at the definition but also at where it came from. People have a tendency to use definitions as explanations for the phenomena they describe, but this fallacy involves circular reasoning.

On the Nature of Consciousness

❚ Consciousness is the continually changing stream of mental activity. Variations in consciousness are related to brain activity, as measured by the EEG. Consciousness clearly is adaptive, but the question of exactly why it evolved is open to debate.

Biological Rhythms and Sleep

❚ Sleep is influenced by biological rhythms, especially 24-hour circadian rhythms. Exposure to light resets biological clocks by affecting the activity of the suprachiasmatic nucleus and the pineal gland, which secretes melatonin.

❚ Being out of sync with circadian rhythms is one reason for jet lag and for the unpleasant nature of rotating shift work. Melatonin may have some value in treating jet lag. The negative effects of rotating shifts may be reduced by bright light administration or circadian-friendly scheduling.

The Sleep and Waking Cycle

❚ When you fall asleep, you pass through a series of stages in cycles of approximately 90 minutes. During the REM stage you experience rapid eye movements, a brain wave that is characteristic of waking thought, and the bulk of one's dreaming. The sleep cycle tends to be repeated about four times in a night, as REM sleep gradually becomes more predominant and NREM sleep dwindles.

❚ The REM portion of sleep declines during childhood, leveling off at around 20% during adolescence. During adulthood, slow-wave sleep declines. Culture appears to have little impact on the architecture of sleep, but it does influence sleeping arrangements and napping patterns. Hypotheses about the evolutionary bases of sleep focus on energy conservation, reduced exposure to predators, and restoration of depleted resources.

❚ Partial sleep deprivation can be a significant problem that appears to contribute to many transportation accidents and mishaps at work. Research on selective sleep deprivation suggests that people need REM sleep and slow-wave sleep. Short sleep duration is associated with a variety of health problems. People who sleep 7–8 hours per day have lower mortality rates than individuals who are long or short sleepers.

❚ Insomnia involves three distinct patterns of sleep difficulty. Sleeping pills generally are a poor solution for insomnia. Other common sleep disorders include narcolepsy, sleep apnea, and somnambulism.

The World of Dreams

❚ Research on dream content indicates that dreams are not as exotic as widely believed, although certain themes are particularly common. The content of one's dreams may be affected by events in one's life and by external stimuli that are experienced during the dream.

❚ Dramatic variations occur across cultures in beliefs about the nature of dreams and their importance, dream recall, dream content, and dream interpretation. The Freudian, cognitive, and activation-synthesis theories of dreaming are all very interesting, but scientists do not really know why people dream.

Hypnosis: Altered Consciousness or Role Playing?

❚ People vary in their susceptibility to hypnosis. Among other things, hypnosis can produce anesthesia, sensory distortions, disinhibition, and posthypnotic amnesia.

Theories of hypnosis view it either as an altered state of consciousness or as a normal state in which subjects assume a hypnotic role.

Meditation: Pure Consciousness or Relaxation?

❚ Evidence suggests that meditation can lead to a potentially beneficial state characterized by suppression of bodily arousal. Research also suggests that meditation may have a variety of long-term benefits. However, some critics suggest that the observed benefits are not unique to meditation and are a product of any effective relaxation procedure.

Altering Consciousness with Drugs

❚ The principal types of psychoactive drugs are narcotics, sedatives, stimulants, hallucinogens, cannabis, alcohol, and MDMA. Although it's possible to describe the typical effects of various drugs, the actual effect on any individual depends on a number of factors, including subjective expectations and tolerance to the drug.

❚ Psychoactive drugs exert their main effects in the brain, where they alter neurotransmitter activity. The mesolimbic dopamine pathway may mediate the reinforcing effects of most abused drugs. Drugs vary in their potential for psychological and physical dependence. Recreational drug use can prove harmful to health by producing an overdose, by causing tissue damage, or by increasing health-impairing behavior.

Reflecting on the Chapter's Themes

❚ Five of our unifying themes were highlighted in this chapter. First, we saw how psychology's study of consciousness reflects concurrent social trends, showing that psychology evolves in a sociohistorical context. Second, we saw how states of consciousness are highly subjective. Third, we saw how culture molds some aspects of sleep and dreaming. Fourth, we learned once again that behavior is governed by multifactorial causation. Fifth, we saw extensive theoretical diversity in this area.

PERSONAL APPLICATION Addressing Practical Questions About Sleep and Dreams

❚ Sleep needs vary, and the value of short naps depends on many factors. People can do many things to avoid or reduce sleep problems. People troubled by transient insomnia should avoid panic, pursue effective relaxation, and try distracting themselves.

❚ Everyone dreams, but some people cannot remember their dreams, probably because of the nature of their sleep cycle. Most theorists believe that dreams require some interpretation, but this may not be as complicated as once assumed.

CRITICAL THINKING APPLICATION Is Alcoholism a Disease? The Power of Definitions

❚ Like many questions, the issue of whether alcoholism should be regarded as a disease is a matter of definition. In evaluating the validity of a definition, one should look not only at the definition but also at where it came from. People have a tendency to use definitions as explanations for the phenomena they describe, but doing so involves circular reasoning.

PSYKTREK PREVIEW

Interestingly, however, when people are isolated in this way they drift toward a 25-hour cycle. As you can see in this chart, which plots one subject's sleep sessions, people tend to go to sleep and awaken about an hour later each day.

© Michel Siffre/National Geographic Image Collection

William Dement

According to William Dement, an influential pioneer in sleep research, REM awakenings produce dream recall about 78% of the time, whereas awakenings from other stages are accompanied by dream recall only about 14% of the time.

Courtesy of William Dement

Check out Module 4a (*Biological Rhythms*) to learn more about how biological

Explore Module 4b (*Sleep*)

1. An EEG would indicate primarily _____ activity while you take this test.
   A. alpha
   B. beta
   C. delta
   D. theta

2. Readjusting your biological clock would be most difficult under which of the following circumstances?
   A. Flying west from Los Angeles to Hawaii
   B. Flying north from Miami to New York
   C. Flying east from Hawaii to Los Angeles
   D. Flying south from New York to Miami

3. As the sleep cycle evolves through the night, people tend to:
   A. spend more time in REM sleep and less time in NREM sleep.
   B. spend more time in NREM sleep and less time in REM sleep.
   C. spend a more or less equal amount of time in REM sleep and NREM sleep.
   D. spend more time in stage 4 sleep and less time in REM sleep.

4. Newborn infants spend about _____ % of their sleep time in REM, and adults spend about _____ % of their sleep time in REM.
   A. 20; 50
   B. 50; 20
   C. 20; 20
   D. 50; 50

5. After being selectively deprived of REM sleep, people typically experience:
   A. hypochondriasis.
   B. Non-REM dysfunction.
   C. emotional breakdowns.
   D. a temporary increase in time spent in REM.

6. Which of the following is not true of sleeping pills?
   A. Sleeping pills are an excellent long-range solution for all types of insomnia.
   B. There is some danger of overdose.
   C. Sleeping pills can make people sluggish and drowsy the next day.
   D. Sleeping pills gradually become less effective with continued use.

7. The activation-synthesis theory of dreaming contends that:
   A. dreams are simply the by-product of bursts of activity in the brain.
   B. dreams provide an outlet for energy invested in socially undesirable impulses.
   C. dreams represent the brain's attempt to purge information taken in during waking hours.
   D. dreams are an attempt to restore a neurotransmitter balance within the brain.

8. A common driving experience is "highway hypnosis," in which one's consciousness seems to be divided between the driving itself and one's conscious train of thought. This phenomenon has been cited to support the idea that hypnosis is:
   A. an exercise in role playing.
   B. a dissociated state of consciousness.
   C. a goal-directed fantasy.
   D. not an altered state of consciousness.

9. Amphetamines work by increasing activity at _____ synapses in a variety of ways.
   A. GABA and glycine
   B. serotonin and dopamine
   C. acetylcholine
   D. norepinephrine and dopamine

10. Which of the following drugs would be most likely to result in a fatal overdose?
    A. LSD
    B. Mescaline
    C. Marijuana
    D. Narcotics

11. Which of the following is a true statement about naps?
    A. Daytime naps invariably lead to insomnia.
    B. Daytime naps are invariably refreshing and an efficient way to rest.
    C. Daytime naps are not very efficient ways to sleep, but their effects are variable and can be beneficial.
    D. Taking many naps during the day can substitute for a full night's sleep.

12. Definitions:
    A. generally emerge out of research.
    B. often have great explanatory value.
    C. generally exert little influence over how people think.
    D. are usually constructed by experts or authorities in a specific field.

Answers

1 B pp. 152–153   5 D p. 161   9 D p. 175
2 C p. 154   6 A p. 163   10 D p. 175
3 A p. 157   7 A p. 167   11 C p. 179
4 B pp. 158–159   8 B p. 170   12 D pp. 182–183

PSYKTREK PREVIEW

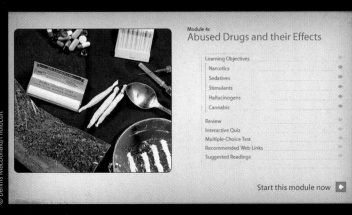

Go to Module 4c (*Abused Drugs and Their Effects*) to get more information about the effects and risks of five categories of widely abused drugs.

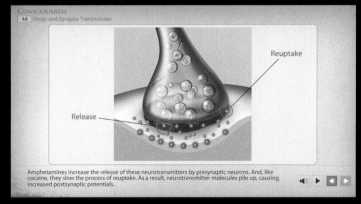

Access Module 4d (*Drugs and Synaptic Transmission*) to view animations of how various drugs exert their effects by altering neurotransmitter activity at specific

6

Learning

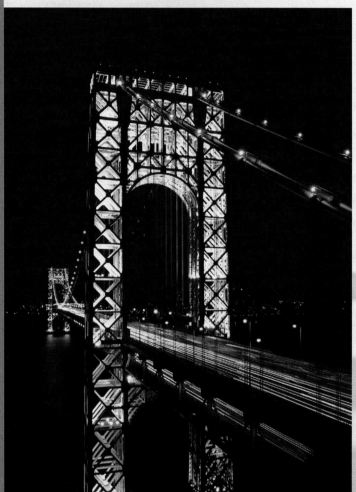

George Washington Bridge, New York © Richard Berenholtz/Corbis

Let's see if you can guess the answer to a riddle. What do the following scenarios have in common?

• In 1953 a Japanese researcher observed a young macaque (a type of monkey) on the island of Koshima washing a sweet potato in a stream before eating it. No one had ever seen a macaque do this before. Soon other members of the monkey's troop were showing the same behavior. Several generations later, macaques on Koshima still wash their potatoes before eating them (De Waal, 2001).

• In 2005 Wade Boggs was elected to baseball's Hall of Fame. Boggs was as renowned for his superstitions as he was for his great hitting. For 20 years Boggs ate chicken every day of the year. Before games he followed a rigorous set of rituals that included stepping on the bases in reverse order, running wind sprints at precisely 17 minutes past the hour, and tossing exactly three pebbles off the field. Every time he stepped up to hit during a game, he drew the Hebrew letter *chai* in the dirt with his bat. For Boggs, the slightest deviation in this routine was profoundly upsetting (Gaddis, 1999; Vyse, 2000).

• Barn swallows in Minnesota have built nests inside a Home Depot warehouse store, safe from the weather and from predators. So how do they get in and out to bring food to their babies when the doors are closed? They flutter around the motion sensors that operate the doors until they open!

• A firefighter in Georgia routinely braves life-threatening situations to rescue people in distress. Yet the firefighter is paralyzed with fear whenever he sees someone dressed as a clown. He has been terrified of clowns ever since the third grade (Ryckeley, 2005).

What common thread runs through these diverse situations? What connects a superstitious ballplayer or a clown-phobic firefighter to potato-washing monkeys and door-opening swallows?

The answer is *learning*. This may surprise you. When most people think of learning, they picture students reading textbooks or novices gaining proficiency in a skill, such as skiing or playing the guitar. To a psychologist, however, *learning* **is any relatively durable change in behavior or knowledge that is due to experience.** Macaques aren't born with the habit of washing their sweet potatoes, nor do swallows begin life knowing how to operate motion sensors. Wade Boggs adopted his superstitious rituals because they seemed to be associated with

success in hitting a baseball. The firefighter in Georgia wasn't born with a fear of clowns, since he only began to be frightened of them in the third grade. In short, all these behaviors are the product of experience—that is, they represent learning.

When you think about it, it would be hard to name a lasting change in behavior that *isn't* due to experience. That is why learning is one of the most fundamental concepts in all of psychology. Learning shapes personal habits, such as nailbiting; personality traits, such as shyness; personal preferences, such as a distaste for formal clothes; and emotional responses, such as reactions to favorite songs. If all your learned responses could somehow be stripped away, little of your behavior would be left. You would not be able to talk, read a book, or cook yourself a hamburger. You would be about as complex and interesting as a turnip.

As the examples at the start of this discussion show, learning is not an exclusively human process. Learning is pervasive in the animal world as well, a fact that won't amaze anyone who has ever owned a dog or seen a trained seal in action. Another insight, however, is considerably more startling: *The principles that explain learned responses in animals explain much of human learning, too.* Thus, the same mechanisms that explain how barn swallows learn to operate an automated door can account for a professional athlete's bizarre superstitions. Indeed, many of the most fascinating discoveries in the study of learning originated in studies of animals.

In this chapter, you will see how fruitful the research into learning has been and how wide ranging its applications are. We will focus most of our attention on a specific kind of learning: conditioning. *Conditioning* involves learning associations between events that occur in an organism's environment (Wade Boggs' eating chicken and having success hitting a baseball is one example). In investigating conditioning, psychologists study learning at a fundamental level. This strategy has paid off with insights that have laid the foundation for the study of more complex forms of learning, such as learning by observation (the kind of learning that may account for the Koshima macaques picking up one monkey's habit of washing her sweet potatoes). In the Personal Application, you'll see how you can harness the principles of conditioning to improve your self-control. The Critical Thinking Application shows how conditioning procedures can be used to manipulate emotions.

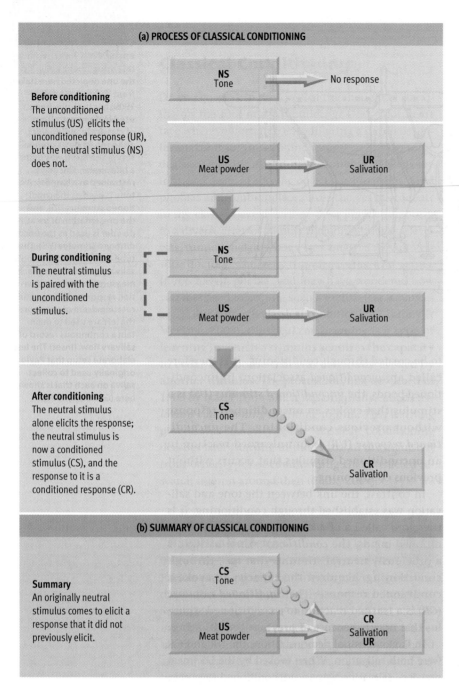

(a) PROCESS OF CLASSICAL CONDITIONING

Before conditioning
The unconditioned stimulus (US) elicits the unconditioned response (UR), but the neutral stimulus (NS) does not.

NS Tone → No response

US Meat powder → UR Salivation

During conditioning
The neutral stimulus is paired with the unconditioned stimulus.

NS Tone

US Meat powder → UR Salivation

After conditioning
The neutral stimulus alone elicits the response; the neutral stimulus is now a conditioned stimulus (CS), and the response to it is a conditioned response (CR).

CS Tone → CR Salivation

(b) SUMMARY OF CLASSICAL CONDITIONING

Summary
An originally neutral stimulus comes to elicit a response that it did not previously elicit.

CS Tone → CR Salivation

US Meat powder → Salivation UR

Figure 6.2

The sequence of events in classical conditioning. (a) Moving downward, this series of three panels outlines the sequence of events in classical conditioning, using Pavlov's original demonstration as an example. **(b)** As we encounter other examples of classical conditioning throughout the book, you will see many diagrams like the one in this panel, which will provide snapshots of specific instances of classical conditioning.

have traditionally been characterized as reflexes and are said to be *elicited* (drawn forth) because most of them are relatively automatic or involuntary. However, research in recent decades has demonstrated that classical conditioning is involved in a wider range of human and animal behavior than previously appreciated, including some types of nonreflexive responding (Allan, 1998; Turkkan, 1989). Finally, a *trial* in classical conditioning consists of any presentation of a stimulus or pair of stimuli. Psychologists are interested in how many trials are required to establish a particular conditioned bond. The number needed to form an association varies considerably. Although classical conditioning gener-

ally proceeds gradually, it can occur quite rapidly, sometimes in just one pairing of the conditioned stimulus and unconditioned stimulus.

Classical Conditioning in Everyday Life 5a

In laboratory experiments on classical conditioning, researchers have generally worked with extremely simple responses. Besides salivation, commonly studied favorites include eyelid closure, knee jerks, and the flexing of various limbs. The study of such simple responses has been productive. However, these responses do not even begin to convey the rich diversity of everyday behavior that is regulated by classical conditioning. Let's look at some examples of classical conditioning drawn from everyday life.

Conditioned Fear and Anxiety 5a

Classical conditioning often plays a key role in shaping emotional responses such as fear and anxiety. Phobias are a good example of such responses. Case studies of patients suffering from phobias suggest that many irrational fears can be traced back to experiences that involve classical conditioning (Antony & McCabe, 2003; Muris &Mercklebach, 2001). It is easy to imagine how such conditioning can occur outside of the laboratory. For example, a student of mine was troubled by a bridge phobia so severe that she couldn't drive on interstate highways because of all the bridges that had to be crossed. She was able to pinpoint the source of her phobia as something that had happened during her childhood. Whenever her family drove to visit her grandmother, they had to cross an old, little-used, rickety, run-down bridge out in the countryside. Her father, in a misguided attempt at humor, made a major production out of these crossings. He would stop short of the bridge and carry on about the enormous danger. Obviously, he thought the bridge was safe or he wouldn't have driven across it. However, the naive young girl was terrified by her father's scare tactics. Thus, the bridge became a conditioned stimulus eliciting great fear (see **Figure 6.3**). Unfortunately, the fear spilled over to all bridges, and 40 years later she was still carrying the burden of this phobia.

Everyday anxiety responses that are less severe than phobias may also be products of classical conditioning. For instance, if you cringe when you hear the sound of a dentist's drill, this response is the result of classical conditioning. In this case, the pain you have experienced from dental drilling is the US. This pain has been paired with the sound of the drill, which became a CS eliciting your cringing behavior.

ping cart (see photo).
sponsor's product off t
dition (Breland & Brela

Extinction

In operant conditio
gradual weakening ar
tendency because the
by reinforcement. Ext
ditioning whenever p
ment is stopped. In la
situation usually oc
stops delivering foo
pressing. When the
brief surge often occu
lowed by a gradual d
approaches zero. The
in the extinction of l
   A key issue in ope
resistance to extinction
reinforcement is ha
occurs when an or
response after deliv
been terminated. T
tinction, the longer
Thus, if a researcher
lever pressing and th
response shows high
ever, if the response
tively little resistanc
   Resistance to ext
of purely theoretica
practical. People oft
in such a way that it
tinction. For instanc
child's studying res
hits a rocky stretch
reinforcement (goo
casino wants to see
if they encounter a

Stimulus Contro
and Discriminat

Operant respondir
consequences, as o
(R-O) associations
that *precede* a respo
havior. When a res
a reinforcer in the
that stimulus come
that the response is
an organism learr
accordingly (Honi
pigeon's disk peck
a small light behi

whether responses lead to the presentation of re-inforcers. Typically, the experimenter manipulates whether positive consequences occur when the ani-mal makes the designated response. The main posi-tive consequence is usually delivery of a small bit of food into a cup mounted in the chamber. Because the animals are deprived of food for a while prior to the experimental session, their hunger virtually ensures that the food serves as a reinforcer.

The key dependent variable in most research on operant conditioning is the subjects' *response rate* over time. An animal's rate of lever pressing or disk pecking in the Skinner box is monitored continu-ously by a device known as a cumulative recorder (see **Figure 6.10**). The *cumulative recorder* creates a graphic record of responding and reinforcement in a Skinner box as a function of time. The recorder works by means of a roll of paper that moves at a steady rate underneath a movable pen. When there is no responding, the pen stays still and draws a straight horizontal line, reflecting the passage of time. When-ever the designated response occurs, however, the pen

Figure 6.9

Reinforcement in operant conditioning. According to Skinner, reinforcement occurs when a response is followed by rewarding consequences and the organism's tendency to make the response increases. The two examples diagrammed here illustrate the basic premise of operant conditioning—that voluntary behavior is controlled by its consequences. These examples involve positive reinforcement; for a comparison of positive and negative reinforcement, see Figure 6.14.

Figure 6.10

Skinner box and cumulative recorder. (a) This diagram highlights some of the key features of an operant chamber, or Skinner box. In this apparatus designed for rats, the response under study is lever pressing. Food pellets, which may serve as reinforcers, are delivered into the food cup on the right. The speaker and light permit manipulations of visual and auditory stimuli, and the electric grid gives the experimenter control over aversive consequences (shock) in the box. **(b)** A cumulative recorder connected to the box keeps a continuous record of responses and reinforcements. A small segment of a cumulative record is shown here. The entire process is automatic as the paper moves with the passage of time; each lever press moves the pen up a step, and each reinforcement is marked with a slash. **(c)** This photo shows the real thing—a rat being conditioned in a Skinner box.

Shaping—an operant technique in which an organism is rewarded for closer and closer approximations of the desired response—is used in teaching both animals and humans. It is the main means of training animals to perform unnatural tricks. Shaping is also the key to training service animals that assist people with disabilities, such as guide dogs for the blind. Breland and Breland's (1961) famous subject, "Priscilla, the Fastidious Pig," is shown on the left. The chimp on the right works in a restaurant in Japan.

their children (Straus & Stewart, 1999), but quite a bit of controversy exists about the wisdom of using physical punishment. Opponents of corporal punishment argue that it produces many unintended and undesirable side effects (Lytton, 1997; McCord, 2005; Straus, 2000). For example, they worry that physical punishment may trigger *strong emotional responses,* including anxiety, anger, and resentment, and that it can generate hostility toward the source of the punishment, such as a parent. Some theorists also argue that children who are subjected to a lot of physical punishment tend to become more aggressive than average. These views were bolstered by a comprehensive review of the empirical research on physical punishment with children. Summarizing the results of 88 studies, Elizabeth Thompson Gershoff (2002) concluded that physical punishment is associated with poor quality parent-child relations; elevated aggression, delinquency, and behavioral problems in youngsters; and an increased likelihood of children being abused. Moreover, she concluded that these effects can carry over into adulthood, as studies find increased aggression, criminal behavior, mental health problems, and child abuse among adults who were physically punished as children. These conclusions about the negative effects of corporal punishment have been echoed in more recent studies (Aucoin, Frick, & Bodin, 2006; Lynch et al., 2006; Mulvaney & Mebert, 2007).

Gershoff's (2002) review was a stinging indictment of physical punishment, but critics have raised some doubts about her conclusions. They argue that her review failed to distinguish between the effects of frequent, harsh, heavy-handed physical punishment and the effects of occasional, mild spankings, used as a backup when other disciplinary strategies fail (Baumrind, Larzelere, & Cowan, 2002). Critics also point out that the evidence linking spanking to negative effects is correlational and that correlation is no assurance of causation (Kazdin & Benjet, 2003). Perhaps spanking causes children to be more aggressive, but it is also plausible that aggressive children cause their parents to rely more on physical punishment (see **Figure 6.17**). Based on objections such as these,

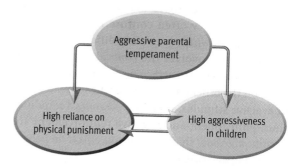

Figure 6.17

The correlation between physical punishment and aggressiveness. As discussed in earlier chapters, a correlation does not establish causation. It seems plausible that extensive reliance on physical punishment causes children to be more aggressive, as many experts suspect. However, it is also possible that highly aggressive children cause their parents to depend heavily on physical punishment. Or, perhaps parents with an aggressive, hostile temperament pass on genes for aggressiveness to their children and prefer to rely on heavy use of physical punishment.

---

concept check 6.5

Distinguishing Between Classical Conditioning and Operant Conditioning

Check your understanding of the usual differences between classical conditioning and operant conditioning by indicating the type of conditioning process involved in each of the following examples. In the space on the left, place a C if the example involves classical conditioning, an O if it involves operant conditioning, or a B if it involves both. The answers can be found in Appendix A.

_____ 1. Whenever Midori takes her dog out for a walk, she wears the same old blue windbreaker. Eventually, she notices that her dog becomes excited whenever she puts on this windbreaker.

_____ 2. The Wailing Creatures are a successful rock band with three hit albums to their credit. They begin their U.S. tour featuring many new, unreleased songs, all of which draw silence from their concert fans. The same fans cheer wildly when the Wailing Creatures play any of their old hits. Gradually, the band reduces the number of new songs it plays and starts playing more of the old standbys.

_____ 3. When Cindy and Mel first fell in love, they listened constantly to the Wailing Creatures' hit song "Transatlantic Obsession." Although several years have passed, whenever they hear this song, they experience a warm, romantic feeling.

_____ 4. For nearly 20 years Ralph has worked as a machinist in the same factory. His new foreman is never satisfied with his work and criticizes him constantly. After a few weeks of heavy criticism, Ralph experiences anxiety whenever he arrives at work. He starts calling in sick more and more frequently to evade this anxiety.

Baumrind et al. (2002) assert that the empirical evidence "does not justify a blanket injunction against mild to moderate disciplinary spanking" (p. 586).

So, what can we conclude about the corporal punishment controversy? It is important to note that the critics of Gershoff's conclusions are not exactly *advocates* of physical punishment. As Holden (2002) points out, "There is unanimous accord among experts that harsh, abusive punishment is detrimental for children" (p. 590). The critics merely think that it is premature to condemn the judicious use of mild spankings, especially when children are too young to understand a verbal reprimand or the withdrawal of privileges. But even the critics would mostly agree that parents should minimize their dependence on physical punishment.

REVIEW of Key Learning Goals

6.6 Operant conditioning largely involves voluntary responses that are governed by their consequences, whereas classical conditioning generally involves involuntary, reflexive responses elicited by stimuli. Although this distinction holds up much of the time, the two types of conditioning jointly and interactively govern some aspects of behavior.

6.7 Skinner pioneered the study of operant conditioning, working mainly with rats and pigeons in Skinner boxes. Reinforcement occurs when an event following a response increases an organism's tendency to emit that response. The key dependent variable in operant conditioning is the rate of response over time, which is tracked by a cumulative recorder. Primary reinforcers are unlearned; secondary reinforcers acquire their reinforcing quality through conditioning.

6.8 Acquisition in operant conditioning often depends on shaping, which involves gradually reinforcing closer and closer approximations of the desired response. Shaping is the key to training animals to perform impressive tricks. In operant conditioning, extinction occurs when reinforcement for a response is terminated and the rate of that response declines. There are variations in resistance to extinction.

6.9 Operant responses are regulated by discriminative stimuli that are cues for the likelihood of obtaining reinforcers. These stimuli are subject to the same processes of generalization and discrimination that occur in classical conditioning.

6.10 Schedules of reinforcement influence patterns of operant responding. Intermittent schedules of reinforcement include fixed-ratio, variable-ratio, fixed-interval, and variable-interval schedules. Intermittent schedules produce greater resistance to extinction than continuous reinforcement. Ratio schedules tend to yield higher rates of response than interval schedules. Shorter intervals and higher ratios are associated with faster responding.

6.11 Positive reinforcement occurs when a response is strengthened because it is followed by the presentation of a rewarding stimulus. Negative reinforcement occurs when a response is strengthened because it is followed by the removal of an aversive stimulus. Some theorists have questioned the value of this distinction.

6.12 In escape learning, an organism acquires a response that decreases or ends aversive stimulation. In avoidance learning, an organism acquires a response that prevents aversive stimulation by learning a signal that serves as a warning of impending noxious stimulation. The process of avoidance learning may shed light on why phobias are so difficult to eliminate.

6.13 Punishment involves aversive consequences that lead to a decline in response strength. Punishment and negative reinforcement are opposite procedures that yield opposite effects on behavior. Issues associated with the application of physical punishment as a disciplinary procedure include emotional side effects, increased aggressive behavior, and behavioral problems. Concerns about these problems make physical punishment a controversial disciplinary strategy.

Changing Directions in the Study of Conditioning

As you learned in Chapter 1, science is constantly evolving and changing in response to new research and new thinking. Such change certainly has occurred in the study of conditioning (Domjan, 1998). In this section, we will examine two major changes in thinking about conditioning that have emerged in recent decades. First, we'll consider the growing recognition that an organism's biological heritage can limit or channel conditioning. Second, we'll discuss the increased appreciation of the role of cognitive processes in conditioning.

Recognizing Biological Constraints on Conditioning

Learning theorists have traditionally assumed that the fundamental laws of conditioning have great generality—that they apply to a wide range of species. Although no one ever suggested that hamsters could learn physics, until the 1960s most psychologists assumed that associations could be conditioned between any stimulus an organism could register and any response it could make. However, findings in recent decades have demonstrated that there are limits to the generality of conditioning principles—limits imposed by an organism's biological heritage.

Conditioned Taste Aversion

A number of years ago, a prominent psychologist, Martin Seligman, dined out with his wife and enjoyed a steak with sauce béarnaise. About 6 hours afterward, he developed a wicked case of stomach flu and endured severe nausea. Subsequently, when he ordered sauce béarnaise, he was chagrined to discover

Key Learning Goals

6.14 Articulate the theoretical significance of conditioned taste aversion and preparedness.

6.15 Explain the importance of ecologically relevant conditioned stimuli, and discuss whether the laws of learning are universal.

6.16 Describe Tolman's research on latent learning and its theoretical importance.

6.17 Understand the theoretical implications of research on signal relations and response-outcome relations.

John Garcia

"Taste aversions do not fit comfortably within the present framework of classical or instrumental conditioning: These aversions selectively seek flavors to the exclusion of other stimuli. Interstimulus intervals are a thousandfold too long."

that its aroma alone nearly made him throw up. Seligman's experience was not unique. Many people develop aversions to food that has been followed by nausea from illness, alcohol intoxication, or food poisoning. However, Seligman was puzzled by what he called his "sauce béarnaise syndrome" (Seligman & Hager, 1972). On the one hand, it appeared to be the straightforward result of classical conditioning. A neutral stimulus (the sauce) had been paired with an unconditioned stimulus (the flu), which caused an unconditioned response (the nausea). Thus, the sauce béarnaise became a conditioned stimulus eliciting nausea (see **Figure 6.18**).

On the other hand, Seligman recognized that his aversion to béarnaise sauce seemed to violate certain basic principles of conditioning. First, the lengthy delay of 6 hours between the CS (the sauce) and the US (the flu) should have prevented conditioning from occurring. In laboratory studies, a delay of more than *30 seconds* between the CS and US makes it difficult to establish a conditioned response, yet this conditioning occurred in just one pairing. Second, why was it that *only* the béarnaise sauce became a CS eliciting nausea? Why not other stimuli that were present in the restaurant? Shouldn't plates, knives, tablecloths, or his wife, for example, also trigger Seligman's nausea?

The riddle of Seligman's sauce béarnaise syndrome was solved by John Garcia (1989) and his colleagues. They conducted a series of studies on *conditioned taste aversion* (Garcia, Clarke, & Hankins, 1973; Garcia & Koelling, 1966; Garcia & Rusiniak, 1980). In these studies, they manipulated the kinds of stimuli preceding the onset of nausea and other noxious experiences in rats, using radiation to artificially induce the nausea. They found that when taste cues were followed by nausea, rats quickly acquired conditioned taste aversions. However, when taste cues were followed by other types of noxious

stimuli (such as shock), rats did *not* develop conditioned taste aversions. Furthermore, visual and auditory stimuli followed by nausea also failed to produce conditioned aversions. In short, Garcia and his co-workers found that it was almost impossible to create certain associations, whereas taste-nausea associations (and odor-nausea associations) were almost impossible to prevent.

What is the theoretical significance of this unique readiness to make connections between taste and nausea? Garcia argues that it is a by-product of the evolutionary history of mammals. Animals that consume poisonous foods and survive must learn not to repeat their mistakes. Natural selection will favor organisms that quickly learn what *not* to eat. Thus, evolution may have biologically programmed some organisms to learn certain types of associations more easily than others.

Preparedness and Phobias

According to Martin Seligman (1971) and other theorists (Öhman, 1979; Öhman, Dimberg, & Öst, 1985), evolution has also programmed organisms to acquire certain fears more readily than others, because of a phenomenon called *preparedness*. *Preparedness* involves species-specific predispositions to be conditioned in certain ways and not others. Seligman believes that preparedness can explain why certain phobias are vastly more common than others. People tend to develop phobias to snakes, spiders, heights, and darkness relatively easily. However, even after painful experiences with hammers, knives, hot stoves, and electrical outlets, phobic fears of these objects are rare. What characteristics do common phobic objects share? Most were once genuine threats to our ancient ancestors. Consequently, a fear response to such objects may have survival value for our species. According to Seligman, evolutionary forces gradually wired the human brain to acquire conditioned fears of these stimuli easily and rapidly.

Laboratory simulations of phobic conditioning have provided some support for the concept of preparedness (Mineka & Öhman, 2002). For example, slides of "prepared" phobic stimuli (snakes, spiders) and neutral or modern fear-relevant stimuli (flowers, mushrooms, guns, knives) have been paired with shock. Consistent with the concept of preparedness, physiological monitoring of the participants indicates that the prepared phobic stimuli tend to produce more rapid conditioning, stronger fear responses, and greater resistance to extinction. Arne Öhman and Susan Mineka (2001) have elaborated on the theory of preparedness, outlining the key elements of what

Figure 6.18

Conditioned taste aversion. Taste aversions can be established through classical conditioning, as in the "sauce béarnaise syndrome." However, as the text explains, taste aversions can be acquired in ways that *seem* to violate basic principles of classical conditioning.

they call an *evolved module for fear learning*. They assert that this evolved module is (1) preferentially activated by stimuli related to survival threats in evolutionary history, (2) automatically activated by these stimuli, (3) relatively resistant to conscious efforts to suppress the resulting fears, and (4) dependent on neural circuitry running through the amygdala.

Arbitrary Versus Ecological Conditioned Stimuli

Michael Domjan (2005) argues that the rapid learning seen in conditioned taste aversion is not all that unique—it is just one example of what happens when *ecologically relevant conditioned stimuli* are studied, as opposed to *arbitrary, neutral stimuli.* Domjan points out that laboratory studies of classical conditioning have traditionally paired a US with a neutral stimulus that is unrelated to the US (such as a bell, tone, or light). This strategy ensured that the association created through conditioning was a newly acquired association rather than the product of previous learning. This approach yielded decades of useful insights about the laws governing classical conditioning, but Domjan argues that there is a gap between this paradigm and the way learning takes place in the real world.

According to Domjan (2005), in natural settings conditioned stimuli generally are not arbitrary cues that are unrelated to the US. In the real world, conditioned stimuli tend to have natural relations to the unconditioned stimuli they predict. For example, a rattlesnake bite is typically preceded by the snake's distinctive rattling sound; copulation among animals is typically preceded by specific mating signals; the consumption of toxic food is normally preceded by a specific taste. If taste-aversion learning appears to "violate" the normal laws of conditioning, it's because these laws have been compiled in unrealistic situations that are not representative of how conditioning unfolds in natural settings.

According to Domjan (2005), over the course of evolution, organisms have developed distinct response systems to deal with crucial tasks, such as finding food and avoiding predators. When a learning task in the laboratory happens to mesh with an animal's evolutionary history, learning is likely to proceed more quickly and easily than when arbitrary stimuli are used (Domjan, Cusato, & Krause, 2004). Thus, biological constraints on learning are not really "constraints" on the general laws of learning. These *species-specific predispositions* are the norm—an insight that eluded researchers for decades because they mostly worked with neutral conditioned stimuli.

People tend to develop phobias to snakes very easily but to hot stoves rarely, even though the latter can be just as painful. Preparedness theory can explain this paradox.

So, what is the current thinking on the idea that the laws of learning are *universal* across various species? The predominant view among learning theorists seems to be that the basic mechanisms of learning are *similar* across species but that these mechanisms have sometimes been modified in the course of evolution as species have adapted to the specialized demands of their environments (Shettleworth, 1998). According to this view, learning is a very general process because the neural substrates of learning and the basic problems confronted by various organisms are much the same across species. For example, it is probably adaptive for virtually any organism to develop the ability to recognize stimuli that signal important events. However, given that different organisms confront different adaptive problems to survive and reproduce, it makes sense that learning has evolved along somewhat different paths in different species (Hollis, 1997; Sherry, 1992).

Recognizing Cognitive Processes in Conditioning

Pavlov, Skinner, and their followers traditionally viewed conditioning as a mechanical process in which stimulus-response associations are "stamped in" by experience. Learning theorists asserted that if creatures such as snails can be conditioned, conditioning can't depend on higher mental pro-

Archives of the History of American Psychology—
The University of Akron

Edward Chace Tolman

*"Learning consists not in
stimulus-response connections
but in the building up in the
nervous system of sets which
function like cognitive maps."*

cesses. This viewpoint did not go entirely unchallenged, as we will discuss momentarily, but mainstream theories of conditioning did not allocate any role to cognitive processes. In recent decades, however, research findings have led theorists to shift toward more cognitive explanations of conditioning. Let's review how this transition gradually occurred.

Latent Learning and Cognitive Maps

The first major "renegade" to chip away at the conventional view of learning was Edward C. Tolman (1932, 1938), an American psychologist who was something of a gadfly for the behaviorist movement in the 1930s and 1940s. Tolman and his colleagues conducted a series of studies that posed some difficult questions for the prevailing views of conditioning. In one landmark study (Tolman & Honzik, 1930), three groups of food-deprived rats learned to run a complicated maze over a series of once-a-day trials (see **Figure 6.19a**). The rats in Group A received a food reward when they got to the end of the maze each day. Because of this reinforcement, their performance in running the maze (measured by how many "wrong turns" they made) gradually improved over the course of 17 days (see **Figure 6.19b**). The rats in Group B did not receive any food reward. Lacking reinforcement for getting to the goal box swiftly, this group made many "errors" and showed only modest improvement in performance. Group C was the critical group; they did not get any reward for their first 10 trials in the maze, but they were rewarded from the 11th trial onward. The rats in this group showed little improvement in performance over the first 10 trials (just like Group B), but after finding food in the goal box on the 11th trial, they

showed sharp improvement on subsequent trials. In fact, their performance was even a little better than that of the Group A rats who had been rewarded after every trial (see **Figure 6.19b**).

Tolman concluded that the rats in Group C had been learning about the maze all along, just as much as the rats in group A, but they had no motivation to demonstrate this learning until a reward was introduced. Tolman called this phenomenon *latent learning*—learning that is not apparent from behavior when it first occurs. *Why did these findings present a challenge for the prevailing view of learning?* First, they suggested that learning can take place in the absence of reinforcement—at a time when learned responses were thought to be stamped in by reinforcement. Second, they suggested that the rats who displayed latent learning had formed a *cognitive map* of the maze (a mental representation of the spatial layout) at a time when cognitive processes were thought to be irrelevant to understanding conditioning even in humans.

Tolman (1948) went on to conduct other studies which suggested that cognitive processes play a role in conditioning. But his ideas were ahead of their time and mostly attracted rebuttals and criticism from the influential learning theorists of his era (Hilgard, 1987). In the long run, however, Tolman's ideas prevailed, as models of conditioning were eventually forced to incorporate cognitive factors.

Signal Relations

One theorist who was especially influential in demonstrating the importance of cognitive factors in classical conditioning was Robert Rescorla (1978, 1980; Rescorla & Wagner, 1972). Rescorla asserts that

Figure 6.19

Latent learning. (a) In the study by Tolman and Honzik (1930), rats learned to run the complicated maze shown here. **(b)** The results obtained by Tolman and Honzik (1930) are summarized in this graph. The rats in Group C showed a sudden improvement in performance when a food reward was introduced on Trial 11. Tolman concluded that the rats in this group were learning about the maze all along, but their learning remained "latent" until reinforcement was made available.

SOURCE: Adapted from Tolman, E. C., & Honzik, C. H. (1930). Introduction and removal of reward and maze performance in rats. *University of California Publications in Psychology, 4,* 257–275.

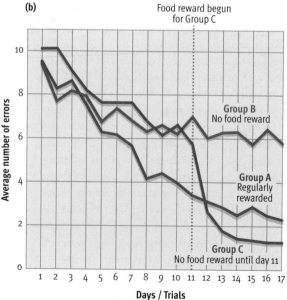

environmental stimuli serve as signals and that some stimuli are better, or more dependable, signals than others. A "good" signal is one that allows accurate prediction of the US. Hence, he has manipulated the *predictive value* of a conditioned stimulus by varying the proportion of trials in which the CS and US are paired. For example, in one study a CS (tone) and US (shock) were paired 100% of the time for one group of rats and only 50% of the time for another group.

What did Rescorla find when he tested the two groups of rats for conditioned fear? He found that the CS elicited a much stronger fear response in the group that had been exposed to the more dependable signal. Many other studies of signal relations have also shown that the predictive value of a CS is an influential factor governing classical conditioning (Rescorla, 1978). These studies suggest that classical conditioning may involve information processing rather than reflexive responding.

Response-Outcome Relations and Reinforcement

Studies of response-outcome relations and reinforcement also highlight the role of cognitive processes in conditioning. Imagine that on the night before an important exam you study hard while repeatedly playing a Norah Jones song. The next morning you earn an A on your exam. Does this result strengthen your tendency to play Norah Jones songs before exams? Probably not. Chances are, you will recognize the logical relation between the response of studying hard and the reinforcement of a good grade, and only the response of studying will be strengthened (Killeen, 1981). Thus, reinforcement is *not* automatic when favorable consequences follow a response. Organisms actively reason out the relations between responses and the outcomes that follow. When a response is followed by a desirable outcome,

the response is more likely to be strengthened if it seems likely that the response *caused* the outcome.

In sum, modern, reformulated models of conditioning view it as a matter of detecting the *contingencies* among environmental events (Matute & Miller, 1998). According to these theories, organisms actively try to figure out what leads to what (the contingencies) in the world around them. The new, cognitively oriented theories of conditioning are quite a departure from older theories that depicted conditioning as a mindless, mechanical process. We can also see this new emphasis on cognitive processes in our next topic, observational learning.

Courtesy of Robert Rescorla

Robert Rescorla

"I encourage students to think of animals as behaving like little statisticians.... They really are very finely attuned to small changes in the likelihood of events."

REVIEW of Key Learning Goals

6.14 Conditioned taste aversions can be readily acquired even when a lengthy delay occurs between the CS and US. Preparedness, or an evolved module for fear learning, appears to explain why people acquire phobias of ancient sources of threat much more readily than modern sources of threat. The findings on conditioned taste aversion and preparedness led to the conclusion that there are biological constraints on conditioning.

6.15 Domjan argues that researchers' focus on arbitrary conditioned stimuli has led to a distorted picture of the principles of conditioning. When ecologically relevant conditioned stimuli are used, learning proceeds more easily and more rapidly. Evolutionary psychologists argue that learning processes vary somewhat across species because different species have to grapple with very different adaptive problems.

6.16 Tolman's studies suggested that learning can take place in the absence of reinforcement, which he called latent learning. His findings suggested that cognitive processes contribute to conditioning, but his work was not influential at the time.

6.17 Rescorla's work on signal relations showed that the predictive value of a CS is an influential factor governing classical conditioning. When a response is followed by a desirable outcome, the response is more likely to be strengthened if it appears to have caused the outcome. Studies of signal relations and response-outcome relations suggest that cognitive processes play a larger role in conditioning than originally believed.

Observational Learning

Can classical and operant conditioning account for all human learning? Absolutely not. Consider how people learn a fairly basic skill such as driving a car. They do not hop naively into an automobile and start emitting random responses until one leads to favorable consequences. On the contrary, most people learning to drive know exactly where to place the key and how to get started. How are these responses acquired? Through *observation*. Most new drivers have years of experience observing oth-

ers drive and they put those observations to work. Learning through observation accounts for a great deal of learning in both animals and humans.

Observational learning occurs when an organism's responding is influenced by the observation of others, who are called models. This process has been investigated extensively by Albert Bandura (1977, 1986). Bandura does not see observational learning as entirely separate from classical and operant conditioning. Instead, he asserts that it greatly extends the

Key Learning Goals

6.18 Explain the nature, importance, and basic processes of observational learning.

6.19 Discuss Bandura's research on TV models and aggression and modern research on the effects of media violence.

Albert Bandura

"Most human behavior is learned by observation through modeling."

Observational learning occurs in both humans and animals. For example, no one trained this dog to "pray" with its owner; the chihuahua just picked up the response through observation. In a similar vein, children acquire a diverse array of responses from role models through observational learning.

reach of these conditioning processes. Whereas previous conditioning theorists emphasized the organism's direct experience, Bandura has demonstrated that both classical and operant conditioning can take place vicariously through observational learning.

Basic Processes

Essentially, observational learning involves being conditioned indirectly by virtue of observing another's conditioning (see **Figure 6.20**). To illustrate, suppose you observe a friend behaving assertively with a car salesperson. You see your friend's assertive behavior reinforced by the exceptionally good buy she gets on the car. Your own tendency to behave assertively with salespeople might well be strengthened as a result. Notice that the reinforcement is experienced by your friend, not you. The good buy should strengthen your friend's tendency to bargain assertively, but your tendency to do so may also be strengthened indirectly.

Bandura has identified four key processes that are crucial in observational learning. The first two—attention and retention—highlight the importance of cognition in this type of learning:

• *Attention.* To learn through observation, you must pay attention to another person's behavior and its consequences.
• *Retention.* You may not have occasion to use an observed response for weeks, months, or even years. Thus, you must store a mental representation of what you have witnessed in your memory.
• *Reproduction.* Enacting a modeled response depends on your ability to reproduce the response by converting your stored mental images into overt behavior.

Figure 6.20
Observational learning. In observational learning, an observer attends to and stores a mental representation of a model's behavior (example: assertive bargaining) and its consequences (example: a good buy on a car). If the observer sees the modeled response lead to a favorable outcome, the observer's tendency to emit the modeled response will be strengthened.

• *Motivation.* Finally, you are unlikely to reproduce an observed response unless you are motivated to do so. Your motivation depends on whether you encounter a situation in which you believe that the response is likely to pay off for you.

Observational Learning and the Media Violence Controversy

The power of observational learning has been at the center of a long-running controversy about the effects of media violence. Ever since television became popular in the 1950s social critics have expressed concern about the amount of violence on TV. In the 1960s, Bandura and his colleagues conducted landmark research on the issue that remains widely cited and influential.

In one classic study, Bandura, Ross, and Ross (1963a) showed how the observation of filmed models can influence the learning of aggressive behavior in children. They manipulated whether or not nursery-school children saw an aggressive model on film and whether the aggressive model experienced positive or negative consequences. Soon after the manipulations, the children were taken to a room where their play was observed through a one-way mirror. Among the toys available in the room were two "Bobo dolls" that served as convenient targets for kicks, punches, and other aggressive responses. Children who had seen the aggressive model rewarded engaged in more aggression toward the toys than children in the other conditions did. This study was one of the earliest experimental demonstrations of a cause-and-effect relationship between exposure to TV depictions of aggression and increased aggressive behavior.

Subsequent research demonstrated that youngsters are exposed to an astonishing amount of violence when they watch TV. The National Television Violence Study, a large-scale study of the content of network and cable television shows conducted in 1994–1997, revealed that 61% of programs contained violence; 44% of violent actors were enticing role models (i.e., the "good guys"); 75% of violent actions occurred without punishment or condemnation; and 51% of violent actions were "sanitized," as they featured no apparent pain (C. A. Anderson et al., 2003).

Does this steady diet of media violence foster increased aggression? Decades of research since Bandura's pioneering work indicate that the answer is "yes" (Bushman & Huesmann, 2001). The short-term effects of media violence have been investigated in hundreds of experimental studies. These studies consistently demonstrate that exposure to TV and movie violence increases the likelihood of physical aggression, verbal aggression, aggressive thoughts, and aggressive emotions in both children and adults (Anderson et al., 2003).

Experimental research indicates that exposure to aggressive content in video games produces similar results (Anderson, 2004; Carnagey, Anderson, & Bartholow, 2007). Moreover, theorists are concerned that violence in video games may have even more detrimental effects than violence in other media. Why? Because video games require a higher level of attention and more active involvement than movies or TV, players clearly identify with the characters that they control, and they are routinely reinforced (within the context of the games) for their violent actions (Carnagey & Anderson, 2004). Unfortunately, the amount of violence in popular games is escalating at an alarming rate, and their depictions of grotesque violence are becoming increasingly realistic (Gentile & Anderson, 2006).

The real-world and long-term effects of media violence have been investigated through correlational research. The findings of these studies show that the more violence children watch on TV, the more aggressive the children tend to be at home and at school (Huesmann & Miller, 1994). Of course, critics point out that this correlation could reflect a variety of causal relationships (see **Figure 6.21**). Perhaps high aggressiveness in children causes an increased interest in violent television shows. However, there are a handful of long-term studies that have followed the same subjects since the 1960s and 1970s that have clarified the causal relations underlying the link between media violence and elevated aggression. These studies show that the extent of youngsters' exposure to media violence in childhood predicts their aggressiveness in adolescence and early adulthood, but not vice versa (Huesman, 1986; Huesman et al., 2003). In other words, high exposure to media violence precedes, and presumably contributes to the causation of, high aggressiveness.

Although many people remain skeptical, the empirical evidence linking media violence to aggression is clear, convincing, and unequivocal. In fact, the strength of the association between media violence and aggression is nearly as great as the correlation between smoking and cancer (Bushman & Anderson, 2001; see **Figure 6.22** on page 216). In any event, the heated debate about media violence shows that observational learning plays an important role in regulating behavior. It represents a third major type of learning that builds on the first two types—classical conditioning and operant conditioning. These three basic types of learning are summarized and compared in the Illustrated Overview on pages 214–215.

Figure 6.21
The correlation between exposure to media violence and aggression. The more violence children watch on TV, the more aggressive they tend to be, but this correlation could reflect a variety of underlying causal relationships. Although watching violent shows probably causes increased aggressiveness, it is also possible that aggressive children are drawn to violent shows. Or perhaps a third variable (such as a genetic predisposition to aggressiveness) leads to both a preference for violent shows and high aggressiveness.

CALVIN AND HOBBES

TYPE OF LEARNING	PROCEDURE	DIAGRAM	RESULT

CLASSICAL CONDITIONING

Ivan Pavlov

A neutral stimulus (for example, a tone) is paired with an unconditioned stimulus (such as food) that elicits an unconditioned response (salivation).

CS Tone

US Meat powder

CR Salivation **UR**

The neutral stimulus becomes a conditioned stimulus that elicits the conditioned response (for example, a tone triggers salivation).

OPERANT CONDITIONING

B. F. Skinner

In a stimulus situation, a response is followed by favorable consequences (reinforcement) or unfavorable consequences (punishment).

Response Press lever

Rewarding or aversive stimulus presented or removed Food delivery or shock

If reinforced, the response is strengthened (emitted more frequently); if punished, the response is weakened (emitted less frequently).

OBSERVATIONAL LEARNING

Albert Bandura

An observer attends to a model's behavior (for example, aggressive bargaining) and its consequences (for example, a good buy on a car).

Response Bargain assertively

Rewarding stimulus presented Good buy on car

The observer stores a mental representation of the modeled response; the observer's tendency to emit the response may be strengthened or weakened, depending on the consequences observed.

TYPICAL KINDS OF RESPONSES	**EXAMPLES IN ANIMALS**	**EXAMPLES IN HUMANS**
Mostly (but not always) involuntary reflexes and visceral responses	Dogs learn to salivate to the sound of a tone that has been paired with meat powder.	Little Albert learns to fear a white rat and other white, furry objects through classical conditioning.
Mostly (but not always) voluntary, spontaneous responses	Trained animals perform remarkable feats because they have been reinforced for gradually learning closer and closer approximations of responses they do not normally emit.	Casino patrons tend to exhibit high, steady rates of gambling, as most games of chance involve complex variable-ratio schedules of reinforcement.
Mostly voluntary responses, often consisting of novel and complex sequences	A dog spontaneously learns to mimic a human ritual.	A young girl performs a response that she has acquired through observation.

© Bettmann/Corbis

Archives of the History of American Psychology, The University of Akron

Courtesy of Animal Behavior Enterprises, Inc. and Marian Bailey

© David Falconer/SuperStock

© AP Images/Itsuo Inouye

© Tom Morrison/Stone/Getty Images

Classical Conditioning

■ Classical conditioning explains how a neutral stimulus can acquire the capacity to elicit a response originally evoked by another stimulus. This kind of learning was originally described by Ivan Pavlov, who conditioned dogs to salivate when a tone was presented. Many kinds of everyday responses are regulated through classical conditioning, including phobias, anxiety responses, pleasant emotional responses, and physiological responses.

■ Stimulus contiguity plays a key role in the acquisition of new conditioned responses. A conditioned response may be weakened and extinguished entirely when the CS is no longer paired with the US. In some cases, spontaneous recovery occurs, and an extinguished response reappears after a period of nonexposure to the CS.

■ Conditioning may generalize to additional stimuli that are similar to the original CS. The opposite of generalization is discrimination, which involves not responding to stimuli that resemble the original CS. Higher-order conditioning occurs when a CS functions as if it were a US, to establish new conditioning.

Operant Conditioning

■ Operant conditioning, which was pioneered by B. F. Skinner, involves largely voluntary responses that are governed by their consequences. The key dependent variable in operant conditioning is the rate of response over time. New operant responses can be shaped by gradually reinforcing closer and closer approximations of the desired response.

■ In operant conditioning, when reinforcement is terminated, the response rate usually declines and extinction may occur. Operant responses are regulated by discriminative stimuli that are cues for the likelihood of obtaining reinforcers.

■ The central process in reinforcement is the strengthening of a response. Primary reinforcers are unlearned. In contrast, secondary reinforcers acquire their reinforcing quality through conditioning.

■ Schedules of reinforcement influence patterns of operant responding. Intermittent schedules produce greater resistance to extinction than similar continuous schedules. Ratio schedules tend to yield higher rates of response than interval schedules. Shorter intervals and higher ratios are associated with faster responding.

■ Responses can be strengthened through either the presentation of positive reinforcers or the removal of negative reinforcers. Negative reinforcement regulates escape and avoidance learning. Punishment involves unfavorable consequences that lead to a decline in response strength. Evidence suggests that physical punishment is associated with a variety of undesirable side effects, including increased aggression, but there is some debate about the issue.

Changing Directions in the Study of Conditioning

■ The findings on conditioned taste aversion and preparedness have led to the recognition that there are species-specific biological constraints on conditioning. Domjan argues that researchers' focus on arbitrary conditioned stimuli has led to a distorted picture of the principles of conditioning. Some evolutionary psychologists argue that learning processes vary somewhat across species.

■ Tolman's studies of latent learning suggested that cognitive processes contribute to conditioning, but his work was not influential at the time. Studies of signal relations in classical conditioning and response-outcome relations in operant conditioning demonstrated that cognitive processes play a larger role in conditioning than originally believed.

Observational Learning

■ Observational learning was first described by Albert Bandura. In observational learning, an organism is conditioned by watching a model's conditioning. Both classical and operant conditioning can occur through observational learning, which depends on the processes of attention, retention, reproduction, and motivation.

■ Research on observational learning has played a central role in the debate about the effects of media violence for many decades. This research suggests that media violence contributes to increased aggression among children and adults.

Reflecting on the Chapter's Themes

■ Two of our key themes were especially apparent in the coverage of learning and conditioning. One theme involves the interaction of heredity and the environment in governing behavior. The other involves the way progress in psychology affects society at large.

PERSONAL APPLICATION Achieving Self-Control Through Behavior Modification

■ The first step in self-modification is to specify the overt target behavior to be increased or decreased. The second step involves gathering baseline data about the initial rate of the target response and identifying any typical antecedents and consequences associated with the behavior.

■ The third step is to design a program. If you are trying to increase the strength of a response, you'll depend on positive reinforcement. A number of strategies can be used to decrease the strength of a response, including reinforcement, control of antecedents, and punishment. The fourth step is to execute and evaluate your program, and then determine when you will phase it out.

CRITICAL THINKING APPLICATION Manipulating Emotions: Pavlov and Persuasion

■ Advertisers routinely pair their products with stimuli that seem likely to elicit positive emotional responses or other specific feelings. The business practice of taking customers out to dinner or to major events also takes advantage of Pavlovian conditioning. Politicians also work to pair themselves with positive events. The best defense is to become more aware of efforts to manipulate your emotions.

PSYKTREK PREVIEW

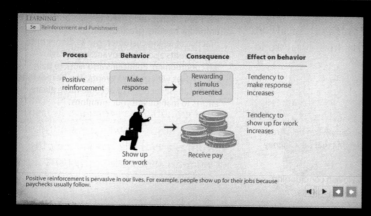

Explore the Unit 5 modules (5a through 5f) to improve your understanding of the principles of classical conditioning and operant conditioning.

Go to the Video Selector to watch historic footage of influential behavioral theorists, including Ivan Pavlov, B. F. Skinner, and Albert Bandura.

1. After repeated pairings of a tone with meat powder, Pavlov found that a dog will salivate when the tone is presented. Salivation to the tone is a(n):
   A. unconditioned stimulus.
   B. unconditioned response.
   C. conditioned stimulus.
   D. conditioned response.

2. Sam's wife always wears the same black nightgown whenever she is "in the mood" for sexual relations. Sam becomes sexually aroused as soon as he sees his wife in the nightgown. For Sam, the nightgown is a(n):
   A. unconditioned stimulus.
   B. unconditioned response.
   C. conditioned stimulus.
   D. conditioned response.

3. Watson and Rayner (1920) conditioned "Little Albert" to fear white rats by banging a hammer on a steel bar as he played with a white rat. Later, it was discovered that Albert feared not only white rats but white stuffed toys and Santa's beard as well. Albert's fear of these other objects can be attributed to:
   A. shaping.
   B. stimulus generalization.
   C. stimulus discrimination.
   D. an overactive imagination.

4. The phenomenon of higher-order conditioning shows that:
   A. only a genuine, natural US can be used to establish a CR.
   B. auditory stimuli are easier to condition than visual stimuli.
   C. visual stimuli are easier to condition than auditory stimuli.
   D. an already established CS can be used in the place of a natural US.

5. In a Skinner box, the dependent variable is usually:
   A. the force with which the lever is pressed or the disk is pecked.
   B. the schedule of reinforcement used.
   C. the rate of responding.
   D. the speed of the cumulative recorder.

6. A primary reinforcer has _____ reinforcing properties; a secondary reinforcer has _____ reinforcing properties.
   A. biological; acquired
   B. conditioned; unconditioned
   C. weak; potent
   D. immediate; delayed

7. The steady, rapid responding of a person playing a slot machine is an example of the pattern of responding typically generated on a _____ schedule of reinforcement.
   A. fixed-ratio
   B. variable-ratio
   C. fixed-interval
   D. variable-interval

8. Positive reinforcement _____ the rate of responding; negative reinforcement _____ the rate of responding.
   A. increases; decreases
   B. decreases; increases
   C. increases; increases
   D. decreases; decreases

9. Research on avoidance learning suggests that conditioned fear acquired through _____ conditioning plays a key role.
   A. classical
   B. operant
   C. reinforcement
   D. intermittent

10. The studies by Garcia and his colleagues demonstrate that rats easily learn to associate a taste CS with a(n) _____ US.
    A. shock
    B. visual
    C. auditory
    D. nausea-inducing

11. Albert Bandura:
    A. was the first to describe species-specific learning tendencies.
    B. was the founder of behaviorism.
    C. pioneered the study of classical conditioning.
    D. pioneered the study of observational learning.

12. In designing a self-modification program, control of antecedents should be used:
    A. by people who are in poor physical condition.
    B. only when your usual reinforcers are unavailable.
    C. when you want to decrease the frequency of a response.
    D. when you are initially not capable of making the target response.

Answers

1 D pp. 189–191 5 C pp. 196–197 9 A p. 204
2 C pp. 189–191 6 A p. 200 10 D p. 208
3 B pp. 193–194 7 B p. 201 11 D pp. 211–212
4 D pp. 194–195 8 C p. 203 12 C p. 219

PSYKTREK PREVIEW

Go to the Video Selector to view famous subjects of behavioral research, including Priscilla the Pig, Little Albert, and Skinner's Ping-Pong playing pigeons.

Discover the power of shaping by trying Simulation 4 (*Shaping in Operant Conditioning*), which allows you to shape Morphy, the virtual rat, to press a lever

7

Human Memory

Venice, Italy © Hermera Technologies/Jupiter Images

If you live in the United States, you've undoubtedly handled thousands upon thousands of American pennies. Surely, then, you remember what a penny looks like—or do you? Take a look at **Figure 7.1**. Which drawing corresponds to a real penny?

Did you have a hard time selecting the real one? If so, you're not alone. Nickerson and Adams (1979) found that most people can't recognize the real penny in this collection of drawings. And their surprising finding was not a fluke. Undergraduates in England showed even worse memory for British coins (Jones, 1990). How can that be? Why do most of us have so poor a memory for an object we see every day?

Let's try another exercise. A definition of a word follows. It's not a particularly common word, but there's a good chance that you're familiar with it. Try to think of the word.

Definition: Favoritism shown or patronage granted by persons in high office to relatives or close friends.

If you can't think of the word, perhaps you can remember what letter of the alphabet it begins with, or what it sounds like. If so, you're experiencing the *tip-of-the-tongue phenomenon,* in which forgotten information feels like it's just out of reach. In this case, the word you may be reaching for is *nepotism.* You've probably endured the tip-of-the-tongue phenomenon while taking exams. You blank out on a term that you're sure you know. You may feel as if you're on the verge of remembering the term, but you can't quite come up with it. Later, perhaps while you're driving home, the term suddenly comes to you. "Of course," you may say to yourself, "how could I forget that?" That's an interesting question. Clearly, the term was stored in your memory.

As these examples suggest, memory involves more than taking in information and storing it in some mental compartment. In fact, psychologists probing the workings of memory have had to grapple with three enduring questions: (1) How does information get *into* memory? (2) How is information *maintained* in memory? (3) How is information *pulled back out* of memory? These three questions correspond to the three key processes involved in memory (see **Figure 7.2**): *encoding* (getting information in), *storage* (maintaining it), and *retrieval* (getting it out).

Figure 7.1

A simple memory test. Nickerson and Adams (1979) presented these 15 versions of an object most people have seen hundreds or thousands of times and asked, "Which one is correct?" Can you identify the real penny?

SOURCE: Nickerson, R. S., & Adams, M. J. (1979). Long-term memory for a common object. *Cognitive Psychology, 11,* 287–307. Copyright © 1979 by Elsevier Science USA. Reproduced with permission from the publisher.

Process	Encoding	Storage	Retrieval
Definition	Involves forming a memory code	Involves maintaining encoded information in memory over time	Involves recovering information from memory stores
Analogy to information processing by a computer	Entering data through keyboard	Saving data in file on hard disk	Calling up file and displaying data on monitor

Figure 7.2

Three key processes in memory. Memory depends on three sequential processes: encoding, storage, and retrieval. Some theorists have drawn an analogy between these processes and elements of information processing by computers, as depicted here. The analogies for encoding and retrieval work pretty well, but the storage analogy is somewhat misleading. When information is stored on a hard drive, it remains unchanged indefinitely, and you can retrieve an exact copy. As you will learn in this chapter, memory storage is a much more dynamic process. Memories change over time and are rough reconstructions rather than exact copies of past events.

Encoding involves forming a memory code. For example, when you form a memory code for a word, you might emphasize how it looks, how it sounds, or what it means. Encoding usually requires attention, which is why you may not be able to recall exactly what a penny looks like—most people don't pay much attention to the appearance of a penny. As you'll see throughout this chapter, memory is largely an active process. For the most part, you're unlikely to remember something unless you make a conscious effort to do so. *Storage* involves maintaining encoded information in memory over time. Psychologists have focused much of their memory research on trying to identify just what factors help or hinder memory storage. But, as the tip-of-the-tongue phenomenon shows, information storage isn't enough to guarantee that you'll remember something. You need to be able to get informa-

tion out of storage. *Retrieval* involves recovering information from memory stores. Research issues concerned with retrieval include the study of how people search memory and why some retrieval strategies are more effective than others.

Most of this chapter is devoted to an examination of memory encoding, storage, and retrieval. As you'll see, these basic processes help explain the ultimate puzzle in the study of memory: why people forget. After our discussion of forgetting, we will take a brief look at the physiological bases of memory. Finally, we will discuss the theoretical controversy about whether there are separate memory systems for different types of information. The chapter's Personal Application provides some practical advice on how to improve your memory. The Critical Thinking Application discusses some reasons that memory is less reliable than people assume it to be.

Encoding: Getting Information into Memory

Key Learning Goals

7.1 Clarify the role of attention in memory, and discuss the effects of divided attention.

7.2 Describe the three types of encoding discussed by Craik and Lockhart and how depth of processing relates to memory.

7.3 Explain how elaboration and visual imagery can enrich encoding.

Have you ever been embarrassed because you couldn't remember someone's name? Perhaps you realized only 30 seconds after meeting someone that you had already "forgotten" his or her name. More often than not, this familiar kind of forgetting results from a failure to form a memory code for the name. When you're introduced to people, you're often busy sizing them up and thinking about what you're going to say. With your attention diverted in this way, names go in one ear and out the other. You don't remember them because they are never encoded for storage.

This problem illustrates that encoding is an important process in memory. In this section, we discuss the role of attention in encoding, types of encoding, and ways to enrich the encoding process.

The Role of Attention

Although there are some fascinating exceptions, you generally need to pay attention to information if you intend to remember it (Lachter, Forster, & Ruthruff, 2004; Mulligan, 1998). For example, if you sit through a class lecture but pay little attention to it, you're unlikely to remember much of what the professor had to say. *Attention* involves focusing awareness on a narrowed range of stimuli or events. Psychologists routinely refer to "selective attention," but the words are really redundant. Attention *is* selection of input.

If you pause to devote a little attention to the matter, you'll realize that selective attention is critical to everyday functioning. If your attention were distributed equally among all stimulus inputs, life would be utter chaos. If you weren't able to filter out most of the potential stimulation around you, you wouldn't be able to read a book, converse with a friend, or even carry on a coherent train of thought.

The importance of attention to memory is apparent when participants are asked to focus their attention on two or more inputs simultaneously. Studies indicate that when participants are forced to divide their attention between memory encoding and some other task, large reductions in memory performance are seen (Craik, 2001; Craik & Kester, 2000). Actually, the negative effects of divided attention are not limited to memory. Divided attention can have a negative impact on the performance of quite a variety of tasks, especially when the tasks are complex or unfamiliar (Pashler, Johnston, & Ruthruff, 2001).

Although people tend to think that they can multitask with no deterioration in performance, research suggests that the human brain can effectively handle only one attention-consuming task at a time (Lien, Ruthruff, & Johnston, 2006). When people multitask, they are really switching their attention back and forth among tasks, rather than processing them simultaneously. That may be fine in many circumstances, but the cost of divided attention does have profound implications for the advisability of driving while conversing on a cell phone. Carefully controlled research clearly demonstrates that cell phone conversations undermine people's driving performance, even when hands-free phones are used (Horrey & Wickens, 2006; Kass, Cole, & Stanny, 2007; Strayer, Drews, & Crouch, 2006). For example, one study of a simulated driving task found that cellular conversations increased the chances of missing traffic signals and slowed down reactions to signals that were detected, as shown in **Figure 7.3** (Strayer & Johnston, 2001).

Levels of Processing   SIM5, 6a

Attention is critical to the encoding of memories, but attention comes in many forms. You can attend to things in different ways, focusing on different aspects of the stimulus input. According to some theorists, these qualitative differences in *how* people attend to information are the main factors influencing how much they remember. For example, Fergus Craik and Robert Lockhart (1972) argue that different rates of forgetting occur because some methods of encoding create more durable memory codes than others.

Craik and Lockhart propose that incoming information can be processed at different levels. For instance, they maintain that in dealing with verbal information, people engage in three progressively deeper levels of processing: structural, phonemic, and semantic encoding (see **Figure 7.4**). *Structural encoding* is relatively shallow processing that emphasizes the physical structure of the stimulus. For example, if words are flashed on a screen, structural encoding registers such things as how the words are printed (capital, lowercase, and so on) or their length (how many letters). Further analysis may result in *phonemic encoding*, which emphasizes what a word sounds like. Phonemic encoding involves naming or saying (perhaps silently) the words. Finally, *semantic encoding* emphasizes the *meaning* of verbal input; it involves thinking about the objects and actions the words represent. *Levels-of-processing theory* proposes that deeper levels of processing result in longer-lasting memory codes.

In one experimental test of levels-of-processing theory, Craik and Tulving (1975) compared the durability of structural, phonemic, and semantic encoding. They directed subjects' attention to particular aspects of briefly presented stimulus words by asking them questions about various characteristics of the words (examples are shown in **Figure 7.4**). The questions were designed to engage the participants in different levels of processing. The key hypothesis was that retention of the stimulus words would increase as subjects moved from structural to phonemic to

Figure 7.3

Divided attention and driving performance. Working on a simulated driving task, subjects in a study by Strayer and Johnston (2001) were supposed to brake as promptly as possible when they saw red lights, while participating or not participating in a phone conversation. (a) The data on the left show that participants missed the red lights more than twice as often when engaged in a cell phone conversation. (b) The data on the right show that participants' reaction time to red lights was slower with the cell phone.

Adapted from Strayer, D. L., & Johnston, W. A. (2001). Driven to distraction: Dual task studies of simulated driving and conversing on a cellular phone. *Psychological Science, 12* (6), 462–465. Copyright © 2001 Association for Psychological Science. Reprinted by permission of Blackwell Publishing.

semantic encoding. After responding to 60 words, the participants received an unexpected test of their memory for the words. As predicted, the subjects' recall was low after structural encoding, notably better after phonemic encoding, and highest after semantic encoding. The hypothesis that deeper processing leads to enhanced memory has been replicated in many studies (Craik, 2002; Lockhart & Craik, 1990). Levels-of-processing theory has been enormously influential; it has shown that memory involves more than just storage and has inspired a great deal of

Figure 7.4

Levels-of-processing theory. According to Craik and Lockhart (1972), structural, phonemic, and semantic encoding—which can be elicited by questions such as those shown on the right—involve progressively deeper levels of processing.

Level of processing	Type of encoding	Example of questions used to elicit appropriate encoding
Shallow processing	*Structural encoding:* emphasizes the physical structure of the stimulus	Is the word written in capital letters?
Intermediate processing	*Phonemic encoding:* emphasizes what a word sounds like	Does the word rhyme with weight?
Deep processing	*Semantic encoding:* emphasizes the meaning of verbal input	Would the word fit in the sentence: "He met a _____ on the street"?

Depth of processing

Alan Baddeley

"The concept of working memory proposes that a dedicated system maintains and stores information in the short term, and that this system underlies human thought processes."

and serves as an interface between working memory and long-term memory. The two key characteristics that originally defined short-term memory—small capacity and short storage duration—are still present in the concept of working memory. However, Baddeley's model accounts for evidence that STM handles a greater variety of functions and depends on more complicated processes than previously thought.

Baddeley's model of working memory has generated an enormous volume of research. For example, research has shown that people vary in how well they can juggle information in their working memory while fending off distractions (Engle, 2001). Interestingly, these variations in *working memory capacity* seem to influence people's ability to control the focus of their attention. People with greater working memory capacity exhibit greater selectivity and flexibility in their deployment of attention (Colflesh & Conway, 2007). Greater working memory capacity also correlates positively with measures of high-level cognitive abilities, such as reading comprehension, complex reasoning, and even intelligence (Conway, Kane, & Engle, 2003; Oberauer et al., 2007). This finding has led some theorists to conclude that working memory capacity is critical to complex cognitive processes and intelligence (Lepine, Barrouillet, & Camos, 2005). Unfortunately, working memory capacity tends to decline gradually during late adulthood (Otsuka & Osaka, 2005; Zacks, Hasher, & Li, 2000). This erosion may play a critical role in age-related decreases in performance on a variety of cognitive tasks (see Chapter 10).

Long-Term Memory 6b

Long-term memory (LTM) is an unlimited capacity store that can hold information over lengthy periods of time. Unlike sensory and short-term memory, which decay rapidly, LTM can store information indefinitely. Long-term memories are durable. Some information may remain in LTM across an entire lifetime.

One point of view is that all information stored in long-term memory is stored there *permanently.* According to this view, forgetting occurs only because people sometimes cannot retrieve needed information from LTM. To draw an analogy, imagine that memories are stored in LTM like marbles in a barrel. According to this view, none of the marbles ever leak out. When you forget, you just aren't able to dig out the right marble, but it's there—somewhere. An alternative point of view assumes that some memories stored in LTM do vanish forever. According to this

"The matters about which I'm being questioned, Your Honor, are all things I should have included in my long-term memory but which I mistakenly inserted in my short-term memory."

view, the barrel is leaky and some of the marbles roll out, never to return.

The existence of *flashbulb memories* is one piece of evidence that has been cited to support the notion that LTM storage may be permanent. At first glance, *flashbulb memories,* **which are unusually vivid and detailed recollections of momentous events,** provide striking examples of seemingly permanent storage (Brown & Kulik, 1977). Many American adults, for instance, can remember exactly where they were, what they were doing, and how they felt when they learned that President John F. Kennedy had been shot. You may have a similar recollection related to the 1997 death of Princess Diana or the terrorist attacks that took place in New York and Washington, DC on September 11, 2001.

Does the evidence on flashbulb memories provide adequate support for the idea that LTM storage is permanent? No. Research eventually showed that flashbulb memories are neither as accurate nor as special as once believed (Neisser & Harsch, 1992). Like other memories, they become less detailed and less accurate with time (Pezdek, 2003; Weaver & Krug, 2004). Recent research suggests that it is not extraordinary accuracy or longevity that distinguish flashbulb memories. Rather, what makes them special is that people subjectively feel that these memories are exceptionally vivid, that people have exceptional confidence (albeit misplaced) in their accuracy, and that more emotional intensity is attached to them (Talarico & Rubin, 2003, 2007). So,

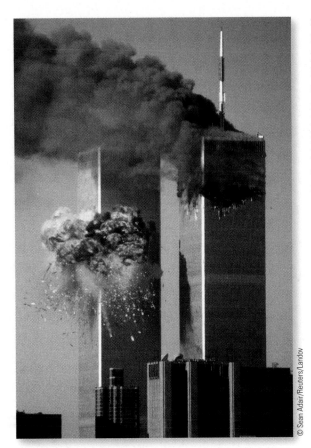

Flashbulb memories are vivid and detailed recollections of momentous events. For example, many people will long remember exactly where they were and how they felt when they learned about the terrorist attacks on the World Trade Center.

perhaps flashbulb memories are "special," but not in the way originally envisioned.

Returning to the question at hand, the research findings on flashbulb memories clearly conflict with the hypothesis that memory storage is permanent. Although the possibility cannot be ruled out completely, there is no convincing evidence that memories are stored away permanently and that forgetting is all a matter of retrieval failure (Payne & Blackwell, 1998; Schacter, 1996).

How Is Knowledge Represented and Organized in Memory? 6b

Over the years memory researchers have wrestled endlessly with another major question relating to memory storage: How is knowledge represented and organized in memory? In other words, what forms do mental representations of information take? Most theorists seem to agree that they probably take a variety of forms, depending on the nature of the material that needs to be tucked away in memory. For example, memories of visual scenes, of how to perform actions (such as typing or hitting a backhand stroke in tennis), and of factual information (such as definitions or dates in history) are probably represented and organized in very different ways. Most of the theorizing to date has focused on how factual knowledge may be represented in memory. In this section, we'll look at a small sample of the organizational structures that have been proposed for semantic information.

Schemas 6b

Imagine that you've just visited Professor Smith's office, which is shown in the photo below. Take a brief look at the photo and then cover it up. Now pretend that you want to describe Professor Smith's office to a friend. Write down what you saw in the office (the picture).

After you finish, compare your description with the picture. Chances are, your description will include elements—filing cabinets, for instance—that were *not* in the office. This common phenomenon demonstrates how *schemas* can influence memory.

A *schema* is an organized cluster of knowledge about a particular object or event abstracted from previous experience with the object or event. For example, college students have schemas for what professors' offices are like. When Brewer and Treyens (1981) tested the recall of 30 subjects who had briefly visited the office shown in the photo, most subjects recalled the desks and chairs, but few recalled the wine bottle or the picnic basket, which aren't part of a typical office schema. Moreover, 9 subjects in

Professor Smith's office is shown in this photo. Follow the instructions in the text to learn how Brewer and Treyens (1981) used it in a study of memory.

concept check 7.1

Comparing the Memory Stores

Check your understanding of the three memory stores by filling in the blanks in the table below. The column on the left lists three features of the memory stores that can be compared. The answers can be found in the back of the book in Appendix A.

Feature	Sensory memory	Short-term memory	Long-term memory
Main encoding format	*copy of input*		*Largely semantic*
Storage capacity	*limited*		
Storage duration		*10–20 seconds*	

web link 7.2

Memory Principles

This brief overview of practical guidelines for improving recall of academic material is maintained by Carolyn Hopper at Middle Tennessee State University. The site succinctly outlines ten basic principles. You'll also find other worthwhile materials to help improve study techniques.

the Brewer and Treyens study falsely recalled that the office contained books. Perhaps you made the same mistake.

These results and other studies (Tuckey & Brewer, 2003) suggest that *people are more likely to remember things that are consistent with their schemas than things that are not.* Although this principle seems applicable much of the time, the inverse is also true: *People sometimes exhibit better recall of things that violate their schema-based expectations* (Koriat, Goldsmith, & Pansky, 2000; Neuschatz et al., 2002). If information really clashes with a schema, it may attract extra attention and deeper processing and thus become more

memorable. For example, if you saw a slot machine in a professor's office, you would probably remember it. In short, the impact of schemas on memory can be difficult to predict, but either way it is apparent that information stored in memory is often organized around schemas (Brewer, 2000).

Semantic Networks

Much of people's knowledge seems to be organized into semantic networks (Collins & Loftus, 1975). A *semantic network* consists of nodes representing concepts, joined together by pathways that link related concepts. **Figure 7.9** shows a small semantic network. The ovals are the nodes, and the words inside the ovals are the interlinked concepts. The lines connecting the nodes are the pathways. A more detailed figure would label the pathways to show how the concepts are related to one another. However, in this instance the relations should be fairly clear. For example, *fire engine* is linked to *red* because of its color, to *vehicle* because it's a vehicle, and to *house* because fires often occur in houses. The length of each pathway represents the degree of association between two concepts. Shorter pathways imply stronger associations.

Semantic networks have proven useful in explaining why thinking about one word (such as *butter*) can make a closely related word (such as *bread*) easier to remember (Meyer & Schvaneveldt, 1976). According to Collins and Loftus (1975), when people think about a word, their thoughts naturally go to related words. These theorists call this process *spreading activation within a semantic network.* They assume that activation spreads out along the pathways of the semantic network surrounding the word. They also theorize that the strength of this activation decreases as it travels outward, much as ripples decrease in size as they radiate outward from a rock tossed into a pond. Consider again the semantic network shown in **Figure 7.9**. If subjects see the word *red,* words that are closely linked to it (such as *orange*) should be easier to recall than words that have longer links (such as *sunrises*).

Connectionist Networks

Connectionist models of memory take their inspiration from how neural networks appear to handle information. The human brain appears to depend extensively on *parallel distributed processing*—that is, simultaneous processing of the same information that is spread across networks of neurons. Based on this insight and basic findings about how neurons operate, *connectionist,* or *parallel distributed processing (PDP), models* assume that cognitive pro-

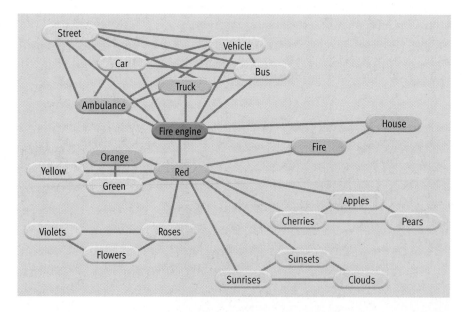

Figure 7.9

A semantic network. Much of the organization of long-term memory depends on networks of associations among concepts. In this highly simplified depiction of a fragment of a semantic network, the shorter the line linking any two concepts, the stronger the association between them. The coloring of the concept boxes (the shades of red) represents activation of the concepts. This is how the network might look just after a person hears the words *fire engine.*

SOURCE: Adapted from Collins, A. M., & Loftus, E. F. (1975). A spreading activation theory of semantic processing. *Psychological Review, 82*, 407–428. Copyright © 1975 by the American Psychological Association. Adapted by permission of the authors.

cesses depend on patterns of activation in highly interconnected computational networks that resemble neural networks (McClelland, 2000; McClelland & Rogers, 2003; McClelland & Rumelhart, 1985). A PDP system consists of a large network of interconnected computing units, or *nodes,* that operate much like neurons. These nodes may be inactive or they may send either excitatory or inhibitory signals to other units. Like an individual neuron, a specific node's level of activation reflects the weighted balance of excitatory and inhibitory inputs from many other units.

Given this framework, *PDP models assert that specific memories correspond to particular patterns of activation in these networks* (McClelland, 1992). Connectionist networks bear some superficial resemblance to semantic networks, but there is a crucial difference. In semantic networks, specific nodes represent specific concepts or pieces of knowledge. In connectionist networks, on the other hand, a piece of knowledge is represented by a particular *pattern* of activation across an entire network. Thus, the information lies in the strengths of the *connections,* which is why the PDP approach is called "connectionism."

In summary, memory storage is a complex matter, involving several memory stores and a variety of organizational devices. Let's now turn to the process of memory retrieval.

REVIEW of Key Learning Goals

7.4 The sensory store preserves information in its original form, probably for only a fraction of a second. Some theorists view stimulus persistence as more like an echo than a memory.

7.5 STM can maintain unrehearsed information for about 10–20 seconds. In a classic paper, George Miller argued that short-term memory has a limited capacity, which is widely assumed to be about seven plus or minus two items of information, although one recent estimate suggests that the capacity of STM is four plus or minus one. The capacity of STM can be increased by combining stimuli into higher-order units called chunks.

7.6 Short-term memory appears to involve more than a simple rehearsal loop and has been reconceptualized as working memory by Alan Baddeley. Working memory includes the phonological loop, the visuospatial sketchpad, a central executive system, and an episodic buffer. Individual differences in working memory capacity correlate with measures of many cognitive abilities. Working memory capacity tends to decline gradually during late adulthood.

7.7 Long-term memory is an unlimited capacity store that may hold information indefinitely. The existence of flashbulb memories suggests that LTM storage may be permanent, but the evidence is not convincing. Research has shown that flashbulb memories are not as durable or accurate as claimed.

7.8 A schema is an organized cluster of knowledge about a particular object or event. Semantic networks consist of concepts joined by pathways. Research suggests that activation spreads along the paths of semantic networks to activate closely associated words. Parallel distributed processing models of memory assert that specific memories correspond to particular patterns of activation in connectionist networks.

Retrieval: Getting Information out of Memory

Entering information into long-term memory is a worthy goal, but it is an insufficient one if you can't get the information back out again when you need it. Fortunately, recall often occurs without much effort. But occasionally a planned search of LTM is necessary. For instance, imagine that you were asked to recall the names of all 50 states in the United States. You would probably conduct your memory search systematically, recalling states in alphabetical order or by geographical location. Although this example is rather simple, retrieval is a complex process, as you'll see in this section.

Using Cues to Aid Retrieval

At the beginning of this chapter we discussed the *tip-of-the-tongue phenomenon*—the temporary inability to remember something you know, accompanied by a feeling that it's just out of reach.

The tip-of-the-tongue phenomenon is a common experience that occurs about once a week, although its occurrence increases with age (A. Brown, 1991; Burke & Shafto, 2004). It clearly represents a failure in retrieval. However, the exact mechanisms underlying this failure are the subject of debate, as a number of explanations have been proposed for the tip-of-the-tongue phenomenon (Schwartz, 1999, 2002).

Fortunately, memories can often be jogged with *retrieval cues*—stimuli that help gain access to memories—such as hints, related information, or partial recollections. This was apparent when Roger Brown and David McNeill (1966) studied the tip-of-the-tongue phenomenon. They gave participants definitions of obscure words and asked them to think of the words. Our example at the beginning of the chapter (the definition for *nepotism*) was taken from their study. Brown and McNeill found that subjects groping for obscure words were correct in guessing

Key Learning Goals

7.9 Explain the tip-of-the-tongue phenomenon and how retrieval cues and context cues influence retrieval.

7.10 Understand the reconstructive nature of memory, and summarize research on the misinformation effect.

7.11 Apply the concept of source monitoring to everyday memory errors.

Elizabeth Loftus

"One reason most of us, as jurors, place so much faith in eyewitness testimony is that we are unaware of how many factors influence its accuracy."

web link 7.3

Mind Tools—Tools for Improving Your Memory

The Mind Tools site details practical techniques to help people improve their cognitive efficiency in many areas. The subpage dedicated to memory functioning offers an excellent collection of suggestions for ways to enhance memory.

Marcia Johnson

"Our long-term goal is to develop ways of determining which aspects of mental experience create one's sense of a personal past and one's conviction (accurate or not) that memories, knowledge, beliefs, attitudes, and feelings are tied to reality in a veridical fashion."

the first letter of the missing word 57% of the time. This figure far exceeds chance and shows that partial recollections are often headed in the right direction.

Reinstating the Context of an Event

Let's test your memory: What did you have for breakfast two days ago? If you can't immediately answer, you might begin by imagining yourself sitting at the breakfast table (or wherever you usually have breakfast). Trying to recall an event by putting yourself back in the context in which it occurred involves working with *context cues* to aid retrieval.

Context cues often facilitate the retrieval of information (Smith, 1988). Most people have experienced the effects of context cues on many occasions. For instance, when people return after a number of years to a place where they used to live, they typically are flooded with long-forgotten memories. Or consider how often you have gone from one room to another to get something (scissors, perhaps), only to discover that you can't remember what you were after. However, when you return to the first room (the original context), you suddenly recall what it was ("Of course, the scissors!"). These examples illustrate the potentially powerful effects of context cues on memory. The technique of reinstating the context of an event has been used effectively in legal investigations to enhance eyewitness recall (Chandler & Fisher, 1996). The eyewitness may be encouraged to retrieve information about a crime by replaying the sequence of events.

Reconstructing Memories

When you retrieve information from long-term memory, you're not able to pull up a "mental videotape" that provides an exact replay of the past. To some extent, your memories are sketchy *reconstructions* of the past that may be distorted and may include details that did not actually occur (Roediger, Wheeler, & Rajaram, 1993).

Research by Elizabeth Loftus (1979, 1992, 2005) and others on the *misinformation effect* has shown that reconstructive distortions show up frequently in eyewitness testimony. The ***misinformation effect*** occurs when participants' recall of an event they witnessed is altered by introducing misleading postevent information. For example, in one study Loftus and Palmer (1974) showed participants a videotape of an automobile accident. Participants were then "grilled" as if they were providing eyewitness testimony, and biasing information was introduced. Some subjects were asked, "How fast were the cars going when they *hit* each other?" Other subjects

were asked, "How fast were the cars going when they *smashed into* each other?" A week later, participants' recall of the accident was tested and they were asked whether they remembered seeing any broken glass in the accident (there was none). Subjects who had earlier been asked about the cars *smashing into* each other were more likely to "recall" broken glass. Why would they add this detail to their reconstructions of the accident? Probably because broken glass is consistent with their schemas for cars *smashing* together (see **Figure 7.10**). The misinformation effect, which has been replicated in "countless studies," is a remarkably reliable phenomenon that "challenged prevailing views about the validity of memory" (Zaragoza, Belli, & Payment, 2007, p. 37). Indeed, the effect is difficult to escape, as even subjects who have been forewarned can be swayed by postevent misinformation (Loftus, 2005).

Other research on the reconstructive nature of memory has demonstrated that the simple act of retelling a story can introduce inaccuracies into memory (Marsh, 2007). When people retell stories, they tend to make a number of "adjustments" that depend on their goals, their audience, and the social context. Think about it, we tell stories to entertain others, to inform others, to impress others, to gain sympathy from our friends, and so forth. Depending on our goals, we may streamline a story, embellish the facts, exaggerate our role, omit important situational considerations, and so forth. Not surprisingly, when participants in one study were asked to evaluate the accuracy of recent retellings, they admitted that 42% were "inaccurate" and that another one-third contained "distortions" (Marsh & Tversky, 2004). When retelling their stories, people may be aware that they are being a little loose with the facts, but what is interesting is that their intentional distortions can reshape their subsequent recollections of the same events. Somehow, the "real" story and the storyteller's "spin" on it probably begin to blend imperceptibly. So, even routine retellings of events can contribute to the malleability of memory.

Source Monitoring

The misinformation effect appears to be due, *in part,* to the unreliability of source monitoring (Mitchell & Johnson, 2000). ***Source monitoring*** is the process of making inferences about the origins of memories. Marcia Johnson and her colleagues maintain that source monitoring is a crucial facet of memory retrieval that contributes to many of the mistakes that people make in reconstructing their experiences (Johnson, 1996, 2006; Johnson, Hashtroudi, & Lindsay, 1993). According to Johnson, memories are not tagged with labels that specify their sources. Thus, when people pull up specific memory records, they have to make decisions *at the time of retrieval* about where the memories came from (example: "Did I read that in the *New York Times* or *Rolling Stone*?"). Much of the time, these decisions are so easy and automatic, people make them without being consciously aware of the source-monitoring process. In other instances, however, they may consciously struggle to pinpoint the source of a memory. A *source-monitoring error* occurs when a memory derived from one source is misattributed to another source. For example, you might attribute something that your roommate said to your psychology professor, or something you heard on *Oprah* to your psychology textbook. Inaccurate memories that reflect source-monitoring errors may seem quite compelling, and people often feel quite confident about their authenticity even though the recollections really are inaccurate (Lampinen, Neuschatz, & Payne, 1999).

Source-monitoring errors appear to be commonplace and may shed light on many interesting memory phenomena. For instance, in studies of eyewitness suggestibility, some subjects have gone so far as to insist that they "remember" seeing something that was only verbally suggested to them. Most theories have a hard time explaining how people can have memories of events that they never actually saw or experienced, but this paradox doesn't seem all that perplexing when it is explained as a source-monitoring error (Lindsay et al., 2004).

Leading question asked during witness testimony	Possible schemas activated	Response of subjects asked one week later, "Did you see any broken glass?" (There was none.)
"About how fast were the cars going when they hit each other?"		"Yes"—14%
"About how fast were the cars going when they smashed into each other?"		"Yes"—32%

Figure 7.10
The misinformation effect. In an experiment by Loftus and Palmer (1974), participants who were asked leading questions in which cars were described as *hitting* or *smashing* each other were prone to recall the same accident differently one week later, demonstrating the reconstructive nature of memory.

REVIEW of Key Learning Goals

7.9 The tip-of-the-tongue phenomenon is the temporary inability to remember something you know, which feels just out of reach. It clearly represents a failure in retrieval. Memories can be jogged by retrieval cues. Reinstating the context of an event can also facilitate recall.

7.10 Memories are not exact replicas of past experiences, as memory is partially reconstructive. Research by Elizabeth Loftus on the misinformation effect shows that information learned after an event can alter one's memory of the event. Even the simple act of retelling a story can introduce inaccuracies into memory.

7.11 Source monitoring is the process of making attributions about the origins of memories. According to Johnson, source-monitoring errors appear to be common and may explain why people sometimes "recall" something that was only verbally suggested to them or confuse their sources of information.

Forgetting: When Memory Lapses

Forgetting gets a "bad press" that it may not deserve. People tend to view forgetting as a failure, weakness, or deficiency in cognitive processing. Although forgetting important information *can* be frustrating, some memory theorists argue that forgetting is actually adaptive. How so? Imagine how cluttered your memory would be if you never forgot anything. According to Daniel Schacter (1999), people need to forget information that is no longer relevant, such as out-of-date phone numbers, discarded passwords, lines that were memorized for a tenth-grade play, and where you kept your important papers three apartments ago. Forgetting can reduce competition among memories that can cause confusion. In a recent exploration of this hypothesis, scientists used brain-imaging technology

to track neural markers of cognitive effort in a series of tasks in which participants memorized pairs of words (Kuhl et al., 2007). They found that the forgetting of word pairs deemed "irrelevant" made it easier to remember the "relevant" word pairs and reduced the "demands" placed on crucial neural circuits. In a nutshell, they found that forgetting helped subjects remember the information they needed to remember.

Although forgetting may be adaptive in the long run, the fundamental question of memory research remains: Why do people forget information that they would like to remember? There isn't one simple answer to this question. Research has shown that forgetting can be caused by defects in encoding, storage, retrieval, or some combination of these processes.

Key Learning Goals

7.12 Describe Ebbinghaus's forgetting curve and three measures of retention.

7.13 Assess ineffective encoding and decay as potential causes of forgetting.

7.14 Evaluate interference and factors in the retrieval process as potential causes of forgetting.

7.15 Summarize evidence for the view that most recovered memories of childhood sexual abuse are genuine.

7.16 Summarize evidence for the view that most recovered memories of childhood sexual abuse are inaccurate.

Hermann Ebbinghaus

"Left to itself every mental content gradually loses its capacity for being revived. . . . Facts crammed at examination time soon vanish."

How Quickly We Forget: Ebbinghaus's Forgetting Curve

6d

The first person to conduct scientific studies of forgetting was Hermann Ebbinghaus. He published a series of insightful memory studies way back in 1885. Ebbinghaus studied only one subject—himself. To give himself lots of new material to memorize, he invented *nonsense syllables*—consonant-vowel-consonant arrangements that do not correspond to words (such as BAF, XOF, VIR, and MEQ). He wanted to work with meaningless materials that would be uncontaminated by his previous learning.

Ebbinghaus was a remarkably dedicated researcher. For instance, in one study he went through over 14,000 practice repetitions, as he tirelessly memorized 420 lists of nonsense syllables (Slamecka, 1985). He tested his memory of these lists after various time intervals. **Figure 7.11** shows what he found. This diagram, called a *forgetting curve,* graphs retention and forgetting over time. Ebbinghaus's forgetting curve shows a sharp drop in retention during the first few hours after the nonsense syllables were memorized. He forgot more than 60% of the syllables in less than 9 hours! Thus, he concluded that most forgetting occurs very rapidly after learning something.

That's a depressing conclusion. What is the point of memorizing information if you're going to forget it all right away? Fortunately, subsequent research showed that Ebbinghaus's forgetting curve was unusually steep (Postman, 1985). Forgetting usually isn't as swift or as extensive as Ebbinghaus thought. One problem was that he was working with such meaningless material. When participants memorize more meaningful material, such as prose or poetry, forgetting curves aren't nearly as steep. Studies of how well people recall their high school classmates suggest that forgetting curves for autobiographical information are much shallower (Bahrick, 2000). Also, different methods of measuring forgetting yield varied estimates of how quickly people forget. This variation underscores the importance of the methods used to measure forgetting, the matter we turn to next.

Measures of Forgetting

SIM5, SIM6, 6d

To study forgetting empirically, psychologists need to be able to measure it precisely. Measures of forgetting inevitably measure retention as well. *Retention* refers to the proportion of material retained (remembered). In studies of forgetting, the results may be reported in terms of the amount forgotten or the amount retained. In these studies, the *retention interval* is the length of time between the presentation of materials to be remembered and the measurement of forgetting. Psychologists use three methods to measure forgetting/retention: recall, recognition, and relearning (Lockhart, 1992).

Who is the current U.S. secretary of state? What movie won the Academy Award for best picture last year? These questions involve recall measures of retention. A *recall measure* requires participants to reproduce information on their own without any cues. If you were to take a recall test on a list of 25 words you had memorized, you would simply be told to write down on a blank sheet of paper as many of the words as you could remember.

In contrast, in a recognition test you might be shown a list of 100 words and asked to choose the 25 words that you had memorized. A *recognition measure* of retention requires participants to select previously learned information from an array of options. Subjects not only have cues to work with, they have the answers right in front of them. In educational testing, multiple-choice, true-false, and matching questions are recognition measures; essay questions and fill-in-the-blanks questions are recall measures.

If you're like most students, you probably prefer multiple-choice tests over essay tests. This preference is understandable, because evidence shows that recognition measures tend to yield higher scores than recall measures of memory for the same information (Lockhart, 2000). This tendency was demonstrated many years ago in a study by Luh (1922), who measured subjects' retention of nonsense syllables with both a recognition test and a recall test. He found that participants' performance on the recognition measure was far superior to their performance on the recall measure. There are two ways of looking at this disparity between recall and recognition tests. One view is that recognition tests are especially *sensitive* measures of retention. The other view is that recognition tests are excessively easy measures of retention.

Figure 7.11

Ebbinghaus's forgetting curve for nonsense syllables. From his experiments on himself, Ebbinghaus (1885) concluded that forgetting is extremely rapid immediately after the original learning and then levels off. Although this generalization remains true, subsequent research has shown that forgetting curves for nonsense syllables are unusually steep.

Actually, there is no guarantee that a recognition test will be easier than a recall test. Although this tends to be the case, the difficulty of recognition tests can vary greatly, depending on the number, similarity, and plausibility of the options provided as possible answers. To illustrate, see whether you know the answer to the following multiple-choice question:

The capital of Washington is:
  a. Seattle   *c. Tacoma*
  b. Spokane   *d. Olympia*

Most students who aren't from Washington find this a fairly difficult question. The answer is Olympia. Now take a look at the next question:

The capital of Washington is:
  a. London   *c. Tokyo*
  b. New York   *d. Olympia*

Virtually anyone can answer this question because the incorrect options are readily dismissed. Although this illustration is a bit extreme, it shows that two recognition measures of the same information can vary dramatically in difficulty.

The third method of measuring forgetting is relearning. A **relearning measure of retention requires a participant to memorize information a second time to determine how much time or effort is saved by having learned it before.** To use this method, a researcher measures how much time (or how many practice trials) a person needs in order to memorize something. At a later date, the participant is asked to relearn the information. The researcher measures how much more quickly the material is memorized the second time. Participants' *savings scores* provide an estimate of their retention. For example, if it takes you 20 minutes to memorize a list the first time and only 5 minutes to memorize it a week later, you've saved 15 minutes. Your savings score of 75% (15/20 = 3/4 = 75%) suggests that you have retained 75% and forgotten the remaining 25% of the information. Relearning measures can detect retention that is overlooked by recognition tests (Crowder & Greene, 2000).

Why We Forget

Measuring forgetting is only the first step in the long journey toward explaining why forgetting occurs. In this section, we explore the possible causes of forgetting, looking at factors that may affect encoding, storage, and retrieval processes.

Ineffective Encoding

A great deal of forgetting may only *appear* to be forgetting. The information in question may never have been inserted into memory in the first place. Since you can't really forget something you never learned, this phenomenon is sometimes called *pseudoforgetting*. We opened the chapter with an example of pseudoforgetting. People usually assume that they know what a penny looks like, but most have actually failed to encode this information. Pseudoforgetting is usually attributable to *lack of attention*.

Even when memory codes are formed for new information, subsequent forgetting may be the result of ineffective or inappropriate encoding (Brown & Craik, 2000). The research on levels of processing shows that some approaches to encoding lead to more forgetting than others (Craik & Tulving, 1975). For example, if you're distracted while you read your textbooks, you may be doing little more than saying the words to yourself. This is an example of *phonemic encoding*, which is inferior to *semantic encoding* for retention of verbal material.

Decay

Instead of focusing on encoding, decay theory attributes forgetting to the impermanence of memory storage. **Decay theory proposes that forgetting occurs because memory traces fade with time.** The implicit assumption is that decay occurs in the physiological mechanisms responsible for memories. According to decay theory, the mere passage of time produces forgetting. This notion meshes nicely with commonsense views of forgetting.

As we saw earlier, decay *does* appear to contribute to the loss of information from the sensory and short-term memory stores. However, the critical task for theories of forgetting is to explain the loss of information from long-term memory. Researchers have *not* been able to demonstrate that decay causes LTM forgetting (Slamecka, 1992).

If decay theory is correct, the principal cause of forgetting should be the passage of time. In studies of long-term memory, however, researchers have repeatedly found that time passage is not as influential as what happens during the time interval. Research has shown that forgetting depends not on the amount of time that has passed since learning but on the amount, complexity, and type of information that subjects have had to absorb *during* the retention interval. The negative impact of competing information on retention is called *interference*. Although theorists have not given up entirely on the intuitively plausible principle of decay (Altmann & Gray, 2002), research on LTM forgetting has been dominated by the concept of interference.

Interference   6d

Interference theory proposes that people forget information because of competition from other material. Although demonstrations of decay in long-term memory have remained elusive, hundreds of studies have shown that interference influences forgetting (Anderson & Neely, 1996; Bjork, 1992). In many of these studies, researchers have controlled interference by varying the similarity between the original material given to subjects (the test material) and the material studied in the intervening period. Interference is assumed to be greatest when intervening material is most similar to the test material. Decreasing the similarity should reduce interference and cause less forgetting. This is exactly what McGeoch and McDonald (1931) found in an influential study (see **Figure 7.12**). They had participants memorize test material that consisted of a list of two-syllable adjectives. They varied the similarity of intervening learning by having subjects then memorize one of five lists. In order of decreasing similarity to the test material, they were synonyms of the test words, antonyms of the test words, unrelated adjectives, nonsense syllables, and numbers. Later, subjects' recall of the test material was measured. **Figure 7.12** shows that as the similarity of the intervening material decreased, the amount of forgetting also decreased—because of reduced interference.

There are two kinds of interference: *retroactive* and *proactive* (Jacoby, Hessels, & Bopp, 2001). *Retroactive interference* occurs when new information impairs the retention of previously learned information. Retroactive interference occurs between the original learning and the retest on that learning (see **Figure 7.13**). For example, the interference manipulated by McGeoch and McDonald (1931) was retroactive interference. In contrast, *proactive interference* occurs when previously learned information interferes with the retention of new information. Proactive interference is rooted in learning that comes before exposure to the test material. For example, when you get a new phone number, your old number (previous learning) may create proactive interference that hampers your recall of your new number. The evidence indicates that both types of interference can have powerful effects on how much you forget.

Retrieval Failure   6d

People often remember things that they were unable to recall at an earlier time. This phenomenon may be obvious only during struggles with the tip-of-the-tongue phenomenon, but it happens frequently. In fact, a great deal of forgetting may be due to breakdowns in the process of retrieval.

Why does an effort to retrieve something fail on one occasion and succeed on another? That's a tough question. One theory is that retrieval failures may be more likely when a mismatch exists between retrieval cues and the encoding of the information you're searching for. According to Tulving and Thomson (1973), a good retrieval cue is consistent with the original encoding of the information to be recalled. If the sound of a word—its phonemic quality—was emphasized during encoding, an effective retrieval cue should emphasize the sound of the word. If the meaning of the word was emphasized during encoding, semantic cues should be best. A general statement of the principle at work here was formulated by Tulving and Thomson (1973). The *encoding specificity principle* states that the value of a retrieval cue depends on how well it corresponds to the memory code. This principle provides one explanation for the inconsistent success of retrieval efforts.

Motivated Forgetting   6d

A century ago, Sigmund Freud (1901) came up with an entirely different explanation for retrieval fail-

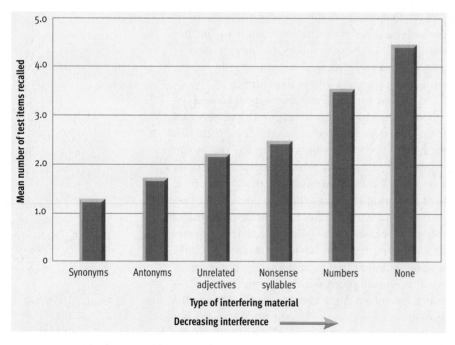

Figure 7.12

Effects of interference. According to interference theory, more interference from competing information should produce more forgetting. McGeoch and McDonald (1931) controlled the amount of interference with a learning task by varying the similarity of an intervening task. The results were consistent with interference theory. The amount of interference is greatest at the left of the graph, as is the amount of forgetting. As interference decreases (moving to the right on the graph), retention improves.

ures. As we noted in Chapter 1, Freud asserted that people often keep embarrassing, unpleasant, or painful memories buried in their unconscious. For example, a person who was deeply wounded by perceived slights at a childhood birthday party might suppress all recollection of that party. In his therapeutic work with patients, Freud recovered many such buried memories. He theorized that the memories were there all along, but their retrieval was blocked by unconscious avoidance tendencies.

The tendency to forget things one doesn't want to think about is called *motivated forgetting*, or to use Freud's terminology, *repression*. In Freudian theory, **repression** refers to keeping distressing thoughts and feelings buried in the unconscious (see Chapter 11). A number of experiments suggest that people don't remember anxiety-laden material as readily as emotionally neutral material, just as Freud proposed (Guenther, 1988; Reisner, 1998). Thus, when you forget unpleasant things such as a dental appointment, a promise to help a friend move, or a term paper deadline, motivated forgetting may be at work.

The Repressed Memories Controversy

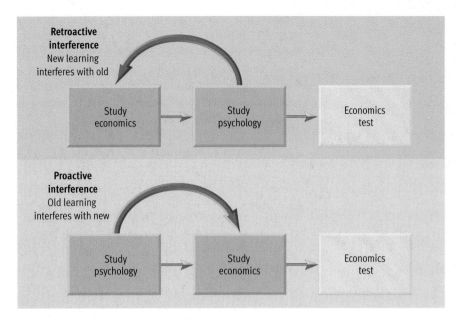

Figure 7.13

Retroactive and proactive interference. Retroactive interference occurs when learning produces a "backward" effect, reducing recall of previously learned material. Proactive interference occurs when learning produces a "forward" effect, reducing recall of subsequently learned material. For example, if you were to prepare for an economics test and then study psychology, the interference from the psychology study would be retroactive interference. However, if you studied psychology first and then economics, the interference from the psychology study would be proactive interference.

Although the concept of repression has been around for a century, interest in this phenomenon has surged in recent years, thanks to a spate of prominent reports involving the return of long-lost memories of sexual abuse and other traumas during childhood. The media have been flooded with reports of adults accusing their parents, teachers, and neighbors of horrible child abuse decades earlier, based on previously repressed memories of these travesties. For the most part, these parents, teachers, and neighbors have denied the allegations. Many of the accused have seemed genuinely baffled by the charges, which have torn some previously happy families apart (Gudjonsson, 2001; McHugh et al., 2004). In an effort to make sense of the charges, some accused parents have argued that their children's recollections are false memories created inadvertently by well-intentioned therapists through the power of suggestion. What do psychologists and psychiatrists have to say about the authenticity of repressed memories? They are sharply divided on the issue.

Support for Repressed Memories

Many psychologists and psychiatrists, especially clinicians involved in the treatment of psychological disorders, accept recovered memories of abuse at face value (Banyard & Williams, 1999; Briere & Conte, 1993; Legault & Laurence, 2007; Skinner, 2001; Terr, 1994; Whitfield, 1995). They assert that sexual abuse

in childhood is far more widespread than most people realize. For example, one large-scale survey (MacMillan et al., 1997), using a random sample of 9953 residents of Ontario, found that 12.8% of the females and 4.3% of the males reported that they had been victims of sexual abuse during childhood. Supporters further assert that there is ample evidence that it is common for people to bury traumatic incidents in

concept check 7.2

Figuring Out Forgetting

Check your understanding of why people forget by identifying the probable causes of forgetting in each of the following scenarios. Choose from (a) motivated forgetting (repression), (b) decay, (c) ineffective encoding, (d) proactive interference, (e) retroactive interference, or (f) retrieval failure. You will find the answers in Appendix A.

_____ 1. Ellen can't recall the reasons for the Webster-Ashburton Treaty because she was daydreaming when it was discussed in history class.

_____ 2. Rufus hates his job at Taco Heaven and is always forgetting when he is scheduled to work.

_____ 3. Ray's new assistant in the shipping department is named Jason Timberlake. Ray keeps calling him Justin, mixing him up with the singer Justin Timberlake.

_____ 4. Tania studied history on Sunday morning and sociology on Sunday evening. It's Monday, and she's struggling with her history test because she keeps mixing up prominent historians with influential sociologists.

their unconscious (Del Monte, 2000; Wilsnack et al., 2002). For instance, in a recent study of psychiatric patients hospitalized for posttraumatic or dissociative disorders (see Chapter 13), one-third of those who reported childhood sexual abuse said that they had experienced complete amnesia for the abuse at some point in their lives (Chu et al., 1999).

Skepticism of Repressed Memories

In contrast, many other psychologists, especially memory researchers, have expressed skepticism about the recent upsurge of recovered memories of abuse (Kihlstrom, 2004; Laney & Loftus, 2005; Loftus, 1998, 2003; McNally, 2003, 2007). The skeptics do *not* argue that people are lying about their previously repressed memories. Rather, they maintain that some suggestible people wrestling with emotional problems have been convinced by persuasive therapists that their emotional problems must be the result of abuse that occurred years before. Critics blame a small minority of therapists who presumably have good intentions but who operate under the questionable assumption that most or even all psychological problems are attributable to childhood sexual abuse (Lindsay & Read, 1994; Loftus & Davis, 2006; Spanos, 1994). Using hypnosis, dream interpretation, and leading questions, they supposedly prod and probe patients until they inadvertently create the memories of abuse that they are searching for (Lynn et al., 2003; Thayer & Lynn, 2006).

Psychologists who doubt the authenticity of repressed memories support their analysis by pointing to discredited cases of recovered memories (Brown, Goldstein, & Bjorklund, 2000). For example, with the help of a church counselor, one woman recovered memories of how her minister father had repeatedly raped her, got her pregnant, and then aborted the pregnancy with a coat-hanger, but sub-sequent evidence revealed that the woman was still a virgin and that her father had had a vasectomy years before (Brainerd & Reyna, 2005). The skeptics also point to published case histories that clearly involved suggestive questioning and to cases in which patients have recanted recovered memories of sexual abuse after realizing that these memories were implanted by their therapists (Loftus, 1994; Shobe & Schooler, 2001). Another problem for memory researchers is that some recovered memories have described incidents of abuse that occurred before the victim reached age 3. However, when adults are asked to recall their earliest memories, their oldest recollections typically don't go back that far (Bruce, Dolan, & Phillips-Grant, 2000; Hayne, 2007).

Those who question the accuracy of repressed memories also point to findings on the misinformation effect, research on source-monitoring errors, and a number of other demonstrations of the relative ease of creating "memories" for events that never happened (Lindsay et al., 2004; Loftus & Cahill, 2007; Strange, Clifasefi, & Garry, 2007). For example, working with college students, Ira Hyman and his colleagues have managed to implant recollections of fairly substantial events (such as spilling a punch bowl at a wedding, being in a grocery store when the fire sprinkler system went off, being hospitalized for an earache) in about 25% of their subjects, just by asking them to elaborate on events supposedly reported by their parents (Hyman, Husband, & Billings, 1995; Hyman & Kleinknecht, 1999). Other studies have succeeded in implanting false memories of nearly drowning (Heaps & Nash, 2001) and of being attacked by a vicious animal (Porter, Yuille, & Lehman, 1999) in many participants. Moreover, subjects in these studies often feel very confident about their false memories, which frequently generate strong emotional reactions and richly detailed "recollections" (Loftus & Bernstein, 2005). The newest wrinkle in this line of research involves using Photoshop to doctor photographs to show participants taking a childhood ride in a hot air balloon. Even with no supportive information supplied, exposing subjects to these bogus photos led 50% of the participants to develop "memories" of their balloon experience (Garry & Gerrie, 2005).

In a similar vein, building on much earlier work by James Deese (1959), Henry Roediger and Kathleen McDermott (1995, 2000) have devised a simple laboratory paradigm involving the learning of word lists that is remarkably reliable in producing memory illusions. In this procedure, now known as the *Deese-Roediger-McDermott (DRM) paradigm*, a series of lists of 15 words are presented to participants, who are asked to recall the words immediately after each list is presented and are given a recognition measure of

Tom Rutherford (shown here with his wife, Joyce) received a $1 million settlement in a suit against a church therapist and a Springfield, Missouri, church in a false memory case. Under the church counselor's guidance, the Rutherfords' daughter, Beth, had "recalled" childhood memories of having been raped repeatedly by her minister father, gotten pregnant, and undergone a painful coat-hanger abortion. Her father lost his job and was ostracized. After he later revealed he'd had a vasectomy when Beth was age 4, and a physical exam revealed that at age 23 she was still a virgin, the memories were shown to be false.

their retention at the end of the session. The trick is that each list consists of a set of words (such as *bed, rest, awake, tired*) that are strongly associated with another target word that is not on the list (in this case, *sleep*). When subjects *recall* the words on each list, they remember the nonpresented target word over 50% of the time, and when they are given the final *recognition* test, they typically indicate that about 80% of the nonstudied target words were presented in the lists (see **Figure 7.14**).

The memory illusions created in this experiment may seem trivial in comparison to the vivid, detailed recollections of previously forgotten sexual abuse that have generated the repressed memories controversy. But these false memories can be reliably created in normal, healthy participants in a matter of minutes, with little effort and no pressure or misleading information. Thus, this line of research provides a dramatic demonstration of how easy it is to get people to remember that they saw something they really didn't see (McDermott, 2007; Neuschatz et al., 2007).

Rebuttals to the Skeptics

Of course, psychologists who believe in recovered memories have mounted rebuttals to the arguments raised by the skeptics. For example, Kluft (1999) argues that a recantation of a recovered memory of abuse does not prove that the memory was false. Gleaves (1994) points out that individuals with a

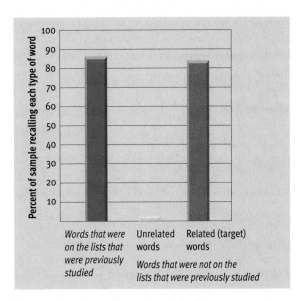

Figure 7.14

The prevalence of false memories observed by Roediger and McDermott (1995). The graph shown here summarizes the recognition test results in Study 1 conducted by Roediger and McDermott (1995). Participants correctly identified words that had been on the lists that they had studied 86% of the time and only misidentified unrelated words that had not been on the lists 2% of the time, indicating that they were paying careful attention to the task. Nonetheless, they mistakenly reported that they "remembered" related target words that were not on the lists 84% of the time—a remarkably high prevalence of false memories.

history of sexual abuse often vacillate between denying and accepting that the abuse occurred. Harvey (1999) argues that laboratory demonstrations showing that it is easy to create false memories have involved trivial memory distortions that are a far cry from the emotionally wrenching recollections of sexual abuse that have generated the recovered memories controversy. Moreover, even if one accepts the assertion that therapists *can* create false memories of abuse in their patients, some critics have noted that there is virtually no direct evidence

web link 7.4

False Memory Syndrome Foundation (FMSF) Online

This site marshals evidence that recovered memories of childhood abuse are often false, therapist induced, and grounded in shoddy and nonobjective scientific claims. Dealing with perhaps the most bitterly contested topic in current psychology, the FMSF has elicited fierce opposition.

DOONESBURY

on how often this situation occurs and no empirical basis for the claim that there has been an *epidemic* of such cases (Berliner & Briere, 1999; Leavitt, 2001; Wilsnack et al., 2002).

Conclusions

Although both sides seem genuinely concerned about the welfare of the people involved, the debate about recovered memories of sexual abuse has grown increasingly bitter and emotionally charged. So, what can we conclude about the recovered memories controversy? It seems pretty clear that therapists can unknowingly create false memories in their patients and that a significant portion of recovered memories of abuse are the product of suggestion. But it also seems likely that some cases of recovered memories are authentic (Brewin, 2007; Smith & Gleaves, 2007). At this point, we don't have adequate data to estimate what proportion of recovered memories of abuse fall in each category (Lindsay & Read, 2001). Thus, the matter needs to be addressed with great caution. On the one hand, people should be extremely careful about accepting recovered memories of abuse in the absence of convincing corroboration. On the other hand, recovered memories of abuse cannot be summarily dismissed, and it would be tragic if the repressed memories controversy made people overly skeptical about the all-too-real problem of childhood sexual abuse.

The repressed memories controversy deserves one last comment regarding its impact on memory research and scientific conceptions of memory. The controversy has helped inspire a great deal of research that has increased our understanding of just how fragile, fallible, malleable, and subjective human memory can be. Indeed, the implicit dichot-

omy underlying the repressed memories debate—that some memories are true, whereas others are false—is misleading and oversimplified. Research demonstrates that all human memories are imperfect reconstructions of the past that are subject to many types of distortion.

web link 7.5

The Recovered Memory Project

Directed by Professor Russ Cheit (Brown University), this site takes issue with the point of view that most recovered memories of abuse are false memories. It provides descriptions of "corroborated" cases of recovered memories and links to scientists and research articles that are sympathetic to those who believe in repressed memories.

In Search of the Memory Trace: The Physiology of Memory

Key Learning Goals

7.17 Distinguish between two types of amnesia, and identify the anatomical structures implicated in memory.

7.18 Describe evidence on neural circuits and memory, including work on long-term potentiation and neurogenesis.

For decades, neuroscientists have ventured forth in search of the physiological basis for memory. On several occasions scientists have been excited by new leads, only to be led down blind alleys. For example, in the 1960s James McConnell rocked the world of science when he reported that he had chemically transferred a specific memory from one flatworm to another. McConnell (1962) created a conditioned reflex (contraction in response to light) in flatworms and then transferred RNA (a basic molecular constituent of all living cells) from trained worms to untrained worms. The untrained worms showed evidence of "remembering" the conditioned reflex. McConnell boldly speculated that in the future, chemists might be able to formulate pills containing the information for Physics 201 or History 101! Unfortunately, the RNA transfer studies proved difficult to replicate (Rilling, 1996). Today, 45 years after McConnell's "breakthrough," we are still a long way from breaking the chemical code for memory.

Investigators continue to explore a variety of leads about the physiological bases for memory. In light of past failures, these lines of research should probably be viewed with guarded optimism. Nonetheless, in this section we'll look at some of the more promising research.

The Anatomy of Memory   6c

Cases of amnesia (extensive memory loss) resulting from head injury are a useful source of clues about the anatomical bases of memory. There are two basic types of amnesia: retrograde and anterograde (see **Figure 7.15**). In *retrograde amnesia* a person loses memories for events that occurred prior to the injury. For example, a 25-year-old gymnast who sustains a head trauma might find three years, seven years, or perhaps her entire lifetime erased. In *anterograde amnesia* a person loses memories for events that occur after the injury. For instance, after her accident, the injured gymnast might suffer impaired ability to remember people she meets, where she has parked her car, and so on.

Because victims' current memory functioning is impaired, cases of anterograde amnesia have been especially rich sources of information about the brain and memory. One well-known case, that of a man referred to as H.M., was followed by Brenda Milner and her colleagues from 1953 until his death in 2008 (Corkin, 1984, 2002; Scoville & Milner, 1957). H.M. had surgery to relieve debilitating epileptic seizures. Unfortunately, the surgery inadvertently wiped out most of his ability to form long-term memories. H.M.'s short-term memory remained fine, but he had no recollection of anything that had happened since 1953 (other than about the most recent 20 seconds of his life). He did not recognize the doctors treating him, he couldn't remember routes to and from places, and he didn't know his own age. H.M. was unable to remember what he did yesterday, let alone what he had done for the previous 55 years. In his elderly years he couldn't even recognize a current photo of himself, as aging had changed his appearance considerably.

H.M.'s memory losses were originally attributed to the removal of his *hippocampus* (see **Figure 7.16**), although theorists now understand that other nearby structures that were removed also contributed to H.M.'s dramatic memory deficits (Delis & Lucas, 1996). Based on decades of additional research, scientists now believe that the entire *hippocampal region* plus the adjacent *parahippocampal region* are critical for many types of long-term memory (Zola & Squire, 2000). Many scientists now refer to this broader memory complex as the *medial temporal lobe memory system* (Squire, Clark, & Bayley, 2004). Given its apparent role in long-term memory, it is interesting to note that the hippocampal region is one of the first

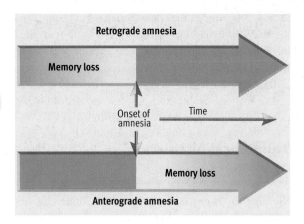

Figure 7.15
Retrograde versus anterograde amnesia. In retrograde amnesia, memory for events that occurred prior to the onset of amnesia is lost. In anterograde amnesia, memory for events that occur subsequent to the onset of amnesia suffers.

areas of the brain to sustain significant damage in the course of Alzheimer's disease, which produces severe memory impairment in many people, typically after age 65 (Albert & Moss, 2002).

Do these findings mean that memories are stored in the hippocampal region and adjacent areas? Probably not. Many theorists believe that the medial temporal lobe memory system plays a key role in the *consolidation* of memories (Dudai, 2004). *Consolidation* is a hypothetical process involving the gradual conversion of information into durable memory codes stored in long-term memory. According to this view, memories are consolidated in the hippocampal region and then stored in diverse and widely distributed areas of the cortex (Eichenbaum, 2004; Markowitsch,

Brenda Milner
"Some effects of temporal lobe lesions in man are hard to reconcile with any unitary-process theory of memory."

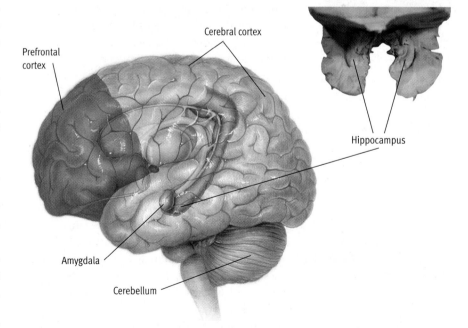

Figure 7.16
The anatomy of memory. All the brain structures identified here have been implicated in efforts to discover the anatomical structures involved in memory. Although its exact contribution to memory remains the subject of debate, the hippocampus is thought to play an especially central role in memory.

2000). This setup allows new memories to become independent of the hippocampal region and to gradually be integrated with other memories already stored in various areas of the cortex (Frankland & Bontempi, 2005). Interestingly, recent research suggests that much of the consolidation process may unfold while people sleep (Stickgold & Walker, 2005).

The Neural Circuitry of Memory

6c

Richard F. Thompson (1989, 1992, 2005) and his colleagues have shown that specific memories may depend on *localized neural circuits* in the brain. In other words, memories may create unique, reusable pathways in the brain along which signals flow. Thompson has traced the pathway that accounts for a rabbit's memory of a conditioned eyeblink response. The key link in this circuit is a microscopic spot in the *cerebellum,* a structure in the hindbrain (see **Figure 7.16**). When this spot is destroyed, the conditioned stimulus no longer elicits the eyeblink response, even though the unconditioned stimulus still does (Steinmetz, 1998). This finding does *not* mean that the cerebellum is the key to all memory. Thompson theorizes that other memories probably create entirely different pathways in other areas of the brain. The key implication of Thompson's work is that it may be possible to map out specific neural circuits that correspond to specific memories.

Another line of research suggests that memory formation results in *alterations in synaptic transmission* at specific sites. Eric Kandel (2001) and his colleagues have studied conditioned reflexes in a simple organism—a sea slug. In research that earned a Nobel prize for Kandel, they showed that reflex learning in the sea slug produces changes in the strength of specific synaptic connections by enhancing the availability and release of neurotransmitters at these synapses (Bailey & Kandel, 2004; Kennedy, Hawkins, & Kandel, 1992). Kandel believes that durable changes in synaptic transmission may be the neural building blocks of more complex memories as well.

Evidence on *long-term potentiation* also supports the idea that memory traces consist of specific neural circuits. *Long-term potentiation (LTP)* is a long-lasting increase in neural excitability at synapses along a specific neural pathway. Researchers produce LTP artificially by sending a burst of high-frequency electrical stimulation along a neural pathway. However, theorists suspect that natural events produce the same sort of potentiated neural circuit when a memory is formed (Abraham, 2006; Lynch, 2004). LTP appears to involve changes in both presynaptic (sending) and postsynaptic (receiving) neu-

rons in neural circuits in the hippocampus (refer to **Figure 7.16**) (Bi & Poo, 2001). The evidence on LTP has inspired promising work on the development of drugs that might enhance memory in humans (Lynch & Gall, 2006).

Recent research suggests that the process of *neurogenesis*—the formation of new neurons—may contribute to the sculpting of neural circuits that underlie memory. As we noted in Chapter 3, scientists have recently discovered that new brain cells are formed constantly in the *dentate gyrus* of the *hippocampus* (Gould, 2004). Animal studies show that manipulations that suppress neurogenesis lead to memory impairments on many types of learning tasks and that conditions that increase neurogenesis are associated with enhanced learning on many tasks (Leuner, Gould, & Shors, 2006). According to Becker and Wojtowicz (2007), newly formed neurons are initially more excitable than mature neurons, so they may be more readily recruited into new neural circuits corresponding to memories. Moreover, neurogenesis provides the brain with a supply of neurons that vary in age, and these variations may somehow allow the brain to "timestamp" some memories. The theorizing about how neurogenesis contributes to memory encoding is highly speculative, but research on neurogenesis is an exciting new line of investigation.

In summary, a number of anatomical structures, neural circuits, and biochemical processes appear to play a role in memory. Does all this sound confusing? It should, because it is. The bottom line is that neuroscientists are still assembling the pieces of the puzzle that will explain the physiological basis of memory. Although they have identified many of the puzzle pieces, they're not sure how the pieces fit together. Their difficulty is probably due to the complex, multifaceted nature of memory. Looking for the physiological basis for memory is only slightly less daunting than looking for the physiological basis for thought itself.

Eric Kandel

"Learning results from changes in the strength of the synaptic connections between precisely interconnected cells."

web link 7.6

The Skeptic's Dictionary: Memory

This site provides a brief but accurate introduction to a host of issues related to memory, with many useful hyperlinks. Topics covered include forgetting, source-monitoring errors, amnesia, and the reliability of memory.

> **REVIEW of Key Learning Goals**
>
> **7.17** In retrograde amnesia, a person loses memory for events prior to the amnesia. In anterograde amnesia, a person shows memory deficits for events subsequent to the onset of the amnesia. Studies of amnesia and other research suggest that the hippocampus and broader medial temporal lobe system play a major role in memory. These areas may be crucial to the consolidation of memories.
>
> **7.18** Richard Thompson's research suggests that memory traces may consist of localized neural circuits. According to Eric Kandel, memory traces reflect alterations in neurotransmitter release at specific synapses. Memories may also depend on long-term potentiation, which is a durable increase in neural excitability at synapses along a specific neural pathway. Neurogenesis may contribute to the sculpting of neural circuits for memories.

Systems and Types of Memory

Some theorists believe that evidence on the physiology of memory is confusing because investigators are unwittingly probing into several distinct memory systems that may have different physiological bases. The various memory systems are distinguished primarily by the types of information they handle.

Declarative Versus Procedural Memory

6c

The most basic division of memory into distinct systems contrasts *declarative memory* with *nondeclarative, or procedural, memory* (Squire, 2004; see **Figure 7.17**). The *declarative memory system* **handles factual information. It contains recollections of** words, definitions, names, dates, faces, events, concepts, and ideas. The *nondeclarative memory system* **houses memory for actions, skills, conditioned responses, and emotional memories. It contains** procedural memories of how to execute such actions as riding a bike, typing, and tying one's shoes. To illustrate the distinction, if you know the rules of tennis (the number of games in a set, scoring, and such), this factual information is stored in declarative memory. If you remember how to hit a serve and swing through a backhand, these perceptual-motor skills are stored in nondeclarative memory.

Support for the distinction between declarative and nondeclarative memory comes from evidence that the two systems seem to operate somewhat differently (Squire, Knowlton, & Musen, 1993). For example, the recall of factual information generally depends on conscious, effortful processes, whereas memory for conditioned reflexes is largely automatic and memories for skills often require little effort and attention (Johnson, 2003). People execute perceptual-motor tasks such as playing the piano or typing with little conscious awareness of what they're doing. In fact, performance on such tasks sometimes deteriorates if people think too much about what they're doing. Another disparity is that the memory for skills (such as typing and bike riding) doesn't decline much over long retention intervals, while declarative memory appears more vulnerable to forgetting.

Although much remains to be learned, researchers have made some progress toward identifying the neural bases of declarative versus procedural memory. Declarative memory appears to be handled by the *medial temporal lobe* memory system and the far-flung areas of the cortex with which it communicates (Eichenbaum, 2003). Pinpointing the neural bases of procedural memory has proven difficult because it consists of more of a hodgepodge of memory functions; however, structures such as the cerebellum and amygdala appear to contribute (Delis & Lucas, 1996; Squire, 2004).

Semantic Versus Episodic Memory

Endel Tulving (1986, 1993, 2002) has further subdivided declarative memory into semantic and episodic memory (see **Figure 7.17**). Both contain factual information, but episodic memory contains *personal facts* and semantic memory contains *general facts*. The *episodic memory system* **is made up of chronological, or temporally dated, recollections of personal experiences. Episodic memory is a record of things** you've done, seen, and heard. It includes information about *when* you did these things, saw them, or heard them. It contains recollections about being in a ninth-grade play, visiting the Grand Canyon, attending a Rolling Stones concert, or going to a movie last weekend. Tulving (2001) emphasizes that the function of episodic memory is "time travel"—that is, to allow one to reexperience the past. He also speculates that episodic memory may be unique to humans.

The *semantic memory system* **contains general knowledge that is not tied to the time when the information was learned. Semantic memory contains**

Key Learning Goals

7.19 Compare and contrast declarative and nondeclarative memory.

7.20 Distinguish between episodic and semantic memory.

7.21 Distinguish between retrospective and prospective memory.

Figure 7.17

Theories of independent memory systems. Theorists have distinguished between declarative memory, which handles facts and information, and nondeclarative memory, which handles motor skills, conditioned responses, and emotional memories. Declarative memory is further subdivided into semantic memory (general knowledge) and episodic memory (dated recollections of personal experiences). The extent to which nondeclarative memory can be usefully subdivided remains the subject of debate.

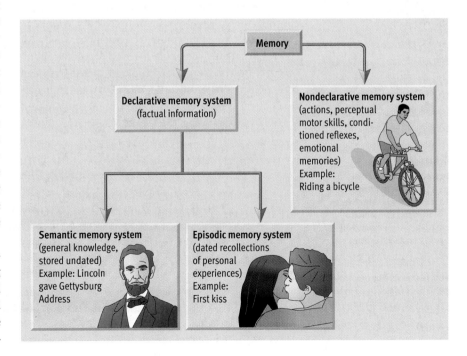

Memory

Declarative memory system (factual information)

Nondeclarative memory system (actions, perceptual motor skills, conditioned reflexes, emotional memories) Example: Riding a bicycle

Semantic memory system (general knowledge, stored undated) Example: Lincoln gave Gettysburg Address

Episodic memory system (dated recollections of personal experiences) Example: First kiss

Endel Tulving

"Memory systems constitute the major subdivisions of the overall organization of the memory complex.... An operating component of a system consists of a neural substrate and its behavioral or cognitive correlates."

information such as Christmas is December 25th, dogs have four legs, the U.S. Supreme Court has nine justices, and Phoenix is located in Arizona. You probably don't remember when you learned these facts. Information like this is usually stored undated. The distinction between episodic and semantic memory can be better appreciated by drawing an analogy to books: Episodic memory is like an autobiography, while semantic memory is like an encyclopedia. The memory deficits seen in some cases of amnesia suggest that episodic and semantic memory are separate systems. For instance, some amnesiacs forget most personal facts, while their recall of general facts is largely unaffected (Wood, Ebert, & Kinsbourne, 1982). However, debate continues about whether episodic and semantic memory have distinct neural bases.

Prospective Versus Retrospective Memory

A 1984 paper with a clever title, "Remembering to Do Things: A Forgotten Topic" (Harris, 1984), introduced yet another distinction between types of memory: *prospective memory* versus *retrospective memory* (see **Figure 7.18**). This distinction does not refer to independent *memory systems* but rather to fundamentally different types of memory tasks. **Prospective memory involves remembering to perform actions in the future.** Examples of prospective memory tasks include remembering to walk the dog, to call someone, to grab the tickets for the big game, and to turn off your lawn sprinkler. In contrast, **retrospective memory involves remembering events from the past or previously learned information.** Retrospective memory is at work when you try to remember who won the Super Bowl last year, when you reminisce about your high school days, or when you try to remember what your professor said in a lecture last week. Prospective memory has been a "forgotten" topic in that it has been the subject of relatively little study. But that has begun to change, as research on prospective memory has increased in recent years (McDaniel & Einstein, 2007).

Researchers interested in prospective memory argue that the topic merits far more study because it plays such a pervasive role in everyday life (Graf & Uttl, 2001). Think about it—a brief trip to attend class at school can be saturated with prospective memory tasks. You may need to remember to pack your notebook, take your cell phone, turn off the coffeemaker, and grab your parking card before you even get out the door. Unfortunately, experiments demonstrate that it is easy to forget such intentions,

Figure 7.18
Retrospective versus prospective memory. Most memory research has explored the dynamics of *retrospective memory,* which focuses on recollections from the past. However, *prospective memory,* which requires people to remember to perform actions in the future, also plays an important role in everyday life.

especially when you are confronted by interruptions and distractions (Einstein et al., 2003). People vary considerably in their ability to successfully carry out prospective memory tasks (Searleman, 1996). Individuals who appear deficient in prospective memory are often characterized as "absent-minded." Research suggests, with some caveats, that older adults are somewhat more vulnerable to problems with prospective memory than younger people are (McDaniel et al., 2003).

REVIEW of Key Learning Goals

7.19 Declarative memory is memory for facts, whereas nondeclarative memory is memory for actions, skills, and conditioned responses. Declarative memory depends more on conscious attention and is more vulnerable to forgetting.

7.20 Tulving subdivided declarative memory into episodic and semantic memory. Episodic memory is made up of temporally dated recollections of personal experiences, much like an autobiography. Semantic memory contains general facts, much like an encyclopedia.

7.21 Prospective memory involves remembering to perform actions in the future. In contrast, retrospective memory involves remembering events from the past or previously learned information. Prospective memory tasks are more common in everyday life than realized. Aging may undermine prospective memory somewhat.

Reflecting on the Chapter's Themes

One of our integrative themes—the idea that people's experience of the world is subjective—stood head and shoulders above the rest in this chapter. Let's briefly review how the study of memory has illuminated this idea.

First, our discussion of attention as inherently selective should have shed light on why people's experience of the world is subjective. To a great degree, what you see in the world around you depends on where you focus your attention. This is one of the

Key Learning Goals

7.22 Identify the three unifying themes highlighted in this chapter.

 Subjectivity of Experience

 Theoretical Diversity

Multifactorial Causation

concept check 7.4

Identifying the Contributions of Major Theorists and Researchers

Check your recall of the principal ideas of important theorists and researchers covered in this chapter by matching the people listed on the left with the appropriate contributions described on the right. If you need help, the crucial pages describing each person's ideas are listed in parentheses. Fill in the letters for your choices in the spaces provided on the left. You'll find the answers in Appendix A.

Major Theorists and Researchers

_____ 1. Richard Atkinson and Richard Shiffrin (p. 229)

_____ 2. Alan Baddeley (pp. 231–232)

_____ 3. Fergus Craik and Robert Lockhart (p. 227)

_____ 4. Hermann Ebbinghaus (p. 238)

_____ 5. Elizabeth Loftus (pp. 236, 242)

_____ 6. Marcia Johnson (pp. 236–237)

_____ 7. Eric Kandel (p. 246)

_____ 8. George Miller (pp. 230–231)

_____ 9. Endel Tulving (pp. 247–248)

Key Ideas and Contributions

a. This 19th-century scholar invented nonsense syllables and showed that forgetting often occurs very rapidly.

b. This expert on short-term memory is famous for a paper titled "The Magical Number Seven, Plus or Minus Two."

c. These researchers developed an influential information-processing model of memory that described three memory stores: sensory memory, short-term memory, and long-term memory.

d. According to this theorist, declarative memory should be subdivided into episodic memory and semantic memory.

e. This researcher developed a four-component model of working memory.

f. These researchers devised levels-of-processing theory, which proposes that deeper levels of processing result in longer-lasting memories.

g. This researcher described the misinformation effect and conducted extensive research on repressed memories.

h. This researcher described the process of source monitoring and the significance of source-monitoring errors.

i. Working with sea slugs, this researcher won a Nobel prize for demonstrating that alterations in synaptic transmission contribute to memory formation.

main reasons why two people can be exposed to the "same" events and walk away with entirely different perceptions. Second, the reconstructive nature of memory should further explain people's tendency to view the world with a subjective slant. When you observe an event, you don't store an exact copy of the event in your memory. Instead, you store a rough, "bare bones" approximation of the event that may be reshaped as time goes by.

A second theme that was apparent in our discussion of memory was psychology's theoretical diversity. We saw illuminating theoretical debates about the nature of memory storage, the causes of forgetting, and the existence of multiple memory systems. Finally, the multifaceted nature of memory demonstrated once again that behavior is governed by multiple causes. For instance, your memory of a specific event may be influenced by your attention to it, your level of processing, your elaboration, how you search your memory store, how you reconstruct the event, and so forth. Given the multifaceted nature of memory, it should come as no surprise that there are many ways to improve memory. We discuss a variety of strategies in the Personal Application section.

REVIEW of Key Learning Goals

7.22 Our discussion of attention and memory enhances understanding of why people's experience of the world is highly subjective. Work on memory also highlights the field's theoretical diversity and shows that behavior is governed by multiple causes.

PERSONAL

APPLICATION

Improving Everyday Memory

Key Learning Goals

7.23 Discuss the importance of rehearsal, distributed practice, and interference in efforts to improve everyday memory.

7.24 Discuss the value of deep processing, good organization, and mnemonic devices in efforts to improve everyday memory.

Answer the following "true" or "false."

___ **1** Memory strategies were recently invented by psychologists.

___ **2** Overlearning of information leads to poor retention.

___ **3** Outlining what you read is not likely to affect retention.

___ **4** Massing practice in one long study session is better than distributing practice across several shorter sessions.

Mnemonic devices are strategies for enhancing memory. They have a long and honorable history. In fact, one of the mnemonic devices covered in this Application— the method of loci—was described in Greece as early as 86–82 B.C. (Yates, 1966). Actually, mnemonic devices were even more crucial in ancient times than they are today. In ancient Greece and Rome, for in-

stance, paper and pencils were not readily available for people to jot down things they needed to remember, so they had to depend heavily on mnemonic devices.

Are mnemonic devices the key to improving one's everyday memory? No. Mnemonic devices clearly can be helpful in some situations (Wilding & Valentine, 1996), but they are not a cure-all. They can be hard to use and hard to apply to many everyday situations. Most books and training programs designed to improve memory probably overemphasize mnemonic techniques (Searleman & Herrmann, 1994). Although less exotic strategies such as increasing rehearsal, engaging in deeper processing, and organizing material are more crucial to everyday memory, we will discuss some popular mnemonics as we proceed through this Application. Along the way, you'll learn that all of our opening true-false statements are false.

Engage in Adequate Rehearsal   SIM5

PSYK TREK

Practice makes perfect, or so you've heard. In reality, practice is not likely to guarantee perfection, but it usually leads to improved retention. Studies show that retention improves with increased rehearsal (Greene, 1992). This improvement presumably occurs because rehearsal helps transfer information into long-term memory. Although the benefits of practice are well known, people have a curious tendency to overestimate their knowledge of a topic and how well they will perform on a subsequent memory test of this knowledge (Koriat & Bjork, 2005).

In addition to checking your mastery, recent research suggests that testing actually enhances retention, a phenomenon dubbed the *testing effect* (Roediger & Karpicke, 2006a). Studies have shown that taking a test on material increases performance on a subsequent test even more than studying for an equal amount of time (see **Figure 7.19**). Why is testing so beneficial? Theorists are not sure yet, but the key may be that testing forces students to engage in deep processing of the material, as well as more appropriate encoding (Roediger & Karpicke, 2006b). In any event, self-testing appears to be an excellent memory tool, which suggests that it would be prudent to take the Practice Tests

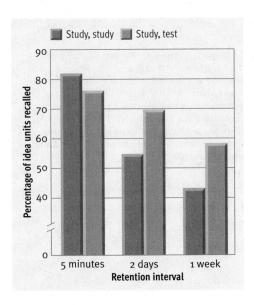

Figure 7.19

The testing effect. In an experiment conducted by Roediger and Karpicke (2006b), participants studied a brief prose passage for 7 minutes. Then, some of them studied it again for 7 minutes while others took a 7-minute test on the material. In the second phase of the study, subjects took another test on the material after either 5 minutes, 2 days, or 1 week. There wasn't much of a performance gap when subjects were tested over a 5-minute retention interval, but the testing group showed a significant advantage in recall when the retention interval was extended to 2 days or 1 week.

SOURCE: Roediger, III, H. L., & Karpicke, J. D. (2006). Test-enhanced learning: Taking memory tests improves long-term retention. *Psychological Science, 17,* 249–255. Copyright © Blackwell Publishing. Reprinted by permission.

in this text or the additional tests available on the website for the book.

Another possible remedy for overconfidence is trying to overlearn material (Driskell, Willis, & Copper, 1992). *Overlearning* refers to continued rehearsal of material after you first appear to have mastered it. In one study, after subjects had mastered a list of nouns (they recited the list without error), Krueger (1929) required them to continue rehearsing for 50% or 100% more trials. Measuring retention at intervals up to 28 days, Krueger found that greater overlearning was related to better recall of the list. Modern studies have also shown that overlearning can enhance performance on an exam that occurs within a week, although the evidence on its long-term benefits (months later) is inconsistent (Peladeau, Forget, & Gagne, 2003; Rohrer et al., 2005).

One other point related to rehearsal is also worth mentioning. If you are memorizing some type of list, be aware of the serial-position effect, which is often observed when subjects are tested on their memory of lists (Murdock, 2001). The *serial-position effect* occurs when subjects show better recall for items at the beginning and end of a list than for items in the middle (see **Figure 7.20**). The reasons for the serial-position effect are complex and need not concern us, but its pragmatic implications are clear: If you need to memorize a list of, say, cranial nerves or past presidents, devote extra practice trials to items in the middle of the list and check your memorization of those items very carefully.

Schedule Distributed Practice and Minimize Interference

Let's assume that you need to study 9 hours for an exam. Should you "cram" all your studying into one 9-hour period (massed practice)? Or is it better to distribute your study among, say, three 3-hour periods on successive days (distributed practice)? The evidence indicates that retention tends to be greater after distributed practice than after massed practice (Rohrer & Taylor, 2006; Seabrook, Brown, & Solity, 2005). Moreover, a recent review of over 300 experiments (Cepeda et al., 2006) showed that the longer the retention interval between studying and testing, the bigger the advantage for massed practice, as shown in **Figure 7.21** on the next page. The same review concluded that the longer the retention interval, the longer the optimal "break" between practice trials. When an upcoming test is more than two days away, the optimal interval between practice periods appears to be around 24 hours. The superiority of distributed practice over massed practice suggests that cramming is an ill-advised approach to studying for exams (Dempster, 1996).

Because interference is a major cause of forgetting, you'll probably want to think about how you can minimize it. This issue is especially important for students, because memorizing information for one course can interfere with the retention of information

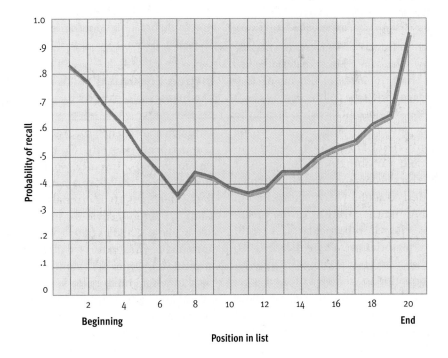

Figure 7.20

The serial-position effect. After learning a list of items to remember, people tend to recall more of the items from the beginning and the end of the list than from the middle, producing the characteristic U-shaped curve shown here. This phenomenon is called the serial-position effect.

SOURCE: Adapted from Rundus, D. (1971). Analysis of rehearsal processes in free recall. *Journal of Experimental Psychology, 89,* 63–77. Copyright © 1971 by the American Psychological Association. Adapted by permission of the author.

Figure 7.21

Effects of massed versus distributed practice on retention. In a review of over 300 experiments on massed versus distributed practice, Cepeda et al. (2006) examined the importance of the retention interval. As you can see, spaced practice was superior to massed practice at all retention intervals, but the gap widened at longer intervals. These findings suggest that distributed practice is especially advantageous when you need or want to remember material over the long haul.

for another course. Thus, the day before an exam in a course, you should study for that course only—if possible. If demands in other courses make that plan impossible, you should study the test material last.

Engage in Deep Processing and Organize Information

Research on levels of processing suggests that how *often* you go over material is less critical than the *depth* of processing that you engage in (Craik & Tulving, 1975). If you expect to remember what you read, you have to fully comprehend its meaning (Einstein & McDaniel, 2004). Many students could probably benefit if they spent less time on rote memorization and devoted more effort to actually paying attention to and analyzing the meaning of their reading assignments. In particular, it is useful to make material *personally* meaningful. When you read your textbooks, try to relate information to your own life and experience. For example, when you read about classical conditioning, try to think of your own responses that are attributable to classical conditioning.

It is also important to understand that retention tends to be greater when information is well organized (Einstein & McDaniel, 2004) Gordon Bower (1970) has shown that hierarchical organization is particularly helpful when it is applicable. Thus, it may be a good idea to *outline* reading assignments for school, since outlining forces you to organize material hierarchically. Consistent with this reasoning, there is some empirical evidence that outlining material from textbooks can enhance retention of that material (McDaniel, Waddill, & Shakesby, 1996).

Enrich Encoding with Mnemonic Devices 6a

Although it's often helpful to make information personally meaningful, it's not always easy to do so. For instance, when you study chemistry you may have a hard time relating to polymers at a personal level. Thus, many mnemonic devices—such as acrostics, acronyms, and narrative methods—are designed to make abstract material more meaningful. Other mnemonic devices depend on visual imagery. As you may recall, Allan Paivio (1986, 2007) believes that visual images create a second memory code and that two codes are better than one.

Acrostics and Acronyms

Acrostics are phrases (or poems) in which the first letter of each word (or line) functions as a cue to help you recall information to be remembered. For instance, you may remember the order of musical notes with the saying "Every Good Boy Does Fine." A slight variation on acrostics is the *acronym*—a word formed out of the first letters of a series of words. Students memorizing the order of colors in the light spectrum often store the name "Roy G. Biv" to remember red, orange, yellow, green, blue, indigo, and violet. Notice that this acronym takes advantage of the principle of chunking. Acrostics and acronyms that individuals create for themselves can be effective memory tools (Hermann, Raybeck, & Gruneberg, 2002).

Narrative Methods

Another useful way to remember a list of words is to create a story that includes the words in the appropriate order. The narrative both increases the meaningfulness of the words and links them in a specific order. Examples of this technique can be seen in **Figure 7.22**. Bower and Clark (1969) found that this procedure greatly enhanced subjects' recall of lists of unrelated words.

Rhymes

Another verbal mnemonic that people often rely on is rhyming. You've probably repeated, "I before E except after C . . ." thousands of times. Perhaps you also remember the number of days in each month with the old

Word lists	Stories
Bird	A man dressed in a *Bird Costume*
Costume	and wearing a *Mailbox* on his
Mailbox	*Head* was seen leaping into
Head	the *River*. A *Nurse* ran out of a
River	nearby *Theater* and applied *Wax*
Nurse	to his *Eyelids*, but her efforts
Theater	were in vain. He died and was
Wax	tossed into the *Furnace*.
Eyelid	
Furnace	
Rustler	A *Rustler* lived in a *Penthouse* on
Penthouse	top of a *Mountain*. His specialty
Mountain	was the three-toed *Sloth*. He
Sloth	would take his captive animals
Tavern	to a *Tavern* where he would
Fuzz	remove *Fuzz* from their *Glands*.
Gland	Unfortunately, all this exposure
Antler	to sloth fuzz caused him to grow
Pencil	*Antlers*. So he gave up his pro-
Vitamin	fession and went to work in a
	Pencil factory. As a precaution
	he also took a lot of *Vitamin* E.

Figure 7.22

Narrative methods of remembering. Bower and Clark (1969) presented participants with 12 lists of words. Subjects in the "narrative group" were asked to recall the words by constructing a story out of them (like the two stories shown here). Subjects in the control group were given no special instructions. Recoding the material in story form dramatically improved recall.

SOURCE: Adapted from Bower, G. H., & Clark, M. C. (1969). Narrative stories as mediators of serial learning. *Psychonomic Science, 14,* 181–182. Copyright © 1969 by the Psychonomic Society. Adapted by permission of the Psychonomic Society and the author.

standby, "Thirty days hath September . . ." Rhyming something to remember it is an old and useful trick.

Link Method   6a

The *link method* involves forming a mental image of items to be remembered in a way that links them together. For instance, suppose that you need to remember some items to pick up at the drugstore: a news magazine, shaving cream, film, and pens. To remember these items, you might visualize a public figure on the magazine cover shaving with a pen while being photographed. The more bizarre you make your image, the more helpful it is likely to be (McDaniel & Einstein, 1986).

Method of Loci   6a

The *method of loci* involves taking an imaginary walk along a familiar path where images of items to be remembered are associated with certain locations. The first step is to commit to memory a series of loci, or places along a path. Usually these loci are specific locations in your home or neighborhood. Then envision each thing you want to remember in one of these locations. Try to form distinctive, vivid images. When you need to remember the items, imagine yourself walking along the path. The various loci on your path should serve as cues for the retrieval of the images that you formed (see **Figure 7.23**). Evidence suggests that the method of loci can be effective in increasing retention (Massen & Vterrodt-Plunnecke, 2006; Moe & De Beni, 2004;). Moreover, this method ensures that items are remembered in their *correct order* because the order is determined by the sequence of locations along the pathway.

REVIEW of Key Learning Goals

7.23 Rehearsal, even when it involves overlearning, facilitates retention. Testing yourself on material also enhances retention. In memorizing lists, one should be wary of the serial-position effect. Distributed practice tends to be more efficient than massed practice. Study sessions should be scheduled in ways that minimize interference.

7.24 Deeper processing of material tends to result in greater retention. Evidence also suggests that organization enhances retention, so outlining texts may be valuable. Meaningfulness can be enhanced through the use of mnemonic devices such as acrostics, acronyms, and narrative methods. The link method and the method of loci are mnemonic devices that depend on the value of visual imagery.

Figure 7.23

The method of loci. In this example from Bower (1970), a person about to go shopping pairs items to remember with familiar places (loci) arranged in a natural sequence: (1) hot dogs/driveway; (2) cat food/garage interior; (3) tomatoes/front door; (4) bananas/coat closet shelf; (5) whiskey/kitchen sink. The shopper then uses imagery to associate the items on the shopping list with the loci, as shown in the drawing: (1) giant hot dog rolls down a driveway; (2) a cat noisily devours cat food in the garage; (3) ripe tomatoes are splattered on the front door; (4) bunches of bananas are hung from the closet shelf; (5) the contents of a bottle of whiskey gurgle down the kitchen sink. As the last panel shows, the shopper recalls the items by mentally touring the loci associated with them.

SOURCE: From Bower, G. H. (1970). Analysis of a mnemonic device. *American Scientist, 58,* 496–499. Copyright © 1970 by Scientific Research Society. Reprinted by permission.

Key Learning Goals

7.25 Understand how hindsight bias and over-confidence contribute to the frequent inaccuracy of eyewitness memory.

Understanding the Fallibility of Eyewitness Accounts

A number of years ago, the Wilmington, Delaware, area was plagued by a series of armed robberies committed by a perpetrator who was dubbed the "gentleman bandit" by the press because he was an unusually polite and well-groomed thief. The local media published a sketch of the gentleman bandit and eventually an alert resident turned in a suspect who resembled the sketch. Much to everyone's surprise, the accused thief was a Catholic priest named Father Bernard Pagano—who vigorously denied the charges. Unfortunately for Father Pagano, his denials and alibis were unconvincing and he was charged with the crimes. At the trial, *seven* eyewitnesses confidently identified Father Pagano as the gentleman bandit. The prosecution was well on its way to a conviction when there was a stunning turn of events—another man, Ronald Clouser, confessed to the police that he was the gentleman bandit. The authorities dropped the charges against Father Pagano, and the relieved priest was able to return to his normal existence (Rodgers, 1982).

This bizarre tale of mistaken identity—which sounds like it was lifted from a movie script—raises some interesting questions about memory. How could seven people "remember" seeing Father Pagnano commit armed robberies that he had nothing to do with? How could they mistake him for Ronald Clouser, when the two really didn't look very similar (see the adjacent photos)? How could the witnesses be so confident when they were so wrong? Perhaps you're thinking that this is just one case and it must be unrepresentative (which would be sound critical thinking). Well, yes, it is a rather extreme example of eyewitness fallibility, but researchers have compiled mountains of evidence that eyewitness testimony is not nearly as reliable or as accurate as widely assumed (Kassin et al., 2001; Wells, Memon, & Penrod, 2006). This finding is ironic in that people are most confident about their assertions when they

can say "I saw it with my own eyes." Television news shows like to use the title "Eyewitness News" to create the impression that they chronicle events with great clarity and accuracy. And our legal system accords special status to eyewitness testimony because it is considered much more dependable than hearsay or circumstantial evidence.

So, why are eyewitness accounts surprisingly inaccurate? Well, a variety of factors and processes contribute to this inaccuracy. Let's briefly review some of the relevant processes that were introduced in the main body of the chapter; then we'll focus on two common errors in thinking that also contribute.

Can you think of any memory phenomena described in the chapter that seem likely to undermine eyewitness accuracy? You could point to the fact that *memory is a reconstructive process,* and eyewitness recall is likely to be *distorted by schemas* that people have for various events. Another consideration is that *witnesses sometimes make source-monitoring errors* and get confused about where they saw a face. For example, one rape victim mixed up her assailant with a guest on a TV show that she was watching when she was attacked. Fortunately, the falsely accused suspect had an airtight alibi, as he could demonstrate that he was on live

television when the rape occurred (Schacter, 1996). Perhaps the most pervasive factor is the misinformation effect (Davis & Loftus, 2007). *Witnesses' recall of events is routinely distorted by information introduced after the event* by police officers, attorneys, news reports, and so forth. In addition to these factors, eyewitness inaccuracy is fueled by *hindsight bias* and *overconfidence effects.*

The Contribution of Hindsight Bias

Hindsight bias is the tendency to mold one's interpretation of the past to fit how events actually turned out. When you know the outcome of an event, this knowledge slants your recall of how the event unfolded and what your thinking was at the time. With the luxury of hindsight, people have a curious tendency to say, "I knew it all along" when explaining events that objectively would have been difficult to foresee. The tendency to exhibit the hindsight bias is normal, pervasive, and surprisingly strong (Guilbault et al., 2004). With regard to eyewitnesses, their recollections may often be distorted by knowing that a particular person has been arrested and accused of the crime in question. For

Although he doesn't look that much like the real "gentleman bandit," who is shown on the left, seven eyewitnesses identified Father Pagano (right) as the gentleman bandit, showing just how unreliable eyewitness accounts can be.

example, Wells and Bradfield (1998) had simulated eyewitnesses select a perpetrator from a photo lineup. The participants' confidence in their identifications tended to be quite modest, which made sense given that the actual perpetrator was not even in the lineup. But when some subjects were told, "Good, you identified the actual suspect," they became highly confident about their identifications, which obviously were incorrect. In another study, participants read identical scenarios about a couple's first date that either had no ending or ended in a rape (described in one additional sentence). The subjects who received the rape ending reconstructed the story to be more consistent with their stereotypes of how rapes occur (Carli, 1999).

The Contribution of Overconfidence

Another flaw in thinking that contributes to inaccuracy in eyewitness accounts is people's tendency to be overconfident about the reliability of their memories. When tested for their memory of general information, people tend to overestimate their accuracy (Koriat & Bjork, 2005; Lichtenstein, Fischhoff, & Phillips, 1982). In studies of eyewitness recall, participants also tend to be overconfident about their recollections. Although jurors tend to be more convinced by eyewitnesses who appear confident, the evidence indicates that there is only a modest correlation between eyewitness confidence and eyewitness accuracy (Shaw, McClure, & Dykstra, 2007). Hence, many convictions of innocent people have been attributed to the impact of testimony from

Although courts give special credence to eyewitness testimony, scientific evidence indicates that eyewitness accounts are less reliable than widely assumed.

highly confident, but mistaken eyewitnesses (Wells, Olson, & Charman, 2002).

Can you learn to make better judgments of the accuracy of your recall of everyday events? Yes, with effort you can get better at making accurate estimates of how likely you are to be correct in the recall of some fact or event. One reason that people tend to be overconfident is that if they can't think of any reasons they might be wrong, they assume they must be right. Thus, overconfidence is fueled by yet another common error in thinking—*the failure to seek disconfirming evidence.* Even veteran scientists fall prey to this weakness, as most people don't seriously consider why they might be wrong about something (Mynatt, Doherty, & Tweney, 1978).

Thus, to make more accurate assessments of what you know and don't know, it helps to engage in a deliberate process of consid-

ering why you might be wrong. Here is an example. Based on your reading of Chapter 1, write down the schools of thought associated with the following major theorists: William James, John B. Watson, and Carl Rogers. After you provide your answers, rate your confidence that the information you just provided is correct. Now, write three reasons that your answers might be wrong and three reasons that they might be correct. Most people will balk at this exercise, arguing that they cannot think of any reasons they might be wrong, but after some resistance, they can come up with several. Such reasons might include "I was half asleep when I read that part of the chapter" or "I might be confusing Watson and James." Reasons for thinking you're right could include "I distinctly recall discussing this with my friend" or "I really worked on those names in Chapter 1." After listing reasons that you might be right and might be wrong, rate your confidence in your accuracy once again. Guess what? Most people are less confident after going through such an exercise than they were before (depending, of course, on the nature of the topic).

The new confidence ratings tend to be more realistic than the original ratings (Koriat, Lichtenstein, & Fischhoff, 1980). Why? Because this exercise forces you to think more deeply about your answers and to search your memory for related information. Most people stop searching their memory as soon as they generate an answer they believe to be correct. Thus, the process of considering reasons you might be wrong about something—a process that people rarely engage in—is a useful critical thinking skill that can reduce overconfidence effects. Better assessment of what you know and don't know can be an important determinant of the quality of the decisions you make and the way you solve problems and reason from evidence.

Table 7.1 Critical Thinking Skills Discussed in This Application

Skill	Description
Understanding the limitations and fallibility of human memory	The critical thinker appreciates that memory is reconstructive and that even eyewitness accounts may be distorted or inaccurate.
Recognizing the bias in hindsight analysis	The critical thinker understands that knowing the outcome of events biases our recall and interpretation of the events.
Recognizing overconfidence in human cognition	The critical thinker understands that people are frequently overconfident about the accuracy of their projections for the future and their recollections of the past.
Understanding the need to seek disconfirming evidence	The critical thinker understands the value of thinking about how or why one might be wrong about something.

REVIEW of Key Learning Goals

7.27 Research indicates that eyewitness memory is not nearly as reliable or as accurate as widely believed. The hindsight bias, which is the tendency to reshape one's interpretation of the past to fit with known outcomes, often distorts eyewitness memory. People tend to be overconfident about their eyewitness recollections.

Encoding: Getting Information into Memory

▌ The multifaceted process of memory begins with encoding. Attention, which facilitates encoding, is inherently selective. Divided attention undermines memory and performance on other tasks.

▌ According to levels-of-processing theory, deeper processing results in better recall of information. Structural, phonemic, and semantic encoding represent progressively deeper and more effective levels of processing.

▌ Elaboration enriches encoding by linking a stimulus to other information. Visual imagery may work in much the same way, creating two memory codes rather than just one.

Storage: Maintaining Information in Memory

▌ Information-processing theories of memory assert that people have three kinds of memory stores: a sensory memory, a short-term memory, and a long-term memory.

▌ Short-term memory has a limited capacity (capable of holding about seven chunks of information) and can maintain unrehearsed information for up to about 20 seconds. Working memory is a more elaborate and multifaceted model of short-term memory, which involves more than a simple rehearsal loop. Variations in working memory capacity are predictive of higher cognitive abilities.

▌ Long-term memory is an unlimited capacity store that may hold information indefinitely. Reports of flashbulb memories suggest that LTM storage may be permanent, but the evidence is not convincing.

▌ Information in LTM can be organized in a variety of ways. A schema is an organized cluster of knowledge about a particular object or sequence of events. Semantic networks consist of concepts joined together by pathways. Parallel distributed processing (PDP) models of memory assert that specific memories correspond to particular patterns of activation in connectionist networks.

Retrieval: Getting Information out of Memory

▌ Recall is often guided by partial information. Reinstating the context of an event can facilitate recall. Memory is highly reconstructive, and information learned after an event can alter one's memory of it, as illustrated by the misinformation effect.

▌ Source monitoring is the process of making attributions about the origins of memories. Source-monitoring errors may explain why people sometimes "recall" something that was only suggested to them.

Forgetting: When Memory Lapses

▌ Ebbinghaus's early studies of nonsense syllables suggested that we forget very rapidly. Subsequent research showed that Ebbinghaus's forgetting curve was exceptionally steep. Forgetting can be measured by asking people to recall, recognize, or relearn information.

▌ Some forgetting, including pseudoforgetting, is attributable to ineffective encoding of information. Decay theory proposes that forgetting occurs spontaneously with the passage of time. It has proven difficult to show that decay occurs in long-term memory.

▌ Interference theory proposes that people forget information because of competition from other material. Evidence that either prior (proactive interference) or subsequent (retroactive interference) learning of material can cause forgetting supports interference theory.

▌ Forgetting is often due to retrieval failure, which may sometimes involve repression. Recent years have seen a surge of reports of recovered memories of sexual abuse in childhood. The authenticity of these recovered memories is the subject of controversy because empirical studies have demonstrated that it is not all that difficult to create inaccurate memories.

In Search of the Memory Trace: The Physiology of Memory

▌ The study of amnesia and other research has implicated the hippocampal region as a key player in memory processes, possibly handling the consolidation of memories. Thompson's research suggests that memory traces may consist of localized neural circuits.

▌ According to Eric Kandel, memory traces reflect alterations in neurotransmitter release at specific synapses. Memories may also depend on long-term potentiation, which is a durable increase in neural excitability at synapses along a specific neural pathway. Neurogenesis may contribute to the sculpting of neural circuits for memories.

Systems and Types of Memory

▌ Declarative memory is memory for facts, while nondeclarative memory is memory for actions and skills. Declarative memory can be subdivided into episodic memory (for personal facts) and semantic memory (for general facts). Retrospective memory involves remembering things from the past, whereas prospective memory involves remembering to do things in the future.

Reflecting on the Chapter's Themes

▌ Our discussion of attention and memory enhances our understanding of why people's experience of the world is highly subjective. Work in this area also shows that behavior is governed by multiple factors and that psychology is marked by theoretical diversity.

PERSONAL APPLICATION Improving Everyday Memory

▌ Rehearsal, even when it involves overlearning, facilitates retention, although one should be wary of the serial-position effect. The process of being tested on material seems to enhance retention of that material. Distributed practice tends to be more efficient than massed practice. It is wise to plan study sessions so as to minimize interference.

▌ Deep processing during rehearsal and good organization enhance recall. Meaningfulness can be enhanced through the use of verbal mnemonics such as acrostics and narrative methods. The link method and the method of loci are mnemonic devices that depend on the value of visual imagery.

CRITICAL THINKING APPLICATION Understanding the Fallibility of Eyewitness Accounts

▌ Research indicates that eyewitness memory is not nearly as reliable or as accurate as widely believed. Two common errors in thinking that contribute to this phenomenon are hindsight bias and overconfidence effects.

PSYKTREK PREVIEW

Visit Module 6a (*Memory Encoding*) and Module 6b (*Memory Storage*) to enhance your mastery of the essential principles of memory.

Explore Module 6c (*Physiology of Memory*) and Module 6d (*Forgetting*) to learn more about the neurological bases of memory and the reasons why we forget.

1. Getting information into memory is called _____ ; getting information out of memory is called _____ .
   A. storage; retrieval
   B. encoding; storage
   C. encoding; retrieval
   D. storage; encoding

2. The word *big* is flashed on a screen. A mental picture of the word big represents a _____ code; the definition "large in size" represents a _____ code; "sounds like pig" represents a _____ code.
   A. structural; phonemic; semantic
   B. phonemic; semantic; structural
   C. structural; semantic; phonemic
   D. phonemic; structural; semantic

3. The capacity of short-term memory is:
   A. about 50,000 words.
   B. unlimited.
   C. about 25 stimuli.
   D. thought to be 7 plus or minus 2 chunks of information, although some theorists suggest it is even less than that.

4. Which statement best represents current evidence on the durability of long-term storage?
   A. All forgetting involves breakdowns in retrieval.
   B. LTM is like a barrel of marbles in which none of the marbles ever leak out.
   C. There is no convincing evidence that all one's memories are stored away permanently.
   D. All long-term memories gradually decay at a constant rate.

5. An organized cluster of knowledge about a particular object or sequence of events is called a:
   A. semantic network.
   B. conceptual hierarchy.
   C. schema.
   D. retrieval cue.

6. The tip-of-the-tongue phenomenon:
   A. is a temporary inability to remember something you know, accompanied by a feeling that it's just out of reach.
   B. is clearly due to a failure in retrieval.
   C. reflects a permanent loss of information from LTM.
   D. is both A and B.

7. Loftus's work on eyewitness testimony has demonstrated that:
   A. memory errors are surprisingly infrequent.
   B. memory errors are mainly due to repression.
   C. information given after an event can alter a person's memory of the event.
   D. information given after an event cannot alter a person's memory of the event.

8. If decay theory is correct:
   A. information can never be permanently lost from long-term memory.
   B. forgetting is simply a case of retrieval failure.
   C. the principal cause of forgetting should be the passage of time.
   D. all of the above.

9. Amnesia in which people lose memories for events that occurred prior to their injury is called _____ amnesia.
   A. anterograde
   B. retrospective
   C. retrograde
   D. episodic

10. Your knowledge that birds fly, that the sun rises in the east, and that 2 + 2 = 4 is contained in your _____ memory.
    A. episodic
    B. procedural
    C. implicit
    D. semantic

11. Dorothy memorized her shopping list. When she got to the store, however, she found she had forgotten many of the items from the middle of the list. This is an example of:
    A. inappropriate encoding.
    B. retrograde amnesia.
    C. proactive interference.
    D. the serial-position effect.

12. The tendency to mold one's interpretation of the past to fit how events actually turned out is called:
    A. the overconfidence effect.
    B. selective amnesia.
    C. retroactive interference.
    D. the hindsight bias.

Answers

1 C pp. 225–226
2 C p. 227
3 D pp. 230–231
4 C pp. 232–233
5 C p. 233
6 D p. 235
7 C pp. 236–237
8 C p. 239
9 C p. 245
10 D pp. 247–248
11 D p. 251
12 D p. 254

PSYKTREK PREVIEW

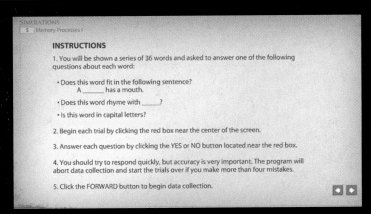

SIMULATIONS
5 | Memory Processes I

INSTRUCTIONS

1. You will be shown a series of 36 words and asked to answer one of the following questions about each word:
   • Does this word fit in the following sentence?
      A _____ has a mouth.
   • Does this word rhyme with _____?
   • Is this word in capital letters?

2. Begin each trial by clicking the red box near the center of the screen.

3. Answer each question by clicking the YES or NO button located near the red box.

4. You should try to respond quickly, but accuracy is very important. The program will abort data collection and start the trials over if you make more than four mistakes.

5. Click the FORWARD button to begin data collection.

SIMULATIONS
6 | Memory Processes II

How do your personal results on the recognition measure compare to those of Roediger and McDermott? CLICK SHOW MY RECOGNITION RESULTS to find out.

Show my recognition results

Your recognition results

Status of words	Distribution of ratings			
	4	3	2	1
Stimulus words (n = 32)	56%	12%	15%	15%
Nonpresented, unrelated words (n = 22)	4%	0%	45%	50%
Nonpresented, target words (n = 12)	91%	8%	0%	0%

The crucial results are those for the nonpresented, target words. As you can see, you incorrectly reported that these words had been stimulus words 99% of the time. Moreover, 91% of the time, you gave a rating of "4" to these words, which means that you were *sure* that the nonpresented words were stimulus words.

EMAIL | PRINT

Go to Simulation 5 (*Memory Processes I*) to participate in a memory experiment that will demonstrate the influence of levels of processing.

Discover how easy it is to develop false memories when you try Simulation 5 (*Memory Processes II*), which allows you to participate in a version of the Deese-

8

Cognition and Intelligence

The Pythonbrug, or "Python Bridge," connecting the Sporenburg Peninsula with Borneo Island, Amsterdam
© Bruno Ehrs/Corbis

Mr. Watson—Mr. Sherlock Holmes," said Stamford, introducing us. "How are you?" he said, cordially, gripping my hand with a strength for which I should hardly have given him credit. "You have been in Afghanistan, I perceive."

"How on earth did you know that?" I asked, in astonishment. (From A Study in Scarlet *by Arthur Conan Doyle)*

If you've ever read any Sherlock Holmes stories, you know that the great detective constantly astonished his loyal companion, Dr. Watson, with his extraordinary deductions. Obviously, Holmes could not arrive at his conclusions without a chain of reasoning. Yet to him even an elaborate reasoning process was a simple, everyday act. Consider his feat of knowing at once, upon first meeting Watson, that the doctor had been in Afghanistan. When asked, Holmes explained his reasoning as follows:

"I knew you came from Afghanistan. From long habit the train of thought ran so swiftly through my mind that I arrived at the conclusion without being conscious of the intermediate steps. There were such steps, however. The train of reasoning ran: 'Here is a gentleman of a medical type, but with the air of a military man. Clearly an army doctor, then. He has just come from the tropics, for his face is dark, and that is not the natural tint of his skin, for his wrists are fair. He has undergone hardship and sickness, as his haggard face says clearly. His left arm has been injured. He holds it in a stiff and unnatural manner. Where in the tropics could an English army doctor have seen much hardship and got his arm wounded? Clearly in Afghanistan.' The whole train of thought did not occupy a second."

Admittedly, Sherlock Holmes's deductive feats are fictional. But even to read about them appreciatively—let alone imagine them, as Sir Arthur Conan Doyle did—is a remarkably complex mental act. Our everyday thought processes seem ordinary to us only because we take them for granted, just as Holmes saw nothing extraordinary in what to him was a simple deduction.

In reality, everyone is a Sherlock Holmes, continually performing magical feats of thought. Even elementary perception—for instance, watching a football game or a ballet—involves elaborate cognitive processes. People must sort through distorted, constantly shifting perceptual inputs and deduce what it is they are seeing out there in the real world. Imagine, then, the complexity of thought required to read a book, fix an automobile, or balance a checkbook. Of course, all this is not to say that human thought processes are flawless or unequaled. You probably own a $10 calculator that can run circles around you when it comes to computing square roots. As we'll see, some of the most interesting research in this chapter focuses on ways in which people's thinking can be limited, simplistic, or outright illogical.

Our topics in this chapter center on *thinking*. In the first half of the chapter, we will summarize research on cognition, or *how people think*, as we look at the subjects of problem solving and decision making. In the second half of the chapter, we will focus on *how well people think*, as measured by tests of intelligence. Thus, the first half of the chapter examines the intricacies of *thinking processes* (cognition), whereas the second half focuses on variations among people in *thinking ability* (intelligence).

The topics of cognition and intelligence have very different histories. As we will discuss later, the first useful tests of general mental ability were created between 1904 and 1916, and intelligence testing flourished throughout the 20th century. In contrast, during the first half of the 20th century, the study of cognition was actively discouraged by the theoretical dominance of behaviorism. Herbert Simon, a pioneer of cognitive psychology, recalls that "you couldn't use a word like *mind* in a psychology journal—you'd get your mouth washed out with soap" (Holden, 1986). Although it wasn't fully recognized until much later, the 1950s brought a "cognitive revolution" in psychology (Baars, 1986). Renegade theorists, such as Simon, began to argue that behaviorists' exclusive focus on overt responses was doomed to yield an incomplete understanding of human functioning. More important, creative new approaches to research on problem solving, decision making, and reasoning led to exciting progress. Thus, it was only in the second half of the 20th century that the study of cognition grew into a robust, influential area of research. We will begin our discussion of cognitive processes by examining the topic of problem solving.

Herbert Simon

"You couldn't use a word like mind *in a psychology journal— you'd get your mouth washed out with soap."*

Problem Solving: In Search of Solutions

Key Learning Goals

8.1 List the three types of problems proposed by Greeno.

8.2 Identify and describe four common barriers to effective problem solving.

8.3 Review a variety of general problem-solving strategies and heuristics.

8.4 Discuss cultural variations in cognitive style as they relate to problem solving.

Look at the two problems below. Can you solve them?

In the Thompson family there are five brothers, and each brother has one sister. If you count Mrs. Thompson, how many females are there in the Thompson family?

Fifteen percent of the people in Topeka have unlisted telephone numbers. You select 200 names at random from the Topeka phone book. How many of these people can be expected to have unlisted phone numbers?

These problems, borrowed from Sternberg (1986, p. 214), are exceptionally simple, but many people fail to solve them. The answer to the first problem is two. The only females in the family are Mrs. Thompson and her one daughter, who is a sister to each of her brothers. The answer to the second problem is none. You won't find any people with unlisted phone numbers in the phone book.

Why do many people fail to solve these simple problems? You'll learn why in a moment, when we discuss barriers to effective problem solving. But first, let's examine a scheme for classifying problems into a few basic types.

Types of Problems   SIM7, 7e

Problem solving refers to active efforts to discover what must be done to achieve a goal that is not readily attainable. Obviously, if a goal is readily attainable, there isn't a problem. But in problem-solving situations, one must go beyond the given information to overcome obstacles and reach a goal. Jim Greeno (1978) has proposed that problems can be categorized into three basic classes:

1. *Problems of inducing structure.* The person must discover the relations among the parts of the prob-

lem. The *series completion problems* and the *analogy problems* in **Figure 8.1** are examples of problems of inducing structure.

2. *Problems of arrangement.* The person must arrange the parts in a way that satisfies some criterion. The parts can usually be arranged in many ways, but only one or a few of the arrangements form a solution. The *string problem* and the *anagrams* in **Figure 8.1** fit in this category.

3. *Problems of transformation.* The person must carry out a sequence of transformations in order to reach a specific goal. The *hobbits and orcs problem* and the *water jar problem* in **Figure 8.1** are examples of transformation problems. Transformation problems can be challenging. Even though you know exactly what the goal is, it's often not obvious how the goal can be achieved.

Greeno's list is not an exhaustive scheme for classifying problems, but it provides a useful system for understanding some of the variety seen in everyday problems.

Barriers to Effective Problem Solving   7e

On the basis of their studies of problem solving, psychologists have identified a number of barriers that frequently impede people's efforts to arrive at solutions. Common obstacles to effective problem solving include a focus on irrelevant information, functional fixedness, mental set, and imposition of unnecessary constraints.

Irrelevant Information   7e

We began our discussion of problem solving with two simple problems that people routinely fail to solve. The catch is that these problems contain *ir-*

DILBERT

A. Analogy
What word completes the analogy?
Merchant : Sell : : Customer : _____
Lawyer : Client : : Doctor : _____

B. String problem
Two strings hang from the ceiling but are too far apart to allow a person to hold one and walk to the other. On the table are a book of matches, a screwdriver, and a few pieces of cotton. How could the strings be tied together?

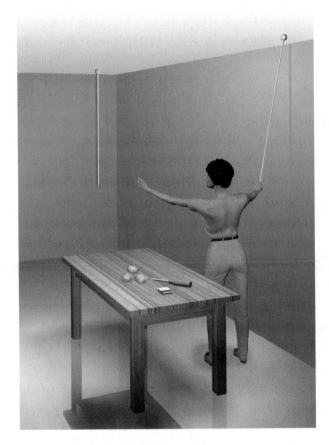

C. Hobbits and orcs problem
Three hobbits and three orcs arrive at a river bank, and they all wish to cross onto the other side. Fortunately, there is a boat, but unfortunately, the boat can hold only two creatures at one time. Also, there is another problem. Orcs are vicious creatures, and whenever there are more orcs than hobbits on one side of the river, the orcs will immediately attack the hobbits and eat them up. Consequently, you should be certain that you never leave more orcs than hobbits on either river bank. How should the problem be solved? It must be added that the orcs, though vicious, can be trusted to bring the boat back! (From Matlin, 1989, p. 319)

D. Water jar problem
Suppose that you have a 21-cup jar, a 127-cup jar, and a 3-cup jar. Drawing and discarding as much water as you like, you need to measure out exactly 100 cups of water. How can this be done?

E. Anagram
Rearrange the letters in each row to make an English word.
RWAET
KEROJ

F. Series completion
What number or letter completes each series?
1 2 8 3 4 6 5 6 _____
A B M C D M _____

Figure 8.1
Six standard problems used in studies of problem solving. Try solving the problems and identifying which class each belongs to before reading further. The problems can be classified as follows. The *analogy problems* and *series completion problems* are problems of inducing structure. The solutions for the analogy problems are *Buy* and *Patient*. The solutions for the series completion problems are *4* and *E*. The *string problem* and the *anagram problems* are problems of arrangement. To solve the string problem, attach the screwdriver to one string and set it swinging as a pendulum. Hold the other string and catch the swinging screwdriver. Then you need only untie the screwdriver and tie the strings together. The solutions for the anagram problems are *WATER* and *JOKER*. The *hobbits and orcs problem* and the *water jar problem* are problems of transformation. The solutions for these two problems are outlined in **Figures 8.2** and **8.3** on the next page.

relevant information that leads people astray. In the first problem, the number of brothers is irrelevant in determining the number of females in the Thompson family. In the second problem, participants tend to focus on the figures of 15% and 200 names. But this numerical information is irrelevant, since all the names came out of the phone book.

Sternberg (1986) points out that people often incorrectly assume that all the numerical information in a problem is necessary to solve it. They therefore try to figure out how to use this information before they even consider whether it's relevant. Focusing on irrelevant information can have adverse effects on reasoning and problem solving (Gaeth & Shanteau, 2000). Thus, effective problem solving requires that you attempt to figure out what information is relevant and what is irrelevant before proceeding.

Functional Fixedness

7e

Another common barrier to successful problem solving is *functional fixedness*—the tendency to perceive an item only in terms of its most common use. Functional fixedness has been seen in the difficulties that people have with the string problem in **Figure 8.1** (Maier, 1931). Solving this problem requires finding a novel use for one of the objects: the screwdriver. Participants tend to think of the screwdriver in terms of its usual functions—turning screws and perhaps prying things open. They have a hard time viewing the screwdriver as a weight. Their rigid way of thinking about the screwdriver illustrates functional fixedness (Dominowski & Bourne, 1994). Ironically, young children appear to be less vulnerable to functional fixedness than older children or adults because they have less knowledge about the conventional uses of various objects (Defeyter & German, 2003).

Mental Set

Rigid thinking is also at work when a mental set interferes with effective problem solving. A *mental set* exists when people persist in using problem-solving strategies that have worked in the past. The effects of mental set were seen in a classic study by Abraham Luchins (1942). Luchins asked subjects to work a series of water jar problems, like the one introduced earlier. Six such problems are outlined in **Figure 8.4**, which shows the capacities of the three jars and the amounts of water to be measured out. Try solving these problems.

Were you able to develop a formula for solving these problems? The first four all require the same strategy, which is described in **Figure 8.3**. You have to fill jar B, draw off the amount that jar A holds once, and draw off the amount that jar C holds twice. Thus, the formula for your solution is $B - A - 2C$. Although there is an obvious and much simpler solution ($A - C$) for the fifth problem (see **Figure 8.9** on page 265), Luchins found that most participants stuck with the more cumbersome strategy that they had used in problems 1–4. Moreover, most subjects couldn't solve the sixth problem in the allotted time, because they kept trying to use their proven strategy, which does not work for this problem. The participants' reliance on their "tried and true" strategy is an illustration of mental set in problem solving. This tendency to let one's thinking get into a rut is a common barrier to successful problem solving (Smith, 1995). Mental set may explain why having expertise in an area sometimes backfires and hampers problem-solving efforts (Leighton & Sternberg, 2003).

Figure 8.2
Solution to the hobbits and orcs problem. This problem is difficult because it is necessary to temporarily work "away" from the goal.

Figure 8.3
The method for solving the water jar problem.
As explained in the text, the correct formula is $B - A - 2C$.

Problem	Capacity of empty jars			Desired amount of water
	A	B	C	
1	14	163	25	99
2	18	43	10	5
3	9	42	6	21
4	20	59	4	31
5	23	49	3	20
6	28	76	3	25

Figure 8.4
Additional water jar problems. Using jars A, B, and C, with the capacities indicated in each row, figure out how to measure out the desired amount of water specified on the far right. The solutions are shown in **Figure 8.9**. (Based on Luchins, 1942)

Unnecessary Constraints

Effective problem solving requires specifying all the constraints governing a problem *without assuming any constraints that don't exist.* An example of a problem in which people place an unnecessary constraint on the solution is shown in **Figure 8.5** (Adams, 1980). Without lifting your pencil from the paper, try to draw four straight lines that will cross through all nine dots. If you struggle with this one, don't feel bad. When a time limit of a few minutes is imposed on this problem, the typical solution rate is 0% (MacGregor et al., 2001). The key factor that makes this a difficult problem is that most people will not draw lines outside the imaginary boundary that surrounds the dots. Notice that this constraint is not part of the problem statement. It's imposed only by the problem solver. Correct solutions, two of which are shown in **Figure 8.10** on page 265, extend outside the imaginary boundary. To solve this problem you need to literally "think outside the box." This popular slogan, spawned by the nine-dot problem, reflects the fact that people often make assumptions that impose unnecessary constraints on problem-solving efforts.

The nine-dot problem is often solved with a burst of insight. *Insight* occurs when people suddenly discover the correct solution to a problem after struggling with it for a while. Problems requiring insight tend to be difficult for a variety of reasons. Difficulties may emerge from (1) how people structure the problem, (2) how they apply prior knowledge, or (3) how much they need to juggle information in working memory (Kershaw & Ohlsson, 2004). For example, in the nine-dot problem, the main barrier to a solution is that people tend to structure the problem poorly by imposing unnecessary boundaries. But people also struggle because their prior knowledge suggests that the "turns" in their lines should occur on the dots (rather than in the white space) and because envisioning all the options strains working memory. Although insight feels like a sudden, "aha" experience to problem solvers, some researchers have questioned whether insight solutions emerge full blown or are preceded by incremental movement toward a solution (Chronicle, MacGregor, & Ormerod, 2004). Recent studies suggest the latter—that insight breakthroughs are often preceded by gradual movement toward a solution that occurs outside of the problem solver's awareness (Novick & Bassok, 2005).

Approaches to Problem Solving

People use a variety of strategies in attempting to solve problems. In this section, we'll examine some general strategies.

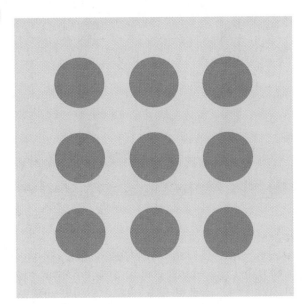

Figure 8.5
The nine-dot problem. Without lifting your pencil from the paper, draw no more than four lines that will cross through all nine dots. For possible solutions, see Figure 8.10.

SOURCE: Adams, J. L. (1980). *Conceptual blockbusting: A guide to better ideas.* New York: W. H. Freeman. Copyright © 1980 by James L. Adams. Reprinted by permission of W. H. Freeman & Co.

Trial and Error and Heuristics

Trial and error is a common, albeit primitive, approach to solving problems. *Trial and error* **involves trying possible solutions sequentially and discarding those that are in error until one works.** Trial and error can be effective when there are relatively few possible solutions to be tried out. However, this method becomes impractical when the number of possible maneuvers is large. Consider, for instance, the problem shown in **Figure 8.6**. The challenge is to move just two matches to create a pattern containing four equal squares. Sure, you could use a trial-and-error approach in moving pairs of matches. But you'd better allocate plenty of time to this effort, as there are over 60,000 possible rearrangements to check out (see **Figure 8.11** on page 265 for the solution).

Because trial and error is inefficient, people often use shortcuts called *heuristics* in problem solving. A *heuristic* **is a guiding principle or "rule of thumb" used in solving problems or making decisions.** Heuristics are often useful, but they don't guarantee success. Helpful heuristics in problem solving include forming subgoals, hill climbing, searching for analogies, and changing the representation of the problem.

Forming Subgoals

It is often useful to tackle problems by formulating *subgoals,* intermediate steps toward a solution (Catrambone, 1998). When you reach a subgoal, you've solved part of the problem. Some problems have fairly obvious subgoals, and research has shown that people take advantage of them. For instance, in analogy problems, the first subgoal usually is to figure out the possible relations between the first two parts of the analogy.

Figure 8.6
The matchstick problem. Move two matches to form four equal squares. You can find the solution in Figure 8.11.

SOURCE: Kendler, H. H. (1974). *Basic psychology.* Menlo Park, CA: Benjamin-Cummings. Copyright © 1974 The Benjamin-Cummings Publishing Co. Adapted by permission of Howard H. Kendler.

Figure 8.7
The tower of Hanoi problem. Your mission is to move the rings from peg A to peg C. You can move only the top ring on a peg and can't place a larger ring above a smaller one. The solution is explained in the text.

CALVIN AND HOBBES

Figure 8.8
The six-coin problem. Your mission is to rearrange the coins so that each coin touches exactly two others. You are limited to three moves. Each move must entail sliding a coin to a position in which it touches exactly two others, without disturbing any coins. A solution is shown in Figure 8.12.

The wisdom of formulating subgoals can be seen in the *tower of Hanoi problem,* depicted in **Figure 8.7**. The terminal goal for this problem is to move all three rings on peg A to peg C, while abiding by two restrictions: Only the top ring on a peg can be moved, and a ring must never be placed above a smaller ring. See whether you can solve the problem before continuing.

Dividing this problem into subgoals facilitates a solution (Kotovsky, Hayes, & Simon, 1985). If you think in terms of subgoals, your first task is to get ring 3 to the bottom of peg C. Breaking this task into sub-subgoals, subjects can figure out that they should move ring 1 to peg C, ring 2 to peg B, and ring 1 from peg C to peg B. These maneuvers allow you to place ring 3 at the bottom of peg C, thus meeting your first subgoal. Your next subgoal—getting ring 2 over to peg C—can be accomplished in just two steps: move ring 1 to peg A and ring 2 to peg C. It should then be obvious how to achieve your final subgoal—getting ring 1 over to peg C.

Hill Climbing

Try the six-coin problem shown in **Figure 8.8**. Some people find it easy, while others struggle with the 7,426 possible sequences of moves (one solution is shown in **Figure 8.12** on page 266). In one recent study, only 32% of participants solved it within 10 minutes (Chronicle et al., 2004). In any event, this problem tends to be approached with the *hill-climbing heuristic,* which entails selecting the alternative at each choice point that appears to lead most directly to one's goal. The name for this heuristic derives from the notion that if you need to climb a hill with many choice points along the pathway (and limited ability to see ahead), one simple strategy would be to always choose the path with the steepest upward slope. The hill-climbing heuristic is a logical strategy that works much of the time, but it can also backfire. Sometimes the optimal solution to a problem involves an indirect pathway or even moving backward, away from one's goal. However, people

tend to be reluctant to make moves that seem to take them away from their goal-state (Robertson, 2001).

Searching for Analogies

Searching for analogies is another of the major heuristics for solving problems (Holyoak, 2005). If you can spot an analogy between problems, you may be able to use the solution to a previous problem to solve a current one. Of course, using this strategy depends on recognizing the similarity between the two problems, which may itself be a challenging problem. Nonetheless, recent studies of real-world problem-solving efforts show that we depend on analogies far more than most people appreciate. For example, one study of biologists' problem solving recorded during their lab meetings found that they used 3–15 analogies per hour (Dunbar & Blanchette, 2001). Another study recorded design engineers during their product development meetings and found that they came up with an average of 11 analogies per hour of deliberation (Christensen & Schunn, 2007).

Unfortunately, people often are unable to recognize that two problems are similar and that an analogy might lead to a solution (Kurtz & Lowenstein, 2007). One reason that people often have difficulty recognizing analogies between problems is that they tend to focus on superficial, surface features of problems rather than their underlying structure (Bassok, 2003). Nonetheless, analogies can be a powerful tool in efforts to solve problems. Try to make use of analogies to solve the following two problems:

Problem 5

Problem 6

Figure 8.9

Solutions to the additional water jar problems. The solution for problems 1–4 is the same as the solution shown in Figure 8.3 (B − A − 2C). This method will work for problem 5, but there also is a simpler solution (A − C), which is the only solution for problem 6. Many subjects exhibit a mental set on these problems, as they fail to notice the simpler solution for problem 5.

Figure 8.10

Two solutions to the nine-dot problem. The key to solving the problem is to recognize that nothing in the problem statement forbids going outside the imaginary boundary surrounding the dots.

SOUCE: Adams, J. L. (1980). *Conceptual blockbusting: A guide to better ideas.* New York: W. H. Freeman. Copyright © 1980 by James L. Adams. Reprinted by permission of W. H. Freeman & Co.

Figure 8.11

Solution to the matchstick problem. The key to solving this problem is to "open up" the figure, something many subjects are reluctant to do because they impose unnecessary constraints on the problem.

SOURCE: Kendler, H. H. (1974). *Basic psychology.* Menlo Park, CA: Benjamin-Cummings. Copyright © 1974 The Benjamin-Cummings Publishing Co. Adapted by permission of Howard H. Kendler.

A teacher had 23 pupils in his class. All but 7 of them went on a museum trip and thus were away for the day. How many students remained in class that day?

Susan gets in her car in Boston and drives toward New York City, averaging 50 miles per hour. Twenty minutes later, Ellen gets in her car in New York City and starts driving toward Boston, averaging 60 miles per hour. Both women take the same route, which extends a total of 220 miles between the two cities. Which car is nearer to Boston when they meet?

These problems, taken from Sternberg (1986, pp. 213 and 215), resemble the ones that opened our discussion of problem solving. Each has an obvious solution that's hidden in irrelevant numerical information. If you recognized this similarity, you probably solved the problems easily. If not, take another look now that you know what the analogy is. Neither problem requires any calculation whatsoever. The answer to the first problem is 7. As for the second problem, when the two cars meet they're in the same place. Obviously, they have to be the same distance from Boston.

Changing the Representation of the Problem

Whether you solve a problem often hinges on how you envision it—your *representation of the problem.*

Many problems can be represented in a variety of ways, such as verbally, mathematically, or spatially. You might represent a problem with a list, a table, an equation, a graph, a matrix of facts or numbers, a hierarchical tree diagram, or a sequential flow-chart (Halpern, 2003). When you fail to make progress with your initial representation of a problem, changing your representation is often a good strategy (Novick & Bassok, 2005). As an illustration, see whether you can solve the *Buddhist monk problem:*

At sunrise, a Buddhist monk sets out to climb a tall mountain. He follows a narrow path that winds around the mountain and up to a temple. He stops frequently to rest and climbs at varying speeds, arriving around sunset. After staying a few days, he begins his return journey. As before, he starts at sunrise, rests often, walks at varying speeds, and arrives around sunset. Prove that there must be a spot along the path that the monk will pass on both trips at precisely the same time of day.

Why should there be such a spot? The monk's walking speed varies. Shouldn't it all be a matter of coincidence if he reaches a spot at the same time each day? Moreover, if there is such a spot, how would you prove it? Participants who represent this problem in terms of verbal, mathematical, or spatial information struggle. Subjects who work with a graphic representation fare much better. The

Figure 8.12

A solution to the six-coin problem. One of the two 3-move sequences that will solve this problem is shown here. According to Chronicle et al. (2004) participants tend to use the hill-climbing heuristic when working on this problem.

best way to represent the problem is to envision the monk (or two different monks) ascending and descending the mountain at the same time. The two monks must meet at some point. If you construct a graph (see **Figure 8.13**) you can vary the speed of the monks' descent in endless ways, but you can see that there's always a place where they meet.

Culture, Cognitive Style, and Problem Solving

Do the varied experiences of people from different cultures lead to cross-cultural variations in problem solving? Yes, at least to some degree, as researchers have found cultural differences in the cognitive style that people exhibit in solving problems.

Richard Nisbett and his colleagues (Nisbett et al., 2001; Nisbett & Miyamoto, 2005) have argued that people from Eastern Asian cultures (such as China, Japan, and Korea) display a *holistic cognitive style* that focuses on context and relationships among elements in a field, whereas people from Western cultures (America and Europe) exhibit an *analytic cognitive style* that focuses on objects and their properties

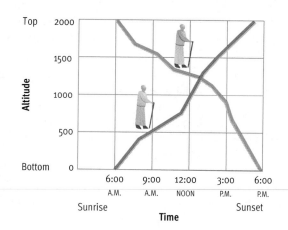

Figure 8.13

Solution to the Buddhist monk problem. If you represent this problem graphically and think in terms of two monks, it is readily apparent that the monk does pass a single spot at the same time each day.

rather than context. To put it simply, *Easterners see wholes where Westerners see parts.*

In one test of this hypothesis, Masuda and Nisbett (2001) presented computer-animated scenes of fish and other underwater objects to Japanese and American participants and asked them to report what

---

concept check 8.1

Thinking About Problem Solving

Check your understanding of problem solving by answering some questions about the following problem. Begin by trying to solve the problem.

The candle problem. Using the objects shown—candles, a box of matches, string, and some tacks—figure out how you could mount a candle on a wall so that it could be used as a light. Work on the problem for a while, then turn to page 268 to see the solution. After you've seen the solution, respond to the following questions. The answers are in Appendix A.

1. If it didn't occur to you that the matchbox could be converted from a container to a platform, this illustrates _____ _____ .

2. While working on the problem, if you thought to yourself, "How can I create a platform attached to the wall?" you used the heuristic of _____ .

3. If it occurred to you suddenly that the matchbox could be used as a platform, this realization would be an example of _____ .

4. If you had a hunch that there might be some similarity between this problem and the string problem in **Figure 8.1** (the similarity is the novel use of an object), your hunch would illustrate the heuristic of _____ _____ _____ .

5. In terms of Greeno's three types of problems, the candle problem is a(n) _____ problem.

they had seen. The initial comments of American subjects typically referred to the focal fish, whereas the initial comments of Japanese subjects usually referred to background elements (see **Figure 8.14**). Furthermore, the Japanese participants made about 70% more statements about context or background and about twice as many statements about relationships between elements in the scenes. Based on these and many other findings, Nisbett et al. (2001) conclude that cultural differences in cognitive style are substantial and that "literally different cognitive processes are often invoked by East Asians and Westerners dealing with the same problem" (p. 305).

Problems are not the only kind of cognitive challenge that people grapple with on a regular basis. Life also seems to constantly demand decisions. As you might expect, cognitive psychologists have shown great interest in the process of decision making, which is our next subject.

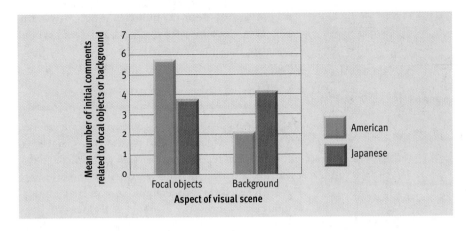

Figure 8.14
Cultural disparities in cognitive style. In one of the studies conducted by Masuda and Nisbett (2001), the participants were asked to describe computer-animated visual scenes. As you can see, the initial comments made by American subjects referred more to focal objects in the scenes, whereas the initial comments made by Japanese subjects referred more to background elements in the scenes. These findings are consistent with the hypothesis that Easterners see wholes (a holistic cognitive style) whereas Westerners see parts (an analytic cognitive style).

REVIEW of Key Learning Goals

8.1 James Greeno distinguished between three broad types of problems: problems of inducing structure, transformation problems, and arrangement problems.

8.2 Common barriers to problem solving include being distracted by irrelevant information, functional fixedness (only seeing an item's most common use), mental set (persisting with strategies that have worked in the past), and placing unnecessary constraints on one's solutions.

8.3 Trial and error involves trying and discarding potential solutions to a problem until one works, whereas a heuristic is a rule of thumb used in searching for solutions to a problem. When people form subgoals, they break a problem into several parts. Hill climbing involves making step-by-step choices that lead most directly to one's goal. Other useful heuristics include searching for analogies between new problems and old problems, and changing the representation of problems.

8.4 Research suggests that there are cultural disparities in typical problem solving strategies. Eastern cultures exhibit a more holistic cognitive style, whereas Western cultures display a more analytic cognitive style. In other words, Easterners see wholes where Westerners see parts.

Decision Making: Choices and Chances

Decisions, decisions. Life is full of them. You decided to read this book today. Earlier today you decided when to get up, whether to eat breakfast, and if so, what to eat. Usually you make routine decisions like these with little effort. But on occasion you need to make important decisions that require more thought. Big decisions—such as selecting a car, a home, or a job—tend to be difficult. The alternatives usually have a number of facets that need to be weighed. For instance, in choosing among several cars, you may want to compare their costs, roominess, fuel economy, handling, acceleration, stylishness, reliability, safety features, and warranties.

Decision making involves evaluating alternatives and making choices among them. Most people try to be systematic and rational in their decision making. However, the work that earned Herbert Simon the 1978 Nobel prize in economics showed that people don't always live up to these goals. Before Simon's work, most traditional theories in economics assumed that people made rational choices to maximize their economic gains. Simon (1957) noted that people have a limited ability to process and evaluate information on numerous facets of possible alternatives. Thus, Simon's *theory of bounded rationality* asserts that people tend to use simple strategies in decision making that focus on only a few facets of available options and often result in "irrational" decisions that are less than optimal.

Spurred by Simon's analysis, psychologists have devoted several decades to the study of how cognitive biases distort people's decision making. The results of this research have sometimes been disturbing, leading one theorist to conclude that people "do a singularly bad job at the business of reasoning, even when they are calm, clearheaded, and under

Key Learning Goals

8.5 Articulate Simon's theory of bounded rationality and Schwartz's notion about choice overload.

8.6 Distinguish the additive and elimination by aspects approaches to making decisions about preferences.

8.7 Understand the nature of risky decision making and the availability and representativeness heuristics.

8.8 Describe base rate neglect and the conjunction fallacy and their causes.

8.9 Explain what is meant by the gambler's fallacy, overestimation of the improbable, and loss aversion.

8.10 Assess evolutionary theorists' evaluation of cognitive research on flaws in human decision strategies.

8.11 Describe the nature of fast and frugal heuristics.

The solution to the candle problem in Concept Check 8.1.

no pressure to perform quickly" (Stich, 1990, pp. 173–174). Let's look at this research—and recent criticism that it has inspired.

Making Choices About Preferences

Many decisions involve choices about *preferences*, which can be made using a variety of strategies. In a fascinating recent analysis, Barry Schwartz (2004) has argued that people in modern societies are overwhelmed by an overabundance of such choices about preferences. For example, Schwartz describes how a simple visit to a local supermarket can require a consumer to choose from 285 varieties of cookies, 61 suntan lotions, 150 lipsticks, and 175 salad dressings. Although increased choice is most tangible in the realm of consumer goods, Schwartz argues that it also extends into more significant domains of life. Today, people tend to have unprecedented opportunities to make choices about how they will be educated, how and where they will work, how their intimate relationships will unfold, and even how they will look (because of advances in plastic surgery). Although enormous freedom of choice sounds attractive, Schwartz (2004) argues that the overabundance of choices in modern life has unexpected costs. He argues that people routinely make errors even when choosing among a handful of alternatives and that errors become much more likely when decisions become more complex. And he explains how having more alternatives increases the potential for rumination and postdecision regret. Ultimately, he argues, the malaise associated with choice overload undermines individuals' happiness and contributes to depression. It is hard to say whether choice over-

People often have to decide between alternative products, such as computers, cars, washers, dryers, and so forth, that are not all that different. Hence they often struggle with their abundant choices.

load is as detrimental to well-being as Schwartz believes, but it is clear that people wrestle with countless choices about preferences, and their reasoning about these decisions is often far from optimal. Let's look at some strategies that people use in making these types of decisions.

Imagine that your friend Boris has found two reasonably attractive apartments and is trying to decide between them. How should he go about selecting between his alternatives? If Boris wanted to use an *additive strategy*, he would list the attributes that influence his decision. Then he would rate the desirability of each apartment on each attribute. For example, let's say that Boris wants to consider four attributes: rent, noise level, distance to campus, and cleanliness. He might make ratings from −3 to +3, like those shown in **Table 8.1**, add up the ratings for each alternative, and select the one with the largest total. Given the ratings in **Table 8.1**, Boris should select apartment B. To make an additive strategy more useful, you can *weight* attributes differently, based on their importance (Shafir & LeBoeuf, 2004). For example, if Boris considers distance to campus to be twice as important as the other considerations, he could multiply his ratings of this attribute by 2. The distance rating would then be +6 for apartment A and −2 for apartment B, and apartment A would become the preferred choice.

People also make choices by gradually eliminating less-attractive alternatives (Slovic, 1990; Tversky, 1972). This strategy is called *elimination by aspects* because it assumes that alternatives are eliminated by evaluating them on each attribute or aspect in turn. Whenever any alternative fails to satisfy some minimum criterion for an attribute, it is eliminated from further consideration.

To illustrate, suppose Juanita is looking for a new car. She may begin by eliminating all cars that cost over $24,000. Then she may eliminate cars that don't average at least 20 miles per gallon of gas. By continuing to reject choices that don't satisfy some minimum criterion on selected attributes, she can gradually eliminate alternatives until only a single

Table 8.1 Application of the Additive Model to Choosing an Apartment

Attribute	Apartment	
	A	B
Rent	+1	+2
Noise level	−2	+3
Distance to campus	+3	−1
Cleanliness	+2	+2
Total	**+4**	**+6**

car remains. The final choice in elimination by aspects depends on the order in which attributes are evaluated, so it's best to evaluate attributes in the order of their importance.

Both the additive and the elimination-by-aspects strategies have advantages, but which strategy do people actually tend to use? Research suggests that when decisions involve relatively few options that need to be evaluated on only a few attributes, people tend to use additive strategies. However, as more options and factors are added to a decision task, people tend to shift to elimination by aspects (Payne & Bettman, 2004).

Taking Chances: Factors Weighed in Risky Decisions

Suppose you have the chance to play a dice game in which you might win some money. You must decide whether it would be to your advantage to play. You're going to roll a fair die. If the number 6 appears, you win $5. If one of the other five numbers appears, you win nothing. It costs you $1 every time you play. Should you participate?

This problem calls for a type of decision making that is somewhat different from making choices about preferences. In selecting alternatives that reflect preferences, people generally weigh known outcomes (apartment A will require a long commute to campus, car B will get 30 miles per gallon, and so forth). In contrast, *risky decision making* involves making choices under conditions of uncertainty. Uncertainty exists when people don't know what will happen. At best, they know, or can estimate, the probability that a particular event will occur.

One way to decide whether to play the dice game would be to figure out the *expected value* of participation in the game. To do so, you would need to calculate the average amount of money you could expect to win or lose each time you play. The value of a win is $4 ($5 minus the $1 entry fee). The value of a loss is −$1. To calculate expected value, you also need to know the probability of a win or loss. Since a die has six faces, the probability of a win is 1 out of 6, and the probability of a loss is 5 out of 6. Thus, on five out of every six trials, you lose $1. On one out of six, you win $4. The game is beginning to sound unattractive, isn't it? We can figure out the precise expected value as follows:

$$\text{Expected value} = (1/6 \times 4) + (5/6 \times -1)$$
$$= 4/6 + (-5/6) = -1/6$$

The expected value of this game is −1/6 of a dollar, which means that you lose an average of about 17 cents per turn. Now that you know the expected value, surely you won't agree to play. Or will you?

If we want to understand why people make the decisions they do, the concept of expected value is not enough. People frequently behave in ways that are inconsistent with expected value (Slovic, Lichtenstein, & Fischoff, 1988). Any time the expected value is negative, a gambler should expect to lose money. Yet a great many people gamble at racetracks and casinos and buy lottery tickets. Although they realize that the odds are against them, they continue to gamble. Even people who don't gamble buy homeowner's insurance, which has a negative expected value. After all, when you buy insurance, your expectation (and hope!) is that you will lose money on the deal.

To explain decisions that violate expected value, some theories replace the objective value of an outcome with its subjective utility (Fischoff, 1988). Subjective utility represents what an outcome is personally worth to an individual. For example, buying a few lottery tickets may allow you to dream about becoming wealthy. Buying insurance may give you a sense of security. Subjective utilities like these vary from one person to another. If we know an individual's subjective utilities, we can better understand that person's risky decision making.

Heuristics in Judging Probabilities

7f

- What are your chances of passing your next psychology test if you study only 3 hours?
- How likely is a major downturn in the stock market during the upcoming year?
- What are the odds of your getting into graduate school in the field of your choice?

These questions ask you to make probability estimates. Amos Tversky and Daniel Kahneman (1982; Kahneman & Tversky, 2000) have conducted extensive research on the *heuristics,* or mental shortcuts, that people use in grappling with probabilities. This research on heuristics earned Kahneman the Nobel prize in economics in 2002 (unfortunately, his collaborator, Amos Tversky, died in 1996).

Availability is one such heuristic. The *availability heuristic* involves basing the estimated probability of an event on the ease with which relevant instances come to mind. For example, you may estimate the divorce rate by recalling the number of divorces among your friends' parents. Recalling specific instances of an event is a reasonable strategy to use in estimating the event's probability. However, if instances occur frequently but you have difficulty

web link 8.1

Online Decision Research Center Experiments

Michael Birnbaum (California State University, Fullerton) presents a range of continuing and completed experiments conducted online that illustrate how people make decisions.

Daniel Kahneman

"The human mind suppresses uncertainty. We're not only convinced that we know more about our politics, our businesses, and our spouses than we really do, but also that what we don't know must be unimportant."

Amos Tversky

"People treat their own cases as if they were unique, rather than part of a huge lottery. You hear this silly argument that 'The odds don't apply to me.' Why should God, or whoever runs this lottery, give you special treatment?"

retrieving them from memory, your estimate will be biased. For instance, it's easier to think of words that begin with a certain letter than words that contain that letter at some other position. Thus, people should tend to respond that there are more words starting with the letter *K* than words having a *K* in the third position. To test this hypothesis, Tversky and Kahneman (1973) selected five consonants (*K, L, N, R, V*) that occur more frequently in the third position of a word than in the first. Subjects were asked whether each of the letters appears more often in the first or third position. Most of the subjects erroneously believed that all five letters were much more frequent in the first than in the third position, confirming the hypothesis.

Representativeness is another guide in estimating probabilities identified by Kahneman and Tversky (1982). **The *representativeness heuristic* involves basing the estimated probability of an event on how similar it is to the typical prototype of that event.** To illustrate, imagine that you flip a coin six times and keep track of how often the result is heads (H) or tails (T). Which of the following sequences is more likely?

1. T T T T T T
2. H T T H T H

People generally believe that the second sequence is more likely. After all, coin tossing is a random affair, and the second sequence looks much more representative of a random process than the first. In reality, the probability of each exact sequence is precisely the same ($1/2 \times 1/2 \times 1/2 \times 1/2 \times 1/2 \times 1/2 = 1/64$). Overdependence on the representativeness heuristic has been used to explain quite a variety of decision-making tendencies (Teigen, 2004), as you will see in the upcoming pages.

Ignoring Base Rates and the Conjunction Fallacy

7f

Steve is very shy and withdrawn, invariably helpful, but with little interest in people or in the world of reality. A meek and tidy soul, he has a need for order and structure and a passion for detail. Do you think Steve is a salesperson or a librarian? (Adapted from Tversky & Kahneman, 1974, p. 1124)

Using the *representativeness heuristic*, participants tend to guess that Steve is a librarian because he resembles their prototype of a librarian (Tversky & Kahneman, 1982). In reality, this is not a very wise guess, because *it ignores the base rates* of librarians and salespeople in the population. Virtually everyone knows that salespeople outnumber librarians by a wide margin (roughly 75 to 1 in the United States). This fact makes it much more likely that Steve is in sales. But in estimating probabilities, people often ignore information on base rates.

Researchers are still debating how common it is for people to neglect base rate information (Birnbaum, 2004; Koehler, 1996), but it does not appear to be a rare event. Moreover, people are particularly bad about applying base rates to themselves. For example, people starting new companies ignore the high failure rate for new businesses, and burglars underestimate the likelihood that they will end up in jail. Thus, in risky decision making, people often think that they can beat the odds. As Amos Tversky put it, "People treat their own cases as if they were unique, rather than part of a huge lottery. You hear this silly argument that 'The odds don't apply to me.' Why should God, or whoever runs this lottery, give you special treatment?" (McKean, 1985, p. 27).

Let's look at another common mistake in decision-related reasoning. Imagine that you're going to meet a man who is an articulate, ambitious, power-hungry wheeler-dealer. Do you think it's more likely that he's a college teacher or a college teacher who's also a politician?

People tend to guess that the man is a "college teacher who's a politician" because the description fits with the typical prototype of politicians. But stop and think for a moment. The broader category of college teachers completely includes the smaller subcategory of college teachers who are politicians (see **Figure 8.15**). The probability of being in the subcategory cannot be higher than the probability of being in the broader category. It's a logical impossibility!

Tversky and Kahneman (1983) call this error the *conjunction fallacy*. The *conjunction fallacy* occurs when people estimate that the odds of two uncertain events happening together are greater than the odds of either event happening alone. The conjunction fallacy has been observed in a number of studies and has generally been attributed to the powerful influence of the representativeness heuristic (Epstein, Donovan, & Denes-Raj, 1999).

The Gambler's Fallacy and Overestimates of the Improbable

7f

Let's look at two more problems that often crop up when people work with probabilities. Consider the following scenario:

Laura is in a casino watching people play roulette. The 38 slots in the roulette wheel include 18 black numbers, 18 red numbers, and 2 green numbers. Hence, on any one

College professors

College professors who are also politicians

Figure 8.15

The conjunction fallacy. People routinely fall victim to the conjunction fallacy, but as this diagram makes obvious, the probability of being in a subcategory (college teachers who are politicians) cannot be higher than the probability of being in the broader category (college teachers). As this case illustrates, it often helps to represent a problem in a diagram.

spin, the probability of red or black is slightly less than 50–50 (.474 to be exact). Although Laura hasn't been betting, she has been following the pattern of results in the game very carefully. The ball has landed in red seven times in a row. Laura concludes that black is long overdue and she jumps into the game, betting heavily on black.

Has Laura made a good bet? Do you agree with Laura's reasoning? Or do you think that Laura misunderstands the laws of probability? As you may have guessed by now, Laura's reasoning is flawed. A great many people tend to believe that Laura has made a good bet (Stanovich, 2003). However, they're wrong. Laura's behavior illustrates the *gambler's fallacy*—the belief that the odds of a chance event increase if the event hasn't occurred recently. People believe that the laws of probability should yield fair results and that a random process must be self-correcting (Burns & Corpus, 2004). These aren't bad assumptions in the long run. However, they don't apply to individual, independent events.

The roulette wheel does not remember its recent results and make adjustments for them. Each spin of the wheel is an independent event. The probability of black on each spin remains at .474, even if red comes up 100 times in a row! The gambler's fallacy reflects the pervasive influence of the *representativeness heuristic*. In betting on black, Laura is predicting that future results will be more representative of a random process. This logic can be used to estimate the probability of black across a *string of spins*. But it doesn't apply to a *specific spin* of the roulette wheel.

Let's examine another issue that frequently crops up in working with probabilities. Various causes of death are paired up below. In each pairing, which is the more likely cause of death?

Asthma or tornadoes?
Accidental falls or gun accidents?
Tuberculosis or floods?
Suicide or murder?

Table 8.2 shows the actual mortality rates for each of the causes of death just listed. As you can see, the first choice in each pair is the more common

web link 8.2

Society for Judgment and Decision Making

The Society for Judgment and Decision Making is an interdisciplinary academic organization dedicated to the study of decision processes. The main attraction for students will be the news section, which profiles recent developments in decision research.

Table 8.2 Actual Mortality Rates for Selected Causes of Death

Cause of Death	Rate	Cause of Death	Rate
Asthma	2,000	Tornadoes	25
Accidental falls	6,021	Firearms accidents	320
Tuberculosis	400	Floods	44
Suicide	11,300	Homicide	6,800

Note: Mortality rates are per 100 million people and are based on the *Statistical Abstract of the United States,* 2001.

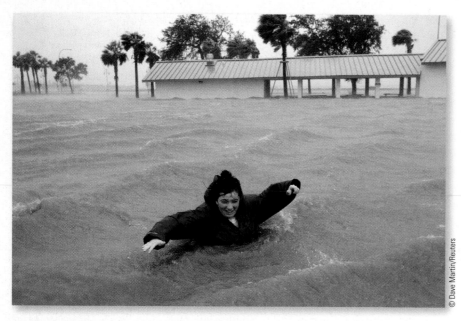

The availability heuristic can be dramatized by juxtaposing the unrelated phenomena of floods and tuberculosis. Many people are killed by floods, but far more die from tuberculosis (see **Table 8.2**). However, since the news media report flood fatalities frequently and prominently but rarely focus on deaths from tuberculosis, people tend to assume that flood-related deaths are more common.

Loss aversion can lead people to pass up excellent opportunities. For instance, subjects tend to decline a theoretical gamble in which they are given an 85% chance of doubling their life savings versus a 15% chance of losing their life savings, which mathematically is vastly more attractive than any bet one could place in a casino (Gilbert, 2006). Loss aversion can influence decisions in many areas of life, including choices of consumer goods, investments, business negotiations, and approaches to health care (Camerer, 2005; Klapper, Ebling, & Temme, 2005). The problem with loss aversion, as Daniel Gilbert and his colleagues have shown, is that people generally overestimate the intensity and duration of the negative emotions that they will experience after all sorts of losses, ranging from losing a job or romantic partner to botching an interview or watching one's team lose in a big game (Gilbert, Driver-Linn, & Wilson, 2002; Kermer et al., 2006).

cause of death. If you guessed wrong for several pairings, don't feel bad. Like many other people, you may be a victim of the tendency to *overestimate the improbable*. People tend to greatly overestimate the likelihood of dramatic, vivid—but infrequent—events that receive heavy media coverage. Thus, the number of fatalities resulting from tornadoes, floods, firearms accidents, and murders is usually overestimated (Slovic, Fischoff, & Lichtenstein, 1982). Fatalities due to asthma and other common diseases, which receive less media coverage, tend to be underestimated. This tendency to exaggerate the improbable has generally been attributed to the operation of the *availability heuristic* (Reber, 2004). Instances of floods, tornadoes, and such are readily available in memory because people are exposed to a great deal of publicity about such events.

The Specter of Regret and Loss Aversion

A surprisingly influential factor in decision making is the need to avoid regret about making a bad decision. People routinely think about how much regret they are likely to experience if the selection of a particular option backfires (Connolly & Zeelenberg, 2002). These estimates of anticipated regret are weighed heavily and often lead people to make overly cautious decisions.

A related phenomenon is *loss aversion*—in general, losses seem likely to have more impact than gains of equal size (Kahneman & Tversky, 1979; Novemsky & Kahneman, 2005). Thus, most people expect that the negative impact of losing $1000 will be greater than the positive impact of wining $1000.

Evolutionary Analyses of Flaws in Human Decision Making

A central conclusion of the last 30 years of research on decision making has been that human decision-making strategies are riddled with errors and biases that yield surprisingly irrational results (Goldstein & Hogarth, 1997; Risen & Gilovich, 2007; Shafir & LeBoeuf, 2002). Theorists have discovered that people have "mental limitations" and have concluded that people are not as bright and rational as they think they are. This broad conclusion has led some evolutionary psychologists to reconsider the work on human decision making, and their take on the matter is quite interesting. First, they argue that traditional decision research has imposed an invalid and unrealistic standard of rationality, which assumes that people should be impeccable in applying the laws of deductive logic and statistical probability while objectively and precisely weighing multiple factors in arriving at decisions (Gigerenzer, 2000). Second, they argue that humans only *seem* irrational because cognitive psychologists have been asking the wrong questions and formulating problems in the wrong ways—ways that have nothing to do with the adaptive problems that the human mind has evolved to solve (Cosmides & Tooby, 1996).

For example, evolutionary psychologists argue that the human mind is wired to think in terms of *raw frequencies* rather than *base rates and probabilities* (Gigerenzer, 1997, 2000). Asking about the probability of a single event occurring is routine in today's world, where we are flooded with statistical data ranging from batting averages to weather predictions. But our ancient ancestors had access to little data other than their own observations, which were accumulating counts of natural frequencies, such as "we had a good hunt three out of the last five times we went to the north plains." Thus, evolutionary theorists assert that many errors in human reasoning, such as neglect of base rates and the conjunction fallacy, should vanish if classic laboratory problems are reformulated in terms of raw frequencies rather than probabilities and base rates. Consistent with this analysis, evolutionary psychologists have shown that some errors in reasoning that are seen in laboratory studies disappear or are decreased when problems are presented in ways that resemble the type of input humans would have processed in ancestral times (Brase, Cosmides, & Tooby, 1998; Gigerenzer & Hoffrage, 1999).

Fast and Frugal Heuristics

To further expand on the evolutionary point of view, Gerd Gigerenzer has argued that humans' reasoning largely depends on "fast and frugal heuristics" that are quite a bit simpler than the complicated mental processes studied in traditional cognitive research (Gigerenzer, 2000, 2004, 2008; Goldstein & Gigerenzer, 1999; Todd & Gigerenzer, 2000, 2007). According to Gigerenzer, organisms from toads to stockbrokers have to make fast decisions under demanding circumstances with limited information. In most instances organisms (including humans) do not have the time, resources, or cognitive capacities to gather all the relevant information, consider all the possible options, calculate all the probabilities and risks, and then make the statistically optimal decision. Instead, they use quick and dirty heuristics that are less than perfect but that work well enough most of the time to be adaptive in the real world.

To explore these fast and frugal heuristics, Gigerenzer and his colleagues have typically studied inferences from *memory,* which challenge participants to search some portion of their general knowledge, rather than inferences from *givens,* which challenge participants to draw logical conclusions from information provided by the experimenter. This research has demonstrated that fast and frugal heuristics can be surprisingly effective. One heuristic that is often used in selecting between alternatives based on some quantitative dimension is the *recognition heuristic,* which works as follows: If one of two alternatives is recognized and the other is not, infer that the recognized alternative has the higher value. Consider the following questions—Which city has more inhabitants: San Diego or San Antonio? Hamburg or

concept check 8.2

Recognizing Heuristics in Decision Making

Check your understanding of heuristics in decision making by trying to identify the heuristics used in the following example. Each numbered element in the anecdote below illustrates a problem-solving heuristic. Write the relevant heuristic in the space on the left. You can find the answers in Appendix A.

_____ 1. Marsha can't decide on a college major. She evaluates all the majors available at her college on the attributes of how much she would enjoy them (likability), how challenging they are (difficulty), and how good the job opportunities are in the field (employability). She drops from consideration any major that she regards as "poor" on any of these three attributes.

_____ 2. When she considers history as a major, she thinks to herself, "Gee, I know four history graduates who are still looking for work," and concludes that the probability of getting a job using a history degree is very low.

_____ 3. She finds that every major gets a "poor" rating on at least one attribute, so she eliminates everything. Because this is unacceptable, she decides she has to switch to another strategy. Marsha finally focuses her consideration on five majors that received just one "poor" rating. She uses a 4-point scale to rate each of these majors on each of the three attributes she values. She totals the ratings and selects the major with the largest sum as her leading candidate.

Munich? In choosing between U.S. cities, American college students weighed a lifetime of facts useful for inferring population and made the correct choice 71% of the time; in choosing between German cities about which they knew very little, the same students depended on the recognition heuristic and chose correctly 73% of the time (Goldstein & Gigerenzer, 2002). Thus, the recognition heuristic allowed students to perform just as well with very limited knowledge as they did with extensive knowledge.

Gigerenzer and his colleagues have studied a variety of other quick, one-reason decision-making strategies and demonstrated that they can yield inferences that are just as accurate as much more elaborate and time-consuming strategies that carefully weigh many factors. And the researchers have demonstrated that people actually use these fast and frugal heuristics in a diverse array of situations (Gigerenzer & Todd, 1999; Rieskamp & Hoffrage, 1999). Thus, the study of fast and frugal heuristics promises to be an intriguing new line of research in the study of human decision making.

How have traditional decision-making theorists responded to the challenge presented by Gigerenzer and other evolutionary theorists? They acknowledge that people often rely on fast and frugal heuristics, but

Gerd Gigerenzer

"These 'fast and frugal' heuristics operate with simple psychological principles that satisfy the constraints of limited time, knowledge, and computational might, rather than those of classical rationality."

web link 8.3

Simple Minds—Smart Choices

This link leads to an article from *Science News* on Gerd Gigerenzer's research, which suggests that decisions can be made quickly and accurately with remarkably simple strategies.

they argue that this finding does not make decades of research on carefully reasoned approaches to decision making meaningless. Rather, they propose *dual-process theories* which posit that people depend on two different modes or systems of thinking when making decisions (De Neys, 2006; Kahneman, 2003; Kahneman & Frederick, 2005; Stanovich & West, 2002). One system consists of quick, simple, effortless, automatic judgments, like Gigerenzer's fast and frugal heuristics, which traditional theorists prefer to characterize as "intuitive thinking." The second system consists of slower, more elaborate, effortful, controlled judgments, like those studied in traditional decision research. According to this view, the second system monitors and corrects the intuitive system as needed and takes over when complicated or important decisions loom. Thus,

traditional theorists maintain that fast and frugal heuristics and reasoned, rule-governed decision strategies exist side by side and that both need to be studied to fully understand decision making.

Although sound decision making and effective problem solving obviously are key aspects of intelligence, there has been relatively little overlap between research on cognition and research on intelligence. As you have seen, cognitive research investigates how people use their intelligence; the focus is on *process*. In contrast, the study of intelligence has usually been approached from a testing perspective, which emphasizes measuring the *amount* of intelligence people have and figuring out why some have more than others. Let's look at how these measurements are made.

REVIEW of Key Learning Goals

8.5 Herbert Simon's theory of bounded rationality suggests that human decision strategies are simplistic and often yield irrational results. Barry Schwartz argues that in modern societies people suffer from choice overload, which leads to rumination, regret, and diminished well-being.

8.6 An additive decision model is used when people make decisions by rating the attributes of each alternative and selecting the alternative that has the highest sum of ratings. When elimination by aspects is used, people gradually eliminate alternatives whose attributes fail to satisfy some minimum criterion.

8.7 Risky decision making involves making choices under conditions of uncertainty. Models of how people make risky decisions focus on the expected value or subjective utility of various outcomes. The availability heuristic involves basing probability estimates on the ease with which relevant examples come to mind. The representativeness heuristics involves basing the estimated probability of an event on how similar it is to the prototype of that event.

8.8 In estimating probabilities, people often ignore information on base rates because of the influence of the representative-

ness heuristic. The conjunction fallacy occurs when people estimate that the odds of two uncertain events happening together are greater than the odds of either event happening alone.

8.9 The gambler's fallacy is the belief that the odds of a chance event increase if the event hasn't occurred recently. People tend to inflate estimates of improbable events that garner heavy coverage in the media, because of the availability heuristic. Most people expect that the negative impact of a loss will be greater than the positive impact of a similar gain, but research shows that people overestimate the impact of losses.

8.10 Evolutionary psychologists maintain that many errors and biases in human reasoning are greatly reduced when problems are presented in ways that resemble the type of input humans would have processed in ancestral times.

8.11 Gerd Gigerenzer argues that people largely depend on fast and frugal decision heuristics that are adaptive in the real world. Research shows that these simple heuristics can be surprisingly effective. Dual-process theories propose that people depend on two different modes of thinking in making decisions: fast and frugal heuristics and effortful, controlled deliberation.

Key Learning Goals

8.12 Summarize the contributions of Binet, Terman, and Wechsler to the evolution of intelligence testing.

8.13 Clarify the meaning of deviation IQ scores on modern intelligence tests.

8.14 Summarize evidence on the reliability and validity of modern IQ test scores.

8.15 Analyze how well intelligence tests predict vocational success.

8.16 Discuss the use of IQ tests in non-Western cultures.

Measuring Intelligence

We'll begin our discussion with a brief overview of the history of intelligence testing, then we will address some practical questions about how intelligence tests work.

A Brief History

7c

Intelligence tests were invented a little over a hundred years ago. The key breakthrough came in 1904, when a commission on education in France asked Alfred Binet to devise a test to identify mentally subnormal children. The commission wanted to single out youngsters in need of special training. It also wanted

to avoid complete reliance on teachers' evaluations, which might often be subjective and biased. In response to this need, Binet and a colleague, Theodore Simon, created the first useful test of general mental ability in 1905. Their scale was a success because it was inexpensive, easy to administer, objective, and capable of predicting children's performance in school fairly well (Siegler, 1992). Thanks to these qualities, its use spread across Europe and America.

The Binet-Simon scale expressed a child's score in terms of "mental level" or "mental age." A child's *mental age* indicated that he or she displayed the mental ability typical of a child of that chronological (actual) age. Thus, a child with a mental age of 6 performed like the average 6-year-old on the test. Binet realized that his scale was a somewhat crude initial effort at measuring mental ability. He revised it in 1908 and again in 1911. Unfortunately, his revising came to an abrupt end with his death in 1911. However, other psychologists continued to build on Binet's work.

In America, Lewis Terman and his colleagues at Stanford University soon went to work on a major expansion and revision of Binet's test. Their work led to the 1916 publication of the Stanford-Binet Intelligence Scale (Terman, 1916). Although this revision was quite loyal to Binet's original conceptions, it incorporated a new scoring scheme based on William Stern's "intelligence quotient" (Minton, 2000). An *intelligence quotient (IQ)* is a child's mental age divided by chronological age, multiplied by 100. IQ scores originally involved actual quotients, calculated as follows:

$$IQ = \frac{Mental\ age}{Chronological\ age} \times 100$$

The IQ ratio placed all children (regardless of age) on the same scale, which was centered at 100 if their mental age corresponded to their chronological age (see **Table 8.3** for examples of IQ calculations).

Terman's technical and theoretical contributions to psychological testing were modest, but he made a convincing case for the educational benefits of testing and became the key force behind American schools' widespread adoption of IQ tests (Chapman, 1988). As a result of his efforts, the Stanford-Binet quickly became the world's foremost intelligence test and the standard of comparison for virtually all intelligence tests that followed (White, 2000). Today, it remains one of the world's most widely used psychological tests.

Further advances in intelligence testing came from the work of David Wechsler (1939), who published the first high-quality IQ test designed specifically for *adults* in 1939. His test, the Wechsler Adult Intelligence Scale (WAIS), introduced two major innovations (Prifitera, 1994). First, Wechsler made his test less dependent on subjects' verbal ability than the Stanford-Binet. He included many items that required nonverbal reasoning. To highlight the distinction between verbal and nonverbal ability, he formalized the computation of separate scores for verbal IQ, performance (nonverbal) IQ, and full-scale (total) IQ. Examples of test items similar to those on the Wechsler scales are presented in **Figure 8.16** on the next page. Second, Wechsler discarded the intelligence quotient in favor of a new scoring scheme based on the *normal distribution*. This scoring system has since been adopted by most other IQ tests, including the Stanford-Binet. Although the term *intelligence quotient* lingers on in our vocabulary, scores on intelligence tests are no longer based on an actual quotient, as you will see momentarily.

Today, psychologists and educators have many IQ tests available for their use. Most IQ testing is conducted by school districts, which are largely free to formulate their own unique testing programs. There is little federal or state policy regarding ideal patterns of testing. Some districts administer group intelligence tests to all students at regular intervals. Others administer individual intelligence tests only on an occasional basis, as needed. Schools use intelligence tests to screen for mental retardation, to group students according to their academic ability ("tracking"), to identify gifted children, and to evaluate educational programs.

What Kinds of Questions Are on Intelligence Tests?

The nature of the questions found on IQ tests varies somewhat from test to test. These variations depend on whether the test is intended for children or adults (or both) and whether the test is designed for individuals or groups. Overall, the questions are fairly diverse in format. The Wechsler scales, with their numerous subtests, provide a representative example of the kinds of items that appear on most IQ tests. As you can see in **Figure 8.16** on the next page, the items in the Wechsler subtests require respondents to furnish information, recognize vocabulary, and demonstrate basic memory. Generally speaking, examinees are required to manipulate words, numbers, and images through abstract reasoning.

Alfred Binet

"The intelligence of anyone is susceptible of development. With practice, enthusiasm, and especially with method one can succeed in increasing one's attention, memory, judgment, and in becoming literally more intelligent than one was before."

Lewis Terman

"It is the method of tests that has brought psychology down from the clouds and made it useful to men; that has transformed the 'science of trivialities' into the 'science of human engineering.'"

David Wechsler

"The subtests [of the WAIS] are different measures of intelligence, not measures of different kinds of intelligence."

Table 8.3 Calculating the Intelligence Quotient

Measure	Child 1	Child 2	Child 3	Child 4
Mental age (MA)	6 years	6 years	9 years	12 years
Chronological age (CA)	6 years	9 years	12 years	9 years
$IQ = \frac{MA}{CA} \times 100$	$\frac{6}{6} \times 100 = 100$	$\frac{6}{9} \times 100 = 67$	$\frac{9}{12} \times 100 = 75$	$\frac{12}{9} \times 100 = 133$

Test	Description	Example
Wechsler Adult Intelligence Scale (WAIS)		
Verbal scale		
Information	Taps general range of information	On what continent is France?
Comprehension	Tests understanding of social conventions and ability to evaluate past experience	Why are children required to go to school?
Arithmetic	Tests arithmetic reasoning through verbal problems	How many hours will it take to drive 150 miles at 50 miles per hour?
Similarities	Asks in what way certain objects or concepts are similar; measures abstract thinking	How are a calculator and a typewriter alike?
Digit span	Tests attention and rote memory by orally presenting series of digits to be repeated forward or backward	Repeat the following numbers backward: 2 4 3 5 1 8 6
Vocabulary	Tests ability to define increasingly difficult words	What does audacity mean?
Performance scale		
Digit symbol	Tests speed of learning through timed coding tasks in which numbers must be associated with marks of various shapes	Shown: Fill in:
Picture completion	Tests visual alertness and visual memory through presentation of an incompletely drawn figure; the missing part must be discovered and named	Tell me what is missing:
Block design	Tests ability to perceive and analyze patterns by presenting designs that must be copied with blocks	Assemble blocks to match this design:
Picture arrangement	Tests understanding of social situations through a series of comic-strip-type pictures that must be arranged in the right sequence to tell a story	Put the pictures in the right order:
Object assembly	Tests ability to deal with part/whole relationships by presenting puzzle pieces that must be assembled to form a complete object	Assemble the pieces into a complete object:

Figure 8.16

Subtests on the Wechsler Adult Intelligence Scale (WAIS). The WAIS is divided into scales that yield separate verbal and performance (nonverbal) IQ scores. The verbal scale consists of six subtests and the performance scale is made up of five subtests. Examples of low-level (easy) test items that closely resemble those on the WAIS are shown on the right.

What Do Modern IQ Scores Mean?

7c

As we discussed, scores on intelligence tests once represented a ratio of mental age to chronological age. However, this system has given way to one based on the normal distribution and the *standard deviation*, a statistical index of variability in a data distribution, which is explained in Appendix B. The *normal distribution* is a symmetrical, bell-shaped curve that represents the pattern in which many characteristics are dispersed in the population. When a trait is normally distributed, most cases fall near the center of the distribution, and the number of cases gradually declines as one moves away from the center in either direction. The normal distribution provides a precise way to measure how people stack up in comparison to one another. The scores under the normal curve are dispersed in a fixed pattern, with the standard deviation serving as the unit of measurement (see **Figure 8.17**). About 68% of the scores in the distribution fall within one standard deviation of the mean, whereas 95% of the scores fall within two standard deviations of the mean. Given this fixed pattern, if you know the mean and standard deviation of a normally distributed trait, you can tell where any score falls in the distribution for the trait. The normal distribution was first discovered by 18th-century astronomers. They found that their measurement errors were distributed in a predictable way that resembled a bell-shaped curve. Since then, research has shown that many human traits, ranging from height to running speed to spatial ability, follow a normal distribution.

Psychologists eventually recognized that intelligence scores also fall into a normal distribution. This insight permitted David Wechsler to devise a more sophisticated scoring system for his tests that has been adopted by virtually all subsequent IQ tests. In this system, raw scores are translated into *deviation IQ scores* that locate respondents precisely within the normal distribution. For most IQ tests, the mean of the distribution is set at 100 and the standard deviation (SD) is set at 15. These choices were made to provide continuity with the original IQ ratio (mental age to chronological age) that was centered at 100. In this system, which is depicted in **Figure 8.17**, a score of 115 means that a person scored exactly one SD (15 points) above the mean. A score of 85 means that a person scored one SD below the mean. A score of 100 means that a person showed average performance. *The key point is that modern IQ scores indicate exactly where you fall in the normal distribution of intelligence.* Thus, a score of 120 does not indicate that you answered 120 questions correctly. Nor does it mean that you have 120 "units" of intelligence. A deviation IQ score places you at a specific point in the normal distribution of intelligence (based on the norms for your age group). Deviation IQ scores can be converted into *percentile scores,* as shown in **Figure 8.17**. A *percentile score* indicates the percentage of people who score at or below the score one has obtained.

web link 8.4

Human Intelligence
A graphic approach to the history of intelligence testing is taken at this site, which uses colored arrows to show academic lineage and connections among various theorists. Maintained by Jonathan Plucker of Indiana University, this site covers all the major intelligence theorists and includes excellent discussions of such topics as the Flynn effect, *The Bell Curve* controversy, and Gardner's theory of multiple intelligences.

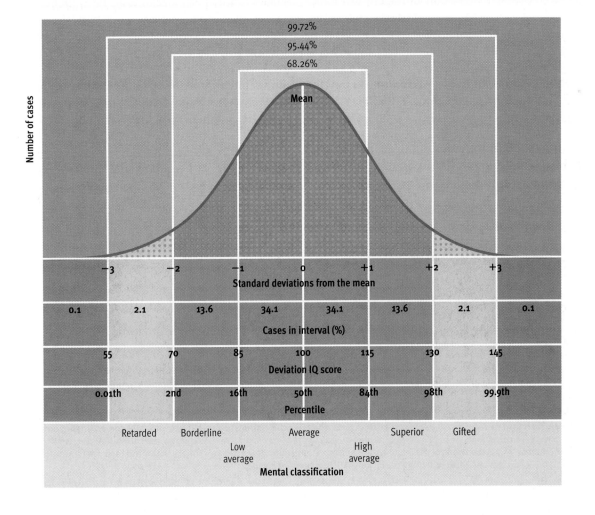

Figure 8.17
The normal distribution. Many characteristics are distributed in a pattern represented by this bell-shaped curve. The horizontal axis shows how far above or below the mean a score is (measured in plus or minus standard deviations). The vertical axis is used to graph the number of cases obtaining each score. In a normal distribution, the cases are distributed in a fixed pattern. For instance, 68.26% of the cases fall between −1 and +1 standard deviation. Modern IQ scores indicate where a person's measured intelligence falls in the normal distribution. On most IQ tests, the mean is set at an IQ of 100 and the standard deviation at 15. Any deviation IQ score can be converted into a percentile score. The mental classifications at the bottom of the figure are descriptive labels that roughly correspond to ranges of IQ scores.

Do Intelligence Tests Have Adequate Reliability? SIM8, 7b

In the jargon of psychological testing, *reliability* refers to the measurement consistency of a test. A reliable test is one that yields similar results on repetition. Like other types of measuring devices, such as a stopwatch or a tire gauge, psychological tests need to be reasonably reliable. Estimates of reliability require the computation of correlation coefficients, which we introduced in Chapter 2. As you may recall, a *correlation coefficient* is a numerical index of the degree of relationship between two variables (see **Figure 8.18**). In gauging a test's reliability, the two variables that are correlated are typically two sets of scores from two administrations of the test. Do IQ tests produce consistent results when people are retested? Yes. Most IQ tests report commendable reliability estimates. The correlations generally range into the .90s (Kaufman, 2000), which is very high. In comparison to most other types of psychological tests, IQ tests are exceptionally reliable.

However, like other tests, they *sample* behavior, and a specific testing may yield an unrepresentative score. Variations in examinees' motivation to take an IQ test or in their anxiety about the test can sometimes produce misleading scores (Hopko et al., 2005; Zimmerman & Woo-Sam, 1984). The most common problem is that low motivation or high anxiety may drag a person's score down on a particular occasion. For instance, a fourth-grader who is made to feel that the test is extremely important may get jittery and be unable to concentrate. The same child might score much higher on a subsequent testing by another examiner who creates a more comfortable atmosphere. Although the reliability of IQ tests is excellent, caution is always in order in interpreting test scores.

Do Intelligence Tests Have Adequate Validity? SIM8, 7b

Even if a test is quite reliable, we still need to be concerned about its validity. *Validity* refers to the ability of a test to measure what it was designed to measure. Validity can be estimated in several ways, depending on the nature of the test (Golden, Sawicki, & Franzen, 1990). In measuring an abstract personal quality such as intelligence, one needs to be concerned about the test's *construct validity*. Do intelligence tests measure what they're supposed to measure? Yes, but this answer has to be qualified very carefully. IQ tests are valid measures of the kind of intelligence that's necessary to do well in academic work. But if the purpose is to assess intelligence in a broader sense, the validity of IQ tests is questionable.

As you may recall, intelligence tests were originally designed with a relatively limited purpose in mind: to predict school performance. This has continued to be the principal purpose of IQ testing. Efforts to document the validity of IQ tests have usually concentrated on their relationship to grades in school. Typically, positive correlations in the .40s and .50s are found between IQ scores and school grades (Kline, 1991; Mackintosh, 1998). Moreover, a recent, huge study of over 70,000 children in England found an even stronger relationship between intelligence and educational achievement. When Deary and colleagues (2007) used a composite measure of intelligence (based on several tests) to predict a composite estimate of educational progress (based on 25 achievement tests) five years later, they found correlations in the vicinity of .70.

These correlations are about as high as one could expect, given that many factors besides a person's intelligence are likely to affect grades and school

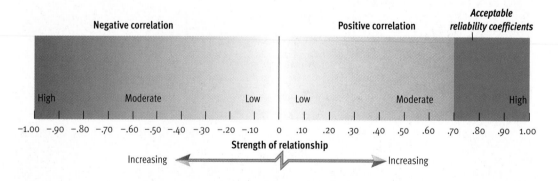

Figure 8.18

Correlation and reliability. As explained in Chapter 2, a positive correlation means that two variables co-vary in the *same* direction; a negative correlation means that two variables co-vary in the *opposite* direction. The closer the correlation coefficient gets to either −1.00 or +1.00, the stronger the relationship. At a minimum, reliability estimates for psychological tests must be moderately high positive correlations. Most reliability coefficients fall between .70 and .95.

progress. For example, school grades may be influenced by a student's motivation or personality, not to mention teachers' subjective biases. Indeed, a recent study reported that measures of students' *self-discipline* are surprisingly strong predictors of students' performance. In two studies of eighth-graders, Duckworth and Seligman (2005) found correlations of .55 and .67 between an elaborate index of self-discipline and students' final GPA. Thus, given all the other factors likely to influence performance in school, IQ tests appear to be reasonably valid indexes of school-related intellectual ability, or academic intelligence.

However, over the years people have mistakenly come to believe that IQ tests measure mental ability in a truly general sense. In reality, IQ tests have always focused on the abstract reasoning and verbal fluency that are essential to academic success. The tests do not tap social competence, practical problem solving, creativity, mechanical ingenuity, or artistic talent.

When Robert Sternberg and his colleagues (1981) asked people to list examples of intelligent behavior, they found that the examples fell into three categories: (1) *verbal intelligence,* (2) *practical intelligence,* and (3) *social intelligence* (see **Figure 8.19**). Thus, people generally recognize three basic types of intelligence.

For the most part, IQ tests assess only the first of these three types. Although IQ tests are billed as measures of *general* mental ability, they actually focus somewhat narrowly on a specific type of intelligence: academic/verbal intelligence (Sternberg, 1998; 2003b).

Do Intelligence Tests Predict Vocational Success?

Vocational success is a vague, value-laden concept that's difficult to quantify. Nonetheless, researchers have attacked this question by examining correlations between IQ scores and specific indicators of vocational success, such as the prestige of subjects' occupations or ratings of subjects' job performance. The data relating IQ to occupational attainment are pretty clear. *People who score high on IQ tests are more likely than those who score low to end up in high-status jobs* (Gottfredson, 2003b; Herrnstein & Murray, 1994; Schmidt & Hunter, 2004). Because IQ tests measure school ability fairly well and school performance is important in attaining certain occupations, this link between IQ scores and job status makes sense. Of course, the correlation between IQ and occupational attainment is moderate. For example, in a meta-analysis of many studies of the issue,

web link 8.5

Educational Psychology Interactive: Intelligence

This site, maintained by Bill Huitt of Valdosta State University, leads to a helpful review of psychological approaches to intelligence and is an excellent resource for other topics in educational psychology.

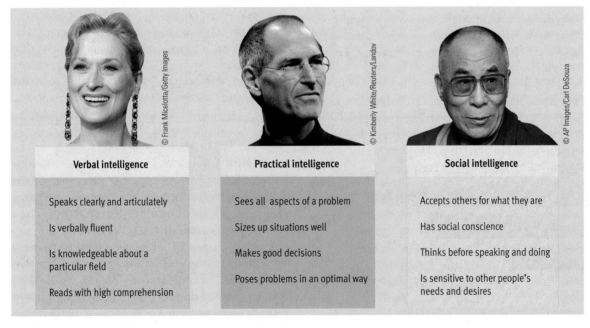

Figure 8.19

Laypersons' conceptions of intelligence. Robert Sternberg and his colleagues (1981) asked participants to list examples of behaviors characteristic of intelligence. The examples tended to sort into three groups that represent the three types of intelligence recognized by the average person: verbal intelligence, practical intelligence, and social intelligence. The three well-known individuals shown here are prototype examples of verbal intelligence (Meryl Streep), practical intelligence (Steve Jobs), and social intelligence (The Dalai Lama).

SOURCE: Adapted from Sternberg, R. J., Conway, B. E., Keton, J. L., & Bernstein, M. (1981). People's conceptions of intelligence. *Journal of Personality and Social Psychology,* *41* (1), 37–55. Copyright © 1981 by the American Psychological Association. Adapted by permission of the author.

The association between intelligence and vocational success is modest for a variety of reasons, including people's motivational idiosyncrasies. Shown here is electronic genius Mark Antman, who prefers to apply his extraordinary intelligence to private projects in his basement workshop rather than have it "exploited" by employment in a technical occupation.

Strenze (2007) found a correlation of .37 between IQ and occupational status. That figure means that there are plenty of exceptions to the general trend. Some people probably outperform brighter colleagues through bulldog determination and hard work. The relationship between IQ and income appears to be somewhat weaker. The meta-analysis by Strenze (2007) reported a correlation of .21 between IQ and income based on 31 studies. In one recent, large-scale study of American baby boomers, the correlation between intelligence and income was .30 (Zagorsky, 2007). These findings suggest that intelli-

gence fosters vocational success, but the strength of the relationship is modest.

There is far more debate about whether IQ scores are effective predictors of performance *within* a particular occupation. On the one hand, research suggests that (a) there is a substantial correlation (about .50) between IQ scores and job performance, (b) this correlation varies somewhat depending on the complexity of a job's requirements but does not disappear even for low-level jobs (see **Figure 8.20**), (c) this association holds up even when workers have more experience at their jobs, and (d) measures of specific mental abilities and personality traits are much less predictive of job performance than measures of intelligence (Gottfredson, 2002; Ones, Viswesvaran, Dilchert, 2005; Schmidt, 2002). On the other hand, critics argue that the reported correlations have usually been corrected for statistical artifacts and that the raw, uncorrected correlations are lower (.30s) (Outtz, 2002). They also note that even a correlation of .50 would provide only modest accuracy in prediction (accounting for about 25% of the variation in job performance) (Goldstein, Zedeck, & Goldstein, 2002; Sternberg & Hedlund, 2002). Concerns have also been raised that when IQ tests are used for job selection they can have an adverse impact on employment opportunities for those in many minority groups who tend to score somewhat lower (on average) on such tests (Murphy, 2002; Outtz, 2002). In the final analysis, there is no question that intelligence is associated with vocational success, but there is room for argument about whether this association is strong enough to justify reliance on IQ testing in hiring employees.

Are IQ Tests Widely Used in Other Cultures?

In other Western cultures with European roots the answer is yes. In most non-Western cultures, the answer is only very little. IQ testing has a long history and continues to be a major enterprise in many Western countries, such as Britain, France, Norway, Canada, and Australia (Irvine & Berry, 1988). However, efforts to export IQ tests to non-Western societies have met with mixed results. The tests have been well received in some non-Western cultures, such as Japan, where the Binet-Simon scales were introduced as early as 1908 (Iwawaki & Vernon, 1988), but they have been met with indifference or resistance in other cultures, such as China and India (Chan & Vernon, 1988; Sinha, 1983). One reason is that some cultures have different conceptions of what intelligence is and value different mental skills (Baral &

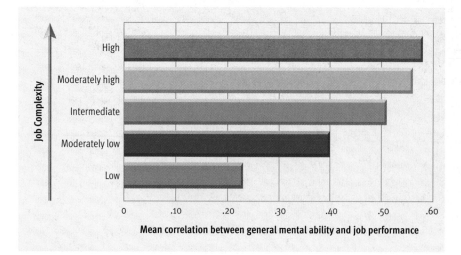

Figure 8.20
Intelligence as a predictor of job performance. Based on a review of 425 studies, Schmidt and Hunter (2004) report that the correlation between general mental ability and job performance depends on the complexity of the job. As jobs become more complicated, intelligence becomes a better predictor of performance. Schmidt and Hunter conclude that these correlations show that IQ tests can be valuable in hiring decisions. However, as the text explains, some other experts have reservations about using intelligence tests in employee selection. (Based on data from Schmidt & Hunter, 2004)

Das, 2004; Sternberg, 2007). Thus, the bottom line is that Western IQ tests do not translate well into the language and cognitive frameworks of many non-Western cultures (Berry, 1994; Sternberg, 2004).

"YOU CAN'T BUILD A HUT, YOU DON'T KNOW HOW TO FIND EDIBLE ROOTS AND YOU KNOW NOTHING ABOUT PREDICTING THE WEATHER. IN OTHER WORDS, YOU DO TERRIBLY ON OUR I.Q. TEST."

ScienceCartoonsPlus.com

REVIEW of Key Learning Goals

8.12 Modern intelligence testing began with the work of Alfred Binet, a French psychologist who published the first useful intelligence test in 1905. Binet's scale measured a child's mental age. Lewis Terman revised the original Binet scale to produce the Stanford-Binet in 1916. It introduced the intelligence quotient and became the standard of comparison for subsequent intelligence tests. David Wechsler devised an improved measure of intelligence for adults, and his IQ test reduced the emphasis on verbal ability. He also introduced a new scoring system based on the normal distribution.

8.13 In the modern scoring system, deviation IQ scores indicate where people fall in the normal distribution of intelligence for their age group. On most tests, the mean is set at 100 and the standard deviation is set at 15.

8.14 IQ tests are exceptionally reliable, with reliability coefficients typically ranging into the .90s. IQ tests are reasonably valid measures of academic intelligence in that they predict school performance fairly well. However, they do not measure intelligence in a truly general sense, as they do not tap social or practical intelligence.

8.15 IQ scores are associated with occupational attainment and income, but the correlations are modest. There is active debate about whether IQ scores predict performance within an occupation well enough to be used in hiring decisions.

8.16 Intelligence testing is largely a Western enterprise, and IQ tests are not widely used in most non-Western cultures. One reason is that different cultures have different conceptions of intelligence.

Heredity and Environment as Determinants of Intelligence

Most early pioneers of intelligence testing maintained that intelligence is inherited (Cravens, 1992). Small wonder, then, that this view lingers in our society. Gradually, however, it has become clear that both heredity and environment influence intelligence (Bartels et al., 2002; Davis, Arden, & Plomin, 2008; Plomin, 2003). Does this mean that the nature versus nurture debate has been settled with respect to intelligence? Absolutely not. Theorists and researchers continue to argue vigorously about which is more important, in part because the issue has such far-reaching social and political implications.

Theorists who believe that intelligence is largely inherited downplay the value of special educational programs for underprivileged groups (Herrnstein & Murray, 1994; Kanazawa, 2006; Rushton & Jensen, 2005). They assert that a child's intelligence cannot be increased noticeably, because genetic destiny cannot be altered. Other theorists take issue with this argument, pointing out that traits with a strong genetic component are not necessarily unchangeable (Flynn, 2007; Sternberg, Grigorenko, & Kidd, 2005). The people in this camp maintain that even more

funds should be devoted to remedial education programs, improved schooling in lower-class neighborhoods, and college financial aid for the underprivileged. Because the debate over the role of heredity in intelligence has direct relevance to important social issues and political decisions, we'll take a detailed look at this complex controversy.

Evidence for Heredity Influence

7d

Researchers have long been aware that intelligence runs in families. However, *family studies* can determine only whether genetic influence on a trait is *plausible*, not whether it is certain. Family members share not just genes, but similar environments. If high intelligence (or low intelligence) appears in a family over several generations, this consistency could reflect the influence of either shared genes or shared environment. Because of this problem, researchers must turn to *twin studies* and *adoption studies* to obtain more definitive evidence on whether heredity affects intelligence.

Key Learning Goals

8.17 Summarize evidence that heredity affects intelligence and discuss the concept of heritability.

8.18 Describe various lines of research that indicate that environment affects intelligence, and explain the concept of reaction range.

8.19 Evaluate heredity and socioeconomic disadvantage as explanations for cultural differences in IQ.

"I don't know anything about the bell curve, but I say heredity is everything."

Twin Studies

7d

The best evidence regarding the role of genetic factors in intelligence comes from studies that compare identical and fraternal twins. The rationale for twin studies is that both identical and fraternal twins normally develop under similar environmental conditions. However, identical twins share more genetic kinship than fraternal twins. Thus, if pairs of identical twins are more similar in intelligence than pairs of fraternal twins, it's presumably because of their greater genetic similarity. (See Chapter 3 for a more detailed explanation of the logic underlying twin studies.)

What are the findings of twin studies regarding intelligence? McGue and colleagues (1993) reviewed the results of over 100 studies of intellectual similarity for various kinds of kinship relations and child-rearing arrangements. The key findings from their review are highlighted in **Figure 8.21**. This figure plots the average correlation observed for various types of relationships. As you can see, the average correlation reported for identical twins (.86) is very high, indicating that identical twins tend to be quite similar in intelligence. The average correlation for fraternal twins (.60) is significantly lower. This correlation indicates that fraternal twins also tend to be similar in intelligence, but noticeably less similar than identical twins. These results support the notion that intelligence is inherited to a considerable degree (Bouchard, 1998; Plomin & Spinath, 2004).

Of course, critics have tried to poke holes in this line of reasoning. They argue that identical twins are more alike in IQ because parents and others treat them more similarly than they treat fraternal twins. This environmental explanation of the findings has some merit. After all, identical twins are always the same sex, and gender influences how a child is raised. However, this explanation seems unlikely in light of the evidence on identical twins reared apart as a result of family breakups or adoption (Bouchard, 1997; Bouchard et al., 1990). *Although reared in different environments,* these identical twins still display greater similarity in IQ (average correlation: .72) than fraternal twins reared together (average correlation: .60).

Figure 8.21

Studies of IQ similarity.
The graph shows the mean correlations of IQ scores for people of various types of relationships, as obtained in studies of IQ similarity. Higher correlations indicate greater similarity. The results show that greater genetic similarity is associated with greater similarity in IQ, suggesting that intelligence is partly inherited (compare, for example, the correlations for identical and fraternal twins). However, the results also show that living together is associated with greater IQ similarity, suggesting that intelligence is partly governed by environment (compare, for example, the scores of siblings reared together and reared apart). (Data from McGue et al., 1993)

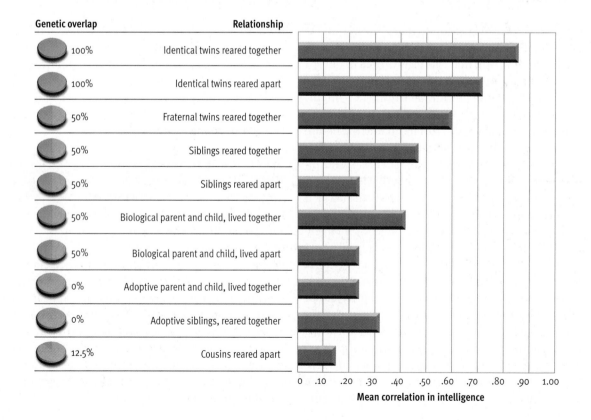

Adoption Studies 7d

Research comparing adopted children to their biological parents also provides evidence about the effects of heredity (and of environment, as we shall see). If adopted children resemble their biological parents in intelligence even though they were not reared by these parents, this finding supports the genetic hypothesis. The relevant studies indicate that there is indeed some measurable similarity between adopted children and their biological parents (Plomin et al., 2008) (refer again to **Figure 8.21**).

Heritability Estimates 7d

Various experts have sifted through mountains of correlational evidence to estimate the *heritability* of intelligence. A *heritability ratio* is an estimate of the proportion of trait variability in a population that is determined by variations in genetic inheritance. Heritability can be estimated for any trait. For example, the heritability of height is estimated to be around 90% (Plomin, 1994). Heritability estimates for intelligence vary (see **Figure 8.22**). At the high end, some theorists estimate that the heritability of IQ ranges as high as 80% (Bouchard, 2004; Jensen, 1980, 1998). That is, they believe that only about 20% of the variation in intelligence is attributable to environmental factors. Estimates at the low end of the spectrum suggest that the heritability of intelligence is around 40% (Plomin, 2003). *In recent years, the consensus estimates of the experts tend to hover around 50%* (Petrill, 2005; Plomin & Spinath, 2004).

However, it's important to understand that heritability estimates have certain limitations (Ceci et al., 1997; Grigorenko, 2000; Reeve & Hakel, 2002). First, a heritability estimate is a *group statistic* based on studies of trait variability within a specific group. A heritability estimate cannot be applied meaningfully to *individuals*. In other words, even if the heritability of intelligence truly is 60%, this does not mean that each individual's intelligence is 60% inherited. Second, the heritability of a specific trait may vary from one group to another depending on a variety of factors. To date, heritability estimates for intelligence have been based largely on research with white, middle-class subjects. Hence, they should be applied only to such groups.

Evidence for Environmental Influence 7d

Heredity unquestionably influences intelligence, but a great deal of evidence indicates that upbringing also affects mental ability. We'll examine three lines of research—concerning adoption, environ-

mental deprivation or enrichment, and generational changes in IQ—that show how life experiences shape intelligence.

Adoption Studies 7d

Research with adopted children provides useful evidence about the impact of experience as well as heredity on intelligence (Locurto, 1990; Loehlin, Horn, & Willerman, 1997). Many of the correlations in **Figure 8.21** reflect the influence of the environment. For example, adopted children show some resemblance to their foster parents in IQ. This similarity is usually attributed to the fact that their foster parents shape their environment. Adoption studies also indicate that siblings reared together are more similar in IQ than siblings reared apart. This is true even for identical twins. Moreover, entirely unrelated children who are raised in the same home also show a significant resemblance in IQ. All of these findings indicate that environment influences intelligence.

Environmental Deprivation and Enrichment

If environment affects intelligence, then children who are raised in substandard circumstances should experience a gradual decrease in IQ as they grow older (since other children will be progressing more rapidly). This *cumulative deprivation hypothesis* was tested decades ago. Researchers studied children consigned to understaffed orphanages and children raised in the poverty and isolation of the back hills of Appalachia (Sherman & Key, 1932; Stoddard, 1943). Generally, investigators *did* find that environmental deprivation led to the predicted decline in IQ scores.

Conversely, children who are removed from a deprived environment and placed in circumstances more conducive to learning tend to benefit from their environmental enrichment (Scarr & Weinberg,

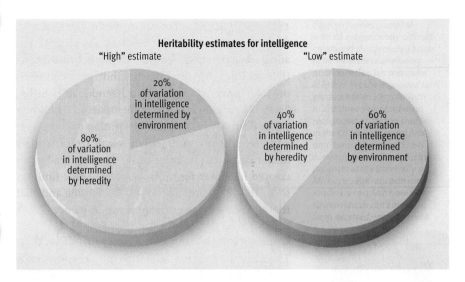

Heritability estimates for intelligence

"High" estimate

20% of variation in intelligence determined by environment

80% of variation in intelligence determined by heredity

"Low" estimate

40% of variation in intelligence determined by heredity

60% of variation in intelligence determined by environment

Figure 8.22

The concept of heritability. A heritability ratio is an estimate of the portion of variation in a trait determined by heredity—with the remainder presumably determined by environment—as these pie charts illustrate. Heritability estimates for intelligence range between a high of 80% and a low of 40%. The consensus estimate tends to hover around 50%. Bear in mind that heritability ratios are *estimates* and have certain limitations that are discussed in the text.

are theoretically interesting, but too weak to give RTs any practical value as an index of intelligence.

Some researchers have also begun to explore the relations between intelligence and brain size. The early studies in this area used various measures of head size as an indicator of brain size. These studies generally found positive but small correlations (average = .15) between head size and IQ (Vernon et al., 2000), leading researchers to speculate that head size is probably a very crude index of brain size. This line of research might have languished, but the invention of sophisticated brain-imaging technologies gave it a huge shot in the arm. Since the 1990s, quite a few studies have examined the correlation between IQ scores and measures of brain volume based on MRI scans (see Chapter 3), yielding an average correlation of about .35 (Anderson, 2003; McDaniel, 2005). One obvious implication of these findings, eagerly embraced by those who tout the influence of heredity on intelligence, is that genetic inheritance gives some people larger brains than others and that larger brain size promotes greater intelligence (Rushton, 2003). However, as always, we must be cautious about interpreting correlational data. As discussed in Chapter 3, research has demonstrated that an enriched environment can produce denser neural networks and heavier brains in laboratory rats (Rosenzweig & Bennett, 1996). Thus, it is also possible that causation runs in the opposite direction—that developing greater intelligence promotes larger brain size, much like weightlifting can promote larger muscles.

Investigating Cognitive Processes in Intelligent Behavior

Investigators interested in intelligence and scholars who have studied cognition have traditionally pursued separate lines of research that only rarely have intersected. However, since the mid-1980s Robert Sternberg (1985, 1988b, 1991) has spearheaded an effort to apply a cognitive perspective to the study of intelligence. His *triarchic theory of human intelligence* consists of three parts: the contextual, experiential, and componential subtheories (see **Figure 8.25**). In his *contextual subtheory*, Sternberg argues that intelligence is a culturally defined concept. He asserts that different manifestations of intelligent behavior are valued in different contexts. In his *experiential subtheory*, Sternberg explores the relationships between experience and intelligence. He emphasizes two factors as the hallmarks of intelligent behavior. The first is the ability to deal effectively with novelty—new tasks, demands, and situations. The second factor is the ability to learn how to handle familiar tasks automatically and effortlessly. Sternberg's *componential subtheory* describes the types of mental processes that intelligent thought depends on (see **Figure 8.25**). This part of the theory has guided ex-

Robert Sternberg

"To understand intelligent behavior, we need to move beyond the fairly restrictive tasks that have been used both in experimental laboratories and in psychometric tests of intelligence."

Figure 8.25

Sternberg's triarchic theory of intelligence. Sternberg's model of intelligence consists of three parts: the contextual subtheory, the experiential subtheory, and the componential subtheory. Much of Sternberg's research has been devoted to the componential subtheory, as he has attempted to identify the cognitive processes that contribute to intelligence. He believes that these processes fall into three groups: metacomponents, performance components, and knowledge-acquisition components. All three component processes contribute to each of three aspects or types of intelligence: analytical intelligence, practical intelligence, and creative intelligence.

tensive research on the specific thinking strategies that contribute to intelligent problem solving.

In more recent extensions of his theory, Sternberg (1999, 2000b, 2003a, 2005b) has asserted that there are three aspects or facets of intelligence: analytical intelligence, creative intelligence, and practical intelligence. *Analytical intelligence* involves abstract reasoning, evaluation, and judgment. It is the type of intelligence that is crucial to most school work and that is assessed by conventional IQ tests. *Creative intelligence* involves the ability to generate new ideas and to be inventive in dealing with novel problems. *Practical intelligence* involves the ability to deal effectively with the kinds of problems that people encounter in everyday life, such as on the job or at home. A big part of practical intelligence involves learning what one needs to know to work efficiently that is not explicitly taught and that often is not even verbalized.

In a series of studies, Sternberg and his colleagues have gathered data suggesting that (1) all three facets of intelligence can be measured reliably, (2) the three facets of intelligence are relatively independent (uncorrelated), and (3) the assessment of all three aspects of intelligence can improve the prediction of intelligent behavior in the real world (Grigorenko & Sternberg, 2001; Henry, Sternberg, & Grigorenko, 2005). Some critics doubt that Sternberg's measures will facilitate better prediction of meaningful outcomes than traditional IQ tests (Gottfredson, 2003a), but that is an empirical question that should be re-

solved by future research. In any event, Sternberg certainly has been an articulate voice arguing for a broader, expanded concept of intelligence, which is a theme that has been echoed by others.

Expanding the Concept of Intelligence

In recent years, many theorists have concluded that traditional IQ tests are too narrow in focus This view has been articulated particularly well by Howard Gardner (1983, 1993, 1999, 2004, 2006). According to Gardner, IQ tests have generally emphasized verbal and mathematical skills, to the exclusion of other important skills. He suggests the existence of a number of relatively independent *human intelligences,* which are listed in **Table 8.4**. To build his list of separate intelligences, Gardner reviewed the evidence on cognitive capacities in normal individuals, people suffering from brain damage, and special populations, such as prodigies and idiot savants. He concluded that humans exhibit eight largely independent intelligences: logical-mathematical, linguistic, musical, spatial, bodily-kinesthetic, interpersonal, intrapersonal, and naturalist. These intelligences obviously include a variety of talents that are not assessed by conventional IQ tests. Gardner is investigating the extent to which these intelligences are largely independent, as his theory asserts. For the most part, he has found that people tend to

Howard Gardner

"It is high time that the view of intelligence be widened to incorporate a range of human computational capacities.... But where is it written that intelligence needs to be determined on the basis of tests?"

Table 8.4 Gardner's Eight Intelligences

Intelligence	End-States	Core Components
Logical-mathematical	Scientist Mathematician	Sensitivity to, and capacity to discern, logical or numerical patterns; ability to handle long chains of reasoning
Linguistic	Poet Journalist	Sensitivity to the sounds, rhythms, and meanings of words; sensitivity to the different functions of language
Musical	Composer Violinist	Abilities to produce and appreciate rhythm, pitch, and timbre; appreciation of the forms of musical expressiveness
Spatial	Navigator Sculptor	Capacities to perceive the visual-spatial world accurately and to perform transformations on one's initial perceptions
Bodily-kinesthetic	Dancer Athlete	Abilities to control one's body movements and to handle objects skillfully
Interpersonal	Therapist Salesperson	Capacities to discern and respond appropriately to the moods, temperaments, motivations, and desires of other people
Intrapersonal	Person with detailed, accurate self-knowledge	Access to one's own feelings and the ability to discriminate among them and draw upon them to guide behavior; knowledge of one's own strengths, weaknesses, desires, and intelligences
Naturalist	Biologist Naturalist	Abilities to recognize and categorize objects and processes in nature

SOURCE: Adapted from Gardner, H., & Hatch, T. (1989). Multiple intelligences go to school: Educational implications of the theory of multiple intelligences. *Educational Researcher, 18* (8), 4–10. American Educational Research Association. Additional information from Gardner (1998).

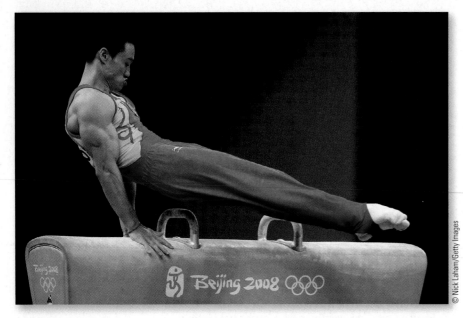

display a mixture of strong, intermediate, and weak abilities, which is consistent with the idea that the various types of intelligence are independent.

Gardner's books have been very popular and his theory clearly resonates with many people (Shearer, 2004). His ideas have had an enormous impact on educators' attitudes and beliefs around the world (Cuban, 2004; Kornhaber, 2004). He has raised thought-provoking questions about what abilities should be included under the rubric of intelligence (Eisner, 2004). However, he has his critics (Hunt, 2001; Klein, 1997; Morgan, 1996; Waterhouse, 2006). Some argue that his use of the term *intelligence* is so broad, encompassing virtually any valued human ability, it makes the term almost meaningless. These critics wonder whether there is any advantage to re-labeling talents such as musical ability and motor coordination as forms of intelligence. Critics also

Should outstanding motor coordination be considered a form of intelligence? Howard Gardner argues for the recognition of eight intelligences, including bodily-kinesthetic intelligence. However, some critics assert that Gardner's view broadens the concept of intelligence to such a degree that it borders on meaningless.

concept check 8.4

Identifying the Contributions of Major Theorists and Researchers

Check your recall of the principal ideas of important theorists and researchers covered in this chapter by matching the people listed on the left with the appropriate contributions described on the right. If you need help, the crucial pages describing each person's ideas are listed in parentheses. Fill in the letters for your choices in the spaces provided on the left. You'll find the answers in Appendix A.

Major Theorists and Researchers

_____ 1. Alfred Binet (pp. 274–275)

_____ 2. Howard Gardner (pp. 289–290)

_____ 3. Arthur Jensen (pp. 285–286)

_____ 4. Daniel Kahneman and Amos Tversky (pp. 269–270)

_____ 5. Sandra Scarr (pp. 284–285)

_____ 6. Herbert Simon (pp. 259, 267)

_____ 7. Robert Sternberg (p. 288)

_____ 8. Lewis Terman (p. 275)

_____ 9. David Wechsler (p. 275)

Key Ideas and Contributions

a. These psychologists conducted pioneering research on the heuristics that people use in risky decision making, such as the availability and representativeness heuristics.

b. This theorist's triarchic theory takes a cognitive approach to intelligence. He argues that there are three key facets of human intelligence: analytical, creative, and practical intelligence.

c. This psychologist developed the Stanford-Binet Intelligence Scale, which originally described children's scores in terms of an intelligence quotient.

d. This French psychologist devised the first successful intelligence test, which expressed a child's score in terms of mental age.

e. This theorist argued that the heritability of intelligence is about 80% and that cultural differences in average IQ scores are primarily a product of heredity.

f. This person developed the first influential intelligence test designed specifically for adults. He also discarded the intelligence quotient in favor of a scoring scheme based on the normal distribution.

g. This theorist argued that there are eight types of human intelligence.

h. This person uses the concept of reaction range to explain the interaction of heredity and environment.

i. This Nobel-winning pioneer of cognitive psychology formulated the theory of bounded rationality.

note that Gardner's theory has not generated much research on the predictive value of measuring individual differences in the eight intelligences he has described. This research would require the development of tests to measure the eight intelligences, but Gardner is not particularly interested in the matter of assessment and he loathes conventional testing. This situation makes it difficult to predict where Gardner's theory will lead, as research is crucial to the evolution of a theory.

web link 8.7

HowardGardner.com

A wealth of resources on Gardner's theory of multiple intelligences can be found at this site, including biographical information on Gardner, seminal and recent papers on his multiple intelligence perspective, and links to other relevant sites.

REVIEW of Key Learning Goals

8.20 Although reaction time indexes of intelligence are being explored, they seem to have little practical utility. Recent research has uncovered a very small positive correlation between head size and intelligence. However, a moderate correlation (.35) has been found between IQ and brain volume estimated from MRI scans.

8.21 Robert Sternberg's triarchic theory uses a cognitive perspective, which emphasizes the need to understand how people use their intelligence. Sternberg emphasizes two factors as hallmarks of intelligence—the ability to deal with novelty and the ability to handle familiar tasks automatically. According to Sternberg, the three facets of successful intelligence are analytical, creative, and practical intelligence.

8.22 Howard Gardner argues that the concept of intelligence should be expanded to encompass a diverse set of eight types of abilities. He believes that these eight intelligences are largely independent of one another. Gardner's critics argue that his use of the term intelligence is so broad, encompassing virtually any human ability, it makes the term almost meaningless.

Reflecting on the Chapter's Themes

Five of our unifying themes surfaced in this chapter. The first is the empirical nature of psychology. For many decades, psychologists paid little attention to cognitive processes, because most of them assumed that thinking is too private to be studied scientifically. During the 1950s and 1960s, however, psychologists began to devise creative new ways to measure mental processes. These innovations, which fueled the cognitive revolution, show that empirical methods are the lifeblood of the scientific enterprise.

Second, our review of cognition and intelligence demonstrated the importance of cultural factors. For example, we learned that there are striking cultural variations in cognitive style. We also saw that intelligence testing is largely a Western phenomenon and that ethnic differences in average intelligence may be largely cultural in origin. Thus, we see once again that if we hope to achieve a sound understanding of behavior, we need to appreciate the cultural contexts in which behavior unfolds.

Third, our coverage showed that intelligence is shaped by a complex interaction of hereditary and environmental factors. We've drawn a similar conclusion before in other chapters where we examined other topics. However, this chapter should have enhanced your appreciation of this idea by illustrating in detail how scientists arrive at this conclusion.

Fourth, we saw more evidence that psychology evolves in a sociohistorical context. Prevailing social attitudes have always exerted some influence on testing practices and the interpretation of test results. In the first half of the 20th century, a strong current of racial and class prejudice was apparent in the United States and Britain. This prejudice supported the idea that IQ tests measured innate ability and that "undesirable" groups scored poorly because of their genetic inferiority. Although these beliefs did not go unchallenged within psychology, their widespread acceptance in the field reflected the social values of the time. Today, the continuing, ferocious debate about the roots of cultural differences in intelligence shows that issues in psychology often have far-reaching social and political implications.

The final theme apparent in this chapter was the subjective nature of human experience, which was prominent in our discussion of peculiarities in human decision making.

Key Learning Goals

8.23 Identify the five unifying themes highlighted in this chapter.

 Empiricism

 Cultural Heritage

 Heredity and Environment

 Sociohistorical Context

 Subjectivity of Experience

REVIEW of Key Learning Goals

8.23 Five of our unifying themes surfaced in the chapter: the empirical nature of psychology, the importance of cultural factors, the interaction of heredity and environment, the way psychology evolves in a sociohistorical context, and the subjectivity of human experience.

Measuring and Understanding Creativity

Key Learning Goals

8.24 Evaluate the role of insight and divergent thinking in creativity.

8.25 Describe creativity tests, and summarize how well they predict creative achievement.

8.26 Clarify the associations between creativity and personality, intelligence, and mental illness.

Answer the following "true" or "false":

___ **1** Creative ideas often come out of nowhere.

___ **2** Creativity usually occurs in a burst of insight.

___ **3** Creativity and intelligence are unrelated.

Intelligence is not the only type of mental ability that psychologists have studied. They have devised tests to explore a variety of mental abilities. Among these, creativity is certainly one of the most interesting. People tend to view creativity as an essential trait for artists, musicians, and writers, but it is important in *many* walks of life. In this Application, we'll discuss psychologists' efforts to measure and understand creativity. As we progress, you'll learn that all the statements above are false.

The Nature of Creativity

What makes thought creative? *Creativity* involves the generation of ideas that are original, novel, and useful. Creative thinking is fresh, innovative, and inventive. But novelty by itself is not enough. In addition to being unusual, creative thinking must be adaptive. It must be appropriate to the situation and problem.

Does Creativity Occur in a Burst of Insight?

It is widely believed that creativity usually involves sudden flashes of insight and great leaps of imagination. Robert Weisberg (1986) calls this belief the "Aha! myth." Undeniably, creative bursts of insight do occur (Feldman, 1988). However, the evidence suggests that major creative achievements gen-

erally are logical extensions of existing ideas, involving long, hard work and many small, faltering steps forward (Weisberg, 1993). Creative ideas do not come out of nowhere. They come from a deep well of experience and training in a specific area, whether it's music, painting, business, or science (Weisberg, 1999, 2006). As Snow (1986) puts it, "Creativity is not a light bulb in the mind, as most cartoons depict it. It is an accomplishment born of intensive study, long reflection, persistence, and interest" (p. 1033).

Does Creativity Depend on Divergent Thinking?

According to many theorists, the key to creativity lies in *divergent thinking*—thinking "that goes off in different directions," as J. P. Guilford (1959) put it. Guilford distinguished between convergent thinking and divergent thinking. In *convergent thinking* one tries to narrow down a list of alternatives to converge on a single correct answer. For example, when you take a multiple-choice exam, you try to eliminate incorrect options until you hit on the correct response. Most training in school encourages convergent thinking. In *divergent thinking* one tries to expand the range of alternatives by generating many possible solutions. Imagine that you work for an advertising agency. To come up with as many slogans as possible for a client's product, you must use divergent thinking. Some of your slogans may be clear losers, and eventually you will have to engage in convergent thinking to pick the best, but coming up with the range of new possibilities depends on divergent thinking.

Thirty years of research on divergent thinking has yielded mixed results. As a whole, the evidence suggests that divergent thinking contributes to creativity, but it clearly does not represent the essence of creativity, as originally proposed (Brown, 1989; Plucker & Renzulli, 1999; Weisberg, 2006). In retrospect, it was unrealistic to expect creativity to depend on a single cognitive skill.

Measuring Creativity SIM8

Although its nature may be elusive, creativity clearly is important in today's world. Creative masterpieces in the arts and literature enrich human existence. Creative inventions fuel technological progress. Thus, it is understandable that psychologists have been interested in measuring creativity with psychological tests.

How Do Psychological Tests Assess Creativity? SIM8

A diverse array of psychological tests have been devised to measure individuals' creativity (Cooper, 1991). Usually, the items on creativity tests give respondents a specific starting point and then require them to generate as many possibilities as they can in a short period of time. Typical items on a creativity test might include the following: (1) List as many uses as you can for a newspaper. (2) Think of as many fluids that burn as you can. (3) Imagine that people no longer need sleep and think of as many consequences as you can. Participants' scores on these tests depend on the *number* of alternatives they generate and on the *originality* and *usefulness* of the alternatives.

How Well Do Tests Predict Creative Productivity?

In general, studies indicate that creativity tests are mediocre predictors of creative achievement in the real world (Hocevar & Bachelor, 1989; Plucker & Renzulli, 1999). Why? One reason is that these tests measure creativity in the abstract, as a *general trait*. However, the accumulation of evidence suggests that *creativity is specific to particular domains* (Amabile, 1996; Feist, 2004; Kaufman & Baer, 2002, 2004). Despite some rare exceptions, creative people usually excel in a single field, in which they typically have considerable training and expertise (Policastro & Gardner, 1999). An innovative physicist might have no potential to be a creative poet. Measuring this person's creativity outside of physics may be meaningless.

Even if better tests of creativity were devised, predicting creative achievement would probably still prove difficult. Why? Because creative achievement depends on many factors besides creativity. Creative productivity over the course of an individual's career will depend on his or her motivation, personality, and intelligence, as well as on situational factors, including training, mentoring, and good fortune (Amabile, 1983; Feldman, 1999; Simonton, 2004).

Correlates of Creativity

What are creative people like? Are they brighter or less well adjusted than average? A great deal of research has been conducted on the correlates of creativity.

Is There a Creative Personality?

Creative people exhibit the full range of personality traits, but investigators have found modest correlations between certain personality characteristics and creativity (Ochse, 1990). Based on a meta-analysis of over 80 studies, Feist (1998) concludes that highly creative people "are more autonomous, introverted, open to new experiences, norm-doubting, self-confident, self-accepting, driven, ambitious, dominant, hostile, and impulsive" (p. 299). At the core of this set of personality characteristics are the related traits of independence and nonconformity. Creative people tend to think for themselves and are less easily influenced by the opinions of others than the average person is. That said, there is no single personality profile that accounts for creativity (Weisberg, 2006).

Are Creativity and Intelligence Related?

Are creative people exceptionally smart? Conceptually, creativity and intelligence represent different types of mental ability. Thus, it's not surprising that correlations between measures of creativity and measures of intelligence are generally weak (Sternberg & O'Hara, 1999). For example, a recent meta-analysis of many studies reported a correlation of only .17 (Kim, 2005). However, some findings suggest that the association between creativity and intelligence is somewhat stronger than that (Silvia, 2008). One widely cited model of the relationship between creativity and intelligence is the *threshold hypothesis* proposed decades ago by pioneering creativity researchers (Barron, 1963; Torrance, 1962). According to this hypothesis, creative achievements require a minimum level of intelligence, so most highly creative people are probably well above average in intelligence. An IQ of 120 has been proposed as the minimum threshold for creative achievement (Lubart, 2003). At this point, all one can conclude is that there appears to be a weak to modest association between IQ and creativity.

Is There a Connection Between Creativity and Mental Illness?

There may be a connection between truly exceptional creativity and mental illness—in particular, mood disorders such as depression. When Nancy Andreasen studied 30 accomplished writers who had been invited as visiting faculty to the prestigious Iowa Writers Workshop, she found that 80% of her sample had suffered a mood disorder at some point in their lives (Andreasen, 1987, 2005). In a similar study of 59 female writers from another writers' conference, Ludwig (1994) found that 56% had experienced depression. These figures are far above the base rate (roughly 15%) for mood disorders in the general population. Other studies have also found an association between creativity and the prevalence of psychological disorders (Frantom & Sherman, 1999; Jamison, 1988; Ludwig, 1998; Post, 1996; Schildkraut, Hirshfeld, & Murphy, 1994). Perhaps the most ambitious examination of the issue has been Arnold Ludwig's (1995) analyses of the biographies of 1,004 people who achieved eminence in 18 fields. He found greatly elevated rates of depression and other disorders among eminent writers, artists, and composers (see **Figure 8.26**). Thus, accumulating empirical data tentatively suggest that there may be a correlation between major creative achievement and vulnerability to mental disorders.

Figure 8.26
Estimated prevalence of psychological disorders among people who achieved creative eminence. Ludwig (1995) studied biographies of 1,004 people who had clearly achieved eminence in one of 18 fields and tried to determine whether each person suffered from any specific mental disorders in their lifetimes. The data summarized here show the prevalence rates for depression and for a mental disorder of any kind for four fields where creativity is often the key to achieving eminence. As you can see, the estimated prevalence of mental illness was extremely elevated among eminent writers, artists, and composers (but not natural scientists) in comparison to the general population, with depression accounting for much of this elevation.

Key Learning Goals

8.27 Understand how appeals to ignorance and reification have cropped up in debates about intelligence.

The Intelligence Debate, Appeals to Ignorance, and Reification

A *fallacy* is a mistake or error in the process of reasoning. Cognitive scientists who study how people think have long lists of common errors that people make in their reasoning processes. One of these fallacies has a curious name, which is the *appeal to ignorance*. It involves misusing the general lack of knowledge or information on an issue (a lack of knowledge is a kind of ignorance) to support an argument. This fallacy often surfaces in the debate about the relative influence of heredity and environment on intelligence. Before we tackle the more difficult issue of how this fallacy shows up in the debate about intelligence, let's start with a simpler example.

Do ghosts exist? This is probably not the kind of question you expected to find in your psychology textbook, but it can clarify the appeal to ignorance. Those who assert that ghosts *do* exist will often support their conclusion by arguing that no one can prove that ghosts do *not* exist; therefore, ghosts must exist. The lack of evidence or inability to show that ghosts do not exist is used to conclude the opposite. Conversely, those who assert that ghosts *do not* exist often rely on the same logic. They argue that no one can prove that ghosts exist; therefore, they must not exist. Can you see what is wrong with these appeals to ignorance? The lack of information on an issue cannot be used to support any conclusion—other than the conclusion that we are too ignorant to draw a conclusion.

One interesting aspect of the appeal to ignorance is that the same appeal can be used to support two conclusions that are diametrically opposed to each other. This paradox is a telltale clue that appeals to ignorance involve flawed reasoning. It is easy to see what is wrong with appeals to ignorance when the opposite arguments (ghosts exist—ghosts do not exist) are presented together and the

lack of evidence on the issue under discussion is obvious. However, when the same fallacy surfaces in more complex debates and the appeal to ignorance is not as blatant, the strategy can be more difficult to recognize. Let's look at how the appeal to ignorance has been used in the debate about intelligence.

As you saw in the main body of the chapter, the debate about the relative contributions of nature and nurture to intelligence is one of psychology's longest-running controversies. This complex debate is exceptionally bitter because it has far-reaching social and political repercussions. In this debate, one argument that has frequently been made is that we have little or no evidence that intelligence can be increased by environmental

(educational) interventions; therefore, intelligence must be mostly inherited. In other words, the argument runs: No one has demonstrated that intelligence is largely shaped by environment, so it must be largely inherited. This argument was part of Jensen's (1969) landmark treatise that greatly intensified the debate about intelligence, and it was one of the arguments made by Herrnstein and Murray (1994) in their controversial book, *The Bell Curve*. What the argument refers to is the evidence that educational enrichment programs such as Head Start, which have been designed to enhance the intellectual development of underprivileged children, generally have not produced substantial, long-term gains in IQ (Neisser et

Do ghosts exist? Littledean Hall, shown here, is said to be the home of 11 ghosts and is reputed to be the most haunted house in Great Britain. Those who believe in ghosts often support their view by arguing that no one can prove that ghosts do not exist. But as the text explains, this appeal to ignorance is logically flawed. This fallacy has also surfaced in some of the debates about the nature of intelligence.

© Simon Marsden/marsdenarchive.com

al., 1996). The programs produce other benefits, including enduring improvements in school achievement, but short-term gains in IQ scores typically have faded by the middle grades (Barnett, 2004). These findings may have some important implications for government policy in the educational arena, but the way in which they have been applied to the nature-nurture debate regarding intelligence has resulted in an appeal to ignorance. In its simplest form, the absence of evidence showing that environmental changes can increase intelligence is used to support the conclusion that intelligence is mostly determined by genetic inheritance. But the absence of evidence (ignorance) cannot be used to argue for or against a position.

By the way, if you have assimilated some of the critical thinking skills discussed in earlier chapters you may be thinking, "Wait a minute. Aren't there alternative explanations for the failure of educational enrichment programs to increase IQ scores?" Yes, one could argue that the programs failed to yield the expected increments in IQ scores because they were poorly planned, poorly executed, too brief, or underfunded (Ramey, 1999; Sigel, 2004). The inability of the enrichment programs to produce enduring increases in IQ does not necessarily imply that intelligence is unchangeable because it is largely a product of heredity. You may also be wondering, "Aren't there contradictory data?" Once again, the answer is yes. Some lesser-known educational enrichment programs attempted with smaller groups of children *have* yielded durable gains in IQ scores or other measures of academic achievement (Ramey & Ramey, 2004; Reynolds et al., 2001; Woodhead, 2004).

The dialogue on intelligence has also been marred by the tendency to engage in reification. *Reification* **occurs when a hypothetical, abstract concept is given a name and then treated as though it were a concrete, tangible object.** Some hypothetical constructs just become so familiar and so taken for granted that we begin to think about them as if they were real. People often fall into this trap with the Freudian personality concepts of id, ego, and superego (see Chapter 11). They begin to think of the *ego*, for instance, as a genuine entity that can be strengthened or controlled, when the ego is really nothing more than a hypothetical abstraction. The concept of intelligence has also been reified in many quarters. Like the ego, intelligence is nothing more than a useful abstraction—a hypothetical construct that is estimated, rather arbitrarily, by a collection of paper-and-pencil measures called IQ tests. Yet people routinely act as if intelligence is a tangible commodity, fighting vitriolic battles over whether it can be measured precisely, whether it can be changed, and whether it can ensure job success. This reification clearly contributes to the tendency for people to attribute excessive importance to the concept of intelligence. It would be wise to remember that intelligence is no more real than the concept of "environment" or "cyberspace" or "the American dream."

Reification has also occurred in the debate about the degree to which intelligence is inherited. Arguments about the heritability coefficient for intelligence often imply that there is a single, true number lurking somewhere "out there" waiting to be discovered. In reality, heritability is a hypothetical construct that can be legitimately estimated in

Reification occurs when we think of hypothetical constructs as if they were real. Like intelligence, the concept of cyberspace has been subject to reification. The fact that cyberspace is merely an abstraction becomes readily apparent when artists are asked to "draw" cyberspace for conference posters or book covers.

several ways that can lead to somewhat different results. Moreover, heritability ratios will vary from one population to the next, depending on the amount of genetic variability and the extent of environmental variability in the populations. No exactly accurate number that corresponds to "true heritability" awaits discovery. Thus, it is important to understand that hypothetical constructs have great heuristic value in the study of complex phenomena such as human thought and behavior, but they do not actually exist in the world—at least not in the same way that a table or a person exists.

Table 8.5 Critical Thinking Skills Discussed in This Application

Skill	Description
Recognizing and avoiding appeals to ignorance	The critical thinker understands that the lack of information on an issue cannot be used to support an argument.
Recognizing and avoiding reification	The critical thinker is vigilant about the tendency to treat hypothetical constructs as if they were concrete things.
Looking for alternative explanations for findings and events	In evaluating explanations, the critical thinker explores whether there are other explanations that could also account for the findings or events under scrutiny.
Looking for contradictory evidence	In evaluating the evidence presented on an issue, the critical thinker attempts to look for contradictory evidence that may have been left out of the debate.

REVIEW of Key Learning Goals

8.27 The appeal to ignorance involves misusing the general lack of knowledge or information on an issue to support an argument. This fallacy has surfaced in the debate about intelligence, wherein it has been argued that because we have little or no evidence that intelligence can be increased by environmental interventions, intelligence must be mostly inherited. Reification occurs when a hypothetical construct, such as intelligence, is treated as though it were a tangible object.

Problem Solving: In Search of Solutions

■ Psychologists have differentiated among several types of problems, including problems of inducing structure, problems of transformation, and problems of arrangement. Common barriers to problem solving include functional fixedness, mental set, getting bogged down in irrelevant information, and placing unnecessary constraints on one's solutions.

■ Besides trial and error, a variety of heuristics are used for solving problems, including forming subgoals, hill climbing, searching for analogies, and changing the representation of a problem. Research suggests that Eastern cultures exhibit a more holistic cognitive style, whereas Western cultures display a more analytic cognitive style.

Decision Making: Choices and Chances

■ Simon's theory of bounded rationality suggests that human decision strategies are simplistic and often yield irrational results. Schwartz argues that in modern societies people suffer from choice overload, which leads to rumination, regret, and diminished well-being.

■ An additive decision model is used when people make decisions by rating the attributes of each alternative and selecting the alternative that has the highest sum of ratings. When elimination by aspects is used, people gradually eliminate alternatives whose attributes fail to satisfy some minimum criterion.

■ People use the representativeness and availability heuristics in estimating probabilities. These heuristics can lead people to ignore base rates and to fall for the conjunction fallacy. The use of the representativeness heuristic contributes to the gambler's fallacy.

■ The availability heuristic underlies the tendency to overestimate the improbable. Most people expect that the negative impact of a loss will be greater than the positive impact of a similar gain, but research shows that people overestimate the impact of losses.

■ Evolutionary psychologists maintain that many errors and biases in human reasoning are greatly reduced when problems are presented in ways that resemble the type of input humans would have processed in ancestral times. Gigerenzer argues that people largely depend on fast and frugal decision heuristics that are adaptive in the real world.

Measuring Intelligence

■ Modern intelligence testing began with the work of Alfred Binet, who devised a scale to measure a child's mental age. Lewis Terman revised the original Binet scale to produce the Stanford-Binet, which became the standard of comparison for subsequent intelligence tests. David Wechsler devised an improved measure of intelligence for adults and a new scoring system based on the normal distribution.

■ Intelligence tests contain a diverse mixture of questions. In the modern scoring system, deviation IQ scores indicate where people fall in the normal distribution of intelligence for their age group. IQ tests are exceptionally reliable. They are reasonably valid measures of academic intelligence, but they do not tap social or practical intelligence.

■ IQ scores are correlated with occupational attainment, and to a lesser degree with income, but doubts have been raised about how well they predict performance within an occupation. IQ tests are not widely used in most non-Western cultures.

Heredity and Environment as Determinants of Intelligence

■ The empirical evidence clearly shows that intelligence is influenced by both heredity and environment. Estimates of the heritability of intelligence range from 40% to 80%, with the consensus centering around 50%. However, heritability ratios have certain limitations. The concept of reaction range posits that heredity places limits on one's intellectual potential and the environment determines where one falls within these limits.

■ Genetic explanations for cultural differences in IQ have been challenged on a variety of grounds. Ethnicity varies with social class, so socioeconomic disadvantage may account for low IQ scores among minority students.

New Directions in the Assessment and Study of Intelligence

■ Biological indexes of intelligence are being explored, but they seem to have little practical utility thus far. Recent studies suggest that there may be a correlation between intelligence and brain size.

■ Research on intelligence increasingly takes a cognitive perspective, which emphasizes the need to understand how people use their intelligence. Sternberg argues that there are three facets of successful intelligence: analytical, creative, and practical intelligence. Many modern theorists, most notably Howard Gardner, argue that the concept of intelligence should be expanded to encompass a greater variety of skills.

Reflecting on the Chapter's Themes

■ Five of our unifying themes surfaced in the chapter: the empirical nature of psychology, the importance of cultural factors, the interaction of heredity and environment, the way psychology evolves in a sociohistorical context, and the subjectivity of human experience.

PERSONAL APPLICATION Measuring and Understanding Creativity

■ Creativity involves the generation of original, novel, and useful ideas. Creativity does not usually involve sudden insight. Divergent thinking can foster creativity, but it does not represent the essence of creativity.

■ Psychologists have developed some clever and useful measures of creativity, but these tests are mediocre predictors of creative productivity in the real world. Creativity is only weakly related to intelligence. Recent evidence suggests that creative geniuses may exhibit heightened vulnerability to psychological disorders.

CRITICAL THINKING APPLICATION The Intelligence Debate, Appeals to Ignorance, and Reification

■ The appeal to ignorance involves misusing the lack of knowledge or information on an issue to support an argument. Reification occurs when a hypothetical construct is treated as though it were a tangible object. The concepts of intelligence and heritability have both been subject to reification.

PSYKTREK PREVIEW

COGNITION AND INTELLIGENCE
7d Heredity, Environment, and Intelligence

"High" estimate — Heredity 80% Environment 20%
"Low" estimate — Heredity 40% Environment 60%
Consensus estimate — Heredity 50% Environment 50%

A "low-end" estimate of the heritability of IQ would suggest that about 40% of the variability in intelligence is determined by genetic factors and about 60% by experience. Experts' consensus estimate of the heritability of intelligence hovers at around 50%.

COGNITION AND INTELLIGENCE
7f Decision Making

Laura is in a casino watching people play roulette. The 38 slots in the roulette wheel include 18 black numbers, 18 red numbers, and 2 green numbers. Hence, on any one spin, the probability of red or black is slightly less than 50-50 (.474 to be exact). The ball has landed in red seven times in a row. Laura concludes that black is long overdue and bets heavily on black. Is Laura's reasoning sound?

Laura's reasoning is sound.
Laura's reasoning is flawed.

Consider the scenario outlined onscreen and then click the options below it to indicate whether Laura has made a good bet.

Review Module 7c (*Understanding IQ Scores*) and Module 7d (*Heredity, Environment, and Intelligence*) to increase your appreciation of how IQ tests work and

Visit Module 7f (*Decision Making*) to learn why people routinely make decisions that are riddled with errors and biases that yield surprisingly irrational results.

1. Problems that require a common object to be used in an unusual way may be difficult to solve because of:
   A. mental set.
   B. irrelevant information.
   C. unnecessary constraints.
   D. functional fixedness.

2. The nine-dot problem:
   A. is often solved suddenly with a burst of insight.
   B. is difficult because people assume constraints that are not part of the problem.
   C. is solved through forming subgoals.
   D. is both a and b.

3. A heuristic is:
   A. a flash of insight.
   B. a guiding principle or "rule of thumb" used in problem solving or decision making.
   C. a methodical procedure for trying all possible solutions to a problem.
   D. a way of making a compensatory decision.

4. According to Nisbett, Eastern cultures tend to favor a(n) _____ cognitive style, whereas Western cultures tend to display a(n) _____ cognitive style.
   A. analytic; holistic
   B. holistic; analytic
   C. logical; emotional
   D. emotional; logical

5. The work of Herbert Simon on decision making showed that:
   A. people generally make rational choices that maximize their gains.
   B. people can evaluate an unlimited number of alternatives effectively.
   C. people tend to focus on only a few aspects of their available options and often make "irrational" decisions as a result.
   D. the more options people consider, the better their decisions tend to be.

6. When you estimate the probability of an event by judging the ease with which relevant instances come to mind, you are relying on:
   A. an additive decision-making model.
   B. the representativeness heuristic.
   C. the availability heuristic.
   D. a noncompensatory model.

7. The belief that the probability of heads is higher after a long string of tails:
   A. is rational and accurate.
   B. is an example of the "gambler's fallacy."
   C. reflects the influence of the representativeness heuristic.
   D. is both B and C.

8. On most modern IQ tests, a score of 115 would be:
   A. about average.
   B. about 15% higher than the average of one's agemates.
   C. an indication of genius.
   D. one standard deviation above the mean.

9. IQ tests have proven to be good predictors of:
   A. social intelligence.
   B. practical problem-solving intelligence.
   C. school performance.
   D. all of the above.

10. Saying that the heritability of intelligence is 60% would mean that:
    A. 60% of a person's intelligence is due to heredity.
    B. 60% of the variability in intelligence scores in a group is estimated to be due to genetic variations.
    C. intelligence is 40% inherited.
    D. heredity affects intelligence in 60% of the members of the group.

11. Evidence indicating that upbringing affects one's mental ability is provided by which of the following findings?
    A. Identical twins are more similar in IQ than fraternal twins.
    B. There is more than a chance similarity between adopted children and their biological parents.
    C. Siblings reared together are more similar in IQ than siblings reared apart.
    D. Identical twins reared apart are more similar in IQ than siblings reared together.

12. According to theories that use the concept of reaction range, the upper limits of an individual's intellectual potential are:
    A. determined during the first year of life.
    B. largely set by heredity.
    C. determined by a person's unique experiences.
    D. determined by one's heritability quotient.

Answers

1 D pp. 261–262 5 C p. 267 9 C pp. 278–279
2 D p. 263 6 C p. 269 10 B p. 283
3 B p. 263 7 D p. 271 11 C pp. 282–283
4 B pp. 266–267 8 D pp. 276–277 12 B pp. 284–285

PSYKTREK PREVIEW

Try Simulation 7 (*Problem Solving*) to see if you can solve the classic hobbits and orcs problem that has been studied by generations of psychologists (it is not

Go to Simulation 8 (*Psychological Testing: Measuring Your Creativity*) to take a genuine psychological test that will give you an estimate of your creative

9

Motivation and Emotion

Golden Gate Bridge, San Francisco © Philip Coblentz/JupiterImages/Brand X/Alamy

It was a bright afternoon in May 1996, and 41-year-old Jon Krakauer was on top of the world—literally. Krakauer had just fulfilled a boyhood dream by climbing Mount Everest, the tallest peak on earth. Clearing the ice from his oxygen mask, he looked down on a sweeping vista of ice, snow, and majestic mountains. His triumph should have brought him intense joy, but he felt strangely detached. "I'd been fantasizing about this moment, and the release of emotion that would accompany it, for many years," he wrote later. "But now that I was finally here, standing on the summit of Mount Everest, I just couldn't summon the energy to care" (Krakauer, 1998, p. 6).

Why were Krakauer's emotions so subdued? A major reason was that he was physically spent. Climbing Mount Everest is an incredibly grueling experience. At just over 29,000 feet, the mountain's peak is at the altitude flown by jumbo jets. Because such high altitudes wreak havoc on the human body, Krakauer and his fellow climbers couldn't even approach the summit until they had spent six weeks acclimating at Base Camp, 17,600 feet above sea level. Even getting that far would test the limits of most people's endurance. At Base Camp, Krakauer found that ordinary bodily functions became painfully difficult. On most nights, he awoke three or four times, gasping for breath and feeling like he was suffocating. His appetite vanished, and his oxygen-starved digestive system failed to metabolize food normally. "My body began consuming itself for sustenance. My arms and legs gradually began to wither to sticklike proportions" (Krakauer, 1998, p. 87).

At this point you may be wondering why anyone would willingly undergo such extreme discomfort, but Base Camp was just the beginning. From Base Camp it is another two vertical miles through the aptly named Death Zone to the summit. Even for a fully acclimated climber, the final leg of the ascent is agonizing. By the time Krakauer reached the summit, every step was labored, every gasping breath hurt. He hadn't slept in 57 hours, and he had two separated ribs from weeks of violent coughing. He was bitterly cold and utterly exhausted. Instead of elation, he felt only apprehension. Even though his oxygen-starved brain was barely functioning, he understood that getting down from the summit would be fully as dangerous as getting up.

Tragically, events proved just how dangerous an assault on Everest can be. During Krakauer's descent, a sudden, howling storm hit the mountain. Winds exceeding 100 miles per hour whipped the snow into a blinding white blur and sent the temperature plummeting. While Krakauer barely escaped with his life, 12 men and women died on the mountain, including several in Krakauer's own party. Some of them

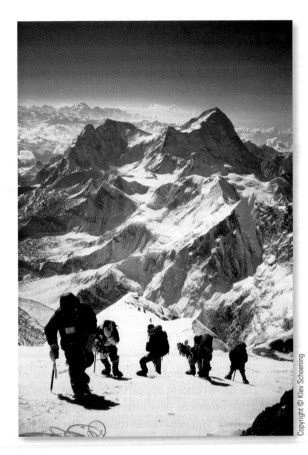

Jon Krakauer (the third person) and other climbers are seen here during their ascent of Mount Everest at an elevation of about 28,200 feet.

perished needlessly because they had fallen victim to "summit fever." Once they got close to the top, they refused to turn back in spite of extreme exhaustion and the obvious threat posed by the storm.

The saga of Jon Krakauer and the other climbers is packed with motivation riddles. Why would people push on toward a goal even at the risk of their lives? Why would they choose to endure such a punishing and hazardous ordeal in the first place? In the case of Mount Everest, perhaps the most obvious motive is simply the satisfaction of conquering the world's tallest peak. When British climber George Leigh Mallory was asked why he wanted to climb Everest in the 1920s, his famous reply was, "Because it is there." Some people seem to have an intense desire to take on the toughest challenges imaginable, to achieve something incredibly difficult. Yet—as is usually the case with human behavior—things are not quite so simple. Krakauer observed that a wide variety of motives drove the climbers and professional expedition leaders he met on Everest, including desires for "minor celebrity, career advancement, ego massage, ordinary bragging rights, filthy lucre," and even a quest for "a state of grace" (Krakauer, 1998, p. 177).

Krakauer's story is also filled with strong emotions. He anticipated that he would experience a transcendent emotional high when he reached the summit of Mount Everest. As it turned out, his

triumph was accompanied more by anxiety than by ecstasy. And though the harrowing events that followed initially left him emotionally numb, he was soon flooded with intense feelings of despair, grief, and guilt over the deaths of his companions. His tale illustrates the intimate connection between motivation and emotion—the topics we examine in this chapter.

Motivational Theories and Concepts

Key Learning Goals
9.1 Compare drive, incentive, and evolutionary approaches to understanding motivation.
9.2 Distinguish between the two major categories of motives found in humans.

Motives are the needs, wants, interests, and desires that propel people in certain directions. In short, *motivation* involves goal-directed behavior. Psychologists have devised a number of theoretical approaches to motivation. Let's look at some of these theories and the concepts they include.

Drive Theories

Many theories view motivational forces in terms of *drives*. The drive concept appears in a diverse array of theories that otherwise have little in common, such as psychoanalytic and behaviorist theories. The concept of drive was derived from Walter Cannon's (1932) observation that organisms seek to maintain *homeostasis, a state of physiological equilibrium or stability*. The body maintains homeostasis in various ways. For example, human body temperature normally fluctuates around 98.6 degrees Fahrenheit (see **Figure 9.1**). If your body temperature rises or drops noticeably, automatic responses occur: If your temperature goes up, you'll perspire; if your temperature goes down, you'll shiver. These reactions are designed to move your temperature back toward 98.6 degrees. Thus, your body reacts to many disturbances in physiological stability by trying to restore equilibrium.

Drive theories apply the concept of homeostasis to behavior. A *drive* is a hypothetical, internal state of tension that motivates an organism to engage in activities that should reduce this tension. These unpleasant states of tension are viewed as disruptions of the preferred equilibrium. According to drive theories, when individuals experience a drive, they're motivated to pursue actions that will lead to *drive reduction*. For example, the hunger motive has usually been viewed as a drive system. If you go without food for a while, you begin to experience some discomfort. This internal tension (the drive) motivates you to obtain food. Eating reduces the drive and restores physiological equilibrium.

Drive theories have been very influential, and the drive concept continues to be widely used in modern psychology. *However, drive theories cannot explain all motivation* (Berridge, 2004). Homeostasis appears irrelevant to some human motives, such as a "thirst for knowledge." Also, motivation may exist without drive arousal. This point is easy to illustrate. Think of all the times that you've eaten when you weren't the least bit hungry. You're driving or walking home from class, amply filled by a solid lunch, when an ice cream parlor beckons seductively. You stop in and have a couple of scoops of your favorite flavor. Not only are you motivated to eat in the absence of internal tension, you may actually cause yourself some internal tension—from overeating. Because drive theories assume that people always try

Figure 9.1
Temperature regulation as an example of homeostasis. The regulation of body temperature provides a simple example of how organisms often seek to maintain homeostasis, or a state of physiological equilibrium. When your temperature moves out of an acceptable range, automatic bodily reactions (such as sweating or shivering) occur that help restore equilibrium. Of course, these automatic reactions may not be sufficient by themselves, so you may have to take other actions (such as turning a furnace up or down) to bring your body temperature back into its comfort zone.

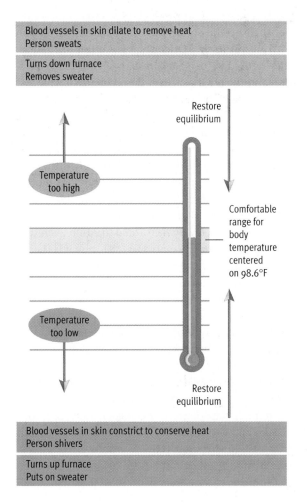

Blood vessels in skin dilate to remove heat
Person sweats

Turns down furnace
Removes sweater

Temperature too high

Restore equilibrium

Comfortable range for body temperature centered on 98.6°F

Temperature too low

Restore equilibrium

Blood vessels in skin constrict to conserve heat
Person shivers

Turns up furnace
Puts on sweater

to reduce internal tension, they can't explain this behavior very well. Incentive theories, which represent a different approach to motivation, can account for this behavior more readily.

Incentive Theories

Incentive theories propose that external stimuli regulate motivational states (Bolles, 1975; McClelland, 1975; Skinner, 1953). An *incentive* is an external goal that has the capacity to motivate behavior. Ice cream, a juicy steak, a monetary prize, approval from friends, an A on an exam, and a promotion at work are all incentives. Some of these incentives may reduce drives, but others may not.

Drive and incentive models of motivation are often contrasted as *push versus pull* theories. Drive theories emphasize how *internal* states of tension *push* people in certain directions. Incentive theories emphasize how *external* stimuli *pull* people in certain directions. According to drive theories, the source of motivation lies *within* the organism. According to incentive theories, the source of motivation lies *outside* the organism, in the environment. Thus, incentive models don't operate according to the principle of homeostasis, which hinges on internal changes in the organism. Rather, incentive theories emphasize environmental factors and downplay the biological bases of human motivation.

Evolutionary Theories

Psychologists who take an evolutionary perspective assert that the motives of humans and of other species are the products of evolution, just as anatomical characteristics are. They argue that natural selection favors behaviors that maximize reproductive success—that is, passing on genes to the next generation. Thus, they explain motives such as affiliation, achievement, dominance, aggression, and sex drive in terms of their adaptive value. If dominance is a crucial motive for a species, they say, it's because dominance provides a reproductive or survival advantage.

Evolutionary analyses of motivation are based on the premise that motives can best be understood in terms of the adaptive problems they have solved over the course of human history. For example, the need for dominance is thought to be greater in men than in women because it could facilitate males' reproductive success in a variety of ways, including (1) females may prefer mating with dominant males, (2) dominant males may poach females from subordinate males, (3) dominant males may intimidate male rivals in competition for sexual access, and (4) dominant males

may acquire more material resources which may increase mating opportunities (Buss, 1999). Consider, also, the *affiliation motive,* or need for belongingness. The adaptive benefits of affiliation for our ancestors probably included help with offspring, collaboration in hunting and gathering, mutual defense, opportunities for sexual interaction, and so forth (Baumeister & Leary, 1995). David Buss (1995) points out that it is not by accident that achievement, power (dominance), and intimacy are among the most heavily studied motives, as the satisfaction of each of these motives is likely to affect one's reproductive success.

The Range and Diversity of Human Motives

Motivational theorists of all persuasions agree on one point: Humans display an enormous diversity of motives. Most theories (evolutionary theories being a notable exception) distinguish between *biological motives* that originate in bodily needs, such as hunger, and *social motives* that originate in social experiences, such as the need for achievement.

People have a limited number of biological needs. According to K. B. Madsen (1968, 1973), most theories identify 10 to 15 such needs, some of which are listed on the left side of **Figure 9.2**. As you can see, most biological motives reflect needs that are essential to survival, such as the needs for food, water, and maintenance of body temperature within an acceptable range.

People all share the same biological motives, but their social motives vary depending on their experiences. For example, we all need to eat, but not everyone has a need for orderliness. Although people have a limited number of biological motives, they can acquire an unlimited number of social motives through learning and socialization. Some examples

Figure 9.2

The diversity of human motives. People are motivated by a wide range of needs, which can be divided into two broad classes: biological motives and social motives. The list on the left (adapted from Madsen, 1973) shows some important biological motive in humans. The list on the right (adapted from Murray, 1938) provides examples of prominent social motives in humans. The distinction between biological and social motives is not absolute.

Examples of Biological Motives in Humans	Examples of Social Motives in Humans
Hunger motive	Achievement motive (need to excel)
Thirst motive	Affiliation motive (need for social bonds)
Sex motive	Autonomy motive (need for independence)
Temperature motive (need for appropriate body temperature)	Nurturance motive (need to nourish and protect others)
Excretory motive (need to eliminate bodily wastes)	Dominance motive (need to influence or control others)
Sleep and rest motive	Exhibition motive (need to make an impression on others)
Activity motive (need for optimal level of stimulation and arousal)	Order motive (need for orderliness, tidiness, organization)
Aggression motive	Play motive (need for fun, relaxation, amusement)

of social motives—from an influential list compiled by Henry Murray (1938)—are shown on the right side of **Figure 9.2**. He theorized that most people have needs for achievement, autonomy, affiliation, dominance, exhibition, and order, among other things. Of course, the strength of these motives varies from person to person, depending on personal history.

Given the range and diversity of human motives, we can only examine a handful in depth. To a large degree, our choices reflect the motives psychologists have studied the most: hunger, sex, and achievement. After our discussion of these motivational systems, we will explore the elements of emotional experience and discuss various theories of emotion.

The Motivation of Hunger and Eating

Key Learning Goals

9.3 Summarize evidence on the physiological factors implicated in the regulation of hunger.

9.4 Explain how food availability, culture, learning, and stress influence hunger.

Why do people eat? Because they're hungry. What makes them hungry? A lack of food. Any grade-school child can explain these basic facts. So hunger is a simple motivational system, right? Wrong! Hunger is deceptive. It only looks simple. Actually, it's a puzzling and complex motivational system. Despite extensive studies of hunger, scientists are still struggling to understand the factors that regulate eating behavior. Let's examine a few of these factors.

Biological Factors in the Regulation of Hunger   2e, 8a

You have probably had embarrassing occasions when your stomach growled loudly at an untimely moment. Someone may have commented, "You must be starving!" Most people equate a rumbling stomach with hunger, and in fact, the first scientific theories of hunger were based on this simple equation. In an elaborate 1912 study, Walter Cannon and A. L. Washburn verified what most people have noticed based on casual observation: There is an association between stomach contractions and the experience of hunger.

Based on this correlation, Cannon theorized that stomach contractions *cause* hunger. However, as we've seen before, correlation is no assurance of causation, and his theory was eventually discredited. Stomach contractions often accompany hunger, but they don't cause it. How do we know? Because later research showed that people continue to experience hunger even after their stomachs have been removed out of medical necessity (Wangensteen & Carlson, 1931). If hunger can occur without a stomach, then stomach contractions can't be the cause of hunger. This realization led to more elaborate theories of hunger that focus on (1) the role of the brain, (2) blood sugar level and digestive factors, and (3) hormones.

Brain Regulation   2e, 8a

Research with laboratory animals eventually suggested that the experience of hunger is controlled in the brain—specifically, in two centers located in the hypothalamus. As we have noted before, the *hypothalamus* is a tiny structure involved in the regulation of a variety of biological needs related to survival (see **Figure 9.3**). Investigators found that when they surgically destroyed animals' *lateral hypothalamus* (*LH*), the animals showed little or no interest in eating, as if their hunger center had been wiped out (Anand & Brobeck, 1951). In contrast, when researchers destroyed animals' *ventromedial nucleus of the hypothalamus* (*VMH*), the animals ate excessively and gained weight rapidly, as if their ability to recognize satiety (fullness) had been neutralized (Brobeck, Tepperman, & Long, 1943). Given these results, investigators concluded that the LH and VMH were the brain's on-off switches for the control of hunger (Stellar, 1954).

However, over the course of several decades, a number of findings complicated this simple picture and undermined the dual-centers model of hunger

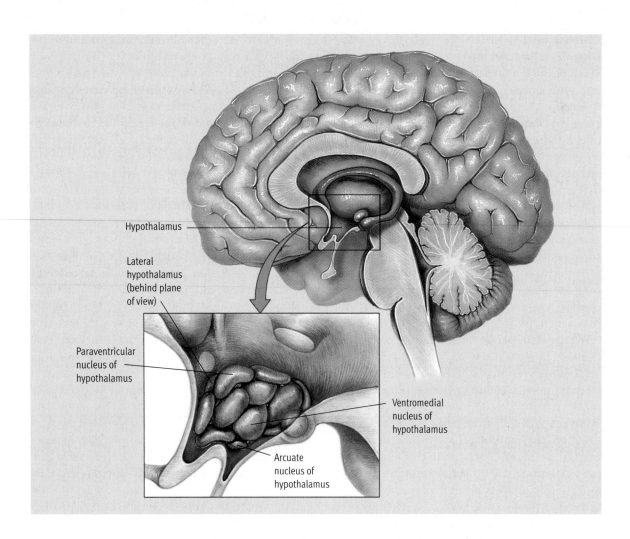

Figure 9.3
The hypothalamus. This small structure at the base of the forebrain plays a role in regulating a variety of human biological needs, including hunger. The detailed blow-up shows that the hypothalamus is made up of a variety of discrete areas. Scientists used to believe that the lateral and ventromedial areas were the brain's on-off centers for eating. However, more recent research suggests that the arcuate and paraventricular areas may be more crucial to the regulation of hunger and that thinking in terms of neural circuits rather than anatomical centers makes more sense.

Hypothalamus

Lateral hypothalamus (behind plane of view)

Paraventricular nucleus of hypothalamus

Ventromedial nucleus of hypothalamus

Arcuate nucleus of hypothalamus

(Valenstein, 1973; Winn, 1995). The current thinking is that the lateral and ventromedial areas of the hypothalamus are elements in the neural circuitry that regulates hunger but are not the key elements and are not simple on-off centers (King, 2006; Meister, 2007). Today, scientists believe that two other areas of the hypothalamus—the *arcuate nucleus* and the *paraventricular nucleus*—play a larger role in the modulation of hunger (Scott, McDade, & Luckman, 2007) (see **Figure 9.3**). In recent years the arcuate nucleus has been singled out as especially important (Becskei, Lutz, & Riediger, 2008; Grill, 2006).

The rat on the left has had its ventromedial hypothalamus lesioned, resulting in a dramatic increase in weight.

© Yoav Levy/PhotoTake

This area in the hypothalamus appears to contain a group of neurons that are sensitive to incoming hunger signals and another group of neurons that respond to satiety signals.

Contemporary theories of hunger focus more on *neural circuits* that pass through areas of the hypothalamus rather than on *anatomical centers* in the brain. These circuits depend on a remarkable variety of neurotransmitters. *Neuropeptide Y* and *serotonin* play prominent roles (Halford & Blundell, 2000; Seeley & Schwartz, 1997), as do *GABA, ghrelin,* and *orexins* (Meister, 2007; Näslund & Hellström, 2007). In recent years scientists have realized that increased levels of ghrelin are particularly crucial in stimulating hunger (Scott et al., 2007). Ghrelin performs double duty as a neurotransmitter in the nervous system and as a hormone in the endocrine system. In both systems, elevated ghrelin levels are associated with increased food intake. Thus, accumulating evidence suggests that the hypothalamus contains a confluence of interacting systems that regulate eating by monitoring a diverse array of physiological processes. Let's examine some other physiological processes that appear to provide input to these systems.

Glucose and Digestive Regulation

8a

Much of the food taken into the body is converted into *glucose*, which circulates in the blood. *Glucose is a simple sugar that is an important source of energy.* Manipulations that decrease blood glucose level can increase hunger. Manipulations that increase glucose level can make people feel full. Based on these findings, Jean Mayer (1955, 1968) proposed that hunger is regulated by the rise and fall of blood glucose levels. His theory proposed that fluctuations in blood glucose level are monitored in the brain by *glucostats*—neurons sensitive to glucose in the surrounding fluid. Like the dual-centers theory, Mayer's theory of hunger gradually ran into several complications, not the least of which was that glucose levels in the blood don't fluctuate all that much (LeMagnen, 1981). Still, it appears likely that hunger is regulated, in part, through glucose mechanisms (Smith & Campfield, 1993).

The digestive system also includes a variety of other mechanisms that influence hunger (Ritter, 2004). It turns out that Walter Cannon was not entirely wrong in hypothesizing that the stomach regulates hunger. After you have consumed food, the stomach can send two types of signals to the brain that inhibit further eating (Deutsch, 1990). The vagus nerve carries information about the stretching of the stomach walls that indicates when the stomach is full. Other nerves carry satiety messages that depend on how rich in nutrients the contents of the stomach are.

Hormonal Regulation

8a

As noted in Chapter 3, *hormones* are the chemical substances released by the endocrine glands. A variety of hormones circulating in the bloodstream also appear to contribute to the regulation of hunger. *Insulin* is a hormone secreted by the pancreas. It must be present for cells to extract glucose from the blood. Indeed, an inadequate supply of insulin is what causes diabetes. Many diabetics are unable to use the glucose in their blood unless they are given insulin injections. In nondiabetic individuals, insulin injections stimulate hunger. Normal secretion of insulin by the pancreas is also associated with increased hunger. And, in landmark research, Judith Rodin (1985) demonstrated that the mere sight and smell of enticing food can stimulate the secretion of insulin. Moreover, insulin levels appear to be sensitive to fluctuations in the body's fat stores (Schwartz et al., 2000). These findings suggest that insulin secretions play a role in the modulation of hunger.

At least two other hormones contribute to the short-term regulation of hunger. After the body goes without food for a while, the stomach secretes ghrelin, which causes stomach contractions and promotes hunger (Cummings, 2006). In contrast, after food is consumed, the upper intestine releases a hormone called CCK that delivers satiety signals to the brain, thus reducing hunger (Moran, 2004; Schwartz & Azzara, 2004)

Finally, evidence indicates that a hormone called *leptin* contributes to the long-term regulation of hunger, as well as the modulation of numerous other bodily functions (Ahima & Osei, 2004). Leptin is produced by fat cells throughout the body and released into the bloodstream. Leptin circulates through the bloodstream and ultimately provides the hypothalamus with information about the body's fat stores (Campfield, 2002). When leptin levels are high, the propensity to feel hungry diminishes. The hormonal signals that influence hunger (the fluctations of insulin, ghrelin, CCK, and leptin) all seem to converge in the hypothalamus, especially the arcuate and paraventricular nuclei (Kuo et al., 2007; Näslund & Hellström, 2007).

If all this sounds confusing, it is, and I haven't even mentioned *all* the physiological processes involved in the regulation of hunger and eating. Frankly, researchers are still struggling to figure out exactly how all these processes work together, as hunger depends on complex interactions among neural circuits, neurotransmitter systems, digestive processes, and hormonal fluctuations (Berthoud & Morrison, 2008).

Environmental Factors in the Regulation of Hunger

8a

Hunger clearly is a biological need, but eating is not regulated by biological factors alone. Studies show that social and environmental factors govern eating to a considerable extent. Three key environmental factors are (1) the availability and palatability of food, (2) learned preferences and habits, and (3) stress.

Food Availability and Related Cues

8a

Most of the research on the physiological regulation of hunger has been based on the assumption that hunger operates as a drive system in which homeostatic mechanisms are at work. However, some theorists emphasize the incentive value of food and argue that humans and other animals are often motivated to eat not by the need to compensate for en-

According to incentive models of hunger, the availability and palatability of food are key factors regulating hunger. An abundance of diverse foods tends to lead to increased eating.

ergy deficits but by the anticipated pleasure of eating (Hetherington & Rolls, 1996; Ramsay et al., 1996). This perspective has been bolstered by evidence that three food variables exert significant influence over food consumption:

• *Palatability.* As you might expect, the better food tastes, the more people consume (de Castro et al., 2000; Pliner & Mann, 2004). This principle is not limited to humans, as the eating behavior of rats and other animals is also influenced by palatability.
• *Quantity available.* A powerful determinant of the amount eaten is the amount available. People tend to consume what is put in front of them. The more people are served, the more they eat (Mrdjenovic & Levitsky, 2005; Rozin et al., 2003). Obviously, the large portions served in modern American restaurants foster increased consumption (Geier, Rozin, & Doros, 2006).
• *Variety.* Humans and animals increase their consumption when a greater variety of foods are available (Raynor & Epstein, 2001; Temple et al., 2008). As you eat a specific food, its incentive value declines. This phenomenon is called *sensory-specific satiety* (Hollis

& Henry, 2007; Raynor, Niemeier, & Wing, 2006). If only a few foods are available, the appeal of all of them can decline quickly. But if many foods are available, people can keep shifting to new foods and end up eating more overall. This principle explains why people are especially likely to overeat at buffets where many foods are available.

Eating can also be triggered by exposure to environmental cues that have been associated with food. You have no doubt had your hunger aroused by television commercials for delicious-looking meals or by seductive odors coming from the kitchen. Consistent with this observation, studies have shown that hunger can be increased by exposure to pictures, written descriptions, and video depictions of attractive foods (Halford et al., 2004; Marcelino et al., 2001; Oakes & Slotterback, 2000). Thus, it's clear that hunger and eating are governed in part by the incentive qualities of food.

Learned Preferences and Habits

8a

Are you fond of eating calves' brains? How about eel or snake? Could I interest you in a grasshopper or some dog meat? Probably not, but these are delicacies in some regions of the world. Arctic Eskimos like to eat maggots! You probably prefer chicken, apples, eggs, lettuce, potato chips, pizza, cornflakes, or ice cream. These preferences are acquired through learning. People from different cultures display very different patterns of food consumption (Rozin, 2007). If you doubt this fact, just visit an ethnic grocery store.

Food preferences are influenced greatly by culture. For example, the fried tarantula shown here would not be a popular treat for most Americans, but it is a delicacy in some cultures.

web link 9.1

The Obesity Society

This nonprofit organization's mission is to change public policy and make obesity a public health priority. It has an incredibly rich and well-organized website. In-depth information is available on the causes, consequences, and treatments of obesity.

Humans do have some innate taste preferences of a general sort. For example, a preference for sweet tastes is present at birth (Mennella & Beauchamp, 1996), and humans' preference for high-fat foods appears to be at least partly genetic in origin (Schiffman et al., 1998). Nonetheless, learning wields a great deal of influence over what people prefer to eat (Rozin, 2007). Taste preferences are partly a function of learned associations formed through *classical conditioning* (Appleton, Gentry, & Shepherd, 2006). For instance, youngsters can be conditioned to prefer flavors paired with pleasant events. Of course, as we learned in Chapter 6, taste aversions can also be acquired through conditioning when foods are followed by nausea (Schafe & Bernstein, 1996).

Eating habits are also shaped by *observational learning* (see Chapter 6). To a large degree, food preferences are a matter of exposure (Cooke, 2007). People generally prefer familiar foods. But geographical, cultural, religious, and ethnic factors limit people's exposure to certain foods. Repeated exposures to a new food usually lead to increased liking. However, as many parents have learned the hard way, forcing a child to eat a specific food can backfire and have a negative effect on the youngster's preference for the required food (Benton, 2004). Learned habits and social considerations also influence *when* and *how much* people eat. For example, a key determinant of when you eat is your memory of how much time has passed since you ate your last meal and what you consumed (Rozin et al., 1998). These expectations about how often and how much you should eat are the product of years of learning.

Stress and Eating

8a

Studies have shown that stress leads to increased eating in a substantial percentage of people (Greeno & Wing, 1994; Laitinen, Ek, & Sovio, 2002). Some studies suggest that stress-induced eating may be especially common among chronic dieters (Heatherton, Striepe, & Wittenberg, 1998). Theorists have suggested that the *negative emotions* often evoked by stress are what promotes additional eating (Macht & Simons, 2000). Some people respond to emotional distress by eating tasty foods because they expect the enjoyable treats to make them feel better (Tice, Bratslavsky, & Baumeister, 2001). Unfortunately, this strategy of emotional regulation does not appear to be very effective, as eating does not usually lead to lasting mood changes (Thayer, 1996). In any event, stress is another environmental factor that can influence hunger, although it's not clear whether the effects are direct or indirect.

REVIEW of Key Learning Goals

9.3 In the brain, the lateral and ventromedial areas of the hypothalamus were once viewed as on-off centers for the control of hunger, but that model proved to be an over-simplification, as the arcuate and paraventricular areas and neural circuits may be more important. Fluctuations in blood glucose also seem to play a role in hunger, but the exact location of the glucostats and their mode of functioning have yet to be determined. Hormonal regulation of hunger depends primarily on insulin, ghrelin, CCK, and leptin.

9.4 Organisms consume more food when it is palatable, when more is available, and when there is greater variety. Cultural traditions also shape food preferences, primarily through variations in exposure to various foods. Learning processes, such as classical conditioning and observational learning, exert a great deal of influence over both what people eat and how much they eat. Stress can stimulate eating.

---

concept check 9.1

Understanding Factors in the Regulation of Hunger

Check your understanding of the effects of the various factors that influence hunger by indicating whether hunger would tend to increase or decrease in each of the situations described below. Indicate your choice by marking an *I* (increase), a *D* (decrease), or a *?* (can't be determined without more information) next to each situation. You'll find the answers in Appendix A at the back of the book.

_____ 1. The ventromedial nucleus of a rat's brain is destroyed.

_____ 2. The glucose level in Marlene's bloodstream decreases.

_____ 3. Norman just ate, but his roommate just brought home his favorite food—a pizza that smells great.

_____ 4. You're offered an exotic, strange-looking food from another culture.

_____ 5. You are eating at a huge buffet where an enormous variety of foods are available.

_____ 6. Elton has been going crazy all day. It seems like everything's happening at once, and he feels totally stressed out. Finally he's been able to break away for a few minutes so he can catch a bite to eat.

Sexual Motivation and Behavior

How does sex resemble food? Sometimes it seems that people are obsessed with both. People joke and gossip about sex constantly. Magazines, novels, movies, and television shows are saturated with sexual activity and innuendo. The advertising industry uses sex to sell everything from mouthwash to designer jeans to automobiles. This intense interest in sex reflects the importance of sexual motivation. In this portion of the chapter, we will examine the physiology of the human sexual response, review evolutionary analyses of human sexual motivation, and discuss the roots of sexual orientation.

The Human Sexual Response

Assuming people are motivated to engage in sexual activity, exactly what happens to them physically? This may sound like a simple question. But scientists really knew very little about the physiology of the human sexual response before William Masters and Virginia Johnson did groundbreaking research in the 1960s. Masters and Johnson used physiological recording devices to monitor the bodily changes of volunteers engaging in sexual activities. Their observations and interviews with their subjects yielded a detailed description of the human sexual response and won them widespread acclaim. Masters and Johnson (1966, 1970) divide the sexual response cycle into four stages: excitement, plateau, orgasm,

and resolution. **Figure 9.4** shows how the intensity of sexual arousal changes as women and men progress through these stages.

During the *excitement phase,* the level of physical arousal usually escalates rapidly. In both sexes, muscle tension, respiration rate, heart rate, and blood pressure increase quickly. *Vasocongestion*—engorgement of blood vessels—produces penile erection and swollen testes in males. In females, vasocongestion leads to a swelling and hardening of the clitoris, expansion of the vaginal lips, and vaginal lubrication. During the *plateau phase,* physiological arousal usually continues to build, but at a much slower pace. When foreplay is lengthy, it's normal for arousal to fluctuate in both sexes.

Orgasm occurs when sexual arousal reaches its peak intensity and is discharged in a series of muscular contractions that pulsate through the pelvic area. The subjective experience of orgasm is very similar for men and women, but women are more likely than men to experience more than one orgasm in a brief time period (pattern C in **Figure 9.4**). That said, women are also more likely than men to engage in intercourse without experiencing an orgasm (see **Figure 9.5** on the next page) (Laumann et al., 1994). Whether these differences reflect attitudes and sexual practices versus physiological processes is open to debate. Evolutionary theorists argue that males' greater orgasmic consistency must be a product of evolution, as it would have obvious adaptive significance for

Key Learning Goals

9.5 Outline the four phases of the human sexual response.

9.6 Discuss parental investment theory and findings on gender differences in sexual activity.

9.7 Describe gender differences in mating preferences and priorities.

9.8 Clarify the nature of sexual orientation, and discuss the prevalence of homosexuality.

9.9 Compare environmental and biological theories of sexual orientation.

William Masters and Virginia Johnson

"The conviction has grown that the most effective treatment of sexual incompatibility involves the technique of working with both members of the family unit."

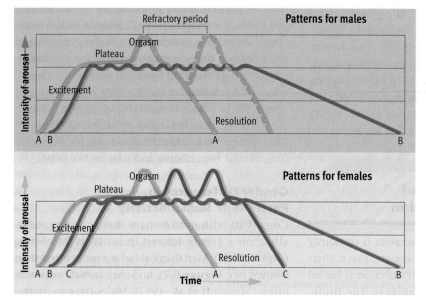

Figure 9.4

The human sexual response cycle. There are similarities and differences between men and women in patterns of sexual arousal. Pattern A, which culminates in orgasm and resolution, is the modal sequence for both sexes, but not something one can count on. Pattern B, which involves sexual arousal without orgasm followed by a slow resolution, is seen in both sexes but is more common among women (see Figure 9.5). Pattern C, which involves multiple orgasms, is seen almost exclusively in women, as men go through a refractory period before they are capable of another orgasm.

SOURCE: Based on Masters, W. H., & Johnson, V. E. (1966). *Human sexual response.* Boston: Little, Brown.

Figure 9.
The gend
gasm co
sexual inte
reach orga
ably than
shown her
the gende
consistenc
Both biolo
tural facto
to this gen
from Laur

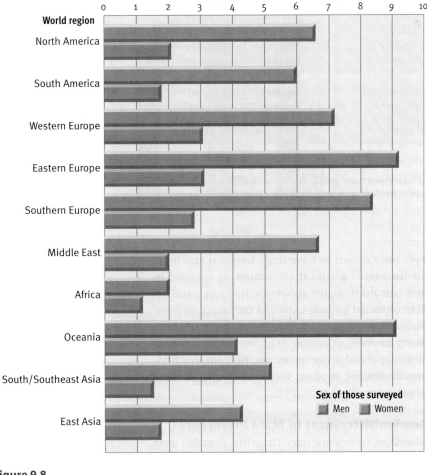

Number of sex partners desired over the next 30 years

Figure 9.8

The gender gap in desire for a variety of sexual partners. Schmitt et al. (2003) gathered cross-cultural data on gender disparities in the number of sex partners desired by people. Respondents were asked about how many sexual partners they ideally would like to have in the next 30 years. As evolutionary theorists would predict, males reported that they would like to have more sexual partners in all ten world regions examined.

SOURCE: Schmitt, D. P., and 118 Members of the International Sexuality Description Project. (2003). Universal sex differences in the desire for sexual variety: Tests from 52 nations, 6 continents, and 13 islands. *Journal of Personality and Social Psychology, 85,* 85–104. Copyright © 2003 by the American Psychological Association. Reprinted by permission of the authors.

web lin

SIECUS

SIECUS stal
ity Informa
Council of
This nonpr
tion has be
nonjudgm
about sexu
founding i
is a rich so
ports, fact
a host of ot
with sexua

web lin

Go Ask Ali

One of the
and most p
of frank inf
Net has bee
Columbia L
Education I
especially t
dergraduat
offers direc
tions about
sexuality ar
alcohol and
tion, emotic
general hea

Courtesy of David M. Buss

David Buss

"Evolutionary psychologists develop hypotheses about the psychological mechanisms that have evolved in humans to solve particular adaptive problems that humans have faced under ancestral conditions."

long-term mating commitments are a normal part of the social landscape in human societies. However, parental investment theory suggests that there should be some glaring disparities between men and women in what they look for in a long-term mate (see **Figure 9.6**).

The adaptive problem for our male ancestors was to find a female with good reproductive potential who would be sexually faithful and effective in nurturing children. Given these needs, evolutionary theory predicts that men should place more emphasis than women on such partner characteristics as youthfulness (which allows for more reproductive years) and attractiveness (which is assumed to be correlated with health and fertility). In contrast, the adaptive problem for our female ancestors was to find a male who could provide material resources

and protect his family and who was dependable and willing to invest his resources in his family. Given these needs, evolutionary theory predicts that women should place more emphasis than men on such partner characteristics as intelligence, ambition, education, income, and social status (which are associated with the ability to provide more material resources). If these evolutionary analyses of sexual motivation are on the mark, gender differences in mating preferences should be virtually universal and thus transcend culture.

To test this hypothesis, David Buss (1989) and 50 scientists from around the world surveyed more than 10,000 people from 37 cultures about what they looked for in a mate. As predicted by parental investment theory, they found that women placed a higher value than men on potential partners' status, ambition, and financial prospects. These priorities were not limited to industrialized or capitalist countries; they were apparent in third-world cultures, socialist countries, and all varieties of economic systems. In contrast, men around the world consistently showed more interest than women in potential partners' youthfulness and physical attractiveness. A number of studies, using diverse samples and a variety of research methods, have replicated the disparities between males and females in mating priorities and preferences (Schmitt, 2005; Shackelford, Schmitt, & Buss, 2005).

Recent research also supports the notion that women pay more attention than men to a potential partner's willingness to invest in children (Brase,

Evolutionary theory posits that men can maximize their reproductive fitness by seeking youthful partners, whereas women can maximize their reproductive success by searching for mates that are rich in material resources that can be invested in children. Obviously, this theory can explain why attractive young women often become romantically involved with much older men who happen to be wealthy.

2006). The gender gap on this dimension occurs in part because men appear to be largely indifferent to females' potential for parental investment. Moreover, men who are perceived to be favorably disposed to investing in children are judged to be more attractive by women. Another study demonstrated that women can gauge males' interest in children surprisingly well just from looking at their faces (Roney et al., 2006).

Criticism and Alternative Explanations

So, the findings on gender differences in sexual motivation mesh very nicely with predictions derived from evolutionary theory. But, in the world of science, everyone is a critic—so you may be wondering: What type of criticism has this line of research generated? One set of concerns centers on the fact that the findings do not paint a flattering picture of human nature. Men end up looking like sordid sexual predators; women come across as cynical, greedy materialists; and evolutionary theory appears to endorse these realities as the inevitable outcome of natural selection. As Buss (1998) acknowledges,

"Much of what I discovered about human mating is not nice" (p. 408). This controversy demonstrates once again that psychological theories can have far-reaching social and political implications, but the sociopolitical fallout has no bearing on evolutionary theory's scientific validity.

However, some critics *have* expressed doubts about the validity of evolutionary explanations of gender differences in sexual motivation. They note that one can easily come up with alternative explanations for the findings. For example, women's emphasis on males' material resources could be a by-product of cultural and economic forces rather than biological forces (Wallen, 1989). Women may have learned to value males' economic clout because their own economic potential has been severely limited in virtually all cultures by a long history of discrimination (Hrdy, 1997; Kasser & Sharma, 1999). In a similar vein, Roy Baumeister, who has convincingly documented that men have stronger sexual motivation than women (Baumeister et al., 2001), has argued that this disparity may be largely the result of extensive cultural processes that serve to suppress female sexuality (Baumeister & Twenge, 2002). Evolutionary theorists counter these arguments by pointing out that the cultural and economic processes at work may themselves be products of evolution. This interesting debate is likely to continue for some time.

The Mystery of Sexual Orientation

Sex must be a contentious topic, as the controversy swirling around evolutionary explanations of gender differences in sexuality is easily equaled by the controversy surrounding the determinants of *sexual orientation*. **Sexual orientation** refers to a person's preference for emotional and sexual relationships with individuals of the same sex, the other sex, or either sex. *Heterosexuals* seek emotional-sexual relationships with members of the other sex, *bisexuals* with members of either sex, and *homosexuals* with members of the same sex. In recent years, the terms *gay* and *straight* have become widely used to refer to homosexuals and heterosexuals, respectively. Although *gay* can refer to homosexuals of either sex, most homosexual women prefer to call themselves *lesbians*.

People tend to view heterosexuality and homosexuality as an all-or-none distinction. However, in a large-scale survey of sexual behavior, Alfred Kinsey and his colleagues (1948, 1953) discovered that many people who define themselves as heterosexuals have had homosexual experiences—and vice versa. Thus, Kinsey and others have concluded that it is more accurate to view heterosexuality and homosexuality as

web link 9.4

The Evolutionary Psychology FAQ

Maintained by Edward Hagen (Institute for Theoretical Biology, Humboldt University, Berlin), this site provides answers to a variety of controversial questions on the subject of evolutionary psychology. Covered questions include: What is an adaptation? How can we identify psychological adaptations? Is evolutionary psychology sexist? If my genes made me do it, am I still responsible? Why do some people hate evolutionary psychology?

Figure 9.9

end points on a continuum (Haslam, 1997). Indeed, Kinsey devised a seven-point scale, shown in **Figure 9.9**, that can be used to characterize individuals' sexual orientation. To reevaluate Kinsey's theory, Robert Epstein (2007) recently collected data via the Internet from over 18,000 people who characterized themselves as gay, straight, or bisexual and then responded to a questionnaire about their sexual desires and experiences. As you can see in **Figure 9.10**, Epstein's data are consistent with the notion that sexual orientation should be viewed as a continuum rather than a matter of discrete categories.

Figure 9.10

New evidence that sexual orientation exists on a continuum. Robert Epstein (2007) conducted a large Internet survey in which 18,000 people characterized themselves as straight, bisexual, or gay and then responded to a questionnaire that placed them on a scale that indexed their sexual orientation. Epstein used a 14-point scale rather than Kinsey's 7-point scale. Given the self-selected nature of the sample, these data cannot tell us much about the exact percentage of people who are gay or bisexual, but the data provide dramatic evidence in support of the notion that sexual orientation exists on a continuum. If sexual orientation *was* an either-or proposition, people's scores would pile up at the two ends of the distribution with little overlap, which clearly is not the case.

SOURCE: Epstein, R. (2007, October/November). Smooth thinking about sexuality. *Scientific American Mind, 18*(5), p. 14. Copyright © 2007 by Robert Epstein. Reprinted by permission of the author. Survey available at http://MySexualOrientation.com

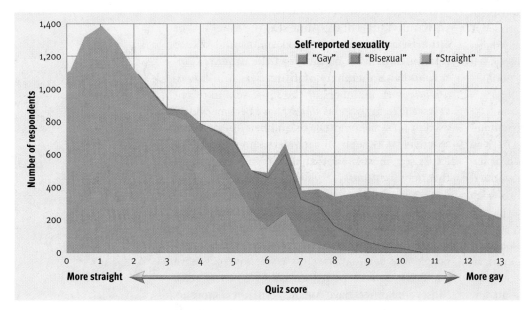

How common is homosexuality? No one knows for sure. Part of the problem is that this question is vastly more complex than it appears at first glance (LeVay, 1996; Savin-Williams, 2006). Given that sexual orientation is best represented as a continuum, where do you draw the lines between heterosexuality, bisexuality, and homosexuality? And how do you handle the distinction between overt behavior and desire? Where, for instance, do you put a person who is married and has never engaged in homosexual behavior but who reports homosexual fantasies and acknowledges being strongly drawn to members of the same sex? The other part of the problem is that many people have extremely prejudicial attitudes about homosexuality, which makes gays cautious and reluctant to give candid information about their sexuality (Herek, 1996, 2000). Small wonder then that estimates of the portion of the population that is homosexual vary widely. A frequently cited estimate of the number of people who are gay is 10%, but recent surveys suggest that this percentage may be an overestimate. Michaels (1996) combined data from two of the better large-scale surveys to arrive at the estimates seen in **Figure 9.11**. As you can see, the numbers are open to varying interpretations, but as a whole they suggest that about 5%–8% of the population could reasonably be characterized as homosexual.

Environmental Theories of Homosexuality

Over the years many environmental theories have been floated to explain the origins of homosexuality, but when tested empirically, these theories have received remarkably little support. For example, psychoanalytic and behavioral theorists, who usually agree on very little, both proposed environmental explanations for the development of homosexuality. The Freudian theorists argued that a male is likely to become

gay when raised by a weak, detached, ineffectual father who is a poor heterosexual role model and by an overprotective, overly attached mother, with whom the boy identifies. Behavioral theorists argued that homosexuality is a learned preference acquired when same-sex stimuli have been paired with sexual arousal, perhaps through chance seductions by adult homosexuals. Extensive research on homosexuals' upbringing and childhood experiences have failed to support either of these theories (Bell, Weinberg, & Hammersmith, 1981).

However, efforts to research homosexuals' personal histories have yielded a number of interesting insights. Extremely feminine behavior in young boys or masculine behavior in young girls does predict the subsequent development of homosexuality (Bailey & Zucker, 1995). For example, 75%–90% of highly feminine young boys eventually turn out to be gay (Blanchard et al., 1995). Consistent with this finding, most gay men and women report that they can trace their homosexual leanings back to their early childhood, even before they understood what sex was really about (Bailey, 2003). Most also report that because of negative parental and societal attitudes about homosexuality, they initially struggled to deny their sexual orientation. Thus, they felt that their homosexuality was not a matter of choice and not something that they could readily change (Breedlove, 1994). Although people's subjective recollections of the past need to be interpreted with caution, these findings suggest that the roots of homosexuality are more biological than environmental.

Biological Theories of Homosexuality

Nonetheless, initial efforts to find a biological basis for homosexuality met with little success. Most theorists originally assumed that hormonal differences between heterosexuals and homosexuals must underlie a person's sexual orientation (Doerr et al., 1976; Dorner, 1988). However, studies comparing circulating hormone levels in gays and straights found only small, inconsistent differences that could not be linked to sexual orientation in any convincing way (Bailey, 2003; Banks & Gartrell, 1995).

Thus, like environmental theorists, biological theorists were frustrated for quite a while in their efforts to explain the roots of homosexuality. However, that picture changed dramatically in the 1990s (Gladue, 1994). For example, in one landmark investigation, Bailey and Pillard (1991) studied gay men who had either a twin brother or an adopted brother. They found that 52% of the participants' identical twins were gay, that 22% of their fraternal twins were gay, and that 11% of their adoptive

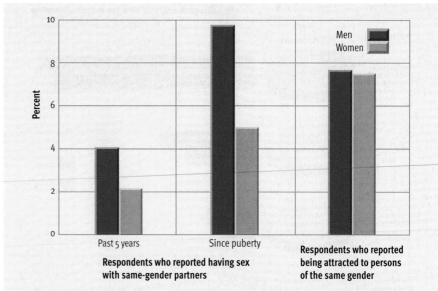

Figure 9.11

How common is homosexuality? The answer to this question is both complex and controversial. Michaels (1996) brought together data from two large-scale surveys to arrive at the estimates shown here. If you look at how many people have actually had a same-sex partner in the last five years, the figures are relatively low, but if you count those who have had a same-sex partner since puberty the figures more than double. Still another way to look at it is to ask people whether they are attracted to others of the same sex (regardless of their actual behavior). This approach suggests that about 8% of the population could be characterized as homosexual.

brothers were gay. A companion study (Bailey et al., 1993) of lesbians yielded a similar pattern of results (see **Figure 9.12** on the next page). Given that identical twins share more genetic overlap than fraternal twins, who share more genes than unrelated adoptive siblings, these results suggest that there is a genetic predisposition to homosexuality (Hyde, 2005b) (see Chapter 3 for an explanation of the logic underlying twin and adoption studies). More-recent twin studies, with larger and more representative samples, have provided further support for the conclusion that heredity influences sexual orientation, although these studies have yielded smaller estimates of genetic influence (Bailey, Dunne, & Martin, 2000; Kendler et al., 2000).

Many theorists suspect that the roots of homosexuality may lie in the organizing effects of prenatal hormones on neurological development (James, 2005). Several lines of research suggest that hormonal secretions during critical periods of prenatal development may shape sexual development, organize the brain in a lasting manner, and influence subsequent sexual orientation (Berenbaum & Snyder, 1995). For example, researchers have found elevated rates of homosexuality among women exposed to abnormally high androgen levels during prenatal development (because their mothers had an adrenal disorder or

web link 9.5

Queer Resources Directory (QRD)

In its 1994 mission statement, the *Queer Resources Directory* described itself as "an electronic research library specifically dedicated to sexual minorities—groups that have traditionally been labeled as 'queer' and systematically discriminated against." Composed of more than 25,000 files and still growing, QRD offers a rich array of resources.

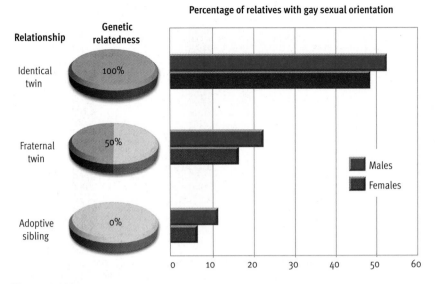

Percentage of relatives with gay sexual orientation

Relationship	Genetic relatedness
Identical twin	100%
Fraternal twin	50%
Adoptive sibling	0%

■ Males
■ Females

0   10   20   30   40   50   60

Figure 9.12

Genetics and sexual orientation. If relatives who share more genetic relatedness show greater similarity on a trait than relatives who share less genetic overlap, this evidence suggests a genetic predisposition to the characteristic. Recent studies of both gay men and lesbian women have found a higher prevalence of homosexuality among their identical twins than their fraternal twins, who, in turn, are more likely to be homosexual than their adoptive siblings. These findings suggest that genetic factors influence sexual orientation. (Data from Bailey & Pillard, 1991; Bailey et. al., 1993)

Some people are befuddled by the fact that actress Anne Heche (left) had a lengthy intimate relationship with comedian Ellen DeGeneres (right), but now has settled into a conventional heterosexual marriage. Although shifts in sexual orientation like this are uncommon among males, research has shown that females' sexual orientation tends to be characterized by more plasticity than that of males. These findings suggest that males' and females' pathways into homosexuality may be somewhat different.

were given a synthetic hormone to reduce the risk of miscarriage) (Breedlove, 1994; Meyer-Bahlburg et al., 1995). Several other independent lines of research suggest that abnormalities in prenatal hormonal secretions may foster a predisposition to homosexuality (Mustanski, Chivers, & Bailey, 2002).

Despite the recent breakthroughs, much remains to be learned about the determinants of sexual orientation. The fact that identical twins of gay subjects turn out to be gay only about half the time suggests that the genetic predisposition to homosexuality is not overpowering. Environmental influences probably contribute to the development of homosexuality (Bem, 1996, 1998), but the nature of these environmental factors remains a matter of speculation.

Another complication is that the pathways to homosexuality may be somewhat different for males as opposed to females (Gladue, 1994). Females' sexuality appears to be characterized by more *plasticity* than males' sexuality (Baumeister, 2000, 2004). In other words, women's sexual behavior may be more easily shaped and modified by sociocultural factors. For example, although sexual orientation is assumed to be a stable characteristic, research shows that lesbian and bisexual women often change their sexual orientation over the course of their adult years (Diamond, 2003, 2007). And, in comparison to gay males, lesbians are less likely to trace their homosexuality

back to their childhood and more likely to indicate that their attraction to the same sex emerged during adulthood (Tolman & Diamond, 2001). These findings suggest that sexual orientation may be more fluid and malleable in women than in men.

Once again, though, we can see that the nature versus nurture debate can have far-reaching social and political implications. Homosexuals have long been victims of extensive—and in many instances legal—discrimination. In most jurisdictions, gays cannot legally formalize their unions in marriage; they are not allowed to openly join the United States military forces; and they are barred from some jobs (for example, many school districts will not hire gays as classroom teachers). However, if research were to show that being gay is largely a matter of biological destiny, much like being black or female or short, many of the arguments against equal rights for gays would disintegrate. Why ban gays from teaching, for instance, if their sexual preference cannot "rub off" on their students? Many individuals' opinions about gay rights may be swayed by the outcome of the nature-nurture debate on the roots of homosexuality.

Figure 9.13

Figure 9.13

Measuring motives with the Thematic Apperception Test (TAT). Subjects taking the TAT tell or write stories about what is happening in a scene, such as this one showing a man at work. The two stories shown here illustrate strong affiliation motivation and strong achievement motivation. The italicized parts of the stories are thematic ideas that would be identified by a TAT scorer.

Source: Stories reprinted by permission of Dr. David McClelland.

Affiliation arousal

George is an engineer who is working late. He is *worried that his wife will be annoyed* with him for neglecting her. She has been *objecting* that he cares more about his work than his wife and family. He seems *unable to satisfy* both his boss and his wife, but he *loves her* very much and will do his best to *finish up* fast and get home to her.

Achievement arousal

George is an engineer who *wants to win* a competition in which the man with the *most practicable drawing* will be awarded the contract to build a bridge. He is taking a moment to think *how happy he will be* if he wins. He has been *baffled by how to make such a long span strong*, but he remembers to *specify a new steel alloy* of great strength, submits his entry, but does not win, and is *very unhappy*.

Do people high in achievement need always tackle the biggest challenges available? Not necessarily. A curious finding has emerged in laboratory studies in which subjects have been asked to choose the difficulty level of a task to work on. Participants high in the need for achievement tend to select tasks of intermediate difficulty (McClelland & Koestner, 1992). For instance, in a study in which subjects playing a ring-tossing game were allowed to stand as close to or as far away from the target peg as they wanted, high achievers tended to prefer a moderate degree of challenge (Atkinson & Litwin, 1960). Research on the situational determinants of achievement behavior has suggested a reason.

Situational Determinants of Achievement Behavior

8b

Your achievement drive is not the only determinant of how hard you work. Situational factors can also influence achievement strivings. John Atkinson (1974, 1981, 1992) has elaborated extensively on McClelland's original theory of achievement motivation and has identified some important situational determinants of achievement behavior. Atkinson theorizes that the tendency to pursue achievement in a particular situation depends on the following factors:

• The strength of one's *motivation* to *achieve* success, which is viewed as a stable aspect of personality.
• One's estimate of the *probability of success* for the task at hand. Such estimates vary from task to task.
• The *incentive value* of success, which depends on the tangible and intangible rewards for success on the specific task.

The last two variables are situational determinants of achievement behavior. That is, they vary from one situation to another. According to Atkinson, the pursuit of achievement increases as the probability of success and incentive value of success go up.

Let's apply Atkinson's model to a simple example. According to his theory, your tendency to pursue a good grade in calculus should depend on your general motivation to achieve success, your estimate of the probability of getting a good grade in the class, and the value you place on getting a good grade. Thus, given a certain motivation to achieve success, you will pursue a good grade in calculus less vigorously if your professor gives impossible exams (thus lowering your expectancy of success) or if a good grade in calculus is not required for your major (lowering the incentive value of success).

The joint influence of these situational factors may explain why high achievers prefer tasks of intermediate difficulty. Atkinson notes that the probability of success and the incentive value of success on tasks are interdependent to some degree. As tasks get easier, success becomes less satisfying. As tasks get harder, success becomes more satisfying but becomes less likely. When the probability and incentive value of success are weighed together, moderately challenging tasks seem to offer the best overall value.

We turn next to the study of emotion. Motivation and emotion are often intertwined (Zurbriggen & Sturman, 2002). On the one hand, *emotion can cause motivation.* For example, *anger* about your work schedule may motivate you to look for a new job. *Jealousy* of an ex-girlfriend may motivate you to ask out her roommate. On the other hand, *motivation can cause emotion.* For example, your motivation to win a photography contest may lead to great *anxiety* during the judging and either *elation* if you win or *gloom* if you don't. Although motivation and emotion are closely related, they're *not* the same thing. We'll analyze the nature of emotion in the next section.

REVIEW of Key Learning Goals

9.10 Achievement, which was first investigated by David McClelland, involves the need to excel, especially in competition with others. The need for achievement is usually measured with a projective test called the TAT.

9.11 People who are relatively high in the need for achievement work harder and more persistently than others. They delay gratification well and pursue competitive careers. However, in choosing challenges they often select tasks of intermediate difficulty.

9.12 Situational factors also influence achievement behavior. The pursuit of achievement tends to increase when the probability of success and the incentive value of success are high. The joint influence of these factors may explain why people high in achievement need tend to prefer challenges of intermediate difficulty.

The Elements of Emotional Experience

The most profound and important experiences in life are saturated with emotion. Think of the *joy* that people feel at weddings, the *grief* they feel at funerals, the *ecstasy* they feel when they fall in love. Emotions also color everyday experiences. For instance, you might experience *anger* when a professor treats you rudely, *dismay* when you learn that your car needs expensive repairs, and *happiness* when you see that you aced your economics exam. In some respects, emotions lie at the core of mental health. The two most common complaints that lead people to seek psychotherapy are *depression* and *anxiety*. Clearly, emotions play an important role in people's lives. Reflecting this reality, modern psychologists have increased their research on emotion in recent decades (Barrett et al., 2007; Cacioppo & Gardner, 1999).

Exactly what is an emotion? Everyone has plenty of personal experience with emotion, but it's an elusive concept to define (LeDoux, 1995). Emotion includes cognitive, physiological, and behavioral components, which are summarized in the following definition: *Emotion* involves (1) a subjective conscious experience (the cognitive component) accompanied by (2) bodily arousal (the physiological component) and (3) characteristic overt expressions (the behavioral component). That's a pretty complex definition. Let's take a closer look at each of these three components of emotion.

The Cognitive Component: Subjective Feelings

8c

More than 550 words in the English language refer to emotions (Averill, 1980). Ironically, however, people often have difficulty describing their emotions (Zajonc, 1980). Emotion is a highly personal, subjective experience. In studying the cognitive component of emotions, psychologists generally rely on subjects' verbal reports of what they're experiencing. These reports indicate that emotions are potentially intense internal feelings that sometimes seem to have a life of their own. People can't switch their

Key Learning Goals

9.13 Describe the cognitive component of emotion.

9.14 Understand the physiological and neural bases of emotions.

9.15 Explain how emotions are reflected in facial expressions, and describe the facial feedback hypothesis.

9.16 Review cross-cultural similarities and variations in emotional experience.

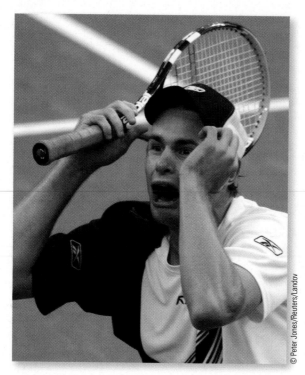
Emotions involve automatic reactions that can be difficult to control.

been neglected? Fredrickson and Branigan (2001) note that there appear to be fewer positive than negative emotions and that positive emotions are less clearly differentiated from each other than negative emotions. Another consideration is that negative emotions appear to have more powerful effects than positive ones (Baumeister et al., 2001). Although these factors probably have contributed, the neglect of positive emotions is symptomatic of a broad and deeply rooted bias in the field of psychology, which has historically focused on pathology, weaknesses, and suffering (and how to heal these conditions) rather than on health, strengths, and resilience (Fredrickson, 2002). In recent years, the architects of the positive psychology movement have set out to shift the field's focus away from negative experiences (Seligman, 2002; Seligman & Csikszentmihalyi, 2000). The advocates of *positive psychology* argue for increased research on contentment, well-being, human strengths, and positive emotions. One outgrowth of this movement has been increased interest in the dynamics of happiness. We will discuss this research in the upcoming Personal Application.

emotions on and off like a bedroom light. If it were that simple, you could choose to be happy whenever you wanted. As Joseph LeDoux puts it, "Emotions are things that happen to us rather than things we will to occur" (1996, p. 19). Although some degree of emotional control is actually possible (Thayer, 1996), emotions tend to involve automatic reactions that are difficult to regulate (Öhman & Wiens, 2003).

People's cognitive appraisals of events in their lives are key determinants of the emotions they experience (Ellsworth & Scherer, 2003; Lazarus, 1995). A specific event, such as giving a speech, may be a highly threatening and thus anxiety-arousing occasion for one person but a "ho-hum," routine matter for another. The conscious experience of emotion includes an *evaluative* aspect. People characterize their emotions as pleasant or unpleasant (Barrett et al., 2007; Lang, 1995). These evaluative reactions can be automatic and subconscious (Ferguson & Bargh, 2004). Of course, individuals often experience "mixed emotions" that include both pleasant and unpleasant qualities (Cacioppo & Berntson, 1999). For example, an executive just given a promotion with challenging new responsibilities may experience both happiness and anxiety.

For the most part, researchers have paid more attention to negative emotions than positive ones (Fredrickson, 1998). Why have positive emotions

The Physiological Component: Diffuse and Multifaceted   8c

Emotional processes are closely tied to physiological processes, but the interconnections are enormously complex. The biological bases of emotions are diffuse and multifaceted, involving many areas in the brain and many neurotransmitter systems, as well as the autonomic nervous system and the endocrine system.

Autonomic Arousal 8c

Imagine your reaction as your car spins out of control on an icy highway. Your fear is accompanied by a variety of physiological changes. Your heart rate and breathing accelerate. Your blood pressure surges, and your pupils dilate. The hairs on your skin stand erect, giving you "goose bumps," and you start to perspire. Although your reactions may not always be as obvious as in this scenario, *emotions are accompanied by physical arousal* (Cacioppo et al., 1993). Surely you've experienced a "knot in your stomach" or a "lump in your throat" thanks to anxiety.

Much of the physiological arousal associated with emotion occurs through the actions of the *autonomic nervous system* (Janig, 2003), which regulates the activity of glands, smooth muscles, and blood vessels (see **Figure 9.14**). As you may recall from Chapter 3,

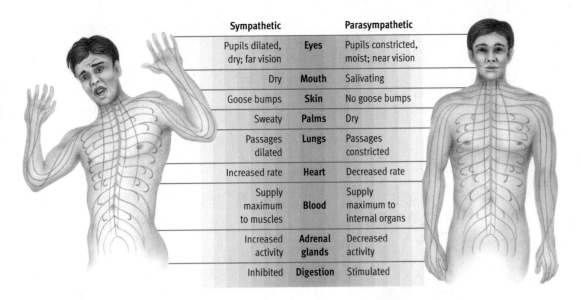

Sympathetic		Parasympathetic
Pupils dilated, dry; far vision	**Eyes**	Pupils constricted, moist; near vision
Dry	**Mouth**	Salivating
Goose bumps	**Skin**	No goose bumps
Sweaty	**Palms**	Dry
Passages dilated	**Lungs**	Passages constricted
Increased rate	**Heart**	Decreased rate
Supply maximum to muscles	**Blood**	Supply maximum to internal organs
Increased activity	**Adrenal glands**	Decreased activity
Inhibited	**Digestion**	Stimulated

Figure 9.14

Emotion and autonomic arousal. The autonomic nervous system (ANS) is composed of the nerves that connect to the heart, blood vessels, smooth muscles, and glands (consult Chapter 3 for more information). The ANS is divided into the *sympathetic division,* which mobilizes bodily resources in response to stress, and the *parasympathetic division,* which conserves bodily resources. Emotions are frequently accompanied by sympathetic ANS activation, which leads to goose bumps, sweaty palms, and the other physical responses listed on the left side of the diagram.

the autonomic nervous system is responsible for the highly emotional *fight-or-flight response,* which is largely modulated by the release of adrenal *hormones* that radiate throughout the body. Hormonal changes clearly play a crucial role in emotional responses to stress and may contribute to many other emotions as well (Baum, Grunberg, & Singer, 1992).

The connection between emotion and autonomic arousal provides the basis for the *polygraph,* or *lie detector,* a device that records autonomic fluctuations while a subject is questioned. The polygraph was invented in 1915 by psychologist William Marston—who also dreamed up the comic book superhero Wonder Woman (Knight, 2004). A polygraph can't actually detect lies. It's really an emotion detector. It monitors key indicators of autonomic arousal, typically heart rate, blood pressure, respiration rate, and *galvanic skin response (GSR),* which is an increase in the electrical conductivity of the skin that occurs when sweat glands increase their activity. The assumption is that when people lie, they experience emotion (presumably anxiety) that produces noticeable changes in these physiological indicators (see **Figure 9.15** on the next page). The polygraph examiner asks a subject a number of nonthreatening questions to establish the person's baseline on these autonomic indicators. Then the examiner asks the critical questions (for example, "Were you at home on the night of the burglary?") and observes whether the subject's autonomic arousal changes.

The polygraph has been controversial since its invention (Grubin & Madsen, 2005). Polygraph advocates claim that lie detector tests are about 85%–90% accurate and that the validity of polygraph testing has been demonstrated in empirical studies, but these claims clearly are not supported by the evidence (Iacono & Lykken, 1997; Iacono & Patrick, 1999). Methodologically sound research on the validity of polygraph testing is surprisingly sparse (largely because it is difficult research to do), and the limited evidence is not very impressive (Branaman & Gallagher, 2005; Lykken, 1998; Saxe & Ben-Shakhar, 1999). Part of the problem is that people who are telling the truth may experience emotional arousal when they respond to incriminating questions. Thus, polygraph tests sometimes lead to accusations against people who are innocent. Another problem is that some people can lie without experiencing anxiety or autonomic arousal. The heart of the problem, as Leonard Saxe (1994) notes, is that "there is no evidence of a unique physiological reaction to deceit" (p. 71). The polygraph *is* a potentially useful tool that can help police check out leads and alibis. However, polygraph results are not reliable enough to be submitted as evidence in most types of courtrooms.

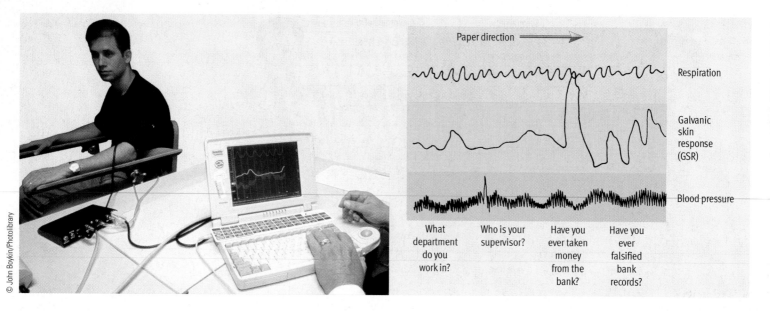

Paper direction

Respiration

Galvanic skin response (GSR)

Blood pressure

| What department do you work in? | Who is your supervisor? | Have you ever taken money from the bank? | Have you ever falsified bank records? |

© John Boykin/Photolibrary

Figure 9.15

Emotion and the polygraph. A lie detector measures the autonomic arousal that most people experience when they tell a lie. After using nonthreatening questions to establish a baseline, a polygraph examiner looks for signs of arousal (such as the sharp change in GSR shown here) on incriminating questions. Unfortunately, as your text explains, the polygraph is not a very dependable index of whether people are lying.

Neural Circuits

8c

The autonomic responses that accompany emotions are ultimately controlled in the brain. The hypothalamus, amygdala, and adjacent structures

Figure 9.16

The amygdala and fear. Emotions are controlled by a constellation of interacting brain systems, but the amygdala appears to play a particularly crucial role. According to LeDoux (1996), sensory inputs that can trigger fear (such as seeing a snake while out walking) arrive in the thalamus and then are routed along a fast pathway (shown in green) directly to the amygdala, and along a slow pathway (shown in blue) which allows the cortex time to think about the situation. Activity in the fast pathway also elicits the autonomic arousal and hormonal responses that are part of the physiological component of emotion. (Adapted from LeDoux, 1994)

Thalamus

Shortcut facilitates instant response

Visual cortex

Amygdala

Endocrine response: Hormonal secretions

Autonomic arousal

in the *limbic system* have long been viewed as the seat of emotions in the brain (Izard & Saxton, 1988; MacLean, 1993). Although these structures do contribute to emotion, the limbic system is not a clearly defined anatomical system (see Chapter 3), and research has shown that a variety of brain structures that lie outside the limbic system play a variety of roles in the regulation of emotion (Berridge, 2003).

Recent evidence suggests that the *amygdala* plays a particularly central role in the acquisition of conditioned fears (LaBar & LeDoux, 2003; Phelps, 2006). According to Joseph LeDoux (1996, 2000), sensory inputs capable of eliciting emotions arrive in the thalamus, which simultaneously routes the information along two separate pathways: to the nearby amygdala and to areas in the cortex (see **Figure 16**). The amygdala processes the information quickly, and if it detects a threat it almost instantly triggers activity in the hypothalamus that leads to the autonomic arousal and hormonal responses associated with emotion. The processing in this pathway is extremely fast, so that emotions may be triggered even before the cortex has had a chance to really "think" about the input. LeDoux believes that this rapid-response pathway evolved because it is a highly adaptive warning system that can "be the difference between life and death." Consistent with LeDoux's theory, evidence indicates that the amygdala can process emotion independent of cognitive awareness (Phelps, 2005). Research linking the amygdala to emotion has mainly focused on fear, but recent evidence suggests that the amygdala may play a role in positive emotions as well (Murray, 2007).

What other areas of the brain are involved in the modulation of emotion? The list is extensive, including the prefrontal cortex, the hippocampus, the lateral hypothalamus, the septum, and the brain stem (Berridge, 2003; Davidson et al., 2003b). Thus, it is clear that *emotion depends on activity in a constellation of interacting brain centers.*

The Behavioral Component: Nonverbal Expressiveness

At the behavioral level, people reveal their emotions through characteristic overt expressions such as smiles, frowns, furrowed brows, clenched fists, and slumped shoulders. In other words, *emotions are expressed in "body language," or nonverbal behavior.*

Facial expressions reveal a variety of basic emotions. In an extensive research project, Paul Ekman and Wallace Friesen have asked participants to identify what emotion a person was experiencing on the basis of facial cues in photographs. They have found that subjects are generally successful in identifying six fundamental emotions: happiness, sadness, anger, fear, surprise, and disgust (Ekman & Friesen, 1975, 1984). Furthermore, the identification of emotions from facial expressions tends to occur quickly and automatically (Tracy & Robins, 2008).

Some theorists believe that muscular feedback from one's own facial expressions contributes to one's conscious experience of emotions (Izard, 1990; Tomkins, 1991). Proponents of the *facial-feedback hypothesis* assert that facial muscles send signals to the brain and that these signals help the brain recognize the emotion that one is experiencing. According to this view, smiles, frowns, and furrowed brows help create the experience of various emotions. Consistent with this idea, studies show that if subjects are instructed to contract their facial muscles to mimic facial expressions associated with certain emotions, they tend to report that they actually experience these emotions to some degree (Kleinke, Peterson, & Rutledge, 1998; Levenson, 1992).

Culture and the Elements of Emotion

Are emotions innate reactions that are universal across cultures? Or are they socially learned reactions that are culturally variable? The research on this lingering question has not yielded a simple answer. Investigators have found both remarkable similarities and dramatic differences among cultures in the experience of emotion.

Cross-Cultural Similarities in Emotional Experience

After demonstrating that Western subjects could discern specific emotions from facial expressions, Ekman and Friesen (1975) took their facial-cue photographs on the road to other societies to see whether nonverbal expressions of emotion transcend cultural boundaries. Testing participants in Argentina, Spain, Japan, and other countries, they found considerable cross-cultural agreement in the identification of happiness, sadness, anger, fear, surprise, and disgust based on facial expressions (see **Figure 9.17** on the next page). Still, Ekman and Friesen wondered whether this agreement might be the result of learning rather than biology, given that people in different cultures often share considerable exposure to Western mass media (magazines, newspapers, television, and so forth), which provide many visual depictions of people's emotional reactions. To rule out this possibility, they took their photos to a remote area in New Guinea and showed them to a group of natives (the Fore) who had had virtually no contact with Western culture. Even the people from this preliterate culture did a fair job of identifying the emotions portrayed in the pictures (see **Figure 9.17**). Subsequent comparisons of many other societies have also shown considerable cross-cultural agreement in the judgment of facial expressions (Biehl et al., 1997; Ekman, 1992, 1993; Izard, 1994). Cross-cultural similarities have also been found in the cognitive appraisals that lead to emotions (Matsumoto, Nezlek, & Koopmann, 2007) and in the physiological arousal that accompanies emotional experience (Breugelmans et al., 2005).

Cross-Cultural Differences in Emotional Experience

The cross-cultural similarities in emotional experience are impressive, but researchers have also found many cultural disparities in how people think about and express their emotions (Mesquita, 2003; Mesquita & Leu, 2007). For example, Japanese culture encourages the experience of *socially engaging emotions* (such as friendly feelings, sympathy, and guilt) more than North American culture, and Japanese participants report experiencing these types of emotion more often (Kitayama, Mesquita, & Karasawa, 2006). In contrast, North American culture encourages *socially disengaging emotions* (such as pride and anger) more than Japanese culture, and North American subjects report experiencing these kinds of emotion more.

Fascinating variations have also been observed in how cultures categorize emotions. Some basic

Joseph LeDoux

"In situations of danger, it is very useful to be able to respond quickly. The time saved by the amygdala in acting on the thalamic information, rather than waiting for the cortical input, may be the difference between life and death."

web link 9.6

UCSC Perceptual Science Laboratory

Perceptions of other people, especially of speech and facial expression, serve as a primary focus for research at this laboratory at the University of California, Santa Cruz. The site offers a broad set of resources, including a comprehensive guide to nonverbal facial analysis research being conducted in laboratories worldwide.

Country	Fear	Disgust	Happiness	Anger
		Agreement in judging photos (%)		
United States	85	92	97	67
Brazil	67	97	95	90
Chile	68	92	95	94
Argentina	54	92	98	90
Japan	66	90	100	90
New Guinea	54	44	82	50

Figure 9.17

Cross-cultural comparisons of people's ability to recognize emotions from facial expressions. Ekman and Friesen (1975) found that people in highly disparate cultures showed fair agreement on the emotions portrayed in these photos. This consensus across cultures suggests that facial expressions of emotions may be universal and that they have a strong biological basis.

SOURCE: Data from Ekman, P., & Friesen, W. V. (1975). *Unmasking the Face*. Englewood Cliffs, NJ: Prentice-Hall. © 1975 by Paul Ekman, photographs courtesy of Paul Ekman.

categories of emotion that are universally understood in Western cultures appear to go unrecognized—or at least unnamed—in some non-Western cultures. James Russell (1991) has compiled numerous examples of English words for emotions that have no equivalent in other languages. For example, Tahitians have no word that corresponds to *sadness*. Many non-Western groups, including the Yoruba of Nigeria, the Kaluli of New Guinea, and the Chinese, lack a word for *depression*. The concept of *anxiety* seems to go unrecognized among Eskimos and the Yoruba, and the Quichua of Ecuador lack a word for *remorse*.

Cultural disparities have also been found in regard to nonverbal expressions of emotion. Although the natural facial expressions associated with basic emotions appear to be universal, people can and do learn to control and modify these expressions. *Display rules are norms that regulate the appropriate expression of emotions.* They prescribe when, how, and to whom people can show various emotions. These norms vary from one culture to another (Ekman, 1992), as do attitudes about specific emotions (Eid & Diener, 2001). The Ifaluk of Micronesia, for instance, severely restrict expressions of happiness because they believe that this emotion often leads people to neglect their duties (Lutz, 1987). Japanese culture emphasizes the suppression of negative emotions in public. More so than in other cultures, the Japanese are socialized to mask emotions such as

anger, sadness, and disgust with stoic facial expressions or polite smiling. Thus, nonverbal expressions of emotions vary somewhat across cultures because of culture-specific attitudes and display rules.

REVIEW of Key Learning Goals

9.13 Emotion is made up of cognitive, physiological, and behavioral components. The cognitive component involves subjective feelings that have an evaluative aspect. People's cognitive appraisals of events in their lives determine the emotions they experience. Generally, researchers have paid more attention to negative emotions than positive ones.

9.14 The most readily apparent aspect of the physiological component of emotion is autonomic arousal. This arousal is the basis for the lie detector, which is really an emotion detector. Polygraphs are not all that accurate in assessing individuals' veracity. The amygdala appears to be the hub of an emotion-processing system in the brain that modulates conditioned fears, but a variety of other areas in the brain contribute to the regulation of emotion.

9.15 At the behavioral level, emotions are expressed through body language, with facial expressions being particularly prominent. Ekman and Friesen have found considerable cross-cultural agreement in the identification of emotions based on facial expressions. Advocates of the facial-feedback hypothesis maintain that facial muscles send signals to the brain that help the brain recognize the emotion one is experiencing.

9.16 Cross-cultural similarities have been found in the facial expressions associated with specific emotions, the cognitive appraisals that provoke emotions, and the physiological underpinnings of emotion. However, there are some striking cultural variations in how people categorize their emotions and in the display rules that govern how much people show their emotions.

Theories of Emotion

How do psychologists explain the experience of emotion? A variety of theories and conflicting models exist. Some have been vigorously debated for over a century. As we describe these theories, you'll recognize a familiar bone of contention. Like theories of motivation, theories of emotion differ in their emphasis on the innate biological basis of emotion versus the social, environmental basis.

James-Lange Theory   8d

As we noted in Chapter 1, William James was an early theorist who urged psychologists to explore the functions of consciousness. James (1884) developed a theory of emotion over 100 years ago that remains influential today. At about the same time, he and Carl Lange (1885) independently proposed that the *conscious experience of emotion results from one's perception of autonomic arousal.* Their theory stood common sense on its head. Everyday logic suggests that when you stumble onto a rattlesnake in the woods, the conscious experience of fear leads to autonomic arousal (the fight-or-flight response). The James-Lange theory of emotion asserts the opposite: that the perception of autonomic arousal leads to the conscious experience of fear (see **Figure 9.18**). In other words, while you might assume that your pulse is racing because you're fearful, James and Lange argue that you're fearful because your pulse is racing.

The James-Lange theory emphasizes the physiological determinants of emotion. According to this

Key Learning Goals

9.17 Compare the James-Lange and Cannon-Bard theories of emotion.

9.18 Explain the two-factor theory of emotion and evolutionary theories of emotion.

Figure 9.18

Theories of emotion. Three influential theories of emotion are contrasted with one another and with the commonsense view. The James-Lange theory was the first to suggest that feelings of arousal cause emotion, rather than vice versa. Schachter built on this idea by adding a second factor—interpretation (appraisal and labeling) of arousal.

view, *different patterns of autonomic activation lead to the experience of different emotions.* Hence, people supposedly distinguish emotions such as fear, joy, and anger on the basis of the exact configuration of physical reactions they experience. Decades of research have supported the concept of *autonomic specificity*—that different emotions are accompanied by different patterns of autonomic activation (Janig, 2003; Levenson, 2003). However, the question of whether people identify their emotions from these varied patterns of autonomic activation remains unresolved.

Cannon-Bard Theory

8d

Walter Cannon (1927) found the James-Lange theory unconvincing. Cannon pointed out that physiological arousal may occur without the experience of emotion (if one exercises vigorously, for instance). He also argued that visceral changes are too slow to precede the conscious experience of emotion. Finally, he argued that people experiencing very different emotions, such as fear, joy, and anger, exhibit almost identical patterns of autonomic arousal.

Thus, Cannon espoused a different explanation of emotion. Later, Philip Bard (1934) elaborated on it. The resulting Cannon-Bard theory argues that emotion occurs when the *thalamus* sends signals *simultaneously* to the cortex (creating the conscious experience of emotion) and to the autonomic nervous system (creating visceral arousal). The Cannon-Bard model is compared to the James-Lange model in **Figure 9.18**. Cannon and Bard were off the mark a bit in pinpointing the thalamus as the neural center for emotion. However, many modern theorists agree with the Cannon-Bard view that emotions originate in subcortical brain structures (LeDoux, 1996; Panksepp, 1991; Rolls, 1990) and with the assertion that people do *not* infer their emotions from different patterns of autonomic activation (Frijda, 1999; Wagner, 1989).

Schachter's Two-Factor Theory

8d

In another influential analysis, Stanley Schachter asserted that people look at situational cues to differentiate between alternative emotions. According to Schachter (1964; Schachter & Singer, 1962, 1979), the experience of emotion depends on two factors: (1) autonomic arousal and (2) cognitive interpretation of that arousal. Schachter proposed that when you experience physiological arousal, you search your environment for an explanation (see **Figure 9.18** again). If you're stuck in a traffic jam, you'll probably label your

arousal as anger. If you're taking an important exam, you'll probably label it as anxiety. If you're celebrating your birthday, you'll probably label it as happiness.

Schachter agrees with the James-Lange view that emotion is inferred from arousal. However, he also agrees with the Cannon-Bard position that different emotions yield indistinguishable patterns of arousal. He reconciles these views by arguing that people look to external rather than internal cues to differentiate and label their specific emotions. In essence, Schachter suggests that people think along the following lines: "If I'm aroused and you're obnoxious, I must be angry."

Although the two-factor theory has received support, studies have revealed some limitations as well (Leventhal & Tomarken, 1986). Situations can't mold emotions in just any way at any time. And in searching to explain arousal, people don't limit themselves to the immediate situation (Sinclair et al., 1994). Thus, emotions are not as pliable as the two-factor theory initially suggested.

Evolutionary Theories of Emotion

8d

In recent years, some theorists interested in emotion have returned to ideas espoused by Charles Darwin over a century ago. Darwin (1872) believed that emotions developed because of their adaptive value. Fear, for instance, would help an organism avoid danger and thus would aid in survival. Thus, Darwin viewed human emotions as a product of evolution. This premise serves as the foundation for several modern theories of emotion developed independently by S. S. Tomkins (1980, 1991), Carroll Izard (1984, 1991), and Robert Plutchik (1984, 1993).

These *evolutionary theories* consider emotions to be largely innate reactions to certain stimuli. As such, emotions should be immediately recognizable under most conditions without much thought. After all, primitive animals that are incapable of complex thought seem to have little difficulty in recognizing their emotions. Evolutionary theorists believe that emotion evolved before thought. They assert that thought plays a relatively small role in emotion, although they admit that learning and cognition may have some influence on human emotions. Evolutionary theories generally assume that emotions originate in subcortical brain structures (such as the hypothalamus and most of the limbic system) that evolved before the higher brain areas (in the cortex) associated with complex thought.

Evolutionary theories also assume that evolution has equipped humans with a small number of innate

Stanley Schachter

"Cognitive factors play a major role in determining how a subject interprets his bodily feelings."

emotions with proven adaptive value. Thus, the principal question that evolutionary theories of emotion wrestle with is, *What are the fundamental emotions?* Evolutionary theorists attempt to identify these primary emotions by searching for universals—emotions that are expressed and recognized in the same way in widely disparate cultures. **Figure 9.19** summarizes the conclusions of the leading theorists in this area. As you can see, Tomkins, Izard, and Plutchik have not come up with identical lists, but they show considerable agreement. All three conclude that people exhibit eight to ten primary emotions. Moreover, six of these emotions appear on all three lists: fear, anger, joy, disgust, interest, and surprise.

Silvan Tomkins	Carroll Izard	Robert Plutchik
Fear	Fear	Fear
Anger	Anger	Anger
Enjoyment	Joy	Joy
Disgust	Disgust	Disgust
Interest	Interest	Anticipation
Surprise	Surprise	Surprise
Contempt	Contempt	
Shame	Shame	
	Sadness	Sadness
Distress		
	Guilt	
		Acceptance

Figure 9.19

Primary emotions. Evolutionary theories of emotion attempt to identify primary emotions. Three leading theorists—Silvan Tomkins, Carroll Izard, and Robert Plutchik—have compiled different lists of primary emotions, but this chart shows great overlap among the basic emotions identified by these theorists. (Based on Mandler, 1984)

REVIEW of Key Learning Goals

9.17 Common sense suggests that emotions cause autonomic arousal, but the James-Lange theory asserted that emotion results from one's perception of autonomic arousal. The Cannon-Bard theory countered with the proposal that emotions originate in subcortical areas of the brain.

9.18 According to Schachter's two-factor theory, people infer emotion from arousal and then label the emotion in accordance with their cognitive explanation for the arousal. Evolutionary theories of emotion maintain that emotions are innate reactions that require little cognitive interpretation. Evolutionary theorists seek to identify a small number of innate, fundamental emotions.

concept check 9.3

Identifying the Contributions of Major Theorists and Researchers

Check your recall of the principal ideas of important theorists and researchers covered in this chapter by matching the people listed on the left with the appropriate contributions described on the right. If you need help, the crucial pages describing each person's ideas are listed in parentheses. Fill in the letters for your choices in the spaces provided on the left. You'll find the answers in Appendix A.

Major Theorists and Researchers

_____ 1. David Buss (p. 310)

_____ 2. Walter Cannon (pp. 302, 324)

_____ 3. Paul Ekman and Wallace Friesen (pp. 321–322)

_____ 4. William James (pp. 323–324)

_____ 5. Joseph LeDoux (pp. 320–321)

_____ 6. William Masters and Virginia Johnson (p. 307)

_____ 7. David McClelland (pp. 315–316)

_____ 8. Stanley Schachter (p. 324)

Key Ideas and Contributions

a. This researcher has shown that the amygdala plays a central role in the acquisition of conditioned fears.

b. This research team conducted groundbreaking work on the physiological bases of the human sexual response.

c. This theorist is known for his influential work on the nature and determinants of achievement motivation.

d. This evolutionary psychologist's research showed that women around the world place a higher value than men on potential partners' status and financial prospects, whereas men show more interest than women in partners' youthfulness and attractiveness.

e. This research team demonstrated that subjects can identify six basic emotions from facial expressions and that nonverbal expressions of emotion transcend culture.

f. This individual devised the two-factor theory of emotion, which posits that emotion depends on autonomic arousal and cognitive interpretation of that arousal.

g. This person conducted early research on hunger and argued that emotions originate in subcortical brain structures.

h. This legendary scholar formulated a theory of emotion which proposed that the conscious experience of emotion results from one's perception of autonomic arousal.

Reflecting on the Chapter's Themes

Key Learning Goals

9.19 Identify the five unifying themes highlighted in this chapter.

Cultural Heritage

Sociohistorical Context

Theoretical Diversity

Heredity and Environment

Multifactorial Causation

Five of our organizing themes were particularly prominent in this chapter: the influence of cultural contexts, the dense connections between psychology and society at large, psychology's theoretical diversity, the interplay of heredity and environment, and the multiple causes of behavior.

Our discussion of motivation and emotion demonstrated once again that there are both similarities and differences across cultures in behavior. The neural, biochemical, genetic, and hormonal processes underlying hunger and eating, for instance, are universal. However, cultural factors influence what people prefer to eat and how much they eat. In a similar vein, researchers have found a great deal of cross-cultural similarity in the cognitive, physiological, and expressive elements of emotional experience, but they have also found cultural variations in how people think about and express their emotions. Thus, as we have seen in previous chapters, psychological processes are characterized by both cultural variance and invariance.

Our discussion of the controversies surrounding evolutionary theory and the determinants of sexual orientation show once again that psychology is not an ivory tower enterprise. It evolves in a sociohistorical context that helps shape the debates in the field, and these debates often have far-reaching social and political ramifications for society at large. We ended the chapter with a discussion of various theories of emotion, which showed once again that psychology is characterized by great theoretical diversity.

Finally, we repeatedly saw that biological and environmental factors jointly govern behavior. For example, we learned that eating behavior, sexual behavior, and the experience of emotion all depend on complicated interactions between biological and environmental determinants. Indeed, complicated interactions were seen throughout the entire chapter, demonstrating that if we want to fully understand behavior, we have to take multiple causes into account. We will see more of this complexity in the upcoming Personal Application, where we will continue our discussion of emotion, looking at recent research on the correlates of happiness. In the Critical Thinking Application that follows, we discuss how to carefully analyze the types of arguments found in this chapter—and everyday life.

> **REVIEW of Key Learning Goals**
>
> **9.19** Our look at motivation and emotion showed once again that psychology is characterized by theoretical diversity, that biology and environment shape behavior interactively, that behavior is governed by multiple causes, that psychological processes are characterized by both cultural variance and invariance, and that psychology evolves in a sociohistorical context.

PERSONAL APPLICATION

Key Learning Goals

9.20 Identify factors that do not predict happiness.
9.21 Review information on factors that are moderately or strongly correlated with happiness.
9.22 Explain four conclusions that can be drawn about the dynamics of happiness.

Exploring the Ingredients of Happiness

Answer the following "true" or "false."

___ **1** The empirical evidence indicates that most people are relatively unhappy.
___ **2** Although wealth doesn't *guarantee* happiness, wealthy people are much more likely to be happy than the rest of the population.
___ **3** People who have children are happier than people without children.
___ **4** Good health is an essential requirement for happiness.

The answer to all these questions is "false." These assertions are all reasonable and widely believed hypotheses about the prevalence and correlates of happiness, but they have *not* been supported by empirical research. Due in part to a new emphasis on positive psychology, recent years have brought a surge of interest in the correlates of *subjective well-being*—individuals' personal perceptions of their overall happiness and life satisfaction. The findings of this research are quite interesting. As you have already seen from our true-false questions, many commonsense notions about happiness appear to be inaccurate.

How Happy Are People?

One of these inaccuracies is the apparently widespread assumption that most people are relatively unhappy. Writers, social scientists, and the general public seem to believe that people around the world are predominantly dissatisfied and unhappy, yet empirical surveys consistently find that the vast majority of respondents—even those who are poor or disabled—characterize themselves as fairly happy (Diener & Diener, 1996; Myers & Diener, 1995). When people are asked to rate their happiness, only a small minority place themselves below the neutral point on the various scales used (see **Figure 9.20**). When the average subjective well-being of entire nations is computed, based on almost 1000 surveys, the means cluster toward the positive end of the scale (Tov & Diener, 2007). That's not to say that everyone is equally happy. Researchers find substantial and thought-provoking disparities among people in subjective well-being, which we will analyze momentarily, but the overall picture seems rosier than anticipated.

Factors That Do Not Predict Happiness

Let us begin our discussion of individual differences in happiness by highlighting those things that turn out to be relatively unimportant determinants of subjective well-being. Quite a number of factors that you might expect to be influential appear to bear little or no relationship to general happiness.

Money. There *is* a positive correlation between income and subjective feelings of happiness, but in modern, affluent cultures the association is surprisingly weak (Diener & Seligman, 2004). For example, one study found a correlation of just .13 between income and happiness in the United States (Diener et al., 1993), and another recent investigation yielded an almost identical correlation of .12 (Johnson & Krueger, 2006). On the average, even wealthy people are only marginally happier than those in the middle classes. One reason for this weak association is that there seems to be a disconnect between actual income and how people feel about their financial situation. Recent research (Johnson & Krueger, 2006) suggests that the correlation between actual wealth and people's subjective perceptions of whether they have enough money to meet their needs is surprisingly modest (around .30).

Another problem is that in this era of voracious consumption, pervasive advertising fuels escalating material desires (Frey & Stutzer, 2002; Kasser et al., 2004). When these growing desires outstrip what people can afford, dissatisfaction is likely (Solberg et al., 2002). Interestingly, there is some evidence that people who place an especially strong emphasis on the pursuit of wealth and materialistic goals tend to be somewhat less happy than others (Kasser, 2002; Van Boven, 2005), perhaps in large part because they are so focused on financial success that they don't derive much satisfaction from their family life (Nickerson et al., 2003). Consistent with this view, a recent study (Kahneman et al., 2006) found that higher income was associated with working longer hours and allocating fewer hours to leisure pursuits.

Age. Age and happiness are consistently found to be unrelated. Age accounts for less than 1% of the variation in people's happiness (Inglehart, 1990; Myers & Diener, 1997). The key factors influencing subjective well-being may shift some as people grow older—work becomes less important, health more so—but people's average level of happiness tends to remain remarkably stable over the life span.

Parenthood. Children can be a tremendous source of joy and fulfillment, but they can also be a tremendous source of headaches and hassles. Compared to childless couples, parents worry more and experience more

"Who can say? I suppose I'm as happy as my portfolio will allow me to be."

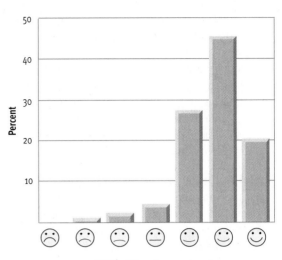

Which of these faces represents the way you feel about life as a whole?

Figure 9.20

Measuring happiness with a nonverbal scale. Researchers have used a variety of methods to estimate the distribution of happiness. For example, in one study in the United States, respondents were asked to examine the seven facial expressions shown and select the one that "comes closest to expressing how you feel about your life as a whole." As you can see, the vast majority of participants chose happy faces. (Data adapted from Myers, 1992)

marital problems (Argyle, 1987). Apparently, the good and bad aspects of parenthood balance each other out, because the evidence indicates that people who have children are neither more nor less happy than people without children (Argyle, 2001).

Intelligence and attractiveness. Intelligence and physical attractiveness are highly valued traits in modern society, but researchers have not found an association between either characteristic and happiness (Diener, 1984; Diener, Wolsic, & Fujita, 1995).

Moderately Good Predictors of Happiness

Research has identified some facets of life that appear to have a *moderate* association with subjective well-being: health, social activity, and religious belief.

Health. Good physical health would seem to be an essential requirement for happiness, but people adapt to health problems. Research reveals that individuals who develop serious, disabling health conditions aren't as unhappy as one might guess (Myers, 1992; Riis et al., 2005). Furthermore, Freedman (1978) argues that good health does not, by itself, produce happiness, because people tend to take good health for granted. Considerations such as these may help to explain why researchers find only a moderate positive correlation (average = .32) between health status and subjective well-being (Argyle, 1999).

Social Activity.   Humans are social animals, and interpersonal relations do appear to contribute to people's happiness. Those who are satisfied with their social support and friendship networks and those who are socially active report above-average levels of happiness (Diener & Seligman, 2004; Myers, 1999). And people who are exceptionally happy tend to report greater satisfaction with their social relations than those who are average or low in subjective well-being (Diener & Seligman, 2002).

Religion.   The link between religiosity and subjective well-being is modest, but a number of large-scale surveys suggest that people with heartfelt religious convictions are more likely to be happy than people who characterize themselves as nonreligious (Abdel-Khalek, 2006; Myers, 2008).

Strong Predictors of Happiness

The list of factors that turn out to have fairly strong associations with happiness is surprisingly short. The key ingredients of happiness appear to involve love, work, and personality.

Love and Marriage.   Romantic relationships can be stressful, but people consistently rate being in love as one of the critical ingredients of happiness (Myers, 1999). Furthermore, although people complain a lot about their marriages, the evidence indicates that marital status is a key correlate of happiness. Among both men and women, married people are happier than people who are single or divorced (see **Figure 9.21**; Myers & Diener, 1995), and this relationship holds around the world in widely different cultures (Diener et al., 2000). However, the causal relations underlying this correlation

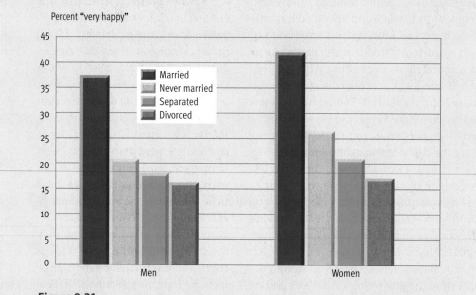

Figure 9.21

Happiness and marital status. This graph shows the percentage of adults characterizing themselves as "Very happy" as a function of marital status (Myers, 1999). Among both women and men, happiness shows up more in those who are married, as opposed to those who are separated, who are divorced, or who have never married. These data and many other findings suggest that marital satisfaction is a key ingredient of happiness.

SOURCE: Myers, D. G. (1999). Close relationships and quality of life. In D. Kahneman, E. Diener, & N. Schwarz (Eds.), *Well-being: The foundations of hedonic psychology.* New York: Russell Sage Foundation. Copyright © 1999. Reprinted by permission of the Russell Sage Foundation.

are unclear. It may be that happiness causes marital satisfaction more than marital satisfaction promotes happiness.

Work.   Given the way people often complain about their jobs, one might not expect work to be a key source of happiness, but it is. Although less critical than love and marriage, job satisfaction has a substantial association with general happiness (Judge & Klinger, 2008; Warr, 1999). Studies also show that unemployment has strong negative effects on subjective well-being (Lucas et al., 2004). It is difficult to sort out whether job satisfaction causes happiness or vice versa, but evidence suggests that causation flows both ways (Argyle, 2001).

Genetics and Personality.   The best predictor of individuals' future happiness is their past happiness (Diener & Lucas, 1999). Some people seem destined to be happy and others unhappy, regardless of their triumphs or setbacks. Evidence suggests that happiness does not depend on external circumstances—buying a nice house, getting pro-

moted—as much as internal factors, such as one's outlook on life (Lyubomirsky, Sheldon, & Schkade, 2005). With this reality in mind, researchers have investigated whether there might be a hereditary basis for variations in happiness. These studies suggest that people's genetic predispositions account for a substantial portion of the variance in happiness, perhaps as much as 50% (Lyubomirsky et al., 2005; Stubbe et al., 2005). How can one's genes influence one's happiness? Presumably, by shaping one's temperament and personality, which are known to be heritable (Weiss, Bates, & Luciano, 2008). As a result, researchers have begun to look for links between personality and subjective well-being, and they have found some interesting correlations. For example, *extraversion* is one of the better predictors of happiness. People who are outgoing, upbeat, and sociable tend to be happier than others (Fleeson, Malanos, & Achille, 2002). Additional personality correlates of happiness include conscientiousness, agreeableness, self-esteem, and optimism (Lucas, 2008; Lyubomirsky, Tkach, & DiMatteo, 2006).

Research shows that happiness does not depend on people's positive and negative experiences as much as one would expect. Some people, presumably because of their personality, seem destined to be happy in spite of major setbacks, and others seem destined to cling to unhappiness even though their lives seem reasonably pleasant.

Conclusions About Subjective Well-Being

We must be cautious in drawing inferences about the *causes* of happiness, because the available data are correlational (see **Figure 9.22**). Nonetheless, the empirical findings suggest a number of worthwhile insights about the roots of happiness.

First, research on happiness demonstrates that the determinants of subjective well-being are precisely that: subjective. *Objective realities are not as important as subjective feelings.* In other words, your health, your wealth, your job, and your age are not as influential as how you *feel* about your health, wealth, job, and age (Schwarz & Strack, 1999). Second, *when it comes to happiness, everything is relative* (Argyle, 1999; Hagerty, 2000). In other words, you evaluate what you have relative to what the people around you have and relative to what you expected to have. Generally, we compare ourselves with others who are similar to us. Thus, people who are wealthy assess what they have by comparing themselves with their wealthy friends and neighbors. This is one reason that there is little correlation between wealth and happiness.

Third, *research on happiness has shown that people are surprisingly bad at predicting what will make them happy.* We assume that we know what is best for us. But research on *affective forecasting*—efforts to predict one's emotional reactions to future events—suggests otherwise (Gilbert, 2006; Hsee & Hastie, 2006; Wilson & Gilbert, 2005). People routinely overestimate the pleasure that they will derive from buying an expensive automobile, taking an exotic vacation, or earning an important promotion. Likewise, people tend to overestimate the misery that they will endure if they ex-

perience a romantic breakup, don't get into the college they want, or develop a serious illness. Thus, the roadmap to happiness is less clearly marked than widely assumed.

Fourth, *research on subjective well-being indicates that people often adapt to their circumstances.* This adaptation effect is one reason that increases in income don't necessarily bring increases in happiness. **Hedonic adaptation occurs when the mental scale that people use to judge the pleasantness-unpleasantness of their experiences shifts so that their neutral point, or baseline for comparison, changes.** Unfortunately, when people's experiences improve, hedonic adaptation may *sometimes* put them on a *hedonic treadmill*—their neutral point moves upward, so that the improvements yield no real benefits (Kahneman, 1999). However, when people have to grapple with major setbacks, hedonic adaptation probably helps protect their mental and physical health. For example, people who are sent to prison and people who develop debilitating diseases are not as unhappy as one might assume, because they adapt to their changed situations and evaluate events from a new perspective (Frederick & Loewenstein, 1999). That's not to say that hedonic adaptation in the face of life's difficulties is inevitable or complete (Lucas, 2007). Moreover, evidence suggests that people adapt more slowly to negative events than to positive events (Larsen & Prizmic, 2008).

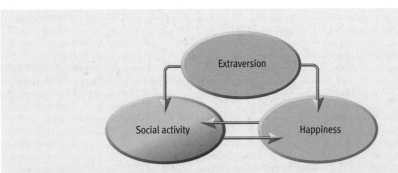

Figure 9.22
Possible causal relations among the correlates of happiness. Although we have considerable data on the correlates of happiness, it is difficult to untangle the possible causal relationships. For example, we know that there is a moderate positive correlation between social activity and happiness, but we can't say for sure whether high social activity causes happiness or whether happiness causes people to be more socially active. Moreover, in light of the research showing that a third variable—extraversion—correlates with both variables, we have to consider the possibility that extraversion causes both greater social activity and greater happiness.

Analyzing Arguments: Making Sense out of Controversy

Key Learning Goals

9.23 Identify the key elements in arguments.

9.24 Recognize common fallacies that often show up in arguments.

Consider the following argument: "Dieting is harmful to your health because the tendency to be obese is largely inherited." What is your reaction to this reasoning? Do you find it convincing? We hope not, as this argument is seriously flawed. Can you see what's wrong? There is no relationship between the conclusion that "dieting is harmful to your health" and the reason given that "the tendency to be obese is largely inherited." The argument is initially seductive because most people know that obesity *is* largely inherited, so the reason provided represents a true statement. But the reason is unrelated to the conclusion advocated. This scenario may strike you as odd, but if you start listening carefully to discussions about controversial issues, you will probably notice that people often cite irrelevant considerations in support of their favored conclusions.

This chapter was loaded with controversial issues that sincere, well-meaning people could argue about for weeks. Are gender differences in mating preferences a product of evolution or of modern economic realities?

Is there a biological basis for homosexuality? Unfortunately, arguments about issues such as these typically are unproductive in terms of moving toward resolution or agreement because most people know little about the rules of argumentation. In this application, we will explore what makes arguments sound or unsound in the hope of improving your ability to analyze and think critically about arguments.

The Anatomy of an Argument

In everyday usage, the word *argument* is used to refer to a dispute or disagreement between two or more people, but in the technical language of rhetoric, an *argument* consists of one or more premises that are used to provide support for a conclusion. *Premises* are the reasons that are presented to persuade someone that a conclusion is true or probably true. *Assumptions* are premises for which no proof or evidence is offered. Assumptions are often left unstated. For example, suppose that your doctor tells you that you should exercise regularly because regular exercise is good for your heart. In this simple argument, the conclusion is "You should exercise regularly." The premise that leads to this conclusion is the idea that "exercise is good for your heart." An

unstated assumption is that everyone wants a healthy heart.

In the language of argument analysis, premises are said to support (or not support) conclusions. A conclusion may be supported by one reason or by many reasons. One way to visualize these possibilities is to draw an analogy between the reasons that support a conclusion and the legs that support a table (Halpern, 2003). As shown in **Figure 9.23**, a table top (conclusion) could be supported by one strong leg (a single strong reason) or many thin legs (lots of weaker reasons). Of course, the reasons provided for a conclusion may fail to support the conclusion. Returning to our table analogy, the table top might not be supported because the legs are too thin (very weak reasons) or because the legs are not attached (irrelevant reasons).

Arguments can get pretty complicated, as they usually have more parts than just premises and conclusions. In addition, there often are *counterarguments*, which are reasons that take support away from a conclusion. And sometimes the most important part of an argument is something that is not there—reasons that have been omitted, either deliberately or not, that would lead to a different conclusion if they were supplied. Given all the complex variations that are possible in arguments, it is impossible to give you

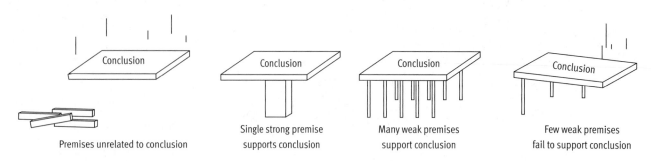

| Premises unrelated to conclusion | Single strong premise supports conclusion | Many weak premises support conclusion | Few weak premises fail to support conclusion |

Figure 9.23

An analogy for understanding the strength of arguments. Halpern (2003) draws an analogy between the premises that support a conclusion and the legs that support a table. She points out that a conclusion may be supported effectively by one strong premise or many weak premises. Of course, the reasons provided for a conclusion may also *fail* to provide adequate support.

SOURCE: Halpern, D. F. (2003). *Thought & knowledge: An introduction to critical thinking.* Mahwah, NJ: Erlbaum. Copyright © 2003 Lawrence Erlbaum Associates. Reprinted by permission.

simple rules for judging arguments, but we can highlight some common fallacies and then provide some criteria you can apply in thinking critically about arguments.

Common Fallacies

As noted in previous chapters, cognitive scientists have compiled lengthy lists of fallacies that people frequently display in their arguments. This section describes five common fallacies. To illustrate each one, we will assume the role of someone arguing that pornographic material on the Internet (cyberporn) should be banned or heavily regulated.

Irrelevant Reasons.   Reasons cannot provide support for an argument unless they are relevant to the conclusion. Arguments that depend on irrelevant reasons—either intentionally or inadvertently—are quite common. You already saw one example at the beginning of this application. The Latin term for this fallacy is *non sequitur,* which literally translates to "it doesn't follow." In other words, the conclusion does not follow from the premise. For example, in the debate about Internet pornography, you might hear the following *non sequitur:* "We need to regulate cyberporn because research has shown that most date rapes go unreported."

Circular Reasoning.   In *circular reasoning* the premise and conclusion are simply restatements of each other. People vary their wording a little so it isn't obvious, but when you look closely, the conclusion is the premise. For example, in arguments about Internet pornography you might hear someone assert, "We need to control cyberporn because it currently is unregulated."

Slippery Slope.   The concept of *slippery slope* argumentation takes its name from the notion that if you are on a slippery slope and you don't dig your heels in, you will slide and slide until you reach bottom. A slippery slope argument typically asserts that if you allow X to happen, things will spin out of control and far worse events will follow. The trick is that no inherent connection exists between X and the events that are predicted to follow. For example, in the debate about medical marijuana, opponents have argued, "If you legalize medical marijuana, the next thing you know cocaine and heroin will be legal." In the debate about cyberporn, a slippery slope argument might go, "If we don't ban cyberporn, the next thing you know, grade school children will be watching smut in their school libraries."

Weak Analogies.   An *analogy* asserts that two concepts or events are similar in some way. Hence, you can draw conclusions about event B because of its similarity to event A. Analogies are useful in thinking about complex issues, but some analogies are weak or inappropriate because the similarity between A and B is superficial, minimal, or irrelevant to the issue at hand. For example, in the debate about Internet erotica, someone might argue, "Cyberporn is morally offensive, just like child molestation. We wouldn't tolerate child molestation, so we shouldn't permit cyberporn."

False Dichotomy.   A *false dichotomy* creates an either-or choice between two outcomes: the outcome advocated and some obviously horrible outcome that any sensible person would want to avoid. These outcomes are presented as the only possible ones, when in reality many other outcomes are possible, including some that lie between the extremes depicted in the false dichotomy. In the debate about Internet pornography, someone might argue, "We can ban cyberporn, or we can hasten the moral decay of modern society."

Evaluating the Strength of Arguments

In everyday life, you frequently need to assess the strength of arguments made by friends, family, co-workers, politicians, media pundits, and so forth. You may also want to evaluate your own arguments when you write papers or speeches for school or prepare presentations for your work. The following questions can help you to make systematic evaluations of arguments (adapted from Halpern, 2003):

- What is the conclusion?
- What are the premises provided to support the conclusion? Are the premises valid?
- Does the conclusion follow from the premises? Are there any fallacies in the chain of reasoning?
- What assumptions have been made? Are they valid assumptions? Should they be stated explicitly?
- What are the counterarguments? Do they weaken the argument?
- Is there anything that has been omitted from the argument?

Table 9.1   Critical Thinking Skills Discussed in This Application

Skill	Description
Understanding the elements of an argument	The critical thinker understands that an argument consists of premises and assumptions that are used to support a conclusion.
Recognizing and avoiding common fallacies, such as irrelevant reasons, circular reasoning, slippery slope reasoning, weak analogies, and false dichotomies	The critical thinker is vigilant about conclusions based on unrelated premises, conclusions that are rewordings of premises, unwarranted predictions that things will spin out of control, superficial analogies, and contrived dichotomies.
Evaluating arguments systematically	The critical thinker carefully assesses the validity of the premises, assumptions, and conclusions in an argument, and considers counterarguments and missing elements.

REVIEW of Key Learning Goals

9.23 An argument consists of one or more premises used to provide support for a conclusion. Assumptions are premises for which no proof is offered. A conclusion may be supported by one or by many reasons.

9.24 Arguments are often marred by fallacies in reasoning, such as irrelevant reasons, weak analogies, or circular reasoning, in which the premise and conclusion are simply restatements of each other. In a slippery slope scenario, people assert that if you allow X to happen, far worse events will follow. False dichotomies create either-or choices when in reality there could be other outcomes.

Motivational Theories and Concepts

▌ Drive theories apply a homeostatic model to motivation. They assume that organisms seek to reduce unpleasant states of tension called drives. In contrast, incentive theories emphasize how external goals energize behavior.

▌ Evolutionary theorists explain motives in terms of their adaptive value. Madsen's list of biological needs and Murray's list of social needs illustrate that a diverse array of motives govern human behavior.

The Motivation of Hunger and Eating

▌ Eating is regulated by a complex interaction of biological and environmental factors. In the brain, the lateral, ventromedial, arcuate, and paraventricular areas of the hypothalamus appear to be involved in the control of hunger, but their exact role is unclear. The control of hunger may depend on neural circuits rather than anatomical centers.

▌ Fluctuations in blood glucose also seem to influence hunger. The stomach can send two types of satiety signals to the brain. Hormonal regulation of hunger depends primarily on insulin, ghrelin, CCK, and leptin secretions.

▌ Incentive-oriented models assert that eating is regulated by the palatability, quantity, and variety of available foods. Learning processes, such as classical conditioning and observational learning, exert a great deal of influence over what people eat and how much they eat. Cultural traditions also shape food preferences. Stress can stimulate eating.

Sexual Motivation and Behavior

▌ The human sexual response cycle can be divided into four stages: excitement, plateau, orgasm, and resolution. Consistent with evolutionary theory, males tend to think about and initiate sex more than females and to have more sexual partners and more interest in casual sex than females.

▌ Gender differences in mating preferences largely transcend cultural boundaries. Males emphasize potential partners' youthfulness and attractiveness, whereas females emphasize potential partners' material resources, financial prospects, and willingness to invest in children.

▌ The determinants of sexual orientation are not well understood. Recent studies suggest that there may be a genetic predisposition to homosexuality and that idiosyncrasies in prenatal hormonal secretions may contribute, but much remains to be learned. Females' sexual orientation may be characterized by greater plasticity than that of males.

Achievement: In Search of Excellence

▌ McClelland pioneered the use of the TAT to measure achievement motivation. People who are relatively high in the need for achievement work harder and more persistently than others, although they often choose to tackle challenges of intermediate difficulty. The pursuit of achievement tends to increase when both the probability of success and the incentive value of success are high.

The Elements of Emotional Experience

▌ Emotion is made up of cognitive, physiological, and behavioral components. The cognitive component involves subjective feelings that have an evaluative aspect. In the peripheral nervous system, the physiological component is dominated by autonomic arousal. In the brain, the amygdala seems to be the hub of the neural circuits that process conditioned fears, but a constellation of brain centers contribute to the experience of emotions.

▌ At the behavioral level, emotions are expressed through body language, with facial expressions being particularly prominent. Ekman and Friesen have found considerable cross-cultural agreement in the identification of emotions based on facial expressions. Cross-cultural similarities have also been found in the cognitive and physiological components of emotion. However, there are some striking cultural variations in how people categorize and display their emotions.

Theories of Emotion

▌ The James-Lange theory asserts that emotion results from one's perception of autonomic arousal. The Cannon-Bard theory counters with the proposal that emotions originate in subcortical areas of the brain.

▌ According to Schachter's two-factor theory, people infer emotion from arousal and then label it in accordance with their cognitive explanation for the arousal. Evolutionary theories of emotion maintain that emotions are innate reactions that require little cognitive interpretation.

Reflecting on the Chapter's Themes

▌ Our look at motivation and emotion showed once again that psychology is characterized by theoretical diversity, that biology and environment shape behavior interactively, that behavior is governed by multiple causes, that psychological processes are characterized by both cultural variance and invariance, and that psychology evolves in a sociohistorical context.

PERSONAL APPLICATION Exploring the Ingredients of Happiness

▌ Factors such as income, age, parenthood, intelligence, and attractiveness are largely uncorrelated with subjective well-being. Physical health, good social relationships, and religious faith appear to have a modest association with feelings of happiness. Strong predictors of happiness include love and marriage, work satisfaction, and personality, which is probably shaped by genetics.

▌ Research on happiness indicates that objective realities are not as important as subjective perceptions and that happiness is relative. Findings also suggest that people are surprisingly bad at predicting what will make them happy and that people adapt to their circumstances.

CRITICAL THINKING APPLICATION Analyzing Arguments: Making Sense out of Controversy

▌ An argument consists of one or more premises used to provide support for a conclusion. Arguments are often marred by fallacies in reasoning, such as irrelevant reasons, circular reasoning, slippery slope scenarios, weak analogies, and false dichotomies. Arguments can be evaluated more effectively by applying systematic criteria.

PsykTrek Preview

Visit Module 8a (*Hunger*) to learn more about the physiological and environmental factors that regulate your fluctuations in hunger.

Follow up with Module 8b (*Achievement Motivation*) for an in-depth analysis of the forces that shape your achievement strivings.

1. Although Jackson had a huge breakfast and felt stuffed, he ate three of the donuts that a colleague brought to a morning meeting. His behavior is consistent with:
   A. incentive theories of motivation.
   B. drive theories of motivation.
   C. evolutionary theories of motivation.
   D. the Cannon-Bard theory of motivation.

2. Results of the early studies of hypothalamic manipulations in animals implied that the lateral hypothalamus and the ventromedial nucleus of the hypothalamus may be on-off centers for the control of:
   A. emotion.
   B. hunger.
   C. thirst.
   D. sex drive.

3. Which of the following statements is false?
   A. Insulin is a hormone secreted by the pancreas.
   B. Insulin must be present for cells to utilize glucose.
   C. Leptin levels correlate with levels of the body's fat stores.
   D. Diabetics have too much insulin.

4. Which of the following has not been found in research on gender differences in sexual interest?
   A. Men think about sex more than women.
   B. Men initiate sex more frequently than women.
   C. Women are more interested in having many partners than men are.
   D. Men are more interested in uncommitted/casual sex than women.

5. Kinsey maintained that sexual orientation:
   A. depends on early classical conditioning experiences.
   B. should be viewed as a continuum.
   C. depends on normalities and abnormalities in the amygdala.
   D. should be viewed as an either-or distinction.

6. One's need for achievement is usually assessed using the:
   A. McClelland Achievement Inventory.
   B. MMPI.
   C. Thematic Apperception Test.
   D. Atkinson Manifest Needs Scale.

7. A polygraph (lie detector) works by:
   A. monitoring physiological indexes of autonomic arousal.
   B. directly assessing the truthfulness of a person's statements.
   C. monitoring the person's facial expressions.
   D. doing all of the above.

8. Which of the following statements about cross-cultural comparisons of emotional experience is true?
   A. The facial expressions associated with various emotions vary widely across cultures.
   B. Some basic emotions go unnamed in some cultures.
   C. People of different cultures categorize emotions in very similar ways.
   D. People of different cultures learn to control their emotional expressions in similar ways.

9. According to the James-Lange theory of emotion:
   A. the experience of emotion depends on autonomic arousal and on one's cognitive interpretation of that arousal.
   B. different patterns of autonomic activation lead to the experience of different emotions.
   C. emotion occurs when the thalamus sends signals simultaneously to the cortex and to the autonomic nervous system.
   D. emotions develop because of their adaptive value.

10. The fact that eating behavior, sexual behavior, and the experience of emotion all depend on interactions between biological and environmental determinants lends evidence to which of the text's organizing themes?
    A. Psychology's theoretical diversity
    B. Psychology's empiricism
    C. People's experience of the world is subjective
    D. The joint influence of heredity and environment

11. Which of the following statements is (are) true?
    A. For the most part, people are pretty happy.
    B. Age is largely unrelated to happiness.
    C. Income is largely unrelated to happiness.
    D. All of the above.

12. The sales pitch "We're the best dealership in town because the other dealerships just don't stack up against us" is an example of:
    A. a false dichotomy.   C. circular reasoning.
    B. semantic slanting.   D. slippery slope.

Answers

1 A pp. 300–301
2 B p. 302
3 D p. 304
4 C pp. 308–309
5 B pp. 311–312
6 C p. 315
7 A p. 319
8 B pp. 321–322
9 B pp. 323–324
10 D p. 326
11 D pp. 326–327
12 C p. 331

PSYKTREK PREVIEW

Using photos of faces such as these, Paul Ekman and Wallace Friesen have found that subjects can reliably identify six basic emotions based on facial cues: happiness, sadness, anger, fear, surprise, and disgust. To check your recognition of emotional expressions, drag and drop the emotions listed on the left onto the appropriate photos.

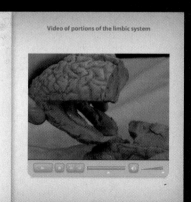

Check out Module 8c (*Elements of Emotion*) and Module 8d (*Theories of Emotion*) to see how psychologists have analyzed the nature and determinants of our emotions.

Go to the Video Selector to see classic footage of rats after hypothalamic stimulation or lesioning, or to see a closeup of the limbic system, the brain's seat of emotion.

10

Human Development Across the Life Span

Vietnam, Lao Cai Province, Sa Pa © Royalty Free/Masterfile

On July 29, 1981, 20-year-old Diana Spencer stood before more than 2,000 guests at St. Paul's Cathedral in London and fumbled through an exchange of wedding vows, nervously transposing two of her husband's middle names. Diana could hardly believe what was happening. Just a few months before, she had been a giggly teenager with a playful sign on her bedroom door that read "Chief Chick." Dubbed "Shy Di" by the hordes of photographers who followed her every move, she had never even had a boyfriend (Morton, 1998). Now she was getting married to Charles, Prince of Wales, the heir to the British throne, in a spectacular wedding ceremony that was televised around the world.

Marriage—let alone to a future king—is a major transition for most people, but for Diana it was only the beginning of an extraordinary series of changes. When Diana became engaged, she was a pretty if slightly pudgy 19-year-old who was just on the threshold of adulthood. A high school dropout, she had few serious interests or ambitions. Her most obvious talent was her rapport with young children, who adored her. Far from a fashion plate, she owned "one long dress, one silk skirt, one smart pair of shoes, and that was it" (Morton, 1998, p. 66).

Yet, like Cinderella, the "fairy tale princess" soon blossomed. "It happened before our very eyes," said one photographer, "the transformation from this shy teenager who hid beneath big hats, and hung her head, into the self-assured woman and mother, confident in her beauty" (Clayton & Craig, 2001, p. 113). The Shy Di who sometimes burst into tears at the sight of crowds became Disco Di, a slender beauty celebrated for her stylish clothes and hairstyles. Then came Dynasty Di, the doting mother of Princes William and Harry. Finally, as her marriage to Charles crumbled and she sought a new and more fulfilling role for herself, still another Diana emerged. Now she was Dedicated Di, a poised and effective spokesperson for important causes, such as the fight against AIDS and the removal of land mines from war-torn areas. No longer a frightened young princess or her husband's beautiful accessory, by her 30s Diana was a seemingly confident and independent woman who could publicly rebuke the royal family for their treatment of her and declare that she would rather be the "Queen of people's hearts" than the Queen of England (Edwards, 1999, p. 342).

Diana's transformations were startling, yet there was also a strong element of continuity in her life. As an adult, Diana continued to display qualities she had shown as a child, including her mischievous sense of humor, her love of swimming and dancing, and even her attachment to stuffed animals (S. B. Smith, 2000). Her childhood feeling of destiny ultimately blossomed into a deep sense of mission that took her to homeless shelters, clinics for lepers, and the bedsides of AIDS patients. Although cynics doubted the genuineness of her empathy for society's "outcasts," she had displayed a similar caring and naturalness as a young teenager dancing with patients in wheelchairs at a hospital for the mentally and physically handicapped (Clayton & Craig, 2001).

Other, more troubling, continuities also marked Diana's turbulent passage through life. Despite her growing mastery of her public roles, privately she remained vulnerable, moody, and insecure. Diana's parents had divorced when she was 6, and fears of abandonment never left her. As a young girl being taken to boarding school, she had begged her father, "If you love me, don't leave me here"—a plea she later echoed in tearful arguments with Prince Charles (Smith, 2000, p. 53). Her childhood feelings of intellectual inferiority continued to plague her as an adult. "A brain the size of a pea I've got," she would say (Clayton & Craig, 2001, p. 22). Throughout her marriage, she suffered bouts of bulimia (an eating disorder) and depression. While she projected a new confidence and maturity after her separation from Prince Charles, some observers felt that she was as needy and insecure as ever. A succession of relationships with men, before and after her divorce, seemed to bring her no closer to the love and security she craved. One biographer argues that in fundamental ways she had changed little, if at all (Smith, 2000). Others, however, believed that a new chapter in her life was just beginning, and that many more changes were undoubtedly in store, when Diana was tragically killed in an auto accident at the age of 36.

What does Princess Diana have to do with developmental psychology? Although her story is obviously unique in many ways, it provides an interesting illustration of the two themes that permeate the study of human development: *transition* and *continuity*. In investigating human development, psychologists study how people evolve through transitions over time. In looking at these transitions, developmental psychologists inevitably find continuity with the past. This continuity may be the most fascinating element in Diana's story. The metamorphosis of the shy, awkward teenager into an elegant, self-assured public figure was a more radical transformation than most people go through. Nonetheless, the threads of continuity connecting Diana's childhood to her adult personality were quite obvious.

Development is the sequence of age-related changes that occur as a person progresses from conception to death. It is a reasonably orderly, cumulative process that includes both the biological and behavioral changes that take place as people

The story of Princess Diana's metamorphosis from an awkward teenager into an elegant, self-assured public figure provides a dramatic demonstration of how human development is marked by both continuity and transition.

grow older. An infant's newfound ability to grasp objects, a child's gradual mastery of grammar, an adolescent's spurt in physical growth, a young adult's increasing commitment to a vocation, and an older adult's transition into the role of grandparent all represent development. These transitions are predictable changes that are related to age.

Traditionally, psychologists have been most interested in development during childhood. Our coverage reflects this emphasis. However, decades of research have clearly demonstrated that development is a lifelong process. In this chapter we divide the life span into four broad periods: (1) the prenatal period, between conception and birth, (2) childhood, (3) adolescence, and (4) adulthood. We'll examine aspects of development that are especially dynamic during each period. Let's begin by looking at events that occur before birth, during prenatal development.

Progress Before Birth: Prenatal Development

Key Learning Goals

10.1 Outline the major events of the three stages of prenatal development.

10.2 Summarize the impact of environmental factors on prenatal development.

Development begins with conception. Conception occurs when fertilization creates a *zygote,* a one-celled organism formed by the union of a sperm and an egg. All the other cells in your body developed from this single cell. Each of your cells contains enduring messages from your parents carried on the *chromosomes* that lie within its nucleus. Each chromosome houses many *genes,* the functional units in hereditary transmission. Genes carry the details of your hereditary blueprints, which are revealed gradually throughout life (see Chapter 3 for more information on genetic transmission).

The *prenatal period* extends from conception to birth, usually encompassing nine months of pregnancy. Significant development occurs before birth. In fact, development during the prenatal period is remarkably rapid. If you were an average-sized newborn and your physical growth had continued during the first year of your life at a prenatal pace, by your first birthday you would have weighed 200 pounds! Fortunately, you didn't grow at that rate—and no human does—because in the final weeks before birth the frenzied pace of prenatal development tapers off dramatically.

In this section, we'll examine the usual course of prenatal development and discuss how environmental events can leave their mark on development even before birth exposes the newborn to the outside world.

The Course of Prenatal Development
9a

The prenatal period is divided into three phases: (1) the germinal stage (the first two weeks), (2) the embryonic stage (two weeks to two months), and (3) the fetal stage (two months to birth). Some key developments in these phases are outlined here.

Germinal Stage
9a

The *germinal stage* is the first phase of prenatal development, encompassing the first two weeks after conception. This brief stage begins when a zygote is created through fertilization. Within 36 hours, rapid cell division begins, and the zygote becomes a microscopic mass of multiplying cells. This mass slowly migrates along the mother's fallopian tube to the uterine cavity. On about the seventh day,

Prenatal development is remarkably rapid. Top left: This 30-day-old embryo is just 6 millimeters in length. Bottom left: At 14 weeks, the fetus is approximately 2 inches long. Note the well-developed fingers. The fetus can already move its legs, feet, hands, and head and displays a variety of basic reflexes. Right: After 4 months of prenatal development, facial features are beginning to emerge.

the cell mass begins to implant itself in the uterine wall. This process takes about a week and is far from automatic. Many zygotes are rejected at this point. As many as one in five pregnancies end with the woman never being aware that conception has occurred (Simpson, 2002).

During the implantation process, the placenta begins to form (Buster & Carson, 2002). **The *placenta* is a structure that allows oxygen and nutrients to pass into the fetus from the mother's bloodstream and bodily wastes to pass out to the mother.** This critical exchange takes place across thin membranes that block the passage of blood cells, keeping the fetal and maternal bloodstreams separate.

Embryonic Stage 9a

The *embryonic stage* is the second stage of prenatal development, lasting from two weeks until the end of the second month. During this stage, most of the vital organs and bodily systems begin to form in the developing organism, which is now called an *embryo*. Structures such as the heart, spine, and brain emerge gradually as cell division becomes more specialized. Although the embryo is typically only about an inch long at the end of this stage, it's already beginning to look human. Arms, legs, hands, feet, fingers, toes, eyes, and ears are already discernible.

The embryonic stage is a period of great vulnerability because virtually all the basic physiological structures are being formed. If anything interferes with normal development during the embryonic phase, the effects can be devastating. Most miscarriages occur during this period (Simpson, 2002). Most major structural birth defects also result from problems that occur during the embryonic stage (Simpson & Niebyl, 2002).

Fetal Stage 9a

The *fetal stage* is the third stage of prenatal development, lasting from two months through birth. Some highlights of fetal development are summarized in **Figure 10.1**. The first two months of the fetal stage bring rapid bodily growth, as muscles and bones begin to form (Moore & Persaud, 2003). The developing organism, now called a *fetus*, becomes capable of physical movements as skeletal structures harden. Organs formed in the embryonic stage continue to grow and gradually begin to function. The sense of hearing, for example, is functional by around 20–24 weeks (Hepper, 2003).

During the final three months of the prenatal period, brain cells multiply at a brisk pace. A layer of fat is deposited under the skin to provide insulation, and the respiratory and digestive systems mature (Adolph & Berger, 2005). All of these changes ready the fetus for life outside the cozy, supportive environment of its mother's womb. Sometime between 22 weeks and 26 weeks the fetus reaches the *age of viability*—**the age at which a baby can survive in the event of a premature birth.** Thanks to advances in medical technology, the age of viability has declined in recent decades in modern societies. At 22–23 weeks the probability of survival is still pretty slim (14%–26%), but it climbs steadily over the next month to an 80%–83% survival rate at 26 weeks (Iams, 2002).

Environmental Factors and Prenatal Development

Although the fetus develops in the protective buffer of the womb, events in the external environment can affect it indirectly through the mother because the developing organism and its mother are linked

Figure 10.1
Overview of fetal development. This chart outlines some of the highlights of development during the fetal stage.

Formation of brain; differentiation of ovaries and testes

Can smile and frown; circulatory system working

Heartbeat is strong; mother feels movement

Hiccups begin; hair forms

Visual and auditory senses functional; eyes open

Body fat is added; brain specialization

Periods of sleep and wakefulness

Rapid increase in weight; gains immunity from mother

Birth

9   12   16   20   24   28   32   36   38
                                                Full term

Weeks since conception

concept check 10.1

Understanding the Stages of Prenatal Development

Check your understanding of the stages of prenatal development by filling in the blanks in the chart below. The first column contains descriptions of a main event from each of the three stages. In the second column, write the name of the stage; in the third column, write the term used to refer to the developing organism during that stage; and in the fourth column, write the time span (in terms of weeks or months) covered by the stage. The answers are in Appendix A at the back of the book.

Event	Stage	Term for organism	Time span
1. Uterine implantation			
2. Muscle and bone begin to form			
3. Vital organs and body systems begin to form			

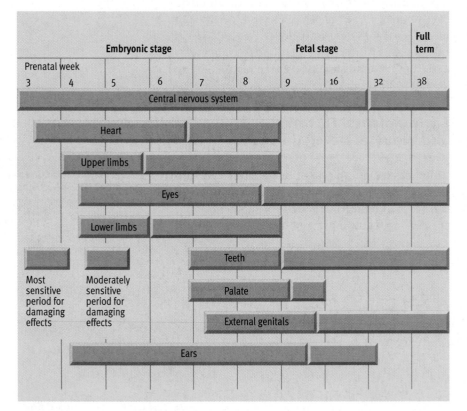

Figure 10.2

Periods of vulnerability in prenatal development. Generally, structures are most susceptible to damage when they are undergoing rapid development. The red regions of the bars indicate the most sensitive periods for various organs and structures, while the purple regions indicate periods of continued, but lessened, vulnerability. As a whole, sensitivity is greatest in the embryonic stage, but some structures remain vulnerable throughout prenatal development.

SOURCE: Adapted from Moore, K. L., & Persaud, T. V. N. (2008). *Before we are born: Essentials of embryology and birth defects.* Philadelphia: W. B. Saunders/Elsevier. Copyright © 2008 Elsevier Science (USA). All rights reserved. Reprinted by permission.

via the placenta. **Figure 10.2** shows the periods of prenatal development during which various structures are most vulnerable to damage.

Maternal nutrition is very important, as the developing fetus needs a variety of essential nutrients. Severe maternal malnutrition increases the risk of birth complications and neurological deficits for the newborn (Coutts, 2000; Fifer, Monk, & Grose-Fifer, 2001). The impact of moderate malnutrition is more difficult to gauge (Guerrini, Thomson, & Gurling, 2007). However, research suggests that moderate malnutrition can have negative effects decades after a child's birth. For example, prenatal malnutrition has been linked to vulnerability to schizophrenia and other psychiatric disorders in adolescence and early adulthood (Susser, Brown, & Matte, 1999) And low birth weight is associated with an increased risk of heart disease, diabetes, and obesity in middle adulthood (Forsen et al., 2000; Roseboom, de Rooij, & Painter, 2006).

Another major source of concern is the mother's consumption of drugs. Unfortunately, most drugs consumed by a pregnant woman can slip through the membranes of the placenta. Virtually all "recreational" drugs can be harmful, with sedatives, narcotics, cocaine, and methamphetamine being particularly dangerous (Finnegan & Kandall, 2005; Singer et al., 2002). Problems can even be caused by drugs prescribed for legitimate medical reasons and by some over-the-counter drugs (Niebyl, 2002). Tobacco use during pregnancy is also problematic. Smoking appears to increase a mother's risk for miscarriage, stillbirth, and prematurity, and newborns' risk for sudden infant death syndrome (Shea & Steiner, 2008), as well as attention deficits, hyperactivity, and conduct problems (Button, Maughan, & McGuffin, 2007).

Alcohol consumption during pregnancy also carries serious risks. It has long been clear that *heavy* drinking by a mother can be hazardous to a fetus. *Fetal alcohol syndrome* is a collection of congenital (inborn) problems associated with excessive alcohol use during pregnancy. Typical problems manifested in childhood include microcephaly (a small head), heart defects, irritability, hyperactivity, and delayed motor development (Hannigan & Armant, 2000; Pellegrino & Pellegrino, 2008). Fetal alcohol syndrome is the most common known cause of mental retardation (Niccols, 2007). Furthermore, many children fall short of the criteria for fetal alcohol syndrome but still show serious impairments attributable to their mothers' drinking during pregnancy (Willford, Leech, & Day, 2006). The best evidence on this issue comes from a long-running study begun in 1974 in Seattle, which was recently summarized by Ann Streissguth (2007). This study has followed roughly 500 offspring of mothers who engaged in varied amounts of drinking during their pregnancy. When the youngsters were 14, higher prenatal alcohol intake was found to be associated with deficits in IQ, reaction time, motor skills, attention span, and math skills, and with increased impulsive, antisocial, and delinquent behavior. At ages 21 and 25, prenatal alcohol intake was found to predict an increased incidence of alcohol problems and psychiatric disorders. Clearly, even normal drinking during pregnancy can have enduring and substantial negative effects.

The placenta screens out quite a number of infectious agents, but not all. Thus, many maternal illnesses can interfere with prenatal development. Diseases such as measles, rubella (German measles), syphilis, and chickenpox can be hazardous to the fetus (Duff, 2002). The nature of any damage depends, in part, on when the mother contracts the illness. The HIV virus that causes AIDS can also be transmitted by pregnant women to their offspring. The transmission of AIDS may occur prenatally through the placenta, during delivery, or through breastfeeding. Up through the mid-1990s, about 20%–30% of HIV-positive pregnant women passed the virus on to their babies, but improved antiretroviral drugs (given to the mother) and more cautious obstetrical care have reduced this figure to about 2%

in the United States (Cotter & Potter, 2006). Yet another risk is that a variety of genital infections, such as gonorrhea, chlamydia, and herpes, can be transmitted to newborns during delivery (Duff, 2002). These common diseases can be very dangerous.

Science has a long way to go before it uncovers all the factors that shape development before birth. For example, the effects of fluctuations in maternal emotions are not well understood. Nonetheless, it's clear that critical developments unfold quickly during the prenatal period. In the next section, you'll learn that development continues at a brisk pace during the early years of childhood.

> **REVIEW of Key Learning Goals**
>
> **10.1** Prenatal development proceeds through the germinal (first two weeks), embryonic (2 weeks to 2 months), and fetal stages (2 months to birth) as the zygote becomes differentiated into a human organism. The embryonic stage is a period of great vulnerability, as most physiological structures are being formed. The fetal stage brings rapid growth as physiological systems mature.
>
> **10.2** Maternal malnutrition during the prenatal period has been linked to birth complications and other subsequent problems. Maternal use of illicit drugs can be dangerous to the unborn child. Even normal social drinking and routine tobacco use can be hazardous during prenatal development. A variety of maternal illnesses can interfere with prenatal development.

The Wondrous Years of Childhood

A certain magic is associated with childhood. Young children have an extraordinary ability to captivate adults' attention. Legions of parents apologize repeatedly to friends and strangers alike as they talk on and on about the cute things their kids do. Most wondrous of all are the rapid and momentous developmental changes of the childhood years. Helpless infants become curious toddlers almost overnight. Before parents can catch their breath, these toddlers are schoolchildren engaged in spirited play with young friends. Then, suddenly, they're insecure adolescents, worrying about dates, part-time jobs, cars, and college. The whirlwind transitions of childhood often seem miraculous.

Of course, the transformations that occur in childhood only *seem* magical. In reality, they reflect an orderly, predictable, gradual progression. In this section you'll see what psychologists have learned about this progression. We'll examine various aspects of development that are especially dynamic during childhood. Let's begin by looking at motor development.

Exploring the World: Motor Development

Motor development refers to the progression of muscular coordination required for physical activities. Basic motor skills include grasping and reaching for objects, manipulating objects, sitting up, crawling, walking, running, and so forth.

Basic Principles

A number of principles are apparent in motor development (Adolph & Berger, 2005). One is the *cephalocaudal trend*—the head-to-foot direction of motor development. Children tend to gain control over the upper part of their bodies before the lower

Key Learning Goals

10.3 Understand general principles and cultural variations in motor development.

10.4 Describe Harlow's and Bowlby's views on attachment and research on patterns of attachment.

10.5 Trace the development of human language during childhood.

10.6 Describe the basic tenets of Erikson's theory and his stages of childhood personality development.

10.7 Outline Piaget's stages of cognitive development, and discuss criticism of Piaget's theory.

10.8 Describe Vygotsky's sociocultural theory, and evaluate the notion that some cognitive abilities may be innate.

10.9 Outline Kohlberg's stages of moral development, and discuss criticism of Kohlberg's theory.

part. You've seen this trend in action if you've seen an infant learn to crawl. Infants gradually shift from using their arms for propelling themselves to using their legs. The *proximodistal trend* is the center-outward direction of motor development. Children gain control over their torso before their extremities. Thus, infants initially reach for things by twisting their entire body, but gradually they learn to extend just their arms.

Early progress in motor skills has traditionally been attributed almost entirely to the process of maturation. *Maturation* **is development that reflects the gradual unfolding of one's genetic blueprint.** It is a product of genetically programmed physical changes that come with age—as opposed to experience and learning. However, research that has taken a closer look at the *process* of motor development suggests that infants are active agents rather than passive organisms waiting for their brain and limbs to mature (Thelen, 1995). According to this view, the driving force behind motor development is infants' ongoing exploration of their world and their need to master specific tasks (such as grasping a larger toy or looking out a window). Progress in motor development is attributed to infants' experimentation and their learning and remembering the consequences of their activities. Although modern researchers acknowledge that maturation facilitates motor development, they argue that its contribution has been overestimated (Bertenthal & Clifton, 1998).

Understanding Developmental Norms

Parents often pay close attention to early motor development, comparing their child's progress with developmental norms. *Developmental norms* **indicate the typical (median) age at which individuals display various behaviors and abilities.** Developmental norms are useful benchmarks as long as parents don't expect their children to progress exactly at the pace specified in the norms. Some parents get unnecessarily alarmed when their children fall behind developmental norms. What these parents overlook is that developmental norms are group *averages*. Variations from the average are entirely normal. This normal variation stands out in **Figure 10.3**, which indicates the age at which 25%, 50%, and 90% of youngsters can demonstrate various motor skills. As **Figure 10.3** shows, a substantial portion of children don't achieve a particular milestone until long after the average time cited in norms.

Cultural Variations and Their Significance

Cross-cultural research has highlighted the dynamic interplay between experience and maturation in motor development. Relatively rapid motor development has been observed in some cultures that provide special practice in basic motor skills. For example, soon after birth the Kipsigis people of Kenya begin active efforts to train their infants to sit up, stand, and walk. Thanks to this training, Kipsigis children achieve these developmental milestones

Figure 10.3

Milestones in motor development. The left edge, interior mark, and right edge of each bar indicate the age at which 25%, 50%, and 90% of infants have mastered each motor skill shown. Developmental norms typically report only the median age of mastery (the interior mark), which can be misleading in light of the variability in age of mastery apparent in this chart.

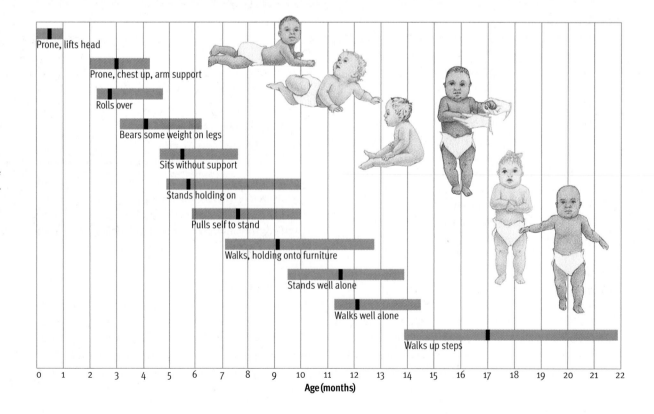

Prone, lifts head
Prone, chest up, arm support
Rolls over
Bears some weight on legs
Sits without support
Stands holding on
Pulls self to stand
Walks, holding onto furniture
Stands well alone
Walks well alone
Walks up steps

Age (months)
0 1 2 3 4 5 6 7 8 9 10 11 12 13 14 15 16 17 18 19 20 21 22

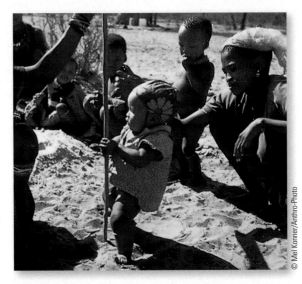

Tribes across the world use a variety of methods to foster rapid development of motor abilities in their children. The Kung San of the Kalahari, Botswana, teach their young to dance quite early, using poles to develop the kinesthetic sense of balance.

(but not others) about a month earlier than babies in the United States (Super, 1976). In contrast, relatively slow motor development has been found in some cultures that discourage motor exploration. For example, among the Ache, a nomadic people living in the rain forests of Paraguay, safety concerns dictate that children under age 3 rarely venture more than 3 feet from their mothers, who carry them virtually everywhere. As a result of these constraints, Ache children are delayed in acquiring a variety of motor skills and typically begin walking about a year later than other children (Kaplan & Dove, 1987). Cultural variations in the emergence of basic motor skills demonstrate that environmental factors can accelerate or slow early motor development.

Early Emotional Development: Attachment   9e

Attachment refers to the close emotional bonds of affection that develop between infants and their caregivers. Researchers have shown a keen interest in how infant-mother attachments are formed early in life. Children eventually form attachments to many people, including their fathers, siblings, grandparents, and others (Cassidy, 1999). However, a child's first important attachment usually occurs with his or her mother because she is typically the principal caregiver in the early months of life (Lamb et al., 1999).

Contrary to popular belief, infants' attachment to their mothers is *not* instantaneous. Initially, babies show relatively little in the way of a special preference for their mother. At 2–3 months of age, infants may smile and laugh more when they interact with their mother, but they can be handed over to strangers such as babysitters with relatively little difficulty. This situation gradually changes, and by about 6–8 months of age, infants begin to show a pronounced preference for their mother's company and often protest when separated from her (Lamb, Ketterlinus, & Fracasso, 1992). This is the first manifestation of *separation anxiety*—emotional distress seen in many infants when they are separated from people with whom they have formed an attachment. Separation anxiety, which may occur with other familiar caregivers as well as the mother, typically peaks at around 14–18 months and then begins to decline.

Theories of Attachment   9e

Why do children gradually develop a special attachment to their mothers? This question sounds simple enough, but it has been the subject of a lively theoretical dialogue. Behaviorists have argued that the infant-mother attachment develops because mothers are associated with the powerful, reinforcing event of being fed. Thus, the mother becomes a conditioned reinforcer. However, this reinforcement theory of attachment came into question as a result of Harry Harlow's famous studies of attachment in infant rhesus monkeys (Harlow, 1958, 1959).

Harlow removed monkeys from their mothers at birth and raised them in the laboratory with two types of artificial "substitute mothers." One type of artificial mother was made of terrycloth and could provide "contact comfort" (see the photo below). The

Harry Harlow

"The little we know about love does not transcend simple observation, and the little we write about it has been written better by poets and novelists."

Even if fed by a wire surrogate mother, the Harlows' infant monkeys cuddled up with a terrycloth surrogate that provided contact comfort. When threatened by a frightening toy, the monkeys sought security from their terrycloth mothers.

John Bowlby

"The only relevant criterion by which to consider the natural adaptedness of any particular part of present-day man's behavioural equipment is the degree to which and the way in which it might contribute to population survival in man's primeval environment."

other type was made of wire. Half of the monkeys were fed from a bottle attached to a wire mother and the other half were fed by a cloth mother. The young monkeys' attachment to their substitute mothers was tested by introducing a frightening stimulus, such as a strange toy. If reinforcement through feeding were the key to attachment, the frightened monkeys should have scampered off to the mother that had fed them. This was not the case. The young monkeys scrambled for their cloth mothers, even if they were *not* fed by them.

Harlow's work made a simple reinforcement explanation of attachment unrealistic for animals, let alone for more complex human beings. Attention then turned to an alternative explanation of attachment proposed by John Bowlby (1969, 1973, 1980). Bowlby was impressed by the importance of contact comfort to Harlow's monkeys and by the apparently unlearned nature of this preference. Influenced by evolutionary theories, Bowlby argued that there must be a biological basis for attachment. According to his view, infants are biologically programmed to emit behavior (smiling, cooing, clinging, and so on) that triggers an affectionate, protective response from adults. Bowlby also asserted that adults are programmed by evolutionary forces to be captivated by this behavior and to respond with warmth, love, and protection. Obviously, these characteristics would be adaptive in terms of promoting children's survival. Bowlby's theory has guided most of the research on attachment over the last several decades, including Mary Ainsworth's influential work on patterns of attachment.

Patterns of Attachment

Infant-mother attachments vary in quality. Mary Ainsworth and her colleagues (1978) found that these attachments fall into three categories. Fortunately, most infants develop a *secure attachment*. They play and explore comfortably with their mother present, become visibly upset when she leaves, and are quickly calmed by her return. However, some children display a pattern called *anxious-ambivalent attachment* (also called *resistant attachment*). They appear anxious even when their mothers are near and protest excessively when she leaves, but they are not particularly comforted when she returns. Children in the third category seek little contact with their mothers and often are not distressed when she leaves, a condition labeled *avoidant attachment*.

Maternal behaviors appear to have considerable influence over the type of attachment that emerges between an infant and mother (Ainsworth et al., 1978; Posada et al., 2007). Mothers who are sensitive

and responsive to their children's needs are more likely to promote secure attachments than mothers who are relatively insensitive or inconsistent in their responding (Nievar & Becker, 2008; van den Boom, 2001). However, infants are not passive bystanders as this process unfolds. They are active participants who influence the process with their crying, smiling, fussing, and babbling. Difficult infants who spit up most of their food, make bathing a major battle, and rarely smile may sometimes slow the process of attachment (van IJzendoorn & Bakermans-Kranenburg, 2004). Thus, the type of attachment that emerges between an infant and mother may depend on the nature of the infant's temperament as well as the mother's sensitivity (Kagan & Fox, 2006).

How stable are the various patterns of attachment over time? The results of research on attachment stability vary considerably, depending on the way attachment is measured, the nature of the sample, and the time interval examined (Thompson, 1998, 2000). Overall, attachment types tend to be moderately stable through childhood and into adulthood (Ammaniti, Speranza, & Fedele, 2005; Fraley, 2002). When changes in attachment type are seen, they often reflect changed circumstances in youngsters' lives, such as increases in family stress or alterations in parental support.

Evidence suggests that the quality of the attachment relationship can have important consequences for children's subsequent development. Based on their attachment experiences, children develop *internal working models* of the dynamics of close relationships, that influence their future interactions with a wide range of people (Bretherton & Munholland, 1999). Infants with a relatively secure attachment *tend* to become resilient, sociable, competent toddlers with high self-esteem (Ranson & Urichuk, 2006; Thompson, 1999). In their preschool years, they display more persistence, curiosity, self-reliance, and leadership and have better peer relations (Weinfield et al., 1999), while experiencing fewer negative emotions and more positive emotions (Kochanska, 2001). In middle childhood, those who had secure attachments in infancy exhibit higher levels of positive moods, healthier strategies for coping with stress, and better regulation of their emotions (Kerns et al., 2007). Studies have also found a relationship between secure attachment and more advanced cognitive development during childhood and adolescence (Ranson & Urichuk, 2006). However, it is worth noting that all the relevant data on attachment effects are correlational (experimenters cannot manipulate caregiver-infant attachments), so we cannot assume that secure attachment *causes* all these favorable outcomes. Secure attachment could co-vary with other

Mary Salter Ainsworth

"Where familial security is lacking, the individual is handicapped by the lack of what might be called a secure base from which to work."

important factors that contribute to high self-esteem, self-reliance, and so forth.

Culture and Attachment

9e

Separation anxiety emerges in children at about 6–8 months and peaks at about 14–18 months in cultures around the world (Grossmann & Grossmann, 1990). These findings, which have been replicated in quite a variety of non-Western cultures, suggest that attachment is a universal feature of human development. However, studies have found some modest cultural variations in the proportion of infants who fall into the three attachment categories described by Ainsworth. Working mostly with white, middle-class subjects in the United States, researchers have found that 67% of infants display a secure attachment, 21% an avoidant attachment, and 12% an anxious-ambivalent attachment (van IJzendoorn & Sagi, 1999). Interestingly, studies in Japan and Germany have yielded somewhat different estimates of the prevalence of various types of attachment, as shown in **Figure 10.4**. That said, the differences are small, and secure attachment appears to be the predominant type of attachment around the world.

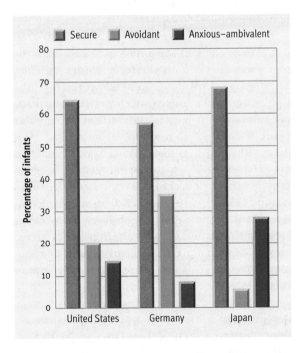

Figure 10.4
Cultural variations in attachment patterns. This graph shows the prevalence of secure, avoidant, and anxious-ambivalent attachment patterns found in specific studies in Germany, Japan, and the United States. As you can see, secure attachment is the most common pattern in all three societies, as it is around the world. However, there are some modest cultural differences in the prevalence of each pattern of attachment, which are probably attributable to cultural variations in childrearing practices. (Data from van IJzendoorn & Kroonenberg, 1988)

Learning to Communicate: Language Development

The early course of language development is similar across very different cultures (Gleitman & Newport, 1996; Slobin, 1992), and language development tends to unfold at roughly the same pace for most children, even though children obviously are reared in diverse home environments. These findings suggest that language development is determined by biological maturation more than personal experience.

Moving Toward Producing Words

Long before infants utter their first words, they are making progress in learning the sound structure of their native language. By 7.5 months, infants begin to recognize common word forms (Houston, Santelmann, & Jusczyk, 2004), and by 8 months many infants show the first signs of understanding the meanings of familiar words (Bates, Devescovi, & Wulfeck, 2001). During the first six months of life, a baby's vocalizations are dominated by crying, cooing, and laughter, which have limited value as a means of communication. Soon, infants are *babbling*. Their babbling gradually becomes more complex and increasingly resembles the language spoken by parents and others in the child's environment (Hoff, 2005). These trends probably reflect ongoing neural development and the maturation of the infant's vocal apparatus (Sachs, 1985), as well as the impact of experience (Kuhl & Meltzoff, 1997).

At around 10 to 13 months of age, most children begin to utter sounds that correspond to words. Most infants' first words are similar in phonetic form and meaning—even in different languages (Waxman, 2002). The initial words resemble the syllables that infants most often babble spontaneously. For example, words such as *dada, mama,* and *papa* are names for parents in many languages because they consist of sounds that are easy to produce.

Using Words

After children utter their first words, their vocabulary grows slowly for the next few months (Dapretto & Bjork, 2000). Toddlers typically can say between 3 and 50 words by 18 months. However, their *receptive vocabulary* is larger than their *productive vocabulary*. That is, they can comprehend more words spoken by others than they can actually produce to express themselves (Dan & Gleason, 2001). Thus, toddlers can *understand* 50 words months before they can *say* 50 words. Children generally acquire nouns before verbs because the meanings of nouns, which often refer to distinct, concrete objects, tend to be easier to encode than the meanings of verbs, which often

web link 10.2

Early Childhood Care and Development

This site's subtitle, International Resources for Early Childhood Development, emphasizes the focus of resources provided: the worldwide (not just North American) challenge of caring for children from birth through age 6 and fulfilling the needs of their families.

refer to more abstract relationships (Poulin-Dubois & Graham, 2007). However, this generalization may not apply to all languages (Bates et al., 2001).

Youngsters' vocabularies soon begin to grow at a dizzying pace, as a *vocabulary spurt* often begins at around 18 months as toddlers realize that everything has a name (Camaioni, 2001; see **Figure 10.5**). By the first grade, the average child has a vocabulary of approximately 10,000 words, which builds to an astonishing 40,000 words by the fifth grade (Anglin, 1993). In building these impressive vocabularies, some 2-year-olds learn as many as 20 new words every week. *Fast mapping* appears to be one factor underlying this rapid growth of vocabulary (Gershkoff-Stowe & Hahn, 2007; Markman, Wasow, & Hansen, 2003). *Fast mapping* **is the process by which children map a word onto an underlying concept after only one exposure.** Thus, children often add words like *tank, board,* and *tape* to their vocabularies after their first encounter with objects that illustrate these concepts.

Of course, these efforts to learn new words are not flawless. Toddlers often make errors, such as overextensions and underextensions (Harley, 2008). An *overextension* **occurs when a child incorrectly uses a word to describe a wider set of objects or actions than it is meant to.** For example, a child might use the word *ball* for anything round—oranges, apples, even the moon. Overextensions usually appear in children's speech between ages 1 and 2½. Specific overextensions typically last up to several months. Toddlers also tend to be guilty of *underextensions,* **which occur when a child incorrectly uses a word to describe a narrower set of objects or actions than it is meant to.** For example, a child might use the word *doll* to refer only to a single, favorite doll. Overextensions and underextensions show that toddlers are actively trying to learn the rules of language—albeit with mixed success.

Combining Words

Children typically begin to combine words into sentences near the end of their second year. Early sentences are characterized as "telegraphic" because they resemble old-fashioned telegrams, which omitted nonessential words because senders were charged by the word (Bochner & Jones, 2003). *Telegraphic speech* **consists mainly of content words; articles, prepositions, and other less critical words are omitted.** Thus, a child might say, "Give doll" rather than "Please give me the doll." Although not unique to the English language, telegraphic speech is not cross-culturally universal, as once thought (de Villiers & de Villiers, 1999).

By the end of their third year, most children can express complex ideas such as the plural or the past tense. However, their efforts to learn the rules of language continue to generate revealing mistakes. *Overregularizations* **occur when grammatical rules are incorrectly generalized to irregular cases where they do not apply.** For example, children will say things like "The girl goed home" or "I hitted the ball." Cross-cultural research suggests that these overregularizations occur in all languages (Slobin, 1985). Most theorists believe that overregularizations demonstrate that children are working actively to master the *rules* of language (Marcus, 1996). Children don't learn the fine points of grammar and usage in a single leap but gradually acquire them in small steps.

Youngsters make their largest strides in language development in their first 4 to 5 years. However, they continue to refine their language skills during their school-age years. They generate longer and more complicated sentences as they receive formal training in written language.

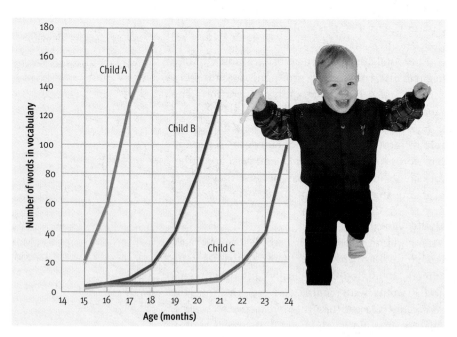

Figure 10.5

The vocabulary spurt. Children typically acquire their first 10–15 words very slowly, but they soon go through a *vocabulary spurt*—a period during which they rapidly acquire many new words. The vocabulary spurt usually begins at around 18 months, but children vary, as these graphs of three toddlers' vocabulary growth show.

SOURCE: Adapted from Goldfield, B. A., & Resnick, J. S. (1990). Early lexical acquisition: Rate, content, and the vocabulary spurt. *Journal of Child Language, 17,* 171–183. Copyright © 1990 by Cambridge University Press. Adapted by permission. Photo: Courtesy of Wayne Weiten

Becoming Unique: Personality Development

9b

How do individuals develop their unique sets of personality traits over time? Many theories have addressed this question. The first major theory of personality development was put together by Sigmund Freud back around the turn of the 20th century. As we'll discuss in Chapter 11, he claimed that the basic foundation of an individual's personality is firmly laid down by age 5. Half a century later, Erik Erikson (1963) proposed a sweeping revision of Freud's theory that has proven influential. Like Freud, Erikson concluded that events in early childhood leave a permanent stamp on adult personality. However, unlike Freud, Erikson theorized that personality continues to evolve over the entire life span.

Building on Freud's earlier work, Erikson devised a stage theory of personality development. As you'll see in this chapter, many theories describe development in terms of stages. A *stage* is a developmental period during which characteristic patterns of behavior are exhibited and certain capacities become established. Stage theories assume that (1) individuals must progress through specified stages in a particular order because each stage builds on the previous stage, (2) progress through these stages is strongly related to age, and (3) development is marked by major discontinuities that usher in dramatic transitions in behavior (see **Figure 10.6**).

Erikson's Stage Theory

9b

Erikson partitioned the life span into eight stages, each characterized by a *psychosocial crisis* involving transitions in important social relationships. According to Erikson, personality is shaped by how individuals deal with these psychosocial crises. Each crisis is a potential turning point that can yield different outcomes. Erikson described the stages in terms of these alternative outcomes, which represent personality traits that people display over the

Figure 10.6

Stage theories of development. Some theories view development as a relatively continuous process, albeit not as smooth and perfectly linear as shown on the left. In contrast, stage theories assume that development is marked by major discontinuities, as shown on the right, that bring fundamental, qualitative changes in capabilities or characteristic behavior.

remainder of their lives. All eight stages in Erikson's theory are charted in **Figure 10.7**. We describe the first four childhood stages here and discuss the remaining stages in the upcoming sections on adolescence and adulthood.

Trust Versus Mistrust. Erikson's first stage encompasses the first year of life, when an infant has to depend completely on adults to take care of its basic needs for such necessities as food, a warm blanket, and changed diapers. If an infant's basic biological needs are adequately met by its caregivers and sound attachments are formed, the child should develop an optimistic, trusting attitude toward the world. However, if the infant's basic needs are taken care of poorly, a more distrusting, insecure personality may result.

Autonomy Versus Shame and Doubt. Erikson's second stage unfolds during the second and third

Erik Erikson

"Human personality in principle develops according to steps predetermined in the growing person's readiness to be driven toward, to be aware of, and to interact with a widening social radius."

Figure 10.7

Erikson's stage theory. Erikson's theory of personality development asserts that people evolve through eight stages over the life span. Each stage is marked by a *psychosocial crisis* that involves confronting a fundamental question, such as "Who am I and where am I going?" The stages are described in terms of alternative traits that are potential outcomes from the crises. Development is enhanced when a crisis is resolved in favor of the healthier alternative (which is listed first for each stage).

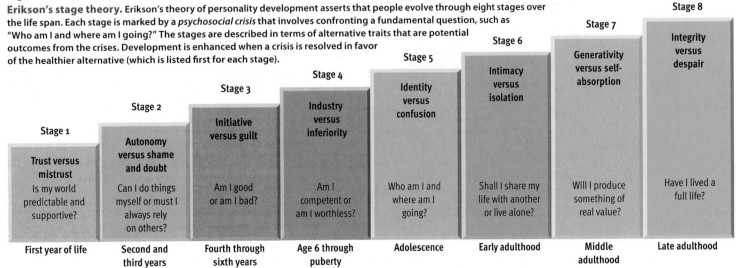

years of life, when parents begin toilet training and other efforts to regulate the child. The child must begin to take some personal responsibility for feeding, dressing, and bathing. If all goes well, he or she acquires a sense of self-sufficiency. But if parents are never satisfied with the child's efforts and if parent-child conflicts are constant, the child may develop a sense of personal shame and self-doubt.

Initiative Versus Guilt. In Erikson's third stage, roughly from ages 3 to 6, the challenge facing children is to function socially within their families. If children think only of their own needs and desires, family members may begin to instill feelings of guilt, and self-esteem may suffer. But if children learn to get along well with siblings and parents, a sense of self-confidence should begin to grow.

Industry Versus Inferiority. In the fourth stage (age 6 through puberty), the challenge of learning to function socially is extended beyond the family to the broader social realm of the neighborhood and school. Children who are able to function effectively in this less nurturant social sphere where productivity is highly valued should develop a sense of competence.

Evaluating Erikson's Theory

The strength of Erikson's theory is that it accounts for both continuity and transition in personality development. It accounts for transition by showing how new challenges in social relations stimulate personality development throughout life. It accounts for continuity by drawing connections between early childhood experiences and aspects of adult personality. One measure of a theory's value is how much research it generates, and Erikson's theory continues to guide a fair amount of research (Thomas, 2005).

On the negative side of the ledger, Erikson's theory provides an "idealized" description of "typical" developmental patterns. Thus, it's not well suited for explaining the enormous personality differences that exist among people. Inadequate explanation of individual differences is a common problem with stage theories of development. This shortcoming surfaces again in the next section, where we'll examine Jean Piaget's stage theory of cognitive development.

The Growth of Thought: Cognitive Development 9c

Cognitive development refers to transitions in youngsters' patterns of thinking, including reasoning, remembering, and problem solving. The

investigation of cognitive development has been dominated by the theory of Jean Piaget (Kessen, 1996). Much of our discussion of cognitive development is devoted to Piaget's theory and the research it generated, although we'll also delve into other approaches to cognitive development.

Overview of Piaget's Stage Theory 9c

Jean Piaget (1929, 1952, 1983) was a Swiss scholar whose own cognitive development was exceptionally rapid. In his early 20s, after he had earned a doctorate in natural science and published a novel, Piaget turned his focus to psychology. He met Theodore Simon, who had collaborated with Alfred Binet in devising the first useful intelligence tests. Working in Simon's Paris laboratory, Piaget administered intelligence tests to many children to develop better test norms. In doing this testing, Piaget was intrigued by the reasoning underlying the children's *wrong* answers. He decided that measuring children's intelligence was less interesting than studying how children *use* their intelligence. In 1921 he moved to Geneva, where he spent the remainder of his life studying cognitive development. Many of his ideas were based on insights gleaned from careful observations of his own three children during their infancy.

Noting that children actively explore the world around them, Piaget asserted that interaction with the environment and maturation gradually alter the way children think. Like Erikson's theory, Piaget's model is a *stage theory* of development. Piaget proposed that children's thought processes go through a series of four major stages: (1) the *sensorimotor period* (birth to age 2), (2) the *preoperational period* (ages 2 to 7), (3) the *concrete operational period* (ages 7 to 11), and (4) the *formal operational period* (age 11 onward). **Figure 10.8** provides an overview of each of these periods. Piaget regarded his age norms as approximations and acknowledged that transitional ages may vary from one child to another.

Sensorimotor Period. One of Piaget's foremost contributions was to greatly enhance our understanding of mental development in the earliest months of life. The first stage in his theory is the *sensorimotor period,* which lasts from birth to about age 2. Piaget called this stage *sensorimotor* because infants are developing the ability to coordinate their sensory input with their motor actions.

The major development during the sensorimotor stage is the gradual appearance of symbolic thought. At the beginning of this stage, a child's behavior is dominated by innate reflexes; infants aren't "thinking" as much as they are simply responding to stimuli.

But by the end of the stage, the child can use mental symbols to represent objects (for example, a mental image of a favorite toy). The key to this transition is the acquisition of the concept of object permanence.

Object permanence develops when a child recognizes that objects continue to exist even when they are no longer visible. Although you surely take the permanence of objects for granted, infants aren't aware of this permanence at first. If you show a 4-month-old child an eye-catching toy and then cover the toy with a pillow, the child will not attempt to search for the toy. Piaget inferred from this observation that the child does not understand that the toy continues to exist under the pillow. The notion of object permanence does not dawn on children overnight. The first signs of this insight usually appear between 4 and 8 months of age, when children will often pursue an object that is *partially* covered in their presence. Progress is gradual, and Piaget believed that children typically don't master the concept of object permanence until they're about 18 months old.

Preoperational Period. During the *preoperational period,* which extends roughly from age 2 to age 7, children gradually improve in their use of mental images. Although progress in symbolic thought continues, Piaget emphasized the *shortcomings* in preoperational thought.

Consider a simple problem that Piaget presented to youngsters. He would take two identical beakers and fill each with the same amount of water. After a child had agreed that the two beakers contained the same amount of water, he would pour the water from one of the beakers into a much taller and thinner beaker (see **Figure 10.9**). He would then ask the child whether the two differently shaped beakers still contained the same amount of water. Confronted with a problem like this, children in the preoperational period generally said "no." They typically focused on the higher water line in the taller beaker and insisted that there was more water in the slender beaker. They had not yet mastered the principle of conservation. *Conservation* is Piaget's term for the awareness that physical quantities remain constant in spite of changes in their shape or appearance.

Why are preoperational children unable to solve conservation problems? According to Piaget, their inability to understand conservation is the result of some basic flaws in preoperational thinking. These flaws include centration, irreversibility, and egocentrism.

Centration is the tendency to focus on just one feature of a problem, neglecting other important aspects. When working on the conservation problem with water, preoperational children tend to con-

centrate on the height of the water while ignoring the width. They have difficulty focusing on several aspects of a problem at once.

Irreversibility is the inability to envision reversing an action. Preoperational children can't mentally "undo" something. For instance, in grappling with the conservation of water, they don't think about what would happen if the water were poured back from the tall beaker into the original beaker.

Egocentrism in thinking is characterized by a limited ability to share another person's viewpoint. Indeed, Piaget felt that preoperational children fail to

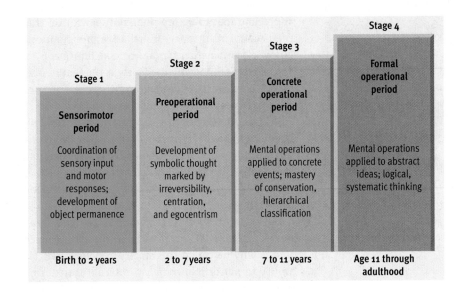

Figure 10.8
Piaget's stage theory. Piaget's theory of cognitive development identifies four stages marked by fundamentally different modes of thinking through which youngsters evolve. The approximate age norms and some key characteristics of thought at each stage are summarized here.

Figure 10.9
Piaget's conservation task. After watching the transformation shown, a preoperational child will usually answer that the taller beaker contains more water. In contrast, the child in the concrete operations period tends to respond correctly, recognizing that the amount of water in beaker C remains the same as the amount in beaker A.

Jean Piaget

"It is virtually impossible to draw a clear line between innate and acquired behavior patterns."

appreciate that there are points of view other than their own. For instance, if you ask a preoperational girl whether her sister has a sister, she'll probably say "no" if they are the only two girls in the family. She's unable to view sisterhood from her sister's perspective (this example also shows irreversibility).

A notable feature of egocentrism is *animism*— **the belief that all things are living,** just like oneself. Thus, youngsters attribute lifelike, human qualities to inanimate objects, asking questions such as, "When does the ocean stop to rest?" or "Why does the wind get so mad?"

As you can see, Piaget emphasized the weaknesses apparent in preoperational thought. Indeed, that is why he called this stage *pre*operational. The ability to perform *operations*—internal transformations, manipulations, and reorganizations of mental structures—emerges in the next stage.

Concrete Operational Period. The development of mental operations marks the beginning of the *concrete operational period,* which usually lasts from about age 7 to age 11. Piaget called this stage *concrete* operations because children can perform operations only on images of tangible objects and actual events.

Among the operations that children master during this stage are reversibility and decentration. *Reversibility* permits a child to mentally undo an action. *Decentration* allows the child to focus on more than one feature of a problem simultaneously. The newfound ability to coordinate several aspects of a problem helps the child appreciate that there are several ways to look at things. This ability in turn leads to a *decline in egocentrism and gradual mastery of conservation* as it applies to liquid, mass, number, volume, area, and length.

As children master concrete operations, they develop a variety of new problem-solving capacities. Let's examine another problem studied by Piaget. Give a preoperational child seven carnations and three daisies. Tell the child the names for the two types of flowers and ask the child to sort them into carnations and daisies. That should be no problem. Now ask the child whether there are more carnations or more daisies. Most children will correctly respond that there are more carnations. Now ask the child whether there are more carnations or more flowers. At this point, most preoperational children will stumble and respond incorrectly that there are more carnations than flowers. Generally, preoperational children can't handle *hierarchical classification* problems that require them to focus simultaneously on two levels of classification. However, the child who has advanced to the concrete operational stage

is not as limited by centration and can work successfully with hierarchical classification problems.

Formal Operational Period. The final stage in Piaget's theory is the *formal operational period,* which typically begins at around 11 years of age. In this stage, children begin to apply their operations to *abstract* concepts in addition to concrete objects. Indeed, during this stage, youngsters come to *enjoy* the contemplation of abstract concepts. Many adolescents spend hours mulling over hypothetical possibilities related to abstractions such as justice, love, and free will.

According to Piaget, youngsters graduate to relatively adult modes of thinking in the formal operations stage. He did *not* mean to suggest that no further cognitive development occurs once children reach this stage. However, he believed that after children achieve formal operations, further developments in thinking are changes in *degree* rather than fundamental changes in the *nature* of thinking.

Adolescents in the formal operational period become more *systematic* in their problem-solving efforts. Children in earlier developmental stages tend to attack problems quickly, with a trial-and-error approach. In contrast, children who have achieved formal operations are more likely to think things through. They envision possible courses of action and try to use logic to reason out the likely consequences of each possible solution before they act. Thus, thought processes in the formal operational period can be characterized as increasingly abstract, systematic, logical, and reflective.

Evaluating Piaget's Theory

Jean Piaget made a landmark contribution to psychology's understanding of children in general and their cognitive development in particular (Beilin, 1992). He founded the field of cognitive development and fostered a new view of children that saw them as active agents constructing their own worlds (Fischer & Hencke, 1996). Above all else, he sought answers to new questions. As he acknowledged in a 1970 interview, "It's just that no adult ever had the idea of asking children about conservation. It was so obvious that if you change the shape of an object, the quantity will be conserved. Why ask a child? The novelty lay in asking the question" (Hall, 1987, p. 56). Piaget's theory guided an enormous volume of productive research that continues through today (Brainerd, 1996; Feldman, 2003). This research has supported many of Piaget's central propositions (Flavell, 1996). In such a far-reaching theory, however, there are bound to be some weak spots. Here are some criticisms of Piaget's theory:

1. In many areas, Piaget appears to have underestimated young children's cognitive development (Birney et al., 2005). For example, researchers have found evidence that children begin to develop object permanence much earlier than Piaget thought, perhaps as early as 3 to 4 months of age (Baillargeon, 2002; Wang, Baillargeon, & Paterson, 2005). Others have marshaled evidence that preoperational children exhibit less egocentrism than Piaget believed (Newcombe & Huttenlocher, 1992).

2. Piaget's model suffers from problems that plague most stage theories. Like Erikson, Piaget had little to say about the variability among children in development (Siegler, 1994). Also, individuals often simultaneously display patterns of thinking that are characteristic of several stages. This "mixing" of stages calls into question the value of organizing development in terms of stages (Bjorklund, 2005; Courage & Howe, 2002).

3. Piaget believed that his theory described universal processes that should lead children everywhere to progress through uniform stages of thinking at roughly the same ages. Subsequent research has shown that the *sequence* of stages is largely invariant, but the *timetable* that children follow in passing through these stages varies considerably across cultures (Dasen, 1994; Rogoff, 2003). Thus, Piaget underestimated the influence of cultural factors on cognitive development. Indeed, it is probably fair to say that Piaget underestimated the importance of environmental factors in general while focusing too heavily on the role of maturation (Birney et al., 2005; Maratsos, 2007).

Vygotsky's Sociocultural Theory

In recent decades, as the limitations and weaknesses of Piaget's ideas have become more apparent, some developmental researchers have looked elsewhere for theoretical guidance. Ironically, the theory that has recently inspired the greatest interest—Lev Vygotsky's *sociocultural theory*—dates back to around the same time that Piaget began formulating his theory (1920s–1930s). Vygotsky was a prominent Russian psychologist whose research ended prematurely in 1934 when he died of tuberculosis at the age of 37. Western scientists had little exposure to his ideas until the 1960s, and it was only in 1986 that a complete version of his principal book (Vygotsky, 1934) was published in English. Working in a perilous political climate in the post-Revolution Soviet Union, Vygotsky had to devise a theory that would not be incompatible with the Marxist social philosophy that ruled communist thinking (Thomas, 2005). Given the constraints placed on his theorizing, one

concept check 10.2

Recognizing Piaget's Stages

Check your understanding of Piaget's theory by indicating the stage of cognitive development illustrated by each of the examples below. For each scenario, fill in the letter for the appropriate stage in the space on the left. The answers are in Appendix A.

    a. Sensorimotor period   **c.** Concrete operational period

    b. Preoperational period   **d.** Formal operational period

_____ **1.** Upon seeing a glass lying on its side, Sammy says, "Look, the glass is tired. It's taking a nap."

_____ **2.** Maria is told that a farmer has nine cows and six horses. The teacher asks, "Does the farmer have more cows or more animals?" Maria answers, "More animals."

_____ **3.** Alice is playing in the living room with a small red ball. The ball rolls under the sofa. She stares for a moment at the place where the ball vanished and then turns her attention to a toy truck sitting in front of her.

might expect that 70 years later his ideas would not resonate with contemporary psychologists in capitalist societies, but the reality is just the opposite, as his theory has become quite influential (Daniels, 2005; Feldman, 2003).

Vygotsky's and Piaget's perspectives on cognitive development have much in common, but they also differ in several important respects (DeVries, 2000; Matusov & Hayes, 2000; Rowe & Wertsch, 2002). First, in Piaget's theory, cognitive development is primarily fueled by the individual child's active exploration of the world around him or her. The child is viewed as the agent of change. In contrast, Vygotsky places enormous emphasis on how children's cognitive development is fueled by social interactions with parents, teachers, and older children who can provide invaluable guidance (Hedegaard, 2005). Second, Piaget viewed cognitive development as a universal process that should unfold in largely the same way across widely disparate cultures. Vygotsky, on the other hand, asserted that culture exerts great influence over how cognitive growth unfolds (Wertsch & Tulviste, 2005). For example, the cognitive skills acquired in literate cultures that rely on schools for training will differ from those acquired in tribal societies with no formal schooling. Third, Piaget viewed children's gradual mastery of language as just another aspect of cognitive development, whereas Vygotsky argued that language acquisition plays a crucial, central role in fostering cognitive development (Kozulin, 2005).

According to Vygotsky, children acquire most of their culture's cognitive skills and problem-solving

Lev Vygotsky

"In the process of development the child not only masters the items of cultural experience but the habits and forms of cultural behaviour, the cultural methods of reasoning."

strategies through collaborative dialogues with more experienced members of their society. He saw cognitive development as more like an *apprenticeship* than a journey of individual discovery. Vygotsky's emphasis on the primacy of language is reflected in his discussion of *private speech*. Preschool children talk aloud to themselves a lot as they go about their activities. Piaget viewed this speech as egocentric and insignificant. Vygotsky argued that children use this private speech to plan their strategies, regulate their actions, and accomplish their goals. As children grow older, this private speech is internalized and becomes the normal verbal dialogue that people have with themselves as they go about their business. Thus, language increasingly serves as the *foundation* for youngsters' cognitive processes.

Vygotsky's sociocultural theory is guiding a great deal of contemporary research on cognitive development (Feldman, 2003). This research has provided empirical support for many of Vygotsky's ideas (Rogoff, 1998; Winsler, 2003). Like Piaget's theory, Vygotsky's perspective promises to enrich our understanding of how children's thinking develops and matures.

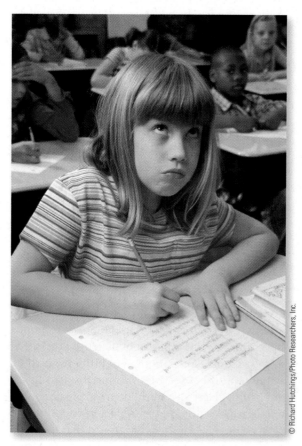

Vygotsky and Piaget differ about the importance of private speech, young children's tendency to talk to themselves as they go about their business. Piaget viewed private speech as insignificant, whereas Vygotsky asserted that children use private speech to regulate their actions and plan their strategies.

Are Some Cognitive Abilities Innate?

The frequent finding that Piaget underestimated infants' cognitive abilities has led to a rash of studies suggesting that infants have a surprising grasp of many complex concepts. Studies have demonstrated that infants understand basic properties of objects and some of the rules that govern them (Baillargeon, 2002, 2004). At 3 to 4 months of age, infants understand that objects are distinct entities with boundaries, that objects move in continuous paths, that one solid object cannot pass through another, that an object cannot pass through an opening that is smaller than the object, and that objects on slopes roll down rather than up (Baillargeon, 2008; Spelke & Newport, 1998).

In this line of research, perhaps the most stunning discovery has been the finding that *infants seem to exhibit surprisingly sophisticated numerical abilities* (Lipton & Spelke, 2004; Wood & Spelke, 2005). If 5-month-old infants are shown a sequence of events in which one object is added to another behind a screen, they expect to see two objects when the screen is removed, and they exhibit surprise when their expectation is violated (see **Figure 10.10**). This expectation suggests that they understand that $1 + 1 = 2$ (Wynn, 1992, 1996). Similar manipulations suggest that infants also understand that $2 - 1 = 1$, that $2 + 1 = 3$, that $3 - 1 = 2$, and other, more complicated calculations (Hauser & Carey, 1998; McCrink & Wynn, 2004; Wynn, 1998).

Again and again in recent years, research has shown that infants appear to understand surprisingly complex concepts that they have had virtually no opportunity to learn about. These findings have led some theorists to conclude that certain basic cognitive abilities are biologically prewired into humans' neural architecture (Spelke & Kinzler, 2007). As you might anticipate, evolutionary theorists maintain that this prewiring is a product of natural selection, and they strive to understand its adaptive significance for our ancient ancestors (Hauser & Carey, 1998; Wynn, 1998).

The Development of Moral Reasoning

In Europe, a woman was near death from cancer. One drug might save her, a form of radium that a druggist in the same town had recently discovered. The druggist was charging $2,000, ten times what the drug cost him to make. The sick woman's husband, Heinz, went to everyone he knew to borrow the money, but he could only get together about half of what it cost. He told the druggist that his wife was dying and asked him to sell it cheaper

or let him pay later. But the druggist said, "No." The husband got desperate and broke into the man's store to steal the drug for his wife. Should the husband have done that? Why? (Kohlberg, 1969, p. 379)

What's your answer to Heinz's dilemma? Would you have answered the same way five years ago? Can you guess what you might have said at age 6? By presenting similar dilemmas to participants and studying their responses, Lawrence Kohlberg (1976, 1984; Colby & Kohlberg, 1987) developed a model of *moral development*. What is morality? That's a complicated question that philosophers have debated for centuries. For our purposes, it will suffice to say that *morality* involves the ability to distinguish right from wrong and to behave accordingly.

Figure 10.10

The procedure used to test infants' understanding of number. To see whether 5-month-old infants have some appreciation of addition and subtraction, Wynn (1992, 1996) showed them sequences of events like those depicted here. If children express surprise (primarily assessed by time spent looking) when the screen drops and they see only one object, this result suggests that they understand that 1 + 1 = 2. Wynn and others have found that infants seem to have some primitive grasp of simple addition and subtraction.

SOURCE: Adapted from Wynn, K. (1992). Addition and subtraction by human infants. *Nature, 358,* 749–750. Copyright © 1992 Macmillan Magazines, Ltd. Reprinted with permission from *Nature* and the author.

Kohlberg's Stage Theory   9d

Kohlberg's model is the most influential of a number of competing theories that attempt to explain how youngsters develop a sense of right and wrong. His work was derived from much earlier work by Piaget (1932). Piaget theorized that moral development is determined by cognitive development. By this he meant that the way individuals think out moral issues depends on their level of cognitive development. This assumption provided the springboard for Kohlberg's research.

Kohlberg's theory focuses on moral *reasoning* rather than overt *behavior*. This point is best illustrated by describing Kohlberg's method of investigation. He presented his participants with thorny moral questions such as Heinz's dilemma, then asked the subjects what the actor in the dilemma should do, and more important, why. It was the *why* that interested Kohlberg. He examined the nature and progression of subjects' moral reasoning.

The result of this work is the stage theory of moral reasoning outlined in **Figure 10.11**. Kohl-berg found that individuals progress through a series of three levels of moral development, each of which can be broken into two sublevels, yielding a total of six stages. Each stage represents a different approach to thinking about right and wrong.

Younger children at the *preconventional level* think in terms of external authority. Acts are wrong because they are punished, or right because they lead to positive consequences. Older children who have reached the *conventional level* of moral reasoning see rules as necessary for maintaining social order. They therefore accept these rules as their own. They "internalize" these rules not to avoid punishment but to be virtuous and win approval from others. Moral thinking at this stage is relatively inflexible. Rules

Lawrence Kohlberg

"Children are almost as likely to reject moral reasoning beneath their level as to fail to assimilate reasoning too far above their level."

Figure 10.11
Kohlberg's stage theory. Kohlberg's model describes three levels of moral reasoning, each of which can be divided into two stages. This chart summarizes some of the key facets in how individuals think about right and wrong at each stage.

Stage 1	Stage 2	Stage 3	Stage 4	Stage 5	Stage 6
Punishment orientation	Naive reward orientation	Good boy/good girl orientation	Authority orientation	Social contract orientation	Individual principles and conscience orientation
Right and wrong is determined by what is punished.	Right and wrong is determined by what is rewarded.	Right and wrong is determined by close others' approval or disapproval.	Right and wrong is determined by society's rules, and laws, which should be obeyed rigidly.	Right and wrong is determined by society's rules, which are viewed as fallible rather than absolute.	Right and wrong is determined by abstract ethical principles that emphasize equity and justice.
Preconventional level		**Conventional level**		**Postconventional level**	

web link 10.4

Parenthood.com

Parents are faced with all sorts of questions about development; this site provides a variety of useful resources for answering some of those questions. Topics tend to be very practical, ranging from potty training to how much back-talk parents should tolerate.

are viewed as absolute guidelines that should be enforced rigidly.

During adolescence, some youngsters move on to the *postconventional level,* which involves working out a personal code of ethics. Acceptance of rules is less rigid, and moral thinking shows some flexibility. Subjects at the postconventional level allow for the possibility that someone might not comply with some of society's rules if they conflict with personal ethics. For example, participants at this level might applaud a newspaper reporter who goes to jail rather than reveal a source of information who was promised anonymity.

Evaluating Kohlberg's Theory

How has Kohlberg's theory fared in research? The central ideas have received reasonable support. Progress in moral reasoning is indeed closely tied to cognitive development (Walker, 1988). Studies also show that youngsters generally do progress through Kohlberg's stages of moral reasoning in the order that he proposed (Walker, 1989). Furthermore, relations between age and level of moral reasoning are in the predicted directions (Rest, 1986). Representative age trends are shown in **Figure 10.12**: As children get older, stage 1 and stage 2 reasoning declines, while stage 3 and stage 4 reasoning

Figure 10.12

Age and moral reasoning. The percentages of different types of moral judgments made by subjects at various ages are graphed here (based on Kohlberg, 1963, 1969). As predicted, preconventional reasoning declines as children mature, conventional reasoning increases during middle childhood, and postconventional reasoning begins to emerge during adolescence. But at each age, children display a mixture of various levels of moral reasoning.

increases. However, there is great variation in the age at which individuals reach specific stages and very few people reach stage 6, which raises doubts about its validity (Lapsley, 2006). Finally, evidence suggests that moral *reasoning* is predictive of moral *behavior,* although the association is modest (Bruggerman & Hart, 1996). That is, youngsters who are at higher stages of moral development are somewhat more likely to be altruistic, conscientious, and honest than youngsters at lower stages (Fabes et al., 1999; Taylor & Walker, 1997). Although these findings support the utility of Kohlberg's model, like all influential theorists, he has his critics. They have raised the following issues:

1. It's not unusual to find that a person shows signs of several adjacent levels of moral reasoning at a particular point in development (Walker & Taylor, 1991). As we noted in the critique of Piaget, this mixing of stages is a problem for virtually all stage theories.

2. Evidence is mounting that Kohlberg's dilemmas may not be valid indicators of moral development in some cultures (Nucci, 2002). Some critics believe that the value judgments built into Kohlberg's theory reflect a liberal, individualistic ideology characteristic of modern Western nations that is much more culture-specific than Kohlberg appreciated (Miller, 2006).

---

concept check 10.3

Analyzing Moral Reasoning

Check your understanding of Kohlberg's theory of moral development by analyzing hypothetical responses to the following moral dilemma.

A midwest biologist has conducted numerous studies demonstrating that simple organisms such as worms and paramecia can learn through conditioning. It occurs to her that perhaps she could condition fertilized human ova, to provide a dramatic demonstration that abortions destroy adaptable, living human organisms. This possibility appeals to her, as she is ardently opposed to abortion. However, there is no way to conduct the necessary research on human ova without sacrificing the lives of potential human beings. She desperately wants to conduct the research, but obviously, the sacrifice of human ova is fundamentally incompatible with her belief in the sanctity of human life. What should she do? Why? [Submitted by a student (age 13) to Professor Barbara Banas at Monroe Community College]

In the spaces on the left of each numbered response, indicate the level of moral reasoning shown, choosing from the following: (a) preconventional level, (b) conventional level, or (c) postconventional level. The answers are in Appendix A.

_____ 1. She should do the research. Although it's wrong to kill, there's a greater good that can be realized through the research.

_____ 2. She shouldn't do the research because people will think that she's a hypocrite and condemn her.

_____ 3. She should do the research because she may become rich and famous as a result.

3. A consensus is building that Kohlberg's theory led to a constricted focus on reasoning about interpersonal conflicts while ignoring many other important aspects of moral development (Walker, 2007). Thus, contemporary researchers are increasingly turning their attention to other dimensions of moral development, including the development of empathy (Eisenberg, Spinrad, & Sadovsky, 2006), the emergence of conscience (Grusec, 2006), the development of prosocial (helping, sharing) behavior (Carlo, 2006), and the significance of moral emotions (such as shame and guilt) (Tangney, Stuewig, & Mashek, 2007).

REVIEW of Key Learning Goals

10.3 Motor development follows cephalocaudal (head-to-foot) and proximodistal (center-outward) trends. Early motor development depends on both maturation and learning. Developmental norms for motor skills and other types of development are only group averages. Cultural variations in the pacing of motor development demonstrate the importance of learning.

10.4 Harry Harlow's work with monkeys undermined the reinforcement explanation of attachment. John Bowlby proposed an evolutionary explanation that has been very influential. Infant-mother attachments fall into three categories: secure, anxious-ambivalent, and avoidant. Research shows that attachment emerges out of an interplay between infant and mother. A secure attachment fosters self-esteem, persistence, curiosity, and self-reliance, among other desirable traits. Cultural variations in childrearing can affect the patterns of attachment seen in a society, but secure attachment is predominant around the world.

10.5 The initial vocalizations by infants are similar across languages, but their babbling gradually begins to resemble the sounds from their surrounding language. Children typically utter their first words around their first birthday. A vocabulary spurt often begins around 18 months. Most children begin to combine words by the end of their second year. Their early sentences are telegraphic. Over the next several years, children gradually learn the complexities of grammar.

10.6 Like other stage theories, Erik Erikson's theory assumes that individuals must progress through a series of specified stages in a particular order and that development is marked by major discontinuities. Erikson's theory of personality development proposes that individuals evolve through eight stages over the life span. In each stage the person wrestles with two opposing tendencies evoked by that stage's psychosocial crisis.

10.7 According to Jean Piaget's theory of cognitive development, the key advance during the sensorimotor period is the child's gradual recognition of the permanence of objects. The preoperational period is marked by certain deficiencies in thinking—notably, centration, irreversibility, and egocentrism. During the concrete operations period, children develop the ability to perform operations on mental representations. The stage of formal operations ushers in more abstract, systematic, and logical thought. Piaget may have underestimated some aspects of children's cognitive development, and his theory, like other stage theories, does not explain individual differences very well.

10.8 Lev Vygotsky's sociocultural theory maintains that children's cognitive development is fueled by social interactions with parents and others and that culture influences how cognitive growth unfolds. Recent research has shown that infants appear to understand surprisingly complex concepts that they have had virtually no opportunity to learn about.

10.9 According to Lawrence Kohlberg, moral reasoning progresses through six stages that are related to age and determined by cognitive development. Age-related progress in moral reasoning has been found in research, although a great deal of overlap occurs between adjacent stages and Kohlberg's theory is more culture-specific than he realized.

The Transition of Adolescence

Adolescence is a bridge between childhood and adulthood. During this time, individuals continue to experience significant changes in cognitive, moral, and social development. However, the most dynamic areas of development during adolescence are physical changes and related transitions in emotional and personality development.

Physiological Changes

Recall for a moment your junior high school days. Didn't it seem that your body grew so fast that your clothes just couldn't "keep up"? This phase of rapid growth in height and weight is called the *adolescent growth spurt*. Brought on by hormonal changes, it typically starts at about age 10 in girls and at about 12 in boys (Archibald, Graber, & Brooks-Dunn, 2003). Scientists are not sure about what triggers the hormonal changes that underlie the adolescent growth spurt, but evidence suggests that rising levels of *leptin,* the recently discovered hormone that reflects the body's fat cell storage (see Chapter 9), may provide the crucial signals (Shalitin & Phillip, 2003).

In addition to growing taller and heavier, children begin to develop the physical features that characterize adults of their respective sexes. These features are termed *secondary sex characteristics*—physical features that distinguish one sex from the other but that are not essential for reproduction. For example, males go through a voice change, develop facial hair, and experience greater skeletal and muscle growth in the upper torso, leading to broader shoulders (see **Figure 10.13** on the next page). Females experience breast growth and a widening of the pelvic bones plus increased fat deposits in this area, resulting in wider hips (Susman & Rogol, 2004).

Key Learning Goals

10.10 Review the physiological changes of puberty and the ramifications of early versus late maturation.

10.11 Summarize research on neural development in adolescence.

10.12 Discuss some common patterns of identity formation in adolescence.

10.13 Articulate the chief characteristics of emerging adulthood as described by Arnett.

ILLUSTRATED OVERVIEW OF HUMAN DEVELOPMENT

STAGE OF DEVELOPMENT

INFANCY (BIRTH–2)

PHYSICAL AND SENSORIMOTOR DEVELOPMENT

Rapid brain growth; 75% of adult brain weight is attained by age 2.

Rapid improvement occurs in visual acuity; depth perception is clearly present by 6 months, perhaps earlier.

Ability to localize sounds is apparent at birth; ability to recognize parent's voice occurs within first week.

Landmarks in motor development: Infants sit without support around 6 months, walk around 12–14 months, run freely around 2 years.

MAJOR STAGE THEORIES

PIAGET	Sensorimotor	
KOHLBERG	Premoral	
ERIKSON	Trust vs. mistrust	Autonomy vs. shame
FREUD (see Chapter 11)	Oral	Anal

COGNITIVE DEVELOPMENT

Object permanence gradually develops.

Infant shows orienting response (pupils dilate, head turns) and attention to new stimulus, habituation (reduced orienting response) to repeated stimulus.

Babbling increasingly resembles spoken language.

First word is used around age 1; vocabulary spurt begins around 18 months; frequent overextensions (words applied too broadly) occur.

SOCIAL AND PERSONALITY DEVELOPMENT

Temperamental individuality is established by 2–3 months; infants tend to be easy, difficult, or slow to warm up.

© George Silver/Corbis

Attachment to caregiver(s) is usually evident around 6–8 months; secure attachment facilitates exploration.

"Stranger anxiety" often appears around 6–8 months; separation anxiety peaks around 14–18 months.

Information compiled by Barbara Hansen Lemme, College of DuPage

EARLY CHILDHOOD (2–6)

Connections among neurons continue to increase in density.

Visual acuity reaches 20/20.

Bladder and bowel control is established.

Hand preference is usually solidified by 3–4 years; coordination improves; children learn to dress themselves.

Preoperational

Preconventional

Initiative vs. guilt

Phallic

Thought is marked by egocentrism (limited ability to view world from another's perspective).

Thought is marked by centration (inability to focus on more than one aspect of a problem at a time) and irreversibility (inability to mentally undo an action).

Telegraphic speech (omitting nonessential words) appears at 2–3 years; syntax is well developed by age 5; vocabulary increases dramatically.

Short-term memory capacity increases from two items at age 2 to five items around age 6–7; attention span improves.

© David Young-Wolff/PhotoEdit

Child realizes that gender does not change and begins to learn gender roles and form gender identity; social behavior is influenced by observational learning, resulting in imitation.

Child progresses from parallel (side-by-side, noninteractive) play to cooperative play.

Social world is extended beyond family; first friendships are formed.

MIDDLE CHILDHOOD (6–12)

In girls, growth spurt begins around age 10, bringing dramatic increases in height and weight.

Levels of pituitary activity and sex hormones increase.

Girls' secondary sex characteristics (such as breast development and widening hips) begin to emerge.

In girls, puberty begins around age 12–13; menstruation starts.

Concrete operational

Conventional

Industry vs. inferiority

Latency

Conservation (understanding that physical qualities can remain constant in spite of transformations in shape) is gradually mastered.

Child develops decentration (ability to focus on more than one feature of a problem at a time) and reversibility (ability to mentally undo an action).

Metalinguistic awareness (ability to reflect on use of language) leads to play with language, use of puns, riddles, metaphors.

Long-term memory improves with increasing use of encoding strategies of rehearsal and organization.

© Jon Feingersh/Corbis

Child experiences great increase in social skills, improved understanding of others' feelings; social world is dominated by same-sex peer relationships.

Role-taking skills emerge; fantasy is basis for thoughts about vocations and jobs.

Altruism tends to increase, aggression tends to decrease; aggression tends to become more verbal rather than physical, hostile more than instrumental.

Continued on next page

ADOLESCENCE (12–20)

YOUNG ADULTHOOD (20–40)

Physical and sensorimotor development
continued

In boys, growth spurt begins around age 12, bringing dramatic increases in height and weight.

Level of pituitary activity and hormones increases.

Boys' secondary sex characteristics (such as voice change and growth of facial hair) begin to emerge.

In boys, puberty begins around age 13–14; boys become capable of ejaculation.

Reaction time and muscular strength peak in early to mid-20s.

Maximum functioning of all body systems, including senses, attained; slow decline begins in 20s.

External signs of aging begin to show in 30s; skin loses elasticity; hair is thinner, more likely to be gray.

Lowered metabolic rate contributes to increased body fat relative to muscle; gain in weight is common.

Major stage theories
continued

Formal operational

Postconventional (if attained)

Identity vs. confusion

Intimacy vs. isolation

Genital

Cognitive development
continued

Deductive reasoning improves; problem solving becomes more systematic, with alternative possibilities considered before solution is selected.

Thought becomes more abstract and reflective; individual develops ability to mentally manipulate abstract concepts as well as concrete objects.

Individual engages in idealistic contemplation of hypotheticals, "what could be."

Long-term memory continues to improve as elaboration is added to encoding strategies.

Intellectual abilities and speed of information processing are stable.

Greater emphasis is on application, rather than acquisition, of knowledge.

There is some evidence of a trend toward dialectical thought (ideas stimulate opposing ideas), leading to more contemplation of contradictions, pros and cons.

Social and personality development
continued

Person experiences increased interactions with opposite-sex peers; dating begins.

Attention is devoted to identify formation, questions such as "Who am I?" and "What do I want out of life?"

Realistic considerations about abilities and training requirements become more influential in thoughts about vocations and jobs.

Energies are focused on intimate relationships, learning to live with marriage partner, starting a family, managing a home.

Trial period is given for occupational choices, followed by stabilization of vocational commitment; emphasis is on self-reliance, becoming one's own person.

For many, close relationship develops with mentor (older person who serves as role model, adviser, and teacher).

© David Young-Wolff/PhotoEdit

© Radius Images/Alamy

MIDDLE ADULTHOOD (40–65)

Changes occur in vision: increased farsightedness and difficulty recovering from glare; slower dark adaptation.

The amount of brain tissue declines, but significance of this neural loss is unclear.

In women, menopause occurs around age 50; in both sexes, sexual activity declines, although capacity for arousal changes only slightly.

Sensitivity to high-frequency sounds decreases, especially in males after age 55.

LATE ADULTHOOD (65 AND OLDER)

Height decreases slightly because of changes in vertebral column; decline in weight also common.

Sensitivity of vision, hearing, and taste noticeably decreases.

Chronic diseases, especially heart disease, cancer, and stroke, increase.

Rate of aging is highly individualized.

Generativity vs. self-absorption

Integrity vs. despair

There is some evidence for a trend toward improved judgment or "wisdom" based on accumulation of life experiences.

Effectiveness of retrieval from long-term memory begins slow decline, usually not noticeable until after age 55.

Individual experiences gradual decline in speed of learning, problem solving, and information processing.

In spite of decreased speed in cognitive processes, intellectual productivity and problem-solving skills usually remain stable.

Individual experiences gradual decline in cognitive speed and effectiveness of working memory.

Intellectual productivity depends on factors such as health and lifestyle; many people in their 60s and 70s remain quite productive.

Decision making tends to become more cautious.

Fluid intelligence often declines, but crystallized intelligence remains stable or increases.

Midlife transition around age 40 leads to reflection, increased awareness of mortality and passage of time, but usually is not a personal crisis.

"Sandwich generation" is caught between needs of aging parents and children reaching adulthood.

Career development peaks; there is some tendency to shift energy from career concerns to family concerns.

Physical changes associated with aging require adjustments that affect life satisfaction.

Marital satisfaction often increases, but eventually death of spouse presents coping challenge.

Living arrangements are a significant determinant of satisfaction, as 60%–90% of time is spent at home.

© Tony Freeman/PhotoEdit

© John Henley/The Stock Market/Corbis

disease have been identified, including regular exercise (Schuit et al., 2001) and frequent participation in stimulating cognitive activities (Snowdon, 2001; Wilson & Bennett, 2003).

Aging and Cognitive Changes

The evidence indicates that general intelligence is fairly stable throughout most of adulthood, with a small decline in *average* test scores often seen after age 60 (Schaie, 1990, 1994, 1996, 2005). However, this seemingly simple assertion masks many complexities and needs to be qualified carefully. First, group averages can be deceptive in that mean scores can be dragged down by a small minority of people who show a decline. For example, when Schaie (1990) calculated the percentage of people who maintain stable performance on various abilities, he found that about 80% showed no decline by age 60 and that about two-thirds were still stable through age 81. Second, some forms of intelligence are more vulnerable to aging than others. Many theorists distinguish between *fluid intelligence,* which involves basic reasoning ability, memory capacity, and speed of information processing, and *crystallized intelligence,* which involves the ability to apply acquired knowledge and skills in problem solving. Research suggests that fluid intelligence is much more likely to decline with age, whereas crystallized intelligence tends to remain stable (Baltes, Staudinger, & Lindenberger, 1999; Horn & Hofer, 1992; Li et al., 2004).

What about memory? Numerous studies report decreases in older adults' memory capabilities (Hoyer & Verhaeghen, 2006). Many researchers maintain that the memory losses associated with normal aging tend to be moderate and are *not* experienced by everyone (Dixon & Cohen, 2003; Shimamura et al., 1995). However, Salthouse (2003, 2004) takes a much more pessimistic view, arguing that age-related decreases in memory are substantial in magnitude, that they begin in early adulthood, and that they affect everyone. One reason for these varied conclusions may be that a variety of memory types can be assessed (see Chapter 7 for a review of various systems of memory). The most reliable decrements are usually seen in *episodic memory* and *working memory,* with less consistent losses observed on tasks involving *procedural memory* and *semantic memory* (Dixon & Cohen, 2003; Hoyer & Verhaeghen, 2006).

In the cognitive domain, aging does seem to take its toll on *speed* first. Many studies indicate that speed in learning, solving problems, and processing information tends to decline with age (Salthouse, 1996). The evidence suggests that the erosion of processing speed may be a gradual, lengthy trend beginning in middle adulthood (see **Figure 10.21**). The general nature of this trend (across differing tasks) suggests that it may be the result of age-related changes in neurological functioning (Salthouse, 2000), but doubts have been raised about this conclusion (Hartley, 2006). Although mental speed declines with age, problem-solving ability remains largely unimpaired if older people are given adequate time to compensate for their reduced speed.

A hot issue in recent years has been whether high levels of mental activity in late adulthood can delay the typical age-related declines in cognitive functioning. This possibility is sometimes referred to as the "use it or lose it" hypothesis. Several lines of evidence seem to provide support for this notion. For example, people who continue to work further into old age, especially people who remain in mentally demanding jobs, tend to show smaller decrements in cognitive abilities than their age-mates (Bosma et al., 2002; Schooler, 2007). Other studies suggest that continuing to engage in intellectually challenging activities in late adulthood serves to buffer against cognitive declines (Hultsch et al., 1999; Kliegel, Zimprich, & Rott, 2004). The evidence is complex and there are skeptics (Salthouse, 2006), but it appears that keeping mentally active may help elderly people delay and diminish the negative effects of aging on cognitive functioning.

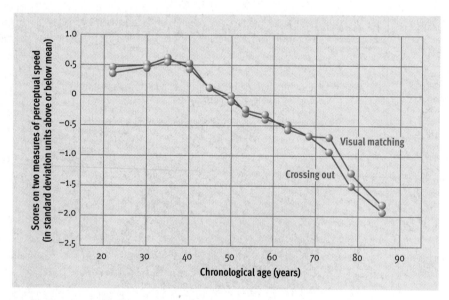

Figure 10.21

Age and mental speed. Many studies have found that mental speed decreases with age. The data shown here, from Salthouse (2000), are based on two perceptual speed tasks. The data points are means for large groups of subjects expressed in terms of how many standard deviations (see Appendix B) they are above or below the mean for all ages (which is set at 0). Similar age-related declines are seen on many tasks that depend on mental speed.

SOURCE: Adapted from Salthouse, T. A. (2000). Aging and measures of processing speed. *Biological Psychology, 54,* 35-54. Reproduced by permission of Elsevier Science.

REVIEW of Key Learning Goals

10.14 During adulthood, personality is marked by both stability and change, as percentile scores remain stable, but mean raw scores change in predictable ways. Warmth, self-confidence, self-control, and emotional stability tend to increase in the adult years. Those who move successfully through the three stages of adulthood posited by Erik Erikson should develop intimacy, generativity, and integrity.

10.15 Many landmarks in adult development involve transitions in family relationships. Difficulty adjusting to marriage is more likely when spouses have different role expectations. The transition to parenthood can be stressful. Parent-adolescent relations are not as contentious as widely assumed. For most parents, the empty nest transition no longer appears to be as difficult as it once was.

10.16 During adulthood, age-related physiological transitions include changes in appearance, sensory losses (especially in vision and hearing), and hormonal changes. Most women experience at least some unpleasant symptoms during menopause, but it is not as problematic as widely suggested.

10.17 Drastic mental decline is not a part of the normal aging process, but dementia is seen in about 15%–20% of people over age 75. Alzheimer's disease accounts for roughly 60% of all cases of dementia. Alzheimer's disease has a subtle onset marked by chronic forgetting of newly learned information, followed by a progressive deterioration over 8–10 years. The causes of this debilitating disease are not well understood, although genetic factors appear to contribute.

10.18 In the cognitive domain, general intelligence is fairly stable, with a small decline in average test scores seen after the age of 60. Fluid intelligence is more likely to decline, whereas crystallized intelligence often remains stable. Many studies have found decreases in older adults' memory capabilities, especially in episodic and working memory. Mental speed declines in late adulthood, but many people remain productive well into old age. Some studies suggest that high levels of mental activity in late adulthood can delay the typical age-related declines in cognitive functioning.

Identifying the Contributions of Major Theorists and Researchers

Check your recall of the principal ideas of important theorists and researchers covered in this chapter by matching the people listed on the left with the appropriate contributions described on the right. If you need help, the crucial pages describing each person's ideas are listed in parentheses. Fill in the letters for your choices in the spaces provided on the left. You'll find the answers in Appendix A.

Major Theorists and Researchers

_____ 1. Mary Ainsworth (p. 342)

_____ 2. John Bowlby (p. 342)

_____ 3. Erik Erikson (pp. 345–346, 356, 358–359)

_____ 4. Harry Harlow (pp. 341–342)

_____ 5. Lawrence Kohlberg (pp. 351–352)

_____ 6. Jean Piaget (pp. 346–349)

_____ 7. Lev Vygotsky (pp. 349–350)

Key Ideas and Contributions

a. This psychologist formulated a six-stage theory of moral development.

b. This Swiss scholar created a groundbreaking theory of cognitive development that described the sensorimotor, preoperational, concrete operational, and formal operational periods.

c. This person expanded on Freud's theory, describing eight stages of development that revolve around psychosocial crises.

d. This researcher found that attachments fall into three categories: secure, anxious-ambivalent, and avoidant.

e. This Russian scholar devised a sociocultural theory of cognitive development which emphasized how social interactions fuel development.

f. This attachment theorist argued that infants are biologically programmed to emit behaviors that trigger an affectionate response from adults.

g. This individual's research with monkeys undermined the behavioral explanation of attachment.

Reflecting on the Chapter's Themes

Five of our seven integrative themes surfaced to some degree in our coverage of human development. We saw theoretical diversity in our discussions of cognitive development and personality development. We saw that psychology evolves in a sociohistorical context, investigating complex, real-world issues—such as transitions in marital roles—that emerge as our society changes. We encountered multifactorial causation of behavior in the development of attachment, among other things. We saw cultural invariance and cultural diversity in our examination of attachment, motor development, cognitive development, and moral development.

But above all else, we saw how heredity and environment jointly mold behavior. We've encountered the dual influence of heredity and environment before, but this theme is rich in complexity, and each chapter draws out different aspects and implica-

tions. Our discussion of development amplified the point that genetics and experience work *interactively* to shape behavior. What does it mean to say that heredity and environment interact? In the language of science, an interaction means that the effects of one variable depend on the effects of another. In other words, heredity and environment do not operate independently. Children with "difficult" temperaments will elicit different reactions from different parents, depending on the parents' personalities and expectations. Likewise, a particular pair of parents will affect different children in different ways, depending on the inborn characteristics of the children. An interplay, or feedback loop, exists between biological and environmental factors.

All aspects of development are shaped jointly by heredity and experience. We often estimate their relative weight or influence, as if we could cleanly

Key Learning Goals

10.19 Identify the five unifying themes highlighted in this chapter.

 Theoretical Diversity

 Sociohistorical Context

 Multifactorial Causation

 Cultural Heritage

 Heredity and Environment

divide behavior into genetic and environmental components. Although we can't really carve up behavior that neatly, such comparisons can be of great theoretical interest, as you'll see in our upcoming Personal Application, which discusses the nature and origins of gender differences in behavior.

PERSONAL APPLICATION

Understanding Gender Differences

Answer the following "true" or "false."

___ **1** Females are more socially oriented than males.

___ **2** Males outperform females on most spatial tasks.

___ **3** Females are more irrational than males.

___ **4** Males are less sensitive to nonverbal cues than females.

___ **5** Females are more emotional than males.

Are there genuine behavioral differences between the sexes similar to those mentioned above? If so, why do these differences exist? How do they develop? These are the complex and controversial questions that we'll explore in this Personal Application.

Before proceeding further, we need to clarify how some key terms are used, as terminology in this area of research has been evolving and remains a source of confusion (Deaux, 1993; Unger & Crawford, 1993). *Sex* refers to the biologically based categories of female and male. In contrast, *gender* refers to culturally constructed distinctions between femininity and masculinity. Individuals are born female or male. However, they become feminine or masculine through complex developmental processes that take years to unfold.

The statements at the beginning of this Application reflect popular gender stereotypes in our society. *Gender stereotypes* are widely held beliefs about females' and males' abilities, personality traits, and social behavior. **Table 10.1** lists some characteristics that are part of the masculine and feminine stereotypes in North American society. The table shows something you may have already noticed on your own. The male stereotype is much more flattering, suggesting that men have virtually cornered the market on competence and rationality. After all, everyone knows that females are more dependent, emotional, irrational, submissive, and talkative than males. Right? Or is that not the case? Let's look at the research.

How Do the Sexes Differ in Behavior?

Gender differences are actual disparities between the sexes in typical behavior or average ability. Mountains of research, literally thousands of studies, exist on gender differences. What does this research show? Are the stereotypes of males and females accurate? Well, the findings are a mixed bag. The research indicates that genuine behavioral differences *do* exist between the sexes and that people's stereotypes are not entirely inaccurate (Eagly, 1995; Swim, 1994). But the differences are fewer in number, smaller in size, and far more complex than stereotypes suggest. As you'll see, only two of the differences mentioned in our opening true-false questions (the even-numbered items) have been largely supported by the research.

Cognitive Abilities

In the cognitive domain, it appears that there are three genuine—albeit very small—gender differences. First, on the average, females

Table 10.1 Elements of Traditional Gender Stereotypes

Masculine	Feminine
Active	Aware of other's feelings
Adventurous	Considerate
Aggressive	Creative
Ambitious	Cries easily
Competitive	Devotes self to others
Dominant	Emotional
Independent	Enjoys art and music
Leadership qualities	Excitable in a crisis
Likes math and science	Expresses tender feelings
Makes decisions easily	Feelings hurt
Mechanical aptitude	Gentle
Not easily influenced	Home oriented
Outspoken	Kind
Persistent	Likes children
Self-confident	Neat
Skilled in business	Needs approval
Stands up under pressure	Tactful
Takes a stand	Understanding

SOURCE: Adapted from Ruble, T. L. (1983). Sex stereotypes: Issues of change in the 70s. *Sex Roles, 9,* 397–402. Copyright © 1983 Plenum Publishing Group. Adapted with kind permission of Springer Science and Business Media.

tend to exhibit slightly better *verbal skills* than males (Halpern et al., 2007). In particular, females seem stronger on tasks that require rapid access to semantic and other information in long-term memory (Halpern, 1997, 2004). Second, starting during high school, males show a slight advantage on tests of *mathematical ability.* When all students are compared, males' advantage is quite small (Hyde, 2005a). However, at the high end of the ability distribution, the gender gap is larger, as far more males than females are found to have exceptional math skills (Halpern et al., 2007). Third, starting in the grade-school years, males tend to score higher than females on most measures of *visual-spatial ability* (Halpern et al., 2007). The size of these gender differences varies from moderate to small depending on the exact nature of the spatial task. Males appear to be strongest on tasks that require visual transformations in working memory (Halpern, 2004).

Social Behavior

In regard to social behavior, research findings support the existence of some additional gender differences. First, studies indicate that males tend to be much more *physically aggressive* than females (Archer, 2005). This disparity shows up early in childhood. Its continuation into adulthood is supported by the fact that men account for a grossly disproportionate number of the violent crimes in our society (Kenrick, Trost, & Sundie, 2004). The findings on *verbal aggression* are more complex, as females appear to exhibit more relational aggression (snide remarks and so forth) (Archer, 2005). Second, there are gender differences in *nonverbal communication*. The evidence indicates that females are more sensitive than males to subtle nonverbal cues (Hall, Carter, & Horgan, 2000; Hampson, van Anders, & Mullin, 2006) and that they pay more attention to interpersonal information (Hall & Mast, 2008). Third, males are more sexually active than females in a variety of ways, and they have more permissive attitudes about casual, premarital, and extramarital sex (Baumeister, Catanese, & Vohs, 2001; Hyde, 2005a; see Chapter 9).

Some Qualifications

Although research has identified some genuine gender differences in behavior, bear in mind that these are group differences that indicate nothing about individuals. Essentially, research results compare the "average man" with the "average woman." However, you are—and every individual is—unique. The average female and male are ultimately figments of our imagination. Furthermore,

the genuine group differences noted are relatively small (Hyde, 2005a). **Figure 10.22** shows how scores on a trait, perhaps verbal ability, might be distributed for men and women. Although the group averages are detectably different, you can see the great variability within each group (sex) and the huge overlap between the two group distributions.

Biological Origins of Gender Differences

What accounts for the development of gender differences? To what degree are they the product of learning or of biology? This question is yet another manifestation of the *nature versus nurture* issue. Investigations of the biological origins of gender differences have centered on the evolutionary bases of behavior, hormones, and brain organization.

Evolutionary Explanations

Evolutionary psychologists argue that gender differences in behavior reflect different natural selection pressures operating on males and females over the course of human history (Archer, 1996; Buss & Kenrick, 1998). For example, as we discussed in Chapter 9, males supposedly are more sexually active and permissive because they invest less than females in the process of procreation and can maximize their reproductive success by seeking many sexual partners (Buss, 1996; Schmitt, 2005). The gender gap in aggression is also explained in terms of reproductive fitness. Because females are more selective about mating than males, males have to engage in more competition for sexual partners than females do. Greater aggressive-

ness is thought to be adaptive for males in this competition for sexual access because it should foster social dominance over other males and facilitate the acquisition of the material resources emphasized by females when evaluating potential partners (Campbell, 2005; Cummins, 2005). Evolutionary theorists assert that gender differences in spatial ability reflect the division of labor in ancestral hunting-and-gathering societies in which males typically handled the hunting and females the gathering. Males' superiority on most spatial tasks has been attributed to the adaptive demands of hunting (Silverman & Choi, 2005; see Chapter 1).

Evolutionary analyses of gender differences are interesting, but controversial. On the one hand, it seems eminently plausible that evolutionary forces could have led to some divergence between males and females in typical behavior. On the other hand, evolutionary hypotheses are highly speculative and difficult to test empirically (Eagly & Wood, 1999; Halpern, 1997). The crucial problem for some critics is that evolutionary analyses are so "flexible" they can be used to explain almost anything. For example, if the situation regarding spatial ability were reversed—if females scored higher than males—evolutionary theorists might attribute females' superiority to the adaptive demands of gathering food, weaving baskets, and making clothes—and it would be difficult to prove otherwise (Cornell, 1997).

The Role of Hormones

Hormones play a key role in sexual differentiation during prenatal development. The high level of androgens (the principal class of male hormones) in males and the low level

Figure 10.22
The nature of gender differences. Gender differences are group differences that indicate little about individuals because of the great overlap between the groups. For a given trait, one gender may score higher on the average, but far more variation occurs within each gender than between the genders.

of androgens in females lead to the differentiation of male and female genital organs. The critical role of prenatal hormones becomes apparent when something interferes with normal prenatal hormonal secretions. About a half-dozen endocrine disorders can cause overproduction or underproduction of specific gonadal hormones during prenatal development. Scientists have also studied children born to mothers who were given an androgenlike drug to prevent miscarriage. The general trend in this research is that females exposed prenatally to abnormally high levels of androgens exhibit more male-typical behavior than other females do and that males exposed prenatally to abnormally low levels of androgens exhibit more female-typical behavior than other males (Collaer & Hines, 1995; Hines, 2004).

These findings suggest that prenatal hormones contribute to the shaping of gender differences in humans. But there are some problems with this evidence (Basow, 1992; Fausto-Sterling, 1992). First, the evidence is much stronger for females than for males. Second, it's always dangerous to draw conclusions about the general population based on small samples of people who have abnormal conditions. Looking at the evidence as a whole, it does seem likely that hormones contribute to gender differences in behavior. However, a great deal remains to be learned.

Differences in Brain Organization

Interpretive problems have also cropped up in efforts to link gender differences to specialization of the cerebral hemispheres in the brain (see **Figure 10.23**). As you may recall from Chapter 3, in most people the left hemisphere is more actively involved in verbal processing, whereas the right hemisphere is more active in visual-spatial processing (Sperry, 1982; Springer & Deutsch, 1998). After these findings surfaced, theorists began to wonder whether this division of labor in the brain might be related to gender differences in verbal and spatial skills. Consequently, they began looking for sex-related disparities in brain organization.

Some thought-provoking findings *have* been reported. For instance, some studies have found that *males tend to exhibit more cerebral specialization than females* (Hellige, 1993b; Voyer, 1996). In other words, there's a trend for males to depend more heavily

Figure 10.23

The cerebral hemispheres and the corpus callosum. In this drawing the cerebral hemispheres have been "pulled apart" to reveal the corpus callosum, the band of fibers that connects the right and left halves of the brain. Research has shown that the right and left hemispheres are specialized to handle different types of cognitive tasks (see Chapter 3), leading some theorists to speculate that patterns of hemispheric specialization might contribute to gender differences in verbal and spatial abilities.

Corpus callosum

than females do on the left hemisphere in verbal processing and more heavily on the right in spatial processing. Differences between males and females have also been found in the size of the corpus callosum, the band of fibers that connects the two hemispheres of the brain. Some studies suggest that *females tend to have a larger corpus callosum* (Bigler et al., 1997), which might allow for better interhemispheric transfer of information, which, in turn, might underlie the less lateralized organization of females' brains (Innocenti, 1994). Thus, some theorists have concluded that differences between the sexes in brain organization are responsible for gender differences in verbal and spatial ability (Geschwind & Galaburda, 1987; Kimura & Hampson, 1993).

This idea is intriguing, but psychologists have a long way to go before they can explain gender differences in terms of right brain/left brain specialization. Studies have not been consistent in finding that males have more specialized brain organization than females (Halpern, 1992; Kinsbourne, 1980), and the

finding of a larger corpus callosum in females has proven controversial (Halpern et al., 2007). Moreover, even if these findings were replicated consistently, no one is really sure just how they would account for the observed gender differences in cognitive abilities.

In summary, researchers have made some intriguing progress in their efforts to document the biological roots of gender differences in behavior. However, the idea that "anatomy is destiny" has proven difficult to demonstrate. Many theorists remain convinced that gender differences are largely shaped by experience. Let's examine their evidence.

Environmental Origins of Gender Differences

All societies make efforts to train children about gender roles. *Gender roles* are expectations about what is appropriate behavior for each sex. Although gender roles are in a period of transition in modern Western society, there are still many disparities in how males and females are brought up. Investigators have identified three key processes involved in the development of gender roles: operant conditioning, observational learning, and self-socialization. First we'll examine these processes. Then we'll look at the principal sources of gender-role socialization: families, schools, and the media.

Operant Conditioning

In part, gender roles are shaped by the power of reward and punishment—the key processes in *operant conditioning* (see Chapter 6). Parents, teachers, peers, and others often reinforce (usually with tacit approval) "gender-appropriate" behavior and respond negatively to "gender-inappropriate" behavior (Bussey & Bandura, 1999; Matlin, 2008). If you're a man, you might recall getting hurt as a young boy and being told that "big boys don't cry." If you succeeded in inhibiting your crying, you may have earned an approving smile or even something tangible like an ice cream cone. The reinforcement probably strengthened your tendency to "act like a man" and suppress emotional displays. If you're a woman, chances are your crying wasn't discouraged as gender-inappropriate. Studies suggest that fathers encourage and reward gender-appropriate behavior in their youngsters more than mothers do and that boys experience more pressure to behave in gender-approriate ways than girls do (Levy, Taylor, & Gelman, 1995).

Observational Learning

Observational learning (see Chapter 6) by children can lead to the imitation of adults' sex-appropriate behavior. Children imitate both males and females, but most children tend to imitate same-sex role models more than opposite-sex role models (Bussey & Bandura, 1984; Frey & Ruble, 1992). Thus, imitation often leads young girls to play with dolls, dollhouses, and toy stoves, while young boys are more likely to tinker with toy trucks, miniature gas stations, or tool kits.

Self-Socialization

Children themselves are active agents in their own gender-role socialization. Several *cognitive theories* of gender-role development emphasize self-socialization (Bem, 1985; Cross & Markus, 1993; Martin & Ruble, 2004). Self-socialization entails three steps. First, children learn to classify themselves as male or female and to recognize their sex as a permanent quality. Second, this self-categorization motivates them to value those characteristics and behaviors associated with their sex. Third, they strive to bring their behavior in line with what is considered gender-appropriate in their culture. In other words, children get involved in their own socialization, working diligently to discover the rules that are supposed to govern their behavior.

Sources of Gender-Role Socialization

There are three main sources of influence in gender-role socialization: families, schools, and the media. Of course, we are now in an era of transition in gender roles, so the generalizations that follow may say more about how you were socialized than about how children will be socialized in the future.

Families. A great deal of gender-role socialization takes place in the home (McHale, Crouter, & Whiteman, 2003; Pomerantz, Ng, & Wang, 2004). For example, fathers engage in more "rough-housing" play with their sons than with their daughters, even in infancy (McBride-Chang & Jacklin, 1993). As children grow, boys and girls are

The socialization of gender roles begins very early, as parents dress their infants in gendered clothing, buy them gender-driven toys, and encourage them to participate in "gender-appropriate" activities.

© Here's Looking at You/Brand X/Jupiter Images

encouraged to play with different types of toys (Wood, Desmarais, & Gugula, 2002). Generally, boys have less leeway to play with "feminine" toys than girls do with "masculine" toys. When children are old enough to help with household chores, the assignments tend to depend on sex (Cunningham, 2001). For example, girls wash dishes and boys mow the lawn.

Schools. Schools and teachers clearly contribute to the socialization of gender roles. The books that children use in learning to read can influence their ideas about what is suitable behavior for males and females (Diekman & Murnen, 2004). Traditionally, males have been more likely to be portrayed as clever, heroic, and adventurous in these books, while females have been more likely to be shown doing domestic chores. Preschool and grade-school teachers frequently reward gender-appropriate behavior in their pupils (Fagot et al., 1985; Ruble & Martin, 1998). Interestingly, teachers tend to pay greater attention to males, helping them, praising them, and scolding them more than females (Sadker & Sadker, 1994). As youngsters progress through the school system, they are often channeled in career directions considered appropriate for their sex (Read, 1991).

Media. Television and other mass media are another source of gender-role socialization (Bussey & Bandura, 2004). Although some improvement has occurred in recent years, television shows have traditionally depicted men and women in stereotypical ways (Galambos, 2004; Signorielli, 2001). Women are often portrayed as submissive, passive, and emotional. Men are more likely to be portrayed as independent, assertive, and competent. Even commercials contribute to the socialization of gender roles (Bretl & Cantor, 1988; Signorielli, McLeod, & Healy, 1994). Women are routinely shown worrying about trivial matters such as the whiteness of their laundry or the shine of their dishes.

Conclusion

As you can see, the findings on gender and behavior are complex and confusing. Nonetheless, the evidence does permit one very general conclusion—a conclusion that you have seen before and will see again. Taken as a whole, the research in this area suggests that biological factors and environmental factors both contribute to gender differences in behavior—as they do to all other aspects of development.

REVIEW of Key Learning Goals

10.20 Gender differences in behavior are fewer in number than gender stereotypes suggest. In the cognitive domain, research reviews suggest that there are genuine gender differences in verbal ability, mathematical ability, and spatial ability. In regard to social behavior, differences have been found in aggression, nonverbal communication, and sexual behavior. But most gender differences in behavior are very small in magnitude.

10.21 Evolutionary theorists maintain that gender differences exist because males and females have confronted different adaptive demands over the course of human history. Extensive evidence suggests that prenatal hormones contribute to human gender differences, but the research is marred by interpretive problems. Research linking gender differences to cerebral specialization is intriguing, but much remains to be learned.

10.22 A vast research literature shows that gender differences are shaped by socialization processes. Operant conditioning, observational learning, and self-socialization contribute to the development of gender differences. Families, schools, and the media are among the main sources of gender-role socialization.

Key Learning Goals

10.23 Clarify and critique the argument that fathers are essential for healthy development.

Are Fathers Essential to Children's Well-Being?

Are fathers essential for children to experience normal, healthy development? This question is currently the subject of heated debate. A number of social scientists have mounted a thought-provoking argument that father absence is the chief factor underlying a variety of modern social ills. For example, David Blankenhorn (1995) argues that "fatherlessness is the most harmful demographic trend of this generation. It is the leading cause of declining child well-being in our society" (p. 1). Expressing a similar view, David Popenoe (1996) maintains that "today's fatherlessness has led to social turmoil—damaged children, unhappy children, aimless children, children who strike back with pathological behavior and violence" (p. 192).

The Basic Argument

What is the evidence for the proposition that fathers are essential to healthy development? Over the last 40 years, the proportion of children growing up without a father in the home has more than doubled. During the same time, we have seen dramatic increases in teenage pregnancy, juvenile delinquency, violent crime, drug abuse, eating disorders, teen suicide, and family dysfunction. Moreover, mountains of studies have demonstrated an association between father absence and an elevated risk for these problems. Summarizing this evidence, Popenoe (1996) asserts that "fatherless children have a risk factor two to three times that of fathered children for a wide range of negative outcomes, including dropping out of high school, giving birth as a teenager, and becoming a juvenile delinquent" (p. 192), which leads him to infer that "fathers have a unique and irreplaceable role to play in child development" (p. 197). Working from this premise, Popenoe concludes, "If present trends continue, our society could be on the verge of committing social suicide" (p. 192). Echoing this dire conclusion, Blankenhorn (1995) comments that "to tolerate the trend of fatherlessness is to accept the inevitability of continued societal recession" (p. 222).

You might be thinking, "What's all the fuss about?" Surely, proclaiming the importance of fatherhood ought to be no more controversial than advocacy for motherhood or apple pie. But the assertion that a father is *essential* to a child's well-being has some interesting political implications. It suggests that heterosexual marriage is the only appropriate context in which to raise children and that other family configurations are fundamentally deficient. Based on this line of reasoning, some people have argued for new laws that would make it more difficult to obtain a divorce and have advocated other policies and programs that would favor traditional families over families headed by single mothers, cohabiting parents, and gay and lesbian parents (Silverstein & Auerbach, 1999). Thus, the question about the importance of fathers is creating a great deal of controversy because it is really a question about alternatives to traditional family structure.

Evaluating the Argument

In light of the far-reaching implications of the view that fathers are essential to normal development, it makes sense to subject this view to critical scrutiny. How could you use critical thinking skills to evaluate this argument? At least three previously discussed ideas seem pertinent.

First, it is important to recognize that the position that fathers are essential for healthy development rests on a foundation of correlational evidence, and as we have seen repeatedly, *correlation is no assurance of causation*. Yes, there has been an increase in fatherlessness that has been paralleled by increases in teenage pregnancy, drug abuse, eating disorders, and other disturbing social problems. But think of all the other changes

Are fathers crucial to children's well-being? This seemingly simple question has sparked heated debate.

© Royalty Free/Corbis

that have occurred in American culture over the last 40 years, such as the decline of organized religion, the growth of mass media, dramatic shifts in sexual mores, and so forth. Increased fatherlessness has co-varied with a host of other cultural trends. Thus, it is highly speculative to infer that father absence is the chief cause of most modern social problems.

Second, it always pays to think about whether there are *alternative explanations* for findings that you might have doubts about. What other factors might account for the association between father absence and children's maladjustment? Think for a moment: What is the most frequent cause of father absence? Obviously, it is divorce. Divorces tend to be highly stressful events that disrupt children's entire lives. Although the evidence suggests that a majority of children seem to survive divorce without lasting, detrimental effects, it is clear that divorce elevates youngsters' risk for a wide range of negative developmental outcomes (Amato, 2001, 2003; Hetherington, 1999, 2003). Given that father absence and divorce are often intertwined, it is possible that the negative effects of divorce account for much of the association between father absence and social problems.

Are there any other alternative explanations for the correlation between fatherlessness and social maladies? Yes, critics point out that the prevalence of father absence co-varies with socioeconomic status. Father absence is much more common in low-income families (Anderson, Kohler, & Letiecq, 2002). Thus, the effects of father absence are entangled to some extent with the many powerful, malignant effects of poverty, which might account for much of the correlation between fatherlessness and negative outcomes (McLoyd, 1998).

A third possible strategy in thinking critically about the effects of father absence would be to look for some of the *fallacies in reasoning* introduced in Chapter 9 (irrelevant reasons, circular reasoning, slippery slope, weak analogies, and false dichotomy). A couple of the quotes from Popenoe and Blankenhorn were chosen to give you an opportunity to detect two of these fallacies in a new context. Take a look at the quotes once again and see whether you can spot the fallacies.

Popenoe's assertion that "if present trends continue, our society could be on the verge of social suicide" is an example of *slippery slope argumentation,* which involves predictions that if one allows X to happen, things will spin out of control and catastrophic events will follow. "Social suicide" is a little vague, but it sounds as if Popenoe is predicting that father absence will lead to the destruction of modern American culture. The other fallacy that you might have spotted was the *false dichotomy* apparent in Blankenhorn's assertion that "to tolerate the trend of fatherlessness is to accept the inevitability of continued societal recession." A false dichotomy creates an either-or choice between the position one wants to advocate (in this case, new social policies to reduce father absence) and some obviously horrible outcome that any sensible person would want to avoid (social decay), while ignoring other possible outcomes that might lie between these extremes.

In summary, we can find a number of flaws and weaknesses in the argument that fathers are *essential* to normal development. However, our critical evaluation of this argument *does not mean that fathers are unimportant.* Many types of evidence suggest that fathers generally make significant contributions to their children's development (Anderson et al., 2002; Phares, 1996; Rohner & Veneziano, 2001). We could argue with merit that fathers typically provide a substantial advantage for children that fatherless children do not have. But there is a crucial distinction between arguing that fathers *promote* normal, healthy development and arguing that fathers are *necessary* for normal, healthy development. If fathers are *necessary,* children who grow up without them could not achieve the same level of well-being as those who have fathers, yet it is clear that a great many children from single-parent homes turn out just fine.

Fathers surely are important, and it seems likely that father absence *contributes* to a variety of problems in modern society. So, why do Blankenhorn (1995) and Popenoe (1996) argue for the much stronger conclusion—that fathers are *essential?* They appear to prefer the stronger conclusion because it raises much more serious questions about the viability of nontraditional family forms. Thus, they seem to want to advance a *political agenda* that champions traditional family values. They are certainly entitled to do so, but when research findings are used to advance a political agenda—whether conservative or liberal—a special caution alert should go off in your head. When a political agenda is at stake, it pays to scrutinize arguments with extra care, because research findings are more likely to be presented in a slanted fashion. The field of psychology deals with a host of complex questions that have profound implications for a wide range of social issues. The skills and habits of critical thinking can help you find your way through the maze of reasons and evidence that hold up the many sides of these complicated issues.

Table 10.2 Critical Thinking Skills Discussed in This Application

Skill	Description
Understanding the limitations of correlational evidence	The critical thinker understands that a correlation between two variables does not demonstrate that there is a causal link between the variables.
Looking for alternative explanations for findings and events	In evaluating explanations, the critical thinker explores whether there are other explanations that could also account for the findings or events under scrutiny.
Recognizing and avoiding common fallacies, such as irrelevant reasons, circular reasoning, slippery slope reasoning, weak analogies, and false dichotomies	The critical thinker is vigilant about conclusions based on unrelated premises, conclusions that are rewordings of premises, unwarranted predictions that things will spin out of control, superficial analogies, and contrived dichotomies.

REVIEW of Key Learning Goals

10.23 Some social scientists have argued that father absence is the chief cause of a number of social problems and that fathers are essential for normal, healthy development. Critics note that all the relevant data are correlational, making causal inferences speculative, and they argue that there are alternative explanations for the association between father absence and negative developmental outcomes.

Progress Before Birth: Prenatal Development

▌ Prenatal development proceeds through the germinal, embryonic, and fetal stages as the zygote is differentiated into a human organism. During this period, development may be affected by maternal drug use, maternal malnutrition, and some maternal illnesses.

The Wondrous Years of Childhood

▌ Motor development follows cephalocaudal (head-to-foot) and proximodistal (center-outward) trends. Developmental norms for motor skills and other types of development are only group averages. Cross-cultural research on the pacing of motor development shows that maturation and experience both are important.

▌ Harlow's work with monkeys undermined the reinforcement explanation of attachment. Bowlby proposed an evolutionary explanation that has been very influential. Separation anxiety usually appears at around 6 to 8 months of age. Research shows that attachment emerges out of an interplay between infant and mother.

▌ Infant-mother attachments fall into three categories: secure, anxious-ambivalent, and avoidant. Cultural variations in childrearing can affect the patterns of attachment seen in a society. Attachment patterns may have lasting effects on individuals. Modest cultural variations in the prevalence of various patterns of attachment are seen, but secure attachment predominates in all cultures.

▌ Children typically utter their first words around their first birthday. Vocabulary growth is slow at first, but a vocabulary spurt often begins at around 18 months. Children begin to combine words by the end of their second year. Their early sentences are telegraphic, in that they omit many nonessential words. Over the next several years, children gradually learn the complexities of grammar.

▌ Erik Erikson's theory of personality development proposes that individuals evolve through eight stages over the life span. Progress through the four childhood stages should yield a trustful, autonomous person with a sense of initiative and industry.

▌ According to Piaget's theory of cognitive development, the key advance during the sensorimotor period is the child's gradual recognition of the permanence of objects. The preoperational period is marked by centration, irreversibility, and egocentrism. During the concrete operations period, children develop the ability to perform operations on mental representations. The stage of formal operations ushers in more abstract, systematic, and logical thought.

▌ Vygotsky's sociocultural theory maintains that cognitive development is fueled by social interactions with parents and others. Vygotsky argued that language is central to cognitive development and that culture exerts great influence over how cognitive growth unfolds. Recent research has shown that infants appear to understand surprisingly complex concepts that they have had virtually no opportunity to learn about, leading some theorists to conclude that basic cognitive abilities are innate.

▌ According to Kohlberg, moral reasoning progresses through three levels that are determined by cognitive development. Age-related progress in moral reasoning has been found, although there is a great deal of overlap between adjacent stages.

The Transition of Adolescence

▌ The growth spurt at puberty involves the development of reproductive maturity and secondary sex characteristics. Neural development continues through adolescence, and the prefrontal cortex is the last area of the brain to fully mature. Adolescents' risk taking may be elevated by their susceptibility to peer influence.

▌ According to Erikson, the key challenge of adolescence is to make some progress toward a sense of identity. Marcia identified four patterns of identity formation. Arnett has argued that emerging adulthood represents a new stage of development falling between adolescence and adulthood.

The Expanse of Adulthood

▌ During adulthood, personality is marked by both stability and change. Many landmarks in adult development involve transitions in family relationships, including adjusting to marriage, parenthood, and the empty nest. During adulthood, age-related physical transitions include changes in appearance, sensory losses, and hormonal changes.

▌ Research suggests that fluid intelligence declines in later adulthood, but crystallized intelligence tends to remain stable. Drastic mental decline is not a part of the normal aging process. However, many adults over age 75 suffer from some form of dementia. In late adulthood, mental speed declines and working memory suffers, but many people remain productive well into old age.

Reflecting on the Chapter's Themes

▌ Five of our seven themes stood out in this chapter, including the value of theoretical diversity, the influence of culture, the importance of sociohistorical context, and the inevitability of multifactorial causation. But above all else, our discussion of development showed how heredity and environment interactively shape behavior.

PERSONAL APPLICATION Understanding Gender Differences

▌ Gender differences in behavior are fewer in number and smaller in magnitude than gender stereotypes suggest. Research reviews suggest that there are genuine gender differences in verbal ability, mathematical ability, spatial ability, aggression, nonverbal communication, and sexual behavior.

▌ Evolutionary explanations of gender differences assert that the adaptive pressures faced by males and females have fostered behavioral disparities. There is research linking gender differences in humans to hormones and brain organization, but the research is marred by interpretive problems. Operant conditioning, observational learning, and self-socialization contribute to the development of gender differences. Families, schools, and the media are among the main sources of gender-role socialization.

CRITICAL THINKING APPLICATION Are Fathers Essential to Children's Well-being?

▌ Some social scientists have argued that father absence is the chief cause of a variety of social problems and that fathers are essential for normal, healthy development. Critics have argued that there are alternative explanations for the association between father absence and negative developmental outcomes.

PSYKTREK PREVIEW

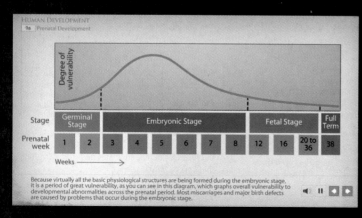

Visit Module 9a (*Prenatal Development*) to learn more about how development unfolds rapidly during the prenatal period.

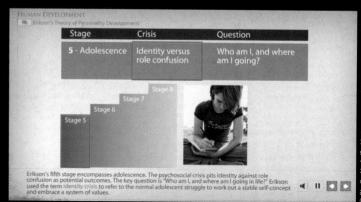

Explore Module 9b (*Erikson's Theory of Personality Development*) to see how Erik Erikson charted the course of human development across eight life stages.

1. The stage of prenatal development during which the developing organism is most vulnerable to injury is the:
   A. zygotic stage.
   C. fetal stage.
   B. germinal stage.
   D. embryonic stage.

2. The cephalocaudal trend in the motor development of children can be described simply as a:
   A. head-to-foot direction.
   C. foot-to-head direction.
   B. center-outward direction.
   D. body-appendages direction.

3. Developmental norms:
   A. can be used to make extremely precise predictions about the age at which an individual child will reach various developmental milestones.
   B. indicate the maximum age at which a child can reach a particular developmental milestone and still be considered "normal."
   C. indicate the average age at which individuals reach various developmental milestones.
   D. involve both A and B.

4. The behavioral, reinforcement explanation of the basis for infant-caregiver attachment was undermined by the research of:
   A. Erik Erikson.
   C. Lawrence Kohlberg.
   B. Harry Harlow.
   D. Lev Vygotsky.

5. The 2-year-old child who refers to every four-legged animal as "doggie" is making which of the following errors?
   A. underextension
   B. overextension
   C. overregularization
   D. underregularization

6. During the second year of life, toddlers begin to take some personal responsibility for feeding, dressing, and bathing themselves in an attempt to establish what Erikson calls a sense of:
   A. superiority.
   C. generativity.
   B. industry.
   D. autonomy.

7. Five-year-old David watches as you pour water from a short, wide glass into a tall, narrow one. He says there is now more water than before. This response demonstrates that:
   A. David understands the concept of conservation.
   B. David does not understand the concept of conservation.
   C. David's cognitive development is "behind" for his age.
   D. both B and C are happening.

8. Which of the following is not one of the criticisms of Piaget's theory of cognitive development?
   A. Piaget may have underestimated the cognitive skills of children in some areas.
   B. Piaget may have underestimated the influence of cultural and environmental factors on cognitive development.
   C. The theory does not clearly address the issue of variability among people in cognitive development.
   D. Evidence for the theory is based on children's answers to questions.

9. If a child's primary reason for not drawing pictures on the living room wall with crayons is to avoid the punishment that would inevitably follow this behavior, she would be said to be at which level of moral development?
   A. Conventional
   C. Preconventional
   B. Postconventional
   D. Unconventional

10. Girls who mature _____ and boys who mature _____ feel more subjective distress about the transition of puberty.
   A. early; early
   C. late; early
   B. early; late
   D. late; late

11. Which cognitive ability is most affected by aging?
   A. Crystallized intelligence
   B. Cognitive speed
   C. Abstract reasoning
   D. Procedural memory

12. Males have been found to differ slightly from females in three well-documented areas of mental abilities. Which of the following is not one of these?
   A. Verbal ability
   C. Intelligence
   B. Mathematical ability
   D. Visual-spatial abilities

Answers

1 D p. 337
2 A p. 339
3 C p. 340
4 B p. 341
5 B p. 344
6 D pp. 345–346
7 B p. 347
8 D pp. 348–349
9 C pp. 351–352
10 B p. 354
11 B p. 366
12 C pp. 368–369

PSYKTREK PREVIEW

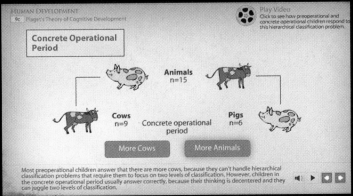

HUMAN DEVELOPMENT
9c Piaget's Theory of Cognitive Development

Concrete Operational Period

Play Video
Click to see how preoperational and concrete operational children respond to this hierarchical classification problem.

Animals n=15
Cows n=9
Concrete operational period
Pigs n=6
More Cows
More Animals

Most preoperational children answer that there are more cows, because they can't handle hierarchical classification problems that require them to focus on two levels of classification. However, children in the concrete operational period usually answer correctly, because their thinking is decentered and they can juggle two levels of classification.

HUMAN DEVELOPMENT
9e Attachment

Harry Harlow   Cloth mother   Wire mother

In the mid-1950s, the behavioral theory of attachment came into question as a result of Harry Harlow's famous studies of attachment in infant rhesus monkeys. Harlow removed newborn monkeys from their mothers at birth and raised them in the laboratory with two types of artificial mothers. Click on the photos shown here to learn about the two types of substitute mothers.

Go to Module 9c (*Piaget's Theory of Cognitive Development*) to enhance your understanding of Jean Piaget's work on children's thinking—and check out two videos showing how young children's reasoning can go awry.

Access Module 9e (*Attachment*) to learn more about the research of Harry Harlow, John Bowlby, and Mary Ainsworth on infant attachment—including a video reenactment of the strange situation procedure.

11

Personality: Theory, Research, and Assessment

Bridge at Multnomah Falls, Columbia River Gorge, Oregon © Rich Reid/National Geographic Image Collection

Richard Branson was sure that he was about to die. He was high above the Atlantic Ocean, alone in a capsule attached to the biggest balloon in the world. Per Lindstrand, the balloon's pilot, was somewhere in the icy waves far below. He and Branson had just become the first people ever to cross the Atlantic in a hot-air balloon, but when an emergency landing at sea failed, Lindstrand had leaped into the water. Before Branson could follow, the balloon had shot back up into the sky. Now Branson—who had never flown in a balloon before his all-too-brief training for the trip—was stranded in midair with no clear idea how to save himself.

Hastily Branson scribbled a note to his family: "I love you." Then he began trying to vent the huge balloon in a desperate attempt to guide it safely earthward. Much to his own surprise, he was able to get close enough to the sea to jump for it. A rescue helicopter plucked him out of the waves. (Lindstrand was saved by a passing fisherman.)

After this frightening brush with death, Branson swore that he would never risk his life so foolishly again. Yet three years later, he and Lindstrand were at it again, this time becoming the first to cross the Pacific in a hot-air balloon. The trip turned into another terrifying ordeal—at one point the balloon caught fire when they were thousands of feet above empty ocean—and once again they were nearly killed. But that didn't stop them from planning their next exploit—trying to become the first hot-air balloonists to fly completely around the world (Branson, 2005; Brown, 1998).

What kind of person has such an insatiable hunger for death-defying adventures? When people describe this side of Richard Branson, they are apt to use words such as *adventurous, brave, daring, impulsive,* and *reckless.* These are the kinds of words used to characterize what we call "personality." And Branson—a self-made billionaire and one of the richest people in the world—may be as famous for his exuberant personality as he is for his immense wealth.

A high school dropout, Branson is the founder of the Virgin group of companies. Among Virgin's 300-plus businesses are such varied enterprises as Virgin Books, Virgin Wines, the airline Virgin Atlantic, and Virgin Galactic, which aims to become the first company to fly tourists into space. Branson is a brash, shrewd, and relentless entrepreneur who loves cutting a deal. But he also loves parties, practical jokes, and flamboyant publicity stunts. Most of all, he relishes finding new fields to conquer. It was typical of Branson—who made his first fortune with a music recording company—to decide that it would be "fun" to start an airline even though he had no knowledge of the business, let alone routes to fly or

Richard Branson, the founder of the Virgin group of companies, clearly manifests a powerful and unusual personality. But everyone has his or her own unique personality, which makes the study of personality a fascinating area of inquiry in psychology.

planes to fly them (Branson, 2005; Brown, 1998). His approach is nicely summed up in the title of his book of life lessons, *Screw It, Let's Do It* (Branson, 2006).

Most people would agree that Richard Branson has an unusual personality. But what exactly *is* personality? And why are personalities so different? Why is one person daring, while another is timid? Why is one person high spirited and outgoing, while another is quiet and shy? Was Richard Branson born with the self-confidence and daring he is renowned for, or were environment and learning critical in shaping his personality? Consider that Branson's parents stressed the importance of being strong and independent, starting at an early age. When Branson was just 4 years old, he relates, his mother "stopped the car a few miles from our house and made me find my own way home across the fields" (Branson, 2005, p. 15). Branson believes that episodes like these nurtured his enduring appetite for "huge, apparently unachievable challenges" (Branson, 2005, p. 219).

Yet can this be the whole explanation? After all, another four-year-old might have simply sat down by the road and cried. Could part of the answer to the riddle of Branson's personality lie in biological inheritance? Branson (2005) describes his mother as a woman of dazzling energy and fierce determination who also has a taste for adventure. During World War II Eve Branson wanted to be a glider pilot even though the job was open only to males. Refusing to take no for an answer, she talked her way into pilot training on the condition that she disguise herself as a boy. Branson's father, Ted, is a quieter sort who nevertheless shares his wife's adventurousness. When Branson dreamed up the idea for Virgin Galactic, an airline offering suborbital spaceflights, Ted said that he intended to be one of the first passengers launched into space—at the age of 90! With parents like these, is being an "adrenaline junkie" wired into Branson's genetic makeup?

Psychologists have approached questions like these from a variety of perspectives. Traditionally, the study of personality has been dominated by "grand theories" that attempt to explain a great many facets of behavior. Our discussion will reflect this emphasis, as we'll devote most of our time to the sweeping theories of Freud, Skinner, Rogers, and several others. In recent decades, however, the study of personality has shifted toward narrower research programs that examine specific issues related to personality. This trend is reflected in our review of biological, cultural, and other contemporary approaches to personality in the last several sections of the chapter. In the Personal Application, we'll examine how psychological tests are used to measure aspects of personality. The Critical Thinking Application will explore how hindsight bias can taint people's analyses of personality.

Key Learning Goals

11.1 Define the construct of personality in terms of consistency and distinctiveness.
11.2 Clarify what is meant by a personality trait, and describe the five-factor model of personality.
11.3 Summarize relations between the Big Five traits and life outcomes.

The Nature of Personality

Personality is a complex hypothetical construct that has been defined in a variety of ways. Let's take a closer look at the concepts of personality and personality traits.

Defining Personality: Consistency and Distinctiveness

What does it mean to say that someone has an optimistic personality? This assertion indicates that the person has a fairly *consistent tendency* to behave in a cheerful, hopeful, enthusiastic way, looking at the bright side of things, across a wide variety of situations. Although no one is entirely consistent in behavior, this quality of *consistency across situations* lies at the core of the concept of personality.

Distinctiveness is also central to the concept of personality. Personality is used to explain why different people do not act the same in similar situations. If you were stuck in an elevator with three people, each might react differently. One might crack jokes to relieve tension. Another might make ominous predictions that "we'll never get out of here." The third person might calmly think about how to escape. These varied reactions to the same situation occur because each person has a different personality. Each person has traits that are seen in other people, but each individual has his or her own distinctive *set* of personality traits.

In summary, the concept of personality is used to explain (1) the stability in a person's behavior over time and across situations (consistency) and (2) the behavioral differences among people reacting to the same situation (distinctiveness). We can combine these ideas into the following definition: *Personality refers to an individual's unique collection of consistent behavioral traits.* Let's explore the concept of *traits* in more detail.

Personality Traits: Dispositions and Dimensions

Everyone makes remarks like "Jan is very *conscientious.*" Or you might assert that "Jamaal is too *timid* to succeed in that job." These descriptive statements refer to personality traits. A *personality trait* is a durable disposition to behave in a particular way in a variety of situations. Adjectives such as *honest, dependable, moody, impulsive, suspicious, anxious, excitable, domineering,* and *friendly* describe dispositions that represent personality traits. People use an enormous number of these trait terms to describe one another's personality. One prominent personality theorist, Gordon Allport (1937, 1961), went through an unabridged dictionary and identified over 4500 personality traits!

Most approaches to personality assume that some traits are more basic than others. According to this notion, a small number of fundamental traits determine other, more superficial traits. For example, a person's tendency to be impulsive, restless, irritable, boisterous, and impatient might all be derived from a more basic tendency to be excitable.

A number of psychologists have taken on the challenge of identifying the basic traits that form the core of personality. For example, Raymond Cattell (1950, 1966, 1990) used the statistical procedure of *factor analysis* to reduce a huge list of personality traits to just 16 basic dimensions of personality. In *factor analysis,* correlations among many variables are analyzed to identify closely related clusters of variables. If the measurements of a number of variables (in this case, personality traits) correlate highly with one another, the assumption is that a single factor is influencing all of them. Cattell concluded that psychologists could thoroughly describe an individual's personality by measuring the 16 traits that he identified in his factor analyses. In the Personal Application, we'll discuss a personality test he designed to assess these traits.

The Five-Factor Model of Personality Traits

Robert McCrae and Paul Costa (1987, 1997, 1999, 2003) have used factor analysis to arrive at an even simpler, *five-factor model of personality* (see **Figure 11.1**). McCrae and Costa maintain that most personality traits are derived from just five higher-order traits that have come to be known as the "Big Five":

- *Extraversion.* People who score high in extraversion, which is called *positive emotionality* by some theorists, are characterized as outgoing, sociable, upbeat, friendly, assertive, and gregarious.
- *Neuroticism.* People who score high in neuroticism, which is characterized as *negative emotionality* in some models, tend to be anxious, hostile, self-conscious, insecure, and vulnerable.
- *Openness to experience.* Openness is associated with curiosity, flexibility, vivid fantasy, imaginativeness, artistic sensitivity, and unconventional attitudes.
- *Agreeableness.* Those who score high in agreeableness tend to be sympathetic, trusting, cooperative, modest, and straightforward.
- *Conscientiousness.* Conscientious people tend to be diligent, disciplined, well-organized, punctual, and dependable. Some theorists refer to this trait as *constraint*.

Correlations have also been found between the Big Five traits and quite a variety of important life outcomes (Ozer & Benet-Martinez, 2006). For instance, higher grades (GPA) in both high school and college are associated with higher conscientiousness, primarily because conscientious students work harder (Noftle & Robins, 2007). Several of the Big Five traits are associated with occupational attainment (career success). Extraversion and conscientiousness are positive predictors of occupational attainment, whereas neuroticism is a negative predictor (Roberts, Caspi, & Moffitt, 2003). The likelihood of divorce can also be predicted by personality traits, as neuroticism elevates the probability of divorce, whereas agreeableness and conscientiousness reduce it (Roberts et al., 2007). Finally, and perhaps most important, two of the Big Five traits are related to health and mortality over the course of the life span. Neuroticism is associated with an elevated prevalence of physical and mental disorders, whereas conscientiousness is correlated with the experience of less illness and with reduced mortality (Goodwin & Friedman, 2006; Martin, Friedman, & Schwartz, 2007). In other words, conscientious people live longer than others!

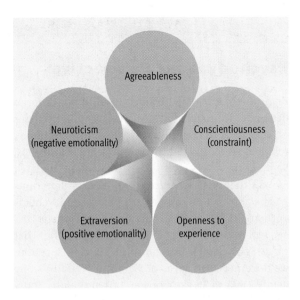

Figure 11.1

The five-factor model of personality. Trait models attempt to break personality down into its basic dimensions. McCrae and Costa (1985, 1987, 1997) maintain that personality can be described adequately with the five higher-order traits identified here, which are widely referred to as the "Big Five."

Like Cattell, McCrae and Costa maintain that personality can be described adequately by measuring the basic traits that they've identified. Their bold claim has been supported in many studies by other researchers, and the Big Five model has become the dominant conception of personality structure in contemporary psychology (John & Srivastava, 1999; McCrae, 2005). However, some theorists have argued that more than five traits are necessary to account for most of the variation seen in human personality (Ashton et al., 2004; Benet & Waller, 1995).

The debate about how many dimensions are necessary to describe personality is likely to continue. As you'll see throughout the chapter, the study of personality is an area in psychology that has a long history of "dueling theories." We'll divide these diverse personality theories into four broad groups that share certain assumptions, emphases, and interests: (1) psychodynamic perspectives, (2) behavioral perspectives, (3) humanistic perspectives, and (4) biological perspectives. We'll begin our discussion of personality theories by examining the life and work of Sigmund Freud.

REVIEW of Key Learning Goals

11.1 The concept of personality focuses on consistency in people's behavior over time and across situations and on what traits make people distinctive from one another. Thus, personality refers to an individual's unique constellation of consistent behavioral traits.

11.2 A personality trait is a durable disposition to behave in a particular way. The five-factor model has become the dominant conception of personality structure. The Big Five personality traits are extraversion, neuroticism, openness to experience, agreeableness, and conscientiousness.

11.3 The Big Five traits are predictive of important life outcomes. For example, occupational attainment is predicted by extraversion, conscientiousness, and neuroticism. Health and mortality are related to neuroticism and conscientiousness.

Key Learning Goals

11.4 Distinguish among the three components of personality and the three levels of awareness in Freud's theory.

11.5 Explain the role of anxiety in Freud's theory, and describe the operation of defense mechanisms.

11.6 Describe Freud's psychosexual stages of development and their importance.

11.7 Summarize the revisions of Freud's theory proposed by Jung and Adler.

11.8 Evaluate the strengths and weaknesses of the psychodynamic approach to personality.

Sigmund Freud

"No one who, like me, conjures up the most evil of those half-tamed demons that inhabit the human beast, and seeks to wrestle with them, can expect to come through the struggle unscathed."

web link 11.1

The Victorian Web

Psychoanalysis initially developed within a late-19th-century context that is comprehensively portrayed in English Professor George Landow's (Brown University) important hypertext archive.

Psychodynamic Perspectives

Psychodynamic theories include all the diverse theories descended from the work of Sigmund Freud that focus on unconscious mental forces. Freud inspired many scholars who followed in his intellectual footsteps. Some of these followers simply refined and updated Freud's theory. Others veered off in new directions and established independent, albeit related, schools of thought. Today, the psychodynamic umbrella covers a large collection of loosely related theories that we can only sample from in this text. In this section, we'll examine the ideas of Sigmund Freud in some detail. Then we'll take a briefer look at the psychodynamic theories of Carl Jung and Alfred Adler.

Freud's Psychoanalytic Theory   10a

Born in 1856, Sigmund Freud grew up in a middle-class Jewish home in Vienna, Austria. He showed an early interest in intellectual pursuits and became an intense, hardworking young man, driven to achieve fame. Freud lived in the Victorian era, which was marked by sexual repression. His life was also affected by World War I, which devastated Europe, and by the growing anti-Semitism of the times. We'll see that the sexual repression and aggressive hostilities that Freud witnessed left their mark on his view of human nature.

Freud was a physician specializing in neurology when he began his medical practice in Vienna toward the end of the 19th century. Like other neurologists in his era, he often treated people troubled by nervous problems such as irrational fears, obsessions, and anxieties. Eventually he devoted himself to the treatment of mental disorders using an innovative procedure he had developed, called *psychoanalysis,* that required lengthy verbal interactions with patients during which Freud probed deeply into their lives.

Freud's (1901, 1924, 1940) *psychoanalytic theory* grew out of his decades of interactions with his clients in psychoanalysis. Psychoanalytic theory attempts to explain personality, motivation, and psychological disorders by focusing on the influence of early childhood experiences, on unconscious motives and conflicts, and on the methods people use to cope with their sexual and aggressive urges.

Most of Freud's contemporaries were uncomfortable with his theory, for at least three reasons. First, in arguing that people's behavior is governed by unconscious factors of which they are unaware, Freud made the disconcerting suggestion that individuals are not masters of their own minds. Second, in claiming that adult personalities are shaped by childhood experiences and other factors beyond one's control, he suggested that people are not masters of their own destinies. Third, by emphasizing the importance of how people cope with their sexual urges, he offended those who held the conservative, Victorian values of his time. Thus, Freud endured a great deal of criticism, condemnation, and outright ridicule, even after his work began to attract favorable attention. Let's examine the ideas that generated so much controversy.

Structure of Personality   10a

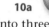

Freud divided personality structure into three components: the id, the ego, and the superego. He saw a person's behavior as the outcome of interactions among these three components.

The *id* is the primitive, instinctive component of personality that operates according to the pleasure principle. Freud referred to the id as the reservoir of psychic energy. By this he meant that the id houses the raw biological urges (to eat, sleep, defecate, copulate, and so on) that energize human behavior. The id operates according to the *pleasure principle,* which demands immediate gratification of its urges. The id engages in *primary-process thinking,* which is primitive, illogical, irrational, and fantasy oriented.

The *ego* is the decision-making component of personality that operates according to the reality principle. The ego mediates between the id, with its forceful desires for immediate satisfaction, and the external social world, with its expectations and norms regarding suitable behavior. The ego considers social realities—society's norms, etiquette, rules, and customs—in deciding how to behave. The ego is guided by the *reality principle,* which seeks to delay gratification of the id's urges until appropriate outlets and situations can be found. In short, to stay out of trouble, the ego often works to tame the unbridled desires of the id.

In the long run, the ego wants to maximize gratification, just as the id does. However, the ego engages in *secondary-process thinking,* which is relatively rational, realistic, and oriented toward problem solving. Thus, the ego strives to avoid negative consequences from society and its representatives (for example, punishment by parents or teachers) by behaving "properly." It also attempts to achieve long-range goals that sometimes require putting off gratification.

While the ego concerns itself with practical realities, the *superego* is the moral component of personality that incorporates social standards about what represents right and wrong. Throughout their lives, but especially during childhood, people receive training about what constitutes good and bad behavior. Many social norms regarding morality are eventually internalized. The superego emerges out of the ego at around 3 to 5 years of age. In some people, the superego can become irrationally demanding in its striving for moral perfection. Such people are plagued by excessive feelings of guilt.

According to Freud, the id, ego, and superego are distributed differently across three levels of awareness, which we'll describe next.

Levels of Awareness

10a

Perhaps Freud's most enduring insight was his recognition of how unconscious forces can influence behavior. He inferred the existence of the unconscious from a variety of observations that he made with his patients. For example, he noticed that "slips of the tongue" often revealed a person's true feelings (hence the expression "Freudian slip"). He also realized that his patients' dreams often expressed hidden desires. Most important, through psychoanalysis he often helped patients discover feelings and conflicts they had previously been unaware of.

Freud contrasted the unconscious with the conscious and preconscious, creating three levels of awareness. The *conscious* consists of whatever one is aware of at a particular point in time. For example, at this moment your conscious may include the train of thought in this text and a dim aware-

ness in the back of your mind that your eyes are getting tired and you're beginning to get hungry. The *preconscious* contains material just beneath the surface of awareness that can easily be retrieved. Examples might include your middle name, what you had for supper last night, or an argument you had with a friend yesterday. The *unconscious* contains thoughts, memories, and desires that are well below the surface of conscious awareness but that nonetheless exert great influence on behavior. Examples of material that might be found in your unconscious include a forgotten trauma from childhood, hidden feelings of hostility toward a parent, and repressed sexual desires.

Freud's conception of the mind is often compared to an iceberg that has most of its mass hidden beneath the water's surface (see **Figure 11.2**). He believed that the unconscious (the mass below the surface) is much larger than the conscious or preconscious. As you can see in **Figure 11.2**, he proposed that the ego and superego operate at all three levels of awareness. In contrast, the id is entirely unconscious, expressing its urges at a conscious level through the ego. Of course, the id's desires for immediate satisfaction often trigger internal conflicts

Freud's psychoanalytic theory was based on decades of clinical work. He treated a great many patients in the consulting room pictured here. The room contains numerous artifacts from other cultures—and the original psychoanalytic couch.

Figure 11.2

Freud's model of personality structure. Freud theorized that people have three levels of awareness: the conscious, the preconscious, and the unconscious. The enormous size of the unconscious is often dramatized by comparing it to the portion of an iceberg that lies beneath the water's surface. Freud also divided personality structure into three components—id, ego, and superego—which operate according to different principles and exhibit different modes of thinking. In Freud's model, the id is entirely unconscious, but the ego and superego operate at all three levels of awareness.

with the ego and superego. These conflicts play a key role in Freud's theory.

Conflict and the Tyranny of Sex and Aggression

"ALL I WANT FROM THEM IS A SIMPLE MAJORITY ON THINGS."

Freud assumed that behavior is the outcome of an ongoing series of internal conflicts. He saw internal battles between the id, ego, and superego as routine. Why? Because the id wants to gratify its urges immediately, but the norms of civilized society frequently dictate otherwise. For example, your id might feel an urge to clobber a co-worker who constantly irritates you. However, society frowns on such behavior, so your ego would try to hold this urge in check. Hence, you would find yourself in conflict. You may be experiencing conflict at this very moment. In Freudian terms, your id may be secretly urging you to abandon reading this chapter so that you can fix a snack and watch some television. Your ego may be weighing this appealing option against your society-induced need to excel in school.

Freud believed that people's lives are dominated by conflict. He asserted that individuals career from one conflict to another. The following scenario provides a concrete illustration of how the three components of personality interact to create constant conflicts:

Imagine lurching across your bed to shut off your alarm clock as it rings obnoxiously. It's 7 A.M. and time to get up for your history class. However, your id (operating according to the pleasure principle) urges you to return to the immediate gratification of additional sleep. Your ego (operating according to the reality principle) points out that you really must go to class since you haven't been able to decipher the history textbook on your own. Your id (in its typical unrealistic fashion) smugly assures you that you will get the A grade that you need and suggests lying back to dream about how impressed your roommates will be. Just as you're relaxing, your superego jumps into the fray. It tries to make you feel guilty about all the money your parents paid in tuition for the class that you're about to skip. You haven't even gotten out of bed yet, but there's already a pitched battle in your psyche.

Freud believed that conflicts centering on sexual and aggressive impulses are especially likely to have far-reaching consequences. Why did he emphasize sex and aggression? Two reasons were prominent in his thinking. First, he thought that sex and aggression are subject to more complex and ambiguous social controls than other basic motives. The norms governing sexual and aggressive behavior are subtle, and people often get inconsistent messages about what's appropriate. Second, he noted that the aggres-

sive and sexual drives are thwarted more regularly than other basic, biological urges. Think about it: If you get hungry or thirsty, you can simply head for a nearby vending machine or a drinking fountain. But if a department store clerk infuriates you, you aren't likely to reach across the counter and slug him or her. Likewise, when you see an attractive person who inspires lustful urges, you don't normally walk up and propose a tryst in a nearby broom closet. There's nothing comparable to vending machines or drinking fountains for the satisfaction of sexual and aggressive urges. Freud ascribed great importance to these needs because social norms dictate that they're routinely frustrated.

Anxiety and Defense Mechanisms

Most internal conflicts are trivial and are quickly resolved. Occasionally, however, a conflict will linger for days, months, or even years, creating internal tension. More often than not, such prolonged and troublesome conflicts involve sexual and aggressive impulses that society wants to tame. These conflicts are often played out entirely in the unconscious. Although you may not be aware of these unconscious battles, they can produce *anxiety* that slips to the surface of conscious awareness.

The arousal of anxiety is a crucial event in Freud's theory of personality functioning (see **Figure 11.3**). Anxiety is distressing, so people try to rid themselves of this unpleasant emotion any way they can. This effort to ward off anxiety often involves the use of defense mechanisms. *Defense mechanisms are largely unconscious reactions that protect a person from unpleasant emotions such as anxiety and guilt.* Typically, they're mental maneuvers that work through self-deception (see **Table 11.1**). Consider *rationalization,* which is creating false but plausible excuses to justify unacceptable behavior. For example, after cheating someone in a business transaction, you might reduce your guilt by rationalizing that "everyone does it."

According to Freud, the most basic and widely used defense mechanism is repression. *Repression* is keeping distressing thoughts and feelings buried in the unconscious. People tend to repress desires that make them feel guilty, conflicts that make them anxious, and memories that are painful. As pointed out in Chapter 7, repression has been called "motivated forgetting." If you forget a dental appointment or the name of someone you don't like, repression may be at work.

Self-deception can also be seen in projection and displacement. *Projection* is attributing one's own thoughts, feelings, or motives to another. Usually, the thoughts one projects onto others are those that would make one feel guilty. For example, if lusting for a co-worker makes you feel guilty, you might attribute any latent sexual tension between the two of you to the *other person's* desire to seduce you. *Displacement* is diverting emotional feelings (usually anger) from their original source to a substitute target. If your boss gives you a hard time at work and you come home and slam the door, kick the dog, and scream at your spouse, you're displacing your anger onto irrelevant targets. Unfortunately, social constraints often force people to hold back their anger, and they end up lashing out at the people they love the most.

Other prominent defense mechanisms include reaction formation, regression, and identification. *Reaction formation* is behaving in a way that's exactly the opposite of one's true feelings. Guilt about sexual desires often leads to reaction formation. Freud theorized that many homophobic males who ridicule homosexuals are defending against their own latent homosexual impulses. The telltale sign of reaction formation is the exaggerated quality of the opposite behavior. *Regression* is a reversion to immature patterns of behavior. When anxious about their self-worth, some adults respond with childish boasting and bragging (as opposed to subtle efforts to impress others). For example, a fired executive having difficulty finding a new job might start making ridiculous statements about his incomparable talents and achievements. Such bragging is regressive when it's marked by massive exaggerations that virtually anyone can see through. *Identification* is bolstering self-esteem by forming an imaginary or real alliance with some person or group.

Youngsters often shore up precarious feelings of self-worth by identifying with rock stars, movie stars, or famous athletes. Adults may join exclusive country clubs or civic organizations as a means of boosting their self-esteem via identification.

Development: Psychosexual Stages

 10a

Freud made the rather startling assertion that the basic foundation of an individual's personality has been laid down by the tender age of 5. To shed light on these crucial early years, Freud formulated a stage theory of development. He emphasized how young children deal with their immature but powerful sexual urges (he used the term *sexual* in a general way to refer to many urges for physical pleasure). According to Freud, these sexual urges shift in focus as children progress from one stage of development to another. Indeed, the names for the stages (oral, anal, genital, and so on) are based on where children are focusing their erotic energy during that period. Thus, *psychosexual* stages are developmental periods with a characteristic sexual focus that leave their mark on adult personality.

Figure 11.3
Freud's model of personality dynamics. According to Freud, unconscious conflicts between the id, ego, and superego sometimes lead to anxiety. This discomfort may lead to the use of defense mechanisms, which may temporarily relieve anxiety.

Table 11.1 Defense Mechanisms, with Examples

Defense Mechanism	Definition	Example
Repression	Keeping distressing thoughts and feelings buried in the unconscious	A traumatized soldier has no recollection of the details of a close brush with death.
Projection	Attributing one's own thoughts, feelings, or motives to another	A woman who dislikes her boss thinks she likes her boss but feels that the boss doesn't like her.
Displacement	Diverting emotional feelings (usually anger) from their original source to a substitute target	After parental scolding, a young girl takes her anger out on her little brother.
Reaction formation	Behaving in a way that is exactly the opposite of one's true feelings	A parent who unconsciously resents a child spoils the child with outlandish gifts.
Regression	A reversion to immature patterns of behavior	An adult has a temper tantrum when he doesn't get his way.
Rationalization	Creating false but plausible excuses to justify unacceptable behavior	A student watches TV instead of studying, saying that "additional study wouldn't do any good anyway."
Identification	Bolstering self-esteem by forming an imaginary or real alliance with some person or group	An insecure young man joins a fraternity to boost his self-esteem.

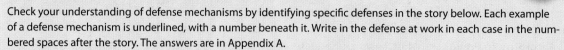
web link 11.2

Sigmund Freud Museum, Vienna, Austria

This online museum, in both English and German versions, offers a detailed chronology of Freud's life and an explanation of the most important concepts of psychoanalysis. The highlights here, though, are the rich audiovisual resources, including photos, amateur movie clips, and voice recordings of Freud.

Freud theorized that each psychosexual stage has its own unique developmental challenges or tasks (see **Table 11.2**). The way these challenges are handled supposedly shapes personality. The notion of *fixation* plays an important role in this process. **Fixation involves a failure to move forward from one stage to another as expected.** Essentially, the child's development stalls for a while. Fixation can be caused by excessive *gratification* of needs at a particular stage or by excessive *frustration* of those needs. Either way, fixations left over from childhood affect adult personality. Generally, fixation leads to an overemphasis on the psychosexual needs prominent during the fixated stage. Freud described a series of five psychosexual stages. Let's examine some of the highlights in this sequence and how fixation might occur.

Oral Stage. The oral stage encompasses the first year of life. During this period, the main source of erotic stimulation is the mouth (in biting, sucking, chewing, and so on). In Freud's view, the way the child's feeding experience is handled is crucial to subsequent development. He attributed considerable importance to the manner in which the child is weaned from the breast or the bottle. According to Freud, fixation at the oral stage could form the basis for obsessive eating or smoking later in life (among many other things).

Anal Stage. In their second year, children get their erotic pleasure from their bowel movements, through either the expulsion or retention of feces. The crucial event at this time is toilet training, which represents society's first systematic effort to regulate the child's biological urges. Severely punitive toilet training leads to a variety of possible outcomes. For example, excessive punishment might produce a latent feeling of hostility toward the "trainer," usually the mother. This hostility might generalize to women as a class. Another possibility is that heavy reliance on punitive measures could lead to an association between genital concerns and the anxiety

Table 11.2 Freud's Stages of Psychosexual Development

Stage	Approximate Ages	Erotic Focus	Key Tasks and Experiences
Oral	0–1	Mouth (sucking, biting)	Weaning (from breast or bottle)
Anal	2–3	Anus (expelling or retaining feces)	Toilet training
Phallic	4–5	Genitals (masturbating)	Identifying with adult role models; coping with Oedipal crisis
Latency	6–12	None (sexually repressed)	Expanding social contacts
Genital	Puberty onward	Genitals (being sexually intimate)	Establishing intimate relationships; contributing to society through working

According to Freud, early childhood experiences such as toilet training (a parental attempt to regulate a child's biological urges) can influence an individual's personality, with consequences lasting throughout adulthood.

that the punishment arouses. This genital anxiety derived from severe toilet training could evolve into anxiety about sexual activities later in life.

Phallic Stage. In the third through fifth years, the genitals become the focus for the child's erotic energy, largely through self-stimulation. During this pivotal stage, the *Oedipal complex* emerges. That is, little boys develop an erotically tinged preference for their mother. They also feel hostility toward their father, whom they view as a competitor for mom's affection. Similarly, little girls develop a special attachment to their father. Around the same time, they learn that little boys have different genitals and supposedly develop *penis envy*. According to Freud, young girls feel hostile toward their mother because they blame her for their anatomical "deficiency." To summarize, in the *Oedipal complex* children manifest erotically tinged desires for their opposite-sex parent, accompanied by feelings of hostility toward their same-sex parent. The name for this syndrome was taken from the Greek myth in which Oedipus, not knowing the identity of his real parents, inadvertently killed his father and married his mother.

According to Freud, the way parents and children deal with the sexual and aggressive conflicts inherent in the Oedipal complex is of paramount importance. The child has to resolve the Oedipal dilemma by purging the sexual longings for the opposite-sex parent and by crushing the hostility felt toward the same-sex parent. In Freud's view, healthy psychosexual development hinges on the resolution of the Oedipal conflict. Why? Because continued hostility toward the same-sex parent may prevent the child from identifying adequately with that parent. Freudian theory predicts that without such identification, many aspects of the child's development won't progress as they should.

Latency and Genital Stages. From around age 5 through puberty, the child's sexuality is largely suppressed—it becomes *latent*. Important events during this *latency stage* center on expanding social contacts beyond the immediate family. With the advent of puberty, the child progresses into the *genital stage*. Sexual urges reappear and focus on the genitals once again. At this point, sexual energy is normally channeled toward peers of the other sex, rather than toward oneself as in the phallic stage.

In arguing that the early years shape personality, Freud did not mean that personality development comes to an abrupt halt in middle childhood. However, he did believe that the foundation for adult personality is solidly entrenched by this time. He maintained that future developments are rooted in early, formative experiences and that significant conflicts in later years are replays of crises from childhood.

In fact, Freud believed that unconscious sexual conflicts rooted in childhood experiences cause most personality disturbances. His steadfast belief in the psychosexual origins of psychological disorders eventually led to bitter theoretical disputes with two of his most brilliant colleagues: Carl Jung and Alfred Adler. Jung and Adler both argued that Freud overemphasized sexuality. Freud summarily rejected their ideas, and the other two theorists felt compelled to go their own way, developing their own psychodynamic theories of personality.

Jung's Analytical Psychology

Carl Jung was born to middle-class Swiss parents in 1875. The son of a Protestant pastor, he was a deeply introverted, lonely child, but an excellent student. Jung had earned his medical degree and was an established young psychiatrist in Zurich when he began to write to Freud in 1906. When the two men had their first meeting, they were so taken by each

Carl Jung

"I am not a Jungian . . . I do not want anybody to be a Jungian. I want people above all to be themselves."

other's insights, they talked nonstop for 13 hours! They exchanged 359 letters before their friendship and theoretical alliance were torn apart in 1913.

Jung called his new approach *analytical psychology* to differentiate it from Freud's psychoanalytic theory. Unlike Freud, Jung encouraged his followers to develop their own theoretical views. Perhaps because of his bitter conflict with Freud, he deplored the way schools of thought often become dogmatic, discouraging creative, new ideas. Although many theorists came to characterize themselves as "Jungians," Jung himself often remarked, "I am not a Jungian" and said, "I do not want anybody to be a Jungian. I want people above all to be themselves" (van der Post, 1975).

Like Freud, Jung (1921, 1933) emphasized the unconscious determinants of personality. However, he proposed that the unconscious consists of two layers. The first layer, called the *personal unconscious,* is essentially the same as Freud's version of the unconscious. The personal unconscious houses material that is not within one's conscious awareness, because it has been repressed or forgotten. In addition, Jung theorized the existence of a deeper layer he called the collective unconscious. The *collective unconscious* is a storehouse of latent memory traces inherited from people's ancestral past. According to Jung, each person shares the collective unconscious with the entire human race (see **Figure 11.4**). It contains the "whole spiritual heritage of mankind's evolution, born anew in the brain structure of every individual" (Jung, quoted in Campbell, 1971, p. 45).

Figure 11.4

Jung's vision of the collective unconscious. Much like Freud, Jung theorized that each person has conscious and unconscious levels of awareness. However, he also proposed that the entire human race shares a collective unconscious, which exists in the deepest reaches of everyone's awareness. He saw the collective unconscious as a storehouse of hidden ancestral memories, called archetypes.

Jung called these ancestral memories *archetypes.* They are not memories of actual, personal experiences. Instead, *archetypes* are emotionally charged images and thought forms that have universal meaning. These archetypal images and ideas show up frequently in dreams and are often manifested in a culture's use of symbols in art, literature, and religion. According to Jung, symbols from very different cultures often show striking similarities because they emerge from archetypes that are shared by the entire human race. For instance, Jung found numerous cultures in which the *mandala,* or "magic circle," has served as a symbol of the unified wholeness of the self. Jung felt that an understanding of archetypal symbols helped him make sense of his patients' dreams. Dream analysis was of great concern to him, as he thought that dreams contain important messages from the unconscious. Like Freud, he depended extensively on dream analysis in his treatment of patients.

Adler's Individual Psychology

Alfred Adler, like Freud, grew up in Vienna in a middle-class Jewish home. He was a sickly child who struggled to overcome rickets (a bone disease caused by vitamin D deficiency) and an almost fatal case of pneumonia. At home, he was overshadowed by an exceptionally bright and successful older brother. Nonetheless, he went on to earn his medical degree, and he practiced ophthalmology and general medicine before his interest turned to psychiatry. He was a charter member of Freud's inner circle—the Vienna Psychoanalytic Society. However, he soon began to develop his own approach to personality, which he called *individual psychology.*

Like Jung, Adler (1917, 1927) argued that Freud had gone overboard in centering his theory on sexual conflicts. According to Adler, the foremost source of human motivation is a striving for superiority. In his view, this striving does not necessarily translate into the pursuit of dominance or high status. Adler saw *striving for superiority* as a universal drive to adapt, improve oneself, and master life's challenges. He noted that young children understandably feel weak and helpless in comparison with more competent older children and adults. These early inferiority feelings supposedly motivate them to acquire new skills and develop new talents. Thus, Adler maintained that striving for superiority is the prime goal of life, rather than physical gratification (as suggested by Freud).

Adler asserted that everyone has to work to overcome some feelings of inferiority—a process he called compensation. *Compensation* involves efforts to overcome imagined or real inferiorities by devel-

Adler's theory has been used to analyze the tragic life of the legendary actress Marilyn Monroe (Ansbacher, 1970). During her childhood, Monroe suffered from parental neglect that left her with acute feelings of inferiority. Her inferiority feelings led her to overcompensate by flaunting her beauty, marrying celebrities (Joe DiMaggio and Arthur Miller), keeping film crews waiting for hours, and seeking the adoration of her fans.

oping one's abilities. Adler believed that compensation is entirely normal. However, in some people inferiority feelings can become excessive, resulting in what is widely known today as an *inferiority complex*—exaggerated feelings of weakness and inadequacy. Adler thought that either parental pampering or parental neglect could cause an inferiority complex. Thus, he agreed with Freud on the importance of early childhood experiences, although he focused on different aspects of parent-child relations.

Evaluating Psychodynamic Perspectives

The psychodynamic approach has provided a number of far-reaching, truly "grand" theories of personality. These theories yielded some bold new insights when they were first presented. Although one might argue about exact details of interpretation, psychodynamic theory and research have demonstrated that (1) unconscious forces can influence behavior,

(2) internal conflict often plays a key role in generating psychological distress, (3) early childhood experiences can influence adult personality, and (4) people use defense mechanisms to reduce their experience of unpleasant emotions (Bornstein, 2003; Solms, 2004; Westen, 1998; Westen & Gabbard, 1999).

In addition to being praised, psychodynamic formulations have also been criticized on several grounds, including the following (Crews, 2006; Eysenck, 1990b; Kramer, 2006; Torrey, 1992):

1. *Poor testability.* Scientific investigations require testable hypotheses. Psychodynamic ideas have often been too vague and conjectural to permit a clear scientific test. For instance, how would you prove or disprove the assertion that the id is entirely unconscious?

2. *Inadequate evidence.* The empirical evidence on psychodynamic theories has often been characterized as "inadequate." Psychodynamic theories depend too heavily on clinical case studies in which it's much too easy for clinicians to see what they expect to see. Reexaminations of Freud's own clinical work suggest that he frequently distorted his patients' case histories to make them mesh with his theory (Esterson, 2001; Powell & Boer, 1995) and that there was a substantial disparity between Freud's writings and his actual therapeutic methods (Lynn & Vaillant, 1998). Insofar as researchers have accumulated evidence on psychodynamic theories, the evidence has provided only modest support for many of the

Alfred Adler

"The goal of the human soul is conquest, perfection, security, superiority."

central hypotheses (Fisher & Greenberg, 1985, 1996; Westen & Gabbard, 1999; Wolitzky, 2006).

3. *Sexism.* Many critics have argued that psychodynamic theories are characterized by a sexist bias against women. Freud believed that females' penis envy made them feel inferior to men. He also thought that females tended to develop weaker superegos and to be more prone to neurosis than men. The sex bias in modern psychodynamic theories has been reduced considerably. Nonetheless, the psychodynamic approach has generally provided a rather male-centered point of view (Lerman, 1986; Person, 1990).

It's easy to ridicule Freud for concepts such as penis envy, and it's easy to point to Freudian ideas that have turned out to be wrong. However, you have to remember that Freud, Jung, and Adler began to fashion their theories over a century ago. It's not entirely fair to compare these theories to other models that are only a decade or two old. Freud and his colleagues deserve great credit for breaking new ground with their speculations about psychodynamics. Standing at a distance a century later, we have to be impressed by the extraordinary impact that psychodynamic theory has had on modern intellectual thought. In psychology as a whole, no other school of thought has been so influential—with the exception of behaviorism, to which we turn next.

Behavioral Perspectives

Behaviorism is a theoretical orientation based on the premise that scientific psychology should study only observable behavior. As we saw in Chapter 1, behaviorism has been a major school of thought in psychology since 1913, when John B. Watson began campaigning for the behavioral point of view. Research in the behavioral tradition has focused largely on learning. For many decades behaviorists devoted relatively little attention to the study of personality. However, their interest in personality began to pick up after John Dollard and Neal Miller (1950) attempted to translate selected Freudian ideas into behavioral terminology. Dollard and Miller showed that behavioral concepts could provide enlightening insights about the complicated subject of personality.

In this section, we'll examine three behavioral views of personality, as we discuss the ideas of B. F. Skinner, Albert Bandura, and Walter Mischel. For

the most part, you'll see that behaviorists explain personality the same way they explain everything else—in terms of learning.

Skinner's Ideas Applied to Personality

10b

As we noted in Chapters 1 and 6, modern behaviorism's most prominent theorist has been B. F. Skinner, an American psychologist who lived from 1904 to 1990. After earning his doctorate in 1931, Skinner spent most of his career at Harvard University. There he achieved renown for his research on learning in lower organisms, mostly rats and pigeons. Skinner's (1953, 1957) principles of *operant conditioning* were never meant to be a theory of personality. However, his ideas have affected thinking in all areas of psychology and have been applied to the explanation of personality. Here we'll examine Skinner's views as they relate to personality structure and development.

Personality Structure: A View from the Outside

10b

Skinner made no provision for internal personality structures similar to Freud's id, ego, and superego because such structures can't be observed. Following in the tradition of Watson, Skinner showed little interest in what goes on "inside" people. He argued that it's useless to speculate about private, unobservable cognitive processes. Instead, he focused on how the external environment molds overt behavior. Indeed, he argued for a strong brand of *determinism*, asserting that behavior is fully determined by environmental stimuli.

How can Skinner's theory explain the consistency that can be seen in individuals' behavior? According to his view, people show some consistent patterns of behavior because they have some stable *response tendencies* that they have acquired through experience. These response tendencies may change in the future, as a result of new experience, but they're enduring enough to create a certain degree of consistency in a person's behavior. Implicitly, then, Skinner viewed an individual's personality as a *collection of response tendencies that are tied to various stimulus situations*. A specific situation may be associated with a number of response tendencies that vary in strength, depending on past conditioning (see **Figure 11.5**).

Personality Development as a Product of Conditioning

10b

Skinner's theory accounts for personality development by explaining how various response tendencies are acquired through learning (Bolling, Terry, & Kohlenberg, 2006). He believed that most human responses are shaped by the type of conditioning that he described: operant conditioning. As we discussed in Chapter 6, Skinner maintained that environmental consequences—reinforcement, punishment, and extinction—determine people's patterns of responding. On the one hand, when responses are followed by favorable consequences (reinforcement), they are strengthened. For example, if your joking at a party pays off with favorable attention, your tendency to joke at parties will increase (see **Figure 11.6**). On the other hand, when responses lead to negative consequences (punishment), they are weakened. Thus, if your impulsive decisions always backfire, your tendency to be impulsive will decline.

Because response tendencies are constantly being strengthened or weakened by new experiences, Skinner's theory views personality development as

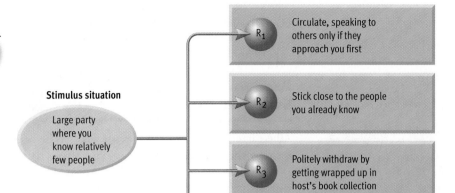

Operant response tendencies

Stimulus situation

Large party where you know relatively few people

R₁ Circulate, speaking to others only if they approach you first

R₂ Stick close to the people you already know

R₃ Politely withdraw by getting wrapped up in host's book collection

R₄ Leave at the first opportunity

Figure 11.5

A behavioral view of personality. Staunch behaviorists devote little attention to the structure of personality because it is unobservable, but they implicitly view personality as an individual's collection of response tendencies. A possible hierarchy of response tendencies for a particular person in specific stimulus situation (a large party) is shown here.

Stimulus context

Party

Telling jokes → Laughter, attention, compliments

Response **Reinforcer**

© David Young-Wolff/PhotoEdit

Figure 11.6

Personality development and operant conditioning. According to Skinner, people's characteristic response tendencies are shaped by reinforcers and other consequences that follow behavior. Thus, if your joking at a party leads to attention and compliments, your tendency to be witty and humorous will be strengthened.

© AP Images

B. F. Skinner

"The practice of looking inside the organism for an explanation of behavior has tended to obscure the variables which are immediately available for a scientific analysis. These variables lie outside the organism, in its immediate environment and in its environmental history.... The objection to inner states is not that they do not exist, but that they are not relevant."

a continuous, lifelong journey. Unlike Freud and many other theorists, Skinner saw no reason to break the developmental process into stages. Nor did he attribute special importance to early childhood experiences.

Bandura's Social Cognitive Theory 10b

Albert Bandura is a modern theorist who has helped reshape the theoretical landscape of behaviorism. He has spent his entire academic career at Stanford University, where he has conducted influential research on behavior therapy and the determinants of aggression.

Bandura is one of several behaviorists who have added a cognitive flavor to behaviorism since the 1960s. Bandura (1977), Walter Mischel (1973), and Julian Rotter (1982) take issue with Skinner's "pure" behaviorism. They point out that humans obviously are conscious, thinking, feeling beings. Moreover, these theorists argue that in neglecting cognitive processes, Skinner ignored the most distinctive and important feature of human behavior. Bandura and like-minded theorists originally call their modified brand of behaviorism *social learning theory*. Today, Bandura refers to his model as *social cognitive theory*.

Bandura (1982, 1986, 1999a, 2006) agrees with the fundamental thrust of behaviorism in that he believes that personality is largely shaped through learning. However, he contends that conditioning is not a mechanical process in which people are passive participants. Instead, he maintains that people actively seek out and process information about their environment to maximize favorable outcomes. In focusing on information processing, he brings unobservable cognitive events into the picture.

Observational Learning 10b

Bandura's foremost theoretical contribution has been his description of observational learning, which we introduced in Chapter 6. *Observational learning* occurs when an organism's responding is influenced by the observation of others. According to Bandura, both classical and operant conditioning can occur indirectly when one person observes another's conditioning. For example, watching your sister get burned by a bounced check upon selling her old stereo could strengthen your tendency to be suspicious of others. Although your sister would be the one actually experiencing the negative consequences, they might also influence

you—through observational learning. Bandura maintains that people's characteristic patterns of behavior are shaped by the *models* that they're exposed to. In observational learning, a *model* is a person whose behavior is observed by another. At one time or another, everyone serves as a model for others. Bandura's key point is that many response tendencies are the product of imitation. According to Bandura, models have a great impact on personality development. Children learn to be assertive, conscientious, self-sufficient, dependable, easygoing, and so forth by observing parents, teachers, relatives, siblings, and peers behaving in these ways.

Self-Efficacy 10b

Bandura discusses how a variety of personal factors (aspects of personality) govern behavior. In recent years, the factor he has emphasized the most is self-efficacy (Bandura, 1990, 1993, 1995). *Self-efficacy* refers to one's belief about one's ability to perform behaviors that should lead to expected outcomes. When self-efficacy is high, individuals feel confident that they can execute the responses necessary to earn reinforcers. When self-efficacy is low, individuals worry that the necessary responses may be beyond their abilities. Perceptions of self-efficacy are subjective and specific to certain kinds of tasks. For instance, you might feel extremely confident about your ability to handle difficult social situations but doubtful about your ability to handle academic challenges.

Perceptions of self-efficacy can influence which challenges people tackle and how well they perform. Studies have found that feelings of greater self-efficacy are associated with reduced procrastination (Steel, 2007), greater success in giving up smoking (Boudreaux et al., 1998), greater adherence to an exercise regimen (Rimal, 2001), more effective weight-loss efforts (Linde et al., 2006), better outcomes in substance abuse treatment (Bandura, 1999a), more success in coping with medical rehabilitation (Waldrop et al., 2001), reduced disability from problems with chronic pain (Hadjistavropoulos et al., 2007), greater persistence and effort in academic pursuits (Zimmerman, 1995), higher levels of academic performance (Chemers, Hu, & Garcia, 2001), reduced vulnerability to anxiety and depression in childhood (Muris, 2002), less jealousy in romantic relationships (Hu, Zhang, & Li, 2005), enhanced performance in athletic competition (Kane et al., 1996), greater receptiveness to technological training (Christoph, Schoenfeld, & Tansky, 1998), greater success in searching for a new job (Saks, 2006), higher work-

Albert Bandura

"Most human behavior is learned by observation through modeling."

web link 11.4

Personality Theories

C. George Boeree (Shippensburg University) provides access to his electronic textbook on personality theories at this site. Behavioral theorists B. F. Skinner and Albert Bandura are discussed extensively, along with many other theorists covered in this chapter.

related performance (Stajkovic & Luthans, 1998), and reduced strain from occupational stress (Grau, Salanova, & Peiro, 2001), among many other things.

Mischel and the Person-Situation Controversy

Walter Mischel was born in Vienna, not far from Freud's home. His family immigrated to the United States in 1939, when he was 9. After earning his doctorate in psychology, he spent many years on the faculty at Stanford, as a colleague of Bandura's. He has since moved to Columbia University. Mischel's (1973, 1984) chief contribution to personality theory has been to focus attention on the extent to which situational factors govern behavior.

According to Mischel, people make responses that they think will lead to reinforcement in the situation at hand. For example, if you believe that hard work in your job will pay off by leading to raises and promotions, you'll probably be diligent and industrious. But if you think that hard work in your job is unlikely to be rewarded, you may behave in a lazy and irresponsible manner. Thus, Mischel's version of social learning theory predicts that people will often behave differently in different situations. Mischel (1968, 1973) reviewed decades of research and concluded that, indeed, people exhibit far less consistency across situations than had been widely assumed. For example, studies show that a person who is honest in one situation may be dishonest in another.

Thus, Mischel's provocative theories have sparked a robust debate about the relative importance of the *person* as opposed to the *situation* in determining behavior. This debate has led to a growing recognition that *both* the person and the situation are important determinants of behavior (Funder, 2001; Roberts & Pomerantz, 2004). As William Fleeson (2004) puts it, "The person-situation debate is coming to an end because both sides of the debate have turned out to

be right" (p. 83). Fleeson reconciles the two opposing views by arguing that each prevails at a different level of analysis. When small chunks of behavior are examined on a moment-to-moment basis, situational factors dominate and most individuals' behavior tends to be highly variable. However, when larger chunks of typical behavior over time are examined, people tend to be reasonably consistent and personality traits prove to be more influential.

Evaluating Behavioral Perspectives

Behavioral theories are firmly rooted in extensive empirical research. Skinner's ideas have shed light on how environmental consequences and conditioning mold people's characteristic behavior. Bandura's social learning theory has expanded the horizons of behaviorism and increased its relevance to the study of personality. Mischel deserves credit for increasing psychology's awareness of how situational factors shape behavior.

Of course, each theoretical approach has its shortcomings, and the behavioral approach is no exception. The behaviorists used to be criticized because they neglected cognitive processes, which clearly are important factors in human behavior. The rise of social cognitive theory blunted this criticism. However, social cognitive theory undermines the foundation on which behaviorism was built—the idea that psychologists should study only observable behavior. Thus, some critics complain that behavioral theories aren't very behavioral anymore. Other critics argue that behaviorists have indiscriminately generalized from animal behavior to human behavior and that in carving personality into stimulus-response bonds, behaviorists have provided a fragmented view of personality (Liebert & Liebert, 1998; Maddi, 1989). Humanistic theorists, whom we shall cover next, have been particularly vocal in criticizing this piecemeal analysis of personality.

Walter Mischel

"It seems remarkable how each of us generally manages to reconcile his seemingly diverse behavior into one self-consistent whole."

REVIEW of Key Learning Goals

11.9 Skinner had little interest in unobservable cognitive processes and embraced a strong determinism. Skinner's followers view personality as a collection of response tendencies tied to specific stimulus situations. They assume that personality development is a lifelong process in which response tendencies are shaped and reshaped by learning, especially operant conditioning.

11.10 Social cognitive theory focuses on how cognitive factors such as expectancies regulate learned behavior. Observational learning occurs when an organism's responding is influenced by the observation of others. High self-efficacy has been related to successful health regimens, academic success, athletic performance, and reduced vulnerability to anxiety, depression, and jealousy, among many other things.

11.11 Mischel has questioned the degree to which people display cross-situational consistency in behavior. Mischel's arguments have increased psychologists' awareness of the situational determinants of behavior. According to Fleeson, situational factors dominate small chunks of behavior, whereas personality traits shape larger chunks of behavior.

11.12 Behavioral approaches to personality are based on rigorous research. They have provided ample insights into how environmental factors and learning mold personalities. The approach has been criticized for its fragmented analysis of personality and for the dilution of modern behavioral approaches.

Humanistic Perspectives

Key Learning Goals

11.13 Identify the impetus for, and assumptions of, humanism.

11.14 Articulate Rogers's views on self-concept, development, and defensive behavior.

11.15 Explain Maslow's hierarchy of needs and summarize his findings on self-actualizing persons.

11.16 Evaluate the strengths and weaknesses of the humanistic approach to personality.

Humanistic theory emerged in the 1950s as something of a backlash against the behavioral and psychodynamic theories that we have just discussed (Cassel, 2000). The principal charge hurled at these two models was that they are dehumanizing (De-Carvalho, 1991). Freudian theory was criticized for its belief that behavior is dominated by primitive, animalistic drives. Behaviorism was criticized for its preoccupation with animal research and for its mechanistic, fragmented view of personality. Critics argued that both schools of thought are too deterministic—that they fail to recognize that humans are free to chart their own courses of action—and that they fail to appreciate the unique qualities of human behavior.

Many of these critics blended into a loose alliance that came to be known as humanism, because of its exclusive focus on human behavior. **Humanism is a theoretical orientation that emphasizes the unique qualities of humans, especially their freedom and their potential for personal growth.** In contrast to most psychodynamic and behavioral theorists, humanistic theorists, such as Carl Rogers and Abraham Maslow, take an optimistic view of human nature. They assume (1) that people can rise above their primitive animal heritage, (2) that people are largely conscious and rational beings who are not dominated by unconscious, irrational conflicts, and (3) that people are not helpless pawns of deterministic forces. Humanistic theorists also maintain that a person's subjective view of the world is more important than objective reality (Wong, 2006). According to this notion, if you think that you're homely or bright or sociable, then this belief will influence your behavior more than the realities of how homely, bright, or sociable you actually are.

Rogers's Person-Centered Theory

Carl Rogers (1951, 1961, 1980) was one of the fathers of the human potential movement. This movement emphasizes self-realization through sensitivity training, encounter groups, and other exercises intended to foster personal growth. Like Freud, Rogers based his personality theory on his extensive therapeutic interactions with many clients. Because of its emphasis on a person's subjective point of view, Rogers called his approach a *person-centered theory.*

The Self

10c

Rogers viewed personality structure in terms of just one construct. He called this construct the *self,* although it's more widely known today as the *self-concept.* **A *self-concept* is a collection of beliefs about one's own nature, unique qualities, and typical behavior.** Your self-concept is your own mental picture of yourself. It's a collection of self-perceptions. For example, a self-concept might include beliefs such as "I'm easygoing" or "I'm sly and crafty" or "I'm pretty" or "I'm hardworking." According to Rogers, individuals are aware of their self-concept. It's not buried in their unconscious.

Rogers stressed the subjective nature of the self-concept. Your self-concept may not be entirely consistent with your experiences. Most people tend to distort their experiences to some extent to promote a relatively favorable self-concept. For example, you may believe that you're quite bright, but your grade transcript might suggest otherwise. Rogers called the gap between self-concept and reality "incongruence." **Incongruence is the degree of disparity between one's self-concept and one's actual experience.** In contrast, if a person's self-concept is reasonably accurate, it's said to be *congruent* with reality (see **Figure 11.7**). Everyone experiences a certain amount of incongruence. The crucial issue is

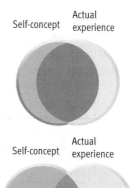

Self-concept | Actual experience

Congruence
Self-concept meshes well with actual experience (some incongruence is probably unavoidable)

Self-concept | Actual experience

Incongruence
Self-concept does not mesh well with actual experience

Figure 11.7

Rogers's view of personality structure. In Rogers's model, the self-concept is the only important structural construct. However, Rogers acknowledged that one's self-concept may not be consistent with the realities of one's actual experience—a condition called incongruence.

Carl Rogers

"I have little sympathy with the rather prevalent concept that man is basically irrational, and that his impulses, if not controlled, will lead to destruction of others and self. Man's behavior is exquisitely rational, moving with subtle and ordered complexity toward the goals his organism is endeavoring to achieve."

how much. As we'll see, Rogers maintained that too much incongruence undermines one's psychological well-being.

Development of the Self

In terms of personality development, Rogers was concerned with how childhood experiences promote congruence or incongruence between one's self-concept and one's experience. According to Rogers, people have a strong need for affection, love, and acceptance from others. Early in life, parents provide most of this affection. Rogers maintained that some parents make their affection *conditional*. That is, it depends on the child's behaving well and living up to expectations. When parental love seems conditional, children often block out of their self-concept those experiences that make them feel unworthy of love. They do so because they're worried about parental acceptance, which appears precarious. At the other end of the spectrum, some parents make their affection *unconditional*. Their children have less need to block out unworthy experiences because they've been assured that they're worthy of affection, no matter what they do.

Rogers believed that unconditional love from parents fosters congruence and that conditional love fosters incongruence. He further theorized that if individuals grow up believing that affection from others is highly conditional, they will go on to distort more and more of their experiences in order to feel worthy of acceptance from a wider and wider array of people.

Anxiety and Defense

According to Rogers, experiences that threaten people's personal views of themselves are the principal cause of troublesome anxiety. The more inaccurate your self-concept is, the more likely you are to have experiences that clash with your self-perceptions. Thus, people with highly incongruent self-concepts are especially likely to be plagued by recurrent anxiety (see **Figure 11.8**).

According to Carl Rogers, unconditional love from parents tends to foster an accurate self-concept that is congruent with reality.

To ward off this anxiety, individuals often behave defensively in an effort to reinterpret their experience so that it appears consistent with their self-concept. Thus, they ignore, deny, and twist reality to protect and perpetuate their self-concept. Consider a young lady who, like most people, considers herself a "nice person." Let's suppose that in reality she is rather conceited and selfish. She gets feedback from both boyfriends and girlfriends that she is a "self-centered, snotty brat." How might she react in order to protect her self-concept? She might ignore or block out those occasions when she behaves selfishly. She might attribute her girlfriends' negative comments to their jealousy of her good looks. Perhaps she would blame her boyfriends' negative remarks on their disappointment because she won't get more serious with them. As you can see, people will sometimes go to great lengths to defend their self-concept.

Maslow's Theory of Self-Actualization

Abraham Maslow, who grew up in Brooklyn, described his childhood as "unhappy, lonely, [and] isolated." To follow through on his interest in psychology, he had to resist parental pressures to go into law. Maslow spent much of his career at Brandeis University, where he created an influential theory of motivation and provided crucial leadership for the

Abraham Maslow

"It is as if Freud supplied to us the sick half of psychology and we must now fill it out with the healthy half."

Figure 11.8
Rogers's view of personality development and dynamics. Rogers's theory of development asserts that conditional love leads to a need to distort experiences, which fosters an incongruent self-concept. Incongruence makes one prone to recurrent anxiety, which triggers defensive behavior, which fuels more incongruence.

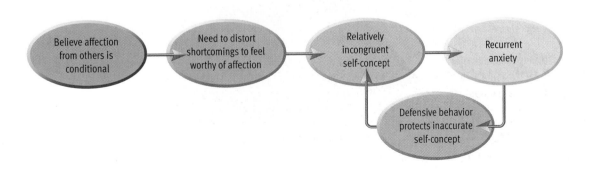

Believe affection from others is conditional → Need to distort shortcomings to feel worthy of affection → Relatively incongruent self-concept → Recurrent anxiety → Defensive behavior protects inaccurate self-concept →

fledgling humanistic movement. Like Rogers, Maslow (1968, 1970) argued that psychology should take an optimistic view of human nature instead of dwelling on the causes of disorders. "To oversimplify the matter somewhat," he said, "it's as if Freud supplied to us the sick half of psychology and we must now fill it out with the healthy half" (1968, p. 5). Maslow's key contributions to personality theory were his analysis of how motives are organized hierarchically and his description of the healthy personality.

Hierarchy of Needs 10c

Maslow proposed that human motives are organized into a *hierarchy of needs*—a systematic arrangement of needs, according to priority, in which basic needs must be met before less basic needs are aroused. This hierarchical arrangement is usually portrayed as a pyramid (see **Figure 11.9**). The needs toward the bottom of the pyramid, such as physiological or security needs, are the most basic. Higher levels in the pyramid consist of progressively less basic needs. When a person manages to satisfy a level of needs reasonably well (complete satisfaction is not necessary), *this satisfaction activates needs at the next level.*

Like Rogers, Maslow argued that humans have an innate drive toward personal growth—that is, evolution toward a higher state of being. Thus, he described the needs in the uppermost reaches of his hierarchy as *growth needs*. These include the needs for knowledge, understanding, order, and aesthetic beauty. Foremost among them is the *need for self-actualization,* which is the need to fulfill one's potential. It is the highest need in Maslow's motiva-

tional hierarchy. Maslow summarized this concept with a simple statement: "What a man *can* be, he *must* be." According to Maslow, people will be frustrated if they are unable to fully utilize their talents or pursue their true interests. For example, if you have great musical talent but must work as an accountant, or if you have scholarly interests but must work as a sales clerk, your need for self-actualization will be thwarted.

The Healthy Personality 10c

Because of his interest in self-actualization, Maslow set out to discover the nature of the healthy personality. Over a period of years, he conducted studies and accumulated case histories. Gradually, he sketched, in broad strokes, a picture of ideal psychological health. According to Maslow, *self-actualizing persons* are people with exceptionally healthy personalities, marked by continued personal growth. Maslow identified various traits characteristic of self-actualizing people. Many of these traits are listed in **Figure 11.10**. In brief, Maslow found that self-actualizers are accurately tuned in to reality and that they're at peace with themselves. He found that they're open and spontaneous and that they retain a fresh appreciation of the world around them. Socially, they're sensitive to others' needs and enjoy rewarding interpersonal relations. However, they're not dependent on others for approval or uncomfortable with solitude. They thrive on their work, and they enjoy their sense of humor. Maslow also noted that they have "peak experiences" (profound emotional highs) more often than others. Finally, he

Figure 11.9

Maslow's hierarchy of needs. According to Maslow, human needs are arranged in a hierarchy, and people must satisfy their basic needs before they can satisfy higher needs. In the diagram, higher levels in the pyramid represent progressively less basic needs. Individuals progress upward in the hierarchy when lower needs are satisfied reasonably well, but they may regress back to lower levels if basic needs are no longer satisfied.

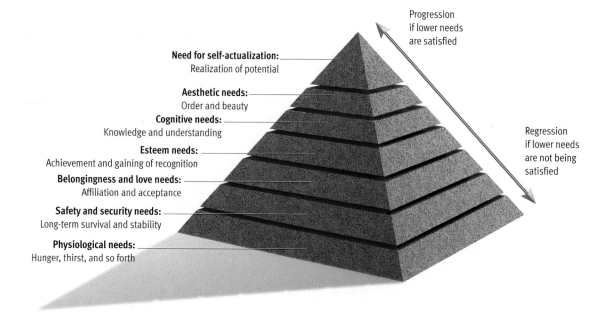

Progression if lower needs are satisfied

Need for self-actualization: Realization of potential

Aesthetic needs: Order and beauty

Cognitive needs: Knowledge and understanding

Esteem needs: Achievement and gaining of recognition

Belongingness and love needs: Affiliation and acceptance

Safety and security needs: Long-term survival and stability

Physiological needs: Hunger, thirst, and so forth

Regression if lower needs are not being satisfied

found that they strike a nice balance between many polarities in personality. For instance, they can be both childlike and mature, both rational and intuitive, both conforming and rebellious.

Evaluating Humanistic Perspectives

The humanists added a refreshing new perspective to the study of personality. Their argument that a person's subjective views may be more important than objective reality has proven compelling. The humanistic approach also deserves credit for making the self-concept an important construct in psychology. Today, theorists of many persuasions use the self-concept in their analyses of personality. Finally, one could argue that the humanists' opti-

mistic, growth- and health-oriented approach laid the foundation for the emergence of the positive psychology movement that is increasingly influential in contemporary psychology (Sheldon & Kasser, 2001; Taylor, 2001).

Of course, the balance sheet has a negative side as well (Burger, 2008; Wong, 2006). Critics argue that (1) many aspects of humanistic theory are difficult to put to a scientific test, (2) humanists have been unrealistically optimistic in their assumptions about human nature and their descriptions of the healthy personality, and (3) more experimental research is needed to catch up with the theorizing in the humanistic camp. This last complaint is precisely the opposite of what we'll encounter in the next section, on biological perspectives, where more theorizing is needed to catch up with the research.

Characteristics of self-actualizing people	
• Clear, efficient perception of reality and comfortable relations with it	• Mystical and peak experiences
• Spontaneity, simplicity, and naturalness	• Feelings of kinship and identification with the human race
• Problem centering (having something outside themselves they "must" do as a mission)	• Strong friendships, but limited in number
• Detachment and need for privacy	• Democratic character structure
• Autonomy, independence of culture and environment	• Ethical discrimination between good and evil
• Continued freshness of appreciation	• Philosophical, unhostile sense of humor
	• Balance between polarities in personality

Figure 11.10

Maslow's view of the healthy personality. Humanistic theorists emphasize psychological health instead of maladjustment. Maslow's description of the characteristics of self-actualizing people evokes a picture of the healthy personality.

SOURCE: Adapted from Potkay, C. R., & Allen, B. P. (1986). *Personality: Theory, research and application*. Pacific Grove, CA: Brooks/Cole. Copyright © 1986 by C. R. Potkay & B. P. Allen. Adapted by permission of the author.

concept check 11.3

Recognizing Key Concepts in Personality Theories

Check your understanding of psychodynamic, behavioral, and humanistic personality theories by identifying key concepts from these theories in the scenarios below. The answers can be found in Appendix A.

1. Thirteen-year-old Sarah watches a TV show in which the leading female character manipulates her boyfriend by acting helpless and purposely losing a tennis match against him. The female lead repeatedly expresses her slogan, "Never let them [men] know you can take care of yourself." Sarah becomes more passive and less competitive around boys her own age.

   Concept: _____

2. Yolanda has a secure, enjoyable, reasonably well-paid job as a tenured English professor at a state university. Her friends are dumbfounded when she announces that she's going to resign and give it all up to try writing a novel. She tries to explain, "I need a new challenge, a new mountain to climb. I've had this lid on my writing talents for years, and I've got to break free. It's something I have to try. I won't be happy until I do."

   Concept: _____

3. Vladimir, who is 4, seems to be emotionally distant from and inattentive to his father. He complains whenever he's left with his dad. In contrast, he cuddles up in bed with his mother frequently and tries very hard to please her by behaving properly.

   Concept: _____

Key Learning Goals

11.17 Outline Eysenck's views of personality structure and development.

11.18 Summarize the find-ings of behavioral genetics research on personality.

11.19 Articulate Buss's and Nettle's evolutionary explana-tions for why the Big Five traits are important.

11.20 Assess the strengths and weaknesses of the biologi-cal approach to personality.

Biological Perspectives

Like many identical twins reared apart, Jim Lewis and Jim Springer found they had been leading eerily similar lives. Separated four weeks after birth in 1940, the Jim twins grew up 45 miles apart in Ohio and were reunited in 1979. Eventually, they discovered that both drove the same model blue Chevrolet, chain-smoked Salems, chewed their fingernails, and owned dogs named Toy. Each had spent a good deal of time vacationing at the same three-block strip of beach in Florida. More impor-tant, when tested for such personality traits as flexibility, self-control, and sociability, the twins responded almost exactly alike. (Leo, 1987, p. 63)

So began a *Time* magazine summary of a major twin study conducted at the University of Minnesota Cen-ter for Twin and Adoption Research. Since 1979 the investigators at this center have been studying the personality resemblance of identical twins reared apart. Not all the twin pairs have been as similar as Jim Lewis and Jim Springer, but many of the paral-lels have been uncanny (Lykken et al., 1992). Identi-cal twins Oskar Stohr and Jack Yufe were separated soon after birth. Oskar was sent to a Nazi-run school in Czechoslovakia, while Jack was raised in a Jew-ish home on a Caribbean island. When they were reunited for the first time during middle age, they showed up wearing similar mustaches, haircuts, shirts, and wire-rimmed glasses! A pair of previously separated female twins both arrived at the Minne-apolis airport wearing seven rings on their fingers. One had a son named Richard Andrew and the other had a son named Andrew Richard!

Could personality be largely inherited? These anecdotal reports of striking resemblances between identical twins reared apart certainly raise this pos-

sibility. In this section we'll discuss Hans Eysenck's theory, which emphasizes the influence of heredity, look at recent behavioral genetics research on the heritability of personality, and outline evolutionary views on personality.

Eysenck's Theory 10d

Hans Eysenck was born in Germany but fled to Lon-don during the era of Nazi rule. He went on to be-come one of Britain's most prominent psychologists. Eysenck (1967, 1982, 1990a) views personality struc-ture as a hierarchy of traits, in which many superficial traits are derived from a smaller number of more basic traits, which are derived from a handful of fundamen-tal higher-order traits, as shown in **Figure 11.11**.

According to Eysenck, "Personality is determined to a large extent by a person's genes" (1967, p. 20). How is heredity linked to personality in Eysenck's model? In part, through conditioning concepts borrowed from behavioral theory (consult Chapter 6 for an overview of classical conditioning). Eysenck theorizes that some people can be conditioned more readily than others because of differences in their physiological func-tioning. These variations in "conditionability" are as-sumed to influence the personality traits that people acquire through conditioning processes.

Eysenck has shown a special interest in explain-ing variations in *extraversion-introversion*. He has proposed that introverts tend to have high levels of physiological arousal, which make them more easily conditioned than extraverts. According to Eysenck, people who condition easily acquire more condi-tioned inhibitions than others. These inhibitions make them more bashful, tentative, and uneasy in

Hans Eysenck

"Personality is determined to a large extent by a person's genes."

By permission from the H. J. Eysenck Memorial Fund

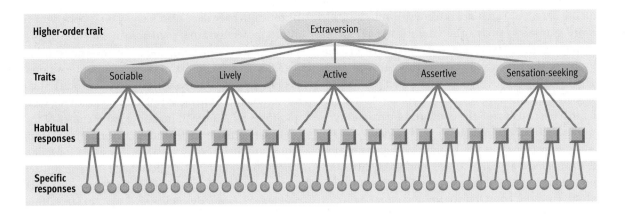

Figure 11.11
Eysenck's model of personality structure. Eysenck described personality structure as a hierarchy of traits. In this scheme, a few higher-order traits, such as extraversion, determine a host of lower-order traits, which determine a person's habitual responses.

SOURCE: Eysenck, H. J. (1976). *The biological basis of personality.* Springfield, IL: Charles C. Thomas. Reprinted by permission of the publisher.

social situations. This social discomfort leads them to turn inward. As a result, they become introverted.

Behavioral Genetics and Personality   10d

Recent research in behavioral genetics has provided impressive support for the idea that personality is largely inherited (Livesley, Jang, & Vernon, 2003; Rowe & van den Oord, 2005). For instance, in twin studies of the Big Five personality traits, identical twins have been found to be much more similar than fraternal twins on all five traits (Loehlin, 1992; see **Figure 11.12**). These findings strongly suggest that genetic factors exert considerable influence over personality.

Some skeptics wonder whether identical twins might exhibit more trait similarity than fraternal twins because they're treated more alike. In other words, they wonder whether environmental factors (rather than heredity) could be responsible for identical twins' greater personality resemblance. This nagging question can be answered only by studying identical twins reared apart, which is why the twin study at the University of Minnesota is so important. The Minnesota study (Tellegen et al., 1988) was the first to administer the same personality test to identical and fraternal twins reared apart, as well as together. Most of the twins reared apart were separated quite early in life (median age of 2.5 months) and remained separated for a long time (median period of almost 34 years).

The results revealed that identical twins reared together were more similar on all three major traits examined in the study than fraternal twins reared together. More telling, though, were the results for the identical twins reared apart. On all three traits,

Figure 11.12
Twin studies of personality. Loehlin (1992) has summarized the results of twin studies that have examined the Big Five personality traits. The N under each trait indicates the number of twin studies that have examined that trait. The chart plots the average correlations obtained for identical and fraternal twins in these studies. As you can see, identical twins have shown greater resemblance in personality than fraternal twins have, suggesting that personality is partly inherited.

Photo: © Daly & Newton/Stone-Getty Images

web link 11.6

The Personality Project

William Revelle, director of the graduate program in personality at Northwestern University's Psychology Department, has assembled a directory to many Internet-based resources in the study of personality.

identical twins reared apart were still substantially more similar to each other than fraternal twins reared together. The *heritability estimates* (see Chapter 8) for the three traits ranged from 40% to 58%. The investigators concluded that their results provided dramatic support for the hypothesis that genetic blueprints shape the contours of personality.

Research on the heritability of personality has inadvertently turned up a surprising finding: *shared family environment* appears to have remarkably little impact on personality. This unexpected finding has been observed quite consistently in behavioral genetics research (Beer, Arnold, & Loehlin, 1998; Rowe & van den Oord, 2005). It is surprising in that social scientists have long assumed that the family environment shared by children growing up together led to some personality resemblance among them. *These findings have led some theorists to conclude that parents don't matter—that they wield very little influence over how their children develop* (Cohen, 1999; Harris, 1998; Rowe, 1994).

Critics have argued with merit that the methods used in behavioral genetics studies have probably underestimated the impact of shared environment on personality (Collins et al., 2000; Stoolmiller, 1999). They also note that shared experiences—such as being raised with authoritarian discipline—may often have different effects on two siblings, which obscures the impact of environment, but is not the same result as having no effect (Turkheimer & Waldron, 2000). And the critics argue that decades of research in developmental psychology have clearly demonstrated that parents have significant influence on their children (Maccoby, 2000). Thus, although the findings on family influence are very thought provoking, the assertion that "parents don't matter" seems premature and overstated.

The Evolutionary Approach to Personality

In the realm of biological perspectives on personality, the most recent development has been the emergence of evolutionary theory. Evolutionary theorists assert that personality has a biological basis because natural selection has favored certain traits over the course of human history (Figueredo et al., 2005). Thus, evolutionary analyses focus on how various personality traits—and the ability to recognize these traits in others—may have contributed to reproductive fitness in ancestral human populations.

For example, David Buss (1991, 1995, 1997) has argued that the Big Five personality traits stand out as important dimensions of personality across a variety of cultures because those traits have had significant adaptive implications. Buss points out that humans historically have depended heavily on groups, which afford protection from predators or enemies, opportunities for sharing food, and a diverse array of other benefits. In the context of these group interactions, people have had to make difficult but crucial judgments about the characteristics of others, asking such questions as: Who will make a good member of my coalition? Who can I depend on when in need? Who will share their resources? Thus, Buss (1995) argues, "those individuals able to accurately discern and act upon these individual differences likely enjoyed a considerable reproductive advantage" (p. 22). According to Buss, the Big Five emerge as fundamental dimensions of personality because humans have evolved special sensitivity to variations in the ability to bond with others (extraversion), the willingness to cooperate and collaborate (agreeableness), the tendency to be reliable and ethical (conscientiousness), the capacity to be an innovative problem solver (openness to experience), and the ability to handle stress (low neuroticism). In a nutshell, Buss argues that the Big Five reflect the most salient features of others' adaptive behavior over the course of evolutionary history.

Daniel Nettle (2006) takes this line of thinking one step further, asserting that the traits themselves (as opposed to the ability to recognize them in others) are products of evolution that were adaptive in ancestral environments. For example, he discusses how extraversion could have promoted mating success, how neuroticism could have fueled competitiveness and avoidance of dangers, how agreeableness could have fostered the effective building of coalitions, and so forth. Nettle also discusses how each of the Big Five traits may have had adaptive costs (extraversion, for example, is associated with risky behavior) as well as benefits. Thus, he argues that evolutionary analyses of personality need to weigh the *trade-offs* between the adaptive advantages and disadvantages of the Big Five traits.

Evaluating Biological Perspectives

Researchers have compiled convincing evidence that biological factors help shape personality, and findings on the meager effects of shared family environment have launched intriguing new approaches to the investigation of personality development. Nonetheless, we must take note of some weaknesses in biological approaches to personality. Critics assert that too much emphasis has been placed on heritability estimates that vary depending on sampling and statistical procedures (Funder, 2001), Critics also note that there's no comprehensive biological theory of personality, so additional theoretical work is needed to catch up with recent empirical findings.

web link 11.7

Great Ideas in Personality

Northwestern University personality psychologist G. Scott Acton demonstrates that scientific research programs in personality generate broad and compelling ideas about what it is to be a human being. He charts the contours of 12 research perspectives, including behaviorism, behavioral genetics, and sociobiology, and backs them up with extensive links to published and online resources associated with each perspective.

REVIEW of Key Learning Goals

11.17 Eysenck views personality structure as a hierarchy of traits. He believes that heredity influences individual differences in physiological functioning that affect how easily people acquire conditioned inhibitions.

11.18 Twin studies of the Big Five personality traits find that identical twins are more similar in personality than fraternal twins, thus suggesting that personality is partly inherited. Estimates for the heritability of personality hover in the vicinity of 50%. Recent research in behavioral genetics has suggested that shared family environment has surprisingly little impact on personality, although a variety of theorists have been critical of this conclusion.

11.19 According to Buss, the ability to recognize and judge others' status on the Big Five traits may have contributed to reproductive fitness. Nettle argues that the Big Five traits themselves (rather than the ability to recognize them) are products of evolution that were adaptive in ancestral times.

11.20 Researchers have compiled convincing evidence that genetic factors exert considerable influence over personality. However, the biological approach has been criticized because of methodological problems with heritability ratios and because it offers no systematic model of how physiology shapes personality.

---

concept check 11.4

Understanding the Implications of Major Theories: Who Said This?

Check your understanding of the implications of the personality theories we've discussed by indicating which theorist is likely to have made the statements below. The answers are in Appendix A.

Choose from the following theorists: Alfred Adler   Albert Bandura   Hans Eysenck
Sigmund Freud   Abraham Maslow   Walter Mischel

Quotes

_____ 1. "If you deliberately plan to be less than you are capable of being, then I warn you that you'll be deeply unhappy for the rest of your life."

_____ 2. "I feel that the major, most fundamental dimensions of personality are likely to be those on which [there is] strong genetic determination of individual differences."

_____ 3. "People are in general not candid over sexual matters . . . they wear a heavy overcoat woven of a tissue of lies, as though the weather were bad in the world of sexuality."

A Contemporary Empirical Approach: Terror Management Theory

So far, our coverage has been largely devoted to grand, panoramic theories of personality. In this section we'll examine a new approach to understanding personality functioning that has a narrower focus than the classic theories of personality. *Terror management theory* emerged as an influential perspective in the 1990s. Although the theory borrows from Freudian and evolutionary formulations, it provides its own unique analysis of the human condition. Developed by Sheldon Solomon, Jeff Greenberg, and Tom Pyszczynski (1991, 2004b), this fresh perspective is currently generating a huge volume of research.

Essentials of Terror Management Theory

One of the chief goals of terror management theory is to explain why people need self-esteem (Solomon, Greenberg, & Pyszczynski, 1991). The theory begins with the assumption that humans share an evolutionary heritage with other animals that includes an instinctive drive for self-preservation. However, unlike other animals, humans have evolved complex cognitive abilities that permit self-awareness and contemplation of the future. These cognitive capacities make humans keenly aware of the inevitability of death—

they appreciate that life can be snuffed out unpredictably at any time. The collision between humans' self-preservation instinct and their awareness of the inevitability of death create the potential for experiencing anxiety, alarm, and terror when individuals think about their mortality (see **Figure 11.13**).

How do humans deal with this potential for terror? According to terror management theory, "What

Key Learning Goals

11.21 Understand the chief concepts and hypotheses of terror management theory.

11.22 Describe how reminders of death influence people's behavior.

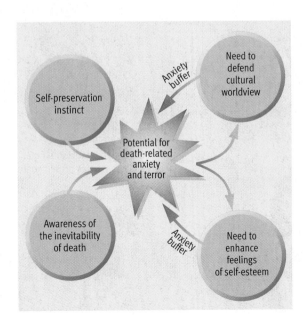

Figure 11.13

Overview of terror management theory. This graphic maps out the relations among the key concepts proposed by terror management theory. The theory asserts that humans' unique awareness of the inevitability of death fosters a need to defend one's cultural worldview and one's self-esteem, which serve to protect one from mortality-related anxiety.

ILLUSTRATED OVERVIEW OF MAJOR THEORIES OF PERSONALITY

THEORIST AND ORIENTATION	SOURCE OF DATA AND OBSERVATIONS	KEY MOTIVATIONAL FORCES

A PSYCHODYNAMIC VIEW

Sigmund Freud

Case studies from clinical practice of psychoanalysis

Sex and aggression; need to reduce tension resulting from internal conflicts

A BEHAVIORAL VIEW

B. F. Skinner

Laboratory experiments, primarily with animals

Courtesy of Professor Rick Stalling and Bradley University. Photo by Duane Zehr.

Pursuit of primary (unlearned) and secondary (learned) reinforcers; priorities depend on personal history

A HUMANISTIC VIEW

Carl Rogers

Case studies from clinical practice of client-centered therapy

© Tom Stewart/Corbis

Actualizing tendency (motive to develop capacities, and experience personal growth) and self-actualizing tendency (motive to maintain self-concept and behave in ways that are consistent with self-concept)

A BIOLOGICAL VIEW

Hans Eysenck

Twin, family, and adoption studies of heritability; factor analysis studies of personality structure

© Daly & Newton/Stone/Getty Images

No specific motivational forces singled out

MODEL OF PERSONALITY STRUCTURE

Three interacting components (id, ego, superego) operating at three levels of consciousness

Collections of response tendencies tied to specific stimulus situations

Operant response tendencies

Self-concept, which may or may not mesh well with actual experience

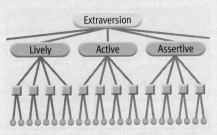

Hierarchy of traits, with specific traits derived from more fundamental, general traits

Extraversion
Lively   Active   Assertive

VIEW OF PERSONALITY DEVELOPMENT

Emphasis on fixation or progress through psycho-sexual stages; experiences in early childhood (such as toilet training) can leave lasting mark on adult personality

© Nancy Sheehan/PhotoEdit

Personality evolves gradually over the life span (not in stages); responses (such as extraverted joking) followed by reinforcement (such as appreciative laughter) become more frequent

© David Young-Wolff/PhotoEdit

Children who receive unconditional love have less need to be defensive; they develop more accurate, congruent self-concept; conditional love fosters incongruence

© blue jean images/Getty Images

Emphasis on unfolding of genetic blueprint with maturation; inherited predispositions interact with learning experiences

ROOTS OF DISORDERS

Unconscious fixations and unresolved conflicts from childhood, usually centering on sex and aggression

Maladaptive behavior due to faulty learning; the "symptom" is the problem, not a sign of underlying disease

Incongruence between self and actual experience (inaccurate self-concept); over-dependence on others for approval and sense of worth

Genetic vulnerability activated in part by environmental factors saves us is culture. Cultures provide ways to view the world—worldviews—that 'solve' the existential crisis engendered by the awareness of death" (Pyszczynski, Solomon, & Greenberg, 2003, p. 16). Cultural worldviews diminish anxiety by providing answers to such universal questions as: Why am I here? What is the meaning of life? Cultures create stories, traditions, and institutions that give their members a sense of being part of an enduring legacy through their contributions to their families, tribes, schools, churches, professions, and so forth. Thus, faith in a cultural worldview can give people a sense of order, meaning, and context that can soothe humans' fear of death.

Where does self-esteem fit into the picture? Self-esteem is viewed as a sense of personal worth that depends on one's confidence in the validity of one's cultural worldview and the belief that one is living up to the standards prescribed by that worldview. "It is the feeling that one is a valuable contributor to a meaningful universe" (Pyszczynski et al., 2004, p. 437). Hence, self-esteem buffers people from the profound anxiety associated with the awareness that we are transient animals destined to die. In other words, self-esteem serves a *terror management* function (refer to **Figure 11.13**).

The notion that self-esteem functions as an *anxiety buffer* has been supported by numerous studies (Pyszczynski et al., 2004). In many of these experiments, researchers have manipulated what they call *mortality salience* by asking subjects to briefly think about their own death. Consistent with the anxiety buffer hypothesis, reminding people of their mortality leads subjects to engage in a variety of behaviors that are likely to bolster their self-esteem, thus reducing anxiety.

Applications of Terror Management Theory

Increasing mortality salience also leads people to work harder at defending their cultural worldview (Arndt, Cook, & Routledge, 2004). For instance, after briefly pondering their mortality, research participants (1) hand out harsher penalties to moral transgressors, (2) respond more negatively to people who criticize their culture, (3) give larger rewards to people who uphold cultural standards, and (4) show more respect for cultural icons, such as a flag (Greenberg et al., 1990; Rosenblatt et al., 1989). This need to defend one's cultural worldview may even fuel prejudice and aggression. Reminding subjects of their mortality leads to (1) more negative evaluations of people from different religious or ethnic backgrounds, (2) more stereotypic thinking about minority group members, and (3) more aggressive

Terror management theory has been applied to a remarkably diverse array of phenomena. For example, it has even been used to explain conspicuous consumption.

behavior toward people with opposing political views (McGregor et al., 1998; Schimel et al., 1999).

Terror management theory yields novel hypotheses regarding many phenomena. For instance, Solomon, Greenberg, and Pyszczynski (2004a) explain excessive materialism in terms of the anxiety-buffering function of self-esteem. Specifically, they argue that "conspicuous possession and consumption are thinly veiled efforts to assert that one is special and therefore more than just an animal fated to die and decay" (p. 134). One study even applied terror management theory to the political process. Cohen et al. (2004) found that mortality salience increases subjects' preference for "charismatic" candidates who articulate a grand vision that makes people feel like they are part of an important movement of lasting significance.

Given its focus on death anxiety, terror management theory has much to say about people's reactions to the contemporary threat of terrorism. Pyszczynski, Solomon, and Greenberg (2003) point out that terrorist attacks are intended to produce a powerful, nationwide manipulation of mortality salience. When mortality salience is elevated, terror management theory predicts that people will embrace their cultural worldviews even more strongly than before. Consistent with this prediction, in the months following the 9/11 terrorist attacks, expressions of patriotism and religious faith increased dramatically. Research on terror management processes has also shown that when death anxiety is heightened, people become less tolerant of opposing views and more prejudiced against those who are different. Consistent with this analysis, in the aftermath of 9/11, individuals who questioned government policies met more hostility than usual. The theory also predicts that reminders of mortality increase the tendency to admire those who uphold cultural standards. More than ever, people need heroes who personify cultural values. This need was apparent after the September 11 terrorist attacks in the way the media made firefighters into larger-than-life heroes.

At first glance, a theory that explains everything from prejudice to compulsive shopping in terms of death anxiety may seem highly implausible. After all, most people do not appear to walk around all day obsessing about the possibility of their death. The architects of terror management theory are well aware of this reality. They explain that the defensive reactions uncovered in their research generally occur when death anxiety surfaces on the fringes of conscious awareness and that these reactions are automatic and subconscious (Pyszczynski, Greenberg, & Solomon, 1999).

REVIEW of Key Learning Goals

11.21 Terror management theory proposes that self-esteem and faith in a cultural worldview shield people from the profound anxiety associated with their mortality. Consistent with this analysis, increasing mortality salience leads people to make efforts to bolster their self-esteem and defend their worldviews.

11.22 Manipulations of mortality salience lead to harsh treatment for moral transgressions, elevated respect for cultural icons, and increased prejudice. Terror management processes can shed light on conspicuous consumption, political preferences, and reactions to terrorism.

Culture and Personality

Are there connections between culture and personality? In recent years psychology's new interest in cultural factors has led to a renaissance of culture-personality research. This research has sought to determine whether Western personality constructs are relevant to other cultures and whether cultural differences can be seen in the prevalence of specific personality traits. As with cross-cultural research in other areas of psychology, these studies have found evidence of both continuity and variability across cultures.

For the most part, continuity has been apparent in cross-cultural comparisons of the *trait structure* of personality. When English language personality scales have been translated and administered in other cultures, the predicted dimensions of personality have emerged from the factor analyses (Paunonen & Ashton, 1998). For example, when scales that tap the Big Five personality traits have been administered and subjected to factor analysis in other cultures, the usual five traits have typically surfaced (Katigbak et al., 2002; McCrae et al., 2005b). Thus, research tentatively suggests that the basic dimensions of personality trait structure may be universal.

On the other hand, some cross-cultural variability is seen when researchers compare the average trait scores of samples from various cultural groups. For example, in a study comparing 51 cultures, McCrae et al. (2005a) found that Brazilians scored relatively high in neuroticism, Australians in extraversion, Germans in openness to experience, Czechs in agreeableness, and Malaysians in conscientiousness, to give but a handful of examples. These findings should be viewed as preliminary, since more data are needed from larger and more carefully selected samples. Nonetheless, the findings suggest that there may be genuine cultural differences on some personality traits. That said, the cultural disparities in average trait scores that were observed were modest in size.

The availability of the data from the McCrae et al. (2005a) study allowed Terracciano et al. (2005) to evaluate the concept of *national character*—the idea that various cultures have widely-recognized prototype personalities. Terracciano and his colleagues asked subjects from many cultures to describe the *typical* member of *their* culture on rating forms guided by the five-factor model. Generally, subjects displayed substantial agreement on these ratings of what was typical for their culture. The averaged ratings, which served as the measures of each culture's national character, were then correlated with the actual mean trait scores for various cultures compiled in the McCrae et al. (2005a) study. The results were definitive—the vast majority of the correlations were extremely low and often even negative. In other words, there was little or no relationship between perceptions of national character and actual trait scores for various cultures (see **Figure 11.14** on the next page). People's beliefs about national character, which often fuel cultural prejudices, turned out to be profoundly inaccurate stereotypes (McCrae & Terracciano, 2006).

Key Learning Goals

11.23 Clarify how researchers have found both cross-cultural similarities and disparities in personality.

11.24 Explain Markus and Kitayama's research on cultural variations in conceptions of self.

Hazel Markus and Shinobu Kitayama

"Most of what psychologists currently know about human nature is based on one particular view—the so-called Western view of the individual as an independent, self-contained, autonomous entity."

Figure 11.14

An example of inaccurate perceptions of national character. Terracciano et al. (2005) found that perceptions of national character (the prototype or typical personality for a particular culture) are largely inaccurate. The data shown here for one culture—Canadians—illustrate this inaccuracy. Mean scores on the Big Five traits for a sample of real individuals from Canada are graphed here in red. Averaged perceptions of national character for Canadians are graphed here in blue. The discrepancy between perception and reality is obvious. Terracciano et al. found similar disparities between views of national character and actual trait scores for a majority of the cultues they studied. (Adapted from McCrae & Terracciano, 2006)

Perhaps the most interesting and influential work on culture and personality has been that of Hazel Markus and Shinobu Kitayama (1991, 1994, 2003) comparing American and Asian conceptions of the self. According to Markus and Kitayama, American parents teach their children to be self-reliant, to feel good about themselves, and to view themselves as special individuals. Children are encouraged to excel in competitive endeavors and to strive to stand out from the crowd. They are told that "the squeaky wheel gets the grease" and that "you have to stand up for yourself." Thus, Markus and Kitayama argue that *American culture fosters an independent view of the self.* American youngsters learn to define themselves in terms of their personal attributes, abilities, accomplishments, and possessions. Their unique strengths and achievements become the basis for their sense of self-worth. Thus, they are prone to emphasize their uniqueness.

Most of us take this individualistic mentality for granted. Indeed, Markus and Kitayama maintain that "most of what psychologists currently know about human nature is based on one particular view—the so-called Western view of the individual as an independent, self-contained, autonomous entity" (1991, p. 224). However, they marshal convincing evidence that this view is *not* universal. They argue that in Asian cultures such as Japan and China, socialization practices foster a more *interdependent view of the self,* which emphasizes the fundamental connectedness of people to each other (see **Figure 11.15**). In these cultures, parents teach their children that they can rely on family and friends, that they should be modest about their personal accomplishments so they don't diminish others' achievements, and that they should view themselves as part of a larger social matrix. Children are encouraged to fit in with others and to avoid standing out from the crowd. A popular adage in Japan reminds children that "the nail that stands out gets pounded down." Hence, Markus and Kitayama assert that Asian youngsters

Figure 11.15

Culture and conceptions of self. According to Markus and Kitayama (1991), Western cultures foster an independent view of the self as a unique individual who is separate from others, as diagrammed on the left. In contrast, Asian cultures encourage an interdependent view of the self as part of an interconnected social matrix, as diagrammed on the right. The interdependent view leads people to define themselves in terms of their social relationships (for instance, as someone's daughter, employee, colleague, or neighbor).

SOURCE: Adapted from Markus, H. R., & Kitayama, S. (1991). Culture and the self: Implications for cognition, emotion, and motivation. *Psychological Review, 98,* 224–253. Copyright © 1991 by the American Psychological Association. Adapted by permission of the author.

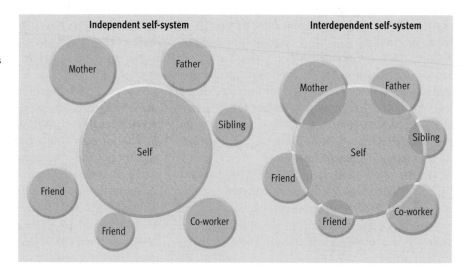

typically learn to define themselves in terms of the groups they belong to. Their harmonious relations with others and their pride in group achievements become the basis for their sense of self-worth. Thus, Asian and American conceptions of self appear to be noticeably different.

REVIEW of Key Learning Goals

11.23 The basic trait structure of personality may be much the same across cultures, as the Big Five traits usually emerge in cross-cultural studies. However, some cultural variability has been seen when researchers compare average trait scores for various cultural groups. Researchers have measured countries' national character, but averaged test data collected from real individuals show that these perceptions of typical personality tend to be inaccurate stereotypes.

11.24 Markus and Kitayama assert that American culture fosters an independent conception of self as a unique individual who is separate from others. In contrast, Asian cultures foster an interdependent view of the self, as part of an interconnected social matrix.

© Chad Ehlers/Photolibrary

Culture can shape personality. Children in Asian cultures, for example, grow up with a value system that allows them to view themselves as interconnected parts of larger social units. Hence, they tend to avoid positioning themselves so that they stand out from others.

concept check 11.5

Identifying the Contributions of Major Theorists and Researchers

Check your recall of the principal ideas of important theorists and researchers covered in this chapter by matching the people listed on the left with the appropriate contributions described on the right. If you need help, the crucial pages describing each person's ideas are listed in parentheses. Fill in the letters for your choices in the spaces provided on the left. You'll find the answers in Appendix A.

Major Theorists and Researchers

_____ 1. Alfred Adler (pp. 386–387)

_____ 2. Albert Bandura (p. 390)

_____ 3. Hans Eysenck (pp. 396–397)

_____ 4. Sigmund Freud (pp. 380–385)

_____ 5. Carl Jung (pp. 385–386)

_____ 6. Abraham Maslow (pp. 393–395)

_____ 7. Walter Mischel (p. 391)

_____ 8. Carl Rogers (pp. 392–393)

_____ 9. B. F. Skinner (pp. 388–390)

Key Ideas and Contributions

a. This humanistic theorist is famous for his hierarchy of needs and his work on self-actualizing persons.

b. This humanist called his approach a person-centered theory. He argued that an incongruent self-concept tends to promote anxiety and defensive behavior.

c. This influential behaviorist explained personality development in terms of operant conditioning, especially the process of reinforcement.

d. This theorist emphasized the importance of unconscious conflicts, anxiety, defense mechanisms, and psychosexual development.

e. This behaviorist sparked a robust debate about the importance of the person as opposed to the situation in determining behavior.

f. This theorist views personality structure as a hierarchy of traits and argues that personality is heavily influenced by heredity.

g. This theorist clashed with Freud and argued that the foremost source of human motivation is a striving for superiority.

h. This psychodynamic theorist is famous for the concepts of the collective unconscious and archetypes.

i. This theorist's social cognitive theory emphasizes observational learning and self-efficacy.

Reflecting on the Chapter's Themes

Key Learning Goals

11.25 Identify the three unifying themes highlighted in this chapter.

Cultural Heritage

Theoretical Diversity

Sociohistorical Context

The preceding discussion of culture and personality obviously highlighted the text's theme that people's behavior is influenced by their cultural heritage. This chapter has also been ideally suited for embellishing on two other unifying themes: psychology's theoretical diversity and the idea that psychology evolves in a sociohistorical context.

No other area of psychology is characterized by as much theoretical diversity as the study of personality, where there are literally dozens of insightful theories. Some of this diversity exists because different theories attempt to explain different facets of behavior. Of course, much of this diversity reflects genuine disagreements on basic questions about personality. These disagreements should be apparent on pages 400–401, where you'll find an Illustrated Overview of the ideas of Freud, Skinner, Rogers, and Eysenck, as representatives of the psychodynamic, behavioral, humanistic, and biological approaches to personality.

The study of personality also highlights the sociohistorical context in which psychology evolves. Personality theories have left many marks on modern culture. The theories of Freud, Adler, and Skinner have had an enormous impact on childrearing practices. The ideas of Freud and Jung have found their way into literature (influencing the portrayal of fictional characters) and the visual arts. For example, Freud's theory helped inspire surrealism's interest in the world of dreams. Maslow's hierarchy of needs and Skinner's affirmation of the value of positive reinforcement have given rise to new approaches to management in the world of business and industry.

Sociohistorical forces also leave their imprint on psychology. This chapter provided many examples of how personal experiences, prevailing attitudes, and historical events have contributed to the evolution of ideas in psychology. For example, Freud's pessimistic view of human nature and his emphasis on the dark forces of aggression were shaped to some extent by his exposure to the hostilities of World War I and prevailing anti-Semitic sentiments. Freud's emphasis on sexuality was surely influenced by the Victorian climate of sexual repression that existed in his youth. Adler's views also reflected the social context in which he grew up. His interest in inferiority feelings and compensation appears to have sprung from his own sickly childhood and the difficulties he had to overcome.

Progress in the study of personality has also been influenced by developments in other areas of psychology. For instance, the enterprise of psychological testing originally emerged out of efforts to measure general intelligence. Eventually, however, the principles of psychological testing were applied to the challenge of measuring personality. In the upcoming Personal Application we discuss the logic and limitations of personality tests.

> **REVIEW of Key Learning Goals**
>
> **11.25** The study of personality illustrates how psychology is characterized by great theoretical diversity. It also demonstrates how ideas in psychology are shaped by sociohistorical forces and how cultural factors influence psychological processes.

PERSONAL APPLICATION · Understanding Personality Assessment

Key Learning Goals

11.26 Describe several prominent personality inventories and evaluate the strengths and weaknesses of self-report inventories.

11.27 Describe and evaluate projective testing, and analyze the emerging role of the Internet in personality assessment.

Answer the following "true" or "false."

___ **1** Responses to personality tests are subject to unconscious distortion.

___ **2** The results of personality tests are often misunderstood.

___ **3** Personality test scores should be interpreted with caution.

___ **4** Personality tests serve many important functions.

If you answered "true" to all four questions, you earned a perfect score. Yes, personality tests are subject to distortion. Admittedly, test results are often misunderstood, and they should be interpreted cautiously. In spite of these problems, however, psychological tests can be quite useful.

Everyone engages in efforts to size up his or her own personality as well as that of others. When you think to yourself that "Mary Ann is shrewd and poised," or when you remark to a friend that "Carlos is timid and submissive," you're making personality assessments. In a sense, then, personality assessment is an ongoing part of daily life. Given the popular interest in personality assessment, it's not surprising that psychologists have devised formal measures of personality.

Personality tests can be helpful in (1) making clinical diagnoses of psychological disorders, (2) vocational counseling, (3) personnel selection in business and industry, and (4) measuring specific personality traits for research purposes. Personality tests can be divided into two broad categories: *self-report inventories* and *projective tests*. In this Personal Application, we'll discuss some representative tests from both categories and discuss their strengths and weaknesses.

Self-Report Inventories   7a

Self-report inventories are personality tests that ask individuals to answer a series of questions about their characteristic behavior. The logic underlying this approach is very simple: Who knows you better? Who has known you longer? Who has more access to your private feelings? We'll look at three examples of self-report scales, the MMPI, the 16PF, and the NEO Personality Inventory.

The MMPI

The most widely used self-report inventory is the Minnesota Multiphasic Personality Inventory (MMPI) (Butcher, 2005, 2006). The MMPI was originally designed to aid clinicians in the diagnosis of psychological disorders. It measures 10 personality traits that, when manifested to an extreme degree, are thought to be symptoms of disorders. Examples include traits such as paranoia, depression, and hysteria.

Are the MMPI clinical scales valid? That is, do they measure what they were designed to measure? Originally, it was assumed that the 10 clinical subscales would provide direct indexes of specific types of disorders. In other words, a high score on the depression scale would be indicative of depression, a high score on the paranoia scale would be indicative of a paranoid disorder, and so forth. However, research revealed that the relations between MMPI scores and various types of mental illness are much more complex than originally anticipated. People with most types of disorders show elevated scores on *several* MMPI subscales. This means that certain score *profiles* are indicative of specific disorders (see **Figure 11.16**). Thus, the interpretation of the MMPI is quite complicated. Nonetheless, the MMPI can be a helpful diagnostic tool for the clinician. The fact that the inventory has been translated into

more than 115 languages is a testimonial to its usefulness (Butcher, 1990).

The 16PF and NEO Personality Inventory   7a

Raymond Cattell (1957, 1965) set out to identify and measure the *basic dimensions* of the *normal* personality. He started with a previously compiled list of 4504 personality traits. This massive list was reduced to 171 traits by weeding out terms that were virtually synonyms. Cattell then used factor analysis to identify clusters of closely related traits. Eventually, he reduced the list of 171 traits to 16 *source traits*. The Sixteen Personality Factor (16PF) Questionnaire (Cattell, 2004; Cattell, Eber, & Tatsuoka, 1970) is a 187-item scale that assesses these 16 basic dimensions of personality which are listed in **Figure 11.17** on the next page.

As we noted in the main body of the chapter, some theorists believe that only five trait dimensions are required to provide a full description of personality. This view led to the creation of the NEO Personality Inventory. Developed by Paul Costa and Robert McCrae (1985, 1992), the NEO Inventory is designed to measure the Big Five traits: neuroticism, extraversion, openness to experience, agreeableness, and conscientiousness. In spite of its relatively short life span, the NEO inventory is widely used in

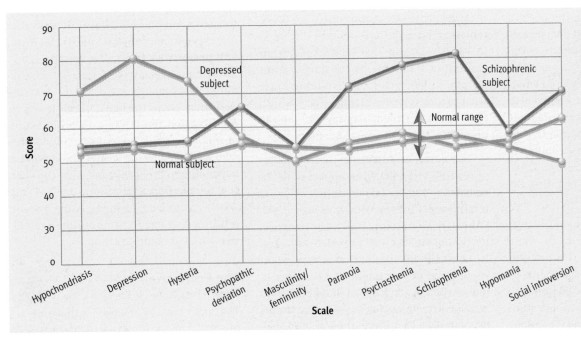

Figure 11.16

MMPI profiles. Scores on the 10 clinical scales of the MMPI are often plotted as shown here to create a profile for a client. The normal range for scores on each subscale is 50 to 65. People with disorders frequently exhibit elevated scores on several clinical scales rather than just one.

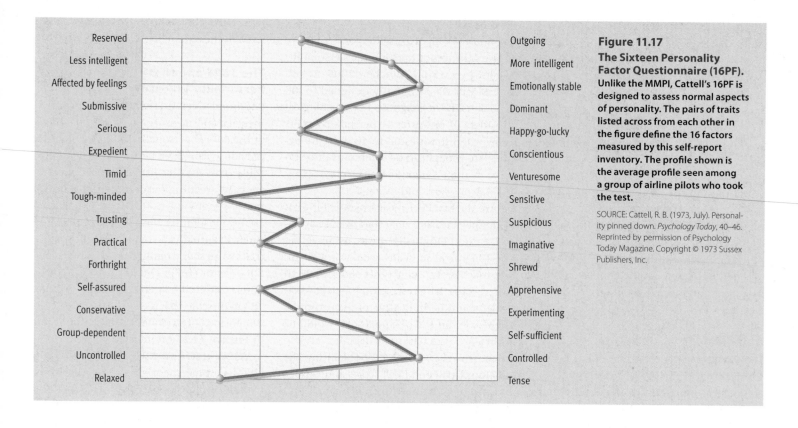

Reserved								Outgoing
Less intelligent								More intelligent
Affected by feelings								Emotionally stable
Submissive								Dominant
Serious								Happy-go-lucky
Expedient								Conscientious
Timid								Venturesome
Tough-minded								Sensitive
Trusting								Suspicious
Practical								Imaginative
Forthright								Shrewd
Self-assured								Apprehensive
Conservative								Experimenting
Group-dependent								Self-sufficient
Uncontrolled								Controlled
Relaxed								Tense

Figure 11.17

The Sixteen Personality Factor Questionnaire (16PF). Unlike the MMPI, Cattell's 16PF is designed to assess normal aspects of personality. The pairs of traits listed across from each other in the figure define the 16 factors measured by this self-report inventory. The profile shown is the average profile seen among a group of airline pilots who took the test.

SOURCE: Cattell, R. B. (1973, July). Personality pinned down. *Psychology Today*, 40–46. Reprinted by permission of Psychology Today Magazine. Copyright © 1973 Sussex Publishers, Inc.

research and clinical work and updated revisions of the scale have been released (McCrae & Costa, 2004, 2007).

Strengths and Weaknesses of Self-Report Inventories

To appreciate the strengths of self-report inventories, consider how else you might inquire about an individual's personality. For instance, if you want to know how assertive someone is, why not just ask the person? Why administer an elaborate 50-item personality inventory that measures assertiveness? The advantage of the personality inventory is that it can provide a more objective and more precise estimate of the person's assertiveness.

Of course, self-report inventories are only as accurate as the information that respondents provide. They are susceptible to several sources of error (Ben-Porath, 2003; Kline, 1995; Paulhus, 1991), including the following:

1. *Deliberate deception.* Some self-report inventories include many questions whose purpose is easy to figure out. This problem makes it possible for some respondents to intentionally fake particular personality traits (Rees & Metcalfe, 2003). Some studies suggest that deliberate faking is a serious

problem when personality scales are used to evaluate job applicants (Birkeland et al., 2006), but other studies suggest that the problem is not all that significant (Hogan, Barrett, & Hogan, 2007).

2. *Social desirability bias.* Without realizing it, some people consistently respond to questions in ways that make them look good. The social desirability bias isn't a matter of deception so much as wishful thinking.

3. *Response sets.* A response set is a systematic tendency to respond to test items in a particular way that is unrelated to the content of the items. For instance, some people, called "yea-sayers," tend to agree with virtually every statement on a test. Other people, called "nay-sayers," tend to disagree with nearly every statement.

Test developers have devised a number of strategies to reduce the impact of deliberate deception, social desirability bias, and response sets (Berry, Wetter, & Baer, 1995; Lanyon & Goodstein, 1997). For instance, it's possible to insert a "lie scale" into a test to assess the likelihood that a respondent is engaging in deception. The best way to reduce the impact of social desirability bias is to identify items that are sensitive to this bias and drop them from the test. Problems

with response sets can be reduced by systematically varying the way in which test items are worded.

Projective Tests 7a

Projective tests, which all take a rather indirect approach to the assessment of personality, are used extensively in clinical work. *Projective tests* ask participants to respond to vague, ambiguous stimuli in ways that may reveal the subjects' needs, feelings, and personality traits. The Rorschach test, for instance, consists of a series of ten inkblots. Respondents are asked to describe what they see in the blots. In the Thematic Apperception Test (TAT), a series of pictures of simple scenes is presented to individuals who are asked to tell stories about what is happening in the scenes and what the characters are feeling. For instance, one TAT card shows a young boy contemplating a violin resting on a table in front of him (see **Figure 11.18** for another example).

The Projective Hypothesis 7a

The "projective hypothesis" is that ambiguous materials can serve as a blank screen

Figure 11.18

The Thematic Apperception Test (TAT). In taking the TAT, a respondent is asked to tell stories about scenes such as this one. The themes apparent in each story can be scored to provide insight about the respondent's personality.

SOURCE: Murray. H. A. (1971). *Thematic Apperception Test*. Cambridge, MA: Harvard University Press. Copyright © 1943 by The President and Fellows of Harvard College, Copyright © 1971 by Henry A. Murray. Reprinted by permission of the publisher.

onto which people project their characteristic concerns, conflicts, and desires (Frank, 1939). Thus, a competitive person who is shown the TAT card of the boy at the table with the violin might concoct a story about how the boy is contemplating an upcoming musical competition at which he hopes to excel. The same card shown to a person high in impulsiveness might elicit a story about how the boy is planning to sneak out the door to go dirt-bike riding with friends.

The scoring and interpretation of projective tests is very complicated. Rorschach responses may be analyzed in terms of content, originality, the feature of the inkblot that determined the response, and the amount of the inkblot used, among other criteria. In fact, six different systems exist for scoring the Rorschach (Adams & Culbertson, 2005). TAT stories are examined in terms of heroes, needs, themes, and outcomes.

Strengths and Weaknesses of Projective Tests

Proponents of projective tests assert that the tests have two unique strengths. First, they are not transparent to respondents. That is, the subject doesn't know how the test provides information to the tester. Hence, it may be difficult for people to engage in intentional deception (Groth-Marnat, 1997). Second, the indirect approach used in these tests may make them especially sensitive to unconscious, latent features of personality.

Unfortunately, the scientific evidence on projective measures is unimpressive (Garb, Florio, & Grove, 1998; Hunsley, Lee, & Wood, 2003; Lanyon & Goodstein, 1997). In a thorough review of the relevant research, Lillienfeld, Wood, and Garb (2000) conclude that projective tests tend to be plagued by inconsistent scoring, low reliability, inadequate test norms, cultural bias, and poor validity estimates. They also assert that, contrary to advocates' claims, projective tests are susceptible to some types of intentional deception (primarily, faking poor mental health). Based on their analysis, Lillienfeld and his colleagues argue that projective tests should be referred to as projective "techniques" or "instruments" rather than tests because "most of these techniques as used in daily clinical practice do not fulfill the traditional criteria for psychological tests" (p. 29). In spite of these problems, projective tests continue to be used by many clinicians. Although the questionable scientific status of these techniques is a very real problem, their continued popularity suggests that they yield subjective information that many clinicians find useful (Viglione & Rivera, 2003).

Personality Testing on the Internet

The emergence of the Internet has had a considerable impact on the process of personality assessment. Self-report inventories are increasingly being administered over the Internet by researchers, clinicians, and companies (Naglieri et al., 2004). Most of the widely used personality scales are available in an online format. The advantages of online testing are substantial (Buchanan, 2007). Tests can be completed quickly, with reduced labor costs, and the data flow directly into interpretive software. Online testing also allows test administrators to collect additional data that would not be available from a traditional paper-and-

pencil test. For instance, they can track answer changing and how long respondents ponder specific questions. Online testing also allows clinicians to deliver assessment services to rural clients who do not have access to local psychologists (Barak & Buchanan, 2004). Given all these advantages, Buchanan (2007) notes that "it is easy to imagine a future where virtually all testing is conducted online" (p. 450).

Are there any disadvantages to online personality assessment? Well, there are issues that merit concern, but they appear to be manageable. The item content of some tests is closely guarded, so security is an issue for some tests (Naglieri et al., 2004). And when personality tests are used for hiring purposes, verifying the identity of the respondent is important. The chief theoretical issue is whether tests delivered online yield results that are equivalent to what is found when the same tests are administered in a paper-and-pencil format. For the most part, research suggests that online tests are equivalent to their offline counterparts, but this issue should be checked empirically whenever a specific test is migrated to an online format (Buchanan, 2007; Epstein & Klinkenberg, 2001). Overall, though, the future of online personality testing appears bright. That said, consumers should remember that the Internet is utterly unregulated, so one can find an abundance of pop psychology tests online that have no scientific or empirical basis (Naglieri et al., 2004).

REVIEW of Key Learning Goals

11.26 Self-report inventories ask subjects to describe themselves. The MMPI is a widely used inventory that measures pathological aspects of personality. The 16PF assesses 16 dimensions of the normal personality. The NEO personality inventory measures the Big Five personality traits. Self-report inventories are vulnerable to certain sources of error, including deception, the social desirability bias, and response sets.

11.27 Projective tests assume that subjects' responses to ambiguous stimuli reveal something about their personality. In the Rorschach test, respondents describe what they see in 10 inkblots, whereas subjects formulate stories about simple scenes when they take the TAT. While the projective hypothesis seems plausible, projective tests' reliability and validity are disturbingly low. Self-report inventories are increasingly being administered over the Internet. The advantages of online testing are substantial, although there are concerns about security and test equivalence.

Hindsight in Everyday Analyses of Personality

Key Learning Goals

11.28 Understand how hindsight bias affects everyday analyses and theoretical analyses of personality.

Consider the case of two close sisters who grew up together: Lorena and Christina. Lorena grew into a frugal adult who is careful about spending her money, only shops when there are sales, and saves every penny she can. In contrast, Christina became an extravagant spender who lives to shop and never saves any money. How do the sisters explain their striking personality differences? Lorena attributes her thrifty habits to the fact that her family was so poor when she was a child that she learned the value of being careful with money. Christina attributes her extravagant spending to the fact that her family was so poor that she learned to really enjoy any money that she might have. Now, it *is* possible that two sisters could react to essentially the same circumstances quite differently, but the more likely explanation is that both sisters have been influenced by *hindsight bias*—the tendency to mold one's interpretation of the past to fit how events actually turned out. We saw how hindsight can distort memory in Chapter 7. Here, we will see how hindsight tends to make people feel as if they are personality experts and how it creates interpretive problems even for scientific theories of personality.

The Prevalence of Hindsight Bias

Hindsight bias is *ubiquitous*, which means that it occurs in many settings, with all sorts of people (Blank, Musch, & Pohl, 2007; Sanna & Schwarz, 2006). Most of the time, people are not aware of the way their explanations are skewed by the fact that the outcome is already known. The experimental literature on hindsight bias offers a rich array of findings on how the knowledge of an outcome biases the way people think about its causes (Fischhoff, 2007; Guilbault et al., 2004). For example, when college students were told the results of a hypothetical

experiment, each group of students could "explain" why the studies turned out the way they did, even though different groups were given opposite results to explain (Slovic & Fischhoff, 1977). The students believed that the results of the studies were obvious when they were told what the experimenter found, but when they were given only the information that was available before the outcome was known, it was not obvious at all. This bias is also called the "I knew it all along" effect because that is the typical refrain of people when they have the luxury of hindsight. Indeed, after the fact, people often act as if events that would have been difficult to predict had in fact been virtually *inevitable*. Looking back at the disintegration of the Soviet Union and the end of the Cold War, for instance, many people today act as though these events were bound to happen, but in reality these landmark events were predicted by almost no one. It appears that outcome knowledge warps judgments in two ways (Erdfelder, Brandt, & Broder, 2007). First, knowing the outcome of an event impairs one's recall of earlier expectations about the event. Second, outcome knowledge shapes how people reconstruct their thinking about the event.

Hindsight bias shows up in many contexts. For example, when a couple announces that they are splitting up, many people in their social circle will typically

claim they "saw it coming." When a football team loses in a huge upset, you will hear many fans claim, "I knew they were overrated and vulnerable." When public authorities make a difficult decision that leads to a disastrous outcome—such as officials' decision not to evacuate New Orleans in preparation for Hurricane Katrina until relatively late—many of the pundits in the press are quick to criticize, often asserting that only incompetent fools could have failed to foresee the catastrophe. Interestingly, people are not much kinder to themselves when they make ill-fated decisions. When individuals make tough calls that lead to negative results—such as buying a car that turns out to be a lemon, or investing in a stock that plummets—they often say things like, "Why did I ignore the obvious warning signs?" or "How could I have been such an idiot?"

Hindsight and Personality

Hindsight bias appears to be pervasive in everyday analyses of personality. Think about it: If you attempt to explain why you are so suspicious, why your mother is so domineering, or why your best friend is so insecure, the starting point in each case will be the personality outcome. It would probably be impossible to reconstruct the past without being swayed by your knowledge of these outcomes. Thus, hindsight

When public officials make tough decisions that backfire, critics are often quick to argue that the officials should have shown greater foresight. This type of hindsight bias has been apparent in discussions of whether New Orleans mayor Ray Nagin (at left) and other state and federal officials should have been more proactive in evacuating New Orleans when Hurricane Katrina loomed as a threat.

© AP Images/Dennis Cook

makes everybody an expert on personality, as we can all come up with plausible explanations for the personality traits of people we know well. Perhaps this is why Judith Harris (1998) ignited a firestorm of protest when she wrote a book arguing that parents have relatively little effect on their children's personalities beyond the genetic material that they supply.

In her book *The Nurture Assumption,* Harris summarizes behavioral genetics research (which we discussed in the main body of the chapter; see p. 398) and other evidence suggesting that family environment has surprisingly little impact on children's personality. There is room for debate on this complex issue (Kagan, 1998; Tavris, 1998), but our chief interest here is that Harris made a cogent, compelling argument that attracted extensive coverage in the press, which generated an avalanche of commentary from angry parents who argued that *parents do matter.* For example, *Newsweek* magazine received 350 letters, mostly from parents who provided examples of how they thought they had influenced their children's personalities. However, parents' retrospective analyses of their children's personality development have to be treated with great skepticism, as they are likely to be distorted by hindsight bias (not to mention the selective recall commonly seen in anecdotal reports).

Unfortunately, hindsight bias is so prevalent, it also presents a problem for scientific theories of personality. For example, the issue of hindsight bias has been raised in many critiques of psychoanalytic theory (Torrey, 1992). Freudian theory was originally built mainly on a foundation of case studies of patients in therapy. Obviously, Freudian therapists who knew what their patients' adult personalities were like probably went looking for the types of childhood experiences hypothesized by Freud (oral fixations, punitive toilet training, Oedipal conflicts, and so forth) in their efforts to explain their patients' personalities.

Another problem with hindsight bias is that once researchers know an outcome, more often than not they can fashion some plausible explanation for it. For instance, Torrey (1992) describes a study inspired by Freudian theory that examined breast-size preferences among men. The original hypothesis was that men who scored higher in dependence—thought to be a sign of oral fixation—would manifest a stronger preference for women with large breasts. When the actual results of the study showed just the opposite—that dependence was associated with a preference for smaller breasts—the finding was attributed to reaction formation (the defense mechanism that involves behaving in a way opposite of one's true feelings). Instead of failing to support Freudian theory, the unexpected findings were simply reinterpreted in a way that was consistent with Freudian theory.

The hindsight bias also presents thorny problems for evolutionary theorists, who generally work backward from known outcomes to reason out how adaptive pressures in humans' ancestral past may have led to those outcomes (Cornell, 1997). Consider, for instance, evolutionary theorists' assertion that the Big Five traits are found to be fundamental dimensions of personality around the world because those specific traits have had major adaptive implications over the course of human history (Buss, 1995; Nettle, 2006). Their explanation makes sense, but what would have happened if some *other traits* had shown up in the Big Five? Would the evolutionary view have been weakened if dominance or paranoia had turned up in the Big Five? Probably not. With the luxury of hindsight, evolutionary theorists surely could have constructed plausible explanations for how these traits promoted reproductive success in the distant past. Thus, hindsight bias is a fundamental feature of human cognition and the scientific enterprise is not immune to this problem.

Other Implications of "20-20 Hindsight"

Our discussion of hindsight has focused on its implications for thinking about personality, but there is ample evidence that hindsight can bias thinking in all sorts of domains. For example, consider the practice of obtaining second opinions on medical diagnoses. The doctor providing the second opinion usually is aware of the first physician's diagnosis, which creates a hindsight bias (Arkes et al., 1981). Second opinions would probably be more valuable if the doctors rendering them were not aware of previous diagnoses. Hindsight also has the potential to distort legal decisions in many types of cases where jurors evaluate defendants' responsibility for known outcomes, such as a failed surgery (Harley, 2007). For example, in trials involving allegations of negligence, jurors' natural tendency to think "how could they have failed to foresee this problem?" may exaggerate the appearance of negligence (LaBine & LaBine, 1996).

Hindsight bias is powerful. The next time you hear of an unfortunate outcome to a decision made by a public official, carefully examine the way news reporters describe the decision. You will probably find that they believe that the disastrous outcome should have been obvious, because they can clearly see what went wrong after the fact. Similarly, if you find yourself thinking, "Only a fool would have failed to anticipate this disaster" or "I would have forseen this problem," take a deep breath and try to review the decision *using only information that was known at the time the decision was being made.* Sometimes good decisions based on the best available information can have terrible outcomes. Unfortunately, the clarity of "20-20 hindsight" makes it difficult for people to learn from their own and others' mistakes.

Table 11.3 Critical Thinking Skill Discussed in This Application

Skill	Description
Recognizing the bias in hindsight analysis	The critical thinker understands that knowing the outcome of events biases one's recall and interpretation of the events.

The Nature of Personality

▌ The concept of personality explains the consistency in people's behavior over time and situations while also explaining their distinctiveness. Personality traits are dispositions to behave in certain ways.

▌ The five-factor model has become the dominant conception of personality structure. The Big Five traits—extraversion, neuroticism, openness to experience, agreeableness, and conscientiousness—are predictive of important life outcomes.

Psychodynamic Perspectives

▌ Freud's psychoanalytic theory emphasizes the importance of the unconscious. Freud described personality structure in terms of three components—the id, ego, and superego—which are routinely involved in an ongoing series of internal conflicts.

▌ Freud theorized that conflicts centering on sex and aggression are especially likely to lead to significant anxiety. According to Freud, anxiety and other unpleasant emotions such as guilt are often warded off with defense mechanisms.

▌ Freud believed that the first five years of life are extremely influential in shaping adult personality. He described a series of five psychosexual stages of development. Certain experiences during these stages can have lasting effects on adult personality.

▌ Jung's most innovative concept was the collective unconscious. Adler's individual psychology emphasizes how people strive for superiority to compensate for feelings of inferiority. Psychodynamic theories have been criticized for their poor testability, their inadequate base of empirical evidence, and their male-centered views.

Behavioral Perspectives

▌ Behavioral theories explain how personality is shaped through learning. Behaviorists see personality as a collection of response tendencies tied to specific stimulus situations. Skinner assumed that personality development is a lifelong process in which response tendencies are shaped by learning.

▌ Social cognitive theory focuses on how cognitive factors regulate learned behavior. Bandura's concept of observational learning accounts for the acquisition of responses from models. Mischel has emphasized the importance of situational factors. The behaviorists have been criticized for their overdependence on animal research and their fragmented analysis of personality.

Humanistic Perspectives

▌ Humanistic theories take an optimistic view of people's conscious, rational ability to chart their own courses of action. Rogers focused on the self-concept as the critical aspect of personality. He maintained that anxiety is attributable to incongruence between one's self-concept and reality.

▌ Maslow theorized that needs are organized hierarchically and that psychological health depends on meeting one's need for self-actualization, which is the need to fulfill one's human potential. Humanistic theories lack a firm base of research, are difficult to put to an empirical test, and may be overly optimistic about human nature.

Biological Perspectives

▌ Eysenck suggests that heredity influences personality by shaping individual differences in physiological functioning that affect how easily people acquire conditioned responses. Twin and adoption studies provide impressive evidence that genetic factors shape personality. Behavioral genetics research also suggests that shared family environment may have surprisingly little impact on personality.

▌ Evolutionary analyses of personality have emphasized how the "Big Five" personality traits may have had significant adaptive value. The biological approach has been criticized because of methodological problems with heritability estimates and because it offers no systematic model of how physiology governs personality.

A Contemporary Empirical Approach: Terror Management Theory

▌ Terror management theory proposes that self-esteem and faith in a cultural worldview shield people from the profound anxiety associated with their mortality. Consistent with this analysis, increasing mortality salience leads people to make efforts to bolster their self-esteem and defend their worldviews. These defensive reactions are automatic and subconscious.

Culture and Personality

▌ Research suggests that the basic trait structure of personality may be much the same across cultures, as the Big Five traits usually emerge in cross-cultural studies. However, there are cultural variations in the mean level of some personality traits.

▌ Perceptions of national character appear to be inaccurate stereotypes. Markus and Kitayama assert that American culture fosters an independent conception of self, whereas Asian cultures foster an interdependent view of the self.

Reflecting on the Chapter's Themes

▌ The study of personality illustrates how psychology is characterized by great theoretical diversity. The study of personality also demonstrates how ideas in psychology are shaped by sociohistorical forces and how cultural factors influence psychological processes.

PERSONAL APPLICATION Understanding Personality Assessment

▌ Self-report inventories, such as the MMPI, 16PF, and NEO Personality Inventory, ask subjects to describe themselves. Self-report inventories are vulnerable to certain sources of error, including deception, the social desirability bias, and response sets.

▌ Projective tests, such as the Rorschach and TAT, assume that subjects' responses to ambiguous stimuli reveal something about their personality. While the projective hypothesis seems plausible, projective tests' reliability and validity are disturbingly low. Personality assessments are increasingly being administered over the Internet.

CRITICAL THINKING APPLICATION Hindsight in Everyday Analyses of Personality

▌ Hindsight bias often leads people to assert that "I knew it all along" in discussing outcomes that they did not actually predict. Thanks to hindsight, people can almost always come up with plausible-sounding explanations for known personality traits. Problems with hindsight bias have been raised in critiques of Freudian theory and evolutionary theory.

PsykTrek Preview

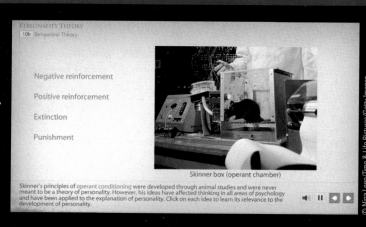

© Nina Leen/Time & Life Pictures/Getty Images

Go to Module 10a (*Freudian Theory*) to review the essentials of Sigmund Freud's controversial psychoanalytic model of personality.

Work through Module 10b (*Behavioral Therapy*) to enhance your understanding of how the behaviorists have analyzed personality and to watch classic footage

1. Harvey Hedonist has devoted his life to the search for physical pleasure and immediate need gratification. Freud would say that Harvey is dominated by:
   A. his ego.
   B. his superego.
   C. his id.
   D. Bacchus.

2. Furious at her boss for what she considers to be unjust criticism, Clara turns around and takes out her anger on her subordinates. Clara may be using the defense mechanism of:
   A. displacement.
   B. reaction formation.
   C. identification.
   D. replacement.

3. Freud believed that most personality disturbances are due to:
   A. the failure of parents to reinforce healthy behavior.
   B. a poor self-concept resulting from excessive parental demands.
   C. unconscious and unresolved sexual conflicts rooted in childhood experiences.
   D. the exposure of children to unhealthy role models.

4. According to Alfred Adler, the prime motivating force in a person's life is:
   A. physical gratification.
   B. existential anxiety.
   C. striving for superiority.
   D. the need for power.

5. Which of the following learning mechanisms does B. F. Skinner see as being the major means by which behavior is learned?
   A. Classical conditioning
   B. Operant conditioning
   C. Observational learning
   D. Insight learning

6. Always having been a good student, Irving is confident that he will do well in his psychology course. According to Bandura's social cognitive theory, Irving would be said to have:
   A. strong feelings of self-efficacy.
   B. a sense of superiority.
   C. strong feelings of narcissism.
   D. strong defense mechanisms.

7. Which of the following did Carl Rogers believe fosters a congruent self-concept?
   A. Conditional love
   B. Appropriate role models
   C. Immediate need gratification
   D. Unconditional love

8. What need was Abraham Maslow expressing when he said, "What a man can be, he must be"?
   A. The need for superiority
   B. The need for unconditional love
   C. The need for self-actualization
   D. The need to achieve

9. The strongest support for the theory that personality is heavily influenced by genetics is provided by strong personality similarity between:
   A. identical twins reared together.
   B. identical twins reared apart.
   C. fraternal twins reared together.
   D. nontwins reared together.

10. In which of the following cultures is an independent view of the self most likely to be the norm?
    A. China
    B. Japan
    C. Korea
    D. United States

11. Which of the following is *not* a shortcoming of self-report personality inventories?
    A. The accuracy of the results is a function of the honesty of the respondent.
    B. Respondents may attempt to answer in a way that makes them look good.
    C. There is sometimes a problem with "yea-sayers" or "nay-sayers."
    D. They are objective measures.

12. In The *Nurture Assumption,* Judith Harris argues that the evidence indicates that family environment has _____ on children's personalities.
    A. largely positive effects
    B. largely negative effects
    C. surprisingly little effect
    D. a powerful effect

Answers

1 C pp. 380–381
2 A p. 383
3 C p. 385
4 C p. 386
5 B pp. 388–389
6 A p. 390
7 D p. 393
8 C p. 394
9 B pp. 397–398
10 D p. 404
11 D p. 408
12 C p. 411

PsykTrek Preview

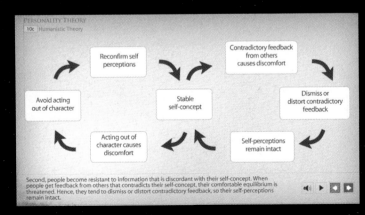

Second, people become resistant to information that is discordant with their self-concept. When people get feedback from others that contradicts their self-concept, their comfortable equilibrium is threatened. Hence, they tend to dismiss or distort contradictory feedback, so their self-perceptions remain intact.

Among the traits Eysenck measured were altruism, empathy, and aggressiveness. Click on each trait to reveal the mean correlations between twins for that trait. Keep in mind that higher correlations mean greater similarity.

Explore Module 10c (*Humanistic Theory*) to get a better handle on the personal-

Visit Module 10d (*Biological Theory*) to learn more about how biological factors

12

Stress, Coping, and Health

A bridge in Kondus Valley, Pakistan © Jimmy Chin/National Geographic/Getty Images

You're in your car headed home from school with a classmate. Traffic is barely moving. A radio report indicates that the traffic jam is only going to get worse. You groan as you fiddle impatiently with the radio dial. Another motorist nearly takes your fender off trying to cut into your lane. Your pulse quickens as you shout insults at the unknown driver, who can't even hear you. You think about the term paper that you have to work on tonight. Your stomach knots up as you think about all the research you still have to do. If you don't finish that paper soon, you won't be able to find any time to study for your math test, not to mention your biology quiz. Suddenly, you remember that you promised the person you're dating that the two of you would get together tonight. There's no way. Another fight looms on the horizon. Your classmate asks how you feel about the tuition increase that the college announced yesterday. You've been trying not to think about it. You're already in debt up to your ears. Your parents are bugging you about changing schools, but you don't want to leave your friends. Your heartbeat quickens as you contemplate the debate you're sure to have with your parents. You feel wired with tension as you realize that the stress in your life never seems to let up.

Many circumstances can create stress. It comes in all sorts of packages: big and small, pretty and ugly, simple and complex. All too often, the package comes as a surprise. In this chapter we'll try to sort out these packages. We'll discuss the nature of stress, how people cope with stress, and the potential effects of stress.

Our examination of the relationship between stress and physical illness will lead us into a broader discussion of the psychology of health. The way people in health professions think about physical illness has changed considerably in the past 20 to 30 years. The traditional view of physical illness as a purely biological phenomenon has given way to a biopsychosocial model of illness (Friedman & Adler, 2007). The *biopsychosocial model* holds that physical illness is caused by a complex interaction of biological, psychological, and sociocultural factors. This model does not suggest that biological factors are unimportant. It simply asserts that these factors operate in a psychological and social context that is also influential.

What has led to this shift in thinking? In part, it's a result of changing patterns of illness. Prior to the 20th century, the principal threats to health were *contagious diseases* caused by infectious agents—diseases such as smallpox, typhoid fever, diphtheria, yellow fever, malaria, cholera, tuberculosis, and polio. Today, none of these diseases are among the leading killers in the United States. They were tamed by improvements in nutrition, public hygiene, sanitation, and medical treatment. Unfortunately, the void left by contagious diseases has been filled all too quickly by *chronic diseases* that develop gradually, such as heart disease, cancer, and stroke (see **Figure 12.1**). Psychosocial

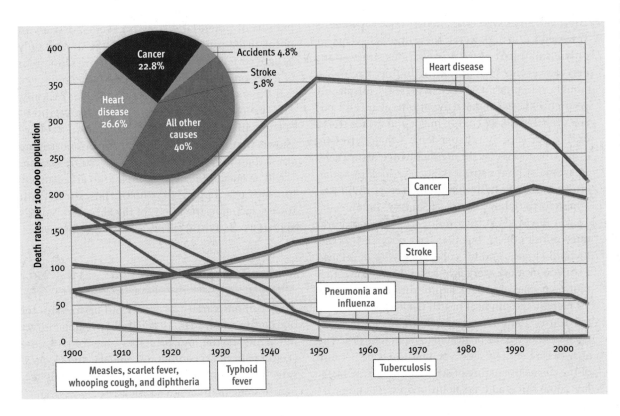

Figure 12.1
Changing patterns of illness. Historical trends in the death rates for various diseases reveal that contagious diseases (shown in blue) have declined as a threat to health. However, the death rates for stress-related chronic diseases (shown in red) have remained quite high. The pie chart (inset) shows the results of these trends: Three chronic diseases (heart disease, cancer, and stroke) account for about 55% of all deaths. Although these chronic diseases remain the chief threat to health in modern societies, it is interesting to note that deaths from heart disease have declined considerably since the 1980s. Many experts attribute much of this decline to improved health habits (Brannon & Feist, 2007), which demonstrates the important link between behavior and health.

SOURCE: Based on data from *National Vital Statistics Reports*, 2008, Vol. 56, No. 10.

factors, such as stress and lifestyle, play a large role in the development of these chronic diseases.

The growing recognition that psychological factors influence physical health eventually led to the emergence of a new specialty in psychology (Friedman & Adler, 2007). *Health psychology* is concerned with how psychosocial factors relate to the promotion and maintenance of health and with the causation, prevention, and treatment of illness. In the second half of this chapter, we'll explore this domain of psychology. In the Personal Application, we'll focus on strategies for enhancing stress management, and in the Critical Thinking Application we'll discuss strategies for improving health-related decision making.

The Nature of Stress

Key Learning Goals

12.1 Evaluate the impact of minor stressors, people's appraisals of stress, and frustration.

12.2 Identify the three basic types of conflict, and discuss which types are most troublesome.

12.3 Summarize evidence on life change and pressure as forms of stress.

The term *stress* has been used in different ways by different theorists. We'll define *stress* as any circumstances that threaten or are perceived to threaten one's well-being and tax one's coping abilities. The threat may be to immediate physical safety, long-range security, self-esteem, reputation, peace of mind, or many other things that one values. This is a complex concept, so let's explore it a little further.

Stress as an Everyday Event

The word *stress* tends to spark images of overwhelming, traumatic crises. People may think of terrorist attacks, hurricanes, military combat, and nuclear accidents. Undeniably, major disasters of this sort are extremely stressful (Stevens, Raphael, & Dobson, 2007; van Griensven et al., 2007; Weisler, Barbee, & Townsend, 2007). However, these unusual events are only a small part of what constitutes stress. Many everyday events such as waiting in line, having car trouble, shopping for Christmas presents, misplacing your checkbook, and staring at bills you can't pay are also stressful. Of course, major and minor stressors are not entirely independent. A major stressful event, such as going through a divorce, can trigger a cascade of minor stressors, such as looking for an attorney, taking on new household responsibilities, and so forth (Pillow, Zautra, & Sandler, 1996).

You might guess that minor stresses would produce minor effects, but that isn't necessarily true. Richard Lazarus and his colleagues, who developed a scale to measure everyday hassles, have shown that routine hassles may have significant harmful effects on mental and physical health (Delongis, Folkman, & Lazarus, 1988; Johnson & Sherman, 1997). Why would minor hassles be related to mental health? The answer isn't entirely clear yet, but it may be because of the *cumulative* nature of stress (Seta, Seta, & McElroy, 2002). Stress adds up. Routine stresses at home, at school, and at work might be fairly benign individually, but collectively they could create great strain.

Appraisal: Stress Lies in the Eye of the Beholder

The experience of feeling stressed depends on what events one notices and how one appraises them (Lazarus, 1999; Semmer, McGrath, & Beehr, 2005). Events that are stressful for one person may be routine for another (Steptoe, 2007). For example, many people find flying in an airplane somewhat stressful, but frequent fliers may not be bothered at all. Some people enjoy the excitement of going out on a date with someone new; others find the uncertainty terrifying.

Often, people aren't very objective in their appraisals of potentially stressful events. A study of hospitalized patients awaiting surgery showed only a slight correlation between the objective seriousness of a person's upcoming surgery and the amount of fear experienced by the patient (Janis, 1958). Clearly, some people are more prone than others to feel threatened by life's difficulties. A number of studies have shown that anxious, neurotic people report more stress than others (Cooper & Bright, 2001; Watson, David, & Suls, 1999), as do people who are relatively unhappy (Cacioppo et al., 2008). Thus, stress lies in the eye (actually, the mind) of the beholder. People's appraisals of stressful events are highly subjective.

Major Types of Stress   11f

An enormous variety of events can be stressful for one person or another. Although they're not entirely independent, the four principal types of stress are (1) frustration, (2) conflict, (3) change, and (4) pressure. As you read about each type, you'll surely recognize some familiar adversaries.

Richard Lazarus

"We developed the Hassle Scale because we think scales that measure major events miss the point. The constant, minor irritants may be much more important than the large, landmark changes."

Courtesy of Richard S. Lazarus

Frustration 11f

As psychologists use the term, *frustration* is experienced whenever the pursuit of some goal is thwarted. In essence, you experience frustration when you want something and you can't have it. Everyone has to deal with frustration virtually every day. Traffic jams, difficult daily commutes, and annoying drivers, for instance, are a routine source of frustration that can elicit anger and aggression (Evans & Wener, 2006; Schaefer, 2005). Fortunately, most frustrations are brief and insignificant. You may be quite upset when you go to a repair shop to pick up your ailing laptop and find that it hasn't been fixed as promised. However, a week later you'll probably have your computer back, and the frustration will be forgotten. Of course, some frustrations—such as failing to get a promotion at work or losing a boyfriend or girlfriend—can be sources of significant stress.

Conflict 11f

Like frustration, conflict is an unavoidable feature of everyday life. The perplexing question "Should I or shouldn't I?" comes up countless times in one's life. *Conflict occurs when two or more incompatible motivations or behavioral impulses compete for expression.* As we discussed in Chapter 11, Sigmund Freud proposed a century ago that internal conflicts generate considerable psychological distress.

Conflicts come in three types, which were originally described by Kurt Lewin (1935) and investigated extensively by Neal Miller (1944, 1959). These three basic types of conflict—approach-approach, avoidance-avoidance, and approach-avoidance—are diagrammed in **Figure 12.2**.

In an *approach-approach conflict* a choice must be made between two attractive goals. The problem, of course, is that you can choose just one of the two goals. For example: You have a free afternoon—should you play tennis or racquetball? You can't afford both the blue sweater and the gray jacket—which should you buy? Among the three kinds of conflict, the approach-approach type tends to be the least stressful. Nonetheless, approach-approach conflicts over important issues may sometimes be troublesome. If you're torn between two appealing college majors or two attractive boyfriends, for example, you may find the decision-making process quite stressful.

In an *avoidance-avoidance conflict* a choice must be made between two unattractive goals. Forced to choose between two repellent alternatives, you are, as they say, "caught between a rock and a hard place." For example, should you continue to collect unemployment checks, or should you take

that boring job at the car wash? Or suppose you have painful backaches. Should you submit to surgery that you dread, or should you continue to live with the pain? Obviously, avoidance-avoidance conflicts are most unpleasant and highly stressful.

In an *approach-avoidance conflict* a choice must be made about whether to pursue a single goal that has both attractive and unattractive aspects. For instance, imagine that you're offered a promotion that will mean a large increase in pay, but you'll have to move to a city that you hate. Approach-avoidance conflicts are common and can be quite stressful. Any time you have to take a risk to pursue some desirable outcome, you're likely to find yourself in an approach-avoidance conflict. Should you risk rejection by approaching that attractive person in class? Should you risk your savings by investing in a new business that could fail? Approach-avoidance conflicts often produce *vacillation* (Miller, 1944). That is, you go back and forth, beset by indecision. You decide to go ahead, then you decide not to, and then you decide to go ahead again.

Change 11f

Thomas Holmes and Richard Rahe have led the way in exploring the idea that life changes—including positive events, such as getting married or getting promoted—represent a key type of stress. *Life changes* are any noticeable alterations in one's living circumstances that require readjustment. Based on their theory, Holmes and Rahe (1967) developed the Social Readjustment Rating Scale (SRRS) to measure life change as a form of stress. The scale assigns numerical values to 43 major life events.

web link 12.1

The Web's Stress Management & Emotional Wellness Page

Ernesto Randolfi (Montana State University) has gathered a comprehensive set of resources dealing with stress management. Topics covered include cognitive restructuring, relaxation techniques, and stress in the workplace and in college life.

Figure 12.2

Types of conflict. Psychologists have identified three basic types of conflict. In approach-approach and avoidance-avoidance conflicts, a person is torn between two goals. In an approach-avoidance conflict, only one goal is under consideration, but it has both positive and negative aspects.

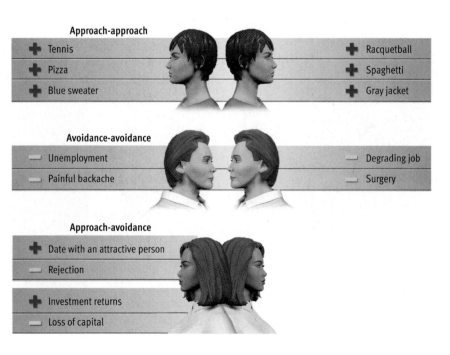

Identifying Types of Conflict

Check your understanding of the three basic types of conflict by identifying the type experienced in each of the following examples. The answers are in Appendix A.

Examples

_____ 1. John can't decide whether to take a boring job in a car wash or to go on welfare.

_____ 2. Desiree wants to apply to a highly selective law school, but she hates to risk the possibility of rejection.

_____ 3. Vanessa has been shopping for a new car and is torn between a nifty little sports car and a classy sedan, both of which she really likes.

Types of conflict

a. approach-approach

b. avoidance-avoidance

c. approach-avoidance

These values are supposed to reflect the magnitude of the readjustment required by each change (see **Table 12.1**). In using the scale, respondents are asked to indicate how often they experienced any of these 43 events during a certain time period (typically, the past year). The numbers associated with each checked event are then added. This total is an index of the amount of change-related stress the person has recently experienced.

The SRRS and similar scales based on it have been used in over 10,000 studies by researchers all over the world (Dohrenwend, 2006). Overall, these studies have shown that people with higher scores tend to be more vulnerable to many kinds of physical illness and to many types of psychological problems as well (Derogatis & Coons, 1993: Scully, Tosi, &

Stress comes in many forms, such as frustration, which obviously becomes vastly more common in times of economic distress. Few things are more frustrating than losing one's job, standing in long unemployment lines, or losing one's house to foreclosure.

Banning, 2000; Surtees & Wainwright, 2007). These results have attracted a great deal of attention, and the SRRS has been reprinted in many popular newspapers and magazines. The attendant publicity has led to the widespread conclusion that life change is inherently stressful.

However, experts have criticized this research, citing problems with the methods used and problems in interpreting the findings (Dohrenwend, 2006; Monroe, 2008; Wethington, 2007). At this point, it's a key interpretive issue that concerns us. A variety of critics have collected evidence showing that the SRRS does not measure *change* exclusively (McLean & Link, 1994; Turner & Wheaton, 1995). In reality, it assesses a wide range of kinds of stressful experiences. Thus, we have little reason to believe that change is *inherently* or *inevitably* stressful. Undoubtedly, some life changes may be quite challenging, but others may be quite benign.

Pressure
11f

At one time or another, most people have remarked that they're "under pressure." What does this mean? *Pressure* **involves expectations or demands that one behave in a certain way.** You are under pressure to *perform* when you're expected to execute tasks and responsibilities quickly, efficiently, and successfully. For example, salespeople are usually under pressure to move merchandise. Professors at research institutions are often under pressure to publish in respected journals. Stand-up comedians are under intense pressure to make people laugh. Pressures to *conform* to others' expectations are also common in our lives. Businessmen are expected to wear suits and ties. Suburban homeowners are expected to keep their yards

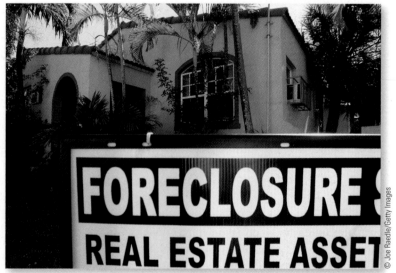

well groomed. Teenagers are expected to respect their parents' values and rules.

Although widely discussed by the general public, the concept of pressure has received scant attention from researchers. However, Weiten (1988b, 1998) has devised a scale to measure pressure as a form of life stress. It assesses self-imposed pressure, pressure from work and school, and pressure from family relations, peer relations, and intimate relations. In research with this scale, a strong relationship has been found between pressure and a variety of psychological symptoms and problems. In fact, pressure has turned out to be more strongly related to measures of mental health than the SRRS and other established measures of stress.

We tend to think of pressure as something imposed on us by outside forces. However, studies of high school and college students find that *pressure is often self-imposed* (Kouzma & Kennedy, 2004; Misra & Castillo, 2004). For example, you might sign up for extra classes to get through school quickly. Or you might actively seek time-consuming leadership responsibilities to impress friends or to build your resume. People frequently put pressure on themselves to get good grades or to rapidly climb the corporate ladder. Actually, self-imposed stress is not unique to

pressure. Research suggests that other forms of stress can also be self-generated (Roberts & Ciesla, 2007). One implication of this finding is that people might have more control over a substantial portion of the stress in their lives than they realize.

concept check 12.2

Recognizing Sources of Stress

Check your understanding of the major sources of stress by indicating which type or types of stress are at work in each of the examples below. Bear in mind that the four basic types of stress are not mutually exclusive. There's some potential for overlap, so a specific experience might include both change and pressure, for instance. The answers are in Appendix A.

Examples

_____ 1. Marie is stuck in line at the bank.

_____ 2. Tamika decides that she won't be satisfied unless she gets straight A's this year.

_____ 3. Jose has just graduated from business school and has taken an exciting new job.

_____ 4. Morris has just been fired from his job and needs to find another.

Types of stress

a. frustration

b. conflict

c. change

d. pressure

Table 12.1 Social Readjustment Rating Scale

Life Event	Mean Value	Life Event	Mean Value
Death of a spouse	100	Change in responsibilities at work	29
Divorce	73	Son or daughter leaving home	29
Marital separation	65	Trouble with in-laws	29
Jail term	63	Outstanding personal achievement	28
Death of a close family member	63	Spouse begins or stops work	26
Personal injury or illness	53	Begin or end school	26
Marriage	50	Change in living conditions	25
Fired at work	47	Revision of personal habits	24
Marital reconciliation	45	Trouble with boss	23
Retirement	45	Change in work hours or conditions	20
Change in health of family member	44	Change in residence	20
Pregnancy	40	Change in school	20
Sex difficulties	39	Change in recreation	19
Gain of a new family member	39	Change in church activities	19
Business readjustment	39	Change in social activities	18
Change in financial state	38	Mortgage or loan for lesser purchase	
Death of a close friend	37	(car, TV, etc.)	17
Change to a different line of work	36	Change in sleeping habits	16
Change in number of arguments with		Change in number of family get-togethers	15
spouse	35	Change in eating habits	15
Mortgage or loan for major purchase		Vacation	13
(home, etc.)	31	Christmas	12
Foreclosure of mortgage or loan	30	Minor violations of the law	11

SOURCE: Adapted from Holmes, T. H., & Rahe, R. (1967). The Social Readjustment Rating Scale. *Journal of Psychosomatic Research, 11*, 213–218. Copyright © 1967 by Elsevier Science Publishing Co. Reprinted by permission.

REVIEW of Key Learning Goals

12.1 Stress involves circumstances and experiences that are perceived as threatening. Stress is a common, everyday event, and even seemingly minor stressors, such as daily hassles, can be problematic. To a large degree, stress is subjective and lies in the eye of the beholder. People's appraisals of events determine what they find stressful. Frustration is a major source of stress. Frustration occurs when an obstacle prevents one from attaining some goal.

12.2 The three principal types of conflict are approach-approach, avoidance-avoidance, and approach-avoidance. The third type is especially stressful. Vacillation is a common response to approach-avoidance conflict.

12.3 A large number of studies with the SRRS suggest that life change is stressful. Although this may be true, it is now clear that the SRRS is a measure of general stress rather than just change-related stress. Two kinds of pressure (to perform and conform) also appear to be stressful.

Key Learning Goals

12.4 Discuss the role of positive emotions in response to stress and the effects of emotional arousal.

12.5 Describe Selye's general adaptation syndrome and other physiological responses to stress.

12.6 Evaluate the adaptive value of giving up, aggression, and self-indulgence as coping responses.

12.7 Explain how defense mechanisms work, and clarify the nature of constructive coping.

---

web link 12.2

Stress Management

University of Nebraska Professor Wesley E. Sime has posted outlines and notes of his lectures on the fundamentals of stress management and on other topics related to stress and its impact on health and performance.

Responding to Stress

The human response to stress is complex and multidimensional. Stress affects the individual at several levels. Consider again the chapter's opening scenario, in which you're driving home in heavy traffic and thinking about overdue papers, tuition increases, and parental pressures. Let's look at some of the reactions that were mentioned. When you groan in reaction to the traffic report, you're experiencing an *emotional response* to stress, in this case annoyance and anger. When your pulse quickens and your stomach knots up, you're exhibiting *physiological responses* to stress. When you shout insults at another driver, your verbal aggression is a *behavioral response* to the stress at hand. Thus, we can analyze a person's reactions to stress at three levels: (1) emotional responses, (2) physiological responses, and (3) behavioral responses. **Figure 12.3** provides an overview of the stress process.

Emotional Responses   11g

When people are under stress, they often react emotionally. Studies that have tracked stress and mood on a daily basis have found intimate relationships between the two (Affleck et al., 1994; van Eck, Nicolson, & Berkhof, 1998).

Emotions Commonly Elicited   11g

No simple one-to-one connections have been found between certain types of stressful events and particular emotions. However, researchers *have* begun to uncover some strong links between *specific cognitive reactions to stress* (appraisals) and specific emotions (Smith & Lazarus, 1993). For example, self-blame tends to lead to guilt, helplessness to sadness, and so forth. Many emotions can be evoked by stressful events, but some are certainly more likely than others. Common emotional responses to stress include (a) annoyance, anger, and rage, (b) apprehension, anxiety, and fear, and (c) dejection, sadness, and grief (Lazarus, 1993; Woolfolk & Richardson, 1978).

Although investigators have tended to focus heavily on the connection between stress and negative emotions, research shows that positive emotions also occur during periods of stress (Folkman, 1997, 2008; Zautra et al., 2005). Although this finding seems counterintuitive, researchers have found that people experience a diverse array of pleasant emotions even while enduring the most dire of circumstances (Folkman et al., 1997). Consider, for example, a study that examined subjects' emotional functioning early in 2001 and again in the weeks following the 9/11 terrorist attacks in the United States (Fredrickson et al., 2003). Like most U.S. citizens, these subjects reported many negative emotions in the aftermath of 9/11, including anger, sadness, and fear. However, within this "dense cloud of anguish" positive emotions also emerged. For example, people felt gratitude for the safety of their loved ones, many took stock and counted their blessings, and quite a few reported renewed love for their friends and family. Fredrickson et al. (2003) also found that the frequency of pleasant emotions correlated positively with a measure of subjects' resilience, whereas the frequency of unpleasant emotions correlated negatively with resilience. Thus, contrary to common sense, positive emotions do *not* vanish during times of severe stress. Moreover, these positive emotions appear to play a key role in helping people bounce back from the difficulties associated with stress (Tugade & Fredrickson, 2004).

How do positive emotions promote resilience in the face of stress? Barbara Fredrickson's (2001, 2005, 2006) *broaden-and-build theory of positive emotions* can shed light on this question. First, positive emotions alter people's mindsets, broadening their scope of attention, and increasing their creativity

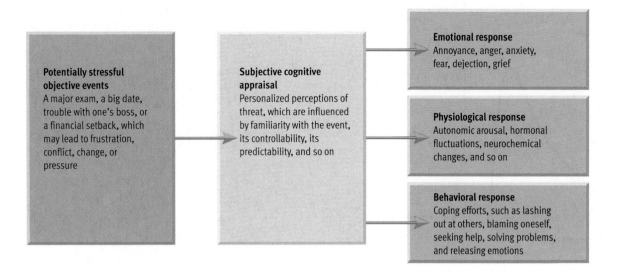

and flexibility in problem solving. Second, positive emotions can undo the lingering effects of negative emotions, and thus short-circuit the potentially damaging physiological responses to stress that we will discuss momentarily. Third, positive emotions can promote rewarding social interactions that help to build valuable social support, enhanced coping strategies, and other enduring personal resources.

Consistent with Fredrickson's model, recent research suggests that positive emotions widen people's scope of attention (Fredrickson & Branigan, 2005), promote healthy coping responses (Folkman, 2008), initiate upward spirals in emotional well-being (Burns et al., 2008), and facilitate flourishing mental health (Fredrickson & Losada, 2005). Studies have also found an association between positive emotion and lower levels of stress hormones (Steptoe et al., 2007) and reduced mortality in some populations (Pressman & Cohen, 2005).

One particularly interesting finding has been that a positive emotional style is associated with an enhanced immune response (Cohen & Pressman, 2006). For example, in a study by Sheldon Cohen and colleagues (2006), healthy volunteers were given nasal drops containing either a rhinovirus (cold virus) or flu virus and were carefully monitored for illness while living in quarantine conditions. The results showed that participants with a positive emotional style were less likely to develop an illness after exposure to either virus. Thus, it appears that the benefits of positive emotions may be more diverse and more far-reaching than widely appreciated.

Effects of Emotional Arousal   11g

Emotional responses are a natural and normal part of life. Even unpleasant emotions serve important purposes. Like physical pain, painful emotions can serve as warnings that one needs to take action. However, strong emotional arousal can also interfere with efforts to cope with stress. For example, there's evidence that high emotional arousal can interfere with attention and memory retrieval and can impair judgment and decision making (Janis, 1993; Lupien & Maheu, 2007; Mandler, 1993).

Although emotional arousal may hurt coping efforts, that isn't *necessarily* the case. The *inverted-U hypothesis* predicts that task performance should improve with increased emotional arousal—up to a point, after which further increases in arousal become disruptive and performance deteriorates (Anderson, 1990; Mandler, 1993). This idea is referred to as the inverted-U hypothesis because when performance is plotted as a function of arousal, the resulting graphs approximate an upside-down U (see **Figure 12.4** on the next page). In these graphs, the level of arousal at which performance peaks is characterized as the *optimal level of arousal* for a task.

This optimal level appears to depend in part on the complexity of the task at hand. The conventional wisdom is that *as a task becomes more complex, the optimal level of arousal (for peak performance) tends to decrease.* This relationship is depicted in **Figure 12.4**. As you can see, a fairly high level of arousal should be optimal on simple tasks (such as driving 8 hours to help a friend in a crisis). However, performance should peak at a lower level of arousal on complex tasks (such as making a major decision in which you have to weigh many factors).

The research evidence on the inverted-U hypothesis is inconsistent and subject to varied interpretations (Neiss, 1988, 1990). Nonetheless, the inverted-U hypothesis provides a plausible model of how emotional arousal could have either beneficial or disruptive effects on coping, depending on the nature of the stressful demands one encounters.

web link 12.3

Centre for Stress Management

This British website houses a diverse collection of brief online articles concerned with many aspects of the stress process. It also features links to many additional sites around the world that provide information on stress.

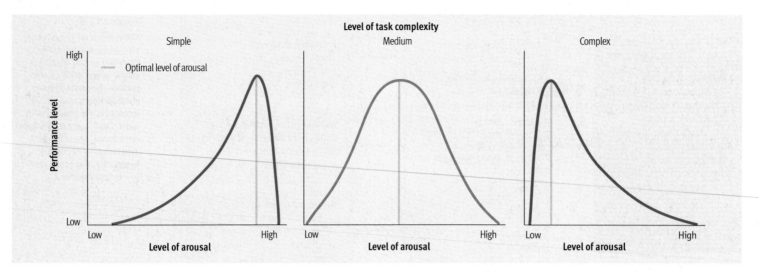

Figure 12.4
Arousal and performance. Graphs of the relationship between emotional arousal and task performance tend to resemble an inverted U, as increased arousal is associated with improved performance up to a point, after which higher arousal leads to poorer performance. The optimal level of arousal for a task depends on the complexity of the task. On complex tasks, a relatively low level of arousal tends to be optimal. On simple tasks, however, performance may peak at a much higher level of arousal.

Hans Selye

"There are two main types of human beings: 'racehorses,' who thrive on stress and are only happy with a vigorous, fast-paced lifestyle; and 'turtles,' who in order to be happy require peace, quiet, and a generally tranquil environment."

Physiological Responses   11g

As we just discussed, stress frequently elicits strong emotional responses. Now we'll look at the important physiological changes that often accompany these emotions.

The General Adaptation Syndrome   11g

Concern about the physical effects of stress was first voiced by Hans Selye (1936, 1956, 1982), a Canadian scientist who launched stress research many decades ago. Selye was born in Vienna but spent his entire professional career at McGill University in Montreal. Beginning in the 1930s, Selye exposed laboratory animals to a diverse array of both physical and psychological stressors (heat, cold, pain, mild shock, restraint, and so on). The patterns of physiological arousal seen in the animals were largely the same, regardless of the type of stress. Thus, Selye concluded that stress reactions are *nonspecific*. In other words, he maintained that the reactions do not vary according to the specific type of stress encountered. Initially, Selye wasn't sure what to call this nonspecific response to a variety of noxious agents. In the 1940s he decided to call it *stress,* and the word has been part of our vocabulary ever since (Russell, 2007).

Selye (1956, 1974) explained stress reactions in terms of the general adaptation syndrome. The *general adaptation syndrome* is a model of the body's stress response, consisting of three stages: alarm, resistance, and exhaustion. In the first stage, an *alarm reaction* occurs when an organism first recognizes the existence of a threat. Physiological arousal occurs as the body musters its resources to combat the challenge. Selye's alarm reaction is essentially the fight-or-flight response described in Chapters 3 and 9.

However, Selye took his investigation of stress a few steps further by exposing laboratory animals to *prolonged stress,* similar to the chronic stress often endured by humans. As stress continues, the organism may progress to the second phase of the general adaptation syndrome, the *stage of resistance.* During this phase, physiological changes stabilize as coping efforts get under way. Typically, physiological arousal continues to be higher than normal, although it may level off somewhat as the organism becomes accustomed to the threat.

DILBERT

If the stress continues over a substantial period of time, the organism may enter the third stage, the *stage of exhaustion*. According to Selye, the body's resources for fighting stress are limited. If the stress can't be overcome, the body's resources may be depleted. Eventually, he thought the organism would experience hormonal exhaustion, although we now know that the crux of the problem is that chronic overactivation of the stress response can have damaging physiological effects on a variety of organ systems (Sapolsky, 2007). These harmful physiological effects can lead to what Selye called "diseases of adaptation."

Brain-Body Pathways 11g

Even in cases of moderate stress, you may notice that your heart has started beating faster, you've begun to breathe harder, and you're perspiring more than usual. How does all this (and much more) happen? It appears that there are two major pathways along which the brain sends signals to the endocrine system (Dallman, Bhatnagar, & Viau, 2007; Tsigos, Kyrou, & Chrousos, 2005). As we noted in Chapter 3, the *endocrine system* consists of glands located at various sites in the body that secrete chemicals called *hormones*. The hypothalamus is the part of the brain that appears to initiate action along these two pathways.

The first pathway (see **Figure 12.5**) is routed through the autonomic nervous system (ANS). Your hypothalamus activates the sympathetic division of the ANS. A key part of this activation involves stimulating the central part of the adrenal glands (the adrenal medulla) to release large amounts of *catecholamines* into the bloodstream. These hormones radiate throughout your body, producing a number of physiological changes. The net result of catecholamine elevation is that your body is mobilized for action (Lundberg, 2007).

The second pathway involves more direct communication between the brain and the endocrine system (see **Figure 12.5**). The hypothalamus sends signals to the so-called master gland of the endocrine system, the pituitary gland. In turn, the pituitary secretes a hormone (ACTH) that stimulates the outer part of the adrenal glands (the adrenal cortex) to release another important set of hormones—*corticosteroids*. These hormones stimulate the release of chemicals that help increase your energy and help inhibit tissue inflammation in case of injury (Munck, 2007).

An important new finding in research on stress and the brain is that stress can interfere with neurogenesis (Mirescu & Gould, 2006). As you may recall from Chapter 3, scientists have recently discovered that the adult brain is capable of *neurogenesis*—the

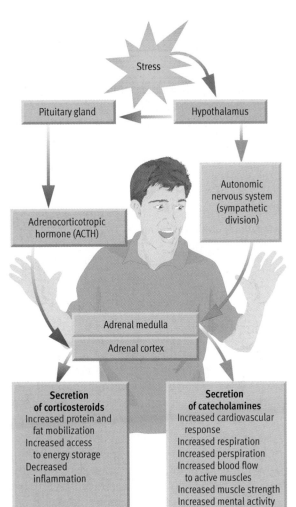

Figure 12.5
Brain-body pathways in stress. In times of stress, the brain sends signals along two pathways. The pathway through the autonomic nervous system controls the release of catecholamine hormones that help mobilize the body for action. The pathway through the pituitary gland and the endocrine system controls the release of corticosteroid hormones that increase energy and ward off tissue inflammation.

formation of new neurons, primarily in key areas in the hippocampus. Neurogenesis appears to enhance learning and memory (see Chapter 7), and in Chapter 14 we will discuss evidence that suppressed neurogenesis may be a key cause of depression (Dranovsky & Hen, 2006). Thus, the capacity of stress to hinder neurogenesis may have important ramifications, which are currently the subject of intense research (Tanapat & Gould, 2006).

Behavioral Responses 11g

Although people respond to stress at several levels, it's clear that behavior is the crucial dimension of their reactions. Most behavioral responses to stress involve coping. *Coping* refers to efforts to master, reduce, or tolerate the demands created by stress. Notice that this definition is neutral as to whether coping efforts are healthful or maladaptive. The popular use of the term often implies that coping is inherently healthful. When people say that someone "coped with her problems," the implication is that she handled them effectively.

web link 12.4

The American Institute of Stress

The American Institute of Stress is a nonprofit organization established in 1978 at the request of stress pioneer Hans Selye. Its Board of Trustees reads like a who's who of stress research. The resources available online are a bit limited, as one has to send for the information packets published by the institute. But there is a very interesting online tribute to Selye.

In reality, however, coping responses may be adaptive or maladaptive (Folkman & Moskowitz, 2004; Kleinke, 2007). For example, if you were flunking a history course at midterm, you might cope with this stress by (1) increasing your study efforts, (2) seeking help from a tutor, (3) blaming your professor, or (4) giving up on the class without really trying. Clearly, the first two of these coping responses would be more adaptive than the last two.

People cope with stress in many ways, but most individuals exhibit certain styles of coping that are fairly consistent across situations (Carver & Scheier, 1994; Jang et al., 2007). Given the immense variety in coping strategies, we can only highlight some of the more common patterns of coping. In this section we'll focus most of our attention on styles of coping that tend to be less than ideal. We'll discuss more healthful coping strategies in the Personal Application on stress management.

Giving Up and Blaming Oneself 11g

When confronted with stress, people sometimes simply give up and withdraw from the battle. Some people routinely respond to stress with fatalism and resignation, passively accepting setbacks that might be dealt with effectively. This syndrome is referred to as *learned helplessness* (Seligman, 1974, 1992). **Learned helplessness is passive behavior produced by exposure to unavoidable aversive events.** Learned helplessness seems to occur when

individuals come to believe that events are beyond their control. As you might guess, giving up is not a highly regarded method of coping. Carver and his colleagues (1989, 1993) have studied this coping strategy, which they refer to as *behavioral disengagement,* and found that it is associated with increased rather than decreased distress. Furthermore, many studies suggest that learned helplessness can contribute to depression (Isaacowitz & Seligman, 2007).

Although giving up is clearly less than optimal in many contexts, new research suggests that when people struggle to pursue goals that turn out to be unattainable, it makes sense for them to cut their losses and disengage from the goal (Wrosch & Scheier, 2003). Recent studies have shown that people who are better able to disengage from unattainable goals report better health and exhibit lower levels of a key stress hormone (Wrosch et al., 2007). They also manifest lower levels of a protein marker associated with inflammation, which is thought to underlie many disease processes (Miller & Wrosch, 2007). Given the way people in our competitive culture tend to disparage the concept of "giving up," the authors note that it might be better to characterize this coping tactic as "goal adjustment."

Blaming oneself is another common response when people are confronted by stressful difficulties. The tendency to become highly self-critical in response to stress has been noted by a number of influential theorists. Albert Ellis (1973, 1987) calls this phenomenon "catastrophic thinking." According to Ellis, catastrophic thinking causes, aggravates, and perpetuates emotional reactions to stress that are often problematic (see the Personal Application for this chapter). Although there is something to be said for recognizing one's weaknesses and taking responsibility for one's failures, Ellis maintains that excessive self-blame can be very unhealthy.

Striking Out at Others 11g

People often respond to stressful events by striking out at others with aggressive behavior. *Aggression* is any behavior that is intended to hurt someone, either physically or verbally. Many years ago, a team of psychologists (Dollard et al., 1939) proposed the *frustration-aggression hypothesis,* which held that aggression is always caused by frustration. Decades of research have supported this idea of a causal link between frustration and aggression (Berkowitz, 1989). However, this research has also shown that there isn't an inevitable, one-to-one correspondence between the two.

Albert Ellis

"People largely disturb themselves by thinking in a self-defeating, illogical, and unrealistic manner."

Courtesy, Albert Ellis Institute

Sigmund Freud theorized that behaving aggressively could get pent-up emotion out of one's system and thus be adaptive. He coined the term *catharsis* **to refer to this release of emotional tension.** The Freudian notion that it is a good idea to vent anger has become widely disseminated and accepted in modern society. Books, magazines, and self-appointed experts routinely advise that it is healthy to "blow off steam" and thereby release and reduce anger. However, experimental research generally has *not* supported the catharsis hypothesis. Indeed, *most studies find just the opposite: Behaving in an aggressive manner tends to fuel more anger and aggression* (Bushman, 2002; Bushman, Baumeister, & Stack, 1999). Other behaviors, such as talking or writing about one's problems, may have some value in releasing pent-up emotions (see the Personal Application), but aggressive behavior is not cathartic.

Indulging Oneself   11g

Stress sometimes leads to reduced impulse control, or *self-indulgence* (Tice, Bratslavsky, & Baumeister, 2001). When troubled by stress, many people engage in excessive or unwise patterns of eating, drinking, smoking, using drugs, spending money, and so forth. It makes sense that when things are going poorly in one area of their lives, people may try to compensate by pursuing substitute forms of satisfaction. Thus, it's not surprising that studies have linked stress to increases in eating (Barker, Williams, & Galambos, 2006), smoking (Kassel, Stroud, & Paronis, 2003), and consumption of alcohol and drugs (Goeders, 2004; Spada & Wells, 2006).

A new manifestation of this coping strategy that has attracted much attention recently is the tendency to immerse oneself in the online world of the Internet. Kimberly Young (1996, 1998) has described a syndrome called *Internet addiction,* which consists of spending an inordinate amount of time on the Internet and inability to control online use. People who exhibit this syndrome tend to feel anxious, depressed, or empty when they are not online (Kandell, 1998). Their Internet use is so excessive, it begins to interfere with their functioning at work, at school, or at home, which leads victims to start concealing the extent of their dependence on the Internet. Although there is active debate about the wisdom of characterizing excessive Internet surfing as an *addiction* (Goldsmith & Shapira, 2006; Griffiths, 1999), it is clear that this new coping strategy is creating very real problems for at least a small portion of Internet users (Morahan-Martin, 2007).

Defensive Coping   10a, 11g

Many people exhibit consistent styles of defensive coping in response to stress (Vaillant, 1994). We noted in the previous chapter that Sigmund Freud originally developed the concept of the *defense mechanism*.

Lashing out at others with verbal aggression tends to be an ineffective coping tactic that often backfires, creating additional stress.

CATHY

YOU WENT OUT AND GOT DRUNK BECAUSE YOU WERE JEALOUS? THAT WAS STUPID.

HOW IS THAT ANY MORE STUPID THAN YOU **EATING** WHEN YOU'RE JEALOUS?

IRVING, I EAT WHEN I'M **DEPRESSED**. I BUY **SHOES** WHEN I'M JEALOUS. I BREAK THE TELEPHONE WHEN I'M ANGRY...

I MANGLE MY FINGERNAILS WHEN I'M LONELY...I THROW THINGS ALL OVER THE HOUSE WHEN I'M HURT...AND I WASTE MONEY ON MAKE-UP WHEN I'M FRUSTRATED.

MEN JUST DON'T KNOW HOW TO COPE.

Though rooted in the psychoanalytic tradition, this concept has gained widespread acceptance from psychologists of most persuasions (Cramer, 2000). Building on Freud's initial insights, modern psychologists have broadened the scope of the concept and added to Freud's list of defense mechanisms.

Defense mechanisms are largely unconscious reactions that protect a person from unpleasant emotions such as anxiety and guilt. Many specific defense mechanisms have been identified. For example, Laughlin (1979) lists 49 different defenses. We described 7 common defense mechanisms in our discussion of Freud's theory in the previous chapter: repression, projection, displacement, reaction formation, regression, rationalization, and identification (consult **Table 11.1**).

The main purpose of defense mechanisms is to shield individuals from the emotional discomfort so often elicited by stress. They accomplish this purpose through *self-deception,* distorting reality so that it doesn't appear so threatening. Defense mechanisms operate at varying levels of awareness, although they're largely unconscious (Cramer, 2001; Erdelyi, 2001).

Generally, defensive coping is less than optimal because avoidance and wishful thinking rarely solve personal problems (Bolger, 1990; Holahan & Moos, 1990). That said, Shelley Taylor and Jonathon Brown (1988, 1994) have reviewed evidence suggesting that "positive illusions" may sometimes be adaptive for mental health. Some of the personal illusions that people create through defensive coping may help them deal with life's difficulties. Roy Baumeister (1989) theorizes that it's all a matter of degree and that there is an "optimal margin of illusion." According to Baumeister, extreme distortions of reality are maladaptive, but small illusions can be beneficial.

Constructive Coping 11g

Our discussion thus far has focused on coping strategies that are less than ideal. Of course, people also exhibit many healthful strategies for dealing with stress. We'll use the term *constructive coping* to refer to relatively healthful efforts that people make to deal with stressful events. No strategy of coping can *guarantee* a successful outcome. Even the best coping responses may turn out to be ineffective in some circumstances. Thus, the concept of constructive coping is simply meant to convey a healthful, positive approach, without promising success.

What makes certain coping strategies constructive? Frankly, it's a gray area in which psychologists' opinions vary to some extent. Nonetheless, a consensus about the nature of constructive coping has emerged from the sizable literature on stress management. Key themes in this literature include the following:

1. Constructive coping involves confronting problems directly. It is task relevant and action oriented. It entails a conscious effort to rationally evaluate your options so that you can try to solve your problems.

2. Constructive coping is based on reasonably realistic appraisals of your stress and coping resources. A little self-deception may sometimes be adaptive, but excessive self-deception and highly unrealistic negative thinking are not.

3. Constructive coping involves learning to recognize, and in some cases inhibit, potentially disruptive emotional reactions to stress.

4. Constructive coping includes making efforts to ensure that your body is not especially vulnerable to the potentially damaging effects of stress.

The principles just described provide a rather general and abstract picture of constructive coping. We'll look at patterns of constructive coping in more detail in the Personal Application, which discusses various stress management strategies that people can use. We turn next to some of the possible outcomes of struggles with stress.

Shelley Taylor

"Rather than perceiving themselves, the world, and the future accurately, most people regard themselves, their circumstances, and the future as considerably more positive than is objectively likely. . . . These illusions are not merely characteristic of human thought; they appear actually to be adaptive, promoting rather than undermining good mental health."

Courtesy of Shelley Taylor

REVIEW of Key Learning Goals

12.4 Stress often triggers emotional reactions, such as anger, fear, and sadness. Fredrickson's broaden-and-build theory asserts that positive emotions broaden thinking and build coping resources. Evidence suggests that positive emotions foster enhanced immune responding and mental and physical health. Emotional arousal may interfere with coping. According to the inverted-U hypothesis, task performance improves with increased arousal up to a point and then declines. The optimal level of arousal on a task depends on the complexity of the task.

12.5 Selye's general adaptation syndrome describes three stages of physiological reactions to stress: alarm, resistance, and exhaustion. Diseases of adaptation may appear during the stage of exhaustion. There are two major pathways along which the brain sends signals to the endocrine system in response to stress, leading to the release of catecholamines and corticosteroids. Stress may suppress neurogenesis in the brain.

12.6 The behavioral response to stress takes the form of coping. Giving up is not a highly regarded approach to coping, but studies suggest that people who are able to disengage from unattainable goals exhibit better health. Aggression tends to fuel more anger and increase rather than decrease stress. Self-indulgence is another coping pattern that tends to be of limited value.

12.7 Defensive coping is quite common. Defense mechanisms protect against emotional distress through self-deception. Some evidence suggests that small positive illusions about one's life may be healthful, but serious distortions are maladaptive. Relatively healthful coping tactics are called constructive coping. Constructive coping is action-oriented and based on realistic appraisals of stress.

Stress and Physical Health

People struggle with many stresses every day. Most stresses come and go without leaving any enduring imprint. However, when stress is severe or when many stressful demands pile up, one's mental or physical health may be affected. In Chapter 13 you'll learn that chronic stress contributes to many types of psychological disorders, including depression, schizophrenia, and anxiety disorders. In this section, we'll discuss the link between stress and physical illness.

Prior to the 1970s, it was thought that stress contributed to the development of only a few physical diseases, such as high blood pressure, ulcers, and asthma, which were called *psychosomatic diseases*. However, in the 1970s, research began to uncover new links between stress and a great variety of diseases previously believed to be purely physiological in origin (Dimsdale et al., 2005; Dougall & Baum, 2001). Let's look at some of this research.

Personality, Hostility, and Heart Disease

Heart disease accounts for about 27% of the deaths in the United States every year. *Coronary heart disease* involves a reduction in blood flow in the coronary arteries, which supply the heart with blood. This type of heart disease accounts for about 90% of heart-related deaths.

Atherosclerosis is the principal cause of coronary heart disease. This condition is characterized by a gradual narrowing of the coronary arteries. A buildup of fatty deposits and other debris on the inner walls of the arteries is the usual cause of this narrowing. Atherosclerosis progresses slowly over a period of years. However, when a narrowed coronary artery is blocked completely (by a blood clot, for instance), the abrupt interruption of blood flow can produce a heart attack. Atherosclerosis is more prevalent in men than women and tends to increase with age. Other established risk factors for atherosclerosis include smoking, lack of exercise, high cholesterol levels, and high blood pressure (Rippe, Angelopoulos, & Zukley, 2007).

Recently, attention has shifted to the possibility that *inflammation* may contribute to atherosclerosis and elevated coronary risk (Miller & Blackwell, 2006). Evidence is mounting that inflammation plays a key role in the initiation and progression of atherosclerosis, as well as the acute complications that trigger heart attacks (Nabi et al., 2008). Fortunately, researchers have found a marker for inflammation—levels of C-reactive protein (CRP) in the blood—that may help physicians estimate individuals' coronary risk more accurately than was previously possible (Kop & Weinstein, 2007; Ridker et al., 2005).

Research on the relationship between *psychological* factors and heart attacks began in the 1960s and 1970s, when a pair of cardiologists, Meyer Friedman and Ray Rosenman (1974), discovered an apparent connection between coronary risk and a syndrome they called the *Type A personality,* which involves self-imposed stress and intense reactions to stress. The *Type A personality* **includes three elements: (1) a strong competitive orientation, (2) impatience and time urgency, and (3) anger and hostility.** Type A's are ambitious, hard-driving perfectionists who are exceedingly time-conscious. They routinely try to do several things at once. They fidget frantically over the briefest delays. Often they are highly competitive, achievement-oriented workaholics who drive themselves with many deadlines. They are easily irritated and are quick to anger. In contrast, **the Type B personality is marked by relatively relaxed, patient, easygoing, amicable behavior.** Type B's are less hurried, less competitive, and less easily angered than Type A's.

Decades of research uncovered a tantalizingly modest correlation between Type A behavior and increased coronary risk. More often than not, studies found a correlation between Type A personality and an elevated incidence of heart disease, but the findings were not as strong nor as consistent as expected (Baker, Suchday, & Krantz, 2007; Myrtek, 2007). However, in recent years, researchers have found a stronger link between personality and coronary risk by focusing on a specific component of the Type A personality: *anger and hostility* (Boyle, Jackson, & Suarez, 2007; Powell & Williams, 2007). For example, in one study of almost 13,000 men and women who had no prior history of heart disease (Williams et al., 2000), investigators found an elevated incidence of heart attacks among participants who exhibited an angry temperament. The participants, who were followed for a median period of 4.5 years, were classified as being low (37.1% of the subjects), moderate (55.2%), or high (7.7%) in the tendency to experience anger.

Key Learning Goals

12.8 Review the evidence linking personality factors, emotional reactions, and depression to coronary heart disease.

12.9 Discuss how stress affects immune functioning, and assess the link between stress and illness.

12.10 Understand how social support moderates the impact of stress.

12.11 Identify two personality factors related to stress resistance and health.

12.12 Explain how stress may have positive effects.

web link 12.5

Mayo Clinic Stress Center

The Mayo Clinic has assembled a rich set of resources related to stress and coping. Topics include stress symptoms, work-related stress, resilience, social support, coping through humor, time management, problem solving, positive thinking, and a host of other subjects.

Among participants with normal blood pressure, the high-anger subjects experienced almost three times as many coronary events as the low-anger subjects (see **Figure 12.6**). The results of this study and many others suggest that hostility may be the crucial toxic element in the Type A syndrome.

Emotional Reactions, Depression, and Heart Disease

Although work on personality risk factors has dominated research on how psychological functioning contributes to heart disease, recent studies suggest that emotional reactions may also be critical. *One line of research has supported the hypothesis that transient mental stress and the resulting emotions that people experience can tax the heart.* Based on anecdotal evidence, cardiologists and laypersons have long voiced suspicions that strong emotional reactions might trigger heart attacks in individuals with coronary disease, but it has been difficult to document this connection. However, advances in cardiac monitoring have facilitated investigation of the issue.

As suspected, laboratory experiments with cardiology patients have shown that brief periods of mental stress can trigger sudden symptoms of heart disease (Baker, Suchday, & Krantz, 2007). Overall, the evidence suggests that mental stress can elicit cardiac symptoms in about 30%–70% of patients with stable coronary disease (Kop, Gottdiener, & Krantz, 2001). Moreover, research indicates that these patients have a higher risk for heart attack than the cardiology patients who do not exhibit symptoms in response to mental stress (Krantz et al., 2000). A

recent study also demonstrated that mental stress can trigger temporary increases in the *inflammation* that is thought to contribute to cardiovascular risk (Kop et al., 2008). Subjects asked to perform stressful tasks in the laboratory showed elevated CRP levels and these reactions were stronger in participants who had a history of coronary disease.

Another line of research has recently implicated depression as a risk factor for heart disease (Goldston & Baillie, 2008). *Depressive disorders,* which are characterized by persistent feelings of sadness and despair, are a fairly common form of mental illness (see Chapter 13). Elevated rates of depression have been found among patients suffering from heart disease in many studies, but most theorists explained this correlation by asserting that being diagnosed with heart disease makes people depressed. Recent evidence, however, suggests that the causal relations may be just the opposite—*that the emotional dysfunction of depression may cause heart disease* (Frasure-Smith & Lesperance, 2005; Thomas, Kalaria, & O'Brien, 2004). For example, Pratt et al. (1996) examined a large sample of people 13 years after they were screened for depression. They found that participants who were depressed at the time of the original study were four times more likely than others to experience a heart attack during the intervening 13 years. Since the participants' depressive disorders preceded their heart attacks, it can't be argued that their heart disease caused their depression. Overall, other studies have found that depression roughly doubles one's chances of developing heart disease (Herbst et al., 2007; Lett et al., 2004). Although the new emphasis is on how depression contributes to heart disease, experts caution that the relationship between the two conditions is surely bidirectional and that heart disease also increases vulnerability to depression (Sayers, 2004).

Stress, Other Diseases, and Immune Functioning

The development of questionnaires to measure life stress has allowed researchers to look for correlations between stress and a variety of diseases. These researchers have uncovered many connections between stress and illness. For example, Zautra and Smith (2001) found an association between life stress and the course of rheumatoid arthritis. Another study found an association between stressful life events and the emergence of lower back pain (Lampe et al., 1998). Other studies have connected stress to the development of diabetes (Landel-Graham, Yount, & Rudnicki, 2003), herpes (Padgett & Sheridan, 2000),

Figure 12.6

Anger and coronary risk. Working with a large sample of healthy men and women who were followed for a median of 4.5 years, Williams et al. (2000) found an association between participants' propensity to get angry and the likelihood of a coronary event. Among subjects who manifested normal blood pressure at the beginning of the study, a moderate anger level was associated with a 36% increase in coronary attacks, and a high level of anger nearly tripled participants' risk for coronary disease.

fibromyalgia (Wood, 2007), and flare-ups of irritable bowel syndrome (Blanchard & Keefer, 2003).

These are just a handful of representative examples of studies relating stress to physical diseases. **Table 12.2** provides a longer list of health problems that have been linked to stress. Many of these stress-illness connections are based on tentative or inconsistent findings, but the sheer length and diversity of the list is remarkable. Why should stress increase the risk for so many kinds of illness? A partial answer may lie in the body's immune functioning.

The *immune response* is the body's defensive reaction to invasion by bacteria, viral agents, or other foreign substances. The immune response works to protect organisms from many forms of disease. A wealth of studies indicate that experimentally induced stress can impair immune functioning *in animals* (Ader, 2001; Rose, 2007). That is, stressors such as crowding, shock, food restriction, and restraint reduce various aspects of immune reactivity in laboratory animals (Prolo & Chiappelli, 2007).

Some studies have also related stress to suppressed immune activity *in humans* (Kiecolt-Glaser & Glaser, 1995). In one study, medical students provided researchers with blood samples so that their immune response could be assessed (Kiecolt-Glaser et al., 1984). They provided a baseline sample a month before final exams and contributed a high-stress sample on the first day of their finals. The subjects also responded to the SRRS to measure recent stress. Reduced levels of immune activity were found during the extremely stressful finals week. Reduced immune activity was also correlated with higher scores on the SRRS. In another study, investigators exposed quarantined volunteers to respiratory viruses that cause the common cold and found that those under high stress were more likely to be infected by the viruses (Cohen, Tyrell, & Smith, 1993).

Although research in recent decades has mainly focused on the link between stress and immune suppression, recent studies have shown that there are other important connections between stress, immune function, and vulnerability to illness. Recent findings suggest that exposure to long-term stress can sometimes foster persistent overproduction of proinflammatory proteins, which can promote chronic inflammation (Robles, Glaser, & Kiecolt-Glaser, 2005). Scientists have only begun to fully appreciate the potential ramifications of this chronic inflammation in recent years. As we noted earlier, inflammation has recently been recognized as a major factor in the development of heart disease. But that's not all. Research has also demonstrated that chronic inflammation contributes to a diverse array of diseases, including arthritis, osteoporosis, respiratory diseases, diabetes, Alzheimer's disease, and some types of cancer (Feuerstein et al., 2007). Thus, chronic inflammation resulting from immune system dysregulation may be another key mechanism underlying the association between stress and a wide variety of diseases.

Table 12.2 Health Problems That May Be Linked to Stress

Health Problem	Representative Evidence
AIDS	Stetler et al. (2005)
Appendicitis	Creed (1989)
Asthma	Lehrer et al. (2002)
Cancer	Dalton & Johansen (2005)
Chronic back pain	Lampe et al. (1998)
Common cold	Cohen (2005)
Complications of pregnancy	Dunkel-Schetter et al. (2001)
Heart disease	Theorell (2005)
Diabetes	Landel-Graham, Yount, & Rudnicki (2003)
Epileptic seizures	Kelly & Schramke (2000)
Hemophilia	Buxton et al. (1981)
Herpes virus	Padgett & Sheridan (2000)
Hyptertension	O'Callahan, Andrews, & Krantz (2003)
Hyperthyroidism	Yang, Liu, & Zang (2000)
Inflammatory bowel disease	Searle & Bennett (2001)
Migraine headaches	Ramadan (2000)
Multiple sclerosis	Mitsonis et al. (2006)
Periodontal disease	Marcenes & Sheiham (1992)
Premenstrual distress	Stanton et al. (2002)
Rheumatoid arthritis	Keefe et al. (2002)
Skin disorders	Arnold (2000)
Stroke	Harmsen et al. (1990)
Ulcers	Levenstein (2002)
Vaginal infections	Williams & Deffenbacher (1983)

Sizing Up the Link Between Stress and Illness

A wealth of evidence shows that stress is related to physical health, and converging lines of evidence suggest that stress contributes to the *causation* of illness (Cohen, Janicki-Deverts, & Miller, 2007). But we have to put this intriguing finding in perspective. Virtually all of the relevant research is correlational, so it can't demonstrate conclusively that stress *causes* illness (Smith & Gallo, 2001; see Chapter 2 for a discussion of correlation and causation). Subjects' elevated levels of stress and illness could both be due to a third variable, perhaps some aspect of personality (see **Figure 12.7**). For instance, some evidence suggests that neuroticism may make people overly prone to interpret events as stressful and overly prone to interpret unpleasant sensations as symptoms of illness, thus inflating the correlation between stress and illness (Watson & Pennebaker, 1989).

In spite of methodological problems favoring inflated correlations, the research in this area consistently indicates that the *strength* of the relationship between stress and health is *modest*. The correlations typically fall in the .20s and .30s (Cohen, Kessler, & Gordon, 1995). Clearly, stress is not an irresistible force that produces inevitable effects on health. Actually, this fact should come as no surprise, as stress is but one factor operating in a complex network of biopsychosocial determinants of health. Other key factors include one's genetic endowment, exposure to infectious agents and environmental toxins, nutrition, exercise, alcohol and drug use, smoking, use of medical care, and cooperation with medical advice. Furthermore, some people handle stress better than others, which is the matter we turn to next.

Factors Moderating the Impact of Stress

Some people seem to be able to withstand the ravages of stress better than others (Holahan & Moos, 1994). Why? Because certain factors can lessen the impact of stress on physical and mental health. We'll look at three such factors—social support, optimism, and conscientiousness—to shed light on individual differences in how well people tolerate stress.

Social Support

Friends may be good for your health! This startling conclusion emerges from studies on social support as a moderator of stress. *Social support* refers to various types of aid and emotional sustenance provided by members of one's social networks. Many studies have found positive correlations between high social support and greater immune functioning (Uchino, Uno, & Holt-Lunstad, 1999). In contrast, the opposite of social support—loneliness and social isolation—was found to predict reduced immune responding in a study of college students (Pressman et al., 2005). In recent decades, a vast number of studies have found evidence that social support is favorably related to physical health (Taylor, 2007; Uchino, 2004), including all-important coronary health (Rutledge et al., 2004). The favorable effects of social support are strong enough to have an impact on participants' mortality! For example, one study followed patients for a mean period of 4.5 years following a nonfatal heart attack and found that higher levels of perceived social support were associated with reduced mortality among patients who did not manifest depression (Lett et al., 2007). Similarly, an Australian study that tracked 1477 participants aged 70 and over for ten years found that people with richer friendship networks lived longer (Giles et al., 2005).

Social support seems to be good medicine for the mind as well as the body, as most studies also find an association between social support and mental health (Davis, Morris, & Kraus, 1998). It appears that

Figure 12.7
The stress-illness correlation. One or more aspects of personality, physiology, or memory could play the role of a postulated third variable in the relationship between high stress and high incidence of illness. For example, neuroticism may lead some subjects to view more events as stressful and to remember more illness, thus inflating the apparent correlation between stress and illness.

In times of stress, seeking support from one's friends is a sensible and helpful coping strategy.

social support serves as a protective buffer during times of high stress, reducing the negative impact of stressful events—and that social support has its own positive effects on health, which may be apparent even when people aren't under great stress (Wills & Fegan, 2001). Interestingly, a recent study has demonstrated that pet owners who view their pets as sources of support also experience health benefits (Allen, Blascovich, & Mendes, 2002).

Optimism and Conscientiousness

Defining *optimism* as a general tendency to expect good outcomes, Michael Scheier and Charles Carver (1985) found a correlation between optimism and relatively good physical health in a sample of college students. Other studies have found that optimism helps people deal more effectively with a diagnosis of breast cancer (Carver et al., 2005) and with a death or onset of illness in one's immediate family (Kivimaki et al. 2005). Why is optimism beneficial to health? Research suggests that optimists cope with stress in more adaptive ways than pessimists (Aspinwall, Richter, & Hoffman, 2001; Nes & Segerstrom, 2006). Optimists are more likely to engage in action-oriented, problem-focused coping. They are more willing than pessimists to seek social support, and they are more likely to emphasize the positive in their appraisals of stressful events. In comparison, pessimists are more likely to deal with stress by giving up or engaging in denial. The potential importance of optimism is illustrated by research which suggests that optimism fosters reduced mortality and greater longevity (Peterson et al., 1998).

Optimism is not the personality trait that has been examined as a possible moderator of physical health. Howard Friedman and his colleagues have found evidence that *conscientiousness,* one of the Big Five personality traits discussed in Chapter 11, may have an impact on physical health (Friedman et al., 1993; Martin, Friedman, & Schwartz, 2007). They have related personality measures to longevity in a sample of individuals who have been followed closely by researchers since 1921. Data were available on six personality traits, which were measured when the subjects were children. The one trait that predicted greater longevity was conscientiousness. Why does conscientiousness promote longevity? According to Friedman (2007), several considerations may contribute, but the key consideration appears to be that conscientiousness fosters better health habits. People who are high in conscientiousness are less likely than others to exhibit unhealthy habits, such as excessive drinking, drug abuse, dangerous driving, smoking, overeating, and risky sexual practices (Bogg & Roberts, 2004; Roberts, Walton, & Bogg, 2005).

Positive Effects of Stress

Our discussion of the link between stress and illness may have given you the impression that the effects of stress are entirely negative, but this most certainly is not the case. Recent years have brought increased interest in the positive aspects of the stress process, including favorable outcomes that follow in the wake of stress (Folkman & Moskowitz, 2000). To some extent, the new focus on the possible benefits of stress reflects a new emphasis on "positive psychology." As we noted in Chapter 1, the advocates of positive psychology argue for increased research on well-being, courage, perseverance, tolerance, and other human strengths and virtues (Seligman, 2003). One of these strengths is resilience in the face of stress (Seligman & Csikszentmihalyi, 2000).

Research on resilience suggests that stress can promote personal growth or self-improvement (Calhoun & Tedeschi, 2006, 2008). For example, studies of people grappling with major health problems show that the majority of respondents report that they derived benefits from their adversity (Tennen & Affleck, 1999). Stressful events sometimes force people to develop new skills, reevaluate priorities, learn new insights, and acquire new strengths. In other words, the adaptation process initiated by stress may lead to personal changes that are changes for the better. Confronting and conquering a stressful challenge may lead to improvements in specific coping abilities and to an enhanced self-concept. Moreover, even if people do not conquer stressors, they may be able to learn from their mistakes. Thus, researchers have begun to explore the growth potential of stressful events (Helgeson, Reynolds, & Tomich, 2006; Park & Fenster, 2004).

Recent studies of resilience also indicate that it is not as uncommon as widely assumed. The predominant view has been that a substantial majority of people who are exposed to traumatic stress tend to suffer severe effects, whereas resilience is unusual, perhaps even rare. However, George Bonanno (2005) and his colleagues (Bonanno et al., 2002, 2005), who have studied the long-term effects of traumatic stressful events, such as bereavement and exposure to combat and terrorism, have found that resilience is seen in as many as 35% to 55% of people (see **Figure 12.8** on the next page). Admittedly, a great many people do endure lasting ill effects from traumatic stress, but resilience is not the rare exception it was once believed to be.

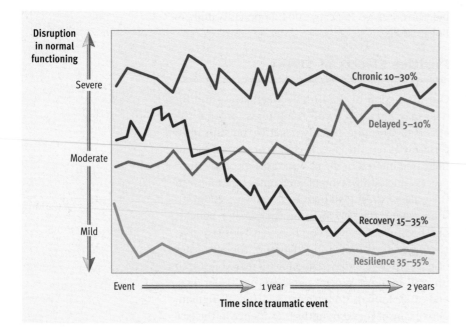

Figure 12.8

Patterns of response to traumatic stress. Bonanno (2005) and colleagues have conducted a number of studies in which they have tracked the adjustment of people after exposure to severe, traumatic stress, such as bereavement. They have identified four patterns of response. Some people experience *chronic disruption* and others show *delayed disruption* of normal functioning, both of which show no abatement after two years. Others show a pattern of *recovery*, wherein initially severe symptoms gradually taper off. Finally, a fourth group exhibits *resilience*, in which relatively modest initial symptoms diminish fairly quickly. The surprising finding in this research is that resilience is the most common of the four patterns, suggesting that resilience is not as rare as previously assumed.

SOURCE: Bonanno, G. A. (2005). Resilience in the face of potential trauma. *Current Directions in Psychological Science, 14,* 135–138. Copyright © 2005 Blackwell Publishing. Reprinted by permission.

Health-Impairing Behavior

Key Learning Goals

12.13 Explain the negative impact of smoking on health.

12.14 Discuss how poor nutrition and lack of exercise are related to physical health.

12.15 Clarify the relationship between behavioral factors and AIDS.

Some people seem determined to dig an early grave for themselves. They do precisely those things that are bad for their health. For example, some people drink heavily even though they know that they're damaging their liver. Others eat all the wrong foods even though they know that they're increasing their risk of a second heart attack. Behavior that's downright *self-destructive* is surprisingly common. In this section we'll discuss how health is affected by smoking, poor nutrition, and lack of exercise, and we'll look at behavioral factors in AIDS. (The health risks of alcohol and drug use are discussed in Chapter 5.)

Smoking

The smoking of tobacco is widespread in our culture. The percentage of people who smoke has declined noticeably since the mid-1960s (see **Figure 12.9**).

Nonetheless, about 24% of adult men and 18% of adult women in the United States continue to smoke regularly. Smokers face a much greater risk of premature death than nonsmokers. For example, the average smoker has an estimated life expectancy *13 to 14 years shorter* than that of a similar nonsmoker (Schmitz & Delaune, 2005). The overall risk is positively correlated with the number of cigarettes smoked and their tar and nicotine content.

Why are mortality rates higher for smokers? Smoking increases the likelihood of developing a surprisingly large range of diseases (Thun, Apicella, & Henley, 2000). Lung cancer and heart disease kill the largest number of smokers. However, smokers also have an elevated risk for oral, bladder, and kidney cancer, as well as cancers of the larynx, esophagus, and pancreas; for arteriosclerosis, hypertension, stroke, and other cardiovascular diseases; and for bronchi-

Figure 12.9

The prevalence of smoking in the United States. This graph shows how the percentage of U.S. adults who smoke has declined steadily since the mid-1960s. Although considerable progress has been made, smoking still accounts for a huge number of premature deaths in the United States each year. (Based on data from the Centers for Disease Control and Prevention)

tis, emphysema, and other pulmonary diseases. Most smokers know about the risks associated with tobacco use, but they tend to underestimate the actual risks as applied to themselves (Ayanian & Cleary, 1999).

Studies show that if people can give up smoking, their health risks decline reasonably quickly (Kenfield et al., 2008; Williams et al., 2002). Evidence suggests that most smokers would like to quit but are reluctant to give up a major source of pleasure, and they worry about craving cigarettes, gaining weight, becoming anxious and irritable, and feeling less able to cope with stress (Grunberg, Faraday, & Rahman, 2001).

Unfortunately, it's difficult to give up cigarettes. People who enroll in formal smoking cessation programs are only slightly more successful than people who try to quit on their own (Swan, Hudman, & Khroyan, 2003). Long-term success rates peak in the vicinity of only 25%, and many studies report lower figures. Nonetheless, the fact that there are nearly 40 million ex-smokers in the United States indicates that it is possible to quit smoking successfully. Interestingly, many people fail several times before they eventually succeed. Research suggests that the readiness to give up smoking builds gradually as people cycle through periods of abstinence and relapse (Prochaska, 1994; Prochaska et al., 2004).

Poor Nutritional Habits

Evidence is accumulating that patterns of nutrition influence susceptibility to a variety of diseases and health problems. Possible connections between eating patterns and diseases include the following:

1. Heavy consumption of foods that elevate serum cholesterol level (eggs, cheeses, butter, shellfish, sausage, and the like) appears to increase the risk of cardiovascular disease (Stamler et al., 2000) (see **Figure 12.10**). Eating habits are only one of several factors that influence serum cholesterol level, but they do make an important contribution.

2. Vulnerability to cardiovascular diseases may also be influenced by other dietary factors. For example, low-fiber diets may increase the likelihood of coronary disease (Timm & Slavin, 2008), and high intake of red and processed meats, sweets, potatoes, and refined grains is associated with increased cardiovascular risk (Hu & Willett, 2002). Recent research indicates that the omega 3 fatty acids found in fish and fish oils offer protection against coronary disease (Din, Newby, & Flapan, 2004).

3. High salt intake is thought to be a contributing factor in the development of high blood pressure, referred to medically as hypertension (Havas, Dickinson, & Wilson, 2007), although there is still some debate about its exact role.

4. High caffeine consumption may elevate one's risk for hypertension (James, 2004) and for coronary disease (Happonen, Voutilainen, & Salonen, 2004), although the negative effects of caffeine appear relatively modest.

5. High-fat diets have been implicated as possible contributors to cardiovascular disease (Melanson, 2007) and to some forms of cancer, especially prostate cancer (Rose, 1997), colon and rectal cancer (Shike, 1999), and breast cancer (Wynder et al.,

web link 12.6

Healthfinder

Through the Department of Health and Human Services, the U.S. government has opened an ambitious online gateway to consumer-oriented information about health in all its aspects. Annotated descriptions are available for all resources identified in no-cost searches of this database.

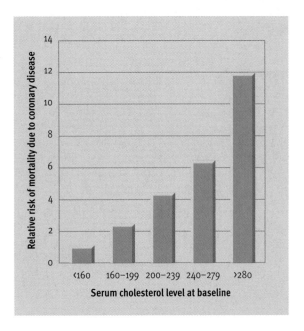

Figure 12.10

The link between cholesterol and coronary risk. In a review of several major studies, Stamler et al. (2000) summarize crucial evidence on the association between cholesterol levels and the prevalence of cardiovascular disease. This graph is based on a sample of over 11,000 men who were aged 18 to 39 at the beginning of the study (1967–1973), when their serum cholesterol level was measured. The data shown here depict participants' relative risk for coronary heart disease during the ensuing 25 years as a function of their initial cholesterol level.

1997). Some studies also suggest that high-fiber diets may reduce one's risk for breast cancer, colon cancer, and diabetes (Timm & Slavin, 2008).

Of course, nutritional habits interact with other factors to determine whether one develops a particular disease. Nonetheless, the examples just described indicate that eating habits are relevant to physical health.

Lack of Exercise

web link 12.7

Exercise and Sport Psychology

For anyone wondering about how psychological science deals with sports and athletics, this site, maintained by Division 47 of the American Psychological Association, is an excellent starting point, especially for those looking for career information.

Considerable evidence links lack of exercise to poor health. Conversely, research indicates that regular exercise is associated with increased longevity (Kokkinos et al., 2008; Lee & Skerrett, 2001). Why would exercise help people live longer? For one thing, an appropriate exercise program can enhance cardiovascular fitness and thereby reduce susceptibility to deadly cardiovascular problems (Zoeller, 2007). Second, exercise may indirectly reduce one's risk for a variety of obesity-related health problems, such as diabetes and respiratory difficulties (Corsica & Perri, 2003). Third, recent studies suggest that exercise can help diminish chronic inflammation, which is thought to contribute to quite a variety of diseases (Flynn, McFarlin, & Markofski, 2007). Fourth, exercise can serve as a buffer that reduces the potentially damaging physical effects of stress (Plante, Caputo, & Chizmar, 2000). This buffering effect

Lack of exercise can undermine physical health in a variety of ways. In contrast, regular, vigorous exercise can buffer the effects of stress, reduce chronic inflammation, and enhance the important process of neurogenesis.

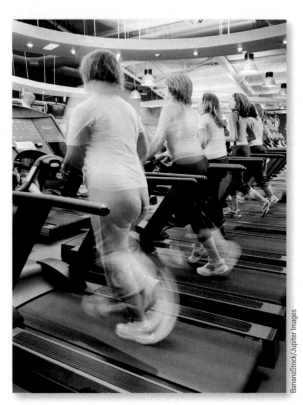

BananaStock/Jupiter Images

may occur because people high in fitness show less physiological reactivity to stress than those who are less fit (Forcier et al., 2006). If these payoffs weren't enough to get people hustling to the gym, recent studies have turned up a new, unexpected benefit of exercise—it can facilitate the generation of new brain cells (Cotman, Berchtold, & Christie, 2007; Pereira et al., 2007). As noted earlier in the chapter (see p. 423), *neurogenesis* appears to be an important process that can be suppressed by stress. The finding that this neurodevelopmental process can be promoted by simple exercise may turn out to have profound implications.

Behavior and HIV/AIDS

At present, some of the most problematic links between behavior and health may be those related to AIDS. AIDS stands for *acquired immune deficiency syndrome,* **a disorder in which the immune system is gradually weakened and eventually disabled by the human immunodeficiency virus (HIV).** Being infected with the HIV virus is *not* equivalent to having AIDS, which is in fact the final stage of the HIV infection process, typically manifested about ten years after the original infection (Treisman, 1999). With the onset of AIDS, one is left virtually defenseless against numerous infectious agents. AIDS inflicts its harm indirectly by opening the door to other diseases. The symptoms of AIDS vary widely depending on the specific constellation of diseases that one develops (Cunningham & Selwyn, 2005). Unfortunately, the worldwide prevalence of this deadly disease continues to increase at an alarming rate, especially in certain regions of Africa (UNAIDS, 2005).

Prior to 1996–1997, the average length of survival for people after the onset of the AIDS syndrome was about 18 to 24 months. Encouraging advances in the treatment of AIDS with drug regimens referred to as *highly active antiretroviral therapy (HAART)* hold out promise for *substantially* longer survival (Anthony & Bell, 2008; Hammer et al., 2006). But these drugs have been rushed into service, and their long-term efficacy is yet to be determined. Medical experts are concerned that the general public has gotten the impression that these treatments have transformed AIDS from a fatal disease to a manageable one, which is a premature conclusion. HIV strains are evolving, and many have developed resistance to the currently available antiretroviral drugs. Moreover, some patients do not respond well to the new drugs, and many patients who are responsive have difficulty sticking to drug regimens that often have adverse side effects (Beusterien et al., 2008; Hammer et al., 2006).

Transmission

The HIV virus is transmitted through person-to-person contact involving the exchange of bodily fluids, primarily semen and blood. The two principal modes of transmission in the United States have been sexual contact and the sharing of needles by intravenous (IV) drug users. In the United States, sexual transmission has occurred primarily among gay and bisexual men, but heterosexual transmission has increased in recent years (Centers for Disease Control, 2006). In the world as a whole, infection through heterosexual relations has been much more common from the beginning. In heterosexual relations, male-to-female transmission is estimated to be about eight times more likely than female-to-male transmission (Ickovics, Thayaparan, & Ethier, 2001). The HIV virus can be found in the tears and saliva of infected individuals, but the concentrations are low and there is no evidence that the infection can be spread through casual contact. Even most forms of noncasual contact, including kissing, hugging, and sharing food with infected individuals, appear safe (Kalichman, 1995).

Misconceptions

Misconceptions about AIDS are widespread. Ironically, the people who hold these misconceptions fall into two polarized camps. On the one hand, a great many people have unrealistic fears that AIDS can be readily transmitted through casual contact with infected individuals. These people worry unnecessarily about contracting AIDS from a handshake, a sneeze, or an eating utensil. They tend to be paranoid about interacting with homosexuals, thus fueling discrimination against gays in regard to housing, employment, and so forth. Some people also believe that it is dangerous to donate blood, when in fact blood *donors* are at no risk whatsoever.

On the other hand, many young heterosexuals who are sexually active with a variety of partners foolishly downplay their risk for HIV, naively assuming that they are safe as long as they avoid IV drug use and sexual relations with gay or bisexual men. They greatly underestimate the probability that their sexual partners previously may have used IV drugs or had unprotected sex with an infected individual. Also, because AIDS is usually accompanied by discernible symptoms, many young people believe that prospective sexual partners who carry the HIV virus will exhibit telltale signs of illness, but that is generally not the case. In reality, many HIV carriers do not know themselves that they are HIV-positive. In a recent study that screened over 5000 men for HIV, 77% of those who tested HIV-positive were previously unaware of their infection

---

AIDS Risk Knowledge Test

Answer the following "true" or "false."

T F **1.** The AIDS virus cannot be spread through kissing.

T F **2.** A person can get the AIDS virus by sharing kitchens and bathrooms with someone who has AIDS.

T F **3.** Men can give the AIDS virus to women.

T F **4.** The AIDS virus attacks the body's ability to fight off diseases.

T F **5.** You can get the AIDS virus by someone sneezing, like a cold or the flu.

T F **6.** You can get AIDS by touching a person with AIDS.

T F **7.** Women can give the AIDS virus to men.

T F **8.** A person who got the AIDS virus from shooting up drugs cannot give the virus to someone by having sex.

T F **9.** A pregnant woman can give the AIDS virus to her unborn baby.

T F **10.** Most types of birth control also protect against getting the AIDS virus.

T F **11.** Condoms make intercourse completely safe.

T F **12.** Oral sex is safe if partners "do not swallow."

T F **13.** A person must have many different sexual partners to be at risk for AIDS.

T F **14.** It is more important to take precautions against AIDS in large cities than in small cities.

T F **15.** A positive result on the AIDS virus antibody test often occurs for people who do not even have the virus.

T F **16.** Only receptive (passive) anal intercourse transmits the AIDS virus.

T F **17.** Donating blood carries no AIDS risk for the donor.

T F **18.** Most people who have the AIDS virus look quite ill.

Answers: 1. T 2. F 3. T 4. T 5. F 6. F 7. T 8. F 9. T 10. F 11. F 12. F 13. F 14. F 15. F 16. F 17. T 18. F

Figure 12.11

A quiz on knowledge of HIV/AIDS. Because misconceptions about HIV infection and AIDS abound, it may be wise to take this brief quiz to test your knowledge of HIV/AIDS. The answers are shown at the bottom of the figure.

SOURCE: Adapted from Kalichman, S. C. (1995). *Understanding AIDS: A guide for mental health professionals.* Washington, DC. Copyright © 1995 American Psychological Association. Reprinted by permission of the publisher and author.

(MacKellar et al., 2005). In sum, many myths about AIDS persist, in spite of extensive efforts to educate the public about this complex and controversial disease. **Figure 12.11** contains a short quiz to test your knowledge of the facts about AIDS.

So far, we've seen that physical health may be affected by stress and by aspects of lifestyle. Next, we'll look at the importance of how people react to physical symptoms, health problems, and health care efforts.

REVIEW of Key Learning Goals

12.13 Smokers have much higher mortality rates than nonsmokers because they are more vulnerable to a host of diseases. Health risks decline reasonably quickly for people who give up smoking, but quitting is difficult and relapse rates are high.

12.14 Poor nutritional habits have been linked to heart disease, hypertension, and cancer, among other things. Regular exercise can reduce one's risk for cardiovascular diseases, diminish chronic inflammation, and buffer the effects of stress. Recent research also indicates that exercise can facilitate neurogenesis.

12.15 Aspects of behavior influence one's risk of AIDS, which is transmitted through person-to-person contact involving the exchange of bodily fluids, primarily semen and blood. Misconceptions about AIDS are common, and the people who hold these misconceptions tend to fall into polarized camps, either overestimating or underestimating their risk of infection.

Identifying the Contributions of Major Theorists and Researchers

Check your recall of the principal ideas of important theorists and researchers covered in this chapter by matching the people listed on the left with the appropriate contributions described on the right. If you need help, the crucial pages describing each person's ideas are listed in parentheses. Fill in the letters for your choices in the spaces provided on the left. You'll find the answers in Appendix A.

Major Theorists and Researchers

_____ 1. Robin DiMatteo
(pp. 436–437)

_____ 2. Albert Ellis
(pp. 424, 440)

_____ 3. Barbara Fredrickson
(pp. 420–421)

_____ 4. Meyer Friedman and
Ray Rosenman (p. 427)

_____ 5. Thomas Holmes and
Richard Rahe (pp. 417–419)

_____ 6. Richard Lazarus (p. 416)

_____ 7. Hans Selye (pp. 422–423)

Key Ideas and Contributions

a. This theorist coined the term stress and described the general adaptation syndrome.

b. This individual showed that everyday hassles can be an important form of stress.

c. This research team devised the Social Readjustment Rating Scale and studied life change as a form of stress.

d. This research team is famous for describing the Type A personality and investigating its role in heart disease.

e. This psychologist's broaden-and-build theory has shed light on how positive emotions can promote resilience in the face of stress.

f. According to this theorist, catastrophic thinking causes, aggravates, and perpetuates emotional reactions to stress that are often unhealthy.

g. This expert on patient behavior has analyzed why people fail to seek medical treatment as promptly as they should.

Reflecting on the Chapter's Themes

Key Learning Goals

12.19 Identify the two unifying themes highlighted in this chapter.

Multifactorial Causation

Subjectivity of Experience

Which of our themes were prominent in this chapter? As you probably noticed, our discussion of stress and health illustrated multifactorial causation and the subjectivity of experience.

Our discussion of the psychology of health provided a particularly complex illustration of multifactorial causation. As we noted in Chapter 1, people are likely to think simplistically, in terms of single causes. In recent years, the highly publicized research linking stress to health has led many people to point automatically to stress as an explanation for illness. In reality, stress has only a modest impact on physical health. Stress can increase the risk for illness, but health is governed by a dense network of factors. Important factors include inherited vulnerabilities, exposure to infectious agents, health-impairing habits, reactions to symptoms, treatment-seeking behavior, compliance with medical advice, optimism, and so-

cial support. In other words, stress is but one actor on a crowded stage. This should be apparent in **Figure 12.12**, which shows the multitude of biopsychosocial factors that jointly influence physical health. It illustrates multifactorial causation in all its complexity.

The subjectivity of experience was demonstrated by the frequently repeated point that stress lies in the eye of the beholder. The same job promotion may be stressful for one person and invigorating for another. One person's pressure is another's challenge. When it comes to stress, objective reality is not nearly as important as subjective perceptions. More than anything else, the impact of stressful events seems to depend on how people view them. The critical importance of stress appraisals will continue to be apparent in our Personal Application on stress management. Many stress-management strategies depend on altering one's appraisals of events.

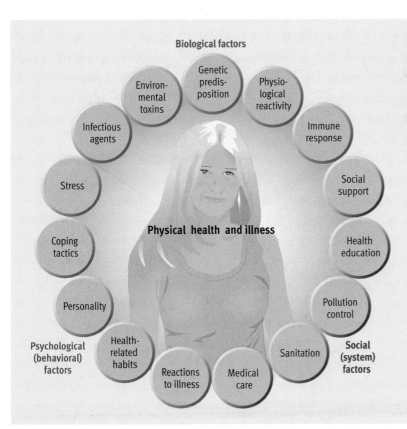

Biological factors

Genetic predisposition
Physiological reactivity
Environmental toxins
Immune response
Infectious agents
Social support
Stress
Health education
Coping tactics
Pollution control
Personality
Sanitation
Psychological (behavioral) factors
Social (system) factors
Health-related habits
Reactions to illness
Medical care

Physical health and illness

Figure 12.12
Biopsychosocial factors in health. Physical health can be influenced by a remarkably diverse set of variables, including biological, psychological, and social factors. The variety of factors that affect health provide an excellent example of multifactorial causation.

REVIEW of Key Learning Goals

12.19 Two of our integrative themes were prominent in this chapter. First, we saw that behavior and health are influenced by multiple causes. Second, we saw that experience is highly subjective, as stress lies in the eye of the beholder.

Improving Coping and Stress Management

Answer the following "true" or "false."

___ **1** The key to managing stress is to avoid or circumvent it.

___ **2** It's best to suppress emotional reactions to stress.

___ **3** Laughing at one's problems is immature.

___ **4** Exercise has little or no impact on stress resistance.

Courses and books on stress management have multiplied at a furious pace in recent decades. They summarize experts' advice on how to cope with stress more effectively. How do these experts feel about the four statements above? As you'll see in this Personal Application, most would agree that all four are false.

The key to managing stress does not lie in avoiding it. Stress is an inevitable element in the fabric of modern life. As Hans Selye (1973) noted, "Contrary to public opinion, we must not—and indeed can't—avoid stress" (p. 693). Thus, most stress-management programs train people to use more effective coping strategies. In this Application, we'll examine a variety of constructive coping tactics, beginning with Albert Ellis's ideas about changing one's appraisals of stressful events.

Key Learning Goals

12.20 Summarize Albert Ellis's ideas about controlling one's emotions.

12.21 Analyze the adaptive value of humor, releasing pent-up emotions, and forgiving others.

12.22 Assess the adaptive value of relaxation and increasing one's fitness.

Reappraisal: Ellis's Rational Thinking

Albert Ellis is a prominent theorist who believes that people can short-circuit their emotional reactions to stress by altering their appraisals of stressful events. Ellis's insights about stress appraisal are the foundation for a widely used system of therapy, called *rational-emotive behavior therapy* (Ellis, 1977, 1987), and several popular books on effective coping (Ellis, 1985, 1999, 2001).

Ellis maintains that *you feel the way you think*. He argues that problematic emotional reactions are caused by negative self-talk, which he calls catastrophic thinking. *Catastrophic thinking* involves unrealistically pessimistic appraisals of stress that exaggerate the magnitude of one's problems. According to Ellis, people unwittingly believe that stressful events cause their emotional turmoil, but he maintains that emotional reactions to personal setbacks are actually caused by overly negative appraisals of stressful events (see **Figure 12.13**).

Ellis theorizes that unrealistic appraisals of stress are derived from irrational assumptions that people hold. He maintains that if you scrutinize your catastrophic thinking, you'll find that your reasoning is based on a logically indefensible premise, such as "I must have approval from everyone" or "I must perform well in all endeavors." These faulty assumptions, which people often hold unconsciously, generate catastrophic thinking and emotional turmoil. How can you reduce your unrealistic appraisals of stress? Ellis asserts that you must learn (1) how to detect catastrophic thinking and (2) how to dispute the irrational assumptions that cause it.

Humor as a Stress Reducer

A number of years ago, the Chicago suburbs experienced their worst flooding in about a century. Thousands of people saw their homes wrecked when two rivers spilled over their banks. As the waters receded, the flood victims returning to their homes were subjected to the inevitable TV interviews. A remarkable number of victims, surrounded by the ruins of their homes, *joked* about their misfortune. When the going gets tough, it may pay to laugh about it. In a study of coping styles, McCrae (1984) found that 40% of his subjects used humor to deal with stress.

Empirical evidence showing that humor moderates the impact of stress has been accumulating over the last 25 years (Abel,

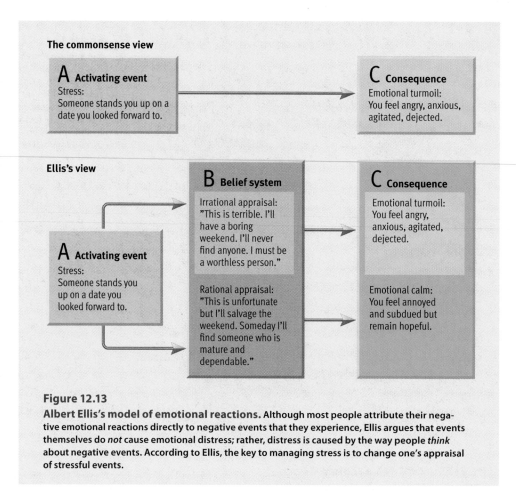

The commonsense view

A Activating event
Stress:
Someone stands you up on a date you looked forward to.

C Consequence
Emotional turmoil:
You feel angry, anxious, agitated, dejected.

Ellis's view

A Activating event
Stress:
Someone stands you up on a date you looked forward to.

B Belief system
Irrational appraisal:
"This is terrible. I'll have a boring weekend. I'll never find anyone. I must be a worthless person."

Rational appraisal:
"This is unfortunate but I'll salvage the weekend. Someday I'll find someone who is mature and dependable."

C Consequence
Emotional turmoil:
You feel angry, anxious, agitated, dejected.

Emotional calm:
You feel annoyed and subdued but remain hopeful.

Figure 12.13
Albert Ellis's model of emotional reactions. Although most people attribute their negative emotional reactions directly to negative events that they experience, Ellis argues that events themselves do *not* cause emotional distress; rather, distress is caused by the way people *think* about negative events. According to Ellis, the key to managing stress is to change one's appraisal of stressful events.

1998; Lefcourt, 2001). How does humor help to reduce the effects of stress and promote wellness? Several explanations have been proposed (see **Figure 12.14**). One possibility is that humor affects appraisals of stressful events (Abel, 2002). Jokes can help people to put a less threatening spin on their trials and tribulations. Another possibility is that humor increases the experience of positive emotions (Martin, 2002), which can help people bounce back from stressful events (Tugade & Fredrickson, 2004). Another hypothesis is that a good sense of humor facilitates rewarding social interactions, which promote social support, which is known to buffer the effects of stress (Martin, 2002). Finally, Lefcourt and colleagues (1995) argue that high-humor people may benefit from not taking themselves as seriously as low-humor people do. As they put it, "If persons do not regard themselves too seriously and do not have an inflated sense of self-importance, then defeats, embarrassments, and even tragedies should have

less pervasive emotional consequences for them" (p. 375).

Releasing Pent-up Emotions and Forgiving Others

As we discussed in the main body of the chapter, stress often leads to emotional arousal. When this happens, there's merit in the commonsense notion that you should try to release the emotions welling up inside. Why? Because the physiological arousal that accompanies emotions can become problematic. For example, research suggests that efforts to actively suppress emotions result in increased stress and autonomic arousal (Butler et al., 2003; Gross, 2001) and ultimately, the experience of more negative emotions and fewer positive emotions (John & Gross, 2007).

Although there's no guarantee of it, you can sometimes reduce your physiological arousal by *expressing* your emotions. For in-

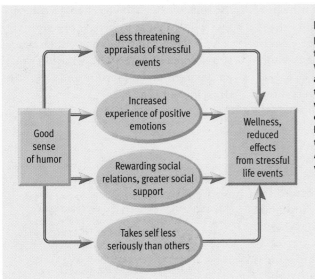

Figure 12.14
Possible explanations for the link between humor and wellness. Research suggests that a good sense of humor buffers the effects of stress and promotes wellness. Four hypothesized explanations for the link between humor and wellness are outlined in the middle column of this diagram. As you can see, humor may have a variety of beneficial effects.

reported by McCollough (2001), the extent to which the women had forgiven their former husbands was positively related to several measures of well-being and inversely related to measures of anxiety and depression. Research also shows that vengefulness is correlated with more rumination and negative emotion and with lower life satisfaction (McCullough et al., 2001). Taken together, these findings suggest that it may be healthful for people to learn to forgive others more readily.

Learning to Relax

Relaxation is a valuable stress-management technique that can soothe emotional turmoil and suppress problematic physiological arousal (McGuigan & Lehrer, 2007; Smith, 2007). The value of relaxation became apparent to Herbert Benson (1975; Benson & Klipper, 1988) as a result of his research on meditation. Benson, a Harvard Medical School cardiologist, believes that relaxation is the key to the beneficial effects of meditation. According to Benson, the elaborate religious rituals and beliefs

stance, evidence is accumulating that writing or talking about life's difficulties can be valuable in dealing with stress (Lyubomirsky, Sousa, & Dickerhoof, 2006; Smyth & Pennebaker, 1999). In one study of college students, half of the subjects were asked to write three essays about their difficulties in adjusting to college, while the other half wrote three essays about superficial topics. The subjects who wrote about their personal problems enjoyed better health in the following months than the other subjects did (Pennebaker, Colder, & Sharp, 1990). Subsequent studies have replicated this finding (Francis & Pennebaker, 1992; Greenberg, Wortman, & Stone, 1996) and shown that emotional disclosure is associated with better immune functioning (Slatcher & Pennebaker, 2005; Smyth & Pennebaker, 2001). So, if you can find a good listener, you may be able to discharge problematic emotions by letting your fears, misgivings, and frustrations spill out in a candid conversation.

People tend to experience hostility and other negative emotions when they feel "wronged"—that is when they believe that the actions of another person were harmful, immoral, or unjust. When people feel wronged, their natural inclination is either to seek revenge or to avoid further contact with the offender (McCullough, 2001). *Forgiving* someone involves counteracting these natural tendencies and releasing the person from further liability for his or

her transgression. Research suggests that forgiving is associated with better adjustment and well-being (McCollough & Witvliet, 2002; Worthington & Scherer, 2004), including enhanced mood and reduced physical symptoms (Bono, McCullough, & Root, 2008). For example, in one study of divorced or permanently separated women

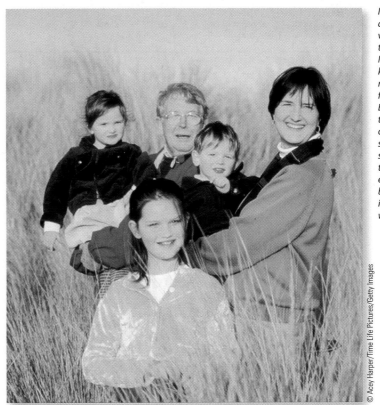

In September 1994, Reg and Maggie Green were vacationing in Italy when their seven-year-old son Nicholas was shot and killed during a highway robbery. In an act of forgiveness that stunned Europe, the Greens chose to donate their son's organs, which went to seven Italians. The Greens, shown here five years after the incident, have weathered their horrific loss better than most, perhaps in part because of their willingness to forgive.

associated with meditation are irrelevant to its effects. After "demystifying" meditation, Benson set out to devise a simple, nonreligious procedure that could provide similar benefits. He calls his procedure the *relaxation response*. From his study of a variety of relaxation techniques, Benson concluded that four factors promote effective relaxation: (1) a quiet, distraction-free environment, (2) a mental device to focus on (such as a sound or word recited repetitively), (3) a passive attitude, and (4) a comfortable position that isn't conducive to sleep. Benson's simple relaxation procedure is described in **Figure 12.15**. For full benefit, it should be practiced daily.

Minimizing Physiological Vulnerability

Your body is intimately involved in your response to stress, and the wear and tear of stress can be injurious to your health. To combat this potential problem, it helps to keep your body in relatively sound shape. The potential benefits of regular exercise are substantial. Regular exercise is associated with increased longevity (Lee & Skerrett, 2001). Moreover, research has shown that you don't have to be a dedicated athlete to benefit from exercise (Blair et al., 1989). Even a moderate amount of exercise reduces your risk of disease (Richardson et al., 2004; see **Figure 12.16**). Successful participation in an exercise program can also lead to improvements in your mood and ability to deal with stress (Hays, 1999; Plante, 1999b).

Embarking on an exercise program is difficult for many people. Exercise is time-consuming, and if you're out of shape, your initial attempts may be painful and discouraging. To avoid these problems, it's wise to (1) select an activity that you find enjoyable, (2) increase your participation gradually, (3) exercise regularly without overdoing it, and (4) reinforce yourself for your efforts (Greenberg, 2002). If you choose a competitive sport (such as basketball or tennis), try to avoid falling into the competition trap. If you become obsessed with winning, you'll put yourself under pressure and *add* to the stress in your life.

REVIEW of Key Learning Goals

12.20 Ellis emphasizes the importance of reappraising stressful events to detect and dispute catastrophic thinking. According to Ellis, emotional distress is often attributable to irrational assumptions that underlie one's thinking.

12.21 Humor may be useful in efforts to redefine stressful situations. In some cases, releasing pent-up emotions may pay off. Stress can also be reduced by learning to be more forgiving toward others.

12.22 Relaxation techniques, such as Benson's relaxation response, can reduce the wear and tear of stress. Physical vulnerability may also be reduced by striving to increase one's fitness through regular exercise. Even moderate levels of exercise can decrease disease risks.

Figure 12.15

Benson's relaxation procedure. Herbert Benson's relaxation procedure is described here. According to Benson, his simple relaxation response can yield benefits similar to meditation. To experience these benefits, you should practice the procedure daily.

SOURCE: Benson, H., & Klipper, M. Z. (1975, 1988). *The relaxation response*. New York: Morrow. Copyright © 1975 by William Morrow & Co. Reprinted by permission of HarperCollins Publishers.

1   Sit quietly in a comfortable position.

2   Close your eyes.

3   Deeply relax all your muscles, beginning at your feet and progressing up to your face. Keep them relaxed.

4   Breathe through your nose. Become aware of your breathing. As you breathe out, say the word "one" silently to yourself. For example, breath in . . . out, "one"; in . . . out, "one"; and so forth. Breathe easily and naturally.

5   Continue for 10 to 20 minutes. You may open your eyes to check the time, but do not use an alarm. When you finish, sit quietly for several minutes, at first with your eyes closed and later with your eyes opened. Do not stand up for a few minutes.

6   Do not worry about whether you are successful in achieving a deep level of relaxation. Maintain a passive attitude and permit relaxation to occur at its own pace. When distracting thoughts occur, try to ignore them by not dwelling on them, and return to repeating "one." With practice, the response should come with little effort. Practice the technique once or twice daily but not within two hours after any meal, since digestive processes seem to interfere with the elicitation of the relaxation response.

© Paul Francis Photo

Low fitness:
Group 1

Medium fitness:
Groups 2 and 3

High fitness:
Groups 4 and 5

Figure 12.16

Physical fitness and mortality. Blair and colleagues (1989) studied death rates among men and women who exhibited low, medium, or high physical fitness. As you can see, fitness was associated with lower mortality rates in both sexes.

SOURCE: Adapted from Blair, S. N., Kohl, W. H., Paffenbarger, R. S., Clark, D. G., Cooper, K. H., & Gibbons, L. W. (1989). Physical fitness and all-cause mortality. *Journal of the American Medical Association, 262,* 2395–2401. Copyright © 1989 American Medical Association. Reprinted by permission.

Participants were divided into five categories based on their fitness, ranging from least fit (group 1) to most fit (group 5).

Thinking Rationally About Health Statistics and Decisions

Key Learning Goals

12.23 Understand important considerations in evaluating health statistics and making health decisions.

With so many conflicting claims about the best ways to prevent or treat diseases, how can anyone ever decide what to do? It seems that every day a report in the media claims that yesterday's health news was wrong. The inconsistency of health news is only part of the problem. We are also overwhelmed by health-related statistics. As mathematics pundit John Allen Paulos (1995) puts it, "Health statistics may be bad for our mental health. Inundated by too many of them, we tend to ignore them completely, to accept them blithely, to disbelieve them closemindedly, or simply to misinterpret their significance" (p. 133).

Personal decisions about health-related issues can be extremely important, even a matter of life and death. Although not always easy, it is particularly important to try to think rationally and systematically about health issues. In this Application, we will discuss a few insights that can help you to think critically about statistics on health risks, then we'll briefly outline a systematic approach to thinking through health decisions.

Evaluating Statistics on Health Risks

News reports seem to suggest that there are links between virtually everything people do, touch, and consume, and some type of physical illness. For example, media have reported that coffee consumption is related to hypertension, that sleep loss is related to mortality, and that a high-fat diet is related to heart disease. Such reports are enough to send even the most subdued person into a panic. Fortunately, your evaluation of data on health risks can become more sophisticated by considering the following factors.

Correlation Is No Assurance of Causation. It is not easy to conduct experiments on health risks, so the vast majority of studies linking lifestyle and demographic factors to diseases are correlational studies. Hence, it pays to remember that no causal link may exist between two variables that happen to be correlated. Thus, when you hear that a factor is related to some disease, try to dig a little deeper and find out *why* scientists think this factor is associated with the disease. The suspected causal factor may be something very different from what was measured.

Statistical Significance Is Not Equivalent to Practical Significance. Reports on health statistics often emphasize that the investigators uncovered "statistically significant" findings. Statistically significant findings are results that are not likely to be due to chance fluctuations. Statistical significance is a useful concept, but it can sometimes be misleading (Matthey, 1998). Medical studies are often based on rather large samples, because they tend to yield more reliable conclusions than small samples. However, when a large sample is used, weak relationships and small differences between groups can turn out to be statistically significant, and these small differences may not have much practical importance. For example, in one study of sodium (salt) intake and cardiovascular disease, which used a sample of over 14,000 participants, He et al. (1999) found a statistically significant link between high sodium intake and the prevalence of hypertension among normal-weight subjects. However, this statistically significant difference was not particularly large. The prevalence of hypertension among subjects with the lowest sodium intake was 19.1% compared to 21.8% for subjects with the highest sodium intake—not exactly a difference worthy of panic.

Base Rates Should Be Considered in Evaluating Probabilities. In evaluating whether a possible risk factor is associated with some disease, people often fail to consider the base rates of these events and draw far-reaching conclusions based on what may be a matter of sheer coincidence. For example, Paulos (1995) discusses how a handful of cases in which cell phone users devel-

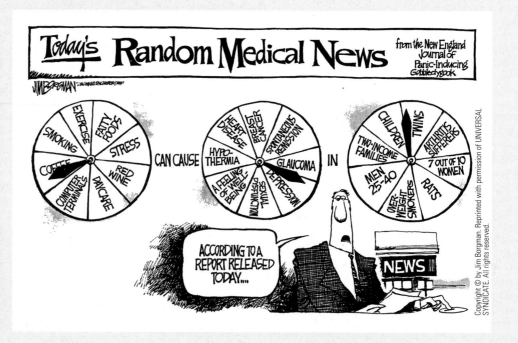

oped brain cancer led to unfounded allegations that cell phones cause brain cancer. Brain cancer is a rare disease, striking only about 6 out of 100,000 Americans per year. But given that many millions of Americans use cell phones, one would expect to find thousands upon thousands of new cases of brain cancer annually among cell phone users. Given the small number of reported cases, Paulos playfully concludes that cell phones must prevent brain cancer.

It is also useful to consider base rates in evaluating percentage increases in diseases. If the base rate of a disease is relatively low, a small increase can sound quite large if it is reported as a percentage. For example, in the He et al. (1999) study, the prevalence of diabetes among subjects with the lowest sodium intake was 2.1% compared to 3.8% for subjects with the highest sodium intake. Based on this small but statistically significant difference, one could say (the investigators did not) that high sodium intake was associated with a 81% increase ([3.8 − 2.1] ÷ 2.1) in the prevalence of diabetes.

Thinking Systematically About Health Decisions

Health decisions are oriented toward the future, which means that there are always uncertainties. And they usually involve weighing potential risks and benefits. None of these variables is unique to health decisions—uncertainty, risks, and benefits play prominent roles in economic and political decisions as well as in personal decisions. To illustrate, let's apply some basic principles of quantitative reasoning to a treatment decision involving whether to prescribe Ritalin for a boy who has been diagnosed with attention deficit disorder (ADD). Keep in mind that the general principles applied in this example can be used for a wide variety of decisions.

Seek Information to Reduce Uncertainty. Gather information and check it carefully for accuracy, completeness, and the presence or absence of conflicting information. For example, is the diagnosis of ADD correct? Look for conflicting information that does not fit with this diagnosis. If the child can sit and read for a long period of time, maybe the problem is an undetected hearing loss that makes him appear to be hyperactive in some situations. As you consider the additional information, begin quantifying the degree of uncertainty or its "flip side," your degree of confidence that the diagnosis is correct. If you decide that you are not confident about the diagnosis, you may be trying to solve the wrong problem.

Make Risk-Benefit Assessments. What are the risks and benefits of Ritalin? How likely is this child to benefit from Ritalin, and just how much improvement can be expected? If the child is 8 years old and unable to read and is miserable in school and at home, any treatment that could reduce his problems deserves serious consideration. As in the first step, the quantification is at an approximate level.

List Alternative Courses of Action. What are the alternatives to Ritalin? How well do they work? What are the risks associated with the alternatives, including the risk of falling further behind in school? Consider the pros and cons of each alternative. A special diet that sometimes works might be a good first step along with the decision to start drug therapy if the child does not show improvement over some time period. What are the relative success rates for different types of treatment for children like the one being considered? In order to answer these questions, you will need to use probability estimates in your decision making.

As you can see from this example, many parts of the problem have been quantified (confidence in the diagnosis, likelihood of improvement, probability of negative outcomes, and so forth). Precise probability values were not used because often the actual numbers are not known. Some of the quantified values reflect value judgments, others reflect likelihoods, and others assess the degree of uncertainty. If you are thinking that the quantification of many unknowns in decision making is a lot of work, you are right. But, it is work worth doing. Whenever there are important decisions to be made about health, the ability to think with numbers will help you reach a better decision. And yes, that assertion is a virtual certainty.

Table 12.3 Critical Thinking Skills Discussed in This Application

Skill	Description
Understanding the limitations of correlational evidence	The critical thinker understands that a correlation between two variables does not demonstrate that there is a causal link between the variables.
Understanding the limitations of statistical significance	The critical thinker understands that weak relationships can be statistically significant when large samples are used in research.
Utilizing base rates in making predictions and evaluating probabilities	The critical thinker appreciates that the initial proportion of some group or event needs to be considered in weighing probabilities.
Seeking information to reduce uncertainty	The critical thinker understands that gathering more information can often decrease uncertainty, and reduced uncertainty can facilitate better decisions.
Making risk-benefit assessments	The critical thinker is aware that most decisions have risks and benefits that need to be weighed carefully.
Generating and evaluating alternative courses of action	In problem solving and decision making, the critical thinker knows the value of generating as many alternatives as possible and assessing their advantages and disadvantages.

The Nature of Stress

▌ Stress involves circumstances and experiences that are perceived as threatening. Stress is a common, everyday event, and even seemingly minor stressors or hassles can be problematic. Whether one feels stressed by events depends on how one appraises them.

▌ Major types of stress include frustration, conflict, change, and pressure. Frustration occurs when an obstacle prevents one from attaining some goal. There are three principal types of conflict: approach-approach, avoidance-avoidance, and approach-avoidance. The third type is especially stressful. Vacillation is a common response to approach-avoidance conflict.

▌ A large number of studies with the SRRS suggest that change is stressful. Although this may be true, it is now clear that the SRRS is a measure of general stress rather than just change-related stress. Two kinds of pressure (to perform and conform) also appear to be stressful.

Responding to Stress

▌ Emotional reactions to stress typically include anger, fear, and sadness, although positive emotions may also occur. Fredrickson's broaden-and-build theory asserts that positive emotions broaden thinking and build coping resources. Evidence suggests that positive emotions foster enhanced immune responding and mental and physical health.

▌ Emotional arousal may interfere with coping. According to the inverted-U hypothesis, the optimal level of arousal on a task depends on the complexity of the task.

▌ Selye's general adaptation syndrome describes three stages in physiological reactions to stress: alarm, resistance, and exhaustion. There are two major pathways along which the brain sends signals to the endocrine system in response to stress. Stress may suppress neurogenesis in the brain.

▌ The behavioral response to stress takes the form of coping. Some coping responses are less than optimal. Among these are giving up, blaming oneself, striking out at others with acts of aggression, and indulging oneself. Defense mechanisms protect against emotional distress through self-deception. Defensive illusions may sometimes be adaptive. Relatively healthy coping tactics are called constructive coping.

Stress and Physical Health

▌ The Type A personality has been implicated as a contributing cause of coronary heart disease. Hostility may be the most toxic element of the Type A syndrome. Transient emotional reactions and depression have also been identified as cardiovascular risk factors.

▌ Researchers have found associations between stress and the onset of a great variety of specific diseases. Stress may play a role in a number of diseases because it can temporarily suppress the effectiveness of the immune system. While there's little doubt that stress can contribute to the development of physical illness, the link between stress and illness is modest.

▌ There are individual differences in how much stress people can tolerate. Social support appears to buffer the negative effects of stress. Two personality traits, optimism and conscientiousness, appear to promote health. Stress may also have positive effects, stimulating personal growth and the acquisition of new strengths. Resilience in the face of severe stress is not as rare as widely assumed.

Health-Impairing Behavior

▌ People frequently display health-impairing lifestyles. Smokers have much higher mortality rates than nonsmokers because they are more vulnerable to a host of diseases. Poor nutritional habits have been linked to a variety of health problems. Lack of exercise elevates one's risk for cardiovascular diseases and perhaps for certain types of cancer.

▌ Aspects of behavior also influence the risk of HIV infection, which is transmitted through person-to-person contact involving the exchange of bodily fluids, primarily semen and blood. Misconceptions about AIDS are common, and the people who hold these misconceptions tend to fall into polarized camps, either overestimating or underestimating the risk of infection.

Reactions to Illness

▌ Ignoring physical symptoms may result in the delay of needed medical treatment. There are many barriers to effective communication between patients and health care providers.

▌ Nonadherence to medical advice is a major problem. The likelihood of noncompliance is greater when instructions are difficult to understand, when recommendations are difficult to follow, and when patients are unhappy with their doctor.

Reflecting on the Chapter's Themes

▌ Two of our integrative themes were prominent in this chapter. First, we saw that behavior and health are influenced by multiple causes. Second, we saw that experience is highly subjective, as stress lies in the eye of the beholder.

PERSONAL APPLICATION Improving Coping and Stress Management

▌ People use a variety of coping strategies, and some are healthier than others. Ellis emphasizes the importance of reappraising stressful events to detect and dispute catastrophic thinking. Using humor to cope with stress may be beneficial in a variety of ways.

▌ In some cases, it may pay to release pent-up emotions by expressing them. Forgiving others' transgressions can also reduce stress. Relaxation techniques, such as Benson's relaxation response, can reduce the wear and tear of stress. Physical vulnerability may also be reduced through regular exercise.

CRITICAL THINKING APPLICATION Thinking Rationally About Health Statistics and Decisions

▌ Evaluations of statistics on health risks can be enhanced by remembering that correlation is no assurance of causation, statistical significance is not equivalent to practical significance, and base rates need to be considered in assessing probabilities.

▌ In trying to think systematically about health decisions, one should seek information to reduce uncertainty, make risk-benefit assessments, and consider alternative courses of action.

PSYKTREK PREVIEW

Visit Module 11f (*Types of Stress*) to improve your understanding of the nature of stress, and to take the Social Readjustment Rating Scale to measure the stress...

Access Module 11g (*Responding to Stress*) to learn more about how people tend to react to stress in both adaptive and maladaptive ways.

1. The notion that health is governed by a complex interaction of biological, psychological, and sociocultural factors is referred to as the:
   A. medical model.
   B. multifactorial model.
   C. biopsychosocial model.
   D. interactive model.

2. The four principal types of stress are:
   A. frustration, conflict, pressure, and anxiety.
   B. frustration, anger, pressure, and change.
   C. anger, anxiety, depression, and annoyance.
   D. frustration, conflict, pressure, and change.

3. You want very badly to ask someone for a date, but you are afraid to risk rejection. You are experiencing:
   A. an approach-avoidance conflict.
   B. an avoidance-avoidance conflict.
   C. optimized arousal.
   D. conformity pressure.

4. Research suggests that a high level of arousal may be most optimal for the performance of a task when:
   A. the task is complex.
   B. the task is simple.
   C. the rewards are high.
   D. an audience is present.

5. The alarm stage of Hans Selye's general adaptation syndrome is essentially the same as:
   A. the fight-or-flight response.
   B. constructive coping.
   C. approach-avoidance conflict.
   D. secondary appraisal.

6. The brain structure responsible for initiating action along the two major pathways through which the brain sends signals to the endocrine system is the:
   A. hypothalamus.
   B. thalamus.
   C. corpus callosum.
   D. medulla.

7. Which of the following is accurate in regard to defense mechanisms?
   A. There are many different defense mechanisms.
   B. They are used to ward off unpleasant emotions.
   C. They work through self-deception.
   D. All of the above are accurate.

8. Which element of the Type A personality seems to be most strongly related to increased coronary risk?
   A. Time consciousness
   B. Perfectionism
   C. Ambitiousness
   D. Hostility

9. Research has found that optimists are more likely than pessimists to:
   A. take their time in confronting problems.
   B. identify the negatives before they identify the positives.
   C. engage in action-oriented, problem-focused coping.
   D. seek social support only after they have exhausted all individual efforts to deal with the problem.

10. Which of the following has *not* been found to be a mode of transmission for the HIV virus?
    A. Sexual contact among homosexual men
    B. The sharing of needles by intravenous drug users
    C. Heterosexual contact
    D. Sharing food

11. The fact that health is governed by a dense network of factors is an illustration of the theme of:
    A. psychology in a sociohistorical context.
    B. the phenomenology of experience.
    C. multifactorial causation.
    D. empiricism.

12. In evaluating health statistics, it is useful to:
    A. remember that statistical significance is equivalent to practical significance.
    B. remember that correlation is a reliable indicator of causation.
    C. consider base rates in thinking about probabilities.
    D. do all of the above.

Answers

1 C p. 415	5 A p. 422	9 C p. 431
2 D p. 416	6 A p. 423	10 D p. 435
3 A p. 417	7 D p. 426	11 C p. 438
4 B pp. 421–422	8 D pp. 427–428	12 C p. 444

PSYKTREK PREVIEW

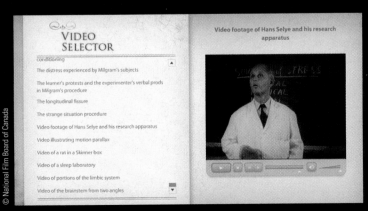

Go to the Video Selector to view historic footage of Hans Selye describing the general adaptation syndrome.

Check out the Unit 8 Critical Thinking Exercise (*Correlation and Causation*) to increase your sophistication about interpreting correlational relationships.

13

Psychological Disorders

Sunshine Skyway Bridge, St. Petersburg, FL © Pete Turner/Image Bank/Getty Images

The government of the United States was overthrown more than a year ago! I'm the president of the United States of America and Bob Dylan is vice president!" So said Ed, the author of a prominent book on journalism, who was speaking to a college journalism class, as a guest lecturer. Ed also informed the class that he had killed both John and Robert Kennedy, as well as Charles de Gaulle, the former president of France. He went on to tell the class that all rock music songs were written about him, that he was the greatest karate expert in the universe, and that he had been fighting "space wars" for 2000 years. The students in the class were mystified by Ed's bizarre, disjointed "lecture," but they assumed that he was putting on a show that would eventually lead to a sensible conclusion. However, their perplexed but expectant calm was shattered when Ed pulled a hatchet from the props he had brought with him and hurled the hatchet at the class! Fortunately, he didn't hit anyone, as the hatchet sailed over the students' heads. At that point,

the professor for the class realized that Ed's irrational behavior was not a pretense. The professor evacuated the class quickly while Ed continued to rant and rave about his presidential administration, space wars, vampires, his romances with female rock stars, and his personal harem of 38 "chicks." (Adapted from Pearce, 1974)

Clearly Ed's behavior was abnormal. Even he recognized that when he agreed later to be admitted to a mental hospital, signing himself in as the "President of the United States of America." What causes such abnormal behavior? Does Ed have a mental illness, or does he just behave strangely? What is the basis for judging behavior as normal versus abnormal? How common are psychological disorders? Are the same mental disorders seen in different cultures? These are just a few of the questions that we will address in this chapter as we discuss psychological disorders and their complex causes.

Abnormal Behavior: Myths and Realities

Misconceptions about abnormal behavior are common. Consequently, we need to clear up some preliminary issues before we describe the various types of disorders. In this section, we will discuss (1) the medical model of abnormal behavior, (2) the criteria of abnormal behavior, and (3) the classification of psychological disorders.

The Medical Model Applied to Abnormal Behavior

In Ed's case, there's no question that his behavior was abnormal. But does it make sense to view his unusual and irrational behavior as an illness? This is a controversial question. **The *medical model* proposes that it is useful to think of abnormal behavior as a disease.** This point of view is the basis for many of the terms used to refer to abnormal behavior, including mental *illness*, psychological *disorder*, and *psychopathology* (*pathology* refers to manifestations of disease). The medical model gradually became the dominant way of thinking about abnormal behavior during the 18th and 19th centuries, and its influence remains strong today.

The medical model clearly represented progress over earlier models of abnormal behavior. Prior to the 18th century, most conceptions of abnormal behavior were based on superstition. People who

behaved strangely were thought to be possessed by demons, to be witches in league with the devil, or to be victims of God's punishment. Their disorders were "treated" with chants, rituals, exorcisms, and such. If individuals' behavior was seen as threatening, they were candidates for chains, dungeons, torture, and death (see **Figure 13.1** on the next page).

The rise of the medical model brought improvements in the treatment of those who exhibited abnormal behavior. As victims of an illness, they were viewed with more sympathy and less hatred and fear. Although living conditions in early asylums were often deplorable, gradual progress was made toward more humane care of the mentally ill. It took time, but ineffective approaches to treatment eventually gave way to scientific investigation of the causes and cures of psychological disorders.

However, in recent decades, some critics have suggested that the medical model may have outlived its usefulness (Boyle, 2007; Kiesler, 1999). A particularly vocal critic has been Thomas Szasz (1974, 1990). He asserts that "strictly speaking, disease or illness can affect only the body; hence there can be no mental illness . . . Minds can be 'sick' only in the sense that jokes are 'sick' or economies are 'sick'" (1974, p. 267). He further argues that abnormal behavior usually involves a deviation from social norms rather than an illness. He contends that

Figure 13.1

Historical conceptions of mental illness. In the Middle Ages people who behaved strangely were sometimes thought to be in league with the devil. The drawing on the right depicts some of the cruel methods used to extract confessions from suspected witches and warlocks. Some psychological disorders were also thought to be caused by demonic possession. The top illustration depicts an exorcism.

SOURCE: (Right) Culver Pictures, Inc. (Top) *St. Catherine of Siena Exorcising a Possessed Woman,* c. 1500–1510 (detail). Girolamo Di Benvenuto. Denver Art Museum Collection, Gift of Samuel H. Kress Foundation Collection, 1967.171 © Denver Art Museum 2009. All rights reserved.

Thomas Szasz

"Minds can be 'sick' only in the sense that jokes are 'sick' or economies are 'sick.'"

such deviations are "problems in living" rather than medical problems. According to Szasz, the medical model's disease analogy converts moral and social questions about what is acceptable behavior into medical questions.

Although Szasz's criticism has some merit, we'll take the position that the disease analogy continues to be useful, although one should remember that it is *only* an analogy. Medical concepts such as *diagnosis, etiology,* and *prognosis* have proven valuable in the treatment and study of abnormality. *Diagnosis* involves distinguishing one illness from another. *Etiology* refers to the apparent causation and developmental history of an illness. A *prognosis* is a forecast about the probable course of an illness. These medically based concepts have widely shared meanings that permit clinicians, researchers, and the public to communicate more effectively in their discussions of abnormal behavior.

Criteria of Abnormal Behavior

If your next-door neighbor scrubs his front porch twice every day and spends virtually all his time cleaning and recleaning his house, is he normal? If your sister-in-law goes to one physician after another seeking treatment for ailments that appear imaginary, is she psychologically healthy? How are we to judge what's normal and what's abnormal? More important, who's to do the judging?

These are complex questions. In a sense, *all* people make judgments about normality in that they all express opinions about others' (and perhaps their own) mental health. Of course, formal diagnoses of psychological disorders are made by mental health professionals. In making these diagnoses, clinicians rely on a variety of criteria, the foremost of which are the following:

1. *Deviance.* As Szasz has pointed out, people are often said to have a disorder because their behavior deviates from what their society considers acceptable. What constitutes normality varies somewhat from one culture to another, but all cultures have such norms. When people violate these standards and expectations, they may be labeled mentally ill. For example, *transvestic fetishism* is a sexual disorder in which a man achieves sexual arousal by dressing in women's clothing. This behavior is regarded as disordered because a man who wears a dress, brassiere, and nylons is deviating from our culture's norms. This example illustrates the arbitrary nature of cultural standards regarding normality, as the same overt behavior (cross-sex dressing) is acceptable for women but deviant for men.

2. *Maladaptive behavior.* In many cases, people are judged to have a psychological disorder because their everyday adaptive behavior is impaired. This is the key criterion in the diagnosis of substance use (drug) disorders. In and of itself, alcohol and drug use is not terribly unusual or deviant. However, when the use of cocaine, for instance, begins to interfere with a person's social or occupational functioning, a substance use disorder exists. In such cases, it is the maladaptive quality of the behavior that makes it disordered.

3. *Personal distress.* Frequently, the diagnosis of a psychological disorder is based on an individual's report of great personal distress. This is usually the criterion met by people who are troubled by depression or anxiety disorders. Depressed people, for instance, may or may not exhibit deviant or maladaptive behavior. Such people are usually labeled as having a disorder when they describe their subjective pain and suffering to friends, relatives, and mental health professionals.

Although two or three criteria may apply in a particular case, people are often viewed as disordered when only one criterion is met. As you may have already noticed, diagnoses of psychological disorders involve *value judgments* about what represents normal or abnormal behavior (Sadler, 2005; Widiger & Sankis, 2000). The criteria of mental illness are not nearly as value-free as the criteria of physical illness. In evaluating physical diseases, people can usually agree that a malfunctioning heart or kidney is pathological, regardless of their personal values. However, judgments about mental illness reflect prevailing cultural values, social trends, and political forces, as well as scientific knowledge (Kutchins & Kirk, 1997, Mechanic, 1999).

Antonyms such as *normal* versus *abnormal* and *mental health* versus *mental illness* imply that people can be divided neatly into two distinct groups: those who are normal and those who are not. In reality, it is often difficult to draw a line that clearly separates normality from abnormality. On occasion, everybody acts in deviant ways, everyone displays some maladaptive behavior, and everyone experiences personal distress. People are judged to have psychological disorders only when their behavior becomes *extremely* deviant, maladaptive, or distressing. Thus, normality and abnormality exist on a continuum. It's a matter of degree, not an either-or proposition (see **Figure 13.2**).

Psychodiagnosis: The Classification of Disorders

 PSYK TREK Sim9

Lumping all psychological disorders together would make it extremely difficult to understand them better. A sound classification system for mental disorders can facilitate empirical research and enhance communication among scientists and clinicians (First, 2003; Zimmerman & Spitzer, 2005). Thus, a great deal of effort has been invested in devising an elaborate system for classifying psychological disorders. This system is outlined in detail in a book published by the American Psychiatric Association, titled the *Diagnostic and Statistical Manual of Mental Disorders*. The current, fourth edition, known as DSM-IV, was released in 1994 and revised in 2000. DSM-IV is a "multiaxial" system that asks for judgments about individuals on five separate dimensions, or "axes." **Figure 13.3** on the next page provides an overview of the entire system and the axes. The diagnoses of disorders are made on Axes I and II. Clinicians record most types of disorders on Axis I. They use Axis II to list long-running personality disorders or mental retardation. People may receive

Figure 13.2

Normality and abnormality as a continuum. No sharp boundary exists between normal and abnormal behavior. Behavior is normal or abnormal in degree, depending on the extent to which one's behavior is deviant, personally distressing, or maladaptive.

concept check 13.1

Applying the Criteria of Abnormal Behavior

Check your understanding of the criteria of abnormal behavior by identifying the criteria met by each of the examples below and checking them off in the table provided. Remember, a specific behavior may meet more than one criterion. The answers are in Appendix A.

Behavioral examples

1. Alan's performance at work has suffered because he has been drinking alcohol to excess. Several co-workers have suggested that he seek help for his problem, but he thinks that they're getting alarmed over nothing. "I just enjoy a good time once in a while," he says.

2. Monica has gone away to college and feels lonely, sad, and dejected. Her grades are fine, and she gets along okay with the other students in the dormitory, but inside she's choked with gloom, hopelessness, and despair.

3. Boris believes that he's Napoleon reborn. He believes that he is destined to lead the U.S. military forces into a great battle to recover California from space aliens.

4. Natasha panics with anxiety whenever she leaves her home. Her problem escalated gradually until she was absent from work so often that she was fired. She hasn't been out of her house in nine months and is deeply troubled by her problem.

Criteria met by each example

	Maladaptive behavior	Deviance	Personal distress
1. Alan	_____	_____	_____
2. Monica	_____	_____	_____
3. Boris	_____	_____	_____
4. Natasha	_____	_____	_____

web link 13.2

National Alliance for the Mentally Ill (NAMI)

NAMI describes itself as "a grassroots, self-help support and advocacy organization of families and friends of people with serious mental illness, and those persons themselves." Its site responds to their needs with extensive and current information about schizophrenia, bipolar disorder, and other severe disorders.

Figure 13.3

Overview of the DSM diagnostic system. Published by the American Psychiatric Association, the *Diagnostic and Statistical Manual of Mental Disorders* is the formal classification system used in the diagnosis of psychological disorders. It is a *multiaxial* system, which means that information is recorded on the five axes described here. (Based on American Psychiatric Association, 1994, 2000)

SOURCE: Adapted with permission from the *Diagnostic and Statistical Manual of Mental Disorders*, DSM-TR Text Revision, Fourth Edition. Copyright © 2000 American Psychiatric Association.

Axis I
Clinical Syndromes

1. **Disorders usually first diagnosed in infancy, childhood, or adolescence**
   This category includes disorders that arise before adolescence, such as attention deficit disorders, autism, enuresis, and stuttering.

2. **Organic mental disorders**
   These disorders are temporary or permanent dysfunctions of brain tissue caused by diseases or chemicals. Examples are delirium, dementia, and amnesia.

3. **Substance-related disorders**
   This category refers to the maladaptive use of drugs and alcohol. This category requires an abnormal pattern of use, as with alcohol abuse and cocaine dependence.

4. **Schizophrenia and other psychotic disorders**
   The schizophrenias are characterized by psychotic symptoms (for example, grossly disorganized behavior, delusions, and hallucinations) and by over six months of behavioral deterioration. This category also includes delusional disorder and schizoaffective disorder.

5. **Mood disorders**
   The cardinal feature is emotional disturbance. These disorders include major depression, bipolar disorder, dysthymic disorder, and cyclothymic disorder.

6. **Anxiety disorders**
   These disorders are characterized by physiological signs of anxiety (for example, palpitations) and subjective feelings of tension, apprehension, or fear. Anxiety may be acute and focused (panic disorder) or continual and diffuse (generalized anxiety disorder).

7. **Somatoform disorders**
   These disorders are dominated by somatic symptoms that resemble physical illnesses. These symptoms cannot be fully accounted for by organic damage. This category includes somatization and conversion disorders and hypochondriasis.

8. **Dissociative disorders**
   These disorders all feature a sudden, temporary alteration or dysfunction of memory, consciousness, and identity, as in dissociative amnesia and dissociative identity disorder.

9. **Sexual and gender-identity disorders**
   There are three basic types of disorders in this category: gender identity disorders (discomfort with identity as male or female), paraphilias (preference for unusual acts to achieve sexual arousal), and sexual dysfunctions (impairments in sexual functioning).

10. **Eating Disorders**
    Eating disorders are severe disturbances in eating behavior characterized by preoccupation with weight concerns and unhealthy efforts to control weight. Examples include anorexia nervosa and bulimia nervosa.

Axis II
Personality Disorders or Mental Retardation

Personality disorders are longstanding patterns of extreme, inflexible personality traits that are deviant or maladaptive and lead to impaired functioning or subjective distress. *Mental retardation* refers to subnormal general mental ability accompanied by deficiencies in adaptive skills, originating before age 18.

Axis III
General Medical Conditions

Physical disorders or conditions are recorded on this axis. Examples include diabetes, arthritis, and hemophilia.

Axis IV
Psychosocial and Environmental Problems

Axis IV is for reporting psychosocial and environmental problems that may affect the diagnosis, treatment, and prognosis of mental disorders (Axes I and II). A psychosocial or environmental problem may be a negative life event, an environmental difficulty or deficiency, a familial or other interpersonal stressor, an inadequacy of social support or personal resources, or another problem that describes the context in which a person's difficulties have developed.

Axis V
Global Assessment of Functioning (GAF) Scale

Code	Symptoms
100	Superior functioning in a wide range of activities
90	Absent or minimal symptoms, good functioning in all areas
80	Symptoms are transient and expectable reactions to psychosocial stressors
70	Some mild symptoms or some difficulty in social, occupational, or school functioning, but generally functioning pretty well
60	Moderate symptoms or difficulty in social, occupational, or school functioning
50	Serious symptoms or impairment in social, occupational, or school functioning
40	Some impairment in reality testing or communication or major impairment in family relations, judgment, thinking, or mood
30	Behavior considerably influenced by delusions or hallucinations, serious impairment in communication or judgment, or inability to function in almost all areas
20	Some danger of hurting self or others, occasional failure to maintain minimal personal hygiene, or gross impairment in communication
10	Persistent danger of severely hurting self or others
1	

diagnoses on both Axes I and II. The remaining axes are used to record supplemental information. A patient's physical disorders are listed on Axis III (General Medical Conditions). On Axis IV (Psychosocial and Environmental Problems), the clinician makes notations regarding the types of stress experienced by the individual in the past year. On Axis V (Global Assessment of Functioning), estimates are made of the individual's current level of adaptive functioning (in social and occupational behavior, viewed as a whole) and of the individual's highest level of functioning in the past year.

Work is currently underway to formulate the next edition (DSM-V) of the diagnostic system (e.g., Banzato, 2004; Spitzer, First, & Wakefield, 2007; Widiger & Simonsen, 2005), which is tentatively scheduled for publication in 2011. Clinical researchers are collecting data, holding conferences, and formulating arguments about whether various syndromes should be added, eliminated, redefined, or renamed. Should complicated grief reactions become a standard diagnostic option (Lichtenthal, Cruess, & Prigerson, 2004)? Should the diagnostic system use the term drug *dependence* or drug *addiction* (O'Brien, Volkow, & Li, 2006)? Should pathological gambling be lumped with impulse-control disorders or addictive disorders (Potenza, 2006)? Should the category of somatoform disorders (see pp. 458–459) be eliminated (Fava et al., 2007)? Should Internet addiction be added to the official list of disorders (Sandoz, 2004)? Vigorous debates about issues such as these will occupy clinical researchers in the upcoming years, and DSM-V may look somewhat different from its predecessors.

We are now ready to start examining the specific types of psychological disorders. Obviously, in this chapter we cannot cover all 200 or so disorders listed in DSM-IV. However, we will introduce most of the major categories of disorders to give you an overview of the many forms abnormal behavior takes. In discussing each set of disorders, we will begin with brief descriptions of the specific subtypes that fall in the category. If data are available, we will discuss the *prevalence* of the disorders in that category (how common they are in the population). Then we'll focus on the *etiology* of that set of disorders.

web link 13.3

Mental Health: A Report of the Surgeon General

In late 1999, the Surgeon General issued the first comprehensive survey of the state of mental health in the United States. This report has provided a crucial foundation of statistics and other information for understanding the needs for mental health care in the 21st century.

REVIEW of Key Learning Goals

13.1 The medical model assumes that it is useful to view abnormal behavior as a disease. This view has been criticized on the grounds that it turns questions about deviance into medical questions, but the model has been useful, as medical concepts such as diagnosis, etiology, and prognosis have proven valuable.

13.2 Three criteria are used in deciding whether people suffer from psychological disorders: deviance, personal distress, and maladaptive behavior. Judgments about abnormality reflect cultural values. Often it is difficult to clearly draw a line between normality and abnormality.

13.3 The DSM is the official psychodiagnostic classification system in the United States. This system asks for information about patients on five axes, or dimensions. Diagnoses of disorders are made on Axes I and II. The current version is DSM-IV, but work is under way on DSM-V.

Anxiety Disorders   Sim9

Everyone experiences anxiety from time to time. It is a natural and common reaction to many of life's difficulties. For some people, however, anxiety becomes a chronic problem. These people experience high levels of anxiety with disturbing regularity. *Anxiety disorders are a class of disorders marked by feelings of excessive apprehension and anxiety.* There are five principal types of anxiety disorders: generalized anxiety disorder, phobic disorder, panic disorder, obsessive-compulsive disorder, and posttraumatic stress disorder. Studies suggest that anxiety disorders are quite common. Over the course of their lives, roughly 19% of people experience an anxiety disorder (Dew, Bromet, & Switzer, 2000; Regier & Burke, 2000).

Generalized Anxiety Disorder   11a

Generalized anxiety disorder is marked by a chronic, high level of anxiety that is not tied to any specific threat. People with this disorder worry constantly about yesterday's mistakes and tomorrow's problems. They worry about minor matters related to family, finances, work, and personal illness. They hope that their worrying will help to ward off negative events (Beidel & Stipelman, 2007), but they nonetheless worry about how much they worry (Barlow et al., 2003). They often dread decisions and brood over them endlessly. Their anxiety is frequently accompanied by physical symptoms, such as trembling, muscle tension, diarrhea, dizziness, faintness, sweating, and heart palpitations. Generalized anxiety disorder tends to have a gradual onset and is seen more frequently in females than males (Brown, 1999). The lifetime prevalence of generalized anxiety disorder appears to be around 5% (Barlow et al., 2003).

Phobic Disorder   11a

In a phobic disorder, an individual's troublesome anxiety has a specific focus. *A phobic disorder is marked by a persistent and irrational fear of an*

Key Learning Goals

13.4 Identify five anxiety disorders and the symptoms associated with each.

13.5 Discuss the role of biological factors and conditioning in the etiology of anxiety disorders.

13.6 Explain how cognitive factors and stress can contribute to the development of anxiety disorders.

object or situation that presents no realistic danger. The following case provides an example of a phobic disorder:

Hilda is 32 years of age and has a rather unusual fear. She is terrified of snow. She cannot go outside in the snow. She cannot even stand to see snow or hear about it on the weather report. Her phobia severely constricts her day-to-day behavior. Probing in therapy revealed that her phobia was caused by a traumatic experience at age 11. Playing at a ski lodge, she was buried briefly by a small avalanche of snow. She had no recollection of this experience until it was recovered in therapy. (Adapted from Laughlin, 1967, p. 227)

As Hilda's unusual snow phobia illustrates, people can develop phobic responses to virtually anything. Nonetheless, certain types of phobias are relatively common, including acrophobia (fear of heights), claustrophobia (fear of small, enclosed places), brontophobia (fear of storms), hydrophobia (fear of water), and various animal and insect phobias (Antony & McCabe, 2003). Many people troubled by phobias realize that their fears are irrational but still are unable to calm themselves when confronted by a phobic object.

Panic Disorder and Agoraphobia

11a

A *panic disorder* is characterized by recurrent attacks of overwhelming anxiety that usually occur suddenly and unexpectedly. These paralyzing attacks are accompanied by physical symptoms of anxiety. After a number of anxiety attacks, victims often become apprehensive, wondering when their next panic will occur. Their concern about exhibiting panic in public may increase to the point where they are afraid to leave home. This fear creates a condition called *agoraphobia*, which is a common complication of panic disorders.

Agoraphobia is a fear of going out to public places (its literal meaning is "fear of the marketplace or open places"). Because of this fear, some people become prisoners confined to their homes, although many will venture out if accompanied by a trusted companion (Hollander & Simeon, 2003). As its name suggests, agoraphobia was originally viewed as a phobic disorder. However, evidence eventually showed that agoraphobia is mainly a complication of panic disorder. About two-thirds of people who suffer from panic disorder are female (Horwath & Weissman, 2000). The onset of panic disorder typically occurs during late adolescence or early adulthood (Pine & McClure, 2005).

web link 13.4

Obsessive Compulsive Foundation

The Obsessive Compulsive Foundation was created to support research, educate the public, and provide help for people suffering from OCD. The site houses newsletters, brochures, and videos on the subject of OCD. Of particular interest are reviews of many books on OCD.

Obsessive-Compulsive Disorder

11a

Obsessions are *thoughts* that repeatedly intrude on one's consciousness in a distressing way. Compulsions are *actions* that one feels forced to carry out. Thus, *obsessive-compulsive disorder (OCD)* is marked by persistent, uncontrollable intrusions of unwanted thoughts (obsessions) and urges to engage in senseless rituals (compulsions). To illustrate, let's examine the bizarre behavior of a man once reputed to be the wealthiest person in the world:

The famous industrialist Howard Hughes was obsessed with the possibility of being contaminated by germs. This led him to devise extraordinary rituals to minimize the possibility of such contamination. He would spend hours methodically cleaning a single telephone. He once wrote a three-page memo instructing assistants on exactly how to open cans of fruit for him. The following is just a small portion of the instructions that Hughes provided for a driver who delivered films to his bungalow. "Get out of the car on the traffic side. Do not at any time be on the side of the car between the car and the curb. . . . Carry only one can of film at a time. Step over the gutter opposite the place where the sidewalk dead-ends into the curb from a point as far out into the center of the road as possible. Do not ever walk on the grass at all, also do not step into the gutter at all. Walk to the bungalow keeping as near to the center of the sidewalk as possible." (Adapted from Barlett & Steele, 1979, pp. 227–237)

Obsessions often center on inflicting harm on others, personal failures, suicide, or sexual acts. People troubled by obsessions may feel that they have lost control of their mind. Compulsions usually involve stereotyped rituals that may temporarily relieve the anxiety produced by one's obsessions. Common examples include constant handwashing; repetitive cleaning of things that are already clean; endless rechecking of locks, faucets, and such; and excessive arranging, counting, and hoarding of things (Pato, Eisen, & Phillips, 2003). Unusual rituals intended to bring good luck are also a common form of compulsive behavior. Although many of us can be compulsive at times, full-fledged obsessive-compulsive disorders occur in roughly 2.5% of people at some time in their lives (Turner et al., 2001). The typical age of onset for OCD is late adolescence, with most cases (75%) emerging before the age of 30 (Kessler et al., 2005a).

Posttraumatic Stress Disorder

Posttraumatic stress disorder (PTSD) involves enduring psychological disturbance attributed to the experience of a major traumatic event. PTSD was first recognized as a disorder in the 1970s in the aftermath of the Vietnam war, when a great many veterans were traumatized by their combat experiences. Research eventually showed that PTSD can be caused by a variety of traumatic events besides harrowing war experiences. For example, PTSD is often seen after a rape or assault, a severe automobile accident, a natural disaster, or the witnessing of someone's death (Koren, Arnon, & Klein, 1999; Stein et al., 1997; Vernberg et al., 1996). Unfortunately, traumatic experiences such as these appear to be much more common than widely assumed. Research suggests that 7%–8% of people have suffered from PTSD at some point in their lives, with prevalence higher among women (10%) than men (5 percent) (Ozer et al., 2003). Currently, there is great concern about the number of military returnees from the Afghanistan and Iraq wars who will develop PTSD (Friedman, 2006). Similar to Vietnam veterans, the preliminary data suggest that these troops are showing greatly elevated rates of PTSD (Hoge et al., 2007). Common symptoms in PTSD include reexperiencing the traumatic event in the form of nightmares and flashbacks, emotional numbing, alienation, problems in social relations, an increased sense of vulnerability, and elevated arousal, anxiety, anger, and guilt (Flannery, 1999; Shalev, 2001).

Research suggests that a variety of factors are predictors of individuals' risk for PTSD in the aftermath of a traumatic event (Keane, Marshall, & Taft, 2006; McNally, 1999; Norris et al., 2001). As you might expect, increased vulnerability is associated with greater personal injuries and losses, greater inten-

As a young man (shown in the photo), Howard Hughes was a handsome, dashing daredevil pilot and movie producer who appeared to be reasonably well adjusted. However, as the years went by, his behavior gradually became more and more maladaptive, as obsessions and compulsions came to dominate his life. In his later years (shown in the drawing), he spent most of his time in darkened rooms, naked, unkempt, and dirty, following bizarre rituals to alleviate his anxieties. (The drawing was done by an NBC artist and was based on descriptions from men who had seen Hughes.)

sity of exposure to the traumatic event, and more exposure to the grotesque aftermath of the event. One key predictor of vulnerability that emerged in a recent review of the relevant research is the *intensity of one's reaction at the time of the traumatic event* (Ozer et al., 2003). Individuals who have especially intense emotional reactions during or immediately after the

Military and other personnel who have served in the wars in Iraq and Afghanistan will almost surely exhibit greatly elevated rates of posttraumatic stress disorder.

traumatic event go on to show elevated vulnerability to PTSD. Vulnerability seems to be greatest among people whose reactions are so intense that they report dissociative experiences (a sense that things are not real, that time is stretching out, that one is watching oneself in a movie).

Etiology of Anxiety Disorders

11a

Like most psychological disorders, anxiety disorders develop out of complicated interactions among a variety of factors. Classical conditioning, observational learning, and cognitive and personality factors appear especially important, but biological factors may also contribute to anxiety disorders.

Biological Factors

11a

In studies that assess the impact of heredity on psychological disorders, investigators look at *concordance rates*. A *concordance rate* indicates the percentage of twin pairs or other pairs of relatives that exhibit the same disorder. If relatives who share more genetic similarity show higher concordance rates than relatives who share less genetic overlap, this finding supports the genetic hypothesis. The results of both *twin studies* (see **Figure 13.4**) and *family studies* (see Chapter 3 for discussions of both methods) suggest that there is a moderate genetic predisposition to anxiety disorders (Hettema, Neale, & Kendler, 2001; McMahon & Kassem, 2005).

Another line of research suggests that *anxiety sensitivity* may make people vulnerable to anxiety disorders (McWilliams et al., 2007; Reiss, 1991; Schmidt, Zvolensky, & Maner, 2006). According to this notion, some people are highly sensitive to the internal physiological symptoms of anxiety and are prone to overreact with fear when they experience these symptoms. Anxiety sensitivity may fuel an inflationary spiral in which anxiety breeds more anxiety, which eventually spins out of control in the form of an anxiety disorder.

Recent evidence suggests that a link may exist between anxiety disorders and neurochemical activity in the brain. As you learned in Chapter 3, *neurotransmitters* are chemicals that carry signals from one neuron to another. Therapeutic drugs (such as Valium or Xanax) that reduce excessive anxiety appear to alter neurotransmitter activity at synapses that release a neurotransmitter called GABA. This finding and other lines of evidence suggest that disturbances in the neural circuits using GABA may play a role in some types of anxiety disorders (Skolnick, 2003). Abnormalities in neural circuits using serotonin have been implicated in PTSD and panic and obsessive-compulsive disorders (Stein & Hugo, 2004). Thus, scientists are beginning to unravel the neurochemical bases for anxiety disorders.

Conditioning and Learning

11a

Many anxiety responses may be *acquired through classical conditioning* and *maintained through operant conditioning* (see Chapter 6). According to Mowrer (1947), an originally neutral stimulus (the snow in Hilda's case, for instance) may be paired with a frightening event (the avalanche) so that it becomes a conditioned stimulus eliciting anxiety (see **Figure 13.5**). Once a fear is acquired through classical conditioning, the person may start avoiding the anxiety-producing stimulus. The avoidance response is negatively reinforced because it is followed by a reduction in anxiety. This process involves operant conditioning (see **Figure 13.5**). Thus, separate conditioning processes may create and then sustain

Figure 13.4

Twin studies of anxiety disorders. The concordance rate for anxiety disorders in identical twins is higher than that for fraternal twins, who share less genetic overlap. These results suggest that there is a genetic predisposition to anxiety disorders. (Data based on Noyes et al., 1987; Slater & Shields, 1969; Torgersen, 1979, 1983)

(a) Classical conditioning: Acquisition of phobic fear

(b) Operant conditioning: Maintenance of phobic fear (negative reinforcement)

Figure 13.5

Conditioning as an explanation for phobias. (a) Many phobias appear to be acquired through classical conditioning when a neutral stimulus is paired with an anxiety-arousing stimulus. **(b)** Once acquired, a phobia may be maintained through operant conditioning. Avoidance of the phobic stimulus reduces anxiety, resulting in negative reinforcement.

specific anxiety responses (Levis, 1989). Consistent with this view, studies find that a substantial portion of people suffering from phobias can identify a traumatic conditioning experience that probably contributed to their anxiety disorder (Antony & McCabe, 2003; Mineka & Zinbarg, 2006).

The tendency to develop phobias of certain types of objects and situations may be explained by Martin Seligman's (1971) concept of *preparedness*. Like many theorists, Seligman believes that classical conditioning creates most phobic responses. *However, he suggests that people are biologically prepared by their evolutionary history to acquire some fears much more easily than others.* His theory would explain why people develop phobias of ancient sources of threat (such as snakes and spiders) much more readily than modern sources of threat (such as electrical outlets or hot irons). As we noted in Chapter 6, Arne Öhman and Susan Mineka (2001) have updated the notion of preparedness, which they call an *evolved module for fear learning.* They maintain that this evolved module is automatically activated by stimuli related to past survival threats in evolutionary history and that it is relatively resistant to intentional efforts to suppress the resulting fears. Consistent with this view, phobic stimuli associated with evolutionary threats tend to produce more rapid conditioning of fears and stronger fear responses (Mineka & Öhman, 2002).

Cognitive Factors   11a

Cognitive theorists maintain that certain styles of thinking make some people particularly vulnerable to anxiety disorders (Craske & Waters, 2005). According to these theorists, some people are more likely to suffer from anxiety problems because they tend to (1) misinterpret harmless situations as threatening, (2) focus excessive attention on perceived threats, and (3) selectively recall information that seems threatening (Beck, 1997; McNally, 1994, 1996). In one intriguing test of the cognitive view, anxious and nonanxious subjects were asked to read 32 sentences that could be interpreted in either a threatening or a nonthreatening manner (Eysenck et al., 1991). For instance, one such sentence was "The doctor examined little Emma's growth," which could mean that the doctor checked her height or the growth of a tumor. As **Figure 13.6** shows, the anxious participants interpreted the sentences in a threatening way more often than the nonanxious participants did. Thus, consistent with our theme that human experience is highly subjective, the cognitive view holds that some people are prone to anxiety disorders because they see threat in every corner of their lives (Aikens & Craske, 2001; Riskind, 2005).

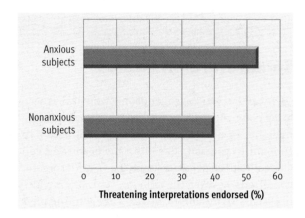

Figure 13.6

Cognitive factors in anxiety disorders. Eysenck and his colleagues (1991) compared how subjects with anxiety problems and nonanxious subjects tended to interpret sentences that could be viewed as threatening or nonthreatening. Consistent with cognitive models of anxiety disorders, anxious subjects were more likely to interpret the sentences in a threatening light.

Stress   11a

Obviously, cases of posttraumatic stress disorder are attributed to individuals' exposure to extremely stressful incidents. Research has also demonstrated that other types of anxiety disorders can be stress related (Beidel & Stipelman, 2007; Sandin et al., 2004). For instance, Faravelli and Pallanti (1989) found that patients with panic disorder had experienced a dramatic increase in stress in the month prior to the onset of their disorder. In another study, Brown and colleagues (1998) found an association between stress and the development of social phobia. Thus, there is reason to believe that high stress often helps precipitate the onset of anxiety disorders.

REVIEW of Key Learning Goals

13.4 Generalized anxiety disorder is marked by chronic, high anxiety, whereas phobic disorder involves irrational fears of specific objects or situations. Panic disorder is demonstrated by recurrent panic attacks and agoraphobia. Obsessive-compulsive disorder is dominated by intrusions of unwanted thoughts and urges, whereas posttraumatic stress disorder consists of disturbance due to the experience of a major traumatic event.

13.5 Studies suggest that there is a weak genetic predisposition to anxiety disorders. These disorders may be more likely in people who are especially sensitive to the physiological symptoms of anxiety. Abnormalities in neurotransmitter activity at GABA or serotonin synapses may also play a role. Many anxiety responses, especially phobias, may be caused by classical conditioning and maintained by operant conditioning, with preparedness influencing which phobias condition most readily.

13.6 Cognitive theorists maintain that certain styles of thinking—especially a tendency to overinterpret harmless situations as threatening—make some people more vulnerable to anxiety disorders. Stress may also predispose people to anxiety disorders.

Somatoform Disorders

Chances are, you have met people who always seem to be complaining about aches, pains, and physical maladies of doubtful authenticity. You may have thought to yourself, "It's all in his head" and concluded that the person exhibited a "psychosomatic" condition. However, the term *psychosomatic* is widely misused. *Psychosomatic diseases* are genuine physical ailments caused in part by psychological factors, especially emotional distress. These diseases, which include maladies such as ulcers, asthma, and high blood pressure, have a genuine organic basis and are not imagined ailments. They are recorded on the DSM axis for physical problems (Axis III). When physical illness appears *largely* psychological in origin, we are dealing with somatoform disorders, which are recorded on Axis I. *Somatoform disorders* are physical ailments that cannot be fully explained by organic conditions and are largely due to psychological factors. Although their symptoms are more imaginary than real, victims of somatoform disorders are *not* simply faking. Deliberate faking of illness for personal gain is another matter altogether, called *malingering*.

We will discuss three specific types of somatoform disorders: somatization disorder, conversion disorder, and hypochondriasis. Diagnostic difficulties make it hard to obtain sound data on the prevalence of somatoform disorders (Bouman, Eifert, & Lejuez, 1999).

(a)   (b)

Figure 13.7
Glove anesthesia. In conversion disorders, the physical complaints are sometimes inconsistent with the known facts of physiology, indicating that the patient's problem is psychological in origin. For instance, in a condition known as glove anesthesia, patients complain of a loss of feeling in one of their hands. The problem with this complaint is that given the patterns of nerve distribution in the arm shown in (a), it is impossible that a loss of feeling would occur in the hand exclusively, as shown in (b). Loss of feeling in the hand would have to be accompanied by some loss of feeling in the nerves in the arm.

Somatization Disorder

Individuals with somatization disorder are often said to "cling to ill health." A *somatization disorder* is marked by a history of diverse physical complaints that appear to be psychological in origin. Somatization disorder occurs mostly in women (Guggenheim, 2000) and often coexists with depression and anxiety disorders (Gureje et al., 1997). Victims report an endless succession of minor physical ailments that seem to wax and wane in response to the stress in their lives (Servan-Schreiber, Kolb, & Tabas, 1999). They usually have a long and complicated history of medical treatment from many doctors. The distinguishing feature of this disorder is the diversity of the victims' physical complaints. Over the years, they report a mixed bag of cardiovascular, gastrointestinal, pulmonary, neurological,

and genitourinary symptoms. The unlikely nature of such a mixture of symptoms occurring together often alerts a physician to the possible psychological basis for the patient's problems.

Conversion Disorder

Conversion disorder is characterized by a significant loss of physical function (with no apparent organic basis), usually in a single organ system. Common symptoms include partial or complete loss of vision, partial or complete loss of hearing, partial paralysis, severe laryngitis or mutism, and loss of feeling or function in limbs. People with conversion disorder are usually troubled by more severe ailments than people with somatization disorder. In some cases of conversion disorder, there are telltale clues about the psychological origins of the illness because the patient's symptoms are not consistent with medical knowledge about their apparent disease. For instance, the loss of feeling in one hand that is seen in "glove anesthesia" is inconsistent with the known facts of neurological organization (see **Figure 13.7**). Conversion disorders tend to have an acute onset triggered by stress (Kirmayer & Looper, 2007).

Hypochondriasis

Hypochondriacs constantly monitor their physical condition, looking for signs of illness. Any tiny alteration from their physical norm leads them to conclude that they have contracted a disease. *Hypochondriasis* (more widely known as *hypochondria*) is characterized by excessive preoccupation with one's health and incessant worry about developing physical illnesses. When hypochondriacs are assured by their physician that they do not have any real illness, they often are skeptical and disbelieving (Starcevic, 2001). They frequently assume that the physician must be incompetent, and they go shopping for another doctor. Hypochondriacs don't subjectively suffer from physical distress so much as they *overinterpret* every conceivable sign of illness. Hypochondria often appears alongside other psychological disorders, especially anxiety disorders and depression (Iezzi, Duckworth, & Adams, 2001). For example, Howard Hughes's obsessive-compulsive disorder was coupled with profound hypochondria.

"Assuming I am a hypochondriac, couldn't that condition be brought on by a brain tumor?"

Etiology of Somatoform Disorders

Inherited aspects of physiological functioning, such as an elevated sensitivity to bodily sensations, may predispose some people to somatoform disorders (Kirmayer & Looper, 2007), but genetic factors do *not* appear to make much of a contribution to the development of these disorders (Hollifield, 2005). The available evidence suggests that these disorders are largely a function of cognitive distortions, personality, and learning.

Cognitive Factors

In recent years, theorists have devoted increased attention to how cognitive peculiarities might contribute to somatoform disorders. For example, Barsky (2001) asserts that some people focus excessive attention on their internal physiological processes and amplify normal bodily sensations into symptoms of distress, which lead them to pursue unnecessary medical treatment. Recent evidence suggests that people with somatoform disorders tend to draw catastrophic conclusions about minor bodily complaints (Salkovskis & Warwick, 2001). They also seem to apply a faulty standard of good health, equating health with a complete absence of symptoms and discomfort, which is unrealistic (Barsky et al., 1993).

Personality Factors

People with certain types of personality traits seem to develop somatoform disorders more readily than others. For example, the personality trait of *neuroticism,* one of the Big Five traits described in Chapter 11, seems to elevate individuals' susceptibility to somatoform disorders (Noyes et al., 2005). Research also suggests that the pathological care-seeking behavior seen in these disorders may be caused by *insecure attachment styles* (see the discussion of at-

tachment in Chapter 10) that are rooted in early experiences with caregivers (Noyes et al., 2003).

The Sick Role

Another consideration is that some people grow fond of the role associated with being sick (Hotopf, 2004; Pilowsky, 1993). Their complaints of physical symptoms may be reinforced by indirect benefits derived from their illness (Schwartz, Slater, & Birchler, 1994). What kinds of benefits are commonly associated with physical illness? One payoff is that becoming ill is a superb way to avoid having to confront life's challenges. Many people with somatoform disorders are avoiding facing up to marital problems, career frustrations, family responsibilities, and the like. After all, when you're sick, others cannot place great demands on you.

Another benefit is that physical problems can provide a convenient excuse when people fail, or worry about failing, in endeavors that are critical to their self-esteem (Organista & Miranda, 1991). Attention from others is yet another payoff that may reinforce complaints of physical illness. When people become ill, they command the attention of family, friends, co-workers, neighbors, and doctors. The sympathy that illness often brings may strengthen the person's tendency to feel ill.

concept check 13.2

Distinguishing Anxiety and Somatoform Disorders

Check your understanding of the nature of anxiety and somatoform disorders by making preliminary diagnoses for the cases described below. Read each case summary and write your tentative diagnosis in the space provided. The answers are in Appendix A.

1. Malcolm religiously follows an exact schedule every day. His showering and grooming ritual takes 2 hours. He follows the same path in walking to his classes every day, and he always sits in the same seat in each class. He can't study until his apartment is arranged perfectly. Although he tries not to, he thinks constantly about flunking out of school. Both his grades and his social life are suffering from his rigid routines.

   Preliminary diagnosis: _____

2. Jane has been unemployed for the last eight years because of poor health. She has suffered through a bizarre series of illnesses of mysterious origin. Troubles with devastating headaches were followed by months of chronic back pain. Then she developed respiratory problems, frequently gasping for breath. Her current problem is stomach pain. Physicians have been unable to find any physical basis for her maladies.

   Preliminary diagnosis: _____

3. Nathan owns a small restaurant that's in deep financial trouble. He dreads facing the possibility that his restaurant will fail. One day, he suddenly loses all feeling in his right arm and the ability to control the arm. He's hospitalized for his condition, but physicians can't find any organic cause for his arm trouble.

   Preliminary diagnosis: _____

REVIEW of Key Learning Goals

13.7 Somatoform disorders are physical ailments that cannot be fully explained by organic conditions. Somatization disorder is characterized by a history of diverse physical complaints, whereas conversion disorder involves a loss of physical function in a single organ system. Hypochondriasis is marked by incessant worry about health concerns.

13.8 These disorders often emerge in people who think irrationally about health, those high in neuroticism, and those who focus excess attention on their internal physiological processes. Somatoform disorders may be a learned avoidance strategy wherein the sick role is reinforced by attention and sympathy.

Key Learning Goals

13.9 Distinguish among three dissociative disorders.

13.10 Discuss the etiology of dissociative identity disorder.

Dissociative Disorders

Dissociative disorders are among the more unusual syndromes that we will discuss. *Dissociative disorders* are a class of disorders in which people lose contact with portions of their consciousness or memory, resulting in disruptions in their sense of identity. We'll describe three dissociative syndromes—dissociative amnesia, dissociative fugue, and dissociative identity disorder—all of them relatively uncommon.

Dissociative Amnesia and Fugue

Dissociative amnesia and fugue are overlapping disorders characterized by serious memory deficits. *Dissociative amnesia* is a sudden loss of memory for important personal information that is too extensive to be due to normal forgetting. Memory losses may occur for a single traumatic event (such as an automobile accident or home fire) or for an extended period of time surrounding the event. Cases of amnesia have been observed after people have experienced disasters, accidents, combat stress, physical abuse, and rape, or after they have witnessed the violent death of a parent, among other things (Arrigo & Pezdek, 1997; Cardena & Gleaves, 2007). In *dissociative fugue,* people lose their memory for their entire lives along with their sense of personal identity. These people forget their name, their family, where they live, and where they work! In spite of this wholesale forgetting, they remember matters unrelated to their identity, such as how to drive a car and how to do math.

Dissociative Identity Disorder

Dissociative identity disorder (DID) involves the coexistence in one person of two or more largely complete, and usually very different, personalities. The name for this disorder used to be *multiple personality disorder,* which still enjoys informal usage. In dissociative identity disorder, the divergences in behavior go far beyond those that people normally display in adapting to different roles in life. People with "multiple personalities" feel that they have more than one identity. Each personality has his or her own name, memories, traits, and physical mannerisms. Although rare, this "Dr. Jekyll and Mr. Hyde" syndrome is frequently portrayed in novels, movies, and television shows. In popular media portrayals, the syndrome is often mistakenly called *schizophrenia*. As you will see later, schizophrenic disorders are entirely different.

In dissociative identity disorder, the various personalities generally report that they are unaware of each other (Eich et al., 1997), although doubts have been raised about the accuracy of this assertion (Allen & Iacono, 2001). The alternate personalities commonly display traits that are quite foreign to the original personality. For instance, a shy, inhibited person might develop a flamboyant, extraverted alternate personality. Transitions between identities often occur suddenly. The disparities between identities can be bizarre, as different personalities may assert that they are different in age, race, gender, and sexual orientation (Kluft, 1996).

Starting in the 1970s, a dramatic increase was seen in the diagnosis of multiple-personality disorder (Kihlstrom, 2001). Only 79 well-documented cases had accumulated up through 1970, but by the late-1990s about 40,000 cases were estimated to have been reported (Lilienfeld & Lynn, 2003). Some theorists believe that these disorders used to be underdiagnosed—that is, they often went undetected (Maldonado & Spiegel, 2003). However, other theorists argue that a handful of clinicians have begun overdiagnosing the condition and that some clinicians even contribute to the emergence of DID (McHugh, 1995; Powell & Gee, 1999). Consistent with this view, a survey of all the psychiatrists in Switzerland found that 90% of them had never seen a case of dissociative identity disorder, whereas three of the psychiatrists had each seen more than 20 patients with dissociative identity disorder (Modestin, 1992). The data from this study suggest that 6 psychiatrists (out of 655 surveyed) accounted for two-thirds of the dissociative identity disorder diagnoses in Switzerland.

Etiology of Dissociative Disorders

Dissociative amnesia and fugue are usually attributed to excessive stress. However, relatively little is known about why this extreme reaction to stress occurs in a tiny minority of people but not in the vast majority who are subjected to similar stress.

The causes of dissociative identity disorder are particularly obscure. Some skeptical theorists, such as Nicholas Spanos (1994, 1996) and others (Gee, Allen, & Powell, 2003; Lilienfeld et al., 1999), believe that people with multiple personalities are engaging in intentional role playing to use mental illness as a face-saving excuse for their personal failings. Spanos also argues that a small minority of therapists help create DID in their patients by subtly encouraging the emergence of alternate personalities. According to Spanos, dissociative identity disorder is a creation of modern North American culture, much as demonic possession was a creation of early Christianity. To bolster his argument, he discusses how DID patients' symptom presentations have been influenced by popular media. For example, the typical multiple-personality patient used to report having two or three personalities, but since the publication of *Sybil* (Schreiber, 1973) and other books describing patients with many personalities, the average number of alternate personalities has climbed to about 15. In a similar vein, there has been a dramatic upsurge in the number of DID patients reporting that they were victims of ritual satanic abuse during childhood that dates back to the publication of *Michelle Remembers* (Smith & Pazder, 1980), a book about a DID patient who purportedly was tortured by a satanic cult.

In spite of these concerns, many clinicians are convinced that dissociative identity disorder is an authentic disorder (Gleaves, May, & Cardena, 2001). They argue that there is no incentive for either patients or therapists to manufacture cases of multiple personalities, which are often greeted with skepticism and outright hostility. They maintain that most cases of dissociative identity disorder are rooted in severe emotional trauma that occurred during childhood (Draijer & Langeland, 1999). A substantial majority of people with dissociative identity disorder report a childhood history of rejection from parents and of physical and sexual abuse (Foote et al., 2006; Scroppo et al., 1998). However, this abuse typically has not been independently verified (Lilienfeld & Lynn, 2003). Moreover, this association would not be unique to DID, as a history of child abuse elevates the likelihood of *many* disorders, especially among females (MacMillan et al., 2001). In the final analysis, little is known about the causes of dissociative identity disorder, which remains a controversial diagnosis (Barry-Walsh, 2005).

REVIEW of Key Learning Goals

13.9 Dissociative amnesia involves sudden memory loss that is too extensive to be due to normal forgetting. In dissociative fugue people also lose their sense of identity. Dissociative identity disorder is marked by the coexistence of two or more very different personalities. Since the 1970s there has been a dramatic and controversial increase in the diagnosis of dissociative identity disorder.

13.10 Some theorists believe that people with dissociative identity disorder are engaging in intentional role playing to use an exotic mental illness as a face-saving excuse for their personal failings. Other theorists view DID as an authentic disorder rooted in emotional trauma that occurred during childhood.

Mood Disorders Sim9

What did Abraham Lincoln, Marilyn Monroe, Kurt Cobain, Vincent van Gogh, Ernest Hemingway, Winston Churchill, Janis Joplin, and Leo Tolstoy have in common? Yes, they all achieved great prominence, albeit in different ways at different times. But, more pertinent to our interest, they all suffered from severe mood disorders. Although mood disorders can be crippling, people with mood disorders may still achieve greatness, because such disorders tend to be *episodic*.

In other words, mood disturbances often come and go, interspersed among periods of normality. These episodes of disturbance can vary greatly in length, but they typically last 3 to 12 months (Akiskal, 2000).

Mood disorders are a class of disorders marked by emotional disturbances of varied kinds that may spill over to disrupt physical, perceptual, social, and thought processes. There are two basic types of mood disorders: bipolar and unipolar (see

Key Learning Goals

13.11 Describe the two major mood disorders and their relation to suicide.

13.12 Clarify how genetic, neurochemical, and neuro-anatomical factors are related to the development of mood disorders.

13.13 Outline the role of cognitive factors, interpersonal problems, and stress in the development of mood disorders.

Mood disorders are common and have affected many successful, well-known people, such as Ashley Judd and Jim Carrey.

Everyone gets depressed once in a while. Thus, the line between normal and abnormal depression can be difficult to draw (Kendler & Gardner, 1998). Ultimately, a subjective judgment is required. Crucial considerations in this judgment include the duration of the depression and its disruptive effects. When a depression significantly impairs everyday adaptive behavior for more than a few weeks, there is reason for concern.

In *major depressive disorder* people show persistent feelings of sadness and despair and a loss of interest in previous sources of pleasure. Negative emotions form the heart of the depressive syndrome, but many other symptoms may also appear. The most common symptoms of depression are summarized and compared with the symptoms of mania in **Table 13.1**. Depressed people often give up activities that they used to find enjoyable. For example, a depressed person might quit going bowling or might give up a favorite hobby like photography. Reduced appetite and insomnia are common. People with depression often lack energy. They tend to move sluggishly and talk slowly. Anxiety, irritability, and brooding are commonly observed. Self-esteem tends to sink as the depressed person begins to feel worthless. Depression plunges people into feelings of hopelessness, dejection, and boundless guilt. The severity of abnormal depression varies considerably.

The onset of depression can occur at any point in the life span, but a substantial majority of cases emerge before age 40 (Hammen, 2003). Depression occurs in children as well as adolescents and adults (Gruenberg & Goldstein, 2003). The vast majority (75%–95%) of people who suffer from depression experience more than one episode over the course of their lifetime (Dubovsky, Davies, & Dubovsky, 2003). In one longitudinal study, after recovery from one's first episode of depression, the cumulative probability of recurrence was 25% after 1 year, 42% after two years, and 60% after 5 years (Solomon et al., 2000).

How common are depressive disorders? Well, estimates of the prevalence of depression vary quite a bit from one study to another because of the previously mentioned difficulty in drawing a line between normal dejection and abnormal depression. That said, depression clearly is a very common disorder. The pooled data from two influential, large-scale studies (see **Figure 13.20** on page 480) yielded a lifetime prevalence estimate of 13%–14%. A recent study of a nationally representative sample of over 9000 adults estimated that the lifetime prevalence of depressive

Figure 13.8). People with *bipolar disorder* experience emotional extremes at both ends of the mood continuum, going through periods of both *depression and mania* (excitement and elation). The mood swings in bipolar disorder can be patterned in many ways. People with *unipolar disorder* experience emotional extremes at just one end of the mood continuum, as they are troubled only by periodic bouts of *depression* (for the most part, patients do not exhibit manic episodes only). Let's look at the symptoms seen in major depressive disorder.

Unipolar mood disorder

Bipolar mood disorder

Figure 13.8

Episodic patterns in mood disorders. Time-limited episodes of emotional disturbance come and go unpredictably in mood disorders. People with unipolar disorder suffer from bouts of depression only, whereas people with bipolar disorder experience both manic and depressive episodes. The time between episodes of disturbance and the length of the episodes varies greatly.

disorder was 16.2% (Kessler et al., 2003). That estimate suggests that over 30 million people in the United States have suffered or will suffer from depression!

Research indicates that the prevalence of depression is about twice as high in women as it is in men (Rihmer & Angst, 2005). The many possible explanations for this gender gap are the subject of considerable debate. The gap does *not* appear to be attributable to differences in genetic makeup (Kessler et al., 2003). A small portion of the disparity may be the result of women's elevated vulnerability to depression at certain points in their reproductive life cycle (Kornstein & Sloan, 2006). Obviously, only women have to worry abut the phenomena of postpartum and postmenopausal depression. Susan Nolen-Hoeksema (2001) argues that women experience more depression than men because they are far more likely to be victims of sexual abuse and somewhat more likely to endure poverty, sexual harassment, role constraints, and excessive pressure to be thin and attractive. In other words, she attributes the higher prevalence of depression among women to their experience of greater stress and adversity. Nolen-Hoeksema also believes that women have a greater tendency than men to *ruminate* about setbacks and problems. Evidence suggests that this tendency to dwell on one's difficulties elevates vulnerability to depression, as we will discuss momentarily.

Bipolar Disorder   11b

Bipolar disorder (formerly known as *manic-depressive disorder*) is marked by the experience of both depressed and manic periods. The symptoms seen in manic periods generally are the opposite of those seen in depression (see **Table 13.1** for a comparison). In a manic episode, a person's mood becomes elevated to the point of euphoria. Self-esteem skyrockets as the person bubbles over with optimism, energy, and extravagant plans. He or she becomes hyperactive and may go for days without sleep. The individual talks rapidly and shifts topics wildly, as his or her mind races at breakneck speed. Judgment is often impaired. Some people in manic periods gamble impulsively, spend money frantically, or become sexually reckless. Like depressive disorder, bipolar disorder varies considerably in severity.

You may be thinking that the euphoria in manic episodes sounds appealing. If so, you are not entirely wrong. In their milder forms, manic states can seem attractive. The increases in energy, self-esteem, and optimism can be deceptively seductive (Goodwin & Jamison, 1990). However, manic periods often carry

Table 13.1 Comparisons of Common Symptoms in Manic and Depressive Episodes

Characteristics	Manic Episode	Depressive Episode
Emotional	Elated, euphoric, very sociable, impatient at any hindrance	Gloomy, hopeless, socially withdrawn, irritable
Cognitive	Characterized by racing thoughts, flight of ideas, desire for action, and impulsive behavior; talkative, self-confident; experiencing delusions of grandeur	Characterized by slowness of thought processes, obsessive worrying, inability to make decisions, negative self-image, self-blame and delusions of guilt and disease
Motor	Hyperactive, tireless, requiring less sleep than usual, showing increased sex drive and fluctuating appetite	Less active, tired, experiencing difficulty in sleeping, showing decreased sex drive and decreased appetite

Source: Sarason, I. G., & Sarason, B. G. (1987). *Abnormal psychology: The problem of maladaptive behavior.* Upper Saddle River, NJ: Prentice-Hall. © 1987 Prentice-Hall, Inc. Reprinted by permission.

a paradoxical negative undercurrent of uneasiness and irritability (Dilsaver et al., 1999). Moreover, mild manic episodes usually escalate to higher levels that become scary and disturbing. Impaired judgment leads many victims to do things that they greatly regret later, as you'll see in the following case history:

Robert, a dentist, awoke one morning with the idea that he was the most gifted dental surgeon in his tri-state area. He decided that he should try to provide services to as many people as possible, so that more people could benefit from his talents. Thus, he decided to remodel his two-chair dental office, installing 20 booths so that he could simultaneously attend to 20 patients. That same day he drew up plans for this arrangement, telephoned a number of remodelers, and invited bids for the work. Later that day, impatient to get rolling on his remodeling, he rolled up his sleeves, got himself a sledgehammer, and began to knock down the walls in his office. Annoyed when that didn't go so well, he smashed his dental tools, washbasins and X-ray equipment. Later, Robert's wife became concerned about his behavior and summoned two of her adult daughters for assistance. The daughters responded quickly, arriving at the family home with their husbands. In the ensuing discussion, Robert—after bragging about his sexual prowess—made advances toward his daughters. He had to be subdued by their husbands. (Adapted from Kleinmuntz, 1980, p. 309)

Although not rare, bipolar disorder is much less common than unipolar disorder. Bipolar disorder affects about 1%–2.5% of the population (Dubovsky et al., 2003). Unlike depressive disorder, bipolar disorder is seen equally often in males and females (Rihmer & Angst, 2005). As **Figure 13.9** on the next page shows, the onset of bipolar disorder is age related, with the age of 25 being the median age of onset (Miklowitz & Johnson, 2007).

web link 13.6

Dr. Ivan's Depression Central

Some might suggest psychiatrist Ivan Goldberg's site would be better titled "Everything You Ever Wanted to Know About Depression." He offers a great depth of resources regarding mood disorders.

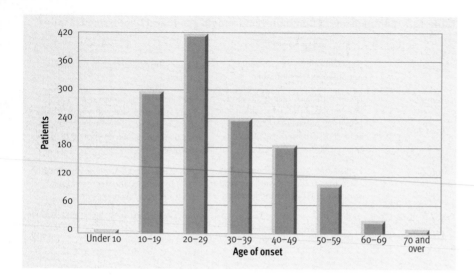

Figure 13.9

Age of onset for bipolar mood disorder. The onset of bipolar disorder typically occurs in adolescence or early adulthood. The data graphed here, which were combined from ten studies, show the distribution of age of onset for 1304 bipolar patients. As you can see, bipolar disorder emerges most frequently during the 20s decade.

SOURCE: Goodwin, F. K., & Jamison, K. R. (1990). *Manic-depressive illness* (p. 132). New York: Oxford University Press. Copyright © 1990 Oxford University Press., Inc. Reprinted by permission.

Mood Disorders and Suicide

A tragic, heartbreaking problem associated with mood disorders is suicide, which is the eleventh leading cause of death in the United States, accounting for about 30,000 deaths annually. Official statistics may underestimate the scope of the problem, as many suicides are disguised as accidents, either by the suicidal person or by the survivors who try to cover up afterward. Moreoover, experts estimate that suicide attempts may outnumber completed suicides by a ratio of as much as 20 to 1 (Sudak, 2005). Anyone can commit suicide, but some groups are at higher risk than others (Carroll-Ghosh, Victor, & Bourgeois, 2003). Evidence suggests that women *attempt* suicide three times more often than men. But men are more likely to actually kill themselves in an attempt, so they *complete* four times as many suicides as women. In regard to age, completed suicides peak in the over-75 age bracket.

With the luxury of hindsight, it is recognized that about 90% of the people who complete suicide suffer from some type of psychological disorder, although in some cases this disorder may not be readily apparent beforehand (Dawkins, Golden, & Fawcett, 2003). As you might expect, suicide rates are highest for people with mood disorders who account for about 60% of completed suicides (Mann & Currier, 2006). Both bipolar disorder and depression are associated with dramatic elevations in suicide rates. Studies suggest that the lifetime risk of completed suicide is about 15%–20% in people with bipolar disorder and about 10% in those who have grappled with depression (Sudak, 2005). Smaller elevations in suicide rates are seen among people who suffer from schizophrenia, alcoholism, and substance abuse (Mann & Currier, 2006). Unfortunately, there is no foolproof way to prevent suicidal persons from taking their own life, but some useful tips are compiled in **Figure 13.10**.

Etiology of Mood Disorders 11b

Quite a bit is known about the etiology of mood disorders, although the puzzle hasn't been assembled completely. There appear to be a number of routes into these disorders, involving intricate interactions among psychological and biological factors.

Genetic Vulnerability 11b

The evidence strongly suggests that genetic factors influence the likelihood of developing major depression or bipolar disorder (Berrettini, 2006; Kelsoe, 2005). *Twin studies* have found a huge disparity between identical and fraternal twins in concordance

---

Suicide Prevention Tips

1. *Take suicidal talk seriously.* When people talk about suicide in vague generalities, it's easy to dismiss it as idle talk and let it go. However, people who talk about suicide are a high-risk group, and their veiled threats should not be ignored. The first step in suicide prevention is to directly ask such people if they're contemplating suicide.

2. *Provide empathy and social support.* It is important to show the suicidal person that you care. People often contemplate suicide because they see the world around them as indifferent and uncaring. Thus, you must demonstrate to the suicidal person that you are genuinely concerned. Suicide threats are often a last-ditch cry for help. It is therefore imperative that you offer to help.

3. *Identify and clarify the crucial problem.* The suicidal person is often confused and feels lost in a sea of frustration and problems. It is a good idea to try to help sort through this confusion. Encourage the person to try to identify the crucial problem. Once it is isolated, the problem may not seem quite so overwhelming.

4. *Do not promise to keep someone's suicidal ideation secret.* If you really feel like someone's life is in danger, don't agree to keep his or her suicidal plans secret to preserve your friendship.

5. *In an acute crisis, do not leave a suicidal person alone.* Stay with the person until additional help is available. Try to remove any guns, drugs, sharp objects, and so forth that might provide an available means to commit suicide.

6. *Encourage professional consultation.* Most mental health professionals have some experience in dealing with suicidal crises. Many cities have suicide prevention centers with 24-hour hotlines. These centers are staffed with people who have been specially trained to deal with suicidal problems. It is important to try to get a suicidal person to seek professional assistance.

Figure 13.10

Preventing suicide. As Sudak (2005) notes, "It is not possible to prevent all suicides or to totally and absolutely protect a given patient from suicide. What is possible is to reduce the likelihood of suicide" (p. 2449). Hence, the advice summarized here may prove useful if you ever have to help someone through a suicidal crisis (Based on American Association of Suicidology, 2007; American Foundation for Suicide Prevention, 2007; Fremouw et al., 1990; Rosenthal, 1988; Shneidman, Farberow, & Litman, 1994).

rates for mood disorders. The concordance rate for identical twins is much higher (see **Figure 13.11**). This evidence suggests that heredity can create a *predisposition* to mood disorders. Environmental factors probably determine whether this predisposition is converted into an actual disorder. The influence of genetic factors appears to be stronger for bipolar disorder than for unipolar disorder (Kieseppa et al., 2004; Merikangas & Risch, 2003).

Neurochemical and Neuroanatomical Factors   11b

Heredity may influence susceptibility to mood disorders by creating a predisposition toward certain types of neurochemical abnormalities in the brain. Correlations have been found between mood disorders and abnormal levels of two neurotransmitters in the brain: norepinephrine and serotonin (Sher & Mann, 2003), although other neurotransmitter disturbances may also contribute (Thase, Jindal, & Howland, 2002). The details remain elusive, but low levels of serotonin appear to be a crucial factor underlying most forms of depression (Flores et al., 2004). A variety of drug therapies are fairly effective in the treatment of severe mood disorders. Most of these drugs are known to affect the availability (in the brain) of the neurotransmitters that have been related to mood disorders (Dubovsky et al., 2003). Since this effect is unlikely to be a coincidence, it bolsters the plausibility of the idea that neurochemical changes produce mood disturbances. That said, after 40 years of enormous research effort, the neurochemical bases of mood disorders remain more mysterious than scientists would like (Delgado & Moreno, 2006).

Studies have also found some interesting correlations between mood disorders and a variety of structural abnormalities in the brain (Flores et al., 2004). Perhaps the best documented correlation is the association between depression and *reduced hippocampal volume* (Campbell et al, 2004; Videbech, 2006). The *hippocampus,* which is known to play a major role in memory consolidation (see Chapter 7), tends to be about 8%–10% smaller in depressed subjects than in normal subjects (Videbech & Ravnkilde, 2004). A fascinating new theory of the biological bases of depression may be able to account for this finding. The springboard for this theory is the recent discovery that the human brain continues to generate new neurons in adulthood, especially in the hippocampal formation (Gage, 2002) (see Chapter 3). This process is called *neurogenesis.* Recent evidence suggests that depression occurs when major life stress causes neurochemical reactions that suppress neurogenesis, resulting in reduced hippocampal volume (B. L. Jacobs, 2004; Warner-Schmidt & Duman, 2006). Ac-

Figure 13.11

Twin studies of mood disorders. The concordance rate for mood disorders in identical twins is much higher than that for fraternal twins, who share less genetic overlap. These results suggest that there is a genetic predisposition to mood disorders. (Data from Gershon, Berrettini, & Goldin, 1989)

cording to this view, the suppression of neurogenesis is the central cause of depression, and antidepressant drugs are successful because they promote neurogenesis (Duman & Monteggia, 2006). A great deal of additional research will be required to fully test this innovative new model of the biological bases of depressive disorders.

Cognitive Factors   11b

A variety of theories emphasize how cognitive factors contribute to depressive disorders (Christensen, Carney, & Segal, 2006). We will discuss Aaron Beck's (1976, 1987) influential cognitive theory of depression in Chapter 14, where his approach to therapy is described. In this section, we'll examine Martin Seligman's *learned helplessness model* of depression and its most recent descendant, *hopelessness theory.* Based largely on animal research, Seligman (1974) proposed that depression is caused by *learned helplessness*—passive "giving up" behavior produced by exposure to unavoidable aversive events (such as uncontrollable shock in the laboratory). He originally considered learned helplessness to be a product of conditioning but eventually revised his theory, giving it a cognitive slant. The reformulated theory of learned helplessness asserted that the roots of depression lie in how people explain the setbacks and other negative events that they experience (Abramson, Seligman, & Teasdale, 1978). According to Seligman (1990), people who exhibit a *pessimistic explanatory style* are especially vulnerable to depression. These people tend to attribute their setbacks to their personal flaws instead of to situational factors, and they tend to draw global, far-reaching conclusions about their personal inadequacies based on these setbacks. *Hopelessness theory* builds on these insights by proposing a sense of hopelessness as the "final pathway" leading to depression and by incorporating additional factors that may interact with

Susan Nolen-Hoeksema

"By adolescence, girls appear to be more likely than boys to respond to stress and distress with rumination—focusing inward on feelings of distress and personal concerns rather than taking action to relieve their distress."

explanatory style to foster this sense of hopelessness (Abramson, Alloy, & Metalsky, 1995).

In accord with this line of thinking, Susan Nolen-Hoeksema (1991, 2000) has found that depressed people who *ruminate* about their depression remain depressed longer than those who try to distract themselves. People who respond to depression with rumination repetitively focus their attention on their feelings of depression, thinking constantly about how sad, lethargic, and unmotivated they are. According to Nolen-Hoeksema (1995), excessive rumination tends to extend and amplify individuals' episodes of depression. She believes that women are more likely to ruminate than men and that this disparity may help explain why depression is more prevalent in women.

In sum, cognitive models of depression maintain that negative thinking is what leads to depression in many people. The principal problem with cognitive theories is their difficulty in separating cause from effect (Rehm, Wagner, & Ivens-Tyndal, 2001). Does negative thinking cause depression? Or does depression cause negative thinking (see **Figure 13.12**)? A *clear* demonstration of a causal link between negative thinking and depression is not possible because it would require manipulating people's explanatory style (which is not easy to change) in sufficient degree to produce full-fledged depressive disorders (which would not be ethical). However, research has provided impressive evidence consistent with a causal link between negative thinking and vulnerability to depression. Lauren Alloy and her colleagues (1999) assessed the explanatory style of a sample of first-year college students who were not depressed at the outset of the study. The students were characterized as being at high risk or low risk for depression based on whether they exhibited a negative cognitive style. The follow-up data over the next 2.5 years on students who had no prior history of depression showed dramatic differences between the two groups in vulnerability to depression. During this relatively brief period, a major depressive disorder emerged in 17% of the high-risk students in comparison to only

1% of the low-risk students. The high-risk subjects also displayed a much greater incidence of minor depressive episodes (39% versus 6%). These findings and other data from the study suggest that negative thinking makes a causal contribution to the development of depressive disorders.

Interpersonal Roots   11b

Behavioral approaches to understanding depression emphasize how inadequate social skills put people on the road to depressive disorders (see **Figure 13.13**) (Coyne, 1999). According to this notion, depression-prone people lack the social finesse needed to acquire many important kinds of reinforcers, such as good friends, top jobs, and desirable spouses. This lack of reinforcers could understandably lead to negative emotions and depression. Consistent with this theory, researchers have found correlations between poor social skills and depression (Petty, Sachs-Ericsson, & Joiner, 2004).

Another interpersonal factor is that depressed people tend to be depressing (Joiner & Katz, 1999). Individuals suffering from depression often are irritable and pessimistic. They complain a lot and aren't particularly enjoyable companions. They also alienate people by constantly asking for reassurances about their relationships and their worth (Burns et al., 2006). As a consequence, depressed people tend to court rejection from those around them (Joiner & Metalsky, 1995). Depressed people thus have fewer sources of social support than nondepressed people. Social rejection and lack of support may in turn ag-

Figure 13.12

Interpreting the correlation between negative thinking and depression. Cognitive theories of depression assume that consistent patterns of negative thinking cause depression. Although these theories are highly plausible, depression could cause negative thoughts, or both could be caused by a third factor, such as neurochemical changes in the brain.

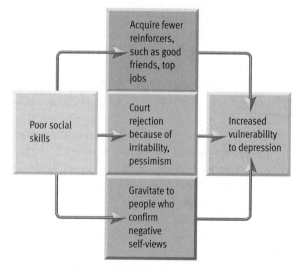

Figure 13.13

Interpersonal factors in depression. Behavioral theories about the etiology of depression emphasize how inadequate social skills may contribute to the development of the disorder through several mechanisms, as diagrammed here.

gravate and deepen a person's depression (Potthoff, Holahan, & Joiner, 1995). Recent evidence suggests that lack of social support may make a larger contribution to depression in women than in men (Kendler, Myers, & Prescott, 2005).

Precipitating Stress   11b

Mood disorders sometimes appear mysteriously in people who are leading benign, nonstressful lives. For this reason, experts used to believe that stress has little influence on mood disorders. However, advances in the measurement of personal stress have altered this picture. The evidence available today suggests the existence of a moderately strong link between stress and the onset of mood disorders (Hammen, 2005; Kendler, Kuhn, & Prescott, 2004). Stress also appears to affect how people with mood disorders respond to treatment and whether they experience a relapse of their disorder (Monroe & Hadjiyannakis, 2002).

REVIEW of Key Learning Goals

13.11 Major depression is marked by profound sadness, slowed thought processes, and loss of interest in previous sources of pleasure. Bipolar disorder involves the experience of both manic episodes and periods of depression. Manic episodes are characterized by inflated self-esteem, high energy, grandiose plans, and racing thoughts. Depression is extremely common, whereas the lifetime prevalence of bipolar disorder is about 1.0%–2.5%. Both types of mood disorders are associated with greatly elevated rates of suicide.

13.12 Evidence indicates that people vary in their genetic vulnerability to mood disorders. These disorders are accompanied by changes in neurochemical activity in the brain. Abnormalities at norepinephrine and serotonin synapses appear particularly critical. Reduced hippocampal volume and suppressed neurogenesis are also associated with depression.

13.13 Cognitive models posit that negative thinking contributes to depression. A pessimistic explanatory style has been implicated, as has a tendency to ruminate about one's problems. Interpersonal inadequacies may contribute to depressive disorders. Poor social skills may lead to a paucity of life's reinforcers and frequent rejection. Mood disorders may also be precipitated by high stress, especially in those who are particularly vulnerable to mood disorders.

web link 13.7

National Institute of Mental Health: For the Public

A wealth of information on psychological disorders is available at this subpage of the National Institute of Mental Health's massive website. Visitors will find detailed online booklets on generalized anxiety disorder, obsessive-compulsive disorder, panic disorder, depression, bipolar disorder, schizophrenia, and other psychological disorders. Brief fact sheets, dense technical reports, and many other resources can also be found here.

Schizophrenic Disorders   Sim9

Literally, *schizophrenia* means "split mind." However, when Eugen Bleuler coined the term in 1911 he was referring to the fragmentation of thought processes seen in the disorder—not to a "split personality." Unfortunately, writers in the popular media often assume that the split-mind notion, and thus schizophrenia, refer to the rare syndrome in which a person manifests two or more personalities. As you have already learned, this syndrome is actually called *multiple-personality disorder* or *dissociative identity disorder*. Schizophrenia is a much more common, and altogether different, type of disorder.

Schizophrenic disorders **encompass a class of disorders marked by delusions, hallucinations, disorganized speech, and deterioration of adaptive behavior.** Prevalence estimates suggest that about 1% of the population may suffer from schizophrenic disorders (Lauriello, Bustillo, & Keith, 2005). That may not sound like much, but it means that in the United States alone several million people may be troubled by schizophrenic disturbances. Moreover, schizophrenia is an extremely costly illness for society, because it is a severe, debilitating illness that tends to have an early onset and often requires lengthy hospital care. Because of these considerations, the financial impact of schizophrenia is estimated to exceed the costs of all types of cancers combined (Buchanan & Carpenter, 2005).

General Symptoms   11c

There are a number of distinct schizophrenic syndromes, but they share some general characteristics that we will examine before looking at the subtypes. Many of these characteristics are apparent in the following case history, adapted from Sheehan (1982).

Sylvia was first diagnosed as schizophrenic at age 15. She has been in and out of many types of psychiatric facilities since then. She has never been able to hold a job for any length of time. During severe flare-ups of her disorder, her personal hygiene deteriorates. She rarely washes, she wears clothes that neither fit nor match, she smears makeup on heavily but randomly, and she slops food all over herself. Sylvia occasionally hears voices talking to her. She tends to be argumentative, aggressive, and emotionally volatile. Over the years, she has been involved in innumerable fights with fellow patients, psychiatric staff members, and strangers. Her thoughts can be highly irrational, as is apparent from the following quote:

"Mick Jagger wants to marry me. If I have Mick Jagger, I don't have to covet Geraldo Rivera. Mick Jagger is St. Nicholas and the Maharishi is Santa Claus. I want to form a gospel rock group called the Thorn Oil, but Geraldo wants me to be the music critic on Eyewitness News, so what can I do? Got to listen to my boyfriend. Teddy

Key Learning Goals

13.14 Review the general characteristics of schizophrenia.

13.15 Outline the classification of schizophrenic subtypes and the course of schizophrenia.

13.16 Explain how genetic vulnerability and neurochemical factors can contribute to schizophrenia.

13.17 Analyze the role of structural abnormalities in the brain and neurodevelopmental processes in the etiology of schizophrenia.

13.18 Summarize how family dynamics and stress may be related to the development of schizophrenia.

Kennedy cured me of my ugliness. I'm pregnant with the son of God. Creedmoor (her hospital) is the headquarters of the American Nazi Party. They're eating the patients here. Archie Bunker wants me to play his niece on his TV show. I'm Joan of Arc. I'm Florence Nightingale. The door between the ward and the porch is the dividing line between New York and California. Forget about Zip Codes. I need shock treatments. The body is run by electricity. My wiring is all faulty." (Adapted from Sheehan, 1982; quotation from pp. 104–105)

Sylvia's case clearly shows that schizophrenic thinking can be bizarre and that schizophrenia can be a severe and crippling disorder. Although no single symptom is inevitably present, the following symptoms are commonly seen in schizophrenia (Ho, Black, & Andreasen, 2003; Lindenmayer & Khan, 2006).

Delusions and Irrational Thought.

Cognitive deficits and disturbed thought processes are the central, defining feature of schizophrenic disorders (Barch, 2003; Heinrichs, 2005). Various kinds of delusions are common. *Delusions are false beliefs that are maintained even though they clearly are out of touch with reality.* For example, one patient's delusion that he was a tiger (with a deformed body) persisted for 15 years (Kulick, Pope, & Keck, 1990). More typically, affected persons believe that their private thoughts are being broadcast to other people, that thoughts are being injected into their mind against their will, or that their thoughts are being controlled by some external force (Maher, 2001). In *delusions of grandeur,* people maintain that they are famous or important. Sylvia expressed an endless array of grandiose delusions, such as thinking that Mick Jagger wanted to marry her, that she had dictated the hobbit stories to J. R. R. Tolkien, and that she was going to win the Nobel prize for medicine. In addition to delusions, the schizophrenic person's train of thought deteriorates. Thinking becomes chaotic rather than logical and linear. A "loosening of associations" occurs, as the person shifts topics in disjointed ways. The quotation from Sylvia illustrates this symptom dramatically. The entire quote involves a wild flight of ideas in which the thoughts mostly have no apparent connection to each other.

Deterioration of Adaptive Behavior.

Schizophrenia usually involves a noticeable deterioration in the quality of the person's routine functioning in work, social relations, and personal care. Friends will often make remarks such as "Hal just isn't himself anymore." This deterioration is readily apparent in Sylvia's inability to get along with others or to function in the work world. It's also apparent in her neglect of personal hygiene.

Distorted Perception.

A variety of perceptual distortions may occur with schizophrenia, the most common being auditory hallucinations, which are reported by about 75% of patients (Combs & Mueser, 2007). *Hallucinations are sensory perceptions that occur in the absence of a real, external stimulus or are gross distortions of perceptual input.* Schizophrenics frequently report that they hear voices of nonexistent or absent people talking to them. Sylvia, for instance, said she heard messages from former Beatle Paul McCartney. These voices often provide an insulting, running commentary on the person's behavior ("You're an idiot for shaking his hand"). They may be argumentative ("You don't need a bath"), and they may issue commands ("Prepare your home for visitors from outer space").

Disturbed Emotion.

Normal emotional tone can be disrupted in schizophrenia in a variety of ways. Some victims show a flattening of emotions. In other words, they show little emotional responsiveness. Others show inappropriate emotional responses that don't jell with the situation or with what they are saying. People with schizophrenia may also become emotionally volatile. This pattern was displayed by Sylvia, who often overreacted emotionally in erratic, unpredictable ways.

Subtypes and Course 11c

Four subtypes of schizophrenic disorders are recognized, including a category for people who don't fit neatly into any of the first three categories. Let's look at the major symptoms of each subtype (Ho et al., 2003; Kirkpatrick & Tek, 2005).

Paranoid Type.

As its name implies, *paranoid schizophrenia is dominated by delusions of persecution, along with delusions of grandeur.* In this common form of schizophrenia, people come to believe that they have many enemies who want to harass and oppress them. They may become suspicious of friends and relatives, or they may attribute the persecution to mysterious, unknown persons. They are convinced that they are being watched and manipulated. To make sense of this persecution, they often develop delusions of grandeur. They believe that they must be enormously important people, frequently seeing themselves as great inventors or as great religious or political leaders. For example, in the case described at the beginning of the chapter, Ed's belief that he was president of the United States was a delusion of grandeur.

Catatonic Type.

Catatonic schizophrenia is marked by striking motor disturbances, ranging from muscular rigidity to random motor activity. Some patients go into an extreme form of withdrawal known as a catatonic stupor. They may remain virtually motionless and seem oblivious to the environment around them for long periods of time. Others go into a state of catatonic excitement. They become hyperactive and incoherent. Some alternate between these dramatic extremes. The catatonic subtype is not particularly common, and its prevalence seems to be declining.

Disorganized Type.

In *disorganized schizophrenia*, a particularly severe deterioration of adaptive behavior is seen. Prominent symptoms include emotional indifference, frequent incoherence, and virtually complete social withdrawal. Aimless babbling and giggling are common. Delusions often center on bodily functions ("My brain is melting out my ears").

Undifferentiated Type.

People who are clearly schizophrenic but who cannot be placed into any of the three previous categories are said to have *undifferentiated schizophrenia*, which is marked by idiosyncratic mixtures of schizophrenic symptoms. The undifferentiated subtype is fairly common.

Positive Versus Negative Symptoms.

Many theorists have raised doubts about the value of dividing schizophrenic disorders into the four subtypes just described (Sanislow & Carson, 2001). Critics note that the catatonic subtype is disappearing and that undifferentiated cases aren't so much a subtype as a hodgepodge of "leftovers." Critics also point out that the subtypes lack meaningful differences in etiology, prognosis, and response to treatment. The absence of such differences casts doubt on the value of the current classification scheme. Because of such problems, Nancy Andreasen (1990) and others (Carpenter, 1992; McGlashan & Fenton, 1992) have proposed an alternative approach to subtyping. This scheme divides schizophrenic disorders into just two categories based on the predominance of negative versus positive symptoms. *Negative symptoms* involve behavioral deficits, such as flattened emotions, social withdrawal, apathy, impaired attention, and poverty of speech. *Positive symptoms* involve behavioral excesses or peculiarities, such as hallucinations, delusions, bizarre behavior, and wild flights of ideas.

Theorists advocating this scheme hoped to find consistent differences between the two subtypes in etiology, prognosis, and response to treatment, and some progress along these lines *has* been made. For example, a predominance of positive symptoms is associated with better adjustment prior to the onset of schizophrenia and greater responsiveness to treatment (Combs & Mueser, 2007; Galderisi et al., 2002).

However, the assumption that patients can be placed into discrete categories based on this scheme has not been supported. Most patients exhibit both types of symptoms and vary only in the degree to which positive or negative symptoms dominate (Black & Andreasen, 1999). Although it seems fair to say that the distinction between positive and negative symptoms is enhancing our understanding of schizophrenia, it has not yielded a classification scheme that can replace the traditional subtypes of schizophrenia.

Course and Outcome.

Schizophrenic disorders usually emerge during adolescence or early adulthood, with 75% of cases manifesting by the age of 30 (Perkins, Miller-Anderson, & Lieberman, 2006). Those who develop schizophrenia usually have a long history of peculiar behavior and cognitive and social deficits, although most do not manifest a full-fledged psychological disorder during childhood (Walker et al., 2004). The emergence of schizophrenia may be sudden, but it usually is insidious and gradual. Once the disorder clearly emerges, its course is variable, but patients tend to fall into three broad groups. Some patients, presumably those with milder disorders, are treated successfully and enjoy a full recovery. Other patients experience a partial recovery and can return to independent living for a time. However, they experience regular relapses over the remainder of their lives. Finally, a third group of patients endure chronic illness marked by relentless deterioration and extensive hospitalization. Estimates of the percentage of patients falling in each category vary. Overall, the preponderance of studies have suggested that only about 20 percent of schizophrenic patients enjoy a full recovery (Perkins et al., 2006; Robinson et al., 2004). However, to some extent, this low recovery rate may reflect the poor to mediocre quality of mental health care available for severe disorders in many countries (see Chapter 14). When comprehensive, well-coordinated, quality care is initiated promptly, higher recovery rates in the vicinity of 50% have been found (Hopper et al., 2007; Liberman & Kopelowicz, 2005). Thus, the outlook for schizophrenia may not need to be as pervasively negative as it has been.

Etiology of Schizophrenia 11c

You can probably identify, at least to some extent, with people who suffer from mood disorders, somatoform disorders, and anxiety disorders. You can probably imagine events that could unfold that might leave you struggling with depression, grappling with anxiety, or worrying about your physical health. But what could possibly have led Ed to believe that he had been fighting space wars and vampires? What could

Nancy Andreasen
"Schizophrenia disfigures the emotional and cognitive faculties of its victims, and sometimes nearly destroys them."

Distinguishing Schizophrenic and Mood Disorders

Check your understanding of the nature of schizophrenic and mood disorders by making preliminary diagnoses for the cases described below. Read each case summary and write your tentative diagnosis in the space provided. The answers are in Appendix A.

1. Max hasn't slept in four days. He's determined to write the "great American novel" before his class reunion, which is a few months away. He expounds eloquently on his novel to anyone who will listen, talking at such a rapid pace that no one can get a word in edgewise. He feels like he's wired with energy and is supremely confident about the novel, even though he's only written 10 to 20 pages. Last week, he charged $5000 worth of new computer equipment, which is supposed to help him write his book.

    Preliminary diagnosis: _____

2. Eduardo maintains that he invented the atomic bomb, even though he was born after its invention. He says he invented it to punish homosexuals, Nazis, and short people. It's short people that he's really afraid of. He's sure that all the short people on TV are talking about him. He thinks that short people are conspiring to make him look like a Republican. Eduardo frequently gets in arguments with people and is emotionally volatile. His grooming is poor, but he says it's okay because he's the Secretary of State.

    Preliminary diagnosis: _____

3. Margaret has hardly gotten out of bed for weeks, although she's troubled by insomnia. She doesn't feel like eating and has absolutely no energy. She feels dejected, discouraged, spiritless, and apathetic. Friends stop by to try to cheer her up, but she tells them not to waste their time on "pond scum."

    Preliminary diagnosis: _____

John Nash, the Nobel prize–winning mathematician whose story was told in the film A Beautiful Mind, has struggled with paranoid schizophrenia since 1959.

account for Sylvia's thinking that she was Joan of Arc or that she had dictated the hobbit novels to Tolkien? As mystifying as these delusions may seem, you'll see that the etiology of schizophrenic disorders is not all that different from the etiology of other psychological disorders. We'll begin our discussion by examining the matter of genetic vulnerability.

Genetic Vulnerability   11c

Evidence is plentiful that hereditary factors play a role in the development of schizophrenic disorders (Sullivan et al., 2006; Tsuang, Glatt, & Faraone, 2003). For instance, in twin studies, concordance rates average around 48% for identical twins, in comparison to about 17% for fraternal twins (Gottesman, 1991, 2001). Studies also indicate that a child born to two schizophrenic parents has about a 46% probability of developing a schizophrenic disorder (as compared to the probability in the general population of about 1%). These and other findings that demonstrate the genetic roots of schizophrenia are summarized in **Figure 13.14**. Overall, the picture is similar to that seen for mood disorders. Several converging lines of evidence indicate that some people inherit a *vulnerability* to schizophrenia (Riley & Kendler, 2005; Schneider & Deldin, 2001).

Neurochemical Factors   11c

Like mood disorders, schizophrenic disorders appear to be accompanied by changes in the activity of one or more neurotransmitters in the brain (Patel, Pinals, & Breier, 2003). The *dopamine hypothesis* asserts that excess dopamine activity is the neurochemical basis for schizophrenia, as presented in **Figure 13.15**. This hypothesis makes sense because most of the drugs that are useful in the treatment of schizophrenia are known to dampen dopamine activity in the brain (Javitt & Laruelle, 2006; Tamminga & Carlsson, 2003). However, the evidence linking schizophrenia to high dopamine levels is riddled with inconsistencies, complexities, and interpretive problems (Abi-Dargham, 2004; Egan & Hyde, 2000). Researchers are currently exploring how interactions between the dopamine and serotonin neurotransmitter systems may contribute to schizophrenia (Patel et al., 2003). Recent research has also suggested that abnormalities in neural circuits using *glutamate* as a neurotransmitter may play a role in schizophrenic disturbance (Tibbo et al., 2004). Thus, investigators are gradually making progress in their search for the neurochemical bases of schizophrenia.

Recent research has suggested that marijuana use during adolescence may help precipitate schizophrenia in young people who have a genetic vulnerability to the disorder (Compton, Goulding, & Walker, 2007; Degenhardt & Hall, 2006). This unexpected finding has generated considerable debate about whether and how cannabis might contribute to the emergence of schizophrenia (Castle, 2008; DeLisi, 2008). The current thinking is that the key chemical ingredient in marijuana (THC) may amplify neurotransmitter activity in dopamine circuits (Degenhardt & Hall, 2006; Di Forti et al., 2007). The data on this issue are still preliminary, and more research will be needed to fully understand the association between marijuana use and schizophrenia.

Structural Abnormalities in the Brain   11c

For decades, studies have suggested that individuals with schizophrenia exhibit a variety of deficits in attention, perception, and information processing (Gold & Green, 2005; Keefe & Eesley, 2006). These cognitive deficits suggested that schizophrenic disorders may be caused by neurological defects (Perry &

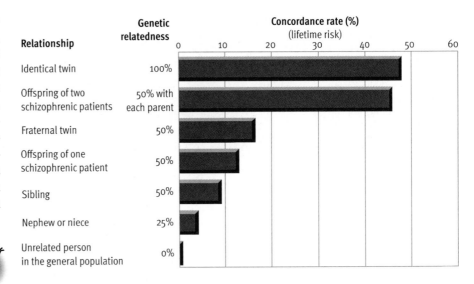

Figure 13.14

Genetic vulnerability to schizophrenic disorders. Relatives of schizophrenic patients have an elevated risk for schizophrenia. This risk is greater among closer relatives. Although environment also plays a role in the etiology of schizophrenia, the concordance rates shown here suggest that there is a genetic vulnerability to the disorder. These concordance estimates are based on pooled data from 40 studies conducted between 1920 and 1987. (Data adapted from Gottesman, 1991)

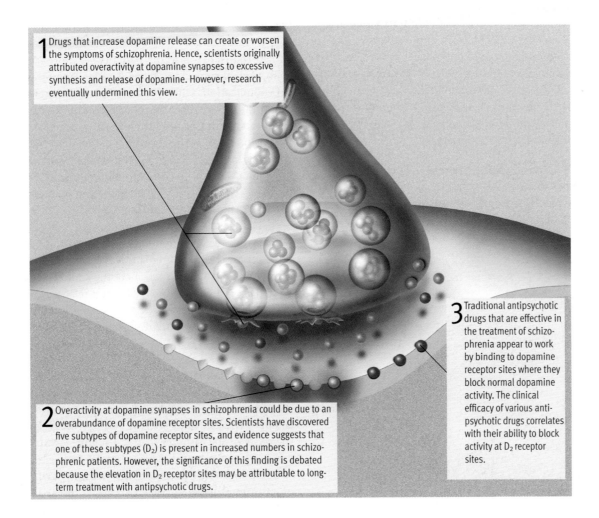

Figure 13.15

The dopamine hypothesis as an explanation for schizophrenia. Decades of research have implicated overactivity at dopamine synapses as a key cause of schizophrenic disorders. However, the evidence on the exact mechanisms underlying this overactivity, which is summarized in this graphic, is complex and open to debate. Recent hypotheses about the neurochemical bases of schizophrenia go beyond the simple assumption that dopamine activity is increased. Moreover, abnormalities in other neurotransmitter systems may also contribute to schizophrenia.

Figure 13.16

Schizophrenia and the ventricles of the brain. Cerebrospinal fluid (CSF) circulates around the brain and spinal cord. The hollow cavities in the brain filled with CSF are called ventricles. The four ventricles in the human brain are depicted here. Studies with CT scans and MRI scans suggest an association between enlarged ventricles in the brain and the occurrence of schizophrenic disturbance.

Right ventricle

Left ventricle

Third ventricle

Fourth ventricle

Figure 13.17

The neurodevelopmental hypothesis of schizophrenia. Recent findings have suggested that insults to the brain sustained during prenatal development or at birth may disrupt crucial maturational processes in the brain, resulting in subtle neurological damage that gradually becomes apparent as youngsters develop. This neurological damage is believed to increase both vulnerability to schizophrenia and the incidence of minor physical anomalies (slight anatomical defects of the head, face, hands, and feet).

Prenatal viral infection

Prenatal malnutrition

Obstetrical complications

Other brain insults

Disruption of normal maturational processes before or at birth

Subtle neurological damage

Increased vulnerability to schizophrenia

Minor physical anomalies

---

cesses of the brain before or at birth (Brown, 1999). According to this hypothesis, insults to the brain during sensitive phases of prenatal development or during birth can cause subtle neurological damage that elevates individuals' vulnerability to schizophrenia years later in adolescence and early adulthood (see **Figure 13.17**). What are the sources of these early insults to the brain? Thus far, research has focused on viral infections or malnutrition during prenatal development and obstetrical complications during the birth process.

The evidence on viral infections has been building since Sarnoff Mednick and his colleagues (1988) discovered an elevated incidence of schizophrenia among individuals who had been in their second trimester of prenatal development during a 1957 influenza epidemic in Finland. Several subsequent studies in other locations have also found a link between exposure to influenza during the second trimester and increased prevalence of schizophrenia (Brown et al., 2004). Another study, which investigated the possible impact of prenatal malnutrition, found an elevated incidence of schizophrenia in a group of people who were prenatally exposed to a severe famine in 1944–45 resulting from a Nazi blockade of food deliveries in the Netherlands during World War II (Susser et al., 1996). Other research has shown that schizophrenic patients are more likely than control subjects to have experienced obstetrical complications when they were born (Kelly et al., 2004; Murray & Bramon, 2005). Finally, research suggests that minor physical anomalies (slight anatomical defects of the head, hands, feet, and face) that would be consistent with prenatal neurological damage are more common among people with schizophrenia than among others (McNeil, Canton-Graae, & Ismail, 2000; Schiffman et al., 2002).

Collectively, these diverse studies argue for a relationship between early neurological trauma and a predisposition to schizophrenia (Mednick et al., 1998). Much remains to be learned about the neurodevelopmental bases of schizophrenia, but this relatively new line of inquiry should increase our understanding of the etiology of schizophrenic disorders.

Braff, 1994). Until recent decades, however, this theory was based more on speculation than on actual research. However, advances in brain imaging technology have yielded mountains of intriguing data since the mid-1980s. The most reliable finding is that CT scans and MRI scans (see Chapter 3) suggest an association between enlarged brain ventricles (the hollow, fluid-filled cavities in the brain depicted in **Figure 13.16**) and schizophrenic disturbance (Belger & Dichter, 2006). Enlarged ventricles are assumed to reflect the degeneration of nearby brain tissue. The significance of enlarged ventricles is hotly debated, however. This structural deterioration could be a *consequence* of schizophrenia, or it could be a contributing *cause* of the illness.

The Neurodevelopmental Hypothesis

11c

The *neurodevelopmental hypothesis* of schizophrenia asserts that schizophrenia is caused in part by various disruptions in the normal maturational pro-

Expressed Emotion

11c

Research on expressed emotion has primarily focused on how this element of family dynamics influences the *course* of schizophrenic illness, after the onset of the disorder (Leff & Vaughn, 1985). *Expressed emotion* is the degree to which a relative of a schizophrenic patient displays highly critical or emotionally overinvolved attitudes toward the patient. Audiotaped interviews of relatives' communication are carefully evaluated for critical comments, resentment toward the patient, and excessive emotional involvement (overprotective, overconcerned attitudes) (Hooley, 2004).

Studies show that a family's expressed emotion is a good predictor of the course of a schizophrenic patient's illness (Hooley, 2007). After release from a hospital, schizophrenic patients who return to a family high in expressed emotion show relapse rates three times that of patients who return to a family low in expressed emotion (Hooley & Hiller, 1998; see **Figure 13.18**). Part of the problem for patients returning to homes high in expressed emotion is that their families probably are sources of stress rather than of social support (Cutting & Docherty, 2000). And as with virtually all mental disorders, schizophrenia is influenced to some extent by life stress.

Precipitating Stress 11c

Most theories of schizophrenia assume that stress plays a key role in triggering schizophrenic disor-

ders (Walker & Tessner, 2008). According to this notion, various biological and psychological factors influence individuals' *vulnerability* to schizophrenia. High stress may then serve to precipitate a schizophrenic disorder in someone who is vulnerable (McGlashan & Hoffman, 2000). Research indicates that high stress can also trigger relapses in patients who have made progress toward recovery (Walker, Mittal, & Tessner, 2008).

Figure 13.18

Expressed emotion and relapse rates in schizophrenia. Schizophrenic patients who return to a home that is high in expressed emotion have higher relapse rates than those who return to a home low in expressed emotion. Thus, unhealthy family dynamics can influence the course of schizophrenia. (Data adapted from Leff & Vaughn, 1981)

web link 13.8

Doctor's Guide to the Internet: Schizophrenia

Produced by a communications and medical education consulting company, the free Doctor's Guide site is updated frequently to provide a current overview of the state of research on schizophrenic disorders. A more detailed set of resources for physicians parallels this site, which is intended primarily for patients and their families.

REVIEW of Key Learning Goals

13.14 Disturbed, irrational thought processes, including delusions, are the defining feature of schizophrenic disorders. Schizophrenia is also characterized by deterioration of everyday adaptive behavior, auditory hallucinations, and disturbed emotion.

13.15 Schizophrenic disorders are classified as paranoid, catatonic, disorganized, or undifferentiated. A classification scheme based on the predominance of positive versus negative symptoms has been proposed but has not supplanted the traditional classification system. Schizophrenic disorders usually emerge during adolescence or young adulthood. The course of the disorder tends to involve chronic deterioration for many patients, but with prompt, effective care recovery is possible.

13.16 Twin studies and other research show that some people inherit a genetic vulnerability to schizophrenia. The

dopamine hypothesis asserts that excess dopamine activity is the neurochemical basis for schizophrenia. The dopamine hypothesis may explain why recent research has uncovered a link between marijuana use and vulnerability to schizophrenia.

13.17 Structural abnormalities in the brain, such as enlarged ventricles, are associated with schizophrenia, but their causal significance is unclear. The neurodevelopmental hypothesis of schizophrenia asserts that schizophrenia is attributable to disruptions in the normal maturational processes of the brain before or at birth that are caused by prenatal viral infections, obstetrical complications, and other insults to the brain.

13.18 Patients who come from homes high in expressed emotion have elevated relapse rates, suggesting that unhealthy family dynamics play a role in schizophrenia. High stress may also contribute to the onset of schizophrenia and to relapse after treatment.

Culture and Pathology

We saw earlier in the chapter that judgments of normality and abnormality are influenced by cultural norms and values. In light of this situation, would it be reasonable to infer that psychological disorders are culturally variable phenomena? Social scientists are sharply divided on the answer to this question. Some embrace a *relativistic view* of psychological disorders, whereas others subscribe to a *universalistic* or *pancultural view* (Tanaka-Matsumi, 2001). Theorists who embrace the *relativistic view* argue that the crite-

ria of mental illness vary greatly across cultures and that there are no universal standards of normality and abnormality. According to the relativists, the DSM diagnostic system reflects an ethnocentric, Western, white, urban, middle- and upper-class cultural orientation that has limited relevance in other cultural contexts. In contrast, those who subscribe to the *pancultural view* argue that the criteria of mental illness are much the same around the world and that basic standards of normality and abnormality are

Key Learning Goals

13.19 Compare the relativistic versus pancultural view of psychological disorders.

13.20 Assess the extent of cultural variability in the existence of mental disorders.

AXIS I CATEGORY

SUBTYPES

PREVALENCE/ WELL-KNOWN VICTIM

ANXIETY DISORDERS

Edvard Munch's *The Scream* expresses overwhelming feelings of anxiety.

National Gallery, Oslo, Norway. SCALA/Art Resource/NY; © 2009 The Munch Museum/The Munch–Ellingsen Group/Artists Rights Society (ARS), NY.

Generalized anxiety disorder: Chronic, high level of anxiety not tied to any specific threat

Phobic disorder: Persistent, irrational fear of object or situation that presents no real danger

Panic disorder: Recurrent attacks of overwhelming anxiety that occur suddenly and unexpectedly

Obsessive-compulsive disorder: Persistent, uncontrollable intrusions of unwanted thoughts and urges to engage in senseless rituals

Posttraumatic stress disorder: Enduring psychological disturbance attributable to the experience of a major traumatic event

0 2 4 6 8 10 12 14 16 18 20

19%

Prevalence

© Bettmann/Corbis

The famous industrialist Howard Hughes suffered from obsessive-compulsive disorder.

MOOD DISORDERS

Musée d'Orsay, Paris. © Erich Lessing/ Art Resource, NY.

Vincent Van Gogh's *Portrait of Dr. Gachet* captures the profound dejection experienced in depressive disorders.

Major depressive disorder: Two or more major depressive episodes marked by feelings of sadness, worthlessness, despair

Bipolar disorder: One or more manic episodes marked by inflated self-esteem, grandiosity, and elevated mood and energy, usually accompanied by major depressive episodes

0 2 4 6 8 10 12 14 16 18 20

15%

Prevalence

Actress Ashley Judd suffered from depression.

© Amy Sussman/Getty Images

SCHIZOPHRENIC DISORDERS

The perceptual distortions seen in schizophrenia probably contributed to the bizarre imagery apparent in this portrait of a cat painted by Louis Wain.

© Derek Bayes/ Aspect Picture Library

Paranoid schizophrenia: Delusions of persecution and delusions of grandeur; frequent auditory hallucinations

Catatonic schizophrenia: Motor disturbances ranging from immobility to excessive, purposeless activity

Disorganized schizophrenia: Flat or inappropriate emotions; disorganized speech and adaptive behavior

Undifferentiated schizophrenia: Idiosyncratic mixtures of schizophrenic symptoms that cannot be placed into above three categories

0 2 4 6 8 10 12 14 16 18 20

1%

Prevalence

© Reuters/Corbis

John Nash, the Nobel Prize-winning mathematician whose story was told in the film *A Beautiful Mind*, has struggled with schizophrenia.

ETIOLOGY: BIOLOGICAL FACTORS

Genetic vulnerability: Twin studies and other evidence suggest a mild genetic predisposition to anxiety disorders.

Concordance rate (%)

Identical twins

Fraternal twins

Anxiety sensitivity: Oversensitivity to physical symptoms of anxiety may lead to overreactions to feelings of anxiety, so anxiety breeds anxiety.

Neurochemical bases: Disturbances in neural circuits releasing GABA may contribute to some disorders; abnormalities at serotonin synapses have been implicated in panic and obsessive-compulsive disorders.

Genetic vulnerability: Twin studies and other evidence suggest a genetic predisposition to mood disorders.

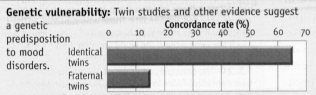

Concordance rate (%)

Identical twins

Fraternal twins

Suppressed neurogenesis: Disruption of neurogenesis may lead to reduced volume in the hippocampus and to depression.

Neurochemical bases: Disturbances in neural circuits releasing norepinephrine may contribute to some mood disorders; abnormalities at serotonin synapses have also been implicated as a factor in depression.

Genetic vulnerability: Twin studies and other evidence suggest a genetic predisposition to schizophrenic disorders.

Concordance rate (%)

Identical twins

Fraternal twins

Neurochemical bases: Overactivity in neural circuits releasing dopamine is associated with schizophrenia; but abnormalities in other neurotransmitter systems may also contribute.

Structural abnormalities in brain: Enlarged brain ventricles are associated with schizophrenia, but they may be an effect rather than a cause of the disorder.

ETIOLOGY: PSYCHOLOGICAL FACTORS

Learning: Many anxiety responses may be acquired through classical conditioning or observational learning; phobic responses may be maintained by operant reinforcement.

CS — Snow

US — Buried in avalanche

CR — Fear
UR

Stress: High stress may help to precipitate the onset of anxiety disorders.

Anxious subjects

Nonanxious subjects

Threatening interpretations endorsed (%)

Cognition: People who misinterpret harmless situations as threatening and who focus excessive attention on perceived threats are more vulnerable to anxiety disorders.

Poor social skills

Acquire fewer reinforcers, such as good friends, top jobs

Court rejection because of irritability, pessimism

Gravitate to people who confirm negative self-views

Increased vulnerability to depression

Negative thinking → Depression

Interpersonal roots: Behavioral theories emphasize how inadequate social skills can result in a paucity of reinforcers and other effects that make people vulnerable to depression.

Stress: High stress can act as precipitating factor that triggers depression or bipolar disorder.

Cognition: Negative thinking can contribute to the development of depression; rumination may extend and amplify depression.

Expressed emotion: A family's expressed emotion is a good predictor of the course of a schizophrenic patient's illness.

Stress: High stress can precipitate schizophrenic disorder in people who are vulnerable to schizophrenia.

Two-year relapse rate (%)

Expressed emotion in patient's family — High

Low

Disruption of normal maturational processes before or at birth → Subtle neurological damage → Increased vulnerability to schizophrenia

The neurodevelopmental hypothesis: Insults to the brain sustained during prenatal development or at birth may disrupt maturational processes in the brain resulting in elevated vulnerability to schizophrenia.

Abnormal Behavior: Myths and Realities

▌ The medical model assumes that it is useful to view abnormal behavior as a disease. This view has been criticized on the grounds that it turns ethical questions about deviance into medical questions. Although there are some problems with the medical model, the concept is useful if one remembers that it is only an analogy.

▌ Three criteria are used in deciding whether people suffer from psychological disorders: deviance, personal distress, and maladaptive behavior. To some extent, judgments about mental illness are value judgments that reflect cultural norms and social trends, as well as scientific knowledge.

▌ DSM-IV is the official psychodiagnostic classification system in the United States. This system asks for information about patients on five axes or dimensions. Researchers are currently working on the development of DSM-V.

Anxiety Disorders

▌ The anxiety disorders include generalized anxiety disorder, phobic disorder, panic disorder, obsessive-compulsive disorder, and posttraumatic stress disorder. These disorders may have a genetic component. Abnormalities in neurotransmitter activity at GABA and serotonin synapses may also play a role.

▌ Many anxiety responses, especially phobias, may be caused by classical conditioning and maintained by operant conditioning. Cognitive theorists maintain that a tendency to overinterpret harmless situations as threatening makes some people vulnerable to anxiety disorders. Stress may also contribute to the development of anxiety disorders.

Somatoform Disorders

▌ Somatoform disorders include somatization disorder, conversion disorder, and hypochondriasis. People with these disorders may focus excessive attention on bodily processes. Somatoform disorders may be a learned avoidance strategy reinforced by attention and sympathy. Neuroticism and insecure attachment may also increase vulnerability to these disorders.

Dissociative Disorders

▌ Dissociative disorders include dissociative amnesia, fugue, and dissociative identity disorder. Dissociative identity disorder may be rooted in emotional trauma that occurred during childhood, although some theorists argue that the disorder typically involves intentional role playing.

Mood Disorders

▌ The principal mood disorders are unipolar depression and bipolar disorder. Mood disorders are episodic. Unipolar depression is much more common than bipolar disorder. Depressive disorders are more common in women than men. Mood disorders are associated with a substantial elevation in suicide rates.

▌ People vary in their genetic vulnerability to mood disorders. These disorders are accompanied by changes in neurochemical activity in the brain. Depression is associated with reduced hippocampal volume and suppressed neurogenesis. Cognitive models posit that negative thinking and rumination contribute to depression. Depression is often rooted in interpersonal inadequacies and setbacks and sometimes is stress related.

Schizophrenic Disorders

▌ Schizophrenic disorders are characterized by deterioration of adaptive behavior, irrational thought, distorted perception, and disturbed mood. Schizophrenic disorders are classified as paranoid, catatonic, disorganized, or undifferentiated. A new classification scheme based on the predominance of positive versus negative symptoms is under study.

▌ Research has linked schizophrenia to genetic vulnerability, changes in neurotransmitter activity, structural abnormalities in the brain, and disruptions in the normal maturational processes of the brain before or at birth. Precipitating stress and unhealthy family dynamics (high expressed emotion) may also contribute to the development of schizophrenia.

Culture and Pathology

▌ The principal categories of psychological disturbance are identifiable in all cultures. However, milder disorders may go unrecognized in some societies, and culture-bound disorders further illustrate the diversity of abnormal behavior around the world.

Reflecting on the Chapter's Themes

▌ This chapter highlighted four of our unifying themes, showing that psychological disorders are governed by multiple causes, that heredity and environment jointly influence mental disorders, that psychology evolves in a sociohistorical context, and that pathology is characterized by both cultural variance and invariance.

PERSONAL APPLICATION Understanding Eating Disorders

▌ The principal eating disorders are anorexia nervosa and bulimia nervosa. Both appear to be largely a product of modern, affluent Westernized culture. Females account for 90%–95% of eating disorders.

▌ There appears to be a genetic vulnerability to eating disorders, which may be mediated by heritable personality traits. Cultural pressures on young women to be thin clearly help foster eating disorders. Unhealthy family dynamics and disturbed thinking can also contribute.

CRITICAL THINKING APPLICATION Working with Probabilities in Thinking About Mental Illness

▌ Probability estimates can be distorted by the representativeness heuristic, which involves basing the estimated probability of an event on how similar it is to the typical prototype of that event. Cumulative probabilities are additive, whereas conjunctive probabilities are always less than the likelihood of the least likely event happening alone. Probability estimates can be biased by the availability heuristic, which involves basing the estimated probability of an event on the ease with which relevant instances come to mind.

PsykTrek Preview

ABNORMAL BEHAVIOR AND THERAPY
11a Anxiety Disorders

Review

GABA

GABA synapse

Recent evidence suggests that disturbances in the neural circuits using GABA may play a role in some types of anxiety disorders, although abnormalities in serotonin circuits have been linked to obsessive-compulsive disorders.

ABNORMAL BEHAVIOR AND THERAPY
11b Mood Disorders

Depression

Diagnostic criteria

Case history

Vincent van Gogh's *Portrait of Dr. Gachet* captures the overpowering dejection experienced by people in episodes of serious depression.

Click on the buttons to view the diagnostic criteria for major depressive disorder and to read a case history.

© Erich Lessing/Art Resource, NY

Visit Module 11a (*Anxiety Disorders*) to dig deeper into the nature and causes of anxiety-dominated disturbances, and see a patient describe his panic attacks.

Increase your understanding of depression and bipolar disorder by working through Module 11b (*Mood Disorders*), which will provide you with detailed diagnostic criteria and case histories for these disorders.

1. According to Thomas Szasz, abnormal behavior usually involves:
   A. behavior that is statistically unusual.
   B. behavior that deviates from social norms.
   C. a disease of the mind.
   D. biological imbalance.

2. Although Sue always feels a high level of dread, worry, and anxiety, she still manages to meet her daily responsibilities. Sue's behavior:
   A. should not be considered abnormal, since her adaptive functioning is not impaired.
   B. should not be considered abnormal, since everyone sometimes experiences worry and anxiety.
   C. can still be considered abnormal, since she feels great personal distress.
   D. both a and b are true.

3. The observation that people acquire phobias of ancient sources of threat (such as snakes) much more readily than modern sources of threat (such as electrical outlets) can best be explained by:
   A. classical conditioning.
   B. operant conditioning.
   C. observational learning.
   D. preparedness/an evolved module for fear learning.

4. Which of the following statements about dissociative identity disorder is true?
   A. The original personality is always aware of the alternate personalities.
   B. Dissociative identity disorder is an alternate name for schizophrenia.
   C. The personalities are typically all quite similar to one another.
   D. Starting in the 1970s, there was a dramatic increase in the diagnosis of dissociative identity disorder.

5. People with unipolar disorder experience _____ ; people with bipolar disorder experience _____ .
   A. alternating periods of depression and mania; mania only
   B. depression only; alternating periods of depression and mania
   C. mania only; alternating periods of depression and mania
   D. alternating periods of depression and mania; depression and mania simultaneously

6. People who consistently come up with _____ explanations for negative events are more prone to depression.
   A. overly optimistic
   B. pessimistic
   C. delusional
   D. dysthymic

7. Mary believes that while she sleeps at night, space creatures are attacking her and invading her uterus, where they will multiply until they are ready to take over the world. Mary was chosen for this task, she believes, because she is the only one with the power to help the space creatures succeed. Mary would most likely be diagnosed as _____ schizophrenic.
   A. paranoid
   B. catatonic
   C. disorganized
   D. undifferentiated

8. As an alternative to the current classification scheme, it has been proposed that schizophrenic disorders be divided into just two categories based on:
   A. whether the prognosis is favorable or unfavorable.
   B. whether the disorder is mild or severe.
   C. the predominance of thought disturbances versus emotional disturbances.
   D. the predominance of negative versus positive symptoms.

9. Most of the drugs that are useful in the treatment of schizophrenia are known to dampen _____ activity in the brain, suggesting that disruptions in the activity of this neurotransmitter may contribute to the development of the disorder.
   A. norepinephrine
   B. serotonin
   C. acetylcholine
   D. dopamine

10. Research suggests that there is an association between schizophrenia and:
    A. atrophied brain ventricles.
    B. enlarged brain ventricles.
    C. hippocampal degeneration.
    D. abnormalities in the cerebellum.

11. Those who embrace a relativistic view of psychological disorders would assert that:
    A. the criteria of mental illness vary greatly across cultures.
    B. there are universal standards of normality and abnormality.
    C. Western diagnostic concepts have validity and utility in other cultural contexts.
    D. both B and C are true.

12. Victims of _____ are more likely to recognize that their eating behavior is pathological; the more life-threatening eating disorder is _____ .
    A. anorexia nervosa; bulimia nervosa
    B. bulimia nervosa; anorexia nervosa
    C. anorexia nervosa; anorexia nervosa
    D. bulimia nervosa; bulimia nervosa

Answers

1 B pp. 449–450
2 C pp. 450–451
3 D p. 457
4 D pp. 460–461
5 B pp. 461–462
6 B pp. 465–466
7 A pp. 468–469
8 D p. 469
9 D pp. 470–471
10 B p. 472
11 A p. 473
12 B p. 478

PSYKTREK PREVIEW

Explore Module 11c (*Schizophrenic Disorders*) for more information on schizophrenic disturbances and their causes.

Try your hand at diagnosing three patients based on video interviews in Simulation 9 (*Clinical Diagnosis*).

14

Treatment of Psychological Disorders

Snow-covered bridge, location unknown © Richard T. Nowitz/National Geographic/Getty Images

The Elements of the Treatment Process
Treatments: How Many Types Are There?
Clients: Who Seeks Therapy?
Therapists: Who Provides Professional Treatment?

Insight Therapies
Psychoanalysis
Client-Centered Therapy
Therapies Inspired by Positive Psychology
Group Therapy
How Effective Are Insight Therapies?

Behavior Therapies
Systematic Desensitization
Aversion Therapy
Social Skills Training
Cognitive-Behavioral Treatments
How Effective Are Behavior Therapies?

Biomedical Therapies
Treatment with Drugs
Electroconvulsive Therapy (ECT)
New Brain Stimulation Techniques

Illustrated Overview of Five Major Approaches to Treatment

Current Trends and Issues in Treatment
Grappling with the Constraints of Managed Care
Increasing Multicultural Sensitivity in Treatment

Institutional Treatment in Transition
Disenchantment with Mental Hospitals
Deinstitutionalization
Mental Illness, the Revolving Door, and Homelessness

Reflecting on the Chapter's Themes

PERSONAL APPLICATION ‖ **Looking for a Therapist**
Where Do You Find Therapeutic Services?
Is the Therapist's Profession or Sex Important?
Is Treatment Always Expensive?
Is the Therapist's Theoretical Approach Important?
What Is Therapy Like?

CRITICAL THINKING APPLICATION ‖ **From Crisis to Wellness—But Was It the Therapy?**

Recap

Practice Test

What do you picture when you hear the term *psychotherapy*? Unless you've had some personal exposure to therapy, your image of it has likely been shaped by portrayals you've seen on television or in the movies. A good example is the 1999 film *Analyze This,* a comedy starring Billy Crystal as psychiatrist Ben Sobol and Robert De Niro as Paul Vitti, a mob boss who is suffering from "panic attacks." Complications develop when Vitti—a man no one says "no" to—demands that Dr. Sobol cure him of his problem before his rivals in crime turn his "weakness" against him.

With his glasses and beard, Billy Crystal's Dr. Sobol resembles many people's picture of a therapist. Like many movie therapists, Dr. Sobol practices "talk therapy." He listens attentively as his patients talk about what is troubling them. Occasionally he offers comments that reflect their thoughts and feelings back to them or that offer some illuminating insight into their problems. We can get a feeling for his approach from a funny scene in which the uneducated Vitti turns Dr. Sobol's techniques on him:

VITTI: *Hey, let's see how you like it. Let's talk about your father.*
SOBOL: *Let's not.*
VITTI: *What kind of work does your father do?*
SOBOL: *It's not important.*
VITTI: *You paused.*
SOBOL: *I did not.*
VITTI: *You just paused. That means you had a feeling, like a thought . . .*
SOBOL: *You know, we're running out of time. Let's not waste it talking about my problems.*
VITTI: *Your father's a problem?*
SOBOL: *No!*
VITTI: *That's what you just said.*
SOBOL: *I did not!*
VITTI: *Now you're upset.*
SOBOL: *(getting upset): I am not upset!*
VITTI: *Yes you are.*
SOBOL: *Will you stop it!*
VITTI: *You know what, I'm getting good at this.*

As in this scene, the film derives much of its humor from popular conceptions—and misconceptions—about therapy. The technique that Vitti makes fun of does resemble one type of therapeutic process. Like Vitti, many people do associate needing therapy with having a shameful weakness. Further, therapy is often of considerable benefit in helping people make significant changes in their lives—even if those changes are not as dramatic as Vitti's giving up his life of crime at the end of the movie. On the other hand, the film's comic exaggerations also highlight some misconceptions about therapy, including the following:

The popular film Analyze This *derived much of its humor from common misconceptions about the process of psychotherapy.*

• Vitti is driven to see a "shrink" because he feels like he's "falling apart." In fact, therapists help people with all kinds of problems. People need not have severe symptoms of mental illness to benefit from therapy.

• Dr. Sobol is a psychiatrist, but most therapists are not. And although Dr. Sobol quotes Freud and the film's plot turns on interpreting a dream (in this case, it's the psychiatrist's dream!), many therapists make little or no use of Freudian techniques.

• Dr. Sobol relies on "talk therapy" to produce insights that will help his patients overcome their troubles. In reality, this approach is only one of the many techniques used by therapists.

• Dr. Sobol "cures" Vitti by getting him to acknowledge a traumatic event in his childhood (the death of his father) that is at the root of his problems. But only rarely does therapy produce a single dramatic insight that results in wholesale change for the client.

In this chapter, we'll take a down-to-earth look at *psychotherapy,* using the term in its broadest sense, to refer to all the diverse approaches used in the treatment of mental disorders and psychological problems. We'll start by discussing some general questions about how treatment is provided. After considering these issues, we'll examine the goals, techniques, and effectiveness of some of the more widely used approaches to therapy and discuss recent trends and issues in treatment, including changes in institutional treatment. In the Personal Application, we'll look at practical questions related to finding and choosing a therapist. And in the Critical Thinking Application we'll address problems involved in determining whether therapy actually helps.

The Elements of the Treatment Process

Key Learning Goals

14.1 Identify the three major categories of therapy, and discuss patterns of treatment seeking.

14.2 Distinguish the various types of mental health professionals involved in the provision of therapy.

Sigmund Freud is widely credited with launching modern psychotherapy. Ironically, the landmark case that inspired Freud was actually treated by one of his colleagues, Josef Breuer. Around 1880, Breuer began to treat a young woman known in the annals of psychiatry as Anna O (her real name, which came out years later, was Bertha Pappenheim). Anna exhibited a variety of physical maladies, including headaches, coughing, and a loss of feeling and movement in her right arm. Much to his surprise, Breuer discovered that Anna's physical symptoms cleared up when he encouraged her to talk about emotionally charged experiences from her past.

When Breuer and Freud discussed the case, they speculated that talking things through had enabled Anna to drain off bottled-up emotions that had caused her symptoms. Breuer found the intense emotional exchange in this treatment not to his liking, so he didn't follow through on his discovery. However, Freud applied Breuer's insight to other patients, and his successes led him to develop a systematic treatment procedure, which he called *psychoanalysis*. Anna O called her treatment "the talking cure." However, as you'll see, psychotherapy isn't always curative, and many modern therapies place little emphasis on talking.

Freud's breakthrough ushered in a century of progress for psychotherapy. Psychoanalysis spawned many offspring as Freud's followers developed their own systems of treatment. Since then, approaches to psychotherapy have steadily grown more numerous, more diverse, and more effective.

Treatments: How Many Types Are There?

In their efforts to help people, psychotherapists use many treatment methods. One expert (Kazdin, 1994) estimates that there may be over 400 different approaches to treatment! Fortunately, we can impose some order on this chaos. As varied as therapists' procedures are, approaches to treatment can be classified into three major categories:

1. *Insight therapies*. Insight therapy is "talk therapy" in the tradition of Freud's psychoanalysis. In insight therapies, clients engage in complex, often lengthy verbal interactions with their therapists. The goal in these discussions is to pursue increased insight regarding the nature of the client's difficulties and to sort through possible solutions.

2. *Behavior therapies*. Behavior therapies are based on the principles of learning, which were introduced in Chapter 6. Instead of emphasizing personal insights, behavior therapists make direct efforts to alter problematic responses (phobias, for instance) and maladaptive habits (drug use, for instance).

3. *Biomedical therapies*. Biomedical approaches to therapy involve interventions into a person's biological functioning. The most widely used procedures are drug therapy and electroconvulsive (shock) therapy. As the name bio*medical* therapies suggests, these treatments have traditionally been provided only by physicians with a medical degree (usually psychiatrists). This situation is changing, however, as psychologists have been campaigning for prescription privileges (Norfleet, 2002; Welsh, 2003). To date psychologists have obtained prescription authority in two states (New Mexico and Louisiana) and they have made legislative progress toward this goal in many other states (Long, 2005). Although some psychologists have argued against pursuing the right to prescribe medication (Heiby, 2002; Robiner et al., 2003), the movement is gathering momentum and seems likely to prevail.

Clients: Who Seeks Therapy?

In the therapeutic triad (therapists, treatments, clients), the greatest diversity of all is seen among the clients. According to the 1999 U.S. Surgeon General's report on mental health (U.S. Department of Health and Human Services, 1999) about 15% of the U.S. population use mental health services in a given year. These people, who do not necessarily have a full-fledged mental disorder, bring to therapy the full range of human problems: anxiety, depression, unsatisfactory interpersonal relations, troublesome habits, poor self-control, low self-esteem, marital conflicts, self-doubt, a sense of emptiness, and feelings of personal stagnation.

People vary considerably in their willingness to seek psychotherapy. One study found that even when people perceive a need for professional assistance, only 59% actually seek professional help (Mojtabai, Olfson, & Mechanic, 2002). As you can see in **Figure 14.1**, women are more likely than men to receive therapy. Treatment is also more likely when people have medical insurance and when they have more education (Olfson et al., 2002; Wang, Lane et al., 2005). *Unfortunately, it appears that many people who need therapy don't receive it* (Kessler et al., 2005b).

The case of Anna O, whose real name was Bertha Pappenheim, provided the inspiration for Sigmund Freud's invention of psychoanalysis.

As **Figure 14.2** shows, only a portion of the people who need treatment get it. People who could benefit from therapy do not seek it for a variety of reasons. Lack of health insurance and cost concerns appear to be major barriers to obtaining needed care for many people. According to the Surgeon General's report, the biggest roadblock is the "stigma surrounding the receipt of mental health treatment." Unfortunately, many people—like Paul Vitti in *Analyze This*—equate seeking therapy with admitting personal weakness.

Therapists: Who Provides Professional Treatment?

Friends and relatives may provide you with excellent advice about your personal problems, but their assistance does not qualify as therapy. Psychotherapy refers to *professional* treatment by someone with special training. However, a common source of confusion about psychotherapy is the variety of "helping professions" involved (Murstein & Fontaine, 1993). Psychology and psychiatry are the principal professions involved in the delivery of psychotherapy, providing the lion's share of mental health care. However, treatment is also provided by other types of therapists. Let's look at these mental health professions.

Psychologists

Two types of psychologists may provide therapy, although the distinction between them is more theoretical than real. *Clinical psychologists* and *counseling psychologists* specialize in the diagnosis and treatment of psychological disorders and everyday behavioral problems. In theory, clinical psychologists' training emphasizes the treatment of full-fledged disorders. In contrast, counseling psychologists' training is supposed to be slanted toward the treatment of everyday adjustment problems in normal people. In practice, however, clinical and counseling psychologists overlap greatly in training, skills, and the clientele they serve. Both types of psychologists must earn a doctoral degree (Ph.D., Psy.D., or Ed.D.). In providing therapy, psychologists use either insight or

Figure 14.2

Psychological disorders and professional treatment. Not everyone who has a psychological disorder receives professional treatment, and not everyone who seeks treatment has a clear disorder. This graph, from the Surgeon General's report on mental health, shows that 15% of the U.S. adult population receive mental health treatment each year. Almost half of these people (7%) do not receive a psychiatric diagnosis, although some of them probably have milder disorders that are not assessed in epidemiological research. This graph also shows that over two-thirds of the people who *do* have disorders do *not* receive professional treatment. (Data from U.S. Department of Health & Human Services, 1999)

Figure 14.1

Therapy utilization rates. Olfson and colleagues (2002) gathered data on the use of nonhospital outpatient mental health services in the United States in relation to various demographic variables. In regard to marital status, utilization rates are particularly high among those who are divorced or separated. The use of therapy is greater among those who have more education, and, in terms of age, utilization peaks in the 35–44 age bracket. Females are more likely to pursue therapy than males are, but utilization rates are extremely low among ethnic minorities.

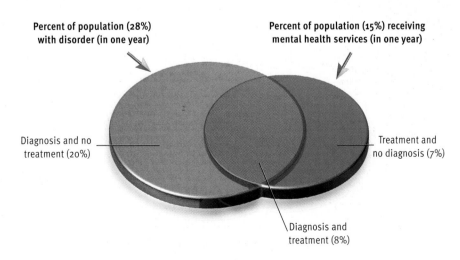

Percent of population (28%) with disorder (in one year)

Percent of population (15%) receiving mental health services (in one year)

Diagnosis and no treatment (20%)

Treatment and no diagnosis (7%)

Diagnosis and treatment (8%)

web link 14.1

Online Dictionary of Mental Health

This thematically arranged "dictionary" at the University of Sheffield (UK) Medical School comprises diverse links related to many forms of psychotherapy, the treatment of psychological disorders, and general issues of mental health.

behavioral approaches. Clinical and counseling psychologists do psychological testing as well as psychotherapy, and many also conduct research.

Psychiatrists

Psychiatrists are physicians who specialize in the diagnosis and treatment of psychological disorders. Many psychiatrists also treat everyday behavioral problems. However, in comparison to psychologists, psychiatrists devote more time to relatively severe disorders (schizophrenia, mood disorders) and less time to everyday marital, family, job, and school problems. Psychiatrists have an M.D. degree. In their treatment efforts, psychiatrists increasingly emphasize drug therapies (Olfson, Marcus, & Pincus, 1999), which the other, nonmedical helping professions generally have not been able to provide.

Other Mental Health Professionals

Several other mental health professions provide psychotherapy services. *Psychiatric social workers* and *psychiatric nurses* often work as part of a treatment team with a psychologist or psychiatrist. Although social workers have traditionally worked in hospitals and social service agencies, many also provide a wide range of therapeutic services as independent practitioners. Many kinds of *counselors* also provide therapeutic services. They often specialize in particular types of problems, such as vocational counseling, marital counseling, rehabilitation counseling, and drug counseling.

Although there are clear differences among the helping professions in education, training, and approach to therapy, their roles in the treatment process overlap considerably. In this chapter, we will refer to psychologists or psychiatrists as needed, but otherwise we'll use the terms *clinician, therapist,* and *mental health professional* to refer to psychotherapists of all kinds, regardless of their professional degree.

Now that we have discussed the basic elements in psychotherapy, we can examine specific approaches to treatment in terms of their goals, procedures, and effectiveness. We'll begin with some representative insight therapies.

REVIEW of Key Learning Goals

14.1 Approaches to treatment are diverse, but they can be grouped into three categories: insight therapies, behavior therapies, and biomedical therapies. Clients bring a wide variety of problems to therapy and do not necessarily have a disorder. People vary in their willingness to seek treatment. Unfortunately, many people who need therapy do not receive it, in part because of the stigma attached to therapy.

14.2 Therapists come from a variety of professional backgrounds. Clinical and counseling psychologists, psychiatrists, clinical social workers, psychiatric nurses, and counselors are the principal providers of therapeutic services. Each of these professions shows different preferences for approaches to treatment. Psychologists typically practice insight or behavior therapy. Psychiatrists rely more heavily on drug therapies.

Key Learning Goals

14.3 Explain the logic of psychoanalysis and the techniques by which analysts probe the unconscious.

14.4 Clarify the nature of resistance and transference in psychoanalysis.

14.5 Understand the role of therapeutic climate and therapeutic process in client-centered therapy.

14.6 Discuss new approaches to insight therapy inspired by the positive psychology movement.

14.7 Articulate how group therapy is generally conducted, and identify some advantages of this approach.

14.8 Assess the efficacy of insight therapies.

Insight Therapies

Many schools of thought offer ideas about how to do insight therapy. Therapists with various theoretical orientations use different methods to pursue different kinds of insights. However, what these varied approaches have in common is that **insight therapies involve verbal interactions intended to enhance clients' self-knowledge and thus promote healthful changes in personality and behavior.** In this section, we'll delve into psychoanalysis, client-centered therapy, and new approaches fostered by the positive psychology movement. We'll also discuss how insight therapy can be done with groups as well as individuals.

Psychoanalysis   11d

After the case of Anna O, Sigmund Freud worked as a psychotherapist for almost 50 years in Vienna.

Through a painstaking process of trial and error, he developed innovative techniques for the treatment of psychological disorders and distress. His system of *psychoanalysis* came to dominate psychiatry for many decades. Although this dominance has eroded in recent years, a diverse collection of psychoanalytic approaches to therapy continue to evolve and to remain influential today (Gabbard, 2005; McWilliams & Weinberger, 2003; Ursano & Silberman, 2003).

Psychoanalysis **is an insight therapy that emphasizes the recovery of unconscious conflicts, motives, and defenses through techniques such as free association and transference.** To appreciate the logic of psychoanalysis, we have to look at Freud's thinking about the roots of mental disorders. Freud mostly treated anxiety-dominated disturbances, such as phobic, panic, obsessive-compulsive, and conversion disorders, which were then called *neuroses*.

Freud believed that neurotic problems are caused by unconscious conflicts left over from early childhood. As explained in Chapter 11, he thought that people depend on defense mechanisms to avoid confronting these conflicts, which remain hidden in the depths of the unconscious (see **Figure 14.3**). However, he noted that defensive maneuvers tend to be only partially successful in alleviating anxiety, guilt, and other distressing emotions. With this model in mind, let's take a look at the therapeutic procedures used in psychoanalysis.

Figure 14.3

Freud's view of the roots of disorders. According to Freud, unconscious conflicts between the id, ego, and superego sometimes lead to anxiety. This discomfort may lead to pathological reliance on defensive behavior.

Probing the Unconscious 11d

Given Freud's assumptions, we can see that the logic of psychoanalysis is quite simple. The analyst attempts to probe the murky depths of the unconscious to discover the unresolved conflicts causing the client's neurotic behavior. In this effort to explore the unconscious, the therapist relies on two techniques: free association and dream analysis.

In *free association* clients spontaneously express their thoughts and feelings exactly as they occur, with as little censorship as possible. In free associating, clients talk about anything that comes to mind, regardless of how trivial, silly, or embarrassing it might be. The analyst studies these free associations for clues about what is going on in the unconscious. In *dream analysis* the therapist interprets the symbolic meaning of the client's dreams. For Freud, dreams were the "royal road to the unconscious," the most direct means of access to patients' innermost conflicts, wishes, and impulses. Psychoanalytic clients are encouraged and trained to remember their dreams, which they describe in therapy.

To better illustrate these matters, let's look at an actual case treated through psychoanalysis (adapted from Greenson, 1967, pp. 40–41). Mr. N was troubled by an unsatisfactory marriage. He claimed to love his wife, but he preferred sexual relations with prostitutes. Mr. N reported that his parents also endured lifelong marital difficulties. His childhood conflicts about their relationship appeared to be related to his problems. Both dream analysis and free association can be seen in the following description of a session in Mr. N's treatment:

Mr. N reported a fragment of a dream. All that he could remember is that he was waiting for a red traffic light to change when he felt that someone had bumped into him from behind. . . . The associations led to Mr. N's love of cars, especially sports cars. He loved the sensation, in particular, of whizzing by those fat, old expensive cars. . . . His father always hinted that he had been a great athlete, but he never substantiated it. . . . Mr. N doubted whether his father could really perform. His father would

flirt with a waitress in a cafe or make sexual remarks about women passing by, but he seemed to be showing off. If he were really sexual, he wouldn't resort to that.

As is characteristic of free association, Mr. N's train of thought meandered about with little direction. Nonetheless, clues about his unconscious conflicts were apparent. What did Mr. N's therapist extract from this session? The therapist saw sexual overtones in the dream fragment, where Mr. N was bumped from behind. The therapist also inferred that Mr. N had a competitive orientation toward his father, based on the free association about whizzing by fat, old expensive cars. As you can see, analysts must *interpret* their clients' dreams and free associations. Contrary to popular belief, analysts generally don't try to dazzle clients with startling revelations. Instead, analysts move forward inch by inch, offering interpretations that should be just out of the client's own reach. Mr. N's therapist eventually offered the following interpretations to his client:

I said to Mr. N near the end of the hour that I felt he was struggling with his feelings about his father's sexual life. He seemed to be saying that his father was sexually not a very potent man. . . . He also recalls that he once found a packet of condoms under his father's pillow when he was an adolescent and he thought, "My father must be going to prostitutes." I then intervened and pointed out that the condoms under his father's pillow seemed to indicate more obviously that his father used the condoms with his mother, who slept in the same bed. However, Mr. N wanted to believe his wish-fulfilling fantasy: mother doesn't want sex with father and father is not very potent. The patient was silent and the hour ended.

As you may have already guessed, the therapist concluded that Mr. N's difficulties were rooted in an Oedipal complex (see Chapter 11). He had unresolved sexual feelings toward his mother and hostile feelings about his father. These unconscious conflicts, rooted in Mr. N's childhood, were distorting his intimate relations as an adult.

Sigmund Freud

"The news that reaches your consciousness is incomplete and often not to be relied on."

National Library of Medicine

web link 14.2

The American Psychoanalytic Association

The website for this professional organization provides a great deal of useful information about psychoanalytic approaches to treatment. The resources include news releases, background information on psychoanalysis, an engine for literature searches, and a bookstore.

Resistance and Transference   11d

How would you expect Mr. N to respond to the therapist's suggestion that he was in competition with his father for the sexual attention of his mother? Obviously, most clients would have great difficulty accepting such an interpretation. Freud fully expected clients to display some resistance to therapeutic efforts. *Resistance* **refers to largely unconscious defensive maneuvers intended to hinder the progress of therapy.** Resistance is assumed to be an inevitable part of the psychoanalytic process (Samberg & Marcus, 2005). Why would clients try to resist the helping process? Because they don't want to face up to the painful, disturbing conflicts that they have buried in their unconscious. Although they have sought help, they are reluctant to confront their real problems. Analysts use a variety of strategies to deal with clients' resistance. Often, a key consideration is the handling of transference.

Transference **occurs when clients start relating to their therapists in ways that mimic critical relationships in their lives.** Thus, a client might start relating to a therapist as if the therapist were an overprotective mother, a rejecting brother, or a passive spouse. In a sense, the client *transfers* conflicting feelings about important people onto the therapist. Psychoanalysts often encourage transference so that clients can reenact relations with crucial people in the context of therapy. These reenactments can help bring repressed feelings and conflicts to the surface, allowing the client to work through them.

Undergoing psychoanalysis is not easy. It can be a slow, painful process of self-examination that routinely requires three to five years of hard work. It tends to be a lengthy process because patients need time to gradually work through their problems and genuinely accept unnerving revelations (Williams, 2005). Ultimately, if resistance and transference can be handled effectively, the therapist's interpreta-

tions should lead the client to profound insights. For instance, Mr. N eventually admitted, "The old boy is probably right, it does tickle me to imagine that my mother preferred me and I could beat out my father. Later, I wondered whether this had something to do with my own screwed-up sex life with my wife." According to Freud, once clients recognize the unconscious sources of conflicts, they can resolve these conflicts and discard their neurotic defenses.

Modern Psychodynamic Treatments

Though still available, classical psychoanalysis as done by Freud is not widely practiced anymore (Kay & Kay, 2003). Freud's psychoanalytic method was geared to a particular kind of clientele that he was seeing in Vienna many years ago. As his followers fanned out across Europe and America, many found it necessary to adapt psychoanalysis to different cultures, changing times, and new kinds of patients (Karasu, 2005). Thus, many variations on Freud's original approach to psychoanalysis have developed over the years. These descendants of psychoanalysis are collectively known as *psychodynamic approaches* to therapy.

Some of these adaptations, such as those by Carl Jung (1917) and Alfred Adler (1927), were sweeping revisions based on fundamental differences in theory. Other variations, such as those devised by Melanie Klein (1948) and Heinz Kohut (1971), involved more subtle changes in theory. Still other revisions (Alexander, 1954; Stekel, 1950) simply involved efforts to modernize and streamline psychoanalytic techniques.

As a result, today we have a rich diversity of psychodynamic approaches to therapy (Magnavita, 2008). Recent reviews of these treatments suggest that interpretation, resistance, and transference continue to play key roles in therapeutic effects (Luborsky & Barrett, 2006). For example, evidence suggests that the amount of resistance manifested in psychodynamic therapy predicts the outcome of therapy. People who exhibit more resistance are less likely to experience a positive outcome and more likely to drop out of therapy (Luborsky & Barrett, 2006). Recent research also suggests that psychodynamic approaches can be helpful in the treatment of a diverse array of disorders, including panic disorder, borderline personality disorder, and substance abuse (Gibbons, Crits-Christoph, & Hearon, 2008).

In psychoanalysis, the therapist encourages the client to reveal thoughts, feelings, dreams, and memories, which can then be interpreted in relation to the client's current problems.

© Bruce Ayres/Stone/Getty Images

Client-Centered Therapy   11d

You may have heard of people going into therapy to "find themselves" or to "get in touch with their real feelings." These now-popular phrases emerged out of the *human potential movement,* which was stimulated in part by the work of Carl Rogers (1951, 1986). Using a humanistic perspective, Rogers devised client-centered therapy (also known as person-centered therapy) in the 1940s and 1950s.

Client-centered therapy is an insight therapy that emphasizes providing a supportive emotional climate for clients, who play a major role in determining the pace and direction of their therapy. Rogers's theory about the principal causes of neurotic anxieties is quite different from the Freudian explanation. As discussed in Chapter 11, Rogers maintains that most personal distress is due to inconsistency, or "incongruence," between a person's self-concept and reality (see **Figure 14.4**). According to his theory, incongruence makes people feel threatened by realistic feedback about themselves from others, and anxiety about such feedback often leads to reliance on defense mechanisms, to distortions of reality, and to stifled personal growth. Excessive incongruence is thought to be rooted in clients' overdependence on others for approval and acceptance.

Given Rogers's theory, client-centered therapists stalk insights that are quite different from the repressed conflicts that psychoanalysts go after. Client-centered therapists help clients realize that they do not have to worry constantly about pleasing others and winning acceptance. They help people restructure their self-concept to correspond better to reality. Ultimately, they try to foster self-acceptance and personal growth.

Therapeutic Climate

11d

According to Rogers, the *process* of therapy is not as important as the emotional *climate* in which the therapy takes place. He believes that it is critical for the therapist to provide a warm, supportive climate in which clients can confront their shortcomings without feeling threatened. The lack of threat should reduce clients' defensive tendencies and thus help them open up. To create this supportive atmosphere, client-centered therapists must provide three conditions: (1) *genuineness* (honest communication),

(2) *unconditional positive regard* (nonjudgmental acceptance of the client), and (3) *accurate empathy* (understanding of the client's point of view).

Therapeutic Process

11d

In client-centered therapy, the client and therapist work together as equals. The therapist provides relatively little guidance and keeps interpretation and advice to a minimum. The therapist's key task is *clarification.* Client-centered therapists try to function like a human mirror, reflecting statements back to their clients, but with enhanced clarity. They help clients become more aware of their true feelings by highlighting themes that may be obscure in the clients' rambling discourse.

By working with clients to clarify their feelings, client-centered therapists hope to gradually build toward more far-reaching insights. In particular, they try to help clients better understand their interpersonal relationships and become more comfortable with their genuine selves. Obviously, these are ambitious goals. Client-centered therapy resembles psychoanalysis in that both seek to achieve a major reconstruction of a client's personality.

Carl Rogers
"To my mind, empathy is in itself a healing agent."

Client-centered therapists emphasize the importance of a supportive emotional climate in therapy. They also work to clarify, rather than interpret, the feelings expressed by their patients.

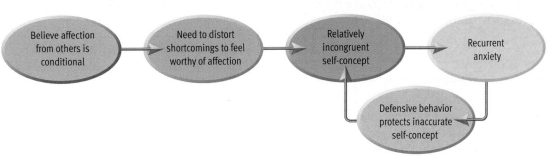

Believe affection from others is conditional → Need to distort shortcomings to feel worthy of affection → Relatively incongruent self-concept → Recurrent anxiety

Defensive behavior protects inaccurate self-concept

Figure 14.4

Rogers's view of the roots of disorders. Rogers's theory asserts that anxiety and self-defeating behavior are rooted in an incongruent self-concept that makes one prone to recurrent anxiety, which triggers defensive behavior, which fuels more incongruence.

Therapies Inspired by Positive Psychology

The growth of the positive psychology movement has begun to inspire new approaches to insight therapy (Duckworth, Steen, & Seligman, 2005). As noted in Chapters 1 and 9, *positive psychology* uses theory and research to better understand the positive, adaptive, creative, and fulfilling aspects of human existence. The advocates of positive psychology maintain that the field has historically focused far too heavily on pathology, weakness, and suffering (and how to heal these conditions) rather than health and resilience (Seligman, 2003; Seligman & Csikszentmihalyi, 2000). They argue for increased research on contentment, well-being, human strengths, and positive emotions.

This philosophical approach has led to new therapeutic interventions. For example, *well-being therapy*, developed by Giovanni Fava and colleagues (Fava, 1999; Ruini & Fava, 2004), seeks to enhance clients' self-acceptance, purpose in life, autonomy, and personal growth. It has been used successfully in the treatment of mood disorders and anxiety disorders (Fava et al., 2005).

Another new approach is *positive psychotherapy*, developed by Martin Seligman and colleagues (Seligman, Rashid, & Parks, 2006). Thus far, positive psychotherapy has been used mainly in the treatment of depression. This approach attempts to get clients to recognize their strengths, appreciate their blessings, savor positive experiences, forgive those who have wronged them, and find meaning in their lives. Preliminary research suggests that positive psychotherapy can be an effective treatment for depression. For example, in one study it was compared to treatment as usual (whatever the therapist would normally do) and treatment as usual with medication. The data shown in **Figure 14.5** compare mean depression scores at the end of the study for participants in these three conditions (Seligman et al., 2006). As you can see, the lowest depression scores were observed in the group that received positive psychotherapy. These innovative interventions spurred by the positive psychology movement are in their infancy, but the early findings seem promising and it will be interesting to see what the future holds.

Group Therapy

Many approaches to insight therapy, such as client-centered therapy, can be conducted on either an individual or group basis. *Group therapy* is the simultaneous treatment of several clients in a group.

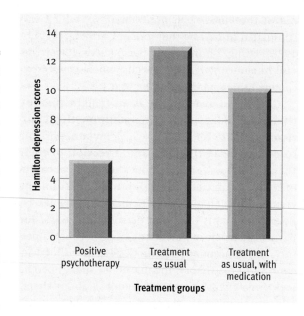

Figure 14.5

Positive psychotherapy for depression. In a study of the efficacy of positive psychotherapy, it was compared to treatment as usual (clinicians delivered whatever treatment they deemed appropriate) and to treatment as usual combined with antidepressant medication. At the end of 12 weeks of treatment, symptoms of depression were measured with the widely used Hamilton Rating Scale for Depression. The mean depression scores for each group are graphed here. As you can see, the positive psychotherapy group showed less depression than the other two treatment groups, suggesting that positive psychotherapy can be an effective intervention for depression.

SOURCE: Adapted from Seligman, M. E. P., Rashid, T., & Parks, A. C. (2006). Positive psychotherapy. *American Psychologist, 61,* 774–788 (Figure 2, p. 784). Copyright © 2006 by the American Psychological Association.

Because of economic pressures in mental health care, the use of group therapy appears likely to grow in future years (Burlingame & McClendon, 2008). Although group therapy can be conducted in a variety of ways, we can provide a general overview of the process (see Alonso, Alonso, & Piper, 2003; Stone, 2003; Vinogradov, Cox, & Yalom, 2003; Wong, 2005).

A therapy group typically consists of 4 to 12 people, with 6 to 8 participants regarded as ideal (Vinogradov et al., 2003). The therapist usually screens the participants, excluding persons who seem likely to be disruptive. Some theorists maintain that judicious selection of participants is crucial to effective group treatment (Salvendy, 1993). In group therapy, participants essentially function as therapists for one another (Stone, 2003). Group members describe their problems, trade viewpoints, share experiences, and discuss coping strategies. Most important, they provide acceptance and emotional support for each other. In this atmosphere, group members work at peeling away the social masks that cover their insecurities. As members come to value one another's opinions, they work hard to display healthy changes. In group treatment, the therapist's responsibilities include selecting participants, setting goals for the group, initiating and maintaining the therapeutic process, and preventing interactions among group members that might be psychologically harmful (Vinogradov et al., 2003). The therapist often plays a relatively subtle role in group therapy, staying in the background and focusing mainly on promoting group cohesiveness.

Group therapies obviously save time and money, which can be critical in understaffed mental hospitals and other institutional settings. Therapists in private practice usually charge less for group than individual therapy, making therapy affordable for more people. However, group therapy is *not* just a less costly substitute for individual therapy (Knauss, 2005; Stone, 2003). Group therapy has unique strengths of its own, and certain kinds of problems are especially well suited to group treatment.

Whether insight therapies are conducted on a group or an individual basis, clients usually invest considerable time, effort, and money. Are these therapies worth the investment? Let's examine the evidence on their effectiveness.

How Effective Are Insight Therapies?

Evaluating the effectiveness of any approach to psychotherapy is a complex matter (Hill & Lambert, 2004; Kendall, Holmbeck, & Verduin, 2004). For one thing, psychological disorders sometimes clear up on their own, a phenomenon called *spontaneous remission*. If a client experiences a recovery after treatment, we cannot automatically assume that the recovery was due to the treatment (see the Critical Thinking Application). Evaluations of insight therapies are especially complicated given that various schools of thought pursue entirely different goals. Judgments of therapeutic outcome in insight therapy tend to be subjective, with little consensus about the best way to assess therapeutic progress. Moreover,

Group treatments have proven particularly helpful when members share similar problems, such as alcoholism, overeating, or having been sexually abused as a child. Many approaches to insight therapy that were originally designed for individuals—such as client-centered therapy—have been adapted for treatment of groups.

concept check 14.1

Understanding Therapists' Conceptions of Disorders

Check your understanding of the three approaches to insight therapy covered in the text by matching each approach with the appropriate explanation of the typical origins of clients' psychological disorders. The answers are in Appendix A.

Theorized causes of disorders

_____ 1. Problems rooted in inadequate attention paid to one's strengths, blessings, and positive experiences

_____ 2. Problems rooted in unconscious conflicts left over from childhood

_____ 3. Problems rooted in inaccurate self-concept and excessive concern about pleasing others

Therapy

a. Psychoanalysis

b. Client-centered therapy

c. Positive psychotherapy

INSIDE WOODY ALLEN

Figure 14.6

Recovery as a function of number of therapy sessions. Based on a national sample of over 6000 patients, Lambert, Hansen, and Finch (2001) mapped out the relationship between recovery and the duration of treatment. These data show that about half of the patients had experienced a clinically significant recovery after 20 weekly sessions of therapy. After 45 sessions of therapy, about 70% had recovered.

SOURCE: Adapted from Lambert, M. J., Hansen, N. B., & Finch, A. E. (2001). Patient-focused research: Using patient outcome data to enhance treatment effects. *Journal of Consulting and Clinical Psychology, 69*, 159–172. Copyright © 2001 by the American Psychological Association. Used by permission of the authors.

ally find the greatest improvement early in treatment (the first 13–18 weekly sessions), with further gains gradually diminishing over time (Lambert, Bergin, & Garfield, 2004). Overall, about 50% of patients show a clinically meaningful recovery within about 20 sessions, and another 20% of patients achieve this goal after about 45 sessions (Lambert & Ogles, 2004) (see **Figure 14.6**). Of course, these broad generalizations mask considerable variability in outcome, but the general trends are encouraging.

people enter therapy with diverse problems of varied severity, so the efficacy of treatment can be evaluated meaningfully only for specific clinical problems.

Despite these difficulties, thousands of outcome studies have been conducted to evaluate the effectiveness of insight therapy. These studies have examined a broad range of clinical problems and used diverse methods to assess therapeutic outcomes, including scores on psychological tests and ratings by family members, as well as therapists' and clients' ratings. These studies consistently indicate that insight therapy *is* superior to no treatment or to placebo treatment and that the effects of therapy are reasonably durable (Kopta et al., 1999; Lambert & Archer, 2006). And when insight therapies are compared head-to-head against drug therapies, they usually show roughly equal efficacy (Arkowitz & Lilienfeld, 2007; Pinquart, Duberstein, & Lyness, 2006). Studies gener-

Behavior Therapies

Behavior therapy is different from insight therapy in that behavior therapists make no attempt to help clients achieve grand insights about themselves. Why not? Because behavior therapists believe that such insights aren't necessary to produce constructive change. For example, consider a client troubled by compulsive gambling. The behavior therapist doesn't care whether this behavior is rooted in unconscious conflicts or parental rejection. What the

client needs is to get rid of the maladaptive behavior. Consequently, the therapist simply designs a program to eliminate the compulsive gambling.

Behavior therapies involve the application of the principles of learning and conditioning to direct efforts to change clients' maladaptive behaviors. Behaviorists devoted little attention to clinical issues until the 1950s, when behavior therapy emerged out of three independent lines of research fostered by B. F. Skinner and his colleagues (Skinner, Solomon, & Lindsley, 1953) in the United States, Hans Eysenck (1959) and his colleagues in Britain, and Joseph Wolpe (1958) and his colleagues in South Africa (Glass & Arnkoff, 1992).

Behavior therapies are based on certain assumptions (Berkowitz, 2003). *First, it is assumed that behavior is a product of learning.* No matter how self-defeating or pathological a client's behavior might be, the behaviorist believes that it is the result of past conditioning. *Second, it is assumed that what has been learned can be unlearned.* Thus, behavior therapists attempt to change clients' behavior by applying the principles of classical conditioning, operant conditioning, and observational learning (see Chapter 6). Behavior therapy involves designing specific procedures for specific types of problems, as you'll see in our discussion of systematic desensitization.

Systematic Desensitization 11e

Devised by Joseph Wolpe (1958), systematic desensitization revolutionized psychotherapy by giving therapists their first useful alternative to traditional "talk therapy" (Fishman & Franks, 1992). *Systematic desensitization is a behavior therapy used to reduce clients' phobic responses.* The treatment assumes that most anxiety responses are acquired through classical conditioning (as discussed in Chapter 13). According to this model, a harmless stimulus (for instance, a bridge) may be paired with a fear-arousing event (lightning striking it), so that it becomes a conditioned stimulus eliciting anxiety. The goal of systematic desensitization is to weaken the association between the conditioned stimulus (the bridge) and the conditioned response of anxiety (see **Figure 14.7**). Systematic desensitization involves three steps.

In the first step, the therapist helps the client build an anxiety hierarchy. The hierarchy is a list of anxiety-arousing stimuli related to the specific source of anxiety, such as flying, academic tests, or snakes. The client ranks the stimuli from the least anxiety arousing to the most anxiety arousing. This ordered list of stimuli is the *anxiety hierarchy.* An example of an anxiety hierarchy for one woman's fear of heights is shown in **Figure 14.8**.

The second step involves training the client in deep muscle relaxation. Various therapists use different relaxation training procedures. Whatever procedures are used, the client must learn to engage in deep, thorough relaxation on command from the therapist.

In the third step, the client tries to work through the hierarchy, learning to remain relaxed while imagining each stimulus. Starting with the least anxiety-arousing stimulus, the client imagines the situation as vividly as possible while relaxing. If the client experiences strong anxiety, he or she drops the imaginary scene and concentrates on relaxation. The client keeps repeating this process until he or she can imagine a scene with little or no anxiety. Once a particular scene is conquered, the client moves on to the next stimulus situation in the anxiety hierarchy. Gradually, over

Joseph Wolpe
"Neurotic anxiety is nothing but a conditioned response."

An Anxiety Hierarchy for Systematic Desensitization	
Degree of fear	
5	I'm standing on the balcony of the top floor of an apartment tower.
10	I'm standing on a stepladder in the kitchen to change a light bulb.
15	I'm walking on a ridge. The edge is hidden by shrubs and treetops.
20	I'm sitting on the slope of a mountain, looking out over the horizon.
25	I'm crossing a bridge 6 feet above a creek. The bridge consists of an 18-inch-wide board with a handrail on one side.
30	I'm riding a ski lift 8 feet above the ground.
35	I'm crossing a shallow, wide creek on an 18-inch-wide board, 3 feet above water level.
40	I'm climbing a ladder outside the house to reach a second-story window.
45	I'm pulling myself up a 30-degree wet, slippery slope on a steel cable.
50	I'm scrambling up a rock, 8 feet high.
55	I'm walking 10 feet on a resilient, 18-inch-wide board, which spans an 8-foot-deep gulch.
60	I'm walking on a wide plateau, 2 feet from the edge of a cliff.
65	I'm skiing an intermediate hill. The snow is packed.
70	I'm walking over a railway trestle.
75	I'm walking on the side of an embankment. The path slopes to the outside.
80	I'm riding a chair lift 15 feet above the ground.
85	I'm walking up a long, steep slope.
90	I'm walking up (or down) a 15-degree slope on a 3-foot-wide trail. On one side of the trail the terrain drops down sharply; on the other side is a steep upward slope.
95	I'm walking on a 3-foot-wide ridge. The slopes on both sides are long and more than 25 degrees steep.
100	I'm walking on a 3-foot-wide ridge. The trail slopes on one side. The drop on either side of the trail is more than 25 degrees.

Figure 14.7

The logic underlying systematic desensitization. Behaviorists argue that many phobic responses are acquired through classical conditioning. For example, a person traumatized by a lightning strike while crossing a bridge might develop a phobia of bridges, as diagrammed here. Systematic desensitization targets the conditioned associations between phobic stimuli and fear responses.

Figure 14.8

Example of an anxiety hierarchy. Systematic desensitization requires the construction of an anxiety hierarchy like the one shown here, which was developed for a woman who had a fear of heights but wanted to go hiking in the mountains.

SOURCE: Rudestam, K. E. (1980). *Methods of self-change: An ABC primer.* Belmont, CA: Wadsworth. Copyright © 1980 by Wadsworth Publishing. Reprinted by permission of the author.

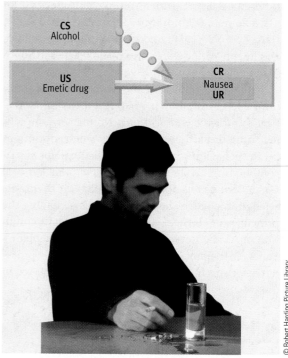

a number of therapy sessions, the client progresses through the hierarchy, unlearning troublesome anxiety responses.

Desensitization to imagined stimuli can be effective by itself, but many behavior therapists advocate following it up with direct exposures to the real anxiety-arousing stimuli (Emmelkamp, 2004). The desensitization process should reduce anxiety enough so that clients will be able to confront situations they used to avoid. Although it seems deceptively simple, systematic desensitization can be quite effective in treating specific anxieties and phobic disorders (Spiegler & Guevremont, 2003).

Aversion Therapy

11e

Aversion therapy uses classical conditioning to create a negative response to a stimulus that has elicited problematic behavior. For example, alcoholics may be given an *emetic drug* (one that causes nausea and vomiting) in conjunction with their favorite drinks during therapy sessions (Landabaso et al., 1999). By pairing the drug with alcohol, the therapist hopes to create a conditioned aversion to alcohol. Aversion therapy takes advantage of the automatic, reflexive nature of responses produced through classical conditioning. Admittedly, alcoholics treated with aversion therapy know that they won't be given an emetic outside of their therapy sessions. However, their reflex response to the stimulus of alcohol may be changed so they respond to it with nausea and distaste (see **Figure 14.9**). Obviously, this response should make it much easier to resist the urge to drink.

Aversion therapy is not a widely used technique, and when used it is usually only one element in a larger treatment program. Troublesome behaviors treated successfully with aversion therapy have included drug and alcohol abuse, sexual deviance, gambling, shoplifting, stuttering, cigarette smoking,

Figure 14.9

Aversion therapy. Aversion therapy uses classical conditioning to create an aversion to a stimulus that has elicited problematic behavior. For example, in the treatment of drinking problems, alcohol may be paired with a nausea-inducing drug to create an aversion to drinking.

and overeating (Bordnick et al., 2004; Emmelkamp, 1994; Grossman & Ruiz, 2004; Maletzky, 2002).

Social Skills Training

Many psychological problems grow out of interpersonal difficulties. Behavior therapists point out that people are not born with social finesse—they acquire social skills through learning. Unfortunately, some people have not learned how to be friendly, how to make conversation, how to express anger appropriately, and so forth. As a result, behavior therapists are increasingly using social skills training in efforts to improve clients' social abilities. This approach to therapy has yielded promising results in the treatment of social anxiety (Herbert et al., 2005), autism (Scattone, 2007), attention deficit disorder (Monastra, 2008) and schizophrenia (Granholm et al., 2008).

Social skills training is a behavior therapy designed to improve interpersonal skills that emphasizes modeling, behavioral rehearsal, and shaping. With *modeling,* clients are encouraged to watch socially skilled friends and colleagues so that they can acquire appropriate responses (eye contact, active listening, and so on) through observation. In *behavioral rehearsal,* the client tries to practice social techniques in structured role-playing exercises. The therapist provides corrective feedback and uses approval to reinforce progress. Eventually, of course, clients try their newly acquired skills in real-world interactions. Usually, they are given specific homework assignments. *Shaping* is used in that clients are gradually asked to handle more complicated and delicate social situations. For example, a nonassertive client may begin by working on making requests of friends. Only much later will he be asked to tackle standing up to his boss at work.

Cognitive-Behavioral Treatments

In Chapter 13, we learned that cognitive factors play a key role in the development of many anxiety and mood disorders. Citing the importance of such findings, behavior therapists started to focus more attention on their clients' cognitions in the 1970s (Arnkoff & Glass, 1992; Hollon & Beck, 2004). *Cognitive-behavioral treatments* use combinations of verbal interventions and behavior modification techniques to help clients change maladaptive patterns of thinking. Some of these treatments, such as Albert Ellis's (1973) *rational-emotive behavior therapy* and Aaron Beck's (1976) *cognitive therapy* emerged out of an insight therapy tradition, whereas other treatments, such as the systems developed by Donald Meichenbaum (1977) and Michael Mahoney (1974), emerged from the behavioral tradition. We will focus on Beck's cognitive therapy as an example of a cognitive-behavioral treatment (see Chapter 12 for a discussion of some of Ellis's ideas).

Cognitive therapy uses specific strategies to correct habitual thinking errors that underlie various types of disorders. In recent years cognitive therapy has been applied fruitfully to a wide range of disorders (Grant, Young, & DeRubeis, 2005; Hollon, Stewart, & Strunk, 2006), but it was originally devised as a treatment for depression. According to cognitive therapists, depression is caused by "errors" in thinking (see **Figure 14.10**). They assert that depression-prone people tend to (1) blame their setbacks on personal inadequacies without considering circumstantial explanations, (2) focus selectively on negative events while ignoring positive events, (3) make unduly pessimistic projections about the future, and (4) draw negative conclusions about their worth as a person based on insignificant events. For instance, imagine that you got a low grade on a minor quiz in a class. If you made the kinds of er-

Negative thinking

- Blame setbacks on personal inadequacies
- Focus selectively on negative events
- Make unduly pessimistic projections about future
- Draw negative conclusions about personal worth

→ Increased vulnerability to depression

Figure 14.10
Beck's view of the roots of disorders. Beck's theory initially focused on the causes of depression, although it was gradually broadened to explain other disorders. According to Beck, depression is caused by the types of negative thinking shown here.

rors in thinking just described, you might blame the grade on your woeful stupidity, dismiss comments from a classmate that it was an unfair test, gloomily predict that you will surely flunk the course, and conclude that you are not genuine college material.

The goal of cognitive therapy is to change clients' negative thoughts and maladaptive beliefs (Kellogg & Young, 2008). To begin, clients are taught to detect their automatic negative thoughts—the self-defeating statements that people are prone to make when analyzing problems. Examples might include "I'm just not smart enough," "No one really likes me," or "It's all my fault." Clients are then trained to subject these automatic thoughts to reality testing. The therapist helps them to see how unrealistically negative the thoughts are.

Cognitive therapy uses a variety of behavioral techniques, such as modeling, systematic monitoring of one's behavior, and behavioral rehearsal (Wright, Beck, & Thase, 2003). For example, cognitive therapists often give their clients "homework assignments" that focus on changing clients' overt behaviors. Clients may be instructed to engage in overt responses on their own, outside of the clinician's office. For example, one shy, insecure young man in cognitive therapy was told to go to a singles bar and engage three different women in conversations for up to five minutes each (Rush, 1984). He was instructed to record his thoughts before and after each of the conversations. This assignment elicited various maladaptive patterns of thought that gave the young man and his therapist plenty to work on in subsequent sessions.

How Effective Are Behavior Therapies?

Behavior therapists have historically placed more emphasis on the importance of measuring therapeutic outcomes than insight therapists have. Thus, there

Aaron Beck

"Most people are barely aware of the automatic thoughts which precede unpleasant feelings or automatic inhibitions."

web link 14.4

Association for Behavioral and Cognitive Therapies

The website for this professional organization has a variety of resources that are relevant to the general public. The most valuable of these resources are the fact sheets on cognitive-behavioral treatments for over 40 common problems and disorders. These fact sheets explain how cognitive-behavioral interventions can be used in the treatment of alcohol abuse, autism, chronic fatigue, eating disorders, insomnia, phobias, schizophrenia, shyness, and a host of other conditions.

web link 14.5

The Beck Institute of Cognitive Therapy and Research

This site offers a diverse array of materials relating to Aaron Beck's cognitive therapy. Resources include newsletters, a referral system, a bookstore, recommended readings for clients, and questions and answers about cognitive therapy.

has been a good deal of research on the effectiveness of behavior therapy (Jacob & Pelham, 2005). Of course, behavior therapies are not well suited to the treatment of some types of problems (vague feelings of discontent, for instance). Furthermore, it's misleading to make global statements about the effectiveness of behavior therapies, because they include many types of procedures designed for very different purposes. For example, the value of systematic desensitization for phobias has no bearing on the value of aversion therapy for sexual deviance. For our pur-

poses, it is sufficient to note that there is favorable evidence on the efficacy of most of the widely used behavioral interventions (Zinbarg & Griffith, 2008). Behavior therapies can make important contributions to the treatment of phobias, obsessive-compulsive disorders, sexual dysfunction, schizophrenia, drug-related problems, eating disorders, psychosomatic disorders, hyperactivity, autism, and mental retardation (Berkowitz, 2003; Emmelkamp, 2004).

concept check 14.2

Understanding Therapists' Goals

Check your understanding of therapists' goals by matching various therapies with the appropriate description. The answers are in Appendix A.

Principal Therapeutic Goals

_____ 1. Elimination of maladaptive behaviors or symptoms

_____ 2. Acceptance of genuine self, personal growth

_____ 3. Recovery of unconscious conflicts, character reconstruction

_____ 4. Detection and reduction of negative thinking

Therapy

a. Psychoanalysis

b. Client-centered therapy

c. Cognitive therapy

d. Behavior therapy

REVIEW of Key Learning Goals

14.9 Behavior therapies use the principles of learning in direct efforts to change specific aspects of behavior. Wolpe's systematic desensitization is a treatment designed to relieve phobias. It involves the construction of an anxiety hierarchy, relaxation training, and step-by-step movement through the hierarchy, pairing relaxation with each phobic stimulus.

14.10 In aversion therapy, a stimulus associated with an unwanted response is paired with an unpleasant stimulus in an effort to eliminate the maladaptive response. Social skills training can improve clients' interpersonal skills through shaping, modeling, and behavioral rehearsal.

14.11 Cognitive-behavioral treatments concentrate on changing the way clients think about events in their lives. Cognitive therapists reeducate clients to detect and challenge automatic negative thoughts that cause depression and anxiety. Cognitive therapy also depends on modeling, behavioral rehearsal, and homework assignments.

14.12 Behavior therapists have historically placed more emphasis on the importance of measuring therapeutic outcomes than insight therapists have. There is ample evidence that behavior therapies are effective in the treatment of a wide variety of disorders.

Biomedical Therapies

Key Learning Goals

14.13 Summarize the therapeutic actions and side effects of antianxiety and antipsychotic drugs.

14.14 Summarize the therapeutic actions and side effects of antidepressant and mood stabilizing drugs.

14.15 Evaluate the overall efficacy of drug treatments, and discuss controversies surrounding pharmaceutical research.

14.16 Describe electroconvulsive therapy, and assess its therapeutic effects and risks.

14.17 Describe the therapeutic use of transcranial magnetic stimulation and direct brain stimulation.

Biomedical therapies are physiological interventions intended to reduce symptoms associated with psychological disorders. These therapies assume that psychological disorders are caused, at least in part, by biological malfunctions. As we discussed in the previous chapter, this assumption clearly has merit for many disorders, especially the more severe ones. We will discuss the two standard biomedical approaches to psychotherapy, drug therapy and electroconvulsive (shock) therapy, and then delve into some experimental, new treatments involving brain stimulation.

Treatment with Drugs   11e

Since the 1950s drug therapy has become increasingly important in the treatment of psychological disorders. Therapeutic drugs fall into four major

groups: antianxiety drugs, antipsychotic drugs, antidepressant drugs, and mood stabilizers.

Antianxiety Drugs   11e

Most of us know someone who pops pills to relieve anxiety. *Antianxiety drugs,* **which reduce tension, apprehension, and nervousness,** are the drugs used in this common coping strategy. The most popular of these drugs are Valium and Xanax (trade names for the generic drugs diazepam and alprazolam, respectively).

Valium, Xanax, and other similar drugs are often called *tranquilizers.* These drugs exert their effects almost immediately, and they can be fairly effective in relieving feelings of anxiety (Dubovsky, 2005). However, their effects are measured in hours, so their impact is relatively short-lived. Antianxiety drugs are routinely prescribed for people with anxiety disorders, but they are also given to millions of people who simply suffer from chronic nervous tension.

All the drugs used to treat psychological disorders have potentially troublesome side effects that show up in some patients but not others. The most common side effects of Valium and Xanax are drowsiness, lightheadedness, cottonmouth, depression, nausea, and constipation. These drugs also have potential for abuse, drug dependence, and overdose, although these risks have probably been exaggerated in the press (Ballenger, 2000; Silberman, 1998). Another drawback is that patients who have been on antianxiety drugs for a while often experience unpleasant withdrawal symptoms when their drug treatment is stopped (Raj & Sheehan, 2004).

Antipsychotic Drugs

Antipsychotic drugs are used primarily in the treatment of schizophrenia. They are also given to people with severe mood disorders who become delusional. *Antipsychotic drugs* are used to gradually reduce psychotic symptoms, including hyperactivity, mental confusion, hallucinations, and delusions. The traditional antipsychotics appear to decrease activity at dopamine synapses, although the exact relationship between their neurochemical effects and their clinical effects remains obscure (Egan & Hyde, 2000; Miyamoto et al., 2003).

Studies suggest that antipsychotic drugs reduce psychotic symptoms in about 70% of patients, albeit in varied degrees (Kane & Marder, 2005). When antipsychotic drugs are effective, they work their magic gradually, as shown in **Figure 14.11**. Patients usually begin to respond within two days to a week. Further improvement may occur for several months. Many schizophrenic patients are placed on antipsychotics indefinitely because these drugs can reduce the likelihood of a relapse into an active schizophrenic episode (Marder & van Kammen, 2005).

Antipsychotic drugs undeniably make a major contribution to the treatment of severe mental disorders, but they are not without problems. They have many unpleasant side effects (Cohen, 1997; Wilkaitis, Mulvihill, & Nasrallah, 2004). Drowsiness, constipation, and cottonmouth are common. Tremors, muscular rigidity, and impaired coordination may also occur. After being released from a hospital, many patients who have been placed on antipsychotics stop their drug regimen because of the side effects. Unfortunately, most patients eventually experience a relapse after they cease taking antipsychotic medication (Gitlin et al., 2001). In addition to their nuisance side effects, antipsychotics may cause a more severe and lasting problem called *tardive dyskinesia*, which

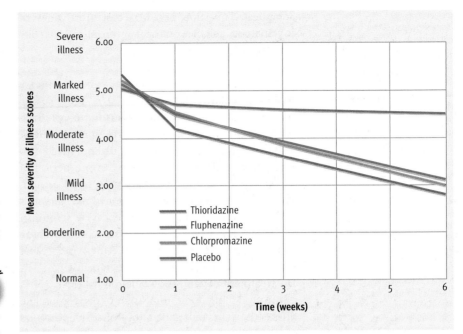

Figure 14.11
The time course of antipsychotic drug effects. Antipsychotic drugs reduce psychotic symptoms gradually, over a span of weeks, as graphed here. In contrast, patients given placebo medication show little improvement.

SOURCE: Cole, J. O., Goldberg, S. C., & Davis, J. M. (1966). Drugs in the treatment of psychosis. In P. Solomon (Ed.), *Psychiatric drugs*. New York: Grune & Stratton. From data in the NIMH-PSC Collaborative Study I. Reprinted by permission of J. M. Davis.

is seen in about 20%–30% of patients who receive long-term treatment with traditional antipsychotics (Marder, 2000). *Tardive dyskinesia* is a neurological disorder marked by involuntary writhing and ticlike movements of the mouth, tongue, face, hands, or feet. Once this debilitating syndrome emerges, there is no cure, although spontaneous remission sometimes occurs after the discontinuation of antipsychotic medication (Pi & Simpson, 2000).

Psychiatrists are currently enthusiastic about a new class of antipsychotic agents called *atypical antipsychotic drugs*. These drugs are roughly as effective as traditional antipsychotics (Fleischhacker, 2002), and they can help some patients who do not respond to conventional antipsychotic medications (Volavka et al., 2002). Moreoever, the atypical antipsychotics produce fewer unpleasant side effects and carry less risk for tardive dyskinesia (Correll, Leucht, & Kane, 2004; Lieberman et al., 2003). Of course, like all powerful drugs, they are not without their risks, as they appear to increase patients' vulnerability to diabetes and cardiovascular problems (Meltzer et al., 2002).

Although they are much more expensive than traditional antipsychotics, the atypical antipsychotics have become the first line of defense in the treatment of schizophrenia (van Kammen & Marder, 2005). However, recent research has generated some controversy regarding this trend. Studies have found that the newer antipsychotics aren't any more effective than the older medications in reducing symptoms and that the side effects of the newer drugs are only marginally less troublesome than the side effects of the older drugs (Lieberman et al., 2005; Stroup, Kraus, & Marder, 2006). These findings raise vexing, complicated questions about the cost effectiveness of psychiatrists' reliance on the newer medications (Lieberman, 2006; Rosenheck, 2006).

Antidepressant Drugs

As their name suggests, *antidepressant drugs* gradually elevate mood and help bring people out of a depression. Like antipsychotic drugs, antidepressants exert their effects gradually over a period of weeks. Today, the most widely prescribed antidepressants are the *selective serotonin reuptake inhibitors (SSRIs),* which slow the reuptake process at serotonin synapses. The drugs in this class, which include Prozac (fluoxetine), Paxil (paroxetine), and Zoloft (sertraline), seem to yield rapid therapeutic gains in the treatment of depression (Shelton & Lester, 2006) while producing fewer unpleasant or dangerous side effects than previous generations of antidepressants (Kelsey, 2005). However, there is some doubt about how effective the SSRIs (and other antidepressants) are in relieving episodes of depression among patients suffering from bipolar disorder (Thase, 2005). Bipolar patients do not seem to respond as well as those who suffer from depression only. And in some cases antidepressants appear to foster a switch back into a manic episode (Altshuler et al., 2006).

A major concern in recent years has been evidence from a number of studies that SSRIs may increase the risk for suicide (Healy & Whitaker, 2003; Holden, 2004). The challenge of collecting definitive data on this issue is much more daunting than one might guess, in part because suicide rates are already elevated among people who exhibit the disorders for which SSRIs are prescribed (Rihmer, 2003; Wessely & Kerwin, 2004). Some researchers have collected data that suggest that suicide rates have *declined* slightly because of widespread prescription of SSRIs (Baldessarini et al., 2007; Gibbons et al., 2006), while others have found no association between SSRIs and suicide (Lapiere, 2003; Simon et al., 2006).

Overall, however, when antidepressants are compared to placebo treatment, the data suggest that antidepressants lead to a slight elevation in the risk of suicidal behavior, from roughly 2% to 4% (Bridge et al., 2007; Dubicka, Hadley, & Roberts, 2006; Hammad, Laughren, & Racoosin, 2006). The increased suicide risk appears to mainly be a problem among a small minority of children and adolescents in the first month after starting antidepressants, especially during the first nine days (Jick, Kaye, & Jick, 2004). Thus, patients starting on SSRIs should be carefully monitored by their physicians and families (Culpepper et al., 2004). Regulatory warnings from the U.S. Food and Drug Administration (FDA) have led to a decline in the prescription of SSRIs among adolescents (Nemeroff et al., 2007). This trend has prompted concern that increases in suicide may occur among untreated individuals. This concern seems legitimate in that suicide risk clearly peaks in the month prior to people beginning treatment for depression, whether that treatment involves SSRIs or psychotherapy (see **Figure 14.12**) (Simon & Savarino, 2007). This pattern presumably occurs because the escalating agony of depression finally prompts people to seek treatment, but it also suggests that getting treatment with

Figure 14.12

Probability of a suicide attempt in relation to the initiation of treatment. Examining medical records for thousands of patients, Simon and Savarino (2007) were able to gather information on the likelihood of a suicide attempt in the months before and after commencing treatment for depression. They compared patients who were put on an antidepressant medication against those who started in some form of insight or behavioral therapy. The data shown here, for young patients under the age of 25, indicate that suicide risk is highest in the month prior to treatment and next highest in the month after treatment is begun for both groups. These findings suggest that elevated suicide rates are not unique to starting on antidepressants and that getting treatment (whether it is medication or psychotherapy) reduces the risk of suicide.

SOURCE: Adapted from Simon, G. E., & Savarino, J. (2007). Suicide attempts among patients starting depression treatments with medications or psychotherapy. *American Journal of Psychiatry, 164,* 1029–1034 (Figure 2, p. 1032). Copyright © 2007 by the American Psychiatric Association. Adapted by permission of the American Psychiatric Association.

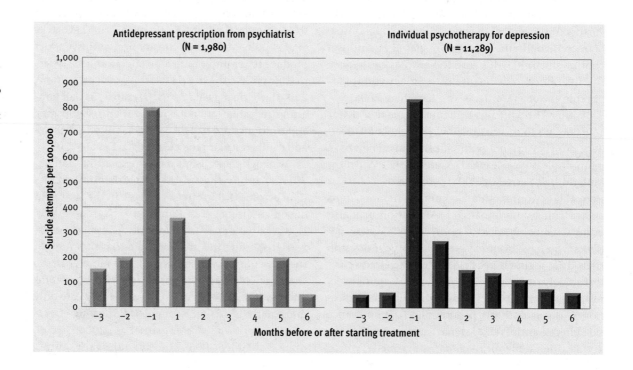

drugs or therapy reduces suicidal risk. In the final analysis, this is a complex issue, but the one thing experts seem to agree on is that adolescents starting on SSRIs should be monitored closely.

The newest class of antidepressants consists of medications that inhibit reuptake at both serotonin and norepinephrine synapses, referred to as SNRIs. The first two drugs in this category are venlafaxine (Effexor) and duloxetine (Celexa). These drugs appear to produce slightly stronger antidepressant effects than the SSRIs (Thase & Denko, 2008). However, targeting two neurotransmitter systems also leads to a broader range of side effects, including troublesome elevations in blood pressure (Thase & Sloan, 2006).

Mood Stabilizers

Mood stabilizers are drugs used to control mood swings in patients with bipolar mood disorders. For many years, *lithium* was the only effective drug in this category. Lithium has proven valuable in preventing *future* episodes of both mania and depression in patients with bipolar illness (Geddes et al., 2004). Lithium can also be used in efforts to bring patients with bipolar illness out of *current* manic or depressive episodes (Keck & McElroy, 2006). However, antipsychotics and antidepressants are more commonly used for these purposes. On the negative side of the ledger, lithium does have some dangerous side effects if its use isn't managed skillfully (Jefferson & Greist, 2005). Lithium levels in the patient's blood must be monitored carefully, because high concentrations can be toxic and even fatal. Kidney and thyroid gland complications are the other major problems associated with lithium therapy.

In recent years a number of alternatives to lithium have been developed. The most popular of these newer mood stabilizers is an anticonvulsant agent called *valproate,* which has become more widely used than lithium in the treatment of bipolar disorders (Thase & Denko, 2008). Valproate appears to be roughly as effective as lithium in efforts to treat current manic episodes and to prevent future affective disturbances (Moseman et al., 2003). The advantage provided by valproate is that it has fewer side effects than lithium and is better tolerated by patients (Bowden, 2004).

Evaluating Drug Therapies

Drug therapies can produce clear therapeutic gains for many kinds of patients. What's especially impressive is that they can be effective with severe disorders that otherwise defy therapeutic endeavors. Nonetheless, drug therapies are controversial. Critics of drug therapy have raised a number of issues (Breggin & Cohen, 2007; Cohen & McCubbin, 1990; Healy,

2004; Lickey & Gordon, 1991; Whitaker, 2002). First, some critics argue that drug therapies are not as effective as advertised and that they often produce superficial, short-lived curative effects. For example, Valium does not really solve problems with anxiety; it merely provides temporary relief from an unpleasant symptom. Moreover, relapse rates are substantial when drug regimens are discontinued. Second, critics charge that many drugs are overprescribed and many patients overmedicated. According to these critics, a number of physicians routinely hand out prescriptions without giving adequate consideration to more complicated and difficult interventions. Third, some critics charge that the damaging side effects of therapeutic drugs are underestimated by psychiatrists and that these side effects are often worse than the illnesses that the drugs are supposed to cure.

Critics maintain that the negative effects of psychiatric drugs are not fully appreciated because the pharmaceutical industry has managed to gain undue influence over the research enterprise as it relates to drug testing (Angell, 2000, 2004; Carpenter, 2002; Healy, 2004; Weber, 2006). Today, most researchers who investigate the benefits and risks of medications and write treatment guidelines have lucrative financial arrangements with the pharmaceutical industry (Bodenheimer, 2000; Choudhry, Stelfox, & Detsky, 2002; Lurie et al., 2006). Their studies are funded by drug companies, and they often receive substantial consulting fees. Unfortunately, these financial ties appear to undermine the objectivity required in scientific research, as studies funded by drug companies are far less likely to report unfavorable results than nonprofit-funded studies (Bekelman, Li, & Gross, 2003; Perlis et al., 2005). Industry-financed drug trials also tend to be much too brief to detect the long-term risks associated with new drugs, and when unfavorable results emerge, the data are often withheld from publication (Antonuccio, Danton, & McClanahan, 2003). Also, research designs are often

"I medicate first and ask questions later."

slanted in a variety of ways so as to exaggerate the positive effects and minimize the negative effects of the drugs under scrutiny (Carpenter, 2002; Chopra, 2003; Moncrieff, 2001). The conflicts of interest that appear to be pervasive in contemporary drug research raise grave concerns that require attention from researchers, universities, and federal agencies.

Electroconvulsive Therapy (ECT)

In the 1930s, a Hungarian psychiatrist named Ladislas von Meduna speculated that epilepsy and schizophrenia could not coexist in the same body. On the basis of this observation, which turned out to be inaccurate, von Meduna theorized that it might be useful to induce epileptic-like seizures in schizophrenic patients. Initially, a drug was used to trigger these seizures. However, by 1938 a pair of Italian psychiatrists (Cerletti & Bini, 1938) demonstrated that it was safer to elicit the seizures with electric shock. Thus, modern electroconvulsive therapy was born.

Electroconvulsive therapy (ECT) is a biomedical treatment in which electric shock is used to produce a cortical seizure accompanied by convulsions. In ECT, electrodes are attached to the skull over the temporal lobes of the brain (see the photo below). A light anesthesia is administered, and the patient is given a variety of drugs to minimize the likelihood of complications, such as spinal fractures. An electric current is then applied for about a second. The current triggers a brief (5–20 seconds) convulsive seizure, during which the patient usually loses consciousness. The patient normally awakens in an hour or two. People typically receive between 6 and 20 treatments as inpatients at a hospital.

The clinical use of ECT peaked in the 1940s and 1950s, before effective drug therapies were widely available. ECT has long been controversial, and its use declined in the 1960s and 1970s. Nonetheless,

the use of ECT has seen a resurgence in recent decades, and it is not a rare form of therapy. Although only about 8% of psychiatrists administer ECT (Hermann et al., 1998), it is estimated that about 100,000 people receive ECT treatments yearly in the United States (Hermann et al., 1995). Some critics argue that ECT is overused because it is a lucrative procedure that boosts psychiatrists' income while consuming relatively little of their time in comparison to insight therapy (Frank, 1990). Conversely, some ECT advocates argue that ECT is underutilized because the public harbors many misconceptions about its risks and side effects (McDonald et al., 2004).

Effectiveness of ECT

The evidence on the therapeutic efficacy of ECT is open to varied interpretations. Proponents maintain that it is a remarkably effective treatment for major depression (Prudic, 2005; Rudorfer, Henry, & Sackeim, 2003). Moreover, they note that many patients who do not benefit from antidepressant medication improve in response to ECT (Nobler & Sackeim, 2006). However, opponents argue that the available studies are flawed and inconclusive and that ECT is probably no more effective than a placebo (Rose et al., 2003). Overall, there does seem to be enough favorable evidence to justify *conservative* use of ECT in treating severe mood disorders in patients who have not responded to medication (Carney & Geddes, 2003; Metzger, 1999). Unfortunately, relapse rates after ECT are distressingly high. Over 50% of patients relapse within 6 to 12 months, although relapse rates can be reduced by giving ECT patients antidepressant drugs (Sackeim et al., 2001).

Risks Associated with ECT

Even ECT proponents acknowledge that memory losses, impaired attention, and other cognitive deficits are common short-term side effects of electroconvulsive therapy (Lisanby et al., 2000; Sackeim et al., 2007). However, ECT proponents assert that these deficits are mild and usually disappear within a month or two (Glass, 2001). An American Psychiatric Association task force (2001) concluded that there is no objective evidence that ECT causes structural damage in the brain or that it has any lasting negative effects on the ability to learn and remember information. In contrast, ECT critics maintain that ECT-induced cognitive deficits are often significant and sometimes permanent (Breggin, 1991; Rose et al., 2003), although their evidence seems to be largely anecdotal. Given the doubts that have been raised about the efficacy and risks of electroconvulsive therapy, it appears that this treatment will remain controversial for some time to come.

This patient is being prepared for electroconvulsive therapy. The mouthpiece keeps the patient from biting her tongue during the electrically induced seizures.

New Brain Stimulation Techniques

Scientists are always on the lookout for new methods of treating psychological disorders that might exhibit greater efficacy or fewer complications than ECT or drug treatments. Some new approaches to treatment involving stimulation of the brain are being explored with promising results, although they remain highly experimental at this time.

One new approach is *transcranial magnetic stimulation,* which was discussed in Chapter 3 as a method for studying brain function. **Transcranial magnetic stimulation (TMS) is a technique that permits scientists to temporarily enhance or depress activity in a specific area of the brain.** In TMS, a magnetic coil mounted on a small paddle is held over specific areas of the head to increase or decrease activity in discrete regions of the cortex (Nahas et al., 2007). Neuroscientists are mostly experimenting with TMS as a treatment for depression. Thus far, treatments delivered to the right and left prefrontal cortex show promise in reducing depressive symptoms (Nobler & Sackeim, 2006; O'Reardon et al., 2007). TMS tends to be well tolerated with minimal side effects. But a great deal of additional research will be necessary before the therapeutic value of TMS can be determined.

The other new approach to treatment is *deep brain stimulation.* In **deep brain stimulation (DBS) a thin electrode is surgically implanted in the brain and connected to an implanted pulse generator so that various electrical currents can be delivered to brain tissue adjacent to the electrode** (George, 2003; see **Figure 14.13**). DBS has proven valuable in the treatment of the motor disturbances associated with Parkinson's disease, tardive dyskinesia, and some seizure disorders (Halpern et al., 2007; Wider et al., 2008). Researchers are currently explor-

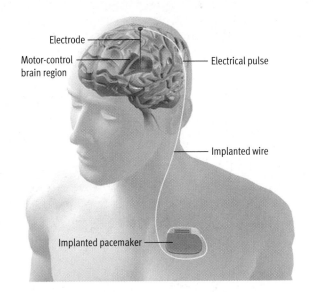

Figure 14.13

Deep brain stimulation. Deep brain stimulation requires a surgical procedure in which a thin electrode (about the width of a human hair) is inserted into deep areas of the brain. The electrode is connected to a pulse generator implanted under the skin of the chest. The placement of the electrode and the type of current generated depend on what condition is being treated. The electrode shown here was implanted in a motor area of the brain to treat the tremors associated with Parkinson's disease. Researchers are experimenting with other electrode placements in efforts to treat depression and obsessive-compulsive disorder.

SOURCE: Adapted from George, M. S. (2003). Stimulating the brain. *Scientific American, 289*(3), 67–73 (p. 70). © Bryan Christie Design.

ing whether DBS may have value in the treatment of depression or obsessive-compulsive disorder (George et al., 2006; Hardesty & Sackeim, 2007). Obviously, this highly invasive procedure requiring brain surgery will never be a frontline therapy for mental disorders, but scientists hope that it may be valuable for treatment-resistant patients who do not benefit from conventional therapies (Kuehn, 2007).

---

concept check 14.3

Understanding Biomedical Therapies

Check your understanding of biomedical therapies by matching each treatment with its chief use. The answers are in Appendix A.

Treatment

_____ 1. Antianxiety drugs

_____ 2. Antipsychotic drugs

_____ 3. Antidepressant drugs

_____ 4. Mood stabilizers

_____ 5. Electroconvulsive therapy (ECT)

Chief Purpose

a. To reduce psychotic symptoms

b. To bring a major depression to an end

c. To suppress tension, nervousness, and apprehension

d. To prevent future episodes of mania or depression in bipolar disorders

THERAPY/FOUNDER

ROOTS OF DISORDERS

PSYCHOANALYSIS

Developed by Sigmund Freud in Vienna, from the 1890s through the 1930s

Intrapsychic conflict (among id, ego, and superego) → Anxiety → Reliance on defense mechanisms

Unconscious conflict resulting from fixations in earlier development cause anxiety, which leads to defensive behavior. The repressed conflicts typically center on sex and aggression.

CLIENT-CENTERED THERAPY

Created by Carl Rogers at the University of Chicago during the 1940s and 1950s

Need to distort shortcomings to feel worthy of affection → Relatively incongruent self-concept → Recurrent anxiety

Defensive behavior protects inaccurate self-concept

Overdependence on acceptance from others fosters incongruence, which leads to anxiety and defensive behavior and thwarts personal growth.

BEHAVIOR THERAPY

Launched primarily by South African Joseph Wolpe's description of systematic desensitization in 1958

Maladaptive patterns of behavior are acquired through learning. For example, many phobias are thought to be created through classical conditioning and maintained by operant conditioning.

CS
Bridge

US
Lightning strikes

CR
Fear
UR

COGNITIVE–BEHAVIORAL TREATMENTS

One approach devised by Aaron Beck at the University of Pennsylvania in the 1960s and 1970s

Pervasive negative thinking about events related to self fosters anxiety and depression, and other forms of pathology.

Blame setbacks on personal inadequacies

Focus selectively on negative events

Make unduly pessimistic projections about future

Draw negative conclusions about personal worth

Increased vulnerability to depression

BIOMEDICAL THERAPY

Many researchers contributed; key breakthroughs in drug treatment made around 1950 by John Cade in Australia, Henri Laborit in France, and Jean Delay and Pierre Deniker, also in France

Most disorders are attributed to genetic predisposition and physiological malfunctions, such as abnormal neurotransmitter activity.
For example, schizophrenia appears to be associated with overactivity at dopamine synapses.

THERAPEUTIC GOALS

THERAPEUTIC TECHNIQUES

Insights regarding unconscious conflicts and motives; resolution of conflicts; personality reconstruction

Free association, dream analysis, interpretation, transference

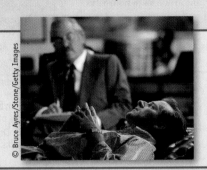

Increased congruence between self-concept and experience; acceptance of genuine self; self-determination and personal growth

Genuineness, empathy, unconditional positive regard, clarification, reflecting back to client

Elimination of maladaptive symptoms; acquisition of more adaptive responses

Desensitization is intended to weaken and replace this association

CS Bridge

US Lightning strikes → **CR** Fear **UR**

Classical and operant conditioning, systematic desensitization, aversive conditioning, social skills training, reinforcement, shaping, punishment, extinction, biofeedback

Reduction of negative thinking; substitution of more realistic thinking

Negative thinking → Depression

Thought stopping, recording of automatic thoughts, refuting of negative thinking, homework assignments

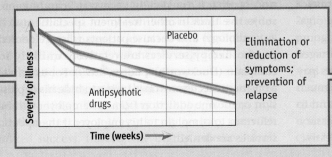

Elimination or reduction of symptoms; prevention of relapse

Antianxiety, antidepressant, antipsychotic, and mood-stabilizing drugs, electroconvulsive therapy

The Elements of the Treatment Process

▌ Approaches to psychotherapy are diverse, but they can be grouped into three categories: insight therapies, behavior therapies, and biomedical therapies. People vary in their willingness to seek treatment, and many people who need therapy do not receive it.

▌ Therapists come from a variety of professional backgrounds. Each of these professions shows different preferences for approaches to treatment. Psychologists typically practice insight or behavior therapy. Psychiatrists tend to depend on drug therapies.

Insight Therapies

▌ Insight therapies involve verbal interactions intended to enhance self-knowledge. In psychoanalysis, free association and dream analysis are used to explore the unconscious. When an analyst's probing hits sensitive areas, resistance can be expected. The transference relationship may be used to overcome this resistance so the client can handle interpretations that lead to insight. Classical psychoanalysis is not widely practiced anymore, but Freud's legacy lives on in a rich diversity of modern psychodynamic therapies.

▌ Rogers's client-centered therapy assumes that neurotic anxieties are derived from incongruence between a person's self-concept and reality. Accordingly, the client-centered therapist tries to provide a supportive climate in which clients can restructure their self-concept. Positive psychotherapy attempts to get clients to recognize their strengths, appreciate their blessings, savor positive experiences, and find meaning in their lives.

▌ Many theoretical approaches to insight therapy have been adapted for use with groups. Group therapists usually play a subtle role, staying in the background and working to promote group cohesiveness.

▌ Evaluating the effectiveness of any approach to therapy is complex and difficult. Nonetheless, the weight of the evidence suggests that insight therapies are superior to no treatment or placebo treatment.

Behavior Therapies

▌ Behavior therapies use the principles of learning in direct efforts to change specific aspects of behavior. Wolpe's systematic desensitization, a treatment for phobias, involves the construction of an anxiety hierarchy, relaxation training, and step-by-step movement through the hierarchy, pairing relaxation with each phobic stimulus.

▌ In aversion therapy, a stimulus associated with an unwanted response is paired with an unpleasant stimulus in an effort to eliminate the maladaptive response. Social skills training can improve clients' interpersonal skills through shaping, modeling, and behavioral rehearsal. Beck's cognitive therapy concentrates on changing the way clients think about events in their lives. There is ample evidence that behavior therapies are effective.

Biomedical Therapies

▌ Biomedical therapies are physiological interventions for psychological problems. The principal types of therapeutic drugs are antianxiety drugs, antipsychotic drugs, antidepressant drugs, and mood stabilizers. Drug therapies can be quite effective, but they have their drawbacks, such as problematic side effects and high relapse rates.

▌ Electroconvulsive therapy (ECT) is used to trigger a cortical seizure that is believed to have therapeutic value for mood disorders, especially depression. There is heated debate about the effectiveness of ECT and about possible risks associated with its use. Transcranial magnetic stimulation may have value in the treatment of depression, and deep brain stimulation is being investigated as a treatment for depression or obsessive-compulsive disorder.

Current Trends and Issues in Treatment

▌ Many clinicians and their clients believe that managed care has restricted access to mental health care and undermined its quality. Unfortunately, there are no simple solutions to these problems.

▌ The highly culture-bound origins of Western therapies have raised doubts about their applicability to other cultures and even to ethnic groups in Western society. Because of cultural and language barriers, therapeutic services are underutilized by ethnic minorities in America.

Institutional Treatment in Transition

▌ Disenchantment with the negative effects of mental hospitals led to the advent of more localized community mental health centers and a policy of deinstitutionalization. Unfortunately, deinstitutionalization has left some unanticipated problems in its wake, including the revolving door problem and increased homelessness.

Reflecting on the Chapter's Themes

▌ Our discussion of psychotherapy highlighted the value of theoretical diversity. Our coverage of therapy also showed once again that cultural factors shape psychological processes.

PERSONAL APPLICATION Looking for a Therapist

▌ Therapeutic services are available in many settings, and such services do not have to be expensive. Therapists' personal skills are more important than their professional degree. In selecting a therapist, it is reasonable to insist on a therapist of one sex or the other.

▌ When different theoretical approaches to therapy are compared, no significant differences are found in their overall effectiveness. However, most experts believe that for specific types of problems, some approaches to therapy are more effective than others. Therapy requires time, hard work, and the courage to confront your problems.

CRITICAL THINKING APPLICATION From Crisis to Wellness—But Was It the Therapy?

▌ People entering therapy are likely to get better even if their treatment is ineffective, because of placebo effects and regression toward the mean. Regression toward the mean occurs when people selected for their extremely high or low scores on some trait are measured a second time and their new scores fall closer to the mean. Regression and placebo effects may help explain why people can often be enthusiastic about phony, ineffectual treatments.

PSYKTREK PREVIEW

Explore Module 11d (*Insight Therapies*) to enhance your understanding of psychoanalysis and client-centered therapy.

Visit Module 11e (*Behavioral and Biomedical Therapies*) to get additional information on systematic desensitization and aversion therapy.

1. One key problem with the provision of psychotherapy is that:
   A. there are too many different approaches to treatment.
   B. there are too many different professions involved.
   C. there is a shortage of qualified therapists.
   D. there are many people who need therapy but do not receive treatment.

2. After undergoing psychoanalysis for several months, Karen has suddenly started "forgetting" to attend her therapy sessions. Karen's behavior is most likely a form of:
   A. resistance.   C. insight.
   B. transference.   D. catharsis.

3. The key task of the client-centered therapist is:
   A. interpretation of the client's thoughts, feelings, memories, and behaviors.
   B. clarification of the client's feelings.
   C. confrontation of the client's irrational thoughts.
   D. modification of the client's problematic behaviors.

4. Evaluating the effectiveness of psychotherapy is complicated and difficult because:
   A. disorders sometimes clear up on their own.
   B. different approaches to treatment pursue entirely different goals.
   C. clients' problems vary in severity.
   D. all of the above are involved.

5. Systematic desensitization is particularly effective for the treatment of _____ disorders.
   A. generalized anxiety   C. obsessive-compulsive
   B. panic   D. phobic

6. Linda's therapist has her practice active listening skills in structured role-playing exercises. Later, Linda is gradually asked to practice these skills with family members, friends, and finally, her boss. Linda is undergoing:
   A. systematic desensitization.   C. a token economy.
   B. cognitive restructuring.   D. social skills training.

7. After being released from a hospital, many schizophrenic patients stop taking their antipsychotic medication because:
   A. their mental impairment causes them to forget.
   B. of the unpleasant side effects.
   C. most schizophrenics don't believe they are ill.
   D. all of the above are involved.

8. Selective serotonin reuptake inhibitors (SSRIs) appear to have value for the treatment of _____ disorders.
   A. depressive   C. dissociative
   B. schizophrenic   D. alcoholic

9. Modern psychotherapy:
   A. was spawned by a cultural milieu that viewed the self as an independent, rational being.
   B. embraces universal cultural values.
   C. has been successfully exported to most non-Western cultures.
   D. both B and C.

10. Many people repeatedly go in and out of mental hospitals. Typically, such people are released because _____ ; they are eventually readmitted because _____ .
    A. they have been stabilized through drug therapy; their condition deteriorates once again because of inadequate outpatient care
    B. they run out of funds to pay for hospitalization; they once again can afford it
    C. they have been cured of their disorder; they develop another disorder
    D. they no longer want to be hospitalized; they voluntarily recommit themselves

11. The type of professional training a therapist has:
    A. is the most important indicator of his or her competence.
    B. should be the major consideration in choosing a therapist.
    C. is not all that important, since talented therapists can be found in all of the mental health professions.
    D. both A and B are true.

12. Which of the following could be explained by regression toward the mean?
    A. You get an average bowling score in one game and a superb score in the next game.
    B. You get an average bowling score in one game and a very low score in the next game.
    C. You get an average bowling score in one game and another average score in the next game.
    D. You get a terrible bowling score in one game and an average score in the next game.

Answers

1 D pp. 486–487
2 A p. 490
3 B p. 491
4 D pp. 493–494
5 D p. 495
6 D pp. 496–497
7 B p. 499
8 A p. 500
9 A p. 507
10 A p. 510
11 C p. 512
12 D pp. 514–515

PSYKTREK PREVIEW

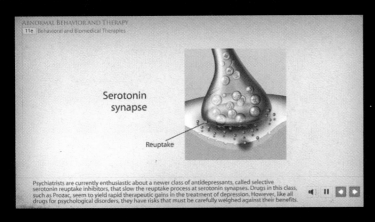

ABNORMAL BEHAVIOR AND THERAPY
11e Behavioral and Biomedical Therapies

Serotonin synapse

Reuptake

Psychiatrists are currently enthusiastic about a newer class of antidepressants, called selective serotonin reuptake inhibitors, that slow the reuptake process at serotonin synapses. Drugs in this class, such as Prozac, seem to yield rapid therapeutic gains in the treatment of depression. However, like all drugs for psychological disorders, they have risks that must be carefully weighed against their benefits.

PERSONALITY THEORY   Critical Thinking ❓

We have seen repeatedly in these Critical Thinking Exercises that our personal experiences can be mistaken when they are based on intuition or automatic processing of information. Furthermore, this phenomenon is not limited to laypeople. Like anyone else, psychologists and other mental health professionals who rely on their clinical experience when testing ideas are susceptible to cognitive distortions and illusions. In particular, it has been argued that clinicians who rely on *projective tests* have been misled by their intuition (Wood et al., 2003). *Projective tests are a category of personality tests in which subjects respond to vague, ambiguous stimuli in ways thought to reveal their inner needs, feelings, and personality traits.* The most widely used projective tests are the Rorschach Test and the Thematic Apperception Test (TAT). In the Rorschach Test, respondents are asked to describe what they see in a series of ten highly ambiguous inkblots. In the TAT, pictures of simple scenes containing one, two, or three people are presented to subjects, who then tell stories about what they think is happening in each scene and what emotions the people are experiencing.

Since the introduction of these tests in the first half of the 20th century, many testing experts have viewed projective tests as pseudoscientific. Despite the extensive criticism, many clinicians continue to believe that their results yield useful information about clients. But scientific researchers have responded that their studies show that clinicians mistakenly place too much faith in the validity of projective tests. The essence of this critique is captured in the following passage from Wood et al. (2003):

If the history of science teaches us anything, it's that common sense and intuition can be undependable barometers of

Increase your understanding of how antianxiety, antipsychotic, and antidepressant drugs exert their effects by accessing Module 11e (Behavioral and Biomedi-

Learn more about the projective tests used in clinical treatment by working through the Unit 10 Critical Thinking Exercise (Illusory Correlation, Consensual

15

Social Behavior

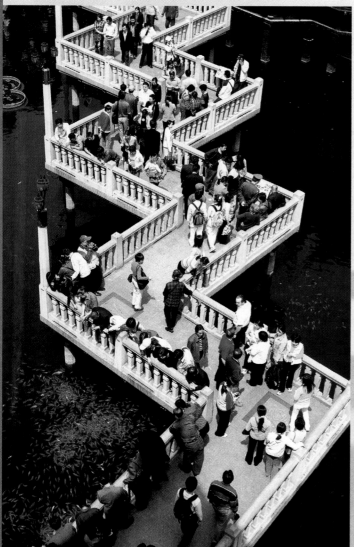

Zigzag Footbridge, Yu Yan Gardens, Shanghai, China © Jose Fuste Raga/Corbis

When Muffy, "the quintessential yuppie," met Jake, "the ultimate working-class stiff," her friends got very nervous.

Muffy is a 28-year-old stockbroker and a self-described "snob" with a group of about ten close women friends. Snobs all. They're graduates of fancy business schools. All consultants, investment bankers, and CPAs. All "cute, bright, fun to be with, and really intelligent," according to Muffy. They're all committed to their high-powered careers, but they all expect to marry someday, too.

Unfortunately, most of them don't date much. In fact, they spend a good deal of time "lamenting the dearth of 'good men.'" You know who the "good men" are. Those are the ones who are "committed to their work, open to the idea of marriage and family, and possessed of a good sense of humor."

Well, lucky Muffy actually met one of those "good men." Jake is a salesman. He comes from a working-class neighborhood. His clothes come from Sears.

He wasn't like the usual men Muffy dated. He treats Muffy the way she's always dreamed of being treated. He listens; he cares; he remembers. "He makes me feel safe and more cherished than any man I've ever known," she says.

So she decided to bring him to a little party of about 30 of her closest friends. . . .

Perhaps it was only Jake's nerves that caused him to commit some truly unforgivable faux pas that night. His sins were legion. Where do we start? First of all, he asked for a beer when everyone else was drinking white wine. He wore a worn turtleneck while everyone else had just removed the Polo tags from their clothing. He smoked. . . .

"The next day at least half of the people who had been at the party called to give me their impressions. They all said that they felt they just had to let me know that they thought Jake 'lacked polish' or 'seemed loud' or 'might not be a suitable match,'" Muffy says.

Now, you may think that Muffy's friends are simply very sensitive, demanding people. A group of princes and princesses who can detect a pea under the fluffiest stack of mattresses. But you'd be wrong. Actually, they've been quite accepting of some of the other men that Muffy has brought to their little parties. Or should we call them inquisitions? Winston, for example, was a great favorite.

"He got drunk, ignored me, and asked for other women's phone numbers right in front of me. But he was six-foot-four, the classic preppie, with blond hair, horn-rimmed glasses, and Ralph Lauren clothes."

And most important of all, he didn't ask for a Pabst Blue Ribbon. So now Muffy is confused. "Jake is the first guy I've been out with in a long time that I've really liked. I was excited about him and my friends knew that. I was surprised by their reaction. I'll admit there's some validity to all their comments, but it's hard to express how violent it was. It made me think about what these women really want in a man. Whatever they say, what they really want is someone they can take to a business dinner. They want someone who comes with a tux. Like a Ken doll."

Muffy may have come to a crossroads in her young life. It's clear that there's no way she can bring Jake among her friends for a while.

"I don't want their reaction to muddy my feelings until I get them sorted out," she says.

It just may be time for Muffy to choose between her man and her friends.

(Excerpt from Tales from the Front by Cheryl Lavin and Laura Kavesh, Copyright © 1988 by Cheryl Lavin and Laura Kavesh. Used by permission of Doubleday, a division of Random House, Inc.)

The preceding account is a real story, taken from a book about intimate relationships titled *Tales from the Front* (Lavin & Kavesh, 1988, pp. 118–121). Muffy is on the horns of a difficult dilemma. Romantic relationships are important to most people, but so are friendships, and Muffy may have to choose between the two. Muffy's story illustrates the significance of social relations in people's lives. It also foreshadows each of the topics that we'll cover in this chapter, as we look at behavior in its social context.

Social psychology is the branch of psychology concerned with the way individuals' thoughts, feelings, and behaviors are influenced by others. Our coverage of social psychology will focus on six broad topics. Let's return to Muffy's story to get a glimpse of the various facets of social behavior that we'll examine in the coming pages:

• *Person perception.* The crux of Muffy's problem is that Jake didn't make a very good impression on her friends. To what extent do people's expectations and stereotypes color their impressions of others?

• *Attribution processes.* Muffy is struggling to understand her friends' rejection of Jake. When she implies that it is due to their snotty elitism, she's engaging in attribution, making an inference about the causes of her friends' behavior. How do people use attributions to explain social behavior?

• *Interpersonal attraction.* Jake and Muffy are different in many important ways—is it true that opposites attract? Does similarity foster liking?

• *Attitudes.* Muffy's girlfriends have negative attitudes about working-class men. How are attitudes formed? What leads to attitude change?

• *Conformity and obedience.* Muffy's friends discourage her from dating Jake, putting her under pressure to conform to their values. What factors influence conformity? Can people be coaxed into doing things that contradict their values?

• *Behavior in groups.* Muffy belongs to a tight-knit group of friends who think along similar lines. Is people's behavior in groups similar to their behavior when alone? Why do people in groups often think alike?

Social psychologists study how people are affected by the actual, imagined, or implied presence of others. Their interest is not limited to individuals' *interactions* with others, as people can engage in social behavior even when they're alone. For instance, if you were driving by yourself on a deserted highway and tossed your trash out your car window, your littering would be a social action. It would defy social norms, reflect your socialization and attitudes, and have repercussions (albeit, small) for other people in your society. Thus, social psychologists often study *individual* behavior in a social context. This interest in understanding individual behavior should be readily apparent in our first section, on person perception.

Person Perception: Forming Impressions of Others

Can you remember the first meeting of your introductory psychology class? What kind of impression did your professor make on you that day? Did your instructor appear to be confident? Easygoing? Pompous? Open-minded? Cynical? Friendly? Were your first impressions supported or undermined by subsequent observations? When you interact with people, you're constantly engaged in *person perception*, **the process of forming impressions of others.** In this section we consider some of the factors that influence, and often distort, people's perceptions of others.

Effects of Physical Appearance   Sim10

"You shouldn't judge a book by its cover." People know better than to let physical attractiveness determine their perceptions of others' personal qualities. Or do they? One recent study showed that good-looking people grab our attention almost immediately and hold it longer than less-attractive individuals do (Maner et al., 2007). And a number of studies have demonstrated that judgments of others' personality are often swayed by their appearance, especially their physical attractiveness. People tend to ascribe desirable personality characteristics to those who are good-looking, seeing them as more sociable, friendly, poised, warm, and well adjusted than those who are less attractive (Eagly et al., 1991; van Leeuwen & Macrae, 2004). In reality, research findings suggest that little correlation exists between attractiveness and personality traits (Feingold, 1992). Why do we inaccurately assume that a connection exists between good looks and personality? One reason is that extremely attractive people are vastly overrepresented in the entertainment media, where they are mostly portrayed in a highly favorable light (Smith, McIntosh, & Bazzini, 1999).

You might guess that physical attractiveness would influence perceptions of competence less than perceptions of personality, but the data suggest otherwise. A review of the relevant research found that people have a surprisingly strong tendency to view good-looking individuals as more competent than less-attractive individuals (Langlois et al., 2000). This bias pays off for good-looking people, as they tend to secure better jobs and earn higher salaries than less-attractive individuals (Collins & Zebrowitz, 1995; Senior et al., 2007). For example, research on attorneys whose law school class photos were evaluated by independent raters found that physical attractiveness boosted income by 10%–12% (Engemann & Owyang, 2005).

Judgments of people's faces seem to be particularly important, as recent evidence suggests that these judgments are associated with important outcomes in the real world. For example, one study found that perceptions of competence based solely on facial appearance predicted the outcomes of U.S. congressional elections surprisingly well (Todorov

"Beauty is life's E-Z Pass."

et al., 2005). Naive participants rated the competence of political candidates from all over the country based on brief exposures to head shots. The candidates who were viewed as more competent ended up winning 72% of Senate races and 67% of House races. In another study, participants rated the competence/power of 100 chief executive officers (CEOs) of large companies based on their facial appearance (Rule & Ambady, 2008). These ratings correlated .34 with the corporate profits of the CEOs' companies. Thus, perceptions of personality based on facial features are associated with objective measures of successful performance in important arenas of life.

Moreover, studies indicate that social perceptions based on facial appearance are formed in the blink of an eye. You might guess that people would need 20–30 seconds to size someone up, but a recent, compelling study demonstrated that it takes only a tenth of a second to draw inferences about individuals based on facial features. Willis and Todorov (2006) asked subjects to assess traits such as competence, trustworthiness, and aggressiveness based on brief exposures (one-tenth of a second, half a second, or one second) to facial photographs. They compared these assessments to judgments of the same photos made by other participants who were given no time constraints and found that the instant judgments were highly correlated with the leisurely judgments. Thus, first impressions based on faces can occur almost instantly.

Stereotypes

Stereotypes can have a dramatic effect on the process of person perception. **Stereotypes are widely held beliefs that people have certain characteristics because of their membership in a particular group.** The most common stereotypes in our society are those based on gender and on membership in ethnic or occupational groups. People who subscribe to traditional *gender stereotypes* tend to assume that women are emotional, submissive, illogical,

and passive, while men are unemotional, dominant, logical, and aggressive. Preconceived notions that Jews are mercenary, blacks have rhythm, Germans are methodical, and Italians are passionate are examples of common *ethnic stereotypes. Occupational stereotypes* suggest that lawyers are manipulative, computer programmers are nerdy, accountants are conforming, artists are moody, and so forth.

Stereotyping is a normal cognitive process that is often automatic and that saves on the time and effort required to get a handle on people individually (Devine & Monteith, 1999; Operario & Fiske, 2001). Stereotypes save energy by simplifying our social world. However, this conservation of energy often comes at some cost in terms of accuracy (Wigboldus, Dijksterhuis, & van Knippenberg, 2003). Stereotypes tend to be broad overgeneralizations that ignore the diversity within social groups and foster inaccurate perceptions of people (Hilton & von Hippel, 1996). Obviously, not all males, Jews, and lawyers behave alike. Most people who subscribe to stereotypes realize that not all members of a group are identical. For instance, they may admit that some men aren't competitive, some Jews aren't mercenary, and some lawyers aren't manipulative. However, people may still tend to assume that males, Jews, and lawyers are *more likely* than others to have these characteristics. Even if stereotypes mean only that people think in terms of slanted *probabilities,* their expectations may lead them to misperceive individuals with whom they interact. As we've noted in previous chapters, perception is subjective, and people often see what they expect to see.

Subjectivity in Person Perception

Stereotypes and other schemas create biases in person perception that often lead to confirmation of people's expectations about others. If any ambiguity exists in someone's behavior, people are likely to interpret what they see in a way that's consistent with their expectations (Olson, Roese, & Zanna, 1996).

DILBERT

People not only see what they expect to see, they also tend to overestimate how often they see it (Johnson & Mullen, 1994; Shavitt et al., 1999). *Illusory correlation* occurs when people estimate that they have encountered more confirmations of an association between social traits than they have actually seen. People also tend to underestimate the number of disconfirmations they have encountered, as illustrated by statements like "I've never met an honest lawyer."

Memory processes can contribute to confirmatory biases in person perception in a variety of ways. Often, individuals selectively recall facts that fit with their schemas and stereotypes (Fiske, 1998; Quinn, Macrae, & Bodenhausen, 2003). Evidence for such a tendency was found in a study by Cohen (1981). In this experiment, subjects watched a videotape of a woman, described as either a waitress or a librarian, who engaged in a variety of activities, including listening to classical music, drinking beer, and watching TV. When asked to recall what the woman did during the filmed sequence, participants tended to remember activities consistent with their stereotypes of waitresses and librarians. For instance, participants who thought the woman was a waitress tended to recall her drinking beer, whereas subjects who thought she was a librarian tended to recall her listening to classical music.

An Evolutionary Perspective on Bias in Person Perception

Why is the process of person perception riddled with bias? Evolutionary psychologists argue that many of the biases seen in social perception were adaptive in humans' ancestral environment (Krebs & Denton, 1997). For example, they argue that person perception is swayed by physical attractiveness because attractiveness was associated with reproductive potential in women and with health, vigor, and the accumulation of material resources in men.

Evolutionary theorists attribute the human tendency to automatically categorize others to our distant ancestors' need to quickly separate friend from foe. They assert that humans are programmed by evolution to immediately classify people as members of an *ingroup*—a group that one belongs to and identifies with, or as members of an *outgroup*—a group that one does not belong to or identify with. This crucial categorization is thought to structure subsequent perceptions. As Krebs and Denton (1997) put it, "It is as though the act of classifying others as ingroup or outgroup members activates two quite different brain circuits" (p. 27). Ingroup members tend to be viewed in a favorable light, whereas outgroup members tend to be viewed in terms of various negative stereotypes. According to Krebs and Denton, these negative stereotypes ("They are inferior; they are all alike; they will exploit us") move outgroups out of our domain of empathy, so we feel justified in not liking them. Thus, evolutionary psychologists assert that much of the bias in person perception is due to cognitive mechanisms that have been wired into the human brain by natural selection.

REVIEW of Key Learning Goals

15.1 People's perceptions of others can be distorted by physical appearance. People tend to attribute desirable characteristics, such as intelligence, competence, warmth, and friendliness, to those who are good-looking. Perceptions of competence based on facial appearance are particularly important. Social perceptions based on facial features can be formed in the blink of an eye.

15.2 Stereotypes are widely held beliefs that others will have certain characteristics because of their membership in a specific group. Gender, age, ethnic, and occupational stereotypes are common. In interacting with others, stereotypes may lead people to see what they expect to see. People also tend to overestimate how often their expectations are confirmed, a phenomenon called the illusory correlation effect.

15.3 Evolutionary psychologists argue that many biases in person perception were adaptive in humans' ancestral past. The human tendency to automatically categorize others may reflect the primitive need to quickly separate friend from foe.

Attribution Processes: Explaining Behavior

It's Friday evening and you're sitting around at home feeling bored. You call a few friends to see whether they'd like to go out. They all say that they'd love to go, but they have other commitments and they can't. Their commitments sound vague, and you feel that their reasons for not going out with you are rather flimsy. How do you explain these rejections?

Do your friends really have commitments? Are they worn out by school and work? Are they just lazy and apathetic about going out? These questions illustrate a process that people engage in routinely: the explanation of behavior. *Attributions* play a key role in these explanatory efforts, and they have significant effects on social relations.

What are attributions? *Attributions* are inferences that people draw about the causes of events, others' behavior, and their own behavior. If you conclude that a friend turned down your invitation because she's overworked, you've made an attribution about the cause of her behavior (and, implicitly, rejected other possible explanations). If you conclude that you're stuck at home with nothing to do because you failed to plan ahead, you've made an attribution about the cause of an event (being stuck at home). If you conclude that you failed to plan ahead because you're a procrastinator, you've made an attribution about the cause of your own behavior. *Why do people make attributions?* Individuals make attributions because they have a strong need to understand their experiences. They want to make sense out of their own behavior, others' actions, and the events in their lives.

Internal Versus External Attributions 12a

Fritz Heider (1958) was the first to describe how people make attributions. He asserted that people tend to locate the cause of behavior either *within a person,* attributing it to personal factors, or *outside a person,* attributing it to environmental factors.

Elaborating on Heider's insight, various theorists have agreed that explanations of behavior and events can be categorized as internal or external attributions (Jones & Davis, 1965; Kelley, 1967; Weiner, 1974). *Internal attributions* ascribe the causes of behavior to personal dispositions, traits, abilities, and feelings. *External attributions* ascribe the causes of behavior to situational demands and environmental constraints. For example, if a friend's business fails, you might attribute it to your friend's lack of business acumen (an internal, personal factor) or to negative trends in the nation's economic climate (an external, situational explanation). Parents who find out that their teenage son has just banged up the car may blame it on his carelessness (an internal attribution) or on slippery road conditions (an external attribution).

Internal and external attributions can have a tremendous impact on everyday interpersonal interactions. Blaming a friend's business failure on poor business judgment as opposed to a poor economy will have a great impact on how you view your friend—not to mention on whether you'll lend him or her money in the future. Likewise, if parents attribute their son's automobile accident to slippery road conditions, they're likely to deal with the event very differently than if they attribute it to his carelessness.

Attributions for Success and Failure 12a

Some psychologists have sought to discover additional dimensions of attributional thinking besides the internal-external dimension. After studying the attributions that people make in explaining success and failure, Bernard Weiner (1980, 1986, 1994) concluded that people often focus on the *stability* of the causes underlying behavior. According to Weiner, the stable-unstable dimension in attribution cuts across the internal-external dimension, creating four types of attributions for success and failure, as shown in **Figure 15.1**.

Let's apply Weiner's model to a concrete event. Imagine that you're contemplating why you failed to get a job that you wanted. You might attribute your setback to internal factors that are stable (lack of ability) or unstable (inadequate effort to put together an eye-catching résumé). Or you might attribute your setback to external factors that are stable (too much outstanding competition) or unstable (bad luck). If you got the job, the explanations you might offer for your success would fall into the same four categories: internal-stable (your excellent ability), internal-unstable (your hard work to assemble a superb résumé), external-stable (lack of top-flight competition), and external-unstable (good luck).

Bias in Attribution 12a

Attributions are only inferences. Your attributions may not be the correct explanations for events.

Fritz Heider

"Often the momentary situation which, at least in part, determines the behavior of a person is disregarded and the behavior is taken as a manifestation of personal characteristics."

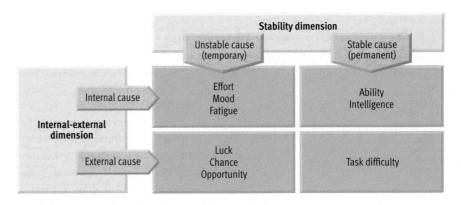

Figure 15.1

Weiner's model of attributions for success and failure. Weiner's model assumes that people's explanations for success and failure emphasize internal versus external causes and stable versus unstable causes. Examples of causal factors that fit into each of the four cells in Weiner's model are shown in the diagram.

SOURCE: Weiner, B., Friese, I., Kukla, A., Reed, L., & Rosenbaum, R. M. (1972). Perceiving the causes of success and failure. In E. E. Jones, D. E. Kanouse, H. H. Kelley, R. E. Nisbett, S. Valins, & B. Weiner (Eds.) *Perceiving the causes of behavior.* Morristown, NJ: General Learning Press. Used by permission of Bernard Weiner.

Analyzing Attributions

Check your understanding of attribution processes by analyzing possible explanations for an athletic team's success. Imagine that the women's track team at your school has just won a regional championship that qualifies it for the national tournament. Around the campus, you hear people attribute the team's success to a variety of factors. Examine the attributions shown below and place each of them in one of the cells of Weiner's model of attribution (just record the letter inside the cell). The answers are in Appendix A.

	Unstable cause (temporary)	Stable cause (permanent)
Internal cause		
External cause		

a. "They won only because the best two athletes on Central State's team were out with injuries—talk about good fortune!"

b. "They won because they have some of the best talent in the country."

c. "Anybody could win this region; the competition is far below average in comparison to the rest of the country."

d. "They won because they put in a great deal of last-minute effort and practice, and they were incredibly fired up for the regional tourney after last year's near miss."

Paradoxical as it may seem, people often arrive at inaccurate explanations even when they contemplate the causes of *their own behavior*. Attributions ultimately represent guesswork about the causes of events, and these guesses tend to be slanted in certain directions. Let's look at the principal biases seen in attribution.

Actor-Observer Bias 12a

Your view of your own behavior can be quite different from the view of someone else observing you. When an actor (the person exhibiting the behavior) and an observer draw inferences about the causes of the actor's behavior, they often make different attributions. The *fundamental attribution error* refers to observers' bias in favor of internal attributions in explaining others' behavior. Of course, in many instances, an internal attribution may not be an "error." However, observers have a curious tendency to overestimate the likelihood that an actor's behavior reflects personal qualities rather than situational factors (Krull, 2001). Why? It is not that people assume that situational factors have little impact on behavior (Gawronski, 2004). Rather, it's that attributing others' behavior to their dispositions is a relatively effortless, almost automatic process, whereas

explaining people's behavior in terms of situational factors requires more thought and effort (see **Figure 15.2**) (Krull & Erickson, 1995). Another factor favoring internal attributions is that many people feel that few situations are so coercive that they negate all freedom of choice (Forsyth, 2004).

To illustrate the gap that often exists between actors' and observers' attributions, imagine that you're visiting your bank and you fly into a rage over a mistake made on your account. Observers who witness your rage are likely to make an internal attribution and infer that you are surly, temperamental, and quarrelsome. They may be right, but if asked, you'd probably attribute your rage to the frustrating situation. Perhaps you're normally a calm, easygoing person, but today you've been in line for 20 minutes, you just straightened out a similar error by the same bank last week, and you're being treated rudely by the teller. Observers often are unaware of situational considerations such as these, so they tend to make internal attributions for another's behavior (Gilbert, 1998).

In contrast, the circumstances that have influenced an actor's behavior tend to be more salient to the actor. Hence, actors are more likely than observers to locate the cause of their behavior in the situation. In general, then, *actors favor external attributions for their behavior, while observers are more likely to explain the same behavior with internal attributions* (Jones & Nisbett, 1971; Krueger, Ham, & Linford, 1996).

That said, a recent study identified an interesting variable that appears to reduce observers' tendency to explain actors' behavior with internal attributions. That variable is whether the observers have experienced the same situation themselves (Balcetis & Dunning, 2008). Dealing with a specific situation gives people an opportunity to learn about the power of external forces in that situation. This knowledge makes them less likely to commit the fundamental attribution error in interpreting the behavior of others in the same situation. For example, people who have been tricked by a con artist, or who have suffered through a foreclosure, generally will be less likely to make internal attributions in explaining why others have experienced a similar fate.

Self-Serving Bias 12a

The self-serving bias in attribution comes into play when people attempt to explain success and failure (Mezulis et al., 2004; Shepperd, Malone, & Sweeny, 2008). The *self-serving bias* is the tendency to attribute one's successes to personal factors and one's failures to situational factors. In explaining *failure*, the usual actor-observer biases are apparent. But in explaining *success*, the usual actor-observer differences are reversed to some degree; actors prefer internal attributions so they can take credit for their triumphs. Interestingly, this bias grows stronger as time passes after an event, so that people tend to take progressively more credit for their successes and less blame for their failures (Burger, 1986).

Culture and Attributions

Do the patterns of attribution observed in subjects from Western societies transcend culture? More research is needed, but the preliminary evidence suggests not. Some interesting cultural disparities have emerged in research on attribution processes.

According to Harry Triandis (1989, 1994, 2001), cultural differences in *individualism* versus *collectivism* influence attributional tendencies as well as other aspects of social behavior. *Individualism* involves putting personal goals ahead of group goals and defining one's identity in terms of personal attributes rather than group memberships. In contrast, *collectivism* involves putting group goals ahead of personal goals and defining one's identity in terms of the groups one belongs to (such as one's family, tribe, work group, social class, caste, and so on). In comparison to individualistic cultures, collectivist cultures place a higher priority on shared values and resources, cooperation, mutual interdependence, and concern for how one's actions will affect other group members. In childrearing, collectivist cultures emphasize the importance of obedience, reliability, and proper behavior, whereas individualistic cultures emphasize the development of independence, self-esteem, and self-reliance.

A variety of factors influence whether societies cherish individualism as opposed to collectivism. Among other things, increases in a culture's affluence, education, urbanization, and social mobility tend to foster more individualism (Triandis, 1994). Many contemporary societies are in transition, but generally speaking, North American and Western European cultures tend to be individualistic, whereas Asian, African, and Latin American cultures tend to be collectivistic (Hofstede, 1980, 1983, 2001) (see **Figure 15.3** on the next page).

How does individualism versus collectivism relate to patterns of attribution? The evidence suggests that collectivist cultures may promote different attributional biases than individualistic cultures do. For example, people from collectivist societies appear to be less susceptible to the *fundamental attribution error* than those from individualistic societies (Choi, Nisbett, & Norenzayan, 1999; Triandis, 2001). And the *self-serving bias* may be particularly prevalent in

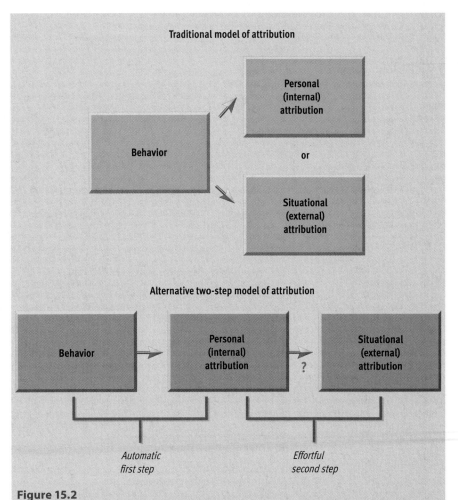

Figure 15.2

An alternative view of the fundamental attribution error. According to Gilbert (1989) and others, the nature of attribution processes favors the *fundamental attribution error*. Traditional models of attribution assume that internal and external attributions are an either-or proposition requiring equal amounts of effort. In contrast, the two-step model of attribution posits that people tend to automatically make internal attributions with little effort, then *may* expend additional effort to adjust for the influence of situational factors, which can lead to an external attribution. Thus, external attributions for others' behavior require more thought and effort, which makes them less common than personal attributions.

Triumphant athletes from cultures high in collectivism typically exhibit different attributional biases than winning athletes from Western societies that are high in individualism. Collectivist cultures tend to promote a self-effacing bias in explaining success, rather than a self-serving bias.

Hofstede's rankings of national cultures' individualism		
Individualistic cultures	**Intermediate cultures**	**Collectivist cultures**
1. United States	19. Israel	37. Hong Kong
2. Australia	20. Spain	38. Chile
3. Great Britain	21. India	40. Singapore
4. Canada	22. Argentina	40. Thailand
4. Netherlands	22. Japan	40. West Africa region
6. New Zealand	24. Iran	42. El Salvador
7. Italy	25. Jamaica	43. South Korea
8. Belgium	26. Arab region	44. Taiwan
9. Denmark	26. Brazil	45. Peru
10. France	28. Turkey	46. Costa Rica
11. Sweden	29. Uruguay	47. Indonesia
12. Ireland	30. Greece	47. Pakistan
13. Norway	31. Philippines	49. Colombia
14. Switzerland	32. Mexico	50. Venezuela
15. West Germany	34. East Africa region	51. Panama
16. South Africa	34. Portugal	52. Ecuador
17. Finland	34. Yugoslavia	53. Guatemala
18. Austria	36. Malaysia	

Figure 15.3

Individualism versus collectivism around the world. Hofstede (1980, 1983, 2001) used survey data from more than 100,000 employees of a large, multinational corporation to estimate the emphasis on individualism versus collectivism in 50 nations and 3 regions. His large, diverse international sample remains unequaled to date. In the figure, cultures are ranked in terms of how strongly they embraced the values of individualism. As you can see, Hofstede's estimates suggest that North American and Western European nations tend to be relatively individualistic, whereas more collectivism is found in Asian, African, and Latin American countries.

SOURCE: Adapted from Hofstede, G. (2001). *Culture's consequences* (2nd ed., p. 215). Thousand Oaks, CA: Sage. Copyright © 2001 Sage Publications. Adapted by permission of Dr. Geert Hofstede.

individualistic, Western societies, where an emphasis on competition and high self-esteem motivates people to try to impress others, as well as themselves (Mezulis et al., 2004). In contrast, Japanese individuals exhibit a *self-effacing bias* in explaining success (Akimoto & Sanbonmatsu, 1999). That is, they tend to attribute their successes to help they receive from others or to the ease of the task, while downplaying the importance of their ability.

Research also suggests that Asians have a greater tendency than Westerners to view events in the context of webs of interdependent social relationships.

This holistic perception of the world leads them to make more complex causal attributions than Westerners. This way of thinking also tends to make Asians more aware of the sometimes indirect and distant consequences of events, what one might refer to as unexpected *ripple effects* (Maddux & Yuki, 2006). For example, when asked about the consequences of a specific event, such as being laid off or being in a car accident, Asian subjects estimate that far more people will be affected than Western participants do.

REVIEW of Key Learning Goals

15.4 Attributions are inferences about the causes of events and behavior. Individuals make attributions to understand their social world. Attributions can be classified as internal or external. Internal attributions ascribe behavior to personal dispositions and traits, whereas external attributions locate the cause of behavior in the environment.

15.5 Weiner's model proposes that attributions for success and failure should be analyzed in terms of the stability of causes, as well as along the internal-external dimension, yielding four possible types of attributions: internal-stable, internal-unstable, external-stable, and external-unstable.

15.6 Observers favor internal attributions to explain another's behavior, which is called the fundamental attribution error, while actors favor external attributions to explain their own behavior. The self-serving bias is the tendency to attribute one's good outcomes to personal factors and one's bad outcomes to situational factors.

15.7 Cultures vary in their emphasis on individualism as opposed to collectivism, and these differences appear to influence attributional tendencies. The fundamental attribution error and the self-serving bias in attribution may be more prevalent in Western cultures that are high in individualism. People in Asian cultures may be more aware of the indirect and distant consequences of events.

concept check 15.2

Recognizing Bias in Social Cognition

Check your understanding of bias in social cognition by identifying various types of errors that are common in person perception and attribution. Imagine that you're a nonvoting student member of a college committee at Southwest State University that is hiring a new political science professor. As you listen to the committee's discussion, you hear examples of (a) the illusory correlation effect, (b) stereotyping, and (c) the fundamental attribution error. Indicate which of these is at work in the excerpts from committee members' deliberations below. The answers are in Appendix A.

_____ **1.** "I absolutely won't consider the fellow who arrived 30 minutes late for his interview. Anybody who can't make a job interview on time is either irresponsible or hopelessly disorganized. I don't care what he says about the airline messing up his reservations."

_____ **2.** "You know, I was very, very impressed with the young female applicant, and I would love to hire her, but every time we add a young woman to the faculty in liberal arts, she gets pregnant within the first year." The committee chairperson, who has heard this line from this professor before replies, "You always say that, so I finally did a systematic check of what's happened in the past. Of the last 14 women hired in liberal arts, only one has become pregnant within a year."

_____ **3.** "The first one I want to rule out is the guy who's been practicing law for the last ten years. Although he has an excellent background in political science, I just don't trust lawyers. They're all ambitious, power-hungry, manipulative cutthroats. He'll be a divisive force in the department."

Interpersonal Attraction: Liking and Loving

"I just don't know what she sees in him. She could do so much better for herself. I suppose he's a nice guy, but they're just not right for each other." Can't you imagine Muffy's friends making these comments in discussing her relationship with Jake? You've probably heard similar remarks on many occasions. These comments illustrate people's interest in analyzing the dynamics of attraction. *Interpersonal attraction refers to positive feelings toward another person.* Social psychologists use this term broadly to encompass a variety of experiences, including liking, friendship, admiration, lust, and love.

Key Factors in Attraction

Many factors influence who is attracted to whom. Here we'll discuss factors that promote the development of liking, friendship, and love. Although these are different types of attraction, the interpersonal dynamics at work in each are surprisingly similar.

Physical Attractiveness

It is often said that "beauty is only skin deep," but the empirical evidence suggests that most people don't really believe this saying (Fitness, Fletcher, & Overall, 2003). The importance of physical attractiveness was demonstrated in a study of college students in which unacquainted men and women were sent off on a "get-acquainted" date (Sprecher & Duck, 1994). The investigators were mainly interested in how communication might affect the process of attraction, but to put this factor in context they also measured participants' perceptions of their date's physical attractiveness and similarity to themselves. They found that the quality of communication during the date did have some effect on females' interest in friendship, but the key determinant of romantic attraction for both sexes was the physical attractiveness of the other person. Consistent with this finding, research has shown, as one might expect, that attractive people of both sexes enjoy greater mating success than their less-attractive peers (Rhodes, Simmons, & Peters, 2005). Many other studies have demonstrated the singular prominence of physical attractiveness in the initial stage of dating and have shown that it continues to influence the course of commitment as relationships evolve (McNulty, Neff, & Karney, 2008; Patzer, 2006). In the realm of romance, being physically attractive appears to be more important for females' desirability (Gottschall, 2007; Regan, 2003).

For example, in a study of college students (Speed & Gangestad, 1997), the correlation between romantic popularity (assessed by peer ratings) and physical attractiveness was higher for females (.76) than for males (.47).

Although people prefer physically attractive partners in romantic relationships, they may consider their own level of attractiveness in pursuing dates. What people want in a partner may be different from what they are willing to settle for (Regan, 1998). **The *matching hypothesis* proposes that males and females of approximately equal physical attractiveness are likely to select each other as partners.** The matching hypothesis is supported by evidence that married couples tend to be very similar in level of physical attractiveness (Feingold, 1988). Interestingly, people expect that individuals who are similar in attractiveness will be more satisfied as couples and less likely to break up (Garcia & Khersonsky, 1996), although a recent study of actual married couples failed to support this notion (McNulty et al., 2008).

Similarity Effects

Is it true that "birds of a feather flock together," or do "opposites attract"? Research provides far more support for the former than the latter. Married and dating couples tend to be similar in age, race, religion, social class, education, intelligence, physical attractiveness, and attitudes (Kalmijn, 1998; Watson et al., 2004). Similarity is also seen among friends. For instance, adult friends tend to be relatively similar

Key Learning Goals

15.8 Evaluate the role of physical attractiveness and similarity in attraction.

15.9 Clarify the role of reciprocity and romantic ideals in attraction.

15.10 Distinguish between passionate and companionate love and between intimacy and commitment.

15.11 Outline the evidence on love as a form of attachment.

15.12 Discuss cultural variations in close relationships and how the Internet has affected romantic relationships.

15.13 Understand evolutionary analyses of mating preferences and tactics.

According to the matching hypothesis, males and females who are similar in physical attractiveness are likely to be drawn together. This type of matching may also influence the formation of friendships.

© Thomas Barwick/Photolibrary

"It would never work out between us, Tom—we're from two totally different tiers of the upper middle class."

in terms of income, education, occupational status, ethnicity, and religion (Blieszner & Adams, 1992). Among romantic couples, similarity in *personality* appears to be modest (Luo & Klohnen, 2005). However, some couples are more similar in personality than others, and this convergence in personality does correlate moderately with relationship satisfaction (Gonzaga, Campos, & Bradbury, 2007).

The most obvious explanation for these correlations is that similarity causes attraction. Laboratory experiments on *attitude similarity,* conducted by Donn Byrne and his colleagues, suggest that similarity *does* cause liking (Byrne, 1997; Byrne, Clore, & Smeaton, 1986). However, research also suggests that attraction can foster similarity (Anderson, Keltner, & John, 2003). For example, Davis and Rusbult (2001) found that dating partners gradually modify their attitudes in ways that make them more congruent, a phenomenon they called *attitude alignment.* Moreover, people in stable, satisfying intimate relationships tend to subjectively overestimate how similar their partners are (Murray et al., 2002). Wanting to believe that they have found a kindred spirit, they tend to assume that their partners are mirrors of themselves.

Reciprocity Effects

In his widely read book *How to Win Friends and Influence People,* Dale Carnegie (1936) suggested that people can gain others' liking by showering them with praise and flattery. However, we've all heard that "flattery will get you nowhere." Which advice is right? The evidence suggests that flattery will get you somewhere, with some people, some of the time.

In interpersonal attraction, *reciprocity* involves liking those who show that they like you. In general, research indicates that we tend to like those who show that they like us and that we tend to see others as liking us more if we like them. Thus, it appears that liking breeds liking and loving promotes loving (Spre-

cher, 1998). Reciprocating attraction generally entails providing friends and intimate partners with positive feedback that results in a *self-enhancement* effect—in other words, you help them feel good about themselves (Sedikides & Strube, 1997). However, studies suggest that people are also interested in *self-verification*—that is, they seek feedback that matches and supports their self-concepts (Bosson & Swann, 2001).

Romantic Ideals

In the realm of romance, people want their partner to measure up to their ideals. These ideals spell out the personal qualities that one hopes to find in a partner, such as warmth, good looks, loyalty, high status, a sense of humor, and so forth. According to Simpson, Fletcher, and Campbell (2001), people routinely evaluate how close their intimate partners come to matching these ideal standards and these evaluations influence how relationships progress. Consistent with this theory, research shows that the more closely individuals' perceptions of their partners match their ideals, the more satisfied they tend to be with their relationship—both in the early stages of dating (Fletcher, Simpson, & Thomas, 2000) and in stable, long-term relationships (Fletcher et al., 1999). Moreover, the size of the discrepancy between ideals and perceptions predicts whether a dating relationship will continue or dissolve (Fletcher et al., 2000; Overall, Fletcher, & Simpson, 2006).

Of course, these evaluations of how a partner compares to one's ideals are subjective, leaving room for distortion. When people are highly invested in a relationship, they can reduce the discrepancy between their ideals and their perceptions either by lowering their standards or by making charitable evaluations of their partners. Research suggests that the latter strategy is more common. For example, in a study of 180 couples, Murray, Holmes, and Griffin (1996) found that most participants viewed their partners more favorably than the partners viewed themselves. Individuals' perceptions of their romantic partners seemed to reflect their ideals for a partner more than reality. Interestingly, research suggests that people are happier in their relationship when they idealize their partners and when their partners idealize them. This line of research suggests that small, positive illusions about one's partner may foster happier and more resilient romantic relationships (Miller, Niehuis, & Huston, 2006; Murray, 2001).

Perspectives on the Mystery of Love

12b

Love has proven to be an elusive subject. It's difficult to define and study because there are many types of love (Berscheid, 2006). Nonetheless, psychologists have begun to make some progress in their study of love. Let's look at their theories and research.

Passionate and Companionate Love 12b

Two pioneers in research on love, Elaine Hatfield and Ellen Berscheid (Berscheid, 1988; Hatfield & Rapson, 1993), proposed that romantic relationships are characterized by two kinds of love: passionate love and companionate love. *Passionate love* is a complete absorption in another that includes tender sexual feelings and the agony and ecstasy of intense emotion. Passionate love has its ups and downs, as it is associated with large swings in positive and negative emotions (Reis & Aron, 2008). *Companionate love* is warm, trusting, tolerant affection for another whose life is deeply intertwined with one's own. Passionate and companionate love *may* coexist, but they don't necessarily go hand in hand. Research suggests that, as a general rule, companionate love is more strongly related to relationship satisfaction than passionate love (Fehr, 2001).

The distinction between passionate and companionate love has been further refined by Robert Sternberg (1988c, 2006), who suggests that love has three facets rather than just two. He subdivides companionate love into intimacy and commitment. *Intimacy* refers to warmth, closeness, and sharing in a relationship. *Commitment* is an intent to maintain a relationship in spite of the difficulties and costs that may arise. Sternberg has mapped out the probable relations between the passage of time and the three components of love, as shown in **Figure 15.4**. He argues that passion reaches its peak in the early phases of love and then erodes. He believes that intimacy and commitment increase with time, although at different rates.

Research suggests that passionate love is a powerful motivational force that produces profound changes in people's thinking, emotion, and behavior (Reis & Aron, 2008). Interestingly, brain-imaging research indicates that when people think about someone they are passionately in love with, these thoughts light up the dopamine circuits in the brain that are known to be activated by cocaine and other addictive drugs (Aron, Fisher, & Mashek, 2005). Perhaps that explains why passionate love sometimes resembles an addiction.

Love as Attachment 12b

Cindy Hazan and Phillip Shaver (1987) have looked not at the types of love but at similarities between adult love and attachment relationships in infancy.

We noted in Chapter 10 that infant-caretaker bonding, or *attachment*, emerges in the first year of life. Early attachments vary in quality, and infants tend to fall into three groups (Ainsworth et al., 1978). Most infants develop a *secure attachment*. However, some are very anxious when separated from their caretaker, a syndrome called *anxious-ambivalent attachment*. A third group of infants, characterized by *avoidant attachment*, never bond very well with their caretaker.

According to Hazan and Shaver, romantic love is an attachment process, and people's intimate relationships in adulthood follow the same form as their attachments in infancy. In their theory, a person who had an anxious-ambivalent attachment in infancy will tend to have romantic relations marked by anxiety and ambivalence in adulthood. In other words, people relive their early bonding experiences with their parents in their romantic relationships in adulthood.

Hazan and Shaver's (1987) initial survey study provided striking support for their theory. They found that adults' love relationships could be sorted into groups that paralleled the three patterns of attachment seen in infants (see **Figure 15.5** on the next page). *Secure adults* found it relatively easy to get close to others and described their love relations as trusting. *Anxious-ambivalent adults* reported a preoccupation with love accompanied by expectations of rejection, and they described their love relations as volatile and marked by jealousy. *Avoidant adults* found it difficult to get close to others and described their love relations as lacking intimacy and trust. Research eventually showed that attachment patterns

Ellen Berscheid

"The emotion of romantic love seems to be distressingly fragile. As a 16th-century sage poignantly observed, 'the history of a love affair is the drama of its fight against time.'"

Elaine Hatfield

"Passionate love is like any other form of excitement. By its very nature, excitement involves a continuous interplay between elation and despair, thrills and terror."

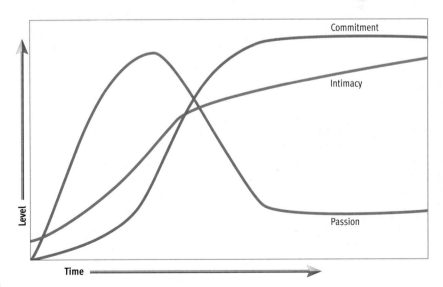

Figure 15.4

Sternberg's view of love over time. In his theory of love, Robert Sternberg (1988c) hypothesizes that the various elements of love progress in different ways over the course of time. According to Sternberg, passion peaks early in a relationship, whereas intimacy and commitment typically continue to build gradually. (Graphs adapted from Trotter, 1986)

Figure 15.5

Attachment and romantic relationships. According to Hazan and Shaver (1987), people's romantic relationships in adulthood are similar in form to their attachment patterns in infancy, which fall into three categories. The three attachment styles seen in adult intimate relations are described here. (Based on Hazan and Shaver, 1986, 1987)

Adult attachment style

Secure
I find it relatively easy to get close to others and am comfortable depending on them and having them depend on me. I don't often worry about being abandoned or about someone getting too close to me.

Avoidant
I am somewhat uncomfortable being close to others; I find it difficult to trust them, difficult to allow myself to depend on them. I am nervous when anyone gets too close, and often love partners want me to be more intimate than I feel comfortable being.

Anxious/ambivalent
I find that others are reluctant to get as close as I would like. I often worry that my partner doesn't really love me or won't want to stay with me. I want to merge completely with another person, and this desire sometimes scares people away.

are reasonably stable over time (Fraley, 2002) and that people's working models of attachment are carried forward from one relationship to the next (Brumbaugh & Fraley, 2006), supporting the notion individuals' infant attachment experiences shape their intimate relations in adulthood.

Understandably, Hazan and Shaver's theory has attracted considerable interest and has generated a number of studies within a relatively short period of time. For example, research has shown that securely attached individuals have more committed, satisfying, well-adjusted, and longer-lasting relationships compared to people with either anxious-ambivalent or avoidant attachment styles (Feeney, 1999). Moreover, studies have shown that people with different attachment styles are predisposed to think, feel, and behave differently in their relationships (Collins & Allard, 2001). For example, anxious-ambivalent people tend to report more intense emotional highs and lows in their romantic relationships. They also report having more conflicts with their partners, that these conflicts are especially stressful, and that these conflicts often have a negative impact on how they feel about their relationship (Campbell et al., 2005). In a similar vein, attachment anxiety promotes *excessive reassurance seeking*—the tendency to persistently ask for assurances from partners that one is worthy of love (Shaver, Schachner, & Mikulincer, 2005). Research also shows that people who are high in attachment anxiety have much more difficulty than others in dealing with the dissolution of romantic relationships (Davis, Shaver, & Vernon, 2003).

Attachment style also appears to be intimately related to people's patterns of sexual interaction. People with secure attachment tend to be more comfortable with their sexuality, more motivated to show love for their partner during sex, more open to sexual exploration, more likely to have sex in the context of committed relationships, and less accepting of casual sex (Cooper et al., 2006; Shaver & Mikulincer, 2006). In contrast, people high in attachment anxiety tend to have sex to reduce their feelings of insecurity and are more likely to consent to unwanted sexual acts and less likely to practice safe sex (Cooper et al., 2006; Schachner & Shaver, 2004). People with an avoidant attachment style tend to engage in more casual sex in an effort to impress their peers, and they are more likely to use sex to manipulate their partners (Schachner & Shaver, 2004; Shaver & Mikulincer, 2006).

Studies have further suggested that attachment patterns may have far-reaching repercussions that extend into many aspects of people's lives besides their romantic relationships. For instance, attachment security promotes compassionate feelings and values and more helping behavior when people are in need (Mikulincer & Shaver, 2005). Researchers have also found correlations between attachment styles and gender roles (Schwartz, Waldo, & Higgins, 2004), religious beliefs (Kirkpatrick, 2005), health habits (Huntsinger & Luecken, 2004), styles of coping with stress (Howard & Medway, 2004), vulnerability to burnout (Pines, 2004), and leadership qualities (Davidovitz et al. 2007). Thus, Hazan and Shaver's innovative ideas about the long-term effects of infant attachment experiences have triggered an avalanche of thought-provoking research.

Culture and Close Relationships

The limited evidence available suggests both similarities and differences among cultures in romantic relationships (Hendrick & Hendrick, 2000; Schmitt, 2005). For the most part, similarities have been seen when research has focused on what people look for in prospective mates—such as mutual attraction, kindness, and intelligence (Buss, 1989, 1994b). Cultures vary, however, in their emphasis on love—especially passionate love—as a prerequisite for marriage. Although romantic love appears to be found in all cultures (Buss, 2006), passionate love as the basis for marriage is an 18th-century invention of Western culture (Stone, 1977). As Hatfield and Rapson (1993) note, "Marriage-for-love represents an ultimate expression of individualism" (p. 2). In contrast, mar-

web link 15.2

Phillip R. Shaver's Homepage

Phillip Shaver of the University of California, Davis, has conducted pioneering and highly influential research on adult attachment style and intimate relationships. His homepage provides a link to his Adult Attachment Lab, where visitors can learn about early and current work and find links to other relevant sites.

riages arranged by families and other go-betweens remain common in cultures high in collectivism, including India, Japan, and China (Hatfield, Rapson, & Martel, 2007). This practice is declining in some societies as a result of Westernization, but in collectivist societies people contemplating marriage still tend to think in terms of "What will my parents and other people say?" rather than "What does my heart say?" (Triandis, 1994). Although romantic love is routinely seen in collectivist societies (Lieberman & Hatfield, 2006), subjects from societies high in individualism tend to report that romantic love is more important for marriage than subjects from collectivist cultures do (Dion & Dion, 2006; Levine et al., 1995).

The Internet and Close Relationships

In recent years the Internet has dramatically expanded opportunities for people to meet and develop close relationships through social networking services (MySpace, Friendster), online dating services, e-mail, chat rooms, and news groups. Some critics worry that this trend will undermine face-to-face interactions and that many people will be lured into dangerous liaisons by unscrupulous people. But research to date generally paints a positive picture of the Internet's impact on people's connections with one another (Whitty, 2008). For example, the Internet offers a wealth of opportunities to interact for those who suffer from physical infirmities or social anxieties (McKenna & Bargh, 2000). Also, Internet groups provide a safer venue than real life for individuals with stigmatized identities (for example, gay people) to interact and receive support.

Although critics are concerned that Internet relationships are superficial, research suggests that virtual relationships are just as intimate as face-to-face ones and are sometimes even closer (Bargh, McKenna, & Fitzsimons, 2002). Moreover, many virtual relationships evolve into face-to-face interactions (Boase & Wellman, 2006). Researchers find that

romantic relationships that begin on the Internet seem to be just as stable over two years as traditional relationships (McKenna, Green, & Gleason, 2002).

The differences between Internet and face-to-face communication may undermine some established principles of relationship development (Bargh & McKenna, 2004). For example, good looks and physical proximity are powerful factors in initial attraction in the real world. On the Internet, where people often form relationships sight-unseen, these factors may be less influential. Online, where people rely on self-disclosure to develop relationships, similarity of interests and values takes on more power than it does in face-to-face relationships. Because the Internet can foster anonymity, people often take greater risks in self-disclosure (Johnson & Paine, 2007).

Anonymity also allows people to construct a virtual identity. Obviously, this can be a problem if one person adopts a fictional persona and another assumes that it is authentic and begins to take the relationship seriously. A related concern is the truthfulness of online daters. In one survey, 25% of online

Marriages based on romantic love are the norm in Western cultures, whereas arranged marriages prevail in collectivist cultures.

JUMP START

daters admitted to using deception (Brym & Lenton, 2001). Yet, a whopping 86% of participants at one online dating site felt that others misrepresented their physical appearance (Gibbs, Ellison, & Heino, 2006). Admittedly, creating an accurate online representation of oneself can be a complex process: People want to put their best self forward to attract potential dates, but they also need to present themselves authentically if they expect to eventually meet face to face (Gibbs, et al., 2006). One study found that online daters dealt with this tension by constructing profiles that reflected their "ideal self" rather than their "actual self" (Ellison, Heino, & Gibbs, 2006). The most common factors that online daters misrepresent are age, appearance, and marital status (Brym & Lenton, 2001).

An Evolutionary Perspective on Attraction

Evolutionary psychologists have a great deal to say about heterosexual attraction. For example, they assert that physical appearance is an influential determinant of attraction because certain aspects of good looks can be indicators of sound health, good genes, and high fertility, all of which can contribute to reproductive potential (Soler et al., 2003; Sugiyama, 2005). Consistent with the evolutionary view, research has found that some standards of attractiveness are more consistent across cultures than previously believed (Sugiyama, 2005). For example, *facial symmetry* seems to be a key element of attractiveness in highly diverse cultures (Fink & Penton-Voak, 2002). Facial symmetry is thought to be valued because a variety of environmental insults and developmental abnormalities are associated with physical asymmetries, which may serve as markers of relatively poor genes or health (Fink et al., 2006).

The most thoroughly documented findings on the evolutionary bases of heterosexual attraction are those on gender differences in mating preferences, which appear to be consistent across highly varied cultures. Consistent with the notion that humans are programmed by evolution to behave in ways that enhance their reproductive fitness, evidence indicates that men generally are more interested than women in seeking youthfulness and physical attractiveness in their mates because these traits should be associated with greater reproductive potential (see Chapter 9). On the other hand, research shows that women place a greater premium on prospective mates' ambition, social status, and financial potential because these traits should be associated with the ability to invest material resources in children (Li et al., 2002; Shackelford, Schmitt, & Buss, 2005). There are some

qualifications to these trends, but even these caveats make evolutionary sense. For example, when women are asked what they prefer in a *short-term partner* (for casual sex) they value physical attractiveness just as much as men (Li & Kenrick, 2006). And very attractive women, aware of their own high mate value, want it all—they want prospective male partners to exhibit excellent economic potential *and* physical attractiveness (Buss & Shackelford, 2008).

Women's menstrual cycles also influence their mating preferences in ways that make evolutionary sense. When women are in mid-cycle approaching ovulation—that is, when they are most fertile—their preferences shift to favor men who exhibit masculine facial and bodily features, attractiveness, and dominance (Gangestad, Thornhill, & Garver-Apgar, 2005; Gangestad et al., 2007; Little, Jones, & Burriss, 2007). Men seem to recognize this shift, as they rate masculine males as more threatening when their partners are in the fertile portion of their menstrual cycle (Burriss & Little, 2006). Interestingly, although ovulation is far from obvious in human females, strippers earn more tip money per night when they are in their most fertile period (Miller, Tybur, & Jordan, 2007). Researchers aren't sure whether male patrons are "detecting" the strippers' heightened fertility or whether the ovulating dancers come on to the customers more because they are more sexually motivated.

Does the gender gap in mating priorities influence the tactics people actually use in pursuing romantic relationships? Yes, evidence indicates that during courtship men tend to emphasize their ma-

BIZARRO

ONE SECOND BEFORE THE BLIND DATE

terial resources, whereas women are more likely to work at enhancing their appearance (Buss, 1988). Interestingly, the tactics used by both sexes may include efforts at deception. One study found that many men and women would be willing to lie about their personality, income, past relationships, career skills, and intelligence to impress a prospective date who was attractive (Rowatt, Cunningham, & Druen, 1999). Consistent with evolutionary theory, women report that they are most upset when men exaggerate their social status, their financial resources, or the depth of their romantic commitment to the woman, whereas men are most upset when women conceal a history of "promiscuity" (Haselton et al., 2005). Females anticipate more deception from prospective dates than males do (Keenan et al., 1997). Perhaps this is the reason women tend to underestimate the strength of men's relationship commitment (Haselton & Buss, 2000). Men do not appear to show a similar bias, but they do show a tendency to overestimate women's sexual interest. These cognitive biases seem to be designed to reduce the probability that ancestral women would consent to sex and then be abandoned and to minimize the likelihood that ancestral men would overlook sexual opportunities (Buss, 2001).

REVIEW of Key Learning Goals

15.8 People tend to like and love others who are physically attractive. The matching hypothesis asserts that people who are similar in physical attractiveness are more likely to be drawn together than those who are not. Byrne's research suggests that similarity causes attraction, although attitude alignment may also be at work.

15.9 Reciprocity involves liking those who show that they like you. In intimate relationships, how well a partner matches up with one's romantic ideals tends to influence the progress of the relationship. But comparisons to one's ideals are subjective, and romantic partners often idealize each other.

15.10 Berscheid and Hatfield distinguished between passionate love (complete absorption with sexual feelings) and companionate love (trusting, tolerant entwinement). Sternberg built on their distinction by dividing companionate love into intimacy (warmth, closeness, and sharing) and commitment (intent to maintain a relationship).

15.11 Hazan and Shaver's theory suggests that love relationships in adulthood mimic attachment patterns in infancy. People tend to fall into three attachment subtypes (secure, avoidant, or anxious-ambivalent) in their romantic relationships.

Those who are secure tend to have more-committed, satisfying relationships. People high in attachment anxiety tend to have sex to reduce their insecurity and tend to have more difficulty than others with romantic breakups. Attachment style is related to many aspects of behavior.

15.12 The characteristics that people seek in prospective mates are much the same around the world. However, cultures vary considerably in their emphasis on passionate love as a prerequisite for marriage. Although critics are concerned that Internet relationships are superficial and open to deception, Internet-initiated relationships appear to be just as intimate and stable as relationships forged offline.

15.13 According to evolutionary psychologists, certain aspects of good looks, such as facial symmetry, influence attraction because they are indicators of reproductive fitness. Consistent with evolutionary theory, men tend to seek youthfulness and attractiveness in their mates, whereas women emphasize prospective mates' financial potential and willingness to invest material resources in children. People's courtship tactics may include deception. Females anticipate more deception than males do.

Attitudes: Making Social Judgments

In our chapter-opening story, Muffy's friends exhibited decidedly negative attitudes about working-class men. Their example reveals a basic feature of attitudes: they're evaluative. Social psychology's interest in attitudes has a much longer history than its interest in attraction. Indeed, in its early days social psychology was defined as the study of attitudes. In this section we'll discuss the nature of attitudes, efforts to change attitudes through persuasion, and theories of attitude change.

What are attitudes? *Attitudes* are positive or negative evaluations of objects of thought. "Objects of thought" may include social issues (capital punishment or gun control, for example), groups (liberals, farmers), institutions (the Lutheran church, the Supreme Court), consumer products (yogurt,

computers), and people (the president, your next-door neighbor).

Components and Dimensions of Attitudes

Social psychologists have traditionally viewed attitudes as being made up of three components: a cognitive component, an affective component, and a behavioral component. However, in recent years it has become apparent that many attitudes do not include all three components (Fazio & Olson, 2003), so it is more accurate to say that *attitudes may include up to three components*. The *cognitive component* of an attitude is made up of the beliefs that people hold about the object of an attitude. The *affective*

Key Learning Goals

15.14 Analyze the structure (components and dimensions) of attitudes.

15.15 Summarize how source, message, and receiver factors influence the process of persuasion.

15.16 Clarify how learning processes and cognitive dissonance can contribute to attitude formation and change.

15.17 Relate the elaboration likelihood model to attitude change.

component consists of the *emotional feelings* stimulated by an object of thought. The *behavioral component* consists of *predispositions to act* in certain ways toward an attitude object. **Figure 15.6** provides concrete examples of how someone's attitude about gun control might be divided into its components.

Attitudes vary along several crucial dimensions, including their *strength, accessibility,* and *ambivalence* (Olson & Maio, 2003). Definitions of *attitude strength* differ, but strong attitudes are generally viewed as ones that are firmly held (resistant to change), that are durable over time, and that have a powerful impact on behavior (Petty, Wheeler, & Tormala, 2003). The *accessibility* of an attitude refers to how often one thinks about it and how quickly it comes to mind. Highly accessible attitudes are quickly and readily available (Fabrigar, MacDonald, & Wegener, 2005). Attitude accessibility is correlated with attitude strength, as highly accessible attitudes *tend* to be strong, but the concepts are distinct and there is no one-to-one correspondence. *Ambivalent attitudes* are conflicted evaluations that include both positive and negative feelings about an object of thought (Fabrigar et al., 2005). When ambivalence is high, an attitude tends to be less predictive of behavior and more pliable in the face of persuasion (Crano & Prislin, 2006).

Trying to Change Attitudes: Factors in Persuasion

Every day you're bombarded by efforts to alter your attitudes. In light of this reality, let's examine some of the factors that determine whether persuasion works.

The process of persuasion includes four basic elements: the source, receiver, message, and channel (see **Figure 15.7**). The *source* is the person who sends a communication, and the *receiver* is the person to whom the message is sent. Thus, if you watch a presidential news conference on TV, the president is the source, and you and millions of other viewers are the receivers. The *message* is the information transmitted by the source, and the *channel* is the medium through which the message is sent. Although the research on communication channels is interesting, we'll confine our discussion to source, message, and receiver variables.

Source Factors

Occasional exceptions to the general rule are seen, but persuasion tends to be more successful when the source has high *credibility* (Pornpitakpan, 2004). What gives a person credibility? Either expertise or trustworthiness. *Expertise* tends to be more influential when an argument is ambiguous or when the receiver is not motivated to pay close attention to the argument (Chaiken & Maheswaran, 1994; Reimer, Mata, & Stoecklin, 2004). People try to convey their expertise by mentioning their degrees, their training, and their experience or by showing an impressive grasp of the issue at hand. Expertise is a plus, but *trustworthiness* can be even more important. Many people tend to accept messages from trustworthy sources with little scrutiny (Priester & Petty, 1995, 2003). Trustworthiness is undermined when a source appears to have something to gain. In contrast, trustworthiness is enhanced when people appear to argue against their own best interests (Hunt, Smith, & Kernan, 1985). *Lik-*

Figure 15.6
The possible components of attitudes. Attitudes may include cognitive, affective, and behavioral components, as illustrated here for a hypothetical person's attitude about gun control.

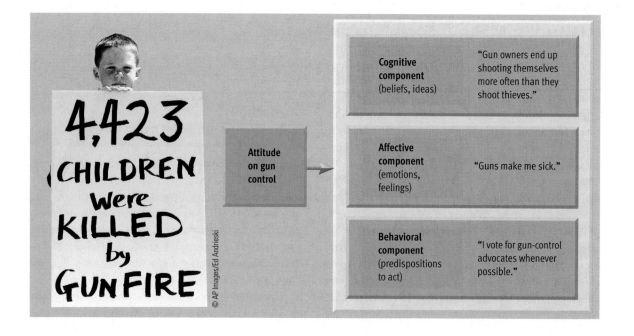

Attitude on gun control

Cognitive component (beliefs, ideas)
"Gun owners end up shooting themselves more often than they shoot thieves."

Affective component (emotions, feelings)
"Guns make me sick."

Behavioral component (predispositions to act)
"I vote for gun-control advocates whenever possible."

© AP Images/Ed Andrieski

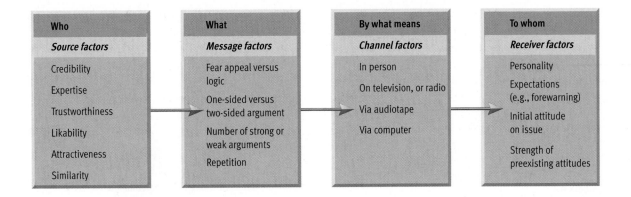

Who	What	By what means	To whom
Source factors	**Message factors**	**Channel factors**	**Receiver factors**
Credibility	Fear appeal versus logic	In person	Personality
Expertise	One-sided versus two-sided argument	On television, or radio	Expectations (e.g., forewarning)
Trustworthiness	Number of strong or weak arguments	Via audiotape	Initial attitude on issue
Likability	Repetition	Via computer	Strength of preexisting attitudes
Attractiveness			
Similarity			

Figure 15.7
Overview of the persuasion process. The process of persuasion essentially boils down to *who* (the source) communicates *what* (the message) *by what means* (the channel) *to whom* (the receiver). Thus, four sets of variables influence the process of persuasion: source, message, channel, and receiver factors. The diagram lists some of the more important factors in each category (including some that are not discussed in the text due to space limitations). (Adapted from Lippa, 1994)

ability also increases the effectiveness of a persuasive source (Johnson, Maio, & Smith-McLallen, 2005). We also respond better to sources who share *similarity* with us in ways that are relevant to the issue at hand (Hilmert, Kulik, & Christenfeld, 2006).

Message Factors

If you were going to give a speech to a local community group advocating a reduction in state taxes on corporations, you'd probably wrestle with a number of questions about how to structure your message. Should you look at both sides of the issue, or should you just present your side? Should you deliver a low-key, logical speech? Or should you try to strike fear into the hearts of your listeners? These questions are concerned with message factors in persuasion.

In general, two-sided arguments seem to be more effective than one-sided presentations (Petty & Wegener, 1998). Just mentioning that an issue has two sides can increase your credibility with an audience. Fear appeals appear to work—if they are successful in arousing fear. Research reveals that many messages intended to induce fear fail to do so. However, studies involving a wide range of issues (nuclear policy, auto safety, dental hygiene, and so on) have shown that messages that are effective in arousing fear tend to increase persuasion (Ruiter, Abraham, & Kok, 2001). Fear appeals are most likely to work when your listeners view the dire consequences that you describe as exceedingly unpleasant, fairly probable if they don't take your advice, and avoidable if they do (Das, de Wit, & Stroebe, 2003).

Receiver Factors

What about the receiver of the persuasive message? Are some people easier to persuade than others? Undoubtedly, but transient factors such as the forewarning a receiver gets about a persuasive effort seem to be more influential than the receiver's personality. Consider, for instance, the old adage that "to be forewarned is to be forearmed." The value of *forewarning* does apply to targets of persuasive efforts (Wood & Quinn, 2003). When you shop for a new car, you *expect* salespeople to work at persuading you, and to some extent this forewarning reduces the impact of their arguments.

Furthermore, studies show that *stronger attitudes are more resistant to change* (Eagly & Chaiken, 1998; Miller & Peterson, 2004). Strong attitudes may be tougher to alter because they tend to be embedded in networks of beliefs and values that might also require change (Erber, Hodges, & Wilson, 1995). Finally, *resistance can promote resistance*. That is, when people successfully resist persuasive efforts to change specific attitudes, they often become more certain about those attitudes (Tormala & Petty, 2002, 2004).

Our review of source, message, and receiver variables has shown that attempting to change attitudes through persuasion involves a complex interplay of factors—and we haven't even looked beneath the surface yet. How do people acquire attitudes in the first place? What dynamic processes within people produce attitude change? We turn to these theoretical issues next.

Theories of Attitude Formation and Change 12c

Many theories have been proposed to explain the mechanisms at work in attitude change, whether or not it occurs in response to persuasion. We'll look at three theoretical perspectives: learning theory, dissonance theory, and the elaboration likelihood model.

Learning Theory 12c

We've seen repeatedly that the concepts of *learning* and *conditioning* can help explain a wide range of phenomena, from conditioned fears to the acquisition of gender roles to the development of personality traits. Now we can add attitude formation and change to our list.

The affective, or emotional, component in an attitude can be created through a special subtype of

web link 15.3

Influence at Work

This site offers an intriguing set of materials that explore a wide variety of social influence phenomena, including persuasion, propaganda, brainwashing, and the tactics that cults use in recruiting. The site is maintained by Kelton Rhodes and Robert Cialdini, perhaps the world's leading authority on social influence strategies.

Understanding Attitudes and Persuasion

Check your understanding of the components of attitudes and the elements of persuasion by analyzing hypothetical political strategies. Imagine you're working on a political campaign and you're invited to join the candidate's inner circle in strategy sessions, as staff members prepare the candidate for upcoming campaign stops. During the meetings, you hear various strategies discussed. For each strategy below, indicate which component of voters' attitudes (cognitive, affective, or behavioral) is being targeted for change, and indicate which element in persuasion (source, message, or receiver factors) is being manipulated. The answers are in Appendix A.

1. "You need to convince this crowd that your program for regulating nursing homes is sound. Whatever you do, don't acknowledge the two weaknesses in the program that we've been playing down. I don't care if you're asked point blank. Just slide by the question and keep harping on the program's advantages." _____ _____

2. "You haven't been smiling enough lately, especially when the TV cameras are rolling. Remember, you can have the best ideas in the world, but if you don't seem likable, you're not gonna get elected. By the way, I think I've lined up some photo opportunities that should help us create an image of sincerity and compassion." _____ _____

3. "This crowd is already behind you. You don't have to alter their opinions on any issue. Get right to work convincing them to contribute to the campaign. I want them lining up to donate money." _____ _____

Figure 15.8

Classical conditioning of attitudes in advertising. Advertisers routinely pair their products with likable celebrities in the hope that their products will come to elicit pleasant emotional responses. As discussed in Chapter 6, this special type of classical conditioning is called *evaluative conditioning*. See the Critical Thinking Application in Chapter 6 for a more in-depth discussion of this practice.

classical conditioning, called evaluative conditioning (Olson & Fazio, 2001, 2002). As we discussed in Chapter 6, *evaluative conditioning* consists of efforts to transfer the emotion attached to a US to a new CS (Kruglanski & Stroebe, 2005; Schimmack & Crites, 2005). Advertisers routinely try to take advantage of evaluative conditioning by pairing their products with stimuli that elicit pleasant emotional responses, such as extremely attractive models, highly likable spokespersons, and cherished events, such as the Olympics (Till & Priluck, 2000). This conditioning process is diagrammed in **Figure 15.8**.

Operant conditioning may come into play when you openly express an attitude, such as "I believe that husbands should do more housework." Some people may endorse your view, while others may jump down your throat. Agreement from other people generally functions as a reinforcer, strengthening your tendency to express a specific attitude (Bohner & Schwarz, 2001). Disagreement often functions as a form of punishment, which may gradually weaken your commitment to your viewpoint.

Another person's attitudes may rub off on you through *observational learning* (Oskamp, 1991). If you hear your uncle say, "Republicans are nothing but puppets of big business" and your mother heartily agrees, your exposure to your uncle's attitude and your mother's reinforcement of your uncle may influence your attitude toward the Republican party. Studies show that parents and their children tend to have similar political attitudes (Sears, 1975), and that college students living in residence halls tend to show some convergence in attitudes (Cullum & Harton, 2007). Observational learning presumably accounts for much of this similarity. The opinions of teachers, coaches, co-workers, talk-show hosts, rock stars, and so forth are also likely to sway people's attitudes through observational learning.

Dissonance Theory 12c

Leon Festinger's *dissonance theory* assumes that inconsistency among attitudes propels people in the direction of attitude change. Dissonance theory burst into prominence in 1959 when Festinger and J. Merrill Carlsmith published a landmark study. Let's look at their findings and at how dissonance theory explains them.

Festinger and Carlsmith (1959) had male college students come to a laboratory and work on excruciatingly dull tasks, such as turning pegs repeatedly. When a subject's hour was over, the experimenter confided that some participants' motivation was being manipulated by telling them that the task was interesting and enjoyable before they started it. Then, after a moment's hesitation, the experimenter asked if the subject could help him out of a jam. His usual helper was delayed and he needed someone to testify to the next "subject" (really an accomplice) that the experimental task was interesting. He offered to pay the subject if he would tell the person in the adjoining waiting room that the task was enjoyable and involving.

This entire scenario was enacted to coax participants into doing something that was inconsistent with their true feelings. Some subjects received a token payment of $1 for their effort, while others received a more substantial payment of $20 (an amount equivalent to about $120 today, in light of inflation). Later, a second experimenter inquired about the participants' true feelings regarding the dull experimental task. **Figure 15.9** summarizes the design of the Festinger and Carlsmith study.

Who do you think rated the task more favorably—the subjects who were paid $1 or those who were paid $20? Both common sense and learning theory would predict that the subjects who received the greater reward ($20) should come to like the task more. In reality, however, the participants who were paid $1 exhibited more favorable attitude change—just as Festinger and Carlsmith had predicted. Why? Dissonance theory provides an explanation.

According to Festinger (1957), *cognitive dissonance* **exists when related attitudes or beliefs are inconsistent—that is, when they contradict each other.** Festinger's model assumes that dissonance is possible only when cognitions are relevant to each other, since unrelated cognitions ("I am hardworking" and "Fire engines are red") can't contradict each other. However, when cognitions are related, they may be consonant ("I am hardworking" and "I'm staying overtime to get an important job done") or dissonant ("I am hardworking" and "I'm playing hooky from work"). When aroused, cognitive dissonance is supposed to create an unpleasant state of tension that motivates people to reduce their dissonance—usually by altering their cognitions.

In the study by Festinger and Carlsmith (1959), the subjects' contradictory cognitions were "The task is boring" and "I told someone the task was enjoyable." The participants who were paid $20 for lying had an obvious reason for behaving inconsistently with their true attitudes, so these subjects experienced little dissonance. In contrast, the participants paid $1 had no readily apparent justification for their lie and experienced high dissonance. To reduce it, they tended to persuade themselves that the

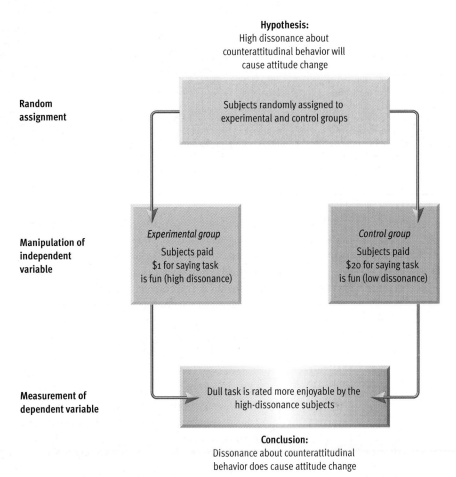

Hypothesis:
High dissonance about counterattitudinal behavior will cause attitude change

Random assignment

Subjects randomly assigned to experimental and control groups

Manipulation of independent variable

Experimental group
Subjects paid $1 for saying task is fun (high dissonance)

Control group
Subjects paid $20 for saying task is fun (low dissonance)

Measurement of dependent variable

Dull task is rated more enjoyable by the high-dissonance subjects

Conclusion:
Dissonance about counterattitudinal behavior does cause attitude change

Figure 15.9
Design of the Festinger and Carlsmith (1959) study. The manipulations of variables and the results of Festinger and Carlsmith's (1959) landmark study of attitude change are outlined here.

task was more enjoyable than they had originally thought. *Thus, dissonance theory sheds light on why people sometimes come to believe their own lies.*

Cognitive dissonance is also at work when people turn attitude somersaults to justify efforts that haven't panned out, a syndrome called *effort justification.* Aronson and Mills (1959) studied effort justification by putting college women through a "severe initiation" before they could qualify to participate in what promised to be an interesting discussion of sexuality. In the initiation, the women had to read obscene passages out loud to a male experimenter. After all that, the highly touted discussion of sexuality turned out to be a boring, taped lecture on reproduction in lower animals. Subjects in the severe initiation condition experienced highly dissonant cognitions ("I went through a lot to get here" and "This discussion is terrible"). How did they reduce their dissonance? Apparently by changing their attitude about the discussion, since they rated it more favorably than participants in two control conditions.

Effort justification may be at work in many facets of everyday life. For example, people who wait for

Leon Festinger

"Cognitive dissonance is a motivating state of affairs. Just as hunger impels a person to eat, so does dissonance impel a person to change his opinions or his behavior."

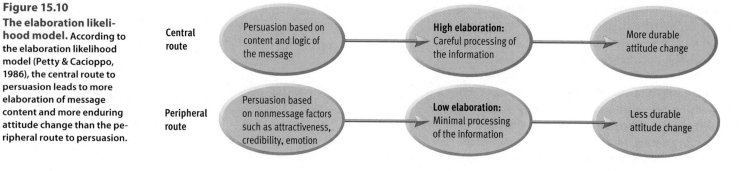

Figure 15.10
The elaboration likelihood model. According to the elaboration likelihood model (Petty & Cacioppo, 1986), the central route to persuasion leads to more elaboration of message content and more enduring attitude change than the peripheral route to persuasion.

Central route: Persuasion based on content and logic of the message → **High elaboration:** Careful processing of the information → More durable attitude change

Peripheral route: Persuasion based on nonmessage factors such as attractiveness, credibility, emotion → **Low elaboration:** Minimal processing of the information → Less durable attitude change

hours to be seated at an exclusive restaurant often praise the restaurant afterward even if they have been served a poorly prepared meal. Rock fans who pay hundreds of dollars for scalped concert tickets will tend to view the concert favorably, even if the artists show up in a stupor and play out of tune.

Dissonance theory has been tested in hundreds of studies with mixed, but largely favorable, results. The dynamics of dissonance appear to underlie many important types of attitude changes (Draycott & Dabbs, 1998; Keller & Block, 1999; Petty et al., 2003). Research has largely supported Festinger's claim that dissonance involves genuine psychological discomfort and even physiological arousal (Visser & Cooper, 2003; Devine et al., 1999). However, dissonance effects are not among the most reliable phenomena in social psychology. Researchers have had difficulty specifying the conditions under which dissonance will occur, and it has become apparent that people can reduce their dissonance in quite a variety of ways besides changing their attitudes (Olson & Stone, 2005; Visser & Cooper, 2003).

Elaboration Likelihood Model 12c

The *elaboration likelihood model* of attitude change, originally proposed by Richard Petty and John Cacioppo (1986), asserts that there are two basic "routes" to persuasion (Petty & Brinol, 2008; Petty & Wegener, 1999). The *central route* is taken when people carefully ponder the content and logic of persuasive messages. The *peripheral route* is taken when persuasion depends on nonmessage factors, such as the attractiveness and credibility of the source, or on conditioned emotional responses (see **Figure 15.10**). For example, a politician who campaigns by delivering carefully researched speeches that thoughtfully analyze complex issues is following the central route to persuasion. In contrast, a politician who depends on marching bands, flag waving, celebrity endorsements, and emotional slogans is following the peripheral route.

Both routes can lead to effective persuasion and attitude change. However, according to the elaboration likelihood model, the durability of attitude change depends on the extent to which people elaborate on (think about) the contents of persuasive communications. Studies suggest that the central route to persuasion leads to more enduring attitude change than the peripheral route (Petty & Wegener, 1998). Research also suggests that attitudes changed through central processes predict behavior better than attitudes changed through peripheral processes (Kruglanski & Stroebe, 2005; Petty, Wegener, & Fabrigar, 1997).

REVIEW of Key Learning Goals

15.14 Attitudes may be made up of cognitive, affective, and behavioral components. The cognitive component consists of beliefs, the affective component of emotional feelings, and the behavioral component of predispositions to act in certain ways. Attitudes also vary along three dimensions: strength, accessibility, and ambivalence.

15.15 A source of persuasion who is credible, expert, trustworthy, likable, and physically attractive tends to be relatively effective in stimulating attitude change. Although there are some situational limitations, two-sided arguments and fear arousal are effective elements in persuasive messages. Persuasion is more difficult when a receiver is forewarned and when strong attitudes are targeted.

15.16 Attitudes may be shaped through classical conditioning, operant conditioning, and observational learning. Festinger's dissonance theory asserts that inconsistent attitudes cause tension and that people alter their attitudes to reduce cognitive dissonance. Dissonance theory has been used to explain attitude change following counterattitudinal behavior and efforts that haven't panned out.

15.17 The elaboration likelihood model holds that the central route to persuasion, which depends on the logic of persuasive messages, tends to yield longer-lasting attitude change than the peripheral route, which depends on non-message factors.

Conformity and Obedience: Yielding to Others

Key Learning Goals

15.18 Review Asch's work on conformity.

15.19 Describe Milgram's research on obedience to authority, and assess the ensuing controversy.

15.20 Discuss cultural variations in conformity and obedience.

15.21 Describe the Stanford Prison Simulation and its implications.

A number of years ago, the area that I lived in experienced a severe spring flood that required the mobilization of the National Guard and several other emergency services. At the height of the crisis, a young man arrived at the scene of the flood, announced that he was from an obscure state agency that no one had ever heard of, and proceeded to take control of the emergency. City work crews, the fire department, local police, municipal officials, and the National Guard followed his orders with dispatch for several days, evacuating entire neighborhoods—until an official thought to check and found out that the man was just someone who had walked in off the street. The imposter, who had had small armies at his beck and call for several days, had no training in emergency services, just a history of unemployment and psychological problems.

After news of the hoax spread, people criticized red-faced local officials for their compliance with the imposter's orders. However, many of the critics probably would have cooperated in much the same way if they had been in the officials' shoes. For most people, willingness to obey an apparent authority figure is the rule, not the exception. In this section, we'll analyze the dynamics of social influence at work in conformity and obedience.

Conformity

12e PSYKTREK

If you keep a well-manicured lawn and praise the talents of the band Coldplay, are you exhibiting conformity? According to social psychologists, it depends on whether your behavior is the result of group pressure. *Conformity* **occurs when people yield to real or imagined social pressure.** For example, if you maintain a well-groomed lawn only to avoid complaints from your neighbors, you're yielding to social pressure. If you like Coldplay because you genuinely enjoy their music, that's *not* conformity. However, if you like Coldplay because it's "hip" and your friends would question your taste if you didn't, then you're conforming.

In the 1950s, Solomon Asch (1951, 1955, 1956) devised a clever procedure that minimized ambiguity about whether subjects were conforming, allowing him to investigate the variables that govern conformity. Let's re-create one of Asch's (1955) classic experiments. The participants are male undergraduates recruited for a study of visual perception. A group of seven subjects are shown a large card with a vertical line on it and then are asked to indicate which of three lines on a second card matches the original "standard line" in length (see **Figure 15.11**). All seven participants are given a turn at the task, and they announce their choice to the group. The subject in the sixth chair doesn't know it, but everyone else in the group is an accomplice of the experimenter, and they're about to make him wonder whether he has taken leave of his senses.

The accomplices give accurate responses on the first two trials. On the third trial, line number 2 clearly is the correct response, but the first five "subjects" all say that line number 3 matches the standard line. The genuine subject is bewildered and can't believe his ears. Over the course of the next 15 trials, the accomplices all give the same incorrect response on 11 of them. How does the real subject respond? The line judgments are easy and unambiguous. So, if the participant consistently agrees with the accomplices, he isn't making honest mistakes—he's conforming.

Averaging across all 50 subjects, Asch (1955) found that the young men conformed on 37% of the trials. The participants varied considerably in their tendency to conform, however. Of the 50 subjects, 13 never caved in to the group, while 14 conformed on more than half the trials. One could argue that the results show that people confronting a unanimous majority generally tend to *resist* the pressure to conform, but given how clear and easy the line judgments were, most social scientists viewed the findings as a dramatic demonstration of humans' propensity to conform (Levine, 1999).

Solomon Asch

"That we have found the tendency to conformity in our society so strong that reasonably intelligent and well-meaning young people are willing to call white black is a matter of concern."

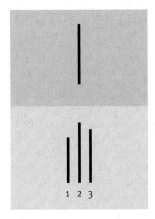

Figure 15.11

Stimuli used in Asch's conformity studies. Subjects were asked to match a standard line (top) with one of three other lines displayed on another card (bottom). The task was easy—until experimental accomplices started responding with obviously incorrect answers, creating a situation in which Asch evaluated subjects' conformity.

SOURCE: Adapted from Asch, S. (1955). Opinion and social pressure. *Scientific American, 193* (5), 31–35. Based on illustrations by Sara Love. Copyright © 1955 by Scientific American, Inc. All rights reserved.

In subsequent studies, *group size* and *group unanimity* turned out to be key determinants of conformity (Asch, 1956). To examine the impact of group size, Asch repeated his procedure with groups that included from 1 to 15 accomplices. Little conformity was seen when a subject was pitted against just 1 person, but conformity increased rapidly as group size went from 2 to 4, peaked at a group size of 7, and then leveled off (see **Figure 15.12**). Thus, Asch reasoned that as groups grow larger, conformity increases—up to a point—a conclusion that has been echoed by other researchers (Cialdini & Trost, 1998).

However, group size made little difference if just one accomplice "broke" with the others, wrecking their unanimous agreement. The presence of another dissenter lowered conformity to about one-quarter of its peak, even when the dissenter made *inaccurate* judgments that happened to conflict with the majority view. Apparently, the participants just needed to hear someone else question the accuracy of the group's perplexing responses. The importance of unanimity in fostering conformity has been replicated in subsequent research (Nemeth & Chiles, 1988).

Obedience 12e

Obedience is a form of compliance that occurs when people follow direct commands, usually from someone in a position of authority. To a surprising extent, when an authority figure says, "Jump!" many people simply ask, "How high?"

Milgram's Studies 12e

Stanley Milgram wanted to study this tendency to obey authority figures. Like many other people after World War II, he was troubled by how readily the citizens of Germany followed the orders of dictator Adolf Hitler, even when the orders required shockingly immoral actions, such as the slaughter of millions of Jews. Milgram, who had worked with Solomon Asch, set out to design a standard laboratory procedure for the study of obedience, much like Asch's procedure for studying conformity. The clever experiment that Milgram devised became one of the most famous and controversial studies in the annals of psychology.

Milgram's (1963) participants were a diverse collection of 40 men from the local community. They were told that they would be participating in a study concerned with the effects of punishment on learning. When they arrived at the lab, they drew slips of paper from a hat to get their assignments. The drawing was rigged so that the subject always became the "teacher" and an experimental accomplice (a likable 47-year-old accountant) became the "learner."

The learner was strapped into an electrified chair through which a shock could be delivered whenever he made a mistake on the task (see **Figure 15.13**). The subject was then taken to an adjoining room that housed the shock generator that he would control in his role as the teacher. Although the apparatus looked and sounded realistic, it was a fake and the learner was never shocked.

As the "learning experiment" proceeded, the accomplice made many mistakes that necessitated shocks. The teacher was instructed to increase the shock level after each wrong answer. At 300 volts, the learner began to pound on the wall between the two rooms in protest and soon stopped responding to the teacher's questions. From this point forward, participants frequently turned to the experimenter for guidance. Whenever they did so, the experimenter firmly indicated that the teacher should continue to give stronger and stronger shocks to the now-silent learner. The dependent variable was the maximum shock the participant was willing to administer before refusing to go on.

As **Figure 15.13** shows, 26 of the 40 subjects (65%) administered all 30 levels of shock. Although they tended to obey the experimenter, many subjects voiced and displayed considerable distress about harming the learner. The horrified participants groaned, bit their lips, stuttered, trembled, and broke into a sweat, but continued administering the shocks. Based on these results, Milgram concluded that obedience to authority was even more common than he or others anticipated. Before the study was conducted, Milgram had described it to 40 psychiatrists and had asked them to predict how much shock subjects would be willing to administer

Figure 15.12
Conformity and group size. This graph shows the percentage of trials on which participants conformed as a function of group size in Asch's research. Asch found that conformity became more frequent as group size increased up to four, peaked at seven, and then leveled off. (Data from Asch, 1955)

SOURCE: Adapted from Asch, S. (1955). Opinion and social pressure. *Scientific American, 193* (5), 31–35. Based on illustrations by Sara Love. Copyright © 1955 by Scientific American, Inc. All rights reserved.

Number of subjects who stopped giving shock

65% of
subjects

Volts

| Slight shock | Moderate shock | Strong shock | Very strong shock | Intense shock | Extreme intensity shock | Danger: severe shock | XXX |

Level of shock (as labeled on Milgram's shock machine)

Figure 15.13
Milgram's experiment on obedience. The photo on the left shows the "learner" being connected to the shock generator during one of Milgram's experimental sessions. The photo on the right shows the fake shock generator used in the study. The surprising results of the Milgram (1963) study are summarized in the bar graph. Although subjects frequently protested, the vast majority (65%) delivered the entire series of shocks to the learner.

to their innocent victims. Most of the psychiatrists had predicted that fewer than 1% of the subjects would continue to the end of the series of shocks!

In interpreting his results, Milgram argued that strong pressure from an authority figure can make decent people do indecent things to others. Applying this insight to Nazi war crimes and other travesties, Milgram asserted that some sinister actions may not be due to actors' evil character so much as to situational pressures that can lead normal people to engage in acts of treachery and violence. Thus, he arrived at the disturbing conclusion that given the right circumstances, any of us might obey orders to inflict harm on innocent strangers.

The Ensuing Controversy   12e

Milgram's study evoked a controversy that continues through today. Some critics argued that Milgram's results wouldn't generalize to the real world (Orne & Holland, 1968). For example, Baumrind (1964) asserted that subjects who agree to participate in a scientific study *expect to obey* orders from an experimenter. Milgram (1964, 1968) replied by pointing out that so do soldiers and bureaucrats in the real world who are accused of villainous acts performed in obedience to authority. "I reject Baumrind's argument that the observed obedience doesn't count because it occurred where it is appropriate," said Milgram (1964). "That is precisely why it *does* count." Overall, the weight of evidence supports the gen-

eralizability of Milgram's results. They were consistently replicated for many years, in diverse settings, with a variety of subjects and procedural variations (Blass, 1999; Miller, 1986).

Critics also questioned the ethics of Milgram's experimental procedures (Baumrind, 1964; Kelman, 1967). They noted that without prior consent, participants were exposed to extensive deception that could undermine their trust in people and severe stress that could leave emotional scars. Milgram's defenders argued that the brief distress experienced by his subjects was a small price to pay for the insights that emerged from his obedience studies. Looking back, however, many psychologists seem to share the critics' concerns about the ethical implications of Milgram's ground-breaking work. His procedure is questionable by contemporary standards of research ethics, and no replications of his obedience study were conducted in the United States from the mid-1970s until recently, when Jerry Burger (2009) crafted a very cautious, *partial* replication that incorporated a variety of additional safeguards to protect the welfare of the participants. Among other things, Burger screened participants with great care, emphasized repeatedly that participants could withdraw from the study at any time, provided instant debriefing, and only enacted Milgram's scenario up through the level of 150 volts. Interestingly, in spite of these extra precautions, Burger's study yielded obedience rates that were only slightly lower than those observed by Milgram 45 years earlier.

Stanley Milgram

"The essence of obedience is that a person comes to view himself as the instrument for carrying out another person's wishes, and he therefore no longer regards himself as responsible for his actions."

Philip Zimbardo

"But in the end, I called off the experiment not because of the horror I saw out there in the prison yard, but because of the horror of realizing that I could have easily traded places with the most brutal guard or become the weakest prisoner full of hatred at being so powerless."

Cultural Variations in Conformity and Obedience

Are conformity and obedience unique to American culture? By no means. The Asch and Milgram experiments have been repeated in many other societies, where they have yielded results roughly similar to those seen in the United States. Thus, the phenomena of conformity and obedience seem to transcend culture.

The replications of Milgram's obedience study have largely been limited to industrialized nations similar to the United States. Many of these studies have reported even *higher* obedience rates than those seen in Milgram's American samples (Smith & Bond, 1994). Thus, the surprisingly high level of obedience observed by Milgram does not appear to be peculiar to the United States. The Asch experiment has been repeated in a more diverse range of societies than the Milgram experiment. Various theorists have hypothesized that collectivistic cultures, which emphasize respect for group norms, cooperation, and harmony, encourage more conformity than individualistic cultures, with their emphasis on independence (Kim & Markus, 1999; Matsumoto, 1994). Consistent with this analysis, replications of the Asch experiment have tended to find somewhat higher levels of conformity in collectivistic cultures than in individualistic cultures (Bond & Smith, 1996; Smith, 2001).

The Power of the Situation: The Stanford Prison Simulation

The research of Asch and Milgram provided dramatic demonstrations of the potent influence that situational factors can have on social behavior. The power of the situation was underscored once again, about a decade after Milgram's obedience research, in another landmark study conducted by Philip Zimbardo, who, ironically, was a high school classmate of Milgram's. Zimbardo and his colleagues designed the Stanford Prison Simulation to investigate why prisons tend to become abusive, degrading violent environments (Haney, Banks, & Zimbardo, 1973; Zimbardo, Haney, & Banks, 1973). Like Milgram, Zimbardo wanted to see how much the power of the situation would shape the behavior of normal, average subjects.

The participants were college students recruited for a study of prison life through a newspaper ad. After 70 volunteers were given an extensive battery of tests and interviews, the researchers chose 24 students who appeared to be physically healthy and psychologically stable to be the subjects. A coin flip determined which of them would be "guards" and which would be the "prisoners" in a simulated prison set up at Stanford University. The prisoners were "arrested" at their homes, handcuffed, and transported to a mock prison on the Stanford campus. Upon arrival, they were ordered to strip, sprayed with a delousing agent, given prison uniforms (smocks), assigned numbers as their identities, and locked up in iron-barred cells. The subjects assigned to be guards were given khaki uniforms, billy clubs, whistles, and reflective sunglasses. They were told that they could run their prison in whatever way they wanted except that they were not allowed to use physical punishment.

What happened? In short order, confrontations occurred between the guards and prisoners and the guards quickly devised a variety of sometimes cruel strategies to maintain total control over their prisoners. Meals, blankets, and bathroom privileges were selectively denied to some prisoners to achieve control. The prisoners were taunted, humiliated, called demeaning names, and forced to beg for opportunities to go to the bathroom. Pointless, petty rules were strictly enforced, and difficult prisoners were punished with hard labor (doing pushups and jumping jacks, cleaning toilets with their bare hands). And the guards creatively turned a 2-foot by 2-foot closet into a "hole" for solitary confinement of rebellious prisoners. Although there was some variation among the guards, collectively they became mean, malicious, and abusive in fulfilling their responsibilities. How did the prisoners react? A few of them showed signs of emotional disturbance and had to be released early, but they mostly became listless, apathetic, and demoralized. The study was designed to run two weeks, but Zimbardo decided to end it prematurely after just six days because he was concerned about the rapidly escalating abuse and degradation of the prisoners. The subjects were debriefed, offered counseling, and sent home.

How did Zimbardo and his colleagues explain the stunning transformations of their subjects? First, they attributed the participants' behavior to the enormous influence of social roles. *Social roles* are widely shared expectations about how people in certain positions are supposed to behave. We have role expectations for salespeople, waiters, ministers, medical patients, students, bus drivers, tourists, flight attendants, and, of course, prison guards and prisoners. The participants had a rough idea of what it meant to act like a guard or a prisoner, and they were gradually consumed by their roles (Haney & Zimbardo, 1998). Second, the researchers attributed

The Abu Ghraib prison scandal in Iraq has sparked renewed interest in the Stanford Prison Simulation. Some of the photos taken of the abuse at Abu Ghraib (right) are stunningly similar to photos from the Stanford study (left). For instance, in both cases, the guards "dehumanized" their prisoners by placing bags over their heads.

their subjects' behavior to the compelling power of situational factors. Before the study began, the tests and interviews showed no measurable differences in personality or character between those randomly assigned to be guards versus prisoners. The stark differences in their behavior had to be due to the radically different situations that they found themselves in. As Haney and Zimbardo (1998) put it, the study "demonstrated the power of situations to overwhelm people and elicit from them unexpectedly cruel, yet 'situationally appropriate' behavior" (p. 719). As a result, Zimbardo, like Milgram before him, concluded that situational pressures can lead normal, decent people to behave in sinister, repugnant ways.

Although the Stanford Prison Simulation was conducted over 35 years ago, renewed interest in the study was sparked by the 2004 Abu Ghraib prison scandal in Iraq. American military personnel with little or no experience in running prisons were found to have engaged in "sadistic, blatant, and wanton criminal abuses" of their Iraqi prisoners (Hersh, 2004). Some of the photos taken of the abuse at Abu Ghraib are eerily reminiscent of photos from the Stanford simulation. The U.S. government blamed these horrific abuses on "a few bad apples" who were presumed to be pathological or morally deficient, writing off the incident as an aberration. Yet the evidence from the Stanford Prison Simulation clearly suggests otherwise. Phil Zimbardo (2004, 2007) argues, and has testified as an expert witness, that it is far more likely that situational pressures led normal, average Americans to commit morally reprehensible abuses. This explanation does *not* absolve the brutal guards of responsibility for their behavior. However,

Zimbardo emphasizes that making scapegoats out of a handful of guards does not solve the real problem, which lies in the system. He maintains that abuses in prisons are more likely than not and can only be reduced if authorities provide extensive training and strong supervision for guards, enact explicit sanctions for abuses, and maintain clear accountability in the chain of command.

web link 15.5

Stanford Prison Experiment
The Stanford Prison Simulation is one of psychology's most renowned studies. At this site, Phil Zimbardo provides a fascinating slide show explaining the study in depth. The site also includes discussion questions, reflections on the study 30 years after it was conducted, and links to a host of related materials. The links include recent writings by Zimbardo that analyze the Abu Ghraib prison scandal.

REVIEW of Key Learning Goals

15.18 Asch found that subjects often conform to the group, even when the group reports inaccurate judgments on a simple line-judging task. Conformity becomes more likely as group size increases, up to a group size of four, then levels off. If a small group isn't unanimous, conformity declines rapidly.

15.19 In Milgram's landmark study of obedience to authority, adult men drawn from the community showed a remarkable tendency, despite their misgivings, to follow orders to shock an innocent stranger. Milgram concluded that situational pressures can make decent people do indecent things. Critics asserted that Milgram's results were not generalizable to the real world and that his methods were unethical. The generalizability of Milgram's findings has stood the test of time, but his work also helped to stimulate stricter ethical standards for research.

15.20 The Asch and Milgram experiments have been replicated in many cultures. These replications have uncovered modest cultural variations in the propensity to conform or to obey an authority figure. Generally, slightly higher rates of conformity and obedience have been found in collectivist cultures.

15.21 The Stanford Prison Simulation, in which normal, healthy students were randomly assigned to be prisoners or guards, demonstrated that social roles and other situational pressures can exert tremendous influence over social behavior. Like Milgram, Zimbardo showed that situational forces can lead normal people to exhibit surprisingly callous, abusive behavior.

Behavior in Groups: Joining with Others

Key Learning Goals

15.22 Clarify the nature of groups and the bystander effect.

15.23 Evaluate evidence on group productivity, including social loafing.

15.24 Explain group polarization and groupthink.

Social psychologists study groups as well as individuals, but exactly what is a group? Are all the divorced fathers living in Baltimore a group? Are three strangers moving skyward in an elevator a group? What if the elevator gets stuck? How about four students from your psychology class who study together regularly? How about a jury working to render a verdict in a trial? The Boston Celtics? Some of these collections of people are groups and others aren't. Let's examine the concept of a group to find out which of these collections qualify.

In social psychologists' eyes, **a group consists of two or more individuals who interact and are interdependent.** The divorced fathers in Baltimore aren't likely to qualify on either count. Strangers sharing an elevator might interact briefly, but they're not interdependent. However, if the elevator gets stuck and they have to deal with an emergency together, they could suddenly become a group. Your psychology classmates who study together qualify as a group, since they interact and depend on each other to achieve shared goals. So do the members of a jury and a sports team such as the Celtics. Historically, most groups have interacted on a face-to-face basis, but advances in telecommunications are rapidly changing that situation. In the era of the Internet, people can interact, become interdependent, and develop a group identity without ever meeting in person (Bargh & McKenna, 2004; McKenna & Bargh, 1998).

Behavior Alone and in Groups: The Case of the Bystander Effect

Imagine that you have a precarious medical condition and that you must go through life worrying about whether someone will leap forward to provide help if the need ever arises. Wouldn't you feel more secure around larger groups? After all, there's "safety in numbers." Logically, as group size increases, the probability of having a good Samaritan on the scene increases. Or does it? We've seen before that human behavior isn't necessarily logical. When it comes to helping behavior, many studies have uncovered an apparent paradox called the *bystander effect:* People are less likely to provide needed help when they are in groups than when they are alone.

Evidence that your probability of getting help *declines* as group size increases was first described by John Darley and Bibb Latané (1968), who were conducting research on the determinants of helping behavior. In the Darley and Latané study, students in individual cubicles connected by an intercom participated in discussion groups of three sizes. Early in the discussion, a student who was an experimental accomplice hesitantly mentioned that he was prone to seizures. Later in the discussion, the same accomplice faked a severe seizure and cried out for help. Although a majority of participants sought assistance for the student, the tendency to seek help *declined* with increasing group size.

Similar trends have been seen in many other experiments, in which over 6000 subjects have had opportunities to respond to apparent emergencies, including fires, asthma attacks, faintings, crashes, and flat tires, as well as less pressing needs to answer a door or to pick up objects dropped by a stranger. Pooling the results of this research, Latané and Nida (1981) estimated that participants who were alone provided help 75% of the time, whereas participants in the presence of others provided help only 53% of the time.

What accounts for the bystander effect? A number of factors may be at work, but the most important appears to be the *diffusion of responsibility* that occurs in a group situation. If you're by yourself when you encounter someone in need of help, the responsibility to provide help rests squarely on your shoulders. However, if other people are present, the responsibility is divided among you, and you may all say to yourselves "Someone else will help." A reduced sense of responsibility may contribute to other aspects of behavior in groups, as we'll see in the next section.

Group Productivity and Social Loafing

Have you ever driven through a road construction project—at a snail's pace, of course—and become irritated because so many workers seem to be just standing around? Maybe the irony of the posted sign "Your tax dollars at work" made you imagine that they were all dawdling. And then again, perhaps not. Individuals' productivity often does decline in larger groups (Latané, Williams, & Harkins, 1979).

Two factors appear to contribute to reduced individual productivity in larger groups. One factor is *reduced efficiency* resulting from the *loss of coordination* among workers' efforts. As you put more people on a yearbook staff, for instance, you'll probably create more and more duplication of effort and increase how often group members end up working at cross purposes.

The second factor contributing to low productivity in groups involves *effort* rather than efficiency. *Social loafing* is a reduction in effort by individuals when they work in groups as compared to when they work by themselves. To investigate social loafing, Latané et al. (1979) measured the sound output produced by subjects who were asked to cheer or clap as loudly as they could. So they couldn't see or hear other group members, participants were told that the study concerned the importance of sensory feedback and were asked to don blindfolds and put on headphones through which loud noise was played. This maneuver permitted a simple deception: Subjects were led to *believe* that they were working alone or in a group of two or six, when in fact *individual* output was actually measured.

When subjects *thought* that they were working in larger groups, their individual output declined. Because lack of coordination could not affect individual output, the participants' decreased sound production had to be attributable to reduced effort. Latané and his colleagues also had the same subjects clap and shout in genuine groups of two and six and found an additional decrease in production that was attributed to loss of coordination. **Figure 15.14** shows how social loafing and loss of coordination combined to reduce productivity as group size increased.

Social loafing and the bystander effect appear to share a common cause: diffusion of responsibility in groups (Comer, 1995; Latané, 1981). As group size increases, the responsibility for getting a job done is divided among more people, and many group members ease up because their individual contribution is less recognizable. Thus, social loafing occurs in situations where individuals can "hide in the crowd."

That said, social loafing is *not* inevitable. For example, people with high achievement motivation are less likely to exhibit social loafing than others (Hart et al., 2004). People who score high on the personality traits of agreeableness and conscientiousness are also less prone to social loafing (Klehe & Anderson, 2007). Social loafing is less likely when individuals' personal contributions to productivity are readily identifiable (Hoigaard & Ingvaldsen, 2006) and when group norms encourage productivity and personal involvement (Hoigaard, Säfvenbom, & Tonnessen, 2006). And social loafing is reduced when people work in smaller and more cohesive groups (Liden et al., 2004). Finally, research suggests that social loafing is less prevalent in collectivistic cultures, which place a high priority on meeting group goals and contributing to one's ingroups (Karau & Williams, 1995; Smith, 2001).

Decision Making in Groups

Productivity is not the only issue that commonly concerns groups. When people join together in groups, they often have to make decisions about what the group will do and how it will use its resources. Whether it's your study group deciding

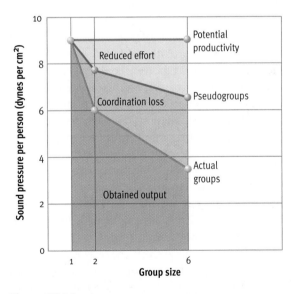

Figure 15.14

The effect of loss of coordination and social loafing on group productivity. The amount of sound produced per person declined noticeably when subjects worked in actual groups of two or six (orange line). This decrease in productivity reflects both loss of coordination and social loafing. Sound per person also declined when subjects merely thought they were working in groups of two or six (purple line). This smaller decrease in productivity is attributed to social loafing.

SOURCE: Adapted from Latané, B., Williams, K., & Harkins, S. (1979). Many hands make light the work: The causes and consequences of social loafing. *Journal of Personality and Social Psychology, 37*, 822–832. Copyright © 1979 by the American Psychological Association. Adapted by permission of the author.

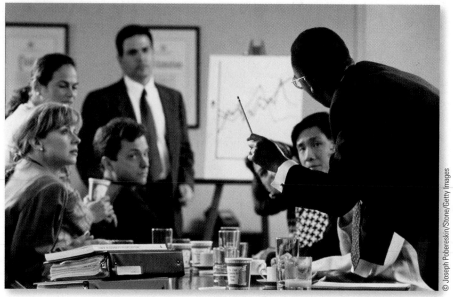

Many types of groups have to arrive at collective decisions. The social dynamics of group decisions are complicated, and a variety of factors can undermine effective decision making.

factions in a group, as its name might suggest. In fact, group polarization can contribute to consensus in a group, as we'll see in our discussion of groupthink.

Groupthink

In contrast to group polarization, which is a normal process in group dynamics, groupthink is more like a "disease" that can infect decision making in groups. *Groupthink* occurs when members of a cohesive group emphasize concurrence at the expense of critical thinking in arriving at a decision. As you might imagine, groupthink doesn't produce very effective decision making. Indeed, groupthink often leads to major blunders that may look incomprehensible after the fact. Irving Janis (1972) first described groupthink in his effort to explain how President John F. Kennedy and his advisers could have miscalculated so badly in deciding to invade Cuba at the Bay of Pigs in 1961. The attempted invasion failed miserably and, in retrospect, seemed remarkably ill-conceived. Applying his many years of research on group dynamics to the Bay of Pigs fiasco, Janis developed a model of groupthink.

When groups get caught up in groupthink, members suspend their critical judgment and the group starts censoring dissent as the pressure to conform increases. Soon, everyone begins to think alike. Moreover, "mind guards" try to shield the group from information that contradicts the group's view. If the group's view is challenged from outside, victims of groupthink tend to think in simplistic "us versus them" terms. Members begin to overestimate the ingroup's unanimity, and they begin to view the outgroup as the enemy. Groupthink also promotes incomplete gathering of information. Like individuals, groups often display a confirmation bias, as they tend to seek and focus on information that supports their initial views (Schulz-Hardt et al., 2000).

What causes groupthink? One key precondition is high group cohesiveness. *Group cohesiveness* refers to the strength of the liking relationships linking group members to each other and to the group itself. Members of cohesive groups are close-knit, are committed, have "team spirit," and are loyal to the group. Cohesiveness itself isn't bad. It can help groups achieve great things. But Janis maintains that the danger of groupthink is greater when groups are highly cohesive. Groupthink is also more likely when a group works in relative isolation, when its power structure is dominated by a strong, directive leader, and when it is under pressure to make a major decision quickly.

Only a handful of experiments have been conducted to test Janis's theory, because the antecedent conditions thought to foster groupthink—such as

what type of pizza to order, a jury deciding on a verdict, or Congress deciding whether to pass a bill, groups make decisions. Social psychologists have discovered some interesting tendencies in group decision making. We'll take a brief look at two of these, *group polarization* and *groupthink*.

Group Polarization

Who leans toward more cautious decisions: individuals or groups? Common sense suggests that groups will work out compromises that cancel out members' extreme views. Hence, the collective wisdom of the group should yield relatively conservative choices. Is common sense correct? To investigate this question, Stoner (1961) asked individual participants to give their recommendations on tough decisions and then asked the same subjects to engage in group discussion to arrive at joint recommendations. When Stoner compared individuals' average recommendation against their group decision generated through discussion, he found that groups arrived at *riskier* decisions than individuals did. Stoner's finding was replicated in other studies (Pruitt, 1971), and the phenomenon acquired the name *risky shift*.

However, investigators eventually determined that groups can shift either way, toward risk or caution, depending on which way the group is leaning to begin with (Friedkin, 1999; Myers & Lamm, 1976). A shift toward a more extreme position, an effect called *polarization,* is often the result of group discussion (Tindale, Kameda, & Hinsz, 2003). Thus, *group polarization* occurs when group discussion strengthens a group's dominant point of view and produces a shift toward a more extreme decision in that direction (see **Figure 15.15**). Group polarization does not involve widening the gap between

web link 15.6

Group Dynamics

Donelson Forsyth of Virginia Commonwealth University maintains this excellent site devoted to the dynamics of group interaction. Topics of interest include group structure, group cohesiveness, influence in groups, conflict in groups, and the history of research on groups. The site also houses a rich set of links to organizations that study groups.

© Joseph Pobereskin/Stone/Getty Images

high decision stress, strong group cohesiveness, and dominating leadership—are difficult to create effectively in laboratory settings (Aldag & Fuller, 1993). The evidence on groupthink consists mostly of retrospective case studies of major decision-making fiascos (Eaton, 2001). Thus, Janis's model of groupthink should probably be characterized as an innovative, sophisticated, intuitively appealing theory that needs to be subjected to much more empirical study (Esser, 1998).

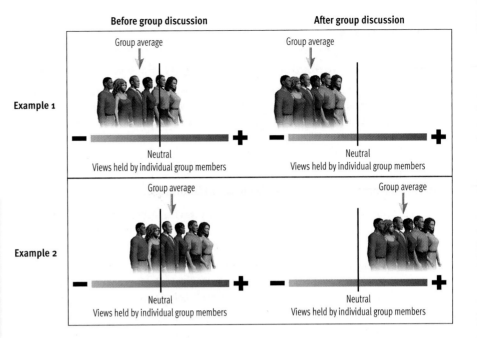

Figure 15.15

Group polarization. Two examples of group polarization are diagrammed here. In the first example (top) a group starts out mildly opposed to an idea, but after discussion sentiment against the idea is stronger. In the second example (bottom), a group starts out with a favorable disposition toward an idea, and this disposition is strengthened by group discussion.

Reflecting on the Chapter's Themes

Our discussion of social psychology has provided a final embellishment on four of our seven unifying themes: psychology's commitment to empiricism, the importance of cultural factors, multifactorial causation, and the extent to which people's experience of the world is highly subjective. Let's consider the virtues of empiricism first.

It's easy to question the need to do scientific research on social behavior, because studies in social psychology often seem to verify common sense. While most people wouldn't presume to devise their own theory of color vision or question the significance of REM sleep, everyone has beliefs about the nature of love, how to persuade others, and the limits of obedience. Thus, when studies demonstrate that credibility enhances persuasion or that good looks facilitate attraction, it's tempting to conclude that social psychologists go to great lengths to document the obvious, and some critics say, "Why bother?"

You saw why in this chapter. Research in social psychology has repeatedly shown that the predic-

tions of logic and common sense are often wrong. Consider just a few examples. Even psychiatric experts failed to predict the remarkable obedience to authority uncovered in Milgram's research. The bystander effect in helping behavior violates cold-blooded mathematical logic. Dissonance research has shown that after a severe initiation, the bigger the letdown, the more favorable people's feelings are. These findings defy common sense.

Thus, research on social behavior provides dramatic illustrations of why psychologists put their faith in empiricism. The moral of social psychology's story is this: Although scientific research often supports ideas based on common sense and logic, we can't count on this result. If psychologists want to achieve sound understanding of the principles governing behavior, they have to put their ideas to an empirical test.

Our coverage of social psychology also demonstrated once again that behavior is characterized by both cultural variance and invariance. Although

Key Learning Goals

15.25 Identify the four unifying themes highlighted in this chapter.

 Empiricism

 Cultural Heritage

 Multifactorial Causation

 Subjectivity of Experience

Person Perception: Forming Impressions of Others

▌ Perceptions of others can be distorted by a variety of factors, including physical appearance. People attribute desirable personality characteristics and competence to those who are good-looking. Perceptions of competence based on facial appearance are particularly important and can be formed in the blink of an eye.

▌ Stereotypes may lead people to see what they expect to see and to overestimate how often they see it. Evolutionary psychologists argue that many biases in person perception were adaptive in humans' ancestral past.

Attribution Processes: Explaining Behavior

▌ Internal attributions ascribe behavior to personal dispositions and traits, whereas external attributions locate the cause of behavior in the environment. Weiner's model proposes that attributions for success and failure should be analyzed in terms of the stability of causes, as well as along the internal-external dimension.

▌ Observers favor internal attributions to explain another's behavior (the fundamental attribution error), while actors favor external attributions to explain their own behavior. The self-serving bias is the tendency to attribute one's good outcomes to personal factors and one's bad outcomes to situational factors. Cultures vary in their emphasis on individualism as opposed to collectivism, and these differences appear to influence attributional tendencies.

Interpersonal Attraction: Liking and Loving

▌ People tend to like and love others who are similar, who reciprocate expressions of affection, and who are physically attractive. Romantic ideals influence the progress of intimate relationships.

▌ Some theorists have distinguished between passionate love and companionate love, which can be subdivided into intimacy and commitment. Hazan and Shaver's theory suggests that love relationships in adulthood mimic attachment patterns in infancy. As a result, people tend to exhibit secure, anxious-ambivalent, or avoidant attachment styles in their romantic relationships.

▌ Cultures vary considerably in their emphasis on passionate love as a prerequisite for marriage. Although critics are concerned that Internet relationships are superficial and open to deception, Internet-initiated relationships appear to be just as intimate and stable as relationships forged offline.

▌ According to evolutionary psychologists, certain aspects of good looks influence attraction because they are indicators of reproductive fitness. Consistent with evolutionary theory, gender differences in mating preferences appear to transcend culture. People's courtship tactics may include deception.

Attitudes: Making Social Judgments

▌ Attitudes may be made up of cognitive, affective, and behavioral components. Attitudes vary in strength, accessibility, and ambivalence. A source of persuasion who is credible, expert, trustworthy, and likable tends to be relatively effective. Two-sided arguments and fear arousal tend to be effective in persuasive efforts. Persuasion is more difficult when a receiver is forewarned.

▌ Attitudes may be shaped through classical conditioning, operant conditioning, and observational learning. Dissonance theory asserts that inconsistent attitudes cause tension and that people alter their attitudes to reduce dissonance. The elaboration likelihood model holds that the central route to persuasion tends to yield longer-lasting attitude change than the peripheral route.

Conformity and Obedience: Yielding to Others

▌ Asch found that conformity in groups becomes more likely as group size increases, up to a point. In Milgram's landmark study of obedience to authority, adult men drawn from the community showed a remarkable tendency, in spite of their misgivings, to follow orders to shock an innocent stranger. The generalizability of Milgram's findings has stood the test of time, but his work also helped to stimulate stricter ethical standards for research.

▌ The Stanford Prison Simulation demonstrated that social roles and other situational pressures can exert tremendous influence over social behavior. Like Milgram, Zimbardo showed that situational forces can lead normal people to exhibit surprisingly callous, abusive behavior.

Behavior in Groups: Joining with Others

▌ People who help someone in need when alone are less likely to provide help when a group is present. The bystander effect occurs primarily because a group creates diffusion of responsibility. Productivity often declines in larger groups because of loss of coordination and social loafing.

▌ Group polarization occurs when a group shifts toward a more extreme decision in the direction it was already leaning. In groupthink, a cohesive group suspends critical judgment in a misguided effort to promote agreement in decision making.

Reflecting on the Chapter's Themes

▌ Social psychology illustrates the value of empiricism because research in this area often proves that common sense is wrong. Additionally, research in social psychology demonstrates that people's experience of the world is highly subjective, that culture shapes behavior, and that multifactorial causation is common.

PERSONAL APPLICATION Understanding Prejudice

▌ Prejudice is a negative attitude toward a group. Prejudice is supported by subjectivity in person perception, stereotyping, and attributional biases. Negative attitudes about groups are often acquired through observational learning and supported by operant conditioning.

▌ Realistic group conflict theory posits that competition between groups fosters prejudice. Threats to social identity can lead to outgroup derogation.

CRITICAL THINKING APPLICATION Analyzing Credibility and Social Influence Tactics

▌ Useful criteria in judging credibility include whether a source has vested interests or appropriate credentials. One should also consider the method used in reaching conclusions and why information might not coincide with conventional wisdom.

▌ To resist manipulative efforts, it helps to be aware of social influence tactics, such as the foot-in-the-door technique, misuse of the reciprocity norm, the lowball technique, and feigned scarcity.

PSYKTREK PREVIEW

Sternberg describes eight different types of relationships that can result from the presence or absence of these components of love. One of these relationship types, nonlove, is not pictured in the diagram because it is defined as the absence of all three components. Click on the terms to learn more about each of the remaining types of relationships.

Learn about love in Module 12b (*Theories of Love*), which will allow you to take

Stereotypes tend to involve broad overgeneralizations that ignore the diversity within groups and foster inaccurate perceptions of people. Obviously, not all Jews, Italians, or females behave alike.

Find out why people are prejudiced by working through Module 12d (*Prejudice*).

1. Stereotypes:
   A. reflect normal cognitive processes that frequently are automatic.
   B. are widely held beliefs that people have certain characteristics because of their membership in a particular group.
   C. tend to be broad overgeneralizations that ignore the diversity within social groups.
   D. are all of the above.

2. You believe that short men have a tendency to be insecure. The concept of illusory correlation implies that you will:
   A. overestimate how often you meet short men who are insecure.
   B. underestimate how often you meet short men who are insecure.
   C. overestimate the frequency of short men in the population.
   D. falsely assume that shortness in men causes insecurity.

3. A father suggests that his son's low marks in school are due to the child's laziness. The father has made _____ attribution.
   A. an external
   B. an internal
   C. a situational
   D. a high consensus

4. The fundamental attribution error refers to the tendency of:
   A. observers to favor external attributions in explaining the behavior of others.
   B. observers to favor internal attributions in explaining the behavior of others.
   C. actors to favor external attributions in explaining the behavior of others.
   D. actors to favor internal attributions in explaining their behavior.

5. Which of the following factors is *not* one that influences interpersonal attraction?
   A. Physical attractiveness
   B. Similarity
   C. Reciprocity
   D. Latitude of acceptance

6. According to Hazan and Shaver (1987):
   A. romantic relationships in adulthood follow the same form as attachment relationships in infancy.
   B. those who had ambivalent attachments in infancy are doomed never to fall in love as adults.
   C. those who had avoidant attachments in infancy often overcompensate by becoming excessively intimate in their adult love relationships.
   D. all of the above are the case.

7. Which of the following variables does *not* tend to facilitate persuasion?
   A. Source credibility
   B. Source trustworthiness
   C. Forewarning of the receiver
   D. A two-sided argument

8. Cognitive dissonance theory predicts that after people engage in behavior that contradicts their true feelings, they will:
   A. convince themselves they really didn't perform the behavior.
   B. change their attitude to make it more consistent with their behavior.
   C. change their attitude to make it less consistent with their behavior.
   D. do nothing.

9. The elaboration likelihood model of attitude change suggests that:
   A. the peripheral route results in more enduring attitude change.
   B. the central route results in more enduring attitude change.
   C. only the central route to persuasion can be effective.
   D. only the peripheral route to persuasion can be effective.

10. The results of Milgram's (1963) study imply that:
   A. in the real world, most people will refuse to follow orders to inflict harm on a stranger.
   B. many people will obey an authority figure even if innocent people get hurt.
   C. most people are willing to give obviously wrong answers when ordered to do so.
   D. most people stick to their own judgment, even when group members unanimously disagree.

11. According to Latané, social loafing is due to:
   A. social norms that stress the importance of positive interactions among group members.
   B. duplication of effort among group members.
   C. diffusion of responsibility in groups.
   D. a bias toward making internal attributions about the behavior of others.

12. Groupthink occurs when members of a cohesive group:
   A. are initially unanimous about an issue.
   B. stress the importance of caution in group decision making.
   C. emphasize concurrence at the expense of critical thinking in arriving at a decision.
   D. shift toward a less extreme position after group discussion.

Answers

1 D p. 521	5 D pp. 527–528	9 B p. 538
2 A p. 522	6 A p. 529	10 B pp. 540–541
3 B p. 523	7 C pp. 534–535	11 C p. 545
4 B p. 524	8 B p. 537	12 C p. 546

PSYKTREK PREVIEW

See Stanley Milgram's subjects cringe in discomfort when they are asked to shock an innocent stranger when you visit Module 12e (*Conformity and Obedience*), which includes three videos from the famous study.

Participate in an experiment on your skills in person perception when you try Simulation 10 (*Social Judgment*).

Answers to Concept Checks

Chapter 1

Concept Check 1.1

1. c. Sigmund Freud (1905, pp. 77–78) arguing that it is possible to probe into the unconscious depths of the mind.

2. a. Wilhelm Wundt (1904 revision of an earlier text, p. v) campaigning for a new, independent science of psychology.

3. b. William James (1890) commenting negatively on the structuralists' efforts to break consciousness into its elements and his view of consciousness as a continuously flowing stream.

Concept Check 1.2

1. b. B. F. Skinner (1971, p. 17) explaining why he believes that freedom is an illusion.

2. c. Carl Rogers (1961, p. 27) commenting on others' assertion that he had an overly optimistic (Pollyannaish) view of human potential and discussing humans' basic drive toward personal growth.

3. a. John B. Watson (1930, p. 103) dismissing the importance of genetic inheritance while arguing that traits are shaped entirely by experience.

Concept Check 1.3

1. c. Thomas and Chess's (1977) well-known New York Longitudinal Study is a landmark in developmental psychology.

2. a. Olds and Milner (1954) made this discovery by accident and thereby opened up a fascinating line of inquiry in physiological psychology.

3. e. Zuckerman (1971) pioneered the study of sensation seeking as a personality trait.

Concept Check 1.4

1. e	2. i	3. h
4. f	5. g	6. c
7. b	8. a	9. d

Chapter 2

Concept Check 2.1

1. IV: Film violence (present versus absent).
   DV: Heart rate and blood pressure (there are two DVs).

2. IV: Courtesy training (training versus no training).
   DV: Number of customer complaints.

3. IV: Stimulus complexity (high versus low) and stimulus contrast (high versus low) (there are two IVs).
   DV: Length of time spent staring at the stimuli.

4. IV: Group size (large versus small).
   DV: Conformity.

Concept Check 2.2

1. b and e. The other three conclusions all equate correlation with causation.

2. a. Negative. As age increases, more people tend to have visual problems and acuity tends to decrease.

   b. Positive. Studies show that highly educated people tend to earn higher incomes and that people with less education tend to earn lower incomes.

   c. Negative. As shyness increases, the size of one's friendship network should decrease. However, research suggests that this inverse association may be weaker than widely believed.

Concept Check 2.3

1. d. Survey. You would distribute a survey to obtain information on subjects' social class, education, and attitudes about nuclear disarmament.

2. c. Case study. Using a case study approach, you could interview people with anxiety disorders, interview their parents, and examine their school records to look for similarities in childhood experiences. As a second choice, you might have people with anxiety disorders fill out a survey about their childhood experiences.

3. b. Naturalistic observation. To answer this question properly, you would want to observe baboons in their natural environment, without interference.

4. a. Experiment. To demonstrate a causal relationship, you would have to conduct an experiment. You would manipulate the presence or absence of food-related cues in controlled circumstances where subjects had an opportunity to eat some food, and monitor the amount eaten.

Concept Check 2.4

Methodological flaw	Study 1	Study 2
Sampling bias	✓	✓
Placebo effects	✓	
Confounding of variables	✓	
Distortions in self-report data		✓
Experimenter bias	✓	

Explanations for Study 1. Sensory deprivation is an unusual kind of experience that may intrigue certain potential subjects, who may be more adventurous or more willing to take risks than the population at large. Using the first 80 students who sign up for this study may not yield a sample that is representative of the population. Assigning the first 40 subjects who sign up to the experimental group may confound these extraneous variables with the treatment (students who sign up most quickly may be the most adventurous). In announcing that he will be examining the detrimental effects of sensory deprivation, the experimenter has created expectations in the subjects. These expectations could lead to placebo effects that have not been

Answers to Concept Checks

Chapter 1

Concept Check 1.1

1. c. Sigmund Freud (1905, pp. 77–78) arguing that it is possible to probe into the unconscious depths of the mind.

2. a. Wilhelm Wundt (1904 revision of an earlier text, p. v) campaigning for a new, independent science of psychology.

3. b. William James (1890) commenting negatively on the structuralists' efforts to break consciousness into its elements and his view of consciousness as a continuously flowing stream.

Concept Check 1.2

1. b. B. F. Skinner (1971, p. 17) explaining why he believes that freedom is an illusion.

2. c. Carl Rogers (1961, p. 27) commenting on others' assertion that he had an overly optimistic (Polly-annaish) view of human potential and discussing humans' basic drive toward personal growth.

3. a. John B. Watson (1930, p. 103) dismissing the importance of genetic inheritance while arguing that traits are shaped entirely by experience.

Concept Check 1.3

1. c. Thomas and Chess's (1977) well-known New York Longitudinal Study is a landmark in developmental psychology.

2. a. Olds and Milner (1954) made this discovery by accident and thereby opened up a fascinating line of inquiry in physiological psychology.

3. e. Zuckerman (1971) pioneered the study of sensation seeking as a personality trait.

Concept Check 1.4

1. e   2. i   3. h

4. f   5. g   6. c

7. b   8. a   9. d

Chapter 2

Concept Check 2.1

1. IV: Film violence (present versus absent).
   DV: Heart rate and blood pressure (there are two DVs).

2. IV: Courtesy training (training versus no training).
   DV: Number of customer complaints.

3. IV: Stimulus complexity (high versus low) and stimulus contrast (high versus low) (there are two IVs).
   DV: Length of time spent staring at the stimuli.

4. IV: Group size (large versus small).
   DV: Conformity.

Concept Check 2.2

1. b and e. The other three conclusions all equate correlation with causation.

2. a. Negative. As age increases, more people tend to have visual problems and acuity tends to decrease.

   b. Positive. Studies show that highly educated people tend to earn higher incomes and that people with less education tend to earn lower incomes.

   c. Negative. As shyness increases, the size of one's friendship network should decrease. However, research suggests that this inverse association may be weaker than widely believed.

Concept Check 2.3

1. d. Survey. You would distribute a survey to obtain information on subjects' social class, education, and attitudes about nuclear disarmament.

2. c. Case study. Using a case study approach, you could interview people with anxiety disorders, interview their parents, and examine their school records to look for similarities in childhood experiences. As a second choice, you might have people with anxiety disorders fill out a survey about their childhood experiences.

3. b. Naturalistic observation. To answer this question properly, you would want to observe baboons in their natural environment, without interference.

4. a. Experiment. To demonstrate a causal relationship, you would have to conduct an experiment. You would manipulate the presence or absence of food-related cues in controlled circumstances where subjects had an opportunity to eat some food, and monitor the amount eaten.

Concept Check 2.4

Methodological flaw	Study 1	Study 2
Sampling bias	✓	✓
Placebo effects	✓	
Confounding of variables	✓	
Distortions in self-report data		✓
Experimenter bias	✓	

Explanations for Study 1. Sensory deprivation is an unusual kind of experience that may intrigue certain potential subjects, who may be more adventurous or more willing to take risks than the population at large. Using the first 80 students who sign up for this study may not yield a sample that is representative of the population. Assigning the first 40 subjects who sign up to the experimental group may confound these extraneous variables with the treatment (students who sign up most quickly may be the most adventurous). In announcing that he will be examining the detrimental effects of sensory deprivation, the experimenter has created expectations in the subjects. These expectations could lead to placebo effects that have not been

controlled for with a placebo group. The experimenter has also revealed that he has a bias about the outcome of the study. Since he supervises the treatments, he knows which subjects are in the experimental and control groups, thus aggravating potential problems with experimenter bias. For example, he might un-intentionally give the control group subjects better instructions on how to do the pursuit-rotor task and thereby slant the study in favor of finding support for his hypothesis.

Explanations for Study 2. Sampling bias is a problem because the researcher has sampled only subjects from a low-income, inner-city neighborhood. A sample ob-tained in this way is not likely to be representative of the population at large. People are sensitive about the issue of racial prejudice, so distortions in self-report data are also likely. Many subjects may be swayed by social desirability bias and rate themselves as less prejudiced than they really are.

Concept Check 2.5
1. c 2. a 3. b

Chapter 3

Concept Check 3.1
1. d. Dendrite. 5. a. Glia.
2. f. Myelin. 6. g. Terminal button.
3. b. Neuron. 7. h. Synapse.
4. e. Axon.

Concept Check 3.2
1. d. Serotonin.
2. b and d. Norepinephrine and serotonin.
3. e. Endorphins.
4. c. Dopamine.
5. a. Acetylcholine.

Concept Check 3.3
1. Left hemisphere damage, probably to Wernicke's area.
2. Deficit in dopamine synthesis in an area of the midbrain.
3. Deterioration of myelin sheaths surrounding axons.
4. Disturbance in dopamine activity.

Please note that neuropsychological assessment is not as simple as this introductory exercise may suggest. There are many possible causes of most disorders, and we discussed only a handful of leading causes for each.

Concept Check 3.4
1. Closer relatives; more distant relatives.
2. Identical twins; fraternal twins.
3. Biological parents; adoptive parents.
4. Genetic overlap or closeness; trait similarity.

Concept Check 3.5
1. c 2. e 3. b
4. a 5. d

Chapter 4

Concept Check 4.1

Dimension	Rods	Cones
1. Physical shape	Elongated	Stubby
2. Number in the retina	125 million	5–6.4 million
3. Area of the retina in which they are dominant receptor	Periphery	Center/fovea
4. Critical to color vision	No	Yes
5. Critical to peripheral vision	Yes	No
6. Sensitivity to dim light	Strong	Weak
7. Speed of dark adaptation	Slow	Rapid

Concept Check 4.2

	Trichromatic	Opponent process
1. Theory proposed by:	Young, Helmholtz	Hering
2. Can/can't account for complementary afterimages	can't	can
3. Explains first/later stage of color processing	first	later
4. Does/doesn't account for need for four terms to describe colors	doesn't	does

Concept Check 4.3
✓ 1. Interposition. The arches in front cut off part of the corridor behind them.

✓ 2. Height in plane. The back of the corridor is higher on the horizontal plane than the front of the corridor is.

✓ 3. Texture gradient. The more distant portions of the hallway are painted in less detail than the closer portions are.

✓ 4. Relative size. The arches in the distance are smaller than those in the foreground.

✓ 5. Light and shadow. Light shining in from the crossing corridor (it's coming from the left) contrasts with shadow elsewhere.

✓ 6. Linear perspective. The lines of the corridor converge in the distance.

Concept Check 4.4

Dimension	Vision	Hearing
1. Stimulus	Light waves	Sound waves
2. Elements of related perceptions	Wavelength/hue Amplitude/ brightness Purity/saturation	Frequency/pitch Amplitude/ loudness Purity/timbre
3. Receptors	Rods and cones	Hair cells
4. Location of receptors	Retina	Basilar membrane
5. Main location of processing in brain	Occipital lobe, visual cortex	Temporal lobe, auditory cortex

Concept Check 4.5

1. c   2. a   3. e

4. b   5. d

Chapter 5

Concept Check 5.1

Characteristic	REM sleep	NREM sleep
1. Type of EEG activity	"Wide awake" brain waves, mostly beta	Varied lots of delta waves
2. Eye movements	Rapid, lateral	Slow or absent
3. Dreaming	Frequent, vivid	Less frequent
4. Depth (difficulty in awakening)	Difficult to awaken	Varied, generally easier to awaken
5. Percentage of total sleep (in adults)	About 20%	About 80%
6. Increases or decreases (as percentage of sleep) during childhood	Percent decreases	Percent increases
7. Timing in sleep (dominates early or late)	Dominates later in cycle	Dominates early in cycle

Concept Check 5.2

1. Beta. Video games require alert information processing, which is associated with beta waves.

2. Alpha. Meditation involves relaxation, which is associated with alpha waves, and studies show increased alpha in meditators.

3. Theta. In stage 1 sleep, theta waves tend to be prevalent.

4. Beta. Dreams are associated with REM sleep, which paradoxically produces "wide awake" beta waves.

5. Beta. If you're a beginner, typing will require alert, focused attention, which should generate beta waves.

Concept Check 5.3

1. c. Stimulants.

2. d. Hallucinogens.

3. b. Sedatives.

4. f. Alcohol.

5. a. Narcotics.

6. e. Cannabis.

Concept Check 5.4

1. d   2. e   3. a

4. f   5. b   6. c

Chapter 6

Concept Check 6.1

1. CS: Fire in fireplace
   US: Pain from burn   CR/UR: Fear

2. CS: Brake lights in rain
   US: Car accident   CR/UR: Tensing up

3. CS: Sight of cat
   US: Cat dander   CR/UR: Wheezing

Concept Check 6.2

1. d. Stimulus generalization.

2. a. Acquisition.

3. f. Higher-order conditioning.

4. e. Stimulus discrimination.

5. c. Spontaneous recovery.

6. b. Extinction.

Concept Check 6.3

1. FR. Each sale is a response and every third response earns reinforcement.

2. VI. A varied amount of time elapses before the response of doing yard work can earn reinforcement.

3. VR. Reinforcement occurs after a varied number of unreinforced casts (time is irrelevant; the more casts Martha makes, the more reinforcers she will receive).

4. CR. The designated response (reading a book) is reinforced (with a gold star) each and every time.

5. FI. A fixed time interval (3 years) has to elapse before Skip can earn a salary increase (the reinforcer).

Concept Check 6.4

1. Punishment.

2. Positive reinforcement.

3. Punishment.

4. Negative reinforcement (for Audrey); the dog is positively reinforced for its whining.

5. Negative reinforcement.

6. Extinction. When Sharma's co-workers start to ignore her complaints, they are trying to extinguish the behavior (which had been positively reinforced when it won sympathy).

Concept Check 6.5

1. Classical conditioning. Midori's blue windbreaker is a CS eliciting excitement in her dog.

2. Operant conditioning. Playing new songs leads to negative consequences (punishment), which weaken the tendency to play new songs. Playing old songs leads to positive reinforcement, which gradually strengthens the tendency to play old songs.

3. Classical conditioning. The song was paired with the passion of new love so that it became a CS eliciting emotional, romantic feelings.

4. Both. Ralph's workplace is paired with criticism so that his workplace becomes a CS eliciting anxiety. Calling in sick is operant behavior that is strengthened through negative reinforcement (because it reduces anxiety).

Concept Check 6.6

1. f	2. b	3. e
4. g	5. h	6. c
7. d	8. a	

Chapter 7

Concept Check 7.1

Feature	Sensory memory	Short-term memory	Long-term memory
1. Main encoding format	Copy of input	Largely phonemic	Largely semantic
2. Storage	Limited capacity	Small (7 ± 2 chunks)	No known limit
3. Storage duration	About ¼ second	Up to 20 seconds	Minutes to years

Concept Check 7.2

1. Ineffective encoding due to lack of attention.

2. Retrieval failure due to motivated forgetting.

3. Proactive interference (previous learning of Justin Timberlake's name interferes with new learning).

4. Retroactive interference (new learning of sociology interferes with older learning of history).

Concept Check 7.3

1. d.   Declarative memory.

2. c.   Long-term memory.

3. a.   Sensory memory.

4. f.   Episodic memory.

5. e.   Nondeclarative memory.

6. g.   Semantic memory.

7. i.   Prospective memory.

8. b.   Short-term memory.

Concept Check 7.4

1. c	2. e	3. f
4. a	5. g	6. h
7. i	8. b	9. d

Chapter 8

Concept Check 8.1

1. Functional fixedness.

2. Forming subgoals.

3. Insight.

4. Searching for analogies.

5. Arrangement problem.

Concept Check 8.2

1. Elimination by aspects.

2. Availability heuristic.

3. Shift to an additive model.

Concept Check 8.3

1. H. Given that the identical twins were reared apart, their greater similarity in comparison to fraternals reared together can only be due to heredity. This comparison is probably the most important piece of evidence supporting the genetic determination of IQ.

2. E. We tend to associate identical twins with evidence supporting heredity, but in this comparison genetic similarity is held constant since both sets of twins are identical. The only logical explanation for the greater similarity in identicals reared together is the effect of their being reared together (environment).

3. E. This comparison is similar to the previous one. Genetic similarity is held constant and a shared environment produces greater similarity than being reared apart.

4. B. This is nothing more than a quantification of the observation that intelligence runs in families. Since families share both genes and environment, either or both could be responsible for the observed correlation.

5. B. The similarity of adopted children to their biological parents can only be due to shared genes, and the similarity of adopted children to their foster parents can only be due to shared environment, so these correlations show the influence of both heredity and environment.

Concept Check 8.4

1. d	2. g	3. e
4. a	5. h	6. i
7. b	8. c	9. f

Chapter 9

Concept Check 9.1

1. I. Early studies indicated that lesioning the ventromedial nucleus of the hypothalamus leads to overeating (although it is an oversimplification to characterize the VMH as the brain's "stop eating" center).

2. I. According to Mayer, hunger increases when the amount of glucose in the blood decreases.

3. I or ?. Food cues generally trigger hunger and eating, but reactions vary among individuals.

4. D. Food preferences are mostly learned, and we tend to like what we are accustomed to eating. Most people will not be eager to eat a strange-looking food.

5. I. People tend to eat more when a variety of foods are available.

6. I. Reactions vary, but stress generally tends to increase eating.

Concept Check 9.2

1. c. Incentive value of success.

2. b. Perceived probability of success.

3. a. Need for achievement.

Concept Check 9.3

1. d   2. g   3. e

4. h   5. a   6. b

7. c   8. f

Chapter 10

Concept Check 10.1

Event	Stage	Organism	Time span
1. Uterine implantation	Germinal	Zygote	0–2 weeks
2. Muscle and bone begin to form	Fetal	Fetus	2 months to birth
3. Vital organs and body systems begin to form	Embryonic	Embryo	2 weeks to 2 months

Concept Check 10.2

1. b. Animism is characteristic of the preoperational period.

2. c. Mastery of hierarchical classification occurs during the concrete operational period.

3. a. Lack of object permanence is characteristic of the sensorimotor period.

Concept Check 10.3

1. c. Commitment to personal ethics is characteristic of postconventional reasoning.

2. b. Concern about approval of others is characteristic of conventional reasoning.

3. a. Emphasis on positive or negative consequences is characteristic of preconventional reasoning.

Concept Check 10.4

1. d   2. f   3. c

4. g   5. a   6. b

7. e

Chapter 11

Concept Check 11.1

1. Regression.

2. Projection.

3. Reaction formation.

4. Repression.

5. Rationalization.

Concept Check 11.2

	Freud	Jung	Adler
1. Archetypes		✓	
2. Physical gratification	✓		
3. Striving for superiority			✓
4. Collective unconscious		✓	
5. Early childhood experiences	✓		✓
6. Dream analysis	✓	✓	
7. Unconscious determinants	✓	✓	

Concept Check 11.3

1. Bandura's observational learning. Sarah imitates a role model from television.

2. Maslow's need for self-actualization. Yolanda is striving to realize her fullest potential.

3. Freud's Oedipal complex. Vladimir shows preference for his opposite-sex parent and emotional distance from his same-sex parent.

Concept Check 11.4

1. Maslow (1971, p. 36) commenting on the need for self-actualization.

2. Eysenck (1977, pp. 407–408) commenting on the biological roots of personality.

3. Freud (in Malcolm, 1980) commenting on the repression of sexuality.

Concept Check 11.5

1. g   2. i   3. f

4. d   5. h   6. a

7. e   8. b   9. c

Chapter 12

Concept Check 12.1

1. b. A choice between two unattractive options.

2. c. Weighing the positive and negative aspects of a single goal.

3. a. A choice between two attractive options.

Concept Check 12.2

1. a. Frustration due to delay.

2. d. Pressure to perform.

3. c. Change associated with leaving school and taking a new job.

4. a. Frustration due to loss of job.

   c. Change in life circumstances.

   d. Pressure to perform (in quickly obtaining new job).

Concept Check 12.3

Pathway 1: hypothalamus, sympathetic division of the ANS, adrenal medulla, catecholamines.

Pathway 2: pituitary, ACTH, adrenal cortex, corticosteroids.

Concept Check 12.4

1. g   2. f   3. e

4. d   5. c   6. b

7. a

Chapter 13

Concept Check 13.1

	Deviance	Maladaptive behavior	Personal distress
1. Alan	_____	✓	_____
2. Monica	_____	_____	✓
3. Boris	✓	_____	_____
4. Natasha	✓	✓	✓

Concept Check 13.2

1. Obsessive-compulsive disorder (key symptoms: frequent rituals, ruminations about school).

2. Somatization disorder (key symptoms: history of physical complaints involving many different organ systems).

3. Conversion disorder (key symptom: loss of function in single organ system).

Concept Check 13.3

1. Bipolar disorder, manic episode (key symptoms: extravagant plans, hyperactivity, reckless spending).

2. Paranoid schizophrenia (key symptoms: delusions of persecution and grandeur, along with deterioration of adaptive behavior).

3. Major depression (key symptoms: feelings of despair, low self-esteem, lack of energy).

Concept Check 13.4

1. c   2. a   3. d

4. b

Chapter 14

Concept Check 14.1

1. c.

2. a.

3. b.

Concept Check 14.2

1. d.   2. b   3. a

4. c

Concept Check 14.3

1. c.

2. a.

3. b.

4. d.

5. b.

Concept Check 14.4

1. c   2. d   3. b

4. a   5. e

Chapter 15

Concept Check 15.1

	Unstable	Stable
Internal	d	b
External	a	c

Concept Check 15.2

1. c. Fundamental attribution error (assuming that arriving late reflects personal qualities).

2. a. Illusory correlation effect (overestimating how often one has seen confirmations of the assertion that young, female professors get pregnant soon after being hired).

3. b. Stereotyping (assuming that all lawyers have certain traits).

Concept Check 15.3

1. *Target:* Cognitive component of attitudes (beliefs about program for regulating nursing homes).

   Persuasion: Message factor (advice to use one-sided instead of two-sided arguments).

2. *Target:* Affective component of attitudes (feelings about candidate).

   Persuasion: Source factor (advice on appearing likable, sincere, and compassionate).

3. *Target:* Behavioral component of attitudes (making contributions).

   Persuasion: Receiver factor (considering audience's initial position regarding the candidate).

Concept Check 15.4

1. False.

2. True.

3. False.

4. True.

5. False.

Concept Check 15.5

1. c   2. d   3. g

4. a   5. b   6. e

7. f

Statistical Methods

Empiricism depends on observation; precise observation depends on measurement; and measurement requires numbers. Thus, scientists routinely analyze numerical data to arrive at their conclusions. Over 2000 empirical studies are cited in this text, and all but a few of the simplest ones required a statistical analysis. **Statistics is the use of mathematics to organize, summarize, and interpret numerical data.** We discussed correlation briefly in Chapter 2, but in this Appendix we look at a variety of statistics.

To illustrate statistics in action, let's assume that we want to test a hypothesis that has generated quite an argument in your psychology class. The hypothesis is that college students who watch a great deal of television aren't as bright as those who watch TV infrequently. For the fun of it, your class decides to conduct a correlational study of itself, collecting survey and psychological test data. Your classmates all agree to respond to a short survey on their TV viewing habits. Because everyone at your school has had to take the SAT, the class decides to use scores on the SAT verbal subtest as an index of how bright students are. All of them agree to allow the records office at the college to furnish their SAT scores to the professor, who replaces each student's name with a subject number (to protect students' right to privacy). Let's see how we could use statistics to analyze the data collected in our pilot study (a small, preliminary investigation).

Graphing Data   1c

After collecting our data, our next step is to organize the data to get a quick overview of our numerical results. Let's assume that there are 20 students in your class, and when they estimate how many hours they spend per day watching TV, the results are as follows:

3	2	0	3	1
3	4	0	5	1
2	3	4	5	2
4	5	3	4	6

One of the simpler things that we can do to organize data is to create a *frequency distribution*—an orderly arrangement of scores indicating the frequency of each score or group of scores. **Figure B.1(a)** shows a frequency distribution for our data on TV viewing. The column on the left lists the possible scores (estimated hours of TV viewing) in order, and the column on the right lists the number of subjects with each score. Graphs can provide an even better overview of the data. One approach is to portray the data in a *histogram,* which is a bar graph that presents data from a frequency distribution. Such a histogram, summarizing our TV viewing data, is presented in **Figure B.1(b)**.

Another widely used method of portraying data graphically is the *frequency polygon*—a line figure used to present data from a frequency distribution. **Figures B.1(c)** and **B.1(d)** show how our TV viewing data can be converted from a histogram to a frequency polygon. In both the bar graph and the line figure, the horizontal axis lists the possible scores and the vertical axis is used to indicate the frequency of each score. This use of the axes is nearly universal for frequency polygons, although sometimes it is reversed in histograms (the vertical axis lists possible scores, so the bars become horizontal).

Figure B.1
Graphing data. (a) Our raw data are tallied into a frequency distribution. (b) The same data are portrayed in a bar graph called a histogram. (c) A frequency polygon is plotted over the histogram. (d) The resultant frequency polygon is shown by itself.

Score	Tallies	Frequency
6	I	1
5	III	3
4	IIII	4
3	TH|	5
2	III	3
1	II	2
0	II	2

(a) Frequency distribution

(b) Histogram

(c) Conversion of histogram into frequency polygon

(d) Frequency polygon

Figure B.2
Measures of central tendency. The mean, median, and mode sometimes yield different results, but they usually converge, as in the case of our TV viewing data.

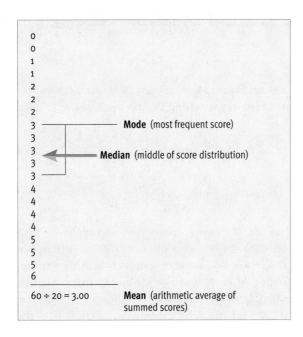

```
0
0
1
1
2
2
2
3 ──────────────── Mode (most frequent score)
3
3 ◄──────────────── Median (middle of score distribution)
3
3
4
4
4
4
5
5
5
6
```
60 ÷ 20 = 3.00   **Mean** (arithmetic average of summed scores)

Our graphs improve on the jumbled collection of scores that we started with, but *descriptive statistics,* which are used to organize and summarize data, provide some additional advantages. Let's see what the three measures of central tendency tell us about our data.

Measuring Central Tendency 1c

In examining a set of data, it's routine to ask "What is a typical score in the distribution?" For instance, in this case we might compare the average amount of TV watching in our sample against national estimates to determine whether our subjects appear to be representative of the population. The three measures of central tendency, the median, the mean, and the mode, give us indications regarding the typical score in a data set. The *median* is the score that falls in the center of a distribution, the *mean* is

the arithmetic average of the scores, and the *mode* is the score that occurs most frequently.

All three measures of central tendency are calculated for our TV viewing data in **Figure B.2**. As you can see, in this set of data, the mean, median, and mode all turn out to be the same score, which is 3. The correspondence among the three measures of central tendency seen in our TV viewing data is quite common, but there are situations in which the mean, median, and mode can yield very different estimates of central tendency. To illustrate, imagine that you're interviewing for a sales position at a company. Unbeknownst to you, the company's five salespeople earned the following incomes in the previous year: $20,000, $20,000, $25,000, $35,000, and $200,000. You ask how much the typical salesperson earns in a year. The sales director proudly announces that her five salespeople earned *a mean* income of $60,000 last year. However, before you order that expensive, new sports car, you had better inquire about the *median* and *modal* income for the sales staff. In this case, one extreme score ($200,000) has inflated the mean, making it unrepresentative of the sales staff's earnings. In this instance, the median ($25,000) and the mode ($20,000) both provide better estimates of what you are likely to earn.

In general, the mean is the most useful measure of central tendency because additional statistical manipulations can be performed on it that are not possible with the median or mode. However, the mean is sensitive to extreme scores in a distribution, which can sometimes make the mean misleading. Thus, lack of agreement among the three measures of central tendency usually occurs when a few extreme scores pull the mean away from the center of the distribution, as shown in **Figure B.3**. The curves plotted in **Figure B.3** are simply "smoothed out" frequency polygons based on data from many subjects. They show that when a distribution is symmetric, the

Figure B.3
Measures of central tendency in skewed distributions. In a symmetrical distribution (a), the three measures of central tendency converge. However, in a negatively skewed distribution (b) or in a positively skewed distribution (c), the mean, median, and mode are pulled apart as shown here. Typically, in these situations the median provides the best index of central tendency.

(a) Symmetrical distribution

(b) Negatively skewed distribution

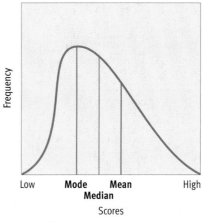

(c) Positively skewed distribution

measures of central tendency fall together, but this is not true in skewed or unbalanced distributions.

Figure B.3(b) shows a *negatively skewed distribution,* in which most scores pile up at the high end of the scale (the negative skew refers to the direction in which the curve's "tail" points). A *positively skewed distribution,* in which scores pile up at the low end of the scale, is shown in **Figure B.3(c)**. In both types of skewed distributions, a few extreme scores at one end pull the mean, and to a lesser degree the median, away from the mode. In these situations, the mean may be misleading and the median usually provides the best index of central tendency.

In any case, the measures of central tendency for our TV viewing data are reassuring, since they all agree and they fall reasonably close to national estimates regarding how much young adults watch TV. Given the small size of our group, this agreement with national norms doesn't *prove* that our sample is representative of the population, but at least there's no obvious reason to believe that they're unrepresentative.

Figure B.4

The standard deviation and dispersion of data. Although both these distributions of golf scores have the same mean, their standard deviations will be different. In (a) the scores are bunched together and there is less variability than in (b), yielding a lower standard deviation for the data in distribution (a).

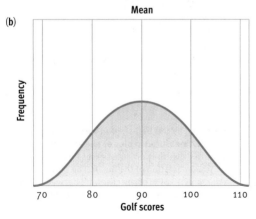

Measuring Variability 1c

Of course, everyone in our sample did not report identical TV viewing habits. Virtually all data sets are characterized by some variability. *Variability* refers to how much the scores tend to vary or depart from the mean score. For example, the distribution of golf scores for a mediocre, erratic golfer would be characterized by high variability, while scores for an equally mediocre but more consistent golfer would show less variability.

The *standard deviation* is an index of the amount of variability in a set of data. It reflects the dispersion of scores in a distribution. This principle is portrayed graphically in **Figure B.4**, where the two distributions of golf scores have the same mean but the top one has less variability because the scores are bunched up in the center (for the consistent golfer). The distribution in **Figure B.4(b)** is characterized by more variability, as the erratic golfer's scores are more spread out. This distribution will yield a higher standard deviation than the distribution in **Figure B.4(a)**.

The formula for calculating the standard deviation is shown in **Figure B.5**, where d stands for each score's deviation from the mean and Σ stands for

TV viewing score (X)	Deviation from mean (d)	Deviation squared (d^2)
0	−3	9
0	−3	9
1	−2	4
1	−2	4
2	−1	1
2	−1	1
2	−1	1
3	0	0
3	0	0
3	0	0
3	0	0
3	0	0
4	+1	1
4	+1	1
4	+1	1
4	+1	1
5	+2	4
5	+2	4
5	+2	4
6	+3	9

$N = 20$

$\Sigma X = 60$ $\Sigma d^2 = 54$

$$\text{Mean} = \frac{\Sigma X}{N} = \frac{60}{20} = 3.0$$

$$\text{Standard deviation} = \sqrt{\frac{\Sigma d^2}{N}} = \sqrt{\frac{54}{20}}$$

$$= \sqrt{2.70} = 1.64$$

Figure B.5

Steps in calculating the standard deviation. (1) Add the scores (ΣX) and divide by the number of scores (N) to calculate the mean (which comes out to 3.0 in this case). **(2)** Calculate each score's deviation from the mean by subtracting the mean from each score (the results are shown in the second column). **(3)** Square these deviations from the mean and total the results to obtain (Σd^2) as shown in the third column. **(4)** Insert the numbers for N and Σd^2 into the formula for the standard deviation and compute the results.

summation. A step-by-step application of this formula to our TV viewing data, shown in **Figure B.5**, reveals that the standard deviation for our TV viewing data is 1.64. The standard deviation has a variety of uses. One of these uses will surface in the next section, where we discuss the normal distribution.

The Normal Distribution

7c

The hypothesis in our study is that brighter students watch less TV than relatively dull students. To test this hypothesis, we're going to correlate TV viewing with SAT scores. But to make effective use of the SAT data, we need to understand what SAT scores mean, which brings us to the normal distribution.

The *normal distribution* is a symmetrical, bell-shaped curve that represents the pattern in which many human characteristics are dispersed in the population. A great many physical qualities (for example, height, nose length, and running speed) and psychological traits (intelligence, spatial reasoning ability, introversion) are distributed in a manner that closely resembles this bell-shaped curve. When a trait is normally distributed, most scores fall near the center of the distribution (the mean) and the number of scores gradually declines as one moves away from the center in either direction (see **Figure B.6**). The normal distribution is *not* a law of nature. It's a mathematical function, or theoretical curve, that approximates the way nature seems to operate.

The normal distribution is the bedrock of the scoring system for most psychological tests, including the SAT. As we discuss in Chapter 8, psychological tests are *relative measures;* they assess how people score on a trait in comparison to other people. The normal distribution gives us a precise way to measure how people stack up in comparison to each other. The scores under the normal curve are dispersed in a fixed pattern, with the standard devia-

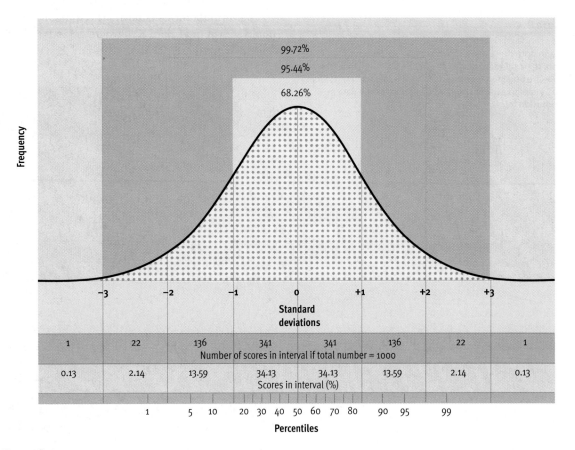

Figure B.6

The normal distribution. Many characteristics are distributed in a pattern represented by this bell-shaped curve (each dot represents a case). The horizontal axis shows how far above or below the mean a score is (measured in plus or minus standard deviations). The vertical axis shows the number of cases obtaining each score. In a normal distribution, most cases fall near the center of the distribution, so that 68.26% of the cases fall within plus or minus 1 standard deviation of the mean. The number of cases gradually declines as one moves away from the mean in either direction, so that only 13.59% of the cases fall between 1 and 2 standard deviations above or below the mean, and even fewer cases (2.14%) fall between 2 and 3 standard deviations above or below the mean.

tion serving as the unit of measurement, as shown in **Figure B.6**. About 68% of the scores in the distribution fall within plus or minus 1 standard deviation of the mean, while 95% of the scores fall within plus or minus 2 standard deviations of the mean. Given this fixed pattern, if you know the mean and standard deviation of a normally distributed trait, you can tell where any score falls in the distribution for the trait.

Although you may not have realized it, you probably have taken many tests in which the scoring system is based on the normal distribution. On the SAT, for instance, raw scores (the number of items correct on each subtest) are converted into standard scores that indicate where you fall in the normal distribution for the trait measured. In this conversion, the mean is set arbitrarily at 500 and the standard deviation at 100, as shown in **Figure B.7**. Therefore, a score of 400 on the SAT verbal subtest means that you scored 1 standard deviation below the mean, while an SAT score of 600 indicates that you scored 1 standard deviation above the mean. Thus, SAT scores tell you how many standard deviations above or below the mean your score was. This system also provides the metric for IQ scales and many other types of psychological tests (see Chapter 8).

Test scores that place examinees in the normal distribution can always be converted to percentile scores, which are a little easier to interpret. A *percentile score* indicates the percentage of people who score at or below the score you obtained. For example, if you score at the 60th percentile, 60% of the people who take the test score the same or below you, while the remaining 40% score above you. There are tables available that permit us to convert any standard deviation placement in a normal distribution into a precise percentile score. **Figure B.6** gives some percentile conversions for the normal curve.

Of course, not all distributions are normal. As we saw in **Figure B.3**, some distributions are skewed in one direction or the other. As an example, consider what would happen if a classroom exam were much too easy or much too hard. If the test were too easy, scores would be bunched up at the high end of the scale, as in **Figure B.3(b)**. If the test were too hard, scores would be bunched up at the low end, as in **Figure B.3(c)**.

Measuring Correlation

1d

To determine whether TV viewing is related to SAT scores, we have to compute a *correlation coefficient*—a numerical index of the degree of rela-

Figure B.7

The normal distribution and SAT scores. The normal distribution is the basis for the scoring system on many standardized tests. For example, on the SAT, the mean is set at 500 and the standard deviation at 100. Hence, an SAT score tells you how many standard deviations above or below the mean you scored. For example, a score of 700 means you scored 2 standard deviations above the mean.

tionship that exists between two variables. As discussed in Chapter 2, a *positive* correlation means that the two variables—say X and Y—covary together. This means that high scores on variable X are associated with high scores on variable Y and that low scores on X are associated with low scores on Y. A *negative* correlation indicates that there is an inverse relationship between two variables. This means that people who score high on variable X tend to score low on variable Y, whereas those who score low on X tend to score high on Y. In our study, we hypothesized that as TV viewing increases, SAT scores will decrease, so we should expect a negative correlation between TV viewing and SAT scores.

The *magnitude* of a correlation coefficient indicates the *strength* of the association between two variables. This coefficient can vary between 0 and ±1.00. The coefficient is usually represented by the letter *r* (for example, *r* = .45). A coefficient near 0 tells us that there is no relationship between two variables. A coefficient of +1.00 or −1.00 indicates that there is a perfect, one-to-one correspondence between two variables. A perfect correlation is found only rarely when working with real data. The closer the coefficient is to either −1.00 or +1.00, the stronger the relationship is.

The direction and strength of correlations can be illustrated graphically in scatter diagrams. A *scatter diagram* is a graph in which paired X and Y scores for each subject are plotted as single points. **Figure B.8** on the next page shows scatter diagrams for positive correlations in the upper half and for

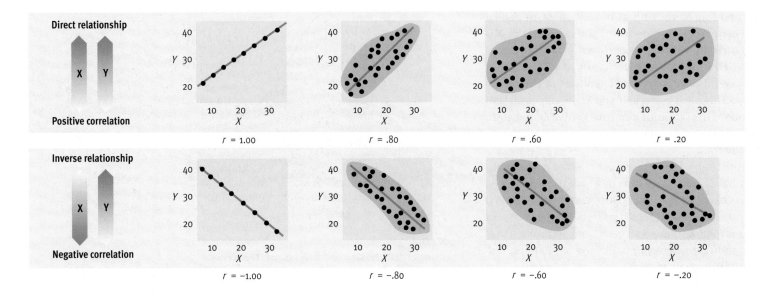

Figure B.8

Scatter diagrams of positive and negative correlations. Scatter diagrams plot paired X and Y scores as single points. Score plots slanted in the opposite direction result from positive (top row) as opposed to negative (bottom row) correlations. Moving across both rows (to the right), you can see that progressively weaker correlations result in more and more scattered plots of data points.

negative correlations in the bottom half. A perfect positive correlation and a perfect negative correlation are shown on the far left. When a correlation is perfect, the data points in the scatter diagram fall exactly in a straight line. However, positive and negative correlations yield lines slanted in the opposite direction because the lines map out opposite types of associations. Moving to the right in **Figure B.8**, you can see what happens when the magnitude of a correlation decreases. The data points scatter farther and farther from the straight line that would represent a perfect relationship.

What about our data relating TV viewing to SAT scores? **Figure B.9** shows a scatter diagram of these data. Having just learned about scatter diagrams, perhaps you can estimate the magnitude of the correlation between TV viewing and SAT scores. The scatter diagram of our data looks a lot like the one seen in the bottom right corner of **Figure B.8**, suggesting that the correlation will be in the vicinity of −.20.

The formula for computing the most widely used measure of correlation—the Pearson product-moment correlation—is shown in **Figure B.10**, along with the

calculations for our data on TV viewing and SAT scores. The data yield a correlation of $r = -.24$. This coefficient of correlation reveals that we have found a weak inverse association between TV viewing and performance on the SAT. Among our subjects, as TV viewing increases, SAT scores decrease, but the trend isn't very strong. We can get a better idea of how strong this correlation is by examining its predictive power.

Correlation and Prediction   1d

As the magnitude of a correlation increases (gets closer to either −1.00 or +1.00), our ability to predict one variable based on knowledge of the other variable steadily increases. This relationship between the magnitude of a correlation and predictability can be quantified precisely. All we have to do is square the correlation coefficient (multiply it by itself) and this gives us the *coefficient of determination*, the percentage of variation in one variable that can be predicted based on the other variable. Thus, a correlation of .70 yields a coefficient of determination of .49 (.70 × .70 = .49), indicating that variable X can account for 49% of the variation in variable Y. **Figure B.11** shows how the coefficient of determination goes up as the magnitude of a correlation increases.

Unfortunately, a correlation of −.24 doesn't give us much predictive power. We can account only for a little over 6% of the variation in variable Y. So, if we tried to predict individuals' SAT scores based on how much TV they watched, our predictions wouldn't be very accurate. Although a low correlation doesn't have much practical, predictive utility, it may still have theoretical value. Just knowing that there is a relationship between two variables can be theoretically interesting. However, we haven't yet addressed

Figure B.9

Scatter diagram of the correlation between TV viewing and SAT scores. Our hypothetical data relating TV viewing to SAT scores are plotted in this scatter diagram. Compare it to the scatter diagrams seen in Figure B.8 and see whether you can estimate the correlation between TV viewing and SAT scores in our data (see the text for the answer).

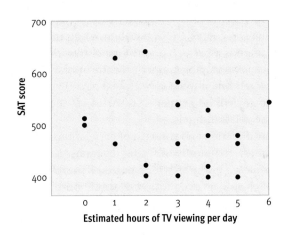

the question of whether our observed correlation is strong enough to support our hypothesis that there is a relationship between TV viewing and SAT scores. To make this judgment, we have to turn to inferential statistics and the process of hypothesis testing.

Hypothesis Testing

Inferential statistics go beyond the mere description of data. *Inferential statistics* are used to interpret data and draw conclusions. They permit researchers to decide whether their data support their hypotheses.

In our study of TV viewing we hypothesized that we would find an inverse relationship between amount of TV watched and SAT scores. Sure enough, that's what we found. However, we have to ask ourselves a critical question: Is this observed correlation large enough to support our hypothesis, or might a correlation of this size have occurred by chance?

We have to ask a similar question nearly every time we conduct a study. Why? Because we are working only with a sample. In research, we observe a limited *sample* (in this case, 20 subjects) to draw conclusions about a much larger *population* (college students in general). There's always a possibility that if we drew a different sample from the population, the results might be different. Perhaps our results are unique to our sample and not generalizable to the larger population. If we were able to collect data on the entire population, we would not have to wrestle with this problem, but our dependence on a sample necessitates the use of inferential statistics to precisely evaluate

Subject number	TV viewing score (X)	X²	SAT score (Y)	Y²	XY
1	0	0	500	250,000	0
2	0	0	515	265,225	0
3	1	1	450	202,500	450
4	1	1	650	422,500	650
5	2	4	400	160,000	800
6	2	4	675	455,625	1350
7	2	4	425	180,625	850
8	3	9	400	160,000	1200
9	3	9	450	202,500	1350
10	3	9	500	250,000	1500
11	3	9	550	302,500	1650
12	3	9	600	360,000	1800
13	4	16	400	160,000	1600
14	4	16	425	180,625	1700
15	4	16	475	225,625	1900
16	4	16	525	275,625	2100
17	5	25	400	160,000	2000
18	5	25	450	202,500	2250
19	5	25	475	225,625	2375
20	6	36	550	302,500	3300
$N = 20$	$\Sigma X = 60$	$\Sigma X^2 = 234$	$\Sigma Y = 9815$	$\Sigma Y^2 = 4,943,975$	$\Sigma XY = 28,825$

Formula for Pearson product-moment correlation coefficient

$$r = \frac{(N)\,\Sigma XY - (\Sigma X)(\Sigma Y)}{\sqrt{[(N)\,\Sigma X^2 - (\Sigma X)^2][(N)\,\Sigma Y^2 - (\Sigma Y)^2]}}$$

$$= \frac{(20)\,(28,825) - (60)\,(9815)}{\sqrt{[(20)\,(234) - (60)^2][(20)\,(4,943,975) - (9815)^2]}}$$

$$= \frac{-12,400}{\sqrt{[1080][2,545,275]}}$$

$$= -.237$$

Figure B.10
Computing a correlation coefficient. The calculations required to compute the Pearson product-moment coefficient of correlation are shown here. The formula looks intimidating, but it's just a matter of filling in the figures taken from the sums of the columns shown above the formula.

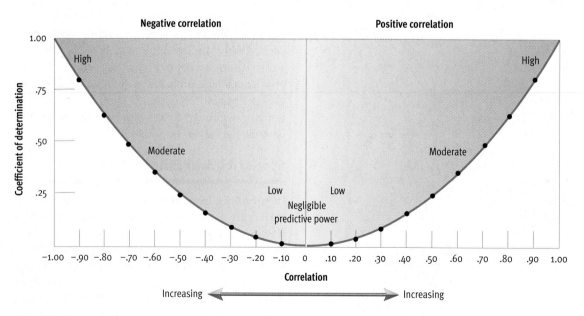

Figure B.11
Correlation and the coefficient of determination. The coefficient of determination is an index of a correlation's predictive power. As you can see, whether positive or negative, stronger correlations yield greater predictive power.

the likelihood that our results are due to chance factors in sampling. Thus, inferential statistics are the key to making the inferential leap from the sample to the population (see **Figure B.12**).

Although it may seem backward, in hypothesis testing we formally test the *null* hypothesis. As applied to correlational data, the **null hypothesis is the assumption that there is no true relationship between the variables observed.** In our study, the null hypothesis is that there is no genuine association between TV viewing and SAT scores. We want to determine whether our results will permit us to *reject* the null hypothesis and thus conclude that our *research hypothesis* (that there is a relationship between the variables) has been supported. Why do we test the null hypothesis instead of the research hypothesis? Because our probability calculations depend on assumptions tied to the null hypothesis. Specifically, we compute the probability of obtaining the results that we have observed if the null hypothesis is indeed true. The calculation of this probability hinges on a number of factors. A key factor is the amount of variability in the data, which is why the standard deviation is an important statistic.

Statistical Significance

When we reject the null hypothesis, we conclude that we have found *statistically significant* results. **Statistical significance is said to exist when the probability that the observed findings are due to chance is very low, usually less than 5 chances in 100.** This means that if the null hypothesis is correct and we conduct our study 100 times, drawing a new sample from the population each time, we will get results such as those observed only 5 times out of 100. If our

calculations allow us to reject the null hypothesis, we conclude that our results support our research hypothesis. Thus, statistically significant results typically are findings that *support* a research hypothesis.

The requirement that there be less than 5 chances in 100 that research results are due to chance is the *minimum* requirement for statistical significance. When this requirement is met, we say the results are significant at the .05 level. If researchers calculate that there is less than 1 chance in 100 that their results are due to chance factors in sampling, the results are significant at the .01 level. If there is less than a 1 in 1000 chance that findings are attributable to sampling error, the results are significant at the .001 level. Thus, there are several *levels* of significance that you may see cited in scientific articles.

Because we are only dealing in matters of probability, there is always the possibility that our decision to accept or reject the null hypothesis is wrong. The various significance levels indicate the probability of erroneously rejecting the null hypothesis (and inaccurately accepting the research hypothesis). At the .05 level of significance, there are 5 chances in 100 that we have made a mistake when we conclude that our results support our hypothesis, and at the .01 level of significance the chance of an erroneous conclusion is 1 in 100. Although researchers hold the probability of this type of error quite low, the probability is never zero. This is one of the reasons that competently executed studies of the same question can yield contradictory findings. The differences may be due to chance variations in sampling that can't be prevented.

What do we find when we evaluate our data linking TV viewing to students' SAT scores? The calculations indicate that, given our sample size and the variability in our data, the probability of obtaining a correlation of −.24 by chance is greater than 20%. That's not a high probability, but it's not low enough to reject the null hypothesis. Thus, our findings are not strong enough to allow us to conclude that we have supported our hypothesis.

Statistics and Empiricism

In summary, conclusions based on empirical research are a matter of probability, and there's always a possibility that the conclusions are wrong. However, two major strengths of the empirical approach are its precision and its intolerance of error. Scientists can give you precise estimates of the likelihood that their conclusions are wrong, and because they're intolerant of error, they hold this probability extremely low. It's their reliance on statistics that allows them to accomplish these goals.

Figure B.12
The relationship between the population and the sample. In research, we are usually interested in a broad population, but we can observe only a small sample from the population. After making observations of our sample, we draw inferences about the population, based on the sample. This inferential process works well as long as the sample is reasonably representative of the population.

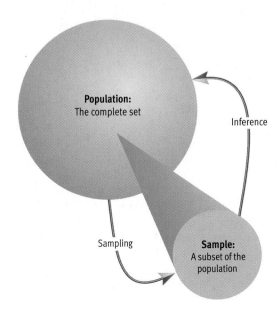

Population:
The complete set

Inference

Sampling

Sample:
A subset of the population

Careers and Areas in Psychology

by Margaret A. Lloyd (Georgia Southern University)

Perhaps you have already heard the disheartening claim, "You can't get a job with a bachelor's degree in psychology." Is there any truth to this assertion? If by "job," you mean working as a professional psychologist, then the saying is true. Psychologists must have a doctoral degree in psychology because the nature of their work requires more extensive education and training than can be gained at the undergraduate level. But it simply is *not* true that you can't get a good entry-level job with a psychology degree.

In the following pages, we will briefly explore the kinds of entry-level jobs that are available to psychology majors as well as some occupations that require graduate degrees. I will also share some pointers to help you compete effectively in the job market and to enhance your chances of getting into graduate school.

Entry-Level Career Options for Psychology Majors

It would be easy to spot entry-level jobs if you could look in the want ads under the heading "psychologist," but as already noted, that tactic won't work. Because the connection between the psychology major (and other liberal arts majors) and relevant entry-level jobs is not as obvious as it is in applied majors (nursing and accounting, for example), identifying relevant entry-level jobs requires some detective work.

Thanks to the Internet, it has become easier to identify job titles of interest. A number of websites have search engines that allow you to locate specific occupations and learn about the relevant skills, educational requirements, salaries, and other useful points (see Web Links C.2, C.3, and C.4).

Because most psychology majors would like jobs in which they can help other people, *counseling* is a popular career option. If you think about it, though, there are many other ways to help people. For example, managers help employees to do their best, child welfare agents help children in trouble, and probation officers help juvenile offenders stay on the right track. Also, in doing your detective work, you should be aware that occupations requiring essentially the same skills are often listed under a variety of titles. Don't overlook a viable option because the title is unfamiliar. **Figure C.1** will give you an idea of the wide range of job options open to psychology majors.

Once you have identified some occupations of interest, compare them on the critical factors of current job openings, salary, and future employment outlook. An excellent resource for this information is the *Occupational Outlook Handbook* (see Web Link C.2). This step is essential if you want to make *informed* occupational choices.

The average starting salary for psychology (and other liberal arts) majors tends to be lower than for most applied majors. In 2007–2008, it was around $30,000 (National Association of Colleges and Employers, 2008). Jobs in business and research command higher salaries than those in human services (counseling and social work, for example). If you are

Potential Jobs for Psychology Majors with a Bachelor's Degree	
Business areas	**Health and human services areas**
customer relations	behavioral analyst
employment interviewer	case worker
human resources recruiter	child welfare agent
insurance agent	director of volunteer services
loan officer	drug counselor
management trainee	family services worker
marketing representative	hospital patient service representative
realtor	nursing home administrator
sales representative	rehabilitation advisor
store manager	residential youth counselor
Law and corrections areas	**Other areas**
case manager	affirmative action officer
corrections officer	college admissions representative
court officer	newspaper reporter
EPA investigator	research assistant
probation/parole officer	technical writer

Figure C.1

Entry-level positions open to psychology majors. A bachelor's degree in psychology can prepare students for a diverse array of entry-level jobs in a variety of occupational areas. The jobs listed here are merely a handful of examples of the entry-level positions for which psychology majors qualify.

web link C.3

The Riley Guide: Employment Opportunities and Job Resources on the Internet

This site, developed by the well-regarded career expert Margaret F. Dikel, complements her excellent book, the *Guide to Internet Job Searching*. Her website contains hundreds of annotated links regarding almost any topic related to employment and careers.

web link C.4

CollegeGrad.com

This website bills itself as "The #1 entry-level job site." Key sections include Preparation (explore careers, résumés, cover letters, and internship preparation), Find the Job (advice, posting résumés, and searching for internships and jobs), and Offers (salary, negotiating, and new job advice). To find jobs in counseling, look under the Community and Social Services category.

like most students, however, your job decision will not be based on money alone. A recent survey regarding what college graduates seek when choosing an employer found that "a high starting salary" was ranked surprisingly low, whereas "enjoying what I do" earned the top ranking (National Association of Colleges and Employers, 2005). Thus, salary is just one of many factors that you should consider in pursuing a job.

Keys to Success in the Entry-Level Job Market

There are three keys to a successful job search. First, you need to have accurate information about the knowledge, skills, and values required for occupations that interest you. You may be surprised to learn that these skills and values are not as job-specific as most people assume. Surveys of employers reveal that a relatively small set of skills and values are considered essential for success in a wide variety of occupations (see **Figure C.2**). You don't have to be a genius to figure out the second key to success: You need to acquire these skills that are prized by employers. The third key to a successful job search is to assemble convincing documentation for prospective employers that you possess these skills and values.

Developing Valuable Skills

To help you acquire these highly rated work skills, you have three excellent skill-building vehicles available: college courses, relevant work experience, and extracurricular activities. Obviously, the earlier in your college career you start your "skills development project," the more time you have to hone your skills.

College courses. Within the constraints of curriculum requirements, choose courses to help you develop occupationally relevant knowledge and skills. Make thoughtful choices across all areas of the curriculum: general education courses, psychology courses, and general electives. The content of courses is an obvious and important aspect of education. Your coursework also provides learning opportunities that are less obvious. In addition to teaching course content, college courses provide numerous opportunities to learn a remarkable variety of skills that can give you a competitive edge in the job market. For example, your courses can help you improve your critical thinking skills, acquire insights into your behavior and that of others, enhance your interpersonal skills, clarify your values, acquaint you with ethical principles, improve your communication abilities, increase your computer

Figure C.2
Qualities employers value in employees. Employers widely agree on the general work skills and values they desire in employees. To be competitive in the job market, workers must have the qualities listed here and document them in cover letters, résumés, and interviews. (Based on Appleby, 2000; Hansen & Hansen, 2003; Landrum & Harrold, 2003)

General Work Skills and Personal Values Employers Seek

Work skills

- **Communication skills.** Almost always rated first, communication skills include being able to write and speak effectively. A third, often overlooked, communication skill is effective listening, including being sensitive enough to hear and relate to the emotions behind another's words.

- **Adaptability/flexibility.** Employers value workers who can adapt to changing conditions and work assignments (learn new skills), deal with ambiguity, and appreciate that there are usually several legitimate perspectives on an issue.

- **Analytical/research skills.** These important skills involve critical thinking; extracting key ideas from written material, graphs, and tables; and solving problems and answering questions.

- **Computer skills.** Employers want workers who are competent in using word-processing, spreadsheet, and database management programs, as well as the Internet and e-mail.

- **Social and teamwork skills.** Today's workers need to interact effectively in one-on-one settings and on teams. They must also be able to work well with co-workers from diverse cultures and backgrounds.

- **Self-management skills.** These critical skills include having self-confidence, being able to work with little supervision, being able to set manageable goals and complete them on time, and being able to manage time effectively. Emotional maturity is also important, especially the ability to cope with undesirable behavior in others and to refrain from petty behavior.

Personal values

- **Integrity/honesty.** Employers greatly value ethical behavior in their employees.

- **Dependability and loyalty.** Workers who come to the workplace prepared to work, who arrive on time, and who show up every day are prized. Employers also value personal and company loyalty in their employees.

- **Positive attitude and motivation/energy.** Valued employees are those who have a "can-do" attitude, bring energy to their work, and are willing to learn new skills and information.

sophistication and information literacy, and bolster your self-management skills (setting and completing goals, managing your time, coping with stress). The psychology major can definitely help you develop the general skills and values that employers seek. **Figure C.3** lists ten learning goals that a psychology major should support, based on the consensus of a national task force. If you compare this list with the list of employers' preferred skills and values in **Figure C.2**, you will see that there is a close match.

Relevant work experience (internships, paid work, and volunteer activities). If you must work while attending school, look for a job that will help you develop useful skills. For example, if you want to be a probation officer, seek out volunteer opportunities to work with adolescents. Many colleges have Volunteer Services offices that match students' interests with community needs. Another excellent resource on how to obtain real-world experience is a short paperback, *Getting from College to Career: 90 Things to Do Before You Join the Real World* (Pollak, 2007). The author, a recent college graduate, offers useful and specific advice on how to shape your college experience to give you a "jump start" on your career.

Extracurricular activities. Involvement in campus clubs and student activities can also help you develop work-related abilities—especially leadership and interpersonal skills. Be careful not to overload yourself with work, volunteering, and extracurricular activities to the detriment of your grades. Good grades are important in obtaining your first job and getting good recommendations from faculty members, and they are *essential* to qualify for graduate school.

Documenting Your Skills

Once you acquire the skills and values employers want, you must be able to document this fact to prospective employers. You do so by preparing résumés and cover letters that showcase your skills. The job interview is another key aspect of this process. Even if you have a bundle of talents, you can easily falter at these critical points. There is a lot to know in developing a competitive résumé, a compelling cover letter, and good interviewing skills. You can learn the essentials at your Career Services office.

Next Steps

It is critical that you start the job search process early—the spring term of your senior year is too late. Attend career fairs, where job recruiters come to your college campus, to learn about job options and what recruiters are looking for. When you are clear about the occupational titles you want to pursue, visit your Career Services office. The staff can get you started off right on your job search.

Career Options at the Master's Level

After working several years in an entry-level position, you may want more challenges, a higher salary, or greater independence. One way to move up the career ladder is to return to school. Alternatively, you may want to attend graduate school directly upon graduation. If you want to extend your knowledge and skills, but do not want to invest the time, effort, and money required for a doctoral degree, then a master's degree may be just the ticket for you. Because counseling is a popular career option among psychology majors, we will focus on three master's-level career options in the mental health area. There are also master's-level careers in other areas of psychology, such as industrial/organizational psychology.

Learning Goals for the Psychology Major

Knowledge, skills, and values consistent with the science and application of psychology

Goal 1. Knowledge base of psychology. Students should show familiarity with the major concepts, theoretical perspectives, empirical findings, and historical trends in psychology.

Goal 2. Research methods in psychology. Students should understand and apply basic research methods in psychology, including research design, data analysis, and interpretation.

Goal 3. Critical thinking skills in psychology. Students should respect and use critical and creative thinking, skeptical inquiry, and, when possible, the scientific approach to solve problems related to behavior and mental processes.

Goal 4. Application of psychology. Students should understand and apply psychological principles to personal, social, and organizational issues.

Goal 5. Values in psychology. Students should be able to weigh evidence, tolerate ambiguity, act ethically, and reflect other values that are the underpinnings of psychology as a discipline.

Knowledge, skills, and values consistent with liberal arts education that are further developed in psychology

Goal 6. Information and technological literacy. Students should demonstrate information competence and the ability to use computers and other technology for many purposes.

Goal 7. Communication skills. Students should be able to communicate effectively in a variety of formats.

Goal 8. Sociocultural and international awareness. Students should recognize, understand, and respect the complexity of sociocultural and international diversity.

Goal 9. Personal development. Students should develop insight into their own and others' behavior and mental processes and apply effective strategies for self-management and self-improvement.

Goal 10. Career planning and development. Students should emerge from the major with realistic ideas about how to implement their psychological knowledge, skills, and values in occupational pursuits in a variety of settings.

Figure C.3

Knowledge, skills, and values supported by the psychology major. Ten learning goals for the undergraduate psychology major have been outlined by a national task force (American Psychological Association, 2007). The first five goals include knowledge, skills, and values developed specifically in the psychology major. The remaining goals consist of knowledge, skills, and values developed in the liberal arts (general education) curriculum and that psychology further advances.

SOURCE: American Psychological Association. (2007). *APA guidelines for the undergraduate psychology major.* Washington, DC: Author. Retrieved May 1, 2008, from http://www.apa.org/ed/psymajorguideline.pdf.

An undergraduate major in psychology is excellent preparation for all these career paths.

Clinical Psychology

Clinical psychologists diagnose and treat people with psychological problems and administer psychological tests. Although most programs in clinical psychology are offered at the doctoral level, there are terminal master's degree programs in clinical psychology and some other subfields. Clinical master's programs typically teach students how to administer selected psychological tests as well as the basics of psychological diagnosis and psychotherapy. Students in these programs receive either an M.A. (Master of Arts) or an M.S. (Master of Science) degree. Upon graduation, they either seek employment or apply to doctoral programs.

Some states license individuals with master's degrees in clinical psychology, but many do not. A license is a quality-control credential that gives individuals legal authority to work independently—that is, without the supervision of a doctoral-level professional. Individuals with a master's degree in clinical psychology may qualify for licenses such as "psychological associate," "professional counselor," or "marriage and family therapist." Note that they are not licensed as "psychologists"—this title is reserved for those with doctoral degrees. Whether licensed or not, these individuals are qualified to work in supervised settings such as community mental health centers.

Clinical Social Work

Unlike social workers or case workers, *clinical social workers* diagnose and treat psychological problems. Clinical social workers are educated in departments or colleges of social work (not psychology departments). The degree that they earn is the M.S.W. (Master of Social Work). They do not do psychological testing, so you should consider majoring in psychology or education if you want to do assessment. They work in community mental health centers, counseling centers, hospitals, and schools. Importantly, all 50 states license clinical social workers at the master's level. This fact makes clinical social work an attractive career option. For more information, see Web Link C.7.

Agency Counseling

Agency counselors provide various types of counseling assistance to clients and may administer a limited number of psychological tests (occupational interest tests, for example). Thus, the work is somewhat like that done by those with a master's degree in clinical psychology. Counselors are educated in departments of education; they receive the M.Ed.

(Master of Education) degree. Most people assume that a degree in education requires one to work in a school setting. Agency counseling (sometimes called "community counseling") is an important exception. If you want to counsel but do not want to work in a school setting, consider this option. Graduates typically work in community mental health centers. They may have a private practice if they obtain a license (typically as a "professional counselor" or "marriage and family therapist").

Career Options at the Doctoral Level

Doctoral-level education and training will give you access to occupations that offer more options and independence as well as higher salaries, compared to those at the master's level. An important consideration is whether you want to emphasize teaching and research or applied work.

Teaching and Research Versus Applied Work

If you want to teach in a university setting, you will probably also be expected to conduct research. If you want to focus solely on teaching, consider a job at a two-year college, as research is not usually required in these institutions. If you are solely interested in doing research, think about working for government agencies (for example, the Centers for Disease Control) or private organizations (for example, the Educational Testing Service). To work in a university psychology department, you will need a Ph.D. (Doctor of Philosophy) in psychology—not a degree in another field such as education or social work. As discussed in Chapter 1, the major research subfields in psychology include cognitive psychology, developmental psychology, educational psychology, experimental psychology, health psychology, personality psychology, physiological psychology, psychometrics, and social psychology. We will discuss some career options in these areas shortly.

In certain subfields, psychologists are qualified to apply their knowledge by offering professional services to the public. These applied areas of specialization include clinical psychology, counseling psychology, industrial/organizational psychology, school psychology, clinical neuropsychology, and forensic psychology. The required degree for most of these areas is typically the Ph.D. (Doctor of Philosophy). The Psy.D. (Doctor of Psychology) is also appropriate in clinical and counseling psychology, and the Ed.D. (Doctor of Education) is awarded in counseling psychology. We will examine career options in these applied areas shortly.

Before looking at the various specialty areas, let's touch on the differences between the Ph.D. and Psy.D. degrees, as students often have questions about this issue. The Ph.D. degree is the terminal (highest) degree offered in all liberal arts and scientific disciplines (psychology, history, physics, and so forth). Thus, the vast majority of college and university professors have the Ph.D. degree. The Psy.D. degree is awarded *only* in psychology and *only* in the professional areas of clinical and counseling psychology—not in other applied areas such as school psychology or industrial/organizational psychology, nor in any of the research subfields (experimental, developmental, or social psychology, for example). The primary difference between the two degrees is the emphasis on research. The Ph.D. degree prepares clinical and counseling psychologists to be both researchers and practitioners. In contrast, Psy.D. programs focus exclusively on preparing clinicians and counselors to be practitioners, although they also strive to make their students highly sophisticated consumers of psychological research. The crux of the difference is that Ph.D. students are required to conduct research to earn their degree, whereas Psy.D. students are not. This means that Ph.D. students typically take a number of courses in research design and statistics and devote much of their time to research projects. Psy.D. programs, on the other hand, tend to require students to spend more time in "hands-on" clinical training.

Another distinction concerns the types of institutions in which the programs are housed. Ph.D. programs in psychology are housed in traditional university psychology departments (as are a few Psy.D. programs), whereas most Psy.D. programs are housed in private, independent, professional schools of psychology. One practical repercussion of this difference is that university-based Ph.D. programs tend to benefit from research grants that permit them to offer many of their students tuition waivers and financial stipends that can greatly reduce the financial cost of graduate training. Lacking this source of revenue, Psy.D. programs are generally able to provide far less financial aid and thus tend to be more expensive than Ph.D. programs. Both types of doctoral programs have their advantages and disadvantages. Ultimately, the choice between pursuing a Ph.D versus a Psy.D. typically hinges on how interested students are in working on original research.

Career Options in Research Areas

To give you a fuller understanding of the breadth of psychology as a field of study, we'll briefly examine the nine major research areas in the discipline and some selected career options in these areas. Psychol-

ogists in these subfields are most likely to work in academic settings, where they teach undergraduate and/or graduate students and conduct research in their areas of interest. Faculty members who teach undergraduates typically do more teaching and less research than faculty who teach graduate students. Most faculty members in psychology do some research, although expectations for research vary depending on the nature of the college.

Cognitive psychology. The field of cognitive psychology is concerned with thinking and mental activity—how people (and animals) acquire, process, retrieve, and apply information. Cognitive psychologists also focus on language, problem solving, concept formation, mental imagery, reasoning, decision making, and creativity. Examples of research topics in the field include the effects of encoding strategies on memory retention, the influence of bilingualism on language development, and the factors that people weigh in making risky decisions. Chapters 7 and 8 in this text provide extensive coverage of cognitive psychology topics. Most cognitive psychologists teach and conduct research in academic settings, but they can also use their expertise in business, government, and military settings (which, typically, pay better than academia). For example, some work in computer programming and artificial intelligence. Others may work in management science, applying their knowledge of problem solving and decision making.

Developmental psychology. Developmental psychologists study how individuals develop physically, intellectually, socially, and emotionally over the lifespan ("from womb to tomb," as some say). Some developmental psychologists focus on just one period of life (for example, childhood or later adulthood), while others study development across the entire lifespan. In a field so broad, the research questions are practically limitless. Examples of research topics include the psychological and social effects of shyness in childhood, conformity to peer pressure in adolescence, and the effects of a spouse's death on the surviving partner. Developmental psychology topics are covered primarily in Chapter 10 of this text, although personality development is discussed in Chapter 11. As for career options, developmental psychologists usually teach and conduct research in academic settings. Some serve as consultants to day-care centers, schools, or social service agencies. Others consult with toy and media companies to ensure that toys, games, television programs, and other media products match the cognitive, social, and physical skills of different-aged children.

web link C.8

APA Online

The American Psychological Association website has two especially useful links for students. Under the Students menu, the Divisions link enables you to access the individual webpages of the many subfields of psychology. The link to the Students page will help you find information about undergraduate psychology honoraries, getting into graduate school, and related topics.

Experimental psychology. The term *experimental psychology* refers to a diverse hodgepodge of topics that made up the core of psychology in the first half-century of its existence, including sensation, perception, learning, motivation, and emotion. Researchers in these areas frequently study animals instead of humans. Although psychologists in all research areas conduct experiments, the name for this area reflects its *heavy* reliance on experimentation and its relatively infrequent use of correlational methods. Examples of research topics include how background factors influence object recognition, how variations in reinforcement patterns affect the acquisition of responses, and how external food cues regulate eating behavior. Chapters 4, 6, and 9 in this text provide many examples of research in experimental psychology. The vast majority of experimental psychologists work in academic settings or research laboratories, although their expertise occasionally leads them into applied fields. For example, experts in perception sometimes work in human engineering.

Physiological psychology. This domain of research, also known as *biopsychology* and *behavioral neuroscience,* explores how behavior is influenced by genetic, neural, and hormonal functioning. Examples of topics include how the hypothalamus contributes to the regulation of eating behavior, how various drugs produce changes in synaptic transmission, and how the pineal gland regulates biological rhythms. Chapter 3 in the text is devoted exclusively to physiological topics, but biopsychology is so basic it shows up in virtually every chapter of the book, for example in discussions of the biological bases of pain perception (Chapter 4), sleep (5), constraints on learning (6) memory (7), intelligence (8), emotion (9), aging (10), personality (11), stress responses (12), psychological disorders (13), and drug treatments for mental disorders (14). Most biopsychologists are employed in academia or research centers, but there are applied specialties, such as *clinical neuropsychology,* which you will read about momentarily.

Personality psychology. This subfield is concerned with understanding and describing people's enduring behavior patterns and the psychological processes that underlie them (personality traits, for example). Personality psychology also focuses on how personality develops and the factors that shape it (heredity and parenting, for example). Some personality psychologists develop psychological tests and other techniques by which to study and evaluate aspects of personality (interests, creativity, and so forth). Examples of research topics include the behavioral

correlates of personality traits, such as extraversion or conscientiousness, the impact of self-efficacy on sports performance, and whether culture influences personality structure. Personality topics are mostly covered in Chapter 11 of this text. Career options for personality psychologists include teaching and conducting research in university settings and working for companies that develop personality tests.

Psychometrics. This area of research is concerned with the precise measurement of behavior and mental processes. Psychologists in this field design psychological tests to measure various aspects of personality, intelligence, and specific abilities. In their work, psychometricians are concerned about ensuring that psychological tests are reliable, valid, and used fairly, among other things. Psychometrics also includes the development of statistical procedures and computer programs to execute these procedures. Examples of research topics include exploring cultural variations in average scores on tests of mental abilities, analyzing the causes of generational changes in measured intelligence, and investigating the relationship between IQ scores and vocational success. Psychometric topics are examined mainly in Chapter 8 of this text but also are considered in the Chapter 11 application on personality testing. Measurement psychologists typically work in academic settings or for companies that develop psychological tests.

Educational psychology. Educational psychologists study the intertwined processes of teaching and learning, including a wide range of relevant factors such as motivation, abilities, learning styles, classroom diversity, curriculum design, instructional methods, and achievement testing. Educational psychologists attempt to understand how students learn and then develop materials and strategies to enhance the teaching process. Examples of research topics include comparing strategies and techniques for teaching reading, analyzing the effects of verbal praise on student motivation, and exploring the effects of mainstreaming on children with various types of disabilities. Educational psychology topics mainly appear in Chapter 8 of this text. Most educational psychologists are trained in departments or colleges of education, as opposed to departments of psychology. They are usually employed in academic settings.

Health psychology. Health psychologists are concerned with the role of psychological factors in the promotion and maintenance of good health, the prevention and treatment of illness, and the formulation of health policy. They study important societal health concerns such as teenage pregnancy,

substance abuse, poor nutrition, and sedentary lifestyles. Examples of research topics include how to enhance the effectiveness of smoking cessation programs, how stress modulates immune system responding, and how to increase adherence to medical advice. Health psychology is covered primarily in Chapter 12 of this text. Health psychologists typically teach and conduct research in universities or medical schools. That said, a fair number of health psychologists are also involved in applied work. They frequently treat patients in hospitals, rehabilitation centers, or other health care settings. For example, they may assist patients with stress management, relaxation training, pain management, or medication compliance. Health psychology may eventually become a distinct applied specialty, but at present most health psychologists in professional practice first obtain degrees in clinical or counseling psychology and then do postdoctoral training in applications of health psychology (Kuther & Morgan, 2007).

Social psychology.

Social psychologists study how other people influence our beliefs, feelings, and behaviors. Some general topics of interest to social psychologists are attitude formation and change, conformity, helping behavior, aggression, prejudice, and interpersonal attraction. Examples of more specific research topics include how physical appearance sways perceptions of personality and competence, how attachment styles influence romantic relationships, how fear appeals work in persuasion, and how culture is related to social loafing. Social psychology is mainly covered in Chapter 15, but the social roots and contexts of behavior surface throughout the book. Examples of social psychology topics in other chapters include the effects of expectations on social perceptions (Chapter 1), the effect of anxiety on the need to be with others (2), the influence of social models on aggressive behavior (6), the sociocultural bases of mating preferences (9), the socialization of gender roles (10), social cognitive approaches to personality (11), the influence of social support on physical health (12), and the relationship between attributional style and depression (13). Most social psychologists work in academic settings, but the applied nature of the subfield also lends itself to work outside academia. For example, some social psychologists consult or work for federal agencies or for businesses that conduct research in marketing and product development.

Career Options in Applied Areas

As noted in Chapter 1, psychology is also made up of various applied subfields. Applied psychology has grown rapidly since World War II sparked a revolution in the training of clinical psychologists. Indeed, today psychologists working in applied fields outnumber those who focus mainly on research by a sizable margin. We will look at six applied areas of specialization: clinical psychology, counseling psychology, clinical neuropsychology, school psychology, forensic psychology, and industrial/organizational psychology.

Clinical psychology.

Clinical psychologists assess, diagnose, and treat people with psychological problems and disorders. They may act as therapists for people experiencing normal psychological crises (grief, for example) or for individuals suffering from severe, chronic disorders (bipolar disorder and schizophrenia, for example). Some clinical psychologists are generalists who work with a wide variety of populations, while others work with specific groups such as children, the elderly, or those with specific disorders (for example, schizophrenia). They may work with individuals or groups. Clinical psychologists are educated in university-based psychology departments or professional schools of psychology. Clinical psychologists can work in a diverse array of settings: academia, hospitals and medical centers, community mental health centers, or private practice. The nature of their work can also be wide ranging: administering and interpreting psychological tests, providing psychotherapy, teaching, conducting research, consulting, and serving in administrative capacities. Clinical psychology is the largest applied area in the field by far, as about two-thirds of applied psychologists are found in this specialty (see Chapter 1). Issues related to clinical psychology are mostly discussed in Chapters 13 and 14 of this text.

Counseling psychology.

Counseling psychologists do many of the same things that clinical psychologists do. However, counseling psychologists *tend* to focus more on persons with normal adjustment problems rather than on those suffering from severe psychological disorders. Also, the testing they do is usually for career counseling rather than for diagnosing serious psychological disorders. Like clinical psychologists, some counseling psychologists are generalists who work with a wide variety of problems and populations, whereas others specialize in family, marital, or career counseling. Counseling psychology programs are offered in psychology departments, in professional schools of psychology, and in colleges or departments of education. Counseling psychologists are employed in private practice, colleges and universities (in the classroom or in counseling centers), community mental health centers, government agencies, and corporations (providing testing and

therapy or serving in administrative roles). Issues related to counseling psychology are mostly discussed in Chapters 13 and 14 of this text.

Clinical neuropsychology. As its name suggests, this relatively new specialization combines clinical psychology (assessment and psychotherapy) and behavioral neuroscience (the study of the neural bases of behavior). Clinical neuropsychologists assess and treat individuals with central nervous system dysfunctions such as traumatic brain injury, stroke, dementia, and seizure disorders. Clinical neuropsychologists must first obtain a doctoral degree in clinical psychology. Because of the specialized nature of their work, they must also complete additional training in clinical neuropsychology during a year-long internship or additional postdoctoral study (Kuther & Morgan, 2007). Clinical neuropsychologists work in a variety of settings, including universities, hospitals, medical centers, and private practice. Topics related to clinical neuropsychology mostly surface in Chapter 3.

School psychology. School psychologists strive to promote the cognitive, emotional, and social development of children in educational settings. They deal with such issues as study skills, time management, family problems, and alcohol and drug problems. School psychologists use psychological tests to assess students' psychoeducational abilities and to understand the nature of their problems. They also counsel students and their parents and often serve as consultants to parents, teachers, and school administrators. School psychologists are typically trained in departments or colleges of education (versus departments of psychology). Many school psychologists have Ph.D. or Ed.D. degrees; others obtain the Ed.S. (education specialist), a degree between a master's and doctoral degree. Most school psychologists work in public school systems, often traveling among schools. Other employment settings include community mental health centers, criminal justice settings, hospitals, and private practice. Some topics related to school psychology can be found in Chapter 8.

Forensic psychology. In forensic psychology, psychological principles are applied to the legal system. Thus forensic psychologists are concerned with child custody decisions and involuntary commitment, among other issues. Increasingly, forensic psychologists play a role in personal injury, medical malpractice, and worker's compensation litigation. Forensic psychologists often serve as expert witnesses in criminal trials and may, occasionally, help develop criminal profiles. Most forensic psychologists are trained as clinical or counseling psychologists. Some forensic psychologists have both doctoral and law degrees. Forensic psychologists may also be involved in developing public policies involving the law and mental health issues. Forensic psychologists work in a variety of settings, including prisons, jails, community mental health centers, and agencies that provide court-related services. Issues related to forensic psychology are discussed briefly in Chapter 13.

Industrial/organizational psychology. Industrial/organizational (I/O) psychology is concerned with the application of psychological principles in the workplace. I/O psychologists are mainly interested in selecting employees, improving organizational effectiveness and the quality of work life, and designing work environments to match people's capacities and limitations. Most I/O psychologists are employed in business and government settings. Many head up or work in human resources departments, guiding personnel selection, employee training and development, and performance evaluation. I/O psychologists may also recommend organizational structures, policies, and procedures that will enhance organizational effectiveness. Others serve as consultants to business and industry. I/O psychologists who are interested in human factors work to help companies design machines and consumer products that mesh with human information processing capacities and response propensities. Some I/O psychologists teach and conduct research in psychology or business departments. Unlike the other professional areas of psychology, I/O psychology is not a mental health specialty requiring licensure, but it is an important, growing, and widely practiced area of applied psychology.

Gaining Admission to Graduate School

The most important requirements for admission to graduate school are high scores on the Graduate Record Exam (GRE), excellent grades, glowing faculty recommendations, and research experience. For the record, it is much harder to gain admission to a doctoral program than a master's program. Common *minimum* scores required on the GRE verbal and quantitative sections for doctoral programs are around 550 to 600 (on each test); for master's programs, they hover around 500. The *minimum* cumulative grade-point average for admission to doctoral programs is typically around 3.2; for a master's program, it is around 3.0. On average, admitted students tend to have GPAs that are quite a bit higher than these minimum figures. Gaining admission to Ph.D. programs in clinical psychology is roughly as

competitive and challenging as gaining admission to medical school. Of course, requirements vary among programs within the two levels. Departments with excellent reputations usually have more stringent requirements.

Early Preparation

Early in your college career you may not know whether you will want to try to gain admission to graduate school. To keep this educational door open until you are sure that you want to close it, keep the following points in mind.

1. *Begin early to develop the knowledge and skills graduate programs seek.* As with the job search, you need to begin early to develop the qualities listed in **Figure C.2**, as they are also important to success in graduate school. In addition, you must hone your verbal, quantitative, and critical thinking skills to a very high degree and be able to demonstrate that you have these skills through your GRE scores, grades, and letters of recommendation. Demonstrating that you have research experience is also important. An excellent way to start is to volunteer to help faculty members with their research. Also note that graduate schools place much less emphasis on extracurricular activities than employers do.

2. *Keep your grades up.* Performing well in all of your classes will help you to learn the information and develop the thinking skills that will permit you to score high on the GRE. It is especially important to do well in your Research Methods and Statistics courses. Good grades will also make you eligible for membership in Psi Chi, the national honor society in psychology.

3. *Position yourself to obtain strong letters of recommendation from three faculty members.* Graduate schools want recommendations only from faculty members. (For employers, recommendations from supervisors and clergy are also acceptable.) Try to take some smaller courses that may enable your professors to get to know you and to become familiar with your work. Otherwise, it will be difficult for them to write good letters of recommendation for you.

Next Steps

You need to prepare your applications for graduate school during the fall term of your senior year. Thus, in your junior year, you should begin identifying the subfield (clinical or social, for instance) in which you want to specialize, as well as schools that interest you. The graduate school application process is complicated and involves dealing with information and issues that are unfamiliar to virtually all students. Thus, it is essential to identify a knowledgeable faculty member in the psychology department at your school to advise you about the admissions process. Although Careers Services' staff members are experts on career issues, they are far less knowledgeable about graduate school admissions. For details about the process of applying to graduate programs in psychology, see Web Link C.1.

Psychology and Environmental Sustainability: Conservation Psychology

by Susan M. Koger (Willamette University) and Britain A. Scott (University of St. Thomas)

What do pollution, deforestation, the extinction of species, and climate change have in common? You might instantly respond, "They're all environmental problems." But is it really the *environment* that has the problems? In fact, what ties all these issues together is their cause: *maladaptive human behavior.* Particularly for the last 150 years, we humans have been behaving in ways that are *unsustainable*, and the effects of our collective actions can no longer be ignored. Humans burn fossil fuels that pollute the air and change the climate, dump wastes into water and soil, overconsume resources (both limited ones, such as oil, and renewable ones, such as wood and seafood), and develop lands that formerly served as habitats for thousands or even millions of other species. If you stop to think about it, these "environmental problems" are really *psychological*. That is, they are caused by destructive behaviors and the underlying thoughts, attitudes, feelings, values, and decisions that lead to these behaviors. Thus, the field of psychology can make a critically important contribution to understanding and solving them (e.g., Clayton & Myers, 2009; Koger & Scott, 2007; Koger & Winter, 2010). As you will see, psychological insights are critical to the achievement of a *sustainable world*—one in which human activities and needs are balanced with those of other species and future generations, taking into account ecological as well as social and economic factors (Schmuck & Schultz, 2002).

Some psychologists have conducted research related to environmental issues for several decades. However, because their work does not fit neatly into a particular subdiscipline of the field, it generally receives little attention in psychology courses, although we are trying to change that (see Web Link D.1). You may have heard of *environmental psychology,* which is the subdiscipline concerned with the study of how individuals are affected by, and interact with, their physical environments. However, the term *environment* in this label does not refer specifically to the natural environment. Only a minority of environmental psychologists study nature-related topics, such as people's cognitive responses to natural settings (Berman, Jonides, & Kaplan, 2008; Kaplan & Kaplan, 1989). Environmental psychologists are more likely to study the effects of noise, crowding, pollution, and urban living on aspects of human behavior.

In the 1990s, holistic thinkers calling themselves *ecopsychologists* began promoting the idea that modern industrialized urban living erodes people's feeling of connectedness to nature, leaving them developmentally deprived and psychologically distressed (Roszak, 1992). Some of these so-called ecopsychologists actually were psychologists, and some were not. A few clinicians have incorporated ecopsychological therapies into their practices to foster mindfulness and a sense of place that may guide people to behave in more environmentally friendly ways (e.g., Clinebell, 1996; Conn, 1995; White & Heerwagen, 1998). Others have promoted wilderness experiences as a means of healing and self-expansion (Greenway, 1995; Harper, 1995) and as a catalyst toward more ecologically sustainable lifestyles (Kals & Ittner, 2003). Empirical research testing ecopsychological ideas has been relatively sparse. In fact, it wasn't until 2009 that the first peer-reviewed research journal, *Ecopsychology*, made its debut. For this reason, ecopsychology has been viewed with skepticism by many mainstream psychologists. However, this situation may be changing with the development of several new attitude scales that assess people's sense of connection to nature; these scales are facilitating new research (Clayton, 2003; Mayer & Frantz, 2004; Schultz, 2000).

Over the past several years, a new discipline has emerged that promises to help tie together the work of nature-oriented environmental psychologists, ecopsychologists, and numerous other researchers grounded in traditional branches of psychology (primarily social, behavioral, and cognitive psychology) who have investigated environmentally relevant behaviors such as energy conservation, recycling, and material consumption. *Conservation psychology* is the study of the interactive relationships between humans and the rest of nature, with a particular focus on how to enhance conservation of natural resources. Conservation psychology is viewed as an applied field "that uses psychological principles, theories, or methods to understand and solve issues related to human aspects of conserva-

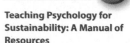

web link D.1

Teaching Psychology for Sustainability: A Manual of Resources

The authors of this appendix have also developed a site that serves as a resource for teachers and students in psychology who are interested in how psychological issues intersect with the challenge of achieving sustainability. Links to discussion topics and activities in 13 areas of psychology (such as learning, development, biopsychology, and so forth) can be found here.

tion" (Saunders, 2003, p. 138). You will note that this definition conceives of humans as *part of nature.* Like ecopsychologists, conservation psychologists believe that much of the current crisis is the result of people's perceiving themselves as separate from, or even above, nature.

In the following sections, we will briefly review the current state of understanding about how humans are negatively affecting the systems upon which we all rely for supporting our very lives. We then go on to illustrate how many of the subdisciplines of psychology can aid in understanding—and hopefully solving—the problems in people's thinking and behavior. (Note: A more thorough discussion of these issues is available in Koger & Winter, 2010.)

The Escalating Environmental Crisis

Unless you've been living in a cave without media access, you are at least somewhat familiar with the environmental issues currently confronting humanity. In fact, you may even feel tired of hearing the "gloom and doom" reports concerning melting ice caps and rising sea levels, toxic chemicals in the air and water, overpopulation, dwindling forests, and species losses. It may all seem too depressing, overwhelming, and perhaps even terrifying. Or perhaps it doesn't seem to have much to do with you personally, and you feel powerless to make any difference. Most people quickly tune out the information and focus their attention on such concerns as family obligations, work or school, paying bills, or enjoying friends. Such a response is understandable and consistent with an evolutionary perspective. Human cognitive and perceptual systems evolved in an environment where any threats to safety were sudden and dramatic, and our ancestors had no need to track gradually worsening problems or assaults that took many years to manifest (Ornstein & Ehrlich, 2000).

As a result, the human species has difficulty responding to slowly developing but potentially calamitous conditions, particularly when the outcomes are likely to occur at distant locations. These characteristics can lead people to discount the danger or take it less seriously than "risks with negative outcomes that occur for sure, now, here, and to us" (Gattig & Hendrickx, 2007, p. 22; Leiserowitz, 2007). Consequently, people have a strong tendency to delay action until problems are large scale and readily apparent rather than working to prevent such conditions. Unfortunately, by then it may be too late.

Despite this "hard-wiring" of the brain, the human species is capable of dramatic and rapid

TOM TOLES

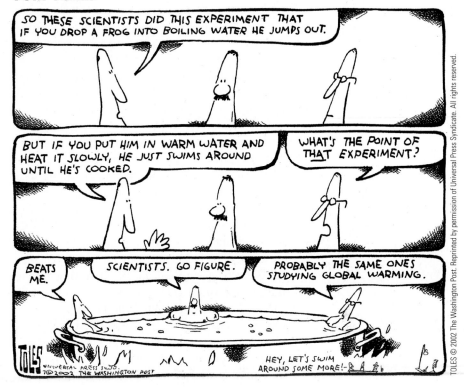

cultural evolution, as the pace of the agricultural, industrial, and technological revolutions reveals (Ehrlich & Ehrlich, 2008; Ornstein & Ehrlich, 2000). For example, as undergraduates, the two of us relied on typewriters for writing papers after engaging in library research with massive printed publication indexes and bound volumes of journals. (Can you imagine?) Now the idea of using anything other than high-speed word processing programs and not relying on the Internet to conduct research seems horribly inefficient and cumbersome. The human capacity for rapid behavioral change could help people reverse current ecological trends, provided they pay sufficient attention and collectively mobilize into action (Smith et al., 2009).

Let's take, for example, the problem of *global climate change.* If you are among the millions of people who have seen Al Gore's film *An Inconvenient Truth* (2006), you know something about what is causing this serious problem. Gases such as carbon dioxide, methane, nitrous oxide, and water vapor trap heat in the atmosphere. The naturally resulting *greenhouse effect* is necessary to stabilize planetary temperatures and maintain a climate suitable for life on this planet. Gas levels vary naturally to some extent, but as you have probably heard, industrialization has created an unprecedented increase in greenhouse gas concentrations since 1750. Simultaneously, our forests, which act as the lungs of the earth by converting carbon dioxide to oxygen, have been rapidly shrinking because of wood extraction, urbanization, and conversion of forests to agricultural land. As a result, carbon dioxide in the Earth's atmosphere is at the "highest level in 650,000 years" (Gardner & Prugh, 2008, p. 3) and is clearly correlated with planetary warming patterns (see **Figure D.1**).

In its most recent report, the Intergovernmental Panel on Climate Change (IPCC) (2007) predicted that the planet could warm as much as 11 degrees Fahrenheit by 2100. To put that number in perspective, during the last ice age the world was only 9 degrees F cooler than it is today. Thus, there is a real possibility of planetary temperature changes of ice age magnitudes within this century. Already, warming trends are evident, based on increased "average air and ocean temperatures, widespread melting of snow and ice, and rising global average sea level" (IPCC, 2007, p. 30). For example, the years between 1995 and 2006 were eleven of the twelve warmest years since 1850 when recording of global temperatures began.

Climate change will affect *ecosystems,* both directly and indirectly, via flooding, drought, wildfires, insect proliferation, and fragmentation of natural systems. As many as 20%–30% of known plant and animal species are estimated to be at an increased risk of extinction as a result of climate change, threatening the *biodiversity* that is necessary to healthy ecosystems (IPCC, 2007). Weather events such as typhoons and hurricanes are likely to become more intense, and while it is impossible to directly associate any particular storm with climate change, the devastation wrought by Hurricane Katrina in 2005 exemplifies what is expected. Coastal

regions such as those containing the cities of New York, Boston, and Miami are at particular risk because of rising sea levels, erosion, and flooding. Densely populated areas, islands, and poor communities are especially vulnerable, and such regions constitute home to nearly half of the planet's population (Gelbspan, 2001). Climate change also carries significant *public health* costs. Millions of people are likely to suffer or die from associated malnutrition, disease (including diarrheal, cardiorespiratory, and infectious illnesses), and injury as a result of extreme weather (IPCC, 2007). Moreover, some scientists think it is far too late to reverse the global warming trends and that the best we can do is try to minimize the likely damage.

Global climate change is only one facet of the current environmental crisis, which has been created by an array of interconnected problems. The bottom line is that the Earth has a limited *carrying capacity,* a biological concept describing the maximum number of any specific population that a habitat can support. If the habitat is isolated and the population cannot migrate to a new habitat, the inhabitants must find a sustainable balance with its resource base. If it doesn't and the population grows too quickly so that it depletes its resources suddenly, the population will crash. In the past, localized crashes in both human and nonhuman populations have occurred in one part of the world without seriously affecting those in another. Today, however, as humans continue to degrade "the great life-supporting systems of the planet's biosphere" (Speth, 1992, p. 27), *global* systems are in crisis and are threatening to "collapse" (Diamond, 2005). Thus, the threat of an ecological catastrophe on a *planetary level* is looming. The Earth is, essentially, a large island, with no way to borrow resources or dump pollution elsewhere.

The Behavioral Foundation of Environmental Problems

As you were reading the preceding paragraphs, did you feel despair? Anxiety? Irritation? Did you scan the material, thinking to yourself that you already knew it? Did you find yourself growing overwhelmed, angry, or afraid? Did you feel defensive or skeptical? Or did you wonder what any of this has to do with you? These *psychological* reactions are important because they affect how such problems are understood and what people are willing to do about them.

Before someone will change his or her behaviors, that person must recognize which behaviors need changing, must know how to change them, and

Figure D.1
Temperature and carbon dioxide trends. This graph shows how both global average temperatures and carbon dioxide levels in the Earth's atmosphere have increased significantly since the Industrial Revolution took off in 1880.

SOURCE: Available at http://www.whrc.org/resources/online_publications/warming_earth/scientific_evidence.htm. Graph design by Michael Ernst, Woods Hole Research Center.

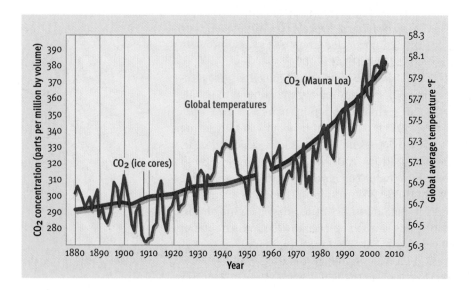

must feel that changing them is a worthwhile expenditure of effort. Most people will not initiate change until they experience a personal crisis (Beddoe et al., 2009), commonly known as "hitting bottom," or until the impacts of risks such as climate change become salient and personally relevant (Weber, 2006).

Does environmental destruction actually have anything to do with individuals? If you don't have children, you might assume that you are not contributing directly to population growth, and you yourself do not produce industrial wastes or log forests. What, then, is *each person* doing to deplete the carrying capacity of the planet to sustain human life? The most obvious answer lies in individuals' extravagant use and misuse of the world's natural resources.

Human influences on the planet can be estimated by using the *ecological footprint*—a measure of how fast a person (or population) consumes resources and generates waste in comparison to how rapidly nature (the habitat) can absorb the waste and replenish the resources. People who live in the United States have the largest *ecological footprints*, consuming considerably more resources and generating more waste than any other people on the planet. Unfortunately, the gap between this ecological footprint and the planet's carrying capacity is growing at an alarming pace (see **Figure D.2**). "If everyone in the world had an ecological footprint equivalent to that of the typical North American or Western European, global society would overshoot the planet's biocapacity three to five fold" (Kitzes et al., 2008, p. 468). In other words, if everyone lived like those in the United States do, three or more planets would be needed to support this lifestyle!

People living in the U.S. are by far the biggest users and wasters of the world's commercial energy. Less than 5% of the planet's population live in the U.S. and the country has only about 3% of the planet's oil supply (Kunstler, 2005), yet U.S. residents use a staggering *25%* of the total commercial supply (Energy Information Administration, 2006): 20,802,160 barrels of oil *per day*. The next largest consumer is China, but consider this: China has *four times* the population of the U.S. and uses only one-third of the amount of oil (6,720,000 barrels per day). Each person in the U.S. uses, on average, more than 30 times the amount of gasoline as the average person in a developing country (World Resources Institute, 2001). This "addiction to oil" is fostering a dangerously unstable international climate. Middle Eastern countries rest on more than 60% of the planet's oil reserves (Kunstler, 2005), inspiring military-based foreign policies that emphasize control and access

(e.g., Klare, 2001; Winter & Cava, 2006). Wars over access to resources including oil will likely become more common.

Amazingly, much of this huge expenditure of energy is wasted (Miller, 2007). People in North America waste over 43% of their energy by selecting energy-inefficient automobiles, appliances, and home heating systems when more efficient choices are available. Energy expert Amory Lovins puts it plainly, "If the United States wants to save a lot of oil and money and increase national security, there are two simple ways to do it: Stop driving Petropigs and stop living in energy sieves" (quoted in Miller, 2007, p. 385).

Those living in the U.S. also overuse and abuse water. The toxic chemicals used in industrial production, as well as those used to kill pests like bugs and weeds, clean houses, and even groom and beautify people and pets, are polluting groundwater, lakes, rivers, and oceans. Demand for water from growing populations in arid locations is lowering reservoirs and aquifers. At least one quarter of the groundwater that is currently withdrawn is not being replenished. For example, Las Vegas has doubled in population since 1990. The city gets 90% of its water from the Colorado River, which is currently experiencing the worst drought in recorded history (Hutchinson, 2007). Already more than *one billion* people on the planet do not have safe drinking water. In contrast, people in the developed world pollute and waste gallons of clean water every time they flush the toilet, while half of the population in developing nations lack access to basic sanitation.

The wasteful use of energy and water are two of the primary contributors to the enormous ecological

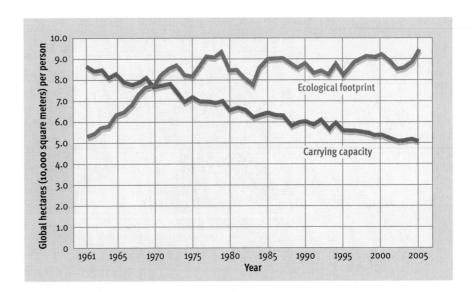

Figure D.2
Trends in the collective ecological footprint of the United States. This graph shows how the ecological footprint of the United States has increased dramatically since the 1960s in relation to the (decreasing) carrying capacity that the Earth's habitat can support. As you can see, the trends are not encouraging.

SOURCE: http://www.footprintnetwork.org/en/index.php/GFN/page/trends/us/. Global Footprint Network 2008 National Footprint Accounts. Reprinted with permission.

web link D.2

Global Footprint Network

The Global Footprint Network is an international think tank working to advance sustainability through the use of the ecological footprint, a tool that measures how much nature exists, how much humans use, and who uses what. You can estimate your personal ecological footprint here.

footprint of the U.S. population. Another major factor is diet. Livestock farming produces more greenhouse gases than transportation (Food and Agriculture Organization of the United Nations, 2006), and it has been estimated that it takes 600 gallons of water to produce one hamburger (Kreith, 1991). U.S. citizens eat four times the amount of meat as the average person in a developing country (World Resources Institute, 2001). The per capita annual meat consumption is 275 pounds in the United States, compared to 115 pounds in China and 11.4 in India (Menzel & D'Alusio, 2005). Most people regularly eat food that is out of season or does not grow in their region. This means that their food must travel long distances to get to them. It is typical in the U.S. for food to travel more than 1500 miles from its source to the dinner table (Pirog & Benjamin, 2003). Furthermore, popular convenience foods are subject to energy-intensive processing and are packaged in containers and wrappers that cannot be reused or recycled. Finally, North Americans waste tremendous amounts of food—about 27% of edible food, which comes to over 3000 pounds *every second* (Kantor, et al., 1997). Most of that food ends up in landfills, and as it rots it releases methane, a greenhouse gas that is 20 times more powerful than carbon dioxide at trapping heat in the atmosphere (U.S. EPA, 2006).

Energy, water, and food are not the only things currently consumed in unsustainable ways. *Overconsumption of consumer goods constitutes the biggest drain on the Earth's carrying capacity.* Many people suffer from *affluenza,* an "unsustainable addiction to overconsumption and materialism" (Miller, 2007, p. 19; de Graaf, Wann, & Naylor, 2005) (see Web Link D.3). Those who are addicted to consumption use shopping in ways similar to overeating, using alcohol and drugs, and surfing the Internet (see Chapter 12). Nearly 20 years ago, it was observed that each person in North America consumes, directly or indirectly, over 100 pounds of raw materials a day (Durning, 1992), vastly more than those in developing countries and even more than people in other developed nations. For example, U.S. residents use "19 times more paper than the average person in a developing country, and most of it becomes trash" (Gardner, 2002, p. 9). Moreover, less than half of the paper used in the U.S. gets recycled (Miller, 2007). And the things people buy—clothes, electronics, cars, furnishings—are produced from materials that leave a long trail of pollution in many third-world countries that is invisible to the U.S. consumer. A pair of pants made of polyester and sold in an American department store may be sewn in a sweatshop in Indonesia, from synthetic material manufactured

web link D.3

Affluenza

Do you suffer from affluenza? Find out at this thought-provoking site that was developed in conjunction with a one-hour show filmed for public television in Oregon. The site includes information on the "diagnosis" and "treatment" of this common condition, as well as an opportunity to order a video of the show.

in Singapore, which comes from oil refined in Mexico. U.S. consumer culture is spreading quickly, so that people in developing countries are aiming for "the good life," hurrying to develop the same extravagant lifestyles modeled in movies, television, advertising, and tourism.

Conspicuous consumption of convenience foods and consumer goods yields astonishing amounts of solid waste. Each person in North America generates more than 4.5 pounds of garbage per day (Miller, 2007), about 10 times their body weight every year. People throw away approximately 2.5 million nonreturnable plastic bottles *every hour* and toss about *25 billion* Styrofoam coffee cups in the garbage each year. Electronic waste, or "e-waste," is growing exponentially. Every year, people living in the U.S. discard an estimated 130 million cell phones and 100 million computers, monitors, and television sets, only recycling about 10% (Miller, 2007). But even careful household recycling will not change the biggest solid waste problem. Commercial and industrial activities generate 98.5% of the waste. Average citizens sponsor this enormous waste production *every time* they buy a product that was inefficiently manufactured, is overly packaged, is not recyclable or biodegradable, and has traveled a long distance to get to them (which describes the vast majority of consumer products, including some that are misleadingly labeled "eco-friendly").

Yet, there is good reason to believe that overconsumption is not delivering the "goods." As you read in Chapter 9, empirical studies suggest that it is not how much stuff people own but the quality of their social relations, the creative fulfillment received from work, and their personality and outlook on life that determine how happy they are. In fact, the race to pay for material possessions is likely to detract from these primary ingredients of happiness. Thus, attempting to meet psychological needs through overconsumption jeopardizes not only physical habitat but also psychological well-being (Kasser & Kanner, 2004). You have no doubt heard of the 3 R's: Reduce, Reuse, Recycle. But effective solutions to environmental problems must start with *Refusing* to buy things that aren't really necessary and choosing sustainably produced options for the things that are (Miller, 2007) (see **Figure D.3**).

The field of psychology has much to offer in terms of understanding and solving the problems causing ecological degradation in today's world. Of course, it would be naive to suggest that any one academic discipline will provide the solution to such a complex interplay of issues as those underlying current

ecological conditions, and it is clear that interdisciplinary collaborations are urgently needed (Smith et al., 2009). However, psychology has a lot to offer for understanding the roots of environmental problems and the psychological forces maintaining them. Individuals have the power to make choices that do not exacerbate environmental problems, and *with ability comes responsibility*. Feeling empowered on one level often inspires people to work at a more global level and thus provides hope for more widespread social change. Bringing psychology to speak to the unspoken pessimism most people share about the

web link   D.4

The Story of Stuff

This site provides a charming but disturbing review of how material goods are produced, distributed and disposed of in ways that are antagonistic to the goal of sustainability.

The UnShopping Card	The UnShopping Card
Do I *really* need this?	**Do I *really* need this?**
Is it made of recycled or renewable materials?	Is it overpackaged?
Is it recyclable or biodegradable?	How long will it last?
	If it breaks, can it be fixed?
Could I borrow, rent or buy it used?	How will I dispose of it?
Is it worth the time I worked to pay for it?	What is its environmental cost?
	Is it a fair trade product?

Figure D.3

An innovative effort to discourage overconsumption.
This "UnShopping Card," developed by the Oregon State University Extension Service, was created to help people think more deliberately about their consumption decisions.

SOURCE: http://www.cof.orst.edu/cof/extended/sustainold/pdf/orderform.pdf. Reprinted by permission of Viviane Simon-Brown, Oregon State University College of Forestry.

web link D.5

Running the Numbers

Visit this site developed by Chris Jordan to see brilliant visual illustrations of the astonishing quantities of consumer goods used in the United States. For example, you can see 15 million sheets of office paper, representing 5 minutes of paper use, or 106,000 aluminum cans for 30 seconds of can consumption. The artwork is clever, creative, and depressing.

future on an overcrowded and overburdened planet makes psychological theory personally and intellectually meaningful and provides insight into how to design a sustainable future. Thus, the following sections will explore several subdisciplines within psychology in terms of how they can be applied to understanding and solving environmentally related behavioral problems.

Insights from Psychoanalytic Theory

As you learned in Chapter 11, part of Sigmund Freud's fame lies in the vigorous criticisms and controversies his theories have inspired. Nonetheless, his emphasis on unconscious conflict and ego anxiety and his description of unconscious defenses that people use to ward off emotional discomfort are particularly relevant to environmental issues. Certainly, acknowledging the probable collapse of the planet's ecosystems *should* trigger powerful negative feelings, including despair, bewilderment, grief, anger, and so on. As one bumper sticker puts it, "If you're not outraged, you're not paying attention!" Emotional defenses explain how people can "know" about environmental problems and yet not change their relevant behaviors.

Freud described several *defense mechanisms* that are particularly useful for understanding people's ecologically unfriendly behaviors. For example, *rationalization* is one of the most common defense mechanisms. Thus, people say, "I have to drive because the bus schedule is too inconvenient," even though they know that cars contribute significantly to air pollution and climate change. *Identification* leads to purchasing unnecessary clothing, electronics, and other items that one's peer group or cultural heroes use and promote. When in *denial,* people claim that the anxiety-provoking material doesn't exist, a tendency that can be bolstered by supporting "evidence" from outside sources. For example, conservative think tanks, funded by industry, have been effective in fostering public denial about the scientific evidence on climate change (Jacques, Dunlap, & Freeman, 2008). Denial about environmental problems includes minimizing their severity, seeing them as irrelevant, and seeing oneself as not responsible (Opotow & Weiss, 2000). Like denial, *reaction formation* is used to deny a painful feeling but in this case *also* gives intense energy to expressing its opposite. For example, the hostility with which Wise Use advocate Ronald Arnold (1993) describes environmentalists as "pathological fools" (p. 42) who buy into "spiritual crap" (p. 30) makes us won-

der about his former role as a Sierra Club official. Finally, *projection* occurs when people perceive in others what they fail to perceive in themselves. One of the authors recalls vehemently grumbling about all the cars on the road during rush hour, only to be reminded by her 3-year-old in the backseat, "But Mommy, you're traffic, too!"

In sum, defenses enable people to make excuses and fail to notice or take responsibility for what they are doing. Consequently, many people ultimately appear apathetic toward fellow human beings, other species, and the future. Yet knowing more about one's personal patterns of defenses may help one to be less habitual in using them. On the other hand, because it takes a lot of patience and time to confront defenses, people may not act soon enough. Psychoanalytic approaches are better at explaining environmentally unfriendly behavior than developing solutions. Fortunately, behavioral theories have more potential for producing meaningful changes in human behavior.

Insights from Behavioral Psychology

Efforts to bring about immediate changes in behavior are better informed by the theories and techniques of behavioral psychology, which focuses on observable behavior in the present rather than its deeper meanings and underlying motivations. As you may recall from Chapter 6, one of the best-known behavioral psychologists, B. F. Skinner, argued that what people do is a function of the consequences of their behavior: reinforcement strengthens response tendencies, whereas punishment weakens them. Toward the end of his career, Skinner took a particular interest in environmental issues. In an address to the American Psychological Association, he criticized the efforts of environmental activists as inconsistent with operant learning principles in that they focused on inspiring guilt, fear, and shame to motivate greener behaviors instead of helping individuals see the potentially reinforcing consequences of sustainable lifestyles (Skinner, 1987). Yet many environmentally damaging behaviors continue to be rewarded by social status, convenience, and low costs. For example, gas-guzzling SUVs are very popular, driving is generally more convenient for running errands rather than biking or using public transit, and gasoline remains relatively cheap for most U.S. citizens. Altering these reinforcement contingencies, such as rewarding bus ridership with tokens redeemable for future trips or movie passes (Everett, Hayward, & Meyers, 1974) or providing *feedback* by praising individuals for reducing the amount of energy they consume (Abrahamse et al., 2005; Lehman & Geller, 2004), can be effective in motivating pro-environmental behaviors. Similarly, *incentives,* such as financial rebates for buying energy-efficient appliances, can motivate such purchases.

Another behavior modification strategy involves altering *antecedent stimuli* to influence behavior (see Chapter 6). *Prompts* and *social modeling* are examples of strategies involving antecedents that have been used to influence environmentally relevant behaviors. *Prompts* signal particular actions. One example is prominently placing aluminum recycling bins in areas where canned soft drinks are consumed (Lehman & Geller, 2004). Another example would be placing signs over light switches, reminding users to turn off the light when they leave a room. Research suggests that the more specific the prompt, the greater its effectiveness. A sign saying "Faculty and students please turn off lights after 5 p.m." is more effective than one reading "Conserve Electricity." Polite prompts are more effective than demanding ones (the word "please" can make a difference), and the closer the prompt is to the point of behavior, the better (a sign over a light switch is more effective than a sign across the room). Thus, polite, salient, and specific reminders can change behavior (Geller, Winett, & Everett, 1982; Lehman & Geller, 2004).

Although providing general information is a technique widely used by environmental groups, distributing slogans, pamphlets, solicitations, or articles is less effective than giving explicit prompts or instructions. For instance, informing maintenance garage managers about specific ways their employees could reduce polluting behaviors at their facility resulted in more positive changes than general information about oil pollution (Daamen et al., 2001). Although common sense suggests the need to educate people about environmental problems, education by itself apparently does little to change behavior. For example, millions of dollars spent on information dissemination resulted in only 2%–3% improvements in energy conservation (Hirst, Berry & Soderstrom, 1981). Because attitudes do not necessarily predict people's actions very well, there is little reason to believe that education alone will change what people actually do, a finding supported by many studies (reviewed by Abrahamse et al., 2005; Gardner & Stern, 2002; Lehman & Geller, 2004). On the other hand, the modeling of environmentally friendly behavior can be effective. For instance, in one study participants were exposed to a video showing a person turning down a thermostat, wearing warmer clothes, and using heavy blankets. With this treatment, viewers reduced their energy use by 28% (Winett et al., 1982). Thus, *modeling* may often work better than simply describing desired behaviors. One of the authors has frequently experienced this phenomenon during walks with friends: when she bends down to pick up litter during the walk, her friends do so as well.

Insights from Social Psychology

Modeling behavior is one way to communicate *social norms*—informal, unwritten "rules" about what is appropriate or typical behavior in a particular setting. Norms can exert a form of social pressure that may lead to conformity, as described in Chapter 15. Some researchers distinguish between *injunctive norms* (what is expected or approved of) and *descriptive norms* (what most people actually do) (Cialdini, Reno, & Kallgren, 1990). In the case of environmentally responsible behaviors, injunctive and descriptive norms are often inconsistent; that is, most people approve of environmentally responsible behaviors but don't actually engage in them. To test the importance of these two types of norms, researchers conducted a series of field experiments on littering. Our society has injunctive norms against littering, but in some situations the descriptive norm is to litter, resulting in some interesting interactions. For example, in an already littered environment, participants were more likely to litter after witnessing a confederate littering. In a clean environment, however, the participants who saw a confederate littering were less likely to litter than those who saw no littering behavior. In both situations the participants' behavior was influenced by the descriptive norms indicated by both the setting and the confederate's behavior (Cialdini et al., 1990). Cialdini (2003) argued that environmental campaigns emphasizing all the bad behaviors people exhibit may backfire, because they inadvertently draw attention to descriptive norms for anti-environmental behavior.

Norms are just one of the influences that subtly or explicitly motivate and direct behavior in the moment. Certainly, internal factors, such as attitudes and values, influence behavior to some extent. For example, people who appreciate the inherent value of nature and other species (those who hold *biocentric values*) are more likely to engage in pro-environmental behaviors such as sharing resources and taking actions to protect other species, landscapes, and natural resources. In contrast, those with

Good intentions do not necessarily result in good behavior. Most people endorse environmentally responsible behaviors such as not littering, but depending on the situation, their actual behavior may be quite different. Social psychology can shed light on these disparities between attitudes and behavior.

egocentric and *materialistic* values that emphasize personal wealth and status tend to exhibit fewer environmentally friendly actions (Schultz et al., 2005). Materialistic values have surged over the last few decades. Data collected on incoming college students over a 30-year period (1966–2007) show that they increasingly value materialism above other values, including finding personal meaning, helping others in difficulty, becoming an authority in one's field, and raising a family (Myers, 2010) (see **Figure D.4**). Still, regardless of the individual differences in people's personalities or attitudes, social psychologists know that situation-specific constraints can make it difficult (or costly, inconvenient, or awkward) for people to act on their pro-environmental values (Kollmus & Agyeman, 2002; Staats, 2003). To paraphrase the founder of experimental social psychology, Kurt Lewin, behavior is a function of the person *and* the situation.

Although most of the research on the "person" is conducted by personality psychologists, social psychologists are interested in the *self-concept* as well as *social identity*. How people define themselves relative to others and to the social environment plays a large part in behavior. Inspired by ecopsychological theories, some social psychologists have recently turned their attention to the notion of the *ecologically connected self*. Theoretically, the more one defines and experiences oneself as *part of nature,* the more one should be interested in and attuned to information about the environment and one's impact on it and the more empathy and caring one should exhibit for other living things (Bragg, 1996). Several recent studies support this idea (e.g., Clayton, 2003; Mayer & Frantz, 2004; Schultz, 2000, 2001). Moreover, the development of an ecologically connected self leads to environmentally appropriate behaviors not out of a sense of self-sacrifice or self-denial, but out of a sense of self-love and common identity. Experiences in nature, particularly during childhood, can foster this positive relationship with nature and other species, as well as pro-environmental behaviors (Chawla, 1988, Kals & Ittner, 2003; Myers, 2007). In contrast, a lack of encounters with unpolluted and undegraded conditions in nature may reduce people's sense of connection and personal responsibility for environmental issues (Kahn, 2007; Pyle, 2002).

A disconnection from nature and egocentric values set the stage for a *social dilemma:* a discrepancy between the interests of oneself and the larger group and the relative short-term and long-term consequences of one's behavior. Many environmental problems result from people acting out of self-interest in the moment, ultimately harming the greater whole. A clear example is commuters' reliance on the convenience of cars rather than using public transit (Joireman, Van Lange & Van Vugt, 2004), thereby contributing to air pollutants and climate-changing gases, as well as traffic problems. Social dilemmas contribute to environmental degradation in several ways (e.g., Gardner & Stern, 2002; Osbaldiston & Sheldon, 2002; Vlek & Steg, 2007):

• First, in *commons dilemmas* (Hardin, 1968), individuals take more than their fair allotment of a shared resource, such as by careless or excessive water use (Van Vugt, 2001).

• Second, in *public goods dilemmas*, individuals do not contribute their fair share to a pooled resource (for instance, by voting down a bill that would increase taxes to fund community bus or train services).

• Third, in *risk dilemmas,* acting from self-interest leads to one contributing more than one's share to the hazards suffered by the greater whole. An example would be the homeowner who pours toxic chemicals (paint thinner or cleaning products) down the drain or uses pesticides (insect or weed sprays) on her lawn. These chemicals ultimately contaminate water, air, and soil throughout the community and cause health hazards ranging from headaches and nausea to attention deficit and learning disabilities, to several forms of cancer (see Koger & Winter, 2010).

• Fourth, *ecological dilemmas* occur when acting from self-interest upsets the larger balance of things, such as when a landowner fills in a wetland on his property, thereby interfering with waterfowl migration.

In these examples, if not in all environmental problems, rewards to the individual are more immediate and compelling than the delayed costs to the population. The likely result is a damaged biosphere, particularly when the adverse consequences of irresponsible behavior are uncertain and solutions depend on the action of large numbers of people (e.g., Staats, 2003). Individuals tend to cooperate with others in working toward a common goal (such as reducing global emissions) if they are convinced of the high probability that they will be personally and adversely affected if the target goals not be reached. In that regard, many studies have shown that people will forgo immediate, personal reinforcers for longer-term group goals, especially if they identify with the group and feel responsible toward it (Dawes, 1980; Gardner & Stern, 2002; Van Vugt, 2002) and if they perceive the long-term benefits of collective action as relevant to them personally as well as to the larger group (Milinski et al., 2008; Ostrom et al., 2007).

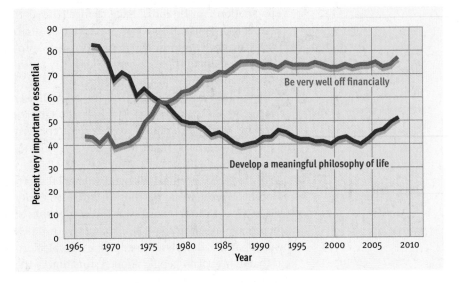

Importantly, environmental social dilemmas differ from some other social dilemmas in that they have a temporal dimension (Joireman, 2005; Osbaldiston & Sheldon, 2002). For example, Joireman, Van Lange, and Van Vugt (2004) studied consumers' automobile-related behaviors and found that having a "future orientation" was more predictive of environmentally responsible behavior than having a "prosocial orientation" (which would typically predict taking the selfless route in a social dilemma).

Insights from Cognitive Psychology

Humans' cognitive and perceptual processes are crucial organizing features of behavior. These mechanisms were shaped by eons of evolution, are modified by personal experiences, and generally function pretty effectively; if they didn't, the species wouldn't have survived for very long. Yet the environments in which perceptual and cognitive systems evolved were very different from those that humans currently encounter. As a result, people tend to focus on threats that are visually noticeable (smoke pouring out of a smokestack) rather than the many largely invisible or slowly acting dangers, such as climate change or pesticides and other toxins in water and food supplies (Ornstein & Ehrlich, 2000).

Thus, from the perspective of cognitive psychology, environmentally destructive behavior is maintained by cognitive biases. For instance, laypeople assess risks in different terms than professionals do, leading the public to express greater levels of concern about local, immediate threats such as hazardous waste and radiation contamination, compared to experts' greater focus on global, longer-term issues, such

Figure D.4
Increasing materialism among college students. An annual survey of the attitudes and values of first-year college students suggests that materialistic values are on the rise. As you can see, the percentage of students who think that it is crucial to "be very well off financially" has almost doubled since the 1960s.

SOURCE: From Myers, D. G. (2008) *Social Psychology*, 9th ed., p. 581. Copyright © 2008 by D. G. Myers. Reprinted by permission of McGraw-Hill, Inc.

as population growth and climate change (Slimak & Dietz, 2006). Thus, although the scientific community has detailed the clear and devastating risks associated with climate change, the public largely maintains a "wait and see" attitude and does not seem to understand the need to drastically and immediately reduce emissions in order to stabilize the climate (Sterman, 2008), although they do report concern about the potential human health risks (Sundblad, Biel, & Gärling, 2007).

Further, the tendency to depend on mental shortcuts called *heuristics,* such as those described in Chapter 8, can lead to errors in assessing the relative risks of environmental hazards and in estimating how one's behavior affects the environment. One mental shortcut that may explain people's underestimation of the risk of climate change is the *availability heuristic.* Individuals may have difficulty imagining the risks associated with climate change because of a lack of vivid, personal experiences with melting icecaps and rising sea levels. On the other hand, dramatic environmental hazards, such as oil spills, feature prominently in people's memories and may, therefore, receive more attention and resources than are warranted relative to other less perceptually vivid, but more insidious, hazards (Gardner & Stern, 2002).

Some cognitive biases help people feel good about themselves in spite of their behavior or circumstances. Several of these biases are relevant when considering how people perceive environmental risk and the impact of their own actions. *Comparative optimism* is a heuristic that leads individuals to believe they are less vulnerable than other people to all types of risks, including environmental threats such air and water pollution or nuclear accidents, even though objectively there is no reason to think the risks are any different for one individual versus another (Pahl et al., 2005). *False consensus* is a cognitive bias that helps people maintain positive self-esteem by convincing themselves that many others engage in the same undesirable behaviors that they do. For example, a water shortage following a tropical storm prompted a temporary shower ban at Princeton University in 1999, which inspired a 5-day field study during and after the ban (Benoît & Norton, 2003). The researchers found that students who defied the shower ban overestimated the prevalence of this socially irresponsible behavior in others. In addition, those who showered were seen by others as caring very little about the greater good, whereas those who did not shower were seen as caring very much. However, self-report data suggested that the attitudinal positions of these two groups were much closer together than either group realized (i.e., both groups cared about the larger group's welfare). *False polarization* is the tendency to perceive the views of those on the opposing side of a partisan debate as more extreme than they really are. All of these tendencies distort the perception of one's behavior relative to others', while they help maintain feelings of safety (comparative optimism), sense of self-esteem (false consensus), and the view of oneself as more reasonable than those who would disagree (false polarization).

Although the use of mental shortcuts is automatic, it is possible to override this tendency when one is sufficiently motivated and not cognitively overloaded by other attentional demands. Humans may be "lazy" thinkers who are prone to biases by default, but they are capable of careful, logical, effortful reasoning. The question is whether "coldly rational" judgments are always superior to emotionally driven ones (Slovic et al., 2004). People's evaluation of the risks and benefits associated with the use of pesticides is based not only on knowledge, but also on how they feel about those risks and benefits (Alhakami & Slovic, 1994). This *affect* (emotion-based) *heuristic* also influences judgments of the risks and benefits of nuclear power. For example, after reading a description of nuclear energy that emphasized the risks of this energy source ("Waste is highly radioactive and contaminated with plutonium, a deadly element"), participants not only raised their estimates of the risks of nuclear power (as would be logically expected) but also *lowered* their estimates of the benefits of nuclear power—even though the description had not said anything about benefits. The researchers explained this change in participants' benefit estimates as being due to an overall increase in negative feelings about nuclear power as a result of reading the description of risks (Finucane et al., 2000). In sum, heuristics may sometimes bias people in an anti-environmental direction and sometimes in a pro-environmental direction. The key may be for each person to increase his or her awareness of the potential for errors in thinking. In this way, individuals can become better environmental decision makers.

Insights from Developmental Psychology

As a discipline, psychology evolved primarily in an urban-industrialized context during the last century. It is probably because of this situation that developmental psychologists have historically overlooked the vital role that nature plays in humans' cognitive, emotional, and social development. Only since the 1990s have some developmental psychologists turned their attention toward topics such as children's relationship with other animals, their understanding of life and ecological systems, their moral reasoning about environmental issues, and the implications of their experiences (or lack thereof) in natural settings.

Developmental psychologists have largely neglected the study of children's relationship with animals, even though animals are a primary focus in children's lives in a variety of forms: as live, stuffed, or imaginary companions; as captive or wild specimens; as zoo attractions; as targets of cruelty; as characters in books and on television; and as roles the children themselves assume. Recently, however, a few developmental psychologists have proposed that in order to fully understand the development of children's perceptual systems, their love relationships and empathy, their play patterns, their fears, and their sense of self, researchers must extend the list of important influences on children to include animals—perhaps even putting animals at the top of the list (Melson, 2001, 2003; Myers, 2007).

Experience with animals makes an important contribution in teaching children about the differences between living and nonliving things. But as you learned in Chapter 10, learning experiences interact with inherited predispositions. The genetic makeup of the brain enables humans to learn certain concepts more easily than others. For instance, *folkbiology* is a term used to describe how people intuitively perceive, categorize, and think about living things. Research on folkbiology suggests that children recognize a "life force" as something unique to biological phenomena and that they make distinctions between living and nonliving things as well as among plants, animals, and humans (Hatano & Inagaki, 1999; Inagaki & Hatano, 2004). Researchers have also begun to address the questions of whether the acquisition of folkbiological knowledge is a continuous developmental process or a discontinuous one, in which a child's view of the world is replaced by a more sophisticated adult understanding (Coley, Solomon, & Shafto, 2002) and whether the acquisition of folkbiological knowledge occurs in the same way across cultures (e.g., Waxman, 2005). Research on children's folkbiology will not only broaden understanding of cognitive development in general but may also help psychologists to better understand why and how adults' unsustainable behaviors may be influenced by *anthropocentric* (human-centered) thinking and ignorance about ecology.

Children make categorical distinctions between humans, nonhuman animals, plants, and nonliving things, but do they make *moral* distinctions between them? Research suggests the answer is "yes." In sev-

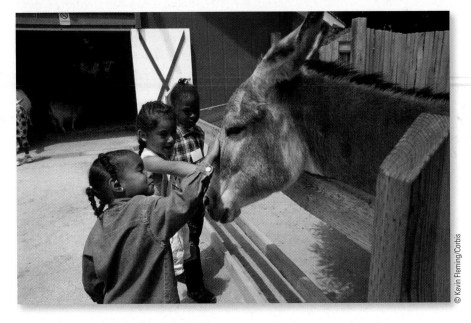

eral cross-cultural studies, children showed strong moral prohibitions against pollution and associated damage to natural systems, including other species. Their concerns reflected anthropocentric values (harm to humans) as well as biocentric values (reviewed in Kahn, 2003). From the biocentric perspective, natural systems have inherent value and rights and deserve respect comparable to humans. Reasoning that involves seeing the similarities between oneself and natural species such as trees can "evoke feelings of empathy for [an] object that permit it to be regarded as something worthy of moral consideration" (Gebhard, Nevers, & Bllmann-Mahecha, 2003, p. 92).

Experiences in nature during childhood help determine whether or not people recognize themselves to

Experience with animals during childhood can have an impact on people's attitudes about nature in general, not to mention their feelings about the importance of preserving endangered species.

be part of nature, feel connected to it, and understand that protecting nature is key to their own survival and well-being (Gebhard et al., 2003; Kals & Ittner, 2003; Searles, 1960). Activists and ecologists often attribute their environmental concern to early personal experiences in nature, family members who modeled appreciation for nature, or feelings of distress over the destruction of a favorite natural place (Chawla, 1998).

Increasingly, child development experts are becoming convinced that children need outdoor experiences to fully develop their emotional, physical, mental, and social capabilities (e.g., Kahn & Kellert, 2002; Louv, 2005). Children need opportunities for spontaneous and independent play or activity in areas that are generally outside human intervention and control (Kellert, 2002; Mergen, 2003; Pyle, 1993). Independent adventure, risk taking, and exploration can foster a sense of mastery, self-sufficiency, and confidence (Derr, 2006). Like adults, children show preferences for natural settings and report that nature offers restoration and relief from stress (e.g., Korpela, 2002; Simmons, 1994). Refuges in the form of forts and dens in natural settings are beloved play spaces for many children, primarily because they represent areas under the children's control (Sobel, 2002).

Children's mental health also suffers when deprived of experiences in nature. Children living in rural communities with more "nearby nature" have less psychological distress, including anxiety, depression, and conduct disorders such as bullying than those living in urban areas (Wells & Evans, 2003). Nature encounters can reduce the adverse effects of trauma and childhood distress on children's feelings of global self-worth. Studies have also demonstrated that symptoms of *attention deficit hyperactivity disorders* can be ameliorated by "green activities" such as camping, fishing, soccer, or a simple "walk in the park" (Faber Tayler et al., 2001; Faber Taylor & Kuo, 2009). Even passive time spent in green settings while relaxing or reading a book outside is negatively correlated with symptoms of attention deficit disorder (Faber Taylor et al., 2001; see also Kuo & Faber Taylor, 2004). While methodological issues may limit some causal inferences (Canu & Gordon, 2005; Kuo & Faber Taylor, 2005), these studies suggest promising research directions and alternative treatment options for the growing problem of attention deficit disorder.

However, many children today experience only degraded and polluted conditions, making identification with nature more difficult (Kahn, 2007; Kals & Ittner, 2003; Pyle, 2002). Further, the average child in the U.S. today spends less than 30 minutes per week engaged in outdoor activities (Hofferth & Curtin, 2005; Hofferth & Sandberg, 2001). More time inside generally means more time in front of a TV or other media sources such as a computer or video game; children are currently spending as many as 6 to 9 hours per day engaged with electronic media (Roberts, Foehr, & Rideout, 2005; Strasburger, 2007). Time with technologies such as television and video games results in less quality time interacting with siblings and parents, less time spent doing homework (as much as an 18% reduction), and less creative play (Vandewater, Bickham, & Lee, 2006), including outdoors. These trends rob children of free time outside and mitigate their understanding of the natural world. Because some investigators have argued that the love of nature and concern about its protection is *only* developed with regular, consistent contact and play outside (Chawla, 1988; Pyle, 2002; Wilson, 1993), children who spend most of their time indoors are less likely to engage in pro-environmental actions.

Perhaps most significant in terms of environmental issues, increased time interacting with media exposes children to an astonishing amount of marketing. The average child sees over 40,000 advertisements on television each year (Linn, 2004). Contemporary advertisers send their messages via television, the Internet, computer games, cell phones, MP3 players, DVDs, virtual world websites, books, and school advertisements (Linn, 2008). This commercialization of childhood constitutes the foundation of the highly destructive consumer culture that depletes resources and degrades the environment (Kasser, 2002; Linn, 2008), in addition to negatively affecting a child's development.

Insights from Health Psychology

You read in Chapter 12 about the physiology of stress and its associated behavioral and health problems. It turns out that many aspects of contemporary environments that are ecologically unsound are also significant human stressors. Noise, traffic, crowding, pollution, and living near toxic industries or waste sites are all associated with increased stress and related symptoms such as anxiety, depression, or anger (Bell et al., 2001; Lima, 2004; Lundberg, 1998), as well as self-reported tension, irritability, distractibility, impaired interpersonal behaviors, and deficits in task performance (Evans & Cohen, 1987; Weil & Rosen, 1997). Urbanized settings are also associated with increased anger, behavioral aggression, and violence (Hartig et al., 2003; Kuo & Sullivan, 2001).

In addition, catastrophic events such as flooding, hurricanes, windstorms, and wildfires such as those predicted to increase from global climate change are very stressful (Few, 2007; Fritze et al., 2008). Loss of loved ones, damage to personal belongings, housing disruption or displacement, and worry about future consequences can all cause *posttraumatic stress disorder* (see Chapter 13) and related problems such as grief, depression and suicide attempts, anxiety, and substance abuse (Fritze et al., 2008).

Furthermore, the manufacture, use, and disposal of tens of thousands of industrial and household chemicals are causing increased rates of cancer, developmental disabilities, and reproductive abnormalities, significant stressors in their own right (e.g., Colborn, Dumanoski, & Myers, 1996; Grandjean & Landrigan, 2006; Koger, Schettler, & Weiss, 2005; Koger & Winter, 2010). The result is deteriorating health of human beings on physical, mental, and social levels, as well as degradation of the planet. Thus, the psychology of health and the environment reminds people that they are inherently interconnected with the rest of the biosphere; the health of human bodies is directly related to the health of the planet Earth.

Not surprisingly, then, people strongly prefer healthy natural settings that include water (lakes, rivers, oceans), plants, trees, and sunlight over urban environments filled with buildings and cars (Kaplan & Kaplan, 1989; Kaplan, 2001; van den Berg, et al., 2007). Further, natural environments can alleviate stress by activating the *parasympathetic nervous system* (Chapter 3), providing recovery from sympathetic (fight or flight) arousal by reducing blood pressure and heart rate (Hartig et al., 2003; Laumann, Gärling, & Stormark, 2003). Studies have found that people with views of nature from their workspace reported fewer headaches, greater job satisfaction, and less job stress (Kaplan, 1993; Kaplan & Kaplan, 1989). Viewing natural settings (through a window or on a video) decreased measures of stress, depression, anger, and tension and increased overall happiness and concentration (van den Berg et al., 2003). Comparably, activities such as gardening, caring for indoor plants, and interacting with animals such as pet dogs can all reduce stress (Frumkin, 2001). Interestingly, restorative experiences in nature can also

web link D.6

The Collaborative on Health and the Environment

The organization that maintains this site works to "advance knowledge and effective action to address growing concerns about the links between human health and environmental factors." The rich resources include access to a searchable database that summarizes research on the links between chemical contaminants and approximately 180 human diseases or conditions.

In recent years, psychologists have conducted some interesting research on the effects of exposure to natural settings (like the top two photos) versus human-created urban environments (like the bottom two photos). This research indicates that natural environments can decrease individuals' response to stress.

help motivate environmentally responsible behavior such as recycling (Hartig, Kaiser, & Bowler, 2001).

In addition to stress reduction, nature can provide recovery from prolonged work and concentration (Berto, 2005; Hartig & Staats, 2006). You can probably relate to the worn-out feeling that accompanies long-term cognitive effort during midterm and final exams. People can suffer from such fatigue even when the work is enjoyable and thus experience reduced productivity. Attentional fatigue often co-occurs with feelings of stress, but natural, *restorative environments* can mitigate the effects of both (Kaplan, 1995; van den Berg et al., 2003). Mental fatigue and other forms of stress can lead people to feel tired, short-tempered, insensitive, and irritable. Thus, to the extent that nature is restorative, it could also help to enhance interpersonal relations and overall life functioning (Herzog & Strevey, 2008).

In sum, natural environments are necessary and healthy not only for children but also for adults. However, while recognizing the value of restorative environments is important, doing so could also lead to exploitation. Saving natural resources only for the ways in which they can benefit humankind is a limited and anthropocentric view. As Greenway (1995) put it, "Perhaps the clearest evidence of our recovery will be that we do not demand that wilderness heal us. We will have learned to let it be. For a wilderness that must heal us is surely a commodity, just as when we can only look at wilderness as a source of endless wealth" (pp. 134–135).

What You Can Personally Do

I am only one. But still I am one.
I cannot do everything, but still I can do something;
And because I cannot do everything,
I will not refuse to do the something that I can do.
(Quote from Edward Everett Hale (1822–1909, original source unknown)

There are many excellent guides available (both online and in print) for how to become more environmentally responsible. You can start by taking the online quiz at http://www.myfootprint.org/ to determine your own ecological footprint and consider ways to alter your daily life based on your quiz results. You might also consider developing a *behavior modification* project (see the Personal Application for Chapter 6) addressing some of your environmentally relevant behaviors.

Six aspects of human lifestyles most significantly and adversely affect the environment (Gardner & Stern, 2008; Miller, 2007): *agriculture, transportation, home energy use, water use, overall resource consumption and waste,* and *toxic chemical production, use, and disposal.* We recommend that you think about these issues and take the following steps toward walking more lightly on the Earth. If you don't feel you can do all of them, select at least a few to get you started on a more sustainable lifestyle, and then add a new one each month.

Agriculture
• Reduce your meat consumption by eating *no meat* one day per week, then increase to two days, and so forth.
• Buy locally grown food for at least one month a year, and then try to increase this.
• Buy organically produced food or grow some of your own.

Transportation
• Walk, bike, carpool, or take mass transit as much as you can.
• If possible, work at home or live near your work or school.
• When you have to drive, note that fuel efficiency can be dramatically increased by reducing your speed, avoiding sudden stops and rapid acceleration, shutting off the engine rather than idling, keeping tires properly inflated, getting regular tune-ups, and turning off your air conditioner.
• Record the distance you drive for one week (baseline), and then try to reduce the amount by 10%. Once you accomplish that, try reducing by 15% or more.
• When you purchase a new car, buy a small, fuel-efficient (greater than 35 mpg) model.

Home energy use
• Turn down the heat by at least a few degrees in winter, and avoid using air conditioning (or turn it up a few degrees).
• Turn off computers, printers, and other appliances when not in use.
• Replace your light bulbs with compact fluorescent bulbs.
• Decrease your energy waste by caulking leaks, adding insulation, and using energy-efficient lights, appliances, and heating/cooling systems.

Water use
• Always turn off the water while brushing your teeth, and consider turning off the water while soaping up, shampooing, or shaving.
• Take quick showers instead of baths.

- Reuse cups and plates when possible, rather than washing after each use.
- Only run dishwashers and clothes-washers with full loads.
- If possible, install water-saving showers and toilets.
- Use the flushing rule: "If it's yellow, let it mellow, if it's brown, flush it down" (urine is sterile).

Resource Consumption
- The two most important ways to reduce consumption and waste are *Refuse* and *Reuse* (refer to the "Unshopping Card" in **Figure D.3**). Refusing and reusing will save you money, as well as reducing your environmental impact. Recycling is important, but it still requires energy and encourages the production and use of more and more stuff. Keep a list of things you refused to buy or reused, and try to expand the list each month.
- *Refusing*: Every time you start to buy something, ask yourself whether you really need it, and if you do, whether you can borrow or rent it. If you must buy it, ask yourself if you are purchasing the most eco-friendly version of whatever it is. (Be aware that many products are misleadingly labeled "eco-friendly.")
- *Reusing*: Examine your lifestyle and figure out which things you can reuse, such as coffee cups, canvas or other bags for groceries, and your own container for getting food to go and for leftovers when you eat out.
- Buy secondhand items of all kinds whenever possible, and give away, donate to charity, or sell items you no longer need or use, rather than throwing them away.
- Junk mail generates an astonishing amount of waste, utilizes an incredible amount of natural resources, and contributes to climate change. Let organizations know that you don't want to receive their newsletters, catalogs, and solicitations, and be sure to recycle mailings you can't refuse.

Toxic Chemicals
- Pesticides are designed to kill bugs (insecticides), weeds (herbicides), rodents, and so forth. They are directly toxic to humans as well, producing cancers and developmental disabilities, among other disor-

ders. Don't use any pesticides in your home, lawn, or garden, and educate others about their impacts on human health and neurological function, as well as detrimental effects on biodiversity.
- Avoid chemical cleansers. Baking soda and vinegar are excellent alternatives to many cleaning products; vinegar is also an effective herbicide (weed killer).
- Many plastics, cosmetics, and personal care products contain chemicals that disrupt normal hormone functions (e.g., phthalates and bisphenol A or BPA). Don't buy bottled water; don't reheat or microwave foods in plastic containers; use fewer, simpler products; and don't trust claims like "dermatologist-tested," "natural," or "organic." Read the ingredient labels and avoid fragrances, dyes, parabens or -paraben, and things you can't pronounce.
- Reduce use of plastics by bringing your own refillable containers, buying in bulk, buying things with minimal packaging, and purchasing products in recyclable and recycled packaging.
- Dispose of household toxic products properly. Many items—paints, pesticides, batteries, and even energy-efficient compact fluorescent light bulbs—contain toxic ingredients. Drop these items off at a local household hazardous waste site.

web link D.7

Environmental Working Group

This nonprofit watchdog organization provides many useful resources (such as "Skin Deep" and "Pots, Pans, and Plastics: A Shopper's Guide to Food Safety") to consumers while simultaneously pushing for national policy change. Their website offers recent research-based information on toxic chemicals and ways to avoid them.

GLOSSARY

A

Absolute refractory period The minimum length of time after an action potential during which another action potential cannot begin.

Achievement motive The need to master difficult challenges, to outperform others, and to meet high standards of excellence.

Acquired immune deficiency syndrome (AIDS) A disorder in which the immune system is gradually weakened and eventually disabled by the human immunodeficiency virus (HIV).

Acquisition The formation of a new conditioned response tendency.

Action potential A brief change in a neuron's electrical charge.

Adaptation An inherited characteristic that increased in a population (through natural selection) because it helped solve a problem of survival or reproduction during the time it emerged. See also *Sensory adaptation.*

Additive color mixing Formation of colors by superimposing lights, putting more light in the mixture than exists in any one light by itself.

Adoption studies Research studies that assess hereditary influence by examining the resemblance between adopted children and both their biological and their adoptive parents.

Affective forecasting Efforts to predict one's emotional reactions to future events.

Afferent nerve fibers Axons that carry information inward to the central nervous system from the periphery of the body.

Afterimage A visual image that persists after a stimulus is removed.

Age of viability The age at which a baby can survive in the event of a premature birth.

Aggression Any behavior that is intended to hurt someone, either physically or verbally.

Agonist A chemical that mimics the action of a neurotransmitter.

Agoraphobia A fear of going out to public places.

Alcohol A variety of beverages containing ethyl alcohol.

Amnesia See *Anterograde amnesia, Retrograde amnesia.*

Anecdotal evidence Personal stories about specific incidents and experiences.

Animism The belief that all things are living.

Anorexia nervosa Eating disorder characterized by intense fear of gaining weight, disturbed body image, refusal to maintain normal weight, and dangerous measures to lose weight.

Antagonist A chemical that opposes the action of a neurotransmitter.

Anterograde amnesia Loss of memories for events that occur after a head injury.

Antianxiety drugs Medications that relieve tension, apprehension, and nervousness.

Antidepressant drugs Medications that gradually elevate mood and help bring people out of a depression.

Antipsychotic drugs Medications used to gradually reduce psychotic symptoms, including hyper-

activity, mental confusion, hallucinations, and delusions.

Anxiety disorders A class of disorders marked by feelings of excessive apprehension and anxiety.

Applied psychology The branch of psychology concerned with everyday, practical problems.

Approach-approach conflict A conflict situation in which a choice must be made between two attractive goals.

Approach-avoidance conflict A conflict situation in which a choice must be made about whether to pursue a single goal that has both attractive and unattractive aspects.

Archetypes According to Jung, emotionally charged images and thought forms that have universal meaning.

Argument One or more premises used to provide support for a conclusion.

Assumptions Premises for which no proof or evidence is offered.

Attachment A close, emotional bond of affection between infants and their caregivers.

Attention Focusing awareness on a narrowed range of stimuli or events.

Attitudes Orientations that locate objects of thought on dimensions of judgment.

Attributions Inferences that people draw about the causes of events, others' behavior, and their own behavior.

Autonomic nervous system (ANS) The system of nerves that connect to the heart, blood vessels, smooth muscles, and glands.

Availability heuristic Basing the estimated probability of an event on the ease with which relevant instances come to mind.

Aversion therapy A behavior therapy in which an aversive stimulus is paired with a stimulus that elicits an undesirable response.

Avoidance-avoidance conflict A conflict situation in which a choice must be made between two unattractive goals.

Avoidance learning Learning that has occurred when an organism engages in a response that prevents aversive stimulation from occurring.

Axon A long, thin fiber that transmits signals away from the neuron cell body to other neurons, or to muscles or glands.

B

Basilar membrane A structure that runs the length of the cochlea in the inner ear and holds the auditory receptors, called hair cells.

Behavior Any overt (observable) response or activity by an organism.

Behavior modification A systematic approach to changing behavior through the application of the principles of conditioning.

Behavior therapies Application of the principles of learning to direct efforts to change clients' maladaptive behaviors.

Behavioral contract A written agreement outlining a promise to adhere to the contingencies of a behavior modification program.

Behaviorism A theoretical orientation based on the premise that scientific psychology should study only observable behavior.

Binocular depth cues Clues about distance based on the differing views of the two eyes.

Biological rhythms Periodic fluctuations in physiological functioning.

Biomedical therapies Physiological interventions intended to reduce symptoms associated with psychological disorders.

Biopsychosocial model A model of illness that holds that physical illness is caused by a complex interaction of biological, psychological, and sociocultural factors.

Bipolar disorder (formerly known as manic-depressive disorder) Mood disorder marked by the experience of both depressed and manic periods.

Bisexuals Persons who seek emotional-sexual relationships with members of either sex.

Bottom-up processing In form perception, progression from individual elements to the whole.

Bounded rationality. See *Theory of bounded rationality.*

Bulimia nervosa Eating disorder characterized by habitually engaging in out-of-control overeating followed by unhealthy compensatory efforts, such as self-induced vomiting, fasting, abuse of laxatives and diuretics, and excessive exercise.

Bystander effect A paradoxical social phenomenon in which people are less likely to provide needed help when they are in groups than when they are alone.

C

Cannabis The hemp plant from which marijuana, hashish, and THC are derived.

Case study An in-depth investigation of an individual subject.

Catastrophic thinking Unrealistically pessimistic appraisals of stress that exaggerate the magnitude of one's problems.

Catatonic schizophrenia A type of schizophrenia marked by striking motor disturbances, ranging from muscular rigidity to random motor activity.

Catharsis The release of emotional tension.

Central nervous system (CNS) The brain and the spinal cord.

Centration The tendency to focus on just one feature of a problem, neglecting other important aspects.

Cephalocaudal trend The head-to-foot direction of motor development.

Cerebellum A relatively large and deeply folded structure located adjacent to the back surface of the brainstem.

Cerebral cortex The convoluted outer layer of the cerebrum.

Cerebral hemispheres The right and left halves of the cerebrum.

Channel The medium through which a message is sent.

Chromosomes Threadlike strands of DNA (deoxyribonucleic acid) molecules that carry genetic information.

Chunk A group of familiar stimuli stored as a single unit.

Circadian rhythms The 24-hour biological cycles found in humans and many other species.

Classical conditioning A type of learning in which a neutral stimulus acquires the ability to evoke a response that was originally evoked by another stimulus.

Client-centered therapy An insight therapy that emphasizes providing a supportive emotional climate for clients, who play a major role in determining the pace and direction of their therapy.

Clinical psychologists Psychologists who specialize in the diagnosis and treatment of psychological disorders and everyday behavioral problems.

Clinical psychology The branch of psychology concerned with the diagnosis and treatment of psychological problems and disorders.

Cochlea The fluid-filled, coiled tunnel in the inner ear that contains the receptors for hearing.

Coefficient of determination The percentage of variation in one variable that can be predicted based on the other variable.

Cognition The mental processes involved in acquiring knowledge.

Cognitive-behavioral treatments A varied combination of verbal interventions and behavioral modification techniques used to help clients change maladaptive patterns of thinking.

Cognitive development Transitions in youngsters' patterns of thinking, including reasoning, remembering, and problem solving.

Cognitive dissonance A psychological state that exists when related cognitions are inconsistent.

Cognitive therapy An insight therapy that emphasizes recognizing and changing negative thoughts and maladaptive beliefs.

Collective unconscious According to Jung, a storehouse of latent memory traces inherited from people's ancestral past.

Collectivism Putting group goals ahead of personal goals and defining one's identity in terms of the groups one belongs to.

Color blindness Deficiency in the ability to distinguish among colors.

Comorbidity The coexistence of two or more disorders.

Companionate love Warm, trusting, tolerant affection for another whose life is deeply intertwined with one's own.

Comparitors People, objects, events, and other standards that are used as a baseline for comparisons in making judgments.

Compensation According to Adler, efforts to overcome imagined or real inferiorities by developing one's abilities.

Complementary colors Pairs of colors that produce gray tones when added together.

Concordance rate The percentage of twin pairs or other pairs of relatives that exhibit the same disorder.

Conditioned reinforcers. See *Secondary reinforcers.*

Conditioned response (CR) A learned reaction to a conditioned stimulus that occurs because of previous conditioning.

Conditioned stimulus (CS) A previously neutral stimulus that has, through conditioning, acquired the capacity to evoke a conditioned response.

Cones Specialized visual receptors that play a key role in daylight vision and color vision.

Conflict A state that occurs when two or more incompatible motivations or behavioral impulses compete for expression.

Conformity The tendency for people to yield to real or imagined social pressure.

Confounding of variables A condition that exists whenever two variables are linked together in a way that makes it difficult to sort out their independent effects.

Conjunction fallacy An error that occurs when people estimate that the odds of two uncertain events happening together are greater than the odds of either event happening alone.

Connectionist models See *Parallel distributed processing (PDP) models.*

Conscious Whatever one is aware of at a particular point in time.

Consciousness One's awareness of internal and external stimuli.

Conservation Piaget's term for the awareness that physical quantities remain constant in spite of changes in their shape or appearance.

Consolidation A hypothetical process involving the gradual conversion of information into durable memory codes stored in long-term memory.

Constructive coping Relatively healthful efforts that people make to deal with stressful events.

Continuous reinforcement Reinforcing every instance of a designated response.

Control group Subjects in a study who do not receive the special treatment given to the experimental group.

Convergent thinking Narrowing down a list of alternatives to converge on a single correct answer.

Conversion disorder A somatoform disorder characterized by a significant loss of physical function (with no apparent organic basis), usually in a single organ system.

Coping Active efforts to master, reduce, or tolerate the demands created by stress.

Corpus callosum The structure that connects the two cerebral hemispheres.

Correlation The extent to which two variables are related to each other.

Correlation coefficient A numerical index of the degree of relationship between two variables.

Counseling psychologists Psychologists who specialize in the treatment of everyday adjustment problems.

Creativity The generation of ideas that are original, novel, and useful.

Critical period A limited time span in the development of an organism when it is optimal for certain capacities to emerge because the organism is especially responsive to certain experiences.

Critical thinking Purposeful, reasoned, goal-directed thinking that involves solving problems, formulating inferences, working with probabilities, and making carefully thought-out decisions.

Cross-sectional study A research design in which investigators compare groups of subjects of differing age who are observed at a single point in time.

Crystallized intelligence Intelligence that involves the ability to apply acquired knowledge and skills in problem solving.

Culture The widely shared customs, beliefs, values, norms, institutions, and other products of a community that are transmitted socially across generations.

Culture-bound disorders Abnormal syndromes found only in a few cultural groups.

Cumulative recorder A graphic record of reinforcement and responding in a Skinner box as a function of time.

D

Dark adaptation The process in which the eyes become more sensitive to light in low illumination.

Data collection techniques Procedures for making empirical observations and measurements.

Decay theory The idea that forgetting occurs because memory traces fade with time.

Decision making The process of evaluating alternatives and making choices among them.

Declarative memory system Memory for factual information.

Deep brain stimulation Approach to treating psychological disorders in which a thin electrode is surgically implanted in the brain and connected to an implanted pulse generator so that various electrical currents can be delivered to brain tissue adjacent to the electrode.

Defense mechanisms Largely unconscious reactions that protect a person from unpleasant emotions such as anxiety and guilt.

Deinstitutionalization Transferring the treatment of mental illness from inpatient institutions to community-based facilities that emphasize outpatient care.

Delusions False beliefs that are maintained even though they are clearly out of touch with reality.

Dementia An abnormal condition marked by multiple cognitive defects that include memory impairment.

Dendrites Branchlike parts of a neuron that are specialized to receive information.

Dependent variable In an experiment, the variable that is thought to be affected by the manipulation of the independent variable.

Depth perception Interpretation of visual cues that indicate how near or far away objects are.

Descriptive statistics Statistics that are used to organize and summarize data.

Development The sequence of age-related changes that occur as a person progresses from conception to death.

Developmental norms The average age at which individuals display various behaviors and abilities.

Deviation IQ scores Scores that locate subjects precisely within the normal distribution, using the standard deviation as the unit of measurement.

Diagnosis Distinguishing one illness from another.

Discrimination Behaving differently, usually unfairly, toward the members of a group.

Discriminative stimuli Cues that influence operant behavior by indicating the probable consequences (reinforcement or nonreinforcement) of a response.

Disorganized schizophrenia A type of schizophrenia in which particularly severe deterioration of adaptive behavior is seen.

Displacement Diverting emotional feelings (usually anger) from their original source to a substitute target.

Display rules Cultural norms that regulate the appropriate expressions of emotions.

Dissociation A splitting off of mental processes into two separate, simultaneous streams of awareness.

Dissociative amnesia A sudden loss of memory for important personal information that is too extensive to be due to normal forgetting.

Dissociative disorders A class of disorders in which people lose contact with portions of their consciousness or memory, resulting in disruptions in their sense of identity.

Dissociative fugue A disorder in which people lose their memory for their entire lives along with their sense of personal identity.

Dissociative identity disorder A type of dissociative disorder characterized by the coexistence in one person of two or more largely complete, and usually very different, personalities. Also called multiple-personality disorder.

Divergent thinking Trying to expand the range of alternatives by generating many possible solutions.

Door-in-the-face technique Making a large request that is likely to be turned down as a way to increase the chances that people will agree to a smaller request later.

Double-blind procedure A research strategy in which neither subjects nor experimenters know which subjects are in the experimental or control groups.

Dream analysis A psychoanalytic technique in which the therapist interprets the symbolic meaning of the client's dreams.

Dual-coding theory Paivio's theory that memory is enhanced by forming semantic and visual codes, since either can lead to recall.

Drive An internal state of tension that motivates an organism to engage in activities that should reduce the tension.

E

Eating disorders Severe disturbances in eating behavior characterized by preoccupation with weight concerns and unhealthy efforts to control weight.

Efferent nerve fibers Axons that carry information outward from the central nervous system to the periphery of the body.

Ego According to Freud, the decision-making component of personality that operates according to the reality principle.

Egocentrism A limited ability to share another person's viewpoint.

Elaboration Linking a stimulus to other information at the time of encoding.

Electrical stimulation of the brain (ESB) Sending a weak electric current into a brain structure to stimulate (activate) it.

Electrocardiograph (EKG) A device that records the contractions of the heart.

Electroconvulsive therapy (ECT) A biomedical treatment in which electric shock is used to produce a cortical seizure accompanied by convulsions.

Electroencephalograph (EEG) A device that monitors the electrical activity of the brain over time by means of recording electrodes attached to the surface of the scalp.

Electromyograph (EMG) A device that records muscular activity and tension.

Electrooculograph (EOG) A device that records eye movements.

Elicit To draw out or bring forth.

Embryonic stage The second stage of prenatal development, lasting from two weeks until the end of the second month.

Emit To send forth.

Emotion A subjective conscious experience (the cognitive component) accommpanied by bodily arousal (the physiological component) and by characteristic overt expression (the behavioral component).

Empiricism The premise that knowledge should be acquired through observation.

Encoding Forming a memory code.

Encoding specificity principle The idea that the value of a retrieval cue depends on how well it corresponds to the memory code.

Endocrine system A group of glands that secrete chemicals into the bloodstream that help control bodily functioning.

Endorphins The entire family of internally produced chemicals that resemble opiates in structure and effects.

Episodic memory system Chronological, or temporally dated, recollections of personal experiences.

Escape learning A type of learning in which an organism acquires a response that decreases or ends some aversive stimulation.

Etiology The apparent causation and developmental history of an illness.

Evaluative conditioning Efforts to transfer the emotion attached to a UCS to a new CS.

Evolutionary psychology Theoretical perspective that examines behavioral processes in terms of their adaptive value for a species over the course of many generations.

Experiment A research method in which the investigator manipulates a variable under carefully controlled conditions and observes whether any changes occur in a second variable as a result.

Experimental group The subjects in a study who receive some special treatment in regard to the independent variable.

Experimenter bias A phenomenon that occurs when a researcher's expectations or preferences about the outcome of a study influence the results obtained.

Expressed emotion The degree to which a relative of a schizophrenic patient displays highly critical or emotionally overinvolved attitudes toward the patient.

External attributions Ascribing the causes of behavior to situational demands and environmental constraints.

Extinction The gradual weakening and disappearance of a conditioned response tendency.

Extraneous variables Any variables other than the independent variable that seem likely to influence the dependent variable in a specific study.

F

Factor analysis Statistical analysis of correlations among many variables to identify closely related clusters of variables.

Family studies Scientific studies in which researchers assess hereditary influence by examining blood relatives to see how much they resemble each other on a specific trait.

Farsightedness A visual deficiency in which distant objects are seen clearly but close objects appear blurry.

Fast mapping The process by which children map a word onto an underlying concept after only one exposure.

Feature analysis The process of detecting specific elements in visual input and assembling them into a more complex form.

Feature detectors Neurons that respond selectively to very specific features of more complex stimuli.

Fetal alcohol syndrome A collection of congenital (inborn) problems associated with excessive alcohol use during pregnancy.

Fetal stage The third stage of prenatal development, lasting from two months through birth.

Fitness The reproductive success (number of descendants) of an individual organism relative to the average reproductive success of the population.

Fixation According to Freud, failure to move forward from one psychosexual stage to another as expected.

Fixed-interval (FI) schedule A reinforcement schedule in which the reinforcer is given for the first response that occurs after a fixed time interval has elapsed.

Fixed-ratio (FR) schedule A reinforcement schedule in which the reinforcer is given after a fixed number of nonreinforced responses.

Flashbulb memories Unusually vivid and detailed recollections of momentous events.

Fluid intelligence Type of intelligence that involves basic reasoning ability, memory capacity, and speed of information processing.

Foot-in-the-door technique Getting people to agree to a small request to increase the chances that they will agree to a larger request later.

Forebrain The largest and most complicated region of the brain, encompassing a variety of structures, including the thalamus, hypothalamus, limbic system, and cerebrum.

Forgetting curve A graph showing retention and forgetting over time.

Fovea A tiny spot in the center of the retina that contains only cones; visual acuity is greatest at this spot.

Free association A psychoanalytic technique in which clients spontaneously express their thoughts and feelings exactly as they occur, with as little censorship as possible.

Frequency distribution An orderly arrangement of scores indicating the frequency of each score or group of scores.

Frequency polygon A line figure used to present data from a frequency distribution.

Frequency theory Theory holding that perception of pitch corresponds to the rate, or frequency, at which the entire basilar membrane vibrates.

Frustration The feeling that people experience in any situation in which their pursuit of some goal is thwarted.

Functional fixedness The tendency to perceive an item only in terms of its most common use.

Functionalism A school of psychology based on the belief that psychology should investigate the function or purpose of consciousness, rather than its structure.

Fundamental attribution error Observers' bias in favor of internal attributions in explaining others' behavior.

G

Galvanic skin response (GSR) An increase in the electrical conductivity of the skin that occurs when sweat glands increase their activity.

Gambler's fallacy The belief that the odds of a chance event increase if the event hasn't occurred recently.

Gender Culturally constructed distinctions between masculinity and femininity.

Gender differences Actual disparities between the sexes in typical behavior or average ability.

Gender roles Expectations about what is appropriate behavior for each sex.

Gender stereotypes Widely held beliefs about males' and females' abilities, personality traits, and behavior.

General adaptation syndrome Selye's model of the body's stress response, consisting of three stages: alarm, resistance, and exhaustion.

Generalized anxiety disorder A psychological disorder marked by a chronic, high level of anxiety that is not tied to any specific threat.

Genes DNA segments that serve as the key functional units in hereditary transmission.

Germinal stage The first phase of prenatal development, encompassing the first two weeks after conception.

Glia Cells found throughout the nervous system that provide various types of support for neurons.

Glucose A simple sugar that is an important source of energy.

Glucostats Neurons sensitive to glucose in the surrounding fluid.

Group Two or more individuals who interact and are interdependent.

Group cohesiveness The strength of the liking relationships linking group members to each other and to the group itself.

Group polarization A phenomenon that occurs when group discussion strengthens a group's dominant point of view and produces a shift toward a more extreme decision in that direction.

Group therapy The simultaneous treatment of several clients in a group.

Groupthink A process in which members of a cohesive group emphasize concurrence at the expense of critical thinking in arriving at a decision.

Gustatory system The sensory system for taste.

H

Hallucinations Sensory perceptions that occur in the absence of a real, external stimulus, or gross distortions of perceptual input.

Hallucinogens A diverse group of drugs that have powerful effects on mental and emotional functioning, marked most prominently by distortions in sensory and perceptual experience.

Health psychology The subfield of psychology concerned with how psychosocial factors relate to the promotion and maintenance of health and with the causation, prevention, and treatment of illness.

Hedonistic adaptation An effect that occurs when the mental scale that people use to judge the pleasantness-unpleasantness of their experiences shifts so that their neutral point, or baseline for comparison, changes.

Heritability ratio An estimate of the proportion of trait variability in a population that is determined by variations in genetic inheritance.

Heterosexuals Persons who seek emotional-sexual relationships with members of the other sex.

Heuristic A strategy, guiding principle, or rule of thumb used in solving problems or making decisions.

Hierarchy of needs Maslow's systematic arrangement of needs according to priority, which assumes that basic needs must be met before less basic needs are aroused.

Higher-order conditioning A type of conditioning in which a conditioned stimulus functions as if it were an unconditioned stimulus.

Hill-climbing heuristic A problem-solving approach that entails selecting the alternative at each choice point that appears to lead most directly to one's goal.

Hindbrain The part of the brain that includes the cerebellum and two structures found in the lower part of the brainstem: the medulla and the pons.

Hindsight bias The tendency to mold one's interpretation of the past to fit how events actually turned out.

Histogram A bar graph that presents data from a frequency distribution.

Homeostasis A state of physiological equilibrium or stability.

Homosexuals Persons who seek emotional-sexual relationships with members of the same sex.

Hormones The chemical substances released by the endocrine glands.

Humanism A theoretical orientation that emphasizes the unique qualities of humans, especially their freedom and their potential for personal growth.

Hypnosis A systematic procedure that typically produces a heightened state of suggestibility.

Hypochondriasis A somatoform disorder characterized by excessive preoccupation with health concerns and incessant worry about developing physical illnesses.

Hypothalamus A structure found near the base of the forebrain that is involved in the regulation of basic biological needs.

Hypothesis A tentative statement about the relationship between two or more variables.

I

Id According to Freud, the primitive, instinctive component of personality that operates according to the pleasure principle.

Identification Bolstering self-esteem by forming an imaginary or real alliance with some person or group.

Illusory correlation A misperception that occurs when people estimate that they have encountered more confirmations of an association between social traits than they have actually seen.

Immune response The body's defensive reaction to invasion by bacteria, viral agents, or other foreign substances.

Impossible figures Objects that can be represented in two-dimensional pictures but cannot exist in three-dimensional space.

Inattentional blindness The failure to see fully visible objects or events in a visual display because one's attention is focused elsewhere.

Incentive An external goal that has the capacity to motivate behavior.

Incongruence The degree of disparity between one's self-concept and one's actual experience.

Independent variable In an experiment, a condition or event that an experimenter varies in order to see its impact on another variable.

Individualism Putting personal goals ahead of group goals and defining one's identity in terms of personal attributes rather than group memberships.

Inferential statistics Statistics that are used to interpret data and draw conclusions.

Ingroup The group that people belong to and identify with.

Insight In problem solving, the sudden discovery of the correct solution following incorrect attempts based primarily on trial and error.

Insight therapies Psychotherapy methods characterized by verbal interactions intended to enhance clients' self-knowledge and thus promote healthful changes in personality and behavior.

Insomnia Chronic problems in getting adequate sleep.

Intelligence quotient (IQ) A child's mental age divided by chronological age, multiplied by 100.

Interference theory The idea that people forget information because of competition from other material.

Intermittent reinforcement A reinforcement schedule in which a designated response is reinforced only some of the time.

Internal attributions Ascribing the causes of behavior to personal dispositions, traits, abilities, and feelings.

Internet addiction Spending an inordinate amount of time on the Internet and being unable to control online use.

Interpersonal attraction Positive feelings toward another.

Introspection Careful, systematic observation of one's own conscious experience.

Irreversibility The inability to envision reversing an action.

J

Journal A periodical that publishes technical and scholarly material, usually in a narrowly defined area of inquiry.

L

Latent content According to Freud, the hidden or disguised meaning of the events in a dream.

Latent learning Learning that is not apparent from behavior when it first occurs.

Learned helplessness Passive behavior produced by exposure to unavoidable aversive events.

Learning A relatively durable change in behavior or knowledge that is due to experience.

Lens The transparent eye structure that focuses the light rays falling on the retina.

Lesioning Destroying a piece of the brain.

Levels-of-processing theory The theory holding that deeper levels of mental processing result in longer-lasting memory codes.

Lie detector See *Polygraph.*

Life changes Any noticeable alterations in one's living circumstances that require readjustment.

Light adaptation The process whereby the eyes become less sensitive to light in high illumination.

Limbic system A densely connected network of structures roughly located along the border between the cerebral cortex and deeper subcortical areas.

Link method Forming a mental image of items to be remembered in a way that links them together.

Long-term memory (LTM) An unlimited capacity store that can hold information over lengthy periods of time.

Long-term potentiation (LTP) A long-lasting increase in neural excitability at synapses along a specific neural pathway.

Lowball technique Getting someone to commit to an attractive proposition before revealing the hidden costs.

M

Major depressive disorder Mood disorder characterized by persistent feelings of sadness and despair and a loss of interest in previous sources of pleasure.

Manic-depressive disorder See *Bipolar disorder*.

Manifest content According to Freud, the plot of a dream at a surface level.

Matching hypothesis The idea that males and females of approximately equal physical attractiveness are likely to select each other as partners.

Maturation Development that reflects the gradual unfolding of one's genetic blueprint.

MDMA A compound drug related to both amphetamines and hallucinogens, especially mescaline; commonly called "ecstasy."

Mean The arithmetic average of the scores in a distribution.

Median The score that falls exactly in the center of a distribution of scores.

Medical model The view that it is useful to think of abnormal behavior as a disease.

Meditation A family of mental exercises in which a conscious attempt is made to focus attention in a nonanalytical way.

Menarche The first occurrence of menstruation.

Mental age In intelligence testing, a score that indicates that a child displays the mental ability typical of a child of that chronological (actual) age.

Mental hospital A medical institution specializing in providing inpatient care for psychological disorders.

Mental set Persisting in using problem-solving strategies that have worked in the past.

Message The information transmitted by a source.

Method of loci A mnemonic device that involves taking an imaginary walk along a familiar path where images of items to be remembered are associated with certain locations.

Midbrain The segment of the brain stem that lies between the hindbrain and the forebrain.

Mirror neurons Neurons that are activated by performing an action or by seeing another monkey or person perform the same action.

Misinformation effect Phenomenon that occurs when participants' recall of an event they witnessed is altered by introducing misleading post-event information.

Mnemonic devices Strategies for enhancing memory.

Mode The score that occurs most frequently in a distribution.

Model A person whose behavior is observed by another.

Monocular depth cues Clues about distance based on the image from either eye alone.

Mood disorders A class of disorders marked by emotional disturbances of varied kinds that may spill over to disrupt physical, perceptual, social, and thought processes.

Mood stabilizers Drugs used to control mood swings in patients with bipolar mood disorders.

Motivation Goal-directed behavior.

Motor development The progression of muscular coordination required for physical activities.

Multiple-personality disorder See *Dissociative identity disorder*.

Myelin sheath Insulating material, derived from glial cells, that encases some axons of neurons.

N

Narcolepsy A disease marked by sudden and irresistible onsets of sleep during normal waking periods.

Narcotics (opiates) Drugs derived from opium that are capable of relieving pain.

Natural selection Principle stating that inherited characteristics that provide a survival or reproductive advantage are more likely than alternative characteristics to be passed on to subsequent generations and thus come to be "selected" over time.

Naturalistic observation A descriptive research method in which the researcher engages in careful, usually prolonged, observation of behavior without intervening directly with the subjects.

Nearsightedness A visual deficiency in which close objects are seen clearly but distant objects appear blurry.

Need for self-actualization The need to fulfill one's potential.

Negative reinforcement The strengthening of a response because it is followed by the removal of an aversive (unpleasant) stimulus.

Negative symptoms Schizophrenic symptoms that involve behavioral deficits, such as flattened emotions, social withdrawal, apathy, impaired attention, and poverty of speech.

Negatively skewed distribution A distribution in which most scores pile up at the high end of the scale.

Neurogenesis The formation of new neurons.

Neurons Individual cells in the nervous system that receive, integrate, and transmit information.

Neurotransmitters Chemicals that transmit information from one neuron to another.

Nondeclarative memory system The repository for memories for actions, skills, conditioned responses, and emotional memories. Also called *procedural memory*.

Non-REM (NREM) sleep Sleep stages 1 through 4, which are marked by an absence of rapid eye movements, relatively little dreaming, and varied EEG activity.

Nonsense syllables Consonant-vowel-consonant arrangements that do not correspond to words.

Normal distribution A symmetric, bell-shaped curve that represents the pattern in which many characteristics are dispersed in the population.

Null hypothesis In inferential statistics, the assumption that there is no true relationship between the variables being observed.

O

Obedience A form of compliance that occurs when people follow direct commands, usually from someone in a position of authority.

Object permanence Recognizing that objects continue to exist even when they are no longer visible.

Observational learning A type of learning that occurs when an organism's responding is influenced by the observation of others, who are called models.

Obsessive-compulsive disorder (OCD) A type of anxiety disorder marked by persistent, uncontrollable intrusions of unwanted thoughts (obsessions) and urges to engage in senseless rituals (compulsions).

Oedipal complex According to Freud, children's manifestation of erotically tinged desires for their opposite-sex parent, accompanied by feelings of hostility toward their same-sex parent.

Olfactory system The sensory system for smell.

Operant conditioning A form of learning in which voluntary responses come to be controlled by their consequences.

Operational definition A definition that describes the actions or operations that will be used to measure or control a variable.

Opiates. See *Narcotics*.

Optic chiasm The point at which the axons from the inside half of each eye cross over and then project to the opposite half of the brain.

Opponent process theory The idea that color perception depends on receptors that make antagonistic responses to three pairs of colors.

Optimism A general tendency to expect good outcomes.

Outgroup People who are not part of the ingroup.

Overextension Mistake in language learning that occurs when a child incorrectly uses a word to describe a wider set of objects or actions than it is meant to.

Overlearning Continued rehearsal of material after one first appears to have mastered it.

Overregulation Mistake in language learning in which a child incorrectly generalizes grammatical rules to irregular cases where they do not apply.

P

Panic disorder A type of anxiety disorder characterized by recurrent attacks of overwhelming anxiety that usually occur suddenly and unexpectedly.

Parallel distributed processing (PDP) models Models of memory that assume cognitive processes depend on patterns of activation in highly interconnected computational networks that resemble neural networks. Also called connectionist models.

Paranoid schizophrenia A type of schizophrenia that is dominated by delusions of persecution along with delusions of grandeur.

Parental investment What each sex invests—in terms of time, energy, survival risk, and forgone opportunities—to produce and nurture offspring.

Parasympathetic division The branch of the autonomic nervous system that generally conserves bodily resources.

Participants The persons or animals whose behavior is systematically observed in a study.

Passionate love A complete absorption in another that includes tender sexual feelings and the agony and ecstasy of intense emotion.

Pavlovian conditioning. See *Classical conditioning*.

Percentile score A figure that indicates the percentage of people who score below the score one has obtained.

Perception The selection, organization, and interpretation of sensory input.

Perceptual constancy A tendency to experience a stable perception in the face of continually changing sensory input.

Perceptual hypothesis An inference about what form could be responsible for a pattern of sensory stimulation.

Perceptual set A readiness to perceive a stimulus in a particular way.

Peripheral nervous system All those nerves that lie outside the brain and spinal cord.

Person perception The process of forming impressions of others.

Personality An individual's unique constellation of consistent behavioral traits.

Personality trait A durable disposition to behave in a particular way in a variety of situations.

Phi phenomenon The illusion of movement created by presenting visual stimuli in rapid succession.

Phobic disorder A type of anxiety disorder marked by a persistent and irrational fear of an object or situation that presents no realistic danger.

Physical dependence The condition that exists when a person must continue to take a drug to avoid withdrawal illness.

Pictorial depth cues Clues about distance that can be given in a flat picture.

Pituitary gland The "master gland" of the endocrine system; it releases a great variety of hormones that fan out through the body, stimulating actions in the other endocrine glands.

Place theory The idea that perception of pitch corresponds to the vibration of different portions, or places, along the basilar membrane.

Placebo effects The fact that subjects' expectations can lead them to experience some change even though they receive an empty, fake, or ineffectual treatment.

Placenta A structure that allows oxygen and nutrients to pass into the fetus from the mother's bloodstream and bodily wastes to pass out to the mother.

Pleasure principle According to Freud, the principle upon which the id operates, demanding immediate gratification of its urges.

Polygenic traits Characteristics that are influenced by more than one pair of genes.

Polygraph A device that records autonomic fluctuations while a subject is questioned, in an effort to determine whether the subject is telling the truth.

Population The larger collection of animals or people from which a sample is drawn and that researchers want to generalize about.

Positive psychology Approach to psychology that uses theory and research to better understand the positive, adaptive, creative, and fulfilling aspects of human existence.

Positive reinforcement Reinforcement that occurs when a response is strengthened because it is followed by the presentation of a rewarding stimulus.

Positive symptoms Schizophrenic symptoms that involve behavioral excesses or peculiarities, such as hallucinations, delusions, bizarre behavior, and wild flights of ideas.

Positively skewed distribution A distribution in which scores pile up at the low end of the scale.

Postsynaptic potential (PSP) A voltage change at the receptor site on a postsynaptic cell membrane.

Posttraumatic stress disorder (PTSD) Disturbed behavior that is attributed to a major stressful event but that emerges after the stress is over.

Preconscious According to Freud, the level of awareness that contains material just beneath the surface of conscious awareness that can easily be retrieved.

Prejudice A negative attitude held toward members of a group.

Premises The reasons presented to persuade someone that a conclusion is true or probably true.

Prenatal period The period from conception to birth, usually encompassing nine months of pregnancy.

Preparedness Species-specific predisposition to be conditioned in certain ways and not others.

Pressure Expectations or demands that one behave in a certain way.

Primary reinforcers Events that are inherently reinforcing because they satisfy biological needs.

Primary sex characteristics The sexual structures necessary for reproduction.

Proactive interference A memory problem that occurs when previously learned information interferes with the retention of new information.

Problem solving Active efforts to discover what must be done to achieve a goal that is not readily available.

Procedural memory system See *Nondeclarative memory system*.

Prognosis A forecast about the probable course of an illness.

Projection Attributing one's own thoughts, feelings, or motives to another.

Projective tests Psychological tests that ask subjects to respond to vague, ambiguous stimuli in ways that may reveal the subjects' needs, feelings, and personality traits.

Prospective memory The ability to remember to perform actions in the future.

Proximodistal trend The center-outward direction of motor development.

Psychiatrists Physicians who specialize in the diagnosis and treatment of psychological disorders.

Psychoactive drugs Chemical substances that modify mental, emotional, or behavioral functioning.

Psychoanalysis An insight therapy that emphasizes the recovery of unconscious conflicts, motives, and defenses through techniques such as free association and transference.

Psychoanalytic theory A theory developed by Freud that attempts to explain personality, motivation, and mental disorders by focusing on unconscious determinants of behavior.

Psychological dependence The condition that exists when a person must continue to take a drug in order to satisfy intense mental and emotional craving for the drug.

Psychological test A standardized measure of a sample of a person's behavior.

Psychology The science that studies behavior and the physiological and cognitive processes that underlie it, and the profession that applies the accumulated knowledge of this science to practical problems.

Psychosexual stages According to Freud, developmental periods with a characteristic sexual focus that leave their mark on adult personality.

Psychosomatic diseases Physical ailments with a genuine organic basis that are caused in part by psychological factors, especially emotional distress.

Puberty The period of early adolescence marked by rapid physical growth and the development of sexual (reproductive) maturity.

Punishment An event that follows a response that weakens or suppresses the tendency to make that response.

Pupil The opening in the center of the iris that helps regulate the amount of light passing into the rear chamber of the eye.

R

Random assignment The design of a study such that all subjects have an equal chance of being assigned to any group or condition.

Rationalization Creating false but plausible excuses to justify unacceptable behavior.

Reaction formation Behaving in a way that's exactly the opposite of one's true feelings.

Reaction range Genetically determined limits on IQ or other traits.

Reactivity Alteration of a subject's behavior due to the presence of an observer.

Reality principle According to Freud, the principle on which the ego operates, which seeks to delay gratification of the id's urges until appropriate outlets and situations can be found.

Recall measure A memory test that requires subjects to reproduce information on their own without any cues.

Receiver The person to whom a message is sent.

Receptive field of a visual cell The retinal area that, when stimulated, affects the firing of that cell.

Reciprocity Liking those who show that they like you.

Reciprocity norm The rule that people should pay back in kind what they receive from others.

Recognition measure A memory test that requires subjects to select previously learned information from an array of options.

Regression A reversion to immature patterns of behavior.

Regression toward the mean Effect that occurs when people who score extremely high or low on some trait are measured a second time and their new score falls closer to the mean (average).

Rehearsal The process of repetitively verbalizing or thinking about information to be stored in memory.

Reification Giving an abstract concept a name and then treating it as though it were a concrete, tangible object.

Reinforcement An event following a response that strengthens the tendency to make that response.

Reinforcement contingencies The circumstances or rules that determine whether responses lead to the presentation of reinforcers.

Relearning measure A memory test that requires a subject to memorize information a second time to determine how much time or effort is saved by having learned it before.

Reliability The measurement consistency of a test (or of other kinds of measurement techniques).

REM sleep A deep stage of sleep marked by rapid eye movements, high-frequency brain waves, and dreaming.

Renewal effect Referring to the phenomenon that occurs if a response is extinguished in a different environment than it was acquired; the extinguished response will reappear if the animal is returned to the original environment where acquisition took place.

Replication The repetition of a study to see whether the earlier results are duplicated.

Representativeness heuristic Basing the estimated probability of an event on how similar it is to the typical prototype of that event.

Repression Keeping distressing thoughts and feelings buried in the unconscious.

Research methods Differing approaches to the observation, measurement, and manipulation and control of variables in empirical studies.

Resistance Largely unconscious defensive maneuvers a client uses to hinder the progress of therapy.

Resistance to extinction In operant conditioning, the phenomenon that occurs when an organism continues to make a response after delivery of the reinforcer for it has been terminated.

Resting potential The stable, negative charge of a neuron when it is inactive.

Retention The proportion of material retained (remembered).

Retina The neural tissue lining the inside back surface of the eye; it absorbs light, processes images, and sends visual information to the brain.

Retinal disparity A cue to the depth based on the fact that objects within 25 feet project images to slightly different locations on the left and right retinas, so the right and left eyes see slightly different views of the object.

Retrieval Recovering information from memory stores.

Retroactive interference A memory problem that occurs when new information impairs the retention of previously learned information.

Retrograde amnesia Loss of memories for events that occurred prior to a head injury.

Retrospective memory The ability to remember events from the past or previously learned information.

Reuptake A process in which neurotransmitters are sponged up from the synaptic cleft by the presynaptic membrane.

Reversible figure A drawing that is compatible with two different interpretations that can shift back and forth.

Risky decision making Making choices under conditions of uncertainty.

Rods Specialized visual receptors that play a key role in night vision and peripheral vision.

S

Sample The collection of subjects selected for observation in an empirical study.

Sampling bias A problem that occurs when a sample is not representative of the population from which it is drawn.

Scatter diagram A graph in which paired X and Y scores for each subject are plotted as single points.

Schedule of reinforcement A specific presentation of reinforcers over time.

Schema An organized cluster of knowledge about a particular object or sequence of events.

Schizophrenic disorders A class of psychological disorders marked by disturbances in thought that spill over to affect perceptual, social, and emotional processes.

Secondary (conditioned) reinforcers Stimulus events that acquire reinforcing qualities by being associated with primary reinforcers.

Secondary sex characteristics Physical features that are associated with gender but that are not directly involved in reproduction.

Sedatives Sleep-inducing drugs that tend to decrease central nervous system activation and behavioral activity.

Self-actualizing persons People with exceptionally healthy personalities, marked by continued personal growth.

Self-concept A collection of beliefs about one's own nature, unique qualities, and typical behavior.

Self-efficacy One's belief about one's ability to perform behaviors that should lead to expected outcomes.

Self-report inventories Personality tests that ask individuals to answer a series of questions about their characteristic behavior.

Self-serving bias The tendency to attribute one's successes to personal factors and one's failures to situational factors.

Semantic memory system General knowledge that is not tied to the time when the information was learned.

Semantic network Concepts joined together by links that show how the concepts are related.

Sensation The stimulation of sense organs.

Sensory adaptation A gradual decline in sensitivity to prolonged stimulation.

Sensory memory The preservation of information in its original sensory form for a brief time, usually only a fraction of a second.

Separation anxiety Emotional distress seen in many infants when they are separated from people with whom they have formed an attachment.

Serial-position effect In memory tests, the fact that subjects show better recall for items at the beginning and end of a list than for items in the middle.

Sex The biologically based categories of male and female.

Sexual orientation A person's preference for emotional and sexual relationships with individuals of the same sex, the other sex, or either sex.

Shaping The reinforcement of closer and closer approximations of a desired response.

Short-term memory (STM) A limited-capacity store that can maintain unrehearsed information for about 20 to 30 seconds.

Skinner box A small enclosure in which an animal can make a specific response that is systematically recorded while the consequences of the response are controlled.

Sleep apnea A sleep disorder characterized by frequent reflexive gasping for air that awakens the sleeper and disrupts sleep.

Slow-wave sleep Sleep stages 3 and 4, during which low-frequency delta waves become prominent in EEG recordings.

Social desirability bias A tendency to give socially approved answers to questions about oneself.

Social loafing A reduction in effort by individuals when they work in groups as compared to when they work by themselves.

Social psychology The branch of psychology concerned with the way individuals' thoughts, feelings, and behaviors are influenced by others.

Social roles Widely shared expectations about how people in certain positions are supposed to behave.

Social skills training A behavior therapy designed to improve interpersonal skills that emphasizes shaping, modeling, and behavioral rehearsal.

Social support Various types of aid and succor provided by members of one's social networks.

Socialization The acquisition of the norms, roles, and behaviors expected of people in a particular society.

Soma The cell body of a neuron; it contains the nucleus and much of the chemical machinery common to most cells.

Somatic nervous system The system of nerves that connect to voluntary skeletal muscles and to sensory receptors.

Somatization disorder A type of somatoform disorder marked by a history of diverse physical complaints that appear to be psychological in origin.

Somatoform disorders A class of psychological disorders involving physical ailments with no authentic organic basis that are due to psychological factors.

Somnambulism Arising and walking about while remaining asleep; sleepwalking.

Source The person who sends a communication.

Source monitoring The process of making attributions about the origins of memories.

Source-monitoring error An error that occurs when a memory derived from one source is misattributed to another source.

Spermarche The first occurrence of ejaculation.

Split-brain surgery A procedure in which the bundle of fibers that connects the cerebral hemispheres (the corpus callosum) is cut to reduce the severity of epileptic seizures.

Spontaneous recovery In classical conditioning, the reappearance of an extinguished response after a period of nonexposure to the conditioned stimulus.

Stage A developmental period during which characteristic patterns of behavior are exhibited and certain capacities become established.

Standard deviation An index of the amount of variability in a set of data.

Standardization The uniform procedures used in the administration and scoring of a test.

Statistical significance The condition that exists when the probability that the observed findings are due to chance is very low.

Statistics The use of mathematics to organize, summarize, and interpret numerical data. See also *Descriptive statistics, Inferential statistics.*

Stereotypes Widely held beliefs that people have certain characteristics because of their membership in a particular group.

Stimulants Drugs that tend to increase central nervous system activation and behavioral activity.

Stimulus discrimination The phenomenon that occurs when an organism that has learned a response to a specific stimulus does not respond in the same way to stimuli that are similar to the original stimulus.

Stimulus generalization The phenomenon that occurs when an organism that has learned a response to a specific stimulus responds in the same way to new stimuli that are similar to the original stimulus.

Storage Maintaining encoded information in memory over time.

Stress Any circumstances that threaten or are perceived to threaten one's well-being and that thereby tax one's coping abilities.

Striving for superiority According to Adler, the universal drive to adapt, improve oneself, and master life's challenges.

Structuralism A school of psychology based on the notion that the task of psychology is to analyze consciousness into its basic elements and to investigate how these elements are related.

Subjective well-being Individuals' perceptions of their overall happiness and life satisfaction.

Subjects See *participants*.

Subtractive color mixing Formation of colors by removing some wavelengths of light, leaving less light than was originally there.

Superego According to Freud, the moral component of personality that incorporates social standards about what represents right and wrong.

Survey A descriptive research method in which researchers use questionnaires or interviews to gather information about specific aspects of subjects' behavior.

Sympathetic division The branch of the autonomic nervous system that mobilizes the body's resources for emergencies.

Synapse A junction where information is transmitted from one neuron to the next.

Synaptic cleft A microscopic gap between the terminal button of a neuron and the cell membrane of another neuron.

Systematic desensitization A behavior therapy used to reduce clients' anxiety responses through counterconditioning.

T

Tardive dyskinesia A neurological disorder marked by chronic tremors and involuntary spastic movements.

Telegraphic speech Referring to a child's early sentences, which consist mainly of content words; articles, prepositions, and other less critical words are omitted.

Terminal buttons Small knobs at the end of axons that secrete chemicals called neurotransmitters.

Testosterone A male sex hormone produced by the testes; women secrete smaller amounts of testosterone from the adrenal cortex and ovary.

Testwiseness The ability to use the characteristics and format of a cognitive test to maximize one's score.

Thalamus A structure in the forebrain through which all sensory information (except smell) must pass to get to the cerebral cortex.

Theory A system of interrelated ideas that is used to explain a set of observations.

Theory of bounded rationality The idea that people tend to use simple strategies in decision making that focus on only a few facets of available options and often result in "irrational" decisions that are less than optimal.

Tip-of-the-tongue phenomenon The temporary inability to remember something you know, accompanied by a feeling that it's just out of reach.

Tolerance A progressive decrease in a person's responsiveness to a drug.

Top-down processing In form perception, a progression from the whole to the elements.

Transcranial magnetic stimulation (TMS) A technique that permits scientists to temporarily enhance or depress activity in a specific area of the brain.

Transference In therapy, the phenomenon that occurs when clients start relating to their therapists in ways that mimic critical relationships in their lives.

Trial In classical conditioning, any presentation of a stimulus or pair of stimuli.

Trial and error Trying possible solutions sequentially and discarding those that are in error until one works.

Trichromatic theory The idea that the human eye has three types of receptors with differing sensitivities to different light wavelengths.

Twin studies A research design in which hereditary influence is assessed by comparing the resemblance of identical twins and fraternal twins with respect to a trait.

Type A personality Personality characterized by (1) a strong competitive orientation, (2) impatience and time urgency, and (3) anger and hostility.

Type B personality Personality characterized by relatively relaxed, patient, easygoing, amicable behavior.

U

Unconditioned response (UCR) An unlearned reaction to an unconditioned stimulus that occurs without previous conditioning.

Unconditioned stimulus (UCS) A stimulus that evokes an unconditioned response without previous conditioning.

Unconscious According to Freud, thoughts, memories, and desires that are well below the surface of conscious awareness but that nonetheless exert great influence on behavior.

Underextensions Mistake that occurs when a child incorrectly uses a word to describe a narrower set of objects or actions than it is meant to

Undifferentiated schizophrenia A type of schizophrenia marked by idiosyncratic mixtures of schizophrenic symptoms.

V

Validity The ability of a test to measure what it was designed to measure.

Variability The extent to which the scores in a data set tend to vary from each other and from the mean.

Variable-interval (VI) schedule A reinforcement schedule in which the reinforcer is given for the first response after a variable time interval has elapsed.

Variable-ratio (VR) schedule A reinforcement schedule in which the reinforcer is given after a variable number of nonreinforced responses.

Variables Any measurable conditions, events, characteristics, or behaviors that are controlled or observed in a study.

Visual illusion An apparently inexplicable discrepancy between the appearance of a visual stimulus and its physical reality.

Z

Zygote A one-celled organism formed by the union of a sperm and an egg.

REFERENCES

Abdel-Khalek, A. M. (2006). Happiness, health, and religiosity: Significant relations. *Mental Health, 9*(1), 85–97.

Abel, E. L. (1998). *Fetal alcohol abuse syndrome.* New York: Plenum.

Abel, M. H. (2002). Humor, stress, and coping strategies. *Humor: International Journal of Humor Research, 15,* 365–381.

Abi-Dargham, A. (2004). Do we still believe in the dopamine hypothesis? New data bring new evidence. *International Journal of Neuropsychopharmacology, 7*(Supplement 1), S1–S5.

Abi-Dargham, A., Gil, R., Krystal, J., Baldwin, R. M., Seibyl, J. P., Bowers, M., van Dyck, C. H., Charney, D. S., Innis, R. B., & Laruelle, M. (1998). Increased striatal dopamine transmission in schizophrenia: Confirmation in a second cohort. *American Journal of Psychiatry, 155,* 761–767.

Aboud, F. E., & Amato, M. (2001). Developmental and socialization influences on intergroup bias. In R. Brown & S. L. Gaertner (Eds.), *Blackwell handbook of social psychology: Intergroup processes.* Malden, MA: Blackwell.

Abraham, W. C. (2006). Memory maintenance. *Current Directions in Psychological Science, 15*(1), 5–8.

Abrahamse, W., Steg, L., Vlek, C., & Rothengatter, T. (2005). A review of intervention studies aimed at household energy conservation. *Journal of Environmental Psychology, 25,* 273–291.

Abramson, L. Y., Alloy, L. B., & Metalsky, J. I. (1995). Hopelessness depression. In J. N. Buchanan & M. E. P. Seligman (Eds.), *Explanatory style.* Hillsdale, NJ: Erlbaum.

Abramson, L. Y., Seligman, M. E. P., & Teasdale, J. (1978). Learned helplessness in humans: Critique and reformulation. *Journal of Abnormal Psychology, 87,* 32–48.

Adam, T. C., & Epel, E. (2007). Stress, eating and the reward system. *Physiology and Behavior, 91,* 449–458.

Adamopoulos, J., & Lonner, W. J. (2001). Culture and psychology at a crossroad: Historical perspective and theoretical analysis. In D. Matsumoto (Ed.), *The handbook of culture and psychology.* New York: Oxford University Press.

Adams, J. L. (1980). *Conceptual blockbusting.* San Francisco: W. H. Freeman.

Adams, R. L., & Culbertson, J. L. (2005). Personality assessment: Adults and children. In B. J. Sadock & V. A. Sadock (Eds.), *Kaplan & Sadock's comprehensive textbook of psychiatry.* Philadelphia: Lippincott Williams & Wilkins.

Ader, R. (2001). Psychoneuroimmunology. *Current Directions in Psychological Science, 10*(3), 94–98.

Ader, R. (2003). Conditioned immunomodulation: Research needs and directions. *Brain, Behavior, and Immunity, 17*(1), S51–S57.

Ader, R., & Cohen, N. (1984). Behavior and the immune system. In W. D. Gentry (Ed.), *Handbook of behavioral medicine.* New York: Guilford.

Ader, R., & Cohen, N. (1993). Psychoneuroimmunology: Conditioning and stress. *Annual Review of Psychology, 44,* 53–85.

Adler, A. (1917). *Study of organ inferiority and its psychical compensation.* New York: Nervous and Mental Diseases Publishing Co.

Adler, A. (1927). *Practice and theory of individual psychology.* New York: Harcourt, Brace & World.

Adler, L. L. (Ed.). (1993). *International handbook on gender roles.* Westport, CT: Greenwood.

Adolph, K. E., & Berger, S. E. (2005). Physical and motor development. In M. H. Bornstein & M. E. Lamb (Eds.), *Developmental science: An advanced textbook.* Mahwah, NJ: Erlbaum.

Affleck, G., Tennen, H., Urrows, S., & Higgins, P. (1994). Person and contextual features of daily stress reactivity: Individual differences in relations of undesirable daily events with mood disturbance and chronic pain intensity. *Journal of Personality and Social Psychology, 66,* 329–340.

Agras, W. S., & Berkowitz, R. I. (1999). Behavior therapies. In R. E. Hales, S. C. Yudofsky, & J. A. Talbott (Eds.), *American Psychiatric Press textbook of psychiatry.* Washington, DC: American Psychiatric Press.

Ahima, R. S., & Osei, S. Y. (2004). Leptin signaling. *Physiology & Behavior, 81,* 223–241.

Aikins, D. E., & Craske, M. G. (2001). Cognitive theories of generalized anxiety disorder. *Psychiatric Clinics of North America, 24*(1), 57–74.

Ainsworth, M. D. S., Blehar, M. C., Waters, E., & Wall, S. (1978). *Patterns of attachment: A psychological study of the strange situation.* Hillsdale, NJ: Erlbaum.

Akerstedt, T., Hume, K., Minors, D., & Waterhouse, J. (1997). Good sleep—its timing and physiological sleep characteristics. *Journal of Sleep Research, 6,* 221–229.

Akimoto, S. A., & Sanbonmatsu, D. M. (1999). Differences in self-effacing behavior between European and Japanese Americans: Effect on competence evaluations. *Journal of Cross-Cultural Psychology, 30,* 159–177.

Akiskal, H. S. (2000). Mood disorders: Clinical features. In B. J. Sadock & V. A. Sadock (Eds.), *Kaplan and Sadock's comprehensive textbook of psychiatry* (7th ed., Vol. 1, pp. 1338–1376). Philadelphia: Lippincott/Williams & Wilkins.

Albee, G. W. (1998). Fifty years of clinical psychology: Selling our soul to the devil. *Applied and Preventive Psychology, 7*(3), 189–194.

Albert, C. M., Ma, J., Rifai, N., Stampfer, M. J., & Ridker, P. M. (2002). Prospective study of C-reactive protein, homocysteine, and plasma lipid levels as predictors of sudden cardiac death. *Circulation, 105,* 2595–2599.

Albert, M. S., & Killiany, R. J. (2001). Age-related cognitive change and brain-behavior relationships. In J. E. Birren & K. W. Schaie (Eds.), *Handbook of the psychology of aging* (5th ed., pp. 160–184). San Diego, CA: Academic Press.

Albert, M. S., & Moss, M. B. (2002). Neuropsychological approaches to preclinical identification of Alzheimer's disease. In L. R. Squire & D. L. Schacter (Eds.), *Neuropsychology of memory.* New York: Guilford.

Alcock, J. (1998). *Animal behavior: An evolutionary approach.* Sunderland, MA: Sinauer Associates.

Alcock, J. (2005). *Animal behavior.* Sunderland, MA: Sinauer Associates.

Aldag, R. J., & Fuller, S. R. (1993). Beyond fiasco: A reappraisal of the groupthink phenomenon and a new model of group decision processes. *Psychological Bulletin, 113,* 533–552.

Aldington, S., Harwood, M., Cox, B., Weatherall, M., Beckert, L., Hansell, A., et al. (2008). Cannabis use and risk of lung cancer: A case-control study. *European Respiratory Journal, 31,* 280–286.

Aldington, S., Williams, M., Nowitz, M., Weatherall, M., Pritchard, A., McNaughton, A., et al. (2007). Effects of cannabis on pulmonary structure, function and symptoms. *Thorax, 62,* 1058–1063.

Aldrich, M. S. (2000). Cardinal manifestations of sleep disorders. In M. H. Kryger, T. Roth, & W. C. Dement (Eds), *Principles and practice of sleep medicine.* Philadelphia: Saunders.

Aldwin, C. M., & Gilmer, D. F. (2004). *Health, illness, and optimal aging: Biological and psychosocial perspectives.* Thousand Oaks, CA: Sage Publications.

Alexander, C. N., Robinson, P., Orme-Johnson, D. W., Schneider, R. H., et al. (1994). The effects of transcendental meditation compared with other methods of relaxation and meditation in reducing risk factors, morbidity, and mortality. *Homeostasis in Health & Disease, 35,* 243–263.

Alexander, F. (1954). Psychoanalysis and psychotherapy. *Journal of the American Psychoanalytic Association, 2,* 722–733.

Alhakami, A. S., & Slovic, P. (1994). A psychological study of the inverse relationship between perceived risk and perceived benefit. *Risk Analysis, 14,* 1085–1096.

Allan, R. W. (1998). Operant-respondent interactions. In W. O'Donohue (Ed.), *Learning and behavior therapy.* Boston: Allyn & Bacon.

Allen, J. J. B., & Iacono, W. G. (2001). Assessing the validity of amnesia in dissociative identity disorder: A dilemma for the DSM and the courts. *Psychology, Public Policy, and Law, 7,* 311–344.

Allen, K., Blascovich, J., & Mendes, W. B. (2002). Cardiovascular reactivity in the presence of pets, friends, and spouses: The truth about cats and dogs. *Psychosomatic Medicine, 64,* 727–739.

Alloy, L. B., Abramson, L. Y., Whitehouse, W. G., Hogan, M. E., Tashman, N. A., Steinberg, D. L., Rose, D. T., & Donovan, P. (1999). Depressogenic cognitive styles: Predictive validity, information processing and personality characteristics, and developmental origins. *Behavioral Research and Therapy, 37,* 503–531.

Allport, G. W. (1937). *Personality: A psychological interpretation.* New York: Holt.

Allport, G. W. (1961). *Pattern and growth in personality.* New York: Holt.

Alonso, A., Alonso, S., & Piper, W. (2003). Group psychotherapy. In G. Stricker & T. A. Widiger (Eds.), *Handbook of psychology, Vol. 8: Clinical psychology.* New York: Wiley.

Altman, I. (1990). Centripetal and centrifugal trends in psychology. In L. Brickman & H. Ellis (Eds.), *Preparing psychologists for the 21st century: Proceedings of the National Conference on Graduate Education in Psychology.* Hillsdale, NJ: Erlbaum.

Altmann, E. M., & Gray, W. D. (2002). Forgetting to remember: The functional relationship of decay and interference. *Psychological Science, 13*(1), 27–33.

Altshuler, L. L., Suppes, T., Black, D. O., Nolen, W. A., Leverich, G., Keck, P. E., Jr., et al. (2006).

Lower switch rate in depressed patients with Bipolar II than Bipolar I disorder treated adjunctively with second-generation antidepressants. *American Journal of Psychiatry, 163,* 313–315.

Amabile, T. M. (1983). *The social psychology of creativity.* New York: Springer-Verlag.

Amabile, T. M. (1996). *Creativity in context.* Boulder, CO: Westview.

Amato, P. R. (2001). The consequences of divorce for adults and children. In R. M. Milardo (Ed.), *Understanding families into the new millenium: A decade in review.* Minneapolis: National Council on Family Relations.

Amato, P. R. (2003). Reconciling divergent perspectives: Judith Wallerstein, quantitative family research and children of divorce. *Family Relations: Interdisciplinary Journal of Applied Family Studies, 52,* 332–339.

Amedi, A., Floel, A., Knecht, S., Zohary, E., & Cohen, L. G. (2004). Transcranial magnetic stimulation of the occipital pole interferes with verbal processing in blind subjects. *Nature Neuroscience, 7,* 1266–1270.

American Association of Suicidology. (2007). *Understanding and helping the suicidal individual.* Retrieved April 12, 2007 from http://www.suicidology .org/associations/1045/files/Understanding.pdf.

American Foundation for Suicide Prevention. (2007). *When you fear someone may take their own life.* Retrieved April 12, 2007 from http://www.afsp .org/index.cfm?page_id=F2F25092-7E90-9BD4 -C4658F1D2B5D19A0

American Psychiatric Association. (1994). *Diagnostic and statistical manual of mental disorders* (4th ed.). Washington, DC: Author.

American Psychiatric Association. (2000). *Diagnostic and statistical manual of mental disorders* (4th ed. Text revision). Washington, DC: Author.

American Psychiatric Association Task Force on Electroconvulsive Therapy. (2001). *The practice of electroconvulsive therapy: Recommendations for treatment* (2nd ed.). Washington, DC: American Psychiatric Association.

American Psychological Association. (1984). *Behavioral research with animals.* Washington, DC: Author.

American Psychological Association. (2002). Ethical principles of psychologists and code of conduct. *American Psychologist, 57,* 1060–1073.

Ammaniti, M., Speranza, A. M., & Fedele, S. (2005). Attachment in infancy and in early and late childhood: A longitudinal study. In K. A. Kerns, & R. A. Richardson (Eds.), *Attachment in middle childhood.* New York: Guilford.

Amodio, D. M., Harmon-Jones, E., Devine, P. G., Curtin, J. J., Hartley, S. L., & Covert, A. E. (2004). Neural signals for the detection of unintentional race bias. *Psychological Science, 15*(2), 88–93.

Anand, B. K., & Brobeck, J. R. (1951). Hypothalamic control of food intake in rats and cats. *Yale Journal of Biology and Medicine, 24,* 123–140.

Anderluh, M. B., Tchanturia, K., Rabe-Hesketh, S., & Treasure, J. (2003). Childhood obsessive-compulsive personality traits in adult women with eating disorders: Defining a broader eating disorder phenotype. *American Journal of Psychiatry, 160,* 242–247.

Anderson, A. E., & Yager, J. (2005). Eating disorders. In B. J. Sadock & V. A. Sadock (Eds.), *Kaplan & Sadock's comprehensive textbook of psychiatry.* Philadelphia: Lippincott Williams & Wilkins.

Anderson, B. (2003). Brain imaging and *g.* In H. Nyborg (Ed.), *The scientific study of general intelligence: Tribute to Arthur R. Jensen.* Oxford, UK: Pergamon.

Anderson, C., Keltner, D., & John, O. P. (2003). Emotional convergence between people over time. *Journal of Personality and Social Psychology, 84,* 1054–1068.

Anderson, C. A. (2004). An update on the effects of playing violent video games. *Journal of Adolescence, 27*(1), 113–122.

Anderson, C. A., Berkowitz, L., Donnerstein, E., Huesman, L. R., Johnson, J. D., Linz, D., Malamuth, N. M. , & Wartella, E. (2003). The influence of media violence on youth. *Psychological Science in the Public Interest, 4*(3), 81–110.

Anderson, E. A., Kohler, J. K., & Letiecq, B. L. (2002). Low-income fathers and "Responsible Fatherhood" programs: A qualitative investigation of participants' experiences. *Family Relations, 51,* 148–155.

Anderson, K. J. (1990). Arousal and the inverted-U hypothesis: A critique of Neiss's "reconceptualizing arousal." *Psychological Bulletin, 107,* 96–100.

Anderson, M. C., & Neely, J. H. (1996). Interference and inhibition in memory retrieval. In E. L. Bjork & R. A. Bjork (Eds.), *Memory.* San Diego: Academic Press.

Anderson-Fye, E. P., & Becker, A. E. (2004). Sociocultural aspects of eating disorders and obesity. In J. K. Thompson (Ed.), *Handbook of eating disorders and obesity.* New York: Wiley.

Andreasen, N. C. (1987). Creativity and mental illness: Prevalence rates in writers and their first-degree relatives. *American Journal of Psychiatry, 144,* 1288–1292.

Andreasen, N. C. (1990). Positive and negative symptoms: Historical and conceptual aspects. In N. C. Andreasen (Ed.), *Modern problems of pharmacopsychiatry: Positive and negative symptoms and syndromes.* Basel: Karger.

Andreasen, N. C. (2001). *Brave new brain: Conquering mental illness in the era of the human genome.* New York: Oxford University Press.

Andreasen, N. C. (2005). *The creating brain: The neuroscience of genius.* New York: Dana Press.

Angell, M. (2000). Is academic medicine for sale? *New England Journal of Medicine, 342,* 1516–1518.

Angell, M. (2004). *The truth about the drug companies: How they deceive us and what to do about it.* New York: Random House.

Anglin, J. M. (1993). Vocabulary development: A morphological analysis. *Monographs of the Society for Research in Child Development, 58.*

Ansbacher, H. (1970, February). Alfred Adler, individual psychology. *Psychology Today,* pp. 42–44, 66.

Anthony, I. C., & Bell, J. E. (2008). The neuropathology of HIV/AIDS. *International Review of Psychiatry, 20*(1), 15–24.

Antonuccio, D. O., Danton, W. G., & McClanahan, T. M. (2003). Psychology in the prescription era: Building a firewall between marketing and science. *American Psychologist, 58,* 1028–1043.

Antony, M. M., & McCabe, R. E. (2003). Anxiety disorders: Social and specific phobias. In A. Tasman, J. Kay, & J. A. Lieberman (Eds.), *Psychiatry.* New York: Wiley.

Apkarian, A. V., Bushnell, M. C., Treede, R., & Zubieta, J. (2005). Human brain mechanisms of pain perception and regulation in health and disease. *European Journal of Pain, 9,* 463–484.

Appelbaum, P. S. (2002). Responses to the presidential debate—The systematic defunding of psychiatric care: A crisis at our doorstep. *American Journal of Psychiatry, 159,* 1638–1640.

Appleton, K. M., Gentry, R. C., & Shepherd, R. (2006). Evidence of a role for conditioning in the development of liking for flavours in humans in everyday life. *Physiology & Behavior, 87,* 478–486.

Aquilino, W. S. (2006). Family relationships and support systems in emerging adulthood. In J. J. Arnett & J. L. Tanner (Eds.), *Emerging adults in America: Coming of age in the 21st century.* Washington, DC: American Psychological Association.

Archer, J. (1996). Sex differences in social behavior: Are the social role and evolutionary explanations compatible? *American Psychologist, 51,* 909–917.

Archer, J. (2005). Are women or men the more aggressive sex? In S. Fein, G. R. Goethals, & M. J. Sansdtrom (Eds.), *Gender and aggression: Interdisciplinary perspectives.* Mahwah, NJ: Erlbaum.

Archibald, A. B., Graber, J. A., & Brooks–Gunn, J. (2003). Pubertal processes and physiological growth in adolescence. In G. R. Adams & M. D. Berzonsky (Eds.), *Blackwell handbook of adolescence.* Malden, MA: Blackwell Publishing.

Arendt, J., & Skene, D. J. (2005). Melatonin as a chronobiotic. *Sleep Medicine Review, 9*(1), 25–39.

Arendt, J., Stone, B., & Skene, D. (2000). Jet lag and sleep disruption. In M. H. Kryger, T. Roth, & W. C. Dement (Eds.), *Principles and practice of sleep medicine.* Philadelphia: Saunders.

Arendt, J., Stone, B., & Skene, D. J. (2005). Sleep disruption in jet lag and other circadian rhythm-related disorders. In M. H. Kryger, T. Roth, & W. C. Dement (Eds.). *Principles and practice of sleep medicine.* Philadelphia: Elsevier Saunders.

Argyle, M. (1987). *The psychology of happiness.* London: Metheun.

Argyle, M. (1999). Causes and correlates of happiness. In D. Kahneman, E. Diener, & N. Schwarz (Eds.), *Well-being: The foundations of hedonic psychology.* New York: Russell Sage Foundation.

Argyle, M. (2001). *The psychology of happiness.* New York: Routledge.

Arkes, H. R., Wortmann, R. L., Saville, P. D., & Harkness, A. R. (1981). Hindsight bias among physicians weighing the likelihood of diagnoses. *Journal of Applied Psychology, 66,* 252–254.

Arkowitz, H., & Lilienfeld, S. O. (2007). The best medicine? How drugs stack up against talk therapy for the treatment of depression. *Scientific American Mind, 18*(5), 80–83.

Armbruster, B. B. (2000). Taking notes from lectures. In R. F. Flippo & D. C. Caverly (Eds.), *Handbook of college reading and study strategy research.* Mahwah, NJ: Erlbaum.

Arndt, J., Cook, A., & Routledge, C. (2004). The blueprint of terror management: Understanding the cognitive architecture of psychological defense against the awareness of death. In J. Greenberg, S. L. Koole, & T. Pyszczynski (Eds.), *Handbook of experimental existential psychology.* New York: Guilford.

Arnett, J. J. (2000). Emerging adulthood: A theory of development from the late teens through the twenties. *American Psychologist, 55,* 469–480.

Arnett, J. J. (2001). Conceptions of the transition to adulthood: Perspectives from adolescence to midlife. *Journal of Adult Development, 8,* 133–143.

Arnett, J. J. (2004). *Emerging adulthood: The winding road from the late teens through the twenties.* New York: Oxford University Press.

Arnett, J. J. (2006). Emerging adulthood: Understanding the new way of coming of age. In J. J. Arnett & J. L. Tanner (Eds.), *Emerging adults in America: Coming of age in the 21st century.* Washington, DC: American Psychological Association.

Arnkoff, D. B., & Glass, C. R. (1992). Cognitive therapy and psychotherapy. In D. K. Freedheim (Ed.), *History of psychotherapy: A century of change.* Washington, DC: American Psychological Association.

Arnold, L. M. (2000). Psychocutaneous disorders. In B. J. Sadock & V. A. Sadock (Eds.), *Kaplan and Sadock's comprehensive textbook of psychiatry* (7th ed., pp. 1818–1827). Philadelphia: Lippincott/Williams & Wilkins.

Arnold, R. (1993). *Ecology wars: Environmentalism as if people mattered.* Bellevue, WA: Meril Press.

Aron, A., Fisher, H., & Mashek, D. J. (2005). Reward, motivation, and emotion systems associated with early–stage intense romantic love. *Journal of Neurophysiology, 94*(1), 327–337.

Aronson, E., & Mills, J. (1959). The effect of severity of initiation on liking for a group. *Journal of Abnormal and Social Psychology, 59,* 177–181.

Arrigo, J. M., & Pezdek, K. (1997). Lessons from the study of psychogenic amnesia. *Current Directions in Psychological Science, 6,* 148–152.

Asch, S. E. (1951). Effects of group pressure on the modification and distortion of judgments. In H. Guetzkow (Ed.), *Groups, Leadership and men.* Pittsburgh: Carnegie Press.

Asch, S. E. (1955). Opinions and social pressures. *Scientific American, 193*(5), 31–35.

Asch, S. E. (1956). Studies of independence and conformity: A minority of one against a unanimous majority. *Psychological Monographs, 70*(9, Whole No. 416).

Aserinsky, E., & Kleitman, N. (1953). Regularly occurring periods of eye mobility and concomitant phenomena during sleep. *Science, 118,* 273–274.

Ashford, J. W., & Mortimer, J. A. (2002). Nonfamilial Alzheimer's disease is mainly due to genetic factors. *Journal of Alzheimer's Disease, 4,* 169–177.

Ashton, M. C., Lee, K., Perugini, M. , Szarota, P., de Vries, R. E., Di Blas, L., Boies, K., & De Raad, B. (2004). A six-factor structure of personality descriptive adjectives: Solutions from psycholexical studies in seven languages. *Journal of Personality and Social Psychology, 86*(2), 356–366.

Aspinwall, L. G., Richter, L., & Hoffman R. R., III. (2001). Understanding how optimism works: An examination of optimists' adaptive moderation of belief and behavior. In E. C. Chang (Ed.), *Optimism and pessimism: Implications for theory, research, and practice* (pp. 217–238). Washington, DC: American Psychological Association.

Assefi, S. L., & Garry, M. (2003). Absolut® memory distortions: Alcohol placebos influence the misinformation effect. *Psychological Science, 14*(1), 77–80.

Atkinson, J. W. (1974). The mainsprings of achievement-oriented activity. In J. W. Atkinson & J. O. Raynor (Eds.), *Motivation and achievement.* New York: Wiley.

Atkinson, J. W. (1981). Studying personality in the context of an advanced motivational psychology. *American Psychologist, 36,* 117–128.

Atkinson, J. W. (1992). Motivational determinants of thematic apperception. In C. P. Smith (Ed.), *Motivation and personality: Handbook of thematic content analysis.* New York: Cambridge University Press.

Atkinson, J. W., & Litwin, G. H. (1960). Achievement motive and test anxiety conceived as motive to approach success and to avoid failure. *Journal of Abnormal and Social Psychology, 60,* 52–63.

Atkinson, R. C., & Shiffrin, R. M. (1968). Human memory: A proposed system and its control processes. In K. W. Spence & J. T. Spence (Eds.), *The psychology of learning and motivation* (Vol. 2). New York: Academic Press.

Atkinson, R. C., & Shiffrin, R. M. (1971). The control of short-term memory. *Scientific American, 225,* 82–90.

Ator, N. A. (2005). Conducting behavioral research: Methodological and laboratory animal welfare issues. In C. K. Akins, S. Panicker, & C. L. Cunningham (Eds.), *Laboratory animals in research and teaching: Ethics, care and methods.* Washington, DC: American Psychological Association.

Aucoin, K. J., Frick, P. J., & Bodin, S. D. (2006). Corporal punishment and child adjustment. *Journal of Applied Developmental Psychology, 27,* 527–541.

Averill, J. A. (1980). A constructivist view of emotion. In R. Plutchik & H. Kellerman (Eds.), *Emotion: Theory, research, and experience: Vol. 1. Theories of emotion.* New York: Academic Press.

Axel, R. (1995, April). The molecular logic of smell. *Scientific American, 273,* 154–159.

Ayanian, J. Z., & Cleary, P. D. (1999). Perceived risks of heart disease and cancer among cigarette smokers. *Journal of the American Medical Association, 281,* 1019–1021.

Ayas, N. T., White, D. P., Manson, J. E., Stampfer, M. J., Speizer, F. E., Malhotra, A., et al. (2003). A prospective study of sleep duration and coronary heart disease in women. *Archives of Internal Medicine, 163,* 205–209.

Ayers, M. S., & Reder, L. M. (1998). A theoretical review of the misinformation effect: Predictions from an activation-based memory model. *Psychonomic Bulletin & Review, 5,* 1–21.

Baars, B. J. (1986). *The cognitive revolution in psychology.* New York: Guilford.

Baddeley, A. D. (1986). *Working memory.* New York: Oxford University Press.

Baddeley, A. D. (1989). The uses of working memory. In P. R. Soloman, G. R. Goethals, C. M. Kelley, & B. R. Stephens (Eds.), *Memory: Interdisciplinary approaches.* New York: Springer-Verlag.

Baddeley, A. D. (1992). Working memory. *Science, 255,* 556–559.

Baddeley, A. D. (2001). Is working memory still working? *American Psychologist, 56,* 851–864.

Baddeley, A. D. (2003). Working memory: Looking back and looking forward. *Nature Reviews Neuroscience, 4,* 829–839.

Baddeley, A. D. (2007). *Working memory, thought, and action.* New York: Oxford University Press.

Baddeley, A. D., & Hitch, G. (1974). Working memory. In G. H. Bower (Ed.), *The psychology of learning and motivation* (Vol. 8). New York: Academic Press.

Bahrick, H. P. (2000). Long-term maintenance of knowledge. In E. Tulving & F. I. M. Craik (Eds.), *The Oxford handbook of memory* (pp. 347–362). New York: Oxford University Press.

Bailey, C. H., & Kandel, E. R. (2004). Synaptic growth and the persistence of long–term memory: A molecular perspective. In M. S. Gazzaniga (Ed.), *The cognitive neurosciences.* Cambridge, MA: MIT Press.

Bailey, J. M. (2003). Biological perspectives on sexual orientation. In L. D. Garnets & D. C. Kimmel (Eds.), *Psychological perspectives on lesbian, gay, and bisexual experiences.* New York: Columbia University Press.

Bailey, J. M., Dunne, M. P., & Martin, N. G. (2000). Genetic and environmental influences on sexual orientation and its correlates in an Australian twin sample. *Journal of Personality and Social Psychology, 78,* 524–536.

Bailey, J. M., & Pillard, R. C. (1991). A genetic study of male homosexual orientation. *Archives of General Psychology, 48,* 1089–1097.

Bailey, J. M., Pillard, R. C., Neale, M. C. I., & Agyei, Y. (1993). Heritable factors influence sexual orientation in women. *Archives of General Psychiatry, 50,* 217–223.

Bailey, J. M., & Zucker, K. J. (1995). Childhood sex-typed behavior and sexual orientation: A conceptual analysis and quantitative review. *Developmental Psychology, 31,* 43–55.

Baillargeon, R. (2002). The acquisition of physical knowledge in infancy: A summary in eight lessons. In U. Goswami (Ed.), *Blackwell handbook of childhood cognitive development.* Malden, MA: Blackwell Publishing.

Baillargeon, R. (2004). Infants' physical world. *Current Directions in Psychological Science, 13*(3), 89–94.

Baillargeon, R. (2008). Innate ideas revisited: For a principle of persistence in infants' physical reasoning. *Perspectives on Psychological Science, 3*(1), 2–13.

Bain, J. (2007). The many faces of testosterone. *Clinical Interventions in Aging, 2,* 567–576.

Bains, J. S., & Oliet, S. H. R. (2007). Glia: They make your memories stick! *Trends in Neuroscience, 30,* 417–424.

Baker, G. J., Suchday, S., & Krantz, D. S. (2007). Heart disease/attack. In G. Fink (Ed.), *Encyclopedia of stress.* San Diego: Elsevier.

Baker, T. B., Piper, M. E., McCarthey, D. E., Majeskie, M. R., & Fiore, M. C. (2004). Addiction motivation reformulated: An affective processing model of negative reinforcement. *Psychological Review, 111,* 33–51.

Balcetis, E., & Dunning, D. A. (2006). See what you want to see: Motivational influences on visual perception. *Journal of Personality and Social Psychology, 91,* 612–625.

Balcetis, E., & Dunning, D. A. (2008). A mile in moccasins: How situational experience diminishes dispositionism in social inference. *Personality and Social Psychology Bulletin, 34*(1), 102–114.

Baldessarini, R. J., Tondo, L., Strombom, I. M., Dominguez, S., Fawcett, J., Licinio, J., Oquendo, M. A., Tollefson, G. D., Valuck, R. J., & Tohen, M. (2007). Ecological studies of antidepressant treatment and suicidal risks. *Harvard Review of Psychiatry, 15,* 133–145.

Baldwin, E. (1993). The case for animal research in psychology. *Journal of Social Issues, 49*(1), 121–131.

Baldwin, W. (2000). Information no one else knows: The value of self-report. In A. A. Stone, J. S. Turkkan, C. A. Bachrach, J. B. Jobe, H. S. Kurtzman, & V. Cain (Eds.), *The science of self-report: Implications for research and practice.* Mahwah, NJ: Erlbaum.

Ball, H. L., Hooker, E., & Kelly, P. J. (2000). Parent-infant co-sleeping: Father's roles and perspectives. *Infant and Child Development, 9*(2), 67–74.

Ballenger, J. C. (2000). Benzodiazepine receptor agonists and antagonists. In B. J. Sadock & V. A. Sadock (Eds.), *Kaplan and Sadock's comprehensive textbook of psychiatry.* Philadelphia: Lippincott/Williams & Wilkins.

Balsam, P. D. (1988). Selection, representation, and equivalence of controlling stimuli. In R. C.

Atkinson, R. J. Herrnstein, G. Lindzey, & R. D. Luce (Eds.), *Stevens' handbook of experimental psychology.* New York: Wiley.

Baltes, P. B., Staudinger, U. M., & Lindenberger, U. (1999). Lifespan psychology: Theory and application to intellectual functioning. *Annual Review of Psychology, 50,* 471–507.

Bandura, A. (1977). *Social learning theory.* Englewood Cliffs, NJ: Prentice-Hall.

Bandura, A. (1982). The psychology of chance encounters and life paths. *American Psychologist, 37,* 747–755.

Bandura, A. (1986). *Social foundations of thought and action: A social-cognitive theory.* Englewood Cliffs, NJ: Prentice-Hall.

Bandura, A. (1990). Perceived self-efficacy in the exercise of personal agency. *Journal of Applied Sport Psychology, 2*(2), 128–163.

Bandura, A. (1993). Perceived self-efficacy in cognitive development and functioning. *Educational Psychologist, 28*(2), 117–148.

Bandura, A. (1995). Exercise of personal and collective efficacy in changing societies. In A. Bandura (Ed.), *Self-efficacy in changing societies.* New York: Cambridge University Press.

Bandura, A. (1999a). Social cognitive theory of personality. In L. A. Pervin & O. P. John (Eds.), *Handbook of personality: Theory and research.* New York: Guilford.

Bandura, A. (1999b). A sociocognitive analysis of substance abuse: An agentic perspective. *Psychological Science, 10*(3), 214–217.

Bandura, A. (2001). Social cognitive theory: An agentic perspective. *Annual Review of Psychology, 52,* 1–26.

Bandura, A. (2006). Toward a psychology of human agency. *Perspectives on Psychological Science, 1,* 164–180.

Bandura, A., Ross, D., & Ross, S. A. (1963a). Imitation of film-mediated aggressive models. *Journal of Abnormal and Social Psychology, 66,* 3–11.

Bandura, A., Ross, D., & Ross. S. A. (1963b). Vicarious reinforcement and imitative learning. *Journal of Abnormal and Social Psychology, 67*(6), 6011–607.

Banich, M. T. (2003). Interaction between the hemispheres and its implications for the processing capacity of the brain. In K. Hugdahl & R. J. Davidson (Eds.), *The asymmetrical brain.* Cambridge, MA: MIT Press.

Banich, M. T., & Heller, W. (1998). Evolving perspectives on lateralization of function. *Current Directions in Psychological Science, 7,* 1.

Banks, A., & Gartell, N. K. (1995). Hormones and sexual orientation: A questionable link. *Journal of Homosexuality, 28,* 247–268.

Banks, S., & Dinges, D. F. (2007). Behavioral and physiological consequences of sleep restriction. *Journal of Clinical Sleep Medicine, 3*(5), 519–528.

Banks, W. A., & Watkins, L. R. (2006). Mediation of chronic pain: Not by neurons alone. *Pain, 124,* 1–2.

Banks, W. P., & Krajicek, D. (1991). Perception. *Annual Review of Psychology, 42,* 305–331.

Banyard, V. L., & Williams, L. M. (1999). Memories for child sexual abuse and mental health functioning: Findings on a sample of women and implications for future research. In L. M. Williams & V. L. Banyard (Eds.), *Trauma & memory.* Thousand Oaks, CA: Sage Publications.

Banzato, C. E. M. (2004). Classification in psychiatry: The move towards ICD-11 and DSM-V. *Current Opinion in Psychiatry, 17,* 497–501.

Barak, A., & Buchanan, T. (2004). Internet-based psychological testing and assessment. In R. Krause, G. Stricker, & J. Zack (Eds.), *Online counseling: A handbook for mental health professionals.* San Diego: Elsevier Academic Press.

Baral, B. D., & Das, J. P. (2004). Intelligence: What is indigenous to India and what is shared? In R. J. Sternberg (Ed.), *International handbook of intelligence.* New York: Cambridge University Press.

Barber, T. X. (1979). Suggested ("hypnotic") behavior: The trance paradigm versus an alternative paradigm. In E. Fromm & R. E. Shor (Eds.), *Hypnosis: Developments in research and new perspectives.* New York: Aldine.

Barber, T. X. (1986). Realities of stage hypnosis. In B. Zilbergeld, M. G. Edelstien, & D. L. Araoz (Eds.), *Hypnosis: Questions and answers.* New York: Norton.

Barch, D. M. (2003). Cognition in schizophrenia: Does working memory work? *Current Directions in Psychological Science, 12*(4), 146–150.

Bard, P. (1934). On emotional experience after decortication with some remarks on theoretical views. *Psychological Review, 41,* 309–329.

Bargh, J. A., & McKenna, K. Y. A. (2004). The Internet and social life. *Annual Review of Psychology, 55,* 573–590.

Bargh, J. A., McKenna, K. Y. A., & Fitzsimons, G. M. (2002). Can you see the real me? Activation and expression of the "true self" on the Internet. *Journal of Social Issues, 58,* 33–48.

Barker, E. T., Williams, R. L., & Galambos, N. L. (2006). Daily spillover to and from binge eating in first-year university females. *Eating Disorders: The Journal of Treatment and Prevention, 14,* 229–242.

Barlett, D. L., & Steele, J. B. (1979). *Empire: The life, legend and madness of Howard Hughes.* New York: Norton.

Barlow, D. H., Pincus, D. B., Heinrichs, N., & Choate, M. L. (2003). Anxiety disorders. In G. Stricker & T. A. Widiger (Eds.), *Handbook of psychology, Vol. 8: Clinical psychology.* New York: Wiley.

Barnes, V. A., Treiber, F., & Davis, H. (2001). The impact of Transcendental Meditation on cardiovascular function at rest and during acute stress in adolescents with high normal blood pressure. *Journal of Psychosomatic Research, 51,* 597–605.

Barnett, S. W. (2004). Does Head Start have lasting cognitive effects? The myth of fade-out. In E. Zigler & S. J. Styfco (Eds.), *The Head Start debates.* Baltimore: Paul H. Brooks Publishing.

Barnier, A. J. (2002). Posthypnotic amnesia for autobiographical episodes: A laboratory model of functional amnesia. *Psychological Science, 13,* 232–237.

Baron, A., & Galizio, M. (2005). Positive and negative reinforcement: Should the distinction be preserved? *Behavior Analyst, 28*(2), 85–98.

Barrett, D. (1988–1989). Dreams of death. *Omega, 19*(2), 95–101.

Barrett, L. F., Mesquita, B., Ochsner, K. N., & Gross, J. J. (2007). The experience of emotion. *Annual Review of Psychology, 58,* 373–403.

Barron, F. (1963). *Creativity and psychological health.* Princeton, NY: Van Nostrand.

Barry, L. J. (2004). Depression: The brain finally gets into the act. *Current Directions in Psychological Science, 13*(3), 104–106.

Barry-Walsh, J. (2005). Dissociative identity disorder. *Australian & New Zealand Journal of Psychiatry, 39*(1-2), 109–110.

Barsky, A. J. (1988). The paradox of health. *New England Journal of Medicine, 318,* 414–418.

Barsky, A. J. (2001). Somatosensory amplification and hypochondriasis. In V. Starcevic & D. R. Lipsitt (Eds.), *Hypochondriasis: Modern perspectives on an ancient malady.* New York: Oxford University Press.

Barsky, A. J., Coeytaux, R. R., Sarnie, M. K., & Cleary, P. D. (1993). Hypochondriacal patients' beliefs about good health. *American Journal of Psychiatry, 150,* 1085–1090.

Bartels, M., Rietveld, M. J. H., Van Baal, G. C. M., & Boomsma, D. I. (2002). Genetic and environmental influences on the development of intelligence. *Behavior Genetics, 32*(4), 237–249.

Bartoshuk, L. M. (1988). Taste. In R. C. Atkinson, R. J. Herrnstein, G. Lindzey, & R. D. Luce (Eds.), *Stevens' handbook of experimental psychology: Perception and motivation* (Vol. 1). New York: Wiley.

Bartoshuk, L. M. (1993a). Genetic and pathological taste variation: What can we learn from animal models and human disease? In D. Chadwick, J. Marsh, & J. Goode (Eds.), *The molecular basis of smell and taste transduction.* New York: Wiley.

Bartoshuk, L. M. (1993b). The biological basis of food perception and acceptance. *Food Quality and Preference, 4,* 21–32.

Bartoshuk, L. M. (2000). Comparing sensory experiences across individuals: Recent psychophysical advances illuminate genetic variation in taste perception. *Chemical Senses, 25,* 447–460.

Bartoshuk, L. M., & Beauchamp, G. K. (1994). Chemical senses. *Annual Review of Psychology, 45,* 419–449.

Bartoshuk, L. M., Duffy, V. B., & Miller, I. J. (1994). PTC/PROP taste: Anatomy, psychophysics, and sex effects. *Physiology & Behavior, 56,* 1165–1171.

Basbaum, A. I., & Jessel, T. M. (2000). The perception of pain. In E. R. Kandel, J. H. Schwartz, & T. M. Jessell (Eds.), *Principles of neural science.* New York: McGraw-Hill.

Basow, S. A. (1992). *Gender: Stereotypes and roles.* Pacific Grove, CA: Brooks/Cole.

Bassok, M. (2003). Analogical transfer in problem solving. In J. E. Davidson & R. J. Sternberg (Eds.), *The psychology of problem solving.* New York: Cambridge University Press.

Basson, M. D., Bartoshuk, L. M., Dichello, S. Z., Panzini, L., Weiffenbach, J. M., & Duffy, V. B. (2005). Association between 6-n-propylthiouracil (PROP) bitterness and colonic neoplasms. *Digestive Diseases Sciences, 50,* 483–489.

Bassuk, E. L., Buckner, J. C., Perloff, J. N., & Bassuk, S. S. (1998). Prevalence of mental health and substance use disorders among homeless and low-income housed mothers. *American Journal of Psychiatry, 155,* 1561–1564.

Bates, E., Devescovi, A., & Wulfeck, B. (2001). Psycholinguistics: A cross-language perspective. *Annual Review of Psychology, 52,* 369–396.

Bates, M. S., Edwards, W. T., & Anderson, K. O. (1993). Ethnocultural influences on variation in chronic pain perception. *Pain, 52*(1), 101–112.

Baudry, M., & Lynch, G. (2001). Remembrance of arguments past: How well is the glutamate receptor hypothesis of LTP holding up after 20 years? *Neurobiology of Learning and Memory, 76,* 284–297.

Bauer, M. S. (2003). Mood disorders: Bipolar (manic-depressive) disorders. In A Tasman, J. Kay, & J. A. Lieberman (Eds.), *Psychiatry*. New York: Wiley.

Baum, A., Grunberg, N. E., & Singer, J. E. (1992). Biochemical measurements in the study of emotion. *Psychological Science, 3*, 56–60.

Baumeister, R. F. (1989). The optimal margin of illusion. *Journal of Social and Clinical Psychology, 8*, 176–189.

Baumeister, R. F. (2000). Gender differences in erotic plasticity: The female sex drive as socially flexible and responsive. *Psychological Bulletin, 126*, 347–374.

Baumeister, R. F. (2004). Gender and erotic plasticity: Sociocultural influences on the sex drive. *Sexual and Relationship Therapy, 19*, 133–139.

Baumeister, R. F., Bratslavsky, E., Finkenauer, C., & Vohs, K. D. (2001). Bad is stronger than good. *Review of General Psychology, 5*, 323–370.

Baumeister, R. F., Catanese, K. R., & Vohs, K. D. (2001). Is there a gender difference in strength of sex drive? Theoretical views, conceptual distinctions and a review of relevant evidence. *Personality and Social Psychology Review, 5*, 242–273.

Baumeister, R. F., & Leary, M. R. (1995). The need to belong: Desire for interpersonal attachments as a fundamental human motivation. *Psychological Bulletin, 117*, 497–529.

Baumeister, R. F., & Twenge, J. M. (2002). Cultural suppression of female sexuality. *Review of General Psychology, 6*, 166–203.

Baumrind, D. (1964). Some thoughts on the ethics of reading Milgram's "Behavioral study of obedience." *American Psychologist, 19*, 421–423.

Baumrind, D. (1985). Research using intentional deception: Ethical issues revisited. *American Psychologist, 40*, 165–174.

Baumrind, D., Larzelere, R. E., & Cowan, P. A. (2002). Ordinary physical punishment: Is it harmful? Comment on Gershoff. *Psychological Bulletin, 128*, 580–589.

Baylis, G. C., & Driver, J. (1995). One-sided edge assignment in vision: 1. Figure-ground segmentation and attention to objects. *Current Directions in Psychological Science, 4*, 140–146.

Beck, A. T. (1976). *Cognitive therapy and the emotional disorders*. New York: International Universities Press.

Beck, A. T. (1987). Cognitive therapy. In J. K. Zeig (Ed.), *The evolution of psychotherapy*. New York: Brunner/Mazel.

Beck, A. T. (1991). Cognitive therapy: A 30-year retrospective. *American Psychologist, 46*, 368–375.

Beck, A. T. (1997). Cognitive therapy: Reflections. In J. K. Zeig (Ed.), *The evolution of psychotherapy: The third conference*. New York: Brunner/Mazel.

Becker, A., & Fay, K. (2006). Sociocultural issues and eating disorders. In S. Wonderlich, J. Mitchell, M. de Zwaan, & H. Steiger (Eds.), *Annual review of eating disorders*. Oxon, England: Radcliffe.

Becker, S., & Wojtowicz, J. M. (2007). A model of hippocampal neurogenesis in memory and mood disorders. *Trends in Cognitive Sciences, 11*(2), 70–76.

Becskei, C., Lutz, T. A., & Riediger, T. (2008). Glucose reverses fasting-induced activation in the arcuate nucleus of mice. *Neuroreport: For Rapid Communication of Neuroscience Research, 19*(1), 105–109.

Beddoe, R., Costanza, R., Farley, JU., Garza, E., Kent, J., Kubiszewski, I., Martinez, L., McCowen, T., Murphy, KI., Myers, N., Ogden, Z., Stapleton, K., & Woodward, J. (2009). Overcoming systematic roadblocks to sustainability: The evolutionary redesign of worldviews, institutions, and technologies. *Proceedings from the National Academy of Science (PNAS), 106*, 2483–2489.

Beeman, M. J., & Chiarello, C. (1998). Complementary right and left hemisphere language comprehension. *Current Directions in Psychological Science, 7*, 2–7.

Beer, J. M., Arnold, R. D., & Loehlin, J. C. (1998). Genetic and environmental influences on MMPI Factor Scales: Joint model fitting to twin and adoption data. *Journal of Personality and Social Psychology, 74*, 818–827.

Beer, J. S., Shimamura, A. P., & Knight, R. T. (2004). Frontal lobe contributions to executive control of cognitive and social behavior. In M. S. Gazzaniga (Ed.), *The cognitive neurosciences*. Cambridge, MA: MIT Press.

Beidel, D. C., & Stipelman, B. (2007). Anxiety disorders. In M. Hersen, S. M. Turner, & D. C. Beidel (Eds.), *Adult psychopathology and diagnosis*. New York: Wiley.

Beilin, H. (1992). Piaget's enduring contribution to developmental psychology. *Developmental Psychology, 28*, 191–204.

Bekelman, J. E., Li, Y., & Gross, C. P. (2003). Scope and impact of financial conflicts of interest in biomedical research. *Journal of the American Medical Association, 289*, 454–465.

Békésy, G. von. (1947). The variation of phase along the basilar membrane with sinusoidal vibrations. *Journal of the Acoustical Society of America, 19*, 452–460.

Belger, A., & Dichter, G. (2006). Structural and functional neuroanatomy. In J. A. Lieberman, T. S. Stroup, & D. O. Perkins (Eds.), *Textbook of schizophrenia*. Washington, DC: American Psychiatric Publishing.

Bell, A. P., Weinberg, M. S., & Hammersmith, S. K. (1981). *Sexual preference: Its development in men and women*. Bloomington: Indiana University Press.

Bell, P. A., Greene, T. C., Fisher, J. D., & Baum, A. (2001). *Environmental psychology* (5th ed). Fort Worth: Harcourt College Publishers.

Bellis, M. A., Downing, J., & Ashton, J. R. (2006). Adults at 12? Trends in puberty and their public health consequences. *Journal of Epidemiology and Community Health, 60*, 910–911.

Belsky, J. (1999). Modern evolutionary theory and patterns of attachment. In J. Cassidy & P. R. Shaver (Eds.), *Handbook of attachment: Theory, research and clinical applications*. New York: Guilford.

Belsky, J. (2007). Experience in childhood and the development of reproductive strategies. *Acta Psychologica Sinica, 39*, 454–468.

Bem, D. J. (1996). Exotic becomes erotic: A developmental theory of sexual orientation. *Psychological Review, 103*, 320–335.

Bem, D. J. (1998). Is EBE theory supported by the evidence? Is it androcentric? A reply to Peplau et al. (1998). *Psychological Review, 105*, 395–398.

Bem, S. L. (1985). Androgyny and gender schema theory: A conceptual and empirical integration. In T. B. Sonderegger (Ed.), *Nebraska symposium on motivation, 1984: Psychology and gender* (Vol. 32). Lincoln: University of Nebraska Press.

Benca, R. M. (2001). Consequences of insomnia and its therapies. *Journal of Clinical Psychiatry, 62*(suppl 10), 33–38.

Bender, D. S., Skodol, A. E., Dyck, I. R., Markowitz, J. C., Shea, M. T., Yen, S., et al. (2007). Ethnicity and mental health treatment utilization by patients with personality disorders. *Journal of Consulting and Clinical Psychology, 75*, 992–999.

Benet, V., & Waller, N. G. (1995). The big seven factor model of personality description: Evidence for its cross-cultural generality in a Spanish sample. *Journal of Personality and Social Psychology, 69*, 701–718.

Benjamin, L. T., Jr. (2000). The psychology laboratory at the turn of the 20th century. *American Psychologist, 55*, 318–321.

Benjamin, L. T., Jr., & Baker, D. B. (2004). *From seance to science: A history of the profession of psychology in America*. Belmont, CA: Wadsworth.

Benjamin, L. T., Jr., & VandenBos, G. R. (2006). The window on psychology's literature: A history of psychological abstracts. *American Psychologist, 61*, 941–954.

Benjamin, L. T., Jr., Cavell, T. A., & Shallenberger, W. R., III. (1984). Staying with initial answers on objective tests: Is it a myth? *Teaching of Psychology, 11*, 133–141.

Benjamin, L. T., Jr., DeLeon, P. H., Freedheim, D. K., & VandenBos, G. R. (2003). Psychology as a profession. In D. K. Freedheim (Ed.), *Handbook of psychology, Vol. 1: History of psychology*. New York: Wiley

Benoît, M., & Norton, M. I. (2003). Perceptions of a fluid consensus: Uniqueness bias, false consensus, false polarization, and pluralistic ignorance in a water conservation crisis. *Personality and Social Psychology Bulletin, 29*, 559–567.

Ben-Porath, Y. S. (2003). Assessing personality and psychopathology with self-report inventories. In J. R. Graham & J. A. Naglieri (Eds.), *Handbook of psychology, Volume 10: Assessment psychology*. New York: Wiley.

Benson, H. (1975). *The relaxation response*. New York: Morrow.

Benson, H., & Klipper, M. Z. (1988). *The relaxation response*. New York: Avon.

Benton, D. (2004). Role of parents in the determination of the food preferences of children and the development of obesity. *International Journal of Obesity, 28*, 858–869.

Berenbaum, S. A., & Snyder, E. (1995). Early hormonal influences on childhood sex-typed activity and playmate preferences: Implications for the development of sexual orientation. *Developmental Psychology, 31*, 31–42.

Berghmans, R. L. P. (2007). Misleading research participants: Moral aspects of deception in psychological research. *Netherlands Journal of Psychology, 63*(1), 14–20.

Berkowitz, L. (1989). Frustration-aggression hypothesis: Examination and reformulation. *Psychological Bulletin, 106*, 59–73.

Berkowitz, R. I. (2003). Behavior therapies. In R. E. Hales & S. C. Yudofsky (Eds.), *Textbook of Clinical Psychiatry*. Washington, DC: American Psychiatric Publishing.

Berliner, L., & Briere, J. (1999). Trauma, memory, and clinical practice. In L. M. Williams & V. L. Banyard (Eds.), *Trauma & memory*. Thousand Oaks, CA: Sage Publications.

Berman, M. G., Jonides, J., & Kaplan, S. (2008). The cognitive benefits of interacting with nature. *Psychological Science, 19*, 1207–1212.

Berndsen, M., Spears, R., van der Plight, J., & McGarty, C. (2002). Illusory correlation and stereotype formation: Making sense of group differences and cognitive biases. In C. McGarty, V. Y. Yzerbyt, & R. Spears (Eds.), *Stereotypes as explanations: The formation of meaningful beliefs about social groups.* New York: Cambridge University Press.

Bernhardt, P. C. (1997). Influences of serotonin and testosterone in aggression and dominance: Convergence with social psychology. *Current Directions in Psychological Science, 6,* 44–48.

Berrettini, W. (2006). Genetics of bipolar and unipolar disorders. In D. J. Stein, D. J. Kupfer, & A. F. Schatzberg (Eds.), *Textbook of mood disorders.* Washington, DC: American Psychiatric Publishing.

Berridge, K. C. (2003). Comparing the emotional brains of humans and other animals. In R. J. Davidson, K. R. Scherer, & H. H. Goldsmith (Eds.), *Handbook of affective sciences.* New York: Oxford University Press.

Berridge, K. C. (2004). Motivation concepts in behavioral neuroscience. *Physiology and Behavior, 81*(2), 179–209.

Berry, D. T. R., Wetter, M. W., & Baer, R. A. (1995). Assessment of malingering. In J. N. Butcher (Ed.), *Clinical personality assessment: Practical approaches.* New York: Oxford University Press.

Berry, J. W. (1994). Cross-cultural variations in intelligence. In R. J. Sternberg (Ed.), *Encyclopedia of human intelligence.* New York: Macmillan.

Berry, J. W., Poortinga, Y., Segall, M., & Dasen, P. (1992). *Cross-cultural psychology.* New York: Cambridge University Press.

Berscheid, E. (1988). Some comments on love's anatomy: Or, whatever happened to old-fashioned lust. In R. J. Sternberg & M. L. Barnes (Eds.), *The psychology of love.* New Haven: Yale University Press.

Berscheid, E. (2006). Searching for the meaning of "love." In R. J. Sternberg & K. Weis (Eds.), *The new psychology of love.* New Haven, CT: Yale University Press.

Bertenthal, B. I., & Clifton, R. K. (1998). Perception and action. In W. Damon (Ed.), *Handbook of child psychology, Vol. 2: Cognition, perception, and language.* New York: Wiley.

Berthoud, H. R., & Morrison, C. (2008). The brain, appetite, and obesity. *Annual Review of Psychology, 59,* 55–92.

Berto, R. (2005). Exposure to restorative environments helps restore attentional capacity. *Journal of Environmental Psychology, 25,* 249–259.

Bertrand, R. M., & Lachman, M. E. (2003). Personality development in adulthood and old age. In R. M. Lerner, M. A. Easterbrooks, & J. Mistry (Eds.), *Handbook of psychology, Vol. 6: Developmental psychology.* New York: Wiley.

Berzonsky, M., & Adams, G. (1999). Commentary: Reevaluating the identity status paradigm: Still useful after 35 years. *Developmental Review, 19,* 557–590.

Beumont, P. J. V. (2002). Clinical presentation of anorexia nervosa and bulimia nervosa. In C. G. Fairburn & K. D. Brownell (Eds.), *Eating disorders and obesity: A comprehensive handbook.* New York: Guilford.

Beusterien, K. M., Davis, E. A., Flood, R., Howard, K., & Jordan, J. (2008). HIV patient insight on adhering to medication: A qualitative analysis. *AIDS Care, 20,* 251–259.

Beutler, L. E. (2002). The dodo bird is extinct. *Clinical Psychology: Science & Practice, 9*(1), 30–34.

Beutler, L. E., Bongar, B., & Shurkin, J. N. (1998). *Am I crazy, or is it my shrink?* New York: Oxford University Press.

Beutler, L. E., Bongar, B., & Shurkin, J. N. (2001). *A consumer's guide to psychotherapy.* New York: Oxford University Press.

Beutler, L. E., Malik, M., Alimohamed, S., Harwood, T. M., Talebi, H., Noble, S., & Wong, E. (2004). Therapist variables. In M. J. Lambert (Ed.), *Bergin and Garfield's handbook of psychotherapy and behavior change.* New York: Wiley.

Bi, G. Q., & Poo, M.-M. (2001). Synaptic modification by correlated activity: Hebb's postulate revisited. *Annual Review of Neuroscience, 24,* 139–166.

Bianchi, S., Milkie, M. A., Sayer, L. C., & Robinson, J. P. (2000). Is anyone doing the housework? Trends in the gender division of household labor. *Social Forces, 79*(1), 191–228.

Biederman, I., Hilton, H. J., & Hummel, J. E. (1991). Pattern goodness and pattern recognition. In G. R. Lockhead & J. R. Pomerantz (Eds.), *The perception of structure.* Washington, DC: American Psychological Association.

Biehl, M., Matsumoto, D., Ekman, P., Hearn, V., Heider, K., Kudoh, T., & Ton, V. (1997). Matsumoto and Ekman's Japanese and Caucasian Facial Expressions of Emotion (JACFEE): Reliability data and cross-national differences. *Journal of Nonverbal Behavior, 21,* 3–21.

Biermann, T., Estel, D., Sperling, W., Bleich, S., Kornhuber, J., & Reulbach, U. (2005). Influence of lunar phases on suicide: The end of a myth? A population-based study. *Chronobiology International, 22,* 1137–1143.

Bigler, E. D., Blatter, D. D., Anderson, C. V., Johnson, S. C., Gale, S. D., Hopkins, R. O., & Burnett, B. (1997). Hippocampal volume in normal aging and traumatic brain injury. *American Journal of Neuroradiology, 18,* 11–23.

Birkeland, S. A., Manson, T. M., Kisamore, J. L., Brannick, M. T., & Smith, M. A. (2006). A meta-analytic investigation of job applicant faking on personality measures. *International Journal of Selection and Assessment, 14,* 317–335.

Birnbaum, M. H. (2004a). Base rates in Bayesian inference. In F. P. Rudiger (Ed.), *Cognitive illusions.* New York: Psychology Press.

Birnbaum, M. H. (2004b). Human research and data collection via the Internet. *Annual Review of Psychology, 55,* 803–832.

Birney, D. P., Citron-Pousty, J. H., Lutz, D. J., & Sternberg, R. J. (2005). The development of cognitive and intellectual abilities. In M. H. Bornstein & M. E. Lamb (Eds.), *Developmental science: An advanced textbook.* Mahwah, NJ: Erlbaum.

Bishop, S. R. (2002). What do we really know about mindfulness-based stress reduction? *Psychosomatic Medicine, 64*(1), 71–83.

Bjork, R. A. (1992). Interference and forgetting. In L. R. Squire (Ed.), *Encyclopedia of learning and memory.* New York: Macmillan.

Bjorklund, D. F. (2005). *Children's thinking: Cognitive development and individual differences.* Belmont, CA: Wadsworth.

Black, D. W., & Andreasen, N. C. (1999). Schizophrenia, schizophreniform disorder, and delusional (paranoid) disorders. In R. E. Hales, S. C. Yudofsky, & J. A. Talbott (Eds.), *American Psychiatric Press textbook of psychiatry* (3rd ed.). Washington, DC: American Psychiatric Press.

Blacker, L. (1999). The launching phase of the life cycle. In B. Carter & M. McGoldrick (Eds.), *The expanded family life cycle: Individual, family, and social perspectives* (3rd ed., pp. 287–306). Boston: Allyn & Bacon.

Blair, C., Gamson, D., Thorne, S., & Baker, D. (2005). Rising mean IQ: Cognitive demand of mathematics education for young children, population

exposure to formal schooling, and the neurobiology of the prefrontal cortex. *Intelligence, 33,* 93–106.

Blair, S. N., Kohl, H. W., Paffenbarger, R. S., Clark, D. G., Cooper, K. H., & Gibbons, L. W. (1989). Physical fitness and all-cause mortality: A prospective study of healthy men and women. *Journal of the American Medical Association, 262,* 2395–2401.

Blakeslee, T. R. (1980). *The right brain.* Garden City, NY: Doubleday/Anchor.

Blanchard, E. B., & Keefer, L. (2003). Irritable bowel syndrome. In A. M. Nezu, C. M. Nezu, & P. A. Geller (Eds.), *Handbook of psychology, Vol. 9: Health psychology.* New York: Wiley.

Blanchard, F. A., Lilly, T., & Vaughn, L. A. (1991). Reducing the expression of racial prejudice. *Psychological Science, 2,* 101–105.

Blanchard, R., Zucker, K. J., Bradley, S. J., & Hume, C. S. (1995). Birth order and siblings sex ratio in homosexual male adolescents and probably prehomosexual feminine boys. *Developmental Psychology, 31,* 22–30.

Blank, H., Musch, J., & Pohl, R. F. (2007). Hindsight bias: On being wise after the event. *Social Cognition, 25*(1), 1–9.

Blankenhorn, D. (1995). *Fatherless America: Confronting our most urgent social problem.* New York: Basic Books.

Blass, T. (1991). Understanding behavior in the Milgram obedience experiment: The role of personality, situations, and their interactions. *Journal of Personality and Social Psychology, 60,* 398–413.

Blass, T. (1999). The Milgram Paradigm after 35 years: Some things we now know about obedience to authority. *Journal of Applied Social Psychology, 29,* 955–978.

Bleuler, E. (1911). *Dementia praecox or the group F schizophrenias.* New York: International Universities Press.

Blieszner, R., & Adams, R. G. (1992). *Adult friendship.* Newbury Park, CA: Sage.

Bliwise, D. L. (2005). Normal aging. In M. H. Kryger, T. Roth, & W. C. Dement (Eds.), *Principles and practice of sleep medicine.* Philadelphia: Elsevier Saunders.

Block, J. R., & Yuker, H. E. (1992). *Can you believe your eyes?: Over 250 illusions and other visual oddities.* New York: Brunner/Mazel.

Block, N. (2002). How heritability misleads us about race. In J. Fish (Ed.), *Race and intelligence: Separating science from myth.* Mahwah, NJ: Erlbaum.

Bloom, B. L. (1984). *Community mental health: A general introduction.* Pacific Grove, CA: Brooks/Cole.

Bloomfield, H. H., & Kory, R. B. (1976). *Happiness: The TM program, psychiatry, and enlightenment.* New York: Simon & Schuster.

Boakes, R. A. (2003). The impact of Pavlov on the psychology of learning in English-speaking countries. *The Spanish Journal of Psychology, 6*(2), 93–98.

Boase, J., & Wellman, B. (2006). Personal relationships: On and off the Internet. In A. L. Vangelisti & D. Perlman (Eds.), *The Cambridge handbook of personal relationships.* New York: Cambridge University Press.

Bochner, S., & Jones, J. (2003). *Child language development: Learning to talk.* London: Whurr Publishers.

Bodenheimer, T. (2000). Uneasy alliance: Clinical investigators and the pharmaceutical industry. *New England Journal of Medicine, 342,* 1539–1544.

Bogg, T., & Roberts, B. W. (2004). Conscientiousness and health-related behaviors: A meta-analysis of the leading behavioral contributors to mortality. *Psychological Bulletin, 130,* 887–919.

Boggild, H., & Knutsson, A. (1999). Shift work, risk factors and cardiovascular disease. *Scandinavian Journal of Work, Environment & Health, 25*(2), 85–99.

Bohner, G., & Schwarz, N. (2001). Attitudes, persuasion, and behavior. In A. Tesser & N. Schwarz (Eds.), *Blackwell handbook of social psychology: Intraindividual processes.* Malden, MA: Blackwell.

Bolger, N. (1990). Coping as a personality process: A prospective study. *Journal of Personality and Social Psychology, 59,* 525–537.

Bolles, R. C. (1975). *Theory of motivation.* New York: Harper & Row.

Bolling, M. Y., Terry, C. M., & Kohlenberg, R. J. (2006). Behavioral theories. In J. C. Thomas & D. L. Segal (Eds.), *Comprehensive handbook of personality and psychopathology.* New York: Wiley.

Boly, M., Faymonville, M.-E., Vogt, B. A., Maquet, P., & Laureys, S. (2007). Hypnotic regulation of consciousness and the pain neuromatrix. In G. A. Jamieson (Ed.), *Hypnosis and conscious states: The cognitive neuroscience perspective.* New York: Oxford University Press.

Bonanno, G. A. (2005). Resilience in the face of potential trauma. *Current Directions in Psychological Science, 14*(3), 135–138.

Bonanno, G. A., Field, N. P., Kovacevic, A., & Kaltman, S. (2002). Self-enhancement as a buffer against extreme adversity: Civil war in Bosnia and traumatic loss in the United States. *Personality and Social Psychology Bulletin, 28,* 184–196.

Bonanno, G. A., Moskowitz, J. T., Papa, A., & Folkman, S. (2005). Resilience to loss in bereaved spouses, bereaved parents, and bereaved gay men. *Journal of Personality and Social Psychology, 88,* 827–843.

Bond, R., & Smith, P. B. (1996). Culture and conformity: A meta-analysis of studies using Asch's line judgment task. *Psychological Bulletin, 119,* 111–137.

Bonnet, M. H. (2000). Sleep deprivation. In M. H. Kryger, T. Roth, & W. C. Dement (Eds.), *Principles and practice of sleep medicine.* Philadelphia: Saunders.

Bonnet, M. H. (2005). Acute sleep deprivation. In M. H. Kryger, T. Roth, & W. C. Dement (Eds.), *Principles and practice of sleep medicine.* Philadelphia: Elsevier Saunders.

Bono, G., McCullough, M. E., & Root, L. M. (2008). Forgiveness, feeling connected to others, and well-being: Two longitudinal studies. *Personality and Social Psychology Bulletin, 34,* 182–195.

Bootzin, R. R., Manber, R., Loewy, D. H., Kuo, T. F., & Franzen, P. L. (2001). Sleep disorders. In P. B. Sutker & H. E. Adams (Eds.), *Comprehensive handbook of psychopathology.* New York: Kluwer Academic/Plenum.

Borbely, A. A., & Achermann, P. (2005). Sleep homeostasis and models of sleep regulation. In M. H. Kryger, T. Roth, & W. C. Dement (Eds.), *Principles and practice of sleep medicine.* Philadelphia: Elsevier Saunders.

Bordnick, P. S., Elkins, R. L., Orr, T. E., Walters, P., & Thyer, B. A. (2004). Evaluating the relative effectiveness of three aversion therapies designed to reduce craving among cocaine abusers. *Behavioral Interventions, 19*(1), 1–24.

Borgida, E., & Nisbett, R. E. (1977). The differential impact of abstract vs. concrete information on decisions. *Journal of Applied Social Psychology, 7,* 258–271.

Boring, E. G. (1966). A note on the origin of the word *psychology. Journal of the History of the Behavioral Sciences, 2,* 167.

Bornstein, R. F. (2003). Psychodynamic models of personality. In T. Millon & M. J. Lerner (Eds.), *Handbook of psychology, Vol. 5: Personality and social psychology.* New York: Wiley.

Bosma, H., van Boxtel, M. P. J., Ponds, R. W. H. M., Houx, P. J., Burdorf, A., & Jolles, J. (2002). Mental work demands protect against cognitive impairment: MAAS prospective cohort study. *Experimental Aging Research, 29*(1), 33–45.

Bosson, J. K., & Swann, W. B. (2001). The paradox of the sincere chameleon: Strategic self-verification in close relationships. In J. H. Harvey & A. Wenzel (Eds.), *Close romantic relationships: Maintenance and enhancement.* Mahwah, NJ: Erlbaum.

Bost, K. K., Cox, M. J., Burchinal, M. R., & Payne, C. (2002). Structural and supporting changes in couples' family and friendship networks across the transition to parenthood. *Journal of Marriage and the Family, 64,* 517–531.

Bouchard, T. J., Jr. (1997). IQ similarity in twins reared apart: Findings and responses to critics. In R. J. Sternberg, & E. L. Grigorenko (Eds.), *Intelligence, heredity, and environment.* New York: Cambridge University Press.

Bouchard, T. J., Jr. (1998). Genetic and environmental influences on adult intelligence and special mental abilities. *Human Biology, 70,* 257–279.

Bouchard, T. J., Jr. (2004). Genetic influence on human psychological traits: A survey. *Current Directions in Psychological Science, 13*(4), 148–151.

Bouchard, T. J., Jr., Lykken, D. T., McGue, M., Segal, N. L., & Tellegen, A. (1990). Sources of human psychological differences: The Minnesota study of twins reared apart. *Science, 250,* 223–228.

Boudreaux, E., Carmack, C. L., Scarinci, I. C., & Brantley, P. J. (1998). Predicting smoking stage of change among a sample of low socioeconomic status, primary care outpatients: Replication and extension using decisional balance and self-efficacy theories. *International Journal of Behavioral Medicine, 5,* 148–165.

Bouman, T. K., Eifert, G. H., & Lejeuz, C. W. (1999). Somatoform disorders. In T. Millon, P. H. Blaney, & R. D. Davis (Eds.), *Oxford textbook of psychopathology* (pp. 444–465). New York: Oxford University Press.

Bourgeois, J. A., Seaman, J. S., & Servis, M. E. (2003). Delirium, dementia, and amnestic disorders. In R. E. Hales & S. C. Yudofsky (Eds.), *Textbook of clinical Psychiatry.* Washington, DC: American Psychiatric Publishing.

Bourguignon, E. (1972). Dreams and altered states of consciousness in anthropological research. In F. L. K. Hsu (Ed.), *Psychological anthropology* (2nd ed.). Cambridge, MA: Schenkman.

Bourhis, R. Y., & Gagnon, A. (2001). Social orientations in the minimal group paradigm. In R. Brown & S. L. Gaertner (Eds.), *Blackwell handbook of social psychology: Intergroup processes.* Malden, MA: Blackwell Publishing.

Bouton, M. E. (2000). A learning theory perspective on lapse, relapse, and the maintenance of behavior change. *Health Psychology, 19,* 57–63.

Bouton, M. E. (2002). Context, ambiguity, and unlearning: Sources of relapse after behavioral extinction. *Biological Psychiatry, 52,* 976–986.

Bouton, M. E. (2004). Context and behavioral processes in extinction. *Learning & Memory, 11,* 485–494.

Bowd, A. D., & Shapiro, K. J. (1993). The case against laboratory animal research in psychology. *Journal of Social Issues, 49*(1), 133–142.

Bowden, C. L. (2004). Valproate. In A. F. Schatzberg & C. B. Nemeroff (Eds.), *Textbook of psychopharmacology.* Washington, DC: American Psychiatric Publishing.

Bower, G. H. (1970). Organizational factors in memory. *Cognitive Psychology, 1,* 18–46.

Bower, G. H. (2000). A brief history of memory research. In E. Tulving & F. I. M. Craik (Eds.), *The Oxford handbook of memory* (pp. 3–32). New York: Oxford University Press.

Bower, G. H., & Clark, M. C. (1969). Narrative stories as mediators of serial learning. *Psychonomic Science, 14,* 181–182.

Bower, G. H., & Springston, F. (1970). Pauses as recoding points in letter series. *Journal of Experimental Psychology, 83,* 421–430.

Bowlby, J. (1969). *Attachment and loss: Vol. 1. Attachment.* New York: Basic Books.

Bowlby, J. (1973). *Attachment and loss: Vol. 2. Separation, anxiety and anger.* New York: Basic Books.

Bowlby, J. (1980). *Attachment and loss: Vol. 3. Sadness and depression.* New York: Basic Books.

Boyle, M. (2007). The problem with diagnosis. *The Psychologist, 20,* 290–292.

Boyle, S. H., Jackson, W. G., & Suarez, E. C. (2007). Hostility, anger, and depression predict increases in C3 over a 10-year period. *Brain, Behavior, and Immunity, 21,* 816–823.

Boynton, R. M. (1990). Human color perception. In K. N. Leibovic (Ed.), *Science of vision.* New York: Springer-Verlag.

Bradshaw, J. L. (1989). *Hemispheric specialization and psychological function.* New York: Wiley.

Bragg, E. A. (1996). Towards ecological self: Deep ecology meets constructionist self-theory. *Journal of Environmental Psychology, 16,* 93–108.

Brainerd, C. J. (1996). Piaget: A centennial celebration. *Psychological Science, 7,* 191–195.

Brainerd, C. J., & Reyna, V. F. (2005). *The science of false memory.* New York: Oxford University Press.

Branaman, T. F., & Gallagher, S. N. (2005). Polygraph testing in sex offender treatment: A review of limitations. *American Journal of Forensic Psychology, 23*(1), 45–64.

Brannon, L., & Feist, J. (2007). *Health psychology: An introduction to behavior and health.* Belmont, CA: Wadsworth.

Branson, R. (2005). *Losing my virginity: The autobiography.* London: Virgin.

Branson, R. (2006). *Screw it, let's do it: Lessons in life.* London: Virgin.

Brase, G. L. (2006). Cues of parental investment as a factor in attractiveness. *Evolution and Human Behavior, 27,* 145–157.

Brase, G. L., Cosmides, L., & Tooby, J. (1998). Individuation, counting, and statistical inference: The role of frequency and whole-object representations in judgment under certainty. *Journal of Experimental Psychology: General, 127,* 3–21.

Bredt, B. M., Higuera-Alhino, D., Hebert, S. J., McCune, J. M., & Abrams, D. I. (2002). Short-term effects of cannabinoids on immune phenotype and function in HIV-1-infected patients. *Journal of Clinical Pharmacology, 42,* 90S–96S.

Breedlove, S. M. (1994). Sexual differentiation of the human nervous system. *Annual Review of Psychology, 45,* 389–418.

Breggin, P. R. (1991). *Toxic psychiatry*. New York: St. Martin's Press.

Breggin, P. R., & Cohen, D. (2007). *Your drug may be your problem: How and why to stop taking psychiatric medications*. New York: Da Capo Lifelong Books.

Brehm, J. W. (1966). *A theory of psychological reactance*. New York: Academic Press.

Brehm, S. S., & Kassin, S. M. (1993). *Social psychology*. Boston: Houghton Mifflin.

Breland, K., & Breland, M. (1961). The misbehavior of organisms. *American Psychologist, 16*, 681–684.

Bretherton, I., & Munholland, K. A. (1999). Internal working models in attachment relationships. In J. Cassidy & P. R. Shaver (Eds.), *Handbook of attachment: Theory, research, and clinical applications*. New York: Guilford.

Bretl, D. J., & Cantor, J. (1988). The portrayal of men and women in U.S. television commercials: A recent content analysis and trend over 15 years. *Sex Roles, 18*, 595–609.

Breugelmans, S. M., Poortinga, Y. H., Ambadar, Z., Setiadi, B., Vaca, J. B., Widiyanto, P., et al. (2005). Body sensations associated with emotions in Raramuri Indians, rural Javanese, and three student samples. *Emotion, 5*, 166–174.

Brewer, W. F. (2000). Bartlett, functionalism, and modern schema theories. *Journal of Mind and Behavior, 21*, 37–44.

Brewer, W. F., & Treyens, J. C. (1981). Role of schemata in memory for places. *Cognitive Psychology, 13*, 207–230.

Brewin, C. R. (2007). Autobiographical memory for trauma: Update on four controversies. *Memory, 15*, 227–248.

Brewster, K. L., & Padavic, I. (2000). Change in gender-ideology, 1977–1996: The contributions of intracohort change and population turnover. *Journal of Marriage and the Family, 62*, 477–487.

Bridge, J. A., & Barbe, R. P. (2004). Reducing hospital readmission in depression and schizophrenia: Current evidence. *Current Opinion in Psychiatry, 17*, 505–511.

Bridge, J. A., Iyengar, S., Salary, C. B., Barbe, R. P., Birmaher, B., Pincus, H. A., et al. (2007). Clinical response and risk for reported suicidal ideation and suicide attempts in pediatric antidepressant treatment: A meta-analysis of randomized controlled trials. *Journal of the American Medical Association, 297*, 1683–1969.

Briere, J., & Conte, J. R. (1993). Self-reported amnesia for abuse in adults molested as children. *Journal of Traumatic Stress, 6*(1), 21–31.

Bringmann, W. G., & Balk, M. M. (1992). Another look at Wilhelm Wundt's publication record. *History of Psychology Newsletter, 24*(3/4), 50–66.

Brislin, R. (2000). *Understanding culture's influence on behavior*. Belmont, CA: Wadsworth.

Broadbent, D. E. (1958). *Perception and communication*. New York: Pergamon Press.

Brobeck, J. R., Tepperman, T., & Long, C. N. (1943). Experimental hypothalamic hyperphagia in the albino rat. *Yale Journal of Biology and Medicine, 15*, 831–853.

Bröder, A. (1998). Deception can be acceptable. *American Psychologist, 53*, 805–806.

Brody, N. (2003). Jensen's genetic interpretation of racial differences in intelligence: Critical evaluation. In H. Nyborg (Ed.), *The scientific study of general intelligence: Tribute to Arthur R. Jensen*. Oxford, UK: Pergamon.

Broughton, R. (1994). Important underemphasized aspects of sleep onset. In R. D. Ogilvie & J. R. Harsh (Eds.), *Sleep onset: Normal and abnormal processes*. Washington, DC: American Psychological Association.

Brown, A. S. (1991). A review of the tip-of-the-tongue experience. *Psychological Bulletin, 109*, 204–223.

Brown, A. S. (1999). New perspectives on the neurodevelopmental hypothesis of schizophrenia. *Psychiatric Annals, 29*(3), 128–130.

Brown, A. S., Begg, M. D., Gravenstein, S., Schaefer, C. S., Wyatt, R. J., Bresnahan, M., Babulas, V. P., & Susser, E. S. (2004). Serologic evidence of prenatal influenza in the etiology of schizophrenia. *Archives of General Psychiatry, 61*, 774–780.

Brown, E. J., Juster, H. R., Heimberg, R. G., & Winning, C. D. (1998). Stressful life events and personality styles: Relation to impairment and treatment outcome in patients with social phobia. *Journal of Anxiety Disorders, 12*, 233–251.

Brown, H. D., & Kosslyn, S. M. (1993). Cerebral lateralization. *Current Opinion in Neurobiology, 3*, 183–186.

Brown, M. (1974). Some determinants of persistence and initiation of achievement-related activities. In J. W. Atkinson & J. O. Raynor (Eds.), *Motivation and achievement*. Washington, DC: Halsted.

Brown, M. (1998). *Richard Branson: The inside story*. London: Headline.

Brown, R., & Kulik, J. (1977). Flashbulb memories. *Cognition, 5*, 73–79.

Brown, R., & McNeill, D. (1966). The "tip-of-the-tongue" phenomenon. *Journal of Verbal Learning and Verbal Behavior, 5*(4), 325–337.

Brown, R. D., Goldstein, E., & Bjorklund, D. F. (2000). The history and zeitgeist of the repressed–false-memory debate: Scientific and sociological perspectives on suggestibility and childhood memory. In D. F. Bjorklund (Ed.), *False-memory creation in children and adults* (pp. 1–30). Mahwah, NJ: Erlbaum.

Brown, R. T. (1989). Creativity: What are we to measure? In J. A. Glover, R. R. Ronning, & C. R. Reynolds (Eds.), *Handbook of creativity*. New York: Plenum.

Brown, S. C., & Craik, F. I. M. (2000). Encoding and retrieval of information. In E. Tulving & F. I. M. Craik (Eds.), *The Oxford handbook of memory* (pp. 93–108). New York: Oxford University Press.

Brown, W. D. (2006). Insomnia: Prevalence and daytime consequences. In T. Lee-Chiong (Ed.), *Sleep: A comprehensive handbook*. Hoboken, NJ: Wiley-Liss.

Brownell, H. H., & Gardner, H. (1981). Hemisphere specialization: Definitions not incantations. *Behavioral and Brain Sciences, 4*, 64–65.

Bruce, D., Dolan, A., & Phillips-Grant, K. (2000). On the transition from childhood amnesia to the recall of personal memories. *Psychological Science, 11*, 360–364.

Bruckner-Gordon, F., Gangi, B. K., & Wallman, G. U. (1988). *Making therapy work: Your guide to choosing, using, and ending therapy*. New York: Harper & Row.

Bruer, J. T. (1999). *The myth of the first three years: A new understanding of early brain development and lifelong learning*. New York: Free Press.

Bruer, J. T. (2002). Avoiding the pediatricians error: How neuroscientists can help educators (and themselves). *Nature Neuroscience, 5*, 1031–1033.

Bruggerman, E. L., & Hart, K. J. (1996). Cheating, lying, and moral reasoning by religious and secular high school students. *Journal of Educational Research, 89*, 340–344.

Brumbaugh, C. C., & Fraley, R. C. (2006). Transference and attachment: How do attachment patterns get carried forward from one relationship to the next? *Personality and Social Psychology Bulletin, 32*, 552–560.

Bryden, M. P. (1982). *Laterality: Functional asymmetry in the intact brain*. New York: Academic Press.

Brym, R., & Lenton, R. (2001). *Love online: A report on digital dating in Canada*. Retrieved from http://www.chass.utoronto.ca/brym/pubs.htm.

Buccino, G., & Riggio, L. (2006). The role of the mirror neuron system in motor learning. *Kinesiology, 38*(1), 5–15.

Buchanan, R. W., & Carpenter, W. T. (2000). Schizophrenia: Introduction and overview. In B. J. Sadock & V. A. Sadock (Eds.), *Kaplan and Sadock's comprehensive textbook of psychiatry* (7th ed., Vol. 1). Philadelphia: Lippincott/Williams & Wilkins.

Buchanan, R. W., & Carpenter, W. T. (2005). Concept of schizophrenia. In B. J. Sadock & V. A. Sadock (Eds.), *Kaplan & Sadock's comprehensive textbook of psychiatry*. Philadelphia: Lippincott Williams & Wilkins.

Buchanan, T. (2000). Potential of the Internet for personality research. In M. H. Birnbaum (Ed.), *Psychological experiments on the Internet*. San Diego: Academic Press.

Buchanan, T. (2007). Personality testing on the Internet: What we know, and what we do not. In A. N. Joinson, K. Y. A. McKenna, T. Postmes, & U-D. Reips (Eds.), *The Oxford handbook of Internet psychology*. New York: Oxford University Press.

Buck, L. B. (2000). Smell and taste: The chemical senses. In E. R. Kandel, J. H. Schwartz, & T. M. Jessell (Eds.), *Principles of neural science*. New York: McGraw-Hill.

Buck, L. B. (2004). Olfactory receptors and coding in mammals. *Nutrition Reviews, 62*, S184–S188.

Buckman, R. (2002). Communications and emotions: Skills and effort are key. *British Medical Journal, 325*, 672.

Bufe, B., Breslin, P. A. S., Kuhn, C., Reed, D. R., Tharp, C. D., Slack, J. P., Kim, U., Drayna, D., & Meyerhof, W. (2005). The molecular basis of individual differences in phenylthiocarbamide and propylthiouracil bitterness perception. *Current Biology, 15*, 322–327.

Bühler, C., & Allen, M. (1972). *Introduction to humanistic psychology*. Pacific Grove, CA: Brooks/Cole.

Bulcroft, R., & Teachman, J. (2004). Ambiguous constructions: Development of a childless or child-free life course. In M. Coleman & L. H. Ganong (Eds.), *Handbook of contemporary families: Considering the past, contemplating the future*. Thousand Oaks, CA: Sage.

Bulik, C. M. (2004). Genetic and biological risk factors. In J. K. Thompson (Ed.), *Handbook of eating disorders and obesity*. New York: Wiley.

Bulik, C. M., Tozzi, F., Anderson, C., Mazzeo, S. E., Aggen, S., & Sullivan, P. F. (2003). The relation between eating disorders and components of perfectionism. *American Journal of Psychiatry, 160*, 366–368.

Burger, J. M. (1986). Temporal effects on attributions: Actor and observer differences. *Social Cognition, 4*, 377–387.

Burger, J. M. (1997). *Personality*. Pacific Grove: Brooks/Cole.

Burger, J. M. (1999). The foot-in-the-door compliance procedure: A multiple process analysis review. *Personality and Social Psychology Review, 3,* 303–325.

Burger, J. M. (2004). *Personality.* Belmont, CA: Wadsworth.

Burger, J. M. (2008). *Personality.* Belmont, CA: Wadsworth.

Burger, J. M. (2009). Replicating Milgram: Would people still obey today? *American Psychologist, 64,* 1-11.

Burgess, A. (2007). On the contribution of neurophysiology to hypnosis research: Current state and future directions. In G. A. Jamieson (Ed.), *Hypnosis and conscious states: The cognitive neuroscience perspective.* New York: Oxford University Press.

Burke, D. M., & Shafto, M. A. (2004). Aging and language production. *Current Directions in Psychological Science, 13*(1), 21–24.

Burlingame, G. M., & McClendon, D. T. (2008). Group therapy. In J. L. Lebow (Ed.), *Twenty-first century psychotherapies: Contemporary approaches to theory and practice.* New York: Wiley.

Burns, A. B., Brown, J. S., Plant, E. A., Sachs-Ericsson, N., & Joiner, T. E. Jr. (2006). On the specific depressotypic nature of excessive reassurance-seeking. *Personality and Individual Differences, 40,* 135–145.

Burns, A. B., Brown, J. S., Sachs-Ericsson, N., Plant, E. A., Curtis, J. T., Fredrickson, B. L., et al. (2008). Upward spirals of positive emotion and coping: Replication, extension, and initial exploration of neurochemical substrates. *Personality and Individual Differences, 44,* 360–370.

Burns, B. D., & Corpus, B. (2004). Randomness and inductions from streaks: "Gambler's fallacy" versus "hot hand." *Psychonomic Bulletin & Review, 11*(1), 179–184.

Burriss, R. P., & Little, A. C. (2006). Effects of partner conception risk phase on male perception of dominance in faces. *Evolution and Human Behavior, 27,* 297–305.

Bursztajn, H. J., & Brodsky, A. (2002). Managed health care: Complications, liability risk, and clinical remedies. *Primary Psychiatry, 9*(4), 37–41.

Bushman, B. J. (2002). Does venting anger feed or extinguish the flame? Catharsis, rumination, distraction, anger, and aggressive responding. *Personality and Social Psychology Bulletin, 28,* 724–731.

Bushman, B. J., & Anderson, C. A. (2001). Media violence and the American public: Scientific facts versus media misinformation. *American Psychologist, 56,* 477–489.

Bushman, B. J., Baumeister, R. F., & Stack, A. D. (1999). Catharsis, aggression, and persuasive influence: Self-fulfilling or self-defeating prophecies? *Journal of Personality and Social Psychology, 76,* 367–376.

Bushman, B. J., & Huesmann, L. R. (2001). Effects of televised violence on aggression. In D. G. Singer & J. L. Singer (Eds.), *Handbook of children and the media.* Thousand Oaks, CA: Sage.

Buss, D. M. (1985). Human mate selection. *American Scientist, 73,* 47–51.

Buss, D. M. (1988). The evolution of human intrasexual competition: Tactics of mate attraction. *Journal of Personality and Social Psychology, 54,* 616–628.

Buss, D. M. (1989). Sex differences in human mate preferences: Evolutionary hypotheses tested in 37 cultures. *Behavioral and Brain Sciences, 12,* 1–49.

Buss, D. M. (1991). Evolutionary personality psychology. *Annual Review of Psychology, 42,* 459–491.

Buss, D. M. (1994a). *The evolution of desire: Strategies of human mating.* New York: Basic Books.

Buss, D. M. (1994b). Mate preferences in 37 cultures. In W. J. Lonner & R. S. Malpass (Eds.), *Psychology and culture.* Boston: Allyn & Bacon.

Buss, D. M. (1995). Evolutionary psychology: A new paradigm for psychological science. *Psychological Inquiry, 6,* 1–30.

Buss, D. M. (1996). The evolutionary psychology of human social strategies. In E. T. Higgins & A. W. Kruglanski (Eds.), *Social psychology: Handbook of basic principles.* New York: Guilford.

Buss, D. M. (1997). Evolutionary foundation of personality. In R. Hogan, J. Johnson, & S. Briggs (Eds.), *Handbook of personality psychology.* San Diego: Academic Press.

Buss, D. M. (1998). The psychology of human mate selection: Exploring the complexity of the strategic repertoire. In C. Crawford, & D. L. Krebs (Eds.), *Handbook of evolutionary psychology: Ideas, issues, and applications.* Mahwah, NJ: Erlbaum.

Buss, D. M. (1999). *Evolutionary psychology: The new science of the mind.* Boston: Allyn & Bacon.

Buss, D. M. (2001). Cognitive biases and emotional wisdom in the evolution of conflict between the sexes. *Current Directions in Psychological Science, 10,* 219–223.

Buss, D. M. (2006). The evolution of love. In R. J. Sternberg & K. Weis (Eds.), *The new psychology of love.* New Haven, CT: Yale University Press.

Buss, D. M., & Kenrick, D. T. (1998). Evolutionary social psychology. In D. T. Gilbert, S. T. Fiske, & G. Lindzey (Eds.), *The handbook of social psychology.* New York: McGraw-Hill.

Buss, D. M., & Reeve, H. K. (2003). Evolutionary psychology and developmental dynamics: Comment on Lickliter and Honeycutt (2003). *Psychological Bulletin, 129,* 848–853.

Buss, D. M., & Schmitt, D. P. (1993). Sexual strategies theory: A contextual evolutionary analysis of human mating. *Psychological Review, 100,* 204–232.

Buss, D. M., & Shackelford, T. K. (2008). Attractive women want it all: Good genes, economic investment, parenting proclivities, and emotional commitment. *Evolutionary Psychology, 6*(1), 134–146.

Bussey, K., & Bandura, A. (1984). Influence of gender constancy and social power on sex-linked modeling. *Journal of Personality and Social Psychology, 47,* 1292–1302.

Bussey, K., & Bandura, A. (1999). Social cognitive theory of gender development and differentiation. *Psychological Review, 106,* 676–713.

Bussey, K., & Bandura, A. (2004). Social cognitive theory of gender development and functioning. In A. H. Eagly, A. E. Beall, & R. J. Sternberg (Eds.), *The psychology of gender.* New York: Guilford.

Buster, J. E., & Carson, S. A. (2002). Endocrinology and diagnosis of pregnancy. In S. G. Gabbe, J. R. Niebyl, & J. L. Simpson (Eds.), *Obstetrics: Normal and problem pregnancies.* New York: Churchill Livingstone.

Butcher, J. N. (1990). *The MMPI-2 in psychological treatment.* New York: Oxford University Press.

Butcher, J. N. (2005). *A beginner's guide to the MMPI-2.* Washington, DC: American Psychological Association.

Butcher, J. N. (2006). *MMPI-2: A practitioner's guide.* Washington, DC: American Psychological Association.

Butler, E. A., Egloff, B., Wilhelm, F. H., Smith, N. C., Erickson, E. A., & Gross, J. J. (2003). The social consequences of expressive suppression. *Emotion, 3*(1), 48–67.

Button, T. M. M., Maughan, B., & McGuffin, P. (2007). The relationship of maternal smoking to psychological problems in the offspring. *Early Human Development, 83,* 727–732.

Buxton, C. E. (1985). American functionalism. In C. E. Buxton (Ed.), *Points of view in the modern history of psychology.* Orlando: Academic Press.

Buxton, M. N., Arkey, Y., Lagos, J., Deposito, F., Lowenthal, F., & Simring, S. (1981). Stress and platelet aggregation in hemophiliac children and their family members. *Research Communications in Psychology, Psychiatry and Behavior, 6*(1), 21–48.

Byne, W., Kemether, E., Jones, L., Haroutunian, V., & Davis, K. L. (1999). The neurochemistry of schizophrenia. In D. S. Charney, E. J. Nestler & B. S. Bunney (Eds.), *Neurobiology of mental illness* (pp. 236–245). New York: Oxford University Press.

Byrne, D. (1997). An overview (and underview) of research and theory within the attraction paradigm. *Journal of Social and Personal Relationships, 14,* 417–431.

Byrne, D., Clore, G. L., & Smeaton, G. (1986). The attraction hypothesis: Do similar attitudes affect anything? *Journal of Personality and Social Psychology, 51,* 1167–1170.

Cacioppo, J. T., & Berntson, G. G. (1999). The affect system: Architecture and operating characteristics. *Current Directions in Psychological Science, 8,* 133–137.

Cacioppo, J. T., & Gardner, W. L. (1999). Emotion. *Annual Review of Psychology, 50,* 191–214.

Cacioppo, J. T., Hawkley, L. C., Kalil, A., Hughes, M. E., Waite, L., & Thisted, R. A. (2008). Happiness and the invisible threads of social connection: The Chicago health, aging, and social relations study. In M. Eid & R. J. Larsen (Eds.), *The science of subjective well-being.* New York: Guilford.

Cacioppo, J. T., Klein, D. J., Berntson, G. G., & Hatfield, E. (1993). The psychophysiology of emotions. In M. Lewis & J. M. Haviland (Eds.), *Handbook of emotions.* New York: Guilford.

Cahn, B. R., & Polich, J. (2006). Meditation states and traits: EEG, ERP, and neuroimaging studies. *Psychological Bulletin, 132,* 180–211.

Cain, W. S. (1988). Olfaction. In R. C. Atkinson, R. J. Herrnstein, G. Lindzey, & R. D. Luce (Eds.), *Stevens' handbook of experimental psychology: Perception and motivation* (Vol. 1). New York: Wiley.

Caine, E. D., & Lyness, J. M. (2000). Delirium, dementia, and amnestic and other cognitive disorders. In B. J. Sadock & V. A. Sadock (Eds.), *Kaplan and Sadock's comprehensive textbook of psychiatry.* Philadelphia: Lippincott/Williams & Wilkins.

Calhoun, L. G., & Tedeschi, R. G. (2006). The foundations of posttraumatic growth: An expanded framework. In L. G. Calhoun & R. G. Tedeschi (Eds.), *Handbook of posttraumatic growth: Research & practice.* Mahwah, NJ: Erlbaum.

Calhoun, L. G., & Tedeschi, R. G. (2008). The paradox of struggling with trauma: Guidelines for practice and directions for research. In S. Joseph & P. A. Linley (Eds.), *Trauma, recovery, and growth: Positive psychological perspectives on posttraumatic stress.* Hoboken, NJ: Wiley.

Callicutt, J. W. (2006). Homeless shelters: An uneasy component of the de facto mental health system. In J. Rosenberg & S. Rosenberg (Eds.), *Community mental health: Challenges for the 21st century.* New York: Routledge.

Cohen, S., Alper, C. M., Doyle, W. J., Treanor, J. J., & Turner, R. B. (2006). Positive emotional style predicts resistance to illness after experimental exposure to Rhinovirus or Influenza A virus. *Psychosomatic Medicine, 68,* 809–815.

Cohen, S., Janicki-Deverts, D., & Miller, G. E. (2007). Psychological stress and disease. *Journal of the American Medical Association, 298,* 1685–1687.

Cohen, S., Kessler, R. C., & Gordon, L. U. (1995). Strategies for measuring stress in studies of psychiatric and physical disorders. In S. Cohen, R. C. Kessler, & L. U. Gordon (Eds.), *Measuring stress: A guide for health and social scientists* (pp. 3–28). New York: Oxford University Press.

Cohen, S., & Pressman, S. D. (2006). Positive affect and health. *Current Directions in Psychological Science, 15*(3), 122–125.

Cohen, S., Tyrrell, D. A. J., & Smith, A. P. (1993). Negative life events, perceived stress, negative affect, and susceptibility to the common cold. *Journal of Personality and Social Psychology, 64,* 131–140.

Colborn, T., Dumanoski, D., & Myers, J. P. (1997). *Our stolen future: Are we threatening our fertility, intelligence, and survival? A scientific detective story.* New York: Plume.

Colby, A., & Kohlberg, L. (1987). *The measurement of moral judgment* (Vols. 1–2). New York: Cambridge University Press.

Coley, J. D., Solomon, G. E. A., & Shafto, P. (2002). The development of folkbiology: A cognitive science perspective on children's understanding of the biological world. In P. H. Kahn, Jr. & S. R. Kellert (Eds.), *Children and nature: Psychological, sociocultural, and evolutionary investigations.* Cambridge, MA: MIT Press.

Colflesh, G. J. H., & Conway, A. R. A. (2007). Individual differences in working memory capacity and divided attention in dichotic listening. *Psychonomic Bulletin & Review, 14,* 699–703.

Collaer, M. L., & Hines, M. (1995). Human behavioral sex differences: A role for gonadal hormones during early development? *Psychological Bulletin, 118,* 55–107.

Collins, A. M., & Loftus, E. F. (1975). A spreading activation theory of semantic processing. *Psychological Review, 82,* 407–428.

Collins, M. A., & Zebrowitz, L. A. (1995). The contributions of appearance to occupational outcomes in civilian and military settings. *Journal of Applied Social Psychology, 25,* 129–163.

Collins, N. L., & Allard, L. M. (2001). Cognitive representations of attachment: The content and function of working models. In G. J. O. Fletcher & M. S. Clark (Eds.), *Blackwell handbook of social psychology: Interpersonal processes.* Malden, MA: Blackwell.

Collins, W. A., & Laursen, B. (2006). Parent-adolescent relationships. In P. Noller & J. A. Feeney (Eds.), *Close relationships: Functions, forms and processes.* Hove, England: Psychology Press.

Collins, W. A., Maccoby, E. E., Steinberg, L., Hetherington, E. M., & Bornstein, M. H. (2000). Contemporary research in parenting: The case for nature and nurture. *American Psychologist, 55,* 218–232.

Collop, N. A. (2006). Polysomnography. In T. Lee-Chiong (Ed.), *Sleep: A comprehensive handbook.* Hoboken, NJ: Wiley-Liss.

Colom, R., Lluis-Font, J. M., & Andres-Pueyo, A. (2005). The generational intelligence gains are caused by decreasing variance in the lower half of the distribution: Supporting evidence for the nutrition hypothesis. *Intelligence, 33,* 83–91.

Coltrane, S. (2001). Research on household labor: Modeling and measuring the social embeddedness of routine family work. In R. M. Milardo (Ed.), *Understanding families into the new millennium: A decade in review* (pp. 427–452). Minneapolis, MN: National Council on Family Relations.

Colwill, R. M. (1993). An associative analysis of instrumental learning. *Current Directions in Psychological Science, 2*(4), 111–116.

Comas-Diaz, L. (2006). Cultural variation in the therapeutic relationship. In C. D. Goodheart, A. E. Kazdin, & R. J. Sternberg (Eds.), *Evidence-based psychotherapy: Where practice and research meet.* Washington, DC: American Psychological Association.

Combs, D. R., & Mueser, K. T. (2007). Schizophrenia. In M. Hersen, S. M. Turner, & D. C. Beidel (Eds.), *Adult psychopathology and diagnosis.* New York: Wiley.

Comer, D. R. (1995). A model of social loafing in real work groups. *Human Relations, 48,* 647–667.

Compas, B. E. (2004). Processes of risk and resilience during adolescence: Linking contexts and individuals. In R. M. Lerner & L. Steinberg (Eds.), *Handbook of adolescent psychology.* New York: Wiley.

Compton, D. M., Dietrich, K. L., & Smith, J. S. (1995). Animal rights activism and animal welfare concerns in the academic setting: Levels of activism and perceived importance of research with animals. *Psychological Reports, 76,* 23–31.

Compton, M. T., Goulding, S. M., & Walker, E. F. (2007). Cannabis use, first-episode psychosis, and schizotypy: A summary and synthesis of recent literature. *Current Psychiatry Reviews, 3,* 161–171.

Conn, S. (1995). When the earth hurts, who responds? In T. Roszak, M. E. Gomes, & A. D. Kanner (Eds.), *Eco-psychology: Restoring the earth, healing the mind.* San Francisco: Sierra Club.

Connolly, T., & Zeelenberg, M. (2002). Regret in decision making. *Current Directions in Psychological Science, 11*(6), 212–216.

Conway, A. R. A., Kane, M. J., & Engle, R. W. (2003). Working memory capacity and its relation to general intelligence. *Trends in Cognitive Sciences, 7,* 547–552.

Conway, L. C., & Schaller, M. (2002). On the verifiability of evolutionary psychological theories: An analysis of the psychology of scientific persuasion. *Personality and Social Psychology Review, 6,* 152–166.

Cooke, L. (2007). The importance of exposure for healthy eating in childhood: A review. *Journal of Human Nutrition and Dietetics, 20,* 294–301.

Cooper, E. (1991). A critique of six measures for assessing creativity. *Journal of Creative Behavior, 25*(3), 194–204.

Cooper, L., & Bright, J. (2001). Individual differences in reactions to stress. In F. Jones & J. Bright (Eds.), *Stress: Myth, theory and research.* Harlow, UK: Pearson Education.

Cooper, M. L., Pioli, M., Levitt, A., Talley, A. E., Micheas, L., & Collins, N. L. (2006). Attachment styles, sex motives, and sexual behavior: Evidence for gender-specific expressions of attachment dynamics. In M. Mikulincer & G. S. Goodman (Eds.), *Dynamics of romantic love: Attachment, caregiving, and sex.* New York: Guilford.

Corballis, M. C. (1991). *The lopsided ape.* New York: Oxford University Press.

Corballis, P. M. (2003). Visuospatial processing and the right-hemisphere interpreter. *Brain & Cognition, 53*(2), 171–176.

Coren, S. (1992). *The left-hander syndrome: The causes and consequences of left-handedness.* New York: Free Press.

Coren, S. (1996). *Sleep thieves: An eye-opening exploration into the science and mysteries of sleep.* New York: Free Press.

Coren, S., & Aks, D. J. (1990). Moon illusion in pictures: A multimechanism approach. *Journal of Experimental Psychology: Human Perception and Performance, 16,* 365–380.

Coren, S., & Girgus, J. S. (1978). *Seeing is deceiving: The psychology of visual illusions.* Hillsdale, NJ: Erlbaum.

Corkin, S. (1984). Lasting consequences of bilateral medial temporal lobectomy: Clinical course and experimental findings in H. M. *Seminars in Neurology, 4,* 249–259.

Corkin, S. (2002). What's new with the amnesic patient H. M.? *Nature Reviews Neuroscience, 3,* 153–159.

Cornell, D. G. (1997). Post hoc explanation is not prediction. *American Psychologist, 52,* 1380.

Correll, C. U., Leucht, S., & Kane, J. M. (2004). Lower risk for tardive dyskinesia associated with second-generation antipsychotics: A systematic review of 1-year studies. *American Journal of Psychiatry, 161,* 414–425.

Corsica, J. A., & Perri, M. G. (2003). Obesity. In A. M. Nezu, C. M. Nezu, & P. A. Geller (Eds.), *Handbook of psychology, Vol. 9: Health psychology.* New York: Wiley.

Cosmides, L. L., & Tooby, J. (1989). Evolutionary psychology and the generation of culture. Part II. Case study: A computational theory of social exchange. *Ethology and Sociobiology, 10,* 51–97.

Cosmides, L., & Tooby, J. (1996). Are humans good intuitive statisticians after all? Rethinking some conclusions from the literature on judgment under uncertainty. *Cognition, 58,* 1–73.

Costa, P. T., Jr., & McCrae, R. R. (1985). *NEO Personality Inventory.* Odessa, FL: Psychological Assessment Resources.

Costa, P. T., Jr., & McCrae, R. R. (1992). *Revised NEO Personality Inventory: NEO PI and NEO Five-Factor Inventory* (Professional Manual). Odessa, FL: Psychological Assessment Resources.

Costa, P. T., Jr., & McCrae, R. R. (1994). Set like plaster? Evidence for the stability of adult personality. In T. F. Heatherton & J. L. Weinberger (Eds.), *Can personality change?* Washington, DC: American Psychological Association.

Costa, P. T., Jr., & McCrae, R. R. (1997). Longitudinal stability of adult personality. In R. Hogan, J. Johnson, & S. Briggs (Eds.), *Handbook of personality psychology.* San Diego: Academic Press.

Côté, J. E. (2006). Emerging adulthood as an institutionalized moratorium: Risks and benefits to identity formation. In J. J. Arnett & J. L. Tanner (Eds.), *Emerging adults in America: Coming of age in the 21st century.* Washington, DC: American Psychological Association.

Cotman, C. W., Berchtold, N. C., & Christie, L.-A. (2007). Exercise builds brain health: Key roles of growth factor cascades and inflammation. *Trends in Neurosciences, 30,* 464–472.

Cotter, A., & Potter, J. E. (2006). Mother to child transmission. In J. Beal, J. J. Orrick, & K. Alfonso (Eds.), *HIV/AIDS: Primary care guide.* Norwalk, CT: Crown House.

Courage, M. L., & Howe, M. L. (2002). From infant to child: The dynamics of cognitive change in the second year of life. *Psychological Bulletin, 128*(2), 250–277.

Coutts, A. (2000). Nutrition and the life cycle. 1: Maternal nutrition and pregnancy. *British Journal of Nursing, 9*, 1133–1138.

Cowan, N. (2001). The magical number 4 in short-term memory: A reconsideration of mental storage capacity. *Behavioral & Brain Sciences, 14*(1), 87–185.

Cowan, N. (2005). *Working memory capacity.* New York: Psychology Press.

Cowart, B. J. (2005). Taste, our body's gustatory gatekeeper. *Cerebrum, 7*(2), 7–22.

Cowart, B. J., & Rawson, N. E. (2001). Olfaction. In E. B. Goldstein (Ed.), *Blackwell handbook of perception.* Malden, MA: Blackwell.

Cowey, A. (1994). Cortical visual areas and the neurobiology of higher visual processes. In M. J. Farah & G. Ratcliff (Eds.), *The neuropsychology of high-level vision: Collected tutorial essays.* Hillsdale, NJ: Erlbaum.

Cox, D., Meyers, E., & Sinha, P. (2004). Contextually evoked object-specific responses in human visual cortex. *Science, 304,* 115–117.

Coyne, J. C. (1999). Thinking interactionally about depression: A radical restatement. In T. E. Joiner & J. C. Coyne (Eds.), *Interpersonal processes in depression* (pp. 369–392). Washington, DC: American Psychological Association.

Craig, J. C., & Rollman, G. B. (1999). Somesthesis. *Annual Review of Psychology, 50,* 305–331.

Craik, F. I. M. (2001). Effects of dividing attention on encoding and retrieval processes. In H. L. Roediger III, J. S. Nairne, I. Neath, & A. M. Surprenant (Eds.), *The nature of remembering: Essays in honor of Robert G. Crowder* (pp. 55–68). Washington, DC: American Psychological Association.

Craik, F. I. M. (2002). Levels of processing: Past, present . . . and future? *Memory, 10*(5–6), 305–318.

Craik, F. I. M., & Kester, J. D. (2000). Divided attention and memory: Impairment of processing or consolidation? In E. Tulving (Ed.), *Memory, consciousness, and the brain: The Tallinn conference* (pp. 38–51). Philadelphia: Psychology Press.

Craik. F. I. M., & Lockhart, R. S. (1972). Levels of processing: A framework for memory research. *Journal of Verbal Learning and Verbal Behavior, 11,* 671–684.

Craik, F. I. M., & Tulving, E. (1975). Depth of processing and the retention of words in episodic memory. *Journal of Experimental Psychology: General, 104,* 268–294.

Cramer, P. (2000). Defense mechanisms in psychology today: Further processes for adaptation. *American Psychologist, 55*(6), 637–646.

Cramer, P. (2001). The unconscious status of defense mechanisms. *American Psychologist, 56,* 762–763.

Crano, W. D., & Prislin, R. (2006). Attitudes and persuasion. *Annual Review of Psychology, 57,* 345–374.

Craske, M. G., & Waters, A. M. (2005). Panic disorders, phobias, and generalized anxiety disorder. *Annual Review of Clinical Psychology, 1,* 197–225.

Cravens, H. (1992). A scientific project locked in time: The Terman Genetic Studies of Genius, 1920s–1950s. *American Psychologist, 47,* 183–189.

Creed, F. (1989). Appendectomy. In G. W. Brown & T. O. Harris (Eds.), *Life events and illness.* New York: Guilford.

Crews, F. (2006). *Follies of the wise: Dissenting essays.* Emeryville, CA: Shoemaker Hoard.

Crits-Christoph, P. (1997). Limitations of the dodo bird verdict and the role of clinical trials in psychotherapy research: Comment on Wampold et al (1997). *Psychological Bulletin, 122,* 216–220.

Crockett, H. (1962). The achievement motive and differential occupational mobility in the United States. *American Sociological Review, 27,* 191–204.

Cross, S. E., & Markus, H. R. (1993). Gender in thought, belief, and action: A cognitive approach. In A. E. Beall & R. J. Sternberg (Eds.), *The psychology of gender.* New York: Guilford.

Crowder, R. G., & Greene, R. L. (2000). Serial learning: Cognition and behavior. In E. Tulving & F. I. M. Craik (Eds.), *The Oxford handbook of memory* (pp. 125–136). New York: Oxford University Press.

Cruz, C., della Rocco, P., & Hackworth, C. (2000). Effects of quick rotating schedules on the health and adjustment of air traffic controllers. *Aviation, Space, & Environmental Medicine, 71,* 400–407.

Csikszentmihalyi, M. (2000). The contribution of flow to positive psychology. In J. E. Gillham (Ed.), *The science of optimism and hope: Research essays in honor of Martin E. P. Seligman.* Philadelphia: Templeton Foundation Press.

Cuban, L. (2004). Assessing the 20-year impact of multiple intelligences on schooling. *Teachers College Record, 106*(1), 140–146.

Cullum, J., & Harton, H. C. (2007). Cultural evolution: Interpersonal influence, issue importance, and the development of shared attitudes in college residence halls. *Personality and Social Psychology Bulletin, 33,* 1327–1339.

Culpepper, L., Davidson, J. R. T., Dietrich, A. J., Goodman, W. K., Kroenke, K., & Schwenk, T. L. (2004). Suicidality as a possible effect of antidepressant treatment. *Journal of Clinical Psychiatry, 65,* 742–749.

Cummings, D. E. (2006). Ghrelin and the short- and long-term regulation of appetite and body weight. *Physiology & Behavior, 89,* 71–84.

Cummins, D. (2005). Dominance, status, and social hierarchies. In D. M. Buss (Ed.), *The handbook of evolutionary psychology.* New York: Wiley.

Cunningham, C. O., & Selwyn, P. A. (2005). HIV-related medical complications and treatment. In J. H. Lowinson, P. Ruiz, R. B. Millman, & J. G. Langrod (Eds.), *Substance abuse: A comprehensive textbook.* Philadelphia: Lippincott/Williams & Williams.

Cunningham, M. (2001). The influence of parental attitudes and behaviors on children's attitudes toward gender and household labor in early adulthood. *Journal of Marriage and the Family, 63,* 111–122.

Cushman, P. (1992). Psychotherapy to 1992: A historically situated interpretation. In D. K. Freedheim (Ed.), *History of psychotherapy: A century of change.* Washington, DC: American Psychological Association.

Cutting, L. P., & Docherty, N. M. (2000). Schizophrenia outpatients' perceptions of their parents: Is expressed emotion a factor? *Journal of Abnormal Psychology, 109,* 266–272.

Czeisler, C. A., Cajochen, C., & Turek, F. W. (2000). Melatonin in the regulation of sleep and circadian rhythms. In M. H. Kryger, T. Roth, & W. C. Dement (Eds.), *Principles and practice of sleep medicine.* Philadelphia: Saunders.

Daamen, D. D. L., Staats, H., Wilke, H. A. M., & Engelen, M. (2001). Improving environmental behavior in companies: The effectiveness of tailored versus nontailored interventions. *Environment and Behavior, 33,* 229–248.

Dahl, R. (2003). Beyond raging hormones: The tinderbox in the teenage brain. *Cerebrum, 5*(3), 7–22.

Daiek, D. B., & Anter, N. M. (2004). *Critical reading for college and beyond.* New York: McGraw Hill.

Dallman, M. F., Bhatnagar, S., & Viau, V. (2007). Hypothalamic-pituitary-adrenal axis. In G. Fink (Ed.), *Encyclopedia of stress.* San Diego: Elsevier.

Dalton, S. O., & Johansen, C. (2005). Stress and cancer: The critical research. In C. L. Cooper (Ed.), *Handbook of stress medicine and health.* Boca Raton, FL: CRC Press.

Daly, M., & Wilson, M. (1985). Child abuse and other risks of not living with both parents. *Ethology and Sociobiology, 6,* 197–210.

Daly, M., & Wilson, M. (1988). *Homicide.* Hawthorne, NY: Aldine.

Dan, B. A., & Gleason, J. B. (2001). Semantic development: Learning the meanings of words. In J. B. Gleason (Ed.), *The development of language* (5th ed.). Boston: Allyn & Bacon.

Daniels, H. (2005). Introduction. In H. Daniels (Ed.), *An introduction to Vygotsky.* New York: Routledge.

Danziger, K. (1990). *Constructing the subject: Historical origins of psychological research.* Cambridge, England: Cambridge University Press.

Dapretto, M., & Bjork, E. (2000). The development of word retrieval abilities in the second year and its relation to early vocabulary growth. *Child Development, 71,* 635–648.

Darley, J. M., & Latané, B. (1968). Bystander intervention in emergencies: Diffusion of responsibility. *Journal of Personality and Social Psychology, 8,* 377–383.

Darwin, C. (1859). *The origin of species.* London: Murray.

Darwin, C. (1871). *Descent of man.* London: Murray.

Darwin, C. (1872). *The expression of emotions in man and animals.* New York: Philosophical Library.

Das, H. H. J., de Wit, J. B. F., & Stroebe, W. (2005). Fear appeals motivate acceptance of action recommendations: Evidence for a positive bias in the processing of persuasive messages. *Personality and Social Psychology Bulletin, 29,* 650–664.

Dasen, P. R. (1994). Culture and cognitive development from a Piagetian perspective. In W. J. Lonner & R. Malpass (Eds.), *Psychology and culture.* Boston: Allyn & Bacon.

Davenport, J. L., & Potter, M. C. (2004). Scene consistency in object and background perception. *Psychological Science, 15,* 559–564.

Davidovitz, R., Mikulincer, M., Shaver, P. R., Izsak, R., & Popper, M. (2007). Leaders as attachment figures: Leaders' attachment orientations predict leadership-related mental representations and followers' performance and mental health. *Journal of Personality and Social Psychology, 93,* 632–650.

Davidson, R. J., Jackson, D. C., & Kalin, N. H. (2000). Emotion, plasticity, context, and regulation: Perspectives from affective neuroscience. *Psychological Bulletin, 126,* 890–909.

Davidson, R. J., Kabat-Zinn, J., Schumacher, J., Rosenkranz, M., Muller, D., Santorelli, S. F., Urbanowski, F., Harrington, A., Bonus, K., & Sheridan, J. F. (2003a). Alterations in brain and immune function produced by mindfulness meditation. *Psychosomatic Medicine, 65,* 564–570.

Davidson, R. J., Pizzagalli, D., Nitschke, J. B., & Kalin, N. H. (2003b). Parsing the subcomponents of emotion and disorders of emotion: Perspectives from affective neuroscience. In R. J. Davidson, K. R. Scherer, & H. H. Goldsmith (Eds.), *Handbook of affective sciences*. New York: Oxford University Press.

Davis, A. S., & Dean, R. S. (2005). Lateralization of cerebral functions and hemispheric specialization: Linking behavior, structure, and neuroimaging. In R. C. D'Amato, E. Fletcher-Janzen, & C. R. Reynolds (Eds.), *Handbook of school neuropsychology*. Hoboken, NJ: Wiley.

Davis, D., & Loftus, E. F. (2007). Internal and external sources of misinformation in adult witness memory. In M. P. Toglia, J. D. Read, D. F. Ross, & R. C. L. Lindsay (Eds.), *Handbook of eyewitness psychology: Volume 1. Memory for events*. Mahwah, NJ: Erlbaum.

Davis, D., Shaver, P. R., & Vernon, M. L. (2003). Physical, emotional, and behavioral reactions to breaking up: The roles of gender, age, emotional involvement, and attachment style. *Personality and Social Psychology Bulletin, 29*, 871–884.

Davis, J. L., & Rusbult, C. E. (2001). Attitude alignment in close relationships. *Journal of Personality and Social Psychology, 81*(1), 65–84.

Davis, M. H., Morris, M. M., & Kraus, L. A. (1998). Relationship-specific and global perceptions of social support: Associations with well-being and attachment. *Journal of Personality and Social Psychology, 74*, 468–481.

Davis, O. S. P., Arden, R., & Plomin, R. (2008). *g* in middle childhood: Moderate genetic and shared environmental influence using diverse measures of general cognitive ability at 7, 9 and 10 years in a large population sample of twins. *Intelligence, 36*,68–80.

Dawes, R. M. (1980). Social dilemmas. *Annual Review of Psychology, 31*, 169–193.

Dawkins, K., Golden, R. N., & Fawcett, J. A. (2003). Therapeutic management of the suicidal patient. In A. Tasman, J. Kay, & J. A. Lieberman (Eds.), *Psychiatry* (pp. 2112–2135). New York: Wiley.

Day, R. H. (1965). Inappropriate constancy explanation of spatial distortions. *Nature, 207*, 891–893.

de Castro, J. M., Bellisle, F., Dalix, A., & Pearcey, S. M. (2000). Palatability and intake relationships in free-living humans: Characterization and independence of influence in North Americans. *Physiology & Behavior, 70*, 343–350.

de Graaf, J., Wann, D., & Naylor, T. H. (2005). *Affluenza: The all-consuming epidemic*. San Francisco: Berrett-Koehler.

De Koninck, J. (2000). Waking experiences and dreaming. In M. H. Kryger, T. Roth, & W. C. Dement (Eds.), *Principles and practice of sleep medicine*. Philadelphia: Saunders.

De Neys, W. (2006). Dual processing in reasoning: Two systems but one reasoner. *Psychological Science, 17*, 428–433.

de Villiers, J. G., & de Villiers, P. A. (1999). Language development. In M. H. Bornstein & M. E. Lamb (Eds.), *Developmental psychology: An advanced textbook*. Mahwah, NJ: Erlbaum.

De Villiers, P. (1977). Choice in concurrent schedules and a quantitative formulation of the law of effect. In W. K. Honig & J. E. R. Staddon (Eds.), *Handbook of operant behavior*. Englewood Cliffs, NJ: Prentice-Hall.

De Waal, F. (2001). *The ape and the sushi master: Cultural reflections of a primatologist*. New York: Basic Books.

de Wijk, R. A., Schab, F. R., & Cain, W. S. (1995). Odor identification. In F. R. Schab & R. G. Crowder (Eds.), *Memory for odors*. Mahwah, NJ: Erlbaum.

Deary, I. J. (2003). Reaction time and psychometric intelligence: Jensen's contributions. In H. Nyborg (Ed.), *The scientific study of general intelligence: Tribute to Arthur R. Jensen*. Oxford, UK: Pergamon.

Deary, I. J., Strand, S., Smith, P., & Fernandes, C. (2007). Intelligence and educational achievement. *Intelligence, 35*, 13–21.

Deaux, K. (1993). Commentary: Sorry, wrong number—A reply to Gentile's call. *Psychological Science, 4*, 125–126.

DeCarvalho, R. J. (1991). *The founders of humanistic psychology*. New York: Praeger.

Deecher, D., Andree, T. H., Sloan, D., & Schechter, L. E. (2008). From menarche to menopause: Exploring the underlying biology of depression in women experiencing hormonal changes. *Psychoneuroendocrinology, 33*(1), 3–17.

Deese, J. (1959). On the prediction of occurrence of particular verbal intrusions in immediate recall. *Journal of Experimental Psychology, 58*, 17–22.

Defeyter, M. A., & German, T. P. (2003). Acquiring an understanding of design: Evidence from children's insight problem solving. *Cognition, 89*(2), 133–155.

DeFrain, J., & Olson, D. H. (1999). Contemporary family patterns and relationships. In M. B. Sussman, S. K. Steinmetz, & G. W. Peterson (Eds.), *Handbook of marriage and the family* (pp. 309–326). New York: Plenum.

Degenhardt, L., & Hall, W. (2006). Is cannabis use a contributory cause of psychosis? *Canadian Journal of Psychiatry, 51*, 556–565.

Del Monte, M. M. (2000). Retrieved memories of childhood sexual abuse. *British Journal of Medical Psychology, 73*, 1–13.

Delgado, P. L., & Moreno, F. A. (2006). Neurochemistry of mood disorders. In D. J. Stein, D. J. Kupfer, & A. F. Schatzberg (Eds.), *Textbook of mood disorders*. Washington, DC: American Psychiatric Publishing.

Delis, D. C., & Lucas, J. A. (1996). Memory. In B. S. Fogel, R. B. Schiffer, & S. M. Rao (Eds.), *Neuropsychiatry*. Baltimore: Williams & Wilkins.

DeLisi, L. E. (2008). The effect of cannabis on the brain: Can it cause brain anomalies that lead to increased risk for schizophrenia? *Current Opinion in Psychiatry, 21*, 140–150.

DeLong, M. R. (2000). The basal ganglia. In E. R. Kandel, J. H. Schwartz, & T. M. Jessell (Eds.), *Principles of neural science* (pp. 853–872). New York: McGraw-Hill.

DeLongis, A., Folkman, S., & Lazarus, R. S. (1988). The impact of daily stress on health and mood: Psychological and social resources as mediators. *Journal of Personality and Social Psychology, 54*, 486–495.

Delprato, D. J., & Midgley, B. D. (1992). Some fundamentals of B. F. Skinner's behaviorism. *American Psychologist, 47*, 1507–1520.

Dement, W. C. (1978). *Some must watch while some must sleep*. New York: Norton.

Dement, W. C. (1992). *The sleepwatchers*. Stanford, CA: Stanford Alumni Association.

Dement, W. C. (2003). Knocking on Kleitman's door: The view from 50 years later. *Sleep Medicine Reviews, 7*(4), 289–292.

Dement, W. C. (2005). History of sleep psychology. In M. H. Kryger, T. Roth, & W. C. Dement (Eds.), *Principles and practice of sleep medicine*. Philadelphia: Elsevier Saunders.

Dement, W. C., & Vaughan, C. (1999). *The promise of sleep*. New York: Delacorte Press.

Dement, W. C., & Wolpert, E. (1958). The relation of eye movements, bodily motility, and external stimuli to dream content. *Journal of Experimental Psychology, 53*, 543–553.

Dempster, F. N. (1996). Distributing and managing the conditions of encoding and practice. In E. L. Bjork & R. A. Bjork (Eds.), *Memory*. San Diego: Academic Press.

Dennerstein, L. (1996). Well-being, symptoms and the menopausal transition. *Maturitas, 23*, 147–157.

Dennis, C., & Ross, L. (2005). Relationships among infant sleep patterns, maternal fatigue, and development of depressive symptomatology. *Birth, 32*, 187–193.

Deregowski, J. B. (1972, November). Pictorial perception and culture.*Scientific American, 227*(5), 83.

Derevensky, J. L., & Gupta, R. (2004). Preface. In J. L. Derevensky & R. Gupta (Eds.), *Gambling problems in youth: Theoretical and applied perspectives* (pp. xxi–xxiv). New York: Kluwer/Plenum.

Derogatis, L. R., & Coons, H. L. (1993). Self-report measures of stress. In L. Goldberger & S. Breznitz (Eds.), *Handbook of stress: Theoretical and clinical aspects* (2nd ed.). New York: Free Press.

Derr, T. (2006). "Sometimes birds sound like fish": Perspectives on children's place experiences. In C. Spencer & M. Blades (Eds.), *Children and their environments: Learning, using and designing spaces*. New York: Cambridge University Press.

Des Jarlais, D. C., Hagan, H., & Friedman, S. R. (2005). Epidemiology and emerging public health perspectives. In J. H. Lowinson, P. Ruiz, R. B. Millman, & J. G. Langrod (Eds.), *Substance abuse: A comprehensive textbook*. Philadelphia: Lippincott/Williams & Wilkins.

Deutsch, J. A. (1990). Food intake: Gastric factors. In E. M. Stricker (Ed), *Handbook of behavioral neurobiology: Vol 10. Neurobiology of food and fluid intake*. New York: Plenum.

DeValois, R. L., & Jacobs, G. H. (1984). Neural mechanisms of color vision. In I. Darian-Smith (Ed.), *The nervous system* (Vol. 3). Baltimore: Williams & Wilkins.

Devine, P. G., & Monteith, M. J. (1999). Automaticity and control in stereotyping. In S. Chaiken & Y. Trope (Eds.), *Dual-process theories in social psychology*. New York: Guilford.

Devine, P. G., Plant, E. A., & Blair, I. V. (2001). Classic and contemporary analysis of racial prejudice. In R. Brown & S. L. Gaertner (Eds.), *Blackwell handbook of social psychology: Intergroup processes*. Malden, MA: Blackwell.

Devine, P. G., Tauer, J. M., Barron, K. E., Elliot, A. J., & Vance, K. M. (1999). Moving beyond attitude change in the study of dissonance-related processes. In E. Harmon-Jones & J. Mills (Eds.), *Cognitive dissonance: Progress on a pivotal theory in social psychology*. Washington, DC: American Psychological Association.

Devlin, B., Fienberg, S. E., Resnick, D. P., & Roeder, K. (2002). Intelligence and success: Is it all in the genes? In J. M. Fish (Ed.), *Race and intelligence: Separating science from myth* (pp. 355–368). Mahwah, NJ: Erlbaum.

DeVries, R. (2000). Vygotsky, Piaget, and education: A reciprocal assimilation of theories and educational practices. *New Ideas in Psychology, 18*(2–3), 187–213.

Dew, M. A., Bromet, E. J., & Switzer, G. E. (2000). Epidemiology. In M. Hersen & A. S. Bellack (Eds.), *Psychopathology in adulthood*. Boston: Allyn & Bacon.

Di Forti, M., Morrison, P. D., Butt, A., & Murray, R. M. (2007). Cannabis use and psychiatric and cognitive disorders: The chicken or the egg? *Current Opinion in Psychiatry, 20*, 228–234.

Di Lorenzo, P. M., & Youngentob, S. L. (2003). Olfaction and taste. In M. Gallagher & R. J. Nelson (Eds.), *Handbook of psychology, Vol. 3: Biological psychology*. New York: Wiley.

Diamond, J. (2005). *Collapse: How societies choose to fail or survive*. London: Allen Lane.

Diamond, L. M. (2003). Was it a phase? Young women's relinquishment of lesbian/bisexual identities over a 5-year period. *Journal of Personality and Social Psychology, 84*, 352–364.

Diamond, L. M. (2007). The evolution of plasticity in female-female desire. *Journal of Psychology & Human Sexuality, 18*, 245–274.

Dick, D. M., & Rose, R. J. (2002). Behavior genetics: What's new? What's next? *Current Directions in Psychological Science, 11*(2), 70–74.

Dickens, W. T., & Flynn, J. R. (2001). Heritability estimates versus large environmental effects: The IQ paradox resolved. *Psychological Review, 108*, 346–369.

Dickens, W. T., & Flynn, J. R. (2006). Black Americans reduce the racial IQ gap: Evidence from standardization samples. *Psychological Science, 17*, 913–920.

Diekman, A. B., & Murnen, S. K. (2004). Learning to be little women and little men: The inequitable gender equality of nonsexist children's literature. *Sex Roles, 50*, 373–385.

Diener, E. (1984). Subjective well-being. *Psychological Bulletin, 93*, 542–575.

Diener, E., & Diener, C. (1996). Most people are happy. *Psychological Science, 7*, 181–185.

Diener, E., Gohm, C. L., Suh, E., & Oishi, S. (2000). Similarity of the relations between marital status and subjective well-being across cultures. *Journal of Cross-Cultural Psychology, 31*, 419–436.

Diener, E., & Lucas, R. E. (1999). Personality and subjective well-being. In D. Kahneman, E. Diener, & N. Schwarz (Eds.), *Well-being: The foundations of hedonic psychology*. New York: Russell Sage Foundation.

Diener, E., Sandvik, E., Seidlitz, L., & Diener, M. (1993). The relationship between income and subjective well-being. Relative or absolute? *Social Indicators Research, 28*, 195–223.

Diener, E., & Seligman, M. E. P. (2002). Very happy people. *Psychological Science, 13*, 81–84.

Diener, E., & Seligman, M. E. P. (2004). Beyond money: Toward an economy of well-being. *Psychological Science in the Public Interest, 5*(1), 1–31.

Diener, E., Wolsic, B., & Fujita, F. (1995). Physical attractiveness and subjective well-being. *Journal of Personality and Social Psychology, 69*, 120–129.

Dillbeck, M. C., & Orme-Johnson, D. W. (1987). Physiological differences between transcendental meditation and rest. *American Psychologist, 42*, 879–881.

Dilsaver, S. C., Chen, Y. R., Shoaib, A. M., & Swann, A. C. (1999). Phenomenology of mania: Evidence for distinct depressed, dysphoric, and euphoric presentations. *American Journal of Psychiatry, 156*, 426–430.

DiMatteo, M. R. (1991). *The psychology of health, illness, and medical care: An individual perspective*. Pacific Grove, CA: Brooks/Cole.

DiMatteo, M. R. (1997). Health behaviors and care decisions: An overview of professional-patient communication. In D. S. Gochman (Ed.), *Handbook of health behavior research II: Provider determinants*. New York: Plenum.

DiMatteo, M. R. (2004a). Social support and patient adherence to medical treatment: A meta analysis. *Health Psychology, 23*, 207–218.

DiMatteo, M. R. (2004b). Variations in patients' adherence to medical recommendations: A quantitative review of 50 years of research. *Medical Care, 42*, 200–209.

DiMatteo, M. R., Giordani, P. J., Lepper, H. S., & Croghan, T. W. (2002). Patient adherence and medical treatment outcomes: A meta-analysis. *Medical Care, 40*, 794–811.

Dimsdale, J. E., Irwin, M., Keefe, F. J., & Stein, M. B. (2005). Stress and anxiety. In B. J. Sadock & V. A. Sadock (Eds.), *Kaplan & Sadock's comprehensive textbook of psychiatry*. Philadelphia: Lippincott Williams & Wilkins.

Din, J. N., Newby, D. E., & Flapan, A. D. (2004). Omega 3 fatty acids and cardiovascular disease—fishing for a natural treatment. *British Medical Journal, 328*, 30–35.

Dinehart, M. E., Hayes, J. E., Bartoshuk, L. M., Lanier, S. L., & Duffy, V. B. (2006). Bitter taste markers explain variability in vegetable sweetness, bitterness, and intake. *Physiology & Behavior, 87*, 304–313.

Dinges, D. F. (1993). Napping. In M.A. Carskadon (Ed.), *Encyclopedia of sleep and dreaming*. New York: Macmillan.

Dinges, D. F., Rogers, N. L., & Baynard, M. D. (2005). Chronic sleep deprivation. In M. H. Kryger, T. Roth, & W. C. Dement (Eds.), *Principles and practice of sleep medicine*. Philadelphia: Elsevier Saunders.

Dinsmoor, J. A. (1998). Punishment. In W. O'Donohue (Ed.), *Learning and behavior therapy*. Boston: Allyn & Bacon.

Dinsmoor, J. A. (2004). The etymology of basic concepts in the experimental analysis of behavior. *Journal of the Experimental Analysis of Behavior, 82*, 311–316.

Dion, K. K., & Dion, K. L. (2006). Individualism, collectivism, and the psychology of love. In R. J. Sternberg & K. Weis (Eds.), *The new psychology of love*. New Haven, CT: Yale University Press.

Dion, K. L. (2003). Prejudice, racism, and discrimination. In T. Millon & M. J. Lerner (Eds.), *Handbook of Psychology, Vol. 5: Personality and social psychology*. New York: Wiley.

Dissell, R. (2005, December 14). Student from Ohio robbed bank to feed gambling habit, lawyer says. *The Plain Dealer*.

Dixon, L., & Goldman, H. (2004). Forty years of progress in community mental health: The role of evidence-based practices. *Administration & Policy in Mental Health, 31*(5), 381–392.

Dixon, M., & Laurence, J. R. (1992). Two hundred years of hypnosis research: Questions resolved? Questions unanswered! In E. Fromm & M. R. Nash (Eds.), *Contemporary hypnosis research*. New York: Guilford.

Dixon, R. A., & Cohen, A. (2003). Cognitive development in adulthood. In R. M. Lerner, M. A. Easterbrooks, & J. Mistry (Eds.), *Handbook of psychology, Vol. 6: Developmental psychology*. New York: Wiley.

Dobzhansky, T. (1937). *Genetics and the origin of species*. New York: Columbia University Press.

Docherty, J. P. (1999). Cost of treating mental illness from a managed care perspective. *Journal of Clinical Psychiatry, 60*, 49–53.

Doerr, P., Pirke, K. M., Kockott, G., & Dittmor, F. (1976). Further studies on sex hormones in male homosexuals. *Archives of General Psychiatry, 33*, 611–614.

Doghramji, P. P. (2001). Detection of insomnia in primary care. *Journal of Clinical Psychiatry, 62*(suppl 10), 18–26.

Dohrenwend, B. P. (2006). Inventorying stressful life events as risk factors for psychopathology: Toward resolution of the problem of intracategory variability. *Psychological Bulletin, 132*, 477–495.

Dolan, M., Anderson, I. M., & Deakin, J. F. W. (2001). Relationship between 5-HT function and impulsivity and aggression in male offenders with personality disorders. *British Journal of Psychiatry, 178*, 352–359.

Dollard, J., & Miller, N. E. (1950). *Personality and psychotherapy: An analysis in terms of learning, thinking and culture*. New York: McGraw-Hill.

Dollard, J., Doob, L. W., Miller, N. E., Mowrer, O. H., & Sears, R. R. (1939). *Frustration and aggression*. New Haven: Yale University Press.

Domhoff, G. W. (2005a). The content of dreams: Methodologic and theoretical implications. In M. H. Kryger, T. Roth, & W. C. Dement (Eds.), *Principles and practice of sleep medicine*. Philadelphia: Elsevier Saunders.

Domhoff, G. W. (2005b). Refocusing the neurocognitive approach to dreams: A critique of the Hobson versus Solms debate. *Dreaming, 15*(1), 3–20.

Dominowski, R. L., & Bourne, L. E., Jr. (1994). History of research on thinking and problem solving. In R. J. Sternberg (Ed.), *Thinking and problem solving*. San Diego: Academic Press.

Domjan, M. (1992). Adult learning and mate choice: Possibilities and experimental evidence. *American Zoologist, 32*, 48–61.

Domjan, M. (1994). Formulation of a behavior system for sexual conditioning. *Psychonomic Bulletin & Review, 1*, 421–428.

Domjan, M. (1998). *The principles of learning and behavior*. Pacific Grove: Brooks/Cole.

Domjan, M. (2005). Pavlovian conditioning: A functional perspective. *Annual Review of Psychology, 56*, 179–206.

Domjan, M., Blesbois, E., & Williams, J. (1998). The adaptive significance of sexual conditioning: Pavlovian control of sperm release. *Psychological Science, 9*, 411–415.

Domjan, M., Cusato, B., & Krause, M. (2004). Learning with arbitrary versus ecological conditioned stimuli: Evidence from sexual conditioning. *Psychonomic Bulletin & Review, 11*, 232–246.

Domjan, M., & Purdy, J. E. (1995). Animal research in psychology: More than meets the eye of the general psychology student. *American Psychologist, 50*, 496–503.

Donahoe, J. W., & Vegas, R. (2004). Pavlovian conditioning: The CS-UR relation. *Journal of Experimental Psychology: Animal Behavior Processes, 30*(1), 17–33.

Dorner, G. (1988). Neuroendocrine response to estrogen and brain differentiation. *Archives of Sexual Behavior, 17*(1), 57–75.

Dorrian, J., & Dinges, D. F. (2006). Sleep deprivation and its effects on cognitive performance. In T.

Lee-Chiong (Ed.), *Sleep: A comprehensive handbook.* Hoboken, NJ: Wiley-Liss.

Doty, R. L. (1991). Olfactory system. In T. V. Getchell, R. L. Doty, L. M. Bartoshuk, & J. B. Snow, Jr. (Eds.), *Smell and taste in health and disease.* New York: Raven.

Doty, R. L. (2001). Olfaction. *Annual Review of Psychology, 52,* 423–452.

Dougall, A. L., & Baum, A. (2001). Stress, health, and illness. In A. Baum, T. A. Revenson, & J. E. Singer (Eds.), *Handbook of health psychology* (pp. 321–338). Mahwah, NJ: Erlbaum.

Douzenis, A., Tsirka, Z., Vassilopoulou, C., & Christodoulou, G. N. (2004). The role of serotonin in neurobiology of aggression. *Psychiatriki, 15*(2), 169–179.

Dovidio, J. F., & Gaertner, S. L. (1999). Reducing prejudice: Combating intergroup biases. *Current Directions in Psychological Science, 8,* 101–105.

Dovidio, J. F., & Gaertner, S. L. (2000). Aversive racism and selection decisions: 1989 and 1999. *Psychological Science, 11,* 315–319.

Dovidio, J. F., & Gaertner, S. L. (2008). New directions in aversive racism research: Persistence and pervasiveness. In C. Willis-Esqueda (Ed.), *Motivational aspects of prejudice and racism.* New York: Springer Science + Business Media.

Dowling, K. W. (2005). The effect of lunar phases on domestic violence incident rates. *The Forensic Examiner, 14*(4), 13–18.

Draganski, B., Gaser, C., Busch, V., Schuierer, G., Bogdahn, U., & May, A. (2004). Changes in grey matter induced by training. *Nature, 427,* 311–312.

Draijer, N., & Langeland, W. (1999). Childhood trauma and perceived parental dysfunction in the etiology of dissociative symptoms in psychiatric inpatients. *American Journal of Psychiatry, 156,* 379–385.

Dranovsky, A., & Hen, R. (2006). Hippocampal neurogenesis: Regulation by stress and antidepressants. *Biological Psychiatry, 59,* 1136–1143.

Draycott, S., & Dabbs, A. (1998). Cognitive dissonance 1: An overview of the literature and its integration into theory and practice of clinical psychology. *British Journal of Clinical Psychology, 37,* 341–353.

Drazen, J. M., & Curfman, G. D. (2002). Financial associations of authors. *New England Journal of Medicine, 346,* 1901–1902.

Drewnowski, A. (1995). Standards for the treatment of obesity. In K. D. Brownell, & C. G. Fairburn (Eds.), *Eating disorders and obesity: A comprehensive handbook.* New York: Guilford.

Driskell, J. E., Willis, R. P., & Copper, C. (1992). Effect of overlearning on retention. *Journal of Applied Psychology, 77*(5), 615–622.

D'Souza, D. C. (2007). Cannabinoids and psychosis. *International Review of Neurobiology, 78,* 289–326.

Dubicka, B., Hadley, S., & Roberts, C. (2006). Suicidal behaviour in youths with depression treated with new-generation antidepressants—Meta-analysis. *British Journal of Psychiatry, 189,* 393–398.

Dubovsky, S. (2005). Benzodiazepine receptor agonists and antagonists. In B. J. Sadock & V. A. Sadock (Eds.), *Kaplan and Sadock's comprehensive textbook of psychiatry.* Philadelphia: Lippincott Williams & Wilkins.

Dubovsky, S. L., Davies, R., & Dubovsky, A. N. (2003). Mood disorders. In R. E. Hales & S. C. Yudofsky (Eds.), *Textbook of clinical psychiatry.* Washington, DC: American Psychiatric Publishing.

Duckworth, A. L., & Seligman, M. E. P. (2005). Self-discipline outdoes IQ in predicting academic performance of adolescents. *Psychological Science, 16,* 939–944.

Duckworth, A. L., Steen, T. A., & Seligman, M. E. P. (2005). Positive psychology in clinical practice. *Annual Review of Clinical Psychology, 1*(1), 629–651.

Duckworth, K., & Borus, J. F. (1999). Population-based psychiatry in the public sector and managed care. In A. M. Nicholi (Ed.), *The Harvard guide to psychiatry.* Cambridge, MA: Harvard University Press.

Dudai, Y. (2004). The neurobiology of consolidation, or, how stable is the engram? *Annual Review of Psychology, 55,* 51–86.

Duff, P. (2002). Maternal and perinatal infection. In S. G. Gabbe, J. R. Niebyl, & J. L. Simpson (Eds.), *Obstetrics: Normal and problem pregnancies.* New York: Churchill Livingstone.

Duffy, V. B. (2004). Associations between oral sensation, dietary behaviors and risk of cardiovascular disease (CVD). *Appetite, 43*(1), 5–9.

Duffy, V. B., Lucchina, L. A., & Bartoshuk, L. M. (2004). Genetic variation in taste: Potential biomarker for cardiovascular disease risk? In J. Prescott & B. J. Tepper (Eds.), *Genetic variations in taste sensitivity: Measurement, significance and implications.* New York: Dekker.

Duffy, V. B., & Peterson, J. M., Bartoshuk, L. M. (2004). Associations between taste genetics, oral sensations and alcohol intake. *Physiology & Behavior, 82,* 435–445.

Duman, R. S., & Monteggia, L. M. (2006). A neurotrophic model for stress-related mood disorders. *Biological Psychiatry, 59,* 1116–1127.

Dunbar, K., & Blanchette, I. (2001). The in vivo/in vitro approach to cognition: The case of analogy. *Trends in Cognitive Sciences, 5,* 334–339.

Dunbar-Jacob, J., & Schlenk, E. (2001). Patient adherence to treatment regimen. In A. Baum, T. A. Revenson, & J. E. Singer (Eds.), *Handbook of health psychology.* Mahwah, NJ: Erlbaum.

Duncan, B. L. (1976). Differential social perception and attribution of intergroup violence: Testing the lower limits of stereotyping of blacks. *Journal of Personality and Social Psychology, 34,* 590–598.

Dunkel-Schetter, C., Gurung, R. A. R., Lobel, M., & Wadhwa, P. D. (2001). Stress processes in pregnancy and birth: Psychological, biological, and sociocultural influences. In A. Baum, T. A. Revenson, & J. E. Singer (Eds.), *Handbook of health psychology* (pp. 495–518). Mahwah, NJ: Erlbaum.

Dunning, D., & Sherman, D. A. (1997). Stereotypes and tacit inference. *Journal of Personality and Social Psychology, 73,* 459–471.

Durmer, J. S., & Dinges, D. F. (2005). Neurocognitive consequences of sleep deprivation. *Seminars in Neurology, 25,* 117–129.

Durning, A. T. (1992). *How much is enough? The consumer society and the future of the earth.* New York: Norton.

Durston, S., Hulshoff, P., Hilleke, E., Casey, B. J., Giedd, J. N., Buitelaar, J. K., & van Engeland, H. (2001). Anatomical MRI of the developing human brain: What have we learned? *Journal of the American Academy of Child and Adolescent Psychiatry, 40,* 1012–1020.

Dwyer, J. (1995). Popular diets. In K. D. Brownell & C. G. Fairburn (Eds.), *Eating disorders and obesity.* New York: Guilford.

Eagly, A. H. (1995). The science and politics of comparing women and men. *American Psychologist, 50,* 145–158.

Eagly, A. H., Ashmore, R. D., Makhijani, M. G., & Longo, L. C. (1991). What is beautiful is good, but . . .: A meta-analytic review of research on the physical attractiveness stereotype. *Psychological Bulletin, 110,* 109–128.

Eagly, A. H., & Chaiken, S. (1995). Attitude strength, attitude structure, and resistance to change. In R. E. Petty & J. A. Krosnick (Eds.), *Attitude strength: Antecedents and consequences.* Mahwah, NJ: Erlbaum.

Eagly, A. H., & Wood, W. (1999). The origins of sex differences in human behavior: Evolved dispositions versus social roles. *American Psychologist, 54,* 408–423.

Easterlin, B. L., & Cardena, E. (1999). Cognitive and emotional differences between short- and long-term Vipassana meditators. *Imagination, Cognition and Personality, 18*(1), 68–81.

Eaton, J. (2001). Management communication: The threat of groupthink. *Corporate Communications, 6,* 183–192.

Ebbinghaus, H. (1885/1964). *Memory: A contribution to experimental psychology* (H. A. Ruger & E. R. Bussemius, Trans.). New York: Dover.

Edinger, J. D., & Means, M. K. (2005). Overview of insomnia: Definitions, epidemiology, differential diagnosis, and assessment. In M. H. Kryger, T. Roth, & W. C. Dement (Eds.), *Principles and practice of sleep medicine.* Philadelphia: Elsevier Saunders.

Edwards, A. (1999). *Ever after: Diana and the life she led.* New York: St. Martin's Press.

Edwards, D. J. A. (2007). Collaborative versus adversarial stances in scientific discourse: Implications for the role of systematic case studies in the development of evidence-based practice in psychotherapy. *Pragmatic Case Studies in Psychotherapy, 3*(1), 6–34.

Edwards, K., & Smith, E. E. (1996). A disconfirmation bias in the evaluation of arguments. *Journal of Personality an Social Psychology, 71,* 5–24.

Efron, R. (1990). *The decline and fall of hemispheric specialization.* Hillsdale, NJ: Erlbaum.

Egan, M. F., & Hyde, T. M. (2000). Schizophrenia: Neurobiology. In B. J. Sadock & V. A. Sadock (Eds.), *Kaplan and Sadock's comprehensive textbook of psychiatry* (7th ed., Vol. 1, pp. 1129–1146). Philadelphia: Lippincott/Williams & Wilkins.

Ehrenberg, O., & Ehrenberg, M. (1994). *The psychotherapy maze: A consumer's guide to getting in and out of therapy.* Northvale, NJ: Jason Aronson.

Ehrlich, P. R., & Ehrlich, A. H. (2008). *The dominant animal: Human evolution and the environment.* Washington, DC: Island Press.

Eich, E., Macaulay, D., Loewenstein, R. J., & Dihle, P. H. (1997). Memory, amnesia, and dissociative identity disorder. *Psychological Science, 8,* 417–422.

Eichenbaum, H. (2003). Memory systems. In M. Gallagher & R. J. Nelson (Eds.), *Handbook of psychology, Vol. 3: Biological psychology.* New York: Wiley.

Eichenbaum, H. (2004). An information processing framework for memory representation by the hippocampus. In M. S. Gazzaniga (Ed.), *The cognitive neurosciences.* Cambridge, MA: MIT Press.

Eid, M., & Diener, E. (2001). Norms for experiencing emotions in different cultures: Inter- and intranational differences. *Journal of Personality and Social Psychology, 81,* 869–885.

Einstein, G. O., & McDaniel, M. A. (1996). Remembering to do things: Remembering a forgotten topic. In D. J. Herrmann, C. McEvoy, C. Hertzog, P. Hertel, & M. K. Johnson (Eds.), *Basic and applied memory research: Practical applications* (Vol. 2). Mahwah, NJ: Erlbaum.

Einstein, G. O., & McDaniel, M. A. (2004). *Memory fitness: A guide for successful aging.* New Haven, CT: Yale University Press.

Einstein, G. O., McDaniel, M. A., Williford, C. L., Pagan, J. L., & Dismukes, R. K. (2003). Forgetting of intentions in demanding situations is rapid. *Journal of Experimental Psychology: Applied, 9*(3), 147–162.

Eisenberg, N., Spinrad, T., & Sadovsky, A. (2006). Empathy-related responding in children. In M. Killen & J. G. Smetana (Eds.), *Handbook of moral development.* Mahwah, NJ: Erlbaum.

Eisner, E. W. (2004). Multiple intelligences. *Teachers College Record, 106*(1), 31–39.

Ekman, P. (1992). Facial expressions of emotion: New findings, new questions. *Psychological Science, 3,* 34–38.

Ekman, P. (1993). Facial expression and emotion. *American Psychologist, 48,* 384–392.

Ekman, P., & Friesen, W. V. (1975). *Unmasking the face.* Englewood Cliffs, NJ: Prentice-Hall.

Ekman, P., & Friesen, W. V. (1984). *Unmasking the face.* Palo Alto: Consulting Psychologists Press.

Ellis, A. (1973). *Humanistic psychotherapy: The rational-emotive approach.* New York: Julian Press.

Ellis, A. (1977). *Reason and emotion in psychotherapy.* Seacaucus, NJ: Lyle Stuart.

Ellis, A. (1985). *How to live with and without anger.* New York: Citadel Press.

Ellis, A. (1987). The evolution of rational-emotive therapy (RET) and cognitive behavior therapy (CBT). In J. K. Zeig (Ed.), *The evolution of psychotherapy.* New York: Brunner/Mazel.

Ellis, A. (1999). *How to make yourself happy and remarkably less disturbable.* Atascadero, CA: Impact Publishers.

Ellis, A. (2001). *Feeling better, getting better: Profound self-help therapy for your emotions.* Atascadero, CA: Impact Publishers.

Ellis, B. J. (2004). Timing of pubertal maturation in girls: An integrated life history approach. *Psychological Bulletin, 130,* 920–958.

Ellison, N., Heino, R., & Gibbs, J. (2006). Managing impressions online: Self-presentation processes in the online dating environment. *Journal of Computer-Mediated Communication, 11,* 415–441.

Ellsworth, P. C., & Scherer, K. R. (2003). Appraisal processes in emotion. In R. J. Davidson, K. R. Scherer, & H. H. Goldsmith (Ed.), *Handbook of affective sciences.* New York: Oxford University Press.

Elpers, J. R. (2001). Public psychiatry. In B. J. Sadock & V. A. Sadock (Eds.), *Kaplan and Sadock's comprehensive textbook of psychiatry* (7th ed., Vol. 2). Philadelphia: Lippincott/Williams & Wilkins.

Emavardhana, T., & Tori, C. D. (1997). Changes in self-concept, ego defense mechanisms, and religiosity following seven-day Vipassana meditation retreats. *Journal for the Scientific Study of Religion, 36,* 194–206.

Emmelkamp, P. M. G. (1994). Behavior therapy with adults. In A. E. Bergin & S. L. Garfield (Eds.), *Handbook of psychotherapy and behavior change* (4th ed.). New York: Wiley.

Emmelkamp, P. M. G. (2004). Behavior therapy with adults. In M. J. Lambert (Ed.), *Bergin and Garfield's handbook of psychotherapy and behavior change.* New York: Wiley.

Energy Information Administration. (2006). *International Energy Annual 2006:* Table 1.2: 1.2 World Petroleum Consumption (Thousand Barrels per Day), 1980–2005. Retrieved June 16, 2009 from http://www.eia.doe.gov/iea/wec.html.

Engemann, K. M., & Owyang, M. T. (2005, April). So much for that merit raise: The link between wages and appearance. *The Regional Economist,* pp. 10–11.

Engen, T. (1987). Remembering odors and their names. *American Scientist, 75,* 497-503.

Engle, R. W. (2001). What is working memory capacity? In H. L. Roediger III, J. S. Nairne, I. Neath, & A. M. Surprenant (Eds.), *The nature of remembering: Essays in honor of Robert G. Crowder.* Washington, DC: American Psychological Association.

Enns, J. T. (2004). *The thinking eye, the seeing brain: Explorations in visual cognition.* New York: Norton.

Epley, N., & Huff, C. (1998). Suspicion, affective response, and educational benefit as a result of deception in psychology research. *Personality and Social Psychology Bulletin, 24,* 759–768.

Epstein, J., & Kinkenberg, W. D. (2001). From Eliza to Internet: A brief history of computerized assessment. *Computers in Human Behavior, 17,* 295–314.

Epstein, R. (2007). Smooth thinking about sexuality: "Gay" and "straight" are misleading terms. *Scientific American Mind, 18*(5), 14.

Epstein, S., Donovan, S., & Denes-Raj, V. (1999). The missing link in the paradox of the Linda conjunction problem: Beyond knowing and thinking of the conjunction rule, the intrinsic appeal of heuristic processing. *Personality and Social Psychology Bulletin, 25,* 204–214.

Erber, M. W., Hodges, S. D., & Wilson, T. D. (1995). Attitude strength, attitude stability, and the effects of analyzing reasons. In R. E. Petty & J. A. Krosnick (Eds.), *Attitude strength: Antecedents and consequences.* Mahwah, NJ: Erlbaum.

Erdelyi, M. H. (2001). Defense processes can be conscious or unconscious. *American Psychologist, 56,* 761–762.

Erdfelder, E., Brandt, M., & Bröder, A. (2007). Recollection biases in hindsight judgments. *Social Cognition, 25,* 114–131.

Erikson, E. (1963). *Childhood and society.* New York: Norton.

Erikson, E. (1968). *Identity: Youth and crisis.* New York: Norton.

Esser, J. K. (1998). Alive and well after twenty-five years: A review of groupthink research. *Organizational Behavior & Human Decision Processes, 73,* 116–141.

Esterson, A. (2001). The mythologizing of psychoanalytic history: Deception and self-deception in Freud's accounts of the seduction theory episode. *History of Psychiatry, 7,* 329–352.

Estes, R. E., Coston, M. L., & Fournet, G. P. (1990). *Rankings of the most notable psychologists by department chairpersons.* Unpublished manuscript.

Estes, W. K. (1999). Models of human memory: A 30-year retrospective. In C. Izawa (Ed.), *On human memory: Evolution, progress, and reflections on the 30th anniversary of the Atkinson-Shiffrin model.* Mahwah, NJ: Erlbaum.

Evans, F. J. (1990). Behavioral responses during sleep. In R. R. Bootzin, J. F. Kihlstrom, & D. L. Schacter (Eds.), *Sleep and cognition.* Washington, DC: American Psychological Association.

Evans, G. W. (2004). The environment of childhood poverty. *American Psychologist, 59*(2), 77–92.

Evans, G. W., & Cohen, S. (1987). Environmental stress. In D. Stokols & I. Altman (Eds.), *Handbook of Environmental Psychology.* New York: Wiley.

Evans, G. W., & Wener, R. E. (2006). Rail commuting duration and passenger stress. *Health Psychology, 25,* 408–412.

Everett, P. B., Hayward, S. C., & Meyers, A. W. (1974). The effects of a token reinforcement procedure on bus ridership. *Journal of Applied Behavior Analysis, 7,* 1–9.

Eysenck, H. J. (1959). Learning theory and behaviour therapy. *Journal of Mental Science, 195,* 61–75.

Eysenck, H. J. (1967). *The biological basis of personality.* Springfield, IL: Charles C. Thomas.

Eysenck, H. J. (1977). *Crime and personality.* London: Routledge & Kegan Paul.

Eysenck, H. J. (1982). *Personality, genetics and behavior: Selected papers.* New York: Praeger.

Eysenck, H. J. (1988). The concept of "intelligence": Useful or useless? *Intelligence, 12*(1), 1–16.

Eysenck, H. J. (1989). Discrimination reaction time and "g": A reply to Humphreys. *Intelligence, 13*(4), 325–326.

Eysenck, H. J. (1990a). Biological dimensions of personality. In L. A. Pervin (Ed.), *Handbook of personality: Theory and research.* New York: Guilford.

Eysenck, H. J. (1990b). *Decline and fall of the Freudian empire.* Washington, DC: Scott-Townsend.

Eysenck, H. J., & Kamin, L. (1981). *The intelligence controversy.* New York: Wiley.

Eysenck, M. W., Mogg, K., May, J., Richards, A., & Mathews, A. (1991). Bias in interpretation of ambiguous sentences related to threat in anxiety. *Journal of Abnormal Psychology, 100,* 144–150.

Faber Taylor, A. & Kuo, F. E. (2009). Children with attention deficits concentrate better after walk in the park. *Journal of Attention Disorders, 12,* 402–409.

Faber Taylor, A., Kuo, F, E., & Sullivan, W. C. (2001). Coping with ADD: the surprising connection to green play settings. *Environment and Behavior, 33,* 54–77.

Fabes, R. A., Carlo, G., Kupanoff, K., & Laible, D. (1999). Early adolescence and prosocial/moral behavior I: The role of individual processes. *Journal of Early Adolescence, 19,* 5–16.

Fabrigar, L. R., MacDonald, T. K., & Wegener, D. T. (2005). The structure of attitudes. In D. Albarracin, B. T. Johnson, & M. P. Zanna (Eds.), *The handbook of attitudes.* Mahwah, NJ: Erlbaum.

Fakhoury, W., & Priebe, S. (2002). The process of deinstitutionalization: An international overview. *Current Opinion in Psychiatry, 15*(2), 187–192.

Falls, W. A. (1998). Extinction: A review of therapy and the evidence suggesting that memories are not erased with nonreinforcement. In W. O'Donohue (Ed.), *Learning and behavior therapy.* Boston: Allyn & Bacon.

Fancher, R. E. (1979). *Pioneers of psychology.* New York: Norton.

Fancher, R. E. (2000). Snapshot of Freud in America, 1899–1999. *American Psychologist, 55,* 1025–1028.

Faraday, A. (1974). *The dream game.* New York: Harper & Row.

Farah, A. (1997). An overview of ECT. *Primary Psychiatry, 4,* 58–62.

Faravelli, C., & Pallanti, S. (1989). Recent life events and panic disorders. *American Journal of Psychiatry, 146,* 622–626.

Fausto-Sterling, A. (1992). *Myths of gender.* New York: Basic Books.

Fava, G. A. (1999). Well-being therapy: Conceptual and technical issues. *Psychotherapy and Psychosomatics, 68*(4), 171–179.

Fava, G. A., Fabbri, S., Sirri, L., & Wise, T. N. (2007). Psychological factors affecting medical condition: A new proposal for DSM-V. *Psychosomatics: Journal of Consultation Liaison Psychiatry, 42*(2), 103–111.

Fava, G. A., Ruini, C., Rafanelli, C., Finos, L., Salmaso, L., Mangelli, L., et al. (2005). Well-being therapy of generalized anxiety disorder. *Psychotherapy and Psychosomatics, 74*(1), 26–30.

Fazio, R. H., & Olson, M. A. (2003). Attitudes: Foundations, functions, and consequences. In M. A. Hogg & J. Cooper (Eds.), *The Sage handbook of social psychology.* Thousand Oaks, CA: Sage.

Feeney, D. M. (1987). Human rights and animal welfare. *American Psychologist, 42,* 593–599.

Feeney, J. A. (1999). Adult romantic attachment and couple relationships. In J. Cassidy & P. R. Shaver (Eds.), *Handbook of attachment: Theory, research, and clinical applications.* New York: Guilford.

Fehr, B. (2001). The status of theory and research on love and commitment. In G. J. O. Fletcher & M. S. Clark (Eds.), *Blackwell handbook of social psychology: Interpersonal processes.* Malden, MA: Blackwell Publishing.

Fein, S., & Spencer, S. J. (1997). Prejudice as self-image maintenance: Affirming the self through derogating others. *Journal of Personality and Social Psychology, 73,* 31–44.

Feingold, A. (1988). Matching for attractiveness in romantic partners and same-sex friends: A meta-analysis and theoretical critique. *Psychological Bulletin, 104,* 226–235.

Feingold, A. (1992). Good-looking people are not what we think. *Psychological Bulletin, 111,* 304–341.

Feist, G. J. (1998). A meta-analysis of personality in scientific and artistic creativity. *Personality and Social Psychology Review, 2,* 290-309.

Feist, G. J. (2004). The evolved fluid specificity of human creativity talent. In R. J. Sternberg, E. L. Grigorenko, & J. L. Singer (Eds.), *Creativity: From potential to realization.* Washington, DC: American Psychological Association.

Feldman, D. H. (1988). Creativity: Dreams, insights, and transformations. In R. J. Sternberg (Ed.), *The nature of creativity: Contemporary psychological perspectives.* Cambridge: Cambridge University Press.

Feldman, D. H. (1999). The development of creativity. In R. J. Sternberg (Ed.), *Handbook of creativity.* New York: Cambridge University Press.

Feldman, D. H. (2003). Cognitive development in childhood. In R. M. Lerner, M. A. Easterbrooks, & J. Mistry (Eds.), *Handbook of psychology, Vol. 6: Developmental psychology.* New York: Wiley.

Fenwick, P. (1987). Meditation and the EEG. In M. A. West (Ed.), *The psychology of meditation.* Oxford: Clarendon Press.

Ferguson, M. J., & Bargh, J. A. (2004). Liking is for doing: The effects of goal pursuit on automatic evaluation. *Journal of Personality and Social Psychology, 87,* 557–572.

Ferguson, T. (1993). Working with your doctor. In D. Goleman & J. Gurin (Eds.), *Mind-body medicine: How to use your mind for better health.* Yonkers, NY: Consumer Reports Books.

Ferris, A. L. (2002). Religion and the quality of life. *Journal of Happiness Studies, 3,* 199–215.

Ferster, C. S., & Skinner, B. F. (1957). *Schedules of reinforcement.* New York: Appleton-Century-Crofts.

Festinger, L. (1957). *A theory of cognitive dissonance.* Stanford, CA: Stanford University Press.

Festinger, L., & Carlsmith, J. M. (1959). Cognitive consequences of forced compliance. *Journal of Abnormal and Social Psychology, 58,* 203–210.

Feuerstein, G. Z., Ruffolo, R. R., Coughlin, C., Wang, J., & Miller, D. (2007). Inflammation. In G. Fink (Ed.), *Encyclopedia of stress.* San Diego: Elsevier.

Few, R. (2007). Health and climatic hazards: Framing social research on vulnerability, Response and adaptation. *Global Environmental Change 17,* 281–295.

Fields, R. D. (2004). The other half of the brain. *Scientific American, 290*(4), 54–61.

Fields, R. D., & Stevens-Graham, B. (2002). New insights into neuron-glia communication. *Science, 298,* 556–562.

Fifer, W. P., Monk, C. E., & Grose-Fifer, J. (2001). Prenatal development and risk. In G. Bremner & A. Fogel (Eds.), *Blackwell handbook of infant development* (pp. 505–542). Malden, MA: Blackwell.

Figueredo, A. J., Sefcek, J. A., Vasquez, G., Brumbach, B. H., King, J. E., & Jacobs, W. J. (2005). Evolutionary personality psychology. In D. M. Buss (Ed.), *The handbook of evolutionary psychology.* New York: Wiley.

Filaire, F., Maso, F., Sagnol, M., Ferrand, C., & Lac, G. (2001). Anxiety, hormonal responses, and coping during a judo competition. *Aggressive Behavior, 27,* 55–63.

Fink, B., & Penton-Voak, I. (2002). Evolutionary psychology of facial attractiveness. *Current Directions in Psychological Science, 11*(5), 154–158.

Fink, B., Neave, N., Manning, J. T., & Grammer, K. (2006). Facial symmetry and judgments of attractiveness, health and personality. *Personality and Individual Differences, 41,* 1253–1262.

Finnegan, L. P., & Kandall, S. R. (2005). Maternal and neonatal effects of alcohol and drugs. In J. H. Lowinson, P. Ruiz, R. B. Millman, & J. G. Langrod (Eds.), *Substance abuse: A comprehensive textbook.* Baltimore: Williams & Wilkins.

Finucane, M. L., Alhakami, A. S., Slovic, P., & Johnson, S. M. (2000). The affect heuristic in judgments of risks and benefits. *Journal of Behavioral Decision Making, 13,* 1–17.

Firestein, S. (2001). How the olfactory system makes sense of scents. *Nature, 413,* 211–218.

First, M. B. (2003). Psychiatric classification. In A. Tasman, J. Kay, & J. A. Lieberman (Eds.), *Psychiatry.* New York: Wiley.

Fischhoff, B. (1988). Judgment and decision making. In R. J. Sternberg & E. E. Smith (Eds.), *The psychology of human thought.* Cambridge: Cambridge University Press.

Fischhoff, B. (2007). An early history of hindsight research. *Social Cognition, 25*(1), 10–13.

Fisher, C., & Fyrberg, D. (1994). College students weigh the costs and benefits of deceptive research. *American Psychologist, 49,* 417–427.

Fisher, S., & Greenberg, R. P. (1985). *The scientific credibility of Freud's theories and therapy.* New York: Columbia University Press.

Fisher, S., & Greenberg, R. P. (1996). *Freud scientifically reappraised: Testing the theories and therapy.* New York: Wiley.

Fisher, S., & Greenberg, R. P. (1997). The curse of the placebo: Fanciful pursuit of a pure biological therapy. In S. Fisher & R. P. Greenberg (Eds.), *From placebo to panacea: Putting psychiatric drugs to the test.* New York: Wiley.

Fishman, D. B. (2007). Seeking an equal place at the therapy research table: An introduction to a series on the pragmatic case study method. *Pragmatic Case Studies in Psychotherapy, 3*(1), 1–5.

Fishman, D. B., & Franks, C. M. (1992). Evolution and differentiation within behavior therapy: A theoretical epistemological review. In D. K. Freedheim (Ed.), *History of psychotherapy: A century of change.* Washington, DC: American Psychological Association.

Fiske, S. T. (1998). Stereotyping, prejudice, and discrimination. In D. T. Gilbert, S. T. Fiske, & G. Lindzey (Eds.), *The handbook of social psychology.* New York: McGraw-Hill.

Fiske, S. T. (2000). Stereotyping, prejudice, and discrimination at the seam between the centuries: Evolution, culture, mind and brain. *European Journal of Social Psychology, 30,* 299–322.

Fiske, S. T. (2004). Mind the gap: In praise of informal sources of formal theory. *Personality and Social Psychology Review, 8*(2), 132–137.

Fitness, J., Fletcher, G., & Overall, N. (2003). Interpersonal attraction and intimate relationships. In M. A. Hogg & J. Cooper (Eds.), *The Sage handbook of social psychology.* Thousand Oaks, CA: Sage.

Flannery, R. B., Jr. (1999). Psychological trauma and posttraumatic stress disorder: A review. *International Journal of Mental Health, 1,* 135–140.

Flavell, J. H. (1996). Piaget's legacy. *Psychological Science, 7,* 200–203.

Fleeson, W. (2004). Moving personality beyond the person-situation debate: The challenge and the opportunity of within-person variability. *Current Directions in Psychological Science, 13*(2), 83–87.

Fleeson, W., Malanos, A. B., & Achille, N. M. (2002). An intraindividual process approach to the relationship between extraversion and positive affect: Is acting extraverted as "good" as being extraverted? *Journal of Personality and Social Psychology, 83,* 1409–1422.

Fleischhacker, W. W. (2002). Second generation antipsychotics. *Psychopharmacology, 162*(1), 90–91.

Fletcher, G. J. O., Simpson, J. A., & Thomas, G. (2000). Ideals, perceptions, and evaluations in early relationship development. *Journal of Personality and Social Psychology, 79,* 933–940.

Fletcher, G. J. O., Simpson, J. A., Thomas, G., & Giles, L. (1999). Ideals in intimate relationships. *Journal of Personality and Social Psychology, 76,* 72–89.

Flett, G. L., Vredenburg, K., & Krames, L. (1995). The stability of depressive symptoms in college students: An empirical demonstration of regression to the mean. *Journal of Psychopathology & Behavioral Assessment, 17,* 403–415.

Flippo, R. F. (2000). *Testwise: Strategies for success in taking tests.* Torrance, CA: Good Apple.

Flippo, R. F., Becker, M. J., & Wark, D. M. (2000). Preparing for and taking tests. In R. F. Flippo & D. C. Caverly (Eds.), *Handbook of college reading and study strategy research.* Mahwah, NJ: Erlbaum.

Flores, B. H., Musselman, D. L., DeBattista, C., Garlow, S. J., Schatzberg, A. F., & Nemeroff, C. B. (2004). Biology of mood disorders. In A. F. Schatzberg & C. B. Nemeroff (Eds.), *Textbook of psychopharmacology.* Washington, DC: American Psychiatric Publishing.

Floyd, J. A., Janisse, J. J., Jenuwine, E. S., & Ager, J. W. (2007). Changes in REM-sleep percentage over the adult lifespan. *Sleep, 30,* 829–836.

Flynn, J. R. (1987). Massive IQ gains in 14 nations: What IQ tests really measure. *Psychological Bulletin, 101,* 171–191.

Flynn, J. R. (1994). IQ gains over time. In R. J. Sternberg (Ed.), *The encyclopedia of human intelligence*. New York: Macmillan.

Flynn, J. R. (1999). Searching for justice: The discovery of IQ gains over time. *American Psychologist, 54*, 5–20.

Flynn, J. R. (2003). Movies about intelligence: The limitations of g. *Current Directions in Psychological Science, 12*(3), 95–99.

Flynn, J. R. (2007). *What is intelligence? Beyond the Flynn effect*. New York: Cambridge University Press.

Flynn, M. G., McFarlin, B. K., & Markofski, M. M. (2007). The anti-inflammatory actions of exercise training. *American Journal of Lifestyle Medicine, 1*, 220–235.

Fodor, E. M., & Carver, R. A. (2000). Achievement and power motives, performance feedback, and creativity. *Journal of Research in Personality, 34*, 380–396.

Foldvary-Schaefer, N. (2006). *Getting a good night's sleep*. Cleveland: Cleveland Clinic Press.

Folkman, S. (1997). Positive psychological states and coping with severe stress. *Social Science and Medicine, 45*, 1207–1221.

Folkman, S. (2008). The case for positive emotions in the stress process. *Anxiety, Stress & Coping: An International Journal, 21*(1), 3–14.

Folkman, S., & Moskowitz, J. T. (2000). Positive affect and the other side of coping. *American Psychologist, 55*, 647–654.

Folkman, S., & Moskowitz, J. T. (2004). Coping: Pitfalls and promise. *Annual Review of Psychology, 55*, 745–774.

Folkman, S., Moskowitz, J. T., Ozer, E. M., & Park, C. L. (1997). Positive meaningful events and coping in the context of HIV/AIDS. In B. H. Gottlieb (Ed.), *Coping with chronic stress* (pp. 293–314). New York: Plenum.

Folsom, D. P., Hawthorne, W., Lindamer, L., Gilmer, T., Bailey, A., Golsham, S., Garcia, P., Unutzer, J., Hough, R., & Jeste, D. V. (2005). Prevalence and risk factors for homelessness and utilization of mental health services among 10,340 patients with serious mental illness in a large public mental health system. *American Journal Psychiatry, 162*, 370–376.

Food and Agriculture Organization of the United Nations. (2006). Livestock's long shadow: Environmental issues and options. Retrieved June 3, 2009 at http://www.fao.org/docrep/010/a0701e/a0701e00.HTM.

Foote, B., Smolin, Y., Kaplan M., Legatt, M. E., & Lipschitz, D. (2006). Prevalence of dissociative disorders in psychiatric outpatients. *American Journal of Psychiatry, 163*, 623–629.

Forcier, K., Stroud, L. R., Papandonatos, G. D., Hitsman, B., Reiches, M., Krishnamoorthy, J., et al. (2006). Links between physical fitness and cardiovascular reactivity and recovery to psychological stressors: A meta-analysis. *Health Psychology, 25*, 723–739.

Formicelli, L. (2001, March-April). Baby blues. *Psychology Today*, p. 24.

Forsén, T., Eriksson, J., Tuomilehto, J., Reunanen, A., Osmond, C., & Barker, D. (2000). The fetal and childhood growth of persons who develop type 2 diabetes. *Annals of Internal Medicine, 133*, 176–182.

Forsyth, D. R. (2004). Inferences about actions performed in constraining contexts: Correspondence bias or correspondent inference? *Current Psychology: Developmental, Learning, Personality, Social , 23*(1), 41–51.

Forsyth, D. R., & Strong, S. R. (1986). The scientific study of counseling and psychotherapy: A unificationist view. *American Psychologist, 41*, 113–119.

Foster, R. G. (2004). Are we trying to banish biological time? *Cerebrum, 6*, 7–26.

Foster, R. G., & Kreitzman, L. (2004). *Rhythms of life: The biological clocks that control the daily lives of every living thing*. New Haven, CT: Yale University Press.

Foulkes, D. (1985). *Dreaming: A cognitive-psychological analysis*. Hillsdale, NJ: Erlbaum.

Foulkes, D. (1996). Dream research: 1953–1993. *Sleep, 19*, 609–624.

Fowers, B. J., & Davidov, B. J. (2006). The virtue of multiculturalism: Personal transformation, character, and openness to the other. *American Psychologist, 61*, 581–594.

Fox, G. L., Bruce, C., & Combs-Orme, T. (2000). Parenting expectations and concerns of fathers and mothers of newborn infants. *Family Relations, 49*(2), 123–131.

Fraley, R. C. (2002). Attachment stability from infancy to adulthood: Meta-analysis and dynamic modeling of developmental mechanisms. *Personality and Social Psychology Review, 6*, 123–151.

Francis, G. (1999). Spatial frequency and visual persistence: Cortical reset. *Spatial Vision, 12*, 31–50.

Francis, L. A., & Birch, L. L. (2005). Maternal influences on daughters' restrained eating behavior. *Health Psychology, 24*, 548–554.

Francis, M. E., & Pennebaker, J. W. (1992). Putting stress into words: The impact of writing on psychological, absentee and self-reported emotional well-being measures. *American Journal of Health Promotion, 6*, 280–287.

Frank, J. D. (1961). *Persuasion and healing*. Baltimore: Johns Hopkins University Press.

Frank, L. K. (1939). Projective methods for the study of personality. *Journal of Psychology, 8*, 343–389.

Frank, L. R. (1990). Electroshock: Death, brain damage, memory loss, and brainwashing. *The Journal of Mind and Behavior, 11*(3/4), 489–512.

Frank, M. G. (2006). The function of sleep. In T. Lee-Chiong (Ed.), *Sleep: A comprehensive handbook*. Hoboken, NJ: Wiley-Liss.

Frankland, P. W., & Bontempi, B. (2005). The organization of recent and remote memories. *Nature Reviews Neuroscience, 6*(2), 119–130.

Frantom, C., & Sherman, M. F. (1999). At what price art? Affective instability within a visual art population. *Creativity Research Journal, 12*, 15–23.

Frasure-Smith, N., & Lesperance, F. (2005). Depression and coronary heart disease: Complex synergism of mind, body, and environment. *Current Directions in Psychological Science, 14*(1), 39–43.

Frederick, S., & Loewenstein, G. (1999). Hedonic adaptation. In D. Kahneman, E. Diener, & N. Schwarz (Eds.), *Well-being: The foundations of hedonic psychology*. New York: Russell Sage Foundation.

Frederickson, B. L. (1998). What good are positive emotions? *Review of General Psychology, 2*, 300–319.

Fredrickson, B. L. (2001). The role of positive emotions in positive psychology: The broaden-and-build theory of positive emotions. *American Psychologist, 56*, 218–226.

Fredrickson, B. L. (2002). Positive emotions. In C. R. Snyder & S. J. Lopez (Eds.), *Handbook of positive psychology* (pp. 120–134). New York: Oxford University Press.

Fredrickson, B. L. (2005). The broaden-and-build theory of positive emotions. In F. A. Huppert, N. Baylis, & B. Keverne (Eds.), *The science of well-being*. New York: Oxford University Press.

Fredrickson, B. L. (2006). The broaden-and-build theory of positive emotions. In M. Csikszentmihalyi, & I. S. Csikszentmihalyi (Eds.), *A life worth living: Contributions to positive psychology*. New York: Oxford University Press.

Fredrickson, B. L., & Branigan, C. (2001). Positive emotions. In T. J. Mayne & G. A. Bonanno (Eds.), *Emotions: Current issues and future directions* (pp. 123–151). New York: Guilford.

Fredrickson, B. L., & Branigan, C. (2005). Positive emotions broaden the scope of attention and thought-action repertoires. *Cognition and Emotion, 19*,313–332.

Fredrickson, B. L., & Losada, M. F. (2005). Positive affect and the complex dynamics of human flourishing. *American Psychologist, 60*, 678–686.

Fredrickson, B. L., Tugade, M. M., Waugh, C. E., & Larkin, G. R. (2003). What good are positive emotions in crises? A prospective study of resilience and emotions following the terrorist attacks on the United States on September 11, 2001. *Journal of Personality and Social Psychology, 84*, 365–376.

Freedman, J. L. (1978). *Happy people*. New York: Harcourt Brace Jovanovich.

Freedman, J. L., & Fraser, S. C. (1966). Compliance without pressure: The foot-in-the-door technique. *Journal of Personality and Social Psychology, 4*, 195–202.

Fremouw, W. J., de Perczel, M., & Ellis, T. E. (1990). *Suicide risk: Assessment and response guidelines*. New York: Pergamon.

Freud, S. (1900/1953). *The interpretation of dreams*. In J. Strachey (Ed.), *The standard edition of the complete psychological works of Sigmund Freud* (Vols. 4 and 5). London: Hogarth.

Freud, S. (1901/1960). *The psychopathology of everyday life*. In J. Strachey (Ed.), *The standard edition of the complete psychological works of Sigmund Freud* (Vol. 6). London: Hogarth.

Freud, S. (1905/1953). *Fragment of an analysis of a case of hysteria*. In J. Strachey (Ed.), *The standard edition of the complete psychological works of Sigmund Freud* (Vol. 7). London: Hogarth.

Freud, S. (1924). *A general introduction to psychoanalysis*. New York: Boni & Liveright.

Freud, S. (1933/1964). *New introductory lectures on psychoanalysis*. In J. Strachey (Ed.), *The standard edition of the complete psychological works of Sigmund Freud* (Vol. 22). London: Hogarth.

Freud, S. (1940). An outline of psychoanalysis. *International Journal of Psychoanalysis, 21*, 27–84.

Frey, B. S., & Stutzer, A. (2002). What can economists learn from happiness research? *Journal of Economic Literature, 40*, 402–435.

Frey, K. S., & Ruble, D. N. (1992). Gender constancy and the cost of sex-typed behavior: A test of the conflict hypothesis. *Developmental Psychology, 28*, 714–721.

Friedkin, N. E. (1999). Choice shift and group polarization. *American Sociological Review, 64*, 856–875.

Friedman, H. S. (2007). Personality, disease, and self-healing. In H. S. Friedman & R. C. Silver (Eds.), *Foundations of health psychology*. New York: Oxford University Press.

Friedman, H. S., & Adler, N. E. (2007). The history and background of health psychology. In H. S. Friedman & R. C. Silver (Eds.), *Foundations of health psychology*. New York: Oxford University Press.

Friedman, H. S., Tucker, J. S., Tomlinson-Keasey, C., Schwartz, J. E., Wingard, D. L., & Criqui, M. H. (1993). Does childhood personality predict longevity? *Journal of Personality and Social Psychology, 65,* 176–185.

Friedman, M. J. (2006). Posttraumatic stress disorder among military returnees from Afghanistan and Iraq. *American Journal of Psychiatry, 163,* 586–593.

Friedman, M., & Rosenman, R. F. (1974). *Type A behavior and your heart.* New York: Knopf.

Frijda, N. H. (1999). Emotions and hedonic experience. In D. Kahneman, E. Diener, & N. Schwarz (Eds.), *Well-being: The foundations of hedonic psychology.* New York: Russell Sage Foundation.

Frishman, L. J. (2001). Basic visual processes. In E. B. Goldstein (Ed.), *Blackwell handbook of perception.* Malden, MA: Blackwell.

Friston, K. J. (2003). Characterizing functional asymmetries with brain mapping. In K. Hugdahl & R. J. Davidson (Eds.), *The asymmetrical brain.* Cambridge, MA: MIT Press.

Fritze, J. G., Blashki, G. A., Burke, S., and Wiseman, J. (2008). Hope, despair and transformation: Climate change and the promotion of mental health and well-being. *International Journal of Mental Health Systems, 2.*

Fromm, E. (1979). The nature of hypnosis and other altered states of consciousness: An ego-psychological theory. In E. Fromm & R. E. Shor (Eds.), *Hypnosis: Developments in research and new perspectives.* New York: Aldine.

Fromm, E. (1992). An ego-psychological theory of hypnosis. In E. Fromm & M. R. Nash (Eds.), *Contemporary hypnosis research.* New York: Guilford.

Frumkin, H. (2001). Beyond toxicity: Human health and the natural environment. *American Journal of Preventive Medicine, 20,* 234–240.

Fuchs, A. H., & Milar, K. S. (2003). Psychology as a science. In D. K. Freedheim (Ed.), *Handbook of psychology, Vol. 1: History of psychology.* New York: Wiley.

Funder, D. C. (2001). Personality. *Annual Review of Psychology, 52,* 197–221.

Furumoto, L., & Scarborough, E. (1986). Placing women in the history of psychology: The first American women psychologists. *American Psychologist, 41,* 35–42.

Gabbard, G. O. (2005). Major modalities: Psychoanalytic/psychodynamic. In G. O. Gabbard, J. S. Beck, & J. Holmes (Eds.), *Oxford textbook of psychotherapy.* New York: Oxford University Press.

Gaddis, C. (1999, August 8). A Boggs life. *Tampa Tribune.* Retrieved at http://rays.tbo.com/rays/MGB-WZ4RSL3E.html.

Gaeth, G. J., & Shanteau, J. (2000). Reducing the influence of irrelevant information on experienced decision makers. In T. Connolly, H. R. Arkes, & K. R. Hammond (Eds.), *Judgment and decision making: An interdisciplinary reader* (2nd ed., pp. 305–323). New York: Cambridge University Press.

Gage, F. H. (2002). Neurogenesis in the adult brain. *Journal of Neuroscience, 22,* 612–613.

Gais, S., & Born, J. (2004). Declarative memory consolidation: Mechanisms acting during human sleep. *Learning & Memory, 11,* 679–685.

Galambos, N. L. (2004). Gender and gender role development in adolescence. In R. M. Lerner & L. Steinberg (Eds.), *Handbook of adolescent psychology.* New York: Wiley.

Galderisi, S., Maj, M., Mucci, A., Cassano, G. B., Invernizzi, G., Rossi, A., Vita, A., Dell'Osso, L., Daneluzzo, E., & Pini, S. (2002). Historical, psychopathological, neurological, and neuropsychological, aspects of deficit schizophrenia: A multicenter study. *American Journal of Psychiatry, 159,* 983–990.

Gallese, V., Fadiga, L., Fogassi, L. , & Rizzolatti, G. (1996). Action recognition in the premotor cortex. *Brain, 119,* 593–609.

Gambone, J. C., Reiter, R. C., & DiMatteo, M. R. (1994). *The PREPARED provider: A guide for improved patient communication.* Beaverton, OR: Mosybl Great Performance.

Gangestad, S. W., Garver-Apgar, C. E., Simpson, J. A., & Cousins, A. J. (2007). Changes in women's mate preferences across the ovulatory cycle. *Journal of Personality and Social Psychology, 92,* 151–163.

Gangestad, S. W., Thornhill, R., & Garver-Apgar, C. E. (2005). Adaptations to ovulation: Implications for sexual and social behavior. *Current Directions in Psychological Science, 14,* 312–316.

Gangwisch, J. E., Heymsfield, S. B., Boden–Albala, B., et al. (2006). Short sleep duration as a risk factor for hypertension: Analyses of the first National Health and Nutrition Examination Survey. *Hypertension, 5,* 833–839.

Gantt, W. H. (1975, April 25). Unpublished lecture, Ohio State University. Cited in D. Hothersall, (1984), *History of psychology.* New York: Random House.

Garb, H. N., Florio, C. M., & Grove, W. M. (1998). The validity of the Rorschach and the Minnesota Multiphasic Personality Inventory: Results form meta-analysis. *Psychological Science, 9,* 402–404.

Garcia, J. (1989). Food for Tolman: Cognition and cathexis in concert. In T. Archer & L. G. Nilsson (Eds.), *Aversion, avoidance, and anxiety: Perspectives on aversively motivated behavior.* Hillsdale, NJ: Erlbaum.

Garcia, J., Clarke, J. C., & Hankins, W. G. (1973). Natural responses to scheduled rewards. In P. P. G. Bateson & P. Klopfer (Eds.), *Perspectives in ethology.* New York: Plenum.

Garcia, J., & Koelling, R. A. (1966). Learning with prolonged delay of reinforcement. *Psychonomic Science, 5,* 121–122.

Garcia, J., & Rusiniak, K. W. (1980). What the nose learns from the mouth. In D. Muller-Schwarze & R. M. Silverstein (Eds.), *Chemical signals.* New York: Plenum.

Garcia, S. D., & Khersonsky, D. (1996). "They make a lovely couple": Perceptions of couple attractiveness. *Journal of Social Behavior and Personality, 11,* 667–682.

Gardner, E. (1975). *Fundamentals of neurology.* Philadelphia: Saunders.

Gardner, E. P., & Kandel, E. R. (2000). Touch. In E. R. Kandel, J. H. Schwartz, & T. M. Jessell (Eds.), *Principles of neural science.* New York: McGraw-Hill.

Gardner, G. (2002). The challenge for Johannesburg: Creating a more secure world. In C. Flavin, H. French, & G. Gardner (Eds.), *State of the World 2002: A Worldwatch Institute Report on Progress Toward a Sustainable Society.* New York: Norton.

Gardner, G., & Prugh, T. (2008). Seeding the sustainable economy. In L. Starke (Ed.), *2008 State of the World: Innovations for a sustainable economy.* New York: Norton.

Gardner, G. & Stern, P. C. (2002). Human reactions to environmental hazards: Perceptual and cognitive processes. In *Environmental problems and human behavior* (2nd ed.). Boston: Allyn & Bacon.

Gardner, G., & Stern, P. C. (2008). The short list: The most effective actions U.S. households can take to curb climate change. *Environment, 50*(5), 12–24.

Gardner, H. (1983). *Frames of mind: The theory of multiple intelligences.* New York: Basic Books.

Gardner, H. (1985). *The mind's new science: A history of the cognitive revolution.* New York: Basic Books.

Gardner, H. (1993). *Multiple intelligences: The theory in practice.* New York: Basic Books.

Gardner, H. (1999). *Intelligence reframed: Multiple intelligences for the 21st century.* New York: Basic Books.

Gardner, H. (2004). Audiences for the theory of multiple intelligences. *Teachers College Record, 106*(1), 212–220.

Gardner, H. (2006). *Multiple intelligences: New horizons.* New York: Basic Books.

Gardner , H., & Hatch, T. (1989). Multiple intelligences go to school: Educational implications of the theory of multiple intelligences. *Educational Researcher, 18* (8), 4–10.

Gardner, M., & Steinberg, L. (2005). Peer influence on risk-taking, risk preference, and risky decision-making in adolescence and adulthood: An experimental study. *Developmental Psychology, 41,* 625–635.

Garnett, N. (2005). Laws, regulations, and guidelines. In C. K. Akins, S. Panicker, & C. L. Cunningham (Eds.), *Laboratory animals in research and teaching: Ethics, care and methods.* Washington, DC: American Psychological Association.

Garry, M., & Gerrie, M. P. (2005). When photographs create false memories. *Current Directions in Psychological Science, 14,* 321–325.

Garvey, C. R. (1929). List of American psychology laboratories. *Psychological Bulletin, 26,* 652–660.

Gaschler, K. (2006, February/March). One person, one neuron? *Scientific American Mind,* pp. 76–80.

Gatchel, R. J., & Maddrey, A. M. (2004). The biopsychosocial perspective of pain. In J. M. Raczynski & L. C. Leviton (Eds.), *Handbook of clinical health psychology Vol. 2: Disorders of behavior and health.* Washington, DC: American Psychological Association.

Gattig, A., & Hendrickx, L. (2007). Judgmental discounting and environmental risk perception: Dimensional similarities, domain differences, and implications for sustainability. *Journal of Social Issues, 63,* 21–39.

Gauthier, I., & Curby, K. M. (2005). A perceptual traffic jam on highway N170: Interference between face and car expertise. *Current Directions in Psychological Science, 14*(1), 30–33.

Gauthier, I., Tarr, M. J., Anderson, A. W., Skudlarski, P., & Gore, J. C. (1999). Activation of the middle fusiform "face area" increases with expertise in recognizing novel objects. *Nature Neuroscience, 2,* 568–573.

Gawronski, B. (2004). Theory-based bias correction in dispositional inference: The fundamental attribution error is dead, long live the correspondence bias. In W. Stroebe & M. Hewstone (Eds.). *European review of social psychology* (Vol. 15). Hove, England: Psychology Press/Taylor & Francis.

Gazzaniga, M. S. (1970). *The bisected brain.* New York: Appleton-Century-Crofts.

Gazzaniga, M. S. (2000). Cerebral specialization and interhemispheric communication. *Brain, 123,* 1293–1326.

Gazzaniga, M. S. (2005). Forty-five years of split-brain research and still going strong. *Nature Reviews Neuroscience, 6,* 653–659.

Gazzaniga, M. S., Bogen, J. E., & Sperry, R. W. (1965). Observations on visual perception after disconnection of the cerebral hemispheres in man. *Brain, 88,* 221–236.

Gebhard, U., Nevers, P., & Billmann-Mahecha, E. (2003). Moralizing trees: Anthropomorphism and identity in children's relationships to nature. In S. Clayton & S. Opotow (Eds.), *Identity and the natural environment: The psychological significance of nature.* Cambridge, MA: MIT Press.

Geddes, J. R., Burgess, S., Hawton, K., Jamison, K., & Goodwin, G. M. (2004). Long-term lithium therapy for bipolar disorder: Systematic review and meta-analysis of randomized controlled trials. *American Journal of Psychiatry, 161,* 217–222.

Geddes, J. R., & Lawrie, S. M. (1995). Obstetrical complications and schizophrenia: A meta-analysis. *British Journal of Psychiatry, 167,* 786–793.

Gee, T., Allen, K., & Powell, R. A. (2003). Questioning premorbid dissociative symptomatology in dissociative identity disorder. *Professional Psychology: Research & Practice, 34*(1), 114–116.

Geier, A. B., Rozin, P., & Doros, G. (2006). Unit bias: A new heuristic that helps explain the effect of portion size on food intake. *Psychological Science, 17,* 521–525.

Geiger, M. A. (1997). An examination of the relationship between answer changing, testwiseness and examination performance. *Journal of Experimental Education, 66,* 49–60.

Gelbspan, R. (2001 May/June). A modest proposal to stop global warming. *Sierra Magazine,* 62–67.

Geller, E. S., Winett, R. A., & Everett, P. B. (1982). *Environmental preservation: New strategies for behavior change.* New York: Pergamon Press.

Geller, J. L. (1992). A historical perspective on the role of state hospitals viewed from the era of the "revolving door." *American Journal of Psychiatry, 149,* 1526–1533.

Gentile, D. A., & Anderson, C. A. (2006). Violent video games: The effects on youth, and public policy implications. In N. Dowd, D. G. Singer, & R. F. Wilson (Eds.), *Handbook of children, culture, and violence.* Thousand Oaks, CA: Sage.

George, M. S. (2003, September). Stimulating the brain. *Scientific American, 289*(3), 66–93.

George, M. S., Bohning, D. E., Lorberbaum, J. P., Nahas, Z., Anderson, B., Borckardt, J. J., et al. (2007). Overview of transcranial magnetic stimulation: History, mechanisms, physics, and safety. In M. S. George & R. H. Belmaker (Eds.), *Transcranial magnetic stimulation in clinical psychiatry.* Washington, DC: American Psychiatric Publishing.

George, M. S., Nahas, Z., Bohning, D. E., Kozel, F. A., Anderson, B., Mu, C., et al. (2006). Vagus nerve stimulation and deep brain stimulation. In D. J. Stein, D. J. Kupfer, & A. F. Schatzberg (Eds.), *Textbook of mood disorders.* Washington, DC: American Psychiatric Publishing.

George, S. A. (2002). The menopause experience: A woman's perspective. *Journal of Obstetric, Gynecologic, and Neonatal Nursing, 31,* 71–85.

Ger, G., & Belk, R. W. (1996). Cross-cultural differences in materialism. *Journal of Economic Psychology, 17,* 55–77.

Gergen, K. J., Gulerce, A., Lock, A., & Misra, G. (1996). Psychological science in cultural context. *American Psychologist, 51,* 496–503.

Gershkoff-Stowe, L., & Hahn, E. R. (2007). Fast mapping skills in the developing lexicon. *Journal of Speech, Language, and Hearing Research, 50,* 682–696.

Gershoff, E. T. (2002). Parental corporal punishment and associated child behaviors and experiences: A meta-analytic and theoretical review. *Psychological Bulletin, 128,* 539–579.

Gershon, E. S., Berrettini, W. H., & Goldin, L. R. (1989). Mood disorders: Genetic aspects. In H. I. Kaplan & B. J. Sadock (Eds.), *Comprehensive textbook of psychiatry* (Vol. 5). Baltimore: Williams & Wilkins.

Geschwind, N., & Galaburda, A. M. (1987). *Cerebral lateralization: Biological mechanisms, associations, and pathology.* Cambridge, MA: MIT Press.

Getchell, T. Y., & Getchell, M. L. (1991). Physiology of olfactory reception and transduction: General principles. In D. G. Laing, R. L. Doty, & W. Breipohl (Eds.), *The human sense of smell.* Berlin: Springer-Verlag.

Ghez, C., & Thach, W. T. (2000). The cerebellum. In E. R. Kandel, J. H. Schwartz & T. M. Jessell (Eds.), *Principles of neural science* (pp. 832–852). New York: McGraw-Hill.

Gibbons, M. B. C., Crits-Christoph, P., & Hearon, B. (2008). The empirical status of psychodynamic therapies. *Annual Review of Clinical Psychology, 4,* 93–108.

Gibbons, R. D., Hur, K., Bhaumik, D. K., & Mann, J. J. (2006). The relationship between antidepressant prescription rates and rate of early adolescent suicide. *American Journal of Psychiatry, 163,* 1898–1904.

Gibbs, J., Ellison, N. B., & Heino, R. D. (2006). Self-presentation in online personals: The role of anticipated future interaction, self-disclosure, and perceived success in Internet dating. *Communication Research, 33,* 152–177.

Giedd, J. N. (2008). The teen brain: Insights from neuroimaging. *Journal of Adolescent Health, 42,* 335–343.

Gigerenzer, G. (1997). Ecological intelligence: An adaption for frequencies. *Psychologische Beitraege, 39,* 107–125.

Gigerenzer, G. (2000). *Adaptive thinking: Rationality in the real world.* New York: Oxford University Press.

Gigerenzer, G. (2004). Fast and frugal heuristics: The tools of bounded rationality. In D. J. Koehler & N. Harvey (Eds.), *Blackwell handbook of judgment and decision making.* Malden, MA: Blackwell Publishing.

Gigerenzer, G. (2008). Why heuristics work. *Perspective on Psychological Science, 3*(1), 20–29.

Gigerenzer, G., & Hoffrage, U. (1999). Overcoming difficulties in Bayesian reasoning: A reply to Lewis and Keren (1999) and Mellers and McGraw (1999). *Psychological Review, 106,* 425–430.

Gigerenzer, G., & Todd, P. M. (1999). Fast and frugal heuristics: The adaptive toolbox. In G. Gigerenzer, P. M. Todd, & ABC Research Group (Eds.), *Simple heuristics that make us smart* (pp. 3–36). New York: Oxford University Press.

Gilbert, A. N., & Firestein, S. (2002). Dollars and scents: Commercial opportunities in olfaction and taste. *Nature Neuroscience, 5,* 1043–1045.

Gilbert, D. T. (1998). Speeding with Ned: A personal view of the correspondence bias. In J. M. Darley & J. Cooper (Ed.), *Attribution and social interaction: The legacy of Edward E. Jones.* Washington, DC: American Psychological Association.

Gilbert, D. T. (2006). *Stumbling on happiness.* New York: Alfred A. Knopf.

Gilbert, D. T., Driver-Linn, E., & Wilson, T. D. (2002). The trouble with Vronsky: Impact bias in the forecasting of future affective states. In L. F. Barrett & S. P (Eds.), *The wisdom in feeling: Psychological processes in emotional intelligence* (pp. 114–143). New York: Guilford.

Giles, L. C., Glonek, G. F. V., Luszcz, M. A., & Andrews, G. R. (2005). Effect of social networks on 10-year survival in very old Australians: The Australian longitudinal study of aging. *Journal of Epidemiology & Community Health, 59,* 574–579.

Giles, T. R., & Marafiote, R. A. (1998). Managed care and the practitioner: A call for unity. *Clinical Psychology: Science & Practice, 5,* 41–50.

Gilgen, A. R. (1982). *American psychology since World War II: A profile of the discipline.* Westport, CT: Greenwood Press.

Gitlin, M. (2002). Pharmacological treatment of depression. In I. H. Gotlib & C. L. Hammen (Eds.), *Handbook of depression.* New York: Guilford.

Gitlin, M., Nuechterlein, K., Subotnik, K. L., Ventura, J., Mintz, J., Fogelson, D. L., Bartzokis, G., & Aravagiri, M. (2001). Clinical outcome following neuroleptic discontinuation in patients with remitted recent-onset schizophrenia. *American Journal of Psychiatry, 158,* 1835–1842.

Gladue, B. A. (1994). The biopsychology of sexual orientation. *Current Directions in Psychological Science, 3,* 150–154.

Glaser, J., & Kahn, K. (2005). Prejudice, discrimination, and the Internet. In Y. Amichai-Hamburger (Ed.), *The social net: Understanding human behavior in cyberspace.* New York: Oxford University Press.

Glass, C. R., & Arnkoff, D. B. (1992). Behavior therapy. In D. K. Freedheim (Ed.), *History of psychotherapy: A century of change.* Washington, DC: American Psychological Association.

Glass, R. M. (2001). Electroconvulsive therapy. *Journal of the American Medical Association, 285,* 1346–1348.

Gleaves, D. H. (1994). On "The reality of repressed memories." *American Psychologist, 49,* 440–441.

Gleaves, D. H., May, M. C., & Cardena, E. (2001). An examination of the diagnostic validity of dissociative identity disorders. *Clinical Psychology Review, 21,* 577–608.

Gleitman, L., & Newport, E. (1996). *The invention of language by children.* Cambridge, MA: MIT Press.

Goeders, N. E. (2004). Stress, motivation, and drug addiction. *Current Directions in Psychological Science, 13*(1), 33–35.

Goff, D. C., & Gudeman, J. E. (1999). The person with chronic mental illness. In A.M. Nicholi (Ed.), *The Harvard guide to psychiatry.* Cambridge, MA: Harvard University Press.

Gogtay, N., Giedd, J. N., Lusk, L., Hayashi, K. M., Rapoport, J. L., Thompson, P. M., et al. (2004). Dynamic mapping of human cortical development during childhood through early adulthood. *Proceedings of the National Academy of Sciences, 101,* 8174–8179.

Gold, J. M., & Green, M. F. (2005). Schizophrenia: Cognition. In B. J. Sadock & V. A. Sadock (Eds.), *Kaplan & Sadock's comprehensive textbook of psychiatry.* Philadelphia: Lippincott Williams & Wilkins.

Gold, M. S., & Jacobs, W. S. (2005). Cocaine and crack: Clinical aspects. In J. H. Lowinson, P. Ruiz, R. B. Millman, & J. G. Langrod (Eds.), *Substance abuse: A comprehensive textbook.* Philadelphia: Lippincott Williams & Wilkins.

Golden, C. J., Sawicki, R. F., & Franzen, M. D. (1990). Test construction. In G. Goldstein & M. Hersen (Eds.), *Handbook of psychological assessment.* New York: Pergamon Press.

Goldenberg, H. (1983). *Contemporary clinical psychology.* Pacific Grove, CA: Brooks/Cole.

Goldsmith, T. D., & Shapira, N. A. (2006). Problematic Internet use. In E. Hollander & D. J. Stein

(Eds.), *Clinical manual of impulse-control disorders* (pp. 291–308). Washington, DC: American Psychiatric Publishing.

Goldstein, D. G., & Gigerenzer, G. (1999). The recognition heuristic: How ignorance makes us smart. In G. Gigerenzer, P. M. Todd, & ABC Research Group (Eds.), *Simple heuristics that make us smart* (pp. 37–58). New York: Oxford University Press.

Goldstein, D. G., & Gigerenzer, G. (2002). Models of ecological rationality: The recognition heuristic. *Psychological Review, 109,* 75–90.

Goldstein, E. B. (1996). *Sensation and perception* (4th ed.). Pacific Grove, CA: Brooks/Cole.

Goldstein, E. B. (2001). Pictorial perception and art. In E. B. Goldstein (Ed.), *Blackwell handbook of perception.* Malden, MA: Blackwell.

Goldstein, E. B. (2008). *Cognitive psychology: Connecting mind, research, and everyday experience.* Belmont, CA: Wadsworth.

Goldstein, H. W., Zedeck, S., & Goldstein, I. L. (2002). *g*: Is this your final answer. *Human Performance, 15,* 123–142.

Goldstein, W. M., & Hogarth, R. M. (1997). Judgement and decision research: Some historical context. In W. M. Goldstein, & R. M. Hogarth (Eds.), *Research on judgement and decision making.* New York: Cambridge University Press.

Goldston, K., & Baillie, A. J. (2008). Depression and coronary heart disease: A review of the epidemiological evidence, explanatory mechanisms and management approaches. *Clinical Psychology Review, 28,* 288–306.

Gonzaga, G. C., Campos, B., & Bradbury, T. (2007). Similarity, convergence, and relationship satisfaction in dating and married couples. *Journal of Personality and Social Psychology, 93,* 34–48.

Gonzalez-Bono, E., Salvador, A., Serrano, M. A., & Ricarte, J. (1999). Testosterone, cortisol and mood in a sports team competition. *Hormones and Behavior, 35,* 55–62.

Goodall, J. (1986). Social rejection, exclusion, and shunning among the Gombe chimpanzees. *Ethology & Sociobiology, 7,* 227–236.

Goodall, J. (1990). *Through a window: My thirty years with the chimpanzees of Gombe.* Boston, MA: Houghton, Mifflin.

Goodenough, D. R. (1991). Dream recall: History and current status of the field. In S. J. Ellman & J. S. Antrobus (Eds.), *The mind in sleep: Psychology and psychophysiology* (2nd ed.). New York: Wiley.

Goodwin, C. J. (1991). Misportraying Pavlov's apparatus. *American Journal of Psychology, 104*(1), 135–141.

Goodwin, F. K., & Jamison, K. R. (1990). *Manic-depressive illness.* New York: Oxford University Press.

Goodwin, R. D., & Friedman, H. S. (2006). Health status and the five-factor personality traits in a nationally representative sample. *Journal of Health Psychology, 11,* 643–654.

Gooley, J. J., & Saper, C. B. (2005). Anatomy of the mammalian circadian system. In M. H. Kryger, T. Roth, & W. C. Dement (Eds.), *Principles and practice of sleep medicine.* Philadelphia: Elsevier Saunders.

Gopnik, A., Meltzoff, A. N., & Kuhl, P. K. (1999). *The scientist in the crib: Minds, brains, and how children learn.* New York: Morrow.

Gordon, H. W. (1990). The neurobiological basis of hemisphericity. In C. Trevarthen (Ed.), *Brain circuits and functions of the mind. Essays in honor of Roger W. Sperry.* Cambridge, MA: Cambridge University Press.

Gordon, J., & Abramov, I. (2001). Color vision. In E. B. Goldstein (Ed.), *Blackwell handbook of perception.* Malden, MA: Blackwell.

Göritz, A. S. (2006). Cash lotteries as incentives in online panels. *Social Science Computer Review, 24,* 445–459.

Göritz, A. S. (2007). Using online panels in psychological research. In A. N. Joinson, K. Y. A. McKenna, T. Postmes, & U–D. Reips (Eds.), *The Oxford handbook of Internet psychology* (pp. 473–486). New York: Oxford University Press.

Goswami, U. (2006). Neuroscience and education: From research to practice? *Nature Reviews Neuroscience, 7*(5), 2–7.

Gottesman, I. I. (1991). *Schizophrenia genesis: The origins of madness.* New York: W. H. Freeman.

Gottesman, I. I. (2001). Psychopathology through a life span-genetic prism. *American Psychologist, 56,* 867–878.

Gottesman, I. I., & Hanson, D. R. (2005). Human development: Biological and genetic processes. *Annual Review of Psychology, 56,* 263–86.

Gottesman, I. I., & Moldin, S. O. (1998). Genotypes, genes, genesis, and pathogenesis in schizophrenia. In M. F. Lenzenweger & R. H. Dworkin (Eds.), *Origins and development of schizophrenia: Advances in experimental psychopathology.* Washington, DC: American Psychological Association.

Gottfredson, L. S. (2002). Where and why *g* matters: Not a mystery. *Human Performance, 15,* 25–46.

Gottfredson, L. S. (2003a). Dissecting practical intelligence theory: Its claims and evidence. *Intelligence, 31,* 343–397.

Gottfredson, L. S. (2003b). *G*, jobs and life. In H. Nyborg (Ed.), *The scientific study of general intelligence: Tribute to Arthur R. Jensen.* Oxford, UK: Pergamon.

Gottfredson, L. S. (2005). What if the hereditarian hypothesis is true? *Psychology, Public Policy, and the Law, 11*(2), 311–319.

Gottlieb, D. J., Punjabi, N. M., Newman, A. B., Resnick, H. E., Redline, S., Baldwin, C. M., & Nieto, F. J. (2005). Association of sleep time with diabetes mellitus and impaired glucose tolerance. *Archives of Internal Medicine, 8,* 863–867.

Gottschall, J. (2007). Greater emphasis on female attractiveness in *Homo sapiens:* A revised solution to an old evolutionary riddle. *Evolutionary Psychology, 5*(1), 347–357.

Gould, E. (2004). Stress, deprivation, and adult neurogenesis. In M. S. Gazzaniga (Ed.), *The cognitive neurosciences* (pp. 139–148). Cambridge, MA: MIT Press.

Gould, R. L. (1975, February). Adult life stages: Growth toward self-tolerance. *Psychology Today,* pp. 74–78.

Gould, S. J. (1993). The sexual politics of classification. *Natural History,* 20–29.

Gould, S. J., & Eldredge, N. (1977). Punctuated equilibria: The tempo and mode of evolution reconsidered. *Paleobiology, 3,* 115–151.

Goulven, J., & Tzourio-Mazoyer, N. (2004). Hemispheric specialization for language. *Brain Research Reviews, 44*(1), 1–12.

Gouras, P. (1991). Color vision. In E. R. Kandel, J. H. Schwartz, & T. M. Jessell (Eds.), *Principles of neural science* (3rd ed.). New York: Elsevier.

Gourevitch, M. N., & Arnsten, J. H. (2005). Medical complications of drug use. In J. H. Lowinson, P. Ruiz, R. B. Millman, & J. G. Langrod (Eds.), *Substance abuse: A comprehensive textbook.* Philadelphia: Lippincott/Williams & Wilkins.

Grady, D. (2006). Management of menopausal symptoms. *New England Journal of Medicine, 355,* 2338–2347.

Graf, P., & Uttl, B. (2001). Prospective memory: A new focus for research. *Consciousness & Cognition: An International Journal, 10,* 437–450.

Granberg, G., & Holmberg, S. (1991). Self-reported turnout and voter validation. *American Journal of Political Science, 35,* 448–459.

Grandjean, P. & Landrigan, P. J. (2006). Developmental neurotoxicity of industrial chemicals. *Lancet, 368,* 2167–2178.

Granholm, E., McQuaid, J. R., Link, P. C., Fish, S., Patterson, T., & Jeste, D. V. (2008). Neuropsychological predictors of functional outcome in cognitive behavioral social skills training for older people with schizophrenia. *Schizophrenia Research, 100,*133–143.

Grant, P., Young, P. R., & DeRubeis, R. J. (2005). Cognitive and behavioral therapies. In G. O. Gabbard, J. S. Beck, & J. Holmes (Eds.), *Oxford textbook of psychotherapy.* New York: Oxford University Press.

Grau, R., Salanova, M., & Peiro, J. M. (2001). Moderator effects of self-efficacy on occupational stress. *Psychology in Spain, 5*(1), 63–74.

Graziano, W. G. (1995). Evolutionary psychology: Old music, but now on CDs? *Psychological Inquiry, 6,* 41–44.

Green, J. P. (1999). Hypnosis, context effects, and recall of early autobiographical memories. *International Journal of Clinical & Experimental Hypnosis, 47,* 284–300.

Greenberg, B. D. (2007). Transcranial magnetic stimulation in anxiety disorders. In M. S. George & R. H. Belmaker (Eds.), *Transcranial magnetic stimulation in clinical psychiatry.* Washington, DC: American Psychiatric Publishing.

Greenberg, J. S. (2002). *Comprehensive stress management: Health and human performance.* New York: McGraw-Hill.

Greenberg, J., Pyszczynski, T., Solomon, S., Rosenblatt, A., Veeder, M., & Kirkland, S. (1990). Evidence for terror management theory II: The effects of mortality salience on reactions to those who threaten or bolster the cultural worldview. *Journal of Personality and Social Psychology, 58,* 308–318.

Greenberg, M. A., Wortman, C. B., & Stone, A. A. (1996). Emotional expression and physical health: Revising traumatic memories or fostering self-regulation? *Journal of Personality and Social Psychology, 71,* 588–602.

Greene, R. L. (1992a). *Human memory: Paradigms and paradoxes.* Hillsdale, NJ: Erlbaum.

Greenfield, P. M. (1998). The cultural evolution of IQ. In U. Neisser (Ed.), *The rising curve: Long-term gains in IQ and related measures.* Washington, DC: American Psychological Association.

Greeno, C. G., & Wing, R. R. (1994). Stress-induced eating. *Psychological Bulletin, 115,* 444–464.

Greeno, J. G. (1978). Nature of problem-solving abilities. In W. K. Estes (Ed.), *Handbook of learning and cognitive processes* (Vol. 5). Hillsdale, NJ: Erlbaum.

Greenough, W. T. (1975). Experiential modification of the developing brain. *American Scientist, 63,* 37–46.

Greenough, W. T., & Volkmar, F. R. (1973). Pattern of dendritic branching in occipital cortex of rats reared in complex environments. *Experimental Neurology, 40,* 491–504.

Greenson, R. R. (1967). *The technique and practice of psychoanalysis* (Vol. 1). New York: International Universities Press.

Greenway, R. (1995). The wilderness effect and ecopsychology. In. T. Roszak, M. E. Gomes, & A. D. Kanner (Eds.), *Eco-psychology: Restoring the earth, healing the mind.* San Francisco: Sierra Club Books.

Gregory, R. J. (1996). *Psychological testing: History, principles, and applications* (2nd ed.). Boston: Allyn & Bacon.

Gregory, R. L. (1973). *Eye and brain.* New York: McGraw-Hill.

Gregory, R. L. (1978). *Eye and brain* (2nd ed.). New York: McGraw-Hill.

Griffith, E. E., Gonzales, C. A., & Blue, H. C. (2003). Introduction to cultural psychiatry. In R. E. Hales & S. C. Yudofsky (Eds.), *Textbook of clinical psychiatry.* Washington, DC: American Psychiatric Publishing.

Griffiths, M. (1999). Internet addiction: Fact or fiction? *Psychologist, 12,* 246–250.

Grigorenko, E. L. (2000). Heritability and intelligence. In R. J. Sternberg (Ed.), *Handbook of intelligence* (pp. 53–91). New York: Cambridge University Press.

Grigorenko, E. L., & Sternberg, R. J. (2001). Analytical, creative, and practical intelligence as predictors of self-reported adaptive functioning: A case study in Russia. *Intelligence, 29,* 57–73.

Grigorenko, E. L., & Sternberg, R. J. (2003). The nature-nurture issue. In A. Slater & G. Bremner (Eds.), *An introduction to development psychology.* Malden, MA: Blackwell Publishers.

Grill, H. J. (2006). Distributed neural control of energy balance: Contributions from hindbrain and hypothalamus. *Obesity, 14*(Suppl5), 216S–221S.

Griner, D., & Smith, T. B. (2006). Culturally adapted mental health intervention: A meta-analytic review. *Psychotherapy: Theory, Research, Practice, Training, 43,* 531–548.

Grinspoon, L., Bakalar, J. B., & Russo, E. (2005). Marihuana: Clinical aspects. In J. H. Lowinson, P. Ruiz, R. B. Millman, & J. G. Langrod (Eds.), *Substance abuse: A comprehensive textbook.* Philadelphia: Lippincott/Williams & Wilkins.

Gross, C. G. (2000). Neurogenesis in the adult brain: Death of a dogma. *Nature Reviews Neuroscience, 1,* 67–73.

Gross, J. J. (1998). Antecedent and response focused emotion regulation: Divergent consequences for experience, expression, and physiology. *Journal of Personality and Social Psychology, 74,* 224–237.

Gross, J. J. (2001). Emotion regulation in adulthood: Timing is everything. *Current Directions in Psychological Science, 10,* 214–219.

Grossman, J. B., & Ruiz, P. (2004). Shall we make a leap-of-faith to disulfiram (Antabuse)? *Addictive Disorders & Their Treatment, 3*(3), 129–132.

Grossman, P., Niemann, L., Schmidt, S., & Walach, H. (2004). Mindfulness-based stress reduction and health benefits: A meta-analysis. *Journal of Psychosomatic Research, 57,* 35–43.

Grossman, R. P., & Till, B. D. (1998). The persistence of classically conditioned brand attitudes. *Journal of Advertising, 27,* 23–31.

Grossman, S. P., Dacey, D., Halaris, A. E., Collier, T., & Routtenberg, A. (1978). Aphagia and adipsia after preferential destruction of nerve cell bodies in hypothalamus. *Science, 202,* 537–539.

Grossmann, K. E., & Grossmann, K. (1990). The wider concept of attachment in cross-cultural research. *Human Development, 33,* 31–47.

Groth-Marnat, G. (1997). *Handbook of psychological assessment.* New York: Wiley.

Grubin, D., & Madsen, L. (2005). Lie detection and the polygraph: A historical review. *Journal of Forensic Psychiatry & Psychology, 16,* 357–369.

Gruenberg, A. M., & Goldstein, R. D. (2003). Mood disorders: Depression. In A. Tasman, J. Kay, & J. A. Lieberman (Eds.), *Psychiatry.* New York: Wiley.

Grunberg, N. E., Faraday, M. M., & Rahman, M. A. (2001). The psychobiology of nicotine self-administration. In A. Baum, T. A. Revenson, & J. E. Singer (Eds.), *Handbook of health psychology* (pp. 249–262). Mahwah, NJ: Erlbaum.

Grusec, J. E. (2006). The development of moral behavior and conscience from a socialization perspective. In M. Killen & J. G. Smetana (Eds.), *Handbook of moral development.* Mahwah, NJ: Erlbaum.

Guarda, A. S., Pinto, A. M., Coughlin, J. W., Hussain, S., Haug, N. A., & Heinberg, L. J. (2007). Perceived coercion and change in perceived need for admission in patients hospitalized for eating disorders. *American Journal of Psychiatry, 164,* 108–114.

Gudjonsson, G. H. (2001). Recovered memories: Effects upon the family and community. In G. M. Davies & T. Dalgleish (Eds.), *Recovered memories: Seeking the middle ground.* Chichester, England: Wiley.

Guéguen, N., Pascual, A., & Dagot, L. (2002). Lowball and compliance to a request: An application in a field setting. *Psychological Reports, 91,* 81–84.

Guenther, K. (1988). Mood and memory. In G. M. Davies & D. M. Thomson (Eds.), *Memory in context: Context in memory.* New York: Wiley.

Guerrini, I., Thomson, A. D., & Gurling, H. D. (2007). The importance of alcohol misuse, malnutrition, and genetic susceptibility on brain growth and plasticity. *Neuroscience & Biobehavioral Reviews, 31,* 212–220.

Guggenheim, F. G. (2000). Somatoform disorders. In B. J. Sadock & V. A. Sadock (Eds.), *Kaplan and Sadock's comprehensive textbook of psychiatry* (7th ed., Vol. 1, pp. 1504–1532). Philadelphia: Lippincott/Williams & Wilkins.

Guilbault, R. L., Bryant, F. B., Brockway, J. H., & Posavac, E. J. (2004). A meta-analysis of research on hindsight bias. *Basic & Applied Social Psychology, 26*(2–3), 103–117.

Guilford, J. P. (1959). Three faces of intellect. *American Psychologist, 14,* 469–479.

Guilleminault, C., & Fromherz, S. (2005). Narcolepsy: Diagnosis and management. In M. H. Kryger, T. Roth, & W. C. Dement (Eds.). *Principles and practice of sleep medicine.* Philadelphia: Elsevier Saunders.

Gunn, S. R., & Gunn, W. S. (2006). Are we in the dark about sleepwalking's dangers? *Cerebrum,* 1–12.

Gureje, O., Simon, G. E., Ustun, T. B., & Goldberg, D. P. (1997). Somatization in cross-cultural perspective: A world health organization study in primary care. *American Journal of Psychiatry, 154,* 989–995.

Guyton, A. C. (1991). *Textbook of medical physiology.* Philadelphia: Saunders.

Güzeldere, G., Flanagan, O., & Hardcastle, V. G. (2000). The nature and function of consciousness: Lessons from blindsight. In M. S. Gazzaniga (Ed.), *The new cognitive neurosciences.* Cambridge, MA: The MIT Press.

Haas, L. (1999). Families and work. In M. B. Sussman, S. K. Steinmetz, & G. W. Peterson (Eds.), *Handbook of marriage and the family* (pp. 571–612). New York: Plenum.

Hadaway, C. K., Marler, P. L., & Chaves, M. (1993). What the polls don't show: A closer look at U.S. church attendance. *American Sociological Review, 58,* 741–752.

Hadjistavropoulos, H., Dash, H., Hadjistavropoulos, T., & Sullivan, T. (2007). Recurrent pain among university students: Contributions of self-efficacy and perfectionism to the pain experience. *Personality and Individual Differences, 42,* 1081–1091.

Hagen, E. H. (2005). Controversial issues in evolutionary psychology. In D. M. Buss (Ed.), *The handbook of evolutionary psychology.* New York: Wiley.

Hagerty, M. R. (2000). Social comparisons of income in one's community: Evidence from national surveys of income and happiness. *Journal of Personality and Social Psychology, 78,* 764–771.

Haggbloom, S. J., Warnick, R., Warnick, J. E., Jones, V. K., Yarbrough, G. L., Russell, T. M., Borecky, C. M., McGahhey, R., Powell III, J. L., Beavers, J., & Monte, E. (2002). The 100 most eminent psychologists of the 20th century. *Review of General Psychology, 6,* 139–152.

Hahn, P. Y., Olson, L. J., & Somers, V. K. (2006). Cardiovascular complications of obstructive sleep apnea. In T. Lee-Chiong (Ed.), *Sleep: A comprehensive handbook.* Hoboken, NJ: Wiley-Liss.

Hales, D. (1987). *How to sleep like a baby.* New York: Ballantine.

Halford, J. C. G., & Blundell, J. E. (2000). Separate systems for serotonin and leptin in appetite control. *Annals of Medicine, 32,* 222–232.

Halford, J. C. G., Gillespie, J., Brown, V., Pontin, E. E., & Dovey, T. M. (2004). Effect of television advertisements for foods on food consumption in children. *Appetite, 42*(2), 221–225.

Hall, C.C.I. (1997). Cultural malpractice: The growing obsolescence of psychology with the changing U.S. population. *American Psychologist, 52,* 642–651.

Hall, C. S. (1966). *The meaning of dreams.* New York: McGraw-Hill.

Hall, C. S. (1979). The meaning of dreams. In D. Goleman & R. J. Davidson (Eds.), *Consciousness: Brain, states of awareness, and mysticism.* New York: Harper & Row.

Hall, E. (1987). *Growing and changing: What the experts say.* New York: Random House.

Hall, J. A., Carter, J. D., & Horgan, T. G. (2000). Gender differences in the nonverbal communication of emotion. In A. Fischer (Ed.), *Gender and emotion.* Cambridge, UK: Cambridge University Press.

Hall, J. A., & Mast, M. S. (2008). Are women always more interpersonally sensitive than men? Impact of goals and content domain. *Personality and Social Psychology Bulletin, 34,* 144–155.

Halmi, K. A. (2002). Physiology of anorexia nervosa and bulimia nervosa. In C. G. Fairburn & K. D. Brownell (Eds.), *Eating disorders and obesity: A comprehensive handbook.* New York: Guilford.

Halmi, K. A. (2003). Eating disorders: Anorexia nervosa, bulimia nervosa, and obesity. In R. E. Hales & S. C. Yudofsky (Eds.), *Textbook of Clinical Psychiatry.* Washington, DC: American Psychiatric Publishing.

Halpern, C., Hurtig, H., Jaggi, J., Grossman, M., Won, M., & Baltuch, G. (2007). Deep brain stimulation in neurologic disorders. *Parkinsonism & Related Disorders, 13*(1), 1–16.

Halpern, D. F. (1992). *Sex differences in cognitive abilities.* Hillsdale, NJ: Erlbaum.

Halpern, D. F. (1997). Sex differences in intelligence: Implications for education. *American Psychologist, 52,* 1091–1102.

Halpern, D. F. (1998). Teaching critical thinking for transfer across domains: Dispositions, skills, structure training, and metacognitive monitoring. *American Psychologist, 53,* 449–455.

Halpern, D. F. (2000). *Sex differences in cognitive abilities.* Mahwah, NJ: Erlbaum.

Halpern, D. F. (2003). *Thought and knowledge: An introduction to critical thinking.* Mahwah, NJ: Erlbaum.

Halpern, D. F. (2004). A cognitive-process taxonomy for sex differences in cognitive abilities. *Current Directions in Psychological Science, 13*(4), 135–139.

Halpern, D. F. (2007). The nature and nurture of critical thinking. In R. J. Sternberg, H. L. Roediger III, & D. F. Halpern (Eds.), *Critical thinking in psychology* (pp. 1–14). New York: Cambridge University Press.

Halpern, D. F., Benbow, C. P., Geary, D. C., Gur, R. C., Hyde, J. S., & Gernsbacher, M. A. (2007). The science of sex differences in science and mathematics. *Psychological Science in the Public Interest, 8,* 1–51.

Hamilton, W. D. (1964). The evolution of social behavior. *Journal of Theoretical Biology, 7,* 1–52.

Hammad, T. A., Laughren, T., & Racoosin, J. (2006). Suicidality in pediatric patients treated with antidepressant drugs. *Archives of General Psychiatry, 63,* 332–339.

Hammen, C. (2003). Mood disorders. In G. Stricker & T. A. Widiger (Eds.), *Handbook of psychology, Vol. 8: Clinical psychology.* New York: Wiley.

Hammen, C. (2005). Stress and depression. *Annual Review of Clinical Psychology, 1,* 293–319.

Hammer, S. M., Saag, M. S., Schechter, M., Montaner, J. S. G., Schooley, R. T., Jacobsen, D. M., et al. (2006). Treatment for adult HIV infection: 2006 recommendations of the international AIDS society–USA panel. *Journal of the American Medical Association, 296,* 827–843.

Hammill, R., Wilson T. D., & Nisbett, R. E. (1980). Insensitivity to sample bias: Generalizing from atypical cases. *Journal of Personality and Social Psychology, 39,* 578–589.

Hampson, E., van Anders, S. M., & Mullin, L. I. (2006). A female advantage in the recognition of emotional facial expressions: Test of an evolutionary hypothesis. *Evolution and Human Behavior, 27,* 401–416.

Haney, C., Banks, W. C., & Zimbardo, P. G. (1973). Interpersonal dynamics in a simulated prison. *International Journal of Criminology and Penology, 1,* 69–97.

Haney, C., & Zimbardo, P. G. (1998). The past and future of U.S. prison policy: Twenty-five years after the Stanford Prison Experiment. *American Psychologist, 53,* 709–727.

Hannigan, J. H., & Armant, D. R. (2000). Alcohol in pregnancy and neonatal outcome. *Seminars in Neonatology, 5,* 243–254.

Happonen, P., Voutilainen, S., & Salonen, J. T. (2004). Coffee drinking is dose dependently related to the risk of acute coronary events in middle-aged men. *Journal of Nutrition, 134,* 2381–2386.

Hardesty, D. E., & Sackeim, H. A. (2007). Deep brain stimulation in movement and psychiatric disorders. *Biological Psychiatry, 31,* 831–835.

Hardin, G. (1968, December). The tragedy of the commons. *Science,* 1243–1248.

Harley, E. M. (2007). Hindsight bias in legal decision making. *Social Cognition, 25,* 48–63.

Harley, T. A. (2008). *The psychology of language: From data to theory.* New York: Psychology Press.

Harlow, H. F. (1958). The nature of love. *American Psychologist, 13,* 673–685.

Harlow, H. F. (1959). Love in infant monkeys. *Scientific American, 200*(6), 68–74.

Harmsen, P., Rosengren, A., Tsipogianni, A., & Wilhelmsen, L. (1990). Risk factors for stroke in middle-aged men in Goteborg, Sweden. *Stroke, 21,* 23–29.

Haroutunian, V., & Davis, K. L. (2003). Psychiatric pathophysiology. In A. Tasman, J. Kay, & J. A. Lieberman (Eds.), *Psychiatry.* New York: Wiley.

Harper, S. (1995). The way of wilderness. In T. Roszak, M. E. Gomes, & A. D. Kanner (Eds.), *Ecopsychology: Restoring the earth, healing the mind.* San Francisco, CA: Sierra Club Books.

Harrington, M. E., & Mistlberger, R. E. (2000). Anatomy and physiology of the mammalian circadian system. In M. H. Kryger, T. Roth, & W. C. Dement (Eds.), *Principles and practice of sleep medicine.* Philadelphia: Saunders.

Harris, J. E. (1984). Remembering to do things: A forgotten topic. In J. E. Harris & P. E. Morris (Eds.), *Everyday memory, actions, and absent-mindedness.* New York: Academic Press.

Harris, J. R. (1998). *The nurture assumption: Why children turn out the way they do.* New York: Free Press.

Harris, J. R. (2000). Context-specific learning, personality, and birth order. *Current Directions in Psychological Science, 9*(5), 174–177.

Hart, J. W., Karau, S. J., Stasson, M. F., & Kerr, N. A. (2004). Achievement motivation, expected co-worker performance, and collective task motivation: Working hard or hardly working? *Journal of Applied Social Psychology, 34,* 984–1000.

Hartig, T., & Staats, H. (2006). The need for psychological restoration as a determinant of environmental preferences. *Journal of Environmental Psychology, 26,* 215–226.

Hartig, T., Evans, G. W., Jamner, L. D., Davis, D. S., & Gärling, T. (2003). Tracking restoration in natural and urban field settings. *Journal of Environmental Psychology, 23,* 109–123.

Hartig, T., Kaiser, F. G., & Bowler, P. A. (2001). Psychological restoration in nature as a positive motivation for ecological behavior. *Environment and Behavior, 33* (4), 590–607.

Hartley, A. (2006). Changing role of the speed of processing construct in the cognitive psychology of human aging. In J. E. Birren & K. W. Schaie (Eds.), *Handbook of the psychology of aging.* San Diego: Academic Press.

Harvey, M. H. (1999). Memory research and clinical practice: A critique of three paradigms and a framework for psychotherapy with trauma survivors. In L. M. Williams & V. L. Banyard (Eds.), *Trauma & memory.* Thousand Oaks, CA: Sage Publications.

Haselton, M. G., & Buss, D. M. (2000). Error management theory: A new perspective on biases in cross-sex mind reading. *Journal of Personality and Social Psychology, 78,* 81–91.

Haselton, M. G., Buss, D. M., Oubaid, V., & Angleitner, A. (2005). Sex, lies, and strategic interference: The psychology of deception between the sexes. *Personality and Social Psychology Bulletin, 31,* 3–23.

Hashimoto, K., Shimizu, E., & Iyo, M. (2005). Dysfunction of glia-neuron communication in pathophysiology of schizophrenia. *Current Psychiatry Reviews, 1,* 151–163.

Haslam, N. (1997). Evidence that male sexual orientation is a matter of degree. *Journal of Personality and Social Psychology, 73,* 862–870.

Hastorf, A., & Cantril, H. (1954). They saw a game: A case study. *Journal of Abnormal and Social Psychology, 49,* 129–134.

Hatano, G., & Inagaki, K. (1999). A developmental perspective on informal biology. In D. L. Medin & S. Atran (Eds.), *Folkbiology.* Cambridge, MA: MIT Press.

Hatfield, E., & Rapson, R. L. (1993). *Love, sex, and intimacy: Their psychology, biology, and history.* New York: HarperCollins.

Hatfield, E., Rapson, R. L., & Martel, L. D. (2007). Passionate love. In S. Kitayama & D. Cohen (Eds.), *Handbook of cultural psychology.* New York: Guilford.

Haugland, G., Siegel, C., Hopper, K., & Alexander, M. J. (1997). Mental illness among homeless individuals in a suburban county. *Psychiatric Services, 48,* 504–509.

Hauser, M., & Carey, S. (1998). Building a cognitive creature from a set of primitives: Evolutionary and developmental insights. In D. D. Cummins & C. Allen (Eds.), *The evolution of mind.* New York: Oxford University Press.

Havas, S., Dickinson, B. D., & Wilson, M. (2007). The urgent need to reduce sodium consumption. *Journal of the American Medical Association, 298,* 1439–1441.

Haworth-Hoeppner, S. (2000). The critical shapes of body image: The role of culture and family in the production of eating disorders. *Journal of Marriage and the Family, 62,* 212–227.

Hayne, H. (2007). Verbal recall of preverbal memories: Implications for the clinic and the courtroom. In M. Garry & H. Hayne (Eds.), *Do justice and let the sky fall: Elizabeth F. Lotus and her contributions to science, law, and academic freedom.* Mahwah, NJ: Erlbaum.

Hays, K. F. (1999). *Working it out: Using exercise in psychotherapy.* Washington, DC: American Psychological Association.

Haywood, T. W., Kravitz, H. M., Grossman, L. S., Cavanaugh, J. L., Jr., Davis, J. M., & Lewis, D. A. (1995). Predicting the "revolving door" phenomenon among patients with schizophrenic, schizoaffective, and affective disorders. *American Journal of Psychiatry, 152,* 861–956.

Hazan, C., & Shaver, P. (1986). *Parental caregiving style questionnaire.* Unpublished questionnaire.

Hazan, C., & Shaver, P. (1987). Romantic love conceptualized as an attachment process. *Journal of Personality and Social Psychology, 52,* 511–524.

He, J., Ogden, L. G., Vupputuri, S., Bazzano, L. A., Loria, C., & Whelton, P. K. (1999). Dietary sodium intake and subsequent risk of cardiovascular disease in overweight adults. *Journal of the American Medical Association, 282,* 2027–2034.

Healy, D. (2004). *Let them eat Prozac: The unhealthy relationship between the pharmaceutical industry and depression.* New York: NYU Press.

Healy, D., & Whitaker, C. (2003). Antidepressants and suicide: Risk-benefit conundrums. *Journal of Psychiatry & Neuroscience, 28*(5), 28.

Heaps, C. M., & Nash, M. (2001). Comparing recollective experience in true and false autobiographical memories. *Journal of Experimental Psychology: Learning, Memory, and Cognition, 27,* 920–930.

Hearst, E. (1988). Fundamentals of learning and conditioning. In R. C. Atkinson, R. J. Herrnstein, G. Lindzey, & R. D. Luce (Eds.), *Stevens' handbook of experimental psychology.* New York: Wiley.

Heatherton, T. F., Striepe, M., & Wittenberg, L. (1998). Emotional distress and disinhibited eating: The role of self. *Personality and Social Psychology Bulletin, 24,* 301–313.

Hedegaard, M. (2005). The zone of proximal development as basis for instruction. In H. Daniels (Ed.), *An introduction to Vygotsky.* New York: Routledge.

Heiby, E. M. (2002). It is time for a moratorium on legislation enabling prescription privileges for psychologists. *Clinical Psychology: Science & Practice, 9*(3), 256–258.

Heider, F. (1958). *The psychology of interpersonal relations.* New York: Wiley.

Heilman, M. E., & Haynes, M. C. (2005). No credit where credit is due: Attributional rationalization of women's success in male-female teams. *Journal of Applied Psychology, 90,* 905–916.

Heinrichs, R. W. (2005). The primacy of cognition in schizophrenia. *American Psychologist, 60,* 229–242.

Helgeson, V. S., Reynolds, K. A., & Tomich, P. L. (2006). A meta-analytic review of benefit finding and growth. *Journal of Consulting and Clinical Psychology, 74,* 797–816.

Hellige, J. B. (1990). Hemispheric asymmetry. *Annual Review of Psychology, 41,* 55–80.

Hellige, J. B. (1993a). Unity of thought and action: Varieties of interaction between left and right cerebral hemispheres. *Current Directions in Psychological Science, 2*(1), 21–25.

Hellige, J. B. (1993b). *Hemispheric asymmetry: What's right and what's left.* Cambridge, MA: Harvard University Press.

Helmholtz, H. von. (1852). On the theory of compound colors. *Philosophical Magazine, 4,* 519–534.

Helmholtz, H. von. (1863). *On the sensations of tone as a physiological basis for the theory of music* (A. J. Ellis, Trans.). New York: Dover.

Helson, R., Jones, C., & Kwan, V. S. Y. (2002). Personality change over 40 years of adulthood: Hierarchical linear modeling analyses of two longitudinal studies. *Journal of Personality & Social Psychology, 83,* 752–766.

Hendrick, S. S., & Hendrick, C. (2000). Romantic love. In S. S. Hendrick & C. Hendrick (Eds.), *Close relationships.* Thousand Oaks, CA: Sage.

Henriksson, M. M., Aro, H. M., Marttunen, M. J., Heikkinen, M. E., Isometsa, E. T., Kuoppasalmi, K. I., & Lonnqvist, J. K. (1993). Mental disorders and comorbidity of suicide. *American Journal of Psychiatry, 150,* 935–940.

Henry, K. R. (1984). Cochlear damage resulting from exposure to four different octave bands of noise at three different ages. *Behavioral Neuroscience, 1,* 107–117.

Henry, P. J., Sternberg, R. J., & Grigorenko, E. L. (2005). Capturing successful intelligence through measures of analytic, creative, and practical skills. In O. Wilhelm & R. W. Engle (Eds.), *Handbook of understanding and measuring intelligence.* Thousand Oaks, CA: Sage.

Hepper, P. (2003). *Prenatal psychological and behavioural development.* Thousand Oaks, CA: Sage.

Herbert, J. D., Gaudiano, B. A., Rheingold, A. A., Myers, V. H., Dalrymple, K., & Nolan, E. M. (2005). Social skills training augments the effectiveness of cognitive behavioral group therapy for social anxiety disorder. *Behavior Therapy, 36,* 125–138.

Herbst, S., Pietrzak, R. H., Wagner, J., White, W. B., & Petry, N. M. (2007). Lifetime major depression is associated with coronary heart disease in older adults: Results from the national epidemiologic survey on alcohol and related conditions. *Psychosomatic Medicine, 69,* 729–734.

Herek, G. M. (1996). Heterosexism and homophobia. In R. P. Cabaj & T. S. Stein (Eds.), *Textbook of homosexuality and mental health.* Washington, DC: American Psychiatric Press.

Herek, G. M. (2000). The psychology of sexual prejudice. *Current Directions in Psychological Science, 9,* 19–22.

Hering, E. (1878). *Zür lehre vom lichtsinne.* Vienna: Gerold.

Herman, J. L. (1994). Presuming to know the truth. *Nieman Reports, 48,* 43–45.

Herman-Giddens, M. E. (2006). Recent data on pubertal milestones in United States children: The secular trend towards earlier development. *International Journal of Andrology, 29,* 241.

Hermann, D., Raybeck, D., & Gruneberg, M. (2002). *Improving memory and study skills: Advances in theory and practice.* Ashland, OH: Hogrefe & Huber.

Hermann, R. C., Dorwart, R. A., Hoover, C. W., & Brody, J. (1995). Variation in ECT use in the United States. *American Journal of Psychiatry, 152,* 869–875.

Hermann, R. C., Ettner, S. L., Dorwart, R. A., Hoover, C. W., & Yeung, E. (1998). Characteristics of psychiatrists who perform ECT. *American Journal of Psychiatry, 155,* 889–894.

Hermans, D., Craske, M. G., Mineks, S., & Lovibond, P. F. (2006). Extinction in human fear conditioning. *Biological Psychiatry, 60,* 361–368.

Hermans, H. J. M., & Kempen, H. J. G. (1998). Moving cultures: The perilous problems of cultural dichotomies in a globalizing society. *American Psychologist, 53,* 1111–1120.

Herrett-Skjellum, J., & Allen, M. (1996). Television programming and sex stereotyping: A meta-analysis. In B. R. Burleson (Ed.), *Communication yearbook 19* (pp. 157–185). Thousand Oaks, CA: Sage.

Herrmann, D., Raybeck, D., & Gruneberg, M. (2002). *Improving memory and study skills: Advances in theory and practice.* Ashland, OH: Hogrefe & Huber.

Herrnstein, R. J., & Murray, C. (1994). *The bell curve: Intelligence and class structure in American life.* New York: Free Press.

Hersh, S. M. (2004, May 10). Torture at Abu Ghraib. *New Yorker, 80*(17), 54–67.

Herz, R. S., & Schooler, J. W. (2002). A naturalistic study of autobiographical memories evoked by olfactory and visual cues: Testing the Proustian hypothesis. *American Journal of Psychology, 115,* 21–32.

Herzog, D. B., & Delinski, S. S. (2001). Classification of eating disorders. In R. H. Striegel-Moore & L. Smolak (Eds.), *Eating disorders* (pp. 31–50). Washington, DC: American Psychological Association.

Herzog, H. A. (2005). Dealing with the animal research controversy. In C. K. Akins, S. Panicker, & C. L. Cunningham (Eds.), *Laboratory animals in research and teaching: Ethics, care and methods.* Washington, DC: American Psychological Association.

Herzog, T. R., & Strevey, S. J. (2008). Contact with nature, sense of humor, and psychological well-being. *Environment and Behavior, 40,* 747–776.

Hetherington, E. M. (1999). Should we stay together for the sake of the children? In E. M. Hetherington (Ed.), *Coping with divorce, single parenting, and remarriage.* Mahwah, NJ: Erlbaum.

Hetherington, E. M. (2003). Intimate pathways: Changing patterns in close personal relationships across time. *Family Relations: Interdisciplinary Journal of Applied Family Studies, 52,* 318–331.

Hetherington, E. M., Reiss, D., & Plomin, R. (1994). *Separate social worlds of siblings: The impact of nonshared environment on development.* Hillsdale, NJ: Erlbaum.

Hetherington, M. M., & Rolls, B. J. (1996). Sensory-specific satiety: Theoretical frameworks and central characteristics. In E. D. Capaldi (Ed.), *Why we eat what we eat: The psychology of eating* (pp. 267–290). Washington, DC: American Psychological Association.

Hettema, J. M., Annas, P., Neale, M. C., Kendler, K. S., & Fredrikson, M. (2003). A twin study of the genetics of fear conditioning. *Archives of General Psychiatry, 6,* 402–707.

Hettema, J. M., Neale, M. C., & Kendler, K. S. (2001). A review and meta-analysis of the genetic epidemiology of anxiety disorders. *American Journal of Psychiatry, 158,* 1568–1578.

Hewson, C. (2003). Conducting research on the Internet. *The Psychologist, 16,* 290–293.

Hewstone, M. (1990). The "ultimate attribution error"? A review of the literature on intergroup causal attribution. *European Journal of Social Psychology, 20,* 311–335.

Higgins, E. T. (2004). Making a theory useful: Lessons handed down. *Personality and Social Psychology Review, 8*(2), 138–145.

Highhouse, S., Beadle, D., Gallo, A., & Miller, L. (1998). Get 'em while they last! Effects of scarcity information in job advertisements. *Journal of Applied Social Psychology, 28,* 779–795.

Hilgard, E. R. (1965). *Hypnotic susceptibility.* New York: Harcourt, Brace & World.

Hilgard, E. R. (1986). *Divided consciousness: Multiple controls in human thought and action.* New York: Wiley.

Hilgard, E. R. (1987). *Psychology in America: A historical survey.* San Diego: Harcourt Brace Jovanovich.

Hilgard, E. R. (1992). Dissociation and theories of hypnosis. In E. Fromm & M. R. Nash (Eds.), *Contemporary hypnosis research.* New York: Guilford.

Hill, C. E., & Lambert, M. J. (2004). Methodological issues in studying psychotherapy processes and outcomes. In M. J. Lambert (Ed.), *Bergin and Garfield's handbook of psychotherapy and behavior change.* New York: Wiley.

Hilmert, C. J., Kulik, J. A., & Christenfeld, N. J. S. (2006). Positive and negative opinion modeling: The influence of another's similarity and dissimilarity. *Journal of Personality and Social Psychology, 90,* 440–452.

Hilton, J. L., & von Hippel, W. (1996). Stereotypes. *Annual Review of Psychology, 47,* 237–271.

Hines, M. (2004). Androgen, estrogen, and gender: Contributions of the early hormone environment to gender-related behavior. In A. H. Eagly, A. E. Beall, & R. J. Sternberg (Eds.), *The psychology of gender.* New York: Guilford.

Hingson, R., & Sleet, D. A. (2006). Modifying alcohol use to reduce motor vehicle injury. In A. C. Gielen, D. A. Sleet, & R. J. DiClemente (Eds.), *Injury*

Kandell, J. J. (1998). Internet addiction on campus: The vulnerability of college students. *CyberPsychology and Behavior, 1*(1), 11–17.

Kane, J. (1991). *Be sick well: A healthy approach to chronic illness.* Oakland, CA: New Harbinger Publications.

Kane, J. M., & Marder, S. R. (2005). Schizophrenia: Somatic treatment. In B. J. Sadock & V. A. Sadock (Eds.), *Kaplan and Sadock's comprehensive textbook of psychiatry.* Philadelphia: Lippincott Williams & Wilkins.

Kane, M. J., & Engle, R. W. (2002). The role of prefrontal cortex in working-memory capacity, executive attention, and general fluid intelligence: An individual-differences perspective. *Psychonomic Bulletin & Review, 9,* 637–671.

Kane, M. J., Brown, L. H., McVay, J. C., Silivia, P. J., Myin-Germeys, I., & Kwapil, T. R. (2007). For whom the mind wanders, and when: An experience-sampling study of working memory and executive control in daily life. *Psychological Science, 18,* 614–621.

Kane, T. D., Marks, M. A., Zaccaro, S. J., & Blair, V. (1996). Self-efficacy, personal goals, and wrestlers' self-regulation. *Journal of Sport & Exercise Psychology, 18,* 36–48.

Kantor, L.S., Lipton, K., Manchester, A., & Oliviera, V. (1997). Estimating and addressing America's food losses. U.S. Department of Agriculture. Retrieved June 4, 2009 from http://www.ers.usda.gov/Publications/FoodReview/Jan1997/Jan97a.pdf.

Kaplan, H., & Dove, H. (1987). Infant development among the Ache of Eastern Paraguay. *Developmental Psychology, 23,* 190–198.

Kaplan, J. T., & Iacoboni, M. (2006). Getting a grip on other minds: Mirror neurons, intention understanding, and cognitive empathy. *Social Neuroscience, 1,* 175–183.

Kaplan, R. (1993). The role of nature in the context of the workplace. *Landscape and Urban Planning, 26,* 193–201.

Kaplan, R. (2001). The nature of the view from home: Psychological benefits. *Environment and Behavior, 33*(4), 507–542.

Kaplan, R., & Kaplan, S. (1989). *The experience of nature: A psychological perspective.* Cambridge, MA: Cambridge University Press.

Kaplan, S. (1995). The restorative benefits of nature: Toward an integrative framework. *Journal of Environmental Psychology, 15,* 169–182.

Karasu, T. B. (2005). Psychoanalysis and psychoanalytic psychotherapy. In B. J. Sadock & V. A. Sadock (Eds.), *Kaplan and Sadock's comprehensive textbook of psychiatry.* Philadelphia: Lippincott Williams & Wilkins.

Karau, S. J., & Williams, K. D. (1993). Social loafing: A meta-analytic review and theoretical integration. *Journal of Personality and Social Psychology, 65,* 681–706.

Kass, S. J., Cole, K. S., & Stanny, C. J. (2007). Effects of distraction and experience on situation awareness and simulated driving. *Transportation Research Part F: Traffic Psychology and Behaviour, 10,* 321–329.

Kassel, J. D., Stroud, L. R., & Paronis, C. A. (2003). Smoking, stress, and negative affect: Correlation, causation, and context across stages of smoking. *Psychological Bulletin, 129,* 270–304.

Kasser, T. (2002). *The high price of materialism.* Cambridge, MA: MIT Press.

Kasser, T., & Kanner, A. D. (2004). *Psychology and consumer culture: The struggle for a good life in a materialistic world.* Washington DC: American Psychological Association.

Kasser, T., Ryan, R. M., Couchman, C. E., & Sheldon, K. M. (2004). Materialistic values: Their causes and consequences. In T. Kasser & A. D. Kanner (Eds.), *Psychology and consumer culture: The struggle for a good life in a materialistic world.* Washington, DC: American Psychological Association.

Kasser, T., & Sharma, Y. S. (1999). Reproductive freedom, educational equality, and females' preference for resource-aquisition characteristics in mates. *Psychological Science, 10,* 374–377.

Kassin, S. M., Tubb, V. A., Hosch, H. M., & Memon, A. (2001). On the "general acceptance" of eyewitness testimony research: A new survey of the experts. *American Psychologist, 56,* 405–416.

Katigbak, M. S., Church, A. T., Guanzon-Lapena, M. A., Carlota, A. J. & del Pilar, G. H. (2002). Are indigenous personality dimensions culture specific? Philippine inventories and the five-factor model. *Journal of Personality and Social Psychology, 82,* 89–101.

Kaufman, A. S. (2000). Tests of intelligence. In R. J. Sternberg (Ed.), *Handbook of intelligence* (pp. 445–476). New York: Cambridge University Press.

Kaufman, J. C., & Baer, J. (2002). Could Steven Spielberg manage the Yankees?: Creative thinking in different domains. *Korean Journal of Thinking & Problem Solving, 12*(2), 5–14.

Kaufman, J. C., & Baer, J. (2004). Hawking's haiku, Madonna's math: Why it is hard to be creative in every room of the house. In R. J. Sternberg, E. L. Grigorenko & J. L. Singer (Eds.), *Creativity: From potential to realization.* Washington, DC: American Psychological Association.

Kaufman, L., & Rock, I. (1962). The moon illusion I. *Science, 136,* 953–961.

Kay, J., & Kay, R. I. (2003). Individual psychoanalytic psychotherapy. In A. Tasman, J. Kay, & J. A. Lieberman (Eds.), *Psychiatry.* New York: Wiley.

Kaye, W. H., Bailer, U. F., Frank, G. K., Wagner, A., & Henry, S. E. (2005). Brain imaging of serotonin after recovery from anorexia and bulimia nervosa. *Physiology and Behavior, 86,* 15–17.

Kazdin, A. (1994). Methodology, design, and evaluation in psychotherapy research. In A. E. Bergin & S. L. Garfield (Eds.), *Handbook of psychotherapy and behavior change* (4th ed.). New York: Wiley.

Kazdin, A. (2001). *Behavior modification in applied settings.* Belmont: Wadsworth.

Kazdin, A., & Benjet, C. (2003). Spanking children: Evidence and issues. *Current Directions in Psychological Science, 12*(3), 99–103.

Keane, T. M., Marshall, A. D., & Taft, C. T. (2006). Posttraumatic stress disorder: Etiology, epidemiology, and treatment outcome. *Annual Review of Clinical Psychology, 2,* 161–197.

Keating, D. P. (2004). Cognitive and brain development. In R. M. Lerner & L. Steinberg (Eds.), *Handbook of adolescent psychology.* New York: Wiley.

Keck, P. E. Jr., & McElroy, S. L. (2006). Lithium and mood stabilizers. In D. J. Stein, D. J. Kupfer, & A. F. Schatzberg (Eds.), *Textbook of mood disorders.* Washington, DC: American Psychiatric Publishing.

Keefauver, S. P., & Guilleminault, C. (1994). Sleep terrors and sleepwalking. In M. H. Kryger, T. Roth, & W. C. Dement (Eds.), *Principles and practice of sleep medicine* (2nd ed.). Philadelphia: Saunders.

Keefe, F. J., Smith, S. J., Buffington, A. L. H., Gibson, J., Studts, J. L., & Caldwell, D. S. (2002). Recent advances and future directions in the biopsychosocial assessment and treatment of arthritis. *Journal of Consulting & Clinical Psychology, 70,* 640–655.

Keefe, R. S. E., & Eesley, C. E. (2006). Neurocognitive impairments. In J. A. Lieberman, T. S. Stroup, & D. O. Perkins (Eds.), *Textbook of schizophrenia.* Washington, DC: American Psychiatric Publishing.

Keenan, J. P., Gallup, G. G. Jr., Goulet, N., & Kulkarni, M. (1997). Attributions of deception in human mating strategies. *Journal of Social Behavior and Personality, 12,* 45–52.

Keesey, R. E., & Powley, T. L. (1975). Hypothalamic regulation of body weight. *American Scientist, 63,* 558–565.

Kehoe, E. J., & Macrae, M. (1998). Classical conditioning. In W. O'Donohue (Ed.), *Learning and behavior therapy.* Boston, Allyn & Bacon.

Keller, P. A., & Block, L. G. (1999). The effect of affect-based dissonance versus cognition-based dissonance on motivated reasoning and health-related persuasion. *Journal of Experimental Psychology: Applied, 5,* 302–313.

Kellert, S. R. (1993). The biological basis for human values of nature. In S. R. Kellert & E. O. Wilson (Eds.), *The biophilia hypothesis.* Washington, DC: Island Press.

Kellert, S. R. (1997). *Kinship to mastery: Biophilia in human evolution and development.* Washington, DC: Island Press.

Kellert, S. R. (2002). Experiencing nature: Affective, cognitive, and evaluative development in children. In P. H. Kahn, Jr. & S. R. Kellert (Eds.), *Children and nature: Psychological, sociocultural, and evolutionary investigations* (pp. 117–151). Cambridge MA: MIT Press.

Kelley, H. H. (1950). The warm-cold variable in first impressions of persons. *Journal of Personality, 18,* 431–439.

Kelley, H. H. (1967). Attributional theory in social psychology. *Nebraska Symposium on Motivation, 15,* 192–241.

Kellogg, S. H., & Young, J. E. (2008). Cognitive Therapy. In J. L. Lebow (Ed.), *Twenty-first century psychotherapies: Contemporary approaches to theory and practice.* New York: Wiley.

Kelly, B. D., Feeney, L., O'Callaghan, E., Browne, R., Byrne, M., Mulryan, N., Scully, A., Morris, M., Kinsella, A., Takei, N., McNeil, T., Walsh, D., & Larkin, C. (2004). Obstetric adversity and age at first presentation with schizophrenia: Evidence of a dose-response relationship. *American Journal of Psychiatry, 161,* 920–922.

Kelly, K. M., & Schramke, C. J. (2000). Epilepsy. In G. Fink (Ed.), *Encyclopedia of stress* (pp. 66–70). San Diego: Academic Press.

Kelman, H. C. (1967). Human use of human subjects: The problem of deception in social psychological experiments. *Psychological Bulletin, 67,* 1–11.

Kelman, H. C. (1982). Ethical issues in different social science methods. In T. L. Beauchamp, R. R. Faden, R. J. Wallace, Jr., & L. Walters (Eds.), *Ethical issues in social science research.* Baltimore: Johns Hopkins University Press.

Kelsey, J. E. (2005). Selective serotonin reuptake inhibitors. In B. J. Sadock & V. A. Sadock (Eds.), *Kaplan and Sadock's comprehensive textbook of psychiatry.* Philadelphia: Lippincott Williams & Wilkins.

Kelsoe, J. (2005). Mood disorders: Genetics. In B. J. Sadock & V. A. Sadock (Eds.), *Kaplan & Sadock's comprehensive textbook of psychiatry.* Philadelphia: Lippincott Williams & Wilkins.

Kendall, P. C., Holmbeck, G., & Verduin, T. (2004). Methodology, design, and evaluation in psychotherapy research. In M. J. Lambert (Ed.), *Bergin and Garfield's handbook of psychotherapy and behavior change*. New York: Wiley.

Kendler, K. S., & Gardner, C. O., Jr. (1998). Boundaries of major depression: An evaluation of DSM-IV criteria. *American Journal of Psychiatry, 155*, 172–177.

Kendler, K. S., Kuhn, J., & Prescott, C. A. (2004). The interrelationship of neuroticism, sex, and stressful life events in the prediction of episodes of major depression. *American Journal of Psychiatry, 161*, 631–636.

Kendler, K. S., Myers, J., & Prescott, C. A. (2005). Sex differences in the relationship between social support and risk for major depression: A longitudinal study of opposite-sex twin pairs. *American Journal of Psychiatry, 162*, 250–256.

Kendler, K. S., Thornton, L. M., Gilman, S. E., & Kessler, R. C. (2000). Sexual orientation in a U.S. national sample of twin and non-twin sibling pairs. *American Journal of Psychiatry, 157*, 1843–1846.

Kenfield, S. A., Stampfer, M. J., Rosner, B. A., & Colditz, G. A. (2008). Smoking and smoking cessation in relation to mortality in women. *Journal of the American Medical Association, 299*, 2037–2047.

Kennedy, T. E., Hawkins, R. D., & Kandel, E. R. (1992). Molecular interrelationships between short- and long-term memory. In L. R. Squire & N. Butters (Eds.), *Neuropsychology of Memory* (2nd ed.). New York: Wiley.

Kenrick, D. T., & Gutierres, S. E. (1980). Contrast effects and judgments of physical attractiveness: When beauty becomes a social problem. *Journal of Personality and Social Psychology, 38*, 131–140.

Kenrick, D. T., Trost, M. R., & Sundie, J. M. (2004). Sex roles as adaptations: An evolutionary perspective on gender differences and similarities. In A. H. Eagly, A. E. Beall, & R. J. Sternberg (Eds.), *The psychology of gender*. New York: Guilford.

Kermer, D. A., Driver-Linn, E., Wilson, T. D., & Gilbert, D. T. (2006). Loss aversion is an affective forecasting error. *Psychological Science, 17*, 649–653.

Kerns, K. A., Abraham, M. M., Schlegelmilch, A., & Morgan, T. A. (2007). Mother-child attachment in later middle-childhood: Assessment approaches and associations with mood and emotion. *Attachment & Human Development, 9*(1), 33–53.

Kershaw, T. C., & Ohlsson, S. (2004). Multiple causes of difficulty in insight: The case of the nine-dot problem. *Journal of Experimental Psychology: Learning, Memory, and Cognition, 30*, 3–13.

Kessen, W. (1996). American psychology just before Piaget. *Psychological Science, 7*, 196–199.

Kessler, R. C., Berglund, P., Demler, O., Jin, R., Koretz, D., Merikangas, K. R., Rush, A. J., Walters, E. E., & Wang, P. S. (2003). The epidemiology of major depressive disorder: Results from the national comorbidity survey replication (NCS-R). *Journal of the American Medical Association, 189*, 3095–3105.

Kessler, R. C., Berglund, P., Demler, O., Jin, R., & Walters, E. E. (2005a). Lifetime prevalence and age-of-onset distributions of DSM-IV disorders in the national comorbidity survey replication. *Archives of General Psychiatry, 62*, 593–602.

Kessler, R. C., Demler, O., Frank, R. G., Olfson, M., Pincus, H. A., Walters, E. E., Wang, P., Wells, K. B., & Zaslavsky, A. M. (2005b). Prevalence and treatment of mental disorders: 1990–2003. *New England Journal of Medicine, 352*, 2515–2523.

Khot, U. N., Khot, M. B., Bajzer, C. T., Sapp, S. K., Ohman, E. M., Brener, S. J., Ellis, S. G., Lincoff, M. A., & Topol, E. J. (2003). Prevalence of conventional risk factors in patients with coronary heart disease. *Journal of the American Medical Association, 290*, 898–904.

Kiecolt-Glaser, J. K., Garner, W., Speicher, C., Penn, G. M., Holliday, J., & Glaser, R. (1984). Psychosocial modifiers of immunocompetence in medical students. *Psychosomatic Medicine, 46*(1), 7–14.

Kiecolt-Glaser, J. K., & Glaser, R. (1995). Measurement of immune response. In S. Cohen, R. C. Kessler, & L. U. Gordon (Eds.), *Measuring stress: A guide for health and social scientists*. New York: Oxford University Press.

Kieseppa, T., Partonen, T., Huakka, J., Kaprio, J., & Lonnqvist, J. (2004). High concordance of bipolar 1 disorder in a nationwide sample of twins. *American Journal of Psychiatry, 161*, 1814–1821.

Kiesler, C. A. (1992). U.S. mental health policy: Doomed to fail. *American Psychologist, 47*, 1077–1082.

Kiesler, C. A. (2000). The next wave of change for psychology and mental health services in the health care revolution. *American Psychologist, 55*, 481–487.

Kiesler, D. J. (1999). *Beyond the disease model of mental disorders*. New York: Praeger Publishers.

Kihlstrom, J. F. (1985). Hypnosis. *Annual Review of Psychology, 36*, 385–418.

Kihlstrom, J. F. (1998). Exhumed memory. In S. J. Lynn, & K. M. McConkey (Eds.), *Truth in memory*. New York: Guilford.

Kihlstrom, J. F. (2001). Dissociative disorders. In P. B. Sutker & H. E. Adams (Eds.), *Comprehensive handbook of psychopathology* (3rd ed., pp. 259–276). New York: Kluwer Academic/Plenum Publishers.

Kihlstrom, J. F. (2004). An unbalanced balancing act: Blocked, recovered, and false memories in the laboratory and clinic. *Clinical Psychology: Science & Practice, 11*(1), 34–41.

Kihlstrom, J. F. (2005). Dissociative disorders. *Annual Review of Clinical Psychology, 1*, 227–253.

Kihlstrom, J. F. (2007). Consciousness in hypnosis. In P. D. Zelazo, M. Moscovitch, & E. Thompson (Eds.), *The Cambridge handbook of consciousness*. New York: Cambridge University Press.

Kihlstrom, J. F., & Cork, R. C. (2007). Consciousness and anesthesia. In M. Velmans & S. Schneider (Eds.), *The Blackwell companion to consciousness*. Malden, MA: Blackwell Publishing.

Killeen, P. R. (1981). Learning as causal inference. In M. L. Commons & J. A. Nevin (Eds.), *Quantitative analyses of behavior, Vol. 1: Discriminative properties of reinforcement schedules*. Cambridge, MA: Ballinger.

Kim, H., & Markus, H. R. (1999). Deviance or uniqueness, harmony or conformity? A cultural analysis. *Journal of Personality and Social Psychology, 77*, 785–800.

Kim, K. H. (2005). Can only intelligent people be creative? *Journal of Secondary Gifted Education, 16*, 57–66.

Kimmel, A. J. (1996). *Ethical issues in behavioral research: A survey*. Cambridge, MA: Blackwell.

Kimura, D. (1973). The asymmetry of the human brain. *Scientific American, 228*, 70–78.

Kimura, D., & Hampson, E. (1993). Neural and hormonal mechanisms mediating sex differences in cognition. In P. A. Vernon (Ed.), *Biological approaches to the study of human intelligence*. Norwood, NJ: Ablex.

King, A. C., Oman, R. F., Brassington, G. S., Bliwise, D. L., & Haskell, W. L. (1997). Moderate-intensity exercise and self-rated quality of sleep in older adults: A randomized controlled trial. *Journal of the American Medical Association, 277*, 32–37.

King, B. M. (2006). The rise, fall, and resurrection of the ventromedial hypothalamus in the regulation of feeding behavior and body weight. *Physiology & Behavior, 87*, 221–244.

King, G. R., & Ellinwood Jr., E. H. (2005). Amphetamines and other stimulants. In J. H. Lowinson, P. Ruiz, R. B. Millman, & J. G. Langrod (Eds.), *Substance abuse: A comprehensive textbook*. Philadelphia: Lippincott/Williams & Wilkins.

King, L. A., & Emmons, R. A. (1990). Conflict over emotional expression: Psychological and physical correlates. *Journal of Personality and Social Psychology, 58*, 864–877.

King, L. A., & Emmons, R. A. (1991). Psychological, physical, and interpersonal correlates of emotional expressiveness, conflict and control. *European Journal of Personality, 5*, 131–150.

Kinnunen, T., Haukkala, A., Korhonen, T., Quiles, Z. N., Spiro, A. I., & Garvey, A. J. (2006). Depression and smoking across 25 years of the normative aging study. *International Journal of Psychiatry in Medicine, 36*, 413–426.

Kinsbourne, M. (1980). If sex differences in brain lateralization exist, they have yet to be discovered. *Behavioral and Brain Sciences, 3*, 241–242.

Kinsbourne, M. (1997). What qualifies a representation for a role in consciousness? In J. D. Cohen & J. W. Schooler (Eds.), *Scientific approaches to consciousness*. Mahwah, NJ: Erlbaum.

Kinsey, A. C., Pomeroy, W. B., & Martin, C. E. (1948). *Sexual behavior in the human male*. Philadelphia: Saunders.

Kinsey, A. C., Pomeroy, W. B., Martin, C. E., & Gebhard, P. H. (1953). *Sexual behavior in the human female*. Philadelphia: Saunders.

Kirkpatrick, B., & Tek, C. (2005). Schizophrenia: Clinical features and psychopathology concepts. In B. J. Sadock & S. V. A (Eds.), *Kaplan & Sadock's comprehensive textbook of psychiatry*. Philadelphia: Lippincott Williams & Wilkins.

Kirkpatrick, L. A. (2005). *Attachment, evolution, and the psychology of religion*. New York: Guilford.

Kirmayer, L. J., & Looper, K. J. (2007). Somatoform disorders. In M. Hersen, S. M. Turner, & D. C. Beidel (Eds.), *Adult psychopathology and diagnosis*. New York: Wiley.

Kirsch, I. (1997). Response expectancy theory and application: A decennial review. *Applied and Preventive Psychology, 6*, 69–79.

Kirsch, I. (2000). The response set theory of hypnosis. *American Journal of Clinical Hypnosis, 42*, 274–292.

Kirsch, I., & Lynn, S. J. (1998). Dissociation theories of hypnosis. *Psychological Bulletin, 123*, 100–115.

Kirsch, I., Mazzoni, G., & Montgomery, G. H. (2007). Remembrance of hypnosis past. *American Journal of Clinical Hypnosis, 49*, 171–178.

Kirschenbaum, H., & Jourdan, A. (2005). The current status of Carl Rogers and the person-centered approach. *Psychotherapy: Theory, Research, Practice, Training, 42*, 37–51.

Kitayama, S., Mesquita, B., & Karasawa, M. (2006). Cultural affordances and emotional experience: Socially engaging and disengaging emotions in Japan and the United States. *Journal of Personality and Social Psychology, 91*, 890–903.

Kitchens, A. (1991). Left brain/right brain theory: Implications for developmental math instruction. *Review of Research in Developmental Education, 8,* 20–23.

Kittler, P. G., & Sucher, K. P. (2008). *Food and culture.* Belmont, CA: Wadsworth.

Kitzes, J., Wackernagel, M., Loh, J., Peller, A., Goldfinger, S., Cheng, D., & Tea, K. (2008). Shrink and share: Humanity's present and future Ecological Footprint. *Philosophical Transactions of the Royal Society of London,* Series B, Biological Sciences, 363, 467–475.

Kivimäki, M., Vahtera, J., Elovainio, M., Helenius, H., Singh-Manoux, A., & Pentti, J. (2005). Optimism and pessimism as predictors of change in health after death or onset of severe illness in family. *Health Psychology, 24,* 413–421.

Klapper, D., Ebling, C., & Temme, J. (2005). Another look at loss aversion in brand choice data: Can we characterize the loss averse consumer? *International Journal of Research in Marketing, 22,* 239–254.

Klare, M. T. (2001). *Resource wars: The new landscape of global conflict.* New York: Henry Holt.

Klehe, U.-C., & Anderson, N. (2007). The moderating influence of personality and culture on social loafing in typical versus maximum performance situations. *International Journal of Selection and Assessment, 15,* 250–262.

Klein, M. (1948). *Contributions to psychoanalysis.* London: Hogarth.

Klein, P. D. (1997). Multiplying the problems of intelligence by eight: A critique of Gardner's theory. *Canadian Journal of Education, 22,* 377–394.

Klein, T. W., Friedman, H., & Specter, S. (1998). Marijuana, immunity and infection. *Journal of Neuroimmunology, 83,* 102–115.

Kleinke, C. L. (2007). What does it mean to cope? In A. Monat, R. S. Lazarus, & G. Reevy (Eds.), *The Praeger handbook on stress and coping.* Westport, CT: Praeger.

Kleinke, C. L., Peterson, T. R., & Rutledge, T. R. (1998). Effects of self-generated facial expressions on mood. *Journal of Personality and Social Psychology, 74,* 272–279.

Kleinmuntz, B. (1980). *Essentials of abnormal psychology.* San Francisco: Harper & Row.

Klerman, E. B., Davis, J. B., Duffy, J. F., Dijk, D., & Kronauer, R. E. (2004). Older people awaken more frequently but fall back asleep at the same rate as younger people. *Sleep: Journal of Sleep & Sleep Disorders Research, 27,* 793–798.

Kliegel, M., Zimprich, D., & Rott, C. (2004). Lifelong intellectual activities mediate the predictive effect of early education on cognitive impairment in centenarians: A retrospective study. *Aging & Mental Health, 8,* 430–437.

Kline, P. (1991). *Intelligence: The psychometric view.* New York: Routledge, Chapman, & Hall.

Kline, P. (1995). A critical review of the measurement of personality and intelligence. In D. H. Saklofske & M. Zeidner (Eds.), *International handbook of personality and intelligence.* New York: Plenum.

Klosch, G., & Kraft, U. (2005). Sweet dreams are made of this. *Scientific American Mind,* 16(2), 38–45.

Kluft, R. P. (1996). Dissociative identity disorder. In L. K. Michelson & W. J. Ray (Eds.), *Handbook of dissociation: Theoretical, empirical, and clinical perspectives.* New York: Plenum.

Kluft, R. P. (1999). True lies, false truths, and naturalistic raw data: Applying clinical research findings to the false memory debate. In L. M. Williams &

V. L. Banyard (Eds.), *Trauma & memory.* Thousand Oaks, CA: Sage Publications.

Klump, K. L., & Culbert, K. M. (2007). Molecular genetic studies of eating disorders: Current status and future directions. *Current Directions in Psychological Science, 16,* 37–41.

Knauss, W. (2005). Group psychotherapy. In G. O. Gabbard, J. S. Beck, & J. Holmes (Eds.), *Oxford textbook of psychotherapy.* New York: Oxford University Press.

Knecht, S., Drager, B., Floel, A., Lohmann, H., Breitenstein, C., Henningsen, H., & Ringelstein, E. B. (2001). Behavioural relevance of atypical language lateralization in healthy subjects. *Brain, 124,* 1657–1665.

Knecht, S., Fioel, A., Drager, B., Breitenstein, C., Sommer, J., Henningsen, H., Ringelstein, E. B., & Pascual-Leone, A. (2002). Degree of language lateralization determines susceptibility to unilateral brain lesions. *Nature Neuroscience, 5,* 695–699.

Knight, J. (2004). The truth about lying. *Nature, 428,* 692–694.

Kochanska, G. (2001). Emotional development in children with different attachment histories: The first three years. *Child Development, 72,* 474–490.

Koehler, J. J. (1996). The base rate fallacy reconsidered: Descriptive, normative, and methodological challenges. *Behavioral Brain Sciences, 19,* 1–53.

Koester, J., & Siegelbaum, S. A. (2000). Propagated signaling: The action potential. In E. R. Kandel, J. H. Schwartz, & T. M. Jessell (Eds.), *Principles of neural science* (pp. 150–174). New York: McGraw-Hill.

Koger, S. M., Schettler, T. & Weiss, B. (2005). Environmental toxicants and developmental disabilities: A challenge for psychologists. *American Psychologist, 60,* 243–255.

Koger, S. M., & Scott, B. A. (2007). Psychology and environmental sustainability: A call for integration. *Teaching of Psychology, 34,* 10–18.

Koger, S. M. & Winter, D. D. (in press/2010). *The Psychology of Environmental Problems (3rd Edition): Psychology for Sustainability.* New York: Taylor & Francis: Psychology Press.

Kohatsu, N. D., Tsai, R., Young, T., VanGilder, R., Burmeister, L. F., Stromquist, A. M., et al. (2006). Sleep duration and body mass index in a rural population. *Archives of Internal Medicine, 166,* 1701–1705.

Kohlberg, L. (1963). The development of children's orientations toward a moral order: I. Sequence in the development of moral thought. *Vita Humana, 6,* 11–33.

Kohlberg, L. (1969). Stage and sequence: The cognitive-developmental approach to socialization. In D. A. Goslin (Ed.), *Handbook of socialization theory and research.* Chicago: Rand McNally.

Kohlberg, L. (1976). Moral stages and moralization: Cognitive-developmental approach. In T. Lickona (Ed.), *Moral development and behavior: Theory, research and social issues.* New York: Holt, Rinehart & Winston.

Kohlberg, L. (1984). *Essays on moral development, Vol. 2: The psychology of moral development.* San Francisco: Harper & Row.

Kohut, H. (1971). *Analysis of the self.* New York: International Universities Press.

Kokkinos, P., Myers, J., Kokkinos, J. P., Pittaras, A., Narayan, P., Manolis, A., et al. (2007). Exercise capacity and mortality in black and white men. *Circulation , 117,* 614–622.

Kolb, B., & Whishaw, I. Q. (1998). Brain plasticity and behavior. *Annual Review of Psychology, 49,* 43–64.

Kolb, B., Gibb, R., & Robinson, T. E. (2003). Brain plasticity and behavior. *Current Directions in Psychological Science, 12,* 1–5.

Kollmuss, A. & Agyeman, J. (2002). Mind the gap: Why do people act environmentally and what are the barriers to pro-environmental behaviour? *Environmental Education Research, 8,* 239–260.

Koob, G. F., & Le Moal, M. (2006). *Neurobiology of addiction.* San Diego: Academic Press.

Kop, W. J., & Weinstein, A. A. (2007). C-reactive protein. In G. Fink (Ed.), *Encyclopedia of stress.* San Diego: Elsevier.

Kop, W. J., Gottdiener, J. S., & Krantz, D. S. (2001). Stress and silent ischemia. In A. Baum, T. A. Revenson, & J. E. Singer (Eds.), *Handbook of health psychology* (pp. 669–682). Mahwah, NJ: Erlbaum.

Kop, W. J., Weissman, N. J., Zhu, J., Bonsall, R. W., Doyle, M., Stretch, M. R., Glaes, S. B., Krantz, D. S., Gottdiener, J. S., & Tracy, R. P. (2008). Effect of acute mental stress and exercise on inflammatory markers in patients with coronary artery disease and healthy controls. *American Journal of Cardiology, 101,* 767–773.

Kopta, S. M., Lueger, R. J., Saunders, S. M., & Howard, K. I. (1999). Individual psychotherapy outcome and process research: Challenges leading to greater turmoil or a positive transition? *Annual Review of Psychology, 50,* 441–69.

Koren, D., Arnon, I., & Klein, E. (1999). Acute stress response and posttraumatic stress disorder in traffic accident victims: A one-year prospective, follow-up study. *American Journal of Psychiatry, 156,* 367–373.

Koriat, A., & Bjork, R. A. (2005). Illusions of competence in monitoring one's knowledge during study. *Journal of Experimental Psychology: Learning, Memory, and Cognition, 31*(2), 187–194.

Koriat, A., Goldsmith, M., & Pansky, A. (2000). Toward a psychology of memory accuracy. *Annual Review of Psychology, 51,* 481–537.

Koriat, A., Lichtenstein, S., & Fischhoff, B. (1980). Reasons for confidence. *Journal of Experimental Psychology, 6,* 107–118.

Korn, J. H. (1987). Judgements of acceptability of deception in psychological research. *Journal of General Psychology, 114,* 205–216.

Korn, J. H. (1997). *Illusions of reality: A history of deception in social psychology.* Albany: State University of New York Press.

Korn, J. H., Davis, R., & Davis, S. F. (1991). Historians' and chairpersons' judgements of eminence among psychologists. *American Psychologist, 46,* 789–792.

Kornhaber, M. L. (2004). Multiple intelligences: From the ivory tower to the dusty classroom—But why? *Teachers College Record, 106*(1), 57–76.

Kornstein, S. G., & Sloan, D. M. E. (2006). Depression and gender. In D. J. Stein, D. J. Kupfer, & A. F. Schatzberg (Eds.), *Textbook of mood disorders.* Washington, DC: American Psychiatric Publishing.

Koropeckyj-Cox, T., & Pendell, G. (2007). The gender gap in attitudes about childlessness in the United States. *Journal of Marriage and Family, 69,* 899–915.

Korpela, K. (2002). Children's environments. In R. B. Bechtel & A. Churchman (Eds.), *Handbook of environmental psychology* (pp. 363–373). Hoboken, NJ: Wiley.

Kostreva, M., McNelis, E., & Clemens, E. (2002). Using a circadian rhythms model to evaluate shift schedules. *Ergonomics, 45,* 739–763.

Kotovsky, K., Hayes, J. R., & Simon, H. A. (1985). Why are some problems hard? Evidence from Tower of Hanoi. *Cognitive Psychology, 17,* 248–294.

Kotulak, R. (1996). *Inside the brain: Revolutionary discoveries of how the mind works.* Kansas City: Andrews McMeel.

Kouzma, N. M., & Kennedy, G. A. (2004). Self-reported sources of stress in senior high school students. *Psychological Reports, 94,* 314–316.

Kozorovitskiy, Y., & Gould, E. (2007). Adult neurogenesis and regeneration in the brain. In Y. Sern (Ed.), *Cognitive reserve: Theory and applications.* Philadelphia: Taylor and Francis.

Kozulin, A. (2005). The concept of activity in Soviet psychology: Vygotsky, his disciples and critics. In H. Daniels (Ed.), *An introduction to Vygotsky.* New York: Routledge.

Kracke, W. (1991). Myths in dreams, thought in images: An Amazonian contribution to the psychoanalytic theory of primary process. In B. Tedlock (Ed.), *Dreaming: Anthropological and psychological interpretations.* Santa Fe, NM: School of American Research Press.

Kracke, W. (1992). Languages of dreaming: Anthropological approaches to the study of dreaming in other cultures. In J. Gackenback & A. Sheik (Eds.), *Dream images: A call to mental arms.* Amityville, NY: Baywood.

Krakauer, D., & Dallenbach, K. M. (1937). Gustatory adaptation to sweet, sour, and bitter. *American Journal of Psychology, 49,* 469–475.

Krakauer, J. (1998). *Into thin air: A personal account of the Mount Everest disaster.* New York: Villard.

Kramer, M. (1994). The scientific study of dreaming. In M. H. Kryger, T. Roth, & W. C. Dement (Eds.), *Principles and practice of sleep medicine* (2nd ed.). Philadelphia: Saunders.

Kramer, P. D. (2006). *Freud: Inventor of the modern mind.* New York: HarperCollins.

Kransny, L., Williams, B. J., Provencal, S., & Ozonoff, S. (2003). Social skills interventions for the autism spectrum: Essential ingredients and a model curriculum. *Child and Adolescent Psychiatric Clinics of North America, 12*(1), 107–122.

Krantz, D. S., Sheps, D. S., Carney, R. M., & Natelson, B. H. (2000). Effects of mental stress in patients with coronary artery disease. *Journal of the American Medical Association, 283,* 1800–1802.

Krebs, D. L., & Denton, K. (1997). Social illusions and self-deception: The evolution of biases in person perception. In J. A. Simpson & D. T. Kenrick (Eds.), *Evolutionary social psychology.* Mahwah, NJ: Erlbaum.

Krieth, M. (1991). Water inputs in California food production. University of California Agricultural Issues Center. Retrieved June 4, 2009 from http://www.sakia.org/cms/fileadmin/content/irrig/general/kreith_1991_water_inputs_in_ca_food_production–excerpt.pdf.

Kristeller, J. L., Baer, R. A., & Quillian-Wolever, R. (2006). Mindfulness-based approaches to eating disorders. In R. A. Baer (Ed.), *Mindfulness-based treatment approaches: Clinician's guide to evidence base and applications* (pp. 75–91). San Diego: Elsevier.

Kroger, J. (2003). Identity development during adolescence. In G. R. Adams & M. D. Berzonsky (Eds.), *Blackwell handbook of adolescence.* Malden, MA: Blackwell Publishing.

Krosnick, J. A. (1999). Survey research. *Annual Review Psychology, 50,* 537–567.

Krosnick, J. A., & Fabrigar, L. R. (1998). *Designing good questionnaires: Insights from psychology.* New York: Oxford University Press.

Krueger, J. (1996). Personal beliefs and cultural stereotypes about racial characteristics. *Journal of Personality and Social Psychology, 71,* 536–548.

Krueger, J., Ham, J. J., & Linford, K. M. (1996). Perceptions of behavioral consistency: Are people aware of the actor-observer effect? *Psychological Science, 7,* 259–264.

Krueger, W. C. F. (1929). The effect of overlearning on retention. *Journal of Experimental Psychology, 12,* 71–78.

Kruglanski, A. W., & Stroebe, W. (2005). The influence of beliefs and goals on attitudes: Issues of structure, function, and dynamics. In D. Albarracin, B. T. Johnson, & M. P. Zanna (Eds.), *The handbook of attitudes.* Mahwah, NJ: Erlbaum.

Krull, D. S. (2001). On partitioning the fundamental attribution error: Dispositionalism and the correspondence bias. In G. B. Moskowitz (Ed.), *Cognitive social psychology: The Princeton Symposium on the legacy and future of social cognition.* Mahwah, NJ: Erlbaum.

Krull, D. S., & Erickson, D. J. (1995). Inferential hopscotch: How people draw social inferences from behavior. *Current Directions in Psychological Science, 4,* 35–38.

Kryger, M. H. (1993). Snoring. In M. A. Carskadon (Ed.), *Encyclopedia of sleep and dreaming.* New York: Macmillan.

Kryger, M. H., Roth, T., & Dement, W. C. (2005). *Principles and practice of sleep medicine.* Philadelphia: Elsevier Saunders.

Kuehn, B. M. (2007). Scientists probe deep brain stimulation: Some promise for brain injury, psychiatric illness. *Journal of the American Medical Association, 298,* 2249–2207.

Kuhl, P. K., & Meltzoff, A. N. (1997). Evolution, nativism and learning in the development of language and speech. In M. Gopnik (Ed.), *The inheritance and innateness of grammars.* New York: Oxford University Press.

Kuhl, B. A., Dudukovic, N. M., Kahn, I., & Wagner, A. D. (2007). Decreased demands on cognitive control reveal the neural processing benefits of forgetting. *Nature Neuroscience, 10,* 908–914.

Kuhn, D. (2006). Do cognitive changes accompany developments in the adolescent brain? *Perspectives on Psychological Science, 1*(1), 59–67.

Kulick, A. R., Pope, H. G., & Keck, P. E. (1990). Lycanthropy and self-identification. *Journal of Nervous & Mental Disease, 178*(2), 134–137.

Kumar, V. M. (2004). Body temperature and sleep: Are they controlled by the same mechanism? *Sleep & Biological Rhythms, 2*(2), 103–125.

Kung, S., & Mrazek, D. A. (2005). Psychiatric emergency department visits on full-moon nights. *Psychiatric Services, 56,* 221–222.

Kunstler, J. H. (2005). *The long emergency: Surviving the end of oil, climate change, and other converging catastrophes of the twenty-first century.* New York: Grove Press.

Kuo, F. E., & Faber Taylor, A. (2004). A potential natural treatment for Attention-Deficit/Hyperactivity Disorder: Evidence from a national study. *American Journal of Public Health, 94,* 1580–1586.

Kuo, F. E., & Faber Taylor, A. (2005). Mother nature as treatment for ADHD: Overstating the benefits of green. Kuo and Faber Taylor respond. *American Journal of Public Health, 95,* 371–372.

Kuo, F. E., & Sullivan, W. C. (2001). Aggression and violence in the inner city: Effects of environment via mental fatigue. *Environment and Behavior, 33*(4), 543–571.

Kuo, Y. T., Parkinson, J. R. C., Chaudhri, O. B., Herlihy, A. H., So, P. W., Dhillo, W. S., et al. (2007). The temporal sequence of gut peptide-CNS interactions tracked in vivo by magnetic resonance imaging. *Journal of Neuroscience, 27,* 12341–12348.

Kupfermann, I., Kandel, E. R., & Iversen, S. (2000). Motivational and addictive states. In E. R. Kandel, J. H. Schwartz, & T. M. Jessell (Eds.), *Principles of neural science.* New York: McGraw-Hill.

Kurtz, K. J., & Loewenstein, J. (2007). Converging on a new role for analogy in problem solving and retrieval: When two problems are better than one. *Memory & Cognition, 35,* 334–342.

Kutchins, H., & Kirk, S. A. (1997). *Making us crazy: DSM—The psychiatric bible and the creation of mental disorders.* New York: Free Press.

Kuther, T., & Morgan, R.D. (2007). *Careers in psychology: Opportunities in a changing world.* Belmont, CA: Wadsworth.

La Cerra, P., & Kurzban, R. (1995). The structure of scientific revolutions and the nature of the adapted mind. *Psychological Inquiry, 6,* 62–65.

La Torre, M. A. (2007). Positive psychology: Is there too much of a push? *Perspectives in Psychiatric Care, 43,* 151–153.

LaBar, K. S., & LeDoux, J. E. (2003). Emotional learning circuits in animals and humans. In R. J. Davidson, K. R. Scherer, & H. H. Goldsmith (Eds.), *Handbook of affective sciences.* New York: Oxford University Press.

LaBine, S. J., & LaBine, G. (1996). Determinations of negligence and the hindsight bias. *Law & Human Behavior, 20,* 501–516.

Labouvie-Vief, G. (2006). Emerging structures of adult thought. In J. J. Arnett & J. L. Tanner (Eds.), *Emerging adults in America: Coming of age in the 21st century.* Washington, DC: American Psychological Association.

Lachman, S. J. (1996). Processes in perception: Psychological transformations of highly structured stimulus material. *Perceptual and Motor Skills, 83,* 411–418.

Lachter, J., Forster, K. I., & Ruthruff, E. (2004). Forty-five years after Broadbent (1958): Still no identification without attention. *Psychological Review, 111,* 880–913.

Lader, M. H. (2002). Managing dependence and withdrawal with newer hypnotic medications in the treatment of insomnia. *Journal of Clinical Psychiatry, 4*(suppl 1), 33–37.

Laitinen, J., Ek, E., & Sovio, U. (2002). Stress-related eating and drinking behavior and body mass index and predictors of this behavior. *Preventive Medicine: An International Journal Devoted to Practice & Theory, 34,* 29–39.

Lakein, A. (1996). *How to get control of your time and your life.* New York: New American Library.

Lamb, H. R. (1998). Deinstitutionalization at the beginning of the new millenium. *Harvard Review of Psychiatry, 6,* 1–10.

Lamb, M. E., Hwang, C. P., Ketterlinus, R. D., & Fracasso, M. P. (1999). Parent-child relationships: Development in the context of the family. In M. H. Bornstein & M. E. Lamb (Eds.), *Developmental psychology and advanced textbook.* Mahwah, NJ: Erlbaum.

Lamb, M. E., Ketterlinus, R. D., & Fracasso, M. P. (1992). Parent-child relationships. In M. H. Bornstein & M. E. Lamb (Eds.), *Developmental psychology: An advanced textbook* (3rd ed.). Hillsdale, NJ: Erlbaum.

Lambert, M. J., & Archer, A. (2006). Research findings on the effects of psychotherapy and their implications for practice. In C. D. Goodheart, A. E. Kazdin, & R. J. Sternberg (Eds.), *Evidence-based psychotherapy: Where practice and research meet* (pp. 111–130). Washington, DC: American Psychological Association.

Lambert, M. J., Bergin, A. E., & Garfield, S. L. (2004). Introduction and historical overview. In M. J. Lambert (Ed.), *Bergin and Garfield's handbook of psychotherapy and behavior change*. New York: Wiley.

Lambert, M. J., Hansen, N. B., & Finch, A. E. (2001). Using patient-focused research: Using patient outcome data to enhance treatment effects. *Journal of Counseling and Clinical Psychology, 69*, 159–172.

Lambert, M. J., & Ogles, B. M. (2004). The efficacy and effectiveness of psychotherapy. In M. J. Lambert (Ed.), *Bergin and Garfield's handbook of psychotherapy and behavior change*. New York: Wiley.

Lampe, A., Soellner, W., Krismer, M., Rumpold, G., Kantner-Rumplmair, W., Ogon, M., & Rathner, G. (1998). The impact of stressful life events on exacerbation of chronic low-back pain. *Journal of Psychosomatic Research, 44*, 555–563.

Lampinen, J. M., Neuschatz, J. S., & Payne, D. G. (1999). Source attributions and false memories: A test of the demand characteristics account. *Psychonomic Bulletin & Review, 6*, 130–135.

Landabaso, M. A., Iraurgi, I., Sanz, J., Calle, R., Ruiz de Apodaka, J., Jimenez-Lerma, J. M., & Gutierrez-Fraile, M. (1999). Naltrexone in the treatment of alcoholism. Two-year follow up results. *European Journal of Psychiatry, 13*, 97–105.

Landel-Graham, J., Yount, S. E., & Rudnicki, S. R. (2003). Diabetes mellitus. In A. M. Nezu, C. M. Nezu, & P. A. Geller (Eds.). *Handbook of psychology, Vol. 9: Health psychology*. New York: Wiley.

Laney, C., & Loftus, E. F. (2005). Traumatic memories are not necessarily accurate memories. *The Canadian Journal of Psychiatry, 50*, 823–828.

Lang, P. J. (1995). The emotion probe: Studies of motivation and attention. *American Psychologist, 50*, 372–385.

Langdon, P. E., Yagueez, L., Brown, J., & Hope, A. (2001). Who walks through the "revolving door" of a British psychiatric hospital? *Journal of Mental Health (UK), 10*, 525–533.

Lange, C. (1885). One leuds beveegelser. In K. Dunlap (Ed.), *The emotions*. Baltimore: Williams & Wilkins.

Langlois, J. H., Kalakanis, L., Rubenstein, A. J., Larson, A., Hallam, M., & Smoot, M. (2000). Maxims or myths of beauty? A meta-analytic and theoretical review. *Psychological Bulletin, 126*, 390–423.

Lanyon, R. I., & Goodstein, L. D. (1997). *Personality assessment*. New York: Wiley.

Lapierre, Y. D. (2003). Suicidality with selective serotonin reuptake inhibitors: Valid claim? *Journal of Psychiatry & Neuroscience, 28*, 340–347.

Lapsley, D. K. (2006). Moral stage theory. In M. Killen & J. G. Smetana (Eds.), *Handbook of moral development*. Mahwah, NJ: Erlbaum.

Lareau, A. (2003). *Unequal childhoods: Class, race, and family life*. Berkeley: University of California Press.

Larsen, R. J., & Prizmic, Z. (2008). Regulation of emotional well-being: Overcoming the hedonic treadmill. In M. Eid & R. J. Larsen (Eds.), *The science of subjective well-being*. New York: Guilford.

Latané, B. (1981). The psychology of social impact. *American Psychologist, 36*, 343–356.

Latané, B., & Nida, S. A. (1981). Ten years of research on group size and helping. *Psychological Bulletin, 89*, 308–324.

Latané, B., Williams, K., & Harkins, S. (1979). Many hands make light the work: The causes and consequences of social loafing. *Journal of Personality and Social Psychology, 37*, 822–832.

Lattal, K. A. (1992). B. F. Skinner and psychology [Introduction to the Special Issue]. *American Psychologist, 27*, 1269–1272.

Latz, S., Wolf, A. W., & Lozoff, B. (1999). Cosleeping in context: Sleep practices and problems in young children in Japan and the United States. *Archives of Pediatrics & Adolescent Medicine, 153*, 339–346.

Lauderdale, D. S., Knutson, K. L., Yan, L. L., Rathouz, P. J., Hulley, S. B., Sidney, S., et al. (2006). Objectively measured sleep characteristics among early-aged adults the CARDIA study. *American Journal of Epidemiology, 164*, 5–16.

Laughlin, H. (1967). *The neuroses*. Washington, DC: Butterworth.

Laughlin, H. (1979). *The ego and its defenses*. New York: Aronson.

Laumann, E. O., Gagnon, J. H., Michael, R. T., & Michaels, S. (1994). *The social organization of sexuality: Sexual practices in the United States*. Chicago: University of Chicago Press.

Laumann, K., Gärling, T. & Stormark, K. M. (2003). Selective attention and heart rate responses to natural and urban environments. *Journal of Environmental Psychology, 23*, 125–134.

Lauriello, J., Bustillo, J. R., & Keith, J. (2005). Schizophrenia: Scope of the problem. In B. J. Sadock & V. A. Sadock (Eds.), *Kaplan & Sadock's comprehensive textbook of psychiatry*. Philadelphia: Lippincott Williams & Wilkins.

Laursen, B., Coy, K. C., & Collins, W. A. (1998). Reconsidering changes in parent-child conflict across adolescence: A meta-analysis. *Child Development, 69*, 817–832.

Lavin, C., & Kavesh, L. (1988). *Tales from the front*. New York: Doubleday.

Lazarus, A. A. (1995). Different types of eclecticism and integration: Let's be aware of the dangers. *Journal of Psychotherapy Integration, 5*, 27–39.

Lazarus, R. S. (1993). Why we should think of stress as a subset of emotion. In L. Goldberger & S. Breznitz (Eds.), *Handbook of stress: Theoretical and clinical aspects* (2nd ed.). New York: Free Press.

Lazarus, R. S. (1999). *Stress and emotion: A new synthesis*. New York: Springer Publishing Company.

Lazarus, R. S. (2003). Does the positive psychology movement have legs? *Psychological Inquiry, 14*(2), 93–109.

Leary, D. E. (2003). A profound and radical change: How William James inspired the reshaping of American psychology. In R. J. Sternberg (Ed.), *The anatomy of impact: What makes the great works of psychology great*. Washington, DC: American Psychological Association.

Leavitt, F. (1995). *Drugs and behavior* (3rd ed.). Thousand Oaks, CA: Sage.

Leavitt, F. (2001). Iatrogenic recovered memories: Examining the empirical evidence. *American Journal of Forensic Psychology, 19*(2), 21–32.

LeBoeuf, R. A., & Shafir, E. B. (2005). Decision making. In K. J. Holyoak & R. G. Morrison (Eds.), *The Cambridge handbook of thinking and reasoning*. New York: Cambridge University Press.

LeDoux, J. E. (1994). Emotion, memory and the brain. *Scientific American, 270*, 50–57.

LeDoux, J. E. (1995). Emotion: Clues from the brain. *Annual Review of Psychology, 46*, 209–235.

LeDoux, J. E. (1996). *The emotional brain*. New York: Simon & Schuster.

LeDoux, J. E. (2000). Emotion circuits in the brain. *Annual Review of Neuroscience, 23*, 155–184.

Lee, I.-M., & Skerrett, P. J. (2001). Physical activity and all-cause mortality: What is the dose-response relation? *Medicine and Science in Sports and Exercise, 33*, S459–S471.

Lee, R. M., & Ramirez, M. (2000). The history, current status, and future of multicultural psychotherapy. In I. Cuellar & F. A. Paniagua (Eds.), *Handbook of multicultural mental health: Assessment and treatment of diverse populations*. San Diego: Academic Press.

Lee, S., & Katzman, M. A. (2002). Cross-cultural perspectives on eating disorders. In C. G. Fairburn & K. D. Brownell (Eds.), *Eating disorders and obesity: A comprehensive handbook*. New York: Guilford.

Lee, Y., Gaskins, D., Anand, A., & Shekhar, A. (2007). Glia mechanisms in mood regulation: A novel model of mood disorders. *Psychopharmacology, 191*, 55–65.

Lee-Chiong, T., & Sateia, M. (2006). Pharmacologic therapy of insomnia. In T. Lee-Chiong (Ed.), *Sleep: A comprehensive handbook*. Hoboken, NJ: Wiley-Liss.

Leeper, R. W. (1935). A study of a neglected portion of the field of learning: The development of sensory organization. *Journal of Genetic Psychology, 46*, 41–75.

Lefcourt, H. M. (2001). The humor solution. In C. R. Snyder (Ed.), *Coping with stress: Effective people and processes* (pp. 68–92). New York: Oxford University Press.

Lefcourt, H. M., Davidson, K., Shepherd, R., Phillips, M., Prkachin, K., & Mills, D. (1995). Perspective-taking humor: Accounting for stress moderation. *Journal of Social and Clinical Psychology, 14*, 373–391.

Leff, J. (2006). Whose life is it anyway? Quality of life for long-stay patients discharged from psychiatric hospitals. In H. Katschnig, H. Freeman, & N. Sartorius (Eds.), *Quality of life in mental disorders*. New York: Wiley.

Leff, J., & Vaughn, C. (1985). *Expressed emotion in families*. New York: Guilford.

Legault, E., & Laurence, J.-R. (2007). Recovered memories of childhood sexual abuse: Social worker, psychologist, and psychiatrist reports of beliefs, practices, and cases. *Australian Journal of Clinical & Experimental Hypnosis, 35*, 111–133.

Lehman, D. R., Chiu, C., & Schaller, M. (2004). Psychology and culture. *Annual Review of Psychology, 55*, 689–714.

Lehman, P. K. & Geller, E. S. (2004). Behavior analysis and environmental protection: Accomplishments and potential for more. *Behavior and Social Issues, 13*, 13–32.

Lehrer, P., Feldman, J., Giardino, N., Song, H., & Schmaling, K. (2002). Psychological aspects of asthma. *Journal of Consulting & Clinical Psychology, 70*, 691–711.

Leibovic, K. N. (1990). Vertebrate photoreceptors. In K. N. Leibovic (Ed.), *Science of vision*. New York: Springer-Verlag.

Leighton, J. P., & Sternberg, R. J. (2003). Reasoning and problem solving. In A. F. Healy & R. W. Proctor (Eds.), *Handbook of psychology, Vol. 4: Experimental psychology*. New York: Wiley.

Leiserowitz, A. (2007). Communicating the risks of global warming: American risk perceptions, affective images, and interpretive communities. In S. C. Moser & L. Dilling (Eds.), *Creating a climate for change: Communicating climate change and facilitating social change* (pp. 44–63). New York: Cambridge University Press.

LeMagnen, J. (1981). The metabolic basis of dual periodicity of feeding in rats. *Behavioral and Brain Sciences, 4,* 561–607.

Lenert, L., & Skoczen, S. (2002). The Internet as a research tool: Worth the price of admission? *Annals of Behavioral Medicine, 24,* 251–256.

Lennie, P. (2000). Color vision. In E. R. Kandel, J. H. Schwartz, & T. M. Jessell (Eds.), *Principles of neural science*. New York: McGraw-Hill.

Leo, J. (1987, January). Exploring the traits of twins. *Time*, p. 63.

Lepine, R., Barrouillet, P., & Camos, V. (2005). What makes working memory spans so predictive of high-level cognition? *Psychonomic Bulletin & Review, 12*(1), 165–170.

Lerman, H. (1986). *A mote in Freud's eye: From psychoanalysis to the psychology of women*. New York: Springer.

Lett, H. S., Blumenthal, J. A., Babyak, M. A., Catellier, D. J., Carney, R. M., Berkman, L. F., et al. (2007). Social support and prognosis in patients at increased psychosocial risk recovering from myocardial infarction. *Health Psychology, 26,* 418–427.

Lett, H. S., Blumenthal, J. A., Babyak, M. A., Sherwood, A., Strauman, T., Robbins, C., & Newman, M. F. (2004). Depression as a risk factor for coronary artery disease: Evidence, mechanisms, and treatment. *Psychosomatic Medicine, 66,* 305–315.

Leuner, B., Gould, E., & Shors, T. J. (2006). Is there a link between adult neurogenesis and learning? *Hippocampus, 16,* 216–224.

LeVay, S. (1996). *Queer science: The use and abuse of research into homosexuality*. Cambridge, MA: MIT Press.

Levenson, R. W. (1992). Autonomic nervous system differences among emotions. *Psychological Science, 3,* 23–27.

Levenson, R. W. (2003). Autonomic specificity and emotion. In R. J. Davidson, K. R. Scherer, & H. H. Goldsmith (Eds.), *Handbook of affective sciences*. New York: Oxford University Press.

Levenstein, S. (2002). Psychosocial factors in peptic ulcer and inflammatory bowel disease. *Journal of Consulting & Clinical Psychology, 70,* 739–750.

Leventhal, H. & Tomarken, A. J. (1986). Emotions: Today's problems. *Annual Review of Psychology, 37,* 565–610.

Levin, S., Henry, P. J., Pratto, F., & Sidanius, J. (2003). Social dominance and social identity in Lebanon: Implications for support of violence against the West. *Group Processes and Intergroup Relations, 6,* 353–368.

Levine, J. M. (1999). Solomon Asch's legacy for group research. *Personality and Social Psychology Review, 3,* 358–364.

Levine, M. P., & Harrison, K. (2004). Media's role in the perpetuation and prevention of negative body image and disordered eating. In J. K. Thompson (Ed.), *Handbook of eating disorders and obesity*. New York: Wiley.

Levine, M. W. (2001). Principles of neural processing. In E. B. Goldstein (Ed.), *Blackwell handbook of perception*. Malden, MA: Blackwell.

Levine, R., & Norenzayan, A. (1999). The pace of life in 31 countries. *Journal of Cross-Cultural Psychology, 30,* 178–205.

Levine, R., Sata, S., Hashimoto, T., & Verma, J. (1995). Love and marriage in eleven cultures. *Journal of Cross-Cultural Psychology, 26,* 554–571.

Levinthal, C. F. (2008). *Drugs, behavior, and modern society*. Boston: Pearson.

Levis, D. J. (1989). The case for a return to a two-factor theory of avoidance: The failure of non-fear interpretations. In S. B. Klein & R. R. Bowrer (Eds.), *Contemporary learning theories: Pavlovian conditioning and the status of traditional learning theory*. Hillsdale NJ: Erlbaum.

Levy, G. D., Taylor, M. G., & Gelman, S. A. (1995). Traditional and evaluative aspects of flexibility in gender roles, social conventions, moral rules, and physical laws. *Child Development, 66,* 515–531.

Levy, J. (1985, May). Right brain, left brain: Fact or fiction. *Psychology Today*, 38–44.

Levy, J., Trevarthen, C., & Sperry, R. W. (1972). Perception of bilateral chimeric figures following hemispheric disconnection. *Brain, 95,* 61–78.

Lewandowsky, S., Duncan, M., & Brown, G. D. A. (2004). Time does not cause forgetting in short-term serial recall. *Psychonomic Bulletin & Review, 11*(5), 771–790.

Lewin, K. (1935). *A dynamic theory of personality*. New York: McGraw-Hill.

Li, N. P., Bailey, J. M., Kenrick, D. T., & Linsenmeier, J. A. W. (2002). The necessities and luxuries of mate preferences: Testing the tradeoffs. *Journal of Personality and Social Psychology, 82,* 947–955.

Li, N. P., & Kenrick, D. T. (2006). Sex similarities and differences in preferences for short-term mates: What, whether, and why. *Journal of Personality and Social Psychology, 90,* 468–489.

Li, S. C., Lindenberger, U., Hommel, B., Aschersleben, G., Prinz, W., & Baltes, P. B. (2004). Transformations in the couplings among intellectual abilities and constituent cognitive processes across the life span. *Psychological Science, 15,* 155–163.

Li, W., Moallem, I., Paller, K. A., & Gottfried, J. A. (2007). Subliminal smells can guide social preferences. *Psychological Science, 18,* 1044–1049.

Liberman, R. P., & Kopelowicz, A. (2005). Recovery from schizophrenia: A concept in search of research. *Psychiatric Services, 56,* 735–742.

Lichtenstein, S., Fischhoff, B., & Phillips, L. (1982). Calibration of probabilities: The state of the art to 1980. In D. Kahneman, P. Slovic, & A. Tversky (Eds.), *Judgment under uncertainty: Heuristics and biases*. Cambridge, England: Cambridge University Press.

Lichtenthal, W. G., Cruess, D. G., & Prigerson, H. G. (2004). A case for establishing complicated grief as a distinct mental disorder in DSM-V. *Clinical Psychology Review, 24,* 637–662.

Lickey, M. E., & Gordon, B. (1991). *Medicine and mental illness: The use of drugs in psychiatry*. New York: W. H. Freeman.

Lickliter, R., & Honeycutt, H. (2003). Developmental dynamics: Toward a biologically plausible evolutionary psychology. *Psychological Bulletin, 129,* 819–835.

Liden, R. C., Wayne, S. J., Jaworski, R. A., & Bennett, N. (2004). Social loafing: A field investigation. *Journal of Management, 30,* 285–304.

Lieberman, D., & Hatfield, E. (2006). Passionate love: Cross-cultural and evolutionary perspectives. In R. J. Sternberg & K. Weis (Eds.), *The new psychology of love*. New Haven, CT: Yale University Press.

Lieberman, J. A. (2006). Comparative effectiveness of antipsychotic drugs. *Archives of General Psychiatry, 63,* 1069–1072.

Lieberman, J. A., Stoup, T. S., McEvoy, J. P., Swartz, M. S., Rosenheck, R. A., & Perkins, D. O. et al. (2005). Effectiveness of antipsychotic drugs in patients with chronic schizophrenia. *New England Journal of Medicine, 353,* 1209–1223.

Lieberman, J. A., Tollefson, G., Tohen, M., Green, A. I., Gur, R. E., Kahn, R., McEvoy, J., Perkins, D., Sharma, T., Zipursky, R., Wei, H., Hamer, R. M., & HGDH Group Study. (2003). Comparative efficacy and safety of atypical and conventional antipsychotic drugs in first-episode psychosis: A randomized double-blind trial of olazapine versus haloperidol. *American Journal of Psychiatry, 160,* 1396–1404.

Liebert, R. M., & Liebert, L. L. (1998). *Liebert & Spiegler's personality strategies and issues*. Pacific Grove: Brooks/Cole.

Lien, M.-C., Ruthruff, E., & Johnston, J. C. (2006). Attentional limitations in doing two tasks at once. *Current Directions in Psychological Science, 15,* 89–93.

Lilienfeld, S. O. (2007). Psychological treatments that cause harm. *Perspectives on Psychological Science, 2,* 53–70.

Lilienfeld, S. O., & Lynn, S. J. (2003). Dissociative identity disorder: Multiple personalities, multiple controversies. In S. O. Lilienfeld, S. J. Lynn, & J. M. Lohr (Eds.), *Science and pseudoscience in clinical psychology*. New York: Guilford.

Lilienfeld, S. O., Lynn, S. J., Kirsch, I., Chaves, J. F., Sarbin, T. R., Ganaway, G. K., & Powell, R. A. (1999). Dissociative identity disorder and the sociocognitive model: Recalling the lessons of the past. *Psychological Bulletin, 125,* 507–523.

Lilienfeld, S. O., Wood, J. M., & Garb, H. N. (2000). The scientific status of projective tests. *Psychological Science in the Public Interest, 1*(2), 27–66.

Lima, M. L. (2004). On the influence of risk perception on mental health: Living near an incinerator. *Journal of Environmental Psychology, 24,* 71–84.

Lin, S. W., & Anthnelli, R. M. (2005). Genetic factors in the risk for substance use disorders. In J. H. Lowinson, P. Ruiz, R. B. Millman, & J. G. Langrod (Eds.), *Substance abuse: A comprehensive textbook*. Philadelphia: Lippincott/Williams & Wilkins.

Linde, J. A., Rothman, A. J., Baldwin, A. S., & Jeffery, R. W. (2006). The impact of self-efficacy on behavior change and weight change among overweight participants in a weight loss trial. *Health Psychology, 25,* 282–291.

Lindenmayer, J. P., & Khan, A. (2006). Psychopathology. In J. A. Lieberman, T. S. Stroup, & D. O. Perkins (Eds.), *Textbook of schizophrenia*. Washington, DC: American Psychiatric Publishing.

Lindgren, H. C. (1969). *The psychology of college success: A dynamic approach*. New York: Wiley.

Lindsay, M., & Lester, D. (2004). *Suicide by cop: Committing suicide by provoking police to shoot you (death, value and meaning)*. Amityville, NY: Baywood Publishing.

Lindsay, P. H., & Norman, D. A. (1977). *Human information processing*. New York: Academic Press.

Lindsay, S. D., & Read, J. D. (2001). The recovered memories controversy: Where do we go from here? In G. M. Davies & T. Dalgleish (Eds.), *Recovered memories: Seeking the middle ground*. Chichester, England: Wiley.

Lindsay, S. D., Allen, B. P., Chan, J. C. K., & Dahl, L. C. (2004). Eyewitness suggestibility and source similarity: Intrusions of details from one event into memory reports of another event. *Journal of Memory & Language, 50*(1), 96–111.

Linn, S. (2004). *Consuming kids: The hostile takeover of childhood.* New York & London: New Press.

Linn, S. (2008). Commercializing childhood: The corporate takeover of kids' lives. (interview by the Multinational Monitor). Retrieved from http://towardfreedom.com/home/content/view/1389/1/

Lippa, R. A. (1994). *Introduction to social psychology.* Pacific Grove, CA: Brooks/Cole.

Lipton, J. S., & Spelke, E. S. (2004). Discrimination of large and small numerosities by human infants. *Infancy, 5,* 271–290.

Lisanby, S. H., Maddox, J. H., Prudic, J., Devanand, D. P., & Sackeim, H. A. (2000). The effects of electroconvulsive therapy on memory of autobiographical and public events. *General Psychiatry, 57,* 581–590.

Little, A. C., Jones, B. C., & Burriss, R. P. (2007). Preferences for masculinity in male bodies change across the menstrual cycle. *Hormones and Behavior, 51,* 633–639.

Little, A. C., & Mannion, H. (2006). Viewing attractive or unattractive same-sex individuals changes self-rated attractiveness and face preferences in women. *Animal Behaviour, 72,* 981–987.

Livesley, W. J., Jang, K. L., & Vernon, P. A. (2003). Genetic basis of personality structure. In T. Millon & M. J. Lerner (Eds.), *Handbook of psychology, Vol. 5: Personality and social psychology.* New York: Wiley.

Lizarraga, M. L. S., & Ganuza, J. M. G. (2003). Improvement of mental rotation in girls and boys. *Sex Roles, 40,* 277–286.

Lockhart, R. S. (1992). Measurement of memory. In L. R. Squire (Ed.), *Encyclopedia of learning and memory.* New York: Macmillan.

Lockhart, R. S. (2000). Methods of memory research. In E. Tulving & F. I. M. Craik (Eds.), *The Oxford handbook of memory* (pp. 45–58). New York: Oxford University Press.

Lockhart, R. S., & Craik, F. I. (1990). Levels of processing: A retrospective commentary on a framework for memory research. *Canadian Journal of Psychology, 44*(1), 87–112.

Locurto, C. (1990). The malleability of IQ as judged from adoption studies. *Intelligence, 14,* 275–292.

Loehlin, J. C. (1992). *Genes and environment in personality development.* Newbury Park, CA: Sage.

Loehlin, J. C. (2000). Group differences in intelligence. In R. J. Sternberg (Ed.), *Handbook of intelligence* (pp. 176–195). New York: Cambridge University Press.

Loehlin, J. C., Horn, J. M., & Willerman, L. (1997). Heredity, environment, and IQ in the Texas Adoption Project. In R. J. Sternberg & E. L. Grigorenko (Eds.), *Intelligence, heredity, and environment.* New York: Cambridge University Press.

Loftus, E. F. (1979). *Eyewitness testimony.* Cambridge, MA: Harvard University Press.

Loftus, E. F. (1992). When a lie becomes memory's truth: Memory distortion after exposure to misinformation. *Current Directions in Psychological Science, 1,* 121–123.

Loftus, E. F. (1994). The repressed memory controversy. *American Psychologist, 49,* 443–445.

Loftus, E. F. (1998). Remembering dangerously. In R. A. Baker (Ed.), *Child sexual abuse and false memory syndrome.* Amherst, NY: Prometheus Books.

Loftus, E. F. (2003). Make believe memories. *American Psychologist, 58,* 864–873.

Loftus, E. F. (2004). Memories of things unseen. *Current Directions in Psychological Science, 13*(4), 145–147.

Loftus, E. F. (2005). Planting misinformation in the human mind: A 30-year investigation of the malleability of memory. *Learning & Memory, 12,* 361–366.

Loftus, E. F., & Bernstein, D. M. (2005). Rich false memories: The royal road to success. In A. F. Healy (Ed.), *Experimental cognitive psychology and its applications.* Washington, DC: American Psychological Association.

Loftus, E. F., & Cahill, L. (2007). Memory distortion: From misinformation to rich false memory. In J. S. Nairne (Ed.), *The foundations of remembering: Essays in honor of Henry L. Roediger III.* New York: Psychology Press.

Loftus, E. F., & Davis, D. (2006). Recovered memories. *Annual Review of Clinical Psychology, 2,* 469–498.

Loftus, E. F., & Palmer, J. C. (1974). Reconstruction of automobile destruction: An example of the interaction between language and memory. *Journal of Verbal Learning and Verbal Behavior, 13,* 585–589.

Logue, A. W. (1991). *The psychology of eating and drinking* (2nd ed.). New York: W. H. Freeman.

Lohmann, R. I. (2007). Dreams and ethnography. In D. Barrett & P. McNamara (Eds.), *The new science of dreaming.* Westport, CT: Praeger.

Long, J. E., Jr. (2005). Power to prescribe: The debate over prescription privileges for psychologists and the legal issues implicated. *Law & Psychology, 29,* 243–260.

Longman, D. G., & Atkinson, R. H. (2002). *College learning and study skills.* Belmont, CA: Wadsworth.

Longman, D. G., & Atkinson, R. H. (2005). *College learning and study skills.* Belmont, CA: Wadsworth.

Lott, B. (1987). *Women's lives.* Pacific Grove, CA: Brooks/Cole.

Lott, B. (2002). Cognitive and behavioral distancing from the poor. *American Psychologist, 57,* 100–110.

Louv, R. (2005). *Last child in the woods: Saving our children from nature-deficit disorder.* Chapel Hill, NC: Algonquin Books.

Lowden, A., Akerstedt, T., & Wibom, R. (2004). Suppression of sleepiness and melatonin by bright light exposure during breaks in night work. *Journal of Sleep Research, 12*(1), 37–43.

Lowinson, J. H., Ruiz, P., Millman, R. B., & Langrod, J. G. (2005). *Substance abuse: A comprehensive textbook.* Philadelphia: Lippincott/Williams & Wilkins.

Lubart, T. I. (2003). In search of creative intelligence. In R. J. Sternberg, J. Lautrey, & T. I. Lubart (Eds.), *Models of intelligence: International perspectives.* Washington, DC: American Psychological Association.

Luborsky, L., & Barrett, M. S. (2006). The history and empirical status of key psychoanalytic concepts. *Annual Review Clinical Psychology, 2,* 1–19.

Luborsky, L., Rosenthal, R., Diguer, L., Andrusyna, T. P., Berman, J. S., Levitt, J. T., Seligman, D. A., & Krause, E. D. (2002). The dodo bird verdict is alive and well—mostly. *Clinical Psychology: Science & Practice, 9,* 2–12.

Luborsky, L., Singer, B., & Luborsky, L. (1975). Comparative studies of psychotherapies: Is it true that everyone has won and all must have prizes? *Archives of General Psychiatry, 32,* 995–1008.

Lucas, A. R., Beard, C. M., O'Fallon, W. M., & Kurland, L. T. (1991). 50-year trends in the incidence of anorexia nervosa in Rochester, Minn.: A population-based study. *American Journal of Psychiatry, 148,* 917–922.

Lucas, R. E. (2007). Adaptation and the set-point model of subjective well-being: Does happiness change after major life events? *Current Directions in Psychological Science, 16,* 75–79.

Lucas, R. E. (2008). Personality and subjective well-being. In M. Eid & R. J. Larsen (Eds.), *The science of subjective well-being.* New York: Guilford.

Lucas, R. E., Clark, A. E., Georgellis, Y., & Diener, E. (2003). Reexamining adaptation and set point model of happiness: Reactions to changes in marital status. *Journal of Personality and Social Psychology, 84,* 527–539.

Lucas, R. E., Clark, A. E., Georgellis, Y., & Diener, E. (2004). Unemployment alters the set point for life satisfaction. *Psychological Science, 15*(1), 8–13.

Lucas, R. E., Diener, E., & Suh, E. (1996). Discriminant validity of well-being measures. *Journal of Personality and Social Psychology, 71,* 616–628.

Luchins, A. S. (1942). Mechanization in problem solving. *Psychological Monographs, 54* (6, Whole No. 248).

Ludwig, A. M. (1994). Mental illness and creative activity in female writers. *American Journal of Psychiatry, 151,* 1650–1656.

Ludwig, A. M. (1995). *The price of greatness: Resolving the creativity and madness controversy.* New York: Guilford.

Ludwig, A. M. (1998). Method and madness in the arts and sciences. *Creativity Research Journal, 11,* 93–101.

Lugaresi, E., Cirignotta, F., Montagna, P., & Sforza, E. (1994). Snoring: Pathogenic, clinical, and therapeutic aspects. In M. H. Kryger, T. Roth, & W. C. Dement (Eds.), *Principles and practice of sleep medicine* (2nd ed.). Philadelphia: Saunders.

Luh, C. W. (1922). The conditions of retention. *Psychological Monographs, 31.*

Lundberg, A. (1998). Environmental change and human health. In A. Lundberg (Ed.), *The Environment and Mental Health: A Guide for Clinicians* (pp. 5–23). Mahwah, NJ: Erlbaum.

Lundberg, U. (2007). Catecholamines. In G. Fink (Ed.), *Encyclopedia of stress.* San Diego: Elsevier.

Luo, S., & Klohen, E. C. (2005). Assortative mating and marital quality in newlyweds: A couple-centered approach. *Journal of Personality and Social Psychology, 88,* 304–326.

Lupien, S. J., & Maheu, F. S. (2007). Memory and stress. In G. Fink (Ed.), *Encyclopedia of stress.* San Diego: Elsevier.

Lurie, P., Almeida, C. M., Stine, N. , Stine, A. R., & Wolfe, S. M. (2006). Financial conflict of interest disclosure and voting patterns at food and drug administration drug advisory committee meetings. *Journal of the American Medical Association, 295,* 1921–1928.

Lutz, C. (1987). Goals, events and understanding in Ifaluk emotion theory. In N. Quinn & D. Holland (Eds.), *Cultural models in language and thought.* Cambridge, England: Cambridge University Press.

Lye, D. N., & Biblarz, T. J. (1993). The effects of attitudes toward family life and gender roles on marital satisfaction. *Journal of Family Issues, 14,* 157–188.

Lykken, D. T. (1998). *A tremor in the blood: Uses and abuses of the lie detector.* New York: Plenum Press.

Lykken, D. T., McGue, M., Tellegen, A., & Bouchard, T. J., Jr. (1992). Emergenesis: Genetic traits that may not run in families. *American Psychologist, 47*, 1565–1577.

Lynch, G., & Gall, C. M. (2006). Ampakines and the threefold path to cognitive enhancement. *Trends in Neurosciences, 29*, 554–562.

Lynch, M. A. (2004). Long-term potentiation and memory. *Psychological Review, 84*, 87–136.

Lynch, S. K., Turkheimer, E., D'Onofrio, B. M., Mendle, J., Emery, R. E., Slutske, W. S., et al. (2006). A genetically informed study of the association between harsh punishment and offspring behavioral problems. *Journal of Family Psychology, 20*, 190–198.

Lynn, D. J., & Vaillant, G. E. (1998). Anonymity, neutrality, and confidentiality in the actual methods of Sigmund Freud: A review of 43 cases, 1907–1939. *American Journal of Psychiatry, 155*, 163–171.

Lynn, M. (1992). Scarcity's enhancement of desirability: The role of naive economic theories. *Basic & Applied Social Psychology, 13*, 67–78.

Lynn, S. J., Kirsch, I., Barabasz, A., Cardena, E., & Patterson, D. (2000). Hypnosis as an empirically supported clinical intervention: The state of the evidence and a look to the future. *International Journal of Clinical & Experimental Hypnosis, 48*, 239–259.

Lynn, S. J., Kirsch, I., Knox, J., Fassler, O., & Lilienfeld, S. O. (2007). Hypnotic regulation of consciousness and the pain neuromatrix. In G. A. Jamieson (Ed.), *Hypnosis and conscious states: The cognitive neuroscience perspective*. New York: Oxford University Press.

Lynn, S. J., Lock, T., Loftus, E. F., Krackow, E., & Lilienfeld, S. O. (2003). The remembrance of things past: Problematic memory recovery techniques in psychotherapy. In S. O. Lilienfeld, S. J. Lynn, & J. M. Lohr (Eds.), *Science and pseudoscience in clinical psychology*. New York: Guilford.

Lynne, S. D., Graber, J. A., Nichols, T. R., & Brooks-Gunn, J., & Botwin, G. J. (2007). Links between pubertal timing, peer influences, and externalizing behaviors among urban students followed through middle school. *Journal of Adolescent Health, 40*(2).

Lytton, H. (1997). Physical punishment is a problem, whether conduct disorder is endogenous or not. *Psychological Inquiry, 8*, 211–214.

Lyubomirsky, S., Sheldon, K. M., & Schkade, D. (2005). Pursuing happiness: The architecture of sustainable change. *Review of General Psychology, 9*, 111–131.

Lyubomirsky, S., Sousa, L., & Dickerhoof, R. (2006). The costs and benefits of writing, talking, and thinking about life's triumphs and defeats. *Journal of Personality and Social Psychology, 90*, 692–708.

Lyubomirsky, S., Tkach, C., & DiMatteo, R. M. (2006). What are the differences between happiness and self-esteem? *Social Indicators Research, 78*, 363–404.

Maas, J. B. (1998). *Power sleep*. New York: Harper Perennial.

Maccoby, E. E. (2000). Parenting and its effects on children: On reading and misreading behavior genetics. *Annual Review of Psychology, 51*, 1–27.

MacCoun, R. J. (1998). Biases in the interpretation and use of research results. *Annual Review Psychology, 49*, 259–287.

MacDonald, K. (1998). Evolution, culture, and the five-factor model. *Journal of Cross-Cultural Psychology, 29*, 119–149.

MacGregor, J. N., Ormerod, T. C., & Chronicle, E. P. (2001). Information-processing and insight: A process model of performance on the nine-dot and related problems. *Journal of Experimental Psychology: Learning, Memory, and Cognition, 27*, 176–201.

Macht, M., & Simons, G. (2000). Emotions and eating in everyday life. *Appetite, 35*, 65–71.

Mack, A. H., Franklin Jr., J. E., & Frances, R. J. (2003). Substance use disorders. In R. E. Hales & S. C. Yudofsky (Eds.), *Textbook of clinical psychiatry*. Washington, DC: American Psychiatric Publishing.

MacKellar, D. A., Valleroy, L. A., Secura, G. M., Behel, S., Bingham, T., Celentano, D. D., Koblin, B. A., LaLota, M., McFarland, W., Shehan, D., Thiede, H., Torian, L. V., & Janssen, R. S., & Young Men's Survey Study Group. (2005). Unrecognized HIV infection, risk behaviors, and perceptions of risk among young men who have sex with men: Opportunities for advancing HIV prevention in the third decade of HIV/AIDS. *Journal of Acquired Immune Deficiency Syndromes, 38*, 603–614.

Mackintosh, N. J. (1998). *IQ and human intelligence*. Oxford: Oxford University Press.

MacLean, A. W., Davies, D. R. T., & Thiele, K. (2003). The hazards and prevention of driving while sleepy. *Sleep Medicine Reviews,7*, 507–521.

MacLean, P. D. (1954). Studies on limbic system ("viosceal brain") and their bearing on psychosomatic problems. In E. D. Wittkower & R. A. Cleghorn (Eds.), *Recent developments in psychosomatic medicine*. Philadelphia: Lippincott.

MacLean, P. D. (1993). Cerebral evolution of emotion. In M. Lewis & J. M. Haviland (Eds.), *Handbook of emotions*. New York: Guilford.

MacMillan, H. L., Fleming, J. E., Streiner, D. L., Lin, E., Boyle, M. H., Jamieson, E., Duku, E. K., Walsh, C. A., Wong, M. Y. Y., & Beardslee, W. R. (2001). Childhood abuse and lifetime psychopathology in a community sample. *American Journal of Psychiatry, 158*, 1878–1883.

MacMillan, H. L., Fleming, J. E., Trocme, N., Boyle, M. H., Wong, M., Racine, Y. A., Beardslee, W. R., & Offord, D. R. (1997). Prevalence of child physical and sexual abuse in the community: Results from the Ontario health supplement. *Journal of the American Medical Association, 278*, 131–135.

Maddi, S. R. (1989). *Personality theories: A comparative analysis*. Chicago, IL: Dorsey Press.

Maddux, W. W., & Yuki, M. (2006). The "ripple effect": Cultural differences in perceptions of the consequences of events. *Personality and Social Psychology Bulletin, 32*, 669–683.

Madon, S., Guyll, M., Aboufadel, K., Montiel, E., Smith, A., Palumbo, P., & Jussim, L. (2001). Ethnic and national stereotypes: The Princeton trilogy revisited and revised. *Personality and Social Psychology Bulletin, 27*, 996–1010.

Madsen, K. B. (1968). *Theories of motivation*. Copenhagen: Munksgaard.

Madsen, K. B. (1973). Theories of motivation. In B. B. Wolman (Ed.), *Handbook of general psychology*. Englewood Cliffs, NJ: Prentice-Hall.

Magnavita, J. J. (2008). Psychoanalytic psychotherapy. In J. L. Lebow (Ed.), *Twenty-first century psychotherapies: Contemporary approaches to theory and practice*. New York: Wiley.

Maguire, W., Weisstein, N., & Klymenko, V. (1990). From visual structure to perceptual function. In K. N. Leibovic (Ed.), *Science of vision*. New York: Springer-Verlag.

Maher, B. A. (2001). Delusions. In P. B. Sutker & H. E. Adams (Eds.), *Comprehensive handbook of psychopathology* (3rd ed., pp. 309–370). New York: Kluwer Academic/Plenum Publishers.

Mahoney, M. J. (1974). *Cognition and behavior modification*. Cambridge, MA: Ballinger.

Mahowald, M. W. (1993). Sleepwalking. In M. A. Carskadon (Ed.), *Encyclopedia of sleep and dreaming*. New York: Macmillan.

Mahowald, M. W., & Schenck, C. H. (2005). Insights from studying human sleep disorders. *Nature, 437*, 1279–1285.

Maier, N. R. F. (1931). Reasoning and learning. *Psychological Review, 38*, 332–346.

Malcolm, J. (1980: Pt. 1 Nov. 24; Pt. 2 Dec. 1). The impossible profession. *The New Yorker*, pp. 55–133, 54–152.

Maldonado, J. R., & Spiegel, D. (2003a). Dissociative disorders. In R. E. Hales & S. C. Yudofsky (Eds.), *Textbook of clinical psychiatry*. Washington, DC: American Psychiatric Publishing.

Maldonado, J. R., & Spiegel, D. (2003b). Hypnosis. In R. E. Hales & S. C. Yudofsky (Eds.), *Textbook of clinical psychiatry*. Washington, DC: American Psychiatry Publishing.

Maletzky, B. M. (2002). The paraphilias: Research and treatment. In P. E. Nathan & J. M. Gorman (Eds.), *A guide to treatments that work*. London: Oxford University Press.

Maltzman, I. (1994). Why alcoholism is a disease. *Journal of Psychoactive Drugs, 26*, 13–31.

Mandler, G. (1984). *Mind and body*. New York: Norton.

Mandler, G. (1993). Thought, memory, and learning: Effects of emotional stress. In L. Goldberger & S. Breznitz (Eds.), *Handbook of stress: Theoretical and clinical aspects* (2nd ed.). New York: Free Press.

Mandler, G. (2002). Origins of the cognitive revolution. *Journal of the History of the Behavioral Sciences, 38*, 339–353.

Maner, J. K., Gailliot, M. T., Rouby, D. A., & Miller, S. L. (2007). Can't take my eyes off you: Attentional adhesion to mates and rivals. *Journal of Personality and Social Psychology, 93*, 389–401.

Mangelsdorf, S., Gunnar, M., Kestenbaum, R., Lang, S., & Andreas, D. (1990). Infant proneness-to-distress temperament, maternal personality, and mother-infant attachment: Associations and goodness of fit. *Child Development, 61*, 830–831.

Mann, J. J., & Currier, D. (2006). Understanding and preventing suicide. In D. J. Stein, D. J. Kupfer, & A. F. Schatzberg (Eds.), *Textbook of mood disorders*. Washington, DC: American Psychiatric Publishing.

Mantovani, A., & Lisanby, S. H. (2007). Transcranial magnetic stimulation in major depression. In M. S. George & R. H. Belmaker (Eds.), *Transcranial magnetic stimulation in clinical psychiatry* (pp. 113–152). Washington, DC: American Psychiatric Publishing.

Maratsos, M. P. (2007). Commentary. *Monographs of the Society for Research in Child Development, 72*, 121–126.

Marcelino, A. S., Adam, A. S., Couronne, T., Koester, E. P., & Sieffermann, J. M. (2001). Internal and external determinants of eating initiation in humans. *Appetite, 36*, 9–14.

Marcenes, W. G., & Sheiham, A. (1992). The relationship between work stress and oral health status. *Social Science and Medicine, 35*, 1511.

Marcia, J. E. (1966). Development and validation of ego identity status. *Journal of Personality and Social Psychology, 3*, 551–558.

Marcia, J. E. (1980). Identity in adolescence. In J. Adelson (Ed.), *Handbook of adolescent psychology.* New York: Wiley.

Marcia, J. E. (1994). The empirical study of ego identity. In H. A. Bosma, T. L. G. Graafsma, H. D. Grotevant, & D. J. de Levita (Eds.), *Identity and development: An interdisciplinary approach.* Thousand Oaks, CA: Sage.

Marcus, G. F. (1996). Why do children say "breaked"? *Current Directions in Psychological Science, 5,* 81–85.

Marder, S. R. (2000). Schizophrenia: Somatic treatment. In B. J. Sadock & V. A. Sadock (Eds.), *Kaplan and Sadock's comprehensive textbook of psychiatry* (7th ed., Vol. 1, pp. 1199–1209). Philadelphia: Lippincott/Williams & Wilkins.

Marder, S. R., & van Kammen, D. P. (2005). Dopamine receptor antagonists (typical antipsychotics). In B. J. Sadock & V. A. Sadock (Eds.), *Kaplan and Sadock's comprehensive textbook of psychiatry.* Philadelphia: Lippincott Williams & Wilkins.

Markman, E. M., Wasow, J. L., & Hansen, M. B. (2003). Use of the mutual exclusivity assumption by young word learners. *Cognitive Psycology, 47,* 241–275.

Markowitsch, H. J. (2000). Neuroanatomy of memory. In E. Tulving & F. I. M. Craik (Eds.), *The Oxford handbook of memory* (pp. 465–484). New York: Oxford University Press.

Marks, I. M. (2004). The Nobel prize award in physiology to Ivan Petrovich Pavlov. *Australian and New Zealand Journal of Psychiatry, 38*(9), 674–677.

Markus, H. R., & Hamedani, M. G. (2007). Sociocultural psychology: The dynamic interdependence among self systems and social systems. In S. Kitayama & D. Cohen (Eds.), *Handbook of cultural psychology.* New York: Guilford.

Markus, H. R., & Kitayama, S. (1991). Culture and the self: Implications for cognition, emotion, and motivation. *Psychological Review, 98,* 224–253.

Markus, H. R., & Kitayama, S. (1994). The cultural construction of self and emotion: Implications for social behavior. In S. Kitayama & H. R. Markus (Eds.), *Emotions and culture: Empirical studies of mutual influence.* Washington, DC: American Psychological Association.

Markus, H. R., & Kitayama, S. (2003). Culture, self, and the reality of the social. *Psychological Inquiry, 14*(3–4), 277–283.

Marsh, E. J. (2007). Retelling is not the same as recalling: Implications for memory. *Current Directions in Psychological Science, 16*(1), 16–20.

Marsh, E. J., & Tversky, B. (2004). Spinning the stories of our lives. *Applied Cognitive Psychology, 18,* 491–503.

Marteau, T. M., & Weinman, J. (2004). Communicating about health threats and treatments. In S. Sutton, A. Baum, & M. Johnston (Ed), *The Sage handbook of health psychology.* Thousand Oaks, CA: Sage.

Martin, C. L., & Ruble, D. (2004). Children's search for gender cues: Cognitive perspectives on gender development. *Current Directions in Psychological Science, 13*(2), 67–70.

Martin, L. R., Friedman, H. S., & Schwartz, J. E. (2007). Personality and mortality risk across the life span: The importance of conscientiousness as a biopsychosocial attribute. *Health Psychology, 26,* 428–436.

Martin, R. A. (2002). IS laughter the best medicine? Humor, laughter, and physical health. *Current Directions in Psychological Science, 11*(6), 216–220.

Martin, R., & Leventhal, H. (2004). Symptom perception and health care-seeking behavior. In J. M. Raczynski & L. C. Leviton (Eds.), *Handbook of clinical health psychology, Vol. 2: Disorders of behavior and health.* Washington, DC: American Psychological Association.

Maslow, A. H. (1954). *Motivation and personality.* New York: Harper & Row.

Maslow, A. H. (1968). *Toward a psychology of being.* New York: Van Nostrand.

Maslow, A. H. (1970). *Motivation and personality.* New York: Harper & Row.

Massaro, D. W., & Loftus, G. R. (1996). Sensory and perceptual storage: Data and theory. In E. L. Bjork & R. A. Bjork (Eds.), *Memory.* San Diego: Academic Press.

Massen, C., & Vaterrodt-Plünnecke, B. (2006). The role of proactive interference in mnemonic techniques. *Memory, 14,* 189–196.

Masters, W. H., & Johnson, V. E. (1966). *Human sexual response.* Boston: Little, Brown.

Masters, W. H., & Johnson, V. E. (1970). *Human sexual inadequacy.* Boston: Little, Brown.

Mastro, D. E., Behm-Morawitz, E., & Kopacz, M. A. (2008). Exposure to television portrayals of Latinos: The implications of aversive racism and social identity theory. *Human Communication Research, 34,* 1–27.

Masuda, T., & Nisbett, R. E. (2001). Attending holistically versus analytically: Comparing the context sensitivity of Japanese and Americans. *Journal of Personality and Social Psychology, 81,* 922–934.

Mathy, R. M., Schillace, M., Coleman, S. M., & Berquist, B. E. (2002). Methodological rigor with Internet samples: New ways to reach underrepresented populations. *Cyber-Psychology and Behavior, 5,* 253–266.

Matlin, M. W. (2008). *The psychology of women.* Belmont, CA: Wadsworth.

Matsumoto, D. (1994). *People: Psychology from a cultural perspective.* Pacific Grove, CA: Brooks/Cole.

Matsumoto, D. (2003). Cross-cultural research. In S. F. Davis (Ed.), *Handbook of research methods in experimental psychology.* Malden, MA: Blackwell Publishers.

Matsumoto, D., & Juang, L. (2008). *Culture and psychology.* Belmont, CA: Wadsworth.

Matsumoto, D., Nezlek, J. B., & Koopmann, B. (2007). Evidence for universality in phenomenological emotion response system coherence. *Emotion, 7,* 57–67.

Matsumoto, D., & Yoo, S. (2006). Toward a new generation of cross-cultural research. *Perspectives on Psychological Science, 1,* 234–250.

Matthey, S. (1998). P<.05—But is it clinically *significant*?: Practical examples for clinicians. *Behaviour Change, 15,* 140–146.

Matusov, E., & Hayes, R. (2000). Sociocultural critique of Piaget and Vygotsky. *New Ideas in Psychology, 18*(2–3), 215–239.

Matute, H., & Miller, R. R. (1998). Detecting causal relations. In W. O'Donohue (Ed.), *Learning and behavior therapy.* Boston, Allyn & Bacon.

Mayer, F. S., & Frantz, C. M. (2004). The connectedness to nature scale: A measure of individuals' feeling in community with nature. *Journal of Environmental Psychology, 24,* 503–515.

Mayer, J. (1955). Regulation of energy intake and the body weight: The glucostatic theory and the li-

postatic hypothesis. *Annals of the New York Academy of Science, 63,* 15–43.

Mayer, J. (1968). *Overweight: Causes and control.* Englewood Cliffs, NJ: Prentice-Hall.

Mays, V. M., Rubin, J., Sabourin, M., & Walker, L. (1996). Moving toward a global psychology: Changing theories and practice to meet the needs of a changing world. *American Psychologist, 51,* 485–487.

McAnarney, E. R. (2008). Adolescent brain development: Forging new links? *Journal of Adolescent Health, 42*(4), 321–323.

McBride-Chang, C., & Jacklin, C. N. (1993). Early play arousal, sex-typed play, and activity level as precursors to later rough-and-tumble play. *Early Education & Development, 4,* 99–108.

McBurney, D. H. (1996). *How to think like a psychologist: Critical thinking in psychology.* Upper Saddle River, NJ: Prentice-Hall.

McBurney, D. H., Zapp, D. J., & Streeter. S. A. (2005). Preferred number of sexual partners: Tails of distributions and tales of mating systems. *Evolution and Human Behavior, 26,* 271–278.

McCarley, R. W. (1994). Dreams and the biology of sleep. In M. H. Kryger, T. Roth, & W. C. Dement (Eds.), *Principles and practice of sleep medicine* (2nd ed.). Philadelphia: Saunders.

McCauley, M. E., Eskes, G., & Moscovitch, M. (1996). The effect of imagery on explicit and implicit tests of memory in young and old people: A double dissociation. *Canadian Journal of Experimental Psychology, 50,* 34–41.

McClelland, D. C. (1975). *Power: The inner experience.* New York: Irvington.

McClelland, D. C. (1985). How motives, skills and values determine what people do. *American Psychologist, 40,* 812–825.

McClelland, D. C. (1987). Characteristics of successful entrepreneurs. *Journal of Creative Behavior, 3,* 219–233.

McClelland, D. C., Atkinson, J. W., Clark, R. A., & Lowell, E. L. (1953). *The achievement motive.* New York: Appleton-Century-Crofts.

McClelland, D. C., & Boyatzis, R. E. (1982). The leadership motive pattern and long-term success in management. *Journal of Applied Psychology, 67,* 737–743.

McClelland, D. C., & Koestner, R. (1992). The achievement motive. In C. P. Smith (Ed.), *Motivation and personality: Handbook of thematic content analysis.* New York: Cambridge University Press.

McClelland, J. L. (1992). Parallel-distributed processing models of memory. In L. R. Squire (Ed.), *Encyclopedia of learning and memory.* New York: Macmillan.

McClelland, J. L. (2000). Connectionist models of memory. In E. Tulving & F. I. M. Craik (Eds.), *The Oxford handbook of memory* (pp. 583–596). New York: Oxford University Press.

McClelland, J. L., & Rogers, T. T. (2003). The parallel distributed processing approach to semantic cognition. *Nature Reviews Neuroscience, 4,* 310–322.

McClelland, J. L., & Rumelhart, D. E. (1985). Distributed memory and the representation of general and specific information. *Journal of Experimental Psychology: General, 114,* 159–188.

McConnell, J. V. (1962). Memory transfer through cannibalism in planarians. *Journal of Neuropsychiatry, 3*(Suppl. 1), 542–548.

McCord, J. (2005). Unintended consequences of punishment. In M. Donnelly & M. A. Straus (Eds.),

Corporal punishment of children in theoretical perspective New Haven, CT: Yale University Press.

McCrae, R. R. (1984). Situational determinants of coping responses: Loss, threat and challenge. *Journal of Personality and Social Psychology, 46,* 919–928.

McCrae, R. R. (2005). Personality structure. In V. A. Derlega, B. A. Winstead, & W. H. Jones (Eds.), *Personality: Contemporary theory and research.* Belmont, CA: Wadsworth.

McCrae, R. R., & Costa, P. T., Jr. (1985). Updating Norman's "adequate taxonomy": Intelligence and personality dimensions in natural language and in questionnaires. *Journal of Personality and Social Psychology, 49,* 710–721.

McCrae, R. R., & Costa, P. T., Jr. (1987). Validation of the five-factor model of personality across instruments and observers. *Journal of Personality and Social Psychology, 52,* 81–90.

McCrae, R. R., & Costa, P. T., Jr. (1997). Personality trait structure as a human universal. *American Psychologist, 52,* 509–516.

McCrae, R. R., & Costa, P. T., Jr. (1999). A five-factor theory of personality. In L. A. Pervin & O. P. John (Eds.), *Handbook of personality: Theory and research.* New York: Guilford.

McCrae, R. R., & Costa, P. T., Jr. (2003). *Personality in adulthood: A five factor theory perspective.* New York: Guilford.

McCrae, R. R., & Costa, P. T., Jr. (2004). A contemplated revision of the NEO five-factor inventory. *Personality and Individual Differences, 36,* 587–596.

McCrae, R. R., & Costa, P. T., Jr. (2007). Brief versions of the NEO-PI-3. *Journal of Individual Differences, 28,* 116–128.

McCrae, R. R., & Terracciano, A. (2006). National character and personality. *Current Directions in Psychological Science, 15,* 156–161.

McCrae, R. R., & Terracciano, A., & the Personality Profiles of Cultures Project. (2005a). Personality profiles of cultures: Aggregate personality traits. *Journal of Personality and Social Psychology, 89,* 407–425.

McCrae, R. R., Terracciano, A., & the Personality Profiles of Cultures Project. (2005b). Universal features of personality traits from the observer's perspective: Data from 50 cultures. *Journal of Personality and Social Psychology, 88,* 547–561.

McCrink, K., & Wynn, K. (2004). Large-number addition and subtraction by 9-month-old infants. *Psychological Science, 15,* 776–781.

McCullough, M. E. (2001). Forgiving. In C. R. Snyder (Ed.), *Coping with stress: Effective people and processes* (pp. 93–113). New York: Oxford University Press.

McCullough, M. E., Bellah, C. G., Kilpatrick, S. D., & Johnson, J. L. (2001). Vengefulness: Relationships with forgiveness, rumination, well-being, and the Big Five. *Personality and Social Psychology Bulletin, 27,* 601–610.

McCullough, M. E., & Witvliet, C. V. (2002). The psychology of forgiveness. In C. R. Synder & S. J. Lopez (Eds.), *Handbook of positive psychology.* New York: Oxford University Press.

McDaniel, M. A. (2005). Big-brained people are smarter: A meta–analysis of the relationship between *in vivo* brain volume and intelligence. *Intelligence, 33,* 337–346.

McDaniel, M. A., & Einstein, G. O. (1986). Bizarre imagery as an effective memory aid: The importance of distinctiveness. *Journal of Experimental Psychology: Learning, Memory & Cognition, 12,* 54–65.

McDaniel, M. A., & Einstein, G. O. (2007). *Prospective memory: An overview and synthesis of an emerging field.* Thousand Oaks, CA: Sage.

McDaniel, M. A., Einstein, G. O., Stout, A. C., & Morgan, Z. (2003). Aging and maintaining intentions over delays: Do it or lose it. *Psychology and Aging, 18,* 823–835.

McDaniel, M. A., Waddill, P. J., & Shakesby, P. S. (1996). Study strategies, interest, and learning from text: The application of material appropriate processing. In D. J. Herrmann, C. McEvoy, C. Hertzog, P. Hertel, & M. K. Johnson (Eds.), *Basic and applied memory research: Theory in context* (Vol. 1). Mahwah, NJ: Erlbaum.

McDermott, K. B. (2007). Inducing false memories through associated lists: A window onto everyday false memories? In J. S. Nairne (Ed.), *The foundations of remembering: Essays in honor of Henry L. Roediger III.* New York: Psychology Press.

McDonald, C., & Murphy, K. C. (2003). The new genetics of schizophrenia. *Psychiatric Clinics of North America, 26*(1), 41–63.

McDonald, W. M., Thompson, T. R., McCall W. V., & Zormuski, C. F. (2004). Electroconvulsive therapy. In A. F. Schatzberg & C. B. Nemeroff (Eds.), *Textbook of psychopharmacology.* Washington, DC: American Psychiatric Publishing.

McEwen, B. S. (2004). How sex and stress hormones regulate the structural and functional plasticity of hippocampus. In M. S. Gazzaniga (Ed.), *The cognitive neurosciences.* Cambridge, MA: MIT Press.

McGeoch, J. A., & McDonald, W. T. (1931). Meaningful relation and retroactive inhibition. *American Journal of Psychology, 43,* 579–588.

McGlashan, T. H., & Fenton, W. S. (1992). The positive-negative distinction in schizophrenia: Review of natural history validators. *Archives of General Psychiatry, 49,* 63–72.

McGlashan, T. H., & Hoffman, R. E. (2000). Schizophrenia: Psychodynamic to neurodynamic theories. In B. J. Sadock & V. A. Sadock (Eds.), *Kaplan and Sadock's comprehensive textbook of psychiatry* (7th ed., Vol. 1, pp. 1159–1168). Philadelphia: Lippincott/Williams & Wilkins.

McGregor, H. A., Lieberman, J. D., Greenberg, J., Solomon, S., Arndt, J., Simon, L., & Pyszczynski, T. (1998). Terror management and aggression: Evidence that mortality salience motivates aggression against worldview-threatening others. *Journal of Personality and Social Psychology, 74,* 590–605.

McGrew, J. H., Wright, E. R., Pescosolido, B. A., & McDonel, E. C. (1999). The closing of Central State Hospital: Long-term outcomes for persons with severe mental illness. *Journal of Behavioral Health Services & Research, 26,* 246–261.

McGue, M., Bouchard, T. J., Jr., Iacono, W. G., & Lykken, D. T. (1993). Behavioral genetics of cognitive ability: A life-span perspective. In R. Plomin & G. E. McClearn (Eds.), *Nature, nurture and psychology.* Washington, DC: American Psychological Association.

McGuigan, F. J., & Lehrer, P. M. (2007). Progressive relaxation: Origins, principles, and clinical applications. In P. M. Lehrer, R. L. Woolfolk, & W. E. Sime (Eds.), *Principles and practice of stress management.* New York: Guilford.

McHale, S. M., Crouter, A. C., & Whiteman, S. D. (2003). The family contexts of gender development in childhood and adolescence. *Social Development, 12,* 125–148.

McHugh, P. R. (1995). Dissociative identity disorder as a socially constructed artifact. *Journal of Practical Psychiatry and Behavioral Health, 1,* 158–166.

McHugh, P. R., Lief, H. I., Freyd, P. P., & Fetkewicz, J. M. (2004). From refusal to reconciliation: Family relationships after an accusation based on recovered memories. *Journal of Nervous and Mental Disease, 192,* 525–531.

McKean, K. (1985, June). Decisions, decisions. *Discover,* pp. 22–31.

McKelvie, P., & Low, J. (2002). Listening to Mozart does not improve children's spatial ability: Final curtains for the Mozart effect. *British Journal of Development Psychology, 20,* 241–258.

McKenna, J. J. (1993). Co-sleeping. In M. A. Carskadon (Ed.), *Encyclopedia of sleep and dreaming.* New York: Macmillan.

McKenna, K. Y. A., & Bargh, J. A. (1998). Coming out in the age of the Internet: Identity "demarginalization" through virtual group participation. *Journal of Personality and Social Psychology, 75,* 681–694.

McKenna, K. Y. A., & Bargh, J. A. (2000). Plan 9 from cyberspace: The implications of the Internet for personality and social psychology. *Personality and Social Psychology Review, 4,* 57–75.

McKenna, K. Y. A., Green, A., & Gleason, M. (2002). Relationship formation on the Internet: What's the big attraction? *Journal of Social Issues, 58,* 9–31.

McKenna, K. Y. A., & Seidman, G. (2005). You, me, and we: Interpersonal processes in electronic groups. In Y. Amichai-Hamburger (Ed.), *The social net: Understanding human behavior in cyberspace.* New York: Oxford University Press.

McLay, R. N., Daylo, A. A., & Hammer, P. S. (2006). No effect of lunar cycle on psychiatric admissions or emergency evaluations. *Military Medicine, 171,* 1239–1242.

McLean, D. E., & Link, B. G. (1994). Unraveling complexity: Strategies to refine concepts, measures, and research designs in the study of life events and mental health. In W. R. Avison & I. H. Gotlib (Eds.), *Stress and mental health: Contemporary issues and prospects for the future.* New York: Plenum.

McLellan, A. T., Lewis, D. C., O'Brien, C. P., & Kleber, H. D. (2000). Drug dependence, a chronic mental illness: Implications for treatment, insurance, and outcome evaluation. *Journal of the American Medical Association, 284,* 1689–1695.

McLoughlin, K., & Paquet, M. (2005, December 14). Gambling led Hogan to robbery, lawyer says. *Lehigh University's The Brown and White.* Retrieved March 21, 2006 from http://www.bw.lehigh.edu/story.asp?ID=19313.

McLoyd, V. C. (1998). Socioeconomic disadvantage and child development. *American Psychologist, 53,* 185–204.

McMahon, F. J., & Kassem, L. (2005). Anxiety disorders: Genetics. In B. J. Sadock & V. A. Sadock (Eds.), *Kaplan & Sadock's comprehensive textbook of psychiatry.* Philadelphia: Lippincott Williams & Wilkins.

McNally, R. J. (1994). Cognitive bias in panic disorder. *Current Directions in Psychological Science, 3,* 129–132.

McNally, R. J. (1996). *Panic disorder: A critical analysis.* New York: Guilford.

McNally, R. J. (1999). Posttraumatic stress disorder. In T. Millon, P. H. Blaney, & R. D. Davis (Eds.), *Oxford textbook of psychopathology* (pp. 144–165). New York: Oxford University Press.

Olson, E. J., & Park, J. G. (2006). Snoring. In T. Lee-Chiong (Ed.), *Sleep: A comprehensive handbook*. Hoboken, NJ: Wiley-Liss.

Olson, J. M., & Maio, G. R. (2003). Persuasion and attitude change. In T. Millon & M. J. Lerner (Eds.), *Handbook of psychology, Vol. 5: Personality and social psychology*. New York: Wiley.

Olson, J. M., Roese, N. J., & Zanna, M. P. (1996). Expectancies. In E. T. Higgins & A. W. Kruglanski (Eds.), *Social psychology: Handbook of basic principles*. New York: Guilford.

Olson, J. M., & Stone, J. (2005). The influence of behavior on attitudes. In D. Albarracin, B. T. Johnson, & M. P. Zanna (Eds.), *The handbook of attitudes*. Mahwah, NJ: Erlbaum.

Olson, M. A., & Fazio, R. H. (2001). Implicit attitude formation through classical conditioning. *Psychological Science, 12*, 413–417.

Olson, M. A., & Fazio, R. H. (2002). Implicit acquisition and manifestation of classically conditioned attitudes. *Social Cognition, 20*(2), 89–104.

Ondeck, D. M. (2003). Impact of culture on pain. *Home Health Care Management & Practice, 15*, 255–257.

Ones, D. S., Viswesvaran, C., & Dilchert, S. (2005). Cognitive ability in selection decisions. In O. Wilhelm & R. W. Engle (Eds.), *Handbook of understanding and measuring intelligence*. Thousand Oaks, CA: Sage.

Operario, D., & Fiske, S. T. (2001). Stereotypes: Content, structures, processes, and context. In R. Brown & S. L. Gaertner (Eds.), *Blackwell handbook of social psychology: Interpersonal processes*. Malden, MA: Blackwell.

Opotow, S. & Weiss, L. (2000). Denial and the process of moral exclusion in environmental conflict. *Journal of Social Issues, 56*, 475–490.

O'Reardon, J. P., Solvason, H. B., Janicak, P. G., Sampson, S., Isenberg, K. E., Nahas, Z., et al. (2007). Efficacy and safety of transcranial magnetic stimulation in the acute treatment of major depression: A multisite randomized controlled trial. *Biological Psychiatry, 62*, 1208–1216.

Organista, P. B., & Miranda, J. (1991). Psychosomatic symptoms in medical outpatients: An investigation of self-handicapping theory. *Health Psychology, 10*, 427–431.

Orme-Johnson, D. W., Schneider, R. H., Son, Y. D., Nidich, S., & Cho, Z.-H. (2006). Neuroimaging of meditation's effect on brain reactivity to pain. *Neuroreport: For Rapid Communication of Neuroscience Research, 17*, 1359–1363.

Orne, M. T. (1951). The mechanisms of hypnotic age regression: An experimental study. *Journal of Abnormal and Social Psychology, 46*, 213–225.

Orne, M. T., & Dinges, D. F. (1989). Hypnosis. In H. I. Kaplan & B. J. Sadock (Eds.), *Comprehensive textbook of psychiatry* (5th ed., Vol. 2). Baltimore: Williams & Wilkins.

Orne, M. T., & Holland, C. C. (1968). On the ecological validity of laboratory deceptions. *International Journal of Psychiatry, 6*, 282–293.

Ornstein, R., & Ehrlich, P. (2000). *New world, new mind: Moving toward conscious evolution*. Cambridge, MA: Malor Books, ISHK.

Ornstein, R. E. (1977). *The psychology of consciousness*. New York: Harcourt Brace Jovanovich.

Ornstein, R. E., & Dewan, T. (1991). *The evolution of consciousness: Of Darwin, Freud, and cranial fire—The origins of the way we think*. New York: Prentice-Hall.

Ortigue, S., Grafton, S. T., & Bianchi-Demicheli, F. (2007). Correlation between insula activation and self-reported quality of orgasm in women. *NeuroImage, 37*, 551–560.

Ortmann, A., & Hertwig, R. (1997). Is deception acceptable? *American Psychologist, 52*, 746–747.

Osbaldiston, R., & Sheldon, K. M. (2002). Social dilemmas and sustainability: Promoting peoples' motivation to "cooperate with the future." In P. Schmuck & W. P. Schultz (Eds.), *Psychology of sustainable development* (pp. 37–58). Boston: Kluwer Academic Press.

Oskamp, S. (1991). *Attitudes and opinions*. Englewood Cliffs, NJ: Prentice-Hall.

Ostovich, J. M., & Sabini, J. (2004). How are sociosexuality, sex drive, and lifetime number of sexual partners related? *Personality and Social Psychology Bulletin, 30*, 1255–1266.

Ostrom, E., Burger, J., Field, C. B., Norgaard, R. B., & Policansky, D. (2007). Revisiting the commons: Local lessons, global challenges. In D. J. Penn & I. Mysterud (Eds.), *Evolutionary perspectives on environmental problems* (pp. 129–140). New Brunswick, NJ: Transaction Publishers.

Otsuka, Y., & Osaka, N. (2005). Working memory in the elderly: Role of prefrontal cortex. *Japanese Psychological Review, 48*, 518–529.

Outtz, J. L. (2002). The role of cognitive ability tests in employment selection. *Human Performance, 15*, 161–171.

Overall, N. C., Fletcher, G. J. O., & Simpson, J.A. (2006). Regulation processes in intimate relationships: The role of ideal standards. *Journal of Personality and Social Psychology, 91*, 662–685.

Ozer, D. J., & Benet-Martínez, V. (2006). Personality and the prediction of consequential outcomes. *Annual Review of Psychology, 57*, 401–421.

Ozer, E. J., Best, S. R., Lipsey, T. L., & Weiss, D. S. (2003). Predictors of posttraumatic stress disorder and symptoms in adults: A meta-analysis. *Psychological Bulletin, 129*, 52–73.

Pace-Schott, E. F. (2005). The neurobiology of dreaming. In M. H. Kryger, T. Roth, & W. C. Dement (Eds.). *Principles and practice of sleep medicine*. Philadelphia: Elsevier Saunders.

Padgett, D. A., & Sheridan, J. F. (2000). Herpesviruses. In G. Fink (Ed.), *Encyclopedia of stress* (pp. 357–363). San Diego: Academic Press.

Pahl, S., Harris, P. R., Todd, H. A., & Rutter, D. R. (2005). Comparative optimism for environmental risks. *Journal of Environmental Psychology, 25*, 1–11.

Paivio, A. (1969). Mental imagery in associative learning and memory. *Psychological Review, 76*, 241–263.

Paivio, A. (1986). *Mental representations: A dual coding approach*. New York: Oxford University Press.

Paivio, A. (2007). *Mind and its evolution: A dual coding theoretical approach*. Mahwah, NJ: Erlbaum.

Paivio, A., Khan, M., & Begg, I. (2000). Concreteness of relational effects on recall of adjective-noun pairs. *Canadian Journal of Experimental Psychology, 54*(3), 149–160.

Paivio, A., Smythe, P. E., & Yuille, J. C. (1968). Imagery versus meaningfulness of nouns in paired-associate learning. *Canadian Journal of Psychology, 22*, 427–441.

Palladino, J. J., & Carducci, B. J. (1984). Students' knowledge of sleep and dreams. *Teaching of Psychology, 11*, 189–191.

Palmer, S. E. (2003). Visual perception of objects. In A. F. Healy & R. W. Proctor (Eds.), *Handbook of psychology, Vol. 4: Experimental psychology*. New York: Wiley.

Palmer, S. E., Rosch, E., & Chase, P. (1981). Canonical perspective and the perception of objects. In J. Long & A. Baddeley (Eds.), *Attention and Performance*. Hillsdale, NJ: Erlbaum.

Palmere, M., Benton, S. L., Glover, J. A., & Ronning, R. (1983). Elaboration and recall of main ideas in prose. *Journal of Educational Psychology, 75*, 898–907.

Palmeri, T. J., & Gauthier, I. (2004). Visual object understanding. *Nature Reviews Neuroscience, 5*, 291-303.

Panksepp, J. (1991). Affective neuroscience: A conceptual framework for the neurobiological study of emotions. In K. T. Strongman (Ed.), *International review of studies on emotion*. Chichester, England: Wiley.

Park, C. L., & Fenster, J. R. (2004). Stress-related growth: Predictors of occurrence and correlates with psychological adjustment. *Journal of Social and Clinical Psychology, 23*, 195–215.

Partinen, M., & Hublin, C. (2005). Epidemiology of sleep disorders. In M. H. Kryger, T. Roth, & W. C. Dement (Eds.). *Principles and practice of sleep medicine*. Philadelphia: Elsevier Saunders.

Pashler, H., Johnston, J. C., & Ruthruff, E. (2001). Attention and performance. *Annual Review of Psychology, 52*, 629–651.

Pasternak, T., Bisley, J. W., & Calkins, D. (2003). Visual processing in the primate brain. In M. Gallagher & R. J. Nelson (Eds.), *Handbook of psychology: Biological psychology*. New York: Wiley.

Patel, J. K., Pinals, D. A., & Breier, A. (2003). Schizophrenia and other psychoses. In A. Tasman, J. Kay, & J. A. Lieberman (Eds.), *Psychiatry*. New York: Wiley.

Patel, S. R., Ayas, N. T., Malhotra, M. R., White, D. P., Schernhammer, E. S., Speizer, F. E., et al. (2004). A prospective study of sleep duration and mortality risk in women. *Sleep: Journal of Sleep and Sleep Disorders Research, 27*, 440–444.

Patel, S. R., Malhotra, A., Gottlieb, D. J., White, P., & Hu, F. B. (2006). Correlates of long sleep deprivation. *Sleep: Journal of Sleep and Sleep Disorders Research, 29*, 881–889.

Pato, M. T., Eisen, J. L., & Phillips, K. A. (2003). Obsessive-compulsive disorder. In A. Tasman, J. Kay, & J. A. Lieberman (Eds.), *Psychiatry*. New York: Wiley.

Patrick, H., Nicklas, T. A., Hughes, S. O., & Morales, M. (2005). The benefits of authoritative feeding style: Caregiver feeding styles and children's food consumption patterns. *Appetite, 44*, 243–249.

Patterson, D. R., & Jensen, M. P. (2003). Hypnosis and clinical pain. *Psychological Bulletin, 129*, 495–521.

Patzer, G. L. (2006). *The power and paradox of physical attractiveness*. Boca Raton, FL: Brown Walker Press.

Paulhus, D. L. (1991). Measurement and control of response bias. In J. P. Robinson, P. Shaver, & L. S. Wrightsman (Eds.), *Measures of personality and social psychological attitudes*. San Diego: Academic Press.

Paulos, J. A. (1995). *A mathematician reads the newspaper*. New York: Doubleday.

Paunonen, S. V. (2003). Big Five factors of personality and replicated predictions of behavior. *Journal of Personality and Social Psychology, 84*, 411–424.

Paunonen, S. V., & Ashton, M. C. (1998). The structured assessment of personality across cultures. *Journal of Cross-Cultural Psychology, 29*, 150–170.

Pavlov, I. P. (1906). The scientific investigation of psychical faculties or processes in the higher animals. *Science, 24*, 613–619.

Pavlov, I. P. (1927). *Conditioned reflexes* (G. V. Anrep, Trans.). London: Oxford University Press.

Payne, D. G., & Blackwell, J. M. (1998). Truth in memory: Caveat emptor. In S. J. Lynn & K. M. McConkey (Eds.), *Truth in memory*. New York: Guilford.

Payne, D. G., & Wenger, M. J. (1996). Practice effects in memory: Data, theory, and unanswered questions. In D. J. Herrmann, C. McEvoy, C. Hertzog, P. Hertel, & M. K. Johnson (Eds.), *Basic and applied memory research: Practical applications* (Vol. 2). Mahwah, NJ: Erlbaum.

Payne, J. W., & Bettman, J. R. (2004). Walking with the scarecrow: The information-processing approach to decision research. In D. J. Koehler & N. Harvey (Ed.), *Blackwell handbook of judgment and decision making*. Malden, MA: Blackwell Publishing.

Pearce, L. (1974). Duck! It's the new journalism. *New Times, 2*(10), 40–41.

Pedersen, P. (1994). A culture-centered approach to counseling. In W. J. Lonner & R. Malpass (Eds.), *Psychology and culture*. Boston: Allyn & Bacon.

Peele, S. (1989). *Diseasing of America: Addiction treatment out of control*. Lexington, MA: Lexington Books.

Peele, S. (2000). What addiction is and is not: The impact of mistaken notions of addiction. *Addiction Research, 8*, 599–607.

Peladeau, N., Forget, J., & Gagne, F. (2003). Effect of paced and unpaced practice on skill application and retention: How much is enough? *American Educational Research Journal, 40*, 769–801.

Pelayo, R., & Lopes, M. C. (2006). Narcolepsy. In T. Lee-Chiong (Ed.), *Sleep: A comprehensive handbook*. Hoboken, NJ: Wiley-Liss.

Pellegrino, J. E., & Pellegrino, L. (2008). Fetal alcohol syndrome and related disorders. In P. J. Accardo (Eds.), *Capute and Accardo's neurodevelopment disabilities in infancy and childhood: Neurodevelopmental diagnosis and treatment*. Baltimore, MD: Paul H. Brookes Publishing.

Peltier, M. E. (1999). Healthcare environments using environmental aroma technology. *The Aroma-Chology Review, 8*(2), 2–3, 12.

Pennebaker, J. W., Colder, M., & Sharp, L. K. (1990). Accelerating the coping process. *Journal of Personality and Social Psychology, 58*, 528–537.

Peplau, L. A. (2003). Human sexuality: How do men and women differ? *Current Directions in Psychological Science, 12*(2), 37–40.

Pereira, A. C., Huddleston, D. E., Brickman, A. M., Sosunov, A. A., Hen, R., McKhann, G. M., et al. (2007). An in vivo correlate of exercise-induced neurogenesis in the adult dentate gyrus. *Proceedings of the National Academy of Sciences, 104*, 5638–5643.

Perkins, D. O., Miller-Anderson, L., & Lieberman, J. A. (2006). Natural history and predictors of clinical course. In J. A. Lieberman, T. S. Stroup, & D. O. Perkins (Eds.), *Textbook of schizophrenia*. Washington, DC: American Psychiatric Publishing.

Perlis, R. H., Perlis, C. S., Wu, Y. , Hwang, C., Joseph, M., & Nierenberg, A. A. (2005). Industry sponsorship and financial conflict of interest in the reporting of clinical trials in psychiatry. *American Journal of Psychiatry, 162*, 1957–1960.

Perone, M., Galizio, M., & Baron, A. (1988). The relevance of animal-based principles in the laboratory study of human operant conditioning. In G.

Davey & C. Cullen (Eds.), *Human operant conditioning and behavior modification*. New York: Wiley.

Perry, W., & Braff, D. L. (1994). Information-processing deficits and thought disorder in schizophrenia. *American Journal of Psychiatry, 151*, 363–367.

Person, E. S. (1990). The influence of values in psychoanalysis: The case of female psychology. In C. Zanardi (Ed.), *Essential papers in psychoanalysis*. New York: New York University Press.

Pert, C. B. (2002). The wisdom of the receptors: Neuropeptides, the emotions, and bodymind. *Advances in Mind-Body Medicine, 18*(1), 30–35.

Pert, C. B., & Snyder, S. H. (1973). Opiate receptor: Demonstration in the nervous tissue. *Science, 179*, 1011–1014.

Perugini, E. M., Kirsch, I., Allen, S. T., Coldwell, E., Meredith, J. M., Montgomery, G. H., & Sheehan, J. (1998). Surreptitious observation of response to hypnotically suggested hallucinations: A test of the compliance hypothesis. *International Journal of Clinical & Experimental Hypnosis, 46*, 191–203.

Peterson, C. (2000). The future of optimism. *American Psychologist, 55*(1), 44–55.

Peterson, C. (2006). *A primer in positive psychology*. New York: Oxford University Press.

Peterson, C., Seligman, M. E. P., Yurko, K. H., Martin, L. R., & Friedman, H. S. (1998). Catastrophizing and untimely death. *Psychological Science, 9*, 127–130.

Peterson, L. R., & Peterson, M. J. (1959). Short-term retention of individual verbal items. *Journal of Experimental Psychology, 58*, 193–198.

Petrie, K. J., & Pennebaker, J. W. (2004). Health-related cognitions. In S. Sutton, A. Baum, & M. Johnston (Eds.), *The Sage handbook of health psychology*. Thousand Oaks, CA: Sage.

Petrill, S. A. (2005). Behavioral genetics and intelligence. In O. Wilhelm & R. W. Engle (Eds.), *Handbook of understanding and measuring intelligence*. Thousand Oaks, CA: Sage.

Petry, N. M. (2005). *Pathological gambling: Etiology, comorbidity, and treatment*. Washington, D.C.: American Psychological Association.

Petty, R. E., & Briñol, P. (2008). Persuasion: From single to multiple to metacognitive processes. *Perspectives on Psychological Science, 3*, 137–147.

Petty, R. E., & Cacioppo, J. T. (1986). Communication and persuasion: Central and peripheral routes to attitude change. New York: Springer-Verlag.

Petty, R. E., & Wegener, D. T. (1998). Attitude change: Multiple roles for persuasion variables. In D. T. Gilbert, S. T. Fiske, & G. Lindzey (Eds.), *The handbook of social psychology*. New York: McGraw-Hill.

Petty, R. E., & Wegener, D. T. (1999). The elaboration likelihood model: Current status and controversies. In S. Chaiken & Y. Trope (Eds.), *Dual-process theories in social psychology*. New York: Guilford.

Petty, R. E., Wegener, D. T., & Fabrigar, L. R. (1997). Attitudes and attitude change. *Annual Review of Psychology, 48*, 609–647.

Petty, R. E., Wheeler, S. C., & Tormala, Z. L. (2003). Persuasion and attitude change. In T. Millon & M. J. Lerner (Eds.), *Handbook of Psychology, Vol. 5: Personality and social psychology*. New York: Wiley.

Petty, S. C., Sachs-Ericsson, N., & Joiner, T. E., Jr. (2004). Interpersonal functioning deficits: Temporary or stable characteristics of depressed individuals. *Journal of Affective Disorders, 81*, 115–122.

Pezdek, K. (2003). Event memory and autobiographical memory for the events of September 11, 2001. *Applied Cognitive Psychology, 17*, 1033–1045.

Pfau, M., Kenski, H. C., Nitz, M., & Sorenson, J. (1990). Efficacy of inoculation strategies in promoting resistance to political attack messages: Application to direct mail. *Communication Monographs, 57*, 25–43.

Pfaus, J. G., Kippin, T. E., & Centeno, S. (2001). Conditioning and sexual behavior: A review. *Hormones & Behavior, 40*, 291–321.

Phares, V. (1996). *Fathers and developmental psychopathology*. New York: Wiley.

Phelps, E. A. (2005). The interaction of emotion and cognition: The relation between the human amygdala and cognitive awareness. In R. R. Hassin, J. S. Uleman, & J. A. Bargh (Eds.), *The new unconscious: Oxford series in social cognition and social neuroscience*. New York: Oxford University Press.

Phelps, E. A. (2006). Emotion and cognition: Insights from studies of the human amygdala. *Annual Review of Psychology, 57*, 27–53.

Phillips, B., & Kryger, M. H. (2005). Management of obstructive sleep apnea-hypopnea syndrome. In M. H. Kryger, T. Roth, & W. C. Dement (Eds.), *Principles and practice of sleep medicine*. Philadelphia: Saunders.

Pi, E. H., & Simpson, G. M. (2001). Medication-induced movement disorders. In B. J. Sadock & V. A. Sadock (Eds.), *Kaplan and Sadock's comprehensive textbook of psychiatry* (7th ed., Vol. 2). Philadelphia: Lippincott/Williams & Wilkins.

Piaget, J. (1929). *The child's conception of the world*. New York: Harcourt, Brace.

Piaget, J. (1932). *The moral judgment of the child*. Glencoe, IL: Free Press.

Piaget, J. (1952). *The origins of intelligence in children*. New York: International Universities Press.

Piaget, J. (1954). *The construction of reality in the child*. New York: Basic Books.

Piaget, J. (1983). Piaget's theory. In P. H. Mussen (Ed.), *Handbook of child psychology* (Vol. 1). New York: Wiley.

Pierce, R. C., & Kumaresan, V. (2006). The mesolimbic dopamine system: The final common pathway for the reinforcing effect of drugs of abuse? *Neuroscience Biobehavioral Reviews, 30*, 215–238.

Pillow, D. R., Zautra, A. J., & Sandler, I. (1996). Major life events and minor stressors: Identifying mediational links in the stress process. *Journal of Personality and Social Psychology, 70*, 381–394.

Pilowsky, I. (1993). Aspects of abnormal illness behaviour. *Psychotherapy and Psychosomatics, 60*, 62–74.

Pine, D. S. (2000). Anxiety disorders: Clinical features. In B. J. Sadock & V. A. Sadock (Eds.), *Kaplan and Sadock's comprehensive textbook of psychiatry* (7th ed., Vol. 1, pp. 1476–1489). Philadelphia: Lippincott/Williams & Wilkins.

Pine, D. S., & McClure, E. B. (2005). Anxiety disorders: Genetics. In B. J. Sadock & V. A. Sadock (Eds.), *Kaplan & Sadock's comprehensive textbook of psychiatry*. Philadelphia: Lippincott Williams & Wilkins.

Pines, A. M. (2004). Adult attachment styles and their relationship to burnout: A preliminary, cross-cultural investigation. *Work & Stress, 18*(1), 66–80.

Pink, D. H. (2005). *A whole new mind: Why right-brainers will rule the future*. New York: Penguin.

Pinquart, M., Duberstein, P. R., & Lyness, J. M. (2006). Treatments for later-life depressive conditions: A meta-analytic comparison of pharmacotherapy and psychotherapy. *American Journal of Psychiatry, 163,* 1493–1501.

Pinyerd, B., & Zipf, W. B. (2005). Puberty—Timing is everything! *Journal of Pediatric Nursing, 20,* 75–82.

Pirog, R. & Benjamin, A. (2003). *Checking the food odometer: Comparing food miles for local versus conventional produce sales to Iowa institutions.* Leopold Center for Sustainable Agriculture, Iowa State University.

Pittman, F., III. (1994, January/February). A buyer's guide to psychotherapy. *Psychology Today,* 50–53, 74–81.

Pizzagalli, D., Shackman, A. J., & Davidson, R. J. (2003). The functional neuroimaging of human emotion: Asymmetric contributions of cortical and subcortical circuitry. In K. Hugdahl & R. J. Davidson (Eds.), *The asymmetrical brain.* Cambridge, MA: MIT Press.

Plante, T. G. (1999a). *Contemporary clinical psychology.* New York: Wiley.

Plante, T. G. (1999b). Could the perception of fitness account for many of the mental and physical health benefits of exercise? *Advances in Mind-Body Medicine, 15,* 291–295.

Plante, T. G., Caputo, D., & Chizmar, L. (2000). Perceived fitness and responses to laboratory-induced stress. *International Journal of Stress Management, 7*(1), 61–73.

Pliner, P., & Mann, N. (2004). Influence of social norms and palatability on amount consumed and food choice. *Appetite, 42,* 227–237.

Plomin, R. (1993). Nature and nurture: Perspective and prospective. In R. Plomin & G. E. McClearn (Eds.), *Nature, nurture and psychology.* Washington, DC: American Psychological Association.

Plomin, R. (1994). Nature, nurture, and development. In R. J. Sternberg (Ed.), *Encyclopedia of human intelligence.* New York: Macmillan.

Plomin, R. (2003). General cognitive ability. In R. Plomin & J. C. DeFries (Eds.), *Behavioral genetics in the postgenomic era.* Washinton, DC: American Psychological Association.

Plomin, R. (2004). Genetics and developmental psychology. *Merrill-Palmer Quarterly, 50,* 341–352.

Plomin, R., DeFries, J. C., McClearn, G. E., & McGuffin, P. (2001). *Behavioral genetics.* New York: Freeman.

Plomin, R., DeFries, J. C., McClearn, G. E., & McGuffin, P. (2008). *Behavioral genetics.* New York: Worth.

Plomin, R., & Spinath, F. M. (2004). Intelligence: Genetics, genes, and genomics. *Journal of Personality & Social Psychology, 86,* 112–129.

Plotkin, H. (1998). *Evolution in mind: An introduction to evolutionary psychology.* Cambridge, MA: Harvard University Press.

Plotkin, H. (2004). *Evolutionary thought in psychology: A brief history.* Malden, MA: Blackwell Publishing.

Plucker, J. A., & Renzulli, J. S. (1999). Psychometric approaches to the study of human creativity. In R. J. Sternberg (Ed.), *Handbook of creativity.* New York: Cambridge University Press.

Plutchik, R. (1984). Emotions: A general psychoevolutionary theory. In K. R. Scherer & P. Ekman (Eds.), *Approaches to emotion.* Hillsdale, NJ: Erlbaum.

Plutchik, R. (1993). Emotions and their vicissitudes: Emotions and psychopathology. In M. Lewis & J. M. Haviland (Eds.), *Handbook of emotions.* New York: Guilford.

Poldrack, R. A., & Willingham, D. T. (2006). Functional neuroimaging of skill learning. In R. Cabeza & A. Kingstone (Eds.), *Handbook of functional neuroimaging of cognition.* Cambridge, MA: MIT Press.

Polger, T. (2007). Rethinking the evolution of consciousness. In M. Velmans & S. Schneider (Eds.), *The Blackwell companion to consciousness.* Malden, MA: Blackwell Publishing.

Policastro, E., & Gardner, H. (1999). From case studies to robust generalizations: An approach to the study of creativity. In R. J. Sternberg (Ed.), *Handbook of creativity.* New York: Cambridge University Press.

Pollak, L. (2007). *Getting from college to career: 90 things to do before you join the real world.* New York: Collins Business.

Pomerantz, E. M., Ng, F. F. Y., & Wang, Q. (2004). Gender socialization: A parent X child model. In A. H. Eagly, A. E. Beall, & R. J. Sternberg (Eds.), *The psychology of gender.* New York: Guilford.

Pomeroy, C., & Mitchell, J. E. (2002). Medical complications of anorexia nervosa and bulimia nervosa. In C. G. Fairburn & K. D. Brownell (Eds.), *Eating disorders and obesity: A comprehensive handbook.* New York: Guilford.

Ponterotto, J. G., & Pedersen, P. B. (1993). *Preventing prejudice: A guide for counselors and educators.* Newbury Park, CA: Sage.

Pope, K. S., Keith-Spiegel, P., & Tabachnick, B. G. (1986). Sexual attraction to clients. *American Psychologist, 41,* 147–158.

Popenoe, D. (1996). *Life without father.* New York: Pressler Press.

Pornpitakpan, C. (2004). The persuasiveness of source credibility: A critical review of five decades' evidence. *Journal of Applied Social Psychology, 34,* 243–281.

Porter, S., Yuille, J. C., & Lehman, D. R. (1999). The nature of real, implanted, and fabricated memories for emotional childhood events: Implications for the recovered memory debate. *Law and Human Behavior, 23,* 517–537.

Posada, G., Kaloustian, G., Richmond, K., & Moreno, A. J. (2007). Maternal secure base support and preschoolers' secure base behavior in natural environments. *Attachment & Human Development, 9,* 393–411.

Post, F. (1996). Verbal creativity, depression and alcoholism: An investigation of one hundred American and British writers. *British Journal of Psychiatry, 168,* 545–555.

Postman, L. (1985). Human learning and memory. In G. A. Kimble & K. Schlesinger (Eds.), *Topics in the history of psychology.* Hillsdale, NJ: Erlbaum.

Potenza, M. N. (2006). Should addictive disorders include non-substance-related conditions? *Addiction, 101*(Suppl 1), 142–151.

Potthoff, J. G., Holahan, C. J., & Joiner, T. E., Jr. (1995). Reassurance-seeking, stress generation, and depressive symptoms: An integrative model. *Journal of Personality and Social Psychology, 68,* 664–670.

Poulin-Dubois, D., & Graham, S. A. (2007). Cognitive processes in early word learning. In E. Hoff & M. Shatz (Eds.), *Blackwell handbook of language development.* Malden, MA: Blackwell.

Powell, L. H., & Williams, K. (2007). Hostility. In G. Fink (Ed.), *Encyclopedia of stress.* San Diego: Elsevier.

Powell, R. A., & Boer, D. P. (1995). Did Freud misinterpret reported memories of sexual abuse as fantasies? *Psychological Reports, 77,* 563–570.

Powell, R. A., & Gee, T. L. (1999). The effects of hypnosis on dissociative identity disorder: A re-examination of the evidence. *Canadian Journal of Psychiatry, 44,* 914–916.

Pratt, L. A., Ford, D. E., Crum, R. M., Armenian, H. K., Gallo, J. J., & Eaton, W. W. (1996). Depression, psychotropic medication, and risk of myocardial infarction: Prospective data from Baltimore ECA follow-up. *Archives of Internal Medicine, 94,* 3123–3129.

Pressman, S. D., & Cohen, S. (2005). Does positive affect influence health? *Psychological Bulletin, 131,* 925–971.

Pressman, S. D., Cohen, S., Miller, G. E., Barkin, A., Rabin, B. S., & Treanor, J. J. (2005). Loneliness, social network size, and immune response to influenza vaccination in college freshman. *Health Psychology, 24,* 297–306.

Priester, J. R., & Petty, R. E. (1995). Source attributions and persuasion; Perceived honesty as a determinant of message scrutiny. *Personality and Social Psychology Bulletin, 21,* 637–654.

Priester, J. R., & Petty, R. E. (2001). Extending the bases of subjective attitudinal ambivalence: Interpersonal and intrapersonal antecedents of evaluative tension. *Journal of Personality and Social Psychology, 80,* 19–34.

Priester, J. R., & Petty, R. E. (2003). The influence of spokesperson trustworthiness on message elaboration, attitude strength, and advertising. *Journal of Consumer Psychology, 13,* 408–421.

Prifitera, A. (1994). Wechsler scales of intelligence. In R. J. Sternberg (Ed.), *Encyclopedia of human intelligence.* New York: Macmillan.

Prochaska, J. O. (1994). Strong and weak principles for progressing from precontemplation to action on the basis of twelve problem behaviors. *Health Psychology, 13,* 47–51.

Prochaska, J. O., Velicer, W. F., Prochaska, J. M., & Johnson, J. L. (2004). Size, consistency, and stability of stage effects for smoking cessation. *Addictive Behaviors, 29,* 207–213.

Proffitt, D. R. (2006a). Distance perception. *Current Directions in Psychological Science, 15,* 131–135.

Proffitt, D. R. (2006b). Embodied perception and the economy of action. *Perspectives on Psychological Science, 1,* 110–122.

Proffitt, D. R., & Caudek, C. (2003). Depth perception and the perception of events. In A. F. Healy & R. W. Proctor (Eds.), *Handbook of psychology, Vol. 4: Experimental psychology.* New York: Wiley.

Proffitt, D. R., Stefanucci, J., Banton, T., & Epstein, W. (2003). The role of effort in perceiving distance. *Psychological Science, 14,* 106–112.

Prolo, P., & Chiappelli, F. (2007). Immune suppression. In G. Fink (Ed.), *Encyclopedia of stress.* San Diego: Elsevier.

Prudic, J. (2005). Electroconvulsive therapy. In B. J. Sadock & V. A. Sadock (Eds.), *Kaplan and Sadock's comprehensive textbook of psychiatry.* Philadelphia: Lippincott Williams & Wilkins.

Prudic, J., & Sackeim, H. A. (1999). Electroconvulsive therapy and suicide risk. *Journal of Clinical Psychiatry, 60,* 104–110.

Pruitt, D. G. (1971). Choice shifts in group discussion: An introductory review. *Journal of Personality and Social Psychology, 20,* 339–360.

Pyle, R. M. (1993). *The thunder tree: Lessons from an urban wildland.* Boston: Houghton Mifflin.

Pyle, R. M. (2002). Eden in a vacant lot: Special places, species and kids in the neighborhood of life. In P. H. Kahn Jr. & S. R. Kellert (Eds.), *Children and* nature: *Psychological, sociocultural, and evolutionary investigations*, (pp. 305–327). Cambridge MA: MIT Press.

Pyszczynski, T., Greenberg, J., & Solomon, S. (1999). A dual-process model of defense against conscious and unconscious death-related thoughts: An extension of terror management theory. *Psychological Review, 106,* 835–845.

Pyszczynski, T., Greenberg, J., Solomon, S., Arndt, J., & Schimel, J. (2004). Why do people need self-esteem? A theoretical and empirical review. *Psychological Bulletin, 130,* 435–468.

Pyszczynski, T., Solomon, S., & Greenberg, J. (2003). *In the wake of 9/11: The psychology of terror.* Washington, DC: American Psychological Association.

Quinn, K. A., Macrae, C. N., & Bodenhausen, G. V. (2003). Stereotyping and impression formation: How categorical thinking shapes person perception. In M. A. Hogg & J. Cooper (Eds.), *The Sage handbook of social psychology.* Thousand Oaks, CA: Sage.

Quiroga, R. Q., Reddy, L., Kreiman, G., Koch, C., & Fried, I. (2005). Invariant visual representation by single neurons in the human brain. *Nature, 435,* 1102–1107.

Quitkin, F. M. (1999). Placebos, drug effects, and study design: A clinician's guide. *American Journal of Psychiatry, 156,* 829–836.

Rachman, S. J. (1992). Behavior therapy. In L. R. Squire (Ed.), *Encyclopedia of learning and memory.* New York: Macmillan.

Raichle, M. E. (2006). Functional neuroimaging: A historical and physiological perspective. In R. Cabeza & A. Kingstone (Eds.), *Handbook of functional neuroimaging of cognition.* Cambridge, MA: MIT Press.

Rains, G. D. (2002). *Principles of human neuropsychology.* New York: McGraw-Hill.

Raj, A., & Sheehan, D. (2004). Benzodiazepines. In A. F. Schatzberg & C. B. Nemeroff (Eds.), *Textbook of psychopharmacology.* Washington, DC: American Psychiatric Publishing.

Rakic, P., Bourgeois, J. P., & Goldman-Rakic, P. S. (1994). Synaptic development of the cerebral cortex: Implications for learning, memory, and mental illness. *Progress in brain research, 102,* 227–243.

Rama, A. N., Cho, S. C., & Kushida, C. A. (2006). Normal human sleep. In T. Lee-Chiong (Ed.), *Sleep: A comprehensive handbook.* Hoboken, NJ: Wiley-Liss.

Ramadan, N. M. (2000). Migraine. In G. Fink (Ed.), *Encyclopedia of stress.* San Diego: Academic Press.

Ramaekers, J. G., Berghaus, G., van Laar, M., & Drummer, O. H. (2004). Dose related risk of motor vehicle crashes after cannabis use. *Drug and Alcohol Dependence, 73,* 109–119.

Ramey, C. T., & Ramey, S. L. (2004). Early educational interventions and intelligence. In E. Zigler & S. J. Styfco (Eds..), *The Head Start debate.* Baltimore: Paul H. Brookes Publishing.

Ramey, S. L. (1999). Head Start and preschool education: Toward continued improvement. *American Psychologist, 54,* 344–346.

Ramsay, D. S., Seeley, R. J., Bolles, R. C., & Woods, S. C. (1996). Ingestive homeostasis: The primacy of learning. In E. D. Capaldi (Ed.), *Why we eat what we eat: The psychology of eating* (pp. 11–29). Washington, DC: American Psychological Association.

Ranson, K. E., & Urichuk, L. J. (2008). The effect of parent-child attachment relationships on child biopsychosocial outcomes: A review. *Early Child Development and Care, 178,* 129–152.

Rauscher, F. H., Shaw, G. L., & Ky, K. N. (1993). Music and spatial task performance. *Nature, 365,* 611.

Rauscher, F. H., Shaw, G. L., & Ky, K. N. (1995). Listening to Mozart enhances spatial-temporal reasoning: Towards a neurophysiological basis. *Neuroscience Letters, 185,* 44–47.

Ray, W. J., & Oathes, D. (2003). Brain imaging techniques. *International Journal of Clinical and Experimental Hypnosis, 51,* 97–104.

Raynor, H. A., & Epstein, L. H. (2001). Dietary variety, energy regulation, and obesity. *Psychological Bulletin, 127,* 325–341.

Raynor, H. A., Niemeier, H. M., & Wing, R. R. (2006). Effect of limiting snack food variety on long-term sensory-specific satiety monotony during obesity treatment. *Eating Disorders, 7,* 1–14.

Raynor, J. O., & Entin, E. E. (1982). Future orientation and achievement motivation. In J. O. Raynor & E. E. Entin (Eds.), *Motivation, career striving, and aging.* New York: Hemisphere.

Read, C. R. (1991). Achievement and career choices: Comparisons of males and females. *Roeper Review, 13,* 188–193.

Reber, R. (2004). Availability. In F. P. Rudiger (Ed.), *Cognitive illusions.* New York: Psychology Press.

Recanzone, G. H. (2000). Cerebral cortical plasticity: Perception and skill acquisition. In M. S. Gazzaniga (Ed.), *The new cognitive neurosciences.* Cambridge, MA: The MIT Press.

Recht, L. D., Lew, R. A., & Schwartz, W. J. (1995). Baseball teams beaten by jet lag. *Nature, 377,* 583.

Rechtschaffen, A. (1994). Sleep onset: Conceptual issues. In R. D. Ogilvie & J. R. Harsh (Eds.), *Sleep onset: Normal and abnormal processes.* Washington, DC: American Psychological Association.

Reed, J. G., & Baxter P. M. (2003). *Library use: A handbook for psychology.* Washington, DC: American Psychological Association.

Rees, C. J., & Metcalfe, B. (2003). The faking of personality questionnaire results: Who's kidding whom? *Journal of Managerial Psychology, 18*(2), 156–165.

Reeve, C. L., & Hakel, M. D. (2002). Asking the right questions about *g. Human Performance, 15,* 47–74.

Refinetti, R. (2006). *Circadian physiology.* Boca Raton, FL: Taylor & Francis.

Regan, P. C. (1998). What if you can't get what you want? Willingness to compromise ideal mate selection standards as a function of sex, mate value, and relationship context. *Personality and Social Psychology Bulletin, 24,* 1294–1303.

Regan, P. C. (2003). *The mating game: A primer on love, sex, and marriage.* Thousand Oaks, CA: Sage.

Regan, T. (1997). The rights of humans and other animals. *Ethics & Behavior, 7*(2), 103–111.

Regier, D. A., & Burke, J. D. (2000). Epidemiology. In B. J. Sadock & V. A. Sadock (Eds.), *Kaplan and Sadock's comprehensive textbook of psychiatry.* Philadelphia: Lippincott/Williams & Wilkins.

Rehm, L. P., Wagner, A., & Ivens-Tyndal, Co. (2001). Mood disorders: Unipolar and bipolar. In P. B. Sutker & H. E. Adams (Eds.), *Comprehensive handbook of psychopathology* (pp. 277–308). New York: Kluwer Academic/Plenum.

Reibel, D. K., Greeson, J. M., Brainard, G. C., & Rosenzweig, S. (2001). Mindfulness-based stress reduction and health-related quality of life in a heterogeneous patient population. *General Hospital Psychiatry, 23*(4), 183–192.

Reichert, T. (2003). The prevalence of sexual imagery in ads targeted to young adults. *Journal of Consumer Affairs, 37,* 403–412.

Reichert, T., & Lambiase, J. (2003). How to get "kissably close": Examining how advertisers appeal to consumers' sexual needs and desires. *Sexuality & Culture: An Interdisciplinary Quarterly, 7*(3), 120–136.

Reichert, T., Heckler, S. E., & Jackson, S. (2001). The effects of sexual social marketing appeals on cognitive processing and persuasion. *Journal of Advertising, 30*(1), 13–27.

Reimer, T., Mata, R., & Stoecklin, M. (2004). The use of heuristics in persuasion: Deriving cues on source expertise from argument quality. *Current Research in Social Psychology, 10*(6).

Reinharz, D., Lesage, A. D., & Contandriopoulos, A. P. (2000). Cost-effectiveness analysis of psychiatric deinstitutionalization. *Canadian Journal of Psychiatry, 45,* 533–538.

Reips, U.-D. (2007). The methodology of Internet-based experiments. In A. N. Joinson, K. Y. A. McKenna, T. Postmes, & U-D. Reips (Eds.), *The Oxford handbook of Internet psychology.* New York: Oxford University Press.

Reis, H. T., & Aron, A. (2008). Love: What is it, why does it matter, and how does it operate? *Perspectives on Psychological Science, 3,* 80–86.

Reisner, A. D. (1998). Repressed memories: True and false. In R. A. Baker (Ed.), *Child sexual abuse and false memory syndrome.* Amherst, NY: Prometheus Books.

Reiss, S. (1991). Expectancy model of fear, anxiety and panic. *Clinical Psychology Review, 11,* 141–154.

Repetto, M., & Gold, M. S. (2005). Cocaine and crack: Neurobiology. In J. H. Lowinson, P. Ruiz, R. B. Millman, & J. G. Langrod (Eds.), *Substance abuse: A comprehensive textbook.* Philadelphia: Lippincott/Williams & Wilkins.

Rescorla, R. A. (1978). Some implications of a cognitive perspective on Pavlovian conditioning. In S. H. Hulse, H. Fowler, & W. K. Honig (Eds.), *Cognitive processes in animal behavior.* Hillsdale, NJ: Erlbaum.

Rescorla, R. A. (1980). *Pavlovian second-order conditioning.* Hillsdale, NJ: Erlbaum.

Rescorla, R. A., & Wagner, A. R. (1972). A theory of Pavlovian conditioning: Variations in the effectiveness of reinforcement and nonreinforcement. In A. H. Black & W. F. Prokasky (Eds.), *Classical conditioning: II. Current research and theory.* New York: Appleton-Century-Crofts.

Rest, J. R. (1986). *Moral development: Advances in research and theory.* New York: Praeger.

Reuter-Lorenz, P. A., & Miller, A. C. (1998). The cognitive neuroscience of human laterality: Lessons from the bisected brain. *Current Directions in Psychological Science, 7,* 15–20.

Reynolds, A. J., Temple, J. T., Robertson, D. L., & Mann, E. A. (2001). Long-term effects of an early childhood intervention on educational achievement and juvenile arrest: A 15-year follow-up of low-income children in public schools. *Journal of the American Medical Association, 285,* 2339–2346.

Rhodes, G., Simmons, L. W., & Peters, M. (2005). Attractiveness and sexual behavior: Does attractiveness enhance mating success? *Evolution and Human Behavior, 26,* 186–201.

Richardson, C. R., Kriska, A. M., Lantz, P. M., & Hayword, R. A. (2004). Physical activity and mortality across cardiovascular disease risk groups. *Medicine and Science in Sports and Exercise, 36,* 1923–1929.

Richardson, G. S. (1993). Circadian rhythms. In M. A. Carskadon (Ed.), *Encyclopedia of sleep and dreaming.* New York: Macmillan.

Richardson, G. S. (2006). Shift work sleep disorder. In T. Lee-Chiong (Ed.), *Sleep: A comprehensive handbook.* Hoboken, NJ: Wiley-Liss.

Richardson, J., Anderson, T., Flaherty, J., & Bell, C. (2003). The quality of mental health care for African Americans. *Culture, Medicine and Psychiatry, 27,* 487–498.

Ridker, P. M., Cannon, C. P., Morrow, D., Rifai, N., Rose, L. M., McCabe, C. H., Pfeffer, M. A., & Braunwald, E. (2005). C-reactive protein levels and outcomes after statin therapy. *New England Journal of Medicine, 6*(352), 20–28.

Rieber, R. W. (1998). The assimilation of psychoanalysis in America: From popularization to vulgarization. In R. W. Rieber & K. D. Salzinger (Eds.), *Psychology: Theoretical-historical perspectives.* Washington, DC: American Psychological Association.

Rieskamp, J., & Hoffrage, U. (1999). When do people use simple heuristics, and how can we tell? In G. Gigerenzer, P. M. Todd, & ABC Research Group (Eds.), *Simple heuristics that make us smart* (pp. 141–168). New York: Oxford University Press.

Riggio, H. R., & Halpern, D. F. (2006). Understanding human thought: Educating students as critical thinkers. In W. Buskist & S. F. Davis (Eds.), *Handbook of the teaching of psychology.* Malden, MA: Blackwell Publishing.

Rihmer, Z. (2003). Do SSRI's increase the risk of suicide among depressives even if they are only taking placebo? *Psychotherapy & Psychosomatics, 72,* 357–358.

Rihmer, Z., & Angst, J. (2005). Mood disorders: Epidemiology. In B. J. Sadock & V. A. Sadock (Eds.), *Kaplan & Sadock's comprehensive textbook of psychiatry.* Philadelphia: Lippincott Williams & Wilkins.

Riis, J., Loewenstein, G., Baron, J., Jepson, C., Fagerlin, A., & Ubel, P. A. (2005). Ignorance of hedonic adaptation to hemodialysis: A study using ecological momentary assessment. *Journal of Experimental Psychology: General, 134*(1), 3–9.

Riley, B. P., & Kendler, K. S. (2005). Schizophrenia: Genetics. In B. J. Sadock & V. A. Sadock (Eds.), *Kaplan & Sadock's comprehensive textbook of psychiatry.* Philadelphia: Lippincott Williams & Wilkins.

Rilling, M. (1996). The mystery of the vanished citations: James McConnell's forgotten 1960s quest for planarian learning, a biochemical engram, and celebrity. *American Psychologist, 51,* 589–598.

Rilling, M. (2000a). How the challenge of explaining learning influenced the origins and development of John B. Watson's behaviorism. *American Journal of Psychology, 113,* 275–301.

Rilling, M. (2000b). John Watson's paradoxical struggle to explain Freud. *American Psychologist, 55,* 301–312.

Rimal R. N. (2001). Longitudinal influences of knowledge and self-efficacy on exercise behavior: Tests of a mutual reinforcement model. *Journal of Health Psychology, 6,* 31–46.

Rippe, J. M., Angelopoulous, T. J., & Zukley, L. (2007). The rationale for intervention to reduce the risk of coronary heart disease. *American Journal of Lifestyle Medicine, 1,* 10–19.

Risen, J., & Gilovich, T. (2007). Informal logical fallacies. In R. J. Sternberg, H. L. Roediger III, & D. F. Halpern (Eds.), *Critical thinking in psychology.* New York: Cambridge University Press.

Riskind, J. H. (2005). Cognitive mechanisms in generalized anxiety disorder: A second generation of theoretical perspectives. *Cognitive Therapy & Research, 29*(1), 1–5.

Ritter, R. C. (2004). Gastrointestinal mechanisms of satiation for food. *Physiology & Behavior, 81,* 249–273.

Rizzolatti, G. (2005). The mirror neuron system and imitation. In S. Hurley, & N. Chater (Eds.), *Perspectives on imitation: From neuroscience to social science: Vol. 1. Mechanisms of imitation and imitation in animals.* Cambridge, MA: MIT Press.

Rizzolatti, G., & Craighero, L. (2004). The mirror-neuron system. *Annual Review of Neuroscience, 27,* 169–192.

Roberts, B. W., Caspi, A., & Moffitt, T. (2003). Work experiences and personality development in young adulthood. *Journal of Personality and Social Psychology, 84,* 582–593.

Roberts, B. W., & DelVecchio, W. F. (2000). The rank-order consistency of personality traits from childhood to old age: A quantitative review of longitudinal studies. *Psychological Bulletin, 126,* 3–25.

Roberts, B. W., Kuncel, N. R., Shiner, R., Caspi, A., & Goldberg, L. R. (2007). The power of personality: The comparative validity of personality traits, socioeconomic status, and cognitive ability for predicting important life outcomes. *Perspectives on Psychological Science, 2,* 313–345.

Roberts, B. W., & Mroczek, D. (2008). Personality trait change in adulthood. *Current Directions in Psychological Science, 17,* 31–35.

Roberts, B. W., & Pomerantz, E. M. (2004). On traits, situations, and their integration: A developmental perspective. *Personality and Social Psychology Review, 8,* 402–416.

Roberts, B. W., Walton, K. E., & Bogg, T. (2005). Conscientiousness and health across the life course. *Review of General Psychology, 9*(2), 156–168.

Roberts, B. W., Walton, K., & Viechtbauer, W. (2006). Patterns of mean-level change in personality traits across the life course: A meta-analysis of longitudinal studies. *Psychological Bulletin, 132,* 1–25.

Roberts, B. W., & Wood, D. (2006). Personality development in the context of the Neo-socioanalytic model of personality. In D. Mroczek & T. Little (Eds.), *Handbook of personality development.* Mahwah, NJ: Erlbaum.

Roberts, D. F., Foehr, U. G., & Rideout, V. (2005). Generation M: Media in the lives of 8–18 year olds (Publication No. 7251). Menlo Park, CA: Henry J. Kaiser Family Foundation.

Roberts, J. E., & Ciesla, J. A. (2007). Stress generation. In G. Fink (Ed.), *Encyclopedia of stress.* San Diego: Elsevier.

Robertson, S. I. (2001). *Problem solving.* East Sussex, England: Psychology Press.

Robiner, W. N., Bearman, D. L., Berman, M., Grove, W. M., Colon, E., Armstrong, J., Mareck, S., & Tanenbaum, R. L. (2003). Prescriptive authority for psychologists: Despite deficits in education and knowledge. *Journal of Clinical Psychology in Medical Settings, 10*(3), 211–212.

Robins, R. W., Gosling, S. D., & Craik, K. H. (1999). An empirical analysis of trends in psychology. *American Psychologist, 54,* 117–128.

Robinson, D. G., Woerner, M. G., McMeniman, M., Mendelowitz, A., & Bilder, R. M. (2004). Symptomatic and functional recovery from a first episode of schizophrenia or schizoaffective disorder. *American Journal of Psychiatry, 161,* 473–479.

Robles, T. F., Glaser, R., & Kiecolt-Glaser, J. K. (2005). Out of balance: A new look at chronic stress, depression, and immunity. *Current Directions in Psychological Science, 14,* 111–115.

Rockey, D. L., Jr., Beason, K. R., Howington, E. B., Rockey, C. M., & Gilbert, J. D. (2005). Gambling by Greek-affiliated college students: An association between affiliation and gambling. *Journal of College Student Development, 46,* 75-87.

Rodgers, J. E. (1982). The malleable memory of eyewitnesses. *Science Digest, 3,* 32–35.

Rodieck, R. W. (1998). *The first steps in seeing.* Sunderland, MA: Sinauer.

Rodin, J. (1985). Insulin levels, hunger, and food intake: An example of feedback loops in body weight regulation. *Health Psychology, 4,* 1–24.

Roediger, H. L., III. (1980). Memory metaphors in cognitive psychology. *Memory & Cognition, 8,* 231–246.

Roediger, H. L., III, Gallo, D. A., & Geraci, L. (2002). Processing approaches to cognition: The impetus from the levels-of-processing framework. *Memory, 10,* 319–332.

Roediger, H. L., III, & Karpicke, J. D. (2006a). Test-enhanced learning: Taking memory tests improves long-term retention. *Psychological Science, 17,* 249–255.

Roediger, H. L., III, & Karpicke, J. D. (2006b). The power of testing memory: Basic research and implications for educational practice. *Perspectives on Psychological Science, 1*(3), 181–210.

Roediger, H. L., III, & McDermott, K. B. (1995). Creating false memories: Remembering words not presented in lists. *Journal of Experimental Psychology: Learning, Memory, and Cognition, 21,* 803–814.

Roediger, H. L., III, & McDermott, K. B. (2000). Tricks of memory. *Current Directions in Psychological Science, 9,* 123–127.

Roediger, H. L., III, Wheeler, M. A., & Rajaram, S. (1993). Remembering, knowing, and reconstructing the past. In D. L. Medin (Ed.), *The psychology of learning and motivation: Advances in research and theory.* San Diego: Academic Press.

Roehrs, T., Carskadon, M. A., Dement, W. C., & Roth, T. (2005). Daytime sleepiness and alertness. In M. H. Kryger, T. Roth, & W. C. Dement (Eds.). *Principles and practice of sleep medicine.* Philadelphia: Elsevier Saunders.

Roehrs, T., & Roth, T. (2000). Hypnotics: Efficacy and adverse effects. In M. H. Kryger, T. Roth, & W. C. Dement (Eds.), *Principles and practice of sleep medicine.* Philadelphia: Saunders.

Roehrs, T., & Roth, T. (2004). "Hypnotic" prescription patterns in a large managed-care population. *Sleep Medicine, 5,* 463–466.

Roffwarg, H. P., Muzio, J. N., & Dement, W. C. (1966). Ontogenetic development of the human sleep-dream cycle. *Science, 152,* 604–619.

Rogers, C. R. (1951). *Client-centered therapy: Its current practice, implications, and theory.* Boston: Houghton Mifflin.

Rogers, C. R. (1961). *On becoming a person: A therapist's view of psychotherapy.* Boston: Houghton Mifflin.

Rogers, C. R. (1980). *A way of being.* Boston: Houghton Mifflin.

Rogers, C. R. (1986). Client-centered therapy. In I. L. Kutash & A. Wolf (Eds.), *Psychotherapist's casebook.* San Francisco: Jossey-Bass.

Rogers, N. L., & Dinges, D. F. (2002). Shiftwork, circadian disruption, and consequences. *Primary Psychiatry, 9*(8), 50.

Rogers, W. T., & Yang, P. (1996). Test-wiseness: Its nature and application. *European Journal of Psychological Assessment, 12,* 247–259.

Rogoff, B. (1990). *Apprenticeship in thinking.* New York: Oxford University Press.

Rogoff, B. (1998). Cognition as a collaborative process. In D. Kuhn & R. S. Siegler (Eds.), *Handbook of child psychology, Vol. 2: Cognition perception, and language.* New York: Wiley.

Rogoff, B. (2003). *The cultural nature of human development.* New York: Oxford University Press.

Rohner, R. P., & Veneziano, R. A. (2001). The importance of father love: History and contemporary evidence. *Review of General Psychology, 5,* 382–405.

Rohrer, D., & Taylor, K. (2006). The effects of overlearning and distributed practice on the retention of mathematics knowledge. *Applied Cognitive Psychology, 20,* 1209–1224.

Rohrer, D., Taylor, K., Pashler, H., Wixted, J. T., & Capeda, N. J. (2005). The effect of overlearning on long-term retention. *Applied Cognitive Psychology, 19,* 361–374.

Rolls, E. T. (1990). A theory of emotion, and its application to understanding the neural basis of emotion. *Cognition and Emotion, 4,* 161–190.

Rolls, E. T., & Tovee, M. T. (1995). Sparseness of the neuronal representation of stimuli in the primate temporal visual cortex. *Journal of Neurophysiology, 73,* 713–726.

Roney, J. R., Hanson, K. N., Durante, K. M., & Maestripieri, D. (2006). Reading men's faces: Women's mate attractiveness judgments track men's testosterone and interest in infants. *Proceedings of the Royal Society, 273,* 2169–2175.

Rose, D. P. (1997). Dietary fatty acids and cancer. *American Journal of Clinical Nutrition, 66,* 998S–1003S.

Rose, D., Wykes, T., Leese, M., Bindman, J., & Fleischmann, P. (2003). Patient's perspectives on electroconvulsive therapy: Systematic review. *British Medical Journal, 326,* 1363–1365.

Rose, H., & Rose, S. E. (2000). *Alas, poor Darwin: Arguments against evolutionary psychology.* New York: Harmony Books.

Rose, N. R. (2007). Neuroimmunomodulation. In G. Fink (Ed.), *Encyclopedia of stress.* San Diego: Elsevier.

Roseboom, T., de Rooij, S., & Painter, R. (2006). The Dutch famine and its long-term consequences for adult health. *Early Human Development, 82,* 485–491.

Rosenberg, E., & DeMaso, D. R. (2008). A doubtful guest: Managed care and mental health. *Child and Adolescent Psychiatric Clinics of North America, 17,* 53–66.

Rosenblatt, A., Greenberg, J., Solomon, S., Pyszczynski, T., & Lyon, D. (1989). Evidence for terror management theory: I. The effect of mortality salience on reactions to those who violate or uphold cultural values. *Journal of Personality and Social Psychology, 57,* 681–690.

Rosenheck, R. A. (2006). Outcomes, costs, and policy caution. *Archives of General Psychiatry, 63,* 1074–1076.

Rosenthal, H. (1988). *Not with my life I don't: Preventing suicide and that of others.* Muncie, IN: Accelerated Development.

Rosenthal, L. (2006). Physiologic processes during sleep. In T. Lee-Chiong (Ed.), *Sleep: A comprehensive handbook.* Hoboken, NJ: Wiley-Liss.

Rosenthal, R. (1976). *Experimenter effects in behavioral research.* New York: Halsted.

Rosenthal, R. (1994). Interpersonal expectancy effects: A 30–year perspective. *Current Directions in Psychological Science, 3,* 176–179.

Rosenthal, R. (2002). Experimenter and clinical effects in scientific inquiry and clinical practice. *Prevention & Treatment, 5*(38).

Rosenthal, R., & Fode, K. L. (1963). Three experiments in experimenter bias. *Psychological Reports, 12,* 491–511.

Rosenzweig, M. R., & Bennet, E. L. (1996). Psychobiology of plasticity: Effects of training and experience on brain and behavior. *Behavioural Brain Research, 78*(5), 57–65.

Rosenzweig, M. R., Krech, D., & Bennett, E. L. (1961). Heredity, environment, brain biochemistry, and learning. In *Current trends in psychological theory.* Pittsburgh: University of Pittsburgh Press.

Rosenzweig, M., Krech, D., Bennett, E. L., & Diamond, M. (1962). Effects of environmental complexity and training on brain chemistry and anatomy: A replication and extension. *Journal of Comparative and Physiological Psychology, 55,* 429–437.

Rosenzweig, S. (1985). Freud and experimental psychology: The emergence of idiodynamics. In S. Koch & D. E. Leary (Eds.), *A century of psychology as a science.* New York: McGraw-Hill.

Ross, B. (1991). William James: Spoiled child of American psychology. In G. A. Kimble, M. Wertheimer, & C. White (Eds.), *Portraits of pioneers in psychology.* Hillsdale, NJ: Erlbaum.

Roszak, T. (1992). *The voice of the earth: An exploration of eco-psychology.* New York: Simon & Schuster.

Roter, D. L., Hall, J. A., Merisca, R., Nordstrom, B., Cretin, D., & Svarstad, B. (1998). Effectiveness of interventions to promote patient compliance. *Medical Care, 36,* 1138–1161.

Rotter, J. B. (1982). *The development and application of social learning theory.* New York: Praeger.

Routh, D. K., & Reisman, J. M. (2003). Clinical psychology. In D. K. Freedheim (Ed.), *Handbook of psychology, Vol. 1: History of psychology.* New York: Wiley.

Rowatt, W. C., Cunningham, M. R., & Druen, P. B. (1999). Lying to get a date: The effect of facial physical attractiveness on the willingness to deceive prospective dating partners. *Journal of Social & Personal Relationships, 16,* 209–223.

Rowe, D. (1994). *The limits of family influence: Genes, experience, and behavior.* New York: Guilford.

Rowe, D., & van den Oord, E. J. C. G. (2005). Genetic and environmental influences. In V. A. Derlega, B. A. Winstead, & W. H. Jones (Eds.), *Personality: Contemporary theory and research.* Belmont, CA: Wadsworth.

Rowe, S. M., & Wertsch, J. V. (2002). Vygotsky's model of cognitive development. In U. Goswami (Ed.), *Blackwell handbook of childhood cognitive development.* Malden, MA: Blackwell Publishing.

Rozin, P. (1990). The importance of social factors in understanding the acquisition of food habits. In E. D. Capaldi & T. L. Powley (Eds.), *Taste, experience, and feeding.* Washington, DC: American Psychological Association.

Rozin, P. (2007). Food and eating. In S. Kitayama & D. Cohen (Eds.), *Handbook of cultural psychology.* New York: Guilford.

Rozin, P., Dow, S., Moscovitch, M., & Rajaram, S. (1998). What causes humans to begin and end a meal? A role for memory for what has been eaten, as evidenced by a study of multiple meal eating in amnesic patients. *Psychological Science, 9,* 392–396.

Rozin, P., Kabnick, K., Pete, E., Fischler, C., & Shields, C. (2003). The ecology of eating: Smaller portion sizes in France than in the United States help explain the French paradox. *Psychological Science, 14,* 450–454.

Ruble, D. N., & Martin, C. L. (1998). Gender development. In W. Damon (Ed.), *Handbook of child psychology (Vol. 3): Social, emotional, and personality development.* New York: Wiley.

Ruble, T. L. (1983). Sex stereotypes: Issues of change in the 70s. *Sex Roles, 9,* 397–402.

Rudorfer, M. V., Henry, M. E., & Sackheim, H. A. (2003). Electroconvulsive therapy. In A. Tasman, J. Kay, & J. A. Lieberman (Eds.), *Psychiatry.* New York: Wiley.

Ruini, C., & Fava, G. A. (2004). Clinical application of well-being therapy. In P. A. Linley & S. Joseph (Eds.), *Positive psychology in practice.* Hoboken, NJ: Wiley.

Ruiter, R. A., Abraham, C., & Kok, G. (2001). Scary warnings and rational precautions: A review of the psychology of fear appeals. *Psychology & Health, 16,* 613–630.

Rule, N. O., & Ambady, N. (2008). The face of success: Inferences from chief executive officers' appearance predict company profits. *Psychological Science, 19,* 109–111.

Runyan, W. M. (2006). Psychobiography and the psychology of science: Understanding relations between the life and work of individual psychologists. *Review of General Psychology, 10,,* 147–162.

Ruscio, J. (2002). *Clear thinking with psychology: Separating sense from nonsense.* Belmont, CA: Wadsworth.

Ruscio, J. (2006). *Clear thinking with psychology: Separating sense from nonsense.* Belmont, CA: Wadsworth.

Rush, A. J. (1984). Cognitive therapy. In T. B. Karasu (Ed.), *The psychiatric therapies.* Washington, DC: American Psychiatric Press.

Rushton, J. P. (2003). Race differences in *g* and the "Jensen effect." In H. Nyborg (Ed.), *The scientific study of general intelligence: Tribute to Arthur R. Jensen.* Oxford, UK: Pergamon.

Rushton, J. P., & Jensen, A. R. (2005). Thirty years of research on race differences in cognitive ability. *Psychology, Public Policy, and Law, 11,* 235–294.

Russell, G. F. M. (1997). The history of bulimia nervosa. In D. M. Garner & P. E. Garfinkel (Eds.), *Handbook of treatment for eating disorders.* New York: Guilford.

Russell, J. A. (1991). Culture and the categorization of emotions. *Psychological Bulletin, 110,* 426–450.

Russell, J. A. (2007). Stress milestones. *Stress: The International Journal on the Biology of Stress, 10*(1), 1–2.

Russo, N. F., & Denmark, F. L. (1987). Contributions of women to psychology. *Annual Review of Psychology, 38,* 279–298.

Rutherford, A. (2000). Radical behaviorism and psychology's public: B. F. Skinner in the popular press, 1934–1990. *History of Psychology, 3,* 371–395.

Rutherford, W. (1886). A new theory of hearing. *Journal of Anatomy and Physiology, 21,* 166–168.

Rutledge, T., Reis, S. E., Olson, M., Owens, J., Kelsey, S. F., Pepine, C. J., Mankad, S., Rogers, W. J., Merz, C. N. B., Sopko, G., Cornell, C. E., Sharaf, B., & Matthews, K. A. (2004). Social networks are associated with lower mortality rates among women with suspected coronary disease: The National Heart, Lung, and Blood Institute–sponsored women's ischemia syndrome evaluation study. *Psychosomatic Medicine, 66,* 882–888.

Rutter, M. (2006). *Genes and behavior: Nature-nurture interplay explained.* Malden, MA: Blackwell Publishing.

Rutter, M. (2007). Gene-environment interdependence. *Developmental Science, 10,* 12–18.

Ryckeley, R. (2005, May). Don't send in the clowns. *The Citizen.*

Ryder, R. D. (2006). Speciesism in the laboratory. In P. Singer (Ed.), *In defense of animals: The second wave.* Malden, MA: Blackwell Publishing.

Sachs, J. (1985). Prelinguistic development. In J. B. Gleason (Ed.), *The development of language.* Columbus: Charles E. Merrill.

Sack, A. T., Hubl, D., Prvulovic, D., Formisano, E., Jandl, M., Zanella, F. E., Maurer, K., Goebel, R., Dierks, T., & Linden, D. E. J. (2002). The experimental combination of r TMS and fMRI reveals the functional relevance of parietal cortex for visuospatial functions. *Cognitive Brain Resarch, 13,* 85–93.

Sackeim, H. A., Haskett, R. F., Mulsant, B. H., Thase, M. E., Mann, J. J., Pettinati, H. M., Greenberg, R. M., Crowe, R. R., Cooper, T. B., & Prudic, J. (2001). Continuation pharmacotherapy in the prevention of relapse following electroconvulsive therapy: A randomized controlled trial. *Journal of the American Medical Association, 285,* 1299–1307.

Sackeim, H. A., Prudic, J., Fuller, R., Keilp, J., Lavori, P. W., & Olfson, M. (2007). The cognitive effects of electroconvulsive therapy in community settings. *Neuropsychopharmacology, 32,* 244–254.

Sacks, O. (1987). *The man who mistook his wife for a hat.* New York: Harper & Row.

Sadker, M., & Sadker, D. (1994). *Failing at fairness: How America's schools cheat girls.* New York: Scribners.

Sadler, J. Z. (2005). *Values and psychiatric diagnosis.* New York: Oxford University Press.

Saks, A. M. (2006). Multiple predictions and criteria of job search success. *Journal of Vocational Behavior, 68,* 400–415.

Salkovskis, P. M., & Warwick, H. M. C. (2001). Meaning, misinterpretations, and medicine: A cognitive-behavioral approach to understanding health anxiety and hypochondriasis. In V. Starcevic & D. R. Lipsitt (Eds.), *Hypochondriasis: Modern perspectives on an ancient malady.* New York: Oxford University Press.

Salmon, P., Sephton, S., Weissbecker, I., Hoover, K., Ulmer, C., & Studts, J. L. (2004). Mindfulness mediation in clinical practice. *Cognitive and Behavioral Practice, 11,* 434–446.

Salthouse, T. A. (1996). The processing-speed theory of adult age differences in cognition. *Psychological Review, 103,* 403–428.

Salthouse, T. A. (2000). Aging and measures of processing speed. *Biological Psychology, 54,* 35–54.

Salthouse, T. A. (2003). Memory aging from 18–80. *Alzheimer Disease & Associated Disorders, 17*(3), 162–167.

Salthouse, T. A. (2004). What and when of cognitive aging. *Current Directions in Psychological Science, 13*(4), 140–144.

Salthouse, T. A. (2006). Mental exercise and mental aging. *Perspectives on Psychological Science, 1,* 68–87.

Salvendy, J. T. (1993). Selection and preparation of patients and organization of the group. In H. I.

Kaplan & B. J. Sadock (Eds.), *Comprehensive group psychotherapy.* Baltimore: Williams & Wilkins.

Samberg, E., & Marcus, E. R. (2005). Process, resistance, and interpretation. In E. S. Person, A. M. Cooper, & G. O. Gabbard (Eds.), *Textbook of psychoanalysis.* Washington, DC: American Psychiatric Publishing.

Sanchez, D. T., Kiefer, A. K., & Ybarra, O. (2006). Sexual submissiveness in women: Costs for sexual autonomy and arousal. *Personality and Social Psychology Bulletin, 32,* 512–524.

Sanchez, I. M., & Turner, S. M. (2003). Practicing psychology in the era of managed care: Implications for practice and training. *American Psychologist, 58*(2), 116–129.

Sanders, M. H., & Givelber, R. J. (2006). Overview of obstructive sleep apnea in adults. In T. Lee-Chiong (Ed.), *Sleep: A comprehensive handbook.* Hoboken, NJ: Wiley-Liss.

Sanderson, W. C., & Barlow, D. H. (1990). A description of patients diagnosed with DSM-III-R generalized anxiety disorder. *Journal of Nervous and Mental Disease, 178,* 588–591.

Sandin, B., Chorot, P., Santed, M. A., & Valiente, R. M. (2004). Differences in negative life events between patients with anxiety disorders, depression and hypochondriasis. *Anxiety, Stress & Coping: An International Journal, 17*(1), 37–47.

Sandoz, J. (2004). Internet addiction. *Annals of the American Psychotherapy Association, 7,* 34.

Sanger, D. J. (2004). The pharmacology and mechanisms of action of new generation, nonbenzodiazepine hypnotic agents. *CNS Drugs, 18*(Suppl1), 9–15.

Sanislow, C. A., & Carson, R. C. (2001). Schizophrenia: A critical examination. In P. B. Sutker & H. E. Adams (Eds.), *Comprehensive handbook of psychopathology* (3rd ed.). New York: Kluwer Academic/Plenum.

Sanna, L. J., & Schwarz, N. (2006). Metacognitive experiences and human judgment: The case of hindsight bias and its debiasing. *Current Directions in Psychological Science, 15,* 172–176.

Saper, C. B. (2000). Brain stem, reflexive behavior, and the cranial nerves. In E. R. Kandel, J. H. Schwartz, & T. M. Jessell (Eds.), *Principles of neural science* (pp. 873–888). New York: McGraw-Hill.

Sapolsky, R. M. (2007). Stress, stress-related disease, and emotion regulation. In J. J. Gross (Ed.), *Handbook of emotion regulation.* New York: Guilford.

Saunders, C. D. (2003). The emerging field of conservation psychology. *Human Ecology Review, 10,* 137–149.

Saunders, C. D., & Myers, O. E. (Eds.) (2003). Conservation psychology [Special issue]. *Human Ecology Review, 10*(2).

Savin-Williams, R. C. (2006). Who's gay? Does it matter? *Current Directions in Psychological Science, 15,* 40–44.

Saxe, L. (1994). Detection of deception: Polygraph and integrity tests. *Current Directions in Psychological Science, 3,* 69–73.

Saxe, L., & Ben-Shakhar, G. (1999). Admissibility of polygraph tests: The application of scientific standards post-Daubert. *Psychology, Public Policy, and Law, 5,* 203–223.

Sayer, L. C. (2005). Gender, time, and inequality: Trends in women's and men's paid work, unpaid work, and free time. *Social Forces, 84,* 285–303.

Sayers, S. L. (2004). Depression and heart disease: The interrelationship between these two common disorders is complex and requires careful diagnostic

and treatment methods. *Psychiatric Annals, 34*(4), 282–288.

Scarr, S., & Weinberg, R. A. (1977). Intellectual similarities within families of both adopted and biological children. *Intelligence, 32,* 170–190.

Scarr, S., & Weinberg, R. A. (1983). The Minnesota adoption studies: Genetic differences and malleability. *Child Development, 54,* 260–267.

Scattone, D. (2007). Social skills interventions for children with autism. *Psychology in the Schools, 44,* 717–726.

Schachner, D. A., & Shaver, P. R. (2004). Attachment dimensions and sexual motives. *Personal Relationships, 11*(2), 179–195.

Schachter, S. (1959). *The psychology of affiliation.* Stanford, CA: Stanford University Press.

Schachter, S. (1964). The interaction of cognitive and physiological determinants of emotional state. In L. Berkowitz (Ed.), *Advances in experimental social psychology* (Vol. 1). New York: Academic Press.

Schachter, S., & Singer, J. E. (1962). Cognitive, social and physiological determinants of emotional state. *Psychological Review, 69,* 379–399.

Schachter, S., & Singer, J. E. (1979). Comments on the Maslach and Marshall-Zimbardo experiments. *Journal of Personality and Social Psychology, 37,* 989–995.

Schacter, D. L. (1996). *Searching for memory: The brain, the mind, and the past.* New York: Basic Books.

Schacter, D. L. (1999). The seven sins of memory: Insights from psychology and cognitive neuroscience. *American Psychologist, 54,* 182–203.

Schacter, D. L. (2001). *The seven sins of memory: How the mind forgets and remembers.* Boston, MA: Houghton Mifflin.

Schaefer, A. (2005). Commuting takes its toll. *Scientific American Mind, 16*(3), 14–15.

Schaeffer, N. C. (2000). Asking questions about threatening topics: A selective overview. In A. A. Stone, J. S. Turkkan, C. A. Bachrach, J. B. Jobe, H. S. Kurtzman, & V. Cain (Eds.), *The science of self-report: Implications for research and practice.* Mahwah, NJ: Erlbaum.

Schafe, G. E., & Bernstein, I. E. (1996). Taste aversion learning. In E. D. Capaldi (Ed.), *Why we eat what we eat: The psychology of eating* (pp. 31–52). Washington, DC: American Psychological Association.

Schafe, G. E., & Ledoux, J. E. (2004). The neural basis of fear. In M. S. Gazzaniga (Ed.), *The cognitive neurosciences.* Cambridge, MA: MIT Press.

Schaie, K. W. (1990). Intellectual development in adulthood. In J. E. Birren & K. W. Schaie (Eds.), *Handbook of the psychology of aging* (3rd ed.). San Diego: Academic Press.

Schaie, K. W. (1994). The course of adult intellectual development. *American Psychologist, 49,* 304–313.

Schaie, K. W. (1996). *Adult intellectual development: The Seattle longitudinal study.* New York: Cambridge University Press.

Schaie, K. W. (2005). *Developmental influences on adult intelligence: The Seattle longitudinal study.* New York: Oxford University Press.

Scheier, M. F., & Carver, C. S. (1985). Optimism, coping and health: Assessment and implications of generalized expectancies. *Health Psychology, 4,* 219–247.

Schieber, F. (2006). Vision and aging. In J. E. Birren & K. W. Schaie (Eds.), *Handbook of the psychology of aging.* San Diego: Academic Press.

Schiff, M., & Lewontin, R. (1986). *Education and class: The irrelevance of IQ genetic studies*. Oxford: Clarendon Press.

Schiffman, J., Ekstrom, M., LaBrie, J., Schulsinger, F., Sorenson, H., & Mednick, S. (2002). Minor physical anomalies and schizophrenia spectrum disorders: A prospective investigation. *American Journal of Psychiatry, 159*, 238–243.

Schiffman, S. S., Graham, B. G., Sattely-Miller, E. A., & Warwick, Z. S. (1998). Orosensory perception of dietary fat. *Current Directions in Psychological Science, 7*, 137–143.

Schildkraut, J. J., Hirshfeld, A. J., & Murphy, J. M. (1994). Mind and mood in modern art, II: Depressive disorders, spirituality, and early deaths in the abstract expressionist artists of the New York School. *American Journal of Psychiatry, 151*, 482–488.

Schimel, J., Simon, L., Greenberg, J., Pyszczynski, T., Solomon, S., Waxmonsky, J., & Arndt, J. (1999). Stereotypes and terror management: Evidence that mortality salience enhances stereotypic thinking and preference. *Journal of Personality and Social Psychology, 77*, 905–926.

Schimmack, U., & Crites, S. L. (2005). The structure of affect. In D. Albarracin, B. T. Johnson, & M. P. Zanna (Eds.), *The handbook of attitudes* . Mahwah, NJ: Erlbaum.

Schmidt, F. L. (2002). The role of general cognitive ability and job performance: Why there cannot be a debate. *Human Performance, 15*, 187–210.

Schmidt, F. L., & Hunter, J. (2004). General mental ability in the world of work: Occupational attainment and job performance. *Journal of Personality and Social Psychology, 86*, 162–173.

Schmidt, N. B., Zvolensky, M. J., & Maner, J. K. (2006). Anxiety sensitivity: Prospective prediction of panic attacks and Axis I pathology. *Journal of Psychiatric Research, 40*, 691–699.

Schmithorst, V. J., Wilke, M., Dardzinski, B. J., & Holland, S. K. (2002). Correlation of white matter diffusivity and anisotropy with age during childhood and adolescence: A cross-sectional diffusion-tensor MR imaging study. *Radiology, 222*, 212–218.

Schmitt, D. P. (2005). Fundamentals of human mating strategies. In D. M. Buss (Ed.), *The handbook of evolutionary psychology*. New York: Wiley.

Schmitt, D. P., & International Sexuality Description Project. (2003). Universal sex differences in the desire for sexual variety: Tests from 52 nations, 6 continents, and 13 islands. *Journal of Personality and Social Psychology, 85*, 85–104.

Schmitt, M. T., & Maes, J. (2002). Stereotypic ingroup bias as self-defense against relative deprivation: Evidence from a longitudinal study of the German unification process. *European Journal of Social Psychology, 32*, 309–326.

Schmitz, J. M., & DeLaune, K. A. (2005). Nicotine. In J. H. Lowinson, P. Ruiz, R. B. Millman, & J. G. Langrod (Eds.), *Substance abuse: A comprehensive textbook*. Philadelphia: Lippincott/Williams & Williams.

Schmuck, P. & Schultz, P. W. (2002). Sustainable development as a challenge for psychology. In P. Schmuck & P. W. Schultz (Eds.), *Psychology of Sustainable Development* (pp. 3–17). Boston: Kluwer Academic Publishers.

Schneider, F., & Deldin, P. J. (2001). Genetics and schizophrenia. In P. B. Sutker & H. E. Adams (Eds.), *Comprehensive handbook of psychopathology* (3rd ed., pp. 371–402). New York: Kluwer Academic/Plenum.

Scholey, A. B., Parrott, A. C., Buchanan, T., Heffernan, T. M., Ling, J., & Rodgers, J. (2004).

Increased intensity of Ecstasy and polydrug usage in the more experienced recreational Ecstasy/MDMA users: A WWW study. *Addictive Behaviors, 29*, 743–752.

Schooler, C. (2007). Use it—and keep it, longer, probably: A reply to Salthouse. *Perspectives on Psychological Science, 2*, 24–29.

Schramm, D. G., Marshall, J. P., Harris, V. W., & Lee, T. R. (2005). After "I do": The newlywed transition. *Marriage and Family Review, 38*, 45–67.

Schreiber, F. R. (1973). *Sybil*. New York: Warner.

Schuit, A. J., Feskens, E. J., Launer, L. J., & Kromhaut, D. (2001). Physical activity and cognitive decline, the role of the apolipoprotein e4 allele. *Medicine and Science in Sports and Exercise, 33*, 772–777.

Schultz, P. W. (2000). Empathizing with nature: The effects of perspective taking on concern for environmental issues. *Journal of Social Issues, 56*, 391406.

Schultz, P. W. (2001). The structure of environmental concern: Concern for self, other people, and the biosphere. *Journal of Environmental Psychology, 21*, 1–13.

Schultz, P. W., Gouveia, V. V., Cameron, L. D., Tankha, G., Schmuck, P., & Franek, M. (2005). Values and their relationship to environmental concern and conservation behavior. *Journal of Cross-Cultural Psychology, 36*, 457–475.

Schulz-Hardt, S., Frey, D., Luethgens, C., & Moscovici, S. (2000). Biased information search in group decision making. *Journal of Personality & Social Psychology, 78*, 655–669.

Schuman, H., & Kalton, G. (1985). Survey methods. In G. Lindzey & E. Aronson (Eds.), *Handbook of social psychology* (3rd ed.). New York: Random House.

Schwartz, B. (2004). *The paradox of choice: Why more is less*. New York: Ecco.

Schwartz, B. L. (1999). Sparkling at the end of the tongue: The etiology of tip-of-the-tongue phenomenology. *Psychonomic Bulletin & Review, 6*, 379–393.

Schwartz, B. L. (2002). *Tip-of-the-tongue states: Phenomenology, mechanism, and lexical retrieval.* Mahwah, NJ: Erlbaum.

Schwartz, B., & Robbins, S. J. (1995). *Psychology of learning and behavior* (4th ed.). New York: Norton.

Schwartz, G. L., & Azzara, A. V. (2004). Sensory neurobiological analysis of neuropeptide modulation of meal size. *Physiology & Behavior , 82*, 81–87.

Schwartz, J. H., & Westbrook, G. L. (2000). The cytology of neurons. In E. R. Kandel, J. H. Schwartz, & T. M. Jessell (Eds.), *Principles of neural science* (pp. 67–104). New York: McGraw-Hill.

Schwartz, J. P., Waldo, M., & Higgins, A. J. (2004). Attachment styles: Relationship to masculine gender role conflict in college men. *Psychology of Men & Masculinity, 5*(2), 143–146.

Schwartz, L., Slater, M. A., & Birchler, G. R. (1994). Interpersonal stress and pain behaviors in patients with chronic pain. *Journal of Consulting and Clinical Psychology, 62*, 861–864.

Schwartz, M. W., Woods, S. C., Porte, D., Seeley, R. J., & Baskin, D. G. (2000). Central nervous system control of food intake. *Nature, 404*, 661–671.

Schwarz, N. (1999). Self-reports: How the questions shape the answers. *American Psychologist, 54*, 93–105.

Schwarz, N., & Strack, F. (1999). Reports of subjective well-being: Judgmental processes and their methodological implications. In D. Kahneman, E.

Diener, & N. Schwarz (Eds.), *Well-being: The foundations of hedonic psychology*. New York: Russell Sage Foundation.

Scott, B. A. & Koger, S. M. (2006). Teaching psychology for sustainability: A manual of resources. Supported by an Instructional Resource Award from the Office of Teaching Resources in Psychology. Available at *http://www.teachgreenpsych.com/*

Scott, V., McDade, D. M., & Luckman, S. M. (2007). Rapid changes in the sensitivity of arcuate nucleus neurons to central ghrelin in relation to feeding status. *Physiology & Behavior, 90*, 180–185.

Scoville, W. B., & Milner, B. (1957). Loss of recent memory after bilateral hippocampal lesions. *Journal of Neurology, Neurosurgery & Psychiatry, 20*, 11–21.

Scroppo, J. C., Drob, S. L., Weinberger, J. L., & Eagle, P. (1998). Identifying dissociative identity disorder: A self-report and projective study. *Journal of Abnormal Psychology, 107*, 272–284.

Scull, A. (1990). Deinstitutionalization: Cycles of despair. *The Journal of Mind and Behavior, 11*(3/4), 301–312.

Scully, J. A., Tosi, H., & Banning, K. (2000). Life event checklists: Revisiting the social readjustment rating scale after 30 years. *Educational & Psychological Measurement, 60*, 864–876.

Seabrook, R., Brown, G. D. A., & Solity, J. E. (2005). Distributed and massed practice: From laboratory to classroom. *Applied Cognitive Psychology, 19*(1), 107–122.

Searle, A., & Bennett, P. (2001). Psychological factors and inflammatory bowel disease: A review of a decade of literature. *Psychology, Health and Medicine, 6*, 121–135.

Searleman, A. (1996). Personality variables and prospective memory performance. In D. J. Herrmann, C. McEvoy, C. Hertzog, P. Hertel, & M. K. Johnson (Eds.), *Basic and applied memory research: Practical applications* (Vol. 2). Mahwah, NJ: Erlbaum.

Searleman, A., & Herrmann, D. (1994). *Memory from a broader perspective*. New York: McGraw-Hill.

Searles, H. F. (1960). *The nonhuman environment in normal development and schizophrenia*. New York: International Universities Press.

Sears, D. O. (1975). Political socialization. In F. I. Greenstein & N. W. Polsby (Eds.), *Handbook of political science* (Vol. 2). Reading, MA: Addison-Wesley.

Sedikides, C., & Strube, M. J. (1997). Self-evaluation: To thine own self be good, to thine own self be sure, to thine own self be true, and to thine own self be better. In M. P. Zanna (Ed.), *Advances in experimental social psychology*. New York: Academic Press.

Seeley, R. J., & Schwartz, M. W. (1997). Regulation of energy balance: Peripheral endocrine signals and hypothalamic neuropeptides. *Current Directions in Psychological Science, 6*, 39–44.

Segall, M. H., Campbell, D. T., Herskovits, M. J. (1966). *The influence of culture on visual perception*. Indianapolis: Bobbs-Merrill.

Segall, M. H., Dasen, P. R., Berry, J. W., & Poortinga, Y. H. (1990). *Human behavior in global perspective: An introduction to cross-cultural psychology*. New York: Pergamon Press.

Segerstrom, S. C., & Miller, G. E. (2004). Psychological stress and the human immune system: A meta-analytic study of 30 years of inquiry. *Psychological Bulletin, 130*, 601–630.

Segerstrom, S. C., Taylor, S. E., Kemeny, M. E., & Fahey, J. L. (1998). Optimism is associated with mood, coping and immune change in response to stress. *Journal of Personality and Social Psychology, 74,* 1646–1655.

Seifer, R. (2001). Socioeconomic status, multiple risks, and development of intelligence. In R. J. Sternberg & E. L. Grigorenko (Eds.), *Environmental effects on cognitive abilities* (pp. 59–82). Mahwah, NJ: Erlbaum.

Seligman, M. E. P. (1971). Phobias and preparedness. *Behavior Therapy, 2,* 307–321.

Seligman, M. E. P. (1974). Depression and learned helplessness. In R. J. Friedman & M. M. Katz (Eds.), *The psychology of depression: Contemporary theory and research.* New York: Wiley.

Seligman, M. E. P. (1990). *Learned optimism.* New York: Pocket Books.

Seligman, M. E. P. (1992). *Helplessness: On depression, development, and death.* New York: Freeman.

Seligman, M. E. P. (1995). The effectiveness of psychotherapy. *American Psychologist, 50,* 965–974.

Seligman, M. E. P. (2002). Positive psychology, positive prevention, and positive therapy. In C. R. Snyder & S. J. Lopez (Eds.), *Handbook of positive psychology* (pp. 3–11). New York: Oxford University Press.

Seligman, M. E. P. (2003). The past and future of positive psychology. In C. L. M. Keyes & J. Haidt (Eds.), *Flourishing: Positive psychology and the life well-lived.* Washington, DC: American Psychological Association.

Seligman, M. E. P., & Csikszentmihalyi, M. (2000). Positive psychology: An introduction. *American Psychologist, 55,* 5–14.

Seligman, M. E. P., & Hager, J. L. (1972, August). Biological boundaries of learning (the sauce béarnaise syndrome). *Psychology Today,* pp. 59–61, 84–87.

Seligman, M. E. P., & Levant, R. F. (1998). Managed care policies rely on inadequate science. *Professional Psychology: Research and Practice, 29,* 211–212.

Seligman, M. E. P., Rashid, T., & Parks, A. C. (2006). Positive psychotherapy. *American Psychologist, 61,* 774–788.

Selye, H. (1936). A syndrome produced by diverse nocuous agents. *Nature, 138,* 32.

Selye, H. (1956). *The stress of life.* New York: McGraw-Hill.

Selye, H. (1973). The evolution of the stress concept. *American Scientist, 61*(6), 672–699.

Selye, H. (1974). *Stress without distress.* New York: Lippincott.

Selye, H. (1982). History and present status of the stress concept. In L. Goldberger & S. Breznitz (Eds.), *Handbook of stress: Theoretical and clinical aspects.* New York: Free Press.

Semmer, N. K., McGrath, J. E., & Beehr, T. A. (2005). Conceptual issues in research on stress and health. In C. L. Cooper (Ed.), *Handbook of stress medicine and health.* Boca Raton, FL: CRC Press.

Senior, C., Thomson, K., Badger, J., & Butler, M. J. R. (2008). Interviewing strategies in the face of beauty: A psychophysiological investigation into the job negotiation process. *Annals of the New York Academy of Sciences, 1118,* 142–162.

Servan-Schreiber, D., Kolb, R., & Tabas, G. (1999). The somatizing patient. *Primary Care, 26,* 225–242.

Seta, J. J., Seta, C. E., & McElroy, T. (2002). Strategies for reducing the stress of negative life experiences: An average/summation analysis. *Personality and Social Psychology Bulletin, 28,* 1574–1585.

Shackelford, T. K., Schmitt, D. P., & Buss, D. M. (2005). Universal dimensions of human mate preferences. *Personality & Individual Differences, 39,* 447–458.

Shafir, E., & LeBoeuf, R. A. (2002). Rationality. *Annual Review of Psychology, 53,* 491–517.

Shafir, E., & LeBoeuf, R. A. (2004). Context and conflict in multiattribute choice. In D. J. Koehler & N. Harvey (Ed), *Blackwell handbook of judgment and decision making.* Malden, MA: Blackwell Publishing.

Shalev, A. Y. (2001). Posttraumatic stress disorder. *Primary Psychiatry, 8*(10), 41–46.

Shalitin, S., & Phillip, M. (2003). Role of obesity and leptin in the pubertal process and pubertal growth—A review. *International Journal of Obesity, 27,* 869–874.

Shank, R. P., Smith-Swintosky, V. L., & Twyman, R. E. (2000). Amino acid neurotransmitters. In B. J. Sadock & V. A. Sadock (Eds), *Comprehensive textbook of psychiatry* (Vol. 1). New York: Lippincott/Williams & Wilkins.

Shapiro, A. F., Gottman, J. M., & Carrère. (2000). The baby and marriage: Identifying factors that buffer against decline in marital satisfaction after the first baby arrives. *Journal of Family Psychology, 14,* 59–70.

Shapiro, D. H., Jr. (1984). Overview: Clinical and physiological comparison of meditation with other self-control strategies. In D. H. Shapiro, Jr., & R. N. Walsh (Eds.), *Meditation: Classic and contemporary perspectives.* New York: Aldine.

Sharpe, D., Adair, J. G., & Roese, N. J. (1992). Twenty years of deception research: A decline in subjects' trust? *Personality and Social Psychology Bulletin, 18,* 585–590.

Sharps, M. J., & Wertheimer, M. (2000). Gestalt perspectives on cognitive science and on experimental psychology. *Review of General Psychology, 4,* 315–336.

Shatz, C. J. (1992, September). The developing brain. *Scientific American,* 60–67.

Shaver, P. R., & Mikulincer, M. (2006). A behavioral systems approach to romantic love relationships: Attachment, caregiving, and sex. In R. J. Sternberg & K. Weis (Eds.), *The new psychology of love.* New Haven, CT: Yale University Press.

Shaver, P. R., Schachner, D. A., & Mikulincer, M. (2005). Attachment style, excessive reassurance seeking, relationship processes, and depression. *Personality and Social Psychology Bulletin, 31*(3), 343–359.

Shavitt, S., Sanbonmatsu, D. M., Smittipatana, S., & Posavac, S. S. (1999). Broadening the conditions for illusory correlation formation: Implications for judging minority groups. *Basic & Applied Social Psychology, 21,* 263–279.

Shaw, J. S. I., McClure, K. A., & Dykstra, J. A. (2007). Eyewitness confidence from the witnessed event through trial. In M. P. Toglia, J. D. Read, D. F. Ross, & R. C. L. Lindsay (Eds.), *Handbook of eyewitness psychology: Volume 1. Memory for events.* Mahwah, NJ: Erlbaum.

Shea, A. K., & Steiner, M. (2008). Cigarette smoking during pregnancy. *Nicotine & Tobacco Research, 10,* 267–278.

Shear, J., & Jevning, R. (1999). Pure consciousness: Scientific exploration of meditation techniques. *Journal of Consciousness Studies, 6,* 189–209.

Shearer, B. (2004). Multiple intelligences theory after 20 years. *Teachers College Record, 106*(1), 2–16.

Shedler, J., Mayman, M., & Manis, M. (1993). The illusion of mental health. *American Psychologist, 48,* 1117–1131.

Sheehan, S. (1982). *Is there no place on earth for me?* Boston: Houghton Mifflin.

Sheldon, K. M., & Kasser, T. (2001). Goals, congruence, and positive well-being: New empirical support for humanistic theories. *Journal of Humanistic Psychology, 41*(1), 30–50.

Shelton, R. C., & Lester, N. (2006). Selective serotonin reuptake inhibitors and newer antidepressants. In D. J. Stein, D. J. Kupfer, & A. F. Schatzberg (Eds.), *Textbook of mood disorders.* Washington, DC: American Psychiatric Publishing.

Shepard, R. N. (1990). *Mind sights.* New York: W. H. Freeman.

Shepperd, J., Malone, W., & Sweeny, K. (2008). Exploring causes of the self-serving bias. *Social and Personality Psychology Compass, 2,* 895–908.

Sher, L., & Mann, J. J. (2003). Psychiatric pathophysiology: Mood disorders. In A. Tasman, J. Kay, & J. A. Lieberman (Eds.), *Psychiatry.* New York: Wiley.

Sherif, M., Harvey, O., White, B., Hood, W., & Sherif, C. (1961). *Intergroup conflict and cooperation: The Robber's Cave experiment.* Norman: University of Oklahoma, Institute of Group Behavior.

Sherman, D. K., Nelson, L. D., & Ross, L. D. (2003). Naive realism and affirmative action: Adversaries are more similar than they think. *Basic and Applied Social Psychology, 25,* 275–289.

Sherman, M., & Key, C. B. (1932). The intelligence of isolated mountain children. *Child Development, 3,* 279–290.

Shermer, M. (1997). *Why people believe weird things: Pseudoscience, superstition, and other confusions of our time.* New York: W. H. Freeman.

Shermer, M. (2004, March). None so blind. *Scientific American,* p. 42.

Sherry, D. F. (1992). Evolution and learning. In L. R. Squire (Ed.), *Encyclopedia of learning and memory.* New York: Macmillan.

Shettleworth, S. J. (1998). *Cognition, evolution, and behavior.* New York: Oxford University Press.

Shike, M. (1999). Diet and lifestyle in the prevention of colorectal cancer: An overview. *American Journal of Medicine, 106*(1A), 11S–15S, 50S–51S.

Shimamura, A. P., Berry, J. M., Mangels, J. A., Rusting, C. L., & Jurica, P. J. (1995). Memory and cognitive abilities in university professors: Evidence for successful aging. *Psychological Science, 6,* 271–277.

Shimp, T. A., Stuart, E. W., & Engle, R. W. (1991). A program of classical conditioning experiments testing variations in the conditioned stimulus and context. *Journal of Consumer Research, 18,* 1–12.

Shneidman, E. S., Farberow, N. L., & Litman, R. E. (1994). *The psychology of suicide: A clinician's guide to evaluation and treatment.* Northvale, NJ: J. Aronson.

Shobe, K. K., & Schooler, J. W. (2001). Discovering fact and fiction: Case-based analyses of authentic and fabricated discovered memories of abuse. In G. M. Davies & T. Dalgleish (Eds.), *Recovered memories: Seeking the middle ground.* Chichester, England: Wiley.

Siebert, A. (1995). *Student success: How to succeed in college and still have time for your friends.* Fort Worth: Harcourt Brace Jovanovich.

Siebert, A., & Karr, M. (2003). *The adult student's guide to survival & success.* Portland, OR: Practical Psychology Press.

Siegel, J. M. (2004). The neurotransmitters of sleep. *Journal of Clinical Psychiatry, 65*(Suppl16), 4–7.

Siegel, S. (2005). Drug tolerance, drug addiction, and drug anticipation. *Current Directions in Psychological Science, 14*, 296–300.

Siegler, R. S. (1992). The other Alfred Binet. *Developmental Psychology, 28*, 179–190.

Siegler, R. S. (1994). Cognitive variability: A key to understanding cognitive development. *Current Directions in Psychological Science, 3*(1), 1–5.

Sigel, I. E. (2004). Head Start—Revisiting a historical psychoeducational intervention: A revisionist perspective. In E. Zigler & S. J. Styfco (Eds.), *The Head Start debate.* Baltimore: Paul H. Brookes Publishing.

Sigman, M., & Whaley, S. E. (1998). The role of nutrition in the development of intelligence. In U. Neisser (Ed.), *The rising curve: Long-term gains in IQ and related measures.* Washington, DC: American Psychological Association.

Signorielli, N. (2001). Television's gender role images and contribution to stereotyping: Past present future. In D. G. Singer & J. L. Singer (Eds.), *Handbook of children and the media.* Thousand Oaks, CA: Sage.

Signorielli, N., McLeod, D., & Healy, E. (1994). Gender stereotypes in MTV commercials: The beat goes on. *Journal of Broadcasting & Electronic Media, 38*, 91–101.

Silberman, E. K. (1998). Psychiatrists' and internists' beliefs. *Primary Psychiatry, 5*, 65–71.

Silver, E., Cirincion, C., & Steadman, H. J. (1994). Demythologizing inaccurate perceptions of the insanity defense. *Law & Human Behavior, 18*, 63–70.

Silverman, I., & Choi, J. (2005). Locating places. In D. M. Buss (Ed.), *The handbook of evolutionary psychology.* New York: Wiley.

Silverman, I., Choi, J., Mackewn, A., Fisher, M., Moro, J., & Olshansky, E. (2000). Evolved mechanisms underlying wayfinding: Further studies on the hunter-gatherer theory of spatial sex differences. *Evolution and Human Behavior, 21*, 201–213.

Silverman, I., & Eals, M. (1992). Sex differences in spatial ability: Evolutionary theory and data. In J. Barkow, L. Cosmides, & J. Tooby (Eds.), *The adapted mind.* New York: Oxford University Press.

Silverman, I., & Phillips, K. (1998). The evolutionary psychology of spatial sex differences. In C. Crawford & D.L. Krebs (Eds.), *Handbook of evolutionary psychology: Ideas, issues, and applications.* Mahwah, NJ: Erlbaum.

Silverstein, L. B., & Auerbach, C. F. (1999). Deconstructing the essential father. *American Psychologist, 54*, 397–407.

Silvia, P. J. (2008). Another look at creativity and intelligence: Exploring higher-order models and probable confounds. *Personality and Individual Differences, 44*, 1012–1021.

Simmons, D. A. (1994). Urban children's preferences for nature: Lessons for environmental education. *Children's Environments, 11*, 194–203.

Simon, G. E., & Savarino, J. (2007). Suicide attempts among patients starting depression treatment with medications or psychotherapy. *American Journal of Psychiatry, 164*, 1029–1034.

Simon, G. E., Savarino, J., Operskalski, B., & Wang, P. S. (2006). Suicide risk during antidepressant treatment. *American Journal of Psychiatry, 163*, 41–47.

Simon, H. A. (1957). *Models of man.* New York: Wiley.

Simon, H. A. (1974). How big is a chunk? *Science, 183*, 482–488.

Simons, D. K., & Chabris, C. F. (1999). Gorillas in our midst: Sustained inattentional blindness for dynamic events. *Perception, 28*, 1059–1074.

Simonton, D. K. (2004). *Creativity in science: Chance, logic, genius, and zeitgeist.* New York: Cambridge University Press.

Simpson, J. A., Fletcher, G. J. O., & Campbell, L. (2001). The structure and function of ideal standards in close relationships. In G. J. O. Fletcher & M. S. Clark (Eds.), *Blackwell handbook of social psychology: Interpersonal processes.* Malden, MA: Blackwell.

Simpson, J. L. (2002). Fetal wastage. In S. G. Gabbe, J. R. Niebyl, & J. L. Simpson (Eds.), *Obstetrics: Normal and problem pregnancies.* New York: Churchill Livingstone.

Simpson, J. L., & Niebyl, J. R. (2002). Occupational and environmental perspectives on birth defects. In S. G. Gabbe, J. R. Niebyl, & J. L. Simpson (Eds.), *Obstetrics: Normal and problem pregnancies.* New York: Churchill Livingstone.

Sinclair, D. (1981). *Mechanisms of cutaneous stimulation.* Oxford, England: Oxford University Press.

Sinclair, R. C., Hoffman, C., Mark, M. M., Martin, L. L., & Pickering, T. L. (1994). Construct accessibility and the misattribution of arousal: Schachter and Singer revisited. *Psychological Science, 5*, 15-19.

Sinclair, S., Dunn, R., & Lowery, B. S. (2005). The relationship between parental racial attitudes and children's implicit prejudice. *Journal of Experimental Social Psychology, 41*, 283–289.

Singer, L. T., Arendt, R., Minnes, S., Farkas, K., Salvator, A., Kirchner, H. L., & Kliegman, R. (2002). Cognitive and motor outcomes of cocaine-exposed infants. *Journal of the American Medical Association, 287*, 1952–1960.

Singer, L. T., Minnes, S., Short, E., Arendt, R., Farkas, K., Lewis, B., Klein, N., Russ, S., Min, M. O., & Kirchner, H. L. (2004). Cognitive outcomes of preschool children with prenatal cocaine exposure. *Journal of the American Medical Association, 291*, 2448–2456.

Singer, W. (2007). Large-scale temporal coordination of cortical activity as a prerequisite for conscious experience. In M. Velmans & S. Schneider (Eds.), *The Blackwell companion to consciousness.* Malden, MA: Blackwell Publishing.

Sinha, D. (1983). Human assessment in the Indian context. In S. H. Irvine & J. W. Berry (Eds.), *Human assessment and cultural factors.* New York: Plenum.

Sivertsen, B., Omvik, S., Pallesen, S., Bjorvatn, B., Havik, O. E., Kvale, G., et al. (2006). Cognitive behavioral therapy vs. Zopiclone for treatment of chronic primary insomnia in older adults: A randomized controlled trial. *Journal of the American Medical Association, 295*, 2851–2858.

SJB. (2006, March 6). Overcoming problem gambling [Why?]. Message posted to http://www.gamcare.org.uk/forum/index.php?tid=7193.

Skinner, A. E. G. (2001). Recovered memories of abuse: Effects on the individual. In G. M. Davies, & T. Dalgleish (Eds.), *Recovered memories: Seeking the middle ground.* Chichester, England: Wiley & Sons.

Skinner, B. F. (1938). *The behavior of organisms.* New York: Appleton-Century-Crofts.

Skinner, B. F. (1953). *Science and human behavior.* New York: Macmillan.

Skinner, B. F. (1957). *Verbal behavior.* New York: Appleton-Century-Crofts.

Skinner, B. F. (1969). *Contingencies of reinforcement.* New York: Appleton-Century-Crofts.

Skinner, B. F. (1971). *Beyond freedom and dignity.* New York: Knopf.

Skinner, B. F. (1984). Selection by consequences. *Behavioral and Brain Sciences, 7*(4), 477–510.

Skinner, B. F. (1987). *Upon further reflection.* Englewood Cliffs, NJ: Prentice-Hall.

Skinner, B. F., Solomon, H. C., & Lindsley, O. R. (1953). *Studies in behavior therapy: Status report I.* Waltham, MA: Unpublished report, Metropolitan State Hospital.

Skitka, L., & Sargis, E. (2005). Social psychological research and the Internet: The promise and peril of a new methodological frontier. In Y. Amichai-Hamburger (Ed.), *The social net: Understanding human behavior in cyberspace.* New York: Oxford University Press.

Skitka, L., & Sargis, E. G. (2006). The Internet as psychological laboratory. *Annual Review of Psychology, 57*, 529–555.

Skolnick, P. (2003). Psychiatric pathophysiology: Anxiety disorders. In A. Tasman, J. Kay, & J. A. Lieberman (Eds.), *Psychiatry.* New York: Wiley.

Slamecka, N. J. (1985). Ebbinghaus: Some associations. *Journal of Experimental Psychology: Learning, Memory and Cognition, 11*, 414–435.

Slamecka, N. J. (1992). Forgetting. In L. R. Squire (Ed.), *Encyclopedia of learning and memory.* New York: Macmillan.

Slatcher, R. B., & Pennebaker, J. W. (2005). Emotional processing of traumatic events. In C. L. Cooper (Ed.), *Handbook of stress medicine and health.* Boca Raton, FL: CRC Press.

Slater, E., & Shields, J. (1969). Genetical aspects of anxiety. In M. H. Lader (Ed.), *Studies of anxiety.* Ashford, England: Headley Brothers.

Slaughter, M. (1990). The vertebrate retina. In K. N. Leibovic (Ed.), *Science of vision.* New York: Springer-Verlag.

Slimak, M. W. & Dietz, T. (2006). Personal values, beliefs, and ecological risk perception. *Risk Analysis, 26*, 1689–1705.

Slobin, D. I. (1985). *A cross-linguistic study of language acquisition.* Hillsdale, NJ: Erlbaum.

Slobin, D. I. (1992). *The crosslinguistic study of language acquisition.* Hillsdale, NJ: Erlbaum.

Slof-Op't Landt, M. C. T., van Furth, E. F., Meulenbelt, I., Slagboom, P. E., Bartels, M., & Boomsma, D. I., et al. (2005). Eating disorders: From twin studies to candidate genes and beyond. *Twin Research and Human Genetics, 8*, 467–482.

Sloman, S. A. (2002). Two systems of reasoning. In T. Gilovich, D. Griffin, & D. Kahneman (Eds.), *Heuristics and biases.* New York: Cambridge University Press.

Slovic, P. (1990). Choice. In D. N. Osherson & E. E. Smith (Eds.), *Thinking: An invitation to cognitive science* (Vol. 3). Cambridge, MA: MIT Press.

Slovic, P., Finucane, M. L., Peters, E., & MacGregor, D. G. (2004). Risk as analysis and risk as feelings: Some thoughts about affect, reason, risk, and rationality. *Risk Analysis, 24*, 311–322.

Slovic, P., & Fischhoff, B. (1977). On the psychology of experimental surprises. *Journal of Experimental Psychology: Human Perception and Performance, 3*, 544–551.

Slovic, P., Fischhoff, B., & Lichtenstein, S. (1982). Facts versus fears: Understanding perceived risk. In D. Kahneman, P. Slovic, & A. Tversky (Eds.), *Judgment under uncertainty: Heuristics and biases.* Cambridge, England: Cambridge University Press.

Slovic, P., Lichtenstein, S., & Fischhoff, B. (1988). Decision making. In R. C. Atkinson, R. J. Herrnstein, G. Lindzey, & R. D. Luce (Eds.), *Stevens' handbook of experimental psychology* (Vol. 2). New York: Wiley.

Small, G. W. (2005). Alzheimer's disease and other dementias. In B. J. Sadock & V. A. Sadock (Eds.), *Kaplan & Sadock's comprehensive textbook of psychiatry.* Philadelphia: Lippincott Williams & Wilkins.

Smedley, S. R., & Eisner, T. (1996). Sodium: A male moth's gift to its offspring. *Proceedings of the National Academy of Sciences, 93,* 809–813.

Smetana, J. G., Campione, B. N., & Metzger, A. (2006). Adolescent development in interpersonal and societal contexts. *Annual Review of Psychology, 57,* 255–284.

Smith, C. A., & Lazarus, R. S. (1993). Appraisal components, core relational themes, and the emotions. *Cognition and Emotion, 7,* 233–269.

Smith, C. P. (1992). Reliability issues. In C. P. Smith (Ed.), *Motivation and personality: Handbook of thematic content analysis.* New York: Cambridge University Press.

Smith, F. J., & Campfield, L. A. (1993). Meal initiation occurs after experimental induction of transient declines in blood glucose. *American Journal of Physiology, 265,* 1423–1429.

Smith, G. T., Spillane, N. S., & Annus, A. M. (2006). Implications of an emerging integration of universal and culturally specific psychologies. *Perspectives on Psychological Science, 1,* 211–233.

Smith, J. C. (1975). Meditation and psychotherapy: A review of the literature. *Psychological Bulletin, 32,* 553–564.

Smith, J. C. (2007). The psychology of relaxation. In P. M. Lehrer, R. L. Woolfolk, & W. E. Sime (Eds.), *Principles and practice of stress management.* New York: Guilford.

Smith, J. W., Positano, S., Stocks, N. & Shearman, D. (2009). *A new way of thinking about our climate crisis: The rational-comprehensive approach.* Lewiston, N.Y.: Edwin Mellen Press.

Smith, L. (2005). Psychotherapy, classism, and the poor: Conspicuous by their absence. *American Psychologist, 60,* 687–696.

Smith, M. J. (2003). Testosterone treatment algorithms in psychiatry. *Psychiatric Annals, 33,* 511–516.

Smith, M., & Pazder, L. (1980). *Michelle remembers.* New York: Pocket Books.

Smith, M. L., & Glass, G. V. (1977). Meta-analysis of psychotherapy outcome studies. *American Psychologist, 32,* 752–760.

Smith, P. B. (2001). Cross-cultural studies of social influence. In D. Matsumoto (Ed.), *The handbook of culture and psychology.* New York: Oxford University Press.

Smith, P. B., & Bond, M. H. (1994). *Social psychology across cultures: Analysis and perspectives.* Boston: Allyn & Bacon.

Smith, S. (1988). Environmental context-dependent memory. In G. M. Davies & D. M. Thomson (Eds.), *Memory in context: Context in memory.* New York: Wiley.

Smith, S. B. (2000). *Diana in search of herself: Portrait of a troubled princess.* New York: Signet.

Smith, S. M. (1995). Getting into and out of mental ruts: A theory of fixation, incubation, and insight. In R. J. Sternberg & J. E. Davidson (Eds.), *The nature of insight* (pp. 229–251). Cambridge, MA: MIT Press.

Smith, S. M., & Gleaves, D. H. (2007). Recovered memories. In M. P. Toglia, J. D. Read, D. F. Ross,

& R. C. L. Lindsay (Eds.), *Handbook of eyewitness psychology: Volume 1. Memory for events.* Mahwah, NJ: Erlbaum.

Smith, S. M., McIntosh, W. D., & Bazzini, D. G. (1999). Are the beautiful good in Hollywood? An investigation of the beauty-and-goodness stereotype on film. *Basic & Applied Social Psychology, 21,* 69–80.

Smith, T. W., & Gallo, L. C. (2001). Personality traits as risk factors for physical illness. In A. Baum, T. A. Revenson, & J. E. Singer (Eds.), *Handbook of health psychology* (pp. 139–174). Mahwah, NJ: Erlbaum.

Smolak, L., & Murnen, S. K. (2001). Gender and eating problems. In R. H. Striegel-Moore & L. Smolak (Eds.), *Eating disorders: Innovative directions in research and practice* (pp. 91–110). Washington, DC: American Psychological Association.

Smyth, J. M., & Pennebaker, J. W. (1999). Sharing one's story: Translating emotional experiences into words as a coping tool. In C. R. Snyder (Ed.), *Coping: The psychology of what works.* New York: Oxford University Press.

Smyth, J. M., & Pennebaker, J. W. (2001). What are the health effects of disclosure? In A. Baum, T. A. Revenson & J. E. Singer (Eds.), *Handbook of health psychology* (pp. 339–348). Mahwah, NJ: Erlbaum.

Snedecor, S. M., Pomerleau, C. S., Mehringer, A. M., Ninowski, R., & Pomerleau, O. F. (2006). Differences in smoking-related variables based on phenylthiocabamide "taster" status. *Addictive Behaviors, 31,* 2309–2312.

Snow, R. E. (1986). Individual differences in the design of educational programs. *American Psychologist, 41,* 1029–1039.

Snowden, L. R., & Hu, T. W. (1996). Outpatient service use in minority-serving mental health programs. *Administration and Policy in Mental Health, 24,* 149–159.

Snowden, L. R., & Yamada, A. (2005). Cultural differences in access to care. *Annual Review of Clinical Psychology, 1,* 143–166.

Snowdon, D. (2001). *Aging with grace: What the Nun Study teaches us about leading longer, healthier, and more meaningful lives.* New York: Bantam Books.

Sobel, D. (2002). *Children's special places: Exploring the role of forts, dens, and bush houses in middle childhood* (The Child in the Cities Series). Detroit, MI: Wayne State University Press.

Sobel, D. A. (1990). A place in the world: Adults' memories of childhood's special places. *Children's Environments Quarterly, 7*(4), 5–12.

Solberg, E. C., Diener, E., Wirtz, D., Lucas, R. E., & Oishi, S. (2002). Wanting, having, and satisfaction: Examining the role of desire discrepancies in satisfaction with income. *Journal of Personality and Social Psychology, 83,* 725–734.

Soldatos, C. R., Allaert, F. A., Ohta, T., & Dikeos, D. G. (2005). How do individuals sleep around the world? Results from a single-day survey in ten countries. *Sleep Medicine, 6,* 5–13.

Soler, C., Nunez, M., Gutierrez, R., Nunez, J., Medina, P., Sancho, M., Alvarez, J., & Nunez, A. (2003). Facial attractiveness in men provides clues to semen quality. *Evolution and Human Behavior, 24,* 199–207.

Solms, M. (2000a). Freudian dream theory today. *Psychologist, 13,* 618–619.

Solms, M. (2000b). Dreaming and REM sleep are controlled by different brain mechanisms. *Behavioral and Brain Sciences, 23,* 843–850.

Solms, M. (2004). Freud returns. *Scientific American, 290*(5), 83–88.

Solomon, D. A., Keller, M. B., Leon, A. C., Mueller, T. I., Lavori, P. W., Shea, M. T., Coryell, W., Warshaw, M., Turvey, C., Maser, J. D., & Endicott, J. (2000). Multiple recurrences of major depressive disorder. *American Journal of Psychiatry, 157,* 229–233.

Solomon, S. G., & Lennie, P. (2007). The machinery of colour vision. *Nature Reviews Neuroscience, 8,* 276–286.

Solomon, S., Greenberg, J., & Pyszczynski, T. (1991). A terror management theory of social behavior: The psychological functions of self-esteem and cultural worldviews. In M. Zanna (Ed.), *Advances in experimental social psychology* (Vol. 24). Orlando, FL: Academic Press.

Solomon, S., Greenberg, J., & Pyszczynski, T. (2004a). Lethal consumption: Death-denying materialism. In T. Kasser, & A. D. Kanner (Eds.), *Psychology and consumer culture: The struggle for a good life in a materialistic world.* Washington, DC: American Psychological Association.

Solomon, S., Greenberg, J., & Pyszczynski, T. (2004b). The cultural animal: Twenty years of terror management. In J. Greenberg, S. L. Koole, & T. Pyszczynski (Eds.), *Handbook of experimental existential psychology.* New York: Guilford.

Solso, R. L. (1994). *Cognition and the visual arts.* Cambridge, MA: MIT Press.

Song, A. W., Huettel, S. A., & McCarthy, G. (2006). Functional neuroimaging: Basic principles of functional MRI. In R. Cabeza & A. Kingstone (Eds.), *Handbook of functional neuroimaging of cognition.* Cambridge, MA: MIT Press.

Song, S., Sjostrom, P. J., Reigl, M., Nelson, S., & Chklovskii, D. B. (2005). Highly nonrandom features of synaptic connectivity in local cortical circuits. *PLoS Biol, 3*(3), 1–13.

Sotiriou, P. E. (2002). *Integrating college study skills: Reasoning in reading, listening, and writing.* Belmont, CA: Wadsworth.

Sousa, D. A. (2000). *How the brain learns: A classroom teacher's guide.* Thousand Oaks, CA: Corwin Press.

Sowell, E. R., Trauner, D. A., Gamst, A., & Jernigan, T. L. (2002). Development of cortical and subcortical brain structures in childhood and adolescence: A structural MRI study. *Developmental Medicine and Child Neurology, 44*(1), 4–16.

Spada, M. M., & Wells, A. (2006). Metacognitions about alcohol use in problem drinkers. *Clinical Psychology & Psychotherapy, 13,* 138–143.

Spangler, W. D. (1992). Validity of questionnaire and TAT measures of need for achievement: Two meta-analyses. *Psychological Bulletin, 112,* 140–154.

Spanos, N. P. (1986). Hypnotic behavior: A social-psychological interpretation of amnesia, analgesia, and "trance logic." *Behavioral & Brain Sciences, 9*(3), 449–467.

Spanos, N. P. (1991). A sociocognitive approach to hypnosis. In S. J. Lynn & J. W. Rhue (Eds.), *Theories of hypnosis: Current models and perspectives* (pp. 324–361). New York: Guilford.

Spanos, N. P. (1994). Multiple identity enactments and multiple personality disorder: A sociocognitive perspective. *Psychological Bulletin, 116,* 143–165.

Spanos, N. P. (1996). *Multiple identities and false memories.* Washington, DC: American Psychological Association.

Speed, A., & Gangestad, S. W. (1997). Romantic popularity and mate preferences: A peer-nomination study. *Personality and Social Psychology Bulletin, 23,* 928–936.

Spelke, E. S., & Kinzler, K. D. (2007). Core knowledge. *Developmental Science, 10*(1), 89–96.

Spelke, E. S., & Newport, E. L. (1998). Nativism, empiricism, and the development of knowledge. In W. Damon (Ed.), *Handbook of child psychology (Vol. 1): Theoretical models of human development*. New York: Wiley.

Spence, I., Wong, P., Rusan, M., & Rastegar, N. (2006). How color enhances visual memory for natural scenes. *Psychological Science, 14*(1), 1–6.

Sperling, G. (1960). The information available in brief visual presentations. *Psychological Monographs, 74*(11, Whole No. 498).

Sperry, R. W. (1982). Some effects of disconnecting the cerebral hemispheres. *Science, 217*, 1223–1226, 1250.

Speth, G. (1992). The global environmental challenge. In Miller, G. T. (1993). *Living in the environment: An introduction to environmental science* (7th ed.). Belmont, CA: Wadsworth.

Spiegel, D. (1995). Hypnosis, dissociation, and trauma: Hidden and overt observers. In J. L. Singer (Ed.), *Repression and dissociation: Implications for personality theory, psychopathology, and health*. Chicago: University of Chicago Press.

Spiegel, D. (2003a). Hypnosis and traumatic dissociation: Therapeutic opportunities. *Journal of Trauma & Dissociation, 4*(3), 73–90.

Spiegel, D. (2003b). Negative and positive visual hypnotic hallucinations: Attending inside and out. *International Journal of Clinical & Experimental Hypnosis, 51*(2), 130–146.

Spiegel, D., Cutcomb, S., Ren, C., & Pribram, K. (1985). Hypnotic hallucination alters evoked potentials. *Journal of Abnormal Psychology, 94*, 249–255.

Spiegel, K., Tasali, E., Penev, P., et al. (2004). Sleep curtailment in healthy young men is associated with decreased leptin levels, elevated ghrelin levels and increased hunger and appetite. *Annals of Internal Medicine, 141*, 846–850.

Spiegler, M. D., & Guevremont, D. C. (2003). *Contemporary behavior therapy*. Belmont, CA: Wadsworth.

Spitzer, R. L., First, M. B., & Wakefield, J. C. (2007). Saving PTSD from itself in DSM-V. *Journal of Anxiety Disorders, 21*(2), 233–241.

Sprecher, S. (1998). Insiders' perspectives on reasons for attraction to a close other. *Social Psychology Quarterly, 61*, 287–300.

Sprecher, S., & Duck, S. (1994). Sweet talk: The importance of perceived communication for romantic and friendship attraction experienced during a get-acquainted date. *Personality and Social Psychology Bulletin, 20*, 391–400.

Sprenger, M. (2001). *Becoming a "wiz" at brain-based teaching: From translation to application*. Thousand Oaks, CA: Corwin Press.

Springer, S. P., & Deutsch, G. (1998). *Left brain, right brain*. New York: W. H. Freeman.

Squire, L. R. (2004). Memory systems of the brain: A brief history and current perspective. *Neurobiology of Learning & Memory, 82*(3), 171–177.

Squire, L. R., Clark, R. E., & Bayley, P. J. (2004). Medial temporal lobe function and memory. In M. S. Gazzaniga (Ed.), *The cognitive neurosciences*. Cambridge, MA: MIT Press.

Squire, L. R., Knowlton, B., & Musen, G. (1993). The structure and organization of memory. *Annual Review of Psychology, 44*, 453–495.

Staats, H. (2003). Understanding proenvironmental attitudes and behavior: An analysis and review of research based on the theory of planned behavior.

In M. Bonnes, T. Lee, & M. Bonaiuto (Eds.), *Psychological theories for environmental issues* (pp. 171–202). Wiltshire, UK: Antony Rowe.

Staats, H., Kieviet, A., & Hartig, T. (2003). Where to recover from attentional fatigue: An expectancy-value analysis of environmental preference. *Journal of Environmental Psychology, 24*, 147–157.

Stajkovic, A. D., & Luthans, F. (1998). Self-efficacy and work-related performance: A meta-analysis. *Psychological Bulletin, 124*, 240–261.

Stamler, J., Daviglus, M. L., Garside, D. B., Dyer, A. R., Greenland, P., & Neaton, J. D. (2000). Relationship of baseline serum cholesterol levels in three large cohorts of younger men to long-term coronary, cardiovascular, and all-cause mortality and to longevity. *Journal of the American Medical Association, 284*, 311–318.

Stanovich, K. E. (2003). The fundamental computational biases of human cognition: Heuristics that (sometimes) impair decision making and problem solving. In J. E. Davidson & R. J. Sternberg (Eds.), *The psychology of problem solving*. New York: Cambridge University Press.

Stanovich, K. E. (2004). *How to think straight about psychology*. Boston: Allyn & Bacon.

Stanovich, K. E., & West, R. F. (2002). Individual differences in reasoning: Implications for the rationality debate. In T. Gilovich, D. Griffin, & D. Kahneman (Eds.), *Heuristics and biases*. New York: Cambridge University Press.

Stanton, A. L., Lobel, M., Sears, S., & DeLuca, R. S. (2002). Psychosocial aspects of selected issues in women's reproductive health: Current status and future directions. *Journal of Consulting & Clinical Psychology, 70*, 751–770.

Starcevic, V. (2001). Clinical features and diagnosis of hypochondriasis. In V. Starcevic & D. R. Lipsitt (Eds.), *Hypochondriasis: Modern perspectives on an ancient malady*. New York: Oxford University Press.

Steel, P. (2007). The nature of procrastination: A meta-analytic and theoretical review of quintessential self-regulatory failure. *Psychological Bulletin, 133*, 65–94.

Steele, K. M. (2003). Do rats show a Mozart effect? *Music Perception, 21*, 251–265.

Steiger, H., Bruce, K. R., & Israel, M. (2003). Eating disorders. In G. Stricker & T. A. Widiger (Eds.), *Handbook of psychology, Vol. 8: Clinical psychology*. New York: Wiley.

Steiger, H., Gauvin, L., Engelberg, M. J., Kin, N. M. K. N. Y., Israel, M., Wonderlich, S. A., et al. (2005). Mood- and restraint-based antecedents to binge episodes in bulimia nervosa: Possible influences of the serotonin system. *Psychological Medicine, 35*, 1553–1562.

Stein, B. E., & Meredith, M. A. (1993). *Vision, touch, and audition: Making sense of it all*. Cambridge, MA: MIT Press.

Stein, B. E., Wallace, M. T., & Stanford, T. R. (2001). Brain mechanisms for synthesizing information from different sensory modalities. In E. B. Goldstein (Ed.), *Blackwell handbook of perception*. Malden, MA: Blackwell.

Stein, D. J., & Hugo, F. J. (2004). Neuropsychiatric aspects of anxiety disorders. In S. C. Yudofsky & R. E. Hales (Eds.), *Essentials of neuropsychiatry and clinical neurosciences*. Washington, DC: American Psychiatric Publishing.

Stein, M. B., Walker, J. R., Hazen, A. L., & Forde, D. R. (1997). Full and partial posttraumatic stress disorder: Findings from a community survey. *American Journal of Psychiatry, 154*, 1114–1119.

Steinberg, L. (2007). Risk taking in adolescence: New perspectives from brain and behavioral science. *Perspectives on Psychological Science, 16*, 55–59.

Steinberg, L., & Morris, A. S. (2001). Adolescent development. *Annual Review of Psychology, 52*, 83–110.

Steinhausen, H. (2002). The outcome of anorexia nervosa in the 20th century. *American Journal of Psychiatry, 159*, 1284–1293.

Steinmetz, J. E. (1998). The localization of a simple type of learning and memory: The cerebellum and classical eyeblink conditioning. *Current Directions in Psychological Science, 7*, 72–77.

Stekel, W. (1950). *Techniques of analytical psychotherapy*. New York: Liveright.

Stellar, E. (1954). The physiology of motivation. *Psychological Review, 61*, 5–22.

Stepanski, E. J., & Wyatt, J. K. (2003). Use of sleep hygiene in the treatment of insomnia. *Sleep Medicine Reviews, 7*(3), 215–225.

Steptoe, A. (2007). Stress effects: Overview. In G. Fink (Ed.), *Encyclopedia of stress*. San Diego: Elsevier.

Steptoe, A., Gibson, E. L., Hamer, M., & Wardle, J. (2007). Neuroendocrine and cardiovascular correlates of positive affect measured by ecological momentary assessment and by questionnaire. *Psychoneuroendocrinology, 32*, 56–64.

Sterman, J. D. (2008). Risk communication on climate: Mental models and mass balance. *Science, 322*, 532–533.

Stern, W. (1914). *The psychological method of testing intelligence*. Baltimore: Warwick & York.

Sternberg, R. J. (1985). *Beyond IQ: A triarchic theory of human intelligence*. New York: Cambridge University Press.

Sternberg, R. J. (1986). *Intelligence applied: Understanding and increasing your intellectual skills*. New York: Harcourt Brace Jovanovich.

Sternberg, R. J. (1988a). A three-facet model of creativity. In R. J. Sternberg (Ed.), *The nature of creativity: Contemporary psychological perspectives*. Cambridge, England: Cambridge University Press.

Sternberg, R. J. (1988b). *The triarchic mind: A new theory of human intelligence*. New York: Viking.

Sternberg, R. J. (1988c). Triangulating love. In R. J. Sternberg & M. L. Barnes (Eds.), *The psychology of love*. New Haven, CT: Yale University Press.

Sternberg, R. J. (1991). Theory-based testing of intellectual abilities: Rationale for the triarchic abilities test. In H. A. H. Rowe (Ed.), *Intelligence: Reconceptualization and measurement*. Hillsdale, NJ: Erlbaum.

Sternberg, R. J. (1998). How intelligent is intelligence testing? *Scientific American Presents Exploring Intelligence, 9*, 12–17.

Sternberg, R. J. (1999). The theory of successful intelligence. *Review of General Psychology, 3*, 292–316.

Sternberg, R. J. (2000a). Creativity is a decision. In A. L. Costa (Ed.), *Teaching for intelligence II* (pp. 85–106). Arlington Heights, IL: Skylight Training.

Sternberg, R. J. (2000b). Successful intelligence: A unified view of giftedness. In C. F. M. van Lieshout & P. G. Heymans (Eds.), *Developing talent across the life span* (pp. 43–65). Philadelphia: Psychology Press.

Sternberg, R. J. (2003a). Construct validity of the theory of successful intelligence. In R. J. Sternberg, J. Lautrey, & T. I. Lubart (Eds.), *Models of intelligence: International perspectives*. Washington, DC: American Psychological Association.

Sternberg, R. J. (2003b). My house is a very, very, very fine house—But it is not the only house. In

H. Nyborg (Ed.), *The scientific study of general intelligence: Tribute to Arthur R. Jensen.* Oxford, UK: Pergamon.

Sternberg, R. J. (2004). Culture and Intelligence. *American Psychologist, 59,* 325–338.

Sternberg, R. J. (2005a). There are no public policy implications: A reply to Rushton and Jensen. *Psychology, Public Policy, and the Law, 11,* 295–301.

Sternberg, R. J. (2005b). The triarchic theory of successful intelligence. In D. P. Flanagan & P. L. Harrison (Eds.), *Contemporary intellectual assessment: Theories, tests and issues* (pp. 103–119). New York: Guillford Press.

Sternberg, R. J. (2006). A duplex theory of love. In R. J. Sternberg & K. Weis (Eds.), *The new psychology of love.* New Haven, CT: Yale University Press.

Sternberg, R. J. (2007). Intelligence and culture. In S. Kitayama & D. Cohen (Eds.), *Handbook of cultural psychology* (pp. 547–568). New York: Guilford.

Sternberg, R. J., Conway, B. E., Ketron, J. L., & Bernstein, M. (1981). People's conceptions of intelligence. *Journal of Personality and Social Psychology, 41,* 37–55.

Sternberg, R. J., Grigorenko, E. L., & Kidd, K. K. (2005). Intelligence, race, and genetics. *American Psychologist, 60,* 45–69.

Sternberg, R. J., & Hedlund, J. (2002). Practical intelligence, g, and work psychology. *Human Performance, 15,* 143–160.

Sternberg, R. J., & O'Hara, L. A. (1999). Creativity and intelligence. In R. J. Sternberg (Ed.), *Handbook of creativity.* New York: Cambridge University Press.

Stetler, C., Murali, R., Chen, E., & Miller, G. E. (2005). Stress, immunity, and disease. In C. L. Cooper (Ed.), *Handbook of stress medicine and health.* Boca Raton, FL: CRC Press.

Steven, M. S., & Blakemore, C. (2004). Cortical plasticity in the adult human brain. In M. S. Gazzaniga (Ed.), *The cognitive neurosciences.* Cambridge, MA: MIT Press.

Stevens, G., Raphael, B., & Dobson, M. (2007). Effects of public disasters and mass violence. In G. Fink (Ed.), *Encyclopedia of stress.* San Diego: Elsevier.

Stevens, S. S. (1955). The measurement of loudness. *Journal of the Acoustical Society of America, 27,* 815–819.

Stewart, W. H., Jr., & Roth, P. L. (2007). A meta-analysis of achievement motivation differences between entrepreneurs and managers. *Journal of Small Business Management, 45,* 401–421.

Stewart-Williams, S. (2004). The placebo puzzle: Putting the pieces together. *Health Psychology, 23,* 198–206.

Stich, S. P. (1990). Rationality. In D. N. Osherson & E. E. Smith (Eds.), *Thinking: An invitation to cognitive science* (Vol. 3). Cambridge, MA: MIT Press.

Stickgold, R. (2001). Toward a cognitive neuroscience of sleep. *Sleep Medicine Reviews, 5,* 417–421.

Stickgold, R. (2005). Why we dream. In M. H. Kryger, T. Roth, & W. C. Dement (Eds.). *Principles and practice of sleep medicine.* Philadelphia: Elsevier Saunders.

Stickgold, R., & Walker, M. P. (2005). Memory consolidation and reconsolidation: What is the role of sleep? *Trends in Neurosciences, 28*(8), 408–415.

Stoddard, G. (1943). *The meaning of intelligence.* New York: Macmillan.

Stone, A. A., Bovbjerg, D. H., Neale, J. M., Napoli, A., Valdimarsdottir, H., Cox, D., Hayden, F. G., & Gwaltney, J. M. (1992). Development of the common cold symptoms following experimental rhino-

virus infection is related to prior stressful events. *Behavioral Medicine, 18,* 115–120.

Stone, L. (1977). *The family, sex and marriage in England 1500–1800.* New York: Harper & Row.

Stone, W. N. (2003). Group psychotherapy. In A. Tasman, J. Kay, & J. A. Lieberman (Eds.), *Psychiatry.* New York: Wiley.

Stoner, J. A. F. (1961). *A comparison of individual and group decisions involving risk.* Unpublished master's thesis, Massachusetts Institute of Technology.

Stoohs, R. A., Blum, H. C., Haselhorst, M., Duchna, H. W., Guilleminault, C., & Dement, W. C. (1998). Normative data on snoring: A comparison between younger and older adults. *European Respiratory Journal, 11,* 451–457.

Stoolmiller, M. (1999). Implications of the restricted range of family environments for estimates of heritability and nonshared environment in behavior-genetic adoption studies. *Psychological Bulletin, 125,* 392–409.

Strahan, E. J., Lafrance, A., Wilson, A. E., Ethier, N., Spencer, S. J., & Zanna, M. P. (2008). Victoria's dirty secret: How sociocultural norms influence adolescent girls and women. *Personality and Social Psychology Bulletin, 34*(2), 288–301.

Strange, D., Clifasefi, S., & Garry, M. (2007). False memories. In M. Garry & H. Hayne (Eds.), *Do justice and let the sky fall: Elizabeth F. Lotus and her contributions to science, law, and academic freedom.* Mahwah, NJ: Erlbaum.

Strasburger, V. C. (2007). First do no harm: Why have parents and pediatricians missed the boat on children and media? *Journal of Pediatrics, 151,* 334–336.

Straus, M. A. (2000). Corporal punishment and primary prevention of physical abuse. *Child Abuse & Neglect, 24,* 1109–1114.

Straus, M. A., & Stewart, J. H. (1999). Corporal punishment by American parents: National data on prevalence, chronicity, severity, and duration, in relation to child family characteristics. *Clinical Child & Family Psychology Review, 2*(2), 55–70.

Strayer, D. L., & Drews, F. A. (2007). Cell-phone-induced driver distraction. *Current Directions in Psychological Science, 16,* 128–131.

Strayer, D. L., & Johnston, W. A. (2001). Driven to distraction: Dual-task studies of simulated driving and conversing on a cellular telephone. *Psychological Science, 12,* 462–466.

Strayer, D. L., Drews, F. A., & Crouch, D. J. (2006). A comparison of the cell phone driver and the drunk driver. *Human Factors, 48,* 381–391.

Streissguth, A. (2007). Offspring effects of prenatal alcohol exposure from birth to 25 years: The Seattle prospective longitudinal study. *Journal of Clinical Psychology in Medical Settings, 14,* 81–101.

Streit, W. J. (2005). Microglia and neuroprotection: Implications for Alzheimer's disease. *Brain Research Reviews, 48,* 234–239.

Strenze, T. (2007). Intelligence and socioeconomic success: A meta-analytic review of longitudinal research. *Intelligence, 35,* 401–426.

Striegel-Moore, R. H., & Bulik, C. M. (2007). Risk factors for eating disorders. *American Psychologist, 62,* 181–198.

Striegel-Moore, R. H., Silberstein, L. R., & Rodin, J. (1993). The social self in bulimia nervosa: Public self-consciousness, social anxiety, and perceived fraudulence. *Journal of Abnormal Psychology, 102.*

Strollo, P. J. Jr., Atwood, C. W. Jr., & Sanders, M. H. (2007). Medical therapy for obstructive sleep apnea-hypopnea syndrome. In M. H. Kryger, T.

Roth, & W. C. Dement (Eds.), *Principles and practice of sleep medicine.* Philadelphia: Saunders.

Stroup, T. S., Kraus, J. E., & Marder, S. R. (2006). Pharmacotherapies. In J. A. Lieberman, T. S. Stroup, & D. O. Perkins (Eds.), *Textbook of schizophrenia.* Washington, DC: American Psychiatric Publishing.

Stubbe, J. H., Posthuma, D., Boomsma, D. I., & de Geus, E. J. C. (2005). Heritability of life satisfaction in adults: A twin study. *Psychological Medicine, 35,* 1581–1588.

Sudak, H. S. (2005). Suicide. In B. J. Sadock & V. A. Sadock (Eds.), *Kaplan & Sadock's comprehensive textbook of psychiatry.* Philadelphia: Lippincott-Williams & Wilkins.

Sue, D. W., & Sue, D. (1999). *Counseling the culturally different: Theory and practice.* New York: Wiley.

Sue, S. (2003). In defense of cultural competency in psychotherapy and treatment. *American Psychologist, 58,* 964–970.

Sue, S., Zane, N., & Young, K. (1994). Research on psychotherapy with culturally diverse populations. In A. E. Bergin & S. L. Garfield (Eds.), *Handbook of psychotherapy and behavior change* (4th ed.). New York: Wiley.

Sufka, K. J., & Price, D. D. (2002). Gate control theory reconsidered. *Brain & Mind, 3,* 277–290.

Sugarman, J. (2007). Practical rationality and the questionable promise of positive psychology. *Journal of Humanistic Psychology, 47,* 175–197.

Sugiyama, L. S. (2005). Physical attractiveness in adaptionist perspective. In D. M. Buss (Ed.), *The handbook of evolutionary psychology.* New York: Wiley.

Sullivan, G. M., & Coplan, J. D. (2000). Anxiety disorders: Biochemical aspects. In B. J. Sadock & V. A. Sadock (Eds.), *Kaplan and Sadock's comprehensive textbook of psychiatry,* (7th ed., Vol. 1). Philadelphia: Lippincott/Williams & Wilkins.

Sullivan, P. F., Neale, M. C., & Kendler, K. S. (2000). Genetic epidemiology of major depression: Review and meta-analysis. *American Journal of Psychiatry, 157,* 1552–1562.

Sullivan, P. F., Owen, M. J., O'Donovan, M. C., & Freedman, R. (2006). Genetics. In J. A. Lieberman, T. S. Stroup, & D. O. Perkins (Eds.), *Textbook of schizophrenia* (pp. 39–54). Washington, DC: American Psychiatric Publishing.

Sundblad, E. L., Biel, A., & Gärling, T. (2007). Cognitive and affective risk judgements related to climate change. *Journal of Environmental Psychology, 27,* 97–106.

Super, C. M. (1976). Environmental effects on motor development: A case of African infant precocity. *Developmental Medicine and Child Neurology, 18,* 561–567.

Surtees, P., & Wainwright, N. (2007). Life events and health. In G. Fink (Ed.), *Encyclopedia of stress.* San Diego: Elsevier.

Susman, E. J., & Rogol, A. (2004). Puberty and psychological development. In R. M. Lerner & L. Steinberg (Eds.), *Handbook of adolescent psychology.* New York: Wiley.

Susman, E. J., Dorn, L. D., & Schiefelbein, V. L. (2003). Puberty, sexuality, and health. In R. M. Lerner, M. A. Easterbrooks, & J. Mistry (Eds.), *Handbook of psychology, Vol. 6: Developmental psychology.* New York: Wiley.

Susser, E. B., Brown, A., & Matte, T. D. (1999). Prenatal factors and adult mental and physical health. *Canadian Journal of Psychiatry, 44,* 326–334.

Susser, E. B., Neugebauer, R., Hoek, H. W., Brown, A. S., Lin, S., Labovitz, D., & Gorman,

J. M. (1996). Schizophrenia after prenatal famine: Further evidence. *Archives of General Psychiatry, 53*, 25–31.

Suzuki, K. (2007). The moon illusion: Kaufman and Rock's (1962) apparent-distance theory reconsidered. *Japanese Psychological Research, 49*, 57–67.

Swan, G. E., Hudmon, K. S., & Khroyan, T. V. (2003). Tobacco dependence. In A. M. Nezu, C. M. Nezu, & P. A. Geller (Eds.), *Handbook of psychology, Vol. 9: Health Psychology.* New York: Wiley.

Swim, J. K. (1994). Perceived versus meta-analytic effect sizes: An assessment of the accuracy of gender stereotypes. *Journal of Personality and Social Psychology, 66*, 21–36.

Swim, J. K., & Sanna, L. J. (1996). He's skilled, she's lucky: A meta-analysis of observers' attributions for women's and men's successes and failures. *Personality and Social Psychology Bulletin, 22*, 507–519.

Szasz, T. (1974). *The myth of mental illness.* New York: Harper & Row.

Szasz, T. (1990). Law and psychiatry: The problems that will not go away. *The Journal of Mind and Behavior, 11*(3/4), 557–564.

Szegedy-Maszak, M. (2005, August 8). In gambling's grip. *Los Angeles Times.* Retrieved March 10, 2006, from http://www.latimes.com/features/printedition/health/la-he-gamble8aug08,1,3002368.story?coll=la-headlines-pe-health.

Tajfel, H., & Turner, J. C. (1979). An integrative theory of intergroup conflict. In W. G. Austin & S. Worchel (Eds.), *The social psychology of intergroup relations.* Monterey, CA: Brooks/Cole.

Takahashi, M., & Kaida, K. (2006). Napping. In T. Lee–Chiong (Ed.), *Sleep: A comprehensive handbook.* Hoboken, NJ: Wiley-Liss.

Takahashi, M., Nakata, A., Haratani, T., Ogawa, Y., & Arito, H. (2004). Post-lunch nap as a worksite intervention to promote alertness on the job. *Ergonomics, 47*, 1003–1013.

Takahashi, T., Sasaki, M., Itoh, H., Yamadera, W., Ozone, M., Obuchi, K., Hayashida, K., Matsunaga, N., & Sano, H. (2002). Melatonin alleviates jet lag symptoms caused by an 11-hour eastward flight. *Psychiatry & Clinical Neurosciences, 56*, 301–302.

Talarico, J. M., & Rubin, D. C. (2003). Confidence, not consistency, characterizes flashbulb memories. *Psychological Science, 14*, 455–461.

Talarico, J. M., & Rubin, D. C. (2007). Flashbulb memories are special after all; in phenomenology, not accuracy. *Applied Cognitive Psychology, 21*, 557–578.

Talbott, J. A. (2004). Deinstitutionalization: Avoiding the disasters of the past. *Psychiatric Services, 55*, 1112–1115.

Talwar, S. K., Xu, S., Hawley, E. S., Weiss, S. A., Moxon, K. A., & Chapin, J. K. (2002). Behavioural neuroscience: Rat navigation guided by remote control. *Nature, 417*, 37–38.

Tamakoshi, A., Ohno, Y., & JACC Study Group. (2004). Self-reported sleep duration as a predictor of all-cause mortality: Results from JACC study, Japan. *Sleep: A Journal of Sleep and Sleep Disorders Research, 27*, 51–54.

Tamminga, C. A. (1999). Principles of the pharmacotherapy of schizophrenia. In D. S. Charney, E. J. Nestler, & B. S. Bunney (Eds.), *Neurobiology of mental illness* (pp. 272–290). New York: Oxford University Press.

Tamminga, C. A., & Carlsson A. (2003). Psychiatric pathophysiology: Schizophrenia. In A. Tasman, J. Kay, & J. A. Lieberman (Eds.), *Psychiatry.* New York: Wiley.

Tanaka, J., Weiskopf, D., & Williams, P. (2001). The role of color in high-level vision. *Trends in Cognitive Sciences, 5*, 211–215.

Tanaka-Matsumi, J. (2001). Abnormal psychology and culture. In D. Matsumoto (Ed.), *The handbook of culture & psychology.* New York: Oxford University Press.

Tanapat, P., & Gould, E. (2007). Neurogenesis. In G. Fink (Ed.), *Encyclopedia of stress.* San Diego: Elsevier.

Tangney, J. P., Stuewig, J., & Mashek, D. J. (2007). Moral emotions and moral behavior. *Annual Review of Psychology, 58*, 345–372.

Tanner, J. L. (2006). Recentering during emerging adulthood: A critical turning point in life span human development. In J. J. Arnett & J. L. Tanner (Eds.), *Emerging adults in America: Coming of age in the 21st century.* Washington, DC: American Psychological Association.

Tart, C. T. (1988). From spontaneous event to lucidity: A review of attempts to consciously control nocturnal dreaming. In J. Gackenbach & S. LaBerge (Eds.), *Conscious mind, sleeping brain: Perspectives on lucid dreaming.* New York: Plenum.

Tashkin, D. P., Baldwin, G. C., Sarafian, T., Dubinett, S., & Roth, M. D. (2002). Respiratory and immunologic consequences of marijuana smoking. *Journal of Clinical Pharmacology, 42*, 71S–81S.

Tavris, C. (1998, September 13). Peer pressure (Review of *The Nurture Assumption*). *The New York Times Book Review, 103*, p. 14.

Taylor, E. (1999). An intellectual renaissance of humanistic psychology. *Journal of Humanistic Psychology, 39*, 7–25.

Taylor, E. (2001). Positive psychology and humanistic psychology: A reply to Seligman. *Journal of Humanistic Psychology, 41*(1), 13–29.

Taylor, J. H., & Walker, L. (1997). Moral climate and the development of moral reasoning: The effects of dyadic discussions between young offenders. *Journal of Moral Education, 26*, 21–43.

Taylor, S. E. (2007). Social support. In H. S. Friedman & R. C. Silver (Eds.), *Foundations of health psychology.* New York: Oxford University Press.

Taylor, S. E., & Brown, J. D. (1988). Illusion and well-being: A social psychological perspective on mental health. *Psychological Bulletin, 103*, 193–210.

Taylor, S. E., & Brown, J. D. (1994). Positive illusions and well-being revisited: Separating fact from fiction. *Psychological Bulletin, 116*, 21–27.

Tedlock, L. B. (1992). Zuni and Quiche dream sharing and interpreting. In B. Tedlock (Ed.), *Dreaming: Anthropological and psychological interpretations.* Santa Fe, NM: School of American Research Press.

Teigen, K. H. (2004). Judgments by representativeness. In F. P. Rudiger (Ed.), *Cognitive illusions.* New York: Psychology Press.

Tellegen, A., Lykken, D. T., Bouchard, T. J., Jr., Wilcox, K. J., Segal, N. L., & Rich, S. (1988). Personality similarity in twins reared apart and together. *Journal of Personality and Social Psychology, 54*, 1031–1039.

Temple, J. L., Giacomelli, A. M., Roemmich, J. N., & Epstein, L. H. (2008). Dietary variety impairs habituation in children. *Health Psychology, 27*, S10–S19.

Tennen, H., & Affleck, G. (1999). Finding benefits in adversity. In C. R. Snyder (Ed.), *Coping: The psychology of what works.* New York: Oxford University Press.

Tepper, B. J., & Nurse, R. J. (1997). Fat perception is related to PROP taster status. *Physiology & Behavior, 61*, 949–954.

Terman, L. M. (1916). *The measurement of intelligence.* Boston: Houghton Mifflin.

Terr, L. (1994). *Unchained memories.* New York: Basic Books.

Terracciano, A., Abdel-Khalak, A. M., Adam, N., Adamovova, L., Ahn, C. K., Ahn, H. N., et al. (2005). National character does not reflect mean personality trait levels in 49 cultures. *Science, 310*, 96–100.

Tessier-Lavigne, M. (2000). Visual processing by the retina. In E. R. Kandel, J. H. Schwartz, & T. M. Jessell (Eds.), *Principles of neural science.* New York: McGraw-Hill.

Teuber, M. (1974). Sources of ambiguity in the prints of Maurits C. Escher. *Scientific American, 231*, 90–104.

Thase, M. E. (2005). Bipolar depression: Issues in diagnosis and treatment. *Harvard Review of Psychiatry, 13*, 257–271.

Thase, M. E., & Denko, T. (2008). Pharmacotherapy of mood disorders. *Annual Review of Clinical Psychology, 4*, 53–91.

Thase, M. E., & Sloan D. M. E. (2006). Venlafaxine. In A. F. Schatzberg & C. B. Nemeroff (Eds.), *Essentials of clinical psychopharmacology.* Washington, DC: American Psychological Association.

Thase, M. E., Jindal, R., & Howland, R. H. (2002). Biological aspects of depression. In I. H. Gotlib & C. L. Hammen (Eds.), *Handbook of depression.* New York: Guilford.

Thayer, A., & Lynn, S. J. (2006). Guided imagery and recovered memory therapy: Considerations and cautions. *Journal of Forensic Psychology Practice, 6*, 63–73.

Thayer, R. E. (1996). *The origin of everyday moods.* New York: Oxford University Press.

Thelen, E. (1995). Motor development: A new synthesis. *American Psychologist, 50*, 79–95.

Theorell, T. (2005). Stress and prevention of cardiovascular disease. In C. L. Cooper (Ed.), *Handbook of stress medicine and health.* Boca Raton, FL: CRC Press.

Thomas, A. J., Kalaria, R. N., & O'Brien, J. T. (2004). Depression and vascular disease: What is the relationship? *Journal of Affective Disorders, 79*(1–3), 81–95.

Thomas, A., & Chess, S. (1977). *Temperament and development.* New York: Brunner/Mazel.

Thomas, D. R. (1992). Discrimination and generalization. In L. R. Squire (Ed.), *Encyclopedia of learning and memory.* New York: Macmillan.

Thomas, R. M. (2005). *Comparing theories of child development.* Belmont, CA: Wadsworth.

Thompson, J. K., & Kinder, B. (2003). Eating disorders. In M. Hersen, & S. Turner (Eds.), *Handbook of adult psychopathology.* New York: Plenum Press.

Thompson, J. K., Roehrig, M., & Kinder, B. N. (2007). Eating disorders. In M. Hersen, S. M. Turner, & D. C. Beidel (Eds.), *Adult psychopathology and diagnosis.* New York: Wiley.

Thompson, J. K., & Stice, E. (2001). Thin-ideal internalization: Mounting evidence for a new risk factor for body-image disturbance and eating pathology. *Current Directions in Psychological Science, 10*(5), 181–183.

Thompson, R. A. (1998). Early socio-personality development. In N. Eisenberg (Ed.), *Handbook of child psychology: Social, emotional, and personality.* New York: Wiley.

Thompson, R. A. (1999). Early attachment and later development. In J. Cassidy & P. R. Shaver (Eds.),

Handbook of attachment: Theory, research, and clinical applications. New York: Guilford.

Thompson, R. A. (2000). The legacy of early attachments. *Child Development, 71,* 145–152.

Thompson, R. A., & Nelson, C. A. (2001). Developmental science and the media: Early brain development. *American Psychologist, 56,* 5–15.

Thompson, R. F. (1989). A model system approach to memory. In P. R. Solomon, G. R. Goethals, C. M. Kelley, & B. R. Stephens (Eds.), *Memory: Interdisciplinary approaches.* New York: Springer-Verlag.

Thompson, R. F. (1992). Memory. *Current Opinion in Neurobiology, 2,* 203–208.

Thompson, R. F. (2005). In search of memory traces. *Annual Review of Psychology, 56,* 1–23.

Thompson, R. F., & Zola, S. M. (2003). In D. K. Freedheim (Ed.), *Handbook of psychology* (Vol. 2): New York: Wiley.

Thorne, B. M., & Henley, T. B. (1997). *Connections in the history and systems of psychology.* Boston: Houghton Mifflin.

Thornhill, R. (1976). Sexual selection and nuptial feeding behavior in *Bittacus apicalis* (Insecta: Mecoptera). *American Naturalist, 110,* 529–548.

Thornton, B., & Maurice, J. K. (199). Physical attractiveness contrast effect and the moderating influence of self-consciousness. *Sex Roles, 40,* 379–392.

Thornton, B., & Moore, S. (1993). Physical attractiveness contrast effect: Implications for self-esteem and evaluations of the social self. *Personality and Social Psychology Bulletin, 19,* 474–480.

Thun, M. J., Apicella, L. F., & Henley, S. J. (2000). Smoking vs. other risk factors as the cause of smoking-attributable deaths: Confounding in the courtroom. *Journal of the American Medical Association, 284,* 706–712.

Tibbo, P., Hanstock, C., Valiakalayil, A., & Allen, P. (2004). 3-T proton MRS investigation and glutamine in adolescents at high genetic risk for schizophrenia. *American Journal of Psychiatry, 161,* 1116–1118.

Tice, D. M., Bratslavsky, E., & Baumeister, R. F. (2001). Emotional distress regulation takes precedence over impulse control: If you feel bad, do it! *Journal of Personality and Social Psychology, 80,* 53–67.

Till, B. D., & Priluck, R. L. (2000). Stimulus generalization in classical conditioning: An initial investigation and extension. *Psychology and Marketing, 17,* 55–72.

Timm, D. A., & Slavin, J. L. (2008). Dietary fiber and the relationship to chronic diseases. *American Journal of Lifestyle Medicine, 2,,* 233–240.

Tindale, R. S., Kameda, T., & Hinsz, V. B. (2003). Group decision making. In M. A. Hogg & J. Cooper (Eds.), *The Sage handbook of social psychology.* Thousand Oaks, CA: Sage.

Titsworth, B. S., & Kiewra, K. A. (2004). Spoken organizational lecture cues and student notetaking as facilitators of student learning. *Contemporary Educational Psychology, 29,* 447–461.

Todd, J. T., & Morris, E. K. (1992). Case histories in the great power of steady misrepresentation. *American Psychologist, 47,* 1441–1453.

Todd, P. M., & Gigerenzer, G. (2000). Precis of simple heuristics that make us smart. *Behavioral & Brain Sciences, 23,* 727–780.

Todd, P. M., & Gigerenzer, G. (2007). Environments that make us smart: Ecological rationality. *Current Directions in Psychological Science, 16,* 167–171.

Todorov, A., Mandisodza, A. N., Goren, A., & Hall, C. C. (2005). Inferences of competence from faces predict election outcomes. *Science, 308,* 1623–1626.

Toga, A. W., Thompson, P. M., & Sowell, E. R. (2006). Mapping brain maturation. *Trends in Neurosciences, 29,* 148–159.

Tolman, D. L., & Diamond, L. M. (2001). Desegregating sexuality research: Cultural and biological perspectives on gender and desire. *Annual Review of Sex Research, 12,* 33–74.

Tolman, E. C. (1932). *Purposive behavior in animals and men.* New York: Appleton-Century-Crofts.

Tolman, E. C. (1938). The determiners of behavior at a choice point. *Psychological Review, 45,* 1–41.

Tolman, E. C. (1948). Cognitive maps in rats and men. *Psychological Review, 55,* 189–208.

Tolman, E. C., & Honzik, C. H. (1930). Introduction and removal of reward, and maze performance in rats. *University of California Publications in Psychology, 4,* 257–275.

Tom, S. M., Fox, C. R., Trepel, C., & Poldrack, R. A. (2007). The neural basis of loss aversion in decision-making under risk. *Science, 315,* 515–518.

Tomkins, S. S. (1980). Affect as amplification: Some modifications in theory. In R. Plutchik & H. Kellerman (Eds.), *Emotion: Theory, research and experience* (Vol. 1). New York: Academic Press.

Tomkins, S. S. (1991). *Affect, imagery, consciousness: 3. Anger and fear.* New York: Springer-Verlag.

Tooby, J., & Cosmides, L. (1989). Evolutionary psychology and the generation of culture: Part 1. Theoretical considerations. *Ethology and Sociobiology, 10,* 29–49.

Torgersen, S. (1979). The nature and origin of common phobic fears. *British Journal of Psychiatry, 119,* 343–351.

Torgersen, S. (1983). Genetic factors in anxiety disorders. *Archives of General Psychiatry, 40,* 1085–1089.

Tormala, Z. L., & Petty, R. E. (2002). What doesn't kill me makes me stronger: The effects of resisting persuasion on attitude certainty. *Journal of Personality and Social Psychology, 83,* 1298–1313.

Tormala, Z. L., & Petty, R. E. (2004). Resistance to persuasion and attitude certainty: The moderating role of elaboration. *Personality and Social Psychology Bulletin, 30,* 1446–1457.

Torrance, E. P. (1962). *Guiding creative talent.* Englewood Cliffs, NJ: Prentice-Hall.

Torrey, E. F. (1992). *Freudian fraud: The malignant effect of Freud's theory on American thought and culture.* New York: Harper Perennial.

Torrey, E. F. (1996). *Out of the shadows.* New York: Wiley.

Toufexis, A. (1990, December 17). Drowsy America. *Time,* pp. 78–85.

Tourangeau, R. (2004). Survey research and societal change. *Annual Review of Psychology, 55,* 775–801.

Tourangeau, R., & Yan, T. (2007). Sensitive questions in surveys. *Psychological Bulletin, 133,* 859–883.

Tov, W., & Diener, E. (2007). Culture and subjective well-being. In S. Kitayama & D. Cohen (Eds.), *Handbook of cultural psychology.* New York: Guilford.

Tower, R. B., & Krasner, M. (2006). Marital closeness, autonomy, mastery, and depressive symptoms in a U.S. Internet sample. *Personal Relationships, 13,* 429–449.

Toyota, H., & Kikuchi, Y. (2004). Self-generated elaboration and spacing effects on incidental memory. *Perceptual and Motor Skills, 99,* 1193–1200.

Toyota, H., & Kikuchi, Y. (2005). Encoding richness of self-generated elaboration and spacing effects on incidental memory. *Perceptual and Motor Skills, 101,* 621–627.

Tracy, J. L., & Robins, R. W. (2008). The automaticity of emotion recognition. *Emotion, 8,* 81–95.

Travis, F. (2001). Autonomic and EEG patterns distinguish transcending from other experiences during Transcendental Meditation practice. *International Journal of Psychophysiology, 42,* 1–9.

Travis, F., & Pearson, C. (2000). Pure consciousness: Distinct phenomenological and physiological correlates of "consciousness itself." *International Journal of Neuroscience, 100*(1-4), 77–89.

Treisman, G. J. (1999). AIDS education for psychiatrists. *Primary Psychiatry, 6*(5), 71–73.

Triandis, H. C. (1989). Self and social behavior in differing cultural contexts. *Psychological Review, 96,* 269–289.

Triandis, H. C. (1994). *Culture and social behavior.* New York: McGraw-Hill.

Triandis, H. C. (2001). Individualism and collectivism: Past, present, and future. In D. Matsumoto (Ed.), *The handbook of culture and psychology.* New York: Oxford University Press.

Triandis, H. C. (2007). Culture and psychology: A history of the study of their relationship. In S. Kitayama & D. Cohen (Eds.), *Handbook of cultural psychology.* New York: Guilford.

Trivers, R. L. (1971). The evolution of reciprocal altruism. *Quarterly Review of Biology, 46,* 35–57.

Trivers, R. L. (1972). Parental investment and sexual selection. In B. Campbell (Ed.), *Sexual selection and the descent of man.* Chicago: Aldine.

Trotter, R. J. (1986, September). The three faces of love. *Psychology Today,* pp. 46–54.

Trujillo, M. (2005). Culture-bound syndromes. In B. J. Sadock & V. A. Sadock (Eds.), *Kaplan & Sadock's comprehensive textbook of psychiatry.* Philadelphia: Lippincott Williams & Wilkins.

Tsai, J. L., Butcher, J. N., Muñoz, R. F., & Vitousek, K. (2001). Culture, ethnicity, and psychopathology. In P. B. Sutker & H. E. Adams (Eds.), *Comprehensive handbook of psychopathology.* New York: Kluwer Academic/Plenum.

Tsigos, C., Kyrou, I., & Chrousos, G. P. (2005). Stress, endocrine manifestations and diseases. In C. L. Cooper (Ed.), *Handbook of stress medicine and health.* Boca Raton, FL: CRC Press.

Tsuang, M. T., Glatt, S. J., & Faraone, S. V. (2003). Genetics and genomics in schizophrenia. *Primary Psychiatry, 10*(3), 37–40, 50.

Tucker, A. M., Dinges, D. F., & Van Dongen, H. P. A. (2007). Trait interindividual differences in the sleep physiology of healthy young adults. *Journal of Sleep Research, 16,* 170–180.

Tuckey, M. R., & Brewer, N. (2003). The influence of schemas, stimulus ambiguity, and interview schedule on eyewitness memory over time. *Journal of Experimental Psychology: Applied, 9,* 101–118.

Tugade, M. M., & Fredrickson, B. L. (2004). Resilient individuals use positive emotions to bounce back from negative emotional experiences. *Journal of Personality and Social Psychology, 86,* 320–333.

Tulving, E. (1986). What kind of a hypothesis is the distinction between episodic and semantic memory? *Journal of Experimental Psychology: Learning, Memory and Cognition, 12,* 307–311.

Tulving, E. (1993). What is episodic memory? *Current Directions in Psychological Science, 2*(3), 67–70.

Tulving, E. (2001). Origin of autonoesis in episodic memory. In H. L. Roediger III, J. S. Nairne, I. Neath, & A. M. Surprenant (Eds.), *The nature of* remembering: Essays in honor of Robert G. Crowder (pp. 17–34). Washington, DC: American Psychological Association.

Tulving, E. (2002). Episodic memory: From mind to brain. *Annual Review of Psychology, 53,* 1–25.

Tulving, E., & Schacter, D. L. (1990). Priming and human memory systems. *Science, 247,* 301–306.

Tulving, E., & Thomson, D. M. (1973). Encoding specificity and retrieval processes in episodic memory. *Psychological Review, 80,* 352–373.

Tunnell, K. D. (2005). The Oxycontin epidemic and crime panic in rural Kentucky. *Contemporary Drug Problems, 32,* 225–258.

Turek, F. W., & Gillette, M. U. (2004). Melatonin, sleep, and circadian rhythms: Rationale for development of specific melatonin agonists. *Sleep Medicine, 5,* 523–532.

Turk, D. C., & Okifuji, A. (2003). Pain management. In A. M. Nezu, C. M. Nezu, & P. A. Geller (Eds.), *Handbook of psychology, Vol. 9: Health psychology.* New York: Wiley.

Turkheimer, E., & Waldron, M. (2000). Nonshared environment: A theoretical, methodological, and quantitative review. *Psychological Bulletin, 126,* 78–108.

Turkheimer, E., Haley, A., Waldron, M., D'Onofrio, B., & Gottesman, I. I. (2003). Socioeconomic status modifies heritability of IQ in young children. *Psychological Science, 14,* 623–628.

Turkkan, J. S. (1989). Classical conditioning: The new hegemony. *Behavioral and Brain Sciences, 12,* 121–179.

Turner, J. C., & Reynolds, K. J. (2001). The social identity perspective in intergroup relations: Theories, themes, and controversies. In R. Brown & S. L. Gaertner (Eds.), *Blackwell handbook of social psychology: Intergroup processes.* Malden, MA: Blackwell Publishing.

Turner, J. G., Hogg, M. A., Oakes, P. J., Reicher, S. D., & Wetherell, M. S. (1987). *Rediscovering the social group: A self-categorization theory.* Oxford, UK: Basil Blackwell.

Turner, J. R., & Wheaton, B. (1995). Checklist measurement of stressful life events. In S. Cohen, R. C. Kessler, & L. U. Gordon (Eds.), *Measuring stress: A guide for health and social scientists.* New York: Oxford University Press.

Turner, S. M., Beidel, D. C., Stanley, M. A., & Heiser, N. (2001). Obsessive-compulsive disorder. In P. B. Sutker & H. E. Adams (Eds.), *Comprehensive textbook of psychiatry* (3rd ed., pp. 155–182). New York: Kluwer Academic/Plenum.

Tversky, A. (1972). Elimination by aspects: A theory of choice. *Psychological Review, 79,* 281–299.

Tversky, A., & Kahneman, D. (1973). Availability: A heuristic for judging frequency and probability. *Cognitive Psychology, 5,* 207–232.

Tversky, A., & Kahneman, D. (1974). Judgments under uncertainty: Heuristics and biases. *Science, 185,* 1124–1131.

Tversky, A., & Kahneman, D. (1982). Judgment under uncertainty: Heuristics and biases. In D. Kahneman, P. Slovic, & A. Tversky (Eds.), *Judgment under uncertainty: Heuristics and biases.* New York: Cambridge University Press.

Tversky, A., & Kahneman, D. (1983). Extensional versus intuitive reasoning: The conjunction fallacy in probability judgment. *Psychological Review, 90,* 283–315.

Twenge, J. M., Campbell, W. K., & Foster, C. A. (2003). Parenthood and marital satisfaction: A meta-analytic review. *Journal of Marriage and the Family, 65,* 574–583.

Uchino, B. N. (2004). *Social support and physical health outcomes: Understanding the health consequences of our relationships.* New Haven, CT: University Press.

Uchino, B. N., Uno, D., & Holt-Lunstad, J. (1999). Social support, physiological processes, and health. *Current Directions in Psychological Science, 8,* 145–148.

UNAIDS. (2005). *AIDS epidemic.* Retrieved from http://www.unaids.org/Epi2005/doc/ EPIupdate2005_html_en/epi05_03_

Underwood, B. J. (1961). Ten years of massed practice on distributed practice. *Psychological Review, 68,* 229–247.

Unger, R. K., & Crawford, M. (1992). *Women and gender: A feminist psychology.* New York: McGraw-Hill.

Ungerleider, L. G., & Haxby, J. V. (1994). "What" and "where" in the human brain. *Current Opinion in Neurobiology, 4,* 157–165.

United Nations. (n.d.). Brundtland Definition—Three-Dimension Concept. United Nations NGO: Sustainability. Retrieved January 28, 2009 from http://www.unngosustainability.org/ CSD_Definitions%20SD.htm

Ursano, R. J., & Silberman, E. K. (1999). Psychoanalysis, psychoanalytic psychotherapy, and supportive psychotherapy. In R. E. Hales, S. C. Yudofsky, & J. A. Talbott (Eds.), *American Psychiatric Press textbook of psychiatry.* Washington, DC: American Psychiatric Press.

Ursano, R. J., & Silberman, E. K. (2003). Psychoanalysis, psychoanalytic psychotherapy, and supportive psychotherapy. In R. E. Hales & S. C. Yudofsky (Eds.), *Textbook of clinical psychiatry.* Washington, DC: American Psychiatric Publishing.

U.S. Department of Health and Human Services. (1999). *Mental health: A report of the Surgeon General.* Washington, DC: U.S. Government Printing Office.

U.S. Environmental Protection Agency. (2006). Climate change. Retrieved electronically June 4, 2009 at http://epa.gov/climatechange/index.html.

Vaillant, G. E. (1994). Ego mechanisms of defense and personality psychopathology. *Journal of Abnormal Psychology, 103,* 44–50.

Valenstein, E. S. (1973). *Brain control.* New York: Wiley.

Van Blerkom, D. L. (2006). *College study skills: Becoming a strategic learner.* Belmont, CA: Wadsworth.

Van Boven, L. (2005). Experientialism, materialism, and the pursuit of happiness. *Review of General Psychology, 9,* 132–142.

Van de Castle, R. L. (1994). *Our dreaming mind.* New York: Ballantine Books.

van den Berg, A. E., Hartig, T., & Staats, H. (2007). Preference for Nature in Urbanized Societies: Stress, Restoration, and the Pursuit of Sustainability. *Journal of Social Issues, 63,* 79–96.

van den Berg, A. E., Koole, S. L., & van der Wulp, N. Y. (2003). Environmental preference and restoration: (How) are they related? *Journal of Environmental Psychology, 23,* 135–146.

van den Boom, D. (2001). First attachments: Theory and research. In G. Bremner & A. Fogel (Eds.), *Blackwell handbook of infant development* (pp. 296–325). Malden, MA: Blackwell Publishing.

van den Boom, D. C. (1994). The influence of temperament and mothering on attachment and exploration: An experimental manipulation of sensitive responsiveness among lower-class mothers and irritable infants. *Child Development, 65,* 1457–1477.

Vandereycken, W. (2002). History of anorexia nervosa and bulimia nervosa. In C. G. Fairburn, & K. D. Brownell (Eds.), *Eating disorders and obesity.* New York: Guilford.

van der Post, L. (1975). *Jung and the story of our time.* New York: Vintage Books.

Vandewater, E., A., Bickham, D. S., & Lee, J. H. (2006). Time well spent? Relating television use to children's free-time activities. *Pediatrics, 117,* 181–191.

Van Dongen, H. P. A., & Dinges, D. F. (2005). Circadian rhythms in sleepiness, alertness, and performance. In M. H. Kryger, T. Roth, & W. C. Dement (Eds.), *Principles and practice of sleep medicine.* Philadelphia: Elsevier Saunders.

Van Dongen, H. P. A., Baynard, M. D., Maislin, G., & Dinges, D. F. (2004). Systematic interindividual differences in neurobehavioral impairment from sleep loss: Evidence of trait-like differential vulnerability. *Sleep: Journal of Sleep & Sleep Disorders Research, 27,* 423–433.

van Eck, M., Nicolson, N. A., & Berkhof, J. (1998). Effects of stressful daily events on mood states: Relationship to global perceived stress. *Journal of Personality and Social Psychology, 75,* 1572–1585.

van Griensven, F., Chakkraband, M. L. S., Thienkrua, W., Pengjuntr, W., Cardozo, B. L., & Tantipiwatanaskul, P. et al. (2007). Mental health problems among adults in tsunami-affected areas in Southern Thailand. *Journal of the American Medical Association, 296,* 537–548.

van Ijzendoorn, M. H., & Bakermans-Kranenburg, M. J. (2004). Maternal sensitivity and infant temperament in the formation of attachment. In G. Bremner & A. Slater (Eds.), *Theories of infant development.* Malden, MA: Blackwell Publishing.

van Ijzendoorn, M. H., & Juffer, F. (2005). Adoption is a successful natural intervention enhancing adopted children's IQ and school performance. *Current Directions in Psychological Science, 14,* 326–330.

van Ijzendoorn, M. H., & Kroonenberg, P. M. (1988). Cross-cultural patterns of attachment: A meta-analysis of the strange situation. *Child Development, 59,* 147–156.

van Ijzendoorn, M. H., & Sagi, A. (1999). Cross-cultural patterns of attachment: Universal and contextual dimensions. In J. Cassidy & P. R. Shaver (Eds.), *Handbook of attachment: Theory, research, and clinical applications.* New York: Guilford.

van Kammen, D. P., & Marder, S. R. (2005). Serotonin-dopamine antagonists (atypical or second-generation antipsychotics). In B. J. Sadock & V. A. Sadock (Eds.), *Kaplan and Sadock's comprehensive textbook of psychiatry* (pp. 2914–2937). Philadelphia: Lippincott Williams & Wilkins.

van Leeuwen, M. L., & Macrae, C. N. (2004). Is beautiful always good? Implicit benefits of facial attractiveness. *Social Cognition, 22,* 637–649.

Van Praag, H., Zhao, X., & Gage, F. H. (2004). Neurogenesis in the adult mammalian brain. In M. S. Gazzaniga (Ed.), *The cognitive neurosciences* (3rd ed.) (pp. 127–137). Cambridge, MA: MIT Press.

Van Vugt, M. (2001). Community identification moderating the impact of financial incentives in a natural social dilemma: Water conservation. *Personality and Social Psychology Bulletin, 27,* 1440–1449.

Van Vugt, M. (2002). Central, individual, or collective control? Social dilemma strategies for natural resource management. *American Behavioral Scientist, 45*(5), 783–800.

Vase, L. R., Riley, I. J., & Price, D. (2002). A comparison of placebo effects in clinical analgesic trials versus studies of placebo analgesia. *Pain, 99,* 443–452.

Vazquez, C., Munoz, M., & Sanz, J. (1997). Lifetime and 12-month prevalence of DSM-III-R mental disorders among the homeless in Madrid: A European study using the CIDI. *Acta Psychiatrica Scandinavica, 95,* 523–530.

Vecera, S. P., & Palmer, S. E. (2006). Grounding the figure: Surface attachment influences figure-ground organization. *Psychonmic Bulletin & Review, 13,* 563–569.

Vecera, S. P., Vogel, E. K., & Woodman, G. F. (2002). Lower region: A new cue for figure-ground assignment. *Journal of Experimental Psychology: General, 131,* 194–205.

Vermeeren, A. (2004). Residual effects of hypnotics: Epidemiology and clinical implications. *CNS Drugs, 18*(5), 297–328.

Vernberg, E. M., La Greca, A. M., Silverman, W. K., & Prinstein, M. J. (1996). Prediction of post-traumatic stress symptoms in children after Hurricane Andrew. *Journal of Abnormal Psychology, 105,* 237–248.

Vernon, P. A., Wickett, J. C., Bazana, G. P., & Stelmack, R. M. (2000). The neuropsychology and psychophysiology of human intelligence. In R. J. Sternberg (Ed.), *Handbook of intelligence.* Cambridge, UK: Cambridge University Press.

Victoroff, J. (2005). Central nervous system changes with normal aging. In B. J. Sadock & V. A. Sadock (Eds.), *Kaplan & Sadock's comprehensive textbook of psychiatry.* Philadelphia: Lippincott Williams & Wilkins.

Videbech, P. (2006). Hippocampus and unipolar depression. *Directions in Psychiatry, 26,* 183–194.

Videbech, P., & Ravnkilde, B. (2004). Hippocampal volume and depression: A meta-analysis of MRI studies. *American Journal of Psychiatry, 161,* 1957–1966.

Viglione, D. J., & Rivera, B. (2003). Assessing personality and psychopathology with projective methods. In J. R. Graham & J. A. Naglieri (Eds.), *Handbook of psychology, Vol. 10: Assessment psychology.* New York: Wiley.

Vinogradov, S., Cox, P. D., & Yalom, I. D. (2003). Group therapy. In R. E. Hales & S. C. Yudofsky (Eds.), *Textbook of clinical psychiatry.* Washington, DC: American Psychiatric Publishing.

Vinters, H. V. (2001). Aging and the human nervous system. In J. E. Birren & K. W. Schaie (Eds.), *Handbook of the psychology of aging* (5th ed., pp. 134–159). San Diego, CA: Academic Press.

Visser, P. S., & Cooper, J. (2003). Attitude change. In M. A. Hogg & J. Cooper (Eds.), *The Sage handbook of social psychology.* Thousand Oaks, CA: Sage.

Vlek, C. & Steg, L. (2007). Human behavior and environmental sustainability: Problems, driving forces, and research topics. *Journal of Social Issues, 63,* 1–19.

Volavka, J., Czobor, P., Sheitman, B., Lindenmayer, J. P., Citrome, L., McEvoy, J. P., Cooper, T. B., Chakos, M., & Lieberman, J. A. (2002). Clozapine, olanzapine, risperidone, haloperidol in the treatment of patients with chronic schizophrenia and schizoaffective disorder. *American Journal of Psychiatry, 159,* 255–262.

Volkow, N. D., Fowler, J. S., & Wang, G. J. (2004). The addicted human brain viewed in the light of imaging studies: Brain circuits and treatment strategies. *Neuropharmacology, 47,* 3–13.

Voyer, D. (1996). On the magnitude of laterality effects and sex differences in functional lateralities. *Laterality, 1,* 51–83.

Voyer, D., Nolan, C., & Voyer, S. (2000). The relation between experience and spatial performance in men and women. *Sex Roles, 43,* 891–915.

Vygotsky, L. S. (1934/1986). *Thought and language.* A. Kozulin (Trans). Cambridge, MA: MIT Press.

Vyse, S. A. (2000). *Believing in magic: The psychology of superstition.* New York: Oxford University Press.

Vythilingam, M., Shen, J., Drevets, W. C., & Innis, R. B. (2005). Nuclear magnetic resonance imaging: Basic principles and recent findings in neuropsychiatric disorders. In B. J. Sadock & V. A. Sadock (Eds.), *Kaplan & Sadock's comprehensive textbook of psychiatry.* Philadelphia: Lippincott Williams & Wilkins.

Wagner, H. (1989). The physiological differentiation of emotions. In H. Wagner & A. Manstead (Eds), *Handbook of social psychophysiology.* New York: Wiley.

Wald, G. (1964). The receptors of human color vision. *Science, 145,* 1007–1017.

Wald, M., Miner, M., & Seftel, A. D. (2008). Male menopause: Fact or fiction? *American Journal of Lifestyle Medicine, 2,* 132.

Waldrop, D., Lightsey, O. R., Ethington, C. A., Woemmel, C. A., & Coke, A. L. (2001). Self-efficacy, optimism, health competence, and recovery from orthopedic surgery. *Journal of Counseling Psychology, 48,* 233–238.

Walker, E., & Tessner, K. (2008). Schizophrenia. *Perspectives on Psychological Science, 3,* 30–37.

Walker, E., Kestler, L., Bollini, A., & Hochman, K. M. (2004). Schizophrenia: Etiology and course. *Annual Review of Psychology, 55,* 401–430.

Walker, E., Mittal, V., & Tessner, K. (2008). Stress and the hypothalamic pituitary adrenal axis in the developmental course of schizophrenia. *Annual Review of Clinical Psychology, 4,* 189–216.

Walker, L. J. (1988). The development of moral reasoning. In R. Vasta (Ed.), *Annals of child development* (Vol. 5). Greenwich, CT: JAI Press.

Walker, L. J. (1989). A longitudinal study of moral reasoning. *Child Development, 60,* 157–166.

Walker, L. J. (2007). Progress and prospects in the psychology of moral development. In G. W. Ladd (Ed.), *Appraising the human developmental sciences: Essays in honor of Merrill-Palmer Quarterly.* Detroit: Wayne State University Press.

Walker, L. J., & Taylor, J. H. (1991). Strange transitions in moral reasoning: A longitudinal study of developmental processes. *Developmental Psychology, 27,* 330–337.

Walker, M. P., & Stickgold, R. (2004). Sleep-dependent learning and memory consolidation. *Neuron, 44,* 121–133.

Walker, M. P., & Stickgold, R. (2006). Sleep, memory, and plasticity. *Annual Review of Psychology, 57,* 139–166.

Walker, M. P., Brakefield, T., Morgan, A., Hobson, J. A., & Stickgold, R. (2002). Practice with sleep makes perfect: Sleep dependent motor skill learning. *Neuron, 35,* 205–211.

Wallace, B., & Fisher, L. E. (1999). *Consciousness and behavior.* Boston: Allyn & Bacon.

Wallen, K. (1989). Mate selection: Economics and affection. *Behavioral and Brain Sciences, 12,* 37–38.

Walraven, J., Enroth-Cugell, C., Hood, D. C., MacLeod, D. I. A., & Schnapf, J. L. (1990). The control of visual sensitivity: Receptoral and post-receptoral processes. In L. Spillmann & J. S. Werner (Eds.), *Visual perception: The neurophysiological foundations.* San Diego: Academic Press.

Walsh, B. T. (2003). Eating disorders. In A. Tasman, J. Kay, & J. A. Lieberman (Eds.), *Psychiatry.* New York: Wiley.

Walsh, B. T., Seidman, S. N., Sysko, R., & Gould, M. (2002). Placebo response studies of major depression: Variable, substantial and growing. *Journal of the American Medical Association, 287,* 1840–1847.

Walsh, J. K., Dement, W. C., & Dinges, D. F. (2005). Sleep medicine, public policy, and public health. In M. H. Kryger, T. Roth, & W. C. Dement (Eds.). *Principles and practice of sleep medicine.* Philadelphia: Elsevier Saunders.

Walsh, R., & Shapiro, S. L. (2006). The meeting of meditative disciplines and Western psychology: A mutually enriching dialogue. *American Psychologist, 61,* 227–239.

Walter, C. A. (2000). The psychological meaning of menopause: Women's experiences. *Journal of Women and Aging, 12*(3–4), 117–131.

Walters, E. E., & Kendler, K. S. (1995). Anorexia nervosa and anorexic-like syndromes in a population-based female twin sample. *American Journal of Psychiatry, 152,* 64–71.

Walther, E., & Grigoriadis, S. (2003). Why sad people like shoes better: The influence of mood on the evaluative conditioning of consumer attitudes. *Psychology & Marketing, 10,* 755–775.

Walther, E., Nagengast, B., & Trasselli, C. (2005). Evaluative conditioning in social psychology: Facts and speculations. *Cognition and Emotion, 19*(2), 175–196.

Walton, K. G., Fields, J. Z., Levitsky, D. K., Harris, D. A., Pugh, N. D., & Schneider, R. H. (2004). Lowering cortisol and CVD risk in postmenopausal women: A pilot study using Transcendental Meditation program. In R. Yehuda, & B. McEwen (Eds.), *Biobehavioral stress response: Protective and damaging effects.* New York: Annals of the New York Academy of Sciences.

Walton, M. E., Devlin, J. T., & Rushworth, M. F. S. (2004). Interactions between decision making and performance monitoring within prefrontal cortex. *Nature Neuroscience, 7,* 1259–1265.

Wampold, B. E. (2001). *The great psychotherapy debate.* Mahwah, NJ: Erlbaum.

Wang, P. S., Lane, M., Olfson, M., Pincus, H. A., Wells, K. B., & Kessler, R. C. (2005). Twelve-month use of mental health services in the United States: Results from the National Comorbidity Survey Replication. *Archives of General Psychiatry, 62,* 629–640.

Wang, S., Baillargeon, R., & Paterson, S. (2005). Detecting continuity violations in infancy: A new account and new evidence from covering and tube events. *Cognition, 95,* 129–173.

Wangensteen, O. H., & Carlson, A. J. (1931). Hunger sensation after total gastrectomy. *Proceedings of the Society for Experimental Biology, 28,* 545–547.

Warner-Schmidt, J. L., & Duman, R. S. (2006). Hippocampal neurogenesis: Opposing effects of stress and antidepressant treatment. *Hippocampus, 16,* 239–249.

Warr, P. (1999). Well-being and the workplace. In D. Kahneman, E. Diener, & N. Schwarz (Eds.), *Well-being: The foundations of hedonic psychology.* New York: Russell Sage Foundation.

Waterhouse, L. (2006). Multiple intelligences, the Mozart effect, and emotional intelligence: A critical review. *Educational Psychologist, 41,* 207–225.

Watkins, L. R. (2007). Immune and glial regulation of pain. *Brain, Behavior, and Immunity, 21,* 519–521.

Watkins, L. R., & Maier, S. F. (2002). Beyond neurons: Evidence that immune and glial cells contribute to pathological pain states. *Physiological Reviews, 82,* 981–1011.

Watkins, L. R., & Maier, S. F. (2003). When good pain turns bad. *Current Directions in Psychological Science, 12,* 232–236.

Watkins, L. R., Hutchinson, M. R., Ledeboer, A., Wieseler-Frank, J., Milligan, E. D., & Maier, S. F. (2007). Glia as the "bad guys": Implications for improving clinical pain control and the clinical utility of opiods. *Brain, Behavior, and Immunity, 21,* 131–146.

Watson, D., David, J. P., & Suls, J. (1999). Personality, affectivity, and coping. In C. R. Snyder (Ed.), *Coping: The psychology of what works.* New York: Oxford University Press.

Watson, D., Klohen, E. C., Casillas, A., Nus Simms, E., Haig, J., & Berry, D. S. (2004). Match makers and deal breakers: Analyses of assortative mating in newlywed couples. *Journal of Personality, 72,* 1029–1068.

Watson, D., & Pennebaker, J. W. (1989). Health complaints, stress, and distress: Exploring the central role of negative affectivity. *Psychological Review, 96,* 234–254.

Watson, D., Suls, J., & Haig, J. (2002). Global self-esteem in relation to structural models of personality and affectivity. *Journal of Personality and Social Psychology, 83,* 185–197.

Watson, D. L., & Tharp, R. G. (2007). *Self-directed behavior: Self-modification for personal adjustment.* Belmont, CA: Wadsworth.

Watson, J. B. (1913). Psychology as the behaviorist views it. *Psychological Review, 20,* 158–177.

Watson, J. B. (1919). *Psychology from the standpoint of a behaviorist.* Philadelphia: Lippincott.

Watson, J. B. (1924). *Behaviorism.* New York: Norton.

Watson, J. B. (1925). *Behaviorism.* New York: Norton.

Watson, J. B. (1930). *Behaviorism.* New York: Norton.

Watson, J. B., & Rayner, R. (1920). Conditioned emotional reactions. *Journal of Experimental Psychology, 3,* 1–14.

Waugh, N. C., & Norman, D. A. (1965). Primary memory. *Psychological Review, 72,* 89–104.

Waxman, S. (2005). Why is the concept "living thing" so elusive? Concepts, languages, and the development of folkbiology. In W. Ahn, R. L. Goldstone, B. C. Love, A. B. Markman, & P. Woolf (Eds.), *Categorization inside and outside the laboratory: Essays in honor of Douglas L. Medin* (pp. 49–67). Washington, DC: American Psychological Association.

Waxman, S. R. (2002). Early word-learning and conceptual development: Everything had a name and each name gave birth to a new thought. In U. Goswami (Ed.), *Blackwell handbook of childhood cognitive development* (pp. 102–126). Malden, MA: Blackwell.

Weaver, C. A., & Krug, K. S. (2004). Consolidation-like effects in flashbulb memories: Evidence from September 11, 2001. *American Journal of Psychology, 117,* 517–530.

Webb, W. B. (1992a). Developmental aspects and a behavioral model of human sleep. In C. Stampi (Ed.), *Why we nap: Evolution, chronobiology, and functions of polyphasic and ultrashort sleep.* Boston: Birkhaeuser.

Webb, W. B. (1992b). *Sleep: The gentle tyrant.* Bolton, MA: Anker.

Webb, W. B., & Dinges, D. F. (1989). Cultural perspectives on napping and the siesta. In D. F. Dinges & R. J. Broughton (Eds.), *Sleep and alertness: Chrono-*

biological, behavioral, and medical aspects of napping. New York: Raven.

Weber, E. U. (2006). Experience-based and description-based perceptions of long-term risk: why global warming does not scare us (yet). *Climatic Change, 77,* 103–120.

Weber, L. J. (2006). *Profits before people?* Bloomington, IN: Indiana University Press.

Wechsler, D. (1939). *The measurement of adult intelligence.* Baltimore: Williams & Wilkins.

Wegner, D. M. (1997). Why the mind wanders. In J. D. Cohen & J. W. Schooler (Eds.), *Scientific approaches to consciousness.* Mahwah, NJ: Erlbaum.

Weil, M. , & Rosen, R. (1997). *Technostress: coping with technology @ work @ home @ play.* New York: Wiley.

Weinberg, R. A. (1989). Intelligence and IQ: Landmark issues and great debates. *American Psychologist, 44,* 98–104.

Weinberger, J. (1995). Common factors aren't so common: The common factors dilemma. *Clinical Psychology: Science and Practice, 2,* 45–69.

Weiner, B. (1980). *Human motivation.* New York: Holt, Rinehart & Winston.

Weiner, B. (1986). *An attributional theory of motivation and emotion.* New York: Springer-Verlag.

Weiner, B. (1994). Integrating social and personal theories of achievement striving. *Review of Educational Research, 64,* 557–573.

Weiner, B. (Ed.). (1974). *Achievement motivation and attribution theory.* Morristown, NJ: General Learning Press.

Weinfield, N. S., Sroufe, L. A., Egeland, B., & Carlson, E. A. (1999). The nature of individual differences in infant-caregiver attachment. In J. Cassidy & P. R. Shaver (Eds.), *Handbook of attachment: Theory, research, and clinical applications.* New York: Guilford.

Weinger, M. B., & Ancoli-Israel, S. (2002). Sleep deprivation and clinical performance. *Journal of the American Medical Association, 287,* 955–957.

Weisberg, R. W. (1986). *Creativity: Genius and other myths.* New York: W. H. Freeman.

Weisberg, R. W. (1993). *Creativity: Beyond the myth of genius.* New York: W. H. Freeman.

Weisberg, R. W. (1999). Creativity and knowledge: A challenge to theories. In R. J. Sternberg (Ed.), *Handbook of creativity.* New York: Cambridge University Press.

Weisberg, R. W. (2006). *Creativity: Understanding innovation in problem solving, science, invention, and the arts.* New York: Wiley.

Weisler, R. H., Barbee, J. G., & Townsend, M. H. (2007). Mental health and recovery in the Gulf Coast after Hurricanes Katrina and Rita. *Journal of the American Medical Association, 296,* 585–588.

Weiss, A., Bates, T. C., & Luciano, M. (2008). Happiness is a personal(ity) thing. *Psychological Science, 19,* 205–210.

Weiten, W. (1984). Violation of selected item-construction principles in educational measurement. *Journal of Experimental Education, 51,* 46–50.

Weiten, W. (1988a). Objective features of introductory psychology textbooks as related to professors' impressions. *Teaching of Psychology, 15,* 10–16.

Weiten, W. (1988b). Pressure as a form of stress and its relationship to psychological symptomatology. *Journal of Social and Clinical Psychology, 6*(1), 127–139.

Weiten, W. (1998). Pressure, major life events, and psychological symptoms. *Journal of Social Behavior and Personality, 13,* 51–68.

Weiten, W. (2002). Wiring the introductory psychology course: How should we harness the Internet? In S. F. Davis & B. Buskist (Eds.), *The teaching of psychology: Essays in honor of Wilbert J. McKeachie and Charles L. Brewer.* Mahwah, NJ: Erlbaum.

Weiten, W., & Diamond, S. S. (1979). A critical review of the jury-simulation paradigm: The case of defendant characteristics. *Law and Human Behavior, 3,* 71–93.

Weiten, W., Guadagno, R. E., & Beck, C. A. (1996). Students' perceptions of textbook pedagogical aids. *Teaching of Psychology, 23,* 105–107.

Weiten, W., & Wight, R. D. (1992). Portraits of a discipline: An examination of introductory psychology textbooks in America. In A. E. Puente, J. R. Matthews, & C. L. Brewer (Eds.), *Teaching psychology in America: A history.* Washington, DC: American Psychological Association.

Wells, G. L., & Bradfield, A. L. (1998). "Good, you identified the suspect": Feedback to eyewitnesses distorts their reports of the witnessing experience. *Journal of Applied Psychology, 83,* 360–376.

Wells, G. L., & Olson, E. A. (2003). Eyewitness testimony. *Annual Review of Psychology, 54,* 277–295.

Wells, G. L., Memon, A., & Penrod, S. D. (2006). Eyewitness evidence: Improving its probative value. *Psychological Science in the Public Interest, 7,* 45–75.

Wells, G. L., Olson, E. A., & Charman, S. D. (2002). The confidence of eyewitnesses in their identifications from lineups. *Current Directions in Psychological Science, 11*(5), 151–154.

Wells, N. M., & Evans, G. W. (2003). Nearby nature: A buffer of life stress among rural children. *Environment and Behavior, 35,* 311–330.

Welsh, R. S. (2003). Prescription privileges: Pro or con. *Clinical Psychology: Science & Practice, 10,* 371–372.

Wenzlaff, R. M., & Wegner, D. M. (2000). Thought suppression. *Annual Review of Psychology, 51,* 51–91.

Wertheimer, M. (1912). Experiment-elle studien über das sehen von bewegung. *Zeitschrift für Psychologie, 60,* 312–378.

Wertsch, J. V., & Tulviste, P. (2005). L. S. Vygotsky and contemporary developmental psychology. In H. Daniels (Ed.), *An introduction to Vygotsky.* New York: Routledge.

Wessely, S., & Kerwin, R. (2004). Suicide risk and the SSRI's. *Journal of the American Medical Association, 292,* 379–381.

Wesson, D. R., Smith, D. E., Ling, W., & Seymour, R. B. (2005). Sedative-hypnotics. In M. H. Kryger, T. Roth, & W. C. Dement (Eds.). *Principles and practice of sleep medicine.* Philadelphia: Elsevier Saunders.

Westen, D. (1998). The scientific legacy of Sigmund Freud: Toward a psychodynamically informed psychological science. *Psychological Bulletin, 124,* 333–371.

Westen, D., & Gabbard, G. O. (1999). Psychoanalytic approaches to personality. In L. A. Pervin & O. P. John (Eds.), *Handbook of personality: Theory and research.* New York: Guilford.

Wethington, E. (2007). Life events scale. In G. Fink (Ed.), *Encyclopedia of stress.* San Diego: Elsevier.

Wexler, B. E., Gottschalk, C. H., Fulbright, R. K., Prohovnik, I., Lacadie, C. M., Rounsaville, B. J., & Gore, J. C. (2001). Functional magnetic resonance imaging of cocaine craving. *American Journal of Psychiatry, 158,* 86–95.

Whitaker, R. (2002). *Mad in America: Bad science, bad medicine, and the enduring mistreatment of the mentally ill.* New York: Perseus Publishing.

Whitbourne, S. K., Zuschlag, M. K., Elliot, L. B., & Waterman, A. S. (1992). Psychosocial development in adulthood: A 22-year sequential study. *Journal of Personality and Social Psychology, 63,* 260–271.

White, R., & Heerwagen, J. (1998). Nature and mental health: Biophilia and biophobia. In A. Lundberg (Ed.), *The environment and mental health: A guide for clinicians* (pp. 175–192). Mahwah, NJ: Lawrence Erlbaum Associates.

White, S. H. (2000). Conceptual foundations of IQ testing. *Psychology, Public Policy, and Law, 6,* 33–43.

Whitfield, C. L. (1995). *Memory and abuse: Remembering and healing the effects of trauma.* Deerfield Beach, FL: Health Communications.

Whitty, M. T. (2008). Liberating or debilitating? An examination of romantic relationships, sexual relationships and friendships on the net. *Computers in Human Behavior, 24,* 1837–1850.

Widiger, T. A., & Sankis, L. M. (2000). Adult psychopathology: Issues and controversies. *Annual Review of Psychology, 51,* 377–404.

Widiger, T. A., & Simonsen, E. (2005). Introduction to the special section: The American Psychiatric Association's research agenda for the DSM-V. *Journal of Personality Disorders, 19,* 103–109.

Wiesel, T. N., & Hubel, D. H. (1965). Extent of recovery from the effects of visual deprivation in kittens. *Journal of Neurophysiology, 28,* 1060–1072.

Wigboldus, D. H. J., Dijksterhuis, A., & van Knippenberg, A. (2003). When stereotypes get in the way: Stereotypes obstruct stereotype-inconsistent trait inferences. *Journal of Personality and Social Psychology, 84,* 470–484.

Wikaitis, J., Mulvihill, T., & Nasrallah, H. A. (2004). Classic antipsychotic medications. In A. F. Schatzberg & C. B. Nemeroff (Eds.), *Textbook of psychopharmacology.* Washington, DC: American Psychiatric Publishing.

Wilder, C., Pollo, C., Bloch, J., Burkhard, P. R., & Vingerhoets, F. J. G. (2008). Long-term outcome of 50 consecutive Parkinson's disease patients treated with subthalamic deep brain stimulation. *Parkinsonism & Related Disorders, 14,* 114–119.

Wilding, J., & Valentine, E. (1996). Memory expertise. In D. J. Herrmann, C. McEvoy, C. Hertzog, P. Hertel, & M. K. Johnson (Eds.), *Basic and applied memory research: Theory in context* (Vol. 1). Mahwah, NJ: Erlbaum.

Willford, J. A., Leech, S. L., & Day, N. L. (2006). Moderate prenatal alcohol exposure and cognitive status of children at age 10. *Alcoholism: Clinical and Experimental Research, 30,* 1051–1059.

Williams, A., & Giles, H. (1998). Communication of ageism. In M. C. Hecht (Ed.), *Communicating prejudice* (pp. 136–160). Thousand Oaks, CA: Sage.

Williams, B. A. (1988). Reinforcement, choice, and response strength. In R. C. Atkinson, R. J. Herrnstein, G. Lindzey, & R. D. Luce (Eds.), *Stevens' handbook of experimental psychology.* New York: Wiley.

Williams, C. G., Gagne, M., Ryan, R. M., & Deci, E. L. (2002). Facilitating autonomous motivation for smoking cessation. *Health Psychology, 21,* 40–50.

Williams, G. C. (1966). *Adaptation and natural selection.* Princeton, NJ: Princeton University Press.

Williams, J. E., Paton, C. C., Siegler, I. C., Eigenbrodt, M. L., Neito, F. J., & Tyroler, H. A. (2000). Anger proneness predicts coronary heart disease risk. *Circulation, 101,* 2034–2039.

Williams, M. H. (1992). Exploitation and inference: Mapping the damage from therapist-patient sexual involvement. *American Psychologist, 47,* 412–421.

Williams, N. A., & Deffenbacher, J. L. (1983). Life stress and chronic yeast infections. *Journal of Human Stress, 9*(1), 26–31.

Williams, P. (2005). What is psychoanalysis? What is a psychoanalyst? In E. S. Person, A. M. Cooper, & G. O. Gabbard (Eds.), *Textbook of psychoanalysis.* Washington, DC: American Psychiatric Publishing.

Williams, R. E., Kaliani, L., DiBenedetti, D. B., Zhou, X., Fehnel, S. E., & Clark, R. V. (2007). Healthcare seeking and treatment for menopausal symptoms in the United States. *Maturitas, 58,* 348–358.

Williams, R. L., & Eggert, A. (2002). Notetaking predictors of test performance. *Teaching of Psychology, 29*(3), 234–237.

Williams, W. M. (1998). Are we raising smarter children today? School-and-home-related influences on IQ. In U. Neisser (Ed.), *The rising curve: Long-term gains in IQ and related measures.* Washington, DC: American Psychological Association.

Williams, W. M., & Ceci, S. J. (1997). Are Americans becoming more or less alike?: Trends in race, class, and ability differences in intelligence. *American Psychologist, 52,* 1226–1235.

Williamson, D. A., Zucker, N. L., Martin, C. K., & Smeets, M. A. M. (2001). Etiology and management of eating disorders. In P. B. Sutker & H. E. Adams (Eds.), *Comprehensive handbook of psychopathology.* New York: Kluwer Academic/Plenum.

Willis, J., & Todorov, A. (2006). First impressions: Making up your mind after a 100-ms exposure to a face. *Psychological Science, 17,* 592–598.

Willis, W. D. (1985). *The pain system. The neural basis of nococeptive transmission in the mammalian nervous system.* Basel: Karger.

Willoughby, T., Motz, M., & Wood, E. (1997). The impact of interest and strategy use on memory performance for child, adolescent, and adult learners. *Alberta Journal of Educational Research, 43,* 127–141.

Wills, T. A., & Fegan, M. (2001). Social networks and social support. In A. Baum, T. A. Revenson, & J. E. Singer (Eds.), *Handbook of health psychology* (pp. 209–234). Mahwah, NJ: Erlbaum.

Wilsnack, S. C., Wonderlich, S. A., Kristjanson, A. F., Vogeltanz-Holm, N. D., & Wilsnack, R. W. (2002). Self-reports of forgetting and remembering childhood sexual abuse in a nationally representative sample of U.S. women. *Child Abuse and Neglect, 26*(2), 139–147.

Wilson, E. O. (1993). Biophilia and the conservation ethic. In S. R. Kellert & E. O. Wilson (Eds.), *The biophilia hypothesis* (pp. 31–41). Washington, DC: Island Press.

Wilson, R. S., & Bennett, D. A. (2003). Cognitive activity and risk of Alzheimer's disease. *Current Directions in Psychological Science, 12*(3), 87–91.

Wilson, T. D., & Gilbert, D. T. (2005). Affective forecasting: Knowing what to want. *Current Directions in Psychological Science, 14,* 131–134.

Windholz, G. (1997). Ivan P. Pavlov: An overview of his life and psychological work. *American Psychologist, 52,* 941–946.

Winett, R. A., Hatcher, J. W., Fort, T. R., Leckliter, I. N., Love, S. Q., Riley, A. W., & Fishback, J. F. (1982). The effects of videotape modeling and daily feedback on residential electricity conservation, home temperature and humidity, perceived comfort, and clothing worn: Winter and summer. *Journal of Applied Behavior Analysis, 15,* 381–402.

Wingfield, A., Tun, P. A., & McCoy, S. L. (2005). Hearing loss in older adulthood: What it is and how it interacts with cognitive performance. *Current Directions in Psychological Science, 14,* 144–148.

Winn, P. (1995). The lateral hypothalmus and motivated behavior: An old syndrome reassessed and a new perspective gained. *Current Directions in Psychological Science, 4,* 182–187.

Winsler, A. (2003). Introduction to special issue: Vygotskian perspectives in early childhood education. *Early Education & Development, 14*(3), 253–269.

Winter, D. D. & Cava, M. M. (2006) The psycho-ecology of armed conflict. *Journal of Social Issues, 62,* 19–40.

Winter, D. D. & Koger, S. M. (2004). *The Psychology of Environmental Problems (2nd Edition).* Mahwah, NJ: Lawrence Erlbaum Associates.

Winters, K. C., Arthur, N., Leitten, W., & Botzet, A. (2004). Gambling and drug abuse in adolescence. In J. L. Derevensky & R. Gupta (Eds.), *Gambling problems in youth: Theoretical and applied perspectives* (pp.57-80). New York: Kluwer/Plenum.

Wise, M. G., Gray, K. F., & Seltzer, B. (1999). Delirium, dementia, and amnestic disorders. In R. E. Hales, S. C. Yudofsky, & J. A. Talbott (Eds.), *The American Psychiatric Press textbook of psychiatry* (3rd ed., pp. 317–362). Washington, DC: American Psychiatric Press.

Wise, R. A. (1999). Animal models of addiction. In D. S. Charney, E. J. Nestler, & B. S. Bunney (Eds.), *Neurobiology of mental illness.* New York: Oxford University Press.

Wise, R. A. (2002). Brain reward circuitry: Insights from unsensed incentives. *Neuron, 36,* 229–240.

Wise, R. J. S., & Price, C. J. (2006). Functional neuroimaging of language. In R. Cabeza & A. Kingstone (Eds.), *Handbook of functional neuroimaging of cognition.* Cambridge, MA: MIT Press.

Witt, J. K., Proffitt, D. R., & Epstein, W. (2004). Perceiving distance: A role of effort and intent. *Perception, 33,* 577–590.

Wittkower, E. D., & Warnes, H. (1984). Cultural aspects of psychotherapy. In J. E. Mezzich & C. E. Berganza (Eds.), *Culture and psychopathology.* New York: Columbia University Press.

Wolford, G., Miller, M. B., & Gazzaniga, M. S. (2004). Split decisions. In M. S. Gazzaniga (Ed.), *The cognitive neurosciences.* Cambridge, MA: MIT Press.

Wolitzky, D. L. (2006). Psychodynamic theories. In J. C. Thomas, & D. L. Segal (Eds.), *Comprehensive handbook of personality and psychopathology.* New York: Wiley.

Wolpe, J. (1958). *Psychotherapy by reciprocal inhibition.* Stanford, CA: Stanford University Press.

Wolpe, J. (1990). *The practice of behavior therapy.* Elmsford, NY: Pergamon Press.

Wonderlich, S. A. (2002). Personality and eating disorders. In C. G. Fairburn & K. D. Brownell (Eds.), *Eating disorders and obesity: A comprehensive handbook.* New York: Guilford.

Wong, L. A. (2006). *Essential study skills.* Boston: Houghton Mifflin.

Wong, N. (2005). Group psychotherapy and combined individual and group psychotherapy. In B. J. Sadock & V. A. Sadock (Eds.), *Kaplan and Sadock's comprehensive textbook of psychiatry.* Philadelphia: Lippincott Williams & Wilkins.

Wong, P. T. P. (2006). Existential and humanistic theories. In J. C. Thomas & D. L. Segal (Eds.), *Comprehensive handbook of personality and psychopathology.* New York: Wiley.

Wood, E., Desmarais, S., & Gugula, S. (2002). The impact of parenting experience on gender stereotyped toy play of children. *Sex Roles, 47*(1–2), 39–49.

Wood, F., Ebert, V., & Kinsbourne, M. (1982). The episodic-semantic memory distinction in memory and amnesia: Clinical and experimental observations. In L. Cermak (Ed.), *Human memory and amnesia*. Hillsdale, NJ: Erlbaum.

Wood, J. N., & Spelke, E. S. (2005). Chronometric studies of numerical cognition in five-month-old infants. *Cognition, 97*, 23–39.

Wood, P. B. (2007). Fibromyalgia. In G. Fink (Ed.), *Encyclopedia of stress*. San Diego: Elsevier.

Wood, W., & Quinn, J. M. (2003). Forewarned and forearmed? Two meta-analytic syntheses of fore-warnings of influence appeals. *Psychological Bulletin, 129*, 119–138.

Woodhead, M. (2004). When psychology informs public policy: The case. In E. Zigler & S. J. Styfco (Eds.), *The Head Start debate*. Baltimore: Paul H. Brookes Publishing.

Woolfolk, R. L., & Richardson, F. C. (1978). *Stress, sanity and survival*. New York: Sovereign/Monarch.

World Resources Institute. (2001). *Facts and figures: Environmental data tables, energy and resource use.* Table ERC.5: Resource Consumption. [Data file]. Available from World Resources Institute website, http://www.wri.org/trends/index.html

Worthen, J. B., & Wade, C. E. (1999). Direction of travel and visiting team athletic performance: Support for a circadian dysrhythmia hypothesis. *Journal of Sport Behavior, 22*, 279–287.

Worthington, E. L., Jr., & Scherer, M. (2004). Forgiveness is an emotion-focused coping strategy that can reduce health risks and promote health resilience: Theory, review, and hypotheses. *Psychology and Health, 19*, 385-405.

Worthington, R. L., Soth-McNett, A. M., & Moreno, M. V. (2007). Multicultural counseling competencies research: A 20-year content analysis. *Journal of Counseling Psychology, 54*, 351–361.

Wright, J. H., Beck, A. T., & Thase, M. E. (2003). Cognitive therapy. In R. E. Hales & S. C. Yudofsky (Eds.), *Textbook of clinical psychiatry*. Washington, DC: American Psychiatric Publishing.

Wrosch, C., & Scheier, M. F. (2003). Personality and quality of life: The importance of optimism and goal adjustment. *Quality of Life Research: An International Journal of Quality of Life Aspects of Treatment, Care & Rehabilitation, 12*, 59–72.

Wrosch, C., Miller, G. E., Scheier, M. F., & de Pontet, S. B. (2007). Giving up on unattainable goals: Benefits for health? *Personality and Social Psychology Bulletin, 33*, 251–265.

Wundt, W. (1874/1904). *Principles of physiological psychology*. Leipzig: Engelmann.

Wynder, E. L., Cohen, L. A., Muscat, J. E., Winters, B., Dwyer, J. T., & Blackburn, G. (1997). Breast cancer: Weighing the evidence for a promoting role of dietary fat. *Journal of the National Cancer Institute, 89*, 766–775.

Wynn, K. (1992). Addition and subtraction by human infants. *Nature, 358*, 749–750.

Wynn, K. (1996). Infants' individuation and enumeration of sequential actions. *Psychological Science, 7*, 164–169.

Wynn, K. (1998). An evolved capacity for number. In D. D. Cummins & C. Allen (Eds.), *The evolution of mind*. New York: Oxford University Press.

Yamamoto, J., Silva, J. A., Justice, L. R., Chang, C. Y., & Leong, G. B. (1993). Cross-cultural psychotherapy. In A. C. Gaw (Ed.), *Culture, ethnicity, and mental illness*. Washington, DC: American Psychiatric Press.

Yang, H., Liu, T., & Zang, D. (2000). A study of stressful life events before the onset of hypothyroidism. *Chinese Mental Health Journal, 14*, 201–202.

Yates, F. A. (1966). *The art of memory*. London: Routledge & Kegan Paul.

Ybarra, O., Stephan, W. G., & Schaberg, L. (2000). Misanthropic memory for the behavior of group members. *Personality and Social Psychology Bulletin, 26*, 1515–1525.

Yeomans, M. R., Tepper, B. J., Rietzschel, J., & Prescott, J. (2007). Human hedonic responses to sweetness: Role of taste genetics and anatomy. *Physiology & Behavior, 91*, 264–273.

Yerkes, R. M., & Morgulis, S. (1909). The method of Pavlov in animal psychology. *Psychological Bulletin, 6*, 257–273.

Yost, W. A. (2000). *Fundamentals of hearing: An introduction*. San Diego, CA: Academic Press.

Young, K. S. (1996, August). *Internet addiction: The emergence of a new clinical disorder*. Paper presented at the meeting of the American Psychological Association: Toronto, Ontario, Canada.

Young, K. S. (1998). *Caught in the net: How to recognize the signs of Internet addiction—and a winning strategy for recovery*. New York: Wiley.

Zacks, R. T., Hasher, L., & Li, K. Z. H. (2000). Human memory. In F. I. M. Craik & T. A. Salthouse (Eds.), *Handbook of aging and cognition*. Mahwah, NJ: Erlbaum.

Zagorsky, J. L. (2007). Do you have to be smart to be rich? The impact of IQ on wealth, income and financial distress. *Intelligence, 35*, 489–501.

Zajonc, R. B. (1980). Feeling and thinking: Preferences need no inferences. *American Psychologist, 35*, 151–175.

Zane, N., Hall, G. C. N., Sue, S., Young, K., & Nunez, J. (2004). Research on psychotherapy with culturally diverse populations. In M. J. Lambert (Ed.), *Bergin and Garfield's handbook of psychotherapy and behavior change*. New York: Wiley.

Zaragoza, M. S., Belli, R. F., & Payment, K. E. (2007). Misinformation effects and the suggestibility of eyewitness memory. In M. Garry & H. Hayne (Eds.), *Do justice and let the sky fall: Elizabeth F. Loftus and her contributions to science, law, and academic freedom*. Mahwah, NJ: Erlbaum.

Zarate, M. A., Garcia, B., Garza, A. A., & Hitlan, R. T. (2004). Cultural threat and perceived realistic group conflict as dual predictors of prejudice. *Journal of Experimental Social Psychology, 40*, 99–105.

Zatzick, D. F. (1999). Managed care and psychiatry. In R. E. Hales, S. C. Yudofsky, & J. A. Talbott (Eds.), *American Psychiatric Press textbook of psychiatry*. Washington, DC: American Psychiatric Press.

Zatzick, D. F., & Dimsdale, J. E. (1990). Cultural variations in response to painful stimuli. *Psychosomatic Medicine, 52*(5), 544–557.

Zautra, A. J., & Smith, B. W. (2001). Depression and reactivity to stress in older women with rheumatoid arthritis and osteoarthritis. *Psychosomatic Medicine, 63*, 687–696.

Zautra, A. J., Affleck, G. G., Tennen, H., Reich, J. W., & Davis, M. C. (2005). Dynamic approaches to emotions and stress in everyday life: Bolger and Zuckerman reloaded with positive as well as negative affects. *Journal of Personality, 73*, 1–28.

Zechmeister, E. B., & Nyberg, S. E. (1982). *Human memory: An introduction to research and theory*. Pacific Grove, CA: Brooks/Cole.

Zeiler, M. (1977). Schedules of reinforcement: The controlling variables. In W. K. Honig & J. E. R. Staddon (Eds.), *Handbook of operant behavior*. Englewood Cliffs, NJ: Prentice-Hall.

Zenhausen, R. (1978). Imagery, cerebral dominance and style of thinking: A unified field model. *Bulletin of the Psychonomic Society, 12*, 381–384.

Zepelin, H. (1993). Internal alarm clock. In M. A. Carskadon (Ed.), *Encyclopedia of sleep and dreaming*. New York: Macmillan.

Zepelin, H., Siegel, J. M., & Tobler, I. (2005). Mammalian sleep. In M. H. Kryger, T. Roth, & W. C. Dement (Eds.). *Principles and practice of sleep medicine*. Philadelphia: Elsevier Saunders.

Zillmer, E. A., Spiers, M. V., & Culbertson, W. C. (2008). *Principles of neuropsychology*. Belmont, CA: Wadsworth.

Zimbardo, P. G. (2004, May 9). Power turns good soldiers into "bad apples." *Boston Globe*. Retrieved from http://www.boston.com/news/globe/editorial_opinion/oped/articles/2004/05/09.

Zimbardo, P. G. (2007). *The Lucifer effect: Understanding how good people turn evil*. New York: Random House.

Zimbardo, P. G., Haney, C., & Banks, W. C. (1973, April 8). The mind is a formidable jailer: A Pirandellian prison. *New York Times Magazine*, Section 6, p. 36.

Zimmerman, B. J. (1995). Self-efficacy and educational development. In A. Bandura (Ed.), *Self-efficacy in changing societies*. New York: Cambridge University Press.

Zimmerman, I. L., & Woo-Sam, J. M. (1984). Intellectual assessment of children. In G. Goldstein & M. Hersen (Eds.), *Handbook of psychological assessment*. New York: Pergamon Press.

Zimmerman, M., & Spitzer, R. L. (2005). Psychiatric classification. In B. J. Sadock & V. A. Sadock (Eds.), *Kaplan & Sadock's comprehensive textbook of psychiatry*. Philadelphia: Lippincott Williams & Wilkins.

Zinbarg, R. E., & Griffith, J. W. (2008). Behavior Therapy. In J. L. Lebow (Ed.), *Twenty-first century psychotherapies: Contemporary approaches to theory and practice*. New York: Wiley.

Zoeller, R. F. Jr. (2007). Physical activity and fitness in the prevention of coronary heart disease and associated risk factors. *American Journal of Lifestyle Medicine, 1*, 29–33.

Zola, S. M., & Squire, L. R. (2000). The medial temporal lobe and the hippocampus. In E. Tulving & F. I. M. Craik (Eds.), *The Oxford handbook of memory* (pp. 485–500). New York: Oxford University Press.

Zorick, F. J., & Walsh, J. K. (2000). Evaluation and management of insomnia: An overview. In M. H. Kryger, T. Roth, & W. C. Dement (Eds.), *Principles and practice of sleep medicine*. Philadelphia: Saunders.

Zrenner, E., Abramov, I., Akita, M., Cowey, A., Livingstone, M., & Valberg, A. (1990). Color perception: Retina to cortex. In L. Spillman & J. S. Werner (Eds.), *Visual perception: The neurophysiological foundations*. San Diego: Academic Press.

Zuckerman, M. (1971). Dimensions of sensation seeking. *Journal of Consulting and Clinical Psychology, 36*, 45–52.

Zull, J. E. (2002). *The art of changing the brain: Enriching teaching by exploring the biology of learning*. Sterling, VA: Stylus.

Zurbriggen, E. L., & Sturman, T. S. (2002). Linking motives and emotions: A test of McClelland's hypothesis. *Personality & Social Psychology Bulletin, 28*, 521–535.

CREDITS

PHOTO CREDITS

This page constitutes an extension of the copyright page. We have made every effort to trace the ownership of all copyrighted material and to secure permission from copyright holders. In the event of any question arising as to the use of any material, we will be pleased to make the necessary corrections in future printings. Thanks are due to the following authors, publishers, and agents for permission to use the material indicated.

Chapter Opener 1. xlviii, 2, 11, 15, 21 © Chad Ehlers/Alamy

Chapter Opener 2. 34, 36, 40, 44, 52, 55, 56, 59 © UrbanEye/Alamy

Chapter Opener 3. 68, 69, 78, 80, 88, 92, 93, 96, 99 © Patrick Byrd/Science Faction/Getty Images

Chapter Opener 4. 106, 108, 119, 130, 134, 139 © DAJ/Getty Images

Chapter Opener 5. 150, 151, 153, 155, 164, 168, 171, 172, 178 © Jean-Pierre Lescourret/Corbis

Chapter Opener 6. 186, 188, 196, 207, 211, 217 © Richard Berenholtz/Corbis

Chapter Opener 7. 224, 226, 229, 235, 237, 244, 247, 249 © Hermera Technologies

Chapter Opener 8. 258, 260, 267, 274, 281, 287, 291 © Bruno Ehrs/Corbis

Chapter Opener 9. 298, 300, 302, 307, 315, 317, 323, 326 © Philip Coblentz/JupiterImages/Brand X/Alamy

Chapter Opener 10. 334, 336, 339, 353, 358, 367 © Royalty Free/Masterfile

Chapter Opener 11. 376, 378, 380, 388, 392, 396, 399, 403, 406 © Rich Reid/National Geographic Image Collection

Chapter Opener 12. 414, 416, 420, 427, 432, 436, 438 © Jimmy Chin/National Geographic/Getty Images

Chapter Opener 13. 448, 449, 453, 458, 460, 461, 467, 473, 476 © Pete Turner/Image Bank/Getty Images

Chapter Opener 14. 484, 486, 488, 494, 498, 506, 508, 511 © Richard T. Nowitz/National Geographic/Getty Images

Chapter Opener 15. 518, 520, 522, 527, 533, 539, 544, 547 © Jose Fuste Raga/Corbis

Table of Contents 1. xxv: © Chad Ehlers/Alamy

Table of Contents 2. xxvi: © UrbanEye/Alamy

Table of Contents 3. xxvii: © Patrick Byrd/Science Faction/Getty Images

Table of Contents 4. xxviii: © DAJ/Getty Images

Table of Contents 5. xxix: © Jean-Pierre Lescourret/Corbis

Table of Contents 6. xxx: © Richard Berenholtz/Corbis

Table of Contents 7. xxxi: © Hermera Technologies

Table of Contents 8. xxxii: © Bruno Ehrs/Corbis

Table of Contents 9. xxxiii: © Philip Coblentz/JupiterImages/Brand X/Alamy

Table of Contents 10. xxxiv: © Royalty Free/Masterfile

Table of Contents 11. xxxv: © Rich Reid/National Geographic Image Collection

Table of Contents 12. xxxvi: © Jimmy Chin/National Geographic/Getty Images

Table of Contents 13. xxxvii: © Pete Turner/Image Bank/Getty Images

Table of Contents 14. xxxviii: © Richard T. Nowitz/National Geographic/Getty Images

Table of Contents 15. xxxix: © Jose Fuste Raga/Corbis

Chapter 1. 1: top, © Dex Images/Corbis 1: bottom, © Wayne Weiten 2: © Chad Ehlers/Alamy 5: Figure 1.2 photos (all) Archives of the History of American Psychology, The University of Akron 8: top, Copyright © 1971 Time Inc. Reprinted by permission. 11: © Chad Ehlers/Alamy 13: © Michael & Patricia Fogden/Corbis 15: © Chad Ehlers/Alamy 16: inset, © White Packert/Iconica/Getty Images 18: (Pavlov lab) Bettmann/Corbis 18: (Freud and others) Compliments of Clark University Archives, Worcester, Massachusetts 18: (Hollingworth) Archives of the History of American Psychology, The University of Akron 18: (Washburn) Archives of the History of American Psychology, The University of Akron 18: (Wright Bros plane) Stock Montage, Inc. 18: (Wundt & others) Archives of the History of American Psychology, The University of Akron 18: (intelligence test) Bettmann/Corbis 18: (lightbulb) The Image Works 18: (telephone) Antman Archives/The Image Works 19: (Atomic bomb) Photo12/The Image Works 19: (Erikson) AP Images 19: bottom, (Kahneman) Courtesy of Daniel Kahneman 19: (Kenneth Clark) © Bettmann Corbis 19: (Loftus) Courtesy of Elizabeth Loftus 19: (Maccoby) Chuck Painter/Stanford News Service 19: (Seligman) Courtesy of Martin E. P. Seligman 19: (Shuttle liftoff) NASA 19: (Vietnam) © AP Images 21: © Chad Ehlers/Alamy 23: © Steve Raymer/Corbis 27: left, © moodboard/CorbisRF 29: inset, © Rob Gage/Taxi/Getty Images 32: left, Archives of the History of American Psychology, The University of Akron 32: right, Reproduced courtesy of The B. F. Skinner Foundation 33: left, Used with permission of Dr. Marianne Olds

Chapter 2. 35: © Corbis Super RF/Alamy 36: © UrbanEye/Alamy 40: © UrbanEye/Alamy 44: © UrbanEye/Alamy 47: © Rob Crandall/Alamy 48: © Michael Nichols/National Geographic Image Collection 50: (pedestrians) © Rob Crandall/Alamy 50: (therapy) photo © David Buffinton/Photodisc Green/Getty Images 50: (waiting) © Studio DL/Corbis/Photolibrary 51: (Goodall) © Michael Nichols/National Geographic Image Collection 52: © UrbanEye/Alamy 53: © StudioDL/Corbis/Photolibrary 54: Courtesy of Robert Rosenthal 55: © UrbanEye/Alamy 56: © UrbanEye/Alamy 58: bottom left, Courtesy of Neal Miller 58: right, © 2005 Foundation for Biomedical Research 58: top left, © William West/AFP/Getty Images 59: © UrbanEye/Alamy 60: Courtesy of Wayne Weiten 64: © Jacob Taposchaner/Photographer's Choice/Getty Images

Chapter 3. 74: Courtesy of Solomon Snyder 75: © Digital Vision/Getty Images 76: © AP Images/Kenneth Lambert 77: Courtesy of Candace Pert 81: top left, Figure 3.08a photo © Henrik Sorensen/Photonica/Getty Images 81: Figure 3.10 © Wellcome Dept of Cognitive Neurology/Science Photo Library/Photo Researchers, Inc. 81: bottom left, Figure 3.9 © ISM-Sovereign/PhotoTake 81: top right, © Dan McCoy/Rainbow 83: top left, Figure 3.12 photo Wadsworth Collection 89: Photo by Bob Paz/Caltech, Courtesy of Roger Sperry 90: Courtesy of Michael S. Gazzaniga 94: © Barbara Penoyar/Photodisc Green/Getty Images 95: Photo courtesy of Tara McKearney 97: © Bettmann/Corbis 98: Courtesy of John Alcock 101: © Ariel Shelley/Corbis 104: right, © Hank Morgan/Photo Researchers, Inc.

Chapter 4. 107: © Steve Cole/Photodisc Green/Getty Images 110: Figure 4.4 photos: Craig McClain 114: Courtesy of David Hubel 115: Figure 4.11 center photo © Doane Gregory/Warner Bros./Bureau L.A. Collection/Corbis 115: Figure 4.11 left photo © Steve Granitz/WireImage/Getty Images 116: right, Figure 4.13b Courtesy of BASF 121: Archives of the History of American Psychology, The University of Akron 122: © Tony Freeman/PhotoEdit 126: bottom center, Figure 4.29 - height/plane: © Chris George/Alamy 126: top right, Figure 4.29 - interposition: © Ron Fehling/Masterfile 126: top left, Figure 4.29 - linear: © RF/Corbis 126: bottom left, Figure 4.29 - relative size: © Jose Fuste Raga/zefa/Corbis 126: top center, Figure 4.29 - texture: © Jean-Marc Truchet/Getty Images 126: bottom right, Figure 4.29 - light/shadow: U.S. Department of Energy 127: Vincent van Gogh (Dutch, 1853–1890), *A Corridor in the Asylum,* late May or early June 1889. Oil color and essence over black chalk on pink laid (Ingres) paper, 25-5/8 × 19-5/16 in. (65.1 × 49.1 cm): The Metropolitan Museum of Art, Bequest of Abby Aldrich Rockefeller, 1948 (48.190.2) Image © 1998 The Metropolitan Museum of Art. Reproduced by permission 129: bottom, © Alan Evrard/Robert Harding/Getty Images 129: top right, © N. R. Rowan/The Image Works 131: inset, Figure 4.37 photo: © Betts Anderson Loman/PhotoEdit 134: Courtesy of Linda Bartoshuk 134: © Michael Mahovlich/Masterfile 140: (massage) © IS713/Image Source Pink/Alamy 140: (sipping wine) © Lisa Woollett/Photofusion Picture Library/Alamy 140: (sunrise) © John White Photos/Alamy 140: (trumpet player) © Photodisc/Getty Images 140: (woman and flowers) © Blend Images/Jamie Grill 142: Figure 4.44: *Maestro della cattura di Cristo, Cattura di Cristo, parte centrale,* Assisi, S. Francisco. Scala/Art Resource, New York 143: Figure 4.45: *Brera Predica di S. Marco Pinaocteca,* by Gentile and Giovanni Bellini in Egitto. Scala/Art Resource, New York 143: top, Figure 4.46: Georges Seurat, French, 1859–1891, *A Sunday Afternoon on La Grande Jatte* - 1884, 1884–86, oil on canvas, 81 3/4 × 121 1/4 in. (207.5 × 308.1 cm)(and detail), Helen Birch Bartlett Memorial Collection, 1926.224 combination of quadrant captures F1,F2, G1, G2. The Art Institute of Chicago. Photography © The Art Institute of Chicago. 144: left, Figure 4.47: Pablo Picasso, *Violin and*

lishers from Henry A. Murray, Thematic Apperception Test, Cambridge, Mass.: Harvard University Press, Copyright © 1943 by The President and Fellows of Harvard College, © 1971 by Henry A. Murray. 410: © AP Images/Dennis Cook 412: right, Nina Leen/Time & Life Pictures/Getty Images

Chapter 12. 416: Courtesy of Richard S. Lazarus 418: left, © AP Images/Phil Coale 418: right, © Joe Raedle/Getty Images 422: © Bettmann/Corbis 424: Courtesy, Albert Ellis Institute 425: © Jeff Smith/The Image Bank/Getty Images 426: Courtesy of Shelley Taylor 428: inset, Figure 12.6 photo Digital Vision/Getty Images 430: © Medio/Photodisc/Getty Images 433: inset, Figure 12.9 photo © Spencer Grant/PhotoEdit 434: © BananaStock/JupiterImages 437: right, Courtesy of University of California, Riverside 437: top, © blue jeans/Getty Images 441: © Acey Harper/Time Life Pictures/Getty Images 442: inset, Figure 12.15 photo © Paul Francis Photo 443: inset, Figure 12.16 (golfer) © Paul Francis Photo 443: inset, Figure 12.16 (joggers) © Michael Newman/PhotoEdit 443: inset, Figure 12.16 (lounge) © C. H. Wooley 447: © National Film Board of Canada

Chapter 13. 450: center right, Culver Pictures, Inc. 450: Figure 13.1 painting: *St. Catherine of Siena Exorcising a Possessed Woman,* c. 1500–1510 (detail). Girolamo Di Benvenuto. Denver Art Museum Collection, Gift of Samuel H. Kress Foundation Collection, 1961.171 © Denver Art Museum 2009. All rights reserved 450:

© David Lees/Corbis 455: top right, © Associated Press/AP 455: top left, © Bettmann/Corbis 455: bottom, © Robert Nickelsberg/Getty Images 462: left, © Amy Sussman/Getty Images 462: right, © Brad Barket/Getty Images 466: Courtesy of Susan Nolen-Hoeksema 469: Courtesy of Nancy Andreasen. M.D. 470: © Reuters/Corbis 474: top left, Munch, Edvard: *The Scream*. National Gallery, Oslo, Norway. SCALA/Art Resource/NY; © 2009 The Munch Museum/The Munch-Ellingsen Group/Artists Rights Society (ARS), NY. REPRODUCTION, INCLUDING DOWNLOADING OF EDVARD MUNCH WORKS IS PROHIBITED BY COPYRIGHT LAWS AND INTERNATIONAL CONVENTIONS WITHOUT THE EXPRESS WRITTEN PERMISSION OF ARTISTS RIGHTS SOCIETY (ARS), NEW YORK." 474: center left, van Gogh, Vincent: *Portrait of Dr. Gachet*. Musee d'Orsay, Paris. © Erich Lessing/Art Resource, NY 474: center right, © Amy Sussman/Getty Images 474: top right, © Bettmann/Corbis 474: bottom left, © Derek Bayes/Aspect Picture Library 474: bottom right, © Reuters/Corbis 478: © Ed Quinn/Corbis 482: van Gogh, Vincent: *Portrait of Dr. Gachet*. Musee d'Orsay, Paris. © Erich Lessing/Art Resource, NY 483: © *PsykTrek 3.0/*Wadsworth

Chapter 14. 485: Warner Bros./Shooting Star 486: bottom, Mary Evans/Sigmund Freud Copyrights 489: National Library of Medicine 490: © Bruce Ayres/Stone/Getty Images 491: Courtesy of Carl Rogers Memorial Library 491: bottom, © Zigy Kaluzny/

Stone/Getty Images 493: © Manchan/Photodisc Red/Getty Images 495: Courtesy of Joseph Wolpe 496: inset, Figure 14.9 photo © Robert Harding Picture Library 496: left, © *Kent News & Picture*/Corbis Sygma 497: Courtesy of Aaron T. Beck 502: © James Wilson/Woodfin Camp & Associates, all rights reserved 504: (Beck) Courtesy of Aaron T. Beck 504: (Freud) National Library of Medicine 504: (Rogers) Courtesy of Center for Studies of the Person 504: (Wolpe) Courtesy of Joseph Wolpe 505: (2nd down) © Zigy Kaluzny/Stone/Getty Images 505: (3rd down) © *Kent News & Picture*/Corbis Sygma 505: (4th down) © Manchan/Photodisc Red/Getty Images 505: (bottom left) © James Wilson/Woodfin Camp & Associates, all rights reserved 505: (bottom right) © PhotoDisc, Inc. 505: (top) © Bruce Ayres/Stone/Getty Images 507: © Michael Newman/PhotoEdit 509: inset, Figure 14–14 (inset) Detail of painting in Harrisburg State Hospital, photo by Ken Smith/LLR Collection 509: right, Figure 14.14 (Asylum) National Library of Medicine 512: © Tom McCarthy/SKA 514: © Issei Kato/Reuters 515: © Tony Freeman/PhotoEdit 516: bottom left, © Peter Aprahamian/Corbis

Chapter 15. 523: University Archives, Spencer Research Library, University of Kansas 525: © Ian Waldie/Getty Images 527: bottom, © Thomas Barwick/Photolibrary 529: Courtesy of Elaine Hatfield 529: top, Courtesy of Ellen Berscheid 531: top, © Najlah Feanny/Corbis 534: inset, Figure 15.6 photo © AP Images/Ed Andrieski 536: inset, Figure 15.8 photo © AP Images/

Jennifer Graylock 537: Courtesy of Prof. Jerry Suls 539: Courtesy of University of Pennsylvania, University Communications 541: inset, Figure 15-13 photos from the film *Obedience* © 1968 by Stanley Milgram; © renewed 1993 by Alexander Milgram, and distributed by Penn State Media Sales. Reprinted by permission of Alexandra Milgram. 541: © 1981 Eric Kroll, courtesy of Alexandra Milgram 542: Courtesy of Philip Zimbardo 543: left, *From A Simulation Study of the Psychology of Imprisonment Conducted at Stanford University,* 1971. Copyright © Philip Zimbardo. Reproduced with permission. 543: right, © AFP/Getty Images 546: © Joseph Pobereskin/Stone/Getty Images 550: © Stephen Ferry/Liaison/Getty Images 553: © Tony Freeman/PhotoEdit 554: left, © Leland Bobbe/Corbis 555: (man wearing tie) © Jack Hollingsworth/Royalty-Free/Corbis 555: (smiling man) © Michael Newman/PhotoEdit 555: (smiling woman) © Reed Kaestner/Corbis 555: (woman on left) © Bill Bachmann/PhotoEdit 555: left, From the film *Obedience* © 1968 by Stanley Milgram; © renewed 1993 by Alexander Milgram, and distributed by Penn State Media Sales. Reprinted by permission of Alexandra Milgram.

Appendices. A-32: © Dan Sullivan/Alamy A-35: top, © Ariel Skelley/Corbis A-35: bottom, © Kevin Fleming/Corbis A-37: bottom right, © EschCollection Royalty-Free/Alamy A-37: top left, © Martyn Osman/Alamy A-37: top right, © Noam Armonn/Alamy A-37: bottom left, © Optic Delight/Alamy

NAME INDEX

A

Aarts, H., 136
Abdel-Khalek, A. M., 328
Abel, M. H., 440
Abi-Dargham, A., 470
Aboud, F. E., 550
Abraham, C., 535
Abraham, W. C., 246
Abrahamse, W., A-31
Abramov, I., 118
Abramson, L. Y., 465, 466
Achermann, P. 161
Achille, N. M., 329
Acton, G. S., 398
Adair, J. G., 57
Adam, T. C., 77
Adamopoulos, J., 13
Adams, G., 356
Adams, H. E., 458
Adams, J. L., 263
Adams, M. J., 225
Adams, R. G., 528
Adams, R. L., 409
Ader, R., 191, 429
Adler, A., 6, 10, 386–387, 406, 490
Adler, L. L., 31
Adler, N. E., 415, 416
Adolph, K. E., 337, 339
Advocat, C. D., 173
Affleck, G., 420, 431
Agyeman, J., A-32
Ahima, R. S., 304
Aikens, D. E., 457
Ainsworth, M. D. S., 342, 529
Ait-Daoud, N., 177, 182
Akerstedt, T., 153
Akimoto, S. A., 526
Akiskal, H. S., 461
Aks, D. J., 129
Albert, M. S., 245, 361
Alcock, J., 98
Aldag, R. I., 547
Aldington, S., 177
Aldrich, M. S., 164
Aldwin, C. M., 360
Alexander, C. N., 172
Alexander, F., 490
Alhakami, A. S., A-34
Allan, R. W., 190, 196
Allard, L. M., 530
Allen, J. J. B., 460, 461
Allen, K., 431
Allen, M., 9
Alloy, L. B., 466
Allport, G., 378
Alonso, A., 492
Alonso, S., 492
Alsop, B., 199
Altman, I., 22
Altmann, E. M., 239
Altshuler, L. L., 500
Amabile, T. M., 292, 293
Amato, M., 550
Amato, P. R., 373
Ambady, N., 521
Amedi, A., 87
Ammaniti, M., 342
Amodio, D. M., 549

Anand

Anand, B. K., 302
Ancoli-Israel, S., 161
Anderluh, M. B., 479
Anderson-Fye, E. P., 479
Anderson, A. E., 478
Anderson, B., 288
Anderson, C., 528
Anderson, C. A., 213, 216
Anderson, E. A., 373
Anderson, I. M., 76
Anderson, K. O., 138
Anderson, M. C., 240
Anderson, N., 545
Andreasen, N. C., 81, 94, 293, 468, 469
Andres-Pueyo, A., 284
Andrews, A. M., 429
Angell, M., 501
Angelopoulos, T. J., 427
Anglin, J. M., 344
Angst, J., 463
Ankney, C. D., 288
Annus , A. M., 12
Ansbacher, H., 387
Anter, N. M., 27
Anthenelli, R. M., 182
Anthony, I. C., 434
Antonuccio, D. O., 501
Antony, M. M., 188, 190, 454, 457
Apicella, L. F., 432
Apkarian, A. V. 77
Appelbaum, P. S., 510
Appleton, K. M., 306
Aquilino, W. S., 357
Archer, A., 494
Archer, J., 92, 369
Archibald, A. B., 353, 354, 355
Arden, R., 281
Arendt, J., 154, 155
Argyle, M., 327, 328
Arkes, H. R., 411
Arkowitz, H., 494
Armant, D. R., 338
Armbruster, B. B., 27
Arndt, J., 402
Arnett, J., 356–357
Arnkoff, D. B., 495, 497
Arnold, L. M., 429
Arnold, R., A-30
Arnold, R. D., 398
Arnon, I., 455
Arnsten, J. H., 176
Aron, A., 529
Aronson, E., 537
Arrigo, J. M., 460
Asch, S., 539–540
Aserinsky, E., 151, 156
Ashford, J. W., 361
Ashton, J. R., 354
Ashton, M. C., 379, 403
Aspinwall, L. G., 431
Assefi, S. L., 53, 174
Atkinson, J., 316
Atkinson, R. C., 229
Atkinson, R. H., 27
Ator, N. A., 59
Atwood, C. W., Jr., 164
Aucoin, K. J., 206

Auerbach

Auerbach, C. F., 372
Averill, J. A., 317
Axel, R., 136
Ayanian, J. Z., 433
Ayas, N. T., 162
Azzara, A. V., 304

B

Baars, B. J., 259
Bachelor, P., 292
Baddely, A., 230, 231–232
Baer, J., 292
Baer, R. A., 172, 408
Bahrick, H. P., 238
Bailey, C. H., 246
Bailey, J. M., 313, 314
Baillargeon, R., 349, 350
Baillie, A. J., 428
Bain, J., 361
Bains, J. S., 71
Bakalar, J. B., 177
Baker, D. B., 11
Baker, G. J., 427, 428
Baker, T. B., 204
Bakermans-Kranenburg, M. J., 342
Balcetis, E., 120, 524
Baldessarini, R. J., 500
Baldwin, E., 58
Baldwin, W., 54
Balk, M. M., 3
Ball, H. L., 160
Ballenger, J. C., 499
Balsam, P. D., 194
Baltes, P. B., 366
Bandura, A., 9, 211–212, 214–215, 370, 371, 390–391
Banich, M. T., 91, 100
Banks, A., 122, 313
Banks, S., 179
Banks, W. A., 71
Banks, W. C., 542
Banning, K., 418
Banyard, V. L., 241
Banzato, C. E. M., 453
Barak, A., 409
Baral, B. D., 280
Barbe, R. P., 510
Barbee, J. G., 416
Barber, T. X., 169, 170
Bard, P., 324
Bargh, J. A., 56, 318, 531, 544
Barker, E. T., 425
Barlett, D. L., 454
Barlow, D. H., 453
Barnes, V. A., 172
Barnett, S. W., 295
Barnier, A. J., 169
Baron, A., 202, 203
Barrett, D., 181
Barrett, L. F., 317, 318
Barrett, M. S., 6 , 490
Barrett, P., 408
Barron, F., 293
Barrouillet, P. 232
Barry-Walsh, J., 461
Barsky, A. J., 436, 459
Bartels, M., 281

Bartholow

Bartholow, B. D., 213
Bartoshuk, L. M., 134, 135, 136
Basbaum, A. I., 77, 138
Basow, S. A., 370
Bassok, M., 263, 264
Basson, M. O., 135
Bassuk, E. L., 510
Bates, E., 343, 344
Bates, M. S., 138
Bates, T. C., 329
Baudry, M., 76
Baum, A., 319, 427
Baumeister, R. F., 301, 306, 309, 311, 314, 318, 369, 425, 426
Baumrind, D., 57, 206, 207, 541
Baxter, P. M., 60
Bayley, P. J., 84, 245
Baylis, G. C., 122
Baynard, M. D., 161
Bazzini, D. G., 520
Beauchamp, G. K., 136, 306
Beck, A. T., 457, 465, 497, 498, 504–505
Becker, A., 478, 479
Becker, M. J., 28
Becker, R. J., 342
Becker, S., 246
Becskei, C., 303
Beddoe, R., A-26
Beehr, T. A., 416
Beeman, M. J., 101
Beer, J. M., 398
Beer, J. S., 87
Begg, I., 228
Behm-Morawitz, E., 550
Beidel, D. C., 453, 457
Beilin, H., 348
Bekelman, J. E., 501
Békésy, G. von, 123
Belger, A., 472
Bell, A. P., 313
Bell, J. E., 434
Bell, P. A., A-36
Belli, R. F., 236
Bellis, M. A., 354
Belsky, J., 354
Bem, D. J., 314
Bem, S. L., 371
Ben-Porath, Y. S., 408
Ben-Shakhar, G., 319
Benca, R. M., 162
Bender, D. S., 507, 508
Benet, V., 379
Benet-Martinez, V., 379
Benjamin, A., A-29
Benjamin, L. T., Jr., 3, 11, 28
Benjet, C., 206
Bennet, D. A., 366
Bennett, E. L., 288
Bennett, P., 429
Benoit, M., A-34
Benson, H., 441–442
Benton, D., 306
Berchtold, N. C., 434
Berenbaum, S. A., 313
Berger, S. E., 337, 339
Berghmans, R. L. D., 57
Bergin, A. E., 494, 514

Caspi, A., 358, 379
Caspi, O., 172
Cassel, R. N., 392
Cassidy, J., 341
Castillo, L. G., 419
Castle, D., 471
Castro, B., 510
Catanese, K. R., 309, 369
Catania, A. C., 196, 200
Catrambone, R., 263
Cattell, J. M., 4
Cattell, R. B., 378, 407
Caudek, C., 125
Cava, M. M., A-28
Cavanaugh, J. C., 361
Cavell, T. A., 28
Caverly, D. C., 27
Ceci, S. J., 283, 287
Centeno, S., 191
Cepeda, N. J., 251
Cerletti, U., 502
Chabris, C. F., 120
Chaiken, S., 534, 535
Chan, J. W. C., 280
Chance, P., 102
Chandler, C. C., 236
Chapman, P. D., 275
Charman, S. D., 255
Chase, P., 125
Chaves, M., 54
Chawla, L., A-32, A-36
Cheit, R., 244
Chemers, M. M., 390
Cherrier, M. M., 93
Chiapelli, F., 429
Chiarello, C., 101
Chiles, C., 540
Chiu, C., 13
Chizmar, L., 434
Cho, S. C., 156
Choi, I., 525
Choi, J., 31, 369
Chomsky, N., 10, 12, 19
Chopra, S. S., 502
Choudhry, N. K., 501
Christensen, A. J., 437
Christensen, B. A., 465
Christensen, B. T., 264
Christensen, C. C., 169
Christensen, L., 57
Christie, L. A., 434
Christoph, R. T., 390
Chronicle, E. P., 263, 264
Chrousos, G. P., 423
Chu, J. A., 242
Chudler, E. H., 64
Chun, M. M., 120
Churchland, P. S., 110
Cialdini, R. B., 146, 221, 535, 553, A-32
Cicero, T. J., 173
Ciesla, J. A., 419
Cilfasefi, S., 242
Clark, K., 19
Clark, M., 19
Clark, M. C., 252, 253
Clark, R. E., 84, 188, 245, 309
Clarke, J. C., 208
Clayton, S., A-24, A-32
Clayton, T., 335
Cleary, P. D., 433
Clemens, E., 155
Clifasefi, S. L., 120
Clifton, R. K., 340

Clinebell, H., A-24
Clore, G. L., 528
Clow, A., 92
Coderre, T. J., 138
Coenen, A., 84
Cohen, A., 366
Cohen, C. E., 522
Cohen, D., 499, 501
Cohen, D. B., 398
Cohen, F., 402
Cohen, N., 191
Cohen, S., 421, 429, 430, A-36
Colborn, T., A-37
Colder, M., 441
Cole, K. S., 227
Cole, R. F., 508
Coley, J. D., A-35
Colflesh, G.J.H., 232
Collaer, M. L., 370
Collins, A. M., 234
Collins, M. A., 520
Collins, N. L., 530
Collins, W. A., 360
Collins, W. R., 398
Collop, N. A., 155
Colom, R., 284
Coltrane, S., 360
Colwill, R. M., 199
Comas-Diaz, L., 508
Comaty, J. E., 173
Combs, D. R., 468, 469
Combs-Orme, T., 360
Comer, D. R., 545
Compas, B. E., 355
Compton, D. M., 58
Compton, M. T., 471
Conn, S., A-24
Connolly, T., 272
Contandriopoulos, A. P., 509
Conte, J. R., 241
Conway, A.R.A., 232
Conway, L. C., 14
Cook, A., 402
Cooke, L., 306
Coons, H. L., 418
Cooper, E., 292
Cooper, J., 538
Cooper, L., 416
Cooper, M., L., 530
Copper, C., 251
Corballis, M. C., 100
Corballis, P. M., 91
Coren, S., 101, 128, 129, 151
Cork, R. C., 152
Corkin, S., 245
Cornell, D. G., 369, 411
Corpus, B., 271
Correll, C. U., 499
Corsica, J. A., 434
Cosmides, L., 10, 14, 272, 273
Costa, P. T., Jr., 358, 379, 407, 408
Coston, M. L., 9
Coté, J. E., 357
Cotman, C. W., 434
Cotter, A., 339
Courage, M. L., 349
Coutts, A., 338
Cowan, N., 231
Cowan, P. A., 206
Cowart, B. J., 134, 136
Cowey, A., 115
Cox, D., 115
Cox, P. D., 492
Coy, K. C., 360

Coyne, J. C., 466
Craig, J. C., 138
Craig, P., 335
Craighero, L., 86
Craik, F.I.M., 226, 227, 239, 252
Craik, K. H., 12
Cramer, P., 426
Crano, W. D., 534
Craske, M. G., 457, 457
Cravens, H., 281
Crawford, M., 368
Creed, F., 429
Crews, F., 387
Crites, S. L., 536
Crits-Cristoph, P., 490, 514
Crockett, H., 315
Cross, S. E., 371
Crouch, D. J., 227
Crouter, A. C., 371
Crowder, R. G., 239
Cruess, D. G., 453
Cruz, C., 154
Csikszentmihalyi, M., 14, 318, 431, 492
Cuban, L., 290
Culbert, K. L., 76
Culbertson, J. L., 409
Culbertson, W. C., 78
Cullum, J., 536
Culpepper, L., 500
Cummings, D. E., 304
Cummins, D., 369
Cunningham, C. O., 434
Cunningham, M., 371
Cunningham, M. R., 533
Curby, K. M., 115
Currer, D., 464
Curtin, S. C., A-36
Cushman, P., 507
Cutting, L. P., 473
Czeisler, C. A., 155

D

D'Alusio, F., A-29
D'Souza, D. C., 177
Daamen, D.D.L., A-31
Dabbs, A., 538
Dagot, L., 553
Dahl, R. 355
Daiek, D. B., 27
Dallenbach, K. M., 135
Dallman, M. F., 423
Dalton, S. O., 429
Daly, M., 10, 14
Dan, B. A., 343
Danton, W. G., 501
Danziger, K., 22
Dapretto, M., 86, 343
Darley, J., 544
Darwin, C., 4, 96, 324
Das, E.H.H., 535
Das, J. P., 281
Dasen, P. R., 349
Davenport, J. L., 124
David, J. P., 416
Davidov, B. J., 13
Davidowitz, R., 530
Davidson, R. J., 91, 172, 321
Davies, D. R. T., 161
Davies, R., 462
Davis, A. S., 100
Davis, D., 242, 254, 530

Davis, H., 172
Davis, J. L., 528
Davis, K. L., 361
Davis, M. N., 430
Davis, O. S. P., 281
Davis, R., 523
Dawes, R. M., A-33
Dawkins, K., 464
Day, N. L., 338
Day, R. H., 127
Daylo, A. A., 64
De Beni, R., 253
de Castro, J. M., 305
de Graaf, J., A-29
De Koninck, J., 165, 166
De Neys, W., 274
de Rooij, S., 338
De Valois, R. L., 118
de Villiers, J. G., 344
de Villiers, P., 202, 344
De Waal, F, 187
de wijk, R. A., 136
de Wit, J.B.F., 535
Deakin, J.F.W., 76
Dean, R. S., 100
Deary, I. J., 278., 287
Deaux, K., 368
DeCarvalho, R. J., 392
Deecher, D., 361
Deese, J., 242
Defeyter, M. A., 262
Deffenbacher, J. L., 429
DeFrain, J., 359
Degenhardt, L., 177, 471
Delaune, K. A., 432
Delay, J., 504
Deldin, P. J., 470
Delgado, P. L., 76
Delinsky, S. S., 477
Delis, D. C., 245, 247
DeLisi, L. E., 471
della Rocca, P., 154
DelMonte, M. M., 242
DeLong, M. R., 75, 84
Delongis, A., 416
Delprato, D. J., 10
DelVecchio, W. F., 358
DeMaso, D. R., 506
Dement, W. C., 151, 155, 156, 157, 158, 159, 160, 161, 163, 166, 180
Dempster, F. N., 251
Deniker, P., 504
Denko, T., 501
Denmark, F. L., 5
Dennerstein, L., 360
Dennis, C., 360
Denton, K., 522
Deregowski, 126
Derevensky, J. L., 2
Derogitis, L. R., 418
Derr, T., A-36
DeRubeis, R. J.,
Des Jarlais, D. C., 177
Descartes, R., 4
Desmarais, S., 371
Detsky, A. S., 501
Deutsch, G., 91, 100, 101, 370
Deutsch, J. A., 304
Devescovi, A., 343
Devine, P. G., 521, 538, 549
Devlin, B., 286
Devlin, J. T., 87
DeVries, R., 349

SUBJECT INDEX

Cannon-Bard theory, 323, 324
carbon dioxide trends, A-26
cardiovascular disease, 427
career success, 315
careers, in psychology, A-15–A-22
caregivers, attachment to, 341
caregiving styles, 529
Carrey, Jim, 462
carrying capacity, A-26, A-27
case studies, 48–49, 50–51, 387
    critical thinking about, 64–65
catastrophic thinking, 424, 440
catatonic schizophrenia, 468–469
catecholamines, 423
catharsis, 425
causation
    correlational research and, 46,
        372–373, 444
    experimental research and, 43
    see also multifactorial causation
CCK, 304
Celexa, 501
cell membrane, of neuron, 71, 72,
    73, 74
cell phones
    cancer and, 445
    driving and, 227
cells
    brain, 87–88
    genetic material in, 93
    in nervous system, 69–70
    in retina, 110–112
center-surround arrangement,
    112, 113, 137
Centers for Disease Control and
    Prevention, 436
central nervous system, 78, 80
    see also brain; spinal cord
central tendency, measures of, A-8
centration, 347
cephalocaudal trend, 339–340
cerebellum, 82–83, 246
cerebral cortex, 83, 85–86
cerebral hemispheres, 85–86,
    88–91, 370
cerebral specialization, 88–91,
    100–101, 370
cerebrospinal fluid (CSF), 80, 472
cerebrum, 83, 85–86
chance, in statistical results, A-14
change, as source of stress,
    417–418
channels, communication, 534
Charles, Prince, 335
chemical senses, 134–136
child abuse
    dissociative identity disorder
        and, 461
    repressed memories of, 241–244
childlessness, 360
childrearing, 398
    cultural differences in, 525
children
    cognitive development in,
        446–350, 362–363
    deciding whether to have, 360
    effect of father absence on,
        372–373
    environment and, A-35–A-36
    environmental deprivation
        and, 286–287
    food preferences in, 306
    fostering independence in, 404
    gender-role socialization of, 371

imitation of models by, 390
language development in,
    343–344
media violence and, 212–213,
    216
moral development in, 350–353
motor development in, 339–343
parental investment in, 308, 309
parental love for, 393
personality development in,
    383–385
physical punishment of,
    205–207
chimpanzees, Goodall's study
    of, 48
chlamydia, 339
chlorpromazine, 499
choice overload, 268
choices
    conflict and, 417
    factors in, 267–274
cholesterol, 427, 433
chromosomes, 93, 336
chronic diseases, 415–416
chronic pain, self-efficacy and,
    390
chunks, in short-term memory,
    231
cicada, 188
cigarettes, 433
    advertising of, 220
circadian rhythms, 153–155
circular reasoning, 183, 331
clarification, in client-centered
    therapy, 491
Clark University, 6
class attendance, grades and, 27
classical conditioning, 188–195
    acquisition in, 192, 193, 200
    in advertising, 220
    of anxiety responses, 456,
        495–496
    of attitudes, 536
    aversion therapy and, 496
    avoidance learning and, 204
    basic processes in, 192–194
    in business negotiations,
        220–221
    discrimination in, 194, 200
    of emotions, 190–191
    in everyday life, 190–192
    extinction in, 192–193, 200
    of food preferences, 306
    generalization in, 193–194, 200
    interaction with operant condi-
        tioning, 204
    observational learning and, 212
    overview of, 214–215
    Pavlov's formulation of, 188–
        190
    of physiological responses, 191
    in politics, 221
    signal relations in, 211
    spontaneous recovery in, 193
    of taste aversion, 207–208
    terminology and procedures
        for, 189–190
classical music, for infants, 102,
    103
claustrophobia, 454
client-centered therapy, 9,
    490–491, 504–505, 513
climate change, A-25–A-26, A-30,
    A-34

clinical neuropsychology, 17, 20,
    A-22
clinical psychologists, 49, 487
clinical psychology, 11, 17, 20,
    A-21
clinical social workers, 488, A-18
clitoris, 307
closure, as Gestalt principle, 122,
    123
Clouser, Ronald, 254
CNS depressants, 173
CNS stimulants, 173
co-sleeping, 160
cocaine, 173, 175, 176
    brain activity and, 82
    neurotransmitters and, 76
    prenatal development and, 338
cochlea, 132, 133
coefficient of determination, A-13
cognition, 11–12, 259
cognitive abilities
    aging and, 366
    gender differences in, 31, 368
cognitive appraisal, of stressful
    events, 420
cognitive-behavioral therapy, 497,
    504–505
cognitive development, 346–350,
    362–365
    attachment style and, 343
    moral development and, 351
    Piaget's stage theory of,
        346–348, 349
    sociocultural theory of,
        349–350
cognitive dissonance, 537–538
cognitive maps, 210
cognitive perspective, 10, 12, 259
    on conditioning, 209–211
    on dreaming, 167
    on emotions, 318
    on gender-role learning, 371
    on intelligence, 288–289
cognitive processes, 12
cognitive psychology, 17, A-19
cognitive style, 101
    culture and, 266–267
    depression and, 465–466
cognitive therapy, 497, 504–505,
    513
Collaborative on Health and the
    Environment, A-37
collective unconscious, 386
collectivism, 525–526, 545
    conformity and, 542
    marriage and, 531
college admissions tests, 45, 46
college students
    gambling by, 1–2
    materialism in, A-33
    as research subjects, 53
colleges, psychology laboratories
    at, 3
color blindness, 117
color circle, 117
color mixing, 116, 117
color solid, 116
color vision, 111, 116–118
commitment, 356, 529
common sense, versus scientific
    approach, 40
communication
    with health providers, 436
    nonverbal, 321, 322

persuasive, 534–535
communities, positive, 14
community counseling, A-18
community mental health
    centers, 512
community mental health
    movement, 508–509
comorbidity, 480
companionate love, 529
comparative optimism, A-34
comparitors, 146–147
compensation, 386–387
competition
    between groups, 550–551
    individualism and, 525
complementary colors, 117
compliance
    with authority, 540–542
    with medical advice, 436–437
composers, mental illness and,
    293, 369
compulsions, 454, 455
concepts, semantic networks of,
    234
conclusions, 330
concordance rate
    for anxiety disorders, 456
    for mood disorders, 464–465
    for schizophrenia, 470, 471
concrete operational period, 346,
    347, 348
conditionability, 396
conditioned reflex, 7
conditioned reinforcers, 200–201
conditioned response (CR), 189,
    190, 191, 192, 194, 195, 204,
    208, 456, 495, 536
conditioned stimulus (CS), 189,
    190, 191, 192, 193, 194, 195,
    204, 204, 208, 209, 211, 456,
    495, 536
conditioning
    biological constraints on,
        207–209
    cognitive processes in, 209–211
    contingencies and, 211
    defined, 187
    evaluative, 220, 536
    personality and, 389–390
    rapid, 208
    see also classical conditioning;
        operant conditioning
cones, 110–111, 112, 118
conflict(s)
    between groups, 550–551
    internal, 382
    as source of stress, 417
    types of, 417
    unconscious, 489
conformity, 519, 539–540
conformity pressure, 418–419
confounding of variables, 42
congruence, 392, 393, 491
conjunction fallacy, 271, 481
conjunctive probabilities, 480,
    481
connectionist models, of
    memory, 234–235
conscientiousness, 358, 379, 397,
    398, 407, 431, 545
conscious, 381
consciousness
    altered, 170
    altering with drugs, 172–177

diazepam, 498
dichromats, 117
diet, quality of, 433–434
dieting, 306
diffusion of responsibility, 544, 545
digestive system, hunger and, 302, 304
disagreements, perceptions in, 37–38
disasters, stress and, 431, 432
discipline, parental, 205–207
disclosure, emotional, 441
disconfirming evidence, 255
discrimination
   in classical conditioning, 194, 200
   in operant conditioning, 199–200
discrimination (social)
   against homosexuals, 314
   prejudice and, 549
discriminative stimuli, 199
disease, biopsychosocial model of, 415
   prenatal development and, 339
   psychosomatic, 427
disinhibition, with hypnosis, 169
disorganized schizophrenia, 469
displacement, 383, 425
display rules, 322
dissociation, with hypnosis, 170
dissociative amnesia, 460
dissociative disorders, 452, 460–461
dissociative identity disorder (DID), 460–461
dissonance theory, 536
distance, perception of, 126, 127
distributed practice, 251, 252
distribution
   normal, A-9–A-10, A-11
   skewed, A-8
divergent thinking, 292
division of labor, 369
divorce, 372, 373
   Big Five traits and, 379
   happiness and, 328
Dix, Dorothea, 508, 509
dizygotic twins, 95
DNA, 93
doctoral degree, in psychology, A-18–A-19
dolphins, 157
door-in-the-face technique, 146
dopamine, 75, 76, 84, 85, 175, 499, 529
dopamine hypothesis, of schizophrenia, 470, 471
double-blind procedure, 54–55
doubt, 346
"downers," 173
Doyle, Arthur Conan, 259
dream analysis, 386, 489
dream interpretation, 242
dreams (dreaming), 164–167
   common questions about, 180–181
   content of, 165–166, 181
   culture and, 166
   interpretation of, 181
   recall for, 181, 166
   REM and, 151, 157
   shocking, 181

symbolism in, 181
   theories of, 166–167
drive reduction, 300
drives, 84, 300
driving, cell phone use and, 227
drowsiness, 161
drug companies, 501–502
drug dependence, 175, 176
drug therapy, 498–502
   deinstitutionalization and, 509
   effectiveness of, 501–502
drug use
   health risks of, 176–177
   during pregnancy, 338
drugs, psychoactive, 172–177
drunk driving, test for, 83
DSM-IV, 451–453
dual-coding theory, 229
dual-process theories, of decision making, 273, 326
duloxetine, 501

E

ear, sensory processing in, 131–132
eardrum, 131, 132
eating behavior
   biological factors in, 302–304
   environmental cues to, 304–305
   observational learning and, 306
   regulation of, 84
   serotonin and, 76
   stress and, 306
eating disorders, 452, 477–479
   etiology of, 479
   meditation and, 172
   prevalence of, 478
eating habits
   poor, 433–434
   sleep and, 180
ecological footprint, A-27–A-28
ecologically connected self, A-32
ecopsychology, A-24
ecosystems, A-26
ecstasy, 174
educational psychology, 17, A-20
EEG, 152–153
efferent nerve fibers, 79
Effexor, 501
efficiency, in groups, 544–545
effort justification, 537–538
egg cell, 93, 336
ego, 380, 381, 382
egocentric values, A-32
egocentrism, 347–348, 349
ejaculation, 307, 354
elaboration, in encoding, 228
elaboration likelihood model, 538
election campaign ads, 221
electrical stimulation of the brain (ESB), 80–81, 85
electroconvulsive therapy (ECT), 502
electroencephalograph (EEG), 152–153
electromyograph (EMG), 155
electrooculograph (EOG), 155, 156
elicited responses, 190
elimination by aspects, 268–269
embryonic stage, 337, 338
emetic drugs, 496

emit, 196
emotion(s), 317–322
   attitudes and, 534, 549
   autonomic nervous system and, 79
   behavioral component of, 321
   Cannon-Bard theory of, 323, 324
   cognitive component of, 317–318
   conditioned, 190–191, 220
   conditioning of, 536
   culture and, 321–322
   defined, 317
   Ellis's model of, 440
   evolutionary perspective on, 324–325
   expressed, 472–473
   facial expressions for, 321, 322
   fundamental, 321, 325
   heart disease and, 428
   James-Lange theory of, 323–324
   limbic system and, 84–85
   manipulation of, 220, 221
   motivation and, 316
   negative, 306, 318, 420, 462, 476
   physiological component of, 318–321
   positive, 14, 318, 420, 421, 440
   release of, 425, 440–441
   in schizophrenia, 468
   socially engaging vs. disengaging, 321
   stress and, 420–421
   suppression of, 440–441
   theories of, 323–325
   two-factor theory of, 323, 324
emotional arousal, 421, 422, 440
emotional development, 341–343
empathy, 353
   mirror neurons and, 86
   of therapist, 491
empiricism, 21, 35, 59, 99
   in social psychology, 547
   statistics and, A-7, A-14
employers, qualities sought in job applicants, A-16
empty nest, 360
encoding, 225, 226–229, 250
   enriching, 228–229, 252–253
   ineffective, 239
encoding specificity principle, 240
endocrine system, 84, 92–93, 304, 423
endorphins, 75, 77, 138–139, 175
energy conservation, A-31
energy consumption, A-27–A-28, A-38
environment
   enriched, 102, 103
   heredity and, 24, 95–96, 99, 284–285, 367
   intelligence and, 283–284
   restorative, A-37–A-38
environmental enrichment, 283–284
environmental fragrancing, 136
environmental sustainability, A-24–A-29
Environmental Working Group, A-39

epilepsy, surgery for, 89
episodic memory system, 247–248, 366
equilibrium, 83, 300
erection, 307
ESB (electrical stimulation of the brain), 80–81, 85
escape learning, 204
Escher, M. C., 144, 145
Eskimos, 322
essay tests, 238
ethics, in research, 56–59, 541
ethnic differences, in IQ scores, 285–287
ethnic groups, mental health services utilization by, 487
ethnic stereotypes, 521, 549
etiology, 450
euphoria
   in bipolar disorders, 463
   with psychoactive drugs, 173
evaluative conditioning, 220, 536
evidence
   anecdotal, 64–64
   disconfirming, 255
   lack of, 294
evolutionary biology, 13
evolutionary perspective, 10, 96–99
   on cognitive abilities, 350
   on color vision, 116
   on conditioned responses, 209
   on conditioned taste aversion, 208
   on consciousness, 152
   criticism of, 14, 311
   Darwin's, 96–97
   on emotion, 324–325
   evaluating, 30–31
   on flaws in decision making, 272–273
   on gender differences, 369–370
   on gender difference in orgasm, 307–308
   on gender differences in taste sensitivity, 135
   hindsight bias and, 411
   on human sexual behavior, 308–311
   on interpersonal attraction, 532–533
   on motivation, 301
   on person perception, 522
   on personality, 398
   on sleep, 160
evolutionary theory, 4
evolved module for fear learning, 209, 457
examples, information retention and, 28
exams, preparing for, 28–29, 251–252
excitatory PSPs, 73, 76
excitement phase, of sexual response cycle, 307
exercise
   lack of, 427, 434
   self-efficacy and, 390
   stress and, 442, 443
exhaustion stage, 422, 423
exorcism, 450
expectations
   in conducting research, 54
   conforming to, 418–419

Integrated Coverage of Evolutionary Psychology

Integrated Coverage of Cultural Factors

(continues on following page)

Integrated Coverage of Issues Related to Gender